Developing Library and
Information Center
Collections

Library Science Text Series

Reference and Information Services: An Introduction. 2d ed. By Richard E. Bopp and Linda C. Smith. 1995.

Developing Library and Information Center Collections. 3d ed. By G. Edward Evans. 1995.

The Collection Program in Schools: Concepts, Practices, and Information Sources. 2d ed. By Phyllis J. Van Orden. 1995.

The Humanities: A Selective Guide to Information Sources. 4th ed. By Ron Blazek and Elizabeth Aversa. 1994.

The School Library Media Manager. By Blanche Woolls. 1994.

Systems Analysis for Librarians and Information Professionals. By Larry N. Osborne and Margaret Nakamura. 1994.

Information Sources in Science and Technology. 2d ed. By C. D. Hurt. 1994.

Introduction to Technical Services. 6th ed. By G. Edward Evans and Sandra M. Heft. 1994.

Library and Information Center Management. 4th ed. By Robert D. Stueart and Barbara B. Moran. 1993.

Introduction to Library Public Services. 5th ed. By G. Edward Evans, Anthony J. Amodeo, and Thomas L. Carter. 1992.

Introduction to Library Services. By Barbara E. Chernik. 1992.

Introduction to United States Government Information Sources. 4th ed. By Joe Morehead and Mary Fetzer. 1992.

Introduction to Cataloging and Classification. Bohdan S. Wynar. 8th ed. By Arlene G. Taylor. 1991.

Immroth's Guide to the Library of Congress Classification. 4th ed. By Lois Mai Chan. 1990.

Library Instruction for Librarians. 2d rev. ed. By Anne F. Roberts and Susan G. Blandy. 1989.

The Social Sciences: A Cross-Disciplinary Guide to Selected Sources. By Nancy L. Herron, General Editor. 1989.

Audiovisual Technology Primer. By Albert J. Casciero and Raymond G. Roney. 1988.

Online Reference and Information Retrieval. 2d ed. By Roger C. Palmer. 1987.

Micrographics. 2d ed. By William Saffady. 1985.

Introduction to Library Automation. By James Rice. 1984.

The Library in Society. By A. Robert Rogers and Kathryn McChesney. 1984.

Developing Library and Information Center Collections

Third Edition

G. Edward Evans

University Librarian
Loyola Marymount University

1995
LIBRARIES UNLIMITED, INC.
Englewood, Colorado

LIBRARIES UNLIMITED, INC.
P.O. Box 6633
Englewood, CO 80155-6633
1-800-237-6124

Library of Congress Cataloging-in-Publication Data

Evans, G. Edward, 1937-
    Developing library and information center collections / G. Edward
Evans. -- 3rd ed.
    xvii, 556 p. 17x25 cm.
    Includes bibliographical references and index.
    ISBN 1-56308-183-0. -- ISBN 1-56308-187-3 (pbk.)
    1. Collection development (Libraries)   2. Information services.
I. Title.
Z687.E918   1995
025.2--dc20
                                                     94-45460
                                                          CIP

Contents

Preface to the First Edition

Collection development is an exciting and challenging area in which to work, and selecting the right materials for the library's community is as intellectually demanding an activity as a librarian will encounter. The selection of library materials is a highly personal process—something that takes a lifetime to learn—and the rewards are great. This book can serve as the starting point in that learning process. Any textbook that attempts to cover all aspects of collection development must give coverage to many topics. This text provides practical information on materials producers and distributors, community survey techniques, policies, materials selection, acquisition, weeding, and evaluation in order to minimize the variables involved in the selection process. Beyond the physical processes of collection development, though, are issues with which a selector should be concerned, as they influence how the collection will and can be developed. Thus, *Developing Library Collections* also delves into library cooperation, copyright (reflecting the changed statutes), and censorship as they affect the process in its entirety.

An author of a collection development textbook should acknowledge that, to a very great degree, the emphasis given each topic is based on a subjective assessment of its importance, reflecting the values and judgments of that author. Certainly, anyone with practical experience in this area knows that selection and collection development are arts, not sciences; and, as with any artistic endeavor, a person wishing to practice the art must devote years to developing the necessary skills. The basic elements of the collection development process—determining what information resources are needed, identifying the appropriate items, acquiring the items, and evaluating the collection—are rather well agreed upon. What is open to debate is how much emphasis to place upon individual steps in the process, and the interrelationship of all the elements.

A person cannot learn selection and collection development only in the classroom. A student will be able to learn the basic elements from this book; whether the student accepts the emphasis placed upon the elements is another matter. With the concepts presented in this book as a base, and using the recommended further readings, however, the student should begin to develop a solidly based, personal approach to selection and collection development.

The purpose of this book is to help library students gain an overall understanding of what is involved in building a collection for a library. Within rather broad limits, one may say that all libraries share certain general characteristics, including the need to assemble a collection of books and other library materials needed by their patrons. This book was written with the intent of emphasizing the similarities between types of libraries in the process of developing a collection.

Unlike any other book on collection development or book selection, *Developing Library Collections* provides an integrated approach to the process of building a library collection for a specific community of users—integrated in the sense that each element in the process is treated as flowing from one to another, and when something occurs in one element, it will have an impact on the others. Thus, as each element is discussed in detail, its relationship with the others will be examined as well, the underlying emphasis always being on the ultimate goal of the process—serving the library's community. To some degree, every chapter in this book has some application to any library. However, some aspects of collection development have more application, or at least are more widely used, in one type of library than another. For example, community analysis has been most widely used in public libraries, and as a result, chapter 4 tends to emphasize community analysis in the public library. Chapters 14 and 15, on weeding and evaluating the collection, deal with issues most pertinent to academic libraries, and this emphasis is reflected in the citations. Nevertheless, every chapter provides information relevant to all types of libraries.

In one sense, this is a jointly authored work. Any librarian who has written or talked about this subject has probably influenced my thinking to some degree. The further readings at the ends of the chapters reflect some of the works that have directly affected my point of view; they are but a fraction of the total waiting to be read. These writings will serve as an excellent starting point for further reading, which will need to continue as long as a librarian is involved in collection development work.

Preface to the Second Edition

The slight change in the title of this book is a reflection of a shift in emphasis from the book and other "information packages" to the information contained in the package. Selection work has always been concerned with the contents of items being considered for a collection. What has happened over the past 15 years is that society has become aware of and concerned about the "value" of information. New systems, often computer based, offer alternative means of providing information for patrons or clients. It appears likely this trend will continue for some time.

In the first edition the first chapter was concerned with definitions and concepts, and so is the first chapter in this edition. However, more emphasis is placed on concepts of information and information transfer. It is virtually a new chapter. Most of the chapters from the first edition have been extensively revised and updated, and additions have been made. The former chapter on selection is now divided into two chapters, on theory and practice. New chapters dealing with serials, government documents, fiscal management, automation, and preservation have been added.

Suggestions for further reading are included in each chapter. Items listed were selected on the basis of ease of availability and currency. (Also, all the items mentioned in a chapter are included regardless of date of publication.) An effort has been made to provide a few references for academic, public, school, and special libraries and information centers in each chapter.

I wish to thank all the individuals who read one or more chapters of this edition and provided many helpful suggestions: Herbert Achlietner, Peter Briscoe, Alan Ericson, William Fisher, Dale Flecker, Doris Frietag, Irene Godden, William McGrath, Assunta Pisanti, Benedict Rugaas, Joel Rutstein, and Sally Williams. Naturally they are not responsible for any of the book's shortcomings. Finally, I want to thank Morris Fry for his copyediting work, Julie Wetherill for the many hours of typing, and Nancy Lambert-Brown for the figures and charts she prepared.

Preface to the Third Edition

This edition reflects the changes that collection management has undergone during the past eight years. There is a new chapter on electronic formats. The additions, deletions, and changes in the presentation grew out of the ideas, suggestions, and comments from a number of people. I started by obtaining input from teachers who used the second edition. Their comments were especially useful. The individuals who took the time to respond in depth and with invaluable input were Robert Broadus, Donald Davis, William Fisher, Elizabeth Futas, Sheila Intner, Bill Katz, Betty Morris, Ronald Powell, James Rice, Judith Serebnick, Phyllis Van Orden, and Adeline Wood Wilkes. I also was fortunate enough to have six people from various types of library environments read the entire manuscript and comment on the material. These readers, who spent long hours reading more than 700 manuscript pages, deserve more thanks than is possible to give in writing. They were Donald Davis (University of Texas, academic libraries and teacher), Bill Fisher (San Jose State University, special libraries and teacher), David Loertscher (Libraries Unlimited, school library media centers), Nancy Pruett (Sandia National Laboratories, special libraries), Brian Reynolds (San Luis Obispo County Library, public libraries), and Margaret Zarnosky (Virginia Polytechnic Institute and State University, academic libraries). Margaret deserves an extra special thank you for her editing efforts, as well as her insightful content comments. Staff members from the Loyola Marymount Library also read many of the chapters. They were Marcia Findley (Assistant University Librarian for Collection Development), Janet Lai (Head of Acquisitions and Serials department), Paula Nielson (Assistant University Librarian for Systems), and Sachi Yagyu (Database Services and Document Delivery). They deserve special recognition for having the courage to read the director's manuscript and make honest comments. Finally, to the others who read one or more chapters, a special thank you: Dr. Elizabeth Eaton (Director, Health Sciences Library, Tufts University), whose suggestions were of immense help in preparing the electronics chapter; Dr. John Richardson (UCLA's library school), who commented on the government information chapter; and Peter Bodell (Director, Information Services, Loyola Marymount University), who provided a computer center perspective.

All the readers' comments greatly improved the manuscript. However, they are not responsible for errors in content. I hope this edition will prove as useful to students and others as did the second edition.

I
Information Age—
Information Society

Reading is the opposite of dissipation;
it is a mental and moral practice of
concentration which leads us to unknown worlds.
—Octavio Paz[1]

In the eight years since the second edition of this book, there have been many developments in the electronic delivery of information. Articles about virtual libraries, or virtual knowledge centers, appear almost monthly in the professional journals (see page 26 for a discussion of "virtuals"). "Interactive multimedia" is the latest concept that some people claim will solve the information problems of society. Authors present images of brave new worlds in which individuals will be able to gain access to any type of information (text, numeric, graphic, or audio) from home, office, or even a traveler's hotel room.

The technologies these authors describe—existing and projected—do hold great promise for assisting in the information transfer process. Taken to the ultimate scenario, one sees a world where a person sits in one's own space and never needs to have direct physical contact with another human being. In fact, Raymond Kurzweil not long ago suggested that we can look forward to virtual physical relations![2] A world without face to face interaction does not appeal to many people, including me. One writer suggests that books and reading are something like horses.[3] That is, in the late nineteenth century, horses were the primary mode of transportation. Today, we still have horses, but primarily for pleasure use and only a few people ride for pleasure.

Perhaps some time in the near future books and reading will be the "horses" of information. However, even if it becomes possible to deliver all information to all individuals everywhere, I believe the interest in the technology misses a key point as reflected in the Paz quotation that went on to state:

> . . . to read is to discover unsuspected paths that lead to our own selves. It is recognition. In the era of advertising and instantaneous communication, how many people are able to read this way? Very few. But the continuity of our civilization lies with them.[4]

What the technologies are best at is delivering information (see pages 260-64). It takes time and personal effort to convert information into knowledge. And with more time, and some luck, into wisdom.

While reading is only one means of acquiring information, it is perhaps the most important. Presently, technologies can only present portions of information on a computer screen that would normally appear on a printed page. Individuals must download or have delivered a paper copy of the material if they wish to consult the information away from the screen. There are a number of problems with this approach to reading. Two of the more significant are the costs entailed in getting information from electronic sources, and users' assumptions about those sources.

As more libraries and information centers pass along some or all of the direct costs of electronic information, the user will attempt to keep the costs as low as possible. This often results in the person taking only a small part of the information in a large file. Without having the full file, the individual is more likely to misinterpret or misunderstand the material. We appear to be entering an age of information bites that could have an even greater impact on society than television's sound bites. Individuals become accustomed to and subsequently demand instant facts, interpretation, and presumed understanding of complex issues in 30 seconds or less. Electronics reinforce the need for speed. (Waiting for a second becomes too long when one is working with a computer.) There is an all too common faith in the electronic sources.

People often assume that if they check for information in an electronic system they have all the information. On one level they know this is a false assumption, but they operate as if it were true. A related assumption is that the information found electronically is the most current and accurate, rather like the past assumption that if the information appeared in a book then it must be true. Somehow libraries and information centers must do more to educate end users about the electronic sources and their limitations.

What does the above have to do with collection development? Everything, I believe. Even if the brave new world of electronic information comes to pass, there will be a need for locally maintained resources, if for no other reason than cost control. Electronic information does not reduce costs but rather shifts them. Securing information from locally maintained databases, for high use sources, will most likely remain less expensive than paying for the information plus the telecommunication charges for accessing a remote database. Knowing who is using what, for what purposes, and how often, as well as knowing what sources exist that can supply the information in the most cost effective way, is the keystone to present and foreseeable collection development work. If, on the other hand, books and reading remain key factors in the transfer of information, the same skills and understanding will still be needed. My personal view is that the future will lie somewhere between the technologists' projections and what exists today. The idea of fiction, essays, literature, poetry, and biographies becoming the "horses" of the information future is most unappealing.

Nature of Information

Some individuals talk as if information is a newly discovered, mysterious, and natural phenomenon. On the other hand, for librarians and others working in information centers, information is neither new nor mysterious; it is the product they have always worked with, an old friend. Both perspectives have an element of truth.

Libraries and their collections (information) have existed for thousands of years. For example, the Red Temple at Uruk, dating about 3000 B.C., contained a library. People recognized the value of information, although in a rather unusual way. For example, monks in European medieval libraries chained many of their books to reading stalls. (There were several reasons for chaining the books, the value of the information being one.) Collecting and organizing information and making it more available to individuals has a long history. However, during the past 15 to 20 years, a major shift in attitude of Western societies toward information has developed.

More organizations and people treat information as an economic product, like petroleum, cardboard boxes, or automobiles. For example, there are many newsletter or special report information services that charge thousands of dollars for one year's service. (Some examples of the cost of information are *Petroleum Argus Telex*, which cost $22,198 in 1995, *Cooper Market Outlook Service* at $15,000 for 1995, and *Decima Quarterly Report* for only $19,885, and one of the most costly 1995 titles was *Information Systems Planning Services* at $56,000.[5]) Combined with this different attitude toward information, is the variety of technological developments that affect the generation, storage, and retrieval of information.

What is happening in the 1990s is, in many ways, similar to what happened with the widespread use of movable type. As Patricia Sabosik noted, the turmoil in today's publishing is almost the same as in the fifteenth century.[6] Just as the printing press shifted access to information from a few to many people, we are seeing a similar shift today. Sabosik suggests the shift today is from libraries to end users. In her view, the libraries are becoming an intermediary to, rather than a storehouse of, information. Certainly some of the shifting she describes has already taken place and is likely to grow in scope; however, the process will probably take a long time to complete. That is, assuming the virtual library, or knowledge center, of the future does become an electronic switching center service.

The net effect of the combination is a new phenomenon that creates problems for libraries and society. Many problems relate to handling the economic aspects of information and access to that information (often written about in terms of ownership versus access). Although a detailed discussion of these problems is beyond the scope of this book, I will mention them where they have an influence on collection development/resource management.

What are some examples of the problems and changes that have taken place? If information is an economic resource, as many people now contend, it has several characteristics that are special, so special as to make information almost unique. Unlike other economic commodities, people share information even after selling it. Sellers always retain the information in some form, if only in a person's memory. There are two economic aspects to the sale of information: 1) the cost of packaging the information, and 2) the cost/value of information contained in the package. When the package is a book, newspaper, magazine, video or audio tape, for example, people tend to think of the package *as* the information. An individual confronted with an online system where one pays for information by the "screen" and yet cannot retain a hard copy, or who is considering paying $30,000 for a quarterly newsletter subscription, quickly begins to appreciate the differences between information and package value.

Another special characteristic of information is that it is neither scarce nor depleting. In fact, the more people use and manipulate it, the more information there is. Many information problems are the result of too much information rather than too little. The problem is locating the necessary information at the right time. To some extent the changes discussed above are contributing to copyright problems (see chapter 18 for a discussion of copyright). *Ownership* of ideas, facts, and information is more of an issue today, unlike in the past when the issue was primarily the *expression* of ideas, facts, and information. Perhaps the ultimate in ownership is the "electronic novel" by William Gibson.[7] This work is a self-contained computer file that erases the data after the user views each "page." There is no going back to review previous pages, to examine how the author expressed an idea, or to reread a passage simply because you enjoyed it—unless you buy another copy! It is frightening to think this might become the next phase of the pricing and ownership struggle. While such an approach solves the issue of sharing information in the traditional sense, most societies could not tolerate such an approach for the majority of the information its citizens produce.

How suppliers will price information is difficult to predict. It seems probable that suppliers will apply the unit cost to smaller and smaller increments of information. Fees based on connect time, per search, per screen, and downloading have not been satisfactory to suppliers or users. Page charges may become the basis for charges, but there would need to be a clear standard of what constitutes a "page" of information. Certainly the CRT screen page contains far less information than typical print book or journal pages, at least with today's technology.

Other characteristics of information that make it a special commodity are transportability, intangibility, compressibility and expandability, storability (in a variety of forms and formats), and manipulability. An ongoing topic of discussion and matter of concern to many people is the "transborder" flow of information. Most of the concern has been about how electronic data flows from one country to another. Hugh Donaghue, a vice president at Control Data Corporation, presented one of several papers on this topic at the 1982 International Federation of Library Associations Conference in Montreal. In his concluding remarks about international library networks, he noted two economic threats could make such networks too costly for libraries to afford unless government exemptions can be obtained. These are: tariffs which may be applied to incoming information and data; and transmission rates based on volume rather than time.[8]

These issues are still as much a major concern for international networking as they were at the time Donaghue voiced them. For libraries in countries that are either less developed or experiencing severe economic problems, there is a third concern: the lack of technology required to participate in international networks.

As more governments consider the idea of information as an economic commodity worth placing tariffs and controls on, and as more of the world's publishers generate and store information in an electronic format, librarians and information specialists must think more in terms of information and less about information packages. This in turn will necessitate rethinking the delivery of services.

Newsletters and journals from library or information associations contain frequent references to new information services or products based on electronic technologies. Several examples of news article headlines from 1992 and 1993 illustrate this trend:

"OhioLINK Online With First 6 of 18 Academic Library Catalogs."[9]

"IAC Issues New Product, Expands CD-ROMs"[10]

" 'Virtual Library' Emerges at Columbia Law Library"[11]

"PLs and Phone Company in CT Offer Information Service"[12]

"*Books In Print* to Be Bowker's First 'Intelligent' Database"[13]

"UMI Unveils New Database Products"[14]

What are some possibilities for the future? A report published in 1984 about California telecommunications in the year 1990 made eight predictions regarding libraries in the state. Most of these predictions could apply to any library in the United States, or any country where telecommunications are undergoing rapid development. I have noted the degree to which those predictions were true for California, as of early 1993, in the following statements:

Prediction #1: Over three quarters of public library records will be machine readable and available through a statewide online network. [Although it is not yet at the 75 percent level, it is over 50 percent and there are multiple networks in existence.]

Prediction #2: Academic and public libraries using online systems will be linked together regardless of their bibliographic utilities memberships. [This is not yet a reality, however, libraries are making progress in this area. There is still a long way to go.]

Prediction #3: Over 75 percent of all interlibrary correspondence will be handled using electronic mail (e-mail) systems, rather than the U.S. Postal Service. [Certainly there is a growing use of online e-mail systems, however, at the moment the real competitor for the postal service is fax equipment. It will be some time before e-mail carries 75 percent of the interlibrary correspondence.]

Prediction #4: Use of videotext will be widespread among California residents (60 percent) and many (40 percent) will gain access to library information through videotext services. [This has not yet taken place.]

Prediction #5: Libraries will use satellite systems heavily. Thirty percent will have receiving equipment installed for use in teleconferencing. [While a number of libraries do have this capability now, less than 10 percent of all California libraries have satellite systems.]

Prediction #6: Cable television services from libraries will expand in both the number of libraries offering services and in the variety of services available. [Because the authors did not predict a percentage, this is true. However, the percentage of libraries offering cable programs is very small.]

Prediction #7: Use of microcomputers continues to grow in libraries, and collections of software will become more common. [This is true, if one counts CD-ROMs as software. Not many libraries have large collections of computer software that circulate. There are, however, an increasing number of print items (books and journals) that include computer disks. The reader is to use the software with the textual material in an integrated fashion.]

Prediction #8: Government information will be less available in print form and will be increasingly distributed online—libraries will be the primary public access point. [This is slowly taking place, although less as online information and more as an electronic format designed for use on a PC.][15]

With some of the above predictions materializing by 1993, others are open to debate. One debate centers on which organization should be the information delivery agent. Should it be a library or a profit-oriented organization? It is not a question of should the service exist, but who will operate the delivery system. Until the question is resolved some of these predictions will remain unfulfilled.

Another interesting set of predictions appeared in the March 1985 issue of *Online*. Jack W. Simpson, president of Mead Data Corporation, wrote a guest editorial in which he listed 10 megatrends for information. Again, my comments appear within the square brackets.

Prediction #1: Information is becoming a strategic weapon. [In some areas it always has been. The difference is we recognize it as such more often today than in the past.]

Prediction #2: Ownership of information is at the root of a growing world conflict between government and private enterprise. [In the United States, the conflict is primarily between the information producers and information users, rather than between government and private enterprise.]

Prediction #3: Information is no longer free. [Perhaps a better way of stating this is to say access to information is becoming less available as a free service for such institutions as libraries. Information has always cost something, if nothing more than the labor to collect and organize it.]

Prediction #4: All high value information will be available in digital form. [This may depend on how a person defines "high value." To date this is a trend, not an accomplished fact.]

Prediction #5: A worldwide "megalibrary" of electronic information is emerging. [Such a library is still well beyond the horizon. There are several databases available internationally; however, the prediction suggests an integrated system which we have yet to see.]

Prediction #6: Intelligent electronic books will evolve to access the "megalibrary." [We are just beginning to see "hand held" electronic books, and currently there is no "megalibrary."]

Prediction #7: New technology will reshape our concepts of privacy, security, and property. [This is an area of concern for everyone. A related issue is who will or does assure the integrity of the information in databases?]

Prediction #8: Exchange of information through shared networks will break down barriers of geography and culture. [The potential exists, but economic conditions and political interests and needs make progress very slow.]

Prediction #9: A conflict over control will occur between end-users and the MIS (management information systems) function. [This is happening more often alongside conflicts between end-users and the owners of information.]

Prediction #10: Librarians and information specialists are becoming a major force in helping end-users interface with the megalibrary. [This is happening and will continue to take place.]

Most of the above predictions could be made today and still appear forward-reaching. While technology changes quickly, people and society are much slower to change. Nevertheless, changes are taking place in the way individuals view, use, and think about information.

The nature of information collections is changing both in terms of formats collected and in ways of providing access to the information. But high tech information services and databases still consist of "collections of information." What to include and what to exclude from the collection must be decided. *Someone* has to acquire the information in some manner, as well as maintain the collection. Maintaining the collection usually involves making certain the information is current and older information is discarded or stored in a manner that indicates the information is old.

If the service is fee based, someone must monitor users' needs and interests to assure the database reflects what the information buyers want. These are the basic steps of collection development, so collection development will not disappear when the "high technology information center" finally becomes a reality. Even Raymond Kurzweil, in spite of his suggestion about "virtual physical relations," acknowledges the librarian will still have the function of selecting materials for the virtual collection.[16]

Whatever form the future megalibrary may take, it is certain that its basis will be a collection of information resources. Unless there is a plan for what the collection will contain, the megalibrary will have limited, if any, value. The purpose of this book is to assist individuals in gaining an understanding of the process of developing an intelligent and useful collection for the end-users of the collection.

Concepts and Terms

Several concepts and terms need defining as I use them in this text. Starting with some basic general terms, such as *information*, and ending with a specific concept such as *collection management*, this section provides a foundation for the remainder of the book. As in the 2d edition, I have tried to present a generic picture of collection development—without tying it to any particular institutional or organizational form (e.g., the library).

Information is the recognition of patterns in the flow of matter and energy reaching an individual or organization. All flows of matter and energy have the capability of carrying patterned signals. Information is present only when a person recognizes the pattern. Each person then develops a set of recognized patterns, and not everyone recognizes the same patterns or necessarily interprets a given pattern in the same way. For example, a strange noise in an automobile may mean nothing to a driver, but to a trained auto mechanic the sound indicates that the "universal joint needs servicing" (information). Two other examples of pattern recognition are "well logs" (records of drilling operations) and "spectrum analysis." To the untrained person a well log is meaningless and of no value. To a geologist or other trained professional, these long strips of paper are an invaluable source of information about subsurface conditions and formations. Depending upon how the person interprets the information, it may save, cost, or earn thousands or even millions of dollars for a company.

For astronomers, colors in a spectrum analysis convey information about the distance, movement, and composition of stars. To the layperson, a spectrum analysis is simply an interesting or pretty display of color.

Involvement in the *information cycle* (see fig. 1.1) is a constant for everyone as matter and energy flow by us. "Objects" emit patterned signals that flow past us (subjects). We identify the signals and evaluate the patterns based on experience. We ignore most of the signals and act only when the pattern provides information. When a person receives an information (action) signal, he or she implements the action that will provide satisfaction.

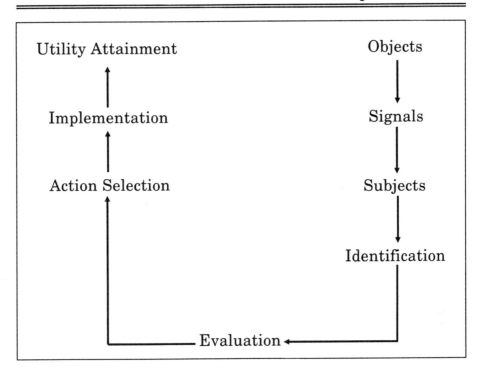

Fig. 1.1. The information cycle.

The information cycle is very similar to the human communication model that most of us learned about in one or more of our undergraduate courses. For human communication to take place, a person must express the information patterns, in a symbolic form, that other people know and understand. True human communication only occurs when two or more people share a symbol-referent system. Figure 1.2, on page 10, illustrates the components of the communication model.

The sender, wishing to communicate with the receiver, has an idea or feeling (a "meaning") which she or he encodes by selecting the appropriate symbols representing the desired meaning. This process creates the message. After encoding, the sender selects the means of delivering the message (channel)—written, oral, pictorial. On the receiver's side, the message arrives and is decoded, and a meaning is assigned to the message. When the process is completed, a communication has taken place; however, this does not necessarily imply that the sender's intended meaning is identical to the meaning the receiver assigned to the message. As is true of the information cycle, a single symbol may have multiple meanings. The more abstract the idea a person wishes to communicate, the more likely it is that "noise" somewhere in the system will distort the two meanings. Some common noise factors for people include differences in education, experiences, and mental state. Normally, the general meaning will be the same, but often the general meaning is not adequate and

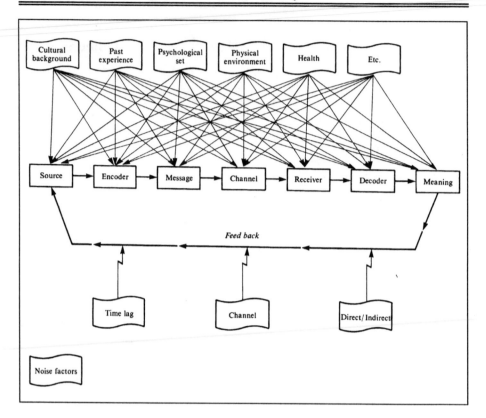

Fig. 1.2. Communication model demonstrating noise factors.

an identical meaning is required. The "feedback" loop provides a mechanism that allows people to clarify meanings, so that closer if not identical meaning and understanding can be achieved. Because an information center or library may work with all forms of human communication, some knowledge of the communication model is helpful in a variety of ways. Later in this volume such issues as conducting needs assessments, developing collection policies, evaluating collections, and handling complaints are examined. All of these activities involve the communication process (model), and remembering to use the feedback loop to verify meaning and to control system "noise" will make the library or information center a more effective service organization.

The term *organization* is used in this volume in two ways. One meaning, and the least often used, refers to the process of arranging information, knowledge, and materials in some logical manner for ease of retrieval. The second and more frequently used meaning relates to people and draws on work by a well-known management writer, Chester Barnard. Barnard's work on human organization is extensive and a simplified explanation of his concept follows.

Human organization, according to Barnard, consists of five basic elements: *size, interdependence, input, throughput,* and *output.*[17] An organization can vary in *size* from one as large as the United States federal government to one as small as two people. The size factor is important for information service work because there is often a tendency not to consider two or three people working together as an organization. Barnard's model does not include any time factor—if all five elements are present, an organization could exist for just a few hours or for centuries. What differentiates a group of two or more people from an organization of two or more people arises from the other elements. *Interdependence* requires the recognition of the existence of one or more shared or common goals. And, that by working together (cooperating), the achievement of these goals will be easier, faster, or in some manner beneficial to everyone in the organization. Disagreement and tension can be and usually are present, but the value of mutually shared benefits holds the organization together. Once the organization sets its goals, it must acquire the material, energy, money, and information (*input*) needed to accomplish the goals. After acquiring the resources, the organization attempts to utilize the resources (*throughput*) effectively to achieve the desired results. The end product of the processing activities is the *output* that the organization disseminates. Output can be as tangible as an automobile or as intangible as ideas that may help people to create a safer environment.

Information is one of the resources organizations acquire to accomplish desired goals. The information will be in one of four forms: *data, text, image,* or *sound.* Most organizations use all four forms, and a library or information center serving the organization should be ready and able to handle all forms of information. More new technologies are drawing these four forms closer together and sometime in the not too distant future there may be an "integrated information resource" (see fig. 1.3 on page 12). The computer is rather like the steam engine at the start of the Industrial Revolution—it is the power source for the integration process. Scanning equipment is becoming more sophisticated and capable of recognizing printed words and converting the recognized patterns into oral presentations (speech synthesizers). Videotext and teletext are other examples of the blending of forms taking place.

Some years ago, S. D. Neill published an article questioning the information role for the library. Neill suggested that the appropriate role is the knowledge center.[18] Which role one selects depends largely on how one defines the concepts. In addition to information, one must define *knowledge* and *wisdom. Knowledge* is the result of linking together a number of pieces of information into meaningful patterns. *Wisdom* is the ability to draw accurate conclusions from the available information and knowledge. Knowledge and wisdom are individual (personal) processes and what may be knowledge for one person may be information for someone else. In my opinion, libraries and information centers can supply information, including recorded knowledge and wisdom. We can inform but it is up to users to gain knowledge and wisdom.

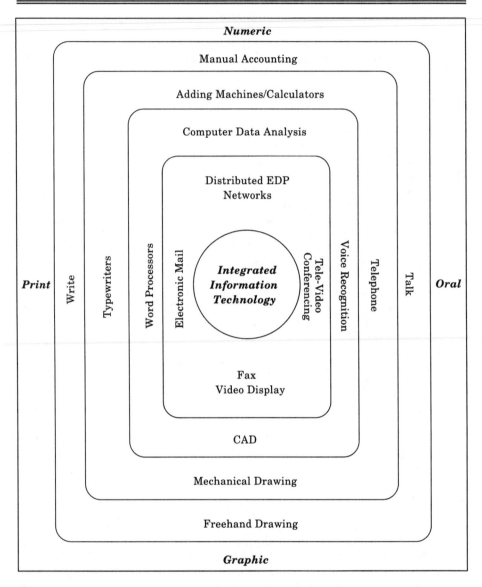

Fig. 1.3. Convergence of information technology and organizational information processing.

Robert S. Taylor proposed a more complex hierarchy. Taylor's "value added hierarchy" consists of five levels: the lowest level is *data*, followed by *information, informing knowledge, productive knowledge,* and *action.* Although his primary concern is with the means by which value is associated with information, a topic beyond the scope of this book, anyone interested in developing collections should read this article. *Informing knowledge* is similar to the definition of knowledge given above. *Productive knowledge* is "a judgmental process, where options are presented and advantages and disadvantages weighed."[19] Personal definitions of various terms (such as data, information, knowledge, and wisdom), as well as one's beliefs about the role of the library or information center, affects the type of collection one builds.

Another important factor is the *organizational environment* of the library or information center. Almost 30 years ago F. Emery and E. L. Trist identified four basic types of organizational environments: *placid-randomized, placid-clustered, disturbed-reactive,* and *turbulent.*[20] Although not directly concerned with information, Emery and Trist's descriptions of the environments do indicate how the environment would affect information work. A *placid-randomized* environment, for example, is one in which the organization assumes both the goals and dangers are basically unchanging. Organizational goals are long term and seldom in need of adjustment. Such organizations assume changes or dangers to its well-being occur randomly and there is little or no predictability as to when such a change or danger will be encountered. A danger is something that would adversely affect the viability of the organization. In such an environment, the organization collects information to meet long-term goals. These goals would be considered very predictable, making collection development relatively easy. Museum collections and archives are examples of organizations operating in a placid-randomized environment; at least this was the case in the past. Today, and for the future, it does not seem likely that many organizations will be operating in such an environment.

Many libraries and information centers operate in a *placid-clustered* environment. Emery and Trist defined this environment as one where goals are primarily long term, but the organization quickly adjusts the goals if there is a significant change in the external factors. In such an environment, the organization assumes dangers and to some extent opportunities arise in clusters. Further, they assume the need to expend some effort in identifying and collecting information about the clusters. With collection development, this means there is a body of relatively unchanging organizational goals, but some time, energy, and money would go toward identifying and collecting information that might affect the goals. Most educational institutions and public libraries are operating in this type of environment. They set long-term goals and rarely change the goals, although they may change short-term objectives. However, they do recognize dangers exist, such as changing public attitudes about the value of social services in general, and library services specifically. Once the questioning starts, it generally expands in scope (clustering) and does not disappear quickly. Also, new service opportunities arise as new technologies become available that may be appropriate for the institution to use, which may counteract some or all of the dangers (e.g., competition) arising from the new technologies.

Disturbed-reactive environments are those in which active competitors to the organization exist. In this environment, having prompt, accurate information about what the competitors are doing, and when possible what they are planning to do, is very important. While the organization has long-term goals, it revises its goals in light of information received about competitors' activities. Business and industrial libraries (special) operate in such an environment. Here four or five years may represent a significant amount of time for long-term collection goals. However, the library or information center devotes significant resources to determining what the competition is doing.

Finally, there is the *turbulent* environment. Not only do competitors exist, but the level of competition becomes a competition for survival. As a result of knowing what others are doing or planning to do, an organization may make a radical change in its basic purposes. Anyone who reads the business section of a newspaper encounters examples of organizations that made successful basic goal changes and those that failed because they did not change. On a slightly less extreme level, an information center or library serving a research and development team experiences occasional abrupt shifts in collecting emphasis, partly due to the knowledge gained from the information collected about the competitions' work and progress. Thus, the organization environment is also an information environment, and the nature of the environment affects the nature of the collection development activities.

With this background we can now look at how organizations and individuals process information. Figure 1.4 is a representation of how this process works; space 1 indicates the totality of matter and energy surrounding an organization or individual. The line separating spaces 1 and 2 represents the boundary between noise and patterned signals (information) as identified by a person or organization. A person or organization identifies only a small portion of the total flow as information. As the information environment changes so does the boundary between 1 and 2. A portion of what the individual or organization identifies as information is of sufficient importance to store it for a short time. Space 3 represents the short-term information storage area. Of that total, the person or organization selects a smaller amount of information for long-term/indefinite retention (space 4). The dotted line within space 4 creates an area labeled 5, which represents the information that a person or organization uses from long storage and disseminates to the external environment.

On an individual level, in the United States anyone who receives mail for any length of time uses the above process. Almost every time a person picks up the mail (the total flow), there is an assortment of material in the delivery. The person recognizes each piece as an attempt at communication. Some material is not within the boundary of information, as defined by the person in question, and is thus noise (space 1). Items in this category go straight into the trash. Other pieces may be about something of interest but not of immediate high interest (space 2). Items in this category go into the trash as well, but there is a slight pause as the person completes the information cycle and selects the desired course of action. A few pieces may relate to something of some interest, and the person sets this material aside for later consideration when there is time. Depending upon the person, days or weeks or even months go by before he or she looks at the material again. More often than not, as a result of a changed environment, this material also ends up in the wastebasket. A few of the items that a person or an entire organization identifies as information receives long-term retention. The person files a few items for safekeeping or later action (for example insurance policies, legal documents, and letters from friends and family) (space 4). Of the total retained in this manner, only a few (usually bills) will require or motivate a person to process the information and respond (space 5).

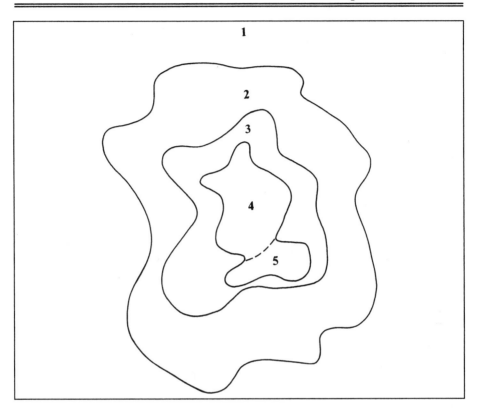

Fig. 1.4. Organizational processing of information: 1) Matter and energy surrounding an organization or individual; 2) Boundary between noise and patterned signals (information); 3) Short-term information storage area; 4) Long-term/indefinite retention of information; 5) Information that an organization or individual uses from long-term storage and disseminates to the external environment.

Libraries and information centers engage in exactly the same process. No organization can take in and process every patterned signal. They all draw some line that separates information from noise. Where the organization draws the line depends upon the nature of its activities and its information environment. The line might be drawn in terms of language, subject matter, depth of treatment, format, or combinations of factors. Even within the defined limits, only a portion of the total information is stored. Organizations acquire and store some items for short periods because their value to the organization is short-term due to changing interests, or because the information becomes dated. Libraries and information centers normally acquire and store more information for long periods of time than the organization will use and/or disseminate to the external environment. The percentage allocated to long-term retention varies among organizations. Organizations operating in a placid-randomized environment normally have a large percentage of retained but unused or disseminated information (50 percent or more). At the other end of the spectrum (turbulent) there should be and usually is very little difference between the two categories. Archives and research libraries are at the high retention/low dissemination end of the spectrum while information centers and libraries in profit organizations are usually the opposite, low retention/high dissemination.

The primary purpose of libraries and information centers is to assist in the transfer of information and the development of knowledge. Figure 1.5 illustrates the process involved using nine circles to represent the transfer

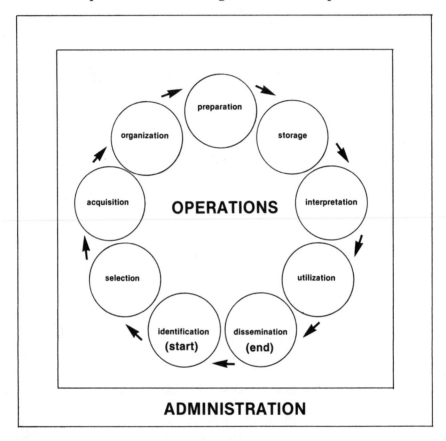

Fig. 1.5. Information transfer work.

cycle. Information transfer is an elaboration of the basic information cycle described earlier. There is the *identification* stage, during which the organization segregates appropriate from inappropriate information. In most instances, there is more appropriate information available than the organization can handle. Thus, there is a need to *select* the most appropriate or important information to *acquire*. After acquisition, the organization *organizes* the information in some manner. Upon completion of the organizing action comes the *preparation* of the information for *storage*, which should mean the information is easily retrievable. Users often need assistance in describing their needs in a manner that leads to locating and retrieving the desired information (*interpretation*). Finally, users draw upon the secured information to aid them in their activities/work (*utilization*) and disseminate the outcome of the work to the internal or external environment or both. In order for the transfer process to function properly, there must be procedures, policies, and people in place to carry out the necessary *operational* steps. As always, there must be coordination and money for the operations to do what they were set up to do; this is the *administrative* and managerial aspect of information work.

The foregoing discussion helps set the stage for this book, which focuses on the process of building information collections for long- and short-term storage. Collection development, or information acquisition, is one area common to both librarianship and information resource management. In the first edition, I defined collection development as "the process of identifying the strengths and weaknesses of a library's materials collection in terms of patron needs and community resources and attempting to correct existing weaknesses, if any." With only minor modifications the definition can apply to both libraries and information collections in any organization. Thus, *collection development* is the process of meeting the information needs of the people (a service population) in a timely and economic manner using information resources locally held as well as from other organizations. This new definition is broader in scope and places emphasis on thoughtful (timely and economic) collection building and on seeking out both internal and external information resources. It is worth noting that Ross Atkinson suggests that the phrases *collection development* and *collection management* are being used interchangeably and that there is no consensus on which term is more comprehensive in scope.[21]

Collection development is a universal process for libraries and information centers. Figure 1.6, on page 18, illustrates the six major components of the process. One can see there is a relationship between figures 1.5 and 1.6 in that collection development involves three of the nine information transfer elements (identification, selection, acquisition). As implied by the circle, collection development is a constant cycle that continues as long as the library or information center exists. All of the elements in the cycle will be discussed in subsequent chapters.

Because of my philosophy of collection development, that is, a focus on meeting the information needs of the community the collection serves, I begin the discussion of collection development with the needs assessment (community analysis) element. The terms *needs assessment, community analysis,* or *patron community* throughout this book mean the group of persons that the library exists to serve. They do *not* only refer to the active users, but also include everyone within the library's or information center's defined service limits. Thus, a community might be an entire political unit (i.e., a nation, region, state, province, county, city, or town), or a more specialized grouping or association (i.e., a university, college, school, government agency, or private organization). Also, the number of patrons that the library is to serve may range from very few to millions. Discussed in chapter 2, data for the analysis comes from a variety of sources, not just staff-generated material. For collection development personnel, the assessment process provides data on what information the clientele needs. It also establishes a valuable mechanism for patron input into the process of collection development. (Note the size of the arrow in figure 1.6 from the community to collection development, the size indicating the level of patron input appropriate for each element.)

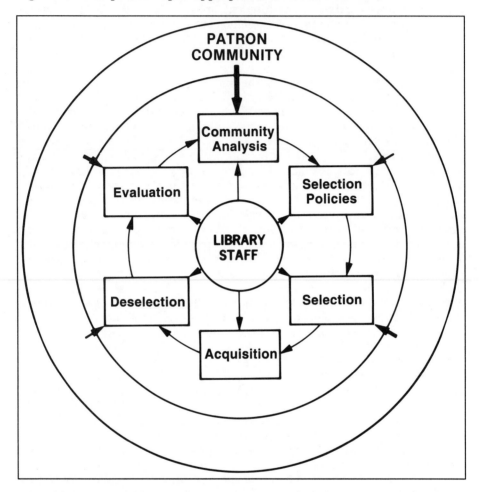

Fig. 1.6. Collection development process.

One use for the data collected for a needs assessment is as part of the preparation for a collection development policy. Clearly delineated policies on both collection development and selection (covered in chapter 3) provide collection development staff with guidelines for choosing items for inclusion in the collection. (Note that collection policies cover a wider range of topics than just selection policies. For example, *selection* policies normally provide only information useful in deciding which items to purchase, while *collection* policies cover that topic and such related issues as gifts, weeding, and cooperation.) Most libraries have some of the required information available for their collection development personnel, although they do not always label it "policy." Some libraries call it an *acquisitions* policy; some a *selection* policy; some a *collection development* policy; and others simply a *statement*. Whatever the local label, the intent is the same: to define the library's goals for its collection(s) and to help staff members select and acquire the most appropriate materials.

At this point the staff begins the procedures for selecting materials (covered in chapters 4, 5, 8, 9, and 10) using whatever written policies or statements its library has prepared. For many people, this is the most interesting element in the collection development process. One constant factor in collection development is there is never enough money available to buy everything that might be of value to the service community. Naturally, this means that someone, usually one or more professional staff members, must decide which items to buy. *Selection* is the process of deciding which materials to acquire for a library collection. It may involve deciding among items that provide information about the same subject; deciding whether the information contained in an item is worth the price; or deciding whether an item could stand up to the use it would receive. In essence, it is a matter of systematically determining quality and value. Selection is a form of decision making. Most of the time it is not just a matter of identifying appropriate materials, but of deciding among items that are essential, important, needed, marginal, nice, or luxurious. Where to place any item in the sequence from essential to luxurious depends, of course, on the individual selector's point of view. It's just a matter of perception. So it is with library materials.

An individual buying an item normally does not have to justify the expenditure to anyone. However, when it is a question of spending the library community's money, whether derived from taxes or a company's budget, the problem is more complex. The question of whose perception of value to use is one of the challenges in collection development. Needs assessments and policies help determine the answer, but a long-standing question in the field is, How much emphasis should selectors place on clientele demand and how much on content quality? Often the question of perception comes up when someone objects to the presence of an item in the collection (see chapter 19).

Once the selectors make their decisions, the acquisition work begins (see chapters 11, 12, and13.) *Acquisition work* is the process of securing materials for the library's collection, whether by purchase, as gifts, or through exchange programs. This is the only point in the collection development process involving little or no community input; it is a fairly straightforward business operation. Once the staff decides to purchase an item, the acquisition department proceeds with the preparation of an order form, the selection of a vendor, eventually recording the receipt of the item, and finally paying the bill (invoice). While details vary, the basic routines remain the same around the world, just as they do in either a manual or automated work environment. (Note that *acquisition* does not always mean buying an item. Gift and exchange programs are also useful means of acquiring needed material.)

After receipt an item goes through a series of internal library operations (beyond the scope of this book) such as cataloging, and is eventually available to the patron community. But over time, nearly every item outlives its original usefulness in the collection. Often the decision is to remove these items from the main collection. The activity of examining items in the library and determining their current value to that library's collection (and to the service community) has several labels, the oldest being *weeding* (see chapter 14). Another term for the process is *deselection* (the opposite of selection). In England, the term is *stock relegation*. When a library decides that a given item is no longer of value, it will dispose of the item (by selling it, giving it away, or even throwing it away). If the item still has some value for the library, the decision may be to transfer the item to a less accessible and usually less expensive storage location.

Evaluation (see chapter 15) is the last element in the collection development process. To some extent, weeding is an evaluative activity, but weeding is also more of an internal library operation. Evaluation of a collection may serve many different purposes, both inside and outside the library. For example, it may help to increase funding for the library. It may aid in the library's gaining some form of recognition, such as high standing in a comparative survey. Or, it may help to determine the quality of the work done by the collection development staff. In order for effective evaluation to occur, one must take the service community's needs into consideration, which leads back to community analysis.

There is little reason to define library materials other than to emphasize that this volume covers various formats, not just books. Different authors writing about library collections use a number of related terms: *print, nonprint, visual materials, audiovisuals, a-v, other media,* and so on. There is no single term encompassing all forms that has gained universal acceptance among librarians. *Library materials* (or simply, materials) is a nonspecific term with respect to format, while being otherwise inclusive. Thus, it is used throughout the text. Library materials may include books, periodicals, pamphlets, reports, manuscripts, microformats, motion pictures, video- or audiotapes, sound recordings, realia, and so forth. In effect, almost any physical object that conveys information, thoughts, or feelings potentially can be part of an information collection.

Two last terms need to be defined: *collection management* and *information resource management*. The terms cover similar activities and differ primarily in organizational context. *Collection management*, as used today, relates to a library environment (in the traditional sense); where the emphasis is on collecting materials produced by other organizations. *Information resource management*, as used today, relates to any organizational context, often without any centralized collection of materials, in which the information resource manager is responsible for identifying and making available both internal and external sources of information. Both terms incorporate all aspects of collection development discussed earlier, plus such managerial aspects as budget planning and control, staffing, and physical facilities. For both collection management and information resource management, the goal is to provide accurate information in a timely and cost-effective manner to all members of the service community.

Collection Development and the Community

Several factors inside and outside the library influence collection development. Among these factors are the library's structure and organization, the production and distribution of the information materials, and the presence of other libraries in the area. Figure 1.7, on page 22, illustrates some of the interrelationships among the library organization, the producers and distributors of materials, and other libraries.

Traditionally, libraries organized their internal activities into public and technical services. Those activities in which the staff has daily contact with patrons are public services; almost all other activities are technical services. Collection development very often bridges this traditional division. With increased automation of library functions the boundaries between public and technical services are disappearing. In fact, they are becoming so undefined that some libraries are doing away with these labels. The library staff responsible for collection development provides information to the acquisition department (usually classed as a technical service), which in turn orders the desired items from the materials producer or a distributor. After receiving the materials and clearing the records, the acquisition department sends the items on to the cataloging department for processing. Eventually, the processed items go on to shelves or into cabinets where the public can use them. Both the public service staff and the patrons using the collections provide input to the collection development staff concerning the value of individual items. The selection staff then considers the input when performing deselection and evaluation activities. The information generated from these sources may eventually influence the library's written policies for collection development.

Materials producers exert many significant influences. Obviously they control what is available for library purchase by their choice of whether or not to produce any given item. (Chapter 6 describes some of the factors considered in making such a decision.) Furthermore, their business requirements occasionally cause libraries to modify their acquisition procedures; however, most producers and vendors are very good about accommodating unusual library requirements. Finally, producers market their products directly to the patron community, thus generating a demand. Patrons often communicate this demand to the library rather than buying the item, thus causing an indirect response to the marketing activities of the materials producers.

Collections and services in other libraries and information centers used by the service population also influence collection development. Cooperative collection development programs enable libraries to provide better service, a wider range of materials, or both. Cooperative projects also can reduce duplication of materials that results from overlapping service communities and patron influence on collection development. For example, a person might engage in business research while in the company's library. The person may take evening classes at an academic institution, using that library for class-related and business-related materials alike. That same individual may also rely on a local public library—because of its convenience—to supply information on both job-related and recreational concerns. Thus, one person's requests for job-related materials could influence three different types of libraries in the same area to collect the same material. Despite numerous advantages, working out effective cooperative programs can still be difficult (see chapter 16 for discussion).

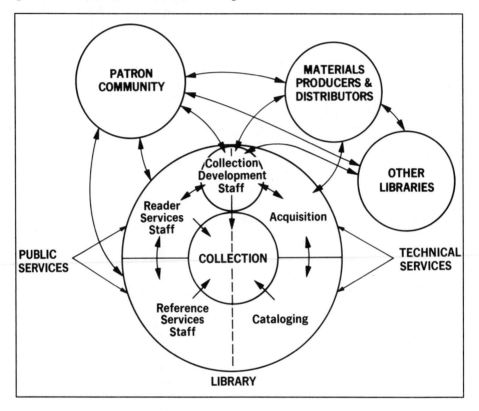

Fig. 1.7. Collection development, the library, and the community.

Collection Development and Institutional Environments

The variety of institutional settings in which one finds information services is large. However, it is possible to discuss a few general categories: education, business, government, and research. These categories share some basic characteristics. They have a specific service population, they collect and preserve materials in a form suitable for use by the service population, and they organize materials in a manner designed to aid in the rapid identification and retrieval of the desired material(s). The definitions given earlier also apply to all of these categories. Differences emerge because of both the specific service population and the limits set by the library's or information center's governing body.

Collection development is a universal process for all types of libraries. But as one moves from one environmental setting to another, differences in emphasis on the various elements of the collection development process become apparent. For example, some education (school) and government (public) libraries tend to place more emphasis on library staff selection activities than do business and research libraries. Also, differences in emphasis occur within a type, so that occasionally a community college library (education) might more closely resemble a large public library (government) in its collection development activities than it does a university library (education). The approach taken in this book is to present an overview, and when necessary note the differences among and within the types.

To some extent, the chapters in this book reflect these differences in emphasis. For several reasons, needs analysis is very important in public and school libraries, as well as in information centers (in a business), and receives less emphasis in college and university libraries. In public libraries, selection is usually the responsibility of librarians, whereas in other types of information centers patrons have a stronger direct voice in the selection process. Public libraries need the information derived from such an analysis in order to build an effective collection; therefore chapter 2 on information needs assessment has a public librarys slant.

The size of a library's service community has a definite bearing on collection development. There are three facts of collection development that are universal:

1. As the size of the service community increases, the degree of divergence in individual information needs increases.

2. As the degree of divergence in individual information needs increases, the need for cooperative programs of information materials sharing increases.

3. It will never be possible to satisfy *all* of the information needs of any individual or class of clientele in the service community.

Even special libraries and information centers, serving a limited number of persons, encounter problems in relation to these laws. Because no two persons are identical, it is impossible for their materials needs and interests to coincide entirely. In the special library environment, the interests of patrons can be and often are very similar, but even within a team of research workers exploring a single problem, individual needs will vary. The needs of a small group are not as homogeneous as they may at first appear.

The element of collection development that varies the least is collection development policy. Simply put, as the collection grows in size, the need for more complex and detailed policy statements increases. Thus, large academic and research libraries generally have the most comprehensive collection policy statements.

Selection is the element in which the greatest variations exist among and within the types. Due to those many variations, it is difficult to identify the many generalizations. However, with that in mind, the following are some general statements about the variations:

1. Public libraries emphasize title-by-title selection, and librarians do the selecting.

2. School libraries also emphasize title-by-title selection. While the media specialist may make the final decision, a committee composed of librarians, teachers, administrators, and parents may have a strong voice in the process.

3. Special and corporate libraries select materials in rather narrow subject fields for specific research and business purposes. Often the client is the primary selector.

4. Academic libraries select materials in subject areas for educational and research purposes, with selection done by several different methods: faculty only, joint faculty/library committees, librarians only, or subject specialists.

The size of the collection is also a factor in determining the who and the how of selection. In small public libraries, most of the librarians do some selection work. (Very often there is only one librarian to do all the professional work.) As the library system grows, adds branches, and expands services, the library director delegates work. More often than not it is the department heads and branch library supervisors who have selection responsibilities. Large metropolitan systems frequently assign selection activities to a committee composed of representatives from all of the service programs, though not always from every branch. This committee generates a list of titles from which individual services and branches select. In essence, the book selection committee does the initial screening and identification work for the system.

A similar relationship of size and selection exists in academic libraries and some special libraries. However, the selectors in these cases, more often than not, are the users—academic faculty or company staff. Even when librarians are responsible for selection in libraries serving institutions with hundreds of subject specialists, the faculty members or researchers have a significant voice in the selection process. Obviously, the in-depth knowledge of a subject specialist can become the deciding factor in making a selection. A common practice in both types of libraries is to hire librarians with graduate degrees in both librarianship and one other subject area. Even then, because of the advanced and sometimes esoteric nature of the research reported in the materials, the library must draw on all of the subject expertise at the institution.

In small academic and special libraries, selection is in the hands of the subject specialist (faculty or researcher), unless the librarian is also an expert in the field. Indeed, small academic institutions often expect the teaching faculty to build the library collection. As budgets for materials increase and as the collection grows proportionally, the librarians become more involved in selection activities.

Eventually a collection will fill all available shelf space. Some time before that happens the library must decide how to reduce the collection size (deselection) or create additional storage space. In school and public libraries, this does not present a great problem; patrons often wear out popular items, freeing up shelf space. Often such libraries buy multiple copies of items. Then, by keeping just one copy after demand drops, they regain some shelf space. Also, only the exceptionally large public libraries have major archival responsibilities; thus, weeding is somewhat easier. Academic and research libraries seldom buy multiple copies or have significant archival responsibilities, making deselection an involved process. Special (business) libraries perform deselection on a regular basis because of space limitations. Often this results in rules for weeding. (For instance, discard all monographs that are five years old.) Rules of this kind help to solve one problem: lack of staff time for deselection. But they may increase the demand for the interlibrary loan of items discarded as a result of this less thoughtful approach to the problem. More research has been performed on weeding/deselection in academic libraries than for all of the other types of libraries combined, and chapter 14 reflects this with its emphasis on academic libraries.

Although the final phase of the process—collection evaluation—takes place in all types of libraries, it is especially significant in libraries serving education organizations. One form of evaluation is by an outside agency that determines the quality of education provided (accreditation) by schools and academic institutions. If nothing more, the agency (government or private) that funds the institution will require periodic assessments, which will invariably include the library and its collection. For such libraries, the evaluation process may have far-reaching effects. Naturally, librarians in educational institutions have a strong interest in improving the evaluation process, and they have written a great deal about the topic. Chapter 15 draws heavily upon this literature, as well as the literature on accreditation.

Every organization and person needs and uses information to survive. The way in which organizations locate, collect, and store information ranges from unstructured chance encounters to a tightly structured, carefully planned process. In the latter case, the organization usually creates a library or information center to handle the work. Collection building requires considerable resources; furthermore, the ways the library organizes, stores, and retrieves the information can be vital to the success of the organization. The definitions in this chapter and the concepts described in this book form the foundation upon which one actively develops a collection of information materials to meet the specific needs of an individual or community.

Collection development is a dynamic process that should involve both the information professional and the service community. Few information professionals question the need or value of client input; the question is how much should there be? The best answer is, as much as the organization can handle and still carry out its basic functions and as much as the community is willing to provide. The following statements are the philosophical foundations of this work.

1. Collection development should be geared primarily to identified needs rather than to abstract standards of quality; however, an identified need can be a long-term need (more than five years into the future), not just an immediate need.

2. Collection development, to be effective, must be responsive to the *total* community's needs, not just to those of the current or the most active users.

3. Collection development should be carried out with knowledge of and participation in cooperative programs at the local, regional, state, national, and international levels.

4. Collection development should consider all information formats for inclusion in the collection.

5. Collection development was, is, and always will be subjective, biased work. A periodic review of the selector's personal biases and their effects on the selection process is the best check against developing a collection that reflects personal interests rather than customer interests.

6. Collection development is not learned entirely in the classroom or from reading. Only through practice, taking risks, and learning from mistakes will a person become proficient in the process of developing a collection.

Summary

Technology is changing the way libraries and information centers go about doing business. A term that gained popularity after 1990 is *virtual library* or *knowledge center*. Recently some writers have used the phrase in ways that negate the original meaning, which was:

> a system by which a user may connect transparently to remote libraries and databases using the local library's online catalog or a university or network computer gateway. Eventually, a user will be able to enter a query, get a cup of coffee, and let the computer check all the databases on the network to retrieve an answer.[22]

Some writers, as noted earlier, suggest the virtual library means the demise of collection development. However, those who understand the concept know that the issue of selection and collection building will remain an important function in whatever environment technology will bring.

One can engage in collection development in libraries and information centers that are formally or informally organized. Although organization labels will vary, the process is the same. Most large organizations now view information and its management and control to be as essential as any other resource they employ. In fact, obtaining the right information at the right time—and being able to analyze and apply it successfully—is crucial to an organization's success and survival. As a result, organizations are training and hiring people who know how to acquire and manage the organization's information resources. While some organizations may not call these individuals librarians—and they may not work in libraries—they need and use many of the same skills librarians traditionally employ in collection building. Whatever environment one works in, collection development is an exciting challenge that requires lifelong learning. One way of keeping up-to-date is to subscribe to a listserve such as Library Collection Development List (COLLDV-L@USC.VM).

Notes

[1] Octavio Paz, *The Other Voice: Essays on Modern Poetry* (San Diego, Calif.: Harcourt Brace Jovanovich, 1991), 88.

[2] Raymond Kurzweil, "The Virtual Library," *Library Journal* 119 (March 15, 1993): 55.

[3] James Lictenberg, "Reading: Does the Future Even Require It?" *Liberal Education* 79 (Winter 1993): 11.

[4] Paz, *The Other Voice*, 88.

[5] EBSCO personal communication.

[6] Patricia Sabosik, "Document Delivery Services: Today's Electronic Scriptoria," *Computers in Libraries* 12 (December 1992): 16-17.

[7] William Gibson, *Agrippa: A Book of the Dead* (New York: Kevin Begos Publishing, 1992).

[8] Hugh Donaghue, "Implications of Transborder Data Flow to Library Networks." (Paper delivered at the 48th International Federation of Library Associations General Conference, Montreal, Quebec, IFLA, 1982): 6.

[9] *Library Hotline* 21 (December 14, 1992): 2.

[10] *Library Hotline* 22 (February 8, 1993): 6.

[11] *Library Hotline* 22 (February 15, 1993): 2.

[12] *Library Hotline* 22 (February 22, 1993): 3.

[13] *Library Hotline* 22 (March 1, 1993): 3.

[14] *Library Hotline* 22 (March 1, 1993): 4.

[15]"Public Sector Telecommunications in California" (San Diego, CA: Center for Communications, San Diego State University, 1983): 27-28.

[16]Kurzweil, "The Virtual Library," 55.

[17]Chester Barnard, *Organization and Management* (Cambridge, MA: Harvard University Press, 1956).

[18]S. D. Neill, "Knowledge or Information—A Crisis of Purpose in Libraries," *Canadian Library Journal* 39 (April 1982): 69-73.

[19]Robert S. Taylor, "Value-Added Process in the Information Cycle," *Journal of the American Society for Information Science* 33 (September 1982): 342.

[20]F. Emery and E. L. Trist, "The Causal Texture of Organizational Environments," *Human Relations* 18 (1965): 21-32.

[21]Ross Atkinson, "The Conditions of Collection Development," in *Collection Management: A New Treatise*. Edited by Charles Osburn and Ross Atkinson. (Greenwich, CT: JAI Press, 1991): 33.

[22]Laverna M. Saunders, "The Virtual Library Today," *Library Administration & Management* 6 (Spring 1992): 66.

Further Reading

General

Adams, R. J. *Communication and Delivery Systems for Librarians*. Brookfield, VT: Ashgate Publishing, 1990.

Altheide, D. L. "Culture of Information." *Journal of Education for Library and Information Science* 31(Fall 1990): 113-21.

Bailey, C.W. "Public-Access Computer Systems." *Information Technology and Libraries* 12 (March 1993): 99-106.

Blake, V. L., and T. T. Surprenant. "Electronic Immigrants in the Information Age: Public Policy Considerations." *Information Society* 7, no. 3 (1990): 223-43.

Branin, J. J. "Information Policies for Collection Development Librarians." *Collection Building* 9, nos. 3/4 (1988): 19-23.

Broadus, R. N. "History of Collection Development." In *Collection Management: A New Treatise*. Edited by C. B. Osburn and R. Atkinson, 3-28. Greenwich, CT: JAI Press, 1991.

Brownrigg, E. B. "Library Telecommunications and Public Policy." In *Telecommunications Networks: Issues and Trends*. Edited by M. E. Jacob. White Plains, NY: Knowledge Industries Publications, 1986.

Bullard, S. R. "Collection Development in the Electronic Age." *Library Acquisitions: Practice and Theory* 13, no. 3 (1989): 209-12.

Cyzyk, M. "Canon Formation, Library Collections, and the Dilemma of Collection Development." *College and Research Libraries* 54 (January 1993): 58-65.

Hammer, D. P. *Information Age.* Metuchen NJ: Scarecrow Press, 1989.

Kohl, David F. *Acquisitions, Collection Development and Collection Use: A Handbook for Library Management.* Santa Barbara, CA: ABC-Clio Information Services, 1985.

Leonard, W. P. "On My Mind: Libraries Without Walls." *Journal of Academic Librarianship* 20 (March 1994): 29-30.

Libraries and the Learning Society. Chicago: American Library Association, 1984.

Lopez, M. D. "Guide for Beginning Bibliographers." *Library Resources & Technical Services* 13 (Fall 1969): 462-70.

McCune, S. M. "What Is the Value of Information?" *Library Acquisitions: Practice and Theory* 13, no. 2 (1989): 161-64.

Moohan, G. "Transborder Data Flow: A Review of Issues and Policies." *Library Review* 37, no. 3 (1988): 27-37.

Osburn, C. "Collection Development and Management." In *Academic Libraries: Research Perspective,* edited by M. J. Lynch and A. Young, 1-37. Chicago: American Library Association, 1990.

Veltman, K. "Electronic Media and Visual Knowledge." *Knowledge Organization* 20, no. 1 (1993): 47-54.

Wallman, K. "Current and Future Stresses on the Information Chain." *Information Reports and Bibliographies* 18, no. 6 (1989): 2-8.

Zink, S. D. "Will Librarians Have a Place in the Information Society?" *Reference Service Review* 19, no. 1 (1991): 76-77.

Academic

Atkinson, R. "Networks, Hypertext, and Academic Information Services." *College and Research Libraries* 54 (May 1993): 199-215.

Basch, R. "Books Online." *Online* 15 (July 1991): 13-27.

Budd, J. M. "It's Not the Principle, It's the Money of the Thing." *Journal of Academic Librarianship* 15 (September 1989): 218-22.

Dougherty, R. M., and A. P. Dougherty. "The Academic Library: A Time of Crisis, Change, and Opportunity." *Journal of Academic Librarianship* 18 (January 1993): 342-46.

Hughes, G. C. "Information Age." *Information Development* 7, no. 2 (1991): 72-74.

Johnson, M. A. "The End of Collection Development As We Know It?" *Technicalities* 12 (August 1992): 5-8.

———. "Visiting Luputa; or the Perils of Preoccupation with Technology." *Technicalities* 12 (December 1992): 5-8.

Kaufman, P. T., and T. J. Miller. "Scholarly Communications: New Realities, Old Values." *Library Hi Tech* 10, no. 3 (1992): 61-78.

St. Clair, G. "Choosing to Choose." *College & Research Libraries* 55 (May 1994): 194-96.

Shaughnessy, T. W. "Library As Information Center: Wishful Thinking or Realistic Role?" *Journal of Library Administration* 12, no. 3 (1990): 3-17.

Public

Ballard, T. "Information Age and the Public Library." *Wilson Library Bulletin* 62 (June 1988): 74-78.

Case, R. N. "And What Do We Do Now?" *Rural Libraries* 14, no. 1 (1994): 59-69.

Curley, A. "Funding for Public Libraries in the 1990s." *Library Journal* 115 (January 1990): 65-67.

Curran, C. "Information Literacy and the Public Library." *Public Libraries* 29 (November/December 1990): 349-53.

Dowlin, K. E. "Public Libraries in the Year 2001." *Information Technology and Libraries* 10 (December 1991): 317-21.

Hendry, J. D. "Public Libraries Versus the Electric Soup." *Library Association Record* 85 (July 1983): 267-68.

Nicholls, P. "The Time Has Come." *CD-ROM Professional* 7 (May/June 1994): 46-52.

Schuman, B. A. "Experience Parlor: Next Evolutionary Step for the American Public Library." *Public Libraries* 12, no. 2 (1992): 35-51.

Usherwood, B. "Privatized Public Library." *Wilson Library Bulletin* 65 (April 1991): 39-41.

Vestheim, G. "Information or Enlightenment?" *Scandinavian Public Library Quarterly* 25, no. 4 (1992): 11-17.

Weiss, M. J. "Clustered America: The Communities We Serve." *Public Libraries* 28 (May/June 1989): 161-65.

School

Aaron, S. L. "Collection Developer's Link to Global Education." *School Media Quarterly* 18 (Fall 1990): 35-43.

——. "Learner-Centered Electronic Schools of the Future." *Bookmark* 50 (Fall 1991): 15-18.

Boardman, E. M. "Don't You Have Something Newer?" *Book Report* 12 (January/February 1994): 27-28.

Brown, J. "Navigating in the 90s: Teacher-Librarian As Change Agent." *Emergency Librarian* 18 (September/October 1990): 19-25.

Callison, D. "Justification for Action in Future School Library Media Programs." *School Library Media Quarterly* 12 (Spring 1984): 205-11.

Durrance, J. C. "Information Needs: Old Song, New Tune." *School Library Media Quarterly* 17 (Spring 1989): 126-30.

Handy, A. E. "Just Do It! Collection Building for the Future." *Book Report* 12 (January/February 1994): 11-13.

Hiland, L. F. "Information and Thinking Skills and Process to Prepare Young Adults for the Information Age." *Library Trends* 37 (Summer 1988): 56-62.

Moe, L. "With Electronic Schools Will School Library/Media Centers Become Dinosaurs?" *Ohio Media Spectrum* 44 (Winter 1992): 93-95.

Saccardi, M. "Interactive Computer: Author and Reader Online." *School Library Journal* 37 (October 1991): 36-38.

Thomas, C. "Building Library Media Collections." *Bookmark* 41 (Fall 1982): 16-19.

Special

Anderson, R. K. G., and S. S. Fuller. "Librarians As Members of Integrated Institutional Information Programs." *Library Trends* 41(Fall 1992): 198-213.

Bunting, A. "Legal Considerations of Document Delivery Services." *Bulletin of the Medical Library Association* 82 (April 1994): 183-87.

Cleveland, H. *The Knowledge Executive: Leadership in an Information Society.* New York: Dutton, 1985.

Hull, P. "Videotext: A New Tool for Libraries." *Special Libraries* 85 (Spring 1994): 81-88.

Lockett, B. A. "Scientific and Technical Librarians: Leaders of the 21st Century." *Science and Technology Libraries* 12 (Summer 1992): 51-66.

Michelson, A., and J. Rothenberg. "Scholarly Communication and Information Technology: Exploring the Impact of Changes in the Research Process on Archives." *American Archivist* 55 (Spring 1992): 236-315.

Mount, E., and W. B. Newman. "Top Secret/Trade Secret: Restricting and Accessing Information." *Collection Building* 7 (Summer 1985): 3-7.

Ojala, M. P. "Decision Points for Company Research." *Online* 17 (January 1993): 79-82.

Panko, W. B., et al. "Networking: An Overview for Leaders of Academic Medical Centers." *Academic Medicine* 68 (July 1993): 528-32.

Seidman, R. K. "Information-Rich, Knowledge-Poor: The Challenge of the Information Society." *Special Libraries* 82 (Winter 1991): 64-67.

Wolpert, A. J. "Libraries in the Year 2001." *Information Technology and Libraries* 10 (December 1991): 331-37.

2
Information Needs Assessment

Knowledge of the service community is the key to effective collection development. It is virtually impossible, and also unnecessary, to collect information about all aspects of the lives of the customers served. However, the more the collection development officers know about the customers' work roles, general interests, education, information or communication behavior, values, and related characteristics, the more likely it is the collection will provide the desired information at the time the service population wants it. Another reason for collecting data about the service population relates to one of the so-called laws of collection development, that is, no collection can meet all the information needs of any one customer or class of customer. With limited resources to serve a wide range of interests, even in a small research and development unit, one must have a solid database of client information in order to prepare an effective collection development plan. The data collected is for planning purposes; it is useful for more than collection development.

Areas in collection development affected by data about customers are policy formulation, selection, and evaluation. Selection officers should base policy formulation and modification on the data collected. Although the data will seldom provide help in the selection of a specific item, it can help establish selection parameters. Any assessment of the collection should include a consideration of how well it meets the expectations and needs of the customers.

Researchers use several terms for the concepts and processes of learning more about a target population: community analysis, information needs analysis, needs analysis, needs assessment, role analysis, user studies, and market analysis. On a general level, the terms are identical, but they differ greatly in the specifics of application and purpose. Community analysis usually refers to a public library's data collection. Sometimes the term planning process more accurately identifies the purpose of the activity. Needs analysis and needs assessment generally apply to the special library, information center, or information brokerage and often refer to an individual or a few individuals. (Both needs analysis and needs assessment are discussed in more detail later in this chapter.) User studies usually denote research projects designed to gain insight into how, why, when, and where people seek information and use information resources. Market analyses are studies of communities or people to assess interest in or reactions to a service or product.

There is a major problem in defining information need, information want, expressed demand, satisfied demand, information behavior, and other related terms. (A good article on this subject is T. D. Wilson's "On

User Studies and Information Needs."[1]) It is far beyond the scope of this chapter to address such problems, however, the terms needs, wants, and demands must be defined for the purpose of this book. Needs are situations (community, institutional, or personal) that require solution; it does not always follow that a need is something the group or person wants. Wants are things for which the group or person is willing to expend time, effort, or money to acquire; it does not always follow that the thing wanted is good for the group or person. Demands are things the group or person wants and is willing to act in concert (writing letters, making telephone calls, testifying, or demonstrating) to acquire. From a library or information center perspective, the ideal outcome of a study is to identify a need that is wanted and demanded. This topic is further explained in the discussion of analyzing survey data.

Conceptual Background

People seek information from both formal and informal systems. Informal systems are of three general types: the flow of matter and energy discussed in chapter 1; friends and colleagues; and organizations not designed as formal information sources. Without question, informal systems provide the bulk of an individual's everyday, or common, information. Daily living activities generate dozens, perhaps hundreds, of information needs ranging from the weather report to the interest rate on loans for buying a home. Depending upon the urgency, a person locates the information with greater or lesser effort, speed, and accuracy. Most of the daily living and activities information requirements are local in nature. Mass-market sources, such as newspapers, radio, and television, answer most local information needs. However, even these sources often serve an area so large or diverse that information is not as precise as some people may require. (For example, in large urban areas major newspapers often publish regional editions.)

As the importance of the information increases, so do the amounts of money, time, and other resources devoted to securing precise, accurate information. A weather forecast (covering 18 to 24 hours) prepared and printed in a newspaper several hours before it is read is adequate for most people. For most people, the weather forecast is of marginal importance, so they expend little time, effort, or money to secure up-to-the-minute, accurate weather information. On the other hand, for airline pilots and those who fly with them, weather information is much more important. As a result, airlines commit significant resources to having the latest, most accurate data. When there is a space shuttle launch, a worldwide meteorological network supplies information. From the individual to the largest organization, all information seekers place a value on each type of information used, often without being fully aware they are doing so. Several factors influence the information's value, such as the role it plays in decision making; the type of information needed (text, numeric, graphic, or audio); and the form of information package. One important factor is accessibility and the effort required to gain access to information. This factor is governed by the law of least effort.

According to the law of least effort, people and organizations expend as little as possible of their available resources (time, money, or effort) to secure information. Frequently when a person is preparing a document, there is a need for more accurate or current information. A typical reaction is to turn first to materials at hand, although the person knows there is only a slight chance that those materials will contain the needed information. Most people try this even when they know where they can secure the appropriate information, just because the known source is in a less convenient location than the materials at hand. In a work environment, individuals ask fellow workers before consulting formal information resources. In a variation on this method, scholars and researchers make frequent and successful use of the so-called invisible college, which is a communication network linking people interested in particular topics. One reason for the success of informal information systems is that the formal information system is slow to distribute data.

It is important for a collection development staff to know what informal sources exist within the service community. In some cases, it is possible to incorporate some of these informal sources into a formal system, thereby providing better service for all customers. Occasionally, such an incorporation improves the quality or retrievability of information. Many libraries and information centers offer referral services that supply names of people or organizations expert in an area and willing to supply information. Equally important is how people use the informal system. This may influence both how one structures a formal information system (e.g., a library collection) and what the collection will contain.

Research on both formal and informal information systems has been ongoing for some time. Generally, the studies fall into one of four broad categories: key informant, community forum, social indicators, and field or user studies. They use and examine terms like information user (who), information need (what and why), information-seeking behavior (how), and information retrieval success and failure (why). We know that a number of variables affect the individual when there is a need for information.

Cultural background is a central factor because it creates the individual's basic values and attitudes toward information. Knowing about the service population's various cultural backgrounds and attitudes about formal information systems is essential in planning effective services and collections. Few formal information systems have a monocultural service population. It is important that collection development officers take the time to study and understand, to some extent, the cultural contexts represented in the service community.

Present and past experience with the political system also affects a person's expectations regarding formal information systems. As the degree of control (government or organizational) increases, there is a corresponding decrease in the variety and range of subjects contained in the formal information system. In a less controlled environment, an individual has every reason to expect the formal information systems to contain a full range of opinions on most, if not all, topics of concern for that system. As people move from one context to another, they carry with them past experiences and a set of expectations. Past experience influences information-seeking behavior just as it does other human behaviors. Again, knowledge of backgrounds in the service population can be helpful in the planning and collection building process.

Group membership, reference groups, and the invisible college all influence how an individual responds to formal information systems. In the work situation, the organization and work responsibilities also enter the picture. Organizations establish special, if not unique, values regarding information. They determine what constitutes information for them, how valuable or important information is, and how much of the organization's resources should go into providing information services. Within that context, departments and work units establish their value systems.

One influential variable is the individual's mind-set. We all have days when things go right and days when nothing seems to work. We also have variations in the intensity of our law of least effort. Some days we accept a close approximation for needed information, and other days no effort is too great to obtain the precise information. Personal mind-set may be the most important variable in how an individual responds to a formal information system. Personal mind-set is unpredictable and is not subject to control by information professionals.

Chapter 1 discusses how legal, economic, political, and technological variables affect information. In the long run, these variables have a great influence on the structure and content of formal information systems. (Chapter 18 discusses specifics concerning current laws governing formal information systems.) Economic considerations are more and more a factor in decision making in the information center environment. Twenty years ago in the United States, few people questioned the idea of a totally subsidized public library or the desirability of having such a library in every community. In the mid 1970s, there was a discussion of costs and benefits in terms of library services and materials. Now there is a more and more frequent discussion of partial, if not full, cost recovery. A future may exist only for for-profit or break-even libraries, in which all public monies spent must be balanced by income from customers. In essence, there will be only neutral or positive cash flow.

Studies of users and the service community can provide information needed for effective planning. As pointed out by T. D. Wilson, studying information behavior is important because

- our concern is with uncovering the facts of the everyday life of the service population;

- by uncovering those facts we strive to understand the needs that push the individual into information-seeking behavior;

- by better understanding those needs we are better able to understand what meaning information has in the everyday life of people; and

- by all of the foregoing we should gain a better understanding of the customer and be able to design more cost-effective information systems.[2]

Though not everyone agrees on what has happened or will happen, based upon the results of several studies, I believe everyone agrees on the need for effective planning.

Fifteen years ago Colin Mick pointed out some issues relating to the difficulties of basing plans on studies of the service population:

> There is now a backlog of nearly 1,000 information needs and use studies, but they provide little information which can be applied to problems involving either the management of information work or the design of information products and services. In short, the reason information innovations are technology and content driven is because information behavior studies have failed to provide information which can be used in the design of systems and services.[3]

In the years that have passed since Mick made this statement, there has been a steady increase in the pool of useful information available. However, Douglas Zweizig, who published several pieces on community analysis, was pessimistic about the real value of such studies:

> Community analysis will not result in direct identification of community information needs. False expectation is associated with community analysis. It is raised by rhetoric that urges community analysis so we may be 'responsive to the information needs of the community' . . . by studying the community, we can diagnose information needs and prescribe appropriate materials and services . . . But the metaphor only serves to conceal our ignorance from even ourselves . . . 'information need' is only our idea, not necessarily something that exists in the minds of our patrons . . . findings have advanced our understanding of individual information seeking but, as libraries are presently organized, the findings do not provide guidance on what programs to plan or what materials to buy.[4]

Despite his cautious view of the value of user or community studies, Dr. Zweizig recognized the importance of conducting and using the results of such studies. Recognizing the limitations and dangers involved is important, and knowing what to do with the results is critical for a successful study. Using a conceptual framework is important. (Mick, Lindsey, and Callahan outline one good model for framing a study.[5])

Practical Aspects

There are several uses for the data collected in a survey, and though one may design a project to meet only one objective, the data may be of value in a later project. Surveys are a starting point, and when properly conducted, provide a database the information center can use for a variety of purposes. Through other techniques of information gathering, and by use of quantitative analysis, collection development staff can more accurately assess information needs. However, first the staff must gain an accurate picture of the service community. During the years I taught at the University of California, Los Angeles (UCLA) library school, many students elected to do their master's thesis on some aspect of collection development, and several did some form of user/community analysis project. As a result of these projects, we identified seven areas where survey data can assist in planning and managing library or information center activities.

One obvious area is collection development. Studies for this purpose range from broad studies identifying basic characteristics of the service population to in-depth analysis of who makes the heaviest use of the collection and why, as well as how people use the materials. One student study was done in response to a statement from the Los Angeles city attorney's office that the Los Angeles Public Library (LAPL) system might be violating several civil rights laws relating to equal access and service. The city attorney's investigation noted a marked difference between branches serving white and nonwhite communities. Differences existed in all areas: staffing, service hours, collection size, amount spent on materials, and space. The branches in nonwhite communities had substantially less in all areas. The investigation showed there was no intent on the part of LAPL to discriminate; the differences resulted from a complex series of events over a long time, primarily a budgeting system based on circulation data. Collections did not change as quickly as the service population. One outcome was some branches had decreased circulation, which translated into lower funding. Failure to consistently monitor changes in the service community also contributed to the problem. The student studied the relationship between branch collections, service area demographic data, and commercial information materials available in the service area. There was a stronger correlation between branch collections than there was between the collections of low-funded branches and their service communities.

Frequently, librarians desire to provide innovative, or at least new, services for customers. Which services and what optimum service levels to offer are difficult questions to address, but data from a properly constructed survey provides decision makers with the basis for predicting user reactions to new or modified services. Should we offer computer software? Should we make computers available for public use? Should we offer online database searching? Can we charge for such searching, and how much? These are but a few of the questions that can arise, and in the absence of sound data from a survey, the decision makers can only guess at the answers. One interesting study of a public library compared four groups' ranking of desired services: the library users, part-time workers in the library (primarily students), clerical and paraprofessional staff, and the professional staff. Professional staff estimates of what would be desirable differed significantly from the users' views, but the part-time employee rankings were very similar to those of the patrons. Although this study was too small in scope to generalize beyond one community, it does suggest that a cautious approach to instituting new services would be wise, especially in the absence of user input.

Two related uses of assessment studies are determining service points and changing physical facilities requirements. With an ever-increasing ability to deliver information electronically, the question of whether there should be service points and, if yes, where to locate them becomes very important. Commitments from funding authorities for capital expenditures for new facilities or long-term leases of space will be harder to secure. Many individuals question mobile delivery services (bookmobiles or media mobiles) because of high energy and maintenance costs. These factors, along with other economic concerns, often suggest that electronic delivery will or would be the best solution. However, electronic delivery has long-term cost implications and raises questions regarding to whom and how the library will provide access to electronic systems. Data from an assessment project will be helpful in making informed decisions.

Many older buildings were not designed with the needs of the disabled and elderly in mind. With steadily improving health care and increased longevity, an increasing number of individuals in the service population will be in one or both of these categories. The passage of the Americans with Disabilities Act of 1990 (ADA) has implications for services in all types of libraries and information centers. Knowing the size of the affected population can help in planning budgets, services, and equipment needs. Complying with ADA regulations will require making changes in public access areas. Modifying existing structures is often more expensive per square foot than new construction. Even the process of making decisions about modifying the library or information center is costly. Data about how many and what types of disabilities are present in the service population will assist in making effective decisions.

The service community clearly varies by type of library. For educational institutions, the primary groups are faculty and students, followed by staff and the general public. Special libraries have a variety of missions that determine the primary clientele, which may range from the entire organization to a single project team. Public libraries have the largest customer base, which presents a great challenge for collection builders.

All libraries and information centers depend on the good will of their customers. Complaints to funding authorities, be they profit or nonprofit, cause the authorities to question the effectiveness of the library or information center. A regular assessment program can be helpful in gauging the service population's attitudes about services and collections. Having current information readily available may make the difference between receiving quick approval of a project or budget or undergoing a long, possibly painful, review and justification process.

As community demographics change, there may be a need to adjust the staffing pattern of the library or information center. Changes in subject expertise (in an academic or business setting); a need for bilingual skills; attention to special population groups (e.g., children, the institutionalized, or the elderly); a need for more technical skills in various electronic fields or in indexing, abstracting, or information consolidation—all of these may require the library or information center to have more staff with different skills and knowledge.

Hiring staff always takes more time than one expects; if you add to the hiring process redefining or restructuring an existing position, the process takes even longer. Survey data about the shifts in the service community can assist in projecting when one should start planning for staff changes. Such projections will allow the library or information center to respond in a timely manner.

All of the areas discussed have cost and budget implications. Funding authorities look with greater favor on budget requests that the library supports with objective data and come from individuals whose past requests were generally accurate. Survey data can prove useful in the budgeting process.

The preceding list of possible uses of the survey data is not exhaustive but illustrates the many processes that can benefit from assessment studies. Again, such surveys can serve multiple purposes, not just collection development.

Needs assessment projects for libraries and information centers and market research for profit organizations share several characteristics. Both types of studies often seek the following types of information:

why a person does or does not use a particular product or service

how the person uses the product or service

where the person acquires and uses the product

what is good and bad about the product or service

what new products or services would be of interest

occasionally, how much the person would be willing to expend, in terms of time, money, or effort, for a product or service

When considering an assessment project, some basic concerns about the outcome will arise. Careful planning using sound research methods will take care of technical issues, such as sample size, pretesting requirements, question bias, and interviewer influence. Questions that can be difficult to answer include:

1. Is the target population knowledgeable or interested enough to respond to complex questions? Would several simple questions covering a complex question be better?

2. Is the cost, in time and energy, of providing adequate background information to individuals lacking the necessary research experience balanced by more or better research data?

3. To what extent will the data accurately reflect the attitudes, opinions, needs, and issues important to respondents instead of information that the respondent thinks the data collectors want?

4. Will the survey process result in unrealistic expectations in both respondents and staff?

Answers to these questions are never fully known until one starts to analyze the survey results. However, by thinking them through in advance, the researchers and library can avoid some of the pitfalls of the process.

It is sometimes possible to locate a recent study conducted for another purpose—unrelated to the library—that contains data useful for the library's current project. In such cases the risk of having data biased by respondents giving answers they think the current project planners want does not exist (although it may have existed for the original study). An example of finding information useful to libraries in an existing nonlibrary study was a survey about lifestyles done by a large advertising agency and analyzed by Madden.[6] One of the more than 200 questions the marketing firm asked was, "How frequently did you use the library in the last year?" Because the survey was performed by an advertising agency, more people answered honestly than would have had a library sent the survey. Still, some bias undoubtedly exists in the data because people tend to think that using the library is a good thing to do, and they respond in a way that will make them look good. Though some librarians did not agree with Madden's conclusions based on the reanalyzed data, no one questions the data. Being aware of studies like this one can save time and effort.

More often than not, you or a consultant will have to develop a customized user or community study. Several sources can assist in formulating a project. Almost any basic textbook on research methods outlines the fundamental techniques of survey research, and many marketing books are helpful. Beyond the fundamental level are more specific aids, including the following:

Association of Research Libraries. *User Studies*—Spec Kit 101. Washington, DC: Association of Research Libraries, February 1984.
The Association of Research Libraries publishes a number of items that are useful for studying the academic environment; this one is of most interest.

Hale, Martha. "Administrators and Information: A Review of Methodologies Used for Diagnosing Information Use." In *Advances in Librarianship*. New York: Academic Press, 1986.
This is an excellent survey article.

Horton, Forest W. *How to Harness Information Resources*. Cleveland, OH: Association for Systems Management, 1974. Information Management Workbook. Washington, DC: Information Management Press, 1983.
Of great interest to special libraries, information brokers, and others in less traditional information center environments.

Kaufman, Roger, and Fenwick English. *Needs Assessment*. Englewood Cliffs, NJ: Educational Technology Publications, 1979.
A useful book that provides an excellent overview of the process. (Still in print.)

Lauffer, Armand. *Assessment Tools for Practitioners, Managers and Trainers*. Newbury Park, CA: Sage Publications, 1982.
A practical guide to assessment methods. (Still in print.)

Nickerns, J. M.; A. J. Purga; and P. P. Noriega. *Research Methods for Needs Assessment*. Washington, DC: University Press of America, 1980.
A sound work for developing a needs assessment project.

Rossmar, Marlene L. *Multicultural Marketing*. New York: American Management Association, 1994.
Written for businesses wishing to become more effective in marketing products to a wider base, this book provides excellent insights that apply to library needs assessments. Particularly good for public libraries.

Warren, Roland L. *Studying Your Community*. New York: Russell Sage Foundation, 1955.
This is an old but useful book for those planning a public library assessment project. (Still in print.)

Full-scale studies are expensive and time-consuming, but they must be done occasionally. Between large projects, libraries and information centers can conduct projects on a smaller scale. Small studies cost less, produce reliable data, and may lengthen the time between large studies. Following are suggestions for the content of both large- and small-scale projects, with focus on how collection development activities may be improved as a result.

Elements of the Study

As soon as the library decides to conduct an assessment project, it must answer several questions, including (1) Who is to collect the information? (2) What information do the planners want? (3) What methods will produce the desired data? and (4) How will the planners use the data?

Who Will Do the Study?

Who or how many people will be responsible for supervising and running the study depends on several factors: financial support (library budget or supplemental funds), the number and qualifications of personnel available (staff members or outside consultants), and the depth and breadth of the study.

Any survey of major proportions must have financial backing sufficient to hire a consultant to assist in planning the study. This is true even if one or more staff members have expertise in designing assessment projects. An outsider's view can be helpful in catching problems insiders are too close to see.

Occasionally, because of limited funding, the survey must be carried out by a committee made up of paid and volunteer workers. In this case, whether or not the library hires a consultant, the involvement of collection development personnel and other staff is essential to the project's success.

Regardless of whether a consultant or volunteers are used to plan the survey, the library must weigh the advantages and disadvantages of using staff to carry out the project. An inexperienced team of staff members can waste inordinate amounts of time and energy. Furthermore, staff members would normally work on the survey during regular working hours, which could cause service and scheduling problems. Also, a staff team may draw conclusions based upon individual members' personal biases concerning a particular area or aspect of the service community, rather than from the research data.

A compromise solution is to hire an outside consultant to formulate the plan which the library staff then implements. A problem with this approach is that the consultant must divide the tasks into units small enough so that personnel who have little experience in conducting surveys can accomplish them. Each project will require weighing the staffing problem against the consequences of failing to conduct any survey.

One way to overcome lack of staff time and experience in assessment work is to build the project into the regular collection development activities. Many larger academic libraries have started moving in this direction by using subject specialists. To some degree this movement is accidental, because the literature about the reasons for and functions of subject specialists gives little indication that formalized survey work is or ever was a primary concern. Instead, the literature suggests subject specialists' activities are contact with faculty, work in conjunction with faculty and specialized users, development of subject areas in the light of institutional and patron needs, syllabus analysis, and citation analysis. In essence, such libraries have laid the foundation for subject specialists to conduct ongoing assessments. A meeting once a year with each faculty member whose subject interest touches on the area of responsibility will maintain close contact with community needs.

Including assessment work in the job description for collection development staff assures an ongoing assessment program. Naturally, it may be difficult to convince funding authorities that adding a major task to existing operations creates a need for additional staff. Incorporating assessment activities in job descriptions may, in effect, increase the staff size by at least one full-time position. In the past, most libraries did not view needs assessment work as a major issue. Now, with stable or shrinking materials budgets, all types of libraries are concerned with making the most effective use of the funds available. Needs assessment data is a key factor in establishing collection priorities and occasionally, choosing among specific items for the collection.

Using the library staff as the assessment team does offer several advantages. The staff collecting the data fully understand how the results will be used. A staff team comes to the task armed with useful information about needs gained through day-to-day work. For example, the staff members have taken requests for or attempted to locate information for customers that is not available in-house.

Another useful outcome of using employees is that the staff on the team gain or increase their commitment to the assessment process and its value as they learn more about the service community. Generally, staff involved in a project show greater willingness to accept and implement the results and to use them daily. In addition, when one uses a staff project team, they need less time to inform the rest of the staff about the results because staff social interaction cuts across departmental boundaries. Using an outside person or firm to conduct the study normally results in one or two presentations to the staff or circulating draft documents for comment. Because of time constraints, the process often leads to staff misunderstandings and, occasionally, resistance to the entire project.

A useful step, especially to secure community support, is to establish an advisory board for the project. The board should represent all the major groups covered by the assessment project (e.g., students, faculty, researchers, administrators, young people, adults, and various ethnic groups). Though the committee must be advisory in nature, it can provide invaluable insight into problems the project team may encounter in collecting data. For example: What are some of the pressing information needs of the target populations? When and where should data gatherers make contact with the sample group? What are some ideas about how to approach people to enlist their full cooperation? In addition to helping answer these questions, the advisory board can help set project priorities and assist in interpreting the collected data. Ideally, the board members and the project team will discuss the project and its goals.

After the library decides who will run the project, it can move on to other issues. This includes developing a clear statement of the study's objectives and a detailed list of the steps to take and the questions to ask. Unclear goals lead to disastrous results and open the way for self-serving interpretations of the data.

What Will Be Studied?

Each type of library or information center will have a slightly different definition of the word community. In the context of the public library, community means the political jurisdiction that the library serves. For academic and school libraries, the community is the parent institution. In the case of special libraries, it is the company, business, institution, or foundation that provides the operating library's funds. In the corporate setting, the community may be a division or unit of the parent company. With these distinctions in mind, it is possible to identify 11 broad categories of data that apply to all types of libraries.

Historical data is useful in several ways. Understanding a community's historical development may lead to a better, and sometimes quicker, understanding of where that community stands today. Although corporate libraries may not have any long-term collection preservation functions, an understanding of the history of the library or information center and its service community can help clarify or restructure current collection development objectives. Historical background information also provides clues about areas of the collection to weed or areas in which it is no longer necessary to acquire material.

Geographical information may answer questions like: In which physical directions is the community growing? (This is an issue for large academic campuses, not just for public libraries.) What is the distribution of population (or departments or offices) over the geographic area? This type of information helps the library staff determine service points, which, in turn, influence the number of duplicate titles that the library needs to acquire. (In most instances, purchasing duplicate copies cuts into the number of titles the library can buy.) This assessment should consider geographic and transportation data, which, because of their interrelatedness, are discussed in the next paragraph.

Transportation availability data, combined with geographic factors, are important in the library's decision-making process regarding how many service points to establish and where to locate them. Merely noting the existence of a bus or shuttle service does not provide enough information for a meaningful analysis. How often is the service provided? What does it cost? What are the hours of service? What is the level of use? Answers to these questions are vital in determining service points and service hours. As noted in the previous paragraph, the number of service points has an impact on plans for developing the collection. Often, large academic and industrial organizations provide their own internal transportation systems, especially in urban areas. The existence of a good internal transportation system may help a library to build a more varied collection. A courier or document delivery system may help alleviate the need for as many (or as large) branch operations. Reduction in the number of branches, while still maintaining the same level of service, can reduce the need for duplicate materials.

Legal research will not be too difficult to do, nor will the amount of data accumulated be large. Nevertheless, there may be legal implications for collection development. In some academic institutions, the teaching faculty has the legal right to expend all book funds. Although there is no longer any American university where the faculty fully exercises this legal authority, cases of limited implementation do exist. Also, this right may exist, but most persons—including the librarians—will have forgotten about it until a problem arises. Preparing for a possible problem is less difficult than dealing with an existing one or with an unexpected surprise. Clear policies about the delegation of selection authority and responsibility may help to avoid a problem and will certainly help to solve those that do arise.

Knowledge of how a community's legal system functions can also be important. Where does authority lie? To which bodies is the library accountable, especially for collection development? Are there any legal restrictions on what the library may buy with monies allocated for collection development? Some jurisdictions, until a few years ago, had regulations making it illegal to buy anything except books, periodicals, and newspapers; other media were supposed to be off-limits. In addition to purchasing, there may be legal restrictions on how long a library must keep material and regulations regarding how one goes about disposing of the material. Libraries that are depositories for government publications are governed by a substantial body of regulations regarding the retention, usage, and disposal of the material. In a corporate information center or archives, there may be government regulations as well as professional guidelines regarding records retention. Some regulations not only specify how the organization must retain the records but in what format (paper, microfilm, or electronic). How does one go about changing the regulations? Knowledge of the library's legal position will help answer the question.

Political information, both formal and informal, has a relationship with legal data, much like the link between geographic and transportation information. On the formal level, questions include: To what extent is the library a political issue? If political parties exist, how do their attitudes toward library and information services differ? What is the distribution of party affiliations in the community? Are some areas of the community more politically conservative or liberal than others? Should library service point collections reflect these philosophical differences? On the informal level, some questions to consider are: How do the politics of the community work? Who influences fiscal decisions? In an academic or special library, what are the politics of the allocation of collection development funds? Answers to most of these questions will not have a direct bearing on which titles go into the collection, but they may influence the way in which the library secures and allocates funds and how much money is available for collection development.

Demographic data is essential in formulating an effective collection development program in all libraries. Basic changes in the composition of the population are inevitable, but only by monitoring the community can collection development staff anticipate changes in the composition of the population. Waiting until change takes place creates an image of an institution that is slow to change. For example, United States academic institutions and their libraries operated for years on the premise that their student bodies would continue to grow in size. Census data in the 1960s indicated a sharp drop in the birth rate which time translates into a smaller pool of potential students. This fact, combined with widespread discontent with the higher education system, should have been a clear indication that continued growth was at least problematic. However, only after several years of declining or stable enrollment did academic institutions and their libraries react to the news, which had been available for more than eighteen years.

Public libraries, on the other hand, must deal with shifts of population out of inner cities. Occasionally, such shifts can change the city's tax base, which affects library revenues. Other changes in the population (e.g., age, education, nationality, and health) have serious implications for developing a collection.

Though Los Angeles is not representative of many cities, the 1990 U.S. Census data suggest its experience may be typical of what is occurring in many cities, at least in terms of ethnic and cultural diversity. The city's experience with demographic shifts illustrates the need to monitor shifting community composition and information needs. One group to become involved with when building an ethnic collection is the Ethnic Materials Information Exchange.[7]

One indication of the cultural diversity of Los Angeles comes from data from the school district (a good source of data for many types of community assessment projects). The district's 1992 data indicated one in six students spoke limited English and, among the homes of 30 percent of the students, 95 different languages were regularly spoken.[8]

Shifts in composition and location of population groupings in Los Angeles affected library service as the city tried to respond to the changes. In 1950, 86 percent of the Los Angeles population was Anglo; by 1990, the Anglo percentage was 37 percent. Meanwhile, the Hispanic percentage rose from 7 percent to 40 percent. Other "minority" groups grew in size during this time as well.

Figures 2.1 through 2.5 (on pages 47-51) illustrate the shift in the west Los Angeles area. The maps were developed using census tracts from the Santa Monica, Westwood, Venice, and Marina del Rey areas. (Note: The racial and ethnic terms used in this discussion and on the maps are those used by the Census Bureau in earlier census reports. The 1990 map uses the same terms for the sake of consistency.)

(Text continues on page 52.)

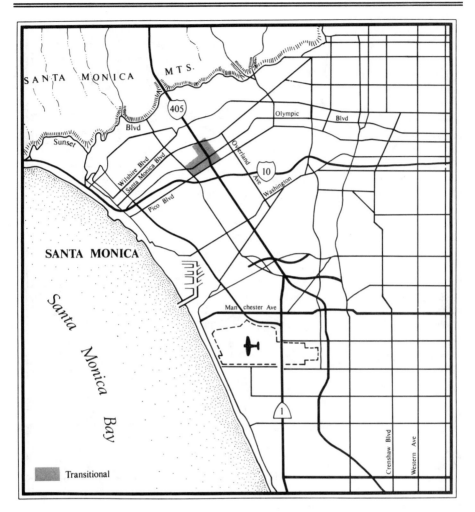

Fig. 2.1. Los Angeles/Santa Monica distribution of ethnic populations, 1950. Map drawn using data from the U.S. Census, 1950.

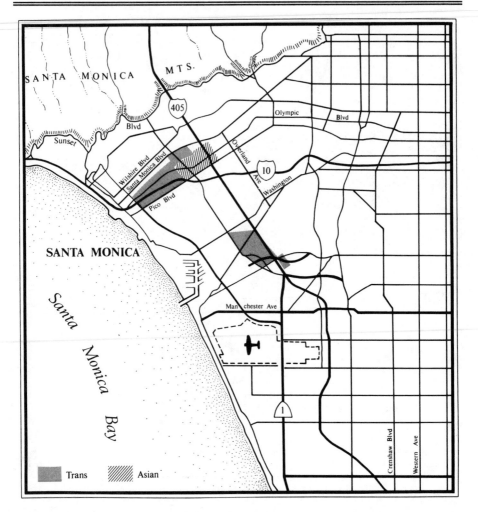

Fig. 2.2. Los Angeles/Santa Monica distribution of ethnic populations, 1960. Map drawn using data from the U.S. Census, 1960.

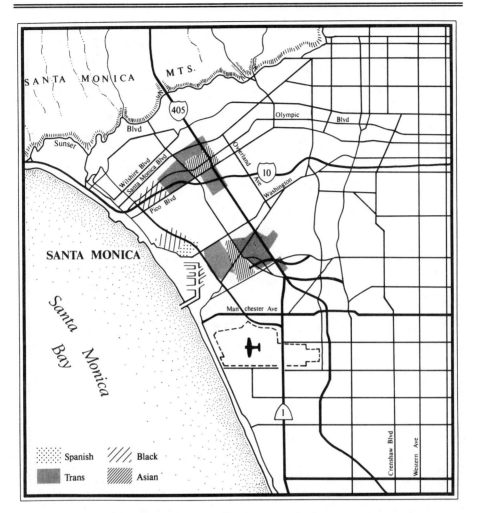

Fig. 2.3. Los Angeles/Santa Monica distribution of ethnic populations, 1970. Map drawn using data from the U.S. Census, 1970.

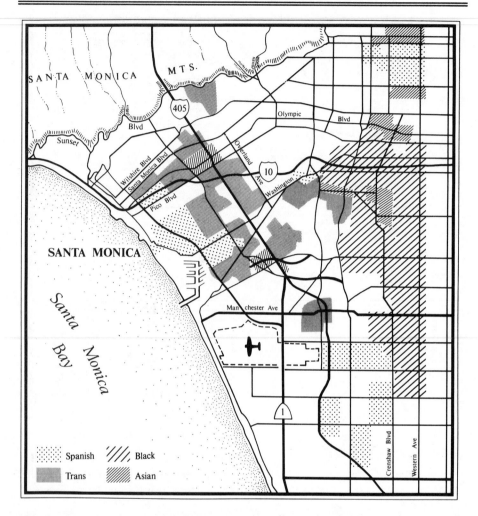

Fig. 2.4. Los Angeles/Santa Monica distribution of ethnic populations, 1980. Map drawn using data from the U.S. Census, 1980.

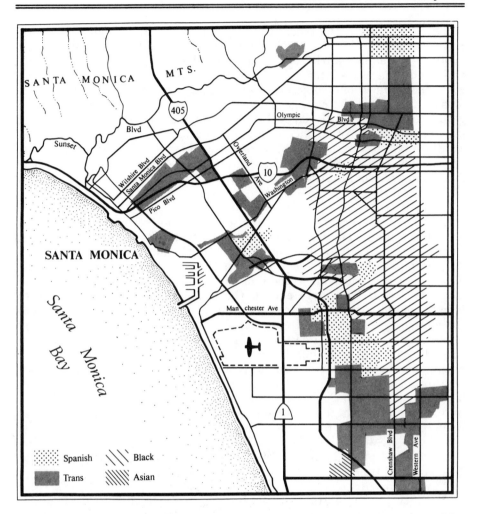

Fig. 2.5. Los Angeles/Santa Monica distribution of ethnic populations, 1990. Map drawn using data from the U.S. Census, 1990.

In 1950, only a few tracts were transitional, that is, with no ethnic grouping dominating. By 1960, the tracts that had been transitional in 1950 were predominantly Asian, and a number of new transitional tracts appeared. Ten years later, additional transitional areas appeared, along with three Black, one Hispanic, and another large block of Asian tracts. Most dramatic is the change between 1970 and 1980, when non-Anglo groups became the majority in Los Angeles. Note that by 1990, many of the areas became Anglo once again. This occurred after large sections of small, single-family homes were replaced by expensive condominiums. Not shown on the maps is the shift of the Anglo population to the suburban areas of Los Angeles to housing developments on what had been agricultural land.

As the city grew out from the core, the Los Angeles Public Library (LAPL) built new branch libraries to serve the new residential areas. Old branches remained in place; unfortunately, so did the original collections. In charging LAPL with discrimination against minority groups, the Los Angeles city attorney's office produced a series of charts showing the great differences in almost all aspects of library service between Anglo and minority areas. To a large extent, the problem arose from a failure to monitor changes in the service community and to adjust the collection to the changing interests and needs of the service population. Like many public library systems, LAPL used circulation data as a major factor in allocating money to branch libraries. That is, as circulation goes up or down, so does the branch's budget. If there is a major shift in the service population and there is no corresponding shift in the collection, there can be a drop in circulation and a drop in funding. When this happens, a library can be caught in a cycle that is difficult, if not impossible, to break. Even if the staff recognizes the problem, there is too little money to effect a change that would adequately reverse the trend. Flexibility in funding is necessary to help break the cycle when the situation has gone on for any length of time.

Two things are clear from this example. First, monitoring the service community and adjusting to the changes is important. Second, major shifts can take place almost overnight, even in a large community. (Ten years in the history of a city of millions of people is almost overnight.) In the case of Los Angeles, an official agency did alert city agencies to the trends and in 1976 predicted quite accurately the 1980 census results. (Predicted Anglo population 49 percent, actual 48 percent; predicted Black population 16 percent, actual 16 percent; and predicted Hispanic population 28 percent, actual 29 percent.) Making use of data from such agencies saves time, money, and work. Unfortunately, budget problems caused Los Angeles to close this office in the late 1970s. However, in most governments there is a planning agency that can supply useful information about community trends. If no such agency exists, it is even more important for the library to undertake community analysis. In such cases, the library may be able to locate a university geography or sociology department that has an interest in demographics and can provide data for an assessment project.

Economic data are useful for both general planning and collection development. Knowledge of the existing economic base of the community and of possible changes may help the library better plan its collection development activities. That is, anticipating increases or decreases in funding can lead to a more even collection, especially for serial publications. An economy based on semiskilled or unskilled workers calls for one type of collection, a skill-based economy calls for another, and an economy based on knowledge workers calls for still another. Communities with a seasonal economy or a predominantly migrant population face several problems. What type of service and which formats would best serve the seasonal population? When you know the answers to these and similar questions, you can begin to build a useful collection.

Communication systems available to the community are important to the library's service mission. Closed circuit and cable television as well as telecommunication systems will become valuable resources for delivering information directly to customers. Already important in the primary and secondary schools, television is becoming a factor in higher education and in the education of the whole community. Public access to cable television—one channel reserved for community use—has had an impact on some libraries. Community reference services combining cable television and telephone are becoming more common, and some libraries offer story hours on cable. Cable television as well as interactive video and teletext will open up new areas of service and patron access, as well as collection development needs. Another developing phenomenon is electronic villages, for example, Blacksburg, Virginia, where the community is connected to the Internet.

Social and educational organizations reflect community values. Though social patterns are slower to change than individual attitudes, the library must consider such pattern shifts in planning an integrated collection building program. Social clubs, unions, and service organizations affect and reflect community interests. The most important group of organizations is educational. An academic institution no longer offers only two-year, four-year, and postgraduate degree programs. Evening adult education classes, day and night degree programs, off-campus classes, and even some remedial high school level courses create complex instructional programs, each facet having different information needs. A public library's concern needs to be broader than public and private primary and secondary schools; it also needs to consider adult vocational programs and higher education. Special libraries in business exist to serve research and development and planning needs; however, other areas, such as in-house training and development, may require library support.

Cultural and recreational organizations also reflect community interests. As is the case with social organizations, these formal groups provide useful clues to highly specialized interest areas with enough community interest to sustain a formal group. Many of these groups, when given library service, join the library's most solid and influential supporters. This category does not apply to special libraries, as there is seldom a question about who their customers are. (For a recent discussion of cultural diversity and needs assessment, see an article by the author in the journal *Collection Building*.[9])

Other *community information services* are, in some respects, the most important elements in the collection development program. If the library identifies several community information sources, and if the various sources can develop a working cooperative agreement, everyone will benefit. All too often public, school, and academic libraries in the same political jurisdiction operate as if they existed in isolation. When a group of publicly supported libraries in a local area fails to develop cooperative programs, considerable resources and service go to waste. The first step in achieving a cooperative arrangement is to know what resources each library holds. In addition to knowing what library resources exist in the community, the librarian should know about other information resources, such as bookstores, video and music stores, newspapers, radio and television stations, and motion picture theaters. Some writers have suggested fewer recreational materials are necessary in the library if other recreational outlets are available to the community.

How and Where Is Data Collected?

Knowing what you need to know is only one-third of the battle. Knowing how to get the information and how to analyze it represents the remaining two-thirds. The fields of social welfare and sociology have developed a number of methods for systematically studying the community. One may divide community studies into four primary types: (1) key informant, (2) community forum, (3) social indicators, and (4) field survey. Libraries can use all of these methods, singly or in combination, depending on the specific project. Combining approaches is a good technique because it helps to insure that valid, unbiased data is obtained. (A good book to review for planning a combined approach is Jack McKillip's *Needs Analysis*.[10])

Key Informant

Key informants are individuals who are in a position to be aware of the needs of the people in the community. Included in this group are public officials, officers of community organizations, business leaders, the clergy, and certain unofficial leaders (those who do not hold office) in the community who are influential and whom other people view as knowledgeable about community affairs. The project team interviews these individuals to ascertain their opinions and ideas concerning the community's information needs. Another term that is sometimes used for key informant is gatekeeper. (A particularly good article on gatekeepers and libraries is by Cheryl Metoyer-Duran.[11])

To be effective, a tested interview schedule needs to be established. A tested interview schedule uses questions the team develops and tests with individuals who have backgrounds or positions similar to the people who will be part of the study. The purposes of pretesting are to learn what types of responses the researcher may expect to receive and whether the answers address the issues addressed by the project. Frequently, researchers get unexpected results from the pretest and find they must develop new questions in order to collect the designated data. Individuals differ in their understanding of what a question really means. Pretesting questions allows a team to reduce the range of interpretation by rewording ambiguous or confusing questions. There should not be too many interviewers, and unless they have had extensive experience in interviewing, they must have thorough training before they begin.

Potential shortcomings of the key informant approach include the fact that key informants do not fully represent the community. Because their selection is not random, the researchers cannot treat the data as if it represents the community population. The opinions of key informants reflect personal biases; their perceptions of a community's information needs may differ from the perceptions of people who do not hold positions of influence. In essence, this type of data supplies subjective but useful information about how people of influence perceive the community information needs.

The key informant approach is relatively easy to prepare and implement. It requires the least amount of time to collect data, and it is very helpful in making key people aware of the information problems of a diverse community. However, when using this approach, one must supplement data from interviews with key informants with published (objective) data and when possible, with a representative cross section of community opinion.

Community Forum

The community forum is a type of town meeting. Again, the advisory committee can be useful in setting up such meetings and encouraging community members to attend. This approach avoids selection bias by the researcher, as anyone in the community can express his or her opinion at a number of public meetings. The key to success for this approach lies in extensive publicity. Libraries may use several mechanisms to encourage people to attend community forums, such as letters to individuals and selected organizations or use of mass media, including newspapers, radio, and television. In a large community, a number of meetings may be necessary in order to keep the groups small enough so people will feel comfortable expressing their opinions. Smaller, more numerous meetings also allow for adequate time to fully hear all points of view. In order to make these meetings useful, the research team must provide some structure for the meetings. A typical approach is to design sets of questions to raise at all the meetings. The team must also leave time to handle questions that arise from the audience. It is usually desirable to have the entire survey team present at all meetings or arrange to tape the meetings.

Two advantages of the community forum are that it is easy to arrange and inexpensive. Forums also help identify individuals who have an interest in improving the quality of library service in their community. When it comes time to implement new programs, the library can call on these people to assist in the work. One glaring disadvantage of the community forum is that people who do not use the library probably will not attend the meetings. If they feel they have no need for the library, why should they spend time talking about its services? Another major disadvantage is that the data obtained are impressionistic and subjective. These data are extremely difficult to categorize and are not readily amenable to systematic analysis. Although these disadvantages are serious, the community forum is useful as a major grassroots democratic process for soliciting opinions, ideas, and criticism from the general population. In the case of exploring options for starting a service to an unserved cultural or ethnic group, the community itself is an essential part of the process.

Social Indicators

Social scientists have developed a method that makes use of social indicators to determine the needs of various segments of a community. "The notion of the city as a constellation of 'natural areas' has . . . proven useful as a method of describing social subdivisions within communities."[12]A natural area is a unit within the community that can be set apart from other units or areas by certain characteristics. Those characteristics, or social indicators, may be geographical features, such as rivers or transportation patterns; sociodemographic characteristics, such as age, sex, income, education, and ethnicity; population factors, including distribution, density, mobility, and migration; the spatial arrangements of institutions; and health and social well-being characteristics, such as condition of housing or suicide rates.[13]

By using descriptive statistics found in public records and reports, the library involved in community analysis can deduce certain information needs of the community's population. By selecting factors that researchers think are highly correlated with those groups in need of information, surveyors may be able to extrapolate the information needs of the whole community. What these social indicators (also called factors, variables, or characteristics) may be is a point of much disagreement among researchers in library and information science. Some social indicators are age, health, sex, employment, education, marital status, income, and location of domicile or work site.

What are the implications of those indicators for library users? Following are some broad generalizations based on library research. Use of libraries and information centers tends to decrease with age, especially among adults over the age of 55. (One reason for decreased use is deteriorating vision and other health problems.) Senior faculty, researchers, and organization officials tend to use libraries and information centers less as they increase in status and age. (They still use information; however, the actual gathering is done by junior or support staff, who tend to be younger.) Women make greater use of libraries and information centers than men, regardless of the library's institutional environment (public, academic, or corporate).

As the number of years of education increases, so does use of libraries, up to about 16 years of formal education. After earning a bachelor's degree, a person's library use curves downward. Apparently, graduate and postgraduate education moves the person into the invisible college network, so there is less need to use formal information systems.

Income level and use of formal information systems also show a J-shaped curve. That is, low income usually translates into low use; use rises through middle and upper-middle income levels; and use sharply decreases at high income. Apparently, persons with high incomes can purchase a large percentage of the information they require.

Generally, as health declines, there is a decrease in the use of formal information systems. However, with proper equipment and special services, libraries can reverse this tendency.

Persons employed in manual labor tend not to use formal information systems. Information use tends to increase in direct relationship to increased levels of skills required to perform the work.

The law of least effort is clearly evident in the finding that as the distance of the residence or work station from the information center increases, there is a corresponding drop in use.

Single persons and married couples with no children tend to use formal information systems less than couples with children, and as the number of children rises, so does use.

After researchers select the indicators, they can start to collect data from a variety of existing sources. The most detailed and accurate source of demographic data is the national census. In the United States, census tract data (a unit for data collections based on geographic areas of a few thousand people) are resources. The major drawback with census data is that it is a complete study done only once every 10 years in the United States. (The Census Bureau does an annual population estimate, but it covers only the county and state levels.) In rapidly changing communities, this is a problem because the statistics are misleading after a few years. However, other sources are available for up-to-date local data. Regional, county, or city planning agencies gather statistics and make projections that can be useful. In addition, school boards, chambers of commerce, social service agencies (public and private), and police departments compile data useful to library researchers.

For actual investigation, the research team must select a unit of analysis, such as census tracts or *block groupings*. Census tracts are one of the most widely used units of analysis for community studies. One obvious reason is that some of the desired data are readily available, and in most cases the geographic area is relatively small. Though the ease of data collecting can serve as a basis for selecting the study unit, the team should never allow ease of data collecting to jeopardize the integrity of the study.

Field Surveys

The field survey approach to community analysis depends on the collection of data from a sample or entire population of people living within a given area. The most common means of collecting data is through interview schedules or questionnaires. The methods most frequently used are telephone interviews, person-to-person interviews, and mailed questionnaires. Each of these methods employs a series of questions. In a community survey for public libraries, questions often elicit data from an individual or household regarding frequency of use of the library, reading habits, economic and/or educational background, or any other information that the library believes will provide insight into need, use, and especially nonuse, of the library.

Researchers must be careful when designing questions so as not to violate an individual's right to privacy. If the person or group designing the questionnaire is not certain of the legality of the questions, advice from reliable legal counsel is required. Questions should have a direct relationship to the objectives of the survey. Those questions that elicit peripheral information lengthen the questionnaire, raise the cost of the survey, overburden the respondent, and create unrealistic expectations. This, in turn, may decrease the response rate and reduce the validity of the findings.

One choice the team must make is between a structured or unstructured format for the questionnaire. Open-ended questions (unstructured format) take more time to answer than fixed-alternative, or closed, questions (structured format). The type of question asked can affect both the response rate and data analysis. Open-ended questions are much more difficult to code and analyze, and there are fewer methods of statistical analysis that one can apply to them. With the structured format, data are homogeneous and are more easily coded and analyzed. The structured format is much easier to use, especially when volunteers are conducting interviews or coding and analyzing the data. However, even when using the structured format, the researcher must carefully prepare instructions to volunteers to assure accurate results.

If the target population does not speak English, it is helpful to have the questionnaire translated into the language of the target population. This can increase participation by showing respondents the team wants their input. Respondents should be offered both versions of the questionnaire; offering only the translated version may be interpreted as an insult. The translation should be done by a native speaker; slang or local usage may not follow formal speech patterns that nonnative speakers tend to use.

The next step in the field survey is to select a sample. According to Warheit, "The selection of the sample depends largely upon the information needed: the unit for analysis, i.e., individuals, households, etc.; the type of data gathering techniques used; and the size it must be to adequately represent the population from which it is drawn."[14]

Cost must be taken into account when selecting a sample. A large sample may call for complex selection methods, and more time will be required to complete the survey. Of course, the use of volunteers can keep the cost down, but the survey method, including sampling, is not a simple procedure. This is an area where the services of a paid consultant are valuable.

A popular method of obtaining information from respondents is through the personal interview. This permits face-to-face contact, stimulates a free exchange of ideas, and usually has a high response rate. The telephone interview, though popular, has the disadvantage of a limit to the amount of time that the interviewer can hold the interest of the respondent. Twenty minutes is about the maximum length for telephone interviews that have a good response rate. With a highly structured interview schedule and a well-trained interviewer, the research team can gather the necessary data efficiently.

Mail surveys require less staffing and training than surveys that depend on personal or telephone interviews. These two advantages can significantly reduce the cost, in both time and money, of conducting a survey. However, there are two significant disadvantages to the mailed survey. First, most mailed surveys have a low response rate. Organizations conducting mail surveys have reported a response rate as low as 35 percent, and such rates can seriously affect the validity and reliability of the collected data. Even with repeated mailings the response is frequently low, and the cost of keeping track of who has or has not responded is high. Second, some persons in the community are unable to respond to anything but the simplest of questions. This may be especially true in bilingual or multilingual communities. Of course, the problem of language can be overcome by printing the questionnaire in all the appropriate languages, but there will still be the problem of the literacy level, regardless of the language used. With an interview, a trained interviewer can detect, from the respondent's verbal and nonverbal signals, when there is something not quite right about a question. One lacks this feedback with the mailed questionnaire. Because of these disadvantages, libraries using the mail survey must carefully design the questionnaire and use the simplest and most succinct language possible while still meeting the established objectives. The libraries should also attempt to determine what an acceptable response rate will be before expending the time and money for a survey that could be of questionable value.

The survey approach, like the other needs assessment approaches, has certain advantages and disadvantages. The primary disadvantage is its cost. Designing a survey of a large sample, extensive interviewing, and advanced statistical analysis, for example, tend to cost more than other methods. Another disadvantage is that many individuals refuse to supply information about themselves or other family members. In many communities, the refusal or nonreturn rate may be so high as to make the data of questionable value.

However, one important advantage of the survey approach is that, if carefully designed and administered, it will produce the most accurate and reliable data for use in determining the information needs of the service community. The other community needs assessment approaches are useful, but they have drawbacks. The key informant approach is not fully representative of the community. The community forum does not attract nonusers. Variables indicating library use and the benefits derived from that use are not fully established for the social indicators approach. When one combines the field survey with one or more of the other methods, the shortfalls of each individual method are mitigated. The combined approach allows the team to compare results from the different methods; especially valuable is the comparison of data from a user study with the data gathered by a field survey.

How Is Data to Be Interpreted?

In some respects, collecting the data is the easy part of the process. Analyzing the data takes time and skill. Analysis begins with tabulating the data. The tabulation method selected depends on how the team collected the data and the capabilities of the agency or group performing the analysis. Tally sheets are one way to start the process. These sheets list each aspect or question of the study, its value or range of responses, and overall totals. After tabulating the data, one can perform elementary statistical analysis, such as averages and standard deviations.

One simple and inexpensive method of analysis is to prepare maps indicating the study units (e.g., census tracts) and the variables or responses analyzed. Adding map overlays improves this method, as they can illustrate distributions of and relationships among the selected variables. This produces the most useful results when there are a small number of variables. Analysis involving a large number of variables requires more sophisticated techniques. Today computers allow the team to employ more sophisticated types of analysis that were costly to perform in the past. However, the team must have sound reasons for using each type of analysis. The ability to do something is not reason enough to do it. It can be just as difficult to draw conclusions from a mass of statistical test results as it is to do from raw data if one has not planned for each test.

Most assessment projects yield large quantities of data that one can manipulate statistically. However, statistics give only one level of probability and statistical significance. The main question—how to interpret the data—remains.

One way to interpret data is in terms of social needs. Some years ago, J. Bradshaw discussed four types of social needs: normative, felt, expressed, and comparative.[15]

Normative needs often are based on expert opinion. One commonly cited normative need is the need to increase the literacy level. Teachers, librarians, and others, in their professional roles, express this normative need. To some degree, the general public accepts this need, but little funding is available to meet it.

Felt needs come from the population or community based on its insight into its problems. How appropriate or realistic felt needs may be is not the issue; they are a reflection of a problem. However, just as normative needs are not always what the community wants, felt needs do not always reflect what is good for the community. Where normative and felt needs conflict, interpretation and compromise come into play.

Expressed needs reflect behavior. Individuals often say they want or need something, but their behavior shows they really want or need something else. Libraries and information centers respond well to expressed needs, that is, they are more likely to meet a greater percentage of the information needs of active customers than the needs of infrequent users. Libraries react to expressed needs by adding more material about the subject to the collection. Though that is not wrong, it does risk unbalanced spending or failure to respond to real, though unexpressed, information needs. The needs assessment project can reveal whether the library is overresponding to active users' needs.

Comparative needs are the result of comparing the target population to other populations. One such comparison might be the number of items checked out, per capita, by the target group versus the overall usage by registered borrowers. When making such comparisons, the services for the two groups need to be the same. One advantage of focusing on comparative needs is that they usually result in some quantitative measures that can be useful in setting goals for new services or programs that may result from the assessment project.

The project team and its advisory board can begin its analysis and interpretation by considering a series of questions. Following is a sample of the types of questions these groups might review before preparing a draft report. Each project generates its own set of questions.

- What are the most important felt needs within the community?

- What are the most important normative needs as identified by the experts?

- Which needs are the most relevant to the mission and experience of the library or information center?

- How can you reconcile the multiple and conflicting needs?

- What is a realistic expectation for resources to respond to the needs?

- What are the clients' costs for each alternative?

- What are the direct and indirect costs to the institution or parent organization for each option?

- What impact or outcome is likely for each alternative? Are they measurable?

- Are time lines feasible to set up an effective program?

- Are the materials available to provide the service?

- How will the option(s) fit into the existing service structure?[16]

To present the findings of the study, the team must select the most suitable format for the community. The factors in the selection relate to the character of the community, the type of survey, and the intended audience. Advanced statistical analysis may be a suitable format for audiences that can understand the assumptions and implications of such tests (e.g., academic and corporate environments). For public libraries, the target audience is more varied, from highly literate to nonliterate. Thus, the team must present the results in such a way that individuals in the community, in public office, and in the library can easily understand the implications. One way to achieve such broad coverage is by employing descriptive summaries, charts, diagrams, and other visual aids.

The examination of the data by several individuals and groups helps the team identify action areas. This can be done by providing the opportunity for group discussions of the preliminary results. For instance, meetings such as those discussed in the section on the community forums provide citizen feedback. If the preliminary conclusions are weak or unsubstantiated, group discussion will reveal it. These discussions will also indicate to the community the areas where action must be taken to improve library services. This type of public discussion can help create a strong commitment among all interested parties to seeing that action is taken to improve services. Another advantage of involving several groups in the analysis is the identification of certain unmet needs and interests of the community that are not the responsibility of the library. Public disclosure of such community problems will bring them to the forefront and possibly motivate an agency or group to assume responsibility for taking corrective action. In this matter, not only will the study help to improve community access to information, but it can also benefit all aspects of community life. After the project staff gathers all the comments, suggestions, and other feedback, it should analyze the conclusions once more in preparation for the final report. The final report should include: the objectives of the study, the methodology used to collect the data, a list of the identified problem areas, and a prioritized list of recommendations.

The most important question to ask following a needs assessment is: Do the present objectives of the library coincide with its new knowledge of the community? Are the objectives in line with the current needs of the community, do they reflect a past need, or are they merely self-serving? The findings of the study should answer the questions, and if the objectives of the library do not reflect the needs and interests of its community, staff recommendations should ensure that the proper changes will occur.

The study may reveal segments of the community that should receive better service. The findings should indicate what areas of library service contributed to the failure to achieve the desired level of service. Hours of service, location of or lack of service points, attitude of staff, and citizens' lack of knowledge about library programs may be the cause of failure. Ways to solve the problems should be recommended. For example, an extensive publicity campaign using newspapers, radio, posters, and bulletins may be effective in informing the community of existing programs.

Recommendations should include those that can be easily and economically implemented as well as those that call for extensive programming changes, but all recommendations should be realistic and economical. Blue sky reports, in which recommendations are uneconomical or unfeasible, seldom receive favorable consideration by those who are responsible for resource allocation. Present and future resources should be a factor in formulating the recommendations. In most countries in the early 1990s, most libraries have little prospect of receiving large infusions of additional funds. Thus, establishing new services necessitates reducing existing services, making it all the more essential that recommendations are realistic.

After a final report is drafted, each unit of the library should examine it for implications for the work unit. Only after all units have completed the review can the selection staff start to assess the impact of the report. After the staff identifies all of the needs and desired changes in programs, it can start formulating a realistic collection development program.

Adjusting the collection development policy is easy to do after the research team identifies the information needs and interests of the community. For example, more older people may have moved into the community, requiring large-print books and materials dealing with living on a limited income. Justifying a change in the collection development policy to reflect the change in service population is easy given accurate survey data.

As soon as the library completes a major needs assessment project, it should establish an ongoing analysis program. Statistical information is easy to keep current, and staff can gather additional information using smaller samples than employed in the original survey. The amount of time and staff effort needed for continuing analysis will be a fraction of that devoted to the original study. This means the staff can continuously adjust the library's objectives, programs, and collection to meet the changing information needs and interests of the service community.

Community Participation

The need for customer participation in needs analysis is substantiated in both the literature of library science and that aspect of social work called community organization. "Community organization refers to various methods . . . whereby a professional . . . helps a community . . . composed of individuals, groups or organizations to engage in planned collective action in order to deal with social problems within a democratic system of values."[17] Practitioners in community organization see "the participation of service users in institutional decisionmaking [as] one means of promoting consumer needs and protecting consumer interests."[18] In other words, in community organization the people of a community are seen as having a definite role in determining the type and quality of services that institutions provide.

Participation of citizens in the operation of public institutions is part of the democratic heritage. Citizens must share in the decision making process of the institutions that exist to serve them. To do otherwise is to undermine the foundations of a free society. However, a select few often try to dictate what they think is best for the general welfare. Consequently, if not mandated by legislation, citizens will demand participation. Libraries are not exempt from this phenomenon. They are beginning to see the writing on the wall regarding community participation in policy-making. Lowell Martin expressed it this way:

> Policy-making for libraries has been mainly in the hands of the professionals; the administrator and staff determine aims and programs for the most part, with trustees furnishing the stamp of approval. This may not be the structure of the future. Our institutions are being questioned, as is the role of professionals within them. If and as libraries become more essential, people will seek a more direct and active voice in what they do.[19]

Ensuring citizen participation in library affairs, especially in community analysis, is not an easy task, and the library will encounter several problems when initiating a program of community participation. For example, it is difficult to find citizens who are both representative of the community and willing to participate. Nevertheless, the greatest problem lies with librarians themselves. Most library administrators, as professionals, believe they have the expertise to run the library without the help of citizens in the community. Not infrequently, library publications report differences of opinion between lay governing boards and librarians. Such individuals contend that citizen participation is extremely time-consuming and actually may hinder the library's overall operation. They also believe that the general population does not have enough knowledge about libraries and librarianship to participate in decision-making functions concerning them.

These objections do have some validity. They can be overcome if the library administration believes that community service is the library's primary function and that citizen input can help improve service. Of course, citizen participation is time-consuming, but most library programs do require large amounts of time to initiate.

The traditional routes of citizen participation, such as library boards, friends of the library groups, and volunteers, often overlook the disadvantaged and the nonusers. These traditional methods do not encourage participation from all segments of the community. By relying on citizens from all segments of the community (as opposed to one or more experts) to participate in the community study, the library solicits diverse opinions and ideas. This broad approach solicits views the library might not learn if it relied solely on users.

Libraries have a democratic responsibility to utilize citizen participation to provide improved library services. By combining citizen participation and community analysis, the library reaches out to the community and fulfills its democratic obligations while at the same time determining what information the community needs and desires. Community study is an essential element in providing sound data which, with other data, can lead to library services that fulfill the information needs of the community. In addition, by utilizing citizen participation in community analysis, the library fulfills the four-fold purpose of gaining publicity, acquiring voluntary help, encouraging the direct expression of needs, and securing the involvement of the people in library affairs. This democratic process will benefit both the library and the community.

Sample Forms

Figure 2.6 and figure 2.8 are examples of forms one can use in conducting a community survey in a small community or a large city. With some rewording, they can be useful in a variety of information environments, not just public libraries. The citizen survey (fig. 2.6, pages 65-66) outlines basic types of information a library may want to collect. Figure 2.7, on page 67, highlights the findings such a survey form might generate. The community profile in figure 2.8, on pages 68-69, is a hypothetical example showing the type of statistical data that one can easily collect from existing data sources. Figure 2.9, on page 70, shows how a library can integrate the findings from a community analysis and information about the collection to evaluate the library's collection and service.

(Text continues on page 71.)

Our Town's Community Survey

The staff and directors of the Our Town Public Library are conducting this survey to evaluate library service and plan for the future. Your input would be greatly appreciated. Thank you.

1. Do you know the location of the Our Town Public Library?   yes   no

2. Have you ever used it?   yes   no
   If no, why not?

3. Is there another library you use regularly?   yes   no

   Which library?

   Why?

4. When is the last time you used the Our Town Public Library?

   _____ In the last week   _____ In the last six months
   _____ In the last month   _____ In the last year
   _____ In the last three months

5. Why do you usually come to the library?

   _____ Keeping up on a subject   _____ Sports or recreation
   _____ Making or fixing something   _____ Personal or family health
   _____ My work or job   _____ Government information (Social
   _____ A hobby   Security, council minutes, etc.)
   _____ Personal interests   _____ To attend a program
   _____ Class or course reading   _____ To bring my children
   _____ A course paper or report   _____ Other _____

6. How often do you find what you are looking for?

   _____ Less than 50% of the time
   _____ 50-75% of the time
   _____ More than 75% of the time

7. Which of these items have you used or checked out from the library?

   _____ Paperback books   _____ Magazines
   _____ CDs   _____ Newspapers
   _____ Cassettes   _____ Children's toys
   _____ Films   _____ Cameras
   _____ Videocassettes   _____ Art prints
   _____ Equipment loan   _____ Maps

8. Which of these services have you used?

   _____ Children's story time   _____ Bookmobile
   _____ Films or lectures   _____ Referral to other places
   _____ Books from other libraries   _____ Adult tutoring
   _____ Books by mail   _____ Library books available at
   _____ Phoning the library to   another place
   answer a reference question

Fig. 2.6 continues on page 66.

9. What two things would increase your use of or satisfaction with the library?

_____ Open more hours
_____ More help with looking for books and materials
_____ More help answering questions
_____ More programs
_____ More magazines

_____ More newspapers
_____ More copies of popular books
_____ More children's books
_____ More teenagers' books
_____ More adult books

Please specify any subject areas in which you would like more books (for example, health, hobbies, science fiction, etc.).

_____

_____

10. What age group are you in?

_____ under 12   _____ 19-39   _____ 65+
_____ 13-18   _____ 40-64

11. Sex   _____ Male   _____ Female

12. Occupation

_____ Agricultural
_____ Business/Professional
_____ Government
_____ Homemaker
_____ Industry/Manufacturing

_____ Military
_____ Retail
_____ Retired
_____ Student
_____ Unemployed

13. What was your approximate household income last year?

_____ $0-$9,999
_____ $10,000-$14,999
_____ $15,000-$24,999
_____ $25,000-$34,999

_____ $35,000-$44,999
_____ $45,000 or more
_____ Don't know

14. Highest education level you have reached

_____ Less than high school
_____ High school graduate

_____ Some college
_____ College graduate

15. Number of people in your household _____

16. Number of library card holders in your household _____

17. How long have you lived in Our Town?

_____ All my life
_____ 20 years or more
_____ 10-20 years

_____ 5-10 years
_____ Less than 5 years
_____ I don't live in Our Town

18. Part of town you live in [in a large town, this could be the zip code. In a smaller town, it could be a small map, and people could indicate which section].

Thank you for taking time to answer this survey. Do you have any other comments or suggestions for us?

Fig. 2.6. Citizen survey. Used with permission of Barbara Doyle and Veronica Storey-Ewoldt.

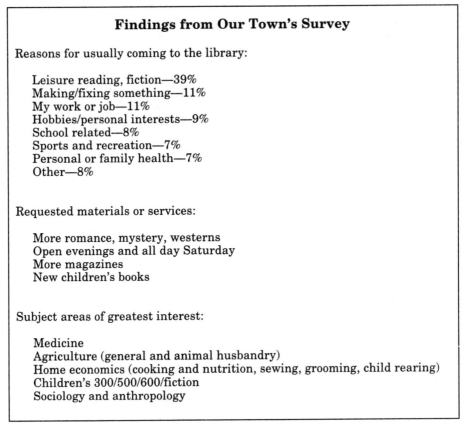

Findings from Our Town's Survey

Reasons for usually coming to the library:

Leisure reading, fiction—39%
Making/fixing something—11%
My work or job—11%
Hobbies/personal interests—9%
School related—8%
Sports and recreation—7%
Personal or family health—7%
Other—8%

Requested materials or services:

More romance, mystery, westerns
Open evenings and all day Saturday
More magazines
New children's books

Subject areas of greatest interest:

Medicine
Agriculture (general and animal husbandry)
Home economics (cooking and nutrition, sewing, grooming, child rearing)
Children's 300/500/600/fiction
Sociology and anthropology

Fig. 2.7. Highlights from a community survey. Used with permission of Barbara Doyle and Veronica Storey-Ewoldt.

Plainsville, Colorado, Community Data Profile

I. Population Description

1. Population

	10 years ago	Present	Anticipated in 10 years
City	7,500	8,000	9,000
County	11,000	12,000	11,500

Is your population growing? Decreasing? Transient? Stable?
   decreasing slightly; pretty stable

2. Demographics

   A. Age levels

   Under 5 _13_ %   13-18 _8_ %   40-64 _27_ %
   5-12 _6_ %   19-39 _35_ %   65+ _11_ %

   B. Family Structure

   Two adults, both work _18_ %   Single parent, children _3_ %
   Two adults, one works _33_ %   Retired _10_ %
   Single adult, no children _12_ %   Other _24_ %

   C. Sex

   Male _40_ %   Female _60_ %

   D. Racial Composition

   Black _1_ %   White _93_ %
   Hispanic _5_ %   Other _1_ %

   Are there notable changes over the past 5-10 years?   no
   Are there anticipated changes in the near future?   no

3. Education—years completed
   Fewer than high school _27_ %   Some college _8_ %
   High school graduate _60_ %   College graduate _5_ %

4. Income
   Average family income $ _22,000_
   Average income per person $ _11,000_
   How does this compare with other communities the size of yours?
      slightly below

5. Occupation

Agricultural	22 %	Military	0 %
Business/Professional	11 %	Retail	17 %
Government	7 %	Retired	3 %
Homemaker	15 %	Student	5 %
Industry/Manufacturing	18 %	Unemployed	2 %

   Who are the major employers in your community?
      junior college, container factory, hospital

   Are there new businesses or industries coming into your community?
      new shopping mall is in planning stages

II. Environmental Description

6. Level of Library Support
   allotted annually from city budget
   Assessed valuation—city   _____
   Assessed valuation—county   _____
   Current mill levy   _____ OR
   Mill rate equivalency   _____
   Is property value increasing or decreasing? increasing a little

		Present	Five years ago	
Annual library budget		$ 25,000	$ 20,000	
Percentage allotted to staff	40%	$ 10,000	$ 9,000	45%
Percentage allotted to materials	8%	$ 2,000	$ 1,600	12.5%
Per capita materials allotment		$ 16¢	$ 14¢	

   Is annual budget increasing or decreasing? increasing
   Is annual budget keeping pace with inflation? no

7. Educational Opportunities (Continuing or adult education programs, community schools, nonprofit institutes, colleges, etc.)
   continuing education classes and nondegree coursework at the junior college. They are beginning a marketing program directed at attracting more part time students

8. Social and Recreational Opportunities (Sports, clubs, associations)
   Lions, Elks, 4-H, Grangers, municipal softball leagues, rifle club, annual rodeo

9. Information Sources (Newspapers, other libraries, radio stations)
   local radio station, weekly newspaper, junior college library

10. Cultural Facilities (Art galleries, music)
    Historical Society Museum, art guild, town marching band

11. Churches (Number, denominations)
    about 25 churches, including Catholic, several Protestant denominations, Jehovah's Witnesses and Pentecostal

12. Institutions (Nursing homes, hospitals, prisons)
    hospitals, nursing homes, county jail

13. People:

    Governing officials

    Superintendent of schools

    Other visible leaders

    Other librarians in the community

14. Physical characteristics (Library accessibility via autos, public transportation; proximity to banks, grocery stores, etc.; transportation patterns)
    large county in terms of square miles; population is widely spread; library is located in center of small downtown area, next to the museum, one block from Safeway; library hours are 10-4, M-Th and 9-12 Sat.

Fig. 2.8. Community profile. Used by permission of Barbara Doyle and Veronica Storey-Ewoldt.

Analysis of Plainsville, Colorado, Community Profile

Total volumes—10,000

7,600	Adult	76%
2,300	Juvenile	23%
100	YA	1%

Each collection is analyzed separately, not including reference or noncirculating items. Based on the community profile information, the following areas are questioned:

Adult:

Agriculture

—Collection is quite old—should be weeded and updated?
—Users are using old materials—but also requesting items on ILL. Because this is important area to community, should we increase acquisitions and attempt to meet more of their needs on site?

Sociology and Anthropology

—Should we decrease acquisitions in this area? Community college is open to public and strong in this area.
—Better to spend some of the dollars on weaker areas of adult collection.

Fiction

—Major use of collection, although readers prefer newer titles— need to allocate dollars to keep new titles available?
—Low ILL—perhaps libraries will not lend or users do not want to wait?
—May need to weed old titles that have not circulated (69% available on shelf despite high circulation)?

Juvenile and YA:

23% of the collection for juveniles for 10% of population
1% for YA for 7% of population

Questions:

—Does school take care of YA needs or are they not interested in library?
—Is too much going into juvenile fiction; is more attention needed to nonfiction areas?
—Do YAs use adult materials—should nonfiction collections be integrated?
—Median age of juvenile nonfiction is old—should be updated and weeded?
—YA use the sports books more than any other area—more attention to this area.
—Perhaps fiction titles are not appropriate.

Fig. 2.9. Analysis of the collection based on community profile. Used by permission of Barbara Doyle and Veronica Storey-Ewoldt.

Information Centers

Normally, in the special library or information center environment the focus is on small groups and individuals. Thus, the techniques used by larger academic or public libraries do not always apply. Currently, information centers employ five basic methods to assess the needs of individuals and small groups: activities, data analysis, decision making, problem solving, and empirical analysis. (F. W. Horton's books, listed on page 40, provide detailed information about these assessment techniques.)

The *activities* approach uses an in-depth interview with an individual or group and has as its objective the outlining of all the activities of a typical day or project. The focus is on decisions made, actions taken, topics discussed, letters or memos written and received, and forms processed. The approach is based on the assumption that daily activities fall into a regular pattern and once that pattern is identified, the information officer can translate the activities into specific information requirements. One problem with the method is that people often forget important but infrequently performed tasks. Another drawback is the tendency to over-emphasize the most recent problems or activities.

Data analysis is a method in which the investigator examines information sources used and materials produced by the person or study group. This approach circumvents the problems of forgetfulness and the overemphasis on recent work. Reports, files, letters, and forms are the focal point of the study. The documents are studied to determine what information was used in creating them. After finishing the examination, the researcher discusses each item in some depth with the person(s) concerned to determine which resources they consulted in preparing the documents. Through this process it is possible to identify unnecessary information sources and to determine unmet needs.

The *decision-making* approach is similar to data analysis, but it focuses on the decision-making process. Again, the researcher is interested in the information used to formulate decisions and the origin of that information. The researcher also looks at the information received but not used. During the interview the researcher explores how the cost of not having the right information or not having it as soon as required impacted the decision-making process. In the profit sector, either or both factors can have serious financial implications for the organization.

The *problem-solving* approach is similar to the decision-making approach, except the focus shifts to problem solving. Frequently, a problem-solving activity cuts across several departments or units and takes more time to complete than a decision-making process. The problem-solving approach provides a better organizational picture more quickly than the decision-making approach does.

All of the approaches depend on the user providing accurate information about what she or he did or did not do. *Empirical studies,* on the other hand, are based on observations of what is done (expressed needs), how users act, and information sources used. If a formal information center exists, it might conduct experiments, such as varying the location of information sources or removing them, to determine whether the users' perceptions of the value of an item translate into use.

Summary

Effective collection development is possible only when it is based on sound knowledge of the service community. All types of libraries should engage in needs assessment. The methods covered in this chapter, though emphasizing the public library environment because of its complex service population, can be modified to work in any type of library or information center environment.

Notes

[1]T. D. Wilson, "On User Studies and Information Needs," *Journal of Documentation* 37 (March 1981): 3-15.

[2]Ibid.

[3]Colin Mick et al., "Toward Usable User Studies," *Journal of the American Society for Information Science* 31 (September 1980): 347-56.

[4]Douglas Zweizig, "Community Analysis," in *Local Public Library Administration,* 2d ed., edited by E. Altman, 38-46 (Chicago: American Library Association, 1980).

[5]Mick et al., "Toward Usable User Studies," 347-56.

[6]Michael Madden, "Marketing Survey Spinoff: Library User/Nonuser Lifestyles," *American Libraries* 10 (February 1979): 78-81.

[7]Ethnic Materials Information Exchange, David Cohen, director. Graduate School of Library and Information Studies, Queens College of the City University of New York.

[8]In such an environment, communication becomes complex, and we are all prone to some cultural biases that can further hinder communication. A good article to read, even if one is not involved in a multicultural assessment project, is Patrick Hall, "Peanuts: A Note on Intercultural Communication," *Journal of Academic Librarianship* 18 (September 1992): 211-13.

[9]G. Edward Evans, "Needs Analysis and Collection Development Policies for Culturally Diverse Populations," *Collection Building* 11, no. 4 (1992): 16-27.

[10]Jack McKillip, *Needs Analysis: Tools for the Human Services and Education* (Beverly Hills, CA: Sage Publications, 1987).

[11]Cheryl Metoyer-Duran, "Information-Seeking Behavior of Gatekeepers in Ethnolinguistic Communities," *Library and Information Science Research* 13 (October-December 1991): 319-46.

[12]G. J. Warheit et al., *Planning for Change: Needs Assessment Approaches* (Rockville, MD: Alcohol, Drug Abuse and Mental Health Administration, n.d.), 48.

[13]Ibid.

[14]Ibid.

[15]J. Bradshaw, "The Concept of Social Need," *New Society* 30 (1972): 640-43.

[16]Evans, "Needs Analysis," 18.

[17]R. M. Kramer and H. Specht, *Readings in Community Organization Practices,* 2d ed. (Englewood Cliffs, NJ: Prentice-Hall, 1975), 6.

[18]G. Brager and H. Specht, *Community Organizing* (New York: Columbia University Press, 1973), 34.

[19]Lowell Martin, "User Studies and Library Planning," *Library Trends* 24 (January 1976): 483-96.

Further Reading

This list presents references for each type of library. Many of the works apply to more than one type of library. To find ideas, methods, or techniques for doing an assessment study, review the entire list.

General

Babbie, E. R. *Practice of Social Research.* 6th ed. Belmont, CA: Wadsworth Publishing, 1992.

Biggs, M. "Discovering How Information Seekers Seek: Methods of Measuring Reference Collection Use." *Reference Librarian* 29 (1990): 103-17.

Billings, H. "Bionic Library." *Library Journal* 116 (October 15, 1991): 38-42.

Bremer, T. A. "Assessing Collection Use by Surveying Users at Randomly Selected Times." *Collection Management* 13, no. 3 (1990): 57-67.

Creelman, J. A., and R. M. Harris. "Coming Out: The Information Needs of Lesbians." *Collection Building* 10, nos. 3/4 (1989): 37-41.

Curly, A., and D. Broderick. "Studying the Library's Community." In *Building Library Collections,* 6th ed., 10-23. Metuchen, NJ: Scarecrow Press, 1985.

Devin, R. B. "Who's Using What." *Library Acquisitions: Practice and Theory* 13, no. 2 (1989): 167-70.

Donahugh, R. H. "Questioning the Questionnaires." *American Libraries* 19 (May 1988): 402-3.

Hannabuss, S. "Importance of User Studies." *Library Review* 36 (Summer 1987): 122-27.

Lawton, B. "Library Instructional Needs Assessment: Designing Survey Instruments." *Research Strategies* 7 (Summer 1989): 119-28.

Newhouse, R. C. "A Library Essential Needs Assessment." *Library Review* 39, no. 2 (1990): 33-36.

Quinn, J., and M. Rogers. "122 Million Library Users Ask for More Technology." *Library Journal* 116 (April 15, 1991): 14-15.

Verhoven, S. M. "User Survey." In *Encyclopedia of Library and Information Science,* vol. 45, 373-99. New York: Decker, 1990.

Academic

Allen, B. "Effects of Academic Background on Statements of Information Need." *Library Quarterly* 60 (April 1990): 120-38.

Broadus, R. N. "Information Needs of Humanities Scholars." *Library & Information Science Research* 9 (April 1987): 113-29.

Crist, M.; P. Daub; and B. MacAdam. "User Studies: A Reality Check and Future Perfect." *Wilson Library Bulletin* 68 (February 1994): 38-41.

Ford, N. "Psychological Determinants of Information Needs: A Small-Scale Study of Higher Education Students." *Journal of Librarianship* 18 (January 1986): 47-61.

Gothenberg, H. "Library Survey: A Research Methodology Rediscovered." *College & Research Libraries* 51 (November 1990): 553-59.

Hardesty, L. "Use of Library Materials at a Small Liberal Arts College: A Replication." *Collection Management* 10, nos. 3/4 (1988): 61-80.

Pasterczyk, C. E. "Checklist for the New Selector." *College & Research Libraries News* 49 (July/August 1988): 434-35.

Richardson, J. M. "Faculty Research Profile Created for Use in a University Library." *Journal of Academic Librarianship* 16 (July 1990): 154-57.

Schlichter, D. J., and J. M. Pemberton. "Emperor's New Clothes? Problems of the User Survey As a Planning Tool in Academic Libraries." *College & Research Libraries* 53 (May 1992): 257-65.

Schloman, B. F.; R. S. Lilly; and W. Hu. "Targeting Liaison Activities: Use of a Faculty Survey in an Academic Library." *RQ* 28 (Summer 1989): 496-505.

Slater, M. "Social Scientists' Information Needs in the 1980s." *Journal of Documentation* 44 (September 1988): 226-37.

Thompson, R. K. H. "Evaluating Academic Library Service." *Technical Service Quarterly* 5, no. 4 (1988): 27-39.

Public

Anderson, L.; L. Luster; and P. Woolridge. "Reading Needs of Older Adults: A Survey." *Wilson Library Bulletin* 67 (November 1992): 41-44.

Davies, A., and I. Kirkpatrick. "To Measure Service: Ask the Library User." *Library Association Record* 96 (February 1994): 88-89.

Davis, M. B. "Developing a Native American Collection." *Wilson Library Bulletin* 67 (December 1992): 33-37.

Dillman, D. "Community Needs and the Rural Library." *Wilson Library Bulletin* 66 (May 1991): 31-33.

Farmer, L. S. J. "Using Research to Improve Library Services." *Public Libraries* 26 (Fall 1987): 130-32.

Fish, J. "Responding to Cultural Diversity: A Library in Transition." *Wilson Library Bulletin* 67 (February 1992): 34-37.

Gaydosh, L. R. "Planning Collection Development in Relation to Community Population Growth." *Public Library Quarterly* 10 (Fall 1991): 3-19.

Kern, S. "Older Adult Needs Assessment Survey." *New Jersey Libraries* 20 (Spring 1987): 18-20.

Marchant, M. "Motivators and User Characteristics: Effects on Service." *Public Libraries* 30 (July/August 1991): 218-25.

Panz, R. "Library Services to Special Population Groups in the 21st Century." *Journal of Library Administration* 11, nos. 1/2 (1989): 151-71.

Smith, B. "Strategies of Collection Development: The Public Library." In *Collection Development: Options for Effective Management,* edited by S. Corrall, 45-55. London: Taylor Graham, 1988.

Spiller, D. J., and M. Baker. "Library Service to Residents of Public Housing Developments." *Public Libraries* 28 (November/December 1989): 358-61.

Vavrek, B. "Assessing Rural Information Needs." In *The Bowker Annual,* 35th ed., 472-78. New York: R. R. Bowker, 1990.

School

Day, C. "Open Discussions As a Market Research Method." *Library Association Record* 93 (June 1991): 389-92.

Dowd, F. S. "Public Library and the Latchkey Problem: A Survey." *School Library Journal* 35 (July 1989): 19-24.

Durrance, J. C. "Information Needs: Old Song, New Tune." *School Library Media Quarterly* 17, no. 3 (1989): 126-30.

Eaton, G. "What the Public Children's Librarian Needs to Know About Location Skills Instruction in Elementary Schools." *Journal of Youth Services in Libraries* 2 (Summer 1989): 357-66.

Feehan, P. "Youth Services: Collection Development Issues." *Collection Building* 10, nos. 1/2 (1990): 55-60.

Grover, R. "A Proposed Model for Diagnosing Information Needs." *School Library Media Quarterly* 21 (Winter 1993): 95-100.

Locke, J. L., and M. M. Kimmel. "Children of the Information Age: Changes and Challenges." *Library Trends* 35 (Winter 1987): 353-68.

Willet, H. G. "Changing Demographics of Children's Services." *Journal of Youth Services in Libraries* 2 (Fall 1988): 40-50.

Wilson, C. M. "Output Measures Identify Problems and Solutions for Middle Schools." *Public Libraries* 29 (January/February 1990): 19-22.

Special

Bichteler, J., and D. Ward. "Information-seeking Behavior of Geoscientists." *Special Libraries* 80 (Summer 1989): 169-78.

Bowden, V. M.; M. E. Kromer; and R. C. Tobia. "Assessment of Physicians' Information Needs." *Bulletin of the Medical Library Association* 82 (April 1994): 196-98.

Covell, D. G.; G. C. Uman; and P. R. Manning. "Information Needs in Office Practice: Are They Being Met?" *Annual of Internal Medicine* 103, no. 4 (1985): 596-99.

French, B. A. "User Needs and Library Services in Agricultural Sciences." *Library Trends* 38 (Winter 1990): 415-41.

Jester, R. E. "To the Ends of the Earth: Librarians and Management Information Needs." *Special Libraries* 83 (Summer 1992): 139-41.

Johnston, M., and J. Weckert. "Selection Advisor: An Expert System for Collection Development." *Information Technology and Libraries* 9 (September 1990): 219-25.

Krikelas, J. "Information-seeking Behavior: Patterns and Concepts." *Drexel Library Quarterly* 19 (Spring 1983): 5-20.

Kuhlthau, C. C. "Inside the Search Process: Information Seeking from the User's Perspective." *Journal of the American Society for Information Science* 42 (June 1991): 361-71.

Lundeen, G. W.; C. Tenopir; and P. Wermager. "Information Needs of Rural Health Care Workers." In *Proceedings of the 56th Annual Meeting of the American Society for Information Science*, 253-69. Medford, NJ: American Society for Information Science/Learned Information, 1993.

Sy, K. J., and P. Walther. "Tracking Issues and Meeting Information Needs in Government Agency Libraries." *Special Libraries* 80 (Summer 1989): 157-63.

Wilson, T. D. "Tools for the Analysis of Business Information Needs." *Aslib Proceedings* 46 (January 1994): 19-23.

3
Collection Development Policies

Collection development policies, selection policies, acquisition policies—are they all one and the same? Given their functions, it is obvious they are not. However, many librarians use the terms interchangeably, perhaps because some of the same information is included in policies variously identified as collection development, selection, or acquisition policies. This assumes, of course, that the library has a written policy. One library school professor who taught collection development told her classes, "On the first day you go to work in collection development ask to see the written policy so you can study it. When they tell you they don't have one, faint. By the way, you need to practice fainting and falling so you don't hurt yourselves—not many libraries have written collection development policies." This is less true in the 1990s than it was in the 1970s and 1980s. Pressures to engage in various types of resource sharing activities have created an environment where it is almost essential for libraries to put into writing how they go about developing their collections.

What Are Collection Development Policies?

Although selection and acquisition policy statements may contain most of the information found in a good collection development policy, they do not cover some important topics. Selection policies often omit references to evaluation, deselection, and intellectual freedom. Acquisition policies tend to focus on the mechanics of acquiring materials instead of the selection process or collection building.

Collection development is the process of making certain that the library meets the information needs of its service population in a timely and economic manner, using information resources produced both in and out of the organization. Effective collection development requires creating a plan to correct collection weaknesses while maintaining its strengths. A collection development policy is the written statement of that plan, providing details to guide the library staff. Thus, a policy statement is a document that represents a plan of action and information used to guide the staff's thinking and decision making. Specifically, the staff consults the collection development policy when considering which subject areas to augment and determining how much emphasis to give each area.

Why Have a Collection Development Policy?

There are hundreds of libraries and information centers that have no written policy and yet have even outstanding collections. Luck plays a strong role in having an excellent collection without having a written policy—that is, the luck of having had individuals charged with the responsibility of building the collection who were highly intelligent and motivated by a deep commitment to the library and its collections. As a result, they stayed at that library for most, if not all, of their careers and had extensive knowledge of the collections' content as well as the needs of the library's service community. In talking to these people one finds that they do have a plan and a policy, although it is not on paper.

Today, it is improbable that a librarian will devote an entire career to a single library. In the United States, career development in librarianship involves moving from one library to another and occasionally changing from one type of library to another.

Besides staff turnover, another trend necessitates a written collection development policy. This trend is the growth in the number of libraries, including so-called instant libraries. (What is an instant library? Consider this: In an advertisement in an American library publication, an institution sought to buy a 15,000-title opening-day collection.) Rapid collection development without a policy or a plan is unlikely to create an excellent collection.

There are still other arguments for a written collection development policy. The most common collection development problem is lack of continuity in both staff and funding. A written policy helps assure continuity and consistency in the collecting program despite changes in staff and funding. Collection development policies are even more important for school libraries because of the many attacks on materials from individuals and groups who seek to limit children's access to certain materials. Even large research libraries are developing written collection development policies, after years of operating successfully (or with the appearance of success) without them. One call for written collection development policies states:

> I am calling on you to formulate written collection policies to articulate the rationale that guides your decisions in the selection, preservation, transfer, and deselection of library materials. At the UCLA Collection Development Forum in June 1988, collection policy statements were identified as a high priority. As a result, the Collection Development Council distributed a format to assure the key components would be included. Some of you have submitted excellent statements since then. This year we need to complete statements for all areas and subjects.[1]

Arguments Against Writing a Collection Development Policy

Why do many libraries fail to formulate or update a collection development policy? One of the major reasons is that a good policy statement requires large quantities of data. It is necessary to know (1) the strengths and weaknesses of your collection; (2) the community you are serving and how it is changing; and (3) other resources available to your patrons locally or accessible through interlibrary loan. Only when you have all of this knowledge in hand are you ready to start developing a collection development policy.

Another reason policies are lacking is that they require a great deal of thought. A policy must change to reflect the changing community; therefore, collection development staff never finishes collecting data and thinking about the changes. Some librarians say it is not worth the trouble: as soon as the plan is on paper, the situation changes so much the plan is out of date. Of course, after the library completes the basic work and writes the policy, updating the policy is not a monumental problem. Updating does take time, but if it is done annually, it is almost painless.

Uses of a Collection Development Policy

A policy statement provides a framework within which individuals can exercise judgment. Unless the library is highly atypical, its collection development work will involve several persons at any one time and a great many persons throughout the library's history. Whenever a number of persons set a policy without written guidelines, slightly different views of the library's purpose will probably emerge. Without written statements, the divergence of opinion can cause confusion. With a collection development policy statement, everyone has a reference point. A written policy allows discussions of differences of opinion based on a common document. In such situations, working agreements are possible even when total agreement is impossible. In a school media center setting, differences of opinion about what should or should not be in the collection can and do lead to the courtroom rather than the classroom.

In an academic situation, with faculty in charge of selection, many points of view come into play. For example, four different anthropology professors might be selectors in four successive years. Lacking a policy statement, each professor would be free to, and sometimes would, buy heavily in a particular area of personal interest. The result might be one year of almost exclusive purchasing of North American ethnology, one of Bantu studies, one of physical anthropology, and one of Oceanic material. Given enough changes in professors and their personal interests, it might be possible to cover the entire field. But, many fields would receive little or no attention during most years. A professor may not stay long enough to fully develop a collection in an area, with the result being that the library cannot claim strength in any one area. If the professors have full authorization for the selection process, the library can do little to keep a bad situation under control.

Special libraries may or may not have a written collection development policy. One reason many do not have a policy is that the mission statement of the library is so specific as to service community, formats, and subject areas collected that a collection policy would be redundant. Where the service population and areas of interest diversify, there is a need to develop a written policy covering all or some of the topics discussed in this chapter. Admittedly, a written policy statement will not solve all problems, because selectors normally have authority to make the final decisions. However, if the library has a document outlining the fields requiring coverage, the policy can serve as a reminder that areas other than the selector's favorites need consideration. Even the small public library will find a written collection development policy useful, especially if there is community involvement in its approval or preparation. Among its many uses, the collection development policy

informs everyone about the nature and scope of the collection

informs everyone of collecting priorities

forces thinking about organizational priorities for the collection

generates some degree of commitment to meeting the organizational goals

sets standards for inclusion and exclusion

reduces the influence of a single selector and personal biases

provides a training and orientation tool for new staff

helps insure a degree of consistency over time and staff turnover

guides staff in handling complaints

aids in weeding and evaluating the collection

aids in rationalizing budget allocations

provides a public relations document

provides a means of assessing overall performance of the collection development program

provides outsiders with information about purpose of collection development (an accountability tool)

Some people suggest the collection development policy would be more practical if it incorporates material that allows the document to serve as a bibliographer's manual. Others suggest preparing minipolicies for specialized service programs. The additional information needed to make the policy a bibliographer's manual will not make the document too long. Providing information about the characteristics of the user population, in addition to simply identifying who the library will serve, will assist newly hired bibliographers in understanding the customer base. Data about what and how the primary customer groups use information materials aids in selecting the right material at the right time. Outlining the character of the various subject fields the library collects, as well as information about the major producers of the materials collected, will assist individuals taking over a new subject responsibility. Including data about review sources will further enhance the usefulness of the manual. Statements about subject and format priorities also are beneficial, especially when combined with an indication of the percentage of the materials budget normally expended on a subject.

Finally, a collection development policy statement can provide a useful means of communicating with patrons. Though a complete policy statement runs to many pages, longer than most patrons care to read, a summary of its major points can be valuable. This is especially true if the patrons have had some say in the policy formulation.

Elements of a Collection Development Policy

What elements belong in a good collection development statement? The following discussion of the three major elements—overview, details of subject areas and formats collected, and miscellaneous issues—illustrates why policy formulation is so time-consuming and why it is critical to success. Certainly all American libraries should consult two American Library Association (ALA) publications, *Guide for Written Collection Policy Statements* and *Guide for Writing a Bibliographer's Manual*. The following discussion parallels the latter document but includes additional considerations not covered in the manual.

Element One: Overview

The first element consists of a clear statement of overall institutional objectives for the library. Statements such as "geared to serve the information needs of the community" have little value or concrete meaning. To ensure that the statement will help selectors and has specific meaning, all of the following factors should be present in the first section:

1. A brief general description of the service community (town, country, school, or business). What is the composition of the community and what changes are occurring? If you have done a thorough job of community analysis (see chapter 2), this part of the policy and many of the following sections will be easy to prepare.

2. Specific identification of the service clientele. Does this include anyone who walks in the door? Probably not, or at least not at the same level as the primary clientele. Who are the primary clients? Does this group include all local citizens, all staff and students of the educational institution, all employees of the business? Will you serve others? If so, to what degree? Will the service to others be free, or will there be a fee? Are there other differences in service for various groups, for example adults, children, faculty, or students? Must patrons come to the library? Will there be service for the disabled, the institutionalized, and

users with below-average reading ability or other communication problems? These are but a sample of the questions one might ask about the service population. There are no universal answers; there is a right answer for a particular library at a particular time, and this answer will change over time.

3. A general statement regarding the parameters of the collection. In what subject fields will the library collect? Are there any limitations on the types of format that the library will acquire, e.g., only printed materials, such as books, periodicals, and newspapers? What are the limits in audiovisual areas? This section should provide an overview of the details covered in the second major element of the policy.

4. A detailed description of the types of programs or patron needs that the collection must meet. In a public library, to what degree is the collection oriented toward educational purposes, that is, toward the support of formal educational programs and self-education? Will the library meet recreational needs? If so, to what degree? Will the collection circulate or is it for on-site reference only?

For public libraries with specialized service programs, this is the place to outline service goals. When developing an ethnic collection, the goals can be different for different groups.

I developed the following list, based on the book *Understanding You and Them,* to illustrate different goals one could have for various purposes. (The target population will decide which goal will be most desirable.)

- The root culture, to help maintain its heritage and social values.

- The experiences of the ethnic group in the United States.

- Survival skills and general information about life in the United States.

- The changing nature of society, with an emphasis on social changes in the root culture.

- Relations with other ethnic groups.

- Materials that reflect the current situation of the group in the United States.

- The future of the group in the American society.

- Educational materials that will help adults and children in various formal and informal educational programs.[2]

Academic libraries need to consider how much emphasis to place on research material in comparison to instructional material. Again, statements about collection goals are appropriate. Gale Hannigan and Janis

Brown suggest five collection development goals in the area of microcomputing. These guidelines can be used in academic or special libraries. The suggested goals are

- to provide computer-based instructional programs to support the clinical years of the medical school curriculum.

- to provide a central facility for expensive resources needed by individuals on an occasional basis, such as interactive videodisc.

- to provide productivity tools (for example, word processing) to increase student computer literacy.

- to provide a facility for evaluation of clinically oriented software.

- to provide end-users with access to computerized databases, either online or CD-ROM.[3]

These goals may appear unrelated to the collection; however, by changing the wording to relate the goals to the service population, they could apply to most academic or special libraries or information centers. In special libraries, the question tends to focus on which classes of users to serve.

1. The general limitations and priorities, including an outline of how the library will develop the collection. To what degree will the library collect retrospective materials? One important issue to cover in this section of the policy is whether the library will buy duplicate copies of an item. If so, what factors will the library use to determine the number of copies to acquire and how long to retain them? One excellent book on the topic of duplicate copies is Michael Buckland's *Book Availability and the Library Users.*[4] This book provides information essential to members and potential members of a collection development staff.

2. A detailed discussion of the library's role in cooperative collection development programs. To be effective, this section must leave no doubt in a reader's mind as to whether the basic philosophy is one of self-sufficiency or cooperation. If the reader is in doubt, it means the policy writers either did not want to make a decision on this critical issue or wanted to avoid taking a public stand. Furthermore, when the library is part of one or more cooperative programs, this section should identify those programs and identify the subject areas for which the library has a major collecting responsibility. For subject areas that the library does not collect, the policy should list the libraries that do collect them.

Element Two: Details of Subject Areas and Formats Collected

The policy writers must break down the collections into constituent subject areas, identify types of material collected, and specify the primary user group for each subject. This may sound like a lot of work— it is. Collection development officers must spend hours talking to customers about what subject areas they use and spend many more hours thinking about what they have learned. After collecting the data someone must assign priorities to each area, perhaps by format within each area. All of this work is done with the goal of achieving a proper balance of subjects, and to supply the information needs of the service community. A complete listing of patron groups and formats could run to several pages if each of the major categories is subdivided. The following list provides the major categories

Patrons

Adults

Young adults

School age children

Preschool children

Physically disabled (e.g., the blind, visually impaired, and persons who use wheelchairs)

Shut-ins and persons in institutions (e.g., hospitals, residential care facilities, and prisons)

Teaching faculty

Researchers

Staff

Undergraduate students

Graduate students

Postgraduate students

Alumni

Formats

Books (hardbound or paperback)

Newspapers

Periodicals (paper, microform, and electronic)

Microforms

Slides

Films and videos

Pictures

Audio recordings

Online resources (Internet and other services)

Musical scores

Pamphlets

Manuscripts and archival material

Maps

Government documents

CD-ROMs and laser disks

Realia

Games and toys

Specimens

Software, databases, and other electronic formats

The lists provide a clear picture of the magnitude of the project, especially when one adds in subject area considerations and changing formats. Although this may seem too time-consuming, remember that few libraries collect all categories, formats, or subjects.

Libraries set priorities, or levels of collecting intensity, in several ways. The ALA guidelines suggest a five-level system: comprehensive, research, study, basic, and minimal. The Research Library Group (RLG), an organization of large research libraries in the United States, developed a multipurpose conspectus that identifies collecting levels. The Association of Research Libraries (ARL) also adopted the conspectus model. European and Canadian academic libraries have or are considering engaging in a conspectus assessment project.

Nonacademic groups have modified the conspectus concept to meet the needs of all types of libraries. Some of these groups include Alaska Statewide Inventory Project, Colorado State Library Project, Illinois Statewide Collection Development Project, Metropolitan Reference and Research Agency of New York, and, most notably, the Pacific Northwest Collection Assessment Project. The conspectus model has become the de facto standard for assigning a numerical value to the existing collections and the level of collecting the library wishes to maintain or achieve. It serves as a tool for both collection policy development and assessment.

The conspectus model helps in formulating a collection policy because it forces collection development staff to engage in detailed subject analysis. Usually, it uses the Library of Congress Classification System, with conversion tables for the Dewey Decimal Classification numbers, as the basis for subject analysis.

The Pacific Northwest model has been successfully employed by more than 200 libraries of all types. It employs the basic conspectus structure but provides a coding system that all types of libraries can use. There are four possible subject level approaches a library may select from:

- 20 major LC divisions (the least detailed and most appropriate for small and medium-sized nonspecialized libraries);

- 200 subject level (this is the level many colleges use);

- 500 field level (the most common level for medium-sized academic and most large public libraries); and

- 5,000 topic level (this is the level one needs to employ with a research collection).

In most of the models, a collection development officer assigns a numerical value to each subject area in terms of both current collecting levels and existing collection strength. With some models the library may also indicate the desired level of collecting, if it differs from existing values. The RLG system of coding employs five values: 0—out of scope; 1—minimal; 2—basic information; 3—instructional level; and 4—research level. The *Pacific Northwest Collection Assessment Manual* offers a finer division of the coding: 1a, 1b, 2a, 2b, 3a (basic), 3b (intermediate), and 3c (advanced).[5]

One of the major concerns or criticisms about the conspectus method relates to how different selectors, in the same or different libraries, apply the codes. It is important that all selectors apply the codes in the same way to ensure some degree of consistency among libraries. Until the *Pacific Northwest Manual* appeared, the process of assigning values was highly subjective. However, the *Pacific Northwest Manual* offers quantitative guidelines to help selectors assign consistent values. The following are the major points:

1. Monographic Coverage in a Division (will vary according to publishing output)

   1a = out-of-scope

   1b (or less) = fewer than 2,500 titles

   2a = 2,500-5,000 titles

   2b = 5,000-8,000 titles

   3a = 8,000-12,000 titles representing a range of monographs

   3b (or more) = more than 12,000 titles representing a wider range than 3a

2. Percentage of Holdings in Major, Standard Subject Bibliographies

1b (or less) = 5% or below
2a = less than 10%
2b = less than 15% holdings of major subject bibliographies
3a = 15-20%
3b = 30-40%
3c = 50-70%
4 (or more) = 75-80%

3. Periodical and Periodical Index Coverage

1b = some general periodicals + *Readers' Guide to Periodical Literature* and/or other major general indexes
2a = some general periodicals + *Readers' Guide to Periodical Literature* and/or other major general indexes
2b = 2a + wider selection of general periodicals + 30% or more of the titles indexed in the appropriate Wilson subject index + access to the index
3a = 50% of the titles indexed in the appropriate Wilson subject index and access to the index(es)
3b = 75% of the titles indexed in the appropriate Wilson subject index and/or other appropriate major subject indexes + access to the indexes + a wide range of basic serials + access to nonbibliographic databases
3c = 3b + 90% of the titles indexed in the appropriate Wilson subject indexes + access to the major indexing and abstracting services in the field[6]

Because the categories are not mutually exclusive, there is a wide margin for interpreting what value one might assign. However, the system is much tighter than the RLG system, which provides no such guidelines.

Elizabeth Futas's interesting article about genre literature suggests one might use categories called recreational, informational, instructional, and reference for genre materials when preparing a policy statement:

The level that makes the most sense for genre literature is the recreational level, which indicates the best current titles on the market. Some of the better known and still read genre authors might fall into one of two other levels available for public library selection, general information level, indicating a large number of current titles, or instructional level, a good selection of current titles and a good selection of retrospective titles. As an example of authors in each, take the Mystery genre:

Level	Author
Recreational	Lillian Jackson Braun, Joe Gores
Informational	Mary Higgins Clark, Ed McBain
Instructional	P. D. James, Elmore Leonard
Reference	Dorothy Sayers, Dashiell Hammett[7]

After the detailed subject information (a complete conspectus) is available, a selector can focus attention on the items appropriate for the collection. Policy statements are only guidelines, with ample room for individual interpretation, but they do narrow the scope of a person's work. Combine the subject intensity section with the patron list and format listing, and the result is a solid framework on which to build a sound collection.

Most subject areas fall into one of the middle intensity ranges. Few libraries have more than one or two topics at the upper levels; libraries usually restrict such categories to a person (e.g., Goethe, or Sir Thomas More) or a narrow topic (e.g., pre-Columbian writing systems or nineteenth century Paris theater).

The next part of the policy is short but important. It identifies where responsibility for collection development lies. Ultimately, responsibility lies with the head of the library, as it does for all library activities. However, unless the library is very small, no one expects the head librarian to perform all the tasks for which she or he is responsible. Because the collections are important to the success of the library's programs, the question of who will actually develop them is vital. The answer requires a careful examination of the needs of the library and the nature of the service community. This section of the collection development policy should contain a clear statement of who will be responsible for selection, what guidelines the selectors are to use in making their decisions, and the basis for evaluating the selectors' performance. Media center selection responsibility can be particularly troublesome because of possible conflicts about who controls collection content—parents, teachers, media specialists or the school board. The United States Supreme Court ruling in *Board of Education* vs. *Pico* limited the power of school boards to add, remove, or limit access to materials. (Chapter 19 contains additional information about the *Island Trees* case.)

Who Shall Select?

Potential selectors include the following:

patrons or users

librarians from public service areas, with no special background or training beyond basic library education

librarians from technical service areas with no special background or training beyond basic library education

subject or service specialists with advanced training in subject or service area

department heads

the head librarian

(A library may utilize one or more of the groups listed.)

How Shall They Select?

Delegation of selection responsibility in any given library depends on the type of library and local conditions. Whatever the decision regarding who will select, it must be in the policy so there will be no question where the responsibility and accountability lies. Selection decisions may be made by

1. independent selectors, with or without a systematic alerting program from the library;

2. committees; and

3. individuals or groups using a centrally prepared list from which selections are made

One can make a few generalizations about differences in where selection responsibility lies in different types of libraries. Many exceptions to these generalizations exist, but broad patterns are apparent in most areas. Educational institution libraries usually have more patron (teachers and students) involvement and greater use of subject specialists than public libraries have. Special or technical library staff often have advanced training in the field in which the library specializes. That staff, with substantial input from the primary customers, are responsible for selection. Public libraries normally use librarians, often department heads from public service areas, as selectors, working through selection committees or from lists prepared by a central agency.

When nonlibrarians have an active voice in the selection process, most of their input relates to the working collection. Usually, members of the library staff have primary responsibility for the reference collection. Thus, users recommend current books and monographs, and librarians do most of the retrospective buying and selecting of serials and other media for the collection.

In addition to specifying how selectors will select, this section of the policy should provide general guidelines concerning what, and what not, to select. Normally, such written guidelines are more important in public libraries and school library media centers than in academic or special libraries. This is because there are more groups with an interest in the content of the collection and concerned about its impact upon the children and young adults using it. Following are some sample selection guideline statements:

Select items useful to clients.

Select and replace items found in standard lists and catalogs.

Select only those items favorably reviewed in two or more selection aids.

Do not select items that received a negative review.

Try to provide both, or all, points of view on controversial subjects.

Do not select textbooks.

Do not select items of a sensational, violent, or inflammatory nature.

Select only items of lasting literary or social value.

Avoid items that, though useful to a client, are more appropriately held by another local library.

The list could go on and on. See chapters 6, 7, and 8 for additional discussion about selection criteria.Whatever criteria the library chooses, the collection development policy must clearly state the criteria to answer questions that may arise about why something is or is not in the collection.

Element Three: Miscellaneous Issues

This section of the collection development policy statement deals with gifts, deselection and discards, evaluation, and complaints and censorship. Each topic is important. However, each can stand alone, and some libraries develop longer, separate policy statements for each. Because they do have some relationship to collection development, the collection policy writers incorporate an abstract or summary of those policies instead of preparing something new.

Gifts

The golden rule for gifts is, do not add a gift unless it is something the library would buy. Selectors must resist the temptation to add an item because it is free. No donated item is ever free. Processing costs are the same for gifts and purchased materials. Expending library resources to add something to the collection just because it was a gift, when it does not match the library's collection profile, is a very poor practice. Applying the same standards to gifts as you do to purchased items will also reduce later weeding problems.

A written gift policy must make it clear whether the library accepts only items matching the collection profile or accepts anything with the proviso that the library may dispose of unwanted items in any manner deemed appropriate. Equally important is a statement regarding conditional gifts. Will the library accept a private collection and house it separately, if the donor provides the funds? Will it accept funds earmarked for certain classes of materials and use them to acquire new materials? If the library is trying to expand the collection through gifts and endowment monies, who will be responsible for this activity? How will the library coordinate the activities? These are some of the major questions that the policy writers should address in a section on gifts.

Gifts and endowment monies are excellent means of developing a collection, provided the library has maximum freedom in their use. There is an important public relations question the library must answer regarding gifts. Is it better to accept all gifts, regardless of the conditions attached to them, or should the library avoid conditional gifts? If there is a clearly reasoned statement as to why the library does not accept conditional gifts, there should be no public relations problem.

Deselection and Discards

Deselection programs vary from library to library, but all libraries eventually must face the issue. Even the largest libraries must decide what materials to store in less accessible facilities; all large libraries have some type of limited-access storage facility. Chapter 14 provides a detailed discussion of this issue. The policy statement records staff decisions regarding the criteria, scope, frequency, and purpose of a deselection program.

At present, deselection questions seldom arise for anything but books and periodicals. In media centers and public libraries where other media are in high demand, especially audio and video recordings, there is a greater need for replacing worn-out items than for weeding unused materials. Multiple copies of bestsellers and other books in high demand are issues in most public and educational libraries. The questions are, how many copies should the library purchase, and for how long should the library retain multiple copies? To some extent, the McNaughton Plan, which provides for short-term rental, can help reduce the cost of popular titles and reduce long-term storage of books in high demand for short periods of time. However, rental plans do not resolve the question of how many extra copies to retain or their retention period.

Questions about multiple copies are not limited to popular or mass-market titles in public libraries. Similar issues arise concerning textbooks in academic libraries. There are no easy solutions to the problem of extra textbooks in educational settings unless the library operates a rental system. Some policy guidelines for academic libraries are:

Buy one copy for every 10 potential readers during a six-month period.

Buy one copy for the general collection and acquire one copy for every five readers during X months for the high-use or rental collection.

Buy one copy for every 10 students for required reserve reading use.

The length of time, number of readers, nature of use, and local conditions influence how many textbooks are purchased and how long they are retained.

Evaluation

Evaluation is essential to collection development. Chapter 15 outlines the major issues and needs the policy should cover. The policy should indicate whether the evaluation process is for internal purposes (i.e., identifying collection strengths and weaknesses), for comparative purposes, or perhaps for reviewing selectors' job performance. Each purpose requires different evaluation techniques or emphases. Making decisions about the how and why of evaluation ahead of time, putting them in writing, and getting them approved will save time and trouble for staff, patrons, funding agencies, and governing bodies.

Complaints and Censorship

The final section of the collection development policy statement outlines the steps to be taken in handling complaints about the collection. Eventually, every library will receive complaints about what is or is not in the collection. It is easier to handle questions about what is not there. (The library can always try to buy a missing item.) The major problem will be complaints about what is in the collection or questions as to why the policy limits collecting areas in a certain way.

When faced by a patron who is livid because of an item's inclusion in the collection, how does one defuse the situation? Passing the buck to the supervisor will only increase the patron's frustration. However, without guidelines for handling this type of situation, it is dangerous to try to solve the problem alone.

Usually, the patron wants the offending item taken out of the collection. The librarian should not promise to remove the item but instead should agree to review it, if the library has an established review procedure. It is necessary to identify who, how, and when the library will handle the review process. Usually, the process begins by asking the patron to fill out a form. Though this response may appear bureaucratic to the patron, it does help identify the exact nature of the complaint. Complaint forms should consist of two parts, one explaining the library's review procedure, the other asking the patron to identify the offending sections or qualities of the item. Because the staff is offering to take action, the patron becomes less angry. (Chapter 19 explores the issues of censorship and intellectual freedom.)

It is important that the library establish procedures for handling complaints before the first complaint arises. Ad hoc decisions in this area can cause community relations problems for the library. In this area, the merits of consistency far outweigh the drawbacks. Whatever system for handling complaints the library chooses must become part of the written collection development policy.

Getting the Policy Approved

After the library staff has invested considerable time preparing a comprehensive collection development policy, it is important that the library's governing board approve it. With board approval, everyone agrees on ground rules for building a collection that will serve the local community.

An ideal policy approval process might consist of the following:

1. The head librarian appoints a staff committee to draft a basic policy statement for submission to the head librarian.

2. The head librarian reviews and comments on the draft and distributes it to the library staff for comments and suggestions.

3. The original committee incorporates the comments and suggestions into a interim draft. Perhaps the committee will call a general meeting to discuss the interim draft before preparing the final version.

4. The head librarian presents the final draft statement to the governing board for review, possible revision, and approval.

5. Between board review and final approval, the library holds an open meeting for patrons to provide feedback about the proposed policy. At the meeting, members of the drafting committee, the head librarian, and representatives of the governing board explain, describe, and if necessary, defend and modify the statement.

6. The final step is to prepare multiple copies of the final statement for the library staff and patrons who request a copy. A good public relations device is to prepare a condensed version for distribution to each new user of the library.

Following these steps ensures community, staff, and administrative consensus about issues before a problem arises. It is much easier to agree on evaluation procedures, review procedures, levels and areas of collecting, and so on in advance than to try to handle them in the heat of a specific disagreement. An approved policy makes it easier to resolve disagreements, because it provides a body of established and agreed-upon rules.

Summary

Collection development is a complex process that is highly subjective and rife with problems and traps for the unwary. A comprehensive written policy, developed with the advice and involvement of all parties concerned, helps regulate the process and makes it less problematic.

Notes

[1]Karin Wittenborg, *Collection Policy Statements* (Internal Document, University Library, University of California, Los Angeles, January 14, 1992).

[2]For a fuller discussion of items in the list, see G. Edward Evans, "Needs Analysis and Collection Development Polices for Culturally Diverse Populations," *Collection Building* 11, no. 4 (1992): 16-27. The list is based on C. E. Cortes, F. Metcalf, and S. Hawke, *Understanding You and Them* (Boulder, CO: Social Science Education Consortium, 1976).

[3]G. Hannigan and Janis F. Brown, *Managing Public Access Microcomputers in Health Sciences Libraries* (Chicago: Medical Library Association, 1992), 90.

[4]Michael Buckland, *Book Availability and the Library Users* (New York: Pergamon Press, 1975).

[5] *Pacific Northwest Collection Assessment Manual*, 4th ed. (Lacey, WA: Western Library Network, 1992).

[6]Ibid., 48.

[7]Elizabeth Futas, "Collection Development of Genre Literature," *Collection Building* 12, nos. 3-4 (1993): 39-45.

Further Reading

General

Bostic, M. J. "A Written Collection Development Policy: To Have and Have Not." *Collection Management* 10, nos. 3/4 (1988): 89-103.

Branin, J. J. "Information Policies for Collection Development Librarians." *Collection Building* 9, nos. 3/4 (1989): 19-23.

Bryant, B., ed. *Guide for Written Collection Policy Statements*. Chicago: American Library Association, 1989.

Bullard, S. R. "Read My Lips: The Politics of Collection Development." *Library Acquisitions: Practice and Theory* 13, no. 3 (1989): 251-53.

Cassell, K. A., and E. Futas. "Collection Development Policies." *Collection Building* 11, no. 2 (1991): 26-29.

Dolive, M. S. "Focusing on the Collection." *Texas Libraries* 50 (Fall 1989): 84-91.

Farrell, D. "Policy and Planning." In *Collection Management: A New Treatise*, edited by C. B. Osburn and R. Atkinson, 51-66. Greenwich, CT: JAI Press, 1991.

Gorman, G. E. "An Embarrassment of Riches, Or Just an Embarrassment?" *Australian Library Review* 8 (November 1991): 381-88.

Hattendorf, L. C. "Art of Reference Collection Development." *RQ* 29 (1989): 219-29.

LaGuardia, C., and S. Bentley. "Electronic Databases: Will Old Collection Development Policies Still Work?" *Online* 16 (July 1992): 60-63.

Losee, R. M., Jr. "Optimality and the Best Collection: The Goals and Rules of Selectors and Collection Managers." *Collection Management* 14, nos. 3/4 (1991): 21-30.

Serebin, R. "Video: Planning Backwards into the Future." *Library Journal* 113 (November 15 1989): 33-36.

Academic

Atkinson, R. "Old Forms, New Forms: The Challenge of Collection Development." *College & Research Libraries* 50 (Summer 1991): 507-20.

Buis, E. "Collection Development Policies: Coordinating Teaching Faculty and Library Staff Interests." *Collection Management* 13, no. 3 (1990): 11-26.

Carpenter, E. J. "Collection Development Policies Based on Approval Plans." *Library Acquisitions: Practice and Theory* 13, no. 1 (1989): 39-43.

Hamilton, P., and H. Feis. "A Model of Cooperative Collection Development Policies for Academic Libraries." *Technicalities* 9 (1989): 9-11.

Public

American Library Association. "Guidelines for Developing Beginning Genealogical Collections and Services." *RQ* 32 (Fall 1992): 31-32.

Feehan, P. "Youth Services Collection Development Issues." *Collection Building* 10, nos. 1/2 (1990): 55-60.

Hamilton, P. A., and T. L. Weech. "Give 'em What They Want or Give 'em What They Should Have." *Illinois Libraries* 69 (April 1987): 284-89.

Jackson, M. E. "Library to Library." *Wilson Library Bulletin* 64 (February 1989): 88-89.

Jacob, M. "Get It in Writing: A Collection Development Plan for the Skokie Public Library." *Library Journal* 115 (September 1, 1990): 166-69.

Little, P. "Collection Development for Bookmobiles." In *The Book Stops Here*, edited by C. S. Alloway, 59-73. Metuchen, NJ: Scarecrow Press, 1990.

Pettas, W. A. "Cooperative Collection Development: The Northern California Experience." *Collection Building* 9, no. 2 (1988): 3-6.

School

Callison, D. "Evolution of School Library Collection Development Policies." *School Library Media Quarterly* 19 (Fall 1990): 27-34.

Caywood, C. "Nonprint Media Selection Guidelines." *Journal of Youth Services in Libraries* 2 (Fall 1988): 90-94.

Gerhardt, L. N. "Matters of Policy." *School Library Journal* 39 (January 1993): 4.

Hopkins, D. M. "Put It in Writing." *School Library Journal* 39 (January 1993): 26-30.

Mancall, J. "(Un)changing Factors in the Searching Environment: Collections, Collectors and Users." *School Library Media Quarterly* 19 (Winter 1991): 84-89.

Special

Beglo, J. "Today Is for Tomorrow." *Art Libraries Journal* 19, no. 1 (1994): 13-15.

Hodge, S. P.; D. Calvin; and G. E. Rike. "Formulating an Integrated Library Government Documents Policy." *Government Information Quarterly* 6, no. 2 (1989): 199-213.

Hoolihand, C. "Collection Development Policies in Medical Rare Book Collections." *Collection Management* 11, no. 3/4 (1989): 167-69.

Ionesco, M. "Regional Cooperation for Research Collections." *Collection Building* 9, no. 2 (1988): 7-11.

Lein, E. "Suggestions for Formulating Collection Development Policy Statements for Music Score Collections." *Collection Management* 9 (Winter 1987): 69-101.

Okpokwasili, N. P., and M. L. Bundy. "A Study of Selection and Acquisition Policies of Agricultural Libraries in the United States." *Libri* 39 (December 1989): 319-30.

Singerman, R. "Charting the Course: University of Florida's Collection Management Policy for Jewish Studies." *Judaica Librarianship* 6 (Spring 1991): 115-19.

Thomas, V. C. "Formulating a Federal Depository Collection Development Statement." *Legal Reference Services Quarterly* 11, no. 1/2 (1991): 111-26.

Wykle, H. H. "Collection Development Policies for Academic Visual Resources Collections." *Art Documentation* 7 (Spring 1988): 22-26.

4
Selection Process: Theory

A central issue in the selection process is whether selectors will emphasize quality or put more importance on potential use when deciding what to buy. Is it an either/or situation? What is the best blend, and how can selectors achieve it? At one end of the spectrum, librarians say a library is the primary means of raising the literary awareness of the community and therefore should contain only the best literature. At the opposite end of the spectrum, librarians say a library is a public institution supported by tax monies and therefore the public should find whatever materials it needs and wants. Of course, another factor is the organizational environment. Different environments call for more or less selection. In many environments, especially in special libraries, selection is limited to acquiring items identified by users.

Quality Versus Demand

Lionel McColvin outlined the issue of community demand as the basis for collection development in his 1925 monograph *The Theory of Book Selection for Public Libraries*. His premises, and those of most librarians who support this concept, are

1. public libraries are established in response to, and in anticipation of, demand; [and]

2. the process of book selection involves both supply and demand: the library's function is to discover and assess community demand, then to satisfy those demands.[1]

To some extent, McColvin's premises apply to any type of library, not only to public libraries.

Advocates of quality selection find excellent support in Helen Haines's *Living with Books*. Although some individuals think her book is oriented toward the public library, it does consider all types of libraries. Haines's premise is that a librarian selects books that will develop and enrich the lives of the library's service community. Obviously, this requires an extensive literary background, including a comprehensive knowledge of classic works. Haines believed the way to meet demand is by selecting the highest quality books. She assumed that people exhibit needs for both ephemeral materials (which can be supplied from sources other than the library) and for materials from "deeper life channels."[2]

Quality and use are not mutually exclusive. However, many individuals are closer to one end or the other of the continuum than they are to the middle. Where librarians fall on that continuum depends on their beliefs about library service and the service community. Thus, at the outset of the discussion of selection, we confront one essential fact about the process: it is a highly personal, highly subjective activity.

A review of some of the major monographs about book selection and collection development provides a good overview of the basic issues and selection criteria, and how these factors change over time. Starting with Lionel McColvin (1925) and ending with William Wortman (1989), this review examines 70 years of writing about book selection. Although monographs in librarianship seldom represent the first appearance of a concept, textbooks attempt to summarize developments and reflect thinking on the subject that is current at the time of publication. This review examines the major U.S. works as well as international titles.

Lionel R. McColvin—*The Theory of Book Selection for Public Libraries* (1925)[3]

McColvin was one of the first to write a major text about book selection and to advocate the principle that libraries should respond to the demands of their communities. McColvin made two assumptions about collection development. First, public libraries (unlike private, national, or general research libraries) exist in response to and in anticipation of demand; they derive their service from demand. Second, the process of book selection involves both supply and demand. Therefore, the library's function is two-fold: 1) to discover and assess demands, and 2) to try to satisfy them.

McColvin's premise is that book representation must be comprehensive of and in proportion to demand, not to subject content. By *comprehensive*, McColvin meant that librarians should make judgments not only on the merits of the demands, but also in relation to the entire body of demands. Thus, representation becomes a matter of proportion, not of volume counts. A large demand may be met by a relatively small number of books, a situation illustrated by the fact that typically 25 to 30 percent of the collection satisfies 60 to 70 percent of the demand. Other factors, such as library budget, space, and availability of titles, also influence the proportion. In addition, intentional duplication (purchasing multiple copies of a title) is important. In McColvin's terms, there is a surprising amount of unintentional duplication, that is, several titles that provide the same basic information with only slight variation. The question is, Would it be better to have only one or two titles in multiple copies or numerous similar titles? At this point, some of the basic criteria for selecting materials come into play. According to McColvin, there are seven basic criteria for selection:

1. The information should be as accurate as possible.

2. The item should be complete and balanced with regard to its subject and intended scope.

3. The author should distinguish between fact and opinion.

4. The information should be current. Often, this is the determining criteria for selection.

5. The writing style and treatment of the subject should be appropriate to the type of demand the book will answer.

6. The title should reflect the cultural values of its country of origin. When the treatment of a subject differs in various countries, accept the treatment from the country of origin.

7. Usually, the physical characteristics are of minor importance, unless there are two books with similar content. With books of similar content, such factors as typeface, illustrations, binding, paper, indexes, bibliographies, and so forth may influence the selection decision.

McColvin suggested that the size of the collection in a particular subject ought to be proportional to the demand for that subject, regardless of a librarian's subjective assessment of the importance of the topic. McColvin recognized that customers' demands are often inconsistent, responses to fads, and changeable. He also recognized that librarians and the public assign relative values to various subject areas. To determine the size of the collection for given subjects, he suggested two numerical values. One value is the relative importance of the subject in terms of local collection needs, such as the subject's rank on a ranked subject list based on local interests. The second numerical value is based on the number of requests the library receives for books about that subject. The librarian multiplies the two numbers to obtain a representative number for that subject area.

McColvin suggested another method for determining the relative value of a subject. This involves ranking a subject from 1 to 10 according to the number of column-inches devoted to the subject in general encyclopedias. (An articulate critic of this approach is Rinaldo Lunati.[4])

Several flaws exist in McColvin's approach to collection development; nevertheless, it represents an attempt to meet demands while, to some degree, considering quality. McColvin's approach (and that of others who follow the demand concept) places heavy emphasis on community analysis for determining changing demands. Some persons have suggested that this approach creates a situation in which the librarian becomes a sociologist and no longer performs real library work. True, community analysis does take time and draws heavily on sociology. However, it is difficult to understand how one can develop an actively used library collection without knowing the community. The suggestion that librarians leave community analysis to sociologists and only use sociological data as the library needs them is faulty. Librarians planning a new library building should not expect a functional building if they leave the project in the hands of an architect. Day-to-day library involvement in the design process, as well as in supervision of the construction, is the only way to help ensure a satisfactory physical facility. The same is true of a community analysis project. Without direct, continual involvement by librarians, the data collected in a community analysis may be less useful. Furthermore, although a building project lasts only a short time, community analysis is ongoing. Unless the library has enough funding to hire a resident sociologist, librarians need to learn how to combine this activity with other library functions. (See chapter 2 for a more detailed discussion of community analysis.)

The socioeconomic emphasis in American and British public librarianship was very strong during the 1920s, 1930s, and late 1940s. Librarians placed considerable emphasis on community studies and on developing programs and services, and in particular, book collections, to meet local needs. During the 1950s and 1960s this emphasis faded; the economic picture was bright, and there was an increasing flow of funds to libraries. Many American academic libraries and a few large public library systems were less concerned with selecting than with collecting everything in sight. (Late in the fiscal year, one such library I worked in received a large appropriation that had to be spent before the end of that fiscal year. Subsequently, the library bought the entire stock of a medium-sized bookstore.) Libraries have now come full circle. Selection is again the key word.

Arthur Bostwick—*The American Public Library* (1929)[5]

Several writers, following McColvin's lead, emphasize the demand concept. Arthur Bostwick discussed the problem from the point of view of American public libraries. As he described the dilemma: let the public have what it wants and run the risk of having the collections fall to what he called an "unacceptably low level," or collect only the best and risk having a library without readers.

Most of the emphasis in McColvin's seven criteria was on nonfiction. Bostwick explored fiction as well. He made a strong case for its inclusion in the public library because recreation is a general need and there is a high demand for recreational reading. Perhaps his emphasis on fiction—which is more difficult to judge than nonfiction, especially when there are questions about style and treatment—caused Bostwick to take one of the more questionable stands on who should be responsible for selection.

Bostwick suggested that the library's board of trustees should have the responsibility for selection, unless the librarian is very knowledgeable. He did not explore the question of who would determine the extent of the librarian's subject knowledge. Even the most cursory review of library literature reveals many cases of disagreements between library boards and librarians about who knows what. (One must remember, however, that Bostwick's book covers all aspects of American public library operation and that the chapter on book selection is only 16 pages long.)

Bostwick also listed required characteristics of selection librarians. Although his list is shorter than some later compilations (especially those of Drury and Haines), it is impressive. Most of the characteristics—forceful, self-confident, sociable, and influential—are those one would expect of any librarian. Bostwick indicated that selectors must depend in part on the judgments of other persons because the range of knowledge and output of material is too large for any one person to manage. If this was true in 1929, it is even more applicable today, when a library subject specialist in fields like chemistry or history cannot be equally knowledgeable in all the subfields.

As so many others have done, Bostwick suggested a middle ground for book selection: the average taste of users. In terms of workload, this solution is no better than the demand approach. Both require extensive sociocultural investigation, the former to determine the community's average taste, and the latter to determine the community's needs. Furthermore, the average taste of users would preclude consideration of the nonuser population as a potential service group. In fact, the focus of attention would remain on the users and their tastes rather than on the entire community. A community-wide focus would identify nonuser groups and possibly provide a mechanism for assessing their interests and needs. That information might suggest new programs or collection development areas for the library.

Francis Drury—*Book Selection* (1930)[6]

Francis Drury's textbook, which focuses on collection development, appeared a year after Bostwick's work. Drury took the position that the value of a book is the basic reason to include it in a collection. He further indicated that selection should operate on the basis of three factors: the books as individual entities, the patrons using the collection, and the library's resources. A one-sentence summary of his philosophy would be: Select the best quality reading material for the greatest number of patrons at the lowest possible price. This is a highly desirable goal for any library.

Drury qualified his concept of the best book in several ways. That is, it could be the best in its field, its use could be "good use," or it could meet certain demands. The best type of reading material, according to Drury, has four qualities: truth, clarity, good taste, and literary merit. Of the four, truth is perhaps the easiest to determine, but even this factor is often a question of perspective; "the truth as I see it" is not an uncommon statement. As for the three remaining factors, clarity is a function of educational level, while individual preference and experience dominate judgments about taste and literary merit. (If this were not so, judicial systems could decide such issues as pornography and libel much more easily.)

Drury outlined a number of guidelines for selectors, with the following suggested keys to selecting the best books

1. Establish suitable standards for judging all books.

2. Apply criteria intelligently, and evaluate the book's contents for inherent worth.

3. Strive to get the best title on any subject, but do not hesitate to add a mediocre title that will be read rather than a superior title that will be unread.

4. Duplicate the best rather than acquire the many.

5. Stock the classics and standards in attractive editions.

6. Select for positive use, not just good books but ones that serve usefully.

7. Develop the local history collection. Patrons will look for these items in the library.

8. Be broadminded and unprejudiced in selection. Represent all sides fairly, but add propagandistic and sectarian titles only as far as use demands.

9. Do select fiction; it has both educational and recreational value.

10. Buy editions in bindings suitable for circulation and borrowing.

11. Know publishers, costs, and values.

12. Know authors and their works. If possible, develop a ranking system for them.

These factors are an interesting mixture of achievable and unachievable goals. "Suitable standards" (guideline 1) and "apply criteria intelligently" (guideline 2) sound good, but what do the phrases mean? If the phrases are open to interpretation, how can there be consistency from library to library, or within libraries where more than one person does the selecting?

The second aspect of Drury's selection philosophy, selecting works for the greatest number of patrons, results in another list of guidelines:

1. Study the library's constituency with an open mind to determine and assess its needs and demands.

2. Develop a selection program that will satisfy community needs and demands and that will develop the community's intellectual level, thereby increasing the sum of its systematic knowledge.

3. Apply the Golden Rule in selecting books for readers.

4. Provide for both actual and potential users. Satisfy the former's general and specific demands as far as possible, and anticipate demands of the latter.

5. Discard and do not add titles for which there is no actual or anticipated demand, except for classics and standards.

6. Use restraint in responding to demands of aggressive patrons, and recognize the inarticulate patron's demands.

7. Buy many works for specialists and community leaders insofar as this does not draw off too much of the book funds required to obtain material for the primary constituency.

8. Do not attempt to complete sets, series, or subject areas unless there is demand for completeness.

These guidelines are general and subjective. However, a group of persons responsible for collection development could use them as a basis for establishing agreed-upon meanings.

The cost aspect is self-explanatory except for one statement: Drury suggests that one not buy any book without first asking whether its purchase deprives the library of a better book in as great or greater demand. This is a useful question, but again, it places great emphasis on quality and does not account for subject matter requirements. Consider a choice between a mediocre title in a new field of anthropology with limited demand and a good title on gardening, which is in high demand. The library has nothing in the new field of anthropology. It has several titles on gardening but not the new title. There is enough money to buy only one of the books. Which title should librarians select? Why?

Drury intended his guidelines to serve as the basis for developing a value system for selecting books. This system, using a permanent and general scale of literary value, presumes selectors are able to judge the merits of any title. Furthermore, the librarian should be able to review, evaluate, and decide what type of library should buy a particular title.

Drury recognized that no one person could possibly know enough about all subjects to assess all new books effectively—assuming that the person would have enough time to read all of them. When one adds in other formats libraries collect, the task becomes even more formidable. American public libraries took Drury's concept to heart. Public librarians spend many hours (of their own time) reviewing new books and discussing their assessments in selection meetings. Personal experience in such meetings suggests that perhaps somewhere in the past, a permanent, general scale of literary values may have existed upon which librarians weighed each book, but somewhere along the way we have misplaced this scale. (This observation is based on listening to two normally friendly individuals argue vigorously and endlessly about the merits of a particular book.) In many ways, *Booklist* (an ALA publication) reflects the same concept. Librarians write and publish reviews of books and other media for librarians, and the journal lists only items recommended for purchase.

The quality approach modifies the basic selection precept of the right book for the right reader at the right time to the best book for all readers all the time. If assessing community needs is complex, think how much more complex is assessing the quality factor. Despite the difficulties, there are many important reasons for buying only the best. One important reason is to make the most effective use of limited collection development funds. The question one must answer is, what is *best*? Does it refer to physical characteristics or content? Not too many years ago, public librarians viewed paperback books as inappropriate for the collection. Some claimed that the material published in paperbacks was too low in quality to justify inclusion in a collection. Others said that it was a question of how long the book would last—after only a few circulations the book would fall apart. Today, paperbacks are a normal part of collections, with libraries selecting both inexpensive reprints of popular titles and high quality original works.

Content, rather than format, is the usual concern of selectors. The main consideration is to maintain the highest literary quality. A collection of the great books and great authors has been the goal of some libraries, which means that raising the community's literary taste was the highest priority for selectors. When using the "buy only the best books" principle, however, one must consider certain fundamental questions. For instance, are there lists of the best books, or can the library develop one? Many such lists exist, for there are dozens of lists titled "Basic Books for . . . ," "Best Books of . . . ," and "All Time Classics" available. Some, such as *Standard Catalog for Public Libraries,* published by H. W. Wilson, carry official standing. Some librarians believe they must acquire all books on such lists before acquiring any additional items. In their view, if a library does not have most, if not all, of the items on such a list, the collection fails to meet the quality standard.

Before using such a list, one should know the answers to several questions concerning its character. What objectives did the compilers have in mind when they developed the list? Who are the compilers, and what are their qualifications for making judgments about what is the best? What are the selection criteria? Does the compilation list several equally good titles for a subject or only one "best" item? Do the list's objectives align with the objectives of the library? The existence of so many similar lists indicates there are differences of opinion about what *best* means. The fact that each individual has a unique value system results in differences of opinion about which books are best. Philosophers have debated value concepts for several thousand years, and there is no resolution in sight. Why should librarians expect to accomplish the task in less than two hundred years?

Authors writing about buying the best recognize that to select the best, a librarian must have an extensive literary background. They recognize that a one- or two-year library school program makes it necessary for future collection developers to come to library school with a literature and subject background. Library schools can sharpen critical skills and teach basics about preparing annotations.

Lasting worth or value is easy to determine for books 100, or even 50, years old. It is more difficult for current books. There is a significant difference between current and retrospective selection, if only in terms of the number of items selectors must consider. The passage of time aids in retrospective collection development. For a variety of reasons, many older titles no longer exist or exist in only limited quantities, and most of those are in libraries' collections. Even a cursory examination of the data regarding the percentage of books published and still available from 1880, 1890, 1920, 1960, and today illustrates how time narrows the choices for selection.

The volume of books published increases each year. If the number of librarians does not increase proportionately, the amount of time available for review per book decreases. No one can examine every new English-language book published each year, much less read them. Less and less time for more and more books means that the librarian must depend on others' judgments about particular items. Consider how long it would take to read 5,000 books, a small number for a selector to review in a year, assuming one had to read every book before ordering it. One would need to read 14 books a day, every day of the year, to get through slightly more than 5,000 books. For most selectors, 5,000 titles only begins to cover their areas of responsibility. It is no wonder selectors must use reviews.

It is important to note that most writers about selection apply the concept of acquiring quality material only to books. They use a different approach for media (as we shall see in chapter 9). Librarians also exclude periodicals, serials, and other printed matter from the quality evaluation process. This is because often, one must accept a particular publication or have nothing at all on that topic in the collection. Another factor, especially with periodicals, is that the evaluation should be ongoing. Periodicals and other serials constantly change in nature: new editors, new contributors, and changing areas of interest all create an environment in which frequent review is necessary. A title once thought to be the best (or worst) may change completely between two issues.

Drury recognized that, despite librarians' best efforts, a considerable number of current selections would not have lasting value. He acknowledged that the removal of obsolete items was part of the normal work of collection development staff. Unfortunately, this aspect of collection development does not receive the attention it should in most library schools and libraries. In spite of the recognition of the necessity of weeding, most libraries ignore the process until lack of collection space reaches crisis proportions.

Perhaps the section of Drury's text that most clearly reveals the difficulties of using the quality approach is his extended discussion of the personality and skills required to become a selector. If Bostwick's list is impressive, Drury's is overwhelming. He identifies more than 24 essential characteristics, ranging from judgment, intelligence, and imagination to accuracy, speed, industriousness, and health. Many of the characteristics are desirable in any employee in any situation. Some are essential for acquisitions personnel but marginal for selectors. Finding persons who exhibit all of Drury's characteristics would be a time-consuming job; the ideal individual would be a paragon of virtues and skills. Developing a means of assessing each person's abilities is almost more difficult than actually carrying out the selection process. Everyone possesses the characteristics identified by Drury; the problem lies in determining the amount and quality.

By the time a person finishes reading Drury, she or he may well conclude: this is all interesting but how can I apply it to the real world of collection development? The answer is that only time, experience, and making mistakes will show the way. As we will see in the next section, Harold Bonny took a more practical approach to collection building.

Harold V. Bonny—A *Manual of Practical Book Selection for Public Libraries* (1939)[7]

Bonny did not claim to add anything new to the theory of book selection, but he did provide excellent practical advice on how to go about building a library collection. Much of the advice focused on knowing the community's tastes and needs. According to Bonny, input into the selection process arises from three sources: the selection librarians, the patrons, and a committee of specialists. He suggested encouraging patrons to recommend titles for the collection and to volunteer to serve on the selection committee. He also suggested the library form a selection committee composed of persons with a variety of subject backgrounds. This committee could suggest appropriate additions to the collection. (In most cases, the committee would not include librarians.)

Another use of the committee would be to assess the value of titles suggested by patrons. Such a committee accomplishes several library goals: it allows community participation in collection development; it helps to ensure a workable level of community input, neither too much nor too little; and it helps to reduce the need for super-librarians who know everything about all subjects. Bonny viewed this committee as advisory, with the final responsibility for selection remaining in the hands of librarians. Although he wrote about public libraries, Bonny's basic concepts apply equally well to all types of libraries. Most educational institutions have an advisory committee for the library. With proper rules governing the committee's powers (whether advisory or decision making), such a committee can be helpful in collection development. Occasionally, special libraries establish a committee of this type because the library staff is too small to handle the workload.

Helen Haines—*Living with Books* (2d ed., 1950)[8]

Living with Books has attained classic status. Haines's general approach to the problem of collection development combines the ideal and the utilitarian. She acknowledged that some of her principles conflict. However, she thought that, when viewed as a whole, the selection process is a dynamic one in which one constantly makes adjustments to achieve some degree of equilibrium. Her basic assumption was that people need and demand not only ephemeral materials, such as popular novels, but also materials for "deeper life channels," which require education and lasting, high quality materials.

Haines outlined two major principles and a number of related ones. The basic principles are

1. Select books that lean toward the development and enrichment of life.

(To accomplish this, one must be familiar with the foundation books, which usually are older titles and valuable current titles. Thus the purpose of collection development seems to be to enlighten—to lessen patterns of mass thinking that may be prevalent but are not conducive to tolerant living—or to help patrons comprehend vital current issues. This purpose seems to place a heavy responsibility burden on the selector, as it requires that person to make judgments about what the community should or should not read.)

2. Make the basis for selection positive, not negative. Every book should be of service, not simply harmless.

Haines's list of related principles is extensive and may leave a person wondering when or how all of it can be done:

Know the community's general and special character and interests.

Be familiar with subjects of current general, national, and local interest.

Represent in the collection all subjects applicable to these conditions.

Make the collection of local history materials useful and extensive.

Provide materials for organized groups whose activities and interests can be related to books.

Provide materials for both actual and potential reader; satisfy existing demands; and anticipate demands suggested by events, conditions, and increasing use.

Avoid selection of books that are not in demand; remove from the collection books that are no longer useful.

Select some books of permanent value regardless of their potential use. Great literary works must remain the foundation of the library.

Practice impartiality in selection. Do not favor certain hobbies or opinions, and in controversial or sectarian subjects, accept gifts if purchase is undesirable.

As much as possible, provide for the needs of specialists. Users who require books as tools have a special claim on the library, as long as the books are not too esoteric.

Strive not for a "complete" collection, but for the best: the best books on a subject, the best books by an author, the most useful volumes of a series. Avoid the practice of acquiring full sets when each volume in the set is not needed.

Prefer an inferior book that will be read over a superior one that will not. With wide and discriminating knowledge, it is usually possible to choose a book with both value and interest.

Keep abreast of current thought and opinion; represent adequately significant and influential scientific, intellectual, and social forces.

As much as possible, maintain promptness and regularity in supplying new books, especially in the case of books that are both good and popular.

In many ways, this list reflects Drury's work, as it should, because Haines essentially updated his book. However, Haines made an even stronger case than Drury for the quality collection. Her selection guidelines modified Drury's, and she turned some of the guidelines into qualitative statements. Haines recognized the impossibility of one person handling all the titles in any major field of interest, and she was one of the first to describe a comprehensive method for dealing with this problem. Her solution was to make extensive use of bibliographic selection aids, supplemented by local input. She listed six types of selection aids, and, though one may not agree with her ranking of their importance, the types do represent what was comprehensive coverage at that time. (Chapter 5 discusses selection aids.) The following list of bibliographic selection tools is in Haines's order of importance:

1. Those issued by library organizations (for example, International Federation of Library Associations [IFLA], Library Association [LA], American Library Association [ALA]).

2. Those issued by individual libraries (for example, British Museum, Library of Congress, *Bibliothèque Nationale*).

3. Those issued by societies and educational institutions (such as UNESCO and the Modern Language Association [MLA]).

4. Those issued by booksellers' organizations (for example, *Publishers Weekly* and *Bookseller*).

5. Those issued by individual publishers (such as catalogs, announcements, and flyers).

6. Those issued by other groups as a service (book reviews in periodicals and newspapers).

Without an extensive knowledge of these aids and without using them constantly, it would be almost impossible to function as an effective book selector. One must spend a considerable amount of time simply getting to know the strengths and weaknesses of the tools. Experience is the only way to get to know authors and publishers; the same is true for selection aids.

Haines went further than earlier writers in recommending a specific system for selection work. Her system is general and may be applied, within limits, in any country and in any type of library. However, Haines did assume the existence of an extensive and effective bibliographic network. She suggested the following procedure:

1. Examine the bibliographic aids on a regular and systematic basis. Examine publisher's flyers and catalogs, lists of new books published or received, and book review sources.

2. Prepare cards for titles that seem to be of potential value; be certain to indicate the source of the information.

3. Solicit and accept recommendations from patrons.

4. Incorporate into one "possible-order" file suggestions from patrons and from bibliographic tools.

5. Search for published reviews of the suggested titles.

6. Sort the suggested titles in the "possible-order" file into two groups: one to order immediately and one to hold. The latter group would include titles for which no review could be found.

7. Transfer cards for titles ordered to an "on-order" file. This will save time and effort by avoiding unintentional duplication.

This is a workable system, but it does place great emphasis on reviews and reviewers, who make judgments about a title without reference to a particular local situation. Naturally, the final decision involves local professional judgment. A particular problem for academic, research, and special libraries is that many of the required titles are highly technical. Reviews of such titles, if they appear at all, slowly appear over a period of years, as much as two or three years after publication. Normally, the library cannot wait that long to decide to buy a particular title. Thus it establishes a local review process.

Published reviews, although of great potential use, must be used with care and understanding. Haines listed four types of reviews:

So-called reviews solely intended to promote the sale of a title. Although often presented in a review format, these are more rightfully termed announcements because the publisher's marketing department prepares them at the time of publication.

Reviews published in library periodicals. Though they publish more reviews per year than most other sources, these periodicals cover only a small percentage of the total annual publishing output. These reviews usually appear shortly after the publication date, and they are seldom long.

Reviews published in mass-market newspapers and periodicals. If the book review editor is knowledgeable, these are useful in identifying titles that may be in high demand. This type of review appears 2-6 months after publication and can be lengthy.

Reviews published in specialized subject publications. Usually written by specialists in the field the book is about, these are scholarly assessments of nonfiction titles of scholarly interest. No fiction is included. These reviews seldom appear sooner than nine months after publication, and may appear even later in the case of specialized titles. These are lengthy, comparative reviews and contain more critical comments than is typical in library journal reviews.

No matter what type of review medium a librarian uses, she or he must get to know the interests and biases of the editors and reviewers. For this reason it is more beneficial to use signed reviews because, over time, one gets to know the reviewers and their biases. Human nature being what it is, we usually respect and accept the opinions of persons who share our biases. Nevertheless, the use of reviews does provide a back-up, an outside opinion that supports a decision concerning a particular title.

If a title receives several reviews, the selector may encounter a wide range of opinion about the item's quality. Some persons find this difference of opinion a problem; they want to buy titles receiving only positive reviews. Mixed reviews require more local judgment, but the differences in viewpoint may provide the required insight to make an informed local decision. It is possible that a reviewer's negative opinion is based on precisely the factor that a library is looking for to balance the coverage of a subject area. Thus, the negative review supports the decision to buy the title.

A major problem is that no single review medium in a country that has an active book trade can review more than a fraction of the annual output. Consequently, some titles receive no reviews, while others seem to get more reviews than their subject matter warrants. There is no satisfactory explanation for this pattern other than review editors work independently and select for review items the editors believe will best serve their readership. The role of the review editor is critical in determining what gets reviewed. An editor receives hundreds of titles and is able to review only a small number. Thus the editor's judgment of what to review is significant. One may never know which titles the editors rejected, but given time and experience, a person will learn which sources review the greatest percentage of titles in a specific area. For most fields, it is necessary to use several sources to achieve any degree of comprehensive coverage.

What constitutes a good review? Haines provided not only a sound discussion about what to look for in a review but also explained how to prepare a good review:

1. There should be a brief, accurate description of the book's subject and contents. This should be factual in presentation and should include information regarding the stated purpose of the book.

2. When appropriate, there should be a comparison to similar works by the same or different authors. This should be factual; however, it is also appropriate for a reviewer to take a personal stand on the quality and utility of the title under review.

3. There should be a straightforward style in the review. The reviewer should not employ an elaborate style or indulge in witticisms at the expense of conveying useful information about the title under review.

4. There should be a limited range of topics reviewed by a single reviewer. A reviewer who attempts to write reviews on almost any subject must be suspect. As a librarian, one needs opinions based on in-depth subject knowledge.

5. There may or may not be a clear statement of recommendation, such as "recommended" or "do not bother to read this one." Regardless of whether such statements are made, the review should be free of bias. Be suspicious of the reviewer who never has anything good or bad to say about any book.

Selectors must use reviews judiciously. No one would ever say you should always or never depend on published reviews. Reviews are useful in the selection process, and with experience, the librarian will learn how to make the most effective use of them.

In summary, Haines' book provides a detailed statement about the whys, wherefores, and hows of selecting quality books. No matter what stand one takes on the issue of demand versus maintaining literary standards, her book is essential reading for anyone wishing to become a book selector.

S. R. Ranganathan—*Library Book Selection* (1952)[9]

One of the post-World War II writers who did all he could to create a more scientific approach to collection development was S. R. Ranganathan. (Without question, Ranganathan was one of the leading thinkers about librarianship. He demonstrated that the central issues and problems of librarianship are international in scope. All librarians ought to read one of Ranganathan's works on cataloging, classification, administration, or collection development.)

In *Library Book Selection*, Ranganathan stated five laws of librarianship, laws that underlie all of his concepts of librarianship and his view of how to build a library collection. The five laws are:

Books are for use.

Every reader his book.

Every book its reader.

Save the reader's time.

A library is a growing organism.

The list is pragmatic. Clearly, his first concern was in developing a library that would be a valuable asset to a particular service community. Utility was the first consideration; after that came quality.

Ranganathan suggested two important means of quality control, useful even when one has only limited knowledge of the content of a specific title. If one knows something about previous works by an author, and assuming the author is writing in the same general field, one will have a clue to the quality of the new work. Using current reviews, when available, and knowledge of prior publications by the same author, the selector can almost always decide about the purchase of an item without examining the title. To avoid problems in using this approach, one must have a sufficiently narrow definition of the phrase *in the same general field*. An example of what can happen when authors change fields is the work of U.S. novelist Allen Drury. As a writer of contemporary political novels, Drury was well known and respected. He also wrote two novels set in ancient Egypt. Unfortunately, they did not match the quality of his contemporary novels. Shifting from a contemporary to a historical setting affected the quality of his work. A librarian might buy fewer of his historical novels than his contemporary ones.

Ranganathan's second suggestion is to study publishing houses. (Though he does not discuss media producers, his basic ideas apply to them as well.) Many times, selection decisions can be based on the reputation of the publisher or producer. Some firms have such an extensive reputation for producing only quality material that 99 percent of the time one is safe in selecting their products unseen and unreviewed. Unfortunately, a few firms have the opposite reputation, and one should never buy anything from them without an extensive, item-by-item review. As with any changing situation, one can never produce the definitive list of good and bad companies. Experience and input from colleagues in other libraries will provide the necessary ongoing assessment. (The next chapter describes one method for using publisher or producer quality to assist in the selection process.)

In addition to the company's overall reputation, one should consider the reputation of any series produced. Frequently, a firm establishes one or more series, each series focused on a limited area of concern (e.g., subject, format, or purpose). For example, this book is in Libraries Unlimited's Library Science Text Series. Some series are house series, that is, handled by a firm's resident staff. Other series have editors who are not full-time members of the firm's staff. This is particularly true in the area of educational materials. Knowledge about series editors, like knowledge of publishers or authors, can help selectors make quick decisions about a certain work.

Ranganathan's book is a complex mixture of practical advice and philosophy. The five laws are straightforward, but he leaves it up to the reader to determine how to implement the laws.

Arthur Curley and Dorothy Broderick—*Building Library Collections* (6th ed., 1985)[10]

Building Library Collections is one of the standard American textbooks on book selection. It first appeared in 1959. Over the years, several individuals contributed to the success of the book. Originally written by Mary D. Carter and Wallace J. Bonk, the book went through several editions; later, Rose Mary Magrill joined the team. With the sixth edition two new authors, Arthur Curley and Dorothy Broderick, took over sole responsibility for the book. The authors are never prescriptive, which is one reason for the book's success. Instead, they present general principles without attempting to create a consistent body of rules. They observe that each librarian's understanding of the library's purpose determines that person's attitude toward and application of various selection principles. To some extent, the size and resources of a particular library further affect the working out of an individual's point of view. Above all, the authors suggest no magic formula for effective selection beyond the use of informed professional judgment. Instead, they emphasize developing a plan of action and viewing the selection task as the building of a collection rather than selecting individual titles.

Their list of principles reiterates the views outlined earlier in this chapter. If they have an emphasis, it is slightly in favor of demand, although they do clearly state they believe basic items and a well-rounded collection are important.

The authors place more emphasis on the impact of the environment (i.e., the type of library) on the selection process than do the other books discussed in this chapter. Their ideas on this subject are worth repeating here:

> Large public libraries with both a heterogeneous community to serve and a reasonable book budget theoretically can apply most of the principles with little modification within the total library system.

> Medium-sized libraries are in a similar position, except that the level of funding usually forces greater care in selection. Mistakes are more costly.

> Small public libraries are most limited, and most can only hope to meet the most significant community demands. These libraries lack both the professional staff and the money to do more.

> College libraries serve a more homogeneous population, or rather, the service goals are more homogeneous. In most cases, demand is the operative principle: college libraries acquire materials needed to support the instructional program, and no one questions the quality of the material if the request originated with a faculty member or department.

University libraries serve a more diverse population than do college libraries, but their populations generally are more homogeneous than those of public libraries. Again, the priority goes to meeting academic and research demands of the faculty and students; after meeting those needs, the collection is rounded out as funds permit.

Community college libraries are closer to public libraries than to academic libraries in terms of the diversity of needs that they must meet. This is due to the wide variety of vocational programs that most community colleges offer. Demand and quality are almost equal factors in this case; limited funds and broad coverage usually mean that the library and faculty must work closely to select the best items for the institution.

Special library collections are extremely homogeneous and develop collections almost solely by demand.

School libraries are unique in that school librarians seldom have sole responsibility for developing the collection. The school system makes the decisions as to what to include; certainly the librarians have input, but their voices are not as strong as in other types of libraries.

David Spiller—*Book Selection: An Introduction to Principles and Practice* (4th ed., 1986)[11]

Book Selection is a standard British work, the first edition of which appeared in 1971. Spiller presents the problem of selection as the means of resolving the conflict between two goals—education and demand. Although his work reveals a slight bias in favor of public libraries, the concepts apply to any type of library.

Spiller believes that two important factors must be present for libraries to meet the educational goal. First, there should be a minimum coverage of all subject fields, achieved with standard works. (A problem exists in determining what those standard works are, as well as who will make the decision about superseded titles.) The second factor is that all but the smallest libraries initially should attempt to stock the standard works in both literature and subject fields for both adults and children. (In this area, Spiller's public library bias is most clear. He does not suggest that his book applies to special libraries or academic libraries; however, much of his material pertains to college libraries, including some references to children's literature.)

He sees demand as a situation in which:

1. Community needs and interests merit more than minimum coverage. Community needs and interests include those of nonusers so that groups that would otherwise be without resources might receive service. (Answering community needs and interests comes only after achieving minimum coverage, however.)

2. Even small public libraries should
   a. change a large proportion of stock frequently to give an indication of the total resources available; and
   b. attempt to serve a wide range of taste in the community rather than limiting choices entirely to popular material.

In Spiller's scheme, demand takes a secondary position to the combination of education and quality. His identification of three main reading areas—factual, cultural, and recreational—further emphasizes his philosophical view. He defines factual reading as purposeful reading, with emphasis on a need for practical information. Cultural reading expands an individual's world view and illuminates some aspect of life. Recreational reading is the least specific area; because alternate sources of recreational reading materials are usually available, the library can provide a smaller range of such materials. Spiller considers the three purposes of reading as independent of each other, but he does indicate that, at times, a reader's purposes may be mixed. Of greater importance to the book selector, Spiller asserts that a single title may serve all three purposes for one or more readers.

The library's relationship to formal and informal educational programs in the community modifies its approach to solving the conflict inherent in education versus demand. The library may choose to complement or support these educational programs. In either case, the identified level of service alters the selection process. Finally, there is a factor not often discussed by other writers: the level and effectiveness of interlibrary loan systems. An extensive and effective interlibrary loan system can have a major impact on how one develops a collection.

According to Spiller, the aim of any educational library service program is increased involvement, that is, broadening the reading interests of present users from occasional, practical use to wider interest in cultural and purposeful reading, and increasing the number and type of clients using the library.

Robert Broadus—*Selecting Materials for Libraries* (2d ed., 1981)[12]

Robert Broadus's *Selecting Materials for Libraries* (first edition published in 1973) is less explicit about principles than most of the other books in this chapter. He provides an inventory of factors or attitudes present in the selection process. The inventory is a mixture of the ideal and the practical. Broadus's philosophy of collection development places first importance on the type of library and then takes up the question of quality and demand. He thinks that the responsiveness of the library to its parent institution is the critical factor in shaping the collection. Intellectually, one can make a distinction between responsiveness and demand. However, on a practical, day-to-day basis, the two are almost indistinguishable.

Broadus sees quality and demand as factors primarily affecting public libraries. He takes the position that public libraries may stress either factor, since most libraries' policies do not fully resolve the issue. Though he presents the case for both sides, his position is that the library should meet both the currently expressed and ultimate needs of the community. To do this the library must make available the best materials because: (1) a small number of persons appreciate quality (this is a demand) and (2) this can help meet future demands for quality items after the library successfully raises the community's concept of quality.

He suggests a number of factors to consider in assessing demand:

Be aware of the impact of publicity that may stimulate demand (for example, an author interviewed on radio or television or a highly favorable review in a local newspaper).

Consider the duration as well as the intensity of the demand. (Consider renting multiple copies of popular titles. The demand for certain titles may decrease after a short time).

Weigh the amount of possible opposition to a title. Controversy stimulates demand.

Include a reasonably high percentage of standards and classics in the collection. Even if they are not extensively used, one can employ them as public relations devices with groups that have concerns about the quality of the collection.

Consider past loans of specific titles and subjects. Past use is one of the most reliable predictors of future use.

Make some provision for serving the needs of potential users in the community. Having made such a provision, advertise it.

Weigh the differences between true demand (which reflects individual needs) and artificial demand (resulting from organized propaganda efforts). This is especially important when assessing differences in reading abilities, ages, living conditions, ethnic backgrounds, and economic conditions.

Broadus's general advice about collection development is somewhat different from that given by other writers:

The maxim "the right book for the right reader at the right time" means accounting for individual readership in the selection policy, as there are various individual needs, interests, and capacities for reading, learning, and enjoyment.

One should base a decision against a particular book on justifiable selection standards concerned with merit and honesty, and it should not infringe on the freedom to read of a majority or minority.

The present status of the collection influences the selection process.

A gap revealed by an unsatisfied demand should be filled for future users.

A balanced collection should be an optimum collection for a given community of users or ought-to-be users.

Insure the presentation of truth by providing materials that express all sides of controversial issues and represent all responsible opinions, although quantitative equality in this matter is not always necessary.

On occasion, strengthen a small part of any special collection, thereby gaining the library a distinction and serving a few people that other libraries cannot serve as well. Belief in balance should not interfere with this aim.

Other collections in the community and particular allegiances the library owes to cooperatives (membership in consortia or networks of various kinds) should influence the selection process.

Written policy statements are desirable, especially for public libraries. They are of use in:

clarifying the dimensions and limits for building the collection (through reference to forms, subjects, and users of materials collected) and

emphasizing patrons' rights, thus legitimately buffering unjust complaints. A written policy can effectively shift the focus of discussion from a certain title to a question of principle.

One of the strengths of Broadus's book is its emphasis on subject field selection (almost half of the book). He provides a sound review of the basic issues in various disciplines and how they influence the selection process.

William A. Katz— *Collection Development: The Selection of Materials for Libraries* (1980)[13]

William Katz, more than any other recent writer on selection, emphasizes the inclusion of all formats in the collection. He devotes more than one third of the book to nonbook materials. Each chapter contains a section on the evaluation of the format covered (recordings, films, periodicals, newspapers, realia, video, and so forth) as well as information about selection aids and acquisition requirements. He also takes a strong stance in favor of the demand principle. "Unless it is a highly unusual situation, demand should override the librarian's negative decision.[14] As with most of Katz's writings, there is a strong emphasis on practical aspects.

An interesting section in the chapter on selection philosophy deals with what he labels the three basic selection philosophies—liberal, traditional, and pluralistic. A person taking a liberal position contends that there must be service to the total community, not only to the active users. Libraries should collect all formats in an effort to cater to all the preferences for securing information. Having a liberal philosophy means having equal concern with educational, recreational, and information-seeking needs of the service community, as well as reversing the passive role of libraries and information centers. It also means using technology and cooperative programs actively to reach people with information. Discussions with students, teachers, and practitioners in the United States and several other countries indicate most librarians subscribe to the liberal position. However, most have trouble translating beliefs into action for a variety of reasons, all too often the primary reason being lack of support from the funding body.

A person with a traditional philosophy takes a cautious approach to service; stay with what works, focus on the active user. Limited funds require maximum effectiveness, and nothing is more effective than doing what we do best, according to the traditionalist. Often, one finds the traditional point of view associated with selecting only quality materials; this is a spinoff of the best-use-of-funds position. Few professionals claim this as their philosophical position, but a surprising number actually implement many elements of the philosophy. Few librarians try to select only the best materials (and thus set a community standard), but many small libraries have so little money for collection development that they can only purchase favorably reviewed items.

The most widely practiced philosophy is that of the pluralist. When funds are more readily available, a more liberal philosophy dominates; when funding remains static, or worse, decreases, traditional approaches reemerge. Most librarians wish for the liberal approach and find themselves practicing the traditional. When we are able to demonstrate to the funding authorities the essential nature of our product and services, we shall be able to continually implement the liberal views.

Richard K. Gardner—*Library Collections: Their Origins, Selection, and Development* (1981)[15]

Although the main strength of Gardner's book is its coverage of the U.S. book trade, including review sources and the book distribution system, the author presents several useful suggestions for selectors. He reviews the issue of demand and value, ending the discussion by stating selectors will have to learn to live with a state of tension between the two factors. He also recalls the standard criteria for judging materials: authoritativeness, accuracy, impartiality, recency of data, adequate scope, depth of coverage, appropriateness, relevance, interest, organization, style, aesthetic qualities, technical aspects, physical characteristics, special features, library potential, and cost. As he indicates, these criteria apply to any information format. A selector can use all the factors only when the item is in hand or when the review or listing provides all the information. Unfortunately, a great many times the selector must make a decision based on less-than-complete information.

Gardner's discussion of selection aids is the most comprehensive of the current selection textbooks. A recommended chapter is the one outlining the review process. His chapter describes all the good and bad aspects of the reviewing process, from the percentage of items reviewed to the qualifications of the reviewers. After reading the chapter, it is clear why one cannot depend solely upon published reviews to build a well-rounded collection. Not only does Gardner provide a sense of the number of items reviewed (a small percentage of the total output), he discusses how review editors select items for review. He details the questions one should attempt to answer before making extensive use of a review source: What is the scope of coverage? What is the editorial bias? Who is the sponsoring organization? Why is it publishing the reviews? Who are the reviewers? Who selects them and how? What is the frequency of publication? What, if any, restrictions do reviewers face in terms of format (e.g., length of the review)? Does the source provide information about titles considered but not selected for review and the basis of those decisions? How quickly do review copies arrive? And, finally, how long do the reviewers have to prepare their reviews? Most of the answers will be easy to find; they are printed in each issue of the publication. Others will take time and effort to answer (e.g., reviewer selection and how soon reviews are printed). Unfortunately, one seldom learns about items considered but rejected.

An interesting example of the problem of review editors' bias in selecting titles for review came to light in 1984. A well-known author, Doris Lessing, undertook a project to illustrate the difficulty first-time authors have in getting reviewed. Lessing wrote a book using the pseudonym Jane Somers. She had two purposes: first, she wanted to highlight how rarely the work of first-time novelists is reviewed. Her experience verified the results of research on the subject. Second, she wanted to have her work reviewed free of reviewer expectations of Doris Lessing. Well-known authors receive repeated reviews because of their popularity, but those reviews almost always carry reviewer expectations that may be inappropriate for the work being reviewed. Moving from one type of writing to another is not easy, or even possible, for many writers, unless they use a pen name to circumvent the expectations of reviewers and readers. The *Time* magazine article that described Lessing's project summed it up in the first sentence: "The trouble with Jane Somers' first novel was not that it was poorly reviewed but that it was scarcely reviewed at all."[16]

Reviewing is an important element in the selection process, and Gardner does an excellent job of describing its components. Selectors, even in a one-person operation, should never depend totally on published reviews. Ultimately, the selector must be responsible for what is and is not in the collection. Telling a patron a desired title or subject is not in the collection because it did not garner a favorable review (or any review) is unlikely to enhance the professional reputation of a librarian or of the profession. Understand the review process, use existing review sources intelligently, contribute to the review sources if so inclined, but do not use reviews as a substitute for personal professional judgment.

William A. Wortman—*Collection Management: Background and Principles* (1989)[17]

Wortman focuses more on management and less on selection than do the other titles discussed in this chapter. His approach to collection management is similar to that taken in this book: it is an integrated process involving several activities. The 24-page chapter about selection devotes only 6 pages to the actual selection process.

Wortman views selection as a three-step process: identifying relevant materials, selecting pertinent materials, and making purchasing decisions.[18] Identifying relevant materials is not as difficult as it may seem to the beginning selector. Many macro decisions limit the scope of a selector's work. A beginning selector should find these macro decisions reflected in the collection development policy. For example, the policy limits subject areas collected, formats included in the collections, depth of treatment (e.g., introductory, advanced, or research), and all of the these limits narrow the amount of material one must consider. Wortman briefly describes some of the basic selection aids, such as *Library Journal* and *Choice* or vendor slips, as places to look for relevant material.

Selecting pertinent material is what the selection process is really about. Most of Wortman's discussion relates to knowing the user community and linking that knowledge to the content of potential purchases. Of all the books covered in this chapter, Wortman's title places the most emphasis on understanding client information requirements.

The decision to buy rests on practical issues, all related to money. Questions the selector must answer are: How much money is available in the materials budget? How much does the item cost? Are there additional costs for the library (such as binding a paperback or copying a disk in a book or disk package)? Will the cost and use be close to balancing? Just because an item is pertinent does not guarantee it will be purchased. This is especially true when material budgets are small.

Wortman's book reflects the trend of viewing collection development as more than selecting materials. His title indicates the broader thinking that now dominates the field.

Summary

Each of the books discussed in this chapter contains a wealth of information for anyone interested in collection development or selection. Because the selection process is subjective, a selector will need to formulate a personal philosophy. In addition to this personal perspective, the type of library, its policies, and its service community influence selection work. The following suggestions concern what a person should do to become a first-rate book selector:

1. Remember that collection development is a dynamic series of interrelated activities, and actual selection is but one of six activities.

2. Take time to learn about the basics of the book trade and audiovisual production.

3. Get to know book editors and producers of audiovisual materials, particularly those in your areas of selection responsibility.

4. Study the publishers who produce the best materials for the library. Examine their catalogs in detail, look for advertisements, learn the names of their editors.

5. Spend time reading reviews in a wide variety of sources. Determine what the review editors and reviewers like and dislike, and compare these findings with what the library requires.

6. Examine the trade and national bibliographies with great care. Determine how accurately they report the materials that the library needs.

7. Knowledge of the library's community is the foundation on which to build its collection. Do not stay in the library and expect to have a useful and used collection. Only by going into the community, meeting people, and becoming involved in its organizations can one develop the necessary feel for community needs.

8. Read as much as possible about the philosophies and processes of book selection, reviewing, and acquisition activities.

9. Make independent personal judgments about specific titles, and compare those judgments with those found in national reviews.

10. Be interested in what is going on in the world, and *read, read, read!*

Notes

[1]Lionel McColvin, *The Theory of Book Selection for Public Libraries* (London: Grafton, 1925).

[2]Helen E. Haines, *Living with Books,* 2d ed. (New York: Columbia University Press, 1950).

[3]McColvin, *Theory of Book Selection.*

[4]Rinaldo Lunati, *La scelta del libro per la formazione e lo sviluppo delle biblioteche* (Firenze, Italy: Leo S. Olschki Editore, 1972).

[5]Arthur Bostwick, *The American Public Library* (New York: Appleton, 1929).

[6]Francis Drury, *Book Selection* (Chicago: American Library Association, 1930).

[7]Harold V. Bonny, *A Manual of Practical Book Selection for Public Libraries* (London: Grafton, 1939).

[8]Haines, *Living with Books.*

[9]S. R. Ranganathan, *Library Book Selection* (New Delhi: India Library Association, 1952).

[10]Arthur Curley and Dorothy Broderick, *Building Library Collections*, 6th ed. (Metuchen, NJ: Scarecrow Press, 1985).

[11]David Spiller, *Book Selection: An Introduction to Principles and Practice*, 4th ed. (London: Clive Bingley, 1986).

[12]Robert Broadus, *Selecting Materials for Libraries*, 2d ed. (New York: H. W. Wilson, 1981).

[13]William A. Katz, *Collection Development: The Selection of Materials for Libraries* (New York: Holt, Rinehart & Winston, 1980).

[14]Ibid., 97.

[15]Richard K. Gardner, *Library Collections: Their Origins, Selection, and Development* (New York: McGraw-Hill, 1981).

[16]R. Zoglin, "The Golden Hoax Book," *Time* 124 (October 1, 1984): 83.

[17]William A. Wortman, *Collection Management: Background and Principles* (Chicago: American Library Association, 1989).

[18]Ibid., 141-44.

Further Reading

General

Budd, J. M. "Best Sellers and Pulitzer Prize Winners: Core or Not?" *Collection Building* 11, no. 1 (1991): 9-13.

Katz, W. "Allure of the New Book Section." *Collection Building* 10, nos. 3/4 (1989): 58-60.

Mancall, J. C. "(Un)changing Factors in the Searching Environment: Collections, Collectors, and Users." *School Library Media Quarterly* 19 (Winter 1991): 84-89.

Osburn, C. B., and R. Atkinson, eds. *Collection Management: A New Treatise.* Greenwich, CT: JAI Press, 1991.

Spiller, D. "Libraries for All?" *Library Association Record* 90 (April 1988): 217-18.

———. "A Strategy for Biography Provision in Public Libraries." *Library Review* 37, no. 1 (1988): 40-44.

Stueart, R. D. *Collection Development.* Greenwich, CT: JAI Press, 1980.

Welsch, E. "A Social Scientific View of Collection Development." *Collection Management* 4 (Fall 1982): 71-84.

Williams. L. B. "Subject Knowledge for Subject Specialists: What the Novice Bibliographer Needs to Know." *Collection Management* 14, nos. 3/4 (1991): 31-47.

Wortman, W. "Collection Management." *Library Resources & Technical Services* 31 (October 1987): 287-305.

Academic

Britten, W. A., and J. D. Webster. "Comparing Characteristics of Highly Circulated Titles for Demand-Driven Collection Development." *College & Research Libraries* 53 (May 1992): 239-48.

Hamaker, C. A. "Management Data for Selection Decisions in Building Library Collections." *Journal of Library Administration* 17, no. 2 (1992): 71-97.

Hannaford, W. "Tilting at Windmills: Selection in College Libraries." *Collection Management* 12, nos. 1/2 (1990): 31-35.

Johnston, M., and J. Weckert. "Selection Advisor: An Expert System for Collection Development." *Information Technology and Libraries* 9 (September 1990): 219-25.

Metz, P. *Landscape of Literatures.* Chicago: American Library Association, 1983.

Stebelman, S. "Role of the Subject Specialists in Reference Collection Development." *RQ* 29 (Winter 1989): 60-62.

Public

Baker, S. L. "Does the Use of a Demand-Oriented Selection Policy Reduce Overall Collection Quality?" *Public Library Quarterly* 5 (Fall 1984): 29-49.

Bob, M. L. "Aspects of Collection Development in Public Library Systems." *Bookmark* 38 (Spring 1980): 374-77.

Genco, B. A. "Mass-Market Books: Their Place in the Library." *School Library Journal* 35 (December 1988): 40-41.

Grim, J. "Growing the Collection." *Wilson Library Bulletin* 68 (February 1994): 31-34.

Hamilton, P. A., and T. L. Weech. "Development and Testing of an Instrument to Measure Attitudes Toward the Quality vs. Demand Debate in Collection Management." *Collection Management* 10, nos. 3/4 (1988): 27-37.

Harmon, C. "Multicultural/Nonsexist Collections: A Closer Look." *Top of the News* 43 (Spring 1987): 303-6.

McGovern, E. M., and H. D. Muller. *They're Never Too Young for Books.* Buffalo, NY: Prometheus Books, 1994.

Quinn, J. "Anatomy of a Collection." *Library Journal* 115 (November 15, 1990): 36-37.

Rawlinson, N. "Give 'em What They Want!" *Library Journal* 115 (June 15, 1990): 77-79.

Serenbnick, J., ed. *Collection Management in Public Libraries.* Chicago: American Library Association, 1986.

Turner, S. "Bad Books for Children—What Are They?" *Emergency Librarian* 16 (May-June 1989): 15-18.

Williams, P. "How Should the Public Library Respond to Public Demand?" *Library Journal* 115 (October 15,1990): 54-56.

School

Broderick, D. M. *Library Work with Children.* New York: H. W. Wilson, 1977.

Dalgneault, A. "Getting to Know the Collection." *Book Report* 9 (September/October 1990): 33-35.

Genco, B. A.; E. K. MacDonald; and B. Hearne. "Juggling Popularity and Quality." *School Library Journal* 37 (March 1991): 115-19.

Graef, R., et al. "Selection Skills and Collection Development in School Libraries." *Book Report* 9 (September/October 1990): 14-15, 17, 19, 23-39.

Issues in Children's Book Selection. New York: R. R. Bowker, 1973.

Loertscher, D. V., and M. L. Ho. *Computerized Collection Development for School Library Media Centers.* Englewood, CO: Libraries Unlimited, 1986.

"Parent Review." *The School Librarian's Workshop* 14 (January 1994): 1-3.

Thomas, L. "Building School Library Media Collections." *Bookmark* 40 (Fall 1982): 16-19.

Van Orden, Phyllis J. *The Collection Program in Schools: Concepts, Practices, and Information Sources.* 2d ed. Englewood, CO: Libraries Unlimited, 1995.

Special

Haymann-Diaz, B. "Establishing a Selection Process Model for an Ethnic Collection in a Prison Library." *Behavioral and Social Sciences Librarian* 8, nos. 1/2 (1989): 33-49.

Hoffmann, E. "Defining Information." *Information Processing and Management* 18, no. 3 (1982): 115-23.

Hurt, C. D. "Important Literature Identification in Science." In *Advances in Librarianship,* vol. 13, 239-58. New York: Academic Press, 1984.

5
Selection Process: Practice

The preceding chapter covered what some writers have identified as the important factors in the selection process. This chapter discusses a more practical side of the process and explores what takes place in the real world of libraries and information centers. It also examines how different environmental settings influence selection work, and describes the major categories of selection and acquisition aids. First, however, a few more basic points about selection need to be covered.

What Happens in Selection

No matter what type of library one works in, there are several steps in the selection process. First, selectors must identify collection needs in terms of subjects and specific types of material. (This is especially important in the absence of a written collection development policy.) The next steps involve determining how much money is available for collection development and allocating a specific amount for each category or subject; developing a plan for identifying potentially useful materials to acquire; and finally, conducting the search for the desired materials. In most situations, the identification of potential acquisitions draws heavily from published lists, catalogs, flyers, announcements, and bibliographies. After securing the list, a person or group assesses the worth of various titles on the same topic. In some cases, only one title is available. When that occurs, only two questions remain. First, is the price reasonable for the level of use that the item will receive? Second, is the item physically suitable for the proposed use? If the answer to both questions is the same (yes or no), the issue is resolved. When the answers are different, one must secure more information about the level of need before ordering the item.

More often than not, one makes the assessment using published information rather than a physical examination of the book. An item-by-item physical examination and reading, listening, or viewing is the ideal. However, most libraries lack the staff resources or the time to secure examination copies and review each title. Typically, school and public libraries devote more time to looking over approval copies than do academic libraries, although university and research libraries do use approval plans.

Most wholesalers and jobbers will provide examination copies if they can reasonably expect that the libraries will purchase most of the titles sent or will order multiple copies of some of the titles. For example, if a librarian requested 100 titles on approval and kept 90, the jobber would probably send other titles on approval. However, if the library kept only 65 titles, it would become necessary to convince the firm there was good reason for this high rejection rate or the firm might cancel the program. (If the library orders multiple copies of most of the retained titles, most vendors would continue to ship approval materials.) The reason is simple: it costs as much to select, pack, and ship an approval order as it does a firm order. (This is true for both the library and vendor.) Thus, the more a library can depend on published selection aids to reduce the need for examination copies, the better off everyone will be. Many academic libraries use a jobber approval program, but the principle remains the same for all types of libraries: the return rate must be low. Vendors will want to reassess a plan if the return rate rises much above 10 percent.

This is a good place to note some common terms used in selection and acquisition work. Four related terms are *standing order, blanket order, approval plan,* and *Till Forbidden.* Although some people use these imprecisely, each has a specific meaning. Serials librarians frequently use *Till Forbidden* to indicate that the publisher or supplier of a journal should automatically renew a subscription without any further approval from the library. This system saves time and money for both the library and publisher or supplier by reducing the amount of paperwork required to maintain subscriptions. (This is discussed in more detail in chapter 7.) *Standing orders* and *blanket orders* are similar; in both cases, the library commits to purchasing everything sent by a publisher or vendor, provided the materials match the terms of a formal agreement. (From a collection management point of view, such orders create a high degree of uncertainty in terms of the total annual cost, although some libraries do set an upper limit on total cost of materials a jobber may send without permission. Using the prior year's cost and an inflation factor is the best one can do to make an estimate, but variations in publishing schedules do cause marked variations in actual costs.) A standing order is normally placed for a series, for example, Academic Press's Studies in Archaeology series, while a blanket order is placed for a subject field, grade level, or country's publications, for example, all books about politics in Latin America, all books for undergraduates, or all the books published in Finnish in Finland. *Approval plans,* as noted above, allow the library to examine items before deciding to buy; they are not firm orders. (Note: A firm order is a legal contract.)

Each of these mechanisms has a role to play in effective and efficient collection development, and each clearly affects selection activities. When selectors know the library needs everything on a subject or all of one type of information material, or when selectors can satisfactorily define the scope and depth of need, a standing or blanket order is best. Such orders free selectors' time for more difficult decision-making activities. If selectors have less precise information about needs but know the library will need large numbers of titles, an approval plan may be best. However, the approval plan requires selectors to examine each shipment to decide which titles to keep and which to return.

Variations in Selection

This section covers some of the variations that occur in selection activities due to various institutional environments. Given the universal nature of information and the diversity of institutional settings in which an information specialist may work during a career, no single method of categorizing institutional environments is completely satisfactory. For convenience of presentation, this section employs the traditional categories of libraries: academic, public, school, and special. There are great differences even within each category, and what follows provides only a broad overview of the thousands of variations that may exist.

Academic Libraries

Community or Junior Colleges

In the United States and many other countries, there are at least two broad types of postsecondary schools: vocational and academic. People usually refer to publicly supported vocational programs in the United States as community or junior colleges. However, most of these institutions have both vocational and academic programs. The academic program is roughly equivalent to the first two years in a college or university and serves as a transfer program to a four-year college or university. Frequently, the quality of education is as good as that of a four-year college. If the transfer program is to succeed in providing the equivalent of the first two years of a four-year undergraduate degree, then the scope of the program must be just as comprehensive as that of the university program.

Collection development officers in a community college library have a challenging job. Not only must they focus on the academic programs, they must give equal attention to a wide range of vocational programs. Unfortunately, from a cost perspective, it is seldom possible to find materials that are useful in both programs. Also, many vocational programs need more visual than print materials, which accounts in part for the fact that American community college libraries tend to be leaders in the use of audiovisual (AV) materials. Strength in the AV collection means that the selection staff must know more about AV selection than their colleagues in other types of academic libraries.

In addition, most community or junior colleges offer extensive adult education or continuing education programs, which all too often have little or no relationship to the degree programs. It is true that most academic institutions offer some form of adult, or nondegree, courses and programs. However, in most community colleges the library, or learning resource center (LRC), must handle all programmatic information needs. Many universities provide a separate library to support the nondegree program. Given the diversity of subjects and levels of user ability, the community college library more resembles the public library than it does its larger relation, the university library.

Some help in establishing collection scope and size is available to the LRC. In 1979, the Junior College Library Section of the Association of College and Research Libraries (part of the American Library Association) published a Statement on Quantitative Standards for Two-Year Learning Resources Programs."[1]

Though the statement does not indicate what to buy, it does help set some limits for what could be a bottomless pit. Distributing copies of such standards may generate more interest in selection and collection building among both the faculty and administration. Faculty involvement in LRC selection work is desirable, just as it is in other educational settings, and such support is just as difficult to secure in LRCs as it is in other educational settings..

LRCs serve a heterogeneous community. Selection is usually item by item, with less use of blanket orders and approval plans than in other types of academic libraries. Collections generally contain at least a few items in all the standard educational formats. Selection personnel generally use a greater variety of selection aids than their colleagues in other types of libraries.

College Libraries

Though college libraries serving primarily bachelor's degree programs are diverse, each serves a highly homogeneous user group. Only the small special library that caters to a company or research group is likely to have a more homogeneous service community. One characteristic of bachelor's degree programs is that, within a particular college, all the students who graduate, regardless of their major, complete some type of general education program. A program of core courses means that students select from a limited number of courses during their first two years. Less variety in course offerings makes selection work for that aspect of the institution's activities less complex. Support of the curriculum is the primary objective of the college library collection. College libraries may offer some collection support for faculty research, but unlike universities, colleges seldom emphasize research. With the curriculum as the focus for collection development activities, selectors have definite limits within which to work. Faculty members frequently play an active role in selection, more so than in the LRC or university context.

Most of the items selected for the American college library are current works in English. College libraries in general have fewer AV materials than do LRCs, but there is a growing trend to include all formats in the collection. Most institutions have a music audio collection and art slides to support the core curriculum survey courses in music and art. Retrospective collection building (identifying and acquiring out-of-print items) is not a major activity in the college library. Many college libraries have rare book rooms and spend a small percentage of their materials budget on rare items. A few college libraries have a strong special collection in a narrow subject field. Even without a rare book or special collection, some retrospective buying takes place. Most of the out-of-print searching and buying activities are to replace worn-out and lost books.

Because of their numbers (more than 900 in the United States) and their long history, college libraries have developed a series of standards, some quantitative and some qualitative. A particularly good review of the standards and the issues surrounding them appears in an article by David Kaser in *Library Trends*.[2] Though standards are of some help in determining collection size, they do not have any influence in selection work, at least on a day-to-day basis.

Without question, the most widely used selection aid in American college libraries is *Choice* (published by the American Library Association). ALA created *Choice* to meet the specific needs of college library collection development officers by reviewing publications aimed at the undergraduate market. Subject experts, including librarians, write the reviews with an emphasis on the subject content and the title's overall suitability for undergraduate, rather than research, use. With small staffs (typically 10-15 people), few college libraries have sufficient subject expertise to evaluate all the potentially useful titles published each year, even with help from the teaching faculty. Because *Choice* annually reviews more than 6,000 titles of "potential use by undergraduates,"[3] and because of its widespread use as a selection aid, several librarians have studied *Choice* to determine whether it is an effective selection aid. For example, do items receiving positive reviews receive more use than titles receiving neutral reviews? One such study concluded that *Choice*

> reviews appear helpful in identifying the most worthy titles, as those most likely to be used repeatedly . . . titles appealing primarily to a more elite audience of specialists ought to be scrutinized if the selector is concerned about maximum use. The question of the level on which the book is written is an important one . . . selecting strictly on the basis of probable popularity runs the risk of developing a collection which could be categorized as 'lightweight' academically.[4]

The authors also note that a collection based on *Choice*'s so-called worthy titles may or may not be a collection that will address the needs of the particular institution.

University Libraries

University and research libraries' interests and needs dominate the professional literature, judging by the number of books and articles published about academic collection development in recent years. This domination arises from several types of numerical superiority. Though these libraries are not as numerous as libraries of other types, the size of their collections and the number of their staff, as well as monies expended per year on operations, far surpass the combined totals for all the other types of libraries. University and research libraries have collections ranging from a few hundred thousand to more than 10 million volumes. As an example, Tozzer Library (Harvard University) is a research library of about 180,000 items, a small library in the world of research libraries. However, it collects only in the fields of anthropology and archaeology. It is, as a result, one of the two largest anthropology libraries in the world. Like all research libraries, Tozzer spends a good deal of money on materials each year, does much work that is retrospective, and collects in most languages.

Collection development and selection work requires more time and attention in university research libraries than in other academic libraries. Typically, there are full-time collection development officers. In other academic libraries, collection development is one of many duties a librarian performs. Looking at the history and development of United States academic libraries, one can see a changing pattern in regard to who does the book selection. In small libraries with limited funds, there is strong faculty involvement; sometimes the faculty has sole responsibility for building the collection. As the collection, institution, and budget grow, there is a shift to more and more librarian involvement and responsibility. At the university and research library level, subject specialists come back into the selection picture, but they are members of the library staff rather than the teaching faculty. Many, if not most, of the persons responsible for collection development in research libraries have one or more subject graduate degrees in addition to a degree in library science. Such individuals are usually responsible for developing the collection in a specific subject or language. There is no single method by which academic libraries divide the universe of knowledge among subject specialists. Local needs and historical precedent determine how the library divides the responsibilities. Some universities use broad areas (social sciences or humanities), others use geographic divisions (Oceania or Latin America), and still others use small subject fields (anthropology or economic botany) and languages (Slavic or Arabic). It is not uncommon to find a mix of all methods.

A significant problem in large university and research library systems with departmental or subject libraries is coordinating collection development activities. Budgets may be large, but there is always more material than money. Unintentional duplication is always a concern, but the biggest problem is determining whose responsibility it is to collect in a given subject. As the number of persons involved goes up and the scope of each person's responsibility diminishes, the danger of missing important items increases. Working together, sending one another announcements, and checking with colleagues about their decisions becomes a major activity for university collection development officers.

University libraries tend to depend heavily on standing and blanket orders as well as approval plans as means of reducing workloads while assuring adequate collection building. Using such programs allows selectors more time for retrospective buying and for tracking down items from countries where the book trade is not well developed. Knowledge of one or more foreign languages is a must if one wishes to be a collection development officer at the university level.

Public Libraries

Diversity is the primary characteristic of public libraries' selection practices (arising from the heterogeneous nature of the communities they serve). Communities of a few hundred people, with a small library open only a few hours per week with no professional or full-time staff, do not follow the same practices that large urban libraries follow. Collection sizes range from several hundred items (Mancos, Colorado) to large research collections of millions of volumes (New York City).

Despite this variety, some generalizations apply to most public libraries. The service population normally consists of many unrelated constituencies: persons from various ethnic groups, of all ages, with various educational backgrounds and levels of skill and knowledge, and with a variety of information needs. All these groups fall within the public library's service population. Community need is the dominant factor in selection, all too often because funding and good sense permit no other choice. Though librarians do the selecting, occasionally they employ a committee format with patron involvement. Growth of the collection is modest because of limited stack space and the removal of worn-out or outdated materials. Most selections are current imprints, with retrospective buying generally limited to replacement titles. Medium and large public libraries commonly collect audio and video recordings as well as a variety of other AV formats. Perhaps the main difference in collection development between public libraries and libraries of other types is the strong emphasis on recreational needs as well as educational and informational materials. Trade publishers count on a strong public library market for most of their new releases. Without the library market, book buyers would see even higher prices, because only a fraction of the new books published would become strong sellers, much less bestsellers.

For larger libraries, there are two important issues in selection: speed and coordination. Most of the larger libraries are systems with a main library and one or more branches. The reading public likes to read new books while they are new, not six to nine months after interest wanes. Often, interest is fleeting, especially in fiction. So, having the new books on the shelf and ready to circulate when the demand arises is important. With several service points, a system needs to control costs. One way to help control cost is to place one order for multiple copies of desired items rather than ordering one now, another later, and still more even later.

Anticipating public interest is a challenge for the public library selector, and it probably would be impossible without several aids. Unquestionably, the most important aid is the selector's inquiring, active mind and the commitment to read, read, read. In addition, one of the most useful aids is *Publishers Weekly* (*PW*). Reading each issue cover to cover provides a wealth of information about what publishers plan to do to market new titles. Clues such as "30,000 first printing; major ad promo; author tour"; "BOMC, Cooking and Crafts Club alternative"; "major national advertising"; "soon to be a TV miniseries"; or "author to appear on the *Tonight Show*" help the selector to identify potentially high-interest items before demand arises. *PW* bases its information on publishers' stated plans, and the information appears well in advance of implementation, so there is time to order and process the items before patrons' requests begin to roll in. Needless to say, not all the highly promoted titles generate the interest the publisher hopes for. Occasionally *PW* has an article that covers publishers' successes and failures.[5] By knowing the community and the publishers, a selector can, in time, predict with reasonable accuracy the high-interest titles. The McNaughton Plan (rental plan) is one way to meet high, short-term demand for multiple copies.

The need to coordinate order placement is one reason many public libraries use selection committees. Such committees, especially if there a representative from each service location, reduce the problem of order coordination. In large systems with dozens of branches and mobile service points, such as the Los Angeles Public Library, total representation is impractical. In such cases, the selection committee develops a recommended buying list, and the service locations have a period of time to order from the list. Though not a perfect system, it does help achieve some degree of coordinated buying and cost control.

Small public libraries do not experience the problems of large libraries. Instead, their problems involve finding the money and time to buy materials. Reviews play a vital role in helping selectors at the small library locate the best possible buys with limited funds. More and more public libraries, including the smallest, depend on some type of cooperative network to help with collection development. Thus, small libraries sometimes can draw on the expertise of the network for identifying appropriate materials and can use selection aids they could never justify having if they were on their own. Some cooperatives engage in joint purchasing to gain discounts on high-volume purchases. In such cases, the smaller libraries use the purchasing list approach that large systems use. Even for small U.S. public libraries that are part of a cooperative, *Booklist* is the most important selection aid. Though *Booklist* contains only recommended titles, it identifies highly recommended titles (called "the best buys"). *Booklist* also reviews a wide range of nonprint materials and reference items.

Another distinctive feature of public library collection development is an emphasis on children's materials. In many public libraries, children's books get the highest use. Most libraries depend on positive reviews when making selection decisions about children's books. Often, the staff examines the title when it arrives to make certain it fits collection guidelines. One of the first specialist positions a growing public library tries to create is for children's materials and services.

(Note: Although there is some overlap between children's materials in schools and those in public libraries, it is not large. In most countries, there are very different requirements for being a school librarian and for being a children's librarian in a public library.)

Two other special features of public library collection development are noteworthy. First, the public library, historically, has been a place to which citizens turn for self-education materials. Self-education needs range from basic language and survival for the recent immigrant, to improving skills gained in schools, to maintaining current knowledge of a subject studied in college. In addition to the true educational function of the preceding, there is the self-help and education aspect exemplified by learning how to repair a car, how to fix a sticky door, how to prepare a special meal, or how to win friends and influence people. Selecting materials for the varied educational wants and desires of a diverse population can be a real challenge and a specialty in itself.

The last feature of note is the selection of genre fiction, a staple in most public library collections. Most people read only a few types of fiction regularly. One of the problems for the selector of genre materials is the lack of reviews; learning about types of fiction and the authors can be a problem. (It might be a good idea for all public librarians to have a course in genre novels while in library school.) A good book that can be of help in learning about such fiction is *Genreflecting: A Guide to Reading Interests in Genre Fiction.*[6] Although one may think all westerns are the same, *Genreflecting* lists 33 distinct themes and the names of authors who specialize in each one. Some readers will devour any western about range wars but will not touch a title about mountain men. Learning about the different categories and their authors is not only fun but useful for anyone developing a public library collection.

School Library Media Centers

Curriculum support dominates school library media center (LMC) collection development. Some similarities exist among community college, college, and school media center selection and collection development. Each emphasizes providing materials directly tied to teaching requirements, and each uses instructor input in the selection process. An emphasis on current material, with limited retrospective buying, is common. Community college and school media centers share the distinction of having the greatest number and variety of AV materials in their collections. Finally, school and community college media centers must serve an immense range of student abilities.

Although similarities do exist, the differences between school media centers and other educational libraries far outweigh the similarities. Take curriculum support, for example. School media centers have limited funds for collection development, in this matter resembling the small public library. With limited funds and limited staff (often there is only one professional on the staff), most of the money goes to purchasing items that directly support specific instructional units.

Library media specialists often build a core collection that provides some breadth and then concentrate on building emphasis collections that target curricular goals. For example, the media specialist might combine textbook and LMC funds to build rotating classroom and LMC collections of fiction and literary nonfiction to support a literature-based reading program. A hands-on math collection of manipulatives and fun math-oriented literature might support a move to meet the National Council of Teachers of Mathematics curriculum standards. Science department and LMC funds could be combined to access the Internet or National Geographic's KIDNET.

In some schools, teachers and LMC staff must plan effectively to assure that scarce funds meet topical requirements and that cooperation with other school, public, and academic libraries will maximize student access to needed materials. All libraries realize that excellent access for children builds expectations for the future and a willingness to fund all types of libraries as intellectual needs expand.

Normally, teachers and media specialists serve on committees that review and select items for purchase. Some parent representation on the committee is desirable. Whatever the committee composition, the media specialist must take the responsibility for identifying potentially useful items, preparing a list of suggestions, and securing examination or preview copies for group consideration. Most importantly, the committee must have a clear sense of collection emphasis, of how the items under consideration support current curriculum, and of how the collection will grow as the curriculum evolves.

More and more schools are equipping entire buildings with new technologies so that each classroom teacher has access to telecommunications, audio, video, and computer equipment. Next on the horizon is the integrating of these technologies to provide true multimedia access and presentations. In these cases, library media specialists must do more than build a centralized collection. In addition, they must build areas in the school for instant access (high-tech teaching stations) or on-call access (we will get the material if you give us advanced warning), or they must help get students to a location where the materials or technology can be used (the school's LMC, the public library, or an academic library).

The collection development policy plays a greater role in school media center operations than it does in other types of libraries. Although selection responsibility lies with the library media specialist, parents and others have legitimate concerns about both formats and content of materials to which children have access. Some parents and religious groups have strong objections to certain ideas in books and journals. Clearly stated, written collection goals and selection criteria allow everyone to operate as efficiently (and safely) as possible.

School library media centers are probably the most closely monitored of all types of libraries. However, public libraries receive their share of monitoring, especially in the area of children's materials. Media centers handle an ongoing flow of questions about and legal challenges to the content of the collection. An illustration of this scrutiny was the tongue-in-cheek *Reader's Guide to Non-Controversial Books* published by the National Committee for Good Reading. This publication listed items that would not be "offensive to any of the cultural or religious values in our society." Its proposed users were to be children, young adults, and "discriminating" adults in the United States. The publication contained 10 blank pages.[7] Concern about controlling, influencing, developing, or expanding (or a number of other labels) children's minds generates challenges. At times, both liberal and conservative pressure groups question why a certain item is or is not in a collection. Written policies and advisory committees are two means of answering such questions.

Published reviews play a significant role in media center selection. Often, school districts secure published reviews and also inspect items before making purchase decisions. The reasons for this are parental and school board interest in the collection's content and the need to spend limited funds on materials that will actually meet teachers' specific needs. The most widely used review sources are ALA's *Booklist*; H. W. Wilson's catalogs, such as the *Children's Catalog*; *School Library Journal*; and Brodart's *Elementary School Library Collection*. To a lesser degree, school libraries also use *Library Journal* and *Wilson Library Bulletin*. Finding reviews that provide adequate coverage of nonprint formats is a challenge; although *Booklist, Library Journal, School Library Journal*, and *Wilson Library Bulletin* all contain some AV reviews, they cover only a small percentage of the total output. Information about grade level and effectiveness in the classroom are two special concerns for the media specialist. Grade level information is generally available, but it is very difficult to locate data about classroom effectiveness. Usually, the time involved in gathering effectiveness data is too great to make it useful in media center collection development.

The term *library media specialist* denotes a person who knows about all types of information formats and the equipment necessary for using the formats. Today, at least in the United States, many school library media centers also serve as computer centers. Selection of instructional computer software is a common responsibility and, not infrequently, so is teaching students and staff how to use computers and software.

Building the school media center collection is probably the most rewarding and the most frustrating of all types of collection building. Normally, the center serves a relatively small population, and each customer is known on a personal level seldom found in other types of libraries. Frustration comes from having too little money to buy all the needed material, understaffing, and the difficulty in finding both appropriate material and necessary reviews.

Special Libraries and Information Centers

Almost any general statement about special libraries and information centers is inaccurate for any individual special library because of the diversity of environmental settings. In a sense, this is a catchall category. As a result, this category may be the largest and the least homogeneous. Dividing this category into three subclasses—scientific and technical, corporate and industrial, and subject and research—allows some useful generalizations. However, even these subclasses are not always mutually exclusive. A hospital library can have both a scientific and a corporate orientation if it has a responsibility to support both the medical and the administrative staff. In teaching hospitals, there is an educational aspect to collection building as well. There may even be a flavor of a public library, if the library offers a patient-service program. Some corporations establish two types of information centers, technical and management; others have a single facility to serve both activities. A geology library in a large research university may have more in common with an energy corporation library than it does with other libraries in its own institution. Large, independent, specialized research libraries, such as the Newberry, Linda Hall, or Folger libraries, fall into a class by themselves, yet they have many of the characteristics of the large university library.

Depending on which commercial mailing list one examines, the count of special libraries in the United States and Canada ranges from 12,000 to more than 19,000. Despite their substantial numbers, special libraries have not influenced professional practice as much as one would expect. This does not mean that special libraries have not made important contributions or developed innovative practices; it merely means that circumstances often make it difficult or impossible for special libraries to share information about their activities in the same manner as other libraries. Their diversity in character and operational environment is one reason for special libraries' modest influence. Another reason is that libraries and information centers in profit-oriented organizations frequently limit the reporting of activities and new systems for proprietary reasons; knowing what a competitor is working on may provide a company with an advantage. Such concerns often limit the amount of cooperative activities in which corporate libraries may engage. One way to learn about an organization's current interests is to study the materials in its library.

One widely shared characteristic of special libraries is lack of space. Limited space for all services, but particularly for collection storage, is a frequent complaint of the special librarian. Although all libraries eventually experience lack of space, a special library seldom expects to expand beyond its assigned area. Deselection becomes, more often than not, a regular part of the special library's cycle. Sound information about the most useful core items for the collection and how long these items will remain useful aids the librarian in providing cost-effective service. Special librarians and information officers make good use of data generated by bibliometric techniques in selecting and maintaining collections of the most needed serials. Bradford's law, Lotka's law, Zipf's law, and citation analysis have contributed to the effective operation of special libraries. Two examples illustrate the use of bibliometric data. Researchers have identified the half-lives of journals for many scientific fields. For example, the half-life of a physics journal is 4.6 years. This means that half of the references in a current physics journal carry a publication date within the last 4.6 years. In addition to half-life, researchers also study journals' impact, importance, or influence. When one knows which journals receive the most bibliometric citations, one can decide which titles to acquire and keep. Like any statistical data, information from bibliometric studies are approximations. Therefore, though helpful in collection building and management, they assist only in decision making and cannot serve as a substitute for professional judgment. (An excellent review of bibliometrics appeared in the Summer 1981 issue of *Library Trends*.[8]) Other libraries will likely make increasing use of these techniques as they come under the economic and space pressures faced by special libraries.

Most special libraries have very current collections and, in terms of collection policy, would be level 4 (research) but without the retrospective element. Despite the heavy emphasis on current materials, the best-known selection aids provide little help to persons responsible for collection building in special libraries. Most of the material acquired for special libraries is very technical and of interest to only a few specialists; as a result, no meaningful market exists for review services. Recommendations of clients and knowledge of their information needs become the key elements in deciding what to buy.

Information center is a reasonable label for most special libraries, because they collect many information formats seldom found in other libraries. For example, special libraries frequently acquire patent and trademark information. In some cases, the library conducts regular searches for new information that may be of interest to the organization and, as is most typical, it makes occasional searches for specific items. Two other classes of unusual information collected by some special libraries are well logs and remote sensing data. Well logs are records of drilling operations and are of interest to most energy companies involved in exploration. Remote sensing data take many forms but are normally from satellite sources; these data, depending on their specific content, can be of interest to farmers, archaeologists, mining engineers, geologists, military officials, and others. Both formats are secured from specialized sources. Most are generally expensive (normally, cost is less important than access and speed of delivery) and require special handling. Some special libraries also handle restricted information. The restricted material may be labeled as classified by law or government agency, or it may take the form of internal documents that are important or sensitive. Staff members working with classified information are usually investigated and given clearances before they begin handling classified material. An interesting book on the handling of special materials is Ellis Mount and Wilda B. Newman's *Top Secret/Trade Secret: Accessing and Safeguarding Restricted Information.*[9]

Special library collections tend to be *now* collections. Their purpose is to meet immediate needs, not future needs. When needed, the library secures historical material through interlibrary loan. Order placement takes place by telephone, and librarians use credit cards to pay for the items. Some special librarians place international telephone calls to order a single item for next-day air express delivery, with the cost of the telephone call and special delivery costs equaling or exceeding the cost of the item ordered. When that happens—and certainly it is not an everyday occurrence—it does give one a sense of how valuable information is in some organizations.

Online database access is something that most special libraries provide. Unlike other libraries that tend to emphasize bibliographic databases, special libraries access numeric, bibliographic, and full-text services. A particular concern for today's special librarian is deciding when to join a database service for occasional access to information and when to acquire a hard copy of the same data. In time, this type of cost-benefit question will probably confront all librarians, but at present, it is primarily an issue for the special librarian.

Needs assessment activities are also a regular part of the special library program, to a greater degree than in other types of libraries. Selective dissemination of information (SDI) is a technique often used in special libraries. By developing and maintaining user interest profiles, the library can continually monitor the information needs and interests of its service population, allowing more effective collection building. The technique also serves as a public relations activity. Every SDI notification serves as a reminder of the library's existence and value. Usually, SDI services are ineffective for large service populations because the services are too costly to operate; however, several commercial firms offer SDI-like services. The Institute for Scientific Information (ISI) is one commercial organization that offers SDI-like services; it also publishes several indexing and abstracting tools to which many special libraries subscribe (e.g., *Science Citation Index* on paper or online). These firms also provide bibliometric data, including information about half-lives and impact, about the titles they cover.

Selection Aids

Everyone involved in collection development recognizes the importance of bibliographies and review sources in building a library collection, even if they are rarely used. One can imagine a situation in which published aids are not used, but in such cases, the size of the library staff would have to increase dramatically or the number of items acquired would drop. The aids provide, to some degree, an overview of the output of publishers and media producers. Imagine the problems a library staff would have if no bibliographies or review sources existed. Each publisher and media producer would flood the library with catalogs and announcements of products; the filing and retrieval system for that material would add significantly to the library's workload. Finding the answer to the question, "How many books exist on vegetable gardening?" would entail going through thousands of catalogs and announcements to cull all relevant items. This merely underscores the fact that, despite their shortcomings and librarians' complaints about specific selection aids, they are time-saving tools essential to the efficient function of the library.

This section describes several categories of selection aids and mentions a few representative titles. All of the aids save time and frustration if one takes the time to study the titles in each one. As with any reference tool, the first step is to read the introductory material that the publisher or producer provides.

This chapter covers eight general categories of selection aids for books as well as a few microform selection tools. Serials and government documents selection aids appear in the chapters about those formats. The categories covered in this chapter are:

1. current sources for in-print books

2. catalogs, flyers, and announcements

3. current reviews

4. national bibliographies

5. recommended, best, and core collection lists

6. subject lists

7. online catalogs

8. microform selection aids

The examples within each category are selective at best. To give complete, worldwide coverage to all the titles in each group would require one or two books at least as long as this one.

Current Sources for In-Print Books

New books (those acquired during the year they are published) represent the majority of the materials acquired by most libraries. In some of the large research or archival libraries, this may not be the case, but even in such libraries, new books represent a large percentage of the total annual acquisitions. Every country in the world with any significant amount of publishing has a publication that attempts to list that nation's books in print. (One source of information about selection aids and dealers in countries in which English is not the native language is *Books in Other Languages* [Canadian Library Association].[10]) Naturally, the degree of success varies, and access to such lists may be easy or difficult. For countries with a high volume of publishing (such as the United States, Great Britain, and other industrialized countries), there may be weekly lists of new books. (An example is Whitaker's *Bookseller*.) Most listings of in-print books provide information about the author, title, publisher, place of publication, date of publication, and price. In addition, the listing may offer information about length; special features; series information; International Standard Book Number (ISBN); and cataloging information, including subject headings. Cataloging information can be helpful in selection because, too often, the title of a book does not provide enough information to allow anyone to make an informed judgment about its content. More often than not, weekly lists facilitate only an author search; a subject search is time-consuming. Monthly lists are also common, offering either first listings or cumulations of weekly lists. Monthly cumulations include *American Book Publishing Record* (R. R. Bowker) and *Books of the Month* (Whitaker). Monthly lists that cumulate weekly lists offer the same information contained in weekly listings. In addition, monthly lists provide several means of access, usually subject, author, and title. In a few countries, prepublication announcements appear in a single source, such as *Forthcoming Books* (R. R. Bowker). *Books of the Month and Books to Come* (Whitaker) combines current and future items for a three-month period. Though such aids can be of some value in planning purchases of new books, two major factors limit their use: 1) announced books do not always appear on schedule, and 2) a few announced titles never appear.

In many countries, an annual list is the only list, or at least the only one that a library outside of the country can acquire. Annual lists range from a few hundred pages to multivolume sets. All contain the basic bibliographic information required to order a specific book (author, title, publisher, date); most include many of the features included in weekly or monthly lists, including author, title, and subject access. Examples of annual lists are *Books in Print* (R. R. Bowker); *Cumulative Book Index* (H. W. Wilson); *British Books in Print, Paperbacks in Print,* and *Whitaker's Cumulative Book List* (Whitaker); *Les Livres Disponibles* (Editions du Cercle de la Librarie); *Libros Espanoles en Venta* (Instituto Nacional del Libro Espanol); and *Verzeichnis Lieferbarer Bucher* (Verlag der Buchhandler-Vereinigung GmbH). Almost every major language in which there is active publishing has an in-print book list.

Most comprehensive in-print lists issued by commercial publishers are not complete. In most cases, the comprehensiveness of the list depends on information submitted by book and media publishers. The in-print list publisher has neither the staff nor the time to attempt to track down all possible titles for inclusion. Thus, if a publisher forgets or does not wish to submit data about a title or group of titles, nothing appears for those items. Because libraries and retail outlets use in-print lists as a buying tool, most larger publishers send in the information, but many smaller publishers do not. One should never assume that because a specific title does not appear in the national in-print list that item is out of print or does not exist. Even if other titles by the same publisher do appear, it is wise to write to the publisher to inquire about the availability of the missing item. Some persons have suggested that a few publishers do not appear in commercial in-print lists because of commercial competition. To date, no evidence suggests that this did or does happen. However, an annual list that is based on copyright deposit data is more likely to be complete than is a commercial list.

National in-print lists are key tools in selection because they identify new materials as they become available. To be effective, individuals involved in selection and acquisition work must be familiar with these tools.

Weekly and monthly lists play a major role in the selection process of large libraries, regardless of type, because reviews are less important in making selection decisions. Reviews are less important because the collecting goal is to achieve broad coverage rather than a selection of the best available items. For small libraries, semiannual and annual listings are the key selection tools because they allow the selector to see a broader spectrum of the current output and help assure a better expenditure of limited funds. There is a slight danger that some items in a less frequent list will be out of print, but for most small libraries, this is hardly a concern because their wish lists far exceed the funds available.

Catalogs, Flyers, and Announcements

Publishers market their products through catalogs and other forms of promotional material. Some publishers use direct mail almost exclusively. They believe that national in-print lists bury their publications among too many others and that such in-print lists do not provide enough information to sell their books. Such publishers distribute catalogs listing all their available products and send out flyers and announcements of new titles. Even publishers who participate in combined in-print lists employ these sales methods.

Generally, such announcements contain more information about a book and its author(s) than do national in-print lists. When one cannot secure a review copy or find a published review, catalogs and flyers can provide useful selection data. It is necessary to use such information with caution. The purpose of the catalogs and flyers is to sell merchandise; though few publishers would lie about an item, advertising copy will present the item in its most favorable light. As the selector becomes familiar with publishers, she or he learns which publishers are objective and which puff their products more than the content warrants.

There are a few unscrupulous individuals who attempt to deceive libraries and individual book buyers. Here is an example: I have a large personal collection of Native American reference works, of which two titles illustrate my point. One is a three-volume set (5½-x-8¼-inches) titled *Dictionary of Indians of North America* with the imprint Scholarly Press, St. Clair Shores, Michigan (1978). The other is a two-volume set (7-x-10¼-inches) titled *Biographical Dictionary of Indians of the Americas* with the imprint American Indian Publishers, Newport Beach, California (1983). The content of both works is identical. The owners of these and many other imprints were convicted of fraud. However, their convictions did nothing to help the many libraries that paid for materials that were never delivered or that duplicated existing material. All one can do when confronted with information about what appears to be a title of high interest from an unfamiliar publisher is to ask for an examination copy and to ask selectors in other libraries if they know the firm. In time, one may associate a company name or location with potential problems. Flyers from unknown publishers offering large discounts for prepaid orders deserve second, third, and fourth looks before committing funds. One may never see the publication or get the money back.

A recent article suggesting Mellen Press is a vanity publisher (rather than a trade publisher) and the subsequent discussion on a collection development listserve also illustrates the need to know publishers.[11] The listserve exchange also shows how quickly information about a problem publisher can spread among selectors.

Libraries that make heavy use of announcements, flyers, and catalogs for selection must set up an efficient storage and retrieval system. In the past, commercial firms have attempted to collect publishers' catalogs and sell the collections to libraries (for example, R. R. Bowker's *Publisher's Trade List Annual* [*PTLA*]). The process has become cumbersome and the collections incomplete. Some years ago, Bowker's *Books in Print* was limited to information from the catalogs in *PTLA*. This is no longer the case. Too many publishers could not afford to be in *PTLA*. Thus, fewer and fewer libraries buy it, depending instead on their own filing system. Of course, the library keeps catalogs only from publishers and dealers that it uses on a regular basis. (See also the discussion of bookseller catalogs, pages 333-45.)

Current Review Sources

Wherever a flourishing book trade exists, so does an equally strong book reviewing system. One can divide book reviews into three types: 1) reviews for persons making their living buying books (trade and professional booksellers and librarians), 2) reviews for subject specialists, and 3) reviews for the general public. Book selectors use all three types, but those of greatest use are the trade and professional reviews. Some differences in emphasis do exist among types of libraries. Special libraries make the least use of reviews, but when they do need a review, the first two categories receive the greatest credence, with a preference for the specialist reviews. Academic and school collection development personnel make extensive use of the first two types of reviews but seldom examine popular reviews. Public libraries frequently consult mass-market review sources along with the other types of sources.

Trade and professional reviews are of two types: those designed to promote and those designed to evaluate. Although the primary market of such trade journals as *Publishers Weekly* (R. R. Bowker) and *Bookseller* (Whitaker) is booksellers (both wholesale and retail), librarians can and do make effective use of their reviews. The reviews alert booksellers to new titles that will receive heavy promotion. Publishers have a reasonably good grasp of which titles will sell well and which will not. Because of this, not all titles are promoted in the same manner, nor with equal funding; this is called *differential marketing*. In differential marketing each title's marketing "allowance" varies based on its anticipated sales, as well as in the approach taken for the title's promotion. A potentially good seller may receive extra promotional effort and funding to cultivate the book into a bestseller. Bookstore owners want to know about such titles ahead of time so they can order enough copies to meet the demand at its peak (usually no more than one or two months). Like book buyers, library patrons want to read bestsellers when they are bestsellers, not after demand subsides. Like bookstore owners, selection personnel read trade reviews to assure that bestsellers are in the collection by the time interest peaks. Trade reviews may miss an unexpected bestseller or predict greater popularity than some books achieve, but they do help selectors identify which items will be in top demand.

Evaluative reviews prepared by librarians or by specialists for librarians are also extremely important in selection, especially in public and school libraries. One will find these reviews in almost all library publications (*Library Journal, Wilson Library Bulletin,* and *LA Record,* for example). Normally, such reviews are descriptive and evaluative; occasionally, they are comparative. Reviews of this type are particularly useful because the reviewers prepare them with library needs in mind.

As useful as they are, current review sources are not without their problems. One of the biggest problems is lack of comprehensive coverage. Although many library publications contain book reviews, only a small percentage of the total annual publishing output is reviewed. Some titles appear to garner more reviews than their content warrants; others never receive a single review. Each *The Bowker Annual: Library and Book Trade Almanac* contains information about the number of titles reviewed. The 1992 volume shows the following pattern for 1991 books.

Booklist	8,254 (down 963 from 1990)
Bulletin of the Center for Children's Books	768 (down 2 from 1990)
Choice	6,592 (down 145 from 1990)
Horn Book Guide	3,300 (up 14 from 1990)
Kirkus Services	4,000 (unchanged)
Library Journal	5,063 (up 593 from 1990)
New York Review of Books*	489 (up 142 from 1990)
New York Times	2,300 (unchanged)
Publishers Weekly	4,524 (down 115 from 1990)

**Not all *New York Review of Books* reviews concern new books.

The Bowker Annual lists 17 review sources that published a total of 47,068 reviews, 10,044 of which appeared in newspapers.[12] The magnitude of the problem of coverage is clear when one realizes that at least 41,920 titles appeared in 1991.[13] If there were minimal overlap (but everyone knows that overlap is fairly extensive) the average number of reviews per title would be 1.27.

Choice covers the largest percentage of new books of primary interest to academic libraries. However, during 1991 publishers released 5,508 titles in the fields of sociology and economics. If one adds history (2,107 new titles), there is a total of more than 7,000 new titles in those three fields alone. With only 6,592 reviews in 1991, *Choice* could not have completely reviewed those three fields, to say nothing of other fields of academic interest.

Another sign of the problem in review coverage of new titles is found in *Book Review Digest*. Each year *BRD* publishes citations to and summaries of 5,000-6,000 new books. A nonfiction title must receive at least two reviews to be included in *BRD*. To find the reviews, *BRD* editors examine leading journals and newspapers that have large book review sections. Even with this large pool of potential sources, only 5,000-6,000 new books out of an annual output of over 40,000 titles meet the inclusion criteria. What are the implications of incomplete review coverage? First, no one source of book reviews covers more than a fraction of the total output. Second, even if every book did get reviewed, there would be only 1.25 reviews per title. Third, many new titles never receive even one review. Even in Great Britain, where there is very high interest in the book trade and a strong tradition of reviewing, most books seldom receive more than one review, and a fairly large number of new books get none.

Another limit on the usefulness of reviews is the speed with which they appear. Most trade reviews appear on or before the publication date; most professional (library) reviews appear several months after publication. One reason for the delay is that librarians and subject specialists write the reviews, one of the strong points of this approach. But first, the title must get to a review editor, who decides which titles ought to be reviewed and identifies an appropriate reviewer. The reviewer may or may not be able to review the item immediately. Eventually, the reviewer returns a review to the editor, who then edits the text and fits the review into the publishing schedule. This is a complex process, but it is necessary to disseminate professional opinions about new titles. For most journals, the only compensation a reviewer receives is the title she or he reviews. Using unpaid reviewers minimizes costs to the journals; hiring professionals to review books would greatly increase the cost to journals,

Some professional journals focus on a particular type of library, for example, *School Library Journal, Choice* (academic), and *Booklist* (public and school). Some materials are useful in more than one type of library, and journal editors try to make their publications useful to several types of libraries. Nevertheless, each journal has a primary emphasis, focusing on certain classes of books and using qualified reviewers who make value judgments about the materials covered.

A few journals (for example, *Booklist*) publish only positive reviews. This approach leaves one wondering why a certain title failed to appear. Was it because of a negative evaluation, or did the editors decide not to review it? Just as the general professional review sources cannot cover every new title, neither can the specialty sources. If a library depends on published reviews, this drawback can be important. One can wait a long time before being reasonably certain that no review will appear, and even then there are nagging questions as to why no review appeared.

When reading reviews, one must consider reviewer competence. Non-fiction titles require reviewers with subject expertise. For general trade books (titles intended for the general reader), it is not essential that the reviewer have in-depth subject knowledge for every book reviewed. When one gets beyond introductory texts and average readers' guides, the need for depth in background increases, until one reaches the level where one expert is reviewing another expert's publication for a few other experts in the field. Most academic disciplines have one or two journals that publish scholarly reviews for the field. Expert reviews of this type could be, but seldom are, of great assistance in developing a collection. A major reason for their lack of usefulness is that the reviews are slow to appear; often, books are one or two years old by the time their review is published. Such delays are unacceptable in libraries with patrons who need up-to-date material. Adding to the problem are scholarly publishers' small press runs (small quantities printed); the item may be out of print by the time a librarian sees its review.

The best source for the broadest coverage of academic titles from the United States is *Choice. Choice* reviewers are subject experts, and the reviews normally appear within a year of publication, often within three or four months after the title's release. To provide wide coverage, the reviews are relatively short, one or two paragraphs; thus, one sacrifices depth to gain coverage and speed.

A final category of review sources focuses upon the interests of the general reader or user of a format (for example, *The New York Times Book Review, Times Literary Supplement, High Fi,* and *Video Review*). Anyone concerned with building a collection geared to current popular interests must examine these publications as a normal part of the selection process.

Editors of popular review sources must keep in touch with current interests and tastes to hold their readership. Because they can only review a small percentage of the new titles, their selections are made with great care and an eye on popular current interests. One knows that thousands of people will read the reviews, and demand for the reviewed titles will likely increase. Because of the need to be up to date, and the fact that most popular press reviewers are paid, reviews of most titles appear within a month or two after the title's release.

It is important to note that many reviewers who write for the popular press are friends of the authors they are reviewing.[14] Thus, one needs to be careful when using popular press reviews for more than identifying titles that may experience high demand.

Data about the number of book reviews published each year make it clear that one will probably face a search problem (Where has that book been reviewed?) if one must use reviews for selection purposes. To some extent, indexing services that cover book reviews help, but they provide little assistance in tracking down the most current titles (from publication date to about eight months old). Two factors account for the problem. First, it takes time to produce and publish a review, and second, after the review appears, it takes the indexing service time to prepare and publish its index. However, for older titles, the indexes can be major time savers. *Book Review Digest (BRD)* and *Book Review Index (BRI)* are two major American tools of this type. *BRI*, which does not include any annotations, lists the reviews that appear in about 325 journals and provides citations to more than 40,000 reviews each year. (Again, one might think that number means every title receives at least one review; not so, as some books receive as many as 20 reviews.) The price of gaining access to review citations is time. Certainly, *BRI* is a useful tool but only for older titles.

In addition to the index publications devoted solely to book reviews, many of the general periodical indexes include book review citations. Selectors need to maintain at least a mental list of these sources, especially if reviews drive the selection process.

A final limit of book reviews is that, as a whole, they are not very critical. A reviewer does not work from the assumption that a book is bad. Rather the expectation is the book will be good, if not great. As a result, the vast majority of reviews are positive or noncommittal. One indexing product on CD-ROM (and used for checking citations for this book) allows one to search "review—favorable" and "review—unfavorable." Of the reviews in the database, 118,923 favorable and only 11,521 unfavorable; 32,903 were "mixed," and 3,107 offered "no opinion."

Certainly reviews are helpful when used with care. Book reviews can and do save libraries valuable staff time because no library has staff with enough time to read and review all of the potentially useful new titles that appear each year. A library should not employ reviews as a substitute for local judgment. Just because review *X* claims an item is great does not mean it fits local needs. Reviews aid in the selection process, but they should never be the sole basis for selection. When selectors gain familiarity with book review editors and with reviewers' biases, these tools become more valuable.

National Bibliographies

In time, most libraries will need to add some out-of-print books. Retrospective collection development is a normal part of academic and research library collection building programs. School and public libraries buy replacement copies of the books that are lost or worn out from use. Special libraries do the least retrospective buying, but they do, on occasion, acquire out-of-print materials. (Chapter 11 discusses sources for acquiring out-of-print books.)

Before buying out-of-print material, one must identify it. There are various sources for identifying authors, titles, publishers, and dates of publication of out-of-print items. One major source is the national bibliography network. Most countries with a book trade (except the United States) have some form of national bibliography. For purposes of this book, a national bibliography is a listing of books published in a country or about a country. One common characteristic of most of these bibliographies is their nonprofit origin. In many cases, the national library or a large research library publishes the bibliography. Some examples are the *British National Bibliography*, *Bibliographie de la France*, *Deutsche Bibliographie*, and *Gambia National Bibliography*.

Frequency of publication varies from weekly to yearly; in some cases, it occurs whenever there is enough material to warrant issuing a volume. In a few countries, the bibliography is based, in part, on books received by the country's copyright office. One bibliography of this sort is the *British National Bibliography* (*BNB*). If such bibliographies also include out-of-print titles added to the library's collection, the bibliography serves as both an in-print and retrospective aid. Several of the national and large research libraries have published or are publishing their public catalogs in multivolume sets (the British Library, Library of Congress, *Bibliothèque Nationale*). If selectors have access to a full set of the public catalog, plus the updated material, they have an almost complete record of official holdings of the library. Because of the size of these libraries, they collect almost everything produced in and about their countries. As a result, their published catalogs serve as national bibliographies. Selectors use them to verify the existence of a particular work and as a source for interlibrary loan (usually as a last resort).

The *National Union Catalog* (*NUC*), published by the Library of Congress, contains entries for libraries other than the Library of Congress. The *NUC* contains information about other libraries that hold a particular book, and in some cases, the book is not even in the Library of Congress collection. The *NUC* is not a true national bibliography because its coverage is not comprehensive. For comprehensive coverage of current titles published in or about the United States, the best sources are national bibliographic utilities such as OCLC or RLIN, the online version of *Books in Print*, and the Library of Congress CDS Alert Service.

A searcher can learn all of the following information from any national bibliography: author, full title, publisher, place and date of publication, pagination, and form of main entry for the book in the library. In most cases, one can locate information about special features of the book, such as whether it contains bibliographies, illustrations, charts, or maps; series information; scope notes; and subject information, including the classification number and subject heading tracings. A few national bibliographies provide the original price of items.

Many large academic and research libraries use the current issues of *NUC*, *BNB*, and other national bibliographies as selection aids. For most libraries, national bibliographies, when they are used, are used for verification rather than selection. No matter what the purpose, selectors must use national bibliographies with care. For example, several years ago, I searched three titles in the then-basic American and British bibliographies: *Publishers Weekly (PW)*, *American Book Publishing Record (BPR)*, *Publisher's Trade List Annual (PTLA)*, *Books in Print (BIP)*, *Subject Guide to Books in Print*, *Paperbound Books in Print*, *Cumulative Book Index (CBI)*, *National Union Catalog (NUC)*, *Bookseller*, *British Books in Print (BBIP)*, *Whitaker's Cumulative Book List (CBL)*, *British National Bibliography (BNB)*, and *British Museum Catalog of Printed Books*. All three titles were monographs that had personal author entries. Two of the titles were available in both hardbound and paper covers, and two of the books were American and one was British.

As indicated by the list of bibliographies searched, both the United States and Great Britain have reasonably comprehensive bibliographic networks for new books. However, despite searching each title through all available approaches (author, title, and sometimes subject) in each bibliography, only two of the fourteen bibliographies listed all three books. This study showed

- American titles are slow to appear in British sources and vice versa

- when a publisher releases a title in England and the United States at the same time, it appears in the trade bibliographies of both countries

- subject entries varied even within the same bibliography

- there is little consistency in the listing of series

- when searching a library's catalog, one must know that library's rules for establishing the main entry

Though most of the sources searched have undergone various changes since the study, the fact remains that there are many factors to keep in mind when using national and trade bibliographies.

Online Databases

Online databases, in the form of both cooperative and individual library catalogs, are, in a way, replacements for national bibliographies. With organizations such as OCLC and RLG providing access to databases of millions of records from thousands of libraries around the world, most libraries do not need access to national bibliographies for collection development. Certainly for retrospective work, national bibliographies are important, and for countries not well represented in the online systems, they are essential. However, for most libraries in the United States, the online databases are much more useful.

For verification work, online databases often prove to be the best single source. Not only can searchers verify the existence of a title, but with proper equipment, they can download the information to the library's acquisition system, thus eliminating the need to key in entries. Further, once the library receives and catalogs the item, the information from the online service can serve as the bibliographic record in the library's online public catalog. Another use of the online databases is in selection. Because systems like OCLC and RLIN provide information about which libraries hold certain titles, it is possible for a selector to determine which local libraries already hold an item under consideration. If resource sharing agreements are in place, and the selector thinks the item will have low use, the decision may be to not purchase the title.

Yet another use of the databases is for collection evaluation. A library can buy CD-ROMs that contain holdings information about a particular group of libraries as well as its own holdings. The data comes from one of the large bibliographic utilities. Using this data, the library can make a variety of comparisons of its holdings against other libraries on the disk. (Chapters 7 and 10 discuss the uses of online databases in more detail.)

Best Books, Recommended Lists, and Core Collections

The previous chapter touched on the problem of generating "best of . . ." lists or lists of items recommended for purchase. Such lists are useful when selectors employ them carefully. A brief examination of the amount of material in such lists will dispel any doubts about the subjectivity of the selection process. Titles like *Public Library Catalog* (H. W. Wilson), *School Librarians' Sourcebook* (R. R. Bowker), *Books for Junior College Libraries* (Books on Demand), or *Handbook of Contemporary Fiction for Public Libraries and School Libraries* (Scarecrow Press) show some overlap but also some differences. The differences arise from the purposes of the lists and the individuals who make the selections. Personal opinions vary, and these lists reflect either one person's opinion or a composite of opinions about the value of a particular title.

Few specialists in collection development would claim that a library ought to hold any title just because of its presence on two or more recommended lists. Consider a list that contains basic books for undergraduate programs in mathematics, published by a national association of mathematics teachers. One would expect a library that serves an undergraduate mathematics program to hold a high percentage of the listed titles. But even in such a case, one should not expect to find every title. Why not? A major reason is the emphasis of the school's program; there may be no need for a particular title. Another reason is that, often, several equally good alternatives exist. A final reason is that the list is out of date on its publication date; almost immediately new titles supersede the titles listed. Also, trying to get a copy of every title on a list can be extremely time-consuming. Unless there is agreement that it is important to secure every title, do not spend the time; retrospective buying requires much more time than buying in-print titles.

Subject Bibliographies

Subject bibliographies suffer from many of the same limitations as lists of best or recommended items: currency and selectivity. When subject experts prepare a bibliography and they write critical evaluations for the items listed, such publications provide useful information for both selection and collection evaluation activities. Only the imagination of the compilers limits the range of subject bibliographies. A quick review of some publishers' catalogs proves that compilers have unlimited imagination. (Two good reviews of subject selection aids for academic libraries are Patricia A. McClung's *Selection of Library Materials in the Humanities, Social Sciences and Sciences*[15] and Beth Shapiro and John Whaley's *Selection of Library Materials in Applied and Interdisciplinary Fields.*[16]) In most broad fields, at least one such bibliography exists, and for most fields several are available. Where there have been multiple editions, it is advisable to check on the amount of change between editions. Do new editions merely add more titles, or is there a real revision, with older, superseded titles dropped and new assessments made of all the items? One should not depend on published reviews but do one's own checking before using such a bibliography as a selection aid.

Using Citation Information for Selection

Many selection aids provide only the basic bibliographic information about an item. Selectors using only citation information select thousands of titles to add to library collections each year. How do they make their decisions from such limited data? Ross Atkinson proposed a model that, in time, may prove useful for neophyte selectors. He based his model on the citation, that is, "any string of natural language signs that refers to or represents, regardless of its textual location, a particular information source or set of sources."[17] Atkinson notes that every selector begins work with a personal "I," the biases and knowledge base that each of us develops over time. The "I" is one element in his model. The citation is a "text" that the "I" reads and judges both from past experience and from the context of the citation. Atkinson proposes three general contexts: syntagmatic, supplemental, and resolution.

Most bibliographic citations follow a convention for the presentation—the content and order—of the entry. (More and more, ANSI Z39.29-1977, American National Standard for Bibliographic References, is the convention selection aids use.) The standard means the selector can expect to see the same pattern in entries in various selection aids. That order provides "information" regarding the item cited (Atkinson's syntagmatic context). With experience, one's judgment about an item may change as one examines each element of the citation.

A selector reading a citation about conditions on the Dakota reservations in South Dakota would make different judgments about the content of the cited item depending on whether the citation read "Washington D.C., 1986" or "Pine Ridge, S.D., 1977." Similarly, the selector's judgment of a title about apartheid would depend on whether its imprint was "Johannesburg, 1993" or "Maseru, 1993." Another example of how an element could modify a judgment is a title implying comprehensive or comparative treatment of a broad or complex subject, with pagination indicating a much shorter book than would be reasonable for the topic. Who authored the title is a key factor in the selection process. Certainly, this context relates to all the factors writers on selection discussed for years: accuracy, currentness, bias, style, etc., but what Atkinson does is provide a framework for understanding how the process operates.

When the citation string includes subject descriptors, profound modification in judgment can occur (Atkinson's supplemental context). An entry in a selection aid may seem appropriate for Tozzer Library (Harvard University) until one encounters the subject heading *juvenile*. Without the supplemental context, it is possible and even probable that the library would order some inappropriate items because of inadequate information. (This is a good reason to follow Ranganathan's rule to know the publishers; even then one may be fooled occasionally.)

John Calhoun and James Bracken[18] proposed an index of publisher quality. (See also a follow-up study by Goedeken.[19]) Although their article describes an index or model for an academic library, it is easy to apply to any type of library. Their concept was very straightforward:

1. Determine the top 50-75 producers/publishers from which the library buys. Select a number of book awards, such as the Caldecott or a best of the year award (e.g., *Choice*'s annual Outstanding Academic Books), or select a frequently updated list of recommended titles (e.g., Bill Katz's *Magazines for* . . .) that are appropriate for the library.

2. Develop a table of award-winning titles by publisher based on the award lists. Total the number of award winners for each publisher over a period of time (e.g., two, three, or five years).

3. Calculate a ratio based on each publisher's average output (during the time period covered by the award lists) and the number of award-winning titles published during that time.

The authors suggested that using this index could improve one's chances of selecting the best books without seeing reviews. For example, a person who blindly selected books from Academic Press stood a 1 in 46.67 chance of picking an award winner; the odds with Basic Books were 1 in 10.97. The effort to collect the data to create the index, though considerable, would familiarize selectors with the publishers from which the library frequently buys as well as the publishers' track records in producing highly recommended titles.

As long as individuals and not machines assign subject headings and classification numbers in selection aids, selectors must realize there is a large element of subjectivity in the process. Normally only one class number appears; the problem is another person might reach a different opinion about the item and assign other headings and classification numbers. If a selector uses several sources with overlapping coverage and they also supply subject assignments, the selector may gain some additional insight as to subject content. However, more often than not, the selector makes her or his decision on only one source of information. One seldom has time to track down entries in several sources, especially if the initial findings are positive.

To return to Atkinson's model (supplemental context), another type of supplemental information is the source in which the citation appears. In national bibliographies, compilers make no value judgments regarding the merits of an item, whereas in a publication like *Booklist*, one knows it contains only recommended items. Thus, each selection aid carries with it a form of supplemental context. And, as Atkinson notes, a patron request may be the supplemental information that determines the selection decision, regardless of any other contextual information. This is especially true in special libraries.

Atkinson's last category, the context of resolution, ties in the selector's personality. This context consists of three elements—archival, communal, and thematic—that relate to a selector's attitudes, knowledge, values, perceptions, and personality. Atkinson defines archival as the selector's knowledge of the collection and its strengths and weaknesses. Communal refers to the knowledge of the clientele and its interests, and thematic refers to the selector's knowledge of the total current output on a topic (theme) area. How these three elements interact is a function of the selector's background, values, and personality as well as of the information environment in which the selector works. Atkinson suggests one of the elements will dominate most of the time. For a school media center or industrial center, the communal context would most likely dominate. In research libraries, the archival context is the most important. For a public library, where funds are scarce and getting the best materials for the available monies is essential, the thematic context is usually the most influential.

The Atkinson model is useful as a way of thinking about selection, and in time, with more research, it may become part of a true theory of selection. Every beginning selector should read his article. (Two other good sources are Charles Schwartz's "Book Selection, Collection Development, and Bounded Rationality"[20] and John Rutledge and Luke Swindler's "The Selection Decision."[21])

To conclude this chapter, I will outline the steps I follow when using selection aids that supply subject information. Most of the time, I select in the area of anthropology and sociology. One quickly learns that, for anthropology, appropriate material can appear under a wide variety of class numbers or subject headings. If one confines one's search to the anthropology class numbers, one will miss important new titles. Thus, one must scan long lists of titles to identify the appropriate title for the library. To do this quickly and effectively, one needs a system for thinking about the titles scanned.

Whenever possible, I start by looking at the subject information with this question in mind: Does this fall within the areas of our collecting? If the answer is yes, then I consider whether the material is of interest to the library's clientele. An affirmative answer to that question raises the third consideration: How much do we already have on this subject (what formats, how old)? If the title remains under consideration at this point, I think about the cost of the item: Can the library afford to acquire it? I also consider quality, taking publisher and author track records into account. If the item is not a one-time purchase, I think about the library's ability to maintain the acquisition. Occasionally, I encounter a reprint of a title already in the collection. Then I must attempt to determine whether there is new material in the reprint (frequently there is a new introduction or other additions); the question is, How much new material is there? Another question is, What is the condition and use pattern of the item in the collection? More and more frequently, there is a question about the need for special handling, as is the case with CD-ROMs or floppy disks that come with traditional books. Two final questions to consider are: What is the source of the information under consideration, that is, review media, publisher's flyer, vendor announcement, trade or professional publication, national bibliography, or other? and, Will the acquisition of the item cause a problem, such as objections, mutilation, or theft?

This approach requires selectors to know the user population, collection content, collection priorities, materials budget status, primary authors and publishers or producers in the selector's areas of responsibility, and review sources and general production levels in the selector's areas of responsibility.

Summary

Although this has been a lengthy discussion, it covers only the high points and basic issues of book selection. Selectors must know the service population, what exists in the collection, types of formats and materials that meet the needs of a given situation, and vendor sources that can supply appropriate materials. In addition, selectors must be able to choose among a variety of items and formats to get the most cost-effective items for a given situation; determine quality and its many variations; balance quantities, qualities and costs; and recognize the real value or nonvalue of gifts. Learning to be a book selector is a lifelong process, and the items listed in the bibliography provide leads to material about various aspects of this challenging, exciting, and rewarding area of information work.

Notes

[1]Junior College Library Section, Association of College and Research Libraries, "Statement on Quantitative Standards for Two-Year Learning Resources Programs" (Chicago: American Library Association, 1979).

[2]David Kaser, "Standards for College Libraries," *Library Trends* 31 (Summer 1982): 7-18.

[3]"Introduction," *Choice* 1 (March 1964).

[4]J. P. Schmitt and S. Saunders, "Assessment of *Choice* as a Tool for Selection," *College & Research Libraries* 44 (September 1983): 375-80.

[5]"The Red and the Black," *Publishers Weekly* 227 (April 19, 1985): 26-30.

[6]Betty Rosenberg and Diane Tixier Herald, *Genreflecting: A Guide to Reading Interests in Genre Fiction*, 4th ed. (Englewood, CO: Libraries Unlimited, 1995).

[7]National Committee for Good Reading, *Reader's Guide to Non-Controversial Books* (Castle Rock, CO: Hi Willow Research and Publishing, 1986).

[8]*Library Trends* 30 (Summer 1981). Edited by William Gray Potter.

[9]Ellis Mount and Wilda B. Newman, *Top Secret/Trade Secret: Accessing and Safeguarding Restricted Information* (New York: Neal-Schuman, 1985).

[10]*Books in Other Languages* (Ottawa: Canadian Library Association, 1970).

[11]Warren St. John, "Vanity's Fare: The Peripatetic Professor and His Peculiarly Profitable Press," *Lingua Franca* 3 (September/October, 1993): 1, 22-25, 62.

[12]*The Bowker Annual* (New York: R. R. Bowker, 1993), 514.

[13]Ibid., 500.

[14]Katherine Dalton, "Books and Book Reviewing, or Why All Press Is Good Press," *Chronicles* 18 (January 1989): 20-22.

[15]Patricia A. McClung, *Selection of Library Materials in the Humanities, Social Sciences and Sciences* (Chicago: American Library Association, 1985).

[16]Beth Shapiro and John Whaley, *Selection of Library Materials in Applied and Interdisciplinary Fields* (Chicago: American Library Association, 1987).

[17]Ross Atkinson, "The Citation as Intertext: Toward a Theory of the Selection Process," *Library Resources & Technical Services* 28 (April/June 1984): 109-19.

[18]John Calhoun and James K. Bracken, "An Index of Publisher Quality for the Academic Library," *College & Research Libraries* 44 (May 1983): 257-59.

[19]Edward Goedeken, "An Index to Publisher Quality Revisited," *Library Acquisitions: Practice and Theory* 17 (Fall 1993): 263-68.

[20]Charles A. Schwartz, "Book Selection, Collection Development, and Bounded Rationality," *College & Research Libraries* 50 (May 1989): 328-43.

[21]John Rutledge and Luke Swindler, "The Selection Decision: Defining Criteria and Establishing Priorities," *College & Research Libraries* 48 (March 1987): 123-31.

Further Reading

General

Batt, F. "Folly of Book Reviews." In *Options for the 80s,* edited by M. D. Kathman and V. F. Massman. Greenwich, CT: JAI Press, 1981. 277-89.

Blake, V. P. "Role of Reviews and Reviewing Media in the Selection Process." *Collection Management* 11, nos. 1/2 (1989): 1-40.

Cline, G. S. "Application of Bradford's Law to Citation Data." *College & Research Libraries* 42 (January 1981): 53-61.

D'Aniello, C. "Bibliography and the Beginning Bibliographer." *Collection Building* 6 (Summer 1984): 11-19.

Dickinson, G. K. *Selection and Evaluation of Electronic Resources.* Englewood, CO: Libraries Unlimited, 1993.

Eaglen, A. "ISBN: A Good Tool Sorely Misused." *Collection Management* 10, nos. 1/2 (1989): 74-77.

Eisenberg, H. "So Many Books, So Little Space: What Makes a Book Review Editor Pick Up a Book?" *Publishers Weekly* 231 (April 10, 1989): 25-30.

Furnham, A. "Book Reviews As a Selection Tool for Librarians: Comments from a Psychologist." *Collection Management* 8 (Spring 1986): 33-43.

Katz, B. "Who Is the Reviewer?" *Collection Building* 7 (Spring 1985): 33-35.

Ryland, J. "Collection Development and Selection: Who Should Do It?" *Library Acquisitions: Practice and Theory* 6, no. 1 (1982): 13-17.

Stiffler, S. A. "Core Analysis in Collection Management." *Collection Management* 5 (Fall/Winter 1983): 135-49.

Academic

Atkinson, R. "Old Forms, New Forms: The Challenge of Collection Development." *College & Research Libraries* 50 (September 1989): 507-20.

Dickinson, D. W. "Rationalist's Critique of Book Selection for Academic Libraries." *Journal of Academic Librarianship* 7 (July 1981): 138-43.

Macleod, B. "*Library Journal* and *Choice*: A Review of Reviews." *Journal of Academic Librarianship* 7 (March 1981): 23-28.

Miller, W., and D. S. Rockwood. "Collection Development from a College Perspective." *College & Research Libraries* 40 (July 1979): 318-24.

Pasterczyk, C. E. "Checklist for the New Selector." *College & Research Libraries News* 49 (July/August 1988): 434-35.

Schmitt, J. P., and S. Saunders. "Assessment of *Choice* As a Tool for Selection." *College & Research Libraries* 44 (September 1983): 375-80.

Public

Baker, S. L. *The Responsive Public Library Collection.* Englewood, CO: Libraries Unlimited, 1993.

Clewis, B. "Selecting Science Books for the General Reader." *Collection Building* 10, nos. 1/2 (1990): 12-15.

Cuesta, Y. J. "From Survival to Sophistication: Hispanic Needs = Library Needs." *Library Journal* 115 (May 15,1990): 26-28.

Haighton, T. *Bookstock Management in Public Libraries.* London: C. Poingley, 1985.

Pearson, J. C. "Sources of Spanish-Language Material." *Library Journal* 115 (May 15, 1990): 29-33.

Scheppke, J. B. "Public Library Book Selection." *Unabashed Librarian,* no. 52 (1984): 5-6.

Serebnick, J. "Book Reviews and the Selection of Potentially Controversial Books in Public Libraries." *Library Quarterly* 51 (October 1981): 390-409.

Swope, D. K. "Quality Versus Demand: Implications for Children's Collections." In *Festschrift in Honor of Dr. Arnulfo D. Trejo,* 66-73. Tucson, AZ: Graduate Library School, University of Arizona, 1984.

School

Altan, S. "Collection Development in Practice in an Independent School." *Catholic Library World* 54 (October 1982): 110-12.

Ekhaml, L. "Peer Review: Student Choices." *School Library Journal* 37 (September 1991): 196.

England, C., and A. M. Fasick. *ChildView: Evaluating and Reviewing Materials for Children.* Englewood, CO: Libraries Unlimited, 1987.

Miller, M. L. "Collection Development in School Library Media Centers: National Recommendations and Reality." *Collection Building* 1 (1987): 25-48.

Reeser, C. "Silk Purse or Sow's Ear: Essential Criteria in Evaluation of Children's Literature." *Idaho Librarian* 34 (October 1982): 157-58.

Van Orden, P. J. *The Collection Program in Schools: Concepts, Practices, and Information Sources.* 2d ed. Englewood, CO: Libraries Unlimited, 1995.

White, Brenda H., ed. *Collection Management for School Library Media Centers.* New York: Haworth Press, 1986.

Special

Bell, J. A., et al. "Faculty Input in Book Selection: A Comparison of Alternative Methods." *Bulletin of the Medical Library Association* 75 (July 1987): 228-33.

Byrd, G. D., et al. "Collection Development Using Interlibrary Loan Borrowing and Acquisitions Statistics." *Medical Library Association Bulletin* 70 (January 1982): 1-9.

Dalton, L., and E. Gartenfeld. "Evaluating Printed Health Information for Consumers." *Medical Library Association Bulletin* 69 (July 1981): 322-24.

Elder, N. J., et al. "Collection Development, Selection, and Acquisitions of Agricultural Materials." *Library Trends* 38 (Winter 1990): 442-73.

Hurt, C. *Information Sources in Science and Technology.* Englewood, CO: Libraries Unlimited, 1988.

McCleary, H. "Practical Guide to Establishing a Business Intelligence Clearing House." *Database* 9 (June 1986): 40-46.

Parker, R. H. "Bibliometric Models for Management of an Information Store." *Information Science* 33 (March 1982): 124-38.

6
Producers of Information Materials

In the past, one could categorize information producers by product: 1) those who produced printed matter (books, periodicals, newspapers, microforms, and the like), and 2) those who produced audiovisual materials. Seldom did a producer work in both areas. Today the situation is different. Though some companies are solely devoted to the production of print or audiovisual materials, most trade book publishers also have one or more electronic or audiovisual lines.

The first portion of this chapter examines publishing, that is, the production of printed material, with comments about the changing nature of the field. The second portion discusses audiovisual production. The chapter provides an overview of the important production characteristics of both types of products with enough depth for one to begin to understand how information producers operate.

Writers have been predicting a paperless society, office, or library for some time. (For example, Frederick W. Lancaster has written extensively about this topic. One of his more wide-ranging titles is *Libraries and Librarians in an Age of Electronics*.[1]) Despite the predictions, printed materials, such as books, newspapers, and journals, are still very much with us and probably will be for some time. Print materials still comprise the largest percentage of items available through most libraries and information centers. A major reason for this is that paper copies still provide the least expensive means of distributing large quantities of timely information to a large number of people. Certainly one can put a long document—even a book—on an electronic network, where any number of individuals can simultaneously read the material. However, though putting large text files on networks is fairly common, many individuals using the material print portions or all of the file to read on paper rather than spending hours in front of a computer. Also, many people are uncomfortable with technology-based information sources. People still like to read in bed, on the subway, at the beach, and other places where technology-based systems are inconvenient, if not impossible, to use. (Try reading a CRT screen in full sunlight at the beach.)

Why Know About Publishing?

What is publishing? Most people think of publishing in terms of books, but actually publishing extends far beyond the activities of book publishers.

Publishing involves many different people and activities: creators of materials (that is, writers and performers), editors and manufacturers, and distributors and salespeople.

In response to the question, "Why bother with details of the trade?" several responses come to mind. When one is going to work day in and day out with an industry, even if one is just buying its products, some knowledge of that industry will make everyone's life a little easier. An understanding of the trade's characteristics—such as how producers determine prices, how they distribute products, and what services one can expect—can improve communication between producers and buyers. Under the best of circumstances, a great deal of communication exists between the library and the trade regarding orders.

All this knowledge provides the librarian with some understanding of, if not sympathy for, the problems of producers. Publishers who depend on library sales know (or should know) a great deal about library problems and operations. They often joke about how uninformed librarians are about the trade. The present strained relationship between libraries and publishers developed, in part, because neither group fully understood nor tried to understand the other's position. (For instance, copyright, discussed in chapter 18, is an area of great controversy.) Yet, we also know that when two parties discuss problems with mutual understanding of the other's position, the working relationship will be more pleasant. Each is more willing to make an occasional concession to the other's needs; this flexibility can, in turn, foster mutually beneficial alliances.

Book selection and collection development courses in library schools usually touch only lightly on publishers and their problems, as teachers often claim there is insufficient time to give more coverage to this important topic. Further, courses in the history of the book trade seldom have time to deal with the contemporary situation, because it is not yet history. Most schools' curricula do not have a place for a course in contemporary production. Even if they did, most students would not have time for it in their one-year course of study. For this reason, students lack information that could prove invaluable,because knowing what happens in publishing can affect the selection process. First, knowing something about publishing helps selectors identify the most likely sources of materials, that is, which among the thousands of producers are most likely to produce the needed material. Second, by keeping up to date with what is happening in publishing, one can anticipate changes in quality and format. Third, librarians may be able to influence publishing decisions, if the publisher is aware that the librarian is knowledgeable about the issues involved in developing profitable books.

The primary concern of publishers is making a profit. Quality and service do matter, but publishers do not exist to provide quality materials and exceptional services at a constant loss, despite what some librarians would like to believe. Publishers are in *business* and must make a profit to stay in business. To do this, they must produce materials that are marketable to a fairly large audience.

Thus, librarians should be among the first to discard the stereotype of the publisher as a retiring, highly sophisticated literary person interested only in creative quality, just as publishers should abandon the view of the librarian as a woman with her hair in a bun, wearing horn-rimmed glasses, with a constant "shush" on her lips.

What Is a Publisher?

What is a publisher? A simple answer is that a publisher supplies the capital and editorial assistance required to transform manuscripts into books and electronic products. (Two exceptions to this are vanity and subsidy presses, discussed later in this section.) Generally, publishers in Western countries perform six basic functions:

1. Tap sources of materials (manuscripts).

2. Raise and supply the capital to make the books.

3. Aid in the development of the manuscript.

4. Contract for the manufacturing (printing and binding) of books.

5. Distribute books, including promotion and advertising.

6. Maintain records of sales, contracts, and correspondence relating to the production and sale of books.

One misconception about publishers is that they actually print books. Printing is seldom done by major publishers; instead, publishers contract with independent printers. A printer does *not* share the risk of the publisher and the author in the production of a book. Printers receive payment for presswork and, in some cases, binding the book, regardless of how well the book sells.

In the past, a book's publisher and printer often were one and the same. A thumbnail sketch of the basic publishing development pattern is pertinent. The pattern seems to be worldwide, and it does have an impact on acquisition and selection work. In the history of publishing, there appear to be three stages of development. These stages have occurred in both Europe and America. They also appear elsewhere in the world.

In stage one, the publishing, printing, and selling of the product are combined in one firm, often in one person or one family. The early giants in Europe acted as publisher, printer, and retail bookseller. These publishers included Froben, Schoffer, Manutius, Caxton, and others. When one examines American publishing history, the same pattern appears on the eastern seaboard and moves west with the frontier; names like Franklin, Green, and Harris fall into this period. Elsewhere in the world, publishing exhibits a similar evolutionary pattern, which is largely a function of how societies organize economic, educational, and human resources. In countries with limited resources, technical skills, and small markets, it is unfeasible, and in many cases impossible, to have specialty publishers in all fields.

From a collection development point of view, stage one development presents many interesting challenges. Research libraries buy materials from around the world, but countries with weak economies and low literacy rates seldom have anything resembling a national bibliography or trade bibliography (mainstays in identifying important titles). As if this were not enough of a challenge, most publishers operating at this level print a limited number of copies of each book. In many cases, they take orders before printing the book. When they do this, they print just a few more copies than the number ordered. Many collection development officers have experienced the frustration of having an order returned with the comment "unavailable, only 200 copies printed." Some books are, in fact, out of print on the date of publication; this frequently occurs in areas where publishing is at the stage one level.

In stage two, specialization begins, with firms emphasizing publishing or printing. New firms, many with a single emphasis, appear. The factors creating this situation relate to available economic, educational, and human resources. Better education creates a greater market for books among both individual and institutional buyers. The retail trade develops at the same time, because the reading public exists countrywide and a single outlet in the country's major population center is no longer adequate. Publishers from this period in American publishing include John Wiley, George Putnam, and the Lippincott Company. In 1807, Charles Wiley joined George Putnam in a bookstore operation in New York City. During the following 150 years, the heirs of the two men built two of the leading publishing houses in the United States. The Lippincott Company started in 1836 as a bookstore; over the years it shifted its emphasis to publishing.

Often, when bookstores begin to develop, a company will decide to create a listing or publication through which publishers inform bookstores about new and existing titles. Collection development librarians expend time and energy trying to track down such systems in countries where the book trade is in stage two. The usual procedure is to establish a good working relationship with a large bookstore, with that shop functioning as a purchasing agent. This may entail signing an agreement to spend a certain amount of money each year with the store, but it normally results in much better coverage, and usually better service, than trying to buy directly from the publishing houses.

The third stage is the complete separation of the three basic functions, as publishers discontinue printing activities. For example, John and James Harper started as printers in 1817. Today, HarperCollins is one of the leading publishers in the United States. It ceased printing years ago. (Two of the last major publishers to retain printing plants are McGraw-Hill and Doubleday.) When publishing reaches stage three, all the trappings we see in contemporary U.S. publishing are evident: specialty publishers, literary agents, trade journals, sales personnel, jobbers and wholesalers, and so forth. Normally, there is something resembling a national bibliography as well as a trade bibliography, both of which are essential for collection development work.

Canadian, U.S., and European publishers have undergone two other changes since reaching the third level of development in publishing. Before 1950, most publishing houses existed as family-owned or privately held firms. With the rapid expansion of the educational market, especially in the United States, most publishers found it impossible to raise enough capital to expand adequately. Slowly at first, and then with increasing frequency, publishers sold stock in the firm to the public. Going public generated several changes in the publishing field, some good and some bad. On the positive side, publishers issued more new material and offered more services. On the negative side, publicly held companies placed an increased emphasis on profitability, with, perhaps, a decline in overall quality. The problems were neither as great nor as bad as the doomsday prophets predicted.

As governments spent more and more money on education in the late 1950s and early 1960s, educational publishing became increasingly profitable. High profitability made publishing an area of interest for large conglomerates looking for diversification, and large electronics and communication firms— RCA, IBM, Xerox, Raytheon, and General Electric, for example—began to buy publishing houses. In the mid-1980s one interesting combination was Time-Life, Inc., and General Electric's General Learning Corporation. This combination had controlling interest in Little, Brown (trade publisher); Silver-Burdett (school textbook publisher); Peter H. Roebuch (television and educational films); New York Graphics; Alva Museum Replicas; Seven Arts Society; Book Find Club; and five publishing houses in England, Spain, Mexico, and France. The combination of Time-Life and General Learning Corporation gave way to Time Warner, Inc., which owns journal and book publishers; book clubs; producers of compact discs, laser discs, and audiotapes; as well as music licensing, motion picture and television production and distribution, and cable television operations. This is fairly complete coverage of the communication channels and popular media formats.

The 1980s were known as a time of "merger mania" in the publishing industry; in the 1990s mergers continue, albeit at a slower rate. Two dated but relevant articles about mergers are Celeste West's "Stalking the Literary Industrial Complex" and "The Question of Size in the Book Industry."[2] Another older, but still valid, article that covers all media is Ben Bagdikan's "Media Brokers."[3] According to one study, in 1987 the top 12 U.S. publishing houses accounted for 56 percent of all domestic and international sales.[4] The data covered all distribution channels: trade, mass-market, school textbook (elementary through high school, also called el-hi), and so forth. In the mid 1990s, if one could get accurate data, the results would probably be much the same.

Bagdikan offered the following fun but worrisome thought:

Is it possible, we're heading
Towards one great climatic wedding
When all but two remain unmerged,
The rest absorbed, acquired or purged.[5]

The potential impact of these new combinations is great. If nothing else, it will mean that market potential will take on even greater importance when publishers select manuscripts to publish. Anyone with a little imagination can envision a future publishing industry that controls what the public may know. To date, little evidence indicates any real change in the quality of books being produced. However, the threat of too few information producers with access to a free market still exists. Selection and acquisition librarians, if they are aware of what is happening in the publishing field and of the implications of changes, should be among the first to note any significant changes.

Changing economic conditions in the late 1980s and early 1990s caused some slowdown in the merger activity. Many companies began divesting their publishing holdings. For example, Xerox Corporation sold many of its publishing holdings, including the R. R. Bowker Company. For other companies, the changing nature of the production and distribution of information meshes nicely with their electronic broadcasting interests. Only time will tell what significance these changes will have.

A fourth stage—electronic publishing—is quickly developing. Some publishers offer information in two or more formats, for example, print and electronic, and others offer some information only in an electronic format. For example, in 1992 Random House entered into a joint venture with Voyager Company (software) and Apple Computer.[6] The group plans to publish both electronic and paper versions of Random House's Modern Library series. The group projects press runs of 7,500-15,000 books and 500-5,000 disks. Digital devices are creating a variety of opportunities for publishers. In a sense, the devices are almost as revolutionary as the introduction of movable type. Digitization is especially useful in the production process; submission of electronic manuscripts containing digitized images also speeds editorial work. The implications of electronic publishing for the bottom line are clear to most publishers, as suggested by Gayle Feldman: "Whether it be CD-ROM opportunities for scholarly presses, document delivery revenue for journal publishers, or multimedia packages for the reference crowd . . . the coffee breaks buzzed with conviction that publishers who ignore new technology do so at their peril."[7]

Insight into the impact on the bottom line appeared in a *Publishers Weekly* (PW) report showing that a completely digital publisher spends an average of $13.60 per page to prepare material for printing. A traditional approach costs slightly over $43 per page.[8]

Today, an increasing percentage of scholarly and research material is available solely in electronic forms. One such title in the field of librarianship is *Libres,* a monthly intended to share research information as well as support and develop knowledge about the electronic environment.[9]

As mentioned in chapter 1, governments are taking a strong interest in the electronic transmission of information. In the United States, it appears likely the Federal Communications Commission will play a regulatory role, at least for systems that employ videotext or teletext. In most other countries, there already is strong government involvement because radio, television, and telephone systems are controlled by the government. If book and other paper-based communication services die, as some predict, there is every reason for concern about intellectual freedom and free expression of divergent ideas because computer systems offer an almost-invisible means of manipulating information and an easily controllable means of distribution.

Types of Publishers

The preceding paragraphs used the terms *house, trade publisher,* and *specialty publisher.* The term *house* originated in the period when publishing was a personal or family operation.

Trade publishers produce a wide range of titles, both fiction and nonfiction, that have wide sales potential. HarperCollins; Alfred A. Knopf; Doubleday; Macmillan; Little, Brown; Thames & Hudson; and Random House are typical trade publishers. Many trade publishers have divisions that resemble specialty publishers, such as children's, textbook, paperback, technical, reference, and so forth. Trade publishers have three markets: bookstores, libraries, and wholesalers. To sell their products, publishers send sales representatives to visit buyers in businesses or institutions in each of the markets. Each successful visit means the sale of a few copies of several titles.

Specialty publishers restrict output to a limited area, subject, or format. Gale Research is an example of a specialty publisher. Specialty publishers' audiences are smaller and more critical than trade publishers' audiences. The categories of specialty publishers include textbook (el-hi and college), paperback, children's, microform, music, cartographic, and subject area.

Textbook publishers, especially those that target the primary and secondary schools, occupy one of the highest risk areas of publishing. Most publishers in this area develop a line of textbooks for several grades, for example, a social studies series. Preparation of such texts requires large amounts of time, energy, and money. Printing costs are high because most school texts feature expensive color plates and other specialized presswork. Such projects require large, up-front investments that must be recouped before a profit can be realized. If enough school districts adopt a text, profits can be substantial, but failure to secure adoption can mean tremendous loss. Larger textbook firms, such as Ginn or Scott, Foresman, & Company, produce several series to help ensure a profit or to cushion against loss. Why would a company take the risk this type of publishing involves? Consider the amount of money spent on textbooks each year: more than $4 billion in 1991. By carefully planning a series with the assistance of educators, and by focusing on marketing, profits can be enormous.

For el-hi material, a single school district's adoption of one textbook series can generate thousands of sales. Because of the scheduling of school textbook adoption practices (usually occurring once a year), textbook publishers can reduce warehousing costs, thus adding to the margin of profit. During the past five years, American school textbook publishers have faced increased pressure to change the content of their publications from a variety of special interest groups[10] (see chapter 19). This pressure adds yet another element of risk to textbook publishing.

Subject specialty houses share some of the characteristics of textbook houses. Many have narrow markets that are easy to identify. Focusing marketing efforts on a limited number of buyers allows specialty publishers to achieve a reasonable return with less risk than a trade publisher takes on a nonfiction title. Specialty houses exist for a variety of fields; examples include art (Harry N. Abrams), music (E. C. Schirmer), scientific (Academic Press), technical (American Technical Publishers), law (West Publishing), and medical (W. B. Saunders). Many specialty books require expensive graphic preparation or presswork. Such presswork increases production costs, which is one of the reasons art, music, and science and technology titles are so costly. Another factor in their cost is the smaller market as compared to the market for a trade title. A smaller market means the publisher must recover production costs from fewer books. Though the level of risk is greater for specialty publishing than for trade publishing, it is much lower than the level of risk that textbook publishers face. Occasionally, especially in the fields of law and medicine, complaints arise that too much control is concentrated in the hands of a few publishers, but it seems questionable whether more publishing houses in either field would change the picture significantly.

Vanity presses differ from other publishing houses in that they receive most of their operating funds from the authors whose works they publish. An example is Exposition Press. Vanity presses always show a profit and never lack material to produce. They offer editing assistance for a fee, and they print as many copies of the book as the author can afford. Distribution is the author's chore. While providing many of the same functions as other publishers, they do not share the same risks.

Private presses are not business operations in the sense that the owners expect to make money. Most private presses are an avocation rather than a vocation for the owners. Examples are Henry Morris, Bird, and Poull Press. In many instances, the owners do not sell their products but give them away. Most private presses are owned by individuals who enjoy fine printing and experimenting with type fonts and design. As one might expect, when the owner gives away the end product (often produced on a hand press) only a few copies are printed. In the past, many developments in type and book design originated with private presses. Some of the most beautiful examples of typographic and book design originated at private presses.

Large research libraries often attempt to secure copies of items produced by private presses and vanity presses. In addition, many authors who use vanity presses give copies of their books to the local libraries, but such gifts usually arrive with no indication that they are gifts. Books arriving in the acquisitions department without packing slips or invoices cause problems. By knowing local publishers, persons in the acquisitions department can make their work easier. If staff members know the local vanity and private presses, they can save time and energy by quickly identifying such possible gift items.

Scholarly publishers, as part of a not-for-profit organization, receive subsidies. Most are part of an academic institution (University of California Press), museum (Museum of the American Indian Heye Foundation), research institution (Battelle Memorial Institute), or learned society (American

Philosophical Society). These presses were founded to produce scholarly books, but many produce a few general interest titles as well. Most scholarly books have limited sales appeal. A commercial, or for-profit, publisher considering a scholarly manuscript has three choices: 1) publish it and try to sell it at a price to ensure costs are recovered; 2) publish it, sell it at a price comparable to commercial titles, and lose money; or 3) do not publish the item. The first two options cost the publisher money and for that reason, most commercial publishers will not publish scholarly books. Because of economic factors and a need to disseminate scholarly information regardless of cost (that is, even if it will lose money) the subsidized (by tax exemption, if nothing else), not-for-profit press exists. As publishing costs have skyrocketed, it has been necessary to fully subsidize some scholarly books, almost in the manner of a vanity press.

Some commercial publishers have questioned whether subsidized presses should be allowed to profit on a title. The commercial publishers wanted scholarly presses to turn over to the commercial houses any work that does more than break even. Proponents of this idea suggested it could be accomplished by auction; if no commercial publisher bid on the title, it could remain with the scholarly press. The commercial publishers' reasoned that scholarly presses receive public support through tax monies or their tax-exempt status. Furthermore, the presses are nonprofit by legal definition. University presses were the primary targets of such claims, which resulted more from a peak in academic library purchases of scholarly works during a period of high funding than from a desire on the part of commercial publishers to publish scholarly books. One seldom hears such claims today, although commercial firms have taken over publishing many journals for professional associations. One outcome of the increase in profit-oriented publishers publishing journals is a very high cost.

To some extent, scholarly presses invited criticism by publishing works aimed at a general audience, that could easily find a commercial publisher. Yet, as costs rise, the presses face pressure from their funding agencies to break even or show a profit on most books or to have a few money makers to carry the losers.

The role of the scholarly press in the economical and open dissemination of knowledge is critical. Every country needs some form of this type of press. Without scholarly presses, important works with limited appeal do not get published. Certainly, there are times when a commercial house is willing to publish a book that will not show a profit because the publisher thinks the book is important, but relying on that type of willingness will, in the long run, mean that many important works will never appear in print.

Like their for-profit counterparts, scholarly presses are making ever-greater use of electronic publishing techniques. Two good survey articles about how electronics are changing scholarly publishing are William Arms's "Scholarly Publishing on the National Networks"[11] and Ann Okerson's "Publishing Through the Network: The 1990s Debutante."[12] Though the

networks hold promise, they also hold the possibility of higher information costs. As Freeman notes,

> If profit rather than commitment to scholarly communication
> becomes the primary goal of those controlling access to the
> Internet, university presses would find themselves unable to
> afford to publish the scholarly works that are the core of their
> activities. Thus the public nature of the Internet must be carefully
> guarded if we want to realize the true benefits of a democratic
> networked environment: broad access to scholarly research and
> information not driven by financial concerns. A diverse range of
> independent, nonprofit publishers is critical to that goal.[13]

Government presses are the world's largest publishers. The combined
annual output of government publications—international (UNESCO),
national (U.S. Government Printing Office), and state, regional, and local (Los
Angeles or State of California)—dwarfs commercial output. In the past,
many people thought of government publications as characterized by poor
physical quality or as uninteresting items that governments gave away.
Today, some government publications rival the best offerings of commercial
publishers and cost much less. (The government price does not fully recover
production costs, so the price can be lower.) Most government publishing
activity goes well beyond the printing of legislative hearings or actions and
occasional executive materials. Often, national governments publish essential and inexpensive (frequently free) materials on nutrition, farming,
building trades, travel, and many other topics. (See chapter 8 for more
detailed information about government publications.)

Paperback publishers produce two types of work: quality trade paperbacks
and mass-market paperbacks. A trade publisher may have a quality paperback division or may issue the paperbound version of a book through the same
division that issued the hardcover edition. The publisher may publish original
paperbacks, that is, a first edition in paperback. Distribution of quality paperbacks is the same as for hardcover books. Mass-market paperback publishers
issue only reprints, or publications that first appeared in hardcover. Their
distribution differs from other book distribution. Their low price is based, in
part, on the concept of mass sales. Therefore, they sell anywhere the publisher
can get someone to handle them. The paperback books on sale in train and bus
stations, airline terminals, corner stores, and kiosks are mass-market paperbacks. These books have a short shelf life compared to hardcovers.

People talk about the paperback revolution, but it is hard to think of
it as a revolution. Certainly the paperback has impacted publishers' and a
few authors' incomes. Also, some readers are unwilling to accept a hardcover when the smaller, compact size of a paperback is more convenient
to use. The low price of a paperback also appeals to book buyers.

Books with paper covers are not new. In some countries all books
come out with paper covers, and buyers must bind the books they wish to
keep. The major difference is that most people think of only the mass-
market paperback as a paperback. The emphasis on popular, previously
published titles issued in new and colorful covers and sold at a low price
is apparent. Those are the elements of the paperback revolution, not the

paper cover nor even the relatively compact form. Nor has the paperback created a whole new group of readers, as some overenthusiastic writers claim. It has merely tapped an existing market for low-cost, popular books.

Contrary to popular belief, using a paper cover rather than a hard cover does not reduce the unit cost of a book by more than 20 or 30 cents. Original paperbacks incur the same costs, except for the cover material, as a hardcover title, which is why their cost is so much higher than reprint paperbacks. The reason the price of paperbacks is so much lower than hardcovers is that most first appeared as hardcovers. The title already sold well in hardcover, or there would be no reason to bring out a paper version, and so the book probably has already shown a profit. This means the publisher has already recovered some of the major production costs. Having recovered most of the editorial costs, it is possible to reduce the price. In addition, releasing a paperback version of a hardcover title allows the publisher to benefit from marketing efforts expended on the hardcover version. Marketing efforts for the hardcover carry over to the paperback, which further reduces publishing costs. Economies of scale, or high sales volume and low per-unit profits, also reduce the price.

Paperbacks are, or can be, an important element in collection development. If the library treats them as expendable and does not give them the same processing it gives hardcovers, paperbacks supply multiple copies of popular works at low cost. Libraries can stretch limited collection development funds farther by making judicious use of paperbacks.

Newspaper and periodical publishers are a different class of publisher. Usually, book publishers depend on persons outside their organization to prepare the material that they publish. Newspaper and periodical publishers retain reporters or writers as members of their staffs. Of course, there are exceptions to the exception. For instance, some popular (and most scholarly) periodicals consist of articles written by persons not employed by the organization that publishes the journal. In general, in newspaper or periodical publishing, one finds the same range of activities found in book publishing. In other words, there are commercial publishers of popular materials, specialty publishers, children's publishers, scholarly or academic publishers, and government publishers. All subcategories share the characteristics of their book publishing counterparts; some are divisions of book publishing organizations.

Supplying current information is the primary objective of newspaper and journal publishers. With books, one can assume that most of the material published is at least six months old at the time of publication. The newspaper or periodical format provides the means for more rapid publishing, from two or three months to less than one day. (A major exception are the scholarly and academic periodicals that frequently are one, two, or more years behind in publishing accepted articles.) To provide the most current information available, the library must acquire the newspapers or periodicals that suit the community's needs and interests. (Chapter 7 discusses problems concerning control and selection of these materials.)

Two other types of publishing activities deserve mention: *associations* and *reprint houses*. Professional and special interest groups and associations frequently establish their own publishing houses. The American Library Association is one such organization. These organizations may publish only a professional journal, but they also may issue books and audiovisual materials. The operating funds come from the association, but the association hopes to recover its costs. Professional associations are often tax-exempt, and thus their publishing activities are similar to those of scholarly presses: limited-appeal titles, small press runs, relatively high prices, and indirect government subsidies. Some associations do not have paid publication staff and use volunteer members instead; they contract with a commercial publisher to print the group's journal, conference proceedings, and other publications. Association publications, whether published by the organization itself or by contract, can provide the library with numerous bibliographic control headaches. For example, they announce titles as forthcoming, but the items never get published. Many publications are papers from meetings and conventions (called "Transactions of . . ." or "Proceedings of . . ."); the titles of such publications frequently change two or three times before they appear in hardcover. Many of these publications do not find their way into trade bibliographies.

Reprint publishers, as the name implies, focus on reprinting items no longer in print. Most of the sales for reprint houses are to libraries and scholars, and many of the titles that these publishers reprint are in the public domain (that is, no longer covered by copyright). The other major source for reprinted material is the purchase of rights to an out-of-print title from another publisher. Although many of the basic costs of creating a book do not exist for the reprint house (editing, design, and royalties, for example), reprints are expensive because of their limited sales appeal. (In the past, some publishers would announce a new release with a prepublication flyer that included an order form. Later, the company would announce the cancellation of the title. Some suspicious librarians suggested that such cancellations were the result of insufficient response to the prepublication announcement.) Sometimes reprints provide as many or more bibliographic headaches for libraries than do association titles. Despite the many problems, reprint houses are an essential source of titles for collection development programs concerned with retrospective materials.

Small presses are important for some libraries. Small presses are thought of as literary presses by some people, including librarians. Anyone reading the annual "Small Press Round-Up" in Library Journal could reasonably reach the same conclusion. The reality is that small presses are as diverse as the international publishing conglomerates. Size is the only real difference; in functions and interests small presses are no different than large trade publishers.

Small Press Record of Books in Print (SPRBIP) annually lists between 15,000 and 17,000 titles from about 1,800 small publishers.[14] Many of these presses are one-person operations, done as a sideline from the publisher's home. Such presses seldom publish more than four titles per year. The listings in SPRBIP show the broad range of subject interests of small presses and shows there are both book and periodical presses in this category. Some people assume that the content of small press publications is poor. This is incorrect, for small presses do not produce, proportionally, any more worthless titles than do the large publishers. Often, it is only through the small press that one can find information on less popular topics. Two examples of very popular books that were originally published by small presses are *Ruby Fruit Jungle* by Rita Mae Brown and the Boston Women's Health Book Collective's *Our Bodies, Ourselves.*

Another factor that sets small presses apart from their larger counterparts is economics: Large publishers have high costs and need substantial sales to recover their costs, but small presses can produce a book for a limited market at a reasonable cost and still expect some profit. Small presses also can produce books more quickly than their larger counterparts.

From a collection development point of view, small presses represent a challenge. Tracking down new releases can present a variety of problems. Locating a correct current address is one common problem. Another is learning about the title before it goes out of print. With *SPRBIP,* Len Fulton of Dustbooks tries to provide access, and he has succeeded to a surprising degree, given the nature of the field. However, waiting for his annual *SPRBIP* may take too long, because small presses frequently move about and their press runs are small, that is, only a limited quantity of books are printed. In essence, few small presses are part of the organized trade or national bibliographic network.

Very few of these presses advertise, and even fewer of their titles receive reviews in national journals. There are two publications that focus on small press titles, *Small Press Review* and *Small Press Book Review.* Lack of reviews is not the result of book review editors discriminating against small press publications. Rather, it is a function of too many small press operators not understanding how items get reviewed and failing to send out review copies.

Collection development librarians interested in small presses have had some commercial help. Quality Books of Northbrook, Illinois (a vendor that in the past was known primarily as a source of remainder books), has become active in the distribution of small press publications. Although it stocks books from only a small percentage of the presses listed in *SPRBIP* (about one-fifth), the fact that it does stock the items is a major feature. Most jobbers say they will attempt to secure a specific title for a library if they do not stock the publication. A librarian could easily devote too much time to an effort to track down a single copy of a $10.95 item from an obscure small press. Librarians interested in small presses, collection development, and access to information need to keep their collective fingers crossed in the hope that Quality Books will find its operation sufficiently profitable and that it will continue to offer the service. (For more information about distributors and vendors, see chapter 12.)

Excellent starting points for learning more about this field are the dated but useful Chandler B. Grannis's *What Happens in Book Publishing?* and Gerald Gross's *Editors on Editing* and *Publishers on Publishing.* (For full citations, refer to the bibliography at the end of this chapter.)

There are a number of reasons why librarians need to know about the producers whose products they purchase. Different classes of publishers perform different functions. Knowing which publishers are good at what function helps to speed the selection process. Some publishers are known for quality material—well written, organized, well edited, and produced as a durable, physical book—and others are not. When selecting material from citation information alone, knowing who does what will make the work easier.

Functions of Publishing

Publishing consists of five basic functions, which apply equally to print and nonprint materials: administration, editorial, production, marketing, and fulfillment. A publisher must be successful in all five areas if the organization is to survive for any length of time. Just because the organization is not for profit does not mean it has any less need for success in each of these areas.

Administration deals with overseeing the activities, ensuring the coordination, and making certain there are adequate funds available to do the desired work.

It is in the editorial area that publishing houses decide what to produce. Acquisition and managing editors discuss and review ideas for books or articles. Large book publishers develop trade lists (a combination of prior publications, manuscripts in production, and titles under contract) to achieve a profit while avoiding unnecessary competition with other publishers. Book selectors ought to learn something about the senior editors in the major publishing houses with which they deal. The editors' opinions about what to accept for publication determine what will be available. As with reviewing, the view of what is good or bad material is personal, so knowing the editors will help in planning selection activities. It is possible to meet many editors at library conventions and to discuss problems, make suggestions, and thus influence what happens in the coming years. This activity is only possible when librarians know 1) the editors and understand their importance in a publishing house and 2) something about the nature of the book trade in general. In addition, librarians can provide valuable marketing information to editors and publishers, again provided that they understand something about the publishing industry beyond its products.

Securing and reviewing manuscripts is a time-consuming activity for most editors. Based on a range of guesses concerning the number of unsolicited manuscripts reviewed for each one accepted, the average suggests that editors reject approximately nine tenths of all unsolicited manuscripts after the first examination. After the first complete reading still more manuscripts are rejected. Even after a careful review by several people, all of whom have favorable reactions, the editor may not accept the manuscript. Three common reasons for this are: 1) the title will not fit into the new list, 2) the sales potential (market) is too low, and 3) the cost of production would be too high.

The annual list is the group of books that a publisher has accepted for publication and plans to release during the next 6-12 months. The backlist comprises titles published in previous years and still available. A strong backlist of steadily selling titles is the dream of most publishers. Editors spend a great deal of time planning their lists. They do not want to have two new books on the same topic appear at the same time unless they complement one another. They want a list that will have good balance and strong sales appeal as well as fit with the titles still in print.

Librarians and readers often complain that commercial publishers are exclusively, or at least overly, concerned with profit and have little concern for quality. What these people forget is that publishing houses are businesses and must show a profit if they are to continue to operate. Even if the presses or publishers are governments, they must try to recover at least some of their costs in some manner, and those costs are constantly increasing. In time, even government publishers must ask, Is this manuscript really worth producing, given its projected production costs? As costs skyrocket, the answer, more and more often, will be no. Society asks publishers to undertake the risk of producing information materials, and it assumes that publishers will receive adequate compensation. In a capitalist system, that compensation involves the right to make a profit on the use of capital. When one can make almost as much profit by placing the capital in a no-risk savings account as it can by risking the loss of all of the capital in a publishing venture, only the compulsive gambler or altruist will try publishing. For noncapitalist systems, the decision whether to continue publishing eventually hinges on the willingness of people to continue to underwrite the expense. Only society can make that decision, but usually, health, safety, and the general good come ahead of books in social priorities.

Production and marketing join with the editorial team to make the final decisions regarding production details. Most publishers can package and price publications in a variety of ways. Some years ago, the Association of University Publishers released an interesting book entitled *One Book Five Ways*. (For a full citation, refer to the bibliography at the end of this chapter.) The book provides a fascinating picture of how five different university presses would handle the same project. In all five functional areas, the presses would have proceeded differently, from contract agreement (administration), copyediting (editorial), physical format (production), pricing and advertising (marketing), to distribution (fulfillment).

Production staff consider issues such as page size, typeface, number and type of illustrative materials, and cover design, as well as typesetting, printing, and binding. Their input and the decision made regarding the physical form of the item play a major role in how much the title will cost. Although electronic and desktop publishing are changing how and who performs some production activities, the basic issues of design, layout, use of illustrations, and use of color remain unchanged.

Marketing departments are responsible for promoting and selling the product. They provide input about the sales potential of the title. Further, this unit often decides how many review copies to distribute and to what review sources. Where, when, or whether to place an ad is the responsibility of the marketing department. All of these decisions influence the cost of the items produced. Many small publishers use direct mail (catalogs and brochures) to market their books. Publishers' sales representatives visit stores, wholesalers, schools, and libraries. When salespeople visit the library or information center, they keep the visits short and to the point.

Each visit represents a cost to the publisher, and the company recovers the cost in some manner, most often in the price of the material. One activity for which most marketing units are responsible is exhibits. For library personnel, convention exhibits are one of the best places to meet publishers' representatives and have some input into the decision-making process. From the publishers' point of view, if the conferees go to the exhibits, conventions can be a cost-effective way of reaching a large number of potential customers in a brief time. Librarians should also remember that the fees exhibitors pay help underwrite the cost of the convention.

Fulfillment activities are those needed to process an order as well as those connected with the warehousing of the materials produced. In many ways, fulfillment is the least controllable cost factor for a publisher. Libraries and information centers sometimes add to the cost of their purchases by requiring special handling of their orders. Keeping special needs to a minimum can help keep prices in check. Speeding up payments to publishers and vendors will also help slow price increases, because the longer a publisher has to carry an outstanding account the more interest has to be paid. Ultimately, most increases in the cost of doing business result in a higher price for the buyer, so whatever libraries can do to help publishers control their fulfillment costs will also help collection development budgets.

For various reasons, despite strong marketing efforts, some publications do not sell as well as expected. When this happens, sooner or later the publisher has to dispose of the material; many times, these become remaindered items. A decision by the Internal Revenue Service has influenced press runs and the speed with which publishers remainder slow-moving warehouse stock (Thor Power Tool Decision; see chapter 18). Remaindered items sell for a small fraction of their actual production costs. Prior to the *Thor* decision, businesses would write down the value of their inventories, or warehouse stock, to a nominal level at the end of the tax year. The resulting loss in the value of the inventory (which was, by and large, on paper only) then became a tax deduction for the company, increasing its profit. Since *Thor,* publishers can take such a deduction only if the material is defective or offered for sale below actual production costs. Under the previous method, publishers could find it profitable to keep slow-selling titles in their warehouses for years. Thus far, efforts to get an exemption from the ruling for publishers have been unsuccessful. At first, the ruling increased the number of remaindered books, but now most publishers have cut back on the size of their print runs in an attempt to match inventories to sales volume. More often than not, this means higher unit costs and retail prices. Despite all the problems for the field, total sales income for book publishing has increased steadily, from $3,177,200 in 1972, to $3,396,000 in 1982, to $16,918,500 in 1992.[15]

One can find data on annual sales in a variety of sources: *PW, The Bowker Annual of Library & Book Trade Almanac,* Standard and Poor's *Industry Surveys,* and so forth. Anyone concerned with collection development must make use of statistical data about publishing to develop intelligent budgets and work plans. Statistical data about the number of new titles available as paperbacks, reprints, and so forth, can be useful in planning the workload for the next fiscal year. For example, perhaps the library will need to hire more staff if the volume of acquisitions increases. Knowing the pricing patterns over a period of years and the expected acquisitions budget allows one to project the workload. The two most accessible sources of publishing statistics for the United States are *PW* and *The Bowker Annual*. Data in both sources, and almost all other printed statistical data about publishing, come from the American Book Producers Association (ABPA). Remember that the statistics represent information drawn from ABPA members, and not all publishers belong to the group. In fact, a great many small and regional publishers do not belong.

Annually, two issues of *PW* report statistical information for the previous year. One issue, published early in the year, contains the preliminary figures; it is late summer or early fall before the revised figures are published. (The reason for the delay in the final figures is that it takes some time for returns from bookstores and wholesalers to arrive back at publishers' warehouses. Most trade publishers allow bookstores to return unsold copies of books, within certain time limits, so it takes time to accurately determine how many copies actually sold.) The information in *The Bowker Annual* provides a condensed version of the *PW* reports, but because it is a hardcover volume, considerable delay in reporting the information is inevitable. For small libraries, which do not need to subscribe to *PW*, and for libraries in which the most current cost information is not necessary, *The Bowker Annual* is an adequate source.

Publishers use a variety of distribution outlets, selling directly to individuals, institutions, retailers, and wholesalers. Distribution is a major problem for both publishers and libraries because of the number of channels and the implications for acquiring a specific publication. Each channel has a different discount, and one accesses them through different sources. Figure 6.1 illustrates in a general way the complexity of the system. Production and distribution of information materials, whether print or nonprint, consist of several elements, all interacting with one another. Writers and creators of the material can and do distribute their output in several ways: directly to the community or public, to agents who in turn pass it on to producers, or directly to the producers. Producers seeking writers often approach agents with publication ideas. The figure illustrates the variety of channels publishers use to distribute their publications to the consumer.

Most publishers use all these sales channels. Wholesalers, direct mail companies, and retail store operators act as middlemen; a retailer may buy from the jobber or directly from the publisher. Each seller will have different discounts for different categories of buyers, ranging from no discount to more than 50 percent. Not only are there a great many choices available to the buyer, but the sources compete with one another. These factors combine to push up the cost of distributing a publication, which in turn increases its list price. With multiple outlets, different discounts, and different credit conditions, the publishing industry has created a cumbersome, uneconomical distribution system.

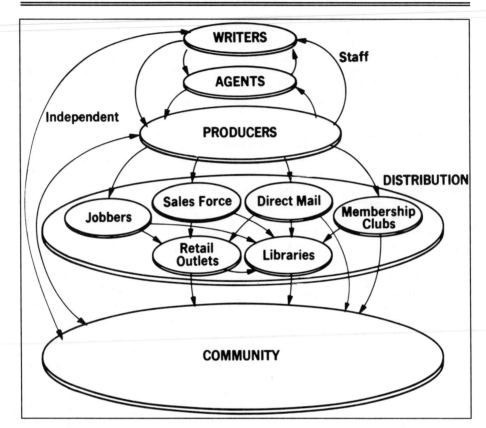

Fig. 6.1. Distribution system.

Selling practices vary by title and publisher; however, one can make a few generalizations. Advertising will help a good book, but it seldom, if ever, makes a success out of a poor book. Publishers use both publicity and advertising, which are two different marketing devices. An interview with the author or a review of the book on a national radio or television program are examples of publicity. Normally free, publicity will do a great deal for the sales of a book. However, the book's topic, or at least its author, must be of national interest or the title will not attract attention. Changes in current events can change a slow-moving book into a bestseller overnight, something that no amount of advertising can accomplish.

Publishers advertise in several ways. First, they use trade advertising directed toward retail outlets and institutional buyers. Second, they make an effort to get items reviewed in major professional and general review media. (Reviews are technically promotion rather than advertising, because one does not pay to have a title reviewed. However, a lead review can be worth more than a full-page advertisement.) Third, they place announcements and ads in professional journals, where the emphasis is on reaching individual buyers, both personal and institutional. Fourth, they employ cooperative advertisements (co-op ads) in the book review sections of many newspapers. A co-op ad is one in which the publisher and a retail store share the advertisement's cost. The publisher determines which titles are eligible for cooperative advertising. Finally, for books with a defined audience for which there is a good mailing list, the publisher often uses a direct mail campaign, again with individuals and institutional buyers as the targets.

This brief overview outlines the most basic elements of publishing. Its purpose is to start a collection development novice thinking about the trade. The next section presents a discussion of audiovisual producers. Unfortunately, because of their diversity, it is not possible in a limited space to parallel the discussion of print publishing.

Producers of Audiovisual Materials

Media producers are a diverse group working with a variety of formats (audio recordings, film, filmstrips, video, models, and so on), making it difficult to generalize about their operations. The following discussion is an attempt to cover all of those audiovisual formats, but it would require a full-length book to describe all the individual variations and exceptions.

Media producers enjoy substantial annual sales to schools and libraries. Indeed, this market is almost the sole sales outlet for the majority of media producers. Two major exceptions are audio and video recordings. The audio and video recording industries are the major sources of "other media" for most libraries. Recorded music, as part of a growing audio collection that includes talking books, is a common feature of libraries, reflecting the fact that a large segment of the general population buys or listens to music. In terms of sales, however, libraries and other institutions represent only a fraction of the music industry's income.

When one considers average circulations per title, video recordings are often the top circulation format, especially in public libraries. Video collections in libraries contain both educational and theatrical film recordings. The sales of motion picture videocassettes are far larger to the general public than to libraries, but libraries (including school media centers) are the largest market for educational video.

One important fact to remember about most media, with the exception of books and filmstrips, is that they require the user to follow the material at a fixed pace—the pace of the machine involved. Certainly, the equipment allows for rewinding and reviewing a section of special importance, and video players can freeze a frame, but the formats make it difficult to skip around as one can do with a book. Selectors must keep this fact in mind when considering these formats for the collection. Will our typical user be able to benefit from the material given the pace of presentation? is a question for selectors to ponder. Interactive video and hypermedia allow for easy random access, and these technologies are most likely to replace many of the traditional media formats libraries have made available. What newer format and technology will replace interactive systems is impossible to guess. Virtual reality is, to many people who follow developments in the field, an enhancement of interactive systems and not really a new system.

Most media producers design products for the average ability or level of knowledge of the target audience. In the case of educational media, the producer assumes the item is for group presentations, with a teacher adding comments and creating a context for the material. Though individuals working alone can benefit from the material, many will get less from the use of the item without some interaction with an instructor. More and more teachers in schools and higher education are assigning media use outside the classroom in the same way they have employed print material to supplement the instructional program. This translates into libraries and media centers receiving requests for bigger and more diverse media collections.

The first major difference between book publishers and media producers is media producers market a product designed primarily for group use, and book publishers market a product designed primarily for individual use. This difference has an influence on how media producers market and distribute their products. Media producers place heavy emphasis on direct institutional sales. Also, there is less use of wholesalers. Though some book jobbers do handle audio and video recordings, a large percentage of media acquisitions are made directly from the producer.

One characteristic of media production that is frequently overlooked is authorship. Most books are the result of the intellectual effort of one or two persons. Textbook publishers frequently commission books. (Perhaps in the age of merger, this approach is becoming more common for trade publications as well.) For media, the process is the opposite. Normally, the producer generates the ideas and seeks the necessary persons to carry out the project if the company's staff cannot handle the project. *This means that the producers have almost total control over the final product.* It is true that book publishers have the final say in what they will publish. The difference is that the book publisher receives hundreds of manuscripts and ideas for books to consider each year, and thus has exposure to ideas and projects that otherwise might not receive consideration. In addition, even if one publisher rejects a manuscript, there is always the chance that another may pick it up. Book publishing has a tradition of being a free marketplace for ideas, whereas this concept is almost nonexistent in the media field. Although this may seem to be a subtle difference, it does have an impact on the type of material produced and, in turn, on the library's collection.

Despite the producers' control, people often think of the media field as one of independence and freedom. One reason for this view is, at least in the past, the relatively low cost of entering it. One hears stories about the individual who started off with a few thousand dollars and some equipment and is now a major producer. One does not hear about the thousands of others who tried and failed. Mediocre equipment and a low advertising budget usually mean a mediocre product and few, if any, sales. The opportunity is there, but the chances of success are only slightly better than for any other business venture. Almost anyone may become a media producer; for example, to become a producer of 35mm slides (educational, art, travel, and so forth), one needs only a 35mm camera, a stock of master images to use to produce slides on demand, and some money for advertising. Success is not likely, but this is all that one needs to become a media producer and be listed in a directory of media sources. In general, the start-up capital (money required to begin operations) is much lower than would be necessary for a book publisher. Good quality professional media production equipment is exceedingly expensive; however, many of the so-called producers do not invest in quality equipment. They depend on commercial laboratories and hope for the best.

Because of a lack of materials and the pressure to have media in schools and libraries, it has been and still is possible to sell copies of extremely poor quality materials because they are all that is available. All too often a selector must purchase an item on the basis of curriculum needs rather than on the basis of quality.

Another characteristic of media producers is that their products have a fairly high cost per unit of information conveyed. Many media items are single-concept materials. (Single-concept films are a special class of educational films that deal with a very narrow concept, such as cell division, and are usually very short, 3-4 minutes long.) Books, on the other hand, have a low cost per unit of information. For example, no single film, videotape, audiotape, or set of 35mm slides can convey the same amount of information about Native Americans as one 300-page book. This feature of the media has great importance for selection, because not every medium is ideal for every purpose. Librarians must know the advantages of each medium and select and acquire items on this basis.

Generally, media products cost more per copy than do books. Color, 16mm, sound films with a 20-minute running time have an average cost of more than $300 per title, or almost $20 per minute. Today, there is a choice of film or videocassette; educational videos are as expensive as films, but most theatrical cassettes are under $80. Sets of 35mm slides range from $5 to more than $100. In general, the kit combinations of media are high profit items. Prices on such combinations run from $20 to more than $100. Also, they are the perfect medium for building-level materials, that is, developing media collections around curriculum needs over time. Because of the cost factor, selectors normally can buy only a few items each year, thus making the selection process important.

Though book publishers use a multitude of outlets to sell their products, media producers use few outlets. With the exception of audio and video stores and a few map shops, there are no retail outlets for "other media." There are no media-of-the-month clubs (except for music recordings and videos), few mail-order houses, and no remainder houses (except for records and some videos). Even wholesalers dealing with all media are few and far between. The main source, and in some cases the only source, is the producer. Because the producers are the basic source, collection development personnel must spend an inordinate amount of time and energy in maintaining lists of producers' addresses. Without such records, schools and libraries almost would have to halt their acquisition of "other media." Because many producers are small and move frequently, updating of addresses is a constant problem for the library. It means that directories more than 12 months old are likely to be out of date.

The one advantage to this situation is that the market for media is clearly identifiable: schools and libraries. Like the specialty publisher, the media producer is better able to focus advertising and sales activities on a small area with a high probability of success. Trade book publishers use a broad spectrum of advertising sources, newspapers, periodicals, flyers, radio, and television. In general, the trade publisher must take a shotgun approach, but specialty publishers and media producers should have a much better idea of their market.

Both books and other media are easy to copy. The difference is in the cost of the item. Most institutions capable of using media also have the capability to duplicate that material. That capability is a concern for producers because it was, and still is, common to request to preview the material before placing a firm order. Previewing can be an opportunity for copying. Awareness of this potential danger may be one factor accounting for the general absence of media wholesalers. The media for which this danger is greatest are tapes (video and audio) and 35mm slides.

The majority of media producers are small-business owners without a large capital reserve. For the small media producer, cash flow is a real problem. Anything that the library can do to help the small media firm control its costs will help to control the unit cost of products as well, for example, using cooperative previewing and keeping order and billing procedures simple.

One other important characteristic of the media field is the speed with which its technology changes. This characteristic is a central problem for everyone concerned, both producers and consumers. Improvements in equipment constantly make existing equipment almost obsolete; occasionally, a new format may, in fact, make equipment obsolete. Given the volatile nature of the field, many users, with good reason, are reluctant to invest heavily in equipment. For the producer, the problem is greater; it means deciding rather quickly whether to go with the new or stay with the old. Staying with the old too long may cut the producer out of the field because of licensing, franchising considerations, or simply not keeping up to date. On the other hand, moving too soon may use up capital on a change that does not last.

Table 6.1 provides an overview of the basic differences between book publishers and media producers, differences that have an impact on collection development. The figure presents broad generalizations to which there are many exceptions.

Table 6.1.

Differences Between Media Producers and Book Publishers

	Media Producers	Book Publishers
Audience	Individual as part of a group	Individual
Idea Authorship	Company generated	Agent generated
Use	Group and sequential, equipment paced	Single and nonsequential, self-paced
Cost per concept	High	Low
Selection process in library	Usually group	Individual
Cost to enter field	Relatively low, except for interactive formats	Moderately high, desktop publishing low
Inventory	Low	High
Market	Clearly defined	Highly variable
Potential sales volume	Low (except audio and video recordings)	Medium
Cost per copy to buy	Moderate	Relatively low
Ease of copying	Easy to copy, high sales price	Easy to copy, low sales price
Distribution	Mostly single source	Multiple source
Changes in format and equipment	Very rapid with high rate of obsolescence	Relatively slow

Producers' Problems and Collection Development

Collection development personnel need to understand some of the important issues and problems facing producers, because those factors inevitably have an impact on the library. Rising costs create problems for everyone, but publishers and media producers have some special problems. Information producers experience pressure from two sides. On the one hand, the rising costs of materials and labor put pressure on them to raise the prices of their products. On the other, if they do raise prices, they must realize that this may cut more deeply into sales, thus cutting into their profits more than the cost increases themselves. The consumer must meet basic needs first, and, during periods of inflation, meeting basic needs cuts into funds available for luxury items. For most individual buyers, books and media are among the first items to be cut.

Producers are likely to continue increasing their prices as the personal buyer market continues to shrink. Institutional buyers will continue to buy materials, but a static materials budget over two or three years, in combination with increasing costs of materials, means that the library buys fewer items each year. Most libraries do not receive large budget increases even during inflationary periods. The increases they do receive do no more than keep pace with inflation; thus, for all practical purposes, the budget is static. These two factors effectively cut the number of items purchased, and producers must carefully weigh these concerns before raising prices. This, in turn, forces them to be more and more selective about the items they produce. They will carry few, if any, materials that do not show a profit.

Resource sharing among libraries is a topic librarians talk about. During periods of tight budgets, many libraries actively cooperate to share materials and resources. Sharing resources helps ensure that items will be available, though accessing them may be inconvenient. However, such cooperation means an overall decline in the market for producers. How to balance market decline and resource sharing has been a knotty problem for producers and librarians for a long time. Librarians must try to achieve real resource sharing and thus control expenditures, and producers worry about how to react to such systems. One approach for the producers is to tie the issue to copyright and the delivery of electronic information, as discussed in chapter 18.

If producers could simplify their distribution system, they could achieve significant savings. Why should the general consumer (individual or institution) be able to purchase an item directly from the producer or from a wholesaler or retailer? The distribution system as it now operates is cumbersome and costly. For book publishers, it is a matter of having a typical marketing system (producer to wholesaler to retailer), but at the same time the system allows any individual customer access to any level of the system to make a purchase. Media producers, on the other hand, use direct sales. Both systems are costly for everyone. The book system requires complex handling procedures at each level because of different classes of customer. For the media system, shipping single-item orders to numerous locations increases the cost of placing and filling an order. The impact on collection development is that more money goes into paperwork and administrative procedures and less is available to collection development. Both producers and librarians must strive to solve this problem.

Perhaps the most difficult question concerns the right to use knowledge resources, or rather, how one may use them. As noted above, copyright has become a central issue among librarians, educators, and other users of knowledge resources on the one hand and the producers on the other. Yet, without copyright, there is little incentive for anyone to produce a work. The problem is how far society can go to provide and protect such incentives and still ensure adequate access to material at a fair price. Libraries want open, free access and use, and producers want limited free access. This issue, of course, has an important role to play in determining how one develops a collection, with electronic information making the issue ever more complex.

Notes

[1]Frederick W. Lancaster, *Libraries and Librarians in an Age of Electronics* (Arlington, VA: Information Resources Press, 1982).

[2]Celeste West, "Stalking the Literary-Industrial Complex," *American Libraries* 13 (May 1982): 298-300; Celeste West, "The Question of Size in the Book Industry," *Publishers Weekly* 214 (July 31, 1978): 25-54.

[3]Ben Bagdikan, "The Media Brokers: Concentration and Ownership of the Press," *Multinational Monitor* (September 1987): 8-12.

[4]John R. Secor, "Growing Crisis of Business Ethics," *Serials Librarian* 13 (October-November 1987): 70.

[5]Bagdikan, "The Media Brokers."

[6]"Modern Library Relaunch to Include Electronic Books," *Publishers Weekly* 239 (May 11, 1992): 10.

[7]Gayle Feldman, "Professional Publishing Goes Electronic," *Publishers Weekly* 239 (May 11, 1992): 31.

[8]Sally Taylor, "The Joys of Electronic Togetherness," *Publishers Weekly* 240 (March 29, 1993): 24.

[9]*Libres*, Kent State University, 1991- , monthly; subscribe at listserv@kentvm.kent.edu.

[10]"State Board of Education Approves New Texts Despite Groups' Protests," *San Fernando Valley Daily News* (October 13, 1990): 1, 23.

[11]William Arms, "Scholarly Publishing on the National Networks," *Scholarly Publishing* 23 (April 1992): 158-69.

[12]Ann Okerson, "Publishing Through the Network: The 1990s Debutante," *Scholarly Publishing* 23 (April 1992): 170-77.

[13]Lisa Freeman, "Big Challenges Face University Presses in the Electronic Age," *Chronicle of Higher Education* (April 28, 1993): A44.

[14]*Small Press Record of Books in Print* (Paradise, CA: Dustbooks, 1975-).

[15]*The Bowker Annual: Library and Book Trade Almanac* (New York: R. R. Bowker, 1992).

Further Reading

General

Arthur Anderson Company. *Book Distribution in the United States*. New York: R. R. Bowker, 1982.

Baker, J. F. "Reinventing the Book Business." *Publishers Weekly* 241 (March 4, 1994): 36-40.

——. "Selling to Libraries: Publishers Learn About a Billion-Dollar Market." *Publishers Weekly* 233 (December 18, 1987): 14-15.

Britt, B. "What Thou Lovest Well Remaindered." *Small Press* 10 (Winter 1991): 52-55.

Bryant, B. "Paper vs. Modem." *Library of Congress Bulletin* 52 (December 13, 1993): 466-67.

Carter, R. A. "Taking Aim at the Library Market." *Publishers Weekly* 237 (June 8, 1990): S6-S12.

Dave, R. *The Private Press*. 2d ed. New York: R. R. Bowker, 1983.

Dessauer, J. P. *Book Publishing: What It Is, What It Does*. 2d ed. New York: R. R. Bowker, 1981.

Dick, J. T. "Laserdisc Redux." *Library Journal* 115 (November 15, 1990): 36-39.

Feldman, T. "Welcome to the Electronic Superhighway." *The Bookseller* 214 (July 10, 1992): 95-97.

Finn, M. "Everything You Need to Know About Trademarks and Publishing." *Publishers Weekly* 239 (January 6, 1991): 41-44.

Graham, G. "Publishers, Librarians and the Eternal Triangle." *Library Acquisitions: Practice and Theory* 15, no. 3 (1991): 261-64.

Grannis, C. B. *What Happens in Publishing?* 2d ed. New York: Columbia University Press, 1967.

Gross, G. *Editors on Editing*. New York: Grossett, 1962.

——. *Publishers on Publishing*. New York: Grossett, 1961.

Hoffert, B. "Getting Published." *Library Journal* 115 (February 15, 1990): 153-56.

Hughes, S. M. "Small Publishers in Texas." *Texas Library Journal* 66 (Spring 1990): 22-26.

Hunter, K. A. "Making the Commercial Transition From Paper to Electronic: Or Publishing in the 'Twilight Zone'." *Collection Management* 15, nos. 1/2 (1992): 129-39.

Kopka, M. "Backlist: How to Use It." *Publishers Weekly* 240 (October 4, 1993): 24-25.

Loe, M. K. H. "Book Culture and Book Business: U.K. vs. the U.S." *Journal of Academic Librarianship* 16 (March 1990): 4-10.

Newlin, B. "Traveling the New Information Superhighway." *Small Press* 12 (Spring 1994): 26-29.

One Book Five Ways. Los Altos, CA: William Kaufmann, Inc., 1977.

Posel, N. R. "High Priced or Over-Priced: They're Every Library's Problem." *Reference Librarian* 19 (1987): 257-67.

Rettig, J. "Do Publishers Have Ears?" *Wilson Library Bulletin* 62 (January 1988): 15-22.

Salace, J. "Video Distribution: The Maze Made Manageable." *Library Journal* 115 (July 1990): 42-44.

Sexton, M. "Replacing the Myths About Marketing to Libraries." *Publishers Weekly* 236 (March 10, 1989): 56-57.

Taylor, S. A. "Joys of Electronic Togetherness." *Publishers Weekly* 240 (March 29, 1993): 24-28.

Weisberg, J. "Rough Trade: The Sad Decline of American Publishing." *New Republic* 204 (June 17, 1991): 16-21.

Academic

Baker, J. F. "Beyond the Ivory Tower." *Publishers Weekly* 239 (June 1, 1992): 26-28.

Berry, H. "Small Presses and Academic Libraries." *Choice* 25 (March 1988): 1044-46.

Berry, J. N. "A New Alliance Aborning?" *Library Journal* 112 (August 1987): 56-60.

Byrd, G. D. "An Economic 'Commons' Tragedy for Research Libraries: Scholarly Journal Publishing and Pricing Trends." *College & Research Libraries* 51 (May 1990): 184-95.

Czeslaw, J. G. "Everything You Need Know About Technology." *Publishing Research Quarterly* 7, no. 4 (1991/92): 3-12.

Day, M. P. "Electronic Publishing and Academic Libraries." *British Journal of Academic Librarianship* 1 (Spring 1986): 53-70.

Graham, G. "Adversaries or Allies?" *Scholarly Publishing* 14 (July 1983): 291-97.

Henon, A. L. "Publish and Perish." *Serials Librarian* 17, nos. 3/4 (1990): 35-41.

Hutton, F. *Early Black Press in America, 1827-1860*. Westport, CT: Greenwood Press, 1993.

Lewis, D. W. "Economics of the Scholarly Journal." *College & Research Libraries* 50 (November 1989): 674-87.

Lustig, S. "UK Academic Library Purchasing Patterns." *The Bookseller* 208 (August 16, 1986): 646-50.

McGinty, S. "Political Science Publishers: What Do the Citations Reveal?" *Collection Management* 11, nos. 3/4 (1989): 93-102.

Moore, T. W. "Believe It or Not, Academic Books Are a Bargain." *Scholarly Publishing* 24 (April 1993): 161-65.

Nixon, W. "University Presses: Highs and Lows." *Publishers Weekly* 236 (September 22, 1989): 18-24.

Public

Burroughs, R. "Book Publishers Focus on Librarian Focus Groups." *Library Journal* 114 (March 15, 1989): 48-49.

———. "Fitting into the Conglomerate Picture (Children's Imprints)." *Publishers Weekly* 236 (July 28, 1989): 138-40.

Dahlin, R. "Category Closeup: Mystery." *Publishers Weekly* 240 (March 8, 1993): 51-52.

Eaglen, A. B. "Publishers' Trade Discounts and Public Libraries." *Library Acquisitions: Practice and Theory* 8, no. 2 (1984): 95-97.

Epstein, H. M. "Strengthening the Partnership." *Publishers Weekly* 238 (May 31, 1991): 33-34.

Hamaker, C. "Least Reading for the Smallest Number at the Highest Price." *American Libraries* 19 (October 1988): 764-68.

Harper, T. "Public Library and Small Presses." *Show-Me Libraries* 34 (October 1982): 8-9.

Hays, K. H. "Sleepy Library Market Awakes." *Library Journal* 115 (November 1, 1990): 22.

Hoffert, B. "Getting People to Read: A Talk with Librarians, Publishers and Booksellers." *Library Journal* 116 (February 15, 1991): 161-65.

———. "A Publisher Checks Out Libraries." *Library Journal* 116 (September 1, 1991): 146-48.

———. "Striking a New Balance of Power." *Library Journal* 117 (February 15, 1992): 124-28.

Johnson, P. "What Publishers Should Know About the Public Library." *Publishers Weekly* 211 (March 28, 1977): 40-42.

Nixon, W. "Art of Publishing Popular Science Books." *Publishers Weekly* 238 (August 23, 1991): 32-35.

Strussy, S. A. "Librarians and the Salesperson: Allies or Enemies?" *Catholic Library World* 57 (May/June 1986): 274-77.

School

Eaglen, A. "Publishers' Sales Strategies: A Questionable Business." *School Library Journal* 34 (February 1988): 19-21.

———. "Shell Game: Publishers, Vendors and the Myth of the Backlist." *School Library Journal* 38 (November 1992): 24-28.

Kayden, M. "Out of Print and Back in Print." *Journal of Youth Services in Libraries* 6 (Spring 1993): 265-69.

Lasky, K. "Creativity in a Boom Industry." *Horn Book Magazine* 67 (November/ December 1991): 705-11.

Lodge, S. "Making of a Crossover: One Book, Two Markets." *Publishers Weekly* 239 (November 23, 1992): 38-42.

Lotz, J. W. "Here Today, Here Tomorrow: Coping with the OP Crisis." *School Library Journal* 35 (July 1989): 25-28.

Nilsen, A. P. "Speaking Loudly for Good Books." *School Library Journal* 37 (September 1991): 180-83.

Roback, D. E., and S. Maughan. "Children's Books." *Publishers Weekly* 240 (February 15, 1993): 26-32.

Roginski, J. W. "When the Publisher Calls: Children's Libraries and Telephone Sales." *School Library Journal* 32 (October 1985): 98-101.

Tangorra, J. "Publishers Refining Strategies for Children's Audio Market." *Publishers Weekly* 237 (February 23, 1990): 186-89.

Special

Albin, M. "Refugee and Exile Publishing in Western Europe." *College & Research Libraries News* 50, no. 5 (May 1989): 381-85.

"Cost Effectiveness of Science Journals." *Publishing Research Quarterly* 8 (Fall 1992): 72-91.

De Kerckhove, D. "What Makes the Classics Classic in the Sciences?" *Bulletin of the American Society for Information Science* 18 (February/March 1991): 13-14.

Drury, N. "Australian Art Books and the International Marketplace." *Art Libraries Journal* 13, no. 4 (1988): 26-28.

Hunter, K. A. "Through a Kaleidoscope Darkly." *Science & Technology Libraries* 12 (Summer 1992): 91-98.

Kawula, J. D. "Similarities Between Legal and Scientific Literature." *Special Libraries* 84 (Spring 1993): 85-89.

Krupp, R. G. "Issues in Acquisition of Science Literature." In *Special Librarianship,* 492-99. Metuchen, NJ: Scarecrow Press, 1980.

Thornton, J. L. *Thornton's Medical Books, Libraries and Collectors: A Study of Bibliography and the Book Trade.* 3d rev. ed. Andershots, England: Gower, 1990.

Walker, R. D., and C. D. Hurt. *Scientific and Technical Literature.* Chicago: American Library Association, 1990.

White, H. S., and B. M. Fry. "Economic Interaction Between Special Libraries and Publishers of Scholarly and Research Journals." *Special Libraries* 68 (March 1977): 109-14.

7
Serials

Individuals use the words *journals, magazines, periodicals*, and *serials*, frequently interchangeably, with no great misunderstanding resulting from the imprecise usage. The *ALA Glossary of Library and Information Science* provides the following definitions of two key terms:

> *Serial*—"a publication issued in successive parts, usually at regular intervals, and, as a rule, intended to be continued indefinitely. Serials include periodicals, annuals (reports, yearbooks, etc.) and memoirs, proceedings, and transactions of societies"

> *Periodical*—"a publication with a distinctive title intended to appear in successive (usually unbound) numbers of parts at stated or regular intervals and, as a rule, for an indefinite time. Each part generally contains articles by several contributors. Newspapers, whose chief function it is to disseminate news, and the memoirs, proceedings, journals, etc. of societies are not considered periodicals"[1]

Definitions in general dictionaries have more overlap:

> *Journal*—"a periodical publication especially dealing with matters of current interest—often used for official or semi-official publications of special groups"

> *Magazine*—"a periodical that usually contains a miscellaneous collection of articles, stories, poems, and pictures and is directed at the general reading public"

> *Periodical*—"a magazine or other publication of which the issues appear at stated or regular intervals—usually for a publication appearing more frequently than annually but infrequently used for a newspaper"

> *Serial*—"a publication (as a newspaper, journal, yearbook, or bulletin) issued as one of a consecutively numbered and indefinitely continued series"[2]

This chapter uses the term *serials* because it represents the broadest spectrum of materials.

Several characteristics unique to serials make this format useful. For many patrons, serials are the most important source of printed information. Serials contain the most current information about a topic, other than what may be available on an electronic bulletin board. Some professional society serial publications are very slow to appear, and scholars in the field will know about the material before it is published in the journal; nevertheless, the journal article will be the first published source of information. (Because of the importance of currency, providing a system that allows patrons to determine the latest issue received is important.) Related to currency is the frequency with which serials update information. For serials, the update interval can be short, for example, newspapers are updated daily. (In contrast, few monographs get updated, and for those titles that go into second or subsequent editions, the updating interval may be several years.) Serial articles are short and focus on narrow subjects; thus readers with a specific information need frequently find that serials provide the desired information more quickly than monographic publications. Finally, serials are often the first printed source of information about a new subject or development. People use serials to learn about new ideas, concepts, and information, and they use monographs to gain a broader or deeper knowledge of a subject.

Serial work is interesting and frustrating. The following quote sums up the work nicely:

> The Publisher is my Tormentor. I shall not smile:
> He maketh me to work all day at my desk.
> He leadeth me astray with misnumbered issues:
> His Roman numerals confound me:
> He changeth titles over and over for His own sake.
> Yea, when I walk through the shadow of missing or irregular
>   issues, I can find no respite, for He has moved.
> He answereth not my letters, nor useth the correct mailing label;
> He starteth not when I ask and quiteth before it is time;
> My work never endeth.
> Rising prices and duplicate issues shall follow me all the days of
>   my life;
> and I shall moan and groan in the library forever.[3]

Selection of Serials

Selection and deselection of serials focuses on three basic issues: titles currently in the collection, titles not in the collection, and new titles. One uses slightly different criteria in assessing each group. When reexamining titles in the collection, subscription price and use patterns are the two primary issues (see page 191 for an explanation of why periodic reexamination is necessary).

Looking at interlibrary loan (ILL) data and citation analysis information helps one decide whether an existing title that is not in the collection ought to be. For new titles, the subject area, cost, and—when available—reviews are the key elements in deciding whether or not to place a subscription.

As with books, one can incorporate some macro selection decisions into the collection development policy for serials. Some possible macro decisions are:

Subscribe to any titles requested by users that match collected subject areas (this rule is often used in special libraries).

Subscribe to any title borrowed through ILL more than X times.

Subscribe to all core titles, as identified through citation analysis, in subject areas collected.

Do not subscribe to unindexed titles.

Do not subscribe to journals that contain unrefereed articles.

The list could go on; the point is, the more macro decisions there are, the easier serials management becomes.

There are other broad generalizations one can make about serials selection. The fields of science, technology, and medicine (commonly abbreviated as STM in the literature) are very dependent on serial publications. At the opposite end of the spectrum are the humanities, which depend more on books than on serials. Between are the social sciences, some of which are more similar to the science disciplines (e.g., psychology, linguistics, physical anthropology), and others of which are more similar to the humanities (e.g., political science, education, and social anthropology). A decision to subscribe to or place a standing order for a serial is a much bigger decision than similar decisions for monographs. Several factors account for the difference. Because serials are ongoing, they can become a standing commitment for the library or information center and thus become a more-or-less fixed element in the materials budget. Because serials arrive in the library or information center in parts, there must be an ongoing process for receiving the parts and maintaining records about what did or did not arrive. Unfortunately, few serials arrive in a form that allows for easy long-term storage or heavy use; therefore, libraries must bind or preserve them. In addition, serials occupy large amounts of storage space, which over time becomes scarce. Gaining access to the contents of most serials usually requires use of indexing and abstracting services, which are in themselves serials. Adding a new indexing or abstracting service typically results in additional work for ILL, unless the library subscribes to all of the titles covered by the service. A serials collection that does not provide for quick, easy, and inexpensive photocopy services will quickly become a collection of covers and advertisements; the articles will disappear. When adding a title that has been published for some time, one must consider the question of back files. Finally, serials change over time. These are the most important differences between selecting a book and a serial.

Unlike a monograph, a serial normally implies a long-term commitment. Subscriptions require renewals, but with most vendor plans, the renewal process is automatic, requiring no action on the part of the collection development staff. When the subscription renewal requires a positive decision by the library staff, the serial holdings are more likely to reflect the current interests of the library's customers. With automatic renewal, there is a substantial chance that the library will continue inappropriate serials long after the serial ceases to meet community needs.

A long-term commitment to a serial results in subscription costs becoming a fixed feature of the budget. With rapidly raising prices and small budget increases, each year serials take up an increasing proportion of the total materials budget. Chapter 13 (fiscal management) provides more information about this problem, but in general, serial prices have been increasing at a much faster rate than general inflation.

Thus, each year the amount of money required to maintain the present serials subscriptions increases at a rate greater than many libraries are able to sustain.

Another fixed cost is processing. When ordering and receiving a monograph, the library incurs a one-time cost. Serials have ongoing receiving and renewal costs, in addition to the cost of placing the initial order. Claiming missing issues is a normal part of maintaining a serials collection. A staff member records each issue when it arrives in the library. When the person notes an issue is missing or a number skipped, the library contacts the publisher or agent to attempt to secure the missing material. (This is called placing a claim). Acting promptly on claims is important because serial publishers print only slightly more copies than the number of subscribers. Serial publishers know a certain percentage of issues sent will go astray in the mail, and they print extra copies to cover the expected claims. However, at times, the number of claims is greater than the number of available copies. When that happens, a number of unlucky libraries receive out-of-print notices. The closer the claim is made to the publication date, the greater the chances are of receiving the missing issue. (The consequences of small print runs appear again when it is time to bind the volume and the library discovers one of the issues is missing. Locating a copy can be time consuming.) Daily serial check-in is a must to avoid missing issues. Automated serial systems help speed routine serials work, including providing automatic claiming, but in a library with a large serials list, one or more full-time staff may work exclusively on processing serials. Clearly, each new serial adds to the workload on an ongoing basis.

By their nature, serials arrive in successive issues, normally as paperbacks. If the library maintains serials for long periods of time or the titles receive relatively heavy use, the library must repackage the serial for more convenient handling. One method is to store the loose issues in a cardboard or metal container (sometimes referred to as a Princeton File) that keeps a limited number of issues together in a vertical position. This makes it easier to shelve the loose issues alongside bound materials. The container must have room on its outfacing side to record the title and issue or volume number of the items in the box. The most common long-term storage treatment is binding. A third alternative, microformat storage, represents an additional cost. Whatever choice is made, there is an ongoing cost to package each serial year after year.

Eventually, finding storage space for collections becomes a problem for all libraries and information centers. Storing long runs of serials can consume large quantities of limited shelf space. Using microforms as the long-term storage format for long runs of low-use serials will help with the space problem for a time. However, microforms also present some problems. Customers usually resist and complain about using microforms, so there is a public relations issue to address when shifting to microforms. Microforms also mean acquiring equipment: microform readers at a minimum, reader-printers the best solution. Libraries usually have at least two types of microform readers, film and fiche. Most machines have several lenses to accommodate various reduction ratios. The library must maintain the equipment and provide users with assistance as needed, especially when it is necessary to change lenses. As the size of the microform collection increases, more equipment will be needed to meet user demands. Finally, microform storage cabinets are heavy when empty and very heavy when full. Libraries may face problems in locating a growing collection of such cabinets if the floor cannot sustain their combined weight. Clearly, microform brings with it new costs and concerns.

Another solution for storage is to move low-use items to a less accessible and less costly facility. Yet another solution is to deselect some titles. As space becomes scarce, decisions about what to keep and for how long become more and more difficult. Given the current nature of most serials, older holdings are prime candidates for remote storage. After making the first, relatively easy decisions about which titles to store, weeding decisions become increasingly complex, take more time, and can lead to conflicts between staff and patrons. This is discussed in more detail in chapter 14.

An important consideration in serials selection is how the patron gains access to the information each issue contains. Going through each issue is not efficient, and few patrons are willing to do this. Many serials produce an annual index, but this is of no help with current issues. An entire industry has developed around providing access to serials. A variety of indexing and abstracting services now provide services that assist in locating information in serials. Naturally, most of these services are expensive and are a hidden cost of building a serials collection. Though Harvard's Tozzer Library (an anthropology library) is atypical, it illustrates the nature of the problem. That library receives more than 1,200 anthropology serials each year. If it did not do its own indexing, the library would have to spend more than $30,000 per year for indexing and abstracting services to achieve only 83 percent coverage of its serial holdings. Tozzer's solution to the indexing problem is to index all the serials it receives. It publishes the index as *Anthropological Literature*, which helps offset the indexing costs.

One selection question is, Should one subscribe only to commercially indexed serials? If a library subscribes to an unindexed title, does the library do anything to help patrons locate information in the new serial? Specialized (subject) indexing services lead to patron requests for titles indexed in the service but not held by the library. The library must then decide whether to add yet another title to the serials list, increase the interlibrary loan (ILL) department's workload, or make patrons unhappy. Copyright law limits the library's ability to use ILL in place of subscribing to a particular title; copyright law imposes legal constraints on the frequency with which one may borrow articles from a single serial title (see chapter 18).

Document delivery services for journal articles are changing the nature of the selection decision. These systems, such as CARL Uncover (originated by the Colorado Alliance of Research Libraries), allow libraries and information centers to offer customers access to thousands of serial titles and their tables of contents. Not only can one identify articles through an index service (presently search capabilities are not very sophisticated), one can order the item as well. The services have taken care of copyright, and the patron receives the full text. There are substantial costs ($10 to $20 per article on average), which the library or customer must pay. Mode of delivery varies from postal service to facsimile, with corresponding price differences. For low-use titles, document delivery (DD) services may be the most cost-effective way to provide service. As of 1993 in the United States, the DD business was small ($60-$70 million) compared to the subscription business (about $1 billion).[4]

Serials tend to increase the volume of photocopying activities. Serial articles are short (seldom more than 25 pages); as a result, many people prefer to photocopy the article and consult the material at their leisure. Also, many libraries do not allow serials, or at least journals, to circulate, which encourages photocopying. The amount of library or information center photocopying is another copyright issue. While the copyright law covers photocopying of monographs, it is the serials photocopying that is the major issue among serial publishers, librarians, and users.

When a library does not start a subscription with volume 1, number 1, the librarian must decide whether and to what extent to acquire back issues or volumes. Are back files needed? Some serial publishers have full runs available, but most do not. Titles widely held by libraries may be available from reprint houses. Back files are expensive, they may be difficult to find, they may require binding, they certainly take up valuable shelf space, and many receive little use.

Serials can and do change over time. New editors, governing boards, or owners make major and minor shifts in the content and orientation. A major shift in emphasis usually is well publicized. As selectors become aware of such shifts, they can reassess the serial. A title change is something librarians frequently complain about, primarily because of internal concerns (see articles by Foggin[5] and Nelson[6]). From a collection development point of view, a title change should be welcome because it probably signals a significant change in the serial's content. For that reason, the selectors should review the changes in content to determine whether the item is still appropriate for the collection. More difficult to identify is the slow shift over a number of years. The final result may be a greater difference in content than a well-publicized major change, but few people will notice the shift. Periodic examination of incoming serials by the selection officers is an excellent method for checking on changes in emphasis.

Given all of the above factors, one can see why the serials selection decision is a major decision. Yet, all too often, libraries treat it as being no different than the decision to acquire a monograph.

Selection Models

There are five basic approaches to selection: cost, citation analysis, worth or use, polling, and core lists. There are many variations, but the five listed form the basis for models for selecting serials. Much of the work done in this area is relatively recent and more the result of having to cancel rather than to start subscriptions.

Cost models of selection are the oldest and have the greatest number of variations. One of the most complex models deals with the real annual cost of a serial. The annual cost consists of six elements: acquisition cost, processing cost, maintenance cost, storage cost, utility or use cost, and subscription price. Acquisition costs include such things as selection, order placement, and time spent in working with the subscription agent or publisher. Processing costs cover check-in, claiming, routing, cataloging or other labeling, adding security strips, and shelving in public service for the first time. Maintenance costs involve binding, microfilming or acquiring microform, selection for remote storage, and possibly discarding. Storage costs entail calculating the linear feet of storage space (either or both shelf and cabinet space) used by the title and the cost of the space. Utility or use costs are the most complex to calculate. They incorporate costs of time for such things as retrieval from a storage location (library staff only), pick up and reshelving, answering questions about the title ("Do you have . . .?" "I can't find . . .", and "What is the latest issue you have?"), and all other required assistance (helping with microform readers, for example). The last, and often the lowest, cost is the subscription price. The sum of these costs represents the real annual cost of the title for the library. Looking over the list of costs makes it clear it will take some time to calculate the individual cost centers. However, once one determines the unit costs (for example, the average time to shelve an issue), it is fairly easy to calculate the cost for a given number of issues of a title. With an annual cost for each title, selectors can determine which titles to continue or discontinue. Several articles describing variations on this approach are included in the bibliography at the end of this chapter.

Like cost models, citation analysis paradigms take several forms. The main objective, from a selection point of view, is to identify frequently cited titles. Citation analysis can help identify a core collection for a field and provide a listing of titles ranked by the frequency with which they are cited. Another collection development use of citation analysis is in evaluating a collection (Could a set of papers/reports have been done using this collection?). Citation analysis information is most useful in large or specialized research collections, although core collection information is valuable to smaller and nonspecialized collections as well.

Certain assumptions about citation analysis are important to understand before deciding to use this approach. The underlying assumption is that the subject content of the cited document relates to that of the citing document. A second assumption is that the number of times a document receives a citation is proportional to the value or intrinsic worth of the document. Another assumption is that all the publications an author cites were, in fact, used. (A related assumption is that the author listed all the sources used.) One other major assumption is that the sources used to secure the citation data are representative of the field under investigation. Those are the major assumptions; there are others. Many people do not accept all the assumptions. If one cannot accept the assumptions, one should not use citation data for collection building.

There are two major sources of citation data: research reports and articles in the professional press, and data from the publishing firm Institute for Scientific Information (ISI). ISI publishes *Science Citation Index (SCI), Social Sciences Citation Index (SSCI)*, and *Humanities Citation Index (HCI)*. These publications provide citation information for many journals. For example, *SSCI* covers almost 1,500 social science titles and provides selective coverage of about 4,500 nonsocial science journals that contain some social science material. On an annual basis, ISI also produces *Journal Citation Reports (JAR)*, which provides a useful analysis of the journals ISI covers. Some of the major features of *JAR* are:

- a listing of the number of articles a title contained for the year

- how many citations were made to articles that appeared in the title through time

- a ratio of articles published to articles cited (impact factor)

- a ratio of articles published during the year to citations to those articles (immediacy index)

- a cited half-life, that is, how far back in time one needs to go to retrieve 50 percent of all citations appearing during a year to all articles that ever appeared in the title

Such information can be helpful in making continuation and storage or deselection decisions.

Using the Bradford Distribution, one can rank titles to develop information for collection policy use as well as making decisions regarding current subscriptions.[7]

The goal of this ranking is to identify all journals containing articles relevant to a given subject and to rank them in order based on the number of relevant articles they publish in a year. The pattern, according to Bradford's Law of Scattering, will show a few journals publish the majority of articles and a large number of journals publish only one or two cited articles. If one equates a basic collection (level 2 in the conspectus concept, see pages 85-86) with holding journals that contain 20 percent of the relevant material, one might subscribe to only three or four titles. For libraries with a comprehensive collection (level 5), the subscription list may contain several hundred titles. For example, Tozzer Library has a current subscription list of more than 1,200 titles for its coverage of anthropology. Journal worth models usually involve some information about title usage along with other data. An article by Dawn Bick and Reeta Sinha describes one of the many worth models,[8] one that is reasonably easy to implement. The model involves cost, use, impact factor, and information about the nature of the publication (core subject, for example) to calculate a cost-benefit ratio.

As one might assume, most of the models require a substantial amount of data collecting. If their only value was in making selection decisions, few libraries would use them. Their major value comes into play when the library must cut subscriptions. Having collected data that is similar for all the titles makes the unpleasant task a little easier. What librarians hoped would be a rare occurrence has, for some libraries, become an almost annual task. Each time, the task becomes more difficult, and the models demonstrate their value.

Polling experts and using lists of recommended journals are other methods for identifying what to buy or keep. Both suffer from being less directly linked to the local situation, unless the experts are local users. One can find lists of journals in relatively narrow subjects, often listed with recommendations, or at least comments, in journals like *Serials Librarian* and *Serials Review*.

What Is a Serial?

About 10 years ago, Fritz Machlup and others developed an 18-part classification system for serials.[9] The following discussion follows their classification system because it covers all types of serials.

The first category is "annual, semiannual, quarterly or occasional reports of corporations, financial institutions, and organizations serving business and finance." Academic libraries serving business and management programs frequently need to acquire this type of serial. Some corporate libraries also actively collect this serial category. Most of the reports available to libraries and information centers are free for the asking. Some organizations will add a library to their distribution list, but others will respond only to requests for the current edition. Collecting in this area is labor-intensive because it requires maintaining files and correspondence, especially if one collects much beyond the large national corporations. Without question, having a computer system that has both word processing and mailing list capabilities will make collecting less tedious, but it will not reduce the need to constantly monitor the program. Corporate annual reports are issued every month. Many companies issue their annual report for their annual meeting of the management board, owner, or stockholders which normally occurs in the month the organization was established. It is difficult to find a satisfactory vendor for this serials category, except for 10-K reports to the Securities and Exchange Commission, which are available on microfiche from Disclosure, Inc. (and, since early 1994, available on the Internet). (A good discussion of the vendors that offer annual report assistance appears in Judith Bernstein's "Corporate Annual Reports: The Commercial Vendors."[10])

A related category is "annuals, biennials, occasional publications, bound or stapled, including yearbooks, almanacs, proceedings, transactions, memoirs, directories and reports of societies and associations." Many libraries collect serials in this class, especially academic, special, and large public libraries. The more libraries that collect a particular society's or association's publications, the more likely it is that a commercial vendor handles a standing order for the material. Although it is possible to secure some of these serials through a vendor, there are a significant number that one must secure directly from the society or association.

Two other labor-intensive collecting categories are 1) "superseding serial services (each new issue superseding previous ones, which are usually discarded) including telephone directories, airplane schedules, catalogs, loose-leaf data sheets, etc.," and 2) "nonsuperseding serial services bound, sewn, stapled, or loose-leaf, including bibliographic and statistical data." One must acquire most of the materials in these classes directly from the publisher. Superseding serials are important but problematic: important because people need the correct or current information, difficult to track and sometimes to secure. Airline schedules, current hotel guides, and other travel-related serial sources have been something of a problem for libraries to acquire. In the past, the publishers would sell the material only to qualified travel agencies. As more and more corporations handle staff travel on their own, it has become easier for libraries to subscribe to such services. In many corporations, the library or information center maintains current travel information. In the United States since the break-up of AT&T, libraries have found it more difficult and expensive to secure telephone directories outside their immediate area.

Loose-leaf services are particularly important in U.S. law libraries and accounting firms. Proper filing and discarding of the material is of critical importance in such an environment because incorrect information can be very costly to a firm (perhaps the clearest way to demonstrate the cost of not having the right information at the right time). With a loose-leaf service, one must make certain that all sections released are received.

Nonsuperseding serials are less of a problem, and some are available from serial jobbers. However, the materials in this class tend to be expensive, and one must order them directly from the publisher. Indexing and abstracting services fall into one of these two classes. All types of libraries need a few of these reference serials. As the serial collection grows, there is an increasing demand from patrons for more indexing and abstracting services.

All types of libraries, with the exception of elementary school media centers, collect newspapers (some subscribe to a local newspaper), another serial category. Almost every small public library receives the local newspaper and one or two newspapers from nearby communities. Large public and academic libraries try to have some national and foreign newspaper coverage. Serial jobbers handle subscriptions to major newspapers for libraries. Thus, it would be possible to place one order with a jobber, such as Faxon or EBSCO, for almost all the major newspapers from around the world. At the time the order is placed, selectors and collection development officers must establish the value of the newspapers' content, in the sense of the demand or need to have the latest issue in the shortest time. For example, one can receive the *London Times* in a variety of packages, each with a different cost: daily airmail edition by air freight, daily airmail edition by airmail (the most expensive option), daily regular edition by air freight, daily regular edition in weekly packets (the least expensive option) or microfilm edition. The *New York Times* offers a wider variety of editions: city edition, late city edition, national edition, New York edition, large-type weekly, same day, next day, two day, weekly packets, and microfilm.

As is clear, subscribing to a newspaper is no simple matter. Depending on the library's clientele, a certain edition and delivery method will provide the right service at the least cost, but determining the right combination takes more time than selecting a book.

Like other serials, newspapers present special storage and access problems. When a library subscribes to several newspapers, a display of recent issues can occupy a large portion of a current issues area. For research libraries, long-term storage is a problem. Bound newspapers tend to be large, heavy, and awkward to handle. The poor quality of newsprint presents preservation problems. Today, most libraries use a microformat for back issue storage, but this adds to the overall subscription cost, because most newspaper companies control the microfilming of their publication. Access is another problem, except for the largest newspapers, because most indexing services cover only the best-known papers.

Newsletters, leaflets, news releases, and similar materials represent yet another serial category of major importance for some libraries. Special libraries are the most likely to become involved in the ongoing collection of this class of serial. Many of the items in this class are very inexpensive or free. Others, especially newsletters, can cost thousands of dollars. In either case, someone must put in time and effort to identify the sources and get on the appropriate mailing lists. Libraries in marketing and public relations firms are likely to be active collectors of this type of material. Any library operating in a disturbed-reactive or turbulent information environment (see pages 13-14) is likely to collect heavily in this class.

Machlup defined two broad groups of serials—magazines and journals, each with several subcategories—as periodicals "published more than once per year."[11] According to Machlup's definition, magazines are mass-market serials, the ones that almost any serial jobber will handle for a library. Machlup divided magazines into five categories: "news weekly or monthly magazines"; "popular magazines (fiction, pictures, sports and games, travel and tourism, fashion, sex, humor, comics, etc.)"; "magazines for popularized science, social, political and cultural affairs, etc."; "magazines for opinion and criticism (social, political, literary, artistic, aesthetic, religious, etc.)"; and "other magazines not elsewhere classified." It is easy to think of magazine titles in each of these categories, with perhaps the exception of the last one. Machlup's other magazines are publications many organizations (and governments) issue for a general or mass market and that promote those groups' services or products. These magazines often contain articles of general interest unrelated to the organization's activities. An example is the airline magazine found in the seat pocket on an airplane. Vendors seldom handle this type of magazine, and few libraries actively collect them.

Machlup similarly divided journals into four subcategories, with one category divided into two smaller units: "nonspecialized journals for the intelligentsia well-informed on literature, art, social affairs, politics, etc."; "learned journals for specialists—primary research journals and secondary research journals (reviews, abstracts, literature surveys, etc.)"; "practical professional journals in applied fields, including technology, medicine, law, agriculture, management, library science, business, and trades"; and "parochial journals of any type but addressed chiefly to a parochial audience (local, regional)." Again, most titles in these categories are available through vendors, although one must place direct orders for some of the more specialized learned journals. Most parochial journals must be purchased directly from the publisher; local history and regional archaeological publications are examples of this class of serial.

The final serial category identified by Machlup was "government publications, reports, bulletins, statistical series, releases, etc. by public agencies, executive, legislative and judiciary, local, state, national, foreign and international." Because this group is covered in the next chapter, no further discussion is offered here.

Identifying Serials

Serials employ a different bibliographic network than that used by monographs. Few of the selection aids for books cover serials. However, there are several general and specialized guides to serial publications. Reviews of serials are few and far between. Bill Katz's column in *Library Journal* is one regular source of serial reviews. In the past, when publishers would supply several free sample copies of a title for the library to examine, the lack of reviews was not a problem. Today, many publishers charge for sample issues, and though it depletes the funds for subscribing to serials and adds to the time it takes to acquire them, it is useful to get sample issues before committing the library to a new serial.

Four useful general guides are *Ulrich's International Periodicals Directory* (R. R. Bowker), *Irregular Serials & Annuals* (R. R. Bowker), *Serials Directory* (EBSCO), and *Standard Periodical Directory* (Oxbridge Communications). All employ a subject arrangement, and entries provide all necessary ordering information. Bowker updates the annual *Ulrich's* with *Ulrich's Update. Standard Periodical Directory* covers American and Canadian titles and has a reputation for providing the best coverage of publications with small circulations, lesser known organizations, and processed materials.

Newspapers, newsletters, and serials published at least five times a year are identifiable in guides like *Gale Directory of Publications and Broadcast Media* (Gale Research) and *Willings' Press Guide* (Thomas Skinner Directories). For literary publications, one should use *International Directory of Little Magazines and Small Presses* (Dustbooks), *MLA International Bibliography* (Modern Language Association), and *L'Annee Philologique* (Societe International de Bibliographie Classique).

All of the above, with the exception of *Ulrich's Update,* have limited value in identifying new titles because they are annuals, which means the information is at least several months old. (As noted earlier, serials change in a variety of ways—titles, frequency, editorial policy, and so on—and keeping up with existing titles is enough of a problem without adding the need to identify newly created serials.) The best source of information about serials acquired by American libraries is the Library of Congress's *New Serial Titles (NST)*, which reflects data in OCLC. The data in *NST* is the result of a cooperative effort called Conversion of Serials (CONSER). One gains a useful sense of the number of existing serial titles when one considers that in 1981, there were 339,000 CONSER records in OCLC; in 1986, there were more than 865,000; and in 1991, the total was well over one million. If one can justify costs, online systems provide the most current information. Certainly OCLC is one source, as are BRS and DIALOG. The latter services have information from *Ulrich's*. Such services are current but costly; $75 per hour is not an uncommon charge, so one must be certain that the speed and currency are essential. Some serial vendors also supply new serial titles information online.

Using a review of serials presents certain difficulties. Most serials that receive reviews are popular magazines rather than learned journals. Given the propensity of serials for change, a completely accurate assessment of a title is possible only when the serial ceases publication and the reviewer can examine all the issues. All that one should expect from a review of a serial is an accurate description of the content of the issue(s) available to the reviewer, usually not more than six issues. What a selector wants from the review is as much information about the purpose, audience, and editorial policy as the reviewer can identify; information about publisher, price, frequency, and other technical matters; and, if appropriate, comparisons to other related serials. Unfortunately, some of those limited data may be lacking, because it is sometimes difficult to determine purpose and editorial policy, even with the volume 1, number 1, issue in hand. Information about the publisher is less important in serials selection than in monograph selection because many times the serial is the publisher's only publication, and only time will reveal the publisher's reliability.

Serials Review (Pierian Press) publishes some reviews prepared by serials librarians and, occasionally, subject experts. The journal started as both a reviewing journal and a professional journal for serials librarians. Today it is primarily a professional journal, with only a few pages of serials reviews in each volume. Occasionally, *Serials Review* reviews an established serial. Such reviews help librarians monitor changes in the editorial policy of titles to which the library subscribes.

Library Journal (R. R. Bowker) offers a regular section focusing on new periodicals. Each issue contains brief annotations describing 6-10 new titles. Because of the breadth of coverage, most types of libraries will find some titles of interest covered in the course of a year. Every few years, Bill Katz, editor of the *Library Journal (LJ)* periodical section, compiles *Magazines for Libraries*,[12] in which he lists 6,000-7,000 recommended titles.

New Magazine Review (New Magazine Review) covers titles of particular interest to public librarians. *Choice* (Association of College and Research Libraries) features a column, "Periodicals for College Libraries." A way to see new titles is to check at book and serial exhibitor booths at professional association meetings.

Serial Vendors

For most libraries, it is not economical to place serial subscriptions directly with the publisher. The amount of work required to monitor expiration dates, place renewals, and approve payments repeatedly for each title is too great. In any sizable serials collection, a few titles will be direct orders to the publisher; however, if a library uses a serials vendor for most orders, there will be more time for other problem-solving activities related to serials.

Serials jobbers tend not to handle monographs, just as book jobbers tend not to handle serials. *Tend* is the key word here, given the variety of serials; in the area of annuals and numbered monograph series, lines become blurred and jobbers overlap. Given the nature of serial publications, one is better served by an experienced serials jobber than by a friendly and willing book jobber who offers to handle the serials list along with book orders. Many serials librarians find it best to use domestic dealers for domestic serials and foreign dealers for foreign titles. Picking a foreign dealer can be a challenge; for American libraries, the American Library Association's *International Subscription Agents: An Annotated Directory* is helpful. The 1994 edition lists agents and provides information about countries and regions covered, types of material serviced, catalogs or listings provided to customers, notes about special services (standing orders for monographs, for example), and name and address. It is advisable to ask other librarians about their experience with the dealers one is considering. If the librarian cannot identify anyone using a dealer, he or she might start by placing one or two subscriptions with the dealer and increase the volume of business if service is satisfactory.

Service is what one is looking for in a serials vendor. In order to provide service, the company must make a profit. How does it do that? In the past, vendors offered discounts. Today, libraries pay a service charge based on a percentage of the total subscription price. Serial vendors have two major and one minor sources of income. One major source is the discount publishers offer vendors. (Publishers offer these discounts because it is more convenient for them to deal with one billing/ordering source rather than subscriptions to many individual subscribers.) Recently, librarians have blamed publishers for rising subscription costs, but a few publishers claim vendors share the blame because vendors are not passing on a share of the discount they receive from the publishers. Whatever the case may be, vendors depend on publishers' discounts to make a profit.

The second major revenue source is the service charge vendors add to their invoices to libraries. The service charge varies from library to library, depending on several factors. It often requires a good deal of work to determine just what the service charge is, in part because, when the subscription list contains thousands of titles, it is unlikely there will be only one invoice, if for no other reason than prices change during the year and supplementary invoices arrive. Sales representatives may not know all the factors involved in calculating the charge and can give only an overview explanation. There may be various rates for various types of publications: in part, the service charge depends on the size of the discount the vendor receives.

Another variable in the calculation of a library's service charge is what services the library uses. Often, there is an extra charge for handling unusual serials, such as government publications. The types and number of management reports the library receives from the vendor also affect the service charge. Title mix is another factor, just as it is with book jobbers. For serial vendors, it is more a matter of knowing which titles generate additional work for the vendor rather than a bookseller's pricing concerns with popular titles (low price/high discount) versus scholarly titles (high price/low discount). If a library has a high percentage of problem titles, its service charge may be somewhat higher than another library with a similar number of subscriptions, costing about the same, but with fewer problem titles.

The setting of the service charge is an art, and the service charge is open to negotiation. A good book on the acquisition aspects of serial work is N. Bernard Basch and Judy McQueen's *Buying Serials*.[13] A minor, but growing, source of income comes from a variety of extra services most agencies offer, such as automation packages, publishing and electronic services (CD-ROMs, for example), or custom lists.

What does the customer receive beyond the basic advantage of one order, one invoice, and one check for multiple subscriptions? Automatic renewal by a vendor saves library staff time, and when the invoice arrives, there is the opportunity to cancel titles no longer needed. Jobbers may offer multiple-year subscription rates that will save the library money. Notifying libraries about discontinuations, mergers, changes in frequency, and other publication alterations is a standard service provided by a serials jobber. The jobber is more likely to learn of changes before a library does, especially if the jobber has placed hundreds of subscriptions with the publisher.

Vendors also provide some assistance in the claiming process (missing issues, breaks in service, and damaged copies). Several of the larger American subscription agents (for example, EBSCO and Readmore) have fully automated serial systems that libraries use to handle their serials management programs, including online claiming. (Faxon supports a back file service, SerialsQuest, that includes data from libraries and dealers.) For libraries with manual claiming systems, most vendors offer two forms of claims: one by which the library notifies the vendor, which in turn contacts the supplier; and one by which the vendor supplies forms for the library to use to contact the publisher. Assistance in claiming has become more important in the past 10-15 years as more and more popular market publishers use fulfillment centers. These centers serve as a publishers' jobber, that is, a center handles a number of different publishers' titles by receiving, entering subscriptions, and sending copies to subscribers. (For such centers, the mailing label is the key to solving problems; until recently, few libraries worried about serials' mailing labels.) Often, the subscription vendor is more effective in resolving a problem with a fulfillment center than is a single library.

Management information is another service serial vendors offer. Their information regarding price changes can be most useful in preparing budget requests. (A sample of this type of data appears in figure 13.4, page 359).

Other types of management information that may be available (at an extra cost) are reports that sort the subscription list by subject or classification category accompanied by the total amount spent for each group, or (if there are several groups) a record of how many titles and how much money were charged to each group.

Most major vendors offer some form of document delivery service, for example EBSCO and Readmore offer CARL Uncover. Such vendors are exploring new services, especially in the areas of current awareness and electronic publishing. They too see the need to change their approach to serials and the services they offer in an electronic environment. EBSCO offers an abstracting service on CD-ROM as well as a CD-ROM with the full text of some widely held journals. Another EBSCO service is access to ADONIS, a biomedical database with full-text articles. In early 1993, EBSCO announced a joint venture with the British Library Document Supply Centre to market a table of contents service as well as the worldwide document delivery service. Other agencies have or are planning similar services.

A good place to learn about the variety of services available, and who offers which services, is national meetings of various library associations. Representatives of most national serial vendors, as well as a number of foreign vendors, attend the ALA annual conventions. They will supply more than enough promotional material to fill a suitcase. Collecting the information (including a formal request to quote), making comparisons, and talking with other librarians about their experiences with various vendors is the best way to go about selecting a vendor for one's library.

Cooperation in Serials Work

No library can acquire and keep all the serials that its patrons need or will at some time request. Knowing who has what serial holdings is important to serials librarians and anyone involved in interlibrary loan activities. The CONSER project and *NST* help to identify holdings in American and Canadian libraries. It is interesting to note that, despite the long-time concern about serial holdings, it was not until early 1986 that a national standard for serials holding statements was adopted in the United States (ANSI Z39.44).

The standard provides for the same data areas, data elements, and punctuation in summary holding statements in both manual and automated systems.

Although the Center for Research Libraries (CRL) (see page 450) is much more than a cooperative serials program, CRL serial holdings have been effective in holding down the amount of duplication of low-use serial titles in American and Canadian research libraries. Bibliographic utilities such as OCLC and RLIN, whose databases include serial holdings, provide a type of union list service that H. W. Wilson's *Union List of Serials* provided so well in the past. To some extent, even vendor-based systems offer a form of union listing. Though it is possible to use such union lists and shared holdings to cover some low-use serial requirements, the librarian must be certain to comply with copyright regulations (see pages 498-99) before deciding not to buy.

Many libraries using the same serials vendor are able to acquire union lists from the vendor. For example, the four largest Catholic universities in California (University of San Francisco, Santa Clara University, Loyola Marymount University, and the University of San Diego) use EBSCO and have a union list produced each year to coordinate serial holdings. The libraries have agreed that when only one institution holds a title, there will be consultation with other libraries before the library drops the title.

Issues and Concerns

Several major issues face libraries today in regard to their serial collections. Cost is perhaps the major concern (cost of subscriptions, processing, storing, changing value of currencies, and tight budgets). Another issue is the delivery of serial information to customers without subscribing to the title by using document delivery or, as some librarians phrase it, "just in time rather than just in case." Related to document delivery are questions about copyright and traditional ILL services; on a percentage basis, ILL does more work with serials than monographs.

Continued growth in the number of serials and their spiraling costs are two issues of grave concern, especially for scholarly journals. Areas of knowledge constantly are being divided into smaller and smaller segments; at the same time, these smaller audiences want more information about the narrower topic. A 1993 announcement from the journal division of Academic Press outlined the problem. It listed one new journal, *Applied Computational Harmonic Analysis*; one journal dividing into two parts: *Journal of Magnetic Resonance—Series A* and *Series B*; and seven titles increasing the number of issues per volume. All these changes carried with them price increases.

Costs of producing a special-interest journal will rise, no matter how many or how few people are interested in reading about the subject. When a journal reaches a certain price level, the number of individual subscribers drops quickly. More often than not any price increase to individual subscribers only makes the problem worse. Increasingly, journal publishers have adopted a dual pricing system, one price for individuals and another, higher price (often double or triple the individual rate) for institutions (read: libraries). The publishers' premise is that an institutional subscription serves the needs of many readers, which justifies the higher price. An interesting ethical question for librarians in general, and collection development personnel in particular is: Is it ethical for a library to regularly accept an individual's gift of a journal that has a high dual rate subscription? (My view is, no, the library should not do that. If not for ethical reasons, there are practical concerns about the regularity with which the person delivers the issues as well as securing missing issues.)

If publishers take the dual pricing concept to its logical conclusion, publishers will demand libraries track the use of each serial and pay an annual service fee based on that number. Or, as one occasionally sees in the literature, publishers will make the title available only on a site-licensed basis. Before dismissing the idea as unrealistic, one should consider two things. First, for years libraries subscribing to H. W. Wilson's periodical indexes have been paying an annual service fee or subscription fee based on the number of journals indexed to which the library subscribes. Second, some countries, including Canada, now have a lending fee, that is, a fee paid to the author for each circulated use of his or her book in a public library (see chapter 18).

There are two types of journal price studies with which collection development staff should become familiar: macro pricing and micro pricing. Macro information deals with subscription prices, rates of increase and projections of coming price increases. One can obtain this type of data about the library's subscription list from the library's serials vendor (see fig. 13.4, page 359). Information about overall price changes appears in several sources for U.S. serials, including *Library Journal*[14] and *American Libraries*.[15] One problem for many libraries is that data about projected price changes that appear at a time when it is of little help in preparing the budget request for the next fiscal year. The data may be useful, but it is about a year behind the budget. That is, one uses 1994 projections for preparing the 1995-1996 budget request. (See chapter 13 for more information about budgeting.)

Micro studies examine cost of the information in the journal, number of articles per volume, number of pages, page size, and cost per one thousand words or characters. Such studies are helpful in the retention and cancellation activities in which more and more libraries must engage on an annual basis. (Finding micro studies takes a little effort; one good article dealing with the subject and presenting some examples is by Barbara Meyers and Janice Fleming.[16]) Not all publishers are pleased to see micro studies published, but such studies do provide useful data for building a cost-effective serials collection. Naturally, one must use these data in conjunction with other information, such as local use patterns.

As journal prices rise and serial budgets fail to keep pace with the increases, collection development staff face the unpleasant task of deciding what to keep and what to drop. No one likes the process, especially the customers. Everyone has her or his favorite candidates for keeping and dropping. A library's first cancellation project may be relatively easy, but after the initial round of cuts, the process becomes progressively more difficult. The usual response is to assist decision makers by developing a model that takes price and use information into account. Price data are easy to acquire, at least at the macro level, but use data are more difficult to come by. Many libraries do not circulate journals, so circulation data are unavailable. In such cases, the library must establish some process for collecting the data. Though one can find a number of articles about journal use data and cancellation work,[17, 18, 19, 20] the true task is to find a method that will work in the local situation.

For the most part, serials will continue to escalate in price, and budgets may or may not keep pace. Clearly, serials will continue to play a major role in meeting customer information needs, and likewise may command a growing share of a limited collection development budget. How far can a library or information center go in cutting back on the acquisition of other formats to maintain the subscription list? Will switching to electronic sources for on-demand material really help with the budget problem or just make matters worse? Answers to such questions vary from institution to institution. Electronic services and document delivery may or may not be a viable answer.

The number of electronic services that include journals grows daily. As of early 1993, there were more than 3,000 titles available in full text online. The total is even larger when one includes CD-ROMs and e-journals, that is, journals that are published online with no paper counterpart. Services range from single titles, such as *Consumer Reports,* to collections of popular titles (*Magazine ASP*) or technical collections (*Comprehensive Core Medical Literature*). At present, there are five types of serials in an electronic format: STM journals (based on a print publication), popular magazines (print based), newspapers (print based), newsletters (print based and electronic) and electronic journals (primarily scholarly, for example, *Current Clinical Trials,* which combines text and graphics).

Two problems with an electronic version of a journal, if it is an ASCII file, is there are no graphics and the page numbers differ from the paper version. Lacking graphics may not matter. However, pagination differences may create citation problems if there is no indication which version of the document the writer used. When the electronic version uses scanned images, which some people say are no different than microforms, the print and electronic versions are identical. One such product is University Microfilms, Incorporated's (UMI) *Business Periodicals Ondisc.* Some major vendors of such products are DIALOG, Mead Data Central, STN, UMI, Information Access Company (IAC), EBSCO, Elsevier, National Library of Medicine, OCLC, and American Chemical Society.

Many libraries and information centers face the problem of buying the journal twice, in paper and electronic formats. Even in a networked environment, it is likely some potential users will not have network access. Does the library ignore these users and provide only the electronic version, or does it offer both versions? One thinks twice about dropping the paper version because some publishers (*Biological Abstracts,* for example) charge a higher fee for the CD-ROM version if the library does not have a paper subscription as well. Often, the higher fee is equal to the price of both subscriptions. With the ADONIS product (biomedical titles), the price of each article printed is based on whether the library has a paper subscription to the journal. Networking the material also entails extra expenses, such as license fees, that can equal or surpass the basic subscription price. Additionally, some products have a per-page or per-view charge that increases the overall cost. For example, UMI has a 10 cents per printed page copyright charge for its full-text material. Libraries should not expect to save money by shifting from paper to electronic formats, unless they also shift some of the costs to the users.

Short of providing full text in electronic form, the library can provide document delivery services backed by indexing and abstracting and table of contents access in electronic form. (A summary article about these services and their 1993 costs is by Ronald Leach and Judith Trible.[21]) Commercial services, such as UMI's Article Clearinghouse and ISI's Genuine Article, provide documents based on their indexing and abstracting services. Newer services are based the tables of contents of a large number of titles (11,000-12,000 titles). Subject searching is generally limited with the table of contents approach; basically, searching is keyword in title. In essence, with table of contents services, one gives up depth of subject access for broader scope in title coverage. Most table of contents services are recent entries into the document delivery field. CARL UnCover 2 is the oldest such service, with OCLC's ContentFirst and ArticleFirst, and RLG's CitaDel the newcomers. As with full text, there are a variety of charges to consider before one can decide to drop a paper subscription.

Summary

Serials are a vital part of any information collection. They are complex and costly, whether paper or electronic. Cost is probably going to remain the primary concern for some time. For the past 15 years, serial prices have had double-digit rate increases, higher than anything else a library adds to its collection. Thus, serials continually take a larger and larger share of the materials budget, or the library must begin to cancel titles and provide access to the information in some other manner. Technology is changing the way libraries handle serials and is making it possible to provide access to more titles. However, technology will not solve the economic concerns of either the publishers and producers or the consumers. How the two groups will solve the problem is impossible to predict. It is likely the serials price problem will be present for some time.

Notes

[1]Heartsill Young, ed., *ALA Glossary of Library and Information Science* (Chicago: American Library Association, 1983).

[2]*Webster's Third New International Dictionary* (Springfield, MA: G & C Merriam, 1976).

[3]Quotation is from a friend's letter. The poet is unknown.

[4]Janice Kuta, "AAP Seminar Explores Document Delivery," *Publishers Weekly* 239 (November 30, 1992): 20.

[5]Carol Foggin, "Title Changes: Another View," *Serials Librarian* 23, no. 1/2 (1992): 71-83.

[6]Nancy Nelson, "Serials Title Changes: What's in a Name?" *Computers in Libraries* 13 (February 1993): 4.

[7]Robert Sivers, "Partitioned Bradford Ranking and the Serials Problem in Academic Libraries," *Collection Building* 8, no. 2 (1986): 12-19.

[8]Dawn Bick and Reeta Sinha, "Maintaining a High-Quality, Cost-Effective Journal Collection," *College & Research Libraries News* 51 (September 1991): 485-90.

[9]F. Machlup et al., *Information Through the Printed Word* (New York: New York University, 1978).

[10]Judith Bernstein, "Corporate Annual Reports: The Commercial Vendors," *College & Research Libraries News* 47 (March 1986): 178-80.

[11]Machlup et al., *Information Through the Printed Word.*

[12]William Katz and Linda Sternberg Katz, *Magazines for Libraries,* 7th ed. (New York: R. R. Bowker, 1992).

[13]N. Bernard Basch and Judy McQueen, *Buying Serials* (New York: Neal-Schuman, 1990).

[14]Kathleen Born and Lee Ketcham, "The Art of Projecting: The Cost of Keeping Periodicals," *Library Journal* 118 (April 15, 1993): 42-48.

[15]Adrian Alexander and Kathryn Hammell Carpenter, "Periodical Price Index for 1993," *American Libraries* 24 (May 1993): 390-93, 434-38.

[16]Barbara Meyers and Janice Fleming, "Price Analysis and the Serial Situation: Trying to Solve an Age-Old Problem," *Journal of Academic Librarianship* 17 (May 1991): 86-92.

[17]Marifran Bustion, John Eltinge, and John Harer, "On the Merits of Direct Observation of Periodical Usage," *College & Research Libraries* 53 (November 1992): 537-50.

[18]Anna Price and Kjestine Carey, "Serials Use Study Raises Questions About Cooperative Ventures," *Serials Review* 19 (Fall 1993): 79-84.

[19]Christie Degener and Marjory Waite, "Using an Automated Serials System to Assist with Collection Review and Cancellations," *Serials Review* 17 (Spring 1991): 13-20.

[20]Maiken Naylor, "A Comparison of Two Methodologies for Counting Current Periodical Use," *Serials Review* 19 (Spring 1993): 27-34, 62.

[21]Ronald G. Leach and Judith E. Trible, "Electronic Document Delivery: New Options for Libraries," *Journal of Academic Librarianship* 18 (January 1993): 359-64.

Further Reading

General

Clasquin, F. F. "Financial Management of Serials and Journals Through Core Lists." *Serials Librarian* 2 (Spring 1978): 287-97.

Diodato, L. W. "Serials Claims: Three Perspectives, Library/Publisher/Vendor." *Serials Librarian* 21, nos. 2/3 (1991): 201-3.

Ganly, J. V., and D. M. Sciattara, eds. *Serials for Libraries.* 2d ed. New York: Neal-Schuman, 1985.

Harrington, S. A. "Serials Specialist Are Hard to Find." *Serials Librarian* 21, no. 1 (1991): 1-11.

International Subscription Agents. 5th ed. Chicago: American Library Association, 1986.

Katz, W. W., and L. S. Katz. *Magazines for Libraries.* 5th ed. New York: R. R. Bowker, 1986.

Keating, L. R. "Replacement Issues: Where Do You Find Them and at What Cost?" *Serials Librarian* 21, nos. 2/3 (1991): 165-68.

Osborn, A. D. *Serial Publications: Their Place and Treatment in Libraries.* 3d ed. Chicago: American Library Association, 1980.

Stein, L. L. "What to Keep and What to Cut?" *Technical Services Quarterly* 10, no. 1 (1992): 3-14.

Tuttle, M. *Introduction to Serials Management.* Greenwich, CT: JAI Press, 1983.

Wilkas, L. *International Subscription Agents.* Chicago: American Library Association, 1994.

Woodward, H. M. "Impact of Electronic Information on Serials Collection Management." *IFLA Journal* 20, no. 1 (1994): 35-45.

Academic

Alexander, A. W., and J. L. Smith. "Annual Survey of Serials Collection Assessment Programs, Practices, and Policies in Academic Libraries." *Journal of Library Administration* 17, no. 2 (1992): 133-48.

Chrzastowski, T. E., and K. A. Schmidt. "Surveying the Damage: Academic Serial Cancellations—1987/88 through 1989/90." *College & Research Libraries* 54 (March 1993): 93-102.

Davis, D. "FirstSearch: Collection Management and Academic Libraries." *OCLC Systems and Services* 9 (Fall 1993): 43-45.

Dow, R. F., et al. "Commentaries on Serials Publishing." *College & Research Libraries* 52 (November 1991): 521-27.

Houbeck, R. L. "Locked in Conversation: College Library Collections and the Pluralist Society." *Journal of Library Administration* 17, no. 2 (1992): 99-131.

Kingma, B. R., and P. B. Eppard. "Journal Price Escalation and the Market for Information." *College & Research Libraries* 53 (November 1992): 523-35.

McCain, K. W. "Some Determinants of Journal Holding Patterns in Academic Libraries." *Library & Information Science Research* 14 (July 1992): 223-43.

Welsch, E. K. "Measures of Social Science Collection Development Costs." *Behavior and Social Science Librarian* 10, no. 2 (1991): 9-26.

Public

Boyer, R. E. "Serials in the Small Public Library." *Library Resources & Technical Services* 29 (April/June 1985): 132-38.

Falk, G. "Increase Your Budget by Convincing Users to Adopt-a-Magazine." *Library Journal* 110 (15 June 1985): 34.

Fyfe, J. "History Journals for a Public Library." *Serials Librarian* 13 (December 1987): 69-75.

Katz, W. *Magazine Selection: How to Build a Community-Oriented Collection.* New York: R. R. Bowker, 1971.

Lenahan, N. M. "Use of Periodicals and Newspapers in a Mid-Sized Public Library." *Serials Librarian* 16, nos. 3/4 (1989): 41-47.

Ostling, E. "Periodicals in Libraries—A Democratic Right." *Scandinavian Public Library Quarterly* 25, no. 2 (1992): 16-17.

Stout, M. A., and B. Stunz. "Creating Core Serial Lists in a Public Library." *Reference Librarian*, nos. 27/28 (1989): 367-78.

Thomas, M. L. "InfoTrac II and Magazine Collections." *CD-ROM Librarian* 4 (May 1989): 31-33.

School

Buboltz, D., and R. Ling-Louie. "A Treeful of Good Reading (Magazines As a Way to Promote Reading)." *Book Report* 10 (January/February 1992): 16-18.

Bury, J. M. "Management of Periodicals in a Small School LMC." In *Collection Management for School Library Media Centers,* edited by Brenda White, 313-49. New York: Haworth Press, 1986.

Clark, M. P. "Young Adult and Children's Periodicals: Selections for the School Media Center." *Serials Review* 7 (October 1981): 7-24.

Drott, M. C., and J. Mancall. "Magazines As Information Sources." *School Media Quarterly* 8 (Summer 1980): 240-44.

Estes-Ricker, B., and J. Johnson. "Relevant Resources: Periodicals in Elementary Schools." *School Library Media Quarterly* 19 (Fall 1990): 53-56.

Richardson, S. K. "Magazines Collections in Elementary School Library Media Centers." In *Library Education and Leadership*, edited by S. Intner and K. Vandergrift, 373-85. Metuchen, NJ: Scarecrow Press, 1990.

Swisher, R., et al. "Magazine Collections in Elementary School Media Centers." *School Library Journal* 37 (November 1991): 40-43.

Special

Amir, H. J., and W. B. Newman. "Information: Unlimited Demands—Limited Funds." *Collection Management* 3 (Spring 1979): 111-19.

Anderson, D. C. "Journal for Academic Veterinary Medical Libraries." *Serials Librarian* 18, nos. 3/4 (1990): 73-86.

Battistella, M. S. "OCLC-SERHOLD Connections: An Evolution in Health Sciences Union Listing." *Bulletin of the Medical Library Association* 79 (October 1991): 370-76.

Bernstein, J. R. "Corporate Annual Reports: The Commercial Vendors." *College & Research Libraries News* 47 (March 1986): 178-80.

Cawkell, A. E. "Evaluating Scientific Journals with Journal Citation Reports." *American Society for Information Science Journal* 29 (January 1978): 41-46.

Cooper, E. R. "Simplified Approaches for Serials Management." *Serials Review* 18, no. 4 (1992): 17-20.

Freehling, D. J. "Cancelling Serials in Academic Law Libraries." *Law Library Journal* 84 (Fall 1992): 707-24.

Humphreys, B. L., and D. E. McCutcheon. "Growth Patterns in the National Library of Medicine's Serials Collection." *Bulletin of the Medical Library Association* 82 (January 1994): 18-22.

Morton, D. "Making the Most of Your Serials Budget." *College & Research Libraries News* 53 (November 1992): 630.

Shalini, R. "Journal Acquisition and Cost Effectiveness in Special Libraries." *International Library Review* 13 (April 1981): 189-94.

Triolo, V. A., and D. Bao. "A Decision Model for Technical Journal Deselection." *Journal of the American Society for Information Science* 44 (April 1993): 148-60.

White, B., and J. Tomlinson. "Library Subscription Scheme at the Institute of Advanced Legal Studies." *Law Librarian* 23 (March 1992): 29-34.

8

Government Information

Government documents and information form a mysterious and frequently misunderstood part of a library's collection. Because of their unique nature, these materials can frighten and confuse librarian and patron alike. Yet, they also can constitute an important, current, and vital part of any collection, and they can provide a wealth of information on almost any topic. People use various labels for this type of material, such as government publication, government information, official document, federal document, agency publication, legislative document, or presidential document. Libraries house the materials in several ways, ranging from a separate collection containing nothing but governmental material to complete integration into the general collection. How the library houses these materials affects their processing, from fully cataloged to partially cataloged, or uncataloged. They are classified using anything from the Library of Congress Classification System or the Superintendent of Documents system to local classification systems. Finally, libraries handle access in several ways. The materials may be included or excluded from indexes, card catalogs, and online catalogs; there may be separate files for government information.

To add to the confusion created by their diverse management, the documents themselves have only one common trait: they are all official publications of some government or international body. Thus, all of them have corporate rather than personal authors, which makes it difficult for patrons to locate a specific publication in a public catalog. If the material is in an online catalog that has subject or keyword searching, clients will identify and use more government information than they will if the material is cataloged in manual files. Government information comes in a variety of sizes, shapes, and media. There are books, technical reports, periodicals, pamphlets, microforms, posters, films, slides, photographs, CD-ROMs, online databases, and maps, to name but a few of the possibilities. They have no special subject focus because they are the product of many diverse branches and agencies of government. Normally, they reflect the concerns of the agency that produced them. Predictably, a document produced by the U.S. Department of Agriculture (USDA) probably deals with a subject related to agriculture, such as livestock statistics, horticulture, or irrigation. The relation may be less direct, because USDA also publishes information about nutrition, forestry, and home economics. However, as remote as the connection may seem, most government publications do have some connection to the issuing agencies' purpose and function. All are official publications of an agency or branch of government.

Compounding the confusion about the nature of government information is the fact that any level of government may issue an official document. Although national government documents are frequently the only official publications easily identified or treated as government publications, all other levels of government—local, regional, state, foreign national, and international—also produce official publications that are government documents. Though national government documents are the most numerous and important in the library's collection, other levels of government publications are also valuable and useful. A library may choose to include only one type or level of document in its government documents section, or it may include several.

The inherent diversity of government agencies and their publications combines with the diverse library management techniques concerning government documents to create bibliographic schizophrenia about government information. However, this immense body of information, available at a modest cost, makes government publications and services a worthwhile collection development information resource.

Government publications are issued by all branches, divisions, and levels of government. They embrace the universe of information and ideas, and there are few subjects outside the scope of government publication. They provide inexpensive, current information about geography, history, space science, statistics, education, environmental matters, earth science, legislation and Congress, banking, business, nutrition, forestry, communication, economics, demographics, weather, cancer research, television, libraries, floods and other hazards, women and minorities, agriculture, cars, regulations, standards and specifications, and almost any other subject imaginable.

The cost of government publications varies among the levels of government and according to purchase plans or depository agreements. However, most government publications cost very little. For example, U.S. law states that the federal government may not make a profit from selling documents. The price, by statute, may only recover publication and overhead costs. This can lead to remarkable bargains for collection development. Where else can one purchase a major reference tool like the annual directory of the federal government, which includes names, addresses, organizational charts, and brief descriptions of the mission and activities of each agency, for $30?[1] Other levels of government follow a similar philosophy concerning pricing and distribution of documents. This makes government publications an inexpensive means of expanding segments of a collection.

Though price and subject coverage are attractive features, the variety in the levels of documents within any subject area also offers many advantages for collection development. The USDA may publish information on nutrition, ranging from bilingual pamphlets to nutritional research studies. The National Aeronautics and Space Administration (NASA) publishes a variety of documents, ranging from space science for school children to extremely technical studies of space flight and the possibilities of extraterrestrial life. Some CD-ROMs issued by federal agencies include the Department of Defense's *Hazardous Materials Information System*, the Department of Commerce's *U.S. Imports of Merchandise*, and the

Central Intelligence Agency's *World Factbook*. Electronic bulletin boards are now part of the government information network (one example is the Department of Commerce's *Economic Bulletin Board*). Information about most subjects related to government is available at a surprising number of reading and use levels that can serve the needs and interests of most age groups.

Perhaps the most attractive feature of government documents is their timeliness. Frequently, they provide the most current information available about popular topics.

Types of Documents

U.S. Federal Documents

The executive, judicial, and legislative branches, as well as executive cabinet-level agencies and independent agencies, issue documents, although presidential statements, reorganization plans, and executive orders are the publications most users want. Two sources for identifying such publications are *Code of Federal Regulations—Title 2 (President)* and *Weekly Compilation of Presidential Documents*. Presidential commission reports belong to this class of publication, as do the *Budget of the United States Government* and *Economic Report of the President Transmitted to the Congress*. Such documents are valuable for academic and general interest purposes, and most large and medium-sized public and academic libraries collect some or all of them. School media centers may collect a few publications that relate to curriculum concerns.

Cabinet-level departments (Department of Agriculture or Department of the Interior, for example) include administrative units, such as agencies and bureaus. Most of these units issue reports, regulations, statistics, and monographs; many issue educational and public relations materials as well. Some sample titles include: *U.S. Statistical Abstract of the United States, Yearbook of Agriculture, Handbook of Labor Statistics,* and *Smokey the Bear Coloring Book*. All types of libraries will find publications of interest from the various units. Special libraries collect many of the technical publications. Most academic libraries collect heavily in this area, but media centers and public libraries are rather selective. One source of information about popular publications in this class is *Guide to Popular U.S. Government Publications*.[2] In addition to cabinet-level agency publications, many independent agencies publish a similar range of items. The Tennessee Valley Authority, Federal Reserve Board, and Central Intelligence Agency are examples of independent agencies.

Cabinet-level and independent agency publications constitute the core of the widely collected federal documents. Many departments and subunits publish general interest periodicals that are very popular with library users. Media centers also find these agencies a good source of inexpensive, high quality visual materials.

Judicial documents are not as numerous as those from the other two branches of government. The best known and most important title is the *Supreme Court Reports,* which contains Supreme Court opinions and decisions. (Note: Private commercial publishers issue the decisions of lower federal courts; these are not government documents.) Although large legal libraries must have the *Supreme Court Reports,* other libraries may find them useful for patrons for historical, political, or personal reasons. As a result, many larger public and academic libraries acquire a set for the general collection, even when there is a good legal library nearby.

Congressional publications are second in number and popularity only to executive publications. In addition to the text of proposed and passed legislation, these publications include materials documenting House and Senate deliberations. Floor debates appear in the *Congressional Record,* assessments of the need for legislation are available in congressional committee reports, testimony before congressional committees appears in documents that bear the words *Hearings of* or *Hearings on,* and there are also several important reference books: *Official Congressional Directory, Senate Manual,* and *House Rules.*

The *Congressional Record* provides a semi-verbatim transcript of the proceedings on the floor of each house of Congress—semi-verbatim, because it is possible for a congressperson to add or delete material in *Congressional Record.* Thus, is not an accurate record of what actually transpired on the floor of Congress. Many libraries, including large public libraries, find there is a strong demand for *Congressional Record.*

House and Senate committee hearings offer a surprising wealth of material for libraries, because most hearings address controversial issues. The reports become a source containing the pros and cons about the subject, as well as information about what groups support or oppose proposed legislation. Often, the hearings contain the first detailed reporting of topics under consideration in Congress. Though such hearings may have immediate general interest for library clients, they also are important for scholars of legislative history.

Reports that accompany bills out of committee form another important information resource for libraries. These reports document recommendations concerning the proposed legislation and background on the need for it. Often these reports are central in interpreting the law after the bill becomes law. Many of the current practices regarding copyright law are the result of interpreting such reports (see chapter 18 for discussion).

Laws of the United States first appear as "slip opinions." They next appear in the chronological list *Statutes at Large,* and they finally are published in codified form in the *United States Code.* For most nonlegal libraries, the *United States Code* is the more useful publication because it provides access by subject and popular name, in addition to placing a specific law in the broad context of other laws on the same subject.

The *Congressional Directory* provides biographical information and current addresses for members of Congress, plus useful information about the executive and judicial branches of government. It is a basic reference work, and many libraries acquire it. Any library with patrons having an interest in the federal government or doing business with the federal government should have a copy. Fewer libraries collect congressional procedure manuals, but these publications do help the public and scholars better understand how the federal legislative process works and assist them in following legislation of interest.

Some collection development officers think of the special congressional publication methods and formats in terms of all or nothing. Certainly it is possible and appropriate for many libraries to acquire all the items mentioned in this discussion, plus many others. But it is also reasonable and possible to select one or two series, such as *Reports* or *Hearings*. It also is possible to collect by subject, for example, all congressional publications about the elderly or Native Americans. In many cases, especially in smaller libraries, it may be appropriate to acquire only a few items of high local interest.

Federal publications are an important source to consider for current information at a modest price. It is not a matter of all or nothing, any more than it is a matter of acquiring all or none of the books and serials on a given topic. Learning more about federal publications and their content will pay dividends in meeting the information needs of a library's community in a timely and cost-effective manner.

State and Local Governments

Documents of state and local government agencies have limited availability in most libraries and information centers. In the last 20 years, most states established or passed legislation to establish depository programs that roughly parallel the federal depository program (see pages 223-25).

These programs distribute various quantities and percentages of state agency publications to designated state document depositories in formats varying from paper to microfiche. The quantity of publications distributed, the format, and the completeness of the depository collection, as well as the types and numbers of designated depository libraries, vary from state to state. Some states established only a few depository sites, but others have extremely liberal depository programs. A few states allow selection of documents for collection development, but others distribute everything on an all-or-nothing basis. Some states provide only paper copies, but others follow the Government Printing Office's lead in making microfiche the preferred format. The type of service provided also varies. A few states offer centralized bibliographic control and a classification system for the documents. Some states carefully select depository materials for distribution; others provide as comprehensive a collection as possible. Out-of-state libraries may or may not become depositories, because some states require depositories to be in-state libraries with a certain profile.

Depository practices and requirements differ from state to state. The statutes of any particular state will provide the frequency and the statutory framework of the depository program. The state library can provide more detailed information about its state depository program, including a list of depositories, sales and acquisition information, and information about which materials are available from a central source and which are available only from individual agencies.

Historically, the most effective method for acquisition of state and local documents has been through direct agency contact. Like the federal government, most state agencies produce and sell publications at or near cost. Often, complimentary copies are available to libraries. One problem in acquisition of state documents has been their short press runs, which results in state documents being out of print practically before they are off the press. Although state and local agencies are usually willing to provide copies of their available publications, they rarely accept standing orders, deposit accounts, and other convenient methods of library acquisitions. Usually, acquisition is possible only on a case-by-case basis, which is time-consuming and frustrating. Frequently, the only way a library learns about a timely document is through a newspaper article or a patron request.

With the advent of state documents depository programs, their bibliographic control has improved. Inclusion of state documents and local documents in a variety of computer-searchable, bibliographic databases also has increased control of documents and has led to greater public exposure and use. However, selection guides for state and local documents are few and far between. They normally have consisted of an assorted collection of checklists and random catalogs. State library checklists of new acquisitions, the very incomplete Library of Congress *Checklist of State Documents,* and occasional lists or indexes produced by various agencies for frequently requested materials (most notably state Geological Survey materials and agricultural experimentation publications, but also occasional legislative studies or special gubernatorial panels or commission indexes) are the traditional means of identifying state publications. With some state depository programs, libraries receive a catalog and index of publications. Though these state productions are frequently inadequate because of budgetary constraints, they do offer a significant improvement over past practice.

Privately published indexes provide additional guidance. CIS's *Statistic Reference File (SRF)*contains a large section of state government published statistics. The *Index to Current Urban Documents* offers both bibliographic control of state and local documents and an optional microfiche collection. Given the poor bibliographic control of state and local documents, these sets, though expensive, sometimes offer the most cost-effective option for collection development.

In general, local government publications offer even fewer selection tools and less bibliographic control than state publications. However, some major publications of special interest, such as long-range county plans, demographic studies, or almost anything with local impact, get local publicity. Often, inexpensive or free copies are available to local libraries. The problems of acquisition roughly parallel those of state documents, that is, no agency mailing lists or standing orders and no effective acquisition options (such as deposit accounts). Furthermore, there is the need to negotiate individually with agencies to acquire reports and short-run publications. The strategic problems are almost identical to those for state documents without the advantage of the state documents depository programs. In many communities, the central public library becomes an unofficial local documents depository, and it may offer support to other libraries seeking local documents.

International Documents

Publications of international agencies vary in availability and acquisition procedure. Major international agencies, such as the United Nations (UN) and its affiliates (agencies like UNESCO, World Bank, Food and Agriculture Organization, International Monetary Fund, and World Health Organization) may offer liberal international depository programs. Others, such as the Organization for Economic Cooperation and Development (OECD), offer a heavily discounted purchase plan in lieu of a true depository agreement. Many larger agencies produce a variety of checklists and archival lists. However, only the UN produces a comprehensive index on a regular basis. The others produce sporadic catalogs and lists. Unfortunately, since the 1950s, the UN index has not included the publications of its affiliates. Thus, bibliographic control, including purchase information, is, in fact, available only for UN publications. Regional or smaller agencies offer less sophisticated bibliographic control and sales assistance. They closely parallel the situation with state documents, that is, standing orders or mailing lists are difficult to establish, and each individual purchase or acquisition requires a specific request and negotiation.

Not many librarians realize that the UN publication program has the second largest print output in the United States; the largest is the U.S. Government Printing Office (GPO).[3] The 1993 edition of *Books in Print of the United Nations System* lists more than 15,000 monographs. One aspect of the UN publishing program that makes it somewhat different from national, state, and local government programs is its mandate to produce science, technology, and medicine (STM) material for developing countries that can pay little for that information. Grants from foundations and other forms of underwriting allow the program to continue operation. Currently (1993), the UN is entering several copublishing ventures with commercial publishers. The commercial houses' marketing operations expand sales, often at a higher price, with the UN and the commercial firms sharing the higher income. In another attempt to increase its revenue, the UN is undertaking a major marketing effort for its publications. The effort may be hampered by the division of publishing activities between New York and Geneva. Both locations handle production and distribution of documents, and some documents are available from only one location. Apparently, the UN hopes to transform its publication program from a government publishing operation to something like a university or scholarly press operation.

Another interesting activity that few librarians are aware of is the UNESCO Collection. This collection of representative works from various countries contains more than 900 titles, most in English and French. Each year, the UNESCO director and member countries select the best titles in all genres from each country. UNESCO then underwrites translation costs and selects a commercial publisher to issue the inexpensive edition. The following gives one a sense of what the collection contains:

upcoming additions to the collection will include an anthology of Ukrainian contemporary poetry in Spanish, complete short stories of Gael Cortazar in French, an anthology of contemporary short stories from South Africa in English, 'memory poems' of America in Spanish, an anthology of contemporary short stories by Turkish women in French, and new Albanian poetry in English.[4]

This UNESCO series can be useful to smaller libraries seeking to expand their collections of international authors. Many of the authors included in the series are Nobel Prize winners.

UNESCO also publishes some excellent reference titles, such as *Statistical Yearbook, World Education Report, World Science Report,* and *Study Abroad.* Some other titles published by agencies related to the UN are the International Labor Organization's (ILO) *Year Book of Labour Statistics*, the UNICEF *State of the World's Children Report,* the Food and Agriculture Organization's (FACE) *State of Food and Agriculture*, and the UN's *Yearbook of the United Nations.*

The international document collection development situation has benefited from the existence of UNIPUB, a private distributor that collects international documents, creates catalogs, and offers the documents for sale from a central facility. This vendor offers a unique opportunity to build an international documents collection from a variety of agencies; UNIPUB provides all the conveniences found in the trade book field, such as standing orders, sales catalogs and subject pamphlets, deposit accounts, and a central sales office. An important fact to keep in mind is UNIPUB handles many intergovernmental agency publications, such as those of FACE, International Atomic Energy Agency, United Nations University Press, General Agreement on Tariffs and Trade (GATT), World Bank, and the International Monetary Fund.

Like state and federal documents, international documents profited from inclusion in computerized bibliographic databases. Privately published indexes, such as CIS's *Index to International Statistics (IIS)*, are among the tools creating some degree of bibliographic control and collection development assistance. As with CIS's state and federal documents program, *IIS* offers companion fiche collections.

Other Countries' National Documents

Most national governments, at least in countries with a reasonably sound economy, issue at least a few documents each year. Most developed countries have a government publications program that rivals that of the United States. They publish the required documents reporting on their activities as well as general information and educational materials. Most governments operate a central agency for producing and issuing their publications, similar to the GPO, and this eases acquisition problems. To gain an overview of government publishing programs in the 20 countries with the highest output, consult J. J. Cherns's old but still useful *Official Publications: An Overview.*[5]

As in the case of U.S. federal materials, libraries can elect to collect legislative, judicial, or executive materials from other national governments. Generally, for legislative material, it is all or nothing for a particular series, for example, the British parliamentary papers or France's *Journal Official*. Frequently, one can acquire, in microformat, sets of retrospective legislative material from commercial vendors or the originating government. Like the U.S. executive branch, foreign executive branch material can be a challenge to collect. More often than not, it is a matter of title-by-title selection from each agency, office, bureau, or other entity. Standing order programs are few and far between.

Very few countries offer depository arrangements for foreign libraries. Some do allow libraries to establish a deposit account; however, variations in exchange rates often cause problems. One method that works, if one wishes to buy a substantial number of publications from a country, is to have a book dealer or vendor in the country purchase the documents. This approach may result in a higher volume of acquisition than the library can handle. As one might expect, there is a wide variation in bibliographic control, from almost total to nonexistent. Anyone involved in an extensive foreign publications collection development program should read the bimonthly *Government Publications Review,* published by Pergamon Press (see the bibliography at the end of this chapter). Pergamon Press also publishes a series, Guides to Official Publications, that is steadily increasing its coverage on a country-by-country basis. Books in this series provide useful acquisition information.

Each type of document has its own place in a collection development program, and each has special acquisition problems, collecting methods, and advantages. Depository programs offer free documents but may pose problems resulting from depository status requirements, such as being open to the public. Or, a library may not wish to assume depository responsibilities in order to acquire documents. This is especially true because there is a wide variety of items available to nondepository libraries.

U.S. Government Printing Office and Other Official Publishers

Governments issue official publications in a variety of ways. A government can establish and operate its own presses, or it can enter into contracts with private firms to supply some or all of its printing needs. The government's central publications office also may be responsible, to some extent, for bibliographic control and sales. The central office may oversee depository libraries, if they exist. On the other hand, there may be no central office for control and coordination of government publications. In that case, publications may be the responsibility of various departments and agencies, which either engage in publishing or use outside contractors. Sales programs and depository library programs are the exception rather than the rule in such a system.

The GPO offers a fairly advanced, centralized operation under the aegis of the Joint Committee on Printing of Congress and the Public Printer of the United States. Though the Superintendent of Documents, who is the Public Printer's assistant, oversees most library-related functions, the Public Printer retains a more than titular position in regard to the actual business of government publication.

The GPO is the world's largest printer. The quantity of materials it must print to perform its statutory duties is more than it can do at its printing shop in Washington, D.C. The daily publication of the *Congressional Record* and the *Federal Register* would challenge the capabilities of average commercial printers, and the GPO prints many, many more items daily. As a result of the demands of publishing for the three branches of the government, including the numerous cabinet-level departments and independent agencies, much work is performed by contractors or performed in printing plants throughout the United States.

In addition to its publishing activities, the GPO offers a variety of services to the government, libraries, and the public. It is a central collection point for all federal publications. Title 44 of the *United States Code* requires that all agencies send copies of their publications to the GPO for cataloging and distribution to depository libraries. In the past, agencies largely ignored their statutory duty when it was inconvenient, for example, when they needed to avoid the cost of a press run large enough to meet the needs of the deposit program. Today, compliance has improved significantly. There will always be a body of fugitive literature that the GPO has never seen and will never see, though it lives on as footnotes in reports and dissertations. However, this figure has dropped from 25 percent of all government publications in 1965 to 5 percent in 1985.

The GPO also is responsible for overseeing the depository program. Under this program, libraries that are willing to meet specific requirements receive publications free of charge on the condition that they house the material and allow free public access to it. Among the responsibilities for administering the depository program are selecting depository sites, selecting materials to send to depositories, inspecting depository sites (checking that the depository sites act in accordance with Title 44 and depository program guidelines), solving problems for depositories, and dealing with libraries that no longer wish to be depositories. In addition, the GPO must issue standards and guidelines for depository libraries.

The GPO administers a sales program, which makes available to the public for a statutorily set price any document that the GPO believes has sales potential or should be available because of great public interest. The sales program includes selection of documents, pricing, handling orders, managing eight regional GPO bookstores, and providing the GPO bookstores with hand-selected, popular merchandise.

Operating a comprehensive bibliographic control program is another GPO function. Part of the GPO's mission is to identify, catalog, and classify *every extant* government publication. To an outside observer, the *Smokey the Bear Coloring Book* (a 5-page promotional item of no long-lasting value) may not seem to deserve this treatment, but the GPO's mission statement indicates that it must catalog, classify, and distribute everything under a depository item number, regardless of content quality. Though this example represents an extreme, it indicates how seriously the GPO views its mission to collect, catalog (by *AACR2* since 1976), and classify (by the Superintendent of Documents system) all available documents. Most documents receive full cataloging and are available on OCLC. Each document receives a classification number within the Superintendent of Documents classification system. Only after completing all these steps are documents ready for distribution to depositories or for the sales program. If, for some reason, a publication is not destined to go into the depository program, the GPO maintains a strict requirement that it catalog and classify the document and enter it into the *Monthly Catalog of United States Government Publications,* unless the document has a security classification. The requirement of bibliographic control is one of the oldest statutory requirements of the GPO, going back to 1895, when the *Documents Catalog* first appeared as a comprehensive bibliographic record of government publications.

Other official publishers do not necessarily follow the GPO's lead. Her Majesty's Stationery Office (HMSO) functions as Great Britain's central publication bureau, and most former British possessions follow suit. European countries follow long-established traditions that vary greatly. Developing countries tend to have no central publications bureau.

Bibliographic Control

United States federal publications have good but incomplete bibliographic control. For retrospective purposes, *Poore's Descriptive Catalogue of Government Publications, 1774-1881; Ames' Comprehensive Index of Publications of the United States Government, 1881-1893; Checklist of United States Public Documents 1789-1969;* and *Congressional Documents: Tables and Indexes, 1789-1893* provide pre-twentieth century coverage. Since 1898, the *Monthly Catalog of United States Government Publications* has been the basic listing of GPO output. Unfortunately, the GPO does not produce all government agency publications. Some of the agencies regularly issue sales catalogs. If a library desires to have almost comprehensive coverage, it must consult a number of sources and write numerous letters. However, for most libraries, the *Monthly Catalog* is adequate. Publications for sale appear in the GPO's *Publication Reference File (PRF).* Any library buying federal publications should probably buy *PRF* (on microfiche) and use it as *Books in Print* is used. For each publication *PRF* provides price, Superintendent of Documents classification number, stock number (essential for purchase from the GPO), bibliographic information, and a brief description. Thorough indexing makes it easy to use for selection and acquisition. Other sources of information about materials include the daily depository shipping lists and *Resources in Education.*

Libraries that buy only a few popular titles will probably find *New Books* or *Government Books* (both free) sufficient to identify appropriate items for the collection. Public libraries will find *Consumer Information Catalog (CIC)* an excellent source for rapid identification of government consumer information. Many of the items listed in *CIC* are free and available from the Consumer Information Center in Pueblo, Colorado. (The center charges a processing fee for two or more free titles.)

The National Technical Information Service (NTIS) issues *Government Reports Announcements and Index.* The NTIS is the source for most reports prepared under government contract, including many reports listed in the *Monthly Catalog.* It is also, on occasion, able to provide copies of out-of-print GPO publications. The future of NTIS as a source of inexpensive government publications is uncertain. There have been extensive discussions about the possibility of converting it to a commercial (for-profit) organization. If that happens, many libraries, particularly special libraries, may find their acquisition funds stretched too far to meet the essential needs of their collections. Perhaps of greater concern is the likelihood that a commercial publisher will not keep the reports available for as long as NTIS currently does.

Acquisitions

Libraries acquire government documents in a variety of ways. Some assume the responsibilities of depository collections if they can. Others purchase documents to match a collection profile. Some have standing orders through official or commercial vendors; others purchase documents individually or acquire most of their documents free of charge.

The federal depository system is the most common depository system in the United States, with more than 1,000 participating libraries. Most states and some international agencies have depository library systems of varying degrees of sophistication. The core of the depository arrangement is an agreement between the library and the government publishing body. According to the agreement, the government publishing body provides publications free of charge; in return, the library makes the publications available to the public. Depository agreements may allow generous latitude in management decisions concerning the depository documents, but the agreements require some form of public access.

Another common method of acquisition is purchase through the agency's official sales program. The agency may or may not offer a standing order program. Some commercial jobbers and bookstores do deal in documents, and some booksellers, especially used or rare booksellers, may stock some documents.

One large vendor of government documents is Bernan Associates of Maryland. Bernan Associates handles federal documents; through UNIPUB, a library may acquire UNESCO, UN, and other international organization publications. One reason for using UNIPUB, rather than the UN sales office in New York, is UNIPUB handles materials that the sales office does not, such as those published by FACE and the International Atomic Energy Agency. Bernan Associates offers several standing order programs.

Of course, many documents are available free of charge from issuing agencies and congressional representatives. They also are available as gifts or exchanges from libraries that have held them for the statutory period and wish to dispose of them or from libraries with extra nondepository or gift copies.

Retrospective Collections

Much of the value of a larger, long-established documents collection revolves around its historical research significance. A historical collection containing old congressional serial set volumes, Smithsonian American Ethnography Bureau publications, early Army Corps of Engineers reports and surveys, State Department surveys, and countless other documents of the United States offer a rare treasure for the scholar, subject specialist, statistician, or curious researcher. Such a collection contains valuable and fascinating primary documents of great public and scholarly merit. However, most functioning documents collections are not in this category, nor should they be.

Most depository libraries collect current documents. This is appropriate, because the primary use of documents focuses on timeliness. In fact, "selective" status allows a collection to be exclusively a current documents collection. Libraries may weed unwanted depository documents after a statutory period of five years, provided they follow proper procedures. This is neither an uncommon nor a bad policy, when the library deselects on the basis of community needs, clientele, space, money, and geographic or regional availability of historical resources. However, for the library that chooses to develop retrospective historical collections, the rewards are substantial.

The major bibliographic tools necessary to deal with pre-1962 publications (chosen because this date marks the beginning of the modern depository program) are listed in this chapter's section about bibliographic control. Each source serves a different function. *Poore's Descriptive Catalogue* and *Ames' Comprehensive Index* describe historic documents but provide little more than bibliographic verification information. *Poore's Descriptive Catalogue* purports to be comprehensive, but it is an incomplete catalog of nearly a century's worth of government publishing. *Ames' Index* offers bibliographic identification and serial set identification where possible, which makes it at least marginally functional as a bibliographic finding tool as well as for verification. The *Monthly Catalog* in its pre-1962 format is difficult to use. However, it is the basic catalog for GPO publications. It began as a sales catalog and in the 1920s, when the Superintendent of Documents added classification numbers, it became a valuable finding tool as well as a verification tool. The *Documents Catalog (1898-1940)*, originally envisioned as the basic bibliographic catalog for U.S. government publications, eventually ceased publication, and it was replaced by the faster appearing *Monthly Catalog*. Cumulative subject and title indexes for the *Monthly Catalog* are available from commercial publishers.

Federal Depository System

The federal depository system has been in effect in some form since Congress distributed the first serial set to libraries in the early nineteenth century. The federal depository system evolved slowly. By the early twentieth century, a number of depositories were in operation, but no bibliographic control (in the sense of a catalog and classification system) existed. Through the first half of the twentieth century, the federal government and depository libraries struggled with growing quantities of documents, mediocre bibliographic control, and an increasing need for the information the documents contained. Finally, in 1962, Congress passed the Depository Library Act, which created the system of depository libraries we know today and statutorily defined their relationship to the GPO.

The depository library system provides the most logical acquisition method for libraries that qualify for depository status. Under Title 44 of the *United States Code,* several types of libraries may qualify for depository status. Public and academic libraries that are willing to allow public access to depository items may receive depository status. Judicial libraries, federal agency libraries, and law school libraries may also qualify for depository status. Corporate or nonfederal special libraries and school media centers generally are unable to meet the requirements and, in most cases, do not wish to be depository sites. Most depository libraries serve either the general public or a branch or agency of government. The GPO selects depositories that will serve the largest public audience. The criteria for selection include willingness to participate in the depository program, to commit resources to it, and to make documents available to the public at no cost or without impediment. Additional criteria address geographic location and the presence of other depositories in the area.

The following items are on the depository basic collection list.

Budget of the United States Government

Catalog of Federal Domestic Assistance

Census Catalog and Guide

Census Population and Housing

Code of Federal Regulations

Congressional Directory

Congressional District Data Book

Congressional Record

County and City Data Book

Federal Register

Historical Statistics of the United States

Monthly Catalog of United States Government Publications

Publications Reference File

Slip Laws (Public)

Statistical Abstract of the United States

Statutes at Large

Subject Bibliographies

United States Code

United States Government Manual

United States Reports

Weekly Compilation of Presidential Documents

The federal government, through the GPO, distributes documents of all three branches of the government free of cost to the depository library. The library must provide adequate staffing, processing, maintenance, and public service. Regular inspection of the depository sites by the GPO ensures compliance with the guidelines. At times, the inspectors seem to focus on minor processing issues, such as stamping each microfiche envelope, but larger issues go unnoted. However, the inspection program does provide some degree of oversight and assures there is public access to the materials on deposit. The GPO does not place restrictions on the overall management or arrangement of the depository collection. The library may use any cataloging and classification system it wishes. In addition, most libraries are free to choose their own collection profile from the enormous range of documents available for selection; these libraries can choose as many or as few types of documents as they wish.

Though the *Guidelines for Depository Libraries* suggests a minimum of 18 percent of available selections, the GPO does not rigidly enforce this suggestion. For example, the Charles Von der Ahe Library at Loyola Marymount University (California) was a depository until 1993. For more than 15 years, the inspection reports strongly suggested the library increase its percentage of accepted documents from 5 percent to at least 28 percent, which is the national average for depositories.[6] The library decided, due to staff and collection space limitations, to drop out of the program. However, after receiving a letter stating the library's intent to drop out of the depository program, the GPO encouraged the library to remain a depository library at the 5 percent level.

Libraries select documents by item number (item numbers denote a moderately broad grouping of documents by general area of interest) and may alter their selections annually. A single item number may include any combination of monographs, series, and periodicals, as well as maps, posters, and other formats. It provides a convenient way to select documents in groups by subject rather than by individual title.

In the past, item numbers consisted of large and unwieldy groups of documents designed for the GPO's convenience rather than the library's collection development needs. Currently, the GPO groups documents under much more specific numbers, which provides a reasonably effective collection development tool. In addition, being able to change selections by dropping numbers annually facilitates collection development. It makes it possible to select a set of documents for inspection and quickly deselect it if the documents are not suitable for the library's collection. Though the library must maintain all documents selected for a statutory period of five years, it may avoid acquiring long runs of unwanted documents by changing its depository profile to a quarterly basis. And it may dispose of the unwanted parts of the collection after the mandatory five-year retention period. Though caution in selection always pays (because it is always easier to add selections than to deselect), the GPO's flexibility in regard to collection profiles significantly aids selection officers in acquiring suitable materials for a specific library.

Most libraries are able to select their acquisitions from the full range of documents offered through the depository program. These libraries form the backbone of the depository system; they are the "selective depositories" because of their ability to selectively acquire and dispose of documents through the depository program. A second type of depository library—the regional library—exists. Each state may have a maximum of two regional depository libraries. These libraries, chosen for both research strength and willingness to serve as regional resources, agree to receive all publications available through the depository program, hold them permanently, and provide ILL service for the region. Because regional status is voluntary, not all states have two or even one regional depository library. A list of current depositories is available in the *Monthly Catalog* and several other sources, including the GPO and individual congressional offices.

Along with the depository collection, the GPO provides bibliographic control in the form of a comprehensive index: the *Monthly Catalog of United States Government Publications*. The GPO also provides a centrally controlled classification system, the Superintendent of Documents (SuDocs) system, a classification scheme using alphanumerics and punctuation to arrange documents within an agency grouping. The GPO also provides *AACR2* cataloging for all documents indexed in the *Monthly Catalog*. Although no library must use any of these features, they make the depository procedure, as well as collection development and maintenance, much easier.

The GPO and Sale of Government Publications

Only publications chosen for the sales program are available from the GPO. These are documents that the GPO has screened and evaluated for sales potential and public interest. The GPO produces these documents in quantities sufficient for sale and adds them to the sales program.

The GPO operates regional bookstores as well as a sales office in Washington, D.C. Publications in the sales program are available for purchase from the central GPO sales office or the regional bookstores. The bookstores exist in several cities, including Atlanta, Denver, Houston, and Los Angeles.

One can order publications listed in *PRF* individually or collectively from the GPO's sales office or through the regional bookstores. GPO deposit accounts are available to minimize purchasing problems. These accounts also apply to NTIS purchases, and NTIS accounts also work for GPO purchases. Additionally, the GPO accepts major credit cards for purchases of GPO publications from Washington, D.C., or regional bookstores.

Most prices are reasonable. For example, the *Statistical Abstract of the United States, 1993* costs $38. This pricing is no accident. According to law, government publications cannot be sold for profit. Pricing may recover the direct publication cost and an overhead percentage.

The GPO sales office offers a series of subject bibliographies based on the current *PRF*, which is republished regularly, adding new publications and deleting out-of-print items. The subject bibliographies are particularly useful as acquisition tools for libraries that have particular subject interests or strengths or for libraries with limited access to the *PRF*. The bibliographies provide patrons with ordering information and an idea of the availability of documents that they might wish to acquire. The GPO sales office also creates a series of sales brochures and catalogs. These range from catalogs to fliers and are available through the GPO sales office and bookstores. Because mailing lists are expensive to maintain, the GPO requires occasional purchases to assure continued receipt of the catalogs.

Other Sources for Federal Documents

Some congressional publications, such as hearings and committee prints, and a few agency publications, may be obtained by contacting the local or Washington, D.C., offices of congressional representatives. Obviously, this is not an appropriate acquisitions technique for large quantities or standing orders, but it can be quite effective for current issues or special subject publications. It is especially effective for acquisition of information about current legislation or information covering a wide range of subjects. School and media centers should take advantage of this source of free government documents. The best method for acquiring recently out-of-print or nonsales publications is to contact the issuing agency directly. The annual *United States Government Manual* provides a list of addresses and telephone numbers for the major and minor agencies of the federal government. Individual contact can produce copies of many federal documents, often free of charge.

Issues Surrounding Government Documents

Without question, the major issue for U.S. libraries with regard to federal information relates to access resulting from privatization. The ALA's *Less Access to Less Information by and About the U. S. Government* details librarians' concerns. In a 1991 article, Herbert Schiller makes a strong statement regarding the societal issues related to the changing view of information, especially government information.[7] Schiller says,

The extent to which, for example, the decision to actually collect data is left to private, profit-seeking firms means that whatever the action taken, is not the result of an assessment of social need but rather a forecast of private gain. . . . The information that is produced in the labs and studies of the faculty is no longer publicly available. . . . Derek Bok, in his final "President's Report" to Harvard University Board of Overseers in the spring of 1991, warned that commercialization may be the greatest threat to American universities. . . . Only data that has commercial value will be collected and retrieved. Democratic participation in government, founded on the right to know and the availability of information, will wither.[8]

The issue remains unresolved.

A related issue is the depository system. As less material is available from the government, there are some who question the need for the system to remain in place. A 1987 article by Bruce Morton outlines the position of those who believe the system is unnecessary.[9] Essentially, their argument is private firms could more effectively package and market government information. They contend the marketing would result in greater, not less, accessibility, as well as greater use of government information by the public. Although this view has few supporters among librarians, it has support in Congress and certainly among members of the information industry. Most librarians, and probably all librarians working with depository material, agree that the basic legislation governing the program needs revision. When one assumes the concern is with government information in all formats rather than just publications, the need for new guidelines is apparent.

Finally there is the issue of electronic information. As more and more of the government's data is available only in electronic formats, smaller libraries are unable to make the information available because they lack the technology. In time, this may become less of a problem. A report issued by the House Committee on Government Operations explores the issues related to electronic information and access; although dated, the report offers a solid overview of the problem.[10] Debbi Schaubman detailed some of the costs related to electronic information, from the relatively expensive electronic bulletin boards (for example, Project Hermes for Supreme Court opinions) to CD-ROMs and tape files.[11] Certainly electronic sources, such as CD-ROMs, enhance searching and retrieval of information; however, they also mean acquisition of equipment and training of staff, both costs for the library. If the library does not have a local area network, work space will quickly disappear as more computers are added to accommodate user demands.

One method of gaining access to more than 130 government databases and bulletin boards is NTIS's FedWorld. The service is available to users using everything from low-end, dial-in computer configurations to MOSAIC/World Wide Web, and FedWorld's graphical user interface works with PCs and Macintosh systems. The NTIS expects to provide access to more than 300 government systems in the near future. At the time this book was prepared, World Wide Web access was http://www.fedworld.gov; the telnet address was fedworld.gov, and for FTP it was ftp.fedworld.gov.

Summary

Government information is an important element in any collection development program. It is fundamentally important for society to have the information easily available, even if people do not use it heavily. All types of libraries can acquire useful information from government agencies at reasonable cost. The idea that private, for-profit firms would provide the variety and depth of information and keep the costs reasonable seems naive. One only has to look at the cost of scholarly serials to see how privatization might affect the cost of government information.

Notes

[1]*1993 U.S. Government Manual* (Washington, DC: Government Printing Office, 1993).

[2]William G. Bailey, *Guide to Popular U.S. Government Publications,* 3d ed. (Englewood, CO: Libraries Unlimited, 1993).

[3]Sally Taylor, "U.N. Publishing, A World of Books," *Publishers Weekly* 240 (March 15, 1993): 37-58.

[4]Ibid., 50.

[5]J. J. Cherns, *Official Publications: An Overview* (Oxford: Pergamon Press, 1979).

[6]Letter from GPO to Charles Von der Ahe Library, Loyola Marymount University, December 1993.

[7]Herbert I. Schiller, "Public Information Goes Corporate," *Library Journal* 116 (October 1, 1991): 44-45.

[8]Ibid., 45.

[9]Bruce Morton, "The Depository Library System: A Costly Anachronism," *Library Journal* 112 (September 15, 1987): 52-54.

[10]Congress, House Committee on Government Operations, *Electronic Collection and Dissemination of Information by Federal Agencies: A Policy Overview* (Washington, DC: Government Printing Office, 1986).

[11]Debbi Schaubman, "Electronic Data from GPO," *Bottom Line* 5 (Spring 1991): 25-29.

Further Reading

General

Dimitrov., T. D., ed. *International Documents for the 80's: Their Role and Use.* Pleasantville, NY: UNIFO, 1982.

Government Publications Review. New York: Pergamon Press, 1974- .

Hernon, P. "Superintendent of Documents Operates an Outdated Vacuum Cleaner." *Government Information Quarterly* 9, no. 2 (1992): 99-105.

Hernon, P., and G. R. Purcell. *Developing Collections of U.S. Government Publications.* Greenwich, CT: JAI Press, 1982.

Higdon, M. A. "Access to Government Information." *Texas Library Journal* 67 (Spring 1991): 9-10.

Hodge, S. P.; D. Calvin; and G. Pike. "Formulating an Integrated Library Documents Collection." *Government Information Quarterly* 6, no. 2 (Spring 1989): 199-213.

Kidd, Y. M. "The Federal Government: Your Virtual Servant." *Inform* 8 (March 1994): 14-16.

Moody, M. "State Documents: Basic Selection Sources." *Collection Building* 7 (Spring 1985): 41-44.

Morehead, J., and M. Fetzer. *Introduction to United States Government Information Sources.* 4th ed. Englewood, CO: Libraries Unlimited, 1992.

Morton, B., and S. D. Zink. "Dissemination and Accessibility of Canadian Government Information." *Government Publications Review* 19 (July/August 1992): 385-96.

Purcell, G. R. "Collection Development for Government Publications." In *Library and Information Science Annual,* vol. 4, edited by B. S. Wynar, 32-39. Englewood, CO: Libraries Unlimited, 1988.

Robinson, W. C. "Evaluation of the Government Documents Collection." *Government Publications Review* 9 (March 1982): 131-41.

Ryan, S. M. "Recent Literature on Government Information." *Journal of Government Information* 21 (March/April 1994): 149-74.

Schuman, P. G. "Making the Case for Access." *RQ* 29 (Winter 1989): 166-70.

Sears, J. L., and M. K. Moody. *Using Government Information Sources.* Phoenix: AZ: Oryx Press, 1994.

Seavy, C. A. "Fixing the Depository Library System." *Journal of Government Information* 21 (March/April 1994): 77-81.

Smith, D. H., ed. *Management of Government Document Collections.* Englewood, CO: Libraries Unlimited, 1993.

Snowhill, L., and R. Meszaros. "New Directions in Federal Information Policy and Dissemination." *Microform Review* 19 (Fall 1990): 181-85.

"United Nations Depository Libraries in the United States and Canada." In *Informing the Nation,* edited by F. J. O'Hara, 532-35. Westport, CT: Greenwood Press, 1990.

"United Nations Documentation." In *Informing the Nation,* edited by F. J. O'Hara, 481-531. Westport, CT: Greenwood Press, 1990.

Academic

Bailey, E. C. "Access to Federal Documents in Small Non-depository Academic Libraries." *Government Publications Review* 8, no. 5 (1981): 405-10.

Gray, C. J. "Sources for Legislative Histories and Status Reports." *Show-Me Libraries* 34 (September 1983): 29-34.

Hallewell, L. "Government Publishing in the Third World." *Government Publications Review* 19 (January/February 1992): 23-58.

Heir, K. M., and M. Moody. "Government Documents in the College Library." In *College Librarianship,* edited by W. Miller and D. S. Rockwood, 214-32. Metuchen, NJ: Scarecrow Press, 1981.

Hernon, P. "Academic Library Reference Service for Publications of Municipal, State and Federal Government." *Government Publications Review* 5, no. 1 (1978): 31-50.

Ruhlin, M. T. "The Gathering Storm: Government Information in CD-ROM Format." *New Jersey Libraries* 24 (Summer 1991): 18-21.

Shil, H. B., and S. K. Peterson. "Is Government Information in Your Library's Future?" *College & Research Libraries News* 50 (September 1989): 649-57.

Public

Documents to the People. Chicago: American Library Association, 1972- .

Jones, D. E. "Serving Everyone: Government Documents to Serve the Physically Handicapped." *Illinois Libraries* 72 (April 1990): 355-59.

Lesko, M. "In Our Information Society, Why Isn't the Public Library the Most Important Building in Our Community?" *Public Libraries* 31 (March/April 1992): 85-87.

Lowe, J. L., and S. Henson. "Government Publications for School and Small Public Libraries." *Collection Management* 11, nos. 3/4 (1989): 141-50.

Moody, M. K. "Source of First Resort." *Library Journal* 117 (May 15, 1992): 36-45.

Morehead, J. H. "Between Infancy and Youth: Children and Government Serials." *Serials Librarian* 4 (Summer 1980): 373-79.

School

Dickmeyer, J. N. "U.S. Government Documents Belong in School Media Centers." *Indiana Media Journal* 3 (Spring 1981): 23-26.

Ekhaml, L., and A. J. Wittig. *U.S. Government Publications for School Library Media Centers*. 2d ed. Englewood, CO: Libraries Unlimited, 1991.

Gonzales-Kirby, D. "Reading with Uncle Sam." *Behavioral & Social Sciences Librarian* 11, no. 2 (1992): 1-38.

Jay, H. L. "Government Documents and Their Use in Schools." In *Collection Management for School Library Media Centers*, edited by Brenda White, 295-312. New York: Haworth Press, 1986.

Keith, D. J. "Introducing Government Documents in Academic Libraries and School Media Centers." *Reference Services Review* 15 (Spring 1987): 51-66.

Swartz, B. J., and K. J. Zimmerman. "Hidden Treasure: Government Documents for Children and Teens." *School Library Journal* 35 (August 1989): 40-43.

Special

Larsgaard, M. L. "Government Cartographic Materials for Earth Sciences/Energy Resources Research." *Information Bulletin* [Western Association of Map Libraries] 21 (June 1990): 172-74.

Morehead, J. H. "Corporate and Government Annual Reports." *Serials Librarian* 5 (Winter 1980): 7-14.

Rockwell, K. "Privatization of U.S. Geological Survey Topographic Maps." *Government Publications Review* 17 (May/June 1990): 40-43.

Sauter, H. E., and R. H Rea. "Place of Research/Classified Reports in a Special Library." In *Special Librarianship,* edited by E. B. Jackson, 509-20. Metuchen, NJ: Scarecrow Press, 1980.

Schmidt, F., and H. W. Welsch. "Acquisition Guide: Technical Reports and Other Non-GPO Publications." *Government Publications Review* 8, no. 4 (1981): 175-79.

Taylor, S. N. "Technical Reports and Non-depository Publications." *Government Publications Review*. [This article, an annual survey, is usually in the November/December issue of *Government Publications Review*.]

9
Audiovisual Materials

With each passing year, as multimedia computer systems combine text, image, and audio, the distinction between books and audiovisuals becomes more blurred. Information that once was available only in printed formats is available in several forms, including books, microfiche, CD-ROM, and online. Book publishers, especially publishers of scholarly journals, are thinking about and, in a few cases publishing, their material electronically (see chapter 6). Many publishers expect to, and are, using CD-ROM packages to distribute reference material. Almost all software mail-order catalogs include one or two CD-ROM packages of reference material. The Library of Congress is experimenting with the use of laser discs (a technology related to CD-ROM) to store the contents of brittle books.

Compact discs and laser discs can hold thousands of pages of text, providing significant storage cost savings. Add to this video, teletext, and machines capable of reading aloud standard typefaces (Reading Edge), and one begins to realize that the integration of information technology described in chapter 1 is becoming a reality. Collections are beginning to reflect these changes, even at academic libraries that have been the least active in audiovisual collection building.

The library's most important products are information and service. If one accepts this philosophy, then the library collection must consist of more than books. Books are, and will be for some time, the least expensive method of conveying large amounts of detailed information to many people at a given time. Television may reach millions of people at one time, but it does not convey detailed information, except in the most exceptional circumstances. A major consideration in building an information collection is how to convey the right information at the right time to the public at the lowest cost.

Books are useful only to persons who are literate. Depending where in the world one is, the percentage of persons who are literate ranges from 1 to 100 percent. Throughout a large portion of the world, less than 50 percent of the population is literate. Even in countries with apparently high literacy rates, such as the United States, there is a difference between the reported and the actual literacy rate. In the United States, many people express concern about functional illiteracy, in which persons may have gone through the required educational system (12 years of schooling) but are unable to read beyond the level reached by the third or fourth year of schooling. Because of functional illiteracy and the many immigrants entering the United States recently, many communities have established literacy programs outside the formal educational system.

Many of these programs operate out of, and with the support of, the public library. Many colleges and universities worry about the inability of entering students to read and write effectively. There is a growing difference in the United States between young people's ability to use and understand the spoken, as opposed to the written, word.

For many purposes, textual material is not the most effective or most reasonable method for conveying a particular message. For teaching, research, and recreation, more and more people consider collections of graphic and audio materials appropriate and useful. Some people still consider these materials less intellectually sound than print, or as toys, or fit for purely recreational purposes, and they resist adding such formats to a collection. However, as the number of people who have used a number of formats in learning about a subject increases, so does the pressure to have all appropriate formats in a collection. Librarians need to remind the public, and sometimes themselves, that libraries are in the information business, not the book business. Certainly, publishers one might consider primarily book publishers now consider themselves in the information business.

Microforms

Where do microformats belong—with books or with audiovisuals? Probably in both places. Most of the guides to microform materials cover microfilm and microfiche that contain previously published information; it is rare for a microformat title to contain original (new) material. The major exception to this is technical reports, which may be available only in microform.

One problem for people doing retrospective selection is finding a hard (that is, a paper) copy of all of the items one might wish to add to the collection. Usually, if one waits long enough (perhaps years), the book or periodical will turn up in an out-of-print shop. Sometimes the need for the item is too great to wait. If reprint dealers do not have the item, then a microform copy may be the answer.

Another reason for using microformats is to save space, especially with low-use back files of serials. (A back file or back run is a set of older volumes of a current serial subscription; for example, if a library's current issues of *Newsweek* begin with volume 92, then volumes 1-91 comprise the back file for that library's *Newsweek* collection.) When a library has long runs of low-use material, it is wasting valuable shelf space by keeping the physical volumes in the library. A serial that occupies several hundred feet of shelving may be reduced to less than a foot of space when converted to a microformat. Naturally, there is a trade-off in space; the more material there is in microformat, the more equipment the library needs to meet patron demand. Some serial librarians use a microformat for back files of popular titles that have a high incidence of mutilation or a habit of disappearing. If the library has a reader-printer (a device that allows a person to read the microform and to push a button to receive a hard copy of the page on the screen), loss and mutilation rates drop.

One major drawback to using microforms to any major degree is patron resistance. Many persons claim that they cannot read anything on a microformat, that it gives them headaches and causes eyestrain and other problems. Occasionally, someone will complain it causes nausea. To date, none of these concerns are supported by research. Usually when the only source for the information is microform, an individual is able to use the material without a problem. Admittedly, it takes time to get used to using microforms; it is more difficult in some formats, such as reels, to locate a specific portion of text than in the traditional book format. Without proper maintenance, the image quality will be poor, and that will cause eyestrain. Equipment breaks down and malfunctions at times, causing user and staff frustration.

Despite these problems, it will become necessary to use more and more microformats as time goes on. The major factor in increased use will be economic. New library buildings will be harder to secure; the prices of hard copies of older materials keep going up; and library book and materials budgets remain about the same or increase at a rate less than the rate of inflation. Thus, it is important to know the guides to microformats. Two guides to in-print microformats are *Guide to Microforms in Print* (Microform Review) and *National Register of Microform Masters* (Library of Congress). Both titles try to be international in scope, cover both commercial and noncommercial sources of supply (for example, libraries and historical associations), and cover more than 16 types of microformats. The *National Register* includes only U.S. suppliers, but the material available is international in scope. *Microform Market Place* (Microform Review) is an international directory of micropublishing, which includes microform jobbers. A major source of reviews of microform series, both current and retrospective, is *Microform Review* (Microform Review). Major producers offer extensive catalogs of what they have available. It is necessary to keep a file of their catalogs, because it is even less common for micropublishers than for book publishers to contribute information to the in-print guides.

General Evaluation Criteria

To a degree, the same factors that determine inclusion or exclusion of books apply to other formats. Obviously, one omits factually incorrect items unless there is a sound reason to buy them. Poorly organized and presented material is seldom likely to become part of the collection. If the quality of a book is difficult to assess, assessing the quality of other media is even more difficult. All of us have seen a film we enjoyed only to hear a friend claim that it is "absolutely *the* worst film" ever made. Thus, subjectivity is a major concern. Though bias also is a problem with literature, we receive more training or exposure to good literature through formal schooling. Few of us receive formal training in evaluating nonprint materials. Basically, the issues of authority, accuracy, effectiveness of presentation or style, and value and usefulness to the community are as valid for all other formats as they are for books.

Before embarking on a program to develop a media collection, one should carefully evaluate each format in terms of its unique utility to the service community. Each format has its strong and weak points, and similar information may be available in a variety of formats. The following paragraphs offer general guidelines for assessing the strengths and weaknesses of various forms.

Formats that involve motion (such as 8mm, 16mm, and 35mm films and videotapes) are among the more expensive formats. Therefore, an important question to ask is whether motion really adds information. There are films in which there is no motion at all, or if there is motion, it may not be relevant to the content. For example, many educational films and videotapes simply alternate shots of one or two persons talking to one another or to the viewers (so-called talking heads); there are no other graphics (or, at least, no graphics that require this expensive mode of presentation). On the other hand, one can read hundreds of pages and look at dozens of still photographs of cell division and not fully understand how it occurs. A short, clearly photographed film combined with a good audio track can sometimes produce a more accurate understanding of the process than one can achieve through hours of reading.

Detailed study is sometimes most effectively carried out with the use of still pictures, charts, or graphs. Another advantage is that the cost of producing and acquiring these formats is much lower than for those that involve motion.

With both motion and still graphic formats, color is an important consideration. Full-color reproduction is more costly than black-and-white reproduction; the question is whether the color is necessary or merely pleasing. In some instances, color is necessary. Certainly, anything that attempts to represent the work of a great artist must have excellent color quality, as is also the case with medical and biological materials.

Audio formats also can provide greater understanding and appreciation of printed material. One's own reading of a poem is never the same as hearing the poet's recitation of the work. Tone, emphasis, inflection, and so forth can change the meaning of a printed text dramatically. On a different level, there are literally millions of people in the world who cannot read music scores and yet get enormous enjoyment from listening to music. Audio recordings are a must in any collection serving the visually impaired. Spoken-word recordings can be an important service for such persons and for commuters who want to listen to a book as they travel.

Other general selection factors include cost, flexibility and manipulation, and patron preference. Audiovisual formats require expensive equipment in addition to rather costly software. When thinking about cost factors, one needs to know what types of equipment patrons own, for example, slide projectors, videotape players, CD or tape players, or record players. If patrons do not own the necessary equipment, can the library supply it free of charge or on a rental basis? Should the library buy the equipment and allow its use only in the library? The librarian also must consider what patrons like and use. Libraries ought not to get into the position of attempting to change patron format preferences. Thus, both cost and patron preference become significant in deciding what to buy or not to buy.

Flexibility and manipulation are inseparable. How and where can one use the format and equipment? With some equipment, the library can produce local programs as well as play back commercial software. Videocassette recorders (VCRs) allow people to perform a variety of recording and playback functions, most of which (like freeze frame) no one uses. Knowing community needs and use patterns may save the library money. Special VCR features may be necessary, nice, or merely gimmicks, depending on the local situation. Ease of operation is very important: Can a person quickly learn to operate the equipment, or does it take extensive training to use it properly?

Types of Media

Any list of current media formats quickly becomes dated as new technologies and new combinations of older forms appear. Just when one thinks he or she has identified the latest developments and decided to invest money in the equipment and software, a new, even more exciting and potentially valuable, format appears. With this in mind, the following list provides a snapshot of media formats of interest to librarians at this writing:

audiotapes (single and multiple track, including audiobooks)

CD recordings

CD-ROM multimedia products

computer programs

films (8mm and 16mm, primarily for older titles not available in a video format)

filmstrips (with or without sound, this is a declining format)

flat pictures (photographs, illustrations, original art work, posters, and the like)

games (usually educational, but some libraries offer a variety of recreational games)

globes (terrestrial and celestial)

maps (flat and relief)

microforms (all types)

mixed-media packages (kits)

printed music (performance and study scores)

realia

slides (35mm and 4-x-4)

specimen collections

video formats (including games)

working models (full and scale)

Considering the range of material, and remembering the special aspects of the media trade, one can understand why collection development in media areas presents some special problems.

Selection Criteria

Once a library decides to follow the media path, how does one select appropriate items? There are four sets of factors to consider—programming, content, technical aspects, and format—with criteria related to each factor. The following paragraphs highlight major selection criteria.

Programming Factors

Programming (that is, use of material) is important in deciding what to acquire. Many articles and books about this topic are available (see the bibliography at the end of this chapter). Programming questions include: Will the medium be used in formal instructional situations? Is it only for recreational use? Who is the primary audience: adults, children, or all ages? Will the item circulate, or will it be available only for in-house use? If used in-house, will it be available to individuals or only to groups? Will group use involve a library staff member or an expert in the field to guide group discussions before or after the item's use? Will the library be a member of a resource sharing network? If so, will the item become part of the shared material pool? Answers to these questions will affect the type of media purchased and the price paid for it. For example, many videos for home use are less expensive than videos for instructional use, even when both packages are the same title.

Content Factors

Content is the next concern in the selection of any format. In the past, audiovisual selection was a group process rather the sole responsibility of one selector. This was especially true in the case of expensive formats. Today, with the prices of videos dropping and increasing numbers of titles needed for the collection, the selection process is more like book selection, that is, an individual process. School media centers still emphasize the group process, in part because of limited funds but also because the possibility of someone objecting to an item's presence in the collection is higher than in other types of libraries. Whether selection is a group or individual process, using an evaluation form is useful. Keeping the forms for several years, for titles rejected as well as those purchased, can save selectors' time. Unlike print material, most media is sequential in nature; this means it takes 50 minutes to review a 50-minute program. An evaluation form indicating that the library reviewed and rejected an item three years ago should help selectors decide whether the item is worth reconsidering. No matter what questions are on the form—and not all items listed in this chapter will be on any one form—one ought to consider all of the following points:

1. What is the primary purpose of the item? If there is a user's guide, does it provide a specific answer to this question?

2. Given the purpose(s) of the item, is the length of the program appropriate? Items can be too short, but more often than not, they are too long.

3. Is the topic a fad, or is it likely to have long-term interest? Long-term interest and lasting value are not always the same.

4. Is the material well organized?

5. Is the story line easy to follow?

6. If the item is of relatively short duration and is an attempt to popularize a subject, does it do this with sufficient accuracy in the sense that the simplification does not cause misunderstandings or worse, create a misrepresentation?

7. When was the material copyrighted? Copyright information can be difficult to find for some formats. Films usually provide this information somewhere in the credits, often in roman numerals. There is no national bibliographic description standard for this information. Sales catalogs may or may not provide the date of production. Unfortunately, a large number of dated products are, or have been, sold as if they were current.

8. Will the visuals or audio date quickly? In many educational films, the subject matter is important but the actors' dress makes the film appear old-fashioned. If one does not present the material as historical, many viewers may miss its true purpose. Audience attention is easily drawn away from the real subject. Needless to say, this ties into the need for accurate copyright information.

9. Are there multiple uses for the item, in addition to those identified by the producer? If there are a number of ways to use the format (with various types of programs or audiences), it is easier to justify spending money on the item.

Technical Factors

Technical issues vary in importance from format to format, but some general considerations apply to several formats. In most instances, judging technical matters is less subjective than judging many other selection criteria. On the other hand, it will take time and guidance from experienced selectors to develop a critical sense of these factors. Most individuals entering the field of library and information work are more attuned to good literature, well-manufactured books, and the various methods of literary review and criticism than the average person. Though our exposure to television, film, and video recordings may be greater than to books, few of us have the background for assessing the technical aspects of these formats. This fact is evident during film and television awards ceremonies—the public interest is in the best film or program and performance categories. It is the rare individual who can name the winners in the technical areas (direction, production, special effects, cinematography, and so forth). Following are some questions to consider regarding technical features:

1. Are the visuals, assuming that there are visuals, necessary?

2. Are the visuals in proper focus, the composition effective, the shots appropriate? (These questions need to be asked because out-of-focus shots, strange angles, and jarring composition may be used to create various moods and feelings.)

3. Is the material edited with skill?

4. Does the background audio material contribute to the overall impact?

5. Is there good synchronization of visuals and audio?

6. How may the format be used—can it be viewed by small or large groups or by both? Can it be viewed in a darkened, semi-lighted, or fully lighted room?

Format Factors

Questions about format factors are:

1. Is the format the best one for the stated purposes of the producer?

2. Is the format the least expensive of those that are appropriate for the content?

3. Will the carrier medium (the base material that supports the image or sound layer) stand up to the amount and type of use that library patrons would give it?

4. If damage occurs, can it be repaired (locally or by the producer), or must one buy a replacement copy? Does it require maintenance and if so, what kind?

5. What are the equipment requirements to use the medium? How portable is the equipment and how heavy?

Additional Considerations

It is possible to group all audiovisual materials into six broad categories: still pictures (filmstrips, slides, microformats, transparencies); video and motion pictures; audio recordings; graphic materials (maps, charts, posters, etc.); three-dimensional (models, realia, dioramas); and other formats (games, software, etc.).

Still Pictures: Filmstrips, Microformats, Slides, and Transparencies

Filmstrips, as noted earlier, were one of the more popular formats with media producers, primarily because of their low production cost and high profit margin. Many book publishers began their ventures into the media field with this format. For some materials, it was the first and only additional format on a topic; more often, it led to other formats.

The filmstrip format is used mostly in primary and secondary schools and undergraduate university instruction. Its use is declining, although many libraries have substantial collections of filmstrips. Perhaps by the time the next edition of this book is published, filmstrips will be only archival or museum specimens. Bibliographic control of this format is good. Material designed for the school market has potential value for the adult seeking self-education.

Filmstrips come in either a sound or silent format. Sound products consist of the filmstrip and an audio recording (usually a cassette tape.) Many of the sound tapes have an electronic signal that indicates it is time for the user to advance the filmstrip to the next frame. There are also sound packages that have the capability of automatically advancing the filmstrip as the recording plays. Such packages require the use of special and more expensive equipment.

Reviews of filmstrips appear in several standard review sources, such as *Booklist*, *Library Journal* (*LJ*), and *School Library Journal* (*SLJ*). More specialized review sources that cover filmstrips with some regularity are *Landers' Film Review*, *Media and Methods*, *Media Review Digest*, and *Science Teacher*.

In a sense, slides are simply filmstrips cut into individual frames and mounted for projection onto a screen. Slides are available in several sizes (2-x-2-inches, 2¼-x-2¼-inches, and 4-x-4-inches) and with different types of mounts (cardboard, plastic, metal, or glass). The larger the size, the better the image will project for large audiences. Mixing different types of mounts may cause problems with projectors or slide trays (too loose or tight a fit). Cardboard mounts are easy to damage, and when damaged, cause projectors to jam. Like filmstrips, there are combined sound and slide packages, primarily for the educational market.

Academic, school, and special libraries are frequent collectors of slides. Academic libraries supporting survey art courses experience heavy student use of their slide collections. Both academic and business libraries in the areas of health sciences, biology, art, architecture, fashion design, interior design, and research and development tend to have large slide collections as well.

Perhaps the greatest problem in collecting slides is the large number of sources, which may produce packages of highly variable quality. A major issue with slides is color quality and the quality of lighting and exposure. Slow exposure using a fine-grained film produces the best quality slides, assuming the photography (focus, composition, and so forth) and film processing were performed competently.

Reviews of slide sets appear, irregularly at best, in such standards as *Booklist*, *LJ*, and *SLJ*. Two more-or-less regular sources of review are *Art and Activities* and *International Bulletin for Photographic Documentation of the Visual Arts*. The latter publication provides updates for Norine Cashman's *Slide Buyers' Guide* (Libraries Unlimited, 6th ed. 1990).

Second only to audio recordings, *microforms* are probably the most common audiovisual format found in libraries. Their popularity as a compact storage medium for printed materials means there is good bibliographic control.

Microform is a blanket term covering several formats: microfilm, microfiche, aperture cards, microprints, and micro-opaques. In addition to various formats, there are variations in size and reduction ratios within a format, for example, an item marked *10x* means the image is 1/10th the size of the original. Currently, producers use five categories of reduction: low (up to 15x), medium (16-30x), high (31-60x), very high (61-90x), and ultra high (greater than 91x). Reduction ratios are important to note because one must, in most cases, change lenses in the reader as one uses microforms at various reduction ratios. Most microform collections contain materials produced using various reduction ratios. Changing lenses is one reason patrons are uncomfortable using microforms. Selectors should try to keep the variations in reduction ratios to a minimum, although there may be few options when it comes to a particular title or collection of titles. One either accepts what the producer selected or forgoes purchasing the item.

Another concern is whether the film treatment is silver halide, diazo, or vesicular. The latter two are less expensive but have relatively short shelf lives, even with good storage and handling conditions. Silver halide, though more expensive, is the option to choose, when there is a choice and long-term retention is an issue. A related issue is the polarity of the film (positive or negative). A negative film produces a black image on a white background (the traditional image people expect) in hard copy. Some of the more expensive reader-printers automatically produce the traditional image, regardless of polarity, and most require the user to select the film's polarity before printing. One more step that many users resent having to undertake.

As noted earlier, there is strong user resistance to microforms. Microformats are best for low-use materials, older materials that need only a black-and-white image, and as second copies of materials with high demand or high loss and mutilation rates. Back files of journals are excellent candidates for storage on microfilm. Color microforms are expensive, and few libraries have equipment capable of making hard color copies from color microforms.

Very little new material initially appears in microform, but it has been and still is a common means of securing copies of out-of-print books, archival material, and other unique items. (Many microform packages use existing material in combinations that create a new product, for example, the Tozzer Library Catalog published by G. K. Hall.[1]) In addition to storing material in compact form, microforms also are useful in disseminating research reports to a large audience at a low unit cost. Some firms publish only in microformats. Their inventory consists of original copy, and they generate another copy when they receive an order. This format will no doubt grow in importance, if for no other reason than its storage capability and the ease of making hard copies. Digitized storage is likely to replace microforms for on-demand publishing, however, this may take some time. The cost of digitized storage space for text and graphics material is still high—even in a compressed format—when compared to microforms. The low cost per unit is another reason that microforms will grow in popularity. A variation is the COM (computer output microform), which is a microform (usually microfiche) created from computer files.

Transparencies and opaque projector materials are used primarily in education. Of all the media choices available, this form is the most group-oriented, designed to aid in the presentation of graphic material to small- and medium-sized groups. Though an individual can use the material, it has no advantage over flat pictures. A library could obtain materials in this format related to adult education classes, especially in the science fields. Plainly, this format has limited value to the individual user, and public libraries seldom collect it. There are a number of guides to educational transparencies, including Mary Sive's *Complete Media Monitor* (Scarecrow Press, 1981) and *Elementary School Library Collection*, 19th edition (Brodart, 1994).

There are some general questions the selector should consider when working with material that features still pictures, whether the format is filmstrips, microformats, slides, or transparencies.

1. Does the lack of movement cause the viewer to misinterpret the meaning?

2. How accurate is the color reproduction? Is the color necessary?

3. Are the mountings and holders compatible with existing library equipment?

4. For filmstrips and microforms, is the sequence of frames logical and easy to follow?

5. If there is an audio track, does it aid in understanding the materials?

6. Are microformat images readable when enlarged? What is the reduction ratio? Does it work with existing library equipment? Can one make hard copies on existing equipment, or must one acquire additional attachments or new hardware?

7. Is the ratio of pictures to narration appropriate? (A frequent problem with slide or tape programs or narrated filmstrips is too few illustrations; this often results in a product that seems to last too long.)

Video and Motion Pictures: 35mm, 16mm, 8mm Films, and Video Formats

In the past, library collections emphasized the 16mm film format; today emphasis is on the videocassette. Usually, selectors can choose a title in video or film format. If the purpose is to use the title with large groups (50 or more people) on a regular basis, the best format is 16mm film. (Projection television sets are getting better all the time, but a 16mm film still provides better image quality for a large group.)

The two formats that most libraries collect are videocassettes and videodiscs. One of the big advantages of videotape is the relative ease with which one can give the same image a new sound track. One U.S. library produced a series of videotapes about how to tune a truck. After producing the master visual tape, the library produced copies with sound tracks in English, Spanish, and several American Indian languages. (One can do this with 16mm sound film as well, but the cost is very high.)

In many libraries, the videocassette collection is one of the fastest-growing and most heavily used areas of the collection. An example of such growth is the Pierce County Library (Tacoma, Washington) collection. At the end of 1992, there were 42,484 tapes in the collection.[2]

Two reasons for the heavy use of video collections are the number of people who own VCRs and the substantial amount of available material that is entertainment-oriented or recreational in nature. Video equipment is relatively easy to use in a playback mode. Certainly, a major appeal is the ability to view motion pictures in one's home with little effort. A feature that is likely to develop is connecting the VCR (or other video playback unit) to a computer to create an interactive system.

From an outreach point of view, videos and other audiovisual items have high potential. As Jean Kreamer stated, "video provides the library gateway for many new patrons, especially those who are functionally illiterate or who might not otherwise be attracted to the more traditional offerings of library collections."[3] In the past, many librarians considered audiovisual materials unacceptable for libraries, except as a means of attracting new people to the library. Once attracted, the librarian's goal was to persuade these patrons to switch from audiovisual items to books, that is, "hook them on books, not AV." Today, most librarians accept audiovisual formats as having a legitimate place in the collection.

On the negative side, videocassettes have a limited life before the image begins to noticeably deteriorate. The reason for that is the VCR heads press against the tape during playback, and the pressure slowly wears off the material that contains the image, especially if the heads are dirty. Blank streaks in the image during playback indicate areas in which all the image-carrying material is gone.

Video equipment, even institutional grade equipment, is fragile. Most video equipment intended for the home market is not suitable for library use. Libraries should buy institutional grade equipment that is capable of withstanding a certain amount of misuse and abuse. That capability translates into higher purchase and maintenance costs.

Perhaps the greatest problem with videocassettes is copyright. What can and cannot a library do with videocassettes? For example, can one use a video sold for home use in a classroom? What is meant by public performance? Public performances are any performances the public may attend, even when there is no fee. Library programs, including story hours and senior discussion groups, as well as programs by any formal group, such as scouts, churches, and service organizations, are public performances. To be safe, in library programs one should not use any video for which the library has not purchased performing rights.

The issue of performance rights is important for classroom use, and this is a growing area of use. According to Lillian Gerhardt, classroom use of videos in educational institutions, elementary through graduate school, is the steadiest growing area of video use.[4]

Not too many years ago, many academicians, like librarians, viewed films and other audiovisual items as inappropriate for instructional use. Comments like, "Didn't have time to do your lecture, right?" or "Are you going out of town?" were common when colleagues learned an instructor planned to show a film or video in class. Today you rarely hear such comments as more and more teachers build video use into their instructional plans. At Loyola Marymount University, the younger faculty are the heaviest users of video for classroom instruction.

Many special libraries also are finding a growing demand for videos. Publications like Ellen Miller and Timothy Hallahan's dated but still valuable *Media Guide for Lawyers*[5] and Bowker's *Law Books and Serials in Print*[6] and *Legal Video Review*[7] indicate a high level of interest in one profession. The same is true of the medical field, where, among other titles, one finds *Media Profiles: The Health Sciences*.[8] In addition, the visual arts, such as architecture, interior design, fashion design, and commercial art, make extensive use of video materials.

Selection of videos is very much like book selection, at least for lower-priced titles. More often than not, one person makes the decision about titles costing less than $100. The decision may be based on information in a producer's catalog or a journal review, as well as a preview of the item. Identifying potentially useful videos is becoming easier and easier. *Bowker's Complete Video Directory*,[9] *Video Source Book,*[10] *Educational Film and Video Locator,*[11] and *Film and Video Finder*[12] all provide long lists of available video titles. Unfortunately, no one source is comprehensive, so one must consult several sources when building a subject collection.

Access to theatrical films is reasonably easy because of the number of retail video stores and their need to have bibliographic control. Documentary film access also is fairly good, in the sense that there are a number of guides available. However, independent filmmakers come and go with great speed; many never appear in a guide, and others remain in the guides long after they are out of business. Keeping current with changes in the independent filmmakers' field could become a full-time occupation for a person, if serious collecting is a goal.

Reviews of videos are becoming common, appearing alongside book reviews in professional journals. *Wilson Library Bulletin, LJ, SLJ,* and *Booklist* cover a number of formats. These publications tend to cover items that have broad appeal, and they do not cover many titles in the course of a year. A sampling of journals that cover a wide range of subjects and levels of treatment are: *American Film Magazine, AV Video, Educational Technology, Educators Curriculum Product Review, EFLA Evaluations, Media and Methods, Photographic Trade News, Sightlines,* and *Videography*.

Some questions to bear in mind when selecting videos and films are:

Does the motion add to the message?

Are variable speed capabilities (fast, normal, slow, and stop) used effectively?

Is the running time appropriate to the content? Too long? Too short?

Do recreational films using performers or animation present an accurate picture of the events depicted?

Is the sound properly synchronized with the visuals?

Audio Recordings: Discs or Tapes

Many audio recording collections that have been in place for any length of time contain a wide variety of formats, including vinyl disks, reel-to-reel tapes, cassette tapes, and compact discs. No other format more clearly demonstrates changing technology. In little more than 40 years, the technology has evolved from 78-rpm disk recordings to 45-rpm and 33 1/3-rpm disks to tape cassettes of various kinds to the compact disc. Each change required new equipment and new recording formats. In libraries that support music programs, it is not uncommon to find fairly large collections of two or three different formats that more or less duplicate one another's content. That is, a library may have all of Bach's symphonies on 33 1/3-rpm vinyl disks, on audiocassette, and on compact disc. The cost of duplicating the information can be substantial; however, users demand the newer format because of the improved quality of sound. (At Loyola Marymount University, a new music department chair demanded the library replace all of the 33 1/3-rpm albums and the audiocassettes with compact discs. To have done so would have cost the library more than $20,000. The library has been replacing the recordings slowly over the last five years but still has about 25 percent of the collection on what the music department chair calls "the dinosaurs.") Unlike secondhand books, there is not a strong used recording trade, making it more difficult to resell or give away materials in the old format. The commercial music and spoken-book trade is reasonably well controlled in a bibliographic sense; certainly there is more control than in any other nonbook format. Where will it go from here? At this writing, tape cassettes and compact discs are the major formats. However, music videos are gaining in popularity and there is talk of CD-ROM or laser disc music videos.

Spoken books are popular in the United States. Public libraries serving patrons that commute by car have trouble keeping up with the demand for the tapes. (Commuters who use public transportation also check out the tapes to use in pocket-sized tape players.) One question selectors need to ask about spoken recordings is, How much did the producer abridge the material? The field has grown to the point that *Publishers Weekly* (*PW*) publishes a regular section about audiotapes, as well as a bestsellers list. Spoken book tapes range from condensed versions of books to unabridged recordings. Recently, one firm announced it would start issuing audiobooks in both CD and tape formats.[13]

Audio tapes have a special value in teaching languages. Language learning is always facilitated by hearing the proper sounds and is further enhanced when the student can practice pronouncing words. Dual-track tapes, with an instructor's voice on a nonerasable track and a learner's recording track, allow for this type of use. Schools and academic libraries supporting language instruction often house the language learning laboratory. Many of these centers, to supplement the program, develop a collection of spoken book titles in the languages taught.

Reviews of popular music recordings are relatively easy to locate in both mass-market and professional publications. *Booklist, LJ, SLJ,* and *Notes* are a few of the professional sources that review sound recordings. *High Fidelity, Stereo Review, Billboard,* and *Downbeat* are mass-market publications one can consult for music reviews. For audiobooks, *PW* publishes a regular section of reviews; occasionally, one can find such reviews in *Booklist* as well.

Regardless of the format, there are some general questions to keep in mind during the selection process:

1. How much use can the format withstand without distorting the quality of the sound?

2. How easily damaged is the format? Can people erase it by mistake?

3. Does the recording provide coverage of the full range of sound frequencies?

4. Is there any distortion of the sound?

5. Is the recording speed constant? (This is seldom a problem with major producers, but it can be significant with smaller producers.)

6. If the recording is multiple channel, were the microphones properly placed to ensure a balanced recording?

7. Was the recording site suitable for the purposes? (For example, if the goal is to produce an excellent recording of a musical composition, then a recording studio or a concert hall with excellent acoustics and no audience, rather than a concert, is the best location. Live performances do not produce the best sound quality.)

Graphic Materials: Flat Pictures, Globes, Maps, Charts, Posters, Prints, and Sheet Music

Flat pictures have been available in library vertical files for years, with the primary users of these materials being teachers and students. With the introduction of rental collections of art reproductions and original prints, the flat picture audience expanded to include adult patrons. Many libraries have found these materials provide one of the most popular services they can offer. Aside from a few UNESCO publications, there is little bibliographic control in this field. Selectors and acquisition staff must learn about producers and maintain files of catalogs to secure these materials in a timely fashion. Once in a great while there are reviews of these formats in *LJ, Booklist,* and *SLJ.*

Globes and maps, although different in form and requiring different handling, usually are available from the same sources as flat pictures. Most libraries have always had a small collection of local maps and atlases, along with a globe or two. Increased leisure time and increased interest in outdoor recreational activities have generated a demand for maps of recreational areas for boaters, campers, and hikers. However, the control of map production is very uneven. There are not many commercial sources of maps, and these are easy to identify. Unfortunately, the largest producers of maps are government agencies. Though federal agency maps are reasonably well controlled, state and local agencies have little central control. Acquisition departments need to develop and maintain their own lists, if map collecting becomes a significant activity.

Some of the selection issues for maps and globes are:

1. Is the level of detail presented appropriate, or is it confusing given the scale of the map?

2. If a color map, are the colors aligned (registered) properly with the lines outlining an area?

3. Are the symbols clearly defined?

4. For world political maps, do the names on the map reflect the current or appropriate names of the countries represented?

5. Will the map or globe be able to withstand the type of use that the library anticipates it will receive?

There are a variety of professional journals that publish reviews to assist selection officers. *American Cartographer, Cartographic Journal* (British), *Canadian Cartographer, Geographical Review* (U. S.), and *Geographical Journal* (Britain) are but a few of the professional journals that publish evaluative reviews. The *Information Bulletin of the Western Association of Map Libraries* also publishes reviews and is a useful source for selection.

An interesting development is the growing use of computer-based (CD-ROM and tape) geographic and demographic data. Geographic information systems will open a new and challenging area of image collecting for many libraries. It will, however, require equipment that is capable of handling the images and color graphics these products contain.

One rather surprising void in public and academic libraries is sheet music. When both recorded music and books about music are available, why is it so difficult to secure the score? Cost is one explanation, but most other media cost more than books. Difficulty in handling (storage and checking in the parts) may be another aspect of the problem, but other media are also difficult to handle in some way. Libraries ought to reconsider this format; music publishers' catalogs are available, and there is frequently a community need.

Most academic music departments would like the library to collect full-size scores (also called complete, open, or performance scores) and miniature scores (pocket or study scores). Music accreditation groups expect to find scores on campus, and because of the problems in maintaining them and controlling their use, the library is the location of choice. One of the biggest factors limiting the growth of score collections, other than cost, is that scores are unbound and need special handling. Because they are and must remain unbound, pages easily get lost and damaged, usually requiring the purchase of another full score. Information about scores appears in the Music Library Association's *A Basic Music Library*[14] guide, and one can find reviews in *Notes*, *Music Review*, *Music and Letters*, and other journals.

Three-Dimensional Objects: Models, Realia, and Dioramas

Models have had a long history of use in education, especially in the sciences. Libraries have not been active collectors, in part because instructors want to keep the models in the laboratories and classrooms for regular use. Students do need to have access to these items for study at times when the labs and classrooms are unavailable. Perhaps computer-generated virtual reality models will provide a satisfactory three-dimensional alternative sometime in the future. For the present, one needs to consider physical models.

One factor limiting the collecting of models is their cost. Good models are expensive, and small institutions may be able to afford only one model for classroom use. Storage of models is another limiting factor because most are bulky and of variable sizes, making it difficult to store them on standard library shelving. Some questions to consider are:

1. Are objects of less than life size reproduced in an appropriate scale?

2. Is the scale sufficient to illustrate the necessary details? Would a two-dimensional representation work just as well?

3. When horizontal and vertical scales must be different, is the distortion so great as to create a false impression?

4. Are the colors accurate?

5. Are the objects durable enough to withstand the type of handling that they will receive?

Reviews of these materials are few and far between. *Booklist* occasionally reviews models. Three curriculum journals, *Curator*, *Instructor*, and *Curriculum Review* also publish model reviews. Libraries usually purchase models from educational supply houses.

Other Formats: Simulations, Games, and Self-Guided Instruction Formats, Software, Laser Products, and Mixed-Media Packages

The idea of buying educational games for library collections is relatively new in the United States, yet libraries in the Scandinavian countries have been lending recreational games for years. Libraries serving teacher education programs and, of course, school media centers usually engage in some game collection building. Teachers, rather than library staff, do almost all of the game selection. One exception is when the school media center staff selects games to assist in bibliographic instruction programs. Until more institutions enter the games market, there will be little incentive to improve bibliographic control. This means that a library wanting to buy games must develop its own file of sources and catalogs.

Simulation learning materials find their greatest use at opposite ends of the educational spectrum—primary and secondary schools and specialized postgraduate programs (e.g., government agencies, especially military, and advanced management training). Some simulations are computer-based, and others are paper-based. Today there is frequent discussion in both the popular and professional press about interactive media and learning. In many ways, this discussion is like the discussions about programmed (self-paced) learning that took place in the 1960s and 1970s. Perhaps interactive materials will succeed where programmed learning failed. Simulations are likely candidates for incorporation into the interactive marketplace. If that happens, perhaps prices will come down (good programs are expensive) and more reviews will appear in print. At present, *Simulations and Games, Simulation/Games for Learning*, and *Simgams* are the most consistent sources of review. Once in a great while *T.H.E., Creative Computing*, and *Man, Society & Technology* publish announcements of new products and, even more infrequently, reviews.

Laser technology and its place in the library and information field is only beginning to be explored. Promises of major developments made in the 1980s have not materialized. While laser disc video recordings offer higher quality picture with no wear to the disk, the format has not grown in popularity as predicted. One reason given is that the technology is playback only and, as long as the videocassette recorder can both play and record a reasonably good picture, buyers will not switch. As a storage unit of printed information, the laser hologram far surpasses microformats. A few technical and research libraries now have small collections of holograms, and most, if not all, of these have been produced in research and development units of companies or in engineering departments of universities. Again, the promise of the perfect storage solution has not materialized. Perhaps the hologram's greatest potential is in combination with other formats, rather than as a separate form. Currently, most of the holograms are scientific or artistic in character. There is nothing resembling a commercial market for holograms at the present time. Therefore, locating information about them is difficult. One source of information is the Museum of Holography in New York City.

Working models, specimen collections, and realia are primarily for the educational market. While a few items are useful for adults who are studying a subject independently, most public libraries acquire them only to supplement school library resources. A number of catalogs and guides to these items exist.

These are but a few of the considerations that must go into the selection of audiovisual formats. As there are few, if any, universal questions to raise when selecting books, so it is with audiovisuals. Selectors will develop their own selection criteria as they gain experience in the field.

Previewing

The actual selection process of audiovisual materials is often a group rather than an individual activity. This is particularly true of films and expensive video sets. To some degree, the cost of the material under consideration, rather than the usual collection development factors, drives the issue. In essence, making a mistake about a 20-minute sound, color, 16mm film or educational video has more serious economic consequences for the library budget than most single mistakes with a book, transparency, or sound recording. Educational videos cost $200-$500 per cassette; in a multiple cassette package, the total cost is substantial. The criteria for selection are highly subjective. Having multiple opinions about a prospective purchase helps avoid costly mistakes. In public libraries and school media centers, an audiovisual selection committee is the typical mechanism employed for securing multiple points of view. In academic libraries, often a single faculty member makes the recommendation, assuming the purchase will use departmental funds, or the head of the library's media program selects titles on the basis of reviews and a knowledge of instructional needs.

How does the audiovisual selection committee differ from the book selection committee? Audiovisual selection committees usually function as a true group decision-making body. Normally, the group previews audiovisual materials under consideration as a group. They view the material from beginning to end. (With book selection, the typical approach is for committee members to divide the items among group members and have individuals give oral reports about each item. Thus, only one member of the committee reviews the item completely.) A group discussion usually takes place after each screening, and each person expresses a reaction to and evaluation of the item. Everyone sees the same material, and group interaction ends in a decision to buy or not to buy. Sometimes, the product may be rerun several times, when there are strong differences in opinion.

An important difference in the two formats affects the selection process. This is the sequential nature of films and video formats. It is not possible to effectively skim a film as one does a book. One must view films and videos at their normal speed to get the proper impression. A 20-minute running time means 20 minutes of previewing time. Simple arithmetic indicates a group previewing 20-minute films could view only 24 films in an eight-hour work day. A book selection committee meeting would be a disaster if only 24 titles were discussed in eight hours. Realistically, no group can preview 24 titles in eight hours, as the figure does not provide for discussion time or for breaks. Finally, it is not feasible to expect people to view materials for four hours straight; they need a break. All of this means, more realistically, the group could preview 10-12 items per day.

Standardization of the evaluation process is probably far away in the media field, but several professional associations have attempted to bring some order to previewing by developing evaluation forms. Until a library decides to commit a major segment of its materials budget to audiovisual formats, librarians can save effort by using one of the association forms. Some of these forms include the UNESCO Film Appraisal Information form, the Educational Film Library Association form, the Council on International Nontheatrical Events, Inc. (CINE), film rating sheet, and the Educational Product Report evaluation form. (The latter form covers more than motion picture formats).

Not only do audiovisual formats cost more to buy, they also cost more to select. Combined, these two cost factors can be significant. Thus, one cannot conclude that, because a library does not have a collection of films or videos, it is reluctant to accept new formats. A significant difference exists between reluctance and the lack of money and qualified staff to select the newer formats. The only question is whether the library is using the monetary factor as an excuse to avoid trying out nonprint formats.

Audiovisual Selection Aids

Despite the desirability of previewing audiovisual materials, published evaluations (especially when combined with previewing) are important in this field. Each year, there is a little more progress toward bibliographic control of the field, including reviews of most formats. Perhaps when multiple published reviews of a majority of formats are available, there will be less and less need for hundreds of audiovisual librarians to spend hours and hours in preview screening rooms.

At this time, no comprehensive source for audiovisual materials similar to *Book Review Digest* or *Book Review Index* exists. *Media Digest* (National Film and Video Center) has developed into the best source for locating reviews in all formats.

Identifying potentially useful audiovisual materials also presents a problem. One series of indexes from the National Information Center for Educational Media (NICEM) focuses on educational materials; however, because NICEM employs a rather broad definition of education, the publications are useful to all types of libraries. With constant revisions to the various publications, several of NICEM's basic titles include

Index to Overhead Transparencies

Index to Educational Audio Tapes

Index to Educational Slides

Index to Educational Video Tapes

Index to Producers and Distributors

Other NICEM indexes exist, and the group also publishes several subject indexes for current topics, such as ecology and ethnic studies. Access Innovations, Inc., recently purchased the NICEM indexes and promises even more publications. With these tools, one can locate basic descriptive information (producer, title, source) and a brief annotation about the content and grade level. In this regard, the series is not unlike many other tools. That is, the indexes describe, rather than analyze or critique, the materials. Lacking critical evaluations, a media librarian must preview items. The NICEM series is, in many ways, the closest one can come to an audiovisual equivalent of *Books in Print*. The NICEM indexes are accessible online through DIALOG under the database file name AV-ON-LINE.

Another service, Educational Media Catalogs on Microfiche (EMCOM), also provides a form of an in-print list. It includes more than 100 microfiche that contain a large number of audiovisual distributors' catalogs. It is probably as comprehensive a source as any, with updates every six months. Because access is by vendor, one has to spend more time searching for material about a topic or in a format than with the NICEM indexes. Although an expensive service, it does relieve the library of having to file and keep up to date hundreds of vendor catalogs.

Although the preceding list of sources provides a general overview, there is a slight emphasis on films. One reason for this is historical. After microforms and phonograph records, motion picture films and videos are the most commonly held audiovisual forms in libraries.

Also, 16mm films and educational videos cost significantly more than either of the other two formats, making previewing all the more important. Because of film's popularity, cost, and longer history of use, film review and evaluation have had more time to become established. Increased popularity of other formats will, in time, make it economically feasible to publish journals covering other audiovisual formats.

Ordering Audiovisual Materials

For all practical purposes, ordering materials in the formats discussed in this chapter is like ordering books and serials, with a few exceptions. One difference is libraries place most of the orders directly with the producer, because there are no general audiovisual jobbers as there are for books and serials. Some book jobbers, such as Baker & Taylor, handle some of the most widely collected formats, for example, videos and audiotapes, but they do not handle the full range of audiovisual materials. Another difference is the need to secure preview copies.

There is a major difference between review copies of books and preview copies of other media. With books, if the purchaser likes what he or she sees, the library keeps it, pays the invoice, and perhaps orders multiple copies at the same time. With audiovisual materials, for a number of reasons (risk of loss, damage, and so forth), the library requests preview copies from the supplier, views the copy, and then generally returns the item. (Some producers now send a new copy and expect the library to keep the copy if it decides to buy the item. Other producers charge for previewing but deduct the charge from the purchase price. A few film vendors ship an approval copy with a 10 percent discount if the library buys the film.) One must request the preview copy well in advance of the preview date. Normally, a librarian writes to the producer or supplier asking for preview copies of certain titles and listing a number of alternative dates. This becomes an issue when previewing with a group, which may cause scheduling problems. One also must know when specific items will be available for previewing. A preview file thus becomes a very important aid in the selection process; it contains a listing of each title requested, the dates requested, scheduled preview dates, and the result of the preview.

One should keep in mind several other factors for previewing as well. A preview copy probably has had some prior use; therefore, the quality will not be as high as that of a new copy. If one can determine from the supplier how often the item went out for previewing, it is possible to gain insight into the durability of the product. In assessing this information (assuming one can get it), the librarian must remember that the preview copy's use was by individuals who know how to properly handle the material (unlike many library users).

After deciding to buy the previewed item, the library returns the preview copy. Upon receiving the new print, a staff member should view the item to be certain it is 1) a new print, 2) the item the library ordered, and 3) technically sound (checking for breaks, sound quality, and quality of processing). Checking for technical soundness upon receipt should be standard procedure for all audiovisual items, not just for previewed items. Generally, other media are not mass produced in the same manner as are books. Many are produced on demand, that is, in response to orders. The producer has several preview copies and a master copy; when an order arrives, the producer uses the master copy to produce a new print.

With some formats, there may be another decision to make: to buy or rent. Normally, the rental fee is 10 percent of the list price. If there are doubts about the level of demand, it may be best to rent a copy. (Ten uses in five years would be more than enough to justify buying the item.) Remember, when calculating the cost, that it will be necessary to include staff time for preparing rental forms, as well as time for mailing and handling activities. In many cases, with film, video, and software, the library is not buying an item in the same sense that it purchases books and serials. Often, the library must sign an agreement that outlines what the library may or may not do with the item. These agreements cover duplication, resale, and, in some cases, place restrictions on where performances are possible. Vendors do enforce these agreements, which are legal contracts, so the librarian must understand what he or she is signing. If something is not clear, or a clause needs modification, the librarian should discuss it with the vendor and the library's legal counsel before signing.

Equipment Issues in Selecting Audiovisual Materials

Part of the expense of developing an audiovisual collection lies in buying and maintaining the equipment required to use the various formats acquired. Increasing standardization in equipment means that the problem of compatibility is not as great as it once was, but newer formats always go through an early stage in which there are competing and incompatible lines of equipment. In those cases in which the library *must* buy a format before standardization has occurred, the librarian should select the line of equipment that has the greatest number of available titles. Do not give a great deal of credence to sales representatives' claims; look at what is, not what may be.

Over the years, companies have offered several video formats (tapes, cassettes, disks). The BETA and VHS cassette systems (incompatible with one another) existed for the home market. Now BETA is no longer a commercial choice, although many individuals still have units at home and think it was the better format. A newer system, the RCA disk system, appeared and failed. Still other disk technologies are being promoted for home and institutional use. From a technical point of view, the disk systems are better than cassettes. How long will the cassette last as a major home video system? No one knows, but many public libraries have heavy investments in videocassettes.

The foregoing discussion highlights two points: 1) standardization takes considerable time to accomplish (assuming it is possible); and 2) the media field is always changing. These two factors combine to make equipment buying expensive and repetitive. To some extent, these factors prevent libraries from building collections.

Several annual guides to equipment are available:

The Audio-Visual Equipment Directory (National Audio-Visual Association, 1953-) is a detailed guide to equipment. Whenever possible, descriptions include information about technical details, operation, and price, as well as accompanying photographs of each piece of equipment. The list is as comprehensive as possible, but it does depend on manufacturers and distributors to supply the information, in much the same manner as *Publishers' Trade List Annual*. The content is descriptive, not evaluative.

EPIE Gram: Equipment (Educational Products Information Exchange, 1967-) provides monthly assessments of materials and equipment. It provides technical data on equipment. Reviews are similar to other review sources but with a stronger technical emphasis.

Library Technology Reports (American Library Association) provides, from time to time, useful evaluations of equipment for the media library (video recorders, computers, and microform equipment have been evaluated). It also publishes articles about the use of a specific type of equipment, as well as testing and evaluation information. Unfortunately, the *LTR* program is not well supported, so it makes no attempt to be comprehensive or to update information previously published.

Consumer information about VCRs, slide projectors, and phonograph record and tape players and recorders is available in popular magazines. The major drawback to these sources is that the equipment is evaluated for home or personal use, rather than institutional use. Institutional use requires the same ease of operation as home use; however, the equipment must be much more durable and able to withstand misuse. Most popular magazines do not examine durability in this light.

All of this means that the selector can do his or her homework in the above sources, and perhaps visit a showroom or convention to examine the equipment and see it demonstrated. However, the final decision is the selector's. Before signing a purchase order for the equipment, any prospective buyer should spend some time and effort in locating a library or educational institution that already has the equipment. Talking with individuals who have used equipment on a daily basis is the best insurance against getting equipment that is continually breaking down. One should find out how easy or how difficult it is to get parts when the unit malfunctions. Can local technicians repair the unit, or is it necessary to return it to the manufacturer? If informants say that, in their experience, the equipment has proved to be durable, reliable, and easy to maintain, it may be what the library needs. If they say less than that, perhaps more searching will save time and trouble in the long run.

Summary

Building a media collection for the library is a time-consuming and expensive undertaking. However, that does not mean it is not worth doing. Previewing and seeking published evaluations of hardware and software do take time. Beyond the cost in time is the cost of the equipment and software. Also, new formats seem to appear every day, threatening to make existing formats obsolete. On the other hand, photography (still and motion), radio, and television have not made the book or any other format obsolete, despite pronouncements of the forthcoming demise of this or that medium. Each new format is capable of doing certain things that no other format can do, but each also has its limitations, and as a result, they supplement rather than replace each other. It is clear there are various preferences in seeking and enjoying information. If the library is to be responsive to the community, it must build a collection of materials that reflects that community's various interests and tastes.

Notes

[1]*Tozzer Library: Author/Subject Catalogs*, 2d ed. Harvard University, Peabody Museum of Archaeology and Ethnology, Tozzer Library (Boston: G. K. Hall, 1988).

[2]Michael Hedges, "Managing an Integrated Video Collection," *Wilson Library Bulletin* 67 (June 1993): 33.

[3]Jean Thibodeaux Kreamer, "Video and Libraries: Introduction," *Wilson Library Bulletin* 67 (June 1993): 31.

[4]Lillian Gerhardt, "Sharpening the AV Focus," *School Library Journal* 37 (April 1991): 4.

[5]Ellen Miller and Timothy Hallahan, eds. *Media Guide for Lawyers* (Owings Mills, MD: National Law Publishing, 1982).

[6]*Law Books and Serials in Print* (New York: R. R. Bowker, 1992).

[7]*Legal Video Review* (Boston: Lawrence R. Cohen Media Library, 1985-).

[8]*Media Profiles: The Health Sciences* (Hoboken, NJ: Olympic Media Information, 1983-).

[9]*Bowker's Complete Video Directory* (New York: R. R. Bowker, 1992).

[10]*Video Source Book* (Syosset, NY: National Video Clearinghouse, 1979-).

[11]Consortium of University Film Centers and R.R. Bowker, *Educational Film and Video Locator* (New York: R. R. Bowker, 1990).

[12]*Film and Video Finder* (Albuquerque, NM: Access Innovations, 1987).

[13]Elizabeth Devereaux, "Audiobooks on CD: Tentative Steps Forward," *Publishers Weekly* 238 (March 1, 1993): 20.

[14]Music Library Association, Committee on Basic Music Collections, *A Basic Music Library* (Chicago: American Library Association, 1983).

Further Reading

General

Annicharies, M. "Playing for Time: Delicate Art of Abridging Audio Books." *Library Journal* 117 (November 15, 1992): 41-44.

Dickinson, G. K. *Selection and Evaluation of Electronic Resources*. Englewood, CO: Libraries Unlimited, 1993.

Ellison, J. W., and P. A. Coty, eds. *Nonbook Media: Collection Management and User Services*. Chicago: American Library Association, 1987.

Hoffert, B. "Books into Bytes." *Library Journal* 117 (September 1, 1992): 130-35.

Kaye, S., and B. Baxter. "Breaking the Sound Barrier." *Library Journal* 119 (May 15, 1994): 34-36.

Langstaff, M. "Selling the New Media." *Publishers Weekly* 238 (May 10, 1993): 42-45.

"Microform Reader/Printers for Libraries." *Library Technology Reports* 27 (July/August 1991): 407-546.

Robinson, S. "Copyright or Wrong: The Public Performance Dilemma." *Wilson Library Bulletin* 66 (April 1992): 76-77.

Rorick, W. C. "Discometrics: A System for Acquiring Scores and Sound Recordings." *Library Journal* 112 (November 15, 1987): 45-47.

Salce, J. "Video Distribution: The Maze Made Manageable." *Library Journal* 115 (July 1990): 42-43.

Scholtz, J. C. *Developing and Maintaining Video Collections in Libraries.* Santa Barbara, CA: ABC-Clio Press, 1989.

Stokell, A., and A. H. Thompson. "In the Crystal Ball." *Audiovisual Librarian* 20 (February 1994): 36-41.

Vlcek, C. W., and R. V. Wiman. *Managing Media Services.* Englewood CO: Libraries Unlimited, 1989.

Zimmerman, B. "The Tangle of Multimedia Rights." *Publishers Weekly* 238 (November 22, 1991): 17-19.

Academic

Bierman, E. G. "Beyond Print: Object Collections in Academic Libraries." *Collection Building* 10, nos. 1/2 (1989): 7-11.

Breen, T. H. "Keeping Pace with the Past." *Microform Review* 10 (Spring 1991): 57-60.

Briody, E. "Microforms: A Brief Narrative of Primary Research in a Secondary Place." *Microform Review* 29 (Spring 1991): 61-66.

Butchart, I. "Management of Collections of Non-print Materials." In *Collection Management in Academic Libraries,* edited by C. Jenkins and M. Morely. Brookfield, VT: Gower, 1991.

"College and University Media Centers News & Views." *Sightlines* 22 (Fall 1989): 4-6.

Cullen, P. "Acquisition of AV Materials in a Higher Educational Institution." *Audiovisual Librarian* 17 (August 1991): 153-57.

Dick, J. "Documentary Delivery." *Library Journal* 119 (May 15, 1994): 38-40.

Renwick, K. "Acquiring A/V in the Academic Arena." *Audiovisual Librarian* 17 (May 1991): 14-18.

Rooker, J. "Federal Copyright Law: How It Affects Academic Video Services." *Indiana Media Journal* 14 (Winter 1992): 23-25.

Thompson, A. H. "University Libraries and Multimedia Development." *Audiovisual Librarian* 15 (November 1989): 203-5.

Tomczyk, C. B. "Academic Media Selection." In *Operations Handbook for Small Academic Libraries*, edited by G. B. McCabe, 269-76. Greenwich, CT: Greenwood Press, 1989.

Public

Ahmad, N. "Collection Development Tools for Media Centres." *Public Library Quarterly* 11, no. 4 (1991): 29-41.

Doran, M. "Libraries or Video Shops? The Need for an Acquisition Policy." *Audiovisual Librarian* 17 (August 1991): 158-61.

Hoppe, D. "Paradise Lost? A Brief History of Alternative Media in Public Libraries." *Wilson Library Bulletin* 68 (March 1994): 26-30.

Kay, K. "Satellite Television and the Public Library." *Audiovisual Librarian* 17 (November 1991): 212-16.

Koepp, D. P. "Map Collections in Public Libraries: A Brighter Future." *Wilson Library Bulletin* 60 (October 1985): 28-32.

Kreamer, J. T. "The Format War." *Wilson Library Bulletin* 67 (November 1992): 38-40.

Palmer, J. B. *KLIATT Audiobook Guide*. Englewood, CO: Libraries Unlimited, 1994.

Sager, D. J. "Evolution of Public Library Audiovisual Services." *Public Libraries* 31 (September/October 1992): 263-69.

Thibodeaux, A. "Audiovisual Selection." *Book Report* 10 (November/December 1991): 40.

Wund, B. "Talking Books." *Small Press* 10 (Spring 1992): 16-17.

School

Considine, D., and G. E. Haley. *Visual Messages: Integrating Imagery into Instruction*. Englewood CO: Libraries Unlimited, 1992.

Dewing, M. *Beyond TV: Activities for Using Video with Children*. Santa Barbara, CA: ABC-Clio, 1992.

Emmens, C. A. *Children's Media Market Place*. 2d ed. New York: Neal-Schuman, 1982.

Kerman, M. "Making Friends with Audiovisuals." *Book Report* 10 (September/October 1991): 16-17.

Knirk, F. G. "New Technology Considerations for Media Facilities." *School Library Media Quarterly* 20 (Summer 1992): 205-10.

Sales, G. C. "Computer Cache: Videodiscs: An Exciting Resource in School Media Centers." *School Library Media Activities Monthly* 8 (December 1991): 255-75.

School Library Media Annual. Englewood, CO: Libraries Unlimited, 1983- .

Triche, C. "Video and Libraries: Video in the School." *Wilson Library Bulletin* 67 (June 1993): 39-40.

Warden, J. M. "Making Tough Decisions About All Those Video Programs." *Ohio Media Spectrum* 43 (Fall 1991): 36-39.

Weaver, C. K. "Captivate the MTV Generation." *School Library Journal* 38 (April 1991): 50.

Special

Bixler, L. S. V. "Evaluation of Criteria for Weeding Non-Print Materials in Health Sciences Libraries." Master's Thesis, Texas Women's University, 1991.

McCormack, T. E. "Media Equipment Selection Methods for Law Libraries." *Law Library Journal* 83 (Spring 1991): 283-88.

———. "Video Technology in the Law Library." *Legal Reference Service Quarterly* 11, nos. 1/2 (1991): 5-37.

Miller, E. J. "Video Collection: Selection and Evaluation." *Law Library Journal* 85 (Summer 1993): 591-98.

Rydeskey, M. M. "Audiovisual Media: Special Library Asset or Bane?" In *Special Librarianship,* edited by E. B. Jackson, 521-29. Metuchen, NJ: Scarecrow Press, 1980.

Singarella, T., et al. "Videodisc Technology Trends in Academic Health Sciences Libraries." *Bulletin of Medical Library Association* 79 (April 1991): 59-67.

Wagers, R. "Online Sources of Competitive Intelligence." *Database* 9 (June 1986): 28-38.

Walters, S. G. "Playing Now at the Law Library." *Legal Reference Service Quarterly* 10, nos. 1/2 (1990): 29-39.

IO
Electronic Materials

Why have a separate chapter on electronic formats? Are they not merely another type of storage medium, like microforms? They are, indeed, another storage format in one sense, because digitized data does allow for compact storage of large quantities of information. Digital formats also allow for data manipulation in ways that are not cost-effective in other formats. Further, the electronic environment allows both free-text and Boolean searching. Downloading information from electronic resources to a user's computer and being able to cut, paste, move, add, and delete as much as desired. Such capabilities make electronic information the preferred information format for many users.

Electronic formats will cause libraries and information centers to concentrate their attention on overall operations in a way never before required. To some degree, it may be a question of the survival of our field. Electronic information producers can deliver the product directly to the user at home or in the office, and increasingly, they are doing so. Proper planning, realistic goals, and intelligent reorganization of operations will ensure libraries an expanding role in the information transfer process in the electronic age.

Electronic delivery of information requires delivery platforms, equipment, software, substantial user support, and time to assess the various services and products that producers offer. Few users have the time, energy, inclination, or funds to handle all these activities effectively. Libraries can and should undertake these tasks. If we do not, someone else will.

To focus discussion and thinking about this important area of information service, this chapter brings together ideas, concepts, and issues related to electronic information collection building that appear in various sections of this book. The chapter's structure follows the basic steps of collection development: background and needs assessment, policy, selection, acquisitions, evaluation, and other issues.

Background and Needs Assessment

The electronic environment creates several dichotomies for libraries and information centers: print versus electronic; ownership versus access; user versus institutional need; free versus fee; and gatekeeper versus user selection. It is not a matter of either/or, rather it is a matter of determining the proper local mix. Clearly, one cannot make the necessary judgments about these issues without knowing the local users, what information they want and need, how and where they use the information, and what monetary and equipment resources are available.

Print and electronic information sources are both complementary and competitive. Users with an interest in historical information and data certainly will require, in most cases, collections of older print material. Few of the electronic products or services provide pre-1970s information, such as back files of periodicals or indexing information. This will change in time, but at the moment recent information is in highest demand, and it is on the highest demand areas that commercial providers focus. One obvious advantage of print sources is they do not malfunction, and one can use them in a variety of locations without having to consider power, network connections, and similar technical issues. Electronic sources have a clear advantage in terms of locating and manipulating information. In any case, it is imperative to have an understanding of the service community's preferences about print and electronic information.

Traditionally, libraries and information centers depended on an ownership of materials model as the primary means of meeting customer information needs. Interlibrary loans (ILL) for books and photocopies of journal articles more or less filled any gaps between the local collections and local needs. Interlibrary loan adheres to the ownership of materials model in that it requires other libraries to own the loaned material. Customers check out ILL materials from their home library and return the materials to the local library when finished; the local library then ships the materials back to the lending source. For all practical purposes, this system operates as if the local library owned the items. Another form of ownership is photocopied ILL journal articles that the user gets to keep. The ILL process is slow, but it preserves the sense of ownership.

Taking the ownership of materials model to an extreme, research libraries once attempted to acquire everything their service community actually did or might need: the goals were impossible to achieve and the attempt was costly. Even in a cooperative collection environment, it was not possible for libraries to own everything their customers wanted or might conceivably want.

Electronic materials and methods of information dissemination present the opportunity for libraries and information centers to provide access to more resources than they can realistically expect to acquire and house. Access can be diverted to a user's home or workplace, allowing end users to make independent choices about what they want, from what source, and how quickly. Access may be a more cost-effective option for the library or information center, even if the organization pays for all searches and documents ordered. (Cost issues are covered later in this chapter.)

User needs have always been the foundation on which libraries and information centers built their collections. Though user needs remain the basis of electronic collection development, institutional budget requirements play a greater role in the electronic environment than in the print environment. Certainly the budget issue was and is a factor in print collections (see chapter 13), but money becomes a central factor for electronic materials collection development. With print materials, after materials are acquired and in the collection, the institution incurs no additional costs based on the number of times each item is used. With many electronic materials, there are incremental costs. On the low end, these costs include replenishing paper and ink cartridges as users print out page after page of citations, abstracts, or full-text documents. Downloading data onto disk or directly to another computer imposes yet another expense, and it may pose problems for some users. Not all patrons can download material, either because they do not know how or because they do not own a computer. (Too often, when people discuss electronic information or technology, they forget about inner-city and rural poor who cannot afford computers or the fees some service centers charge for access.) Single-user licenses cost less than multiple-user fees, and per-page royalty charges can quickly mount. Again, there must be an understanding of the local situation to balance individual information needs against institutional cost control needs.

The balancing of individual and institutional needs raises the issue of free versus fee services. There is the long-standing tradition of free library service. Though maintaining this tradition is the goal of many information professionals, it has been some time since all services were free. Charging for services began with charging for photocopying, and the practice has expanded steadily over the years. In the electronic environment, it is easy to associate service costs with individual customers, and there are a greater variety of costs (for example, charges for per-page or per-screen viewing, connect time, printing, or copyright or royalties). Because it is easier to associate costs with an individual in the electronic environment than it is in the print environment, it is possible to pass the charges on to the customer. To some degree, the new costs are not new, they were hidden or too time-consuming to track in the print world. Again, how far one goes in charging fees depends on the local situation and service community. Libraries supporting educational programs are more likely to absorb the costs for electronic information that directly supports instruction and pass on charges for noninstructional uses. Some institutions, like Loyola Marymount University, have a sliding scale, allowing for a base level of free access and some form of cost sharing as the individual's use increases. Public libraries must consider the economic differences in the community with the goal of assuring that those who cannot afford to pay the fees do not become information-poor. Special libraries may pass costs to project teams or departments to answer an organization's desire to track actual operating costs of various units; in other situations, the costs are considered overhead and are not assigned to any unit other than the information center.

The roles of the library, computing services, telecommunication services, and the customer in electronic information transfer is a topic of debate in electronic discussion groups or conferences, as well as in the literature and in the institution. Who has primary responsibility? If shared, how is it shared? Who decides what will be available? Who supports and maintains the service(s)? None of these questions, nor many related ones, have clear answers. We are in the process of developing models based on experience. Efforts to merge the various institutional players have not proven successful. However, as noted in chapter 1, it is clear that text, numeric, voice, and image data technologies are becoming integrated and, at some point, the institution must come to grips with the need to coordinate the various activities.

One aspect of the debate is, Should there be preselection of electronic materials? In preselection, the library or information center plays the role of gatekeeper, rather than letting users search independently. Although the terms used in the debate are *electronic gophers, servers,* and *gatekeepers,* the fundamental issue is as old as libraries and collection development. Years ago, a favorite examination question in collection development courses was, Is collection development selection or censorship? On one side are those who believe no one should predetermine what resources best fit the organization's mission and profile. Their position is, let the user find what she or he needs without preselection by someone else. The opposite view is that preselection and guidance are in the best interests of both the users and the organization. As in the past, libraries, information centers, and organizations cannot provide access to everything. Thus, choices are inevitable; someone or some group must function as a gate-keeper or, at least, as a cost controller (that is, an information manager). Refusing to perform the gatekeeper function is akin to putting a person in the middle of a multimillion volume storehouse with only a floor plan that is keyed to broad classification groupings and saying to this person, "You are on your own." That will waste not only the individual's time, but also the institution's resources. In a sense, this view is a return to the research library philosophy of the 1950s, 1960s, and early 1970s: "Get everything possible, just in case." A gatekeeper who points the way to potentially useful materials, perhaps by adding pointers to the local gopher, aids the user in the long run and maximizes the benefit of the institution's funding for information services. When the library or information center provides such assistance, it does not deny the user access to other electronic resources available through other services, such as the Internet (assuming the individual has network access and the ability to explore it effectively). The case for some assistance and evaluation is summed up in the following:

> Still in its infancy—with only a hint of its future richness—networked information is currently anarchic and pretty much 'use at your own risk.' One writer characterized Internet as 'awash with information, both useful and banal.' Data files are incomplete and unverified, there is little or no documentation or support, it is difficult to pin down author responsibility, and there are few evaluative resources.[1]

One advantage of electronic collection building, compared with building print collections, is the more effective tracking of the person using the information and what resources she or he used that one can achieve with electronic materials. (Although state-of-the-art online circulation systems allow one to easily get similar information about circulated items, for in-house use, the best one can do is track the items used, not who used them.) Many of the better commercial electronic products have management report software that allows one to learn how and when the users accessed the material. One gets more accurate and complete data with less effort in the electronic environment. It is up to librarians to make effective use of the data to provide the right information at the right time at the right cost.

Electronic Collection Policy

There should be a single collection development policy statement that incorporates electronic materials. Today, it is more likely that a library will have a separate electronic policy that, in time, will become part of the overall collection policy. It is currently easier to address electronic materials without becoming caught up in reviewing the entire policy statement. Also, if the emphasis is on access rather than ownership, many of the print collection policy concerns do not apply (for example, concerns about space or deselection). A starting point for developing a selection policy for electronic materials is the Association for Library Collections and Technical Services acquisition guide.[2]

Loyola Marymount University's (LMU) policy can be found in figure 10.1 (pages 265-71). LMU's policy is similar to those of other libraries; it is not intended to represent a model statement but simply provides an example of the issues one should address.

Formats

One aspect of the collection development policy that does apply to both print and electronic information is determining what formats to collect or make available. For most libraries, this means acquiring one or more of five types of electronic material: full text, numeric data, bibliographic data, software, and image data. Educational institution libraries also collect curricula software or courseware developed in-house.

Of the five main types of electronic resources, at present *full text* is least common. Full text is replete with challenges and options. Presently, some full text is available only online, for example, electronic journals. There were an estimated 127 electronic journals in mid 1994. These so-called journals present a decision point: the library or organization must decide how to provide access, that is, through the library or other gatekeeper or gateway or through direct access. Certainly the technical, legal, and financial issues addressed later in this chapter must be considered, but collection development issues are easily dealt with.

Full-text material comes in three formats: online, CD-ROM, and print. In some cases, there are cost differences when there is both a print and electronic format available. The vendor or publisher frequently has one price for the print version and a different price for the electronic version. If one orders just the electronic version, there is a third price, roughly equal to the sum of the print and electronic rates. An advantage to having both formats occurs during, for example, a power outage when users still have access to the print version.

Text continues on page 272.

Policy for Electronic Resources Management
Charles Von der Ahe Library,
Loyola Marymount University
(DRAFT) April 1994

I. **Role of the Library**
The Von der Ahe Library has a central, established role ". . . to provide information materials and services that will assist the University in achieving its educational and service goals." (Charles Von der Ahe Library, *Mission and Goals*, December 17, 1992.) The Library's top priorities in its mission are: curriculum related materials and services; faculty research materials and services; and administrative support materials and services. The Collection Development Librarian, with contributions from Reference, Systems, and other interested parties, is responsible for recommending collection policy to the University Library administration and coordinating collection development activities in the Library.

II. **Purpose of This Policy**
The Library collects or provides access to appropriate materials in print and nonprint media. Currently electronic formats present libraries with management issues that more traditional formats do not. They may require additional hardware and software to operate or to access. Because these concerns complicate the selection and the accessibility of such materials within the Library, a policy specifically for electronic formats is needed.
This "Policy for Electronic Resources Management" provides context and guidelines for the Library in the selection, acquisition, provision of access to, and maintenance of electronic resources. It does not address specific procedural issues such as funding options or where a particular resource will be located.

III. **Relationships with Related Groups**
Providing access to electronic resources may involve funding, equipment, data storage, location, and remote access decisions affecting many units both within the Library and outside of it. These include the Computer Center, departmental offices, dorm rooms, and other libraries outside the University. The Library seeks to work cooperatively with the above and other concerned groups on such issues as they arise.

IV. **Scope of This Policy**
A. This policy addresses the selection and acquisition of the following types of electronic materials:

  1. *Numeric data files*—data gathering, statistical analysis, numeric and mathematical programs, e.g., SPSS (Statistical Package for the Social Sciences), and ICPSR (Inter-university Consortium for Political and Social Research); statistical compendia, e.g., U.S. Census.

  2. *Textual files*—full texts of encyclopedias, dictionaries, electronic journals, literary texts.

  3. *Bibliographic files*—files with information arranged mainly in fixed fields but can also have free text, e.g., Wilson indexes, ABI Inform, PsycLit, etc.

  4. *Graphic and multimedia files*—map and art databases.

Fig. 10.1 continues on page 266.

B. The Library will consider the purchase of other types of electronic resources as they are developed, in light of their relevance and contribution to the Library's mission.

C. This policy does not cover general purpose applications software such as authoring programs, gateway programs, reference management programs, and productivity programs, which are, or may become, the function of LMUNet; or integrated library management programs (e.g., Innovative).

V. Selection and Acquisition Responsibilities of the Library

A. General Guidelines

1. The Library will select, fund, and make available appropriate electronic resources.

2. The Library will provide monies from its materials budget for the purchase of electronic materials meeting the criteria mentioned later in this document.

3. The Faculty, with collaboration of the Subject Bibliographers, will have the primary responsibility for identifying, selecting, and funding through individual subject funds, the electronic resources they wish to add to the library collection.

4. The Subject Bibliographers will have the primary responsibility for negotiating and coordinating funding for applications programs needed to operate specific electronic resources the Faculty have selected.

5. Electronic resources of campus-wide utility, such as the Wilson databases, may be purchased with general reference funds. The Reference Department will review such recommendations.

6. The fundamental and primary criteria used for measuring the appropriateness of adding a particular electronic resource to the Library's collection will not differ essentially from those criteria used to measure books or any other format. These primary criteria are:

   a. The resource contributes to the Library's mission of providing support for instruction and research.

   b. There is demonstrated demand or a potential audience for the resource.

7. The public services support required to make a resource available should be given early consideration in the selection process. Reference librarians should consult with staff of other library departments that may be affected. Aspects of public services support to be considered are:

   a. The need for staff and user training.

   b. The availability and usefulness of manuals, guides, and tutorials from the producer.

   c. The ease of production of a brief guide, if necessary, by Reference staff.

B. Selection Criteria

1. Policy Concerns

   a. Materials in electronic format should reflect the library's own collection development and acquisitions policies.

   b. The resource offers some value-added enhancement to make it preferable over, or a significant addition to, other print or non-print equivalents. Examples of such enhancements include wider access and greater flexibility in searching.

   c. If the item is an electronic version of a resource in another format, it contains or covers the equivalent information to the extent appropriate and desirable.

   d. User and programmatic needs are a prime consideration. Special attention is given to products that provide coverage of under represented or high-priority subject areas.

   e. Selection procedures and criteria are evaluated and revised regularly.

   f. Before selection, the reputation of the publisher and producer is investigated to make sure of reliability and responsiveness to problems. A list of current customers of the publishers is consulted to verify customer satisfaction.

   g. If currency is important, the resource is updated often enough to be useful.

   h. Reviews are used to assess data's comprehensiveness, scope, and indexing accuracy.

   i. The printed editions of the electronic counterpart will be kept if exact duplication of coverage is not made.

   j. Evaluate the durability of the medium and what the cost-benefit trade off will be between immediate usefulness and potential degradation of electronic data.

   k. The subject area and intellectual level shall be suitable to the clientele of the library.

2. Service or Vendor Concerns

   a. The selection criteria conform with the institution's general plans for establishing a computerized information environment.

   b. Public service staffing and training levels are evaluated in light of the additional information services available to patrons.

   c. The user documentation should be accurate, easy to use, comprehensive, cost-effective, and in convenient locations.

   d. The impact of current library staffing and training, such as cataloging and processing subscriptions in different formats, is assessed.

   e. Vendor reliability and business record indicate continued support for the product via updates or new versions.

   f. Vendor-produced documentation is comprehensive and clearly written.

Fig. 10.1 continues on page 268.

     g. Customer support is available from the vendor during library working hours.

     h. A trial period is available for examining the utility and value of the resource before a final commitment is made with the vendor.

3. Technical Concerns

     a. It is absolutely necessary to have technical support and maintenance of the product.

     b. Software and hardware should be compatible with existing systems in the library and with the systems used by the University so that future networking can be possible.

     c. The evaluation of software focuses on issues that include menu-driven versus command-driven features, override capability in the program's command structure, short initial learning curve, security (tampering and viruses), compatibility with existing hardware and software media.

     d. Search capabilities will include reasonable response time and availability of the following:

> the interruption of search processing
> Boolean searches using logical operators
> phrase searching
> truncating, wild card, or stem searching features
> nesting
> stored searches for reuse
> purging of stored searches
> searching limited by language
> simultaneous searching of all fields
> sorting and displaying of sets
> printing of multiple records and of selected records
> customized formats for printing
> downloading to floppy disk and DBMS
> direct transfer of a search to the online version of the database

     e. Ease of use of the product includes the following:

> introductory screens
> on-screen tutorials
> prompts and menus
> ease of exiting from one point in a search to another, and from the database
> availability of function-specific help
> availability of context-specific on-screen help

f. Hardware-related concerns include reliability, maintenance, compatibility with peripherals, flexibility for other uses or networking, security from theft and tampering. Ascertain that the desired information can be run on currently available computers. Check for:

overall system compatibility; some products will not run on all types of computers

hardware configuration—memory, disk storage, processor speed, etc.

need for software platforms to interface with the data

compatibility of current CD-ROM drives

growth of the database; it may be necessary to add more disk storage, memory, CD-ROM drives

4. Cost Concerns

a. Short-term preservation benefits of optical disc technology are apparent.

b. If print sources or other formats are discontinued, there may be savings. Package discounts are sometimes available when retaining the subscription to the paper or alternate format.

c. If there are cost differentials between online and CD-ROM options, the more cost-effective one is chosen.

d. Purchase or lease options needs are studied to determine the most cost-effective option.

e. Plans for any additional costs for future updates or upgrades are made at the time of the original purchase. This may include additional start-up and maintenance costs that are not reflected in the invoice for the information product. These could include site preparation and hardware shipping and installation.

f. The shelf life of the product's storage medium is weighed against replacement costs.

g. Differences are explored between the availability of vendor or publisher discounts for hardware and software packages (bundles) associated with the product.

h. The following cost requirements are observed:

space for the new equipment and additional electrical and telecommunications wiring

costs for start-up or site preparation

more staff time for technical and training support

costs for supplies such as tables, chairs, printers, paper, ribbons

Fig. 10.1 continues on page 270.

5. Local Needs

   a. Identify which subject areas have a demonstrated need for specific information products in electronic format.

   b. Identify patron and staff groups that will benefit the most from the use of these products.

   c. Make sure the ease of use and depth of information levels are appropriate for the intended user group.

   d. Compare the product under consideration with the scope and cost of other resources, electronic or not, currently available.

   e. Decide whether the new electronic sources go to reference or similar noncirculating collections or to the stacks.

   f. Specify the conditions and procedures used to circulate this material.

   g. Consider the practical consequences of making the selection, such as cancellation of other titles or special equipment needs that may require funding.

   h. The condition of circulation copies of electronic information is assessed for damage or software viruses when the material is returned.

VI. Implementation Responsibilities of the Library

A. The library will comply with the copyright law and promote compliance of the law among its users.

B. The library will optimize access to and utility of electronic resources through the following activities:

   1. Bibliographic control through the cataloging or inventorying of each resource.

   2. Storage for the item, if needed.

   3. Appropriate circulation procedures.

   4. The purchase, maintenance, preparation, and loading of software and hardware necessary to use the resource.

   5. Appropriate staff support and training.

   6. Appropriate user support and training.

C. The library will negotiate and comply with vendor licensing agreements.

   1. In general, it is the responsibility of the Database Coordinator to negotiate and sign licensing agreements. The office of the Coordinator will maintain a file containing copies of all licensing agreements.

   2. Final responsibility for compliance with licensing agreements and day-to-day oversight rests with the Database Coordinator.

   3. The lease will clearly delineate the terms of ownership or lease agreements, including a description of what back files are acquired, the ownership of these back files, how often updates are to be received, and the disposition of superseded files.

4. All licensing, use, or copyright restrictions are indicated so as not to interfere with rights reserved by the publisher.

5. If hardware is included in the purchase, the agreement will state whether the machinery is leased or purchased, whether the seller or buyer is responsible for maintenance, and the terms of service.

6. Product warranties are clearly stated and understood.

7. Before entering into any license agreement, check that local protocols are properly followed to ensure the legality of the contract. Items to be noted are:

   a. Restrictions on the use of the data in regard to the copying, printing, or downloading from the database.

   b. Restrictions on the number of simultaneous users, or the use of the product in local area networks (LAN) or wide area networks (WAN).

   c. Restrictions on the method of access, such as dial-access or Internet.

   d. Conversion of the database to other media.

   e. Limits on use to internal or noncommercial activities.

   f. Limits on the ability to transfer, resell, or reassign the product.

   g. For software, limiting the program to use on one machine by one user at a time.

   h. Restrictions that limit access to the subscriber's patrons and staff.

VII. Deselection

Electronic resources will be reviewed periodically by the selector to assess their continuing value. It shall be the prerogative of the selectors to weed from the collection those electronic materials determined to be no longer of value.

Drafted by Marcia Findley. Assistance in developing this draft policy was derived from the following sources and is gratefully acknowledged:

Guide to Selecting and Acquiring CD-ROMS, Software, and Other Electronic Publications. Chicago: ALA, 1994.

Draft Policy for Electronic Resources Management. Iowa City, IA: University of Iowa Libraries, 1993.

Foulds, M. S., and Foulds, L. R. "CD-ROM Disk Selection and Evaluation." *Reference Services Review*, 18, no. 2 (1990): 27-38.

Fig. 10.1. Sample electronic policy.

What are some of the issues for full text online or on CD-ROM? Online services are evolving but are not noted for being user friendly. Many are command-driven, and, in order to become cost-effective searchers, end users must study manuals or undergo extensive instruction. In many cases, it is more cost-effective for the library or information center to search for the customer, although many users do not think a search done by someone else is satisfactory. Online advocates say one only pays for what one needs. True, but with direct charges for each search, unless one is an experienced user, it is possible (even likely) that the searches will generate much unwanted material and high costs. For example, OCLC's FirstSearch charges by the search. If a library bought 10,000 searches for $5,000, each search would cost 50 cents, whether or not the search terms (spelled correctly or not) produce any hits (useful or not). CD-ROM advocates say it is less expensive, as there is no per-search cost. Of course, a low-use product with a high subscription price will produce a high per-search charge. (*Biosis* costs $10,000 per year. Loyola Marymount University could not justify that cost if it were used only by the biology department's 7 faculty and 100 under-graduates.) This is one more reason for knowing customer interests.

Another question is the definition of full text. Often, in the online version, it means text without graphics. As of 1994, few online databases offered both graphical interfaces and imaged information. The reason is images (charts, tables, and other illustrations) require substantial amounts of disk space and delivery time as well as delivery platforms capable of handling images. CD-ROMs, on the other hand, are making great strides in the imaging area; even MEDLINE is making it easier for users to find information (Knowledge Finder's version of MEDLINE, for example). Windows interfaces, now available with many CD-ROM products, will probably be available soon for online services. Graphics require megabytes of memory and powerful PCs (486 or better), more powerful than most PC owners currently have. In addition, if an end user's modem is limited to transmitting data at 2400 bits per second (bps) or 9600 bps, online imaging is a slow and expensive process. Because of imaging issues, it will probably be some time before online services follow in the footsteps of OCLC's *Clinical Trials* journal.

Numeric databases have been part of library or information center collecting activities for at least 25 years. Generally, libraries acquired these data sets, such as the U.S. Census, as tapes that were mounted on a mainframe. Today, researchers can gain access to such sets online. A disadvantage is that downloading large data sets takes a long time; an advantage is that local ownership speeds the work. A source for numeric data sets is the Inter-university Consortium for Political and Social Research (ICPSR) at the University of Michigan. Hundreds of universities in 22 countries around the world are members of ICPSR. This consortium serves as a central repository and dissemination service for social science electronic data sets. Since its establishment in the early 1960s, ICPSR has collected data sets that cover a broad range of topics.

> Beginning with a few major surveys of the American electorate, the holdings of the Archive have now broadened to include comparable information from diverse settings and for extended periods. Data ranging from nineteenth century French census materials

to recent sessions of the United Nations, from American elections in the 1790s, to the socioeconomic structure of Polish poviats, from characteristics of Knights of Labor Assemblies to expectations of American consumers are contained in the Archive.[3]

Some concerns for any numeric collection building are very large files, format or compatibility issues, and quality of the documentation. In the case of ICPSR, data sets are available as round tapes, 9-track, or diskettes. It is also possible to FTP files online using CDNet (Consortium Data Network) on the Internet. Users electing this mode might pay telecommunication charges, as well as University of Michigan computer services charges. Though avoiding the potential conversion costs, the online approach leaves open the possibility of surprisingly large and unpredictable service and telecommunication charges.

Occasionally, one may encounter a conflict between how long users wish to have access to the data and how long computing services are willing to make the tapes accessible through the campus network. This may result in pressure on the library not only to acquire the data sets but to have in-house CPU capacity to operate the automation system as well as mount the tapes.

Support depends on people with the skills and knowledge to do the technical work as well as on sound documentation. Anyone who has seen the documentation that accompanies many commercial products can imagine the quality of documentation for data sets from researchers whose primary purpose was their own project. If the library is already mounting bibliographic or full-text tapes, it may have staff with appropriate computer operations background. Probably, however, the staff will not have experience with all the various statistical packages on the market (such as SPSS and SAS). Support means institutional costs. Again, there are costs associated with either mode of access (online or tape). Careful consideration of both options and how to handle the charges are essential before moving into the business of acquiring data sets.

Bibliographies, indexes, abstracts, and *tables of contents* are the traditional types of reference materials. As with full text, one has the option of electronic or print for each of these. The debate about CD-ROM versus online access is particularly applicable to these reference materials. Given the greater control publishers have when they distribute information in the CD-ROM format, it is not surprising that this is the producers' preferred format. Through licensing agreements, producers or publishers have greater legal control over the use of their products (see pages 285-88). With the data in electronic form, the publishers or producers can generate more specialized products. An example is SIRS's Discover CD-ROM for the school market, which draws on SIRS's larger CD-ROM database Researcher. Users prefer CD-ROM products over print versions.

User expectations or beliefs about electronic information also creates challenges. Too often, users think the electronic data is both the most current and the most comprehensive. A few years ago I reviewed a book, a revised doctoral dissertation, about the image of Native American women in nineteenth century American literature. The author made several statements that her conclusions were *proven* by the fact that she had done several searches of DIALOG. I quickly located more than 25 citations, from print sources, specific to Native American literature covering the nineteenth century, that disproved her conclusions. Both the author and her doctoral committee failed to recognize the limits of electronic databases. If doctoral level researchers and their committees fail to understand the nature of electronic information, what can one expect from undergraduate students and less sophisticated researchers?

Few libraries actively collect *software* because of copyright problems and the difficulty of maintaining the integrity of the software. (Chapter 18 discusses copyright and circulation issues related to software.) Though it is possible to collect operating systems, few, if any, libraries maintain collections of these programs for public use. Programming tools and languages are two other types of software that are rarely collected. The two areas where some collecting occurs are applications and, as discussed earlier, data files. Libraries are acquiring more and more books that come with software that is integral to using the printed material. School media centers, if they have responsibility for computing services, are the most likely to maintain collections of educational application programs. (Perhaps the safest software to collect is shareware.)

Videodiscs and other imaging technologies are becoming high demand items. Companies like Voyager Company are producing multimedia materials on laser disks, and other companies are using the CD-ROM format for multimedia products. The basic difference is laser disks and videodiscs do not require a computer interface because they are not interactive or multimedia. Which format—laser disk, videodisc, or CD-ROM—will be the most successful is impossible to predict. Laser disks require a television and a special playback unit; their advantage at present is more homes have television sets and playback units can handle disks of various sizes. Multimedia CD-ROMs, though requiring a computer interface, offer a much higher degree of interactivity. One may surmise then that the CD-ROM format will eventually dominate.

Video games are another format that many public and school media centers collect, both focusing on instructional games. A few public libraries have circulating collections of recreational games. Like other technologies, there is a high rate of development, making it expensive to maintain a collection of game cartridges that play on the machines that are, at the moment, state of the art.

Without doubt, libraries and collection development officers will face increasing pressure to add electronic formats. Cost, legal, and selection issues will become more complex. Balancing the various needs will present a challenge for all concerned.

Selection Issues

Loyola Marymount University considers four broad categories of issues when evaluating a new electronic product: content, access, support, and cost. The approach is similar to what other libraries do in this area (see fig. 10.2).

Text continues on page 278.

Boston College Library's
Checklist for CD-ROM Products and Subscriptions

Name of Vendor _____ Date _____

Vendor _____ Phone _____

Address _____

Suggested by _____

Product Description

1. What subject area(s) does the product cover? _____

2. How often is the data updated? _____

3. How accurate is the data? _____

4. How thorough is the indexing? _____

5. How will the product support the curriculum? _____

6. Explain why the product is appropriate for an academic library. _____
   _____

7. Is the content suitable for ready reference, basic inquiry, or in-depth research?
   _____

8. What other patron information needs will this source fill? _____
   _____

9. What is the printed counterpart of this product? _____
   _____

10. What other sources now available in the library cover this subject?
    _____

Technical Considerations

1. Does the software meet High Sierra Group NISO standards for the
   CD-ROM drive? _____

2. Does the product run on hardware presently owned? _____
   If not, what hardware is needed? _____

3. Will the product's operating system be compatible with those systems
   already loaded on the same machine? _____

Fig. 10.2 continues on page 276.

Administrative Considerations

1. Is the product available through outright purchase (data is owned) _____ or lease (data is rented and returned on cancellation)? _____
   _____

2. Can this product be networked? _____ If yes, what are the costs? _____
   _____

3. Is this information available from other vendors? _____

   What is the cost? _____

   Vendor _____ Cost _____

   Vendor _____ Cost _____

   How does the content of this product compare? _____
   _____
   _____

4. In what other electronic formats is the product available? _____
   _____
   _____

   What is the cost? _____

Product Costs

1. What is the initial subscription cost of the product? _____

2. What are the annual costs, if any, for updates? _____

3. What are the costs, if any, for current and archival disks?

   Current _____

   Archival _____

4. What are the licensing costs? _____

5. How much of a discount is applied to the cost if the product is already being purchased in a different format (print, microfiche, etc.)? _____
   _____
   _____

6. What is the cost of the print product? _____

   Do we currently subscribe to the print product? _____

   How many subscriptions? _____

Related Issues

1. Presently, are there enough workstations to support the projected use of the product? _____

2. Will any additional hardware be needed? _____ Cost? _____

3. How many compact discs will be received with this product? _____

4. How many additional compact discs will be added each year? _____

5. What sources could this product replace? _____

   What are content comparisons? _____

6. What percentage of the material covered is owned by Boston College? _____

7. Are there any access restrictions imposed on this product? _____

Vendor Support and Staff Impact

1. What user documentation is available? _____

2. Is there a toll-free hotline and/or other forms of user support? _____

3. Who will provide training and user aids? _____

4. What impact will the purchase have on online searching costs and staff time? _____

Other Considerations

1. Include basic technical specifications for the product.

2. Include a copy of any published evaluation of the product.

3. Include the names of institutions that already own the product.

4. Attach any supporting material available.

Fig. 10.2. Sample checklist for CD-ROMs.

Content

As with any format, content issues should be the first consideration. There is some temptation to acquire an electronic format because it is new, because others have it, because it is attractive or entertaining, because it is multimedia, or because it will interface with existing equipment. None of these are valid reasons for adding a title. Make certain the item matches up with both library and institutional goals. In an ideal situation, the item will match several goals.

Given the relatively high cost of electronic formats, it is important that the material be useful to a large number of potential users. It is not unreasonable to purchase a $50 or $75 book for a single known user and a few potential users. Similarly, a library might subscribe to a $1,000 journal to serve the needs of a department, and in an academic environment, the needs of departmental majors. However, in today's tight budget environment, with the exception of specialized research environments, most libraries would think long and hard about committing $2,000 or more to any product that did not meet multiple user needs.

Though popularity, or high demand, is a basic reason for selecting an item, it also creates some public service concerns. One can lease or buy multiple copies of bestseller books, develop request lists, and have a few rental copies of high demand items. Few libraries or information centers circulate their journals, which usually means current journals are available when a user seeks them.

A single-user license for a CD-ROM product can create queues and substantial paper and ink cartridge or ribbon costs (if there is a printer attached to the computer) as well as equipment maintenance on the heavily used hardware. Thus, though multiple users are an important factor in the selection decision, the consequences of that popularity also must be a factor. A popular item may require purchasing a multiple-user license or several single-user copies to handle the workload. All these options add to the cost.

Content of the product is the key issue, as it is for any addition to the collection. If the product is bibliographic or statistical, how far back in time does the data go? What are the use characteristics of the subject field represented in the product? The idea that older literature in the sciences is obsolete has little research documentation.[4] It is true of all fields that use declines with age (see chapter 14), but that does not mean use, or importance to the field, ceases. Understanding local use patterns will be a key issue in making the selection decision.

More and more full-text and image CD-ROMs are spin-offs of print publications. Some of the products incorporate only a portion of the print version, but others contain everything. The question is, How complete or comprehensive is the product? A rough rule of thumb is if the price is under $200, chances are it is not the full print version, especially if there are extensive graphics in the print edition.

How often is the product updated? Are there plans to add to the back files? If so, how soon will they be added and how far back will they go? These are key questions for products that incorporate bibliographic and abstracting data. Occasionally, vendors advertise greater coverage than the product actually offers. In 1992, I reviewed the initial offering of a bibliographic CD-ROM product that claimed its coverage was from 1520 to 1990. Because one of the search capabilities was by date, I checked the number of items included for several different years, 1986 to 1990 and 1520 to 1526. I was surprised to find there were more items for the sixteenth century than for the last five years. In fact, there were an equal number of items for 1520 and 1990. By checking 1989 and 1990 issues of a quarterly journal covered by the database, I discovered there was limited coverage of late 1980s and 1990s. Indexing of that particular journal ended in mid 1989. The producers did have 93 items from 1990 in the database, so the claim of coverage from 1520 to 1990 was not false. On the other hand, it was not completely accurate because there were at least 1,000 items from 1990 that should have been in the database. The annual updates would improve coverage of the most recent five-year period but would not cover the most recent years, if the first offering was indicative of future indexing practices.

Problems like this make it important to seek out reviews *and* ask for a 30-day trial for new products. Clearly, the public service staff will need to be fully aware of the various product limitations to make the end users equally aware of the situation. This is one excellent reason why library and information center staffs need to continue to serve as interpreters and guides to information services, electronic or print.

In selecting any product for the collection, aspects like quality, accuracy, authoritativeness, and currency of data are factors any collection development officer will consider. With electronic products, these factors can be even more significant than with other formats. Many people have great respect for anything in print (see chapter 14) and transfer that faith to electronic products, which they believe always contain the most current, complete, and accurate information available. This almost-blind end user acceptance of electronic information means selection personnel must be careful in their decisions about electronic formats.

Long-term availability is another concern. Online material sometimes seems to disappear overnight. The person operating a listserv or gopher may simply stop maintaining the service or may make a significant change in a gopher; some users don't learn of the change, and they lose connection. With a print version in the collection, there is a reasonable degree of certainty that the data always will be available.

A real concern is how long will the CD-ROM format be with us? Will full text on CD-ROM become the next problem format, rather like sound recordings? How many times must a library or information center acquire the same information? Will *Time* become available on multiple formats like the sound recordings of Handel's *Water Music*—first a 78-rpm disk, then a 33 1/3-rpm disk, then 8-track tape, then cassette, and now CD? (See chapter 9 for more about this issue.) If one of the library's or information center's goals is to preserve information for future generations, then format viability and support must be a concern. Technologists claim there is nothing to worry about. They say once the information is digitized it can be preserved. What is to say that digitization is the final process? Will systems 50 years in the future have the capability to handle ancient material in an ASCII format? More to the point, who will own that data, and what will it cost to have access? These are questions that have no ready answer. We know print served human kind very well for centuries and can continue to do so without regard to operating systems or hardware delivery platforms.

A final item on the list of content considerations is whether the product offers some value-added advantage over existing print versions. Especially important is any type of customization that the producer offers that more closely links the product's content to the local collections. For example, indexes that are customized to show which indexed titles are locally available would have added value. Almost all electronic products offer easier searching, more search options, and generally faster results than their print counterparts. Because of this, try to find some other value-added feature before committing funds.

Access

Being able to customize the product to indicate local holdings brings us to the second major category of selection issues: *access*. One aspect of access is availability of materials. This issue applies primarily to the indexing, abstracting, and table of contents products. As noted in chapter 7, when the library adds a new indexing or abstracting service, users will be seeing citations to publications not in the local collection. A decision to give users access to the tables of contents of thousands of periodicals will, for most libraries, generate numerous requests for articles from titles not locally available. One should not ignore the impact on ILL service when making this decision.

Document delivery services (DDSs; see chapters 1 and 7) are one option for addressing the demand for materials not locally owned. Often, traditional ILL services are much too slow for users and, in some libraries, are an overworked, understaffed service. Many DDSs permit the end user to decide how much to spend on desired information by allowing the library or information center to establish individual accounts and passwords. The individual may select the mode of delivery in most cases (the faster the service the higher the cost). The variety of sources (26 such services were described in a 1993 *LJ* article[5]) means there is some overlap in coverage. One can and should do cost comparisons before committing to a service. Despite the overlap, no one service is capable of handling all the needs of the user community, so it is likely the library will use several services. There are several advantages to using DDS, starting with the increase in the number of titles accessible to users. Other advantages are cost control, speed of delivery, and copyright compliance. Because the vendors pay the copyright fees, there is no limit on how many articles a library may request from any one title during a calendar year, as there is with traditional ILL. (See chapter 18 for more information about copyright.)

There are three types of DDS: nonprofit organizations, professional societies, and commercial services. Examples of nonprofit DDS are the British Library's Document Supply Centre, OCLC's Dispatch Service, RLG's CitaDel, the Library of Congress's National Translation Center, National Technical Information Service (NTIS), and CARL's UnCover 2. Being offered by a nonprofit does not mean the material is free, merely that the cost of documents may be slightly lower than those from another source. Some providers, such as the British Library, supply the material from their own collections, and others, such as CARL, do so from several library collections; still others, such as OCLC, provide documents from a variety of sources.

Professional societies usually restrict their services to material in their own database. ESL (Engineering Societies Libraries) Information Services is an example of this type of service. As the name suggests, this service focuses on engineering data. Another subject service is Chemical Abstracts Service.

Commercial services range from ADONIS (a CD-ROM product covering 350 top biomedical journals), to companies like Information On Demand that are strong in the area of hard-to-find items, to combinations, such as EBSCO and Dynamic Information.

An example of the combined DDS is EBSCO's new CASIAS™ (Current Awareness Service Individual Article Service) program. This program of table of contents, indexing, and abstracting data, combined with article delivery, uses the British Library's Document Supply Centre's Inside Information (table of contents service) to 10,000 titles, EBSCO's Academic Search and Magazine Search (indexing and abstracts to 2,400 titles), and ADONIS's indexing of 500 biomedical titles, as well as the capability of Dynamic Information in locating hard-to-find items. It seems likely there will be more consolidation like this as well as additions to a growing pool of DDS organizations. Given the rapidly changing environment for DDS suppliers, it is important to closely monitor services selected by the library.

Returning to other access issues, one question that requires an answer is: How compatible is the product with the local network or library automation system? Related to compatibility is the question of licensing, that is, what is the difference in cost between single-user and multiple-user or networking licenses? Also of concern is the type of search engine used by the product. How different is it from other electronic products already locally available? In the past, one could assume Boolean logic searching, but today some vendors are using statistical searching, or weighted terms. (Weighted term searching is a system that retrieves on the basis of word frequency matches of search terms to words in the document and presents the user with the most frequent matches first.) The popularity of the latter system in commercial text imaging and retrieval systems (for example, a records management application) is causing companies like Westlaw and Mead Data Central to use statistical searching engines. Strategies for a successful search are very different for the two search engines. This will translate into extra training for staff and patrons alike.

The overarching access issue is the user. Where (library, office, home), when (during library operating hours, 24 hours per day) and how (local network, Internet, commercial service) does the end user gain access to the information? As a general rule, as accessibility goes up so does the cost. An as yet unavailable ideal solution is having everything available 24 hours a day, from any authorized location, with full cost control capability, and no need for local support.

Support

Support should be considered during the selection process. How much training does a user need to successfully use the product? Having only similar products, or having only a few variations in how one can use products, will mean the public service staff will have less support activity. This leads to the question, How much initial and ongoing staff training is necessary to provide customer support? The answers to these questions depend on the quality of the documentation that accompanies the product.

Usually, a toll-free telephone number for vendor support works well only when the caller has a fair technical knowledge of the product. Usually, this means staff members rather than end users must make the call.

Anyone with public service experience knows that most people follow the directions when everything else fails. Reading introductory material about how to use print resources was never a strong point with general users. They are no more likely to take the time to read instructions for an electronic product, some of which come with extensive user manuals. A rule of thumb is the bigger the manual the more help the public service staff will have to provide. Information about ease of use and size or usefulness of manuals may appear in product reviews (if a review can be found). Some review sources are *Database: Magazine of Electronic Database Reviews, Online and CD-ROM Review, Wilson Library Bulletin,* and *American Reference Books Annual (ARBA).* Often, information about ease of use and size of the manual is available only after the library receives the product. Calling a library that has the product is worthwhile, especially for products costing more than $500. However, your library may receive a later version of the product that incorporates significant changes, so the experiences of libraries with previous versions may not apply to the new version.

Questions about vendor/producer reliability are important to the support issue. Reliability of the producer is a more significant issue with electronic products than it is with print products. Will the toll-free telephone number for customer help remain active? Will new versions result in retraining users or reconfiguring the local system? What is the relationship between vendor support service hours and the library's hours? Just because the producer of the electronic product is one the library staff knows from its nonelectronic products does not mean the transition to the new format will be smooth. It also does not mean the producer will stay with the format or support existing products if the company decides to drop the format. Just as technology changes rapidly, so do the producers of electronic materials.

Some software can be unreliable and troublesome. Invariably, some products have one or more bugs that take time and effort to eliminate. A few seem to have bugs in each new release, and, in a sense, this is better than the occasional bug. Where there is a consistent pattern, one can plan how the debugging will take place instead of encountering unexpected problems. Compatibility of hardware and software is also a key issue in selecting a format for mounting electronic information.

Support issues affect the impact new products have on existing services and activities. Some new products reduce pressure on the staff, for example, the full text of materials frequently requested through ILL.

In some instances, it may be possible to reduce staff work by giving end users thorough training in using a product and assigning users their own accounts and passwords. Other times, there will be a substantial increase of staff workload. In those cases, staff discussions about the impact and the value of the product are an essential part of the decision-making process.

Cost

After addressing questions of content, access, and support, the selection process must also deal with cost. The most obvious costs are the initial cost of the product and ongoing charges for updates. Though the most obvious, these may not be the largest costs in the long run. Networking fees, which are almost always in addition to the base fee or annual fee, may equal or surpass the base fee. Information is an economic good that does not follow traditional pricing models. Producers employ a variety of pricing strategies. This makes it more complicated to calculate what electronic information will cost the library or information center and makes it difficult to accurately compare prices of various products offering similar information. Likewise, it is a time-consuming task to attempt to compare the unit cost of a print periodical subscription and full-text CD-ROM to the cost of securing the article from one of several DDS vendors. As an example, how does one compare McGraw-Hill's *Multimedia Encyclopedia of Mammalian Biology* with the five-volume set *Encyclopedia of Mammals*? Can cost really be a factor in the comparison? To assign a logical monetary value to ease of use and speed of access is difficult. It depends on local circumstances. At best, one can look at the expected use or cost of each format and decide whether the value is reasonable for the library. The sample form in figure 10.3 provides some assistance in making the needed comparisons. (The form was developed by Bart Harloe for the Claremont Colleges.)

Additional cost considerations for one or more electronic formats may include connect and telecommunication charges; display or print charges; downloading charges; customization charges; optional features, such as saved searches; and charges for management reports or software. Even CD-ROM products may impose printing charges; for example, UMI's full-text CD-ROM Business Periodicals Ondisc (BPO) imposes a 10-cent royalty charge for each page printed. When you buy a CD-ROM product, what do you buy? Do you own the material, or do you own only a license to use the material for a period of time? The answers vary by product. Libraries did not send back quarterly issues of print indexing services when the annual volume arrived. However, with most of the CD-ROM indexing products, the library only leases the product and must return superseded discs or make a cut in the edge of the disk to prevent use. Occasionally, the library can arrange to continue to use the previous disk in another area of the library. For example, technical services might use the current version of *BIP* while reference uses the preceding version. With a paper subscription, the library retains all the paper copies after canceling the subscription; with a CD-ROM subscription, the library may have nothing to show for its investment after it cancels the service.

Discipline/Title	Print $	CD-ROM $	CD-ROM Network $	TOTAL	First Search Y/N	Coverage	Lexis/Nexis Y/N	Online* Y/N	Keep Selection Decision Y/N	Sys/Ver
SOCIAL SCIENCES-Group 3										
Eric	271	1,195	---	1,195	Y	(1966-)	N	Y (CDE)		
Education Index	809	1,489	---		Y	(1983-)	N	Y (E)		
Dissertation Abstracts	1,700	1,995	---		N		N	Y (CDES)		
SOCIAL SCIENCES-Group 4										
P.A.I.S.	535	1,600	800	2,400	Y	(Last 10yr)	N	Y (CDE)		
GPO	-	1,495	-		Y	(1976-)	N	Y (DE)		
Index to Legal Per.	225	1,495	-		Y	(1981-)	Y	Y (E)		
ASI/Statistical Master File	6,490	2,595	250+		N		N	N		
CIS/Cong. Master File	4,610	1,845	250+		N		N	Y		
FBIS	2,200	2,550	-		N		N	N		
Popline	-	790	395		N		N	Y?		
Total	16,840	14,070	1,195	3,595		7,000+	3,500+	3,500+		

*C = Classmate D = Dialog E = Epic S = STN

$ Bold highlights Title/Database available at Claremont in 92/93 fiscal year

Fig. 10.3. Sample worksheet to guide decision making. Courtesy of Bart Harloe, St. Lawrence University. Matrix developed at The Libraries of the Claremont Colleges in 1993.

In addition to vendor costs, local costs are a factor in the decision-making process. The computers and other hardware required to use electronic materials are generally more expensive to buy and maintain than other media playback equipment. As programmable units, they are susceptible to system failure, to loss of information because of power fluctuations and inadvertent user error, to tampering by computer hackers, to viruses, and to theft. All of these factors generate additional costs (equipment, security devices, maintenance, and, all too often, replacement).

An estimate of the amount of printing or downloading activity the product will generate is another cost factor. Even without a royalty fee, there are printing costs, assuming the decision is to allow users to print information. Paper, ink, ribbon, and cartridge costs can mount, if there is no effort to control them. Libraries and information centers employ several techniques to control such costs. One obvious method is to assess a printing charge. (There are coin or debit card units that will work with printers.) Another method is to allocate a number of free copies per user, with the staff providing the appropriate number of sheets of paper and charging for additional paper. This approach generates a cost in staff time to provide the paper and, occasionally, put the paper into the printer. Some libraries allow downloading to disk instead of printing. There are several drawbacks to this approach. First, the library must keep on hand a stock of disks to sell. Second, some products do not allow downloading. Another serious disadvantage is not all customers can use downloaded data, which means the library must allow for some printing or risk having a single user tie up a product for extended periods. For popular products, libraries want to keep the customer turnover rate as high as possible, which means offering both printing and downloading. Shareware programs, such as PRNAFILE, provide a way of printing to disk rather than to paper, which is useful for programs that are not set up for downloading. Another method for handling printing costs is to locate a system printer, perhaps connected to a CD-ROM LAN, in a staff area, making it possible to monitor and charge for printing activities. This option generates staff costs and establishes a distribution system that assures each customer gets the right printout. If the institution is networked and has sophisticated software, printing charges, as well as other costs of use, could become automatic debits against individual user accounts.

The overall goal is to select the most cost-effective format that will meet the needs of a large number of users. This is no easy task, given the cost and pricing variables that exist. By seriously considering the factors outlined above, one has a better chance of successfully achieving the goal.

Other Issues

The legal, financial, and technical issues relating to acquisitions work, as well as to other activities and services, are important enough to merit extra emphasis.

The legal issues are copyright and licensing agreements. Copyright involves several topics: fair use, preservation, and production. Electronic (digital) material is easy to transmit, manipulate, and duplicate. These features make the medium popular but also raise copyright questions. According to Mark McGuire, "One of many challenges in the digital realm is the problem of ensuring appropriate compensation in transactions involving intellectual property. Other considerations include: ascertaining and proving liability in information malpractice; safeguarding information integrity; ensuring respect for privacy; and maintaining equitable access to information."[6]

Achieving compliance with these copyright issues provides ongoing challenges for library and information center staffs. Some of the use issues are addressed by the licensing agreements accompanying the product or contract for online services. Rather like photocopying services, the library takes no responsibility for what users do with downloaded data after they leave the library. Whether posting signs regarding copyright in the electronic work area(s) will prove adequate to protect libraries and information centers remains to be seen. In any case, the staff must know what use rights exist for each product.

The entire question of preserving print material by converting to a digital format is slowly being resolved. (See chapter 18 for a discussion of how this issue relates to copyright.) In all likelihood, if the digital material is not publicly accessible, except through the group preserving the material, that will be acceptable to everyone. The ease of manipulating and duplicating electronic data is one of the concerns in the area of preserving materials that are becoming too brittle to handle.

A complex area is that of author responsibility or ownership. Perhaps the idea put forward by McGuire,[7] or something similar, that allows for embedding in the data codes that link various information elements to their original producers, thus identifying authorship as well as assigning responsibility for content, will solve the problem. In addition, such coding could ensure that economic value is equitably attributed to the originators. Such a system would avoid the fair use concerns that Robert Kost identified as the key problem: "We have lost the control necessary for copyright law to be effective. Control over copies is hopeless."[8]

When the library or information center provides equipment or assists with multimedia production, under copyright law, it has some responsibility for assuring that the copied material is public domain or that permission is granted to reproduce the material.

Copyright law requires libraries and information centers that supply public access equipment to post signs reminding users about the need to comply with copyright law. One further step to consider is if the equipment is in a secure area or locked cabinet that requires users to get a key from library staff, the staff person may have the user sign a statement assuming full responsibility for complying with copyright law. Obviously, if the library is producing products, it can make certain compliance occurs. A question arises about accepting multimedia courseware from instructors without some type of protection for the library in the event the developer failed to get the required permission(s).

Licensing agreements are a relatively recent issue for libraries and collection development staff. Initially library staff paid little attention to such agreements. Acquisition staff signed the agreements and returned them without fully understanding what they were signing. As Edward Warro stated,

> When is the last time you stood at the counter of a rental car agency and quibbled over various clauses on your rental agreement? ... To make them even more unappealing to read, the agreements are normally printed in fine gray type on pink paper to maximize eyestrain. There is good reason for the fine print: the people who wrote these agreements would sooner have you die than read them. But if you do read them, you will probably die anyway when you realize what you have been signing.[9]

Anyone involved in the selection or acquisition of electronic materials should read Warro's article.

Topics covered in typical licensing agreements include the lessee's responsibility for security, customer service, payment and delivery, limitations and warranties, termination, indemnification, and assignment. All of these factors can impact the expected use. Though having to add attorney fees to the cost of building a collection is unappealing, the fact is that most of the producers will negotiate changes, and librarians should demand changes that benefit libraries and customers.

The library must maintain a master file of copies of all the licensing agreements and contracts. There should be a contact person who is responsible for knowing the terms of these documents as well as being able to answer or secure answers to questions about the agreements. Compliance is a key issue, and the library or information center must do what it can to ensure compliance. However, some licensing agreements contain language that places on the library (subscriber) responsibility to monitor what users do with material after they leave the premises. Such clauses are beyond any library's or information center's ability to handle, and librarians should insist they be deleted from the agreement.

The key is knowing what is in the agreement before purchasing. As with computer software, the licensing agreement often comes with the product, that is, after the purchase. It is sealed in a package with a warning message to the effect that opening the package constitutes accepting the terms of the agreement inside the package. When considering a product from a new vendor, ask for a copy of the licensing agreement before making a final decision to purchase. This gives the staff an opportunity to review the document. It also provides an opportunity to request changes that the vendor may or may not be willing to make. In any event, it will give the library a chance to consider whether it can live with the conditions of the licensing agreement before committing to the purchase.

Financial and technical considerations are what staff talk about most after they finish with other concerns. In times of tight budgets, which seem to be the norm, high-priced electronic material represents a challenge. Balancing quality, quantity, and cost is the fundamental task of collection development staff. The fact that electronic materials tend to be expensive for single-user agreements, and even more expensive for multiple-user agreements, makes it even more difficult to answer the question: How much benefit to how many users? Does enhanced searching capability justify the purchase? What must be given up in other areas?

Shifting resources from monographs, to serials, to electronics is a finite game for most libraries and information centers. Sometimes, additional funding is available for electronic materials, particularly when funding bodies view it as enhancing the image of the parent institution. As the glamour of electronic material delivered to individual workstations fades, so does the additional funding. Sometimes, the tradeoff involves canceling low-use serials to gain enough money to cover the DDS costs for acquiring both the occasionally needed article from the canceled titles and a few articles from titles never held. The question of formats is also a question of technology and money. Realistically, additional funding will come from direct and indirect charges end users pay. These charges will, at best, cover only the cost of the information, not the support, training, staffing, equipment, and maintenance costs, thus creating an overall net cash drain and cost shift from other areas—often print collection funds.

Because electronic information access offers the potential of end users having full control of their searches and acquisition of data, cost containment may become an important consideration. For example, initial cost will vary depending on how the organization decides to handle its connections with electronic services, such as the Internet. There are three basic options for handling such service: terminal access, SLIP or PPP, and leased line. Terminal access employs someone else's host computer. This approach eliminates host computer overhead and operating costs. Institutional costs are a registration fee, a monthly access charge, and hourly connect charges. (This approach is like that employed by Prodigy, America Online, CompuServe, and other online services.) A major disadvantage of this option is that the hourly connect charges are unknown until the monthly bill arrives. It is not uncommon for active users employing this option to accumulate monthly charges in excess of $700. Unsophisticated searchers, or experienced searchers without software that permits them to do some of the search formulation off-line, can run up large bills. If users do not have to pay the costs, they have little incentive to improve their searching methods or to limit use time.

Employing the serial line Internet protocol (SLIP) or point-to-point protocol (PPP) option provides more control over the connect costs. Many suppliers of these services charge an annual fee for unlimited connect time and no hourly charges. The disadvantage is that the annual fee will vary depending on the number of users. Additional charges are for local host capability for TCP/IP (transmission control protocol/Internet Protocol) as well as the technical expertise to manage the host. Though this capability probably exists in most academic and other large organizations, the question may be, Do the people with the capability have the time and willingness to take on the extra work?

The third access option, with even higher operating costs, is a leased-line connection. With this approach, the organization operates a full-time host connection. The speed and bandwidth of service selected (for example, a T1 line) determines the annual service charge ($10,000 is not uncommon).

However, the real cost in this method is that it requires significant staff support as well as a solid computing program. As one can see, the question of how to provide access is not just a library or information center decision; it involves substantial technical and financial resources. All options have implications for cost. One cost that is sometimes overlooked is user education, training, and support. That cost is ongoing, and depending on the turnover rate of users, can result in a large or small annual cost for training.

Summary

Electronic materials will be an ever-growing part of collections and user expectations. According to Mary Morley and Hazel Woodward,

> In an era of restricted funding, decisions have to be made between the provision of printed and electronic information; between local holdings of material and remote access to external information; between "just in case" as opposed to a "just in time" strategy. Librarians dealing with electronic information are constantly confronted by questions about equipment requirements; pricing polices; bibliographic control; archival access; staffing implication; and user needs.[10]

Balancing these various elements demands constant adjustments in how libraries think about services and the most cost-effective approach. One must keep up to date on changing technology, changing players in the marketplace, and user needs and wants. Further, libraries must do what they can to maintain a balance between producers' economic interests and rights and users' rights to fair use. It will be an ongoing challenge to libraries and information centers for years to come. By engaging in careful planning (including the preparation of an electronic collection policy), employing sound selection criteria, and monitoring the use of the resources, libraries will meet the challenge.

Notes

[1]Peter Jasco. "Tomorrow's Online in Today's CD-ROM: Interfaces and Images," *Online* 18 (March 1994): 41-47.

[2]Association for Library Collections and Technical Services Publications Committee of the Acquisition of Library Materials Section, *Guide to Selecting and Acquiring CD-ROMs, Software and Other Electronic Publications,* ed. Stephen Bosch, Patricia Promis, and Chris Suznet (Chicago: American Library Association, 1994).

[3]Inter-university Consortium for Political and Social Research, *Guide to Resources and Services 1993-1994* (Ann Arbor, MI: ICPSR, 1993), vii.

[4]Thomas W. Cokling and Bonnie Anne Osif, "CD-ROM and Changing Research Patterns," *Online* 18 (May 1994): 71-74.

[5]Mounir Khalil, "Document Delivery: A Better Option," *Library Journal* 118 (February 1, 1993): 43-47.

[6]Mark McGuire, "Secure SGML: A Proposal to the Information Community," *Journal of Scholarly Publishing* 25 (April 1994): 146.

[7]Ibid., 146-56.

[8]Robert Kost, "Technology Giveth . . . Electronic Information and the Future of Copyright," *Serials Review* 18, nos. 1/2 (1992): 69.

[9]Edward A. Warro, "What Have We Been Signing? A Look at Database Licensing Agreements," *Library Administration & Management* 8 (Summer 1994): 173.

[10]*Taming the Electronic Jungle,* ed. Mary Morley and Hazel Woodward (Horsforth, UK: National Acquisitions Group and U. K. Serials Group, 1993), xiii.

Further Reading

General

Antelmon, K., and D. Lagenberg. "Collection Development in the Electronic Library." *Association for Computing Machinery SIGUCCS* 21 (1993): 50-56.

Eaton, E. K. "Information Management Systems Planning: A Process for Health Sciences Libraries and Institutions." In *Advances in Librarianship*, vol. 18, edited by I. Godden, 131-57. New York: Academic Press, 1994.

Flanagan, M. "Database Licensing: A Future View." *Computers in Libraries* 13 (January 1993): 21-22.

Gammon, J. A. "EDI and Acquisitions." *Library Acquisitions: Practice and Theory* 18 (Spring 1994): 113-23.

Hunter, K. "National Site License Model." *Serials Review* 18, nos. 1/2 (1992): 71-72+.

Pack, T. "Electronic Books: A New Spin on the Great American Novel." *CD-ROM Professional* 7 (March 1994): 54-56.

Sasse, M. L., and B. J. Winkler. "Electronic Journals: A Formidable Challenge for Libraries." In *Advances in Librarianship,* vol. 17, edited by I. Godden, 149-73. New York: Academic Press, 1993.

Sutherlan, L. "Copyright and Licensing in the Electronic Environment." *Serials Librarian* 23, nos. 3/4 (1993): 143-47.

Woodward, H. M. "Impact of Electronic Information on Serials Collection Management." *IFLA Journal* 20, no. 1 (1994): 35-45.

Valauskas, E. J. "Reading and Computers: Paper-based or Digital Text: What Is Best?" *Computers in Libraries* 14 (January 1994): 44-47.

Zarnosky, M. "Knowledge Served on a Silver Platter: Planning and Paying for CD-ROMs." *RQ* 32 (Fall): 75-84.

Academic

Atkinson, R. "Crisis and Opportunity: Reevaluating Acquisitions Budgeting in an Age of Transition." *Journal of Library Administration* 19, no. 2 (1993): 35-55.

———. "Networks, Hypertext, and Academic Libraries." *College & Research Libraries* 54 (May 1993): 199-215.

Brett, G. H. "Networked Information Retrieval Tools in the Academic Environment." *Internet Research* 3 (Fall 1993): 26-36.

Dougherty, R. M., and A. P. Dougherty. "Academic Library: A Time of Crisis, Change, and Opportunity." *Journal of Academic Librarianship* 18 (January 1993): 342-46.

Forth, S. "Emerging Technologies." *Journal of Library Administration* 17, no. 4 (1992): 15-23.

Kaufman, P. T., and T. J. Miller. "Scholarly Communication: New Realities, Old Values." *Library Hi Tech* 10, no. 3 (1992): 61-78.

Rutstein, J. S., et al. "Ownership Versus Access: Shifting Perspectives for Libraries." In *Advances in Librarianship*, vol. 17, edited by I. Godden, 33-60. New York: Academic Press, 1993.

Schwartz, C. A. "Scholarly Communication as a Loosely Coupled System." *College & Research Libraries* 55 (March 1994): 101-17.

Wilson, D. L. "Creating Electronic Texts: Scholar Believes New Encoding Guidelines Will Spur a Wave of New Research." *Chronicle of Higher Education* 40 (June 15, 1994): A19, A23.

Public

Batt, C. "Cutting Edge." *Public Library Journal* 7 (July/August 1992): 103-6.

Dervin, B. "Information—Democracy." *Journal of the American Society for Information Science* 45 (July 1994): 367-85.

LaRue, J. "Library Tomorrow." *Computers in Libraries* 13 (Fall 1993): 14-16.

McCune, B. "Leading Technology by the Nose: Denver Public's Booktech 2000." *Wilson Library Bulletin* 68 (November 1993): 33-35.

Newhagen, J. E. "Media Use and Political Efficacy." *Journal of the American Society of Information Science* 45 (July 1994): 386-94.

Rogers, E. M., L. Collins-Jarvis, and J. Schmitz. "The PEN Project in Santa Monica." *Journal of the American Society of Information Science* 45 (July 1994): 401-10.

Valauskas, E. J. "Using Internet in Libraries." *IFLA Journal* 20, no. 1 (1994): 22-28.

School

Bard, N. "Networking CD-ROMs." *Journal of Youth Services Libraries* 6 (Winter 1993): 185-89.

Burleigh, M., and P. Weeg. "KIDLINK: A Challenging and Safe Place for Children Across the World." *Information Development* 9 (Spring 1993): 47-57.

Callison, D. "Impact of New Technologies on School Media Center Facilities and Instruction." *Journal of Youth Services Libraries* 6 (Summer 1993): 414-19.

Caywood, C. "Tunneling Through the Internet." *School Library Journal* 40 (March 1994): 164.

"Hooked on Technology." *Book Report* 11 (November/December 1992): 20-23.

Hughes, D. R. "Appropriate and Distributed Networks: A Model for K-12 Educational Telecommunications." *Internet Research* 3 (Winter 1993): 22-29.

Martinez, M. E. "Access to Information Technologies Among School-Age Children." *Journal of the American Society of Information Science* 45 (July 1994): 395-400.

Sutton, R. E. "Equity and Computers in Schools." *Review of Educational Research* 61 (1991): 475-503.

Special

Ashdown, B. G. "Managing Information As a Corporate Asset." In *Looking to the Year 2000: Papers from the 84th Annual Conference of the Special Library Association,* 21-49. New York: Special Library Association, 1993.

Bennett, V. M., and E. M. Palmer. "Electronic Document Delivery Using Internet." *Bulletin of the Medical Library Association* 82 (April 1994): 163-67.

Brudvig, G. L. "Managing the Sea Change in Science and Technology Libraries." *Science and Technology Libraries* 12 (Summer 1992): 35-50.

Ertel, M. "Electronic Challenge: Providing and Evaluating Information Services." In *Online/CD-ROM '92,* 14th Conference Proceedings, 68-72. Wilton, CT: Eight Bit Books, 1992.

Hoffman, M. M. "Document Supply Service of the AT&T Library Network." In *Looking to the Year 2000: Papers from the 84th Annual Conference of the Special Library Association,* 123-30. New York: Special Library Association, 1993.

Kreizman, K. "Optimizing and Enhancing Information Resources: Development of a Corporate Library Network." In *Looking to the Year 2000: Papers from the 84th Annual Conference of the Special Library Association,* 51-59. New York: Special Library Association, 1993.

Prime, E. "Virtual Library: A Corporate Imperative." *Information Technology and Libraries* 12 (June 1993): 248-50.

Tyler, J. K., and F. A. Brahmi. "Effect of a Local Area MEDLINE Network on Online End-user and Mediated Searching." *Medical Reference Services Quarterly* 12 (Winter 1993): 1-6.

Weinstein, L. "Lifenet/Internet and the Health Science Librarian." *Special Libraries* 85 (Winter 1994): 16-23.

II
Acquisitions

Acquisitions work involves locating and acquiring the items identified as appropriate for the collection. Only in the smallest libraries are the same people likely to do both selection and acquisition work. As the size of the library increases, so does the complexity of selection and acquisition work, which usually results in two separate, interrelated units.

To be fully effective, selection and acquisitions personnel must have a close, cooperative work relationship. Poor coordination will result in wasted effort, slow response time, and high unit costs. Achieving coordination requires that all parties understand the work processes, problems, and value of each other's work. Beyond the obvious purpose of supporting overall library objectives, the acquisitions department has both library-wide goals and departmental goals. One can group library-wide goals into five broad areas of purpose:

assist in developing a knowledge of the book and media trade

assist in the selection and collection development process

assist in processing requests for items to be added to the collection

assist in monitoring the expenditure of collection development funds

assist in maintaining all of the required records, and produce reports regarding the expenditure of funds

By disseminating information from book publishers and from media producers and vendors, the acquisitions department aids in the selection process. Normally, acquisitions departments maintain collections of publishers' catalogs, prepublication announcements, and book dealers' catalogs. They also collect information regarding changes in publishing schedules, new publishers, and new services. Many departments serve as clearinghouses for this type of information for the entire library. Indeed, in larger libraries, the department sometimes operates a limited selective dissemination of information (SDI) system by routing information to selectors based on each individual's subject or area of responsibility.

Processing requests for materials involves several activities to ensure that the library acquires the needed items as quickly and inexpensively as possible. Libraries would waste time and money if they simply forwarded requests to the appropriate publisher or vendor. Inaccurate information, duplicate requests, unavailable material, and similar problems would generate unacceptable costs for both the library and the supplier (and would probably cause considerable ill will). Each acquisitions department develops its own set of procedures to reduce problems of this type. Though there are hundreds of variations, the basic process is the same: preorder searching, ordering, receiving, fiscal managing, and record keeping.

Acquisitions departments also have internal goals. Four common goals are:

1. To acquire material as quickly as possible.

2. To maintain a high level of accuracy in all work procedures.

3. To keep work processes simple to achieve the lowest possible unit cost.

4. To develop close, friendly working relationships with other library units and with vendors.

Internal goals are important to the achievement of the broader, library-wide goals, because all of the department's decisions regarding internal goals will have some impact on other operating units in the library.

Speed is a significant factor in meeting patron demands and determining patron satisfaction. Many patrons want their material immediately. An acquisitions system that requires three or four months to secure items available in local bookstores will create a serious public relations problem. A system that is very fast but has a high error rate will increase operating costs, and will waste time and energy for both departmental staff and suppliers. Studies have shown that, in many medium-sized and large libraries, the costs of acquiring and processing an item are equal to or greater than the price of the item. By keeping procedures simple, and by periodically reviewing workflow, the department can help the library provide better service. Speed, accuracy, and thrift should be the watchwords of acquisitions departments.

Staffing

Staffing patterns play an important role in achieving departmental and library goals. Thoughtful staff planning is one aspect of providing efficient service. Efficient staffing usually involves using four classes of employees: professionals, library media technical assistants (LMTAs), clerks, and part-time help. Persons in each category supply certain skills and knowledge required for the optimum operation of the department.

Librarians provide in-depth knowledge of library operations and the book and media trades. They set departmental objectives and goals, prepare operating plans, develop policies, and supervise departmental operations. They also carry out tasks requiring special skills or knowledge, such as verifying requests for out-of-print items or checking rare or special collection items. If the acquisitions department does not have any selection responsibility (and few do), only the largest departments need to have many professionals. With properly planned procedures, support staff (LMTAs and clerks) can handle a large percentage of the department's activities.

Library media technical assistants are staff who have had some training in librarianship. Many LMTAs are graduates of community college library technician training programs and also hold a bachelor's degree. On the surface, this background appears similar to that of a library school graduate. Acquisitions departments make considerable use of LMTAs in conducting departmental activities. Acquisitions work requires some knowledge of librarianship, yet its structured nature makes it possible to employ LMTAs for most of the work. LMTAs have enough background to perform most functions effectively. Acquisitions typing and filing activities are appropriate for clerical and part-time staff.[1]

Several surveys indicate this staffing pattern is typical of U.S. libraries. One of the more comprehensive studies was that done by Karen Schmidt.[2] Her data showed that support staff perform at least 75 percent of each of the major acquisitions activities (preorder searching, ordering, claiming, and receiving). Another study, by James Coffey, reviewed personnel costs of library acquisitions. His message was that there is a need to carefully consider staffing patterns when one tries to control the cost of acquisitions work.[3]

An interesting aspect of the Schmidt article is her data showing the continuing division of acquisitions and serials work in the majority of the responding libraries.[4] This is despite little difference in the basic activities of the two departments (ordering, claiming, and receiving). Library automation system vendors recognize the large overlap and usually combine the two in one module. A sound review of technical service reorganization efforts, including merging acquisitions and serials departments, is by Gomez and Harrell.[5] There is a trend to merge the departments, as Loyola Marymount University did, when the library installs an integrated automation system. After four years, the merger at LMU is working smoothly. Certainly, one factor in deciding to merge departments is the need to control staffing costs.

As noted earlier, few acquisitions departments have any selection responsibility. Most libraries divide selection responsibility among all librarians and, in some instances, users. Many large public and research libraries employ full-time subject specialists for collection development work. Even in such libraries, the individuals involved in the process must cover broad subject areas or select materials published in many countries. Chapter 1 outlined the six major collection development functions; each function has many elements. Beyond those basic functions, excluding acquisitions, selectors perform ongoing liaison activities with their primary user groups; review gift and exchange materials; review acquisition programs, such as approval plans and standing orders; take part in fund allocation discussions; conduct various user and circulation studies; be involved in deselection decisions; plan and implement collection evaluation studies; and identify needed retrospective materials. When one adds these duties to other full-time activities, as is typical in most libraries, it is not surprising to find that not all the duties are performed as often as everyone wishes. The result is that some activities receive little attention; deselection and user studies are two areas commonly given less time and effort than is desirable. This chapter covers only the basic functions of the acquisitions department staff (see fig. 11.1).

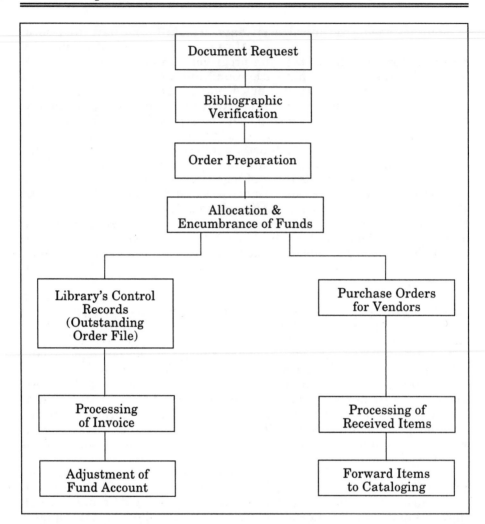

Fig. 11.1. Acquisition process. From *Introduction to Technical Services*, 6th ed., by G. Edward Evans and Sandra M. Heft. Englewood, Colo.: Libraries Unlimited, 1994, p.23.

Request Processing

The first step in acquisitions work is to organize the incoming requests. The form of the request varies from oral requests or a scrawled note on a napkin to a completed formal request card. Eventually, the staff organizes all requests so they can carry out an efficient checking process. Each library will have its own request form, typically a card produced by a library supply firm, such as Gaylord or Brodart. Requests arriving in other forms usually are transferred to a request card, making it easier to conduct the necessary searches. Sometimes, when selectors use a trade or national bibliography (such as *Booklist*), they simply check desired items in the publication, and the searchers work with the entire publication rather than transferring everything to request cards.

Commercially produced request cards cover all the categories of information called for in the *Guidelines for Handling Library Orders for In-Print Monographic Publications*,[6] that is, author, title, publisher, date of publication, edition, ISBN or ISSN, Standard Address Number (SAN), price, and number of copies. Many provide space for other information that is of interest only to libraries, such as requester's name, series, vendor, funding source, and approval signature. For any person not familiar with library or book trade practice, the most confusing item on the request card is the space labeled "date/year." Many nonlibrary requesters often assume the library wants the date they filled out the form, rather than the items' copyright or publication date. Anyone with acquisitions department experience knows how often this confusion takes place. If the form specifically calls for the date of publication, there will be no problem.

Many patrons request items already in the collection because they do not know how to use the public catalog. People occasionally combine or confuse authors' names, titles, publishers, and so on. Therefore, bibliographic searching is the next step in acquisitions work.

Preorder Work

Bibliographic verification or searching consists of two elements. First is establishing the existence of a particular item, that is, verification. Second is establishing whether the library needs to order the item, that is, searching. In verification, the concern is with identifying the correct author, title, publisher, and other necessary ordering data. Searching determines whether the library already owns the item (perhaps received but not yet represented in the public catalog), whether there is a need for a second copy or multiple copies, and whether the item has been ordered but not received. Integrated automated library systems make searching quick and easy, except for determining the need for additional copies. Many systems show ordered and received status in the online public catalog, which tends to reduce the number of requests that duplicate existing orders.

Where to begin the process? The answer depends on the collection development system employed by the library. Though it is true that all requests require searching, it also is true that not all request cards have sufficient correct information to search accurately. If the majority of information comes from bibliographies, dealers' catalogs, publishers' flyers, or forms filled out by selection personnel, then searching may be the most efficient way to start. A survey by Karen Schmidt of per-order searching indicates between 30 percent and 40 percent of nonlibrarian requests are duplicates or for items already in the collection.[7] When a large percentage of the selections are from nonlibrarians, it is advisable to start with the verification process.

One of the major activities for preorder searchers is establishing the correct author (main) entry. Some selectors, usually nonlibrarians, know little about cataloging rules of entry. Even bibliographers may not keep up-to-date on rule changes. Knowing something about main entry rules, as well as how the standard bibliographic sources list titles, will save search time.

Corporate authors, conference papers, proceedings, or transactions are the most troublesome to search. If the department maintains its order files in title rather than main entry order, it may be possible to reduce bibliographic training to a minimum while improving accuracy. Titles generally do not change after publication. On the other hand, catalogers' decisions about the proper main entry may change several times between the time of selection and the time the item is on the shelf. Main entry searching requires a greater knowledge of cataloging rules, which, in turn, requires more time for training searchers and more time spent searching.

If the author main entry search procedure does not verify 60-90 percent of the items, the staff should review the procedure. It is probable that either the requests lack adequate information (requiring additional education or training of requesters), or the staff is searching the wrong verification tools. A title search should verify most, if not all, the requests that cannot be verified by author main entry. Occasionally, it is impossible to verify an item using the submitted information. All the department can do is contact the requester to try to acquire additional information. If the requestor cannot provide additional information, a subject search may produce a verification. The success rate of subject searches is low for several reasons. First, some bibliographies do not provide subject access, making it impossible to search all the commonly used bibliographies. A more critical reason is that the assignment of subject is somewhat arbitrary. Even with a work in hand, two individuals may well provide two different subject categories for the same title. Searchers must look under as many subjects as seem likely and still can never be certain they examined all the appropriate headings. Because of its low success rate, subject verification is a last resort for urgently needed items.

Occasionally, it is necessary to examine three or four sources to establish all of the required order information. One may quickly find the author, title, publisher, date of publication, and price, but it may be difficult to find information determining whether or not the item is in a series. Failure to identify series information may lead to unwanted duplication, for example, one copy received on a series standing order and another copy from a direct order. *Books in Series* (R. R. Bowker) is helpful. However it covers only the United States (37,619 series with more than 326,688 titles).[8]

Both verification and searching procedures involve using several bibliographic tools, the major categories of which are described in chapter 5. Book dealers' catalogs are another helpful source (see chapter 12).

There are several files to check when establishing the library's need for an item. The most obvious starting point is the public catalog or the library's bibliographic database. A searcher should look first under the assumed main entry; if the results are negative and there is some doubt as to validity of the main entry, then a title search is appropriate. Many librarians suggest that checkers begin with the title because there tends to be less variation and doubt. In some libraries, even if there is an online public catalog, there exist a number of other public catalogs to search, for example, special collections or a nonprint catalog, and all should be part of the checking process, if appropriate. Audiovisual materials, government documents, serials, and collections in special libraries often are not fully represented in the online system or card catalog. Other public service files that searchers need to examine are those for lost, missing, or damaged items (replacement files). The searcher would not examine all of these files for all items, but merely for those popular items not marked "added copy" or "replacement."

In the technical services area, searchers have several files to examine to determine whether the item is already somewhere in the acquisitions receiving process. Normally, there are three files to consult if the department has a manual system: the in-process file, the verified requests file (items awaiting typing on order forms), and the standing order file. The in-process file represents books on order, books received but not yet sent to cataloging, and books in the cataloging department. The standing order file represents items that will arrive automatically from a supplier. Because standing order items usually are part of publishers' series, it is important that the checker examine the standing order file after establishing that an item is in a series.

Online systems are available in many libraries to speed preorder checking. *Books in Print* is available in both online and CD-ROM formats, as well as in the traditional print version. Other commercial bibliographic selection aids are available in electronic formats. Bibliographic utilities, such as OCLC, Western Library Network (WLN), and RLIN provide large bibliographic databases that are useful in verification and searching. Integrated automation systems have eased the workload on acquisitions. It is possible to download bibliographic data from a bibliographic utility. With some systems, the staff can use the downloaded data to prepare a computer-generated order form, provide an online status report, and create the basis for local cataloging work. In some libraries, a person responsible for preorder activities may be able to do 90 percent or more of the work at one terminal merely by logging on and off the integrated system and the bibliographic utility.

Ordering

Libraries employ five major acquisitions methods: firm order, standing order, approval plan, deposit or gift, and exchange. Each method has a useful role to play in developing a collection in an efficient, cost-effective manner. Most large and many medium-sized libraries use computer-generated orders and store the data electronically, thus reducing the volume of paper associated with ordering activities. For a few libraries, there is no order form for current trade books, because the libraries handle the entire order process electronically, storing the transaction in both the library's and the supplier's computers. In the future, this may be the way all libraries place their orders; however, for thousands of libraries, the paperless order is far from reality.

Regardless of the method used to order material, the vendor must receive enough information to assure shipment of the correct materials: author, title, publisher, date of publication, price, edition (if there are various editions), number of copies, order number, and any special instructions regarding invoicing or methods of payment. Also, more suppliers are asking for the International Standard Book Number (ISBN) or International Standard Serial Number (ISSN). In time, international standard numbers (ISNs) may be all the library needs to send, because ISNs are unique numbers representing a specific journal or a specific edition of a specific title.

A useful publication for all aspiring collection development officers is *Guidelines for Handling Library Orders for In-Print Monographic Publications.* Written by the Book Dealer–Library Relations Committee of the Resources and Technical Services division of ALA, it reflects the needs of both groups and contains recommendations for establishing and maintaining good working relationships. One suggestion is that libraries use the American National Standards Institute (ANSI) Committee Z39 single title order form, which measures 3-x-5-inches.

At present, there is no equivalent standard for electronic order transmission; however, ANSI Committee Z39 is working on such a standard.

Another standard of ANSI Committee Z39 is the Standard Address Number (SAN). Like the ISBN, the SAN is a unique number (of seven digits) that identifies each address or organization doing business in the American book trade. For example, the SAN of the Charles Von der Ahe Library at Loyola Marymount University is 332-9135; Brodart is 159-9984; and Libraries Unlimited is 202-6767. Perhaps, in time, all that will be necessary to order a title electronically will be three sets of unique numbers: the ISBN or ISSN and the SANs for the supplier and the buyer. Again, such ease of ordering is some time off, if it ever comes. Nevertheless, these unique numbers are useful as a cross-check for accuracy. Keys to SANs appear in a variety of sources, such as the *American Library Directory*, which provides library SANs.

With a manual system, libraries commonly use a multiple copy (fan-fold) order form for placing orders. These forms are available in a number of formats and contain from four to as many as twelve copies. The 3-x-5-inch size is standard in the United States. Normally, each copy is a different color for easy identification. There is no standard dictating a particular color for a certain purpose. A minimum of four copies is typical: (1) outstanding order copy, (2) dealer's copy, (3) claiming copy, and (4) accounting copy. Only the librarians' imagination limits the number of potential uses of additional copies. A few libraries still use ten copies. Some libraries mail two copies to the dealer and keep three or four in the in-process file. In the past, some libraries used one copy to order catalog cards from the Library of Congress or a commercial cataloging service. Today, such use is diminishing as more and more libraries use only online cataloging systems, such as OCLC and, if necessary, order cards from that source. In some larger systems, where selectors are not in close contact with the acquisitions department (as in academic libraries, where faculty members do much of the selecting), an information copy goes to the selector.

The in-process file may contain several copies of the order form. For example, after sending the order, the staff might place five copies in the in-process file. One copy represents on-order status, two are available for possible claims, one is to forward to cataloging with the item when it arrives, and the final one remains in the file, indicating that the book is being processed but is not yet ready for public use. Upon receipt, a staff member pulls all slips except the in-process slip. When the book is ready for circulation, the cataloging department returns a slip to acquisitions to prompt the removal of the in-process slip. Presumably, at this point a set of cards are in the public catalog indicating that the book is available for use.

Claiming and handling supplier reports is one of the more time-consuming and frustrating aspects of the order function. Most multiple-copy order forms have slips for these purposes. Purchasers have every reason to expect American commercial publishers, or vendors supplying titles from such publishers, to deliver or report on the status of the order within 90 days. For American noncommercial publishers (for example, university presses or professional associations), an additional 30 days (120 days total) is common for delivery or a report. Western European titles delivered to the United States normally require 180 days, and from countries with a developing book trade, a year or more is not uncommon. When there is an active collecting program from developing countries, one must expect a certain percentage of nonresponse. Learning how long to wait for delivery or a status report takes experience. (Harvard's Tozzer Library once received a monograph from Bolivia that was ordered five years earlier.)

When dealing with an American publisher, allowing for the normal two-way postal time, it is reasonable to send a second claim in 60 days, if there has been no response. Many order forms have a printed note stating "cancel after x days." Although such statements are legally binding, most libraries send a separate cancellation notice. Certainly, cancellation should not take place until after the normal response time passes, unless there are unusual circumstances, such as unexpected reductions in the budget. Unfortunately, over the past 20 years, many such cuts have taken place, and most vendors have been cooperative about making the adjustments. By establishing a regular cancellation time line, libraries that must expend funds within a fixed period can avoid or reduce the last-minute scramble of canceling outstanding orders and ordering materials that the vendor can deliver in time to use the funds.

Vendors should respond with a meaningful report when they cannot fill an order within a reasonable period. One less-than-helpful report that vendors did and occasionally still do use is "temporarily out of stock" (TOS). How long is temporarily? What has the vendor done to secure the item? Poor or inaccurate reporting costs the library money, as Audrey Eaglen points out in "Trouble in Kiddyland: The Hidden Costs of O.P. and O.S."[9] In periods of rapid inflation, each day the funds remain committed but unexpended erodes buying power because producers and suppliers raise prices without notice. Recommended vendor reports are "not yet received from publisher" (NYR); "out-of-stock, ordering" (OS, ordering); "claiming"; "canceled"; "not yet published" (NYP); "out-of-stock, publisher" (OS, publisher); "out-of-print" (OP); "publication canceled"; "out-of-stock indefinitely" (treat this one as a cancellation); "not our publication"

(NOP); "wrong title supplied"; "defective copy"; and "wrong quantity supplied." After one learns how long a vendor takes to supply items first reported in the recommended manner, it is possible to make an informed decision regarding when to cancel and when to wait for delivery.

Before placing an order, the staff must make three important decisions:

1. Which acquisition method to use.

2. What vendor to use.

3. Where is the money to come from.

The remainder of this chapter explores the methods of acquiring materials. Chapter 12 discusses vendors—when and how to use them and what to expect from them. Chapter 13 covers the fiscal side of acquisitions work.

For most current items, the firm order is the only logical method to use. It is often the best method for the first volume in a series, even if the selectors are thinking about ordering all the items in the series. There is a distinction between thinking about and planning on when considering series items. When the selectors know that the reputation of the publisher or editor of the series is sound, it is probably best to place a standing order. If there is some question about suitability or content of the series, a firm order or approval copy order for the first volume is the better choice. In late 1993, there were a number of e-mail messages on one of the collection development listservs discussing an article in *Lingua Franca* about a publisher that appears to be a vanity house but markets books as part of a series.[10] Getting to know publishers and editors is an important activity for selectors.

Though standing orders (sometimes also called blanket orders) save ordering paperwork, selection staff must periodically review incoming material to assure that the material received is still appropriate. (Review of standing orders and approval materials is normally the responsibility of selector(s), not the acquisitions department.)

Deciding to use the gift or deposit method of acquisition will almost always result in a long delay in receiving the desired item. Verification may establish that the item is a government publication that may be part of the library's depository program, or it may be a new government series that should become part of the program. In either case, one would not issue a firm order but would notify the requester so he or she can decide what to do. Sometimes a library user or board member donates certain materials on a regular basis, making it unnecessary to order the item if there is no immediate demand for the material. Occasionally, an appropriate series or set costs so much a library cannot buy it with regular funding sources. Seeking out a donor to assist with funding or pay for the purchase is not unheard of, but again, there may be substantial delays in acquiring the item. Most often, this takes place with rare books and special collections items. An active (and well-to-do) Friends of the Library group may be the answer to a special purchase situation. Friends groups, used judiciously, can significantly expand the collection and stretch funds.

Gifts and Deposits

Usually, acquisitions departments are the ultimate recipients of unsolicited gifts of books, serials, and other materials (including a variety of molds and insects) that well-meaning people give to the library. Both solicited and unsolicited gifts can be a source of out-of-print materials for replacement, extra copies, and the filling of gaps in the collection. The collection development policy statement on gifts will help acquisitions personnel process the material quickly. A good article outlining all aspects of handling gifts is Mary Bostic's "Gifts to Libraries: Coping Effectively."[11]

Searching gifts is important, because the library should not add unnecessary items, and the processing and storage costs are the same for a gift as for a purchased item. However, a library cannot afford to discard valuable or needed items that arrive as gifts. Older books require careful checking, as variations in printings and editions may determine whether an item is valuable or worthless. (Usually, a second or third printing is less valuable than the first printing of a work.) Searching must be done by persons with extensive training and experience in bibliographic checking.

There are two basic types of exchange activity: the exchange of unwanted duplicate materials, and the exchange of new materials between libraries. Usually, only large research libraries engage in exchanging new materials. In essence, cooperating institutions trade institutional publications. Tozzer Library has exchange agreements with several hundred organizations. These organizations send their publications to Tozzer which, in turn, sends them Peabody Museum publications. Often, this method is the only way a library can acquire an organization's publications. Occasionally, libraries use this system to acquire materials from countries in which there are commercial trade restrictions. Where government trade restrictions make buying and selling of foreign publications difficult or impossible, the cooperating libraries acquire (buy) their local publications for exchange. Exchanges of this type are complex and difficult to manage, and this is a method of last resort. Libraries can exercise better quality control when they trade for known organizational series or titles than when the choice of publications from the organization is more or less left to chance. Exchanges of this type exist on the basis of formal agreements between the cooperating organizations. They play an important role in developing comprehensive subject collections.

Libraries add only a small percentage of gifts to the collection. This means the library must dispose of a great many unwanted items. In some libraries, a separate unit handles unneeded material; this unit usually is called the exchange unit. In most cases, it is the gift unit that handles the disposal work.

Disposition of unwanted gift materials is an activity that almost every library engages in at some time. One method is to list the unwanted items and mail the list to exchange units in other libraries, and the first library to request an item gets it for the shipping cost (usually book rate postage). This method is time-consuming. Another method is to arrange with an out-of-print dealer to take the items, usually as a lot rather than for a per-item price. It is unusual to receive cash; instead, the dealer gives the library a line of credit. The library uses the credit to acquire materials from the dealer. This system works well when the library has specialized materials the dealer wants and when the dealer stocks enough useful material so that the library can use its credit within a reasonable time (less than 18-24 months.) Holding a book sale is yet another method of disposing of unwanted material, one that is gaining in popularity as dealers resist the credit memo system. Staff must select the items for sale, establish a fair price, find a suitable location, and monitor the sale. Depending on the volume of gifts, annual, semiannual, or monthly sales are appropriate. Sales can be an excellent Friends of the Library project that can save some staff time. A few libraries use an ongoing sale tactic, especially when they have limited staff and space and a high volume of unwanted gifts.

Order Placement and Receiving

After selecting a vendor, a staff member assigns an order number and decides which fund to use for payment. Order numbers assist the staff in tracking the order. The assignment process is simply a matter of checking the last order number and using the next number in the sequence. As soon as the department head signs the orders, they are ready for mailing.

Receiving orders, though not difficult, requires careful planning. If not handled properly, receiving can be more complex and time-consuming than ordering. As strange as it may seem, proper unpacking of shipments will save everyone in the department a great deal of time, energy, and frustration. Finding the packing slip or invoice is the key first step in the process. A packing slip lists all the items in a particular shipment. An invoice is an itemized bill, which business offices require before they will issue a voucher or check. For receivers' convenience, most vendors attach a clearly-marked envelope containing the packing slip to the outside of one of the boxes. Unfortunately, a few vendors seem to delight in hiding the slip in strange places. One technique is to enclose the slip inside one of the items, and another favorite hiding place is under a cardboard bottom liner on the bottom of the box. If no packing slip is found, it is essential to keep the items separated from other materials in the receiving area. Mixing shipments can create seemingly endless problems.

A second important step is to check each item against the packing slip as it comes out of the box. This serves as a check on what the shippers think they sent against what the library actually received. Boxes go astray in shipment, shipping room clerks overlook items, and sometimes, items disappear from the library before processing. Checking the physical condition of each item is another step in the receiving process. Defective materials may be returned for credit or replacement without prior approval from the vendor. Imperfections can be of many kinds. With books, typical problems are missing or blank pages or improperly collated texts. Staff members need to check audiotapes and videotapes for gaps, blank or fogged sections, and proper recording speed. Microforms need to be examined to assure the producer processed them properly; sometimes they have fogged, streaked, or spotted areas, and occasionally, there is hypo residue, which can ruin the film. The following list highlights some common receipt problems:

The wrong edition sent. (Note: The checker must be aware of the difference between an edition and a printing. A new edition means there are substantial changes—material added or deleted; a new printing merely indicates the publisher sold out the previous printing and reprinted more copies with no changes in the text.)

Items ordered but not received.

Items not ordered but shipped.

Too many or not enough copies sent.

Imperfect copies received.

Vendors usually are good about accepting returns of unwanted items, even when it turns out to have been the fault of the library—as long as the library has not property marked them.

After determining that the shipment is complete, property marking (such as stamping or embossing) takes place. As noted above, sometimes items disappear, so the sooner property marking takes place the more difficult it will be for materials to vanish without a trace. Property marking takes many forms. Stamping the fore-edge and the title page of books is a common practice. (Rare books are handled differently.) Another method is to accession items, that is, to give each item a unique number. A staff member records the number and title of the item in an accessions book. Today, linking the bar code in an item to its item record in a database accomplishes the same type of inventory control with much less effort.

The last step in processing is approving the invoice for payment. Normally, this requires the signature of the head of the department or that person's representative. Usually, only a completely filled order may be approved for payment. The library bookkeeper passes on the approved invoice to the agency that actually issues the check. Rarely does a library itself write such checks; it is done by the governing agency.

Automatic Acquisitions Activities

Clearly, acquisitions work involves myriad details as well as extensive record keeping. Having detailed and accurate records is essential for effective planning for collection development. Manual systems worked reasonably well in the past and continue to do so in many acquisitions departments. Computerized systems offer greater accuracy, more detail, high speed, a variety of management reports almost impossible to get from a manual system, and faster and wider distribution of results. Figure 11.1 charts the acquisition process. If one knows how computers operate, the potential applications for acquisitions work are clear for all but perhaps the first and last steps. Most commercial computerized acquisitions systems cover all but the first and last steps. Several commercial systems offer an optional module that allows for electronic document requests. There is some debate about which system (manual or automated) allows for the easiest cross-training of acquisitions staff. Someday, when all library clients have their own personal computers and can access the library's computer system, the electronic request process may become standard.

Bibliographic verification was one of the last functions vendors built into commercial computerized acquisitions systems. The key was having access to large bibliographic databases that contained both current imprints (preferably all current imprints) and retrospective imprints. A second limiting factor was the types of searching methods that one could use in each database. Often, the person making a request fails to provide complete or correct information about the desired item. Lacking complete information, searchers must employ a variety of search strategies before securing all the needed information. In the past, most databases provided author and title searching, but subject search capability was lacking. National bibliographic utilities now allow subject searches as well as searches by publisher, date of publication, and series. (An example of a bibliographic utility's extended search service is OCLC's PRISM.)

With each passing year, retrospective search capability improves, but most verification work for pre-1960 imprints is through manual searching. A computer system for the antiquarian and out-of-print book trade (Book-Ease) is available, but it is primarily a word processing and spreadsheet system for individual stores. As more and more dealers use electronic systems that contain catalogs and auction book prices, it will be possible to develop an out-of-print database. That day is in the future, but it is getting closer.

Order preparation, encumbering, account reconciliation, and other accounting functions were among the first activities that vendors automated. Today, most large and medium-sized acquisitions departments have computerized all or most of their bookkeeping functions. Even one-person libraries can be automated if the librarian has access to a personal computer. Existing software allows one to automate the library's bookkeeping routines. Order form preparation is available on commercial systems. Most major book vendors offer some type of electronic ordering. The day is approaching when orders can be accurately and quickly processed using nothing more than ISBNs, ISSNs, and SANs.

Receiving items is not yet fully automated. Many books and some journals have the ISBN or ISSN printed on them in a bar code, thus holding out the prospect of quick and accurate receipt work. The computer checks the bar code number against the outstanding order file and indicates whether the item is on order and how many copies are on order.

The second edition of this book listed 10 functions that would be desirable in any good automated system. The list, revised and expanded, includes:

Verify the bibliographic data for a requested item.

Interface with and have downloading capabilities for national bibliographic utilities.

Verify that the item is not already on order or in process.

Verify price and availability.

Prepare the purchase order.

Send orders electronically.

Encumber the correct amount of money.

Produce claims for late or nondelivered orders.

Maintain and update the on-order or in-process file.

Record receipts of orders and check for completeness of orders.

Prepare payment authorization forms for orders.

Process electronic invoices.

Prepare the necessary financial and statistical reports for the department.

Produce management reports for collection development officers and outside agencies.

Access to large bibliographic databases is essential for verification work. Ideal systems allow for full access to the library's bibliographic utility as well as to every item in its collection. (For many libraries, access to all items in the collection is a dream. Many large libraries will not be able to convert all of their bibliographic records due to the high cost of conversion.) Many people question the cost benefit of such conversion activities because use tends to decline sharply after a few years (see chapter 15). Access to the various bibliographic utilities, to vendor systems (for checking availability and electronic ordering), and to an online in-print database completes the desired system. Bowker's *Books in Print* is available online, on CD-ROM, or on tape, and some vendors allow free searching of an electronic version of *BIP* when the library does a certain volume of business with the vendor. Vendors are also working with bibliographic utilities on interface problems so that it will be possible to search in more than one utility.

Selecting an Automated System

Libraries have a wide variety of computer systems to consider, from PC to mainframe. Each year, usually in April, *Library Journal* publishes a library automation survey article. The 1994 article lists 29 vendors who installed more than 11,000 new systems in 1993, not including more than 6,500 PC-based systems installed in school media centers by two vendors.[12]

The library needs to be cautious and thoughtful in selecting an automated system. One issue to consider is how long there will be support for the selected system. Large companies and bibliographic utilities have been in and out of the automated acquisitions systems business.[13] Long-term support is as important as the ability to move data from one system to another if the library's needs change or the vendor ceases to exist.

There are four general types of organizations offering computer systems and services to libraries. They are:

- Library cooperatives and consortia, which provide for the sharing of materials and expertise. These include organizations like the Research Libraries Group (RLG), which organized its membership to provide the capacity to work together to meet mutual needs through interinstitutional planning and cooperation.

- Nonprofit computerized bibliographic organizations, which provide their services to members for a fee. Examples are OCLC and WLN.

- Commercial vendors with turnkey (that is, ready-to-operate) systems for cataloging, materials control, and acquisition. Dynix, NOTIS, and Innovative Interfaces are commercial organizations that sell integrated library systems.

- Broker networks or library service centers that arrange for cooperating institutions to obtain automated services at discounted prices. AMIGOS Bibliographic Council (Dallas), and SOLINET (Southeastern Library Network) are in this group.

Connectivity among the various systems is an issue. Connectivity among the library's automated system and (1) other computers in the library (PCs and Macs); (2) local area networks and wide area networks that the library must use to distribute library information; (3) information networks, such as the Internet; and (4) national bibliographic utilities, such as OCLC. As noted earlier, there also are concerns regarding the ability to migrate from one system to another (that is, to move bibliographic and patron data from one vendor's system to another). In addition, one must consider how existing applications software (for example, Windows, Lotus, and WordPerfect) will interface with the system. If anything, these concerns are of greater significance than they were in the past.

Future Developments

What about the future of automated acquisition systems? One does not have to be a prophet to predict greater growth in the use of online systems. Furthermore, it is likely that in our lifetime the technical service aspects of the hypothetical total library system will exist with a national online bibliographic database. Steps are being taken in that direction, and some steps are being taken toward an international system.

Undoubtedly, hardware and software technology, especially in the area of the small, relatively inexpensive home computer systems, will make it increasingly possible for local variations to exist and yet allow the library to tie into regional and national systems. The idea that all homes and offices will have terminals that tie into a library's online catalog is no longer a daydream. In fact, OCLC experimented in 1980 with a local (Columbus, Ohio) cable television company to provide subscribers with access to the Columbus and Franklin County public libraries and information about their services and holdings; libraries elsewhere are exploring the idea of home access to bibliographic data. With each new subsystem bringing the total integrated library system closer to reality, collection development can become more effective and efficient. But, despite the marvels of technology, there will always have to be intelligent, widely read, humanistic and service-oriented information professionals making the decisions and planning the systems.

Summary

This chapter touched on only the basic activities and problems in acquisitions work. The following three chapters cover vendors and suppliers, fiscal management related to collection development, and an overview of how automation assists in collection development activities.

Notes

[1]The details regarding support staff acquisition duties are discussed in G. Edward Evans and Sandra Heft, *Introduction to Library Technical Services,* 6th ed. (Englewood, CO: Libraries Unlimited, 1994).

[2]Karen Schmidt, "Acquisition Process in Research Libraries," *Library Acquisitions: Practice and Theory* 11, no. 1 (1987): 35-44.

[3]James Coffey, "Identifying Personnel Costs in Acquisitions," in *Operational Costs in Acquisitions,* edited by J. Coffey, 55-74 (New York: Haworth Press, 1990).

[4]Schmidt, "Acquisition Process in Research Libraries."

[5]Joni Gomez and Jeanne Harrell, "Technical Services Reorganization: Realities and Reactions," *Technical Services Quarterly* 10, no. 2 (1992): 1-15.

[6]*Guidelines for Handling Library Orders for In-Print Monographic Publications,* 2d ed. (Chicago: American Library Association, 1984).

[7]Karen Schmidt, "Cost of Pre-order Searching," in *Operational Costs in Acquisitions,* edited by J. Coffey, 5-20 (New York: Haworth Press, 1990).

[8]*Books in Series* (New York: R. R. Bowker, 1989).

[9]Audrey Eaglen, "Trouble in Kiddyland: The Hidden Costs of O.P. and O.S.," *Collection Building* 6 (Summer 1984): 26-28.

[10]Warren St. John, "Vanity's Fare: The Peripatetic Professor and His Peculiarly Profitable Press," *Lingua Franca* 3 (September/October 1993): 1, 22-25, 62.

[11]Mary Bostic, "Gifts to Libraries: Coping Effectively," *Collection Management* 14, nos. 3/4 (1991): 175-84.

[12]Jose-Marie Griffiths and Kimberly Kertis, "Automated System Marketplace—1994," *Library Journal* 119 (April 1994): 50-59.

[13]"Librarians Attack OCLC for Abandoning Systems," *Library Journal* 111 (April 1, 1986): 21.

Further Reading

General

Alldredge, N. S. "Doing Business in the West." *Library Acquisitions: Practice and Theory* 15, no. 1 (1991): 21-27.

Baker, J. W. "Acquisitions Principles and the Future of Acquisitions." *Library Acquisitions: Practice and Theory* 17, no. 1 (1993): 23-32.

Bushing, M. C. "Acquisitions Ethics." *Library Acquisitions: Practice and Theory* 17, no. 1 (1993): 47-52.

Carter, R. A. "And What Do Librarians Want?" *Publishers Weekly* 237 (June 8, 1990): S12-S16.

Fisher, W. "Education for Acquisitions." *Library Acquisitions: Practice and Theory* 15, no. 1 (1991): 29-31.

Jackson, P. "Business of Acquisitions." *Technicalities* 9 (June 1989): 5-7.

Kennedy, G. A. "Relationships Between Acquisitions and Collection Development." *Library Acquisitions: Practice and Theory* 7, no. 3 (1983): 225-32.

Magrill, R. M., and D. J. Hickey. *Acquisitions Management and Collection Development in Libraries*. Chicago: American Library Association, 1984.

Ogburn, J. L. "Theory in Acquisitions: Defining the Principles Behind Practice." *Library Acquisitions: Practice and Theory* 17, no. 1 (1993): 33-40.

O'Neill, A. L. "Evaluating the Success of Acquisitions Departments." *Library Acquisitions: Practice and Theory* 16, no. 3 (1992): 209-19.

———. "How Richard Abel Co., Inc., Changed the Way We Work." *Library Acquisitions: Practice and Theory* 17, no. 1 (1993): 41-46.

Samore, T. *Acquisition of Foreign Materials for U.S. Libraries*. 2d ed. Metuchen, NJ: Scarecrow Press, 1982.

Schmidt, K. A., ed. *Understanding the Business of Acquisitions*. Chicago: American Library Association, 1990.

Academic

Archer, J. D. "Preorder Searching in Academic Libraries." *Library Acquisitions: Practice and Theory* 7, no. 2 (1983): 139-44.

Atkinson, R. "Acquisitions Librarian As Change Agent in the Transition to the Electronic Library." *Library Resources & Technical Services* 39 (January 1992): 7-20.

Bucknall, C. "Mass Buying Programs." In *Collection Management: A New Treatise,* edited by C. B. Osburn and R. Atkinson, 337-50. Greenwich, CT: JAI Press, 1991.

Clark, M. "Gifts and Exchanges." In *Understanding the Business of Library Acquisitions*, edited by K. A. Schmidt, 167-86. Chicago: American Library Association, 1990.

Diodato, L. W., and V. P. Diodato. "Use of Gifts in a Medium-Sized Academic Library." *Collection Management* 5 (Summer 1983): 53-71.

Hewitt, J. A. "On the Nature of Acquisitions." *Library Resources & Technical Services* 33 (April 1989): 105-22.

Jasper, R. P. "Challenge, Change, and Confidence: The Literature of Acquisitions." *Library Resources & Technical Services* 36 (July 1992): 263-75.

Pritchard, S. M. "Foreign Acquisitions." In *Collection Management: A New Treatise,* edited by C. B. Osburn and R. Atkinson, 351-72. Greenwich, CT: JAI Press, 1991.

Zager, P. A., and O. A. Samadi. "A Knowledge-Based Expert Systems Application in Library Acquisitions." *Library Acquisitions* 16, no. 2 (1992): 145-54.

Public

Bullard, S. R. "Acquisitions-Ache and Its Relief." *American Libraries* 18 (November 1987): 857-60.

Gambles, B. R. "Which Supplier?" *Public Library Journal* 6 (November/December 1991): 153-56.

Hoffert, B. "Paperback Bind." *Library Journal* 116 (July 1991): 51-55.

McLachlan, R. W. "Public Libraries—Shrinking Dollars, Increased Demands." *OCLC Micro* 7 (December 1991): 19-22.

Steinbrenner, J. "Cost-Effectiveness of Book Rental Plans." *Ohio Library Association Bulletin* 49 (April 1979): 5-6.

Vertrees, L. S. "Foreign Acquisitions: Frustration and Fun!" In *Vendors and Library Acquisitions*, edited by W. Katz, 75-81. New York: Haworth Press, 1991.

Schools

Brodie, C. S. "Promotional 'Hotlines.' " *School Library Media Activities Monthly* 7 (April 1991): 42-44.

Kemp, B. *School Library and Media Center Acquisitions Policies and Procedures.* 2d ed. Phoenix, AZ: Oryx Press, 1986.

"Ordering Procedures." In *Media Program in the Elementary and Middle Schools,* edited by J. J. Delaney, 126-44. Hamden, CT: Shoe String Press, 1976.

Pretorius, M. "Strengthen Your Buying Power Through Reviews." *Ohio Media Spectrum* 42 (Spring 1990): 18-22.

Roback, D. E. "Checking Out Children's Books." *Publishers Weekly* 238 (May 31 1991): 38-39.

Tucker, C. "Selection Power." *Ohio Media Spectrum* 42 (Spring 1990): 26-29.

Special

Ali, S. N. "Acquisition of Scientific Literature in Developing Countries." *Information Development* 5 (April 1989): 151-68.

Byrne, N. "Selection and Acquisition in an Art School Library." *Library Acquisitions: Practice and Theory* 7, no. 1 (1983): 7-11.

Cooper, E. R. "Options for the Disposal of Unwanted Donations." *Bulletin of the Medical Library Association* 78 (October 1990): 388-94.

Dickson, L. E. "Law Library Book Orders." *Law Library Journal* 73 (Spring 1980): 446-50.

Moore, E. "Acquisitions in the Special Library." *Scholarly Publishing* 13 (January 1982): 167-73.

Myers, A. K. "Acquiring Minds Want to Know." *Law Library Journal* 83 (Summer 1991): 479-91.

St. Clair, G., and J. Treadwell. "Science and Technology Approval Plans." *Library Resources & Technical Services* 33 (October 1989): 82-92.

Schaffer, E. G. "Georgetown University's Developing Foreign Law Policy." *Legal Reference Service Quarterly* 9, nos. 1/2 (1989): 121-26.

Wineburgh-Freed, M., et al. "Library-Wide Use of a dBase Acquisition System." *Bulletin of the Medical Library Association* 76 (January 1988): 73-74.

12
Distributors and Vendors

Chapter 6 identified three major problems for materials producers: economics, copyright infringement, and distribution. A knowledge of distribution is essential for developing the most cost-effective collection of information materials. Wholesalers, retailers, and remainder houses are major sources of material for the library collection. Often, several different sources can supply the same item. Is there an important difference among these sources? What services does each provide? For example, if one is looking for a book published last year, it is possible to acquire a copy from many of the sources. Would it matter which source is used? How likely is it that all would have the book? For that matter, what function does each source perform?

Jobbers and Wholesalers

Librarians refer to *jobbers* or *vendors* rather than wholesalers. There is a technical difference between a wholesaler and a jobber,[1] but for libraries, the difference is insignificant. Jobbers purchase quantities of books from various publishers, then sell the copies to bookstores and libraries. Because they buy in volume, they receive a substantial discount from publishers. When the jobber sells a book, the purchaser receives a discount off the producer's list price, but it is much lower than the discount that the jobber received. For instance, if the jobber received a 50 percent discount from the producer, the discount given the library will be 15-20 percent. If the library or bookstore orders the book directly from the publisher, the discount may be as high or perhaps even higher.

Discounting is a complex issue in any commercial activity, and it is highly complex in the book trade. Every producer has a discount schedule that is slightly different, if not unique. Some items are net (no discount); usually, these are textbooks, scientific and technical titles, or items of limited sales appeal. Short discounts are normally 20 percent; these are items the producers expect will have limited appeal but with more potential than the net titles. Trade discounts range from 30 to 60 percent or more; items in this category are high-demand items or high-risk popular fiction. Publishers believe that by giving a high discount for fiction, bookstores will stock more copies and thus help promote the title. Jobbers normally receive 50-60 percent discounts, primarily because of their high-volume orders (hundreds of copies per title rather than the tens that most libraries and independent bookstore owners order).

Recently, jobbers have encountered financial problems in the form of rising costs and declining sales. A number of publishers are requiring prepayment or have placed jobbers on a pro forma status. Pro forma status requires prepayment, and suppliers extend credit on the basis of the current performance in payment of bills. Much of the credit and order fulfillment extended by publishers depends on an almost personal relationship with a jobber. This means that libraries must select a jobber with care. It is not inappropriate to check a prospective jobber's financial status (through a rating service, such as Dun and Bradstreet).

What Can Jobbers Do?

Why buy from an indirect source that charges the same or a higher price than the direct source would? Service! Jobbers provide an important service in that they can save a library a significant amount of time and money. Although jobbers do not give high discounts, the time saved by placing a single order for 10 different titles from 10 different publishers (instead of 10 different orders) more than pays for the slightly higher price. Other savings can result from the batch effect of unpacking only one box and authorizing only one payment. Most jobbers also promise to provide fast, accurate service. It is true that a few publishers, if they accept single-copy orders (and most do), handle these orders more slowly than they do large orders. But it is also true that jobbers do not always have a specific title when the library wants it, which means that the library must allow additional time to secure the desired item.

Many jobbers promise 24-hour shipment of items in stock. Do they make good on such claims? Generally, yes; however, the key phrase is *in stock*. Frequently, there are delays of three to four months in receiving a complete order because some titles are not in stock. When talking with jobbers, do not become impressed by numbers quoted in their advertising, for example, "more than 2 million books in stock." What is important is how many titles and which publishers they stock. For various reasons, from economic to personal, some publishers will refuse to deal with a particular jobber. Four important questions to ask any jobber before a library contracts for that firm's services are:

1. Will you give me a list of all the publishers that you do not handle?

2. How does your firm handle a request for a title not in stock?

3. Will you give me a list of series that your firm does not handle?

4. Do you have any service charges on any category of material? (If so, ask if the charge is indicated on the invoice as a separate cost.)

Often, the answer to the first question is difficult to obtain. Sales representatives want to say they can supply any title from any publisher, with only minor exceptions. However, libraries in the same system may simultaneously receive different lists from various representatives of the same firm. The issue is important, and the acquisitions department must resolve the question if it is to operate effectively. Sending an order for a title from a publisher that the jobber cannot handle only delays matters. In some cases, the jobber will report that it is trying to secure the item; this often leads to a later report of failure, making the acquisition process even slower. Buying directly from the publisher is the best approach to this problem, if one knows which publishers the jobber cannot handle.

The second question relates to the speed of service. Some jobbers order a single title from a publisher when it is not in stock. Others say they will do this, but they may wait until they have received multiple requests before placing the order. By placing a multiple-copy order, the jobber receives a better discount. For the library, the delay may be one to several months, because it will take that long for the jobber to accumulate enough individual requests for the title to make up an order of sufficient size. Usually, jobbers that place single-copy orders for a customer offer a lower discount on those items. Again, the acquisitions staff must weigh service and speed against discount. Occasionally, a jobber will have a title in stock after the publisher has listed the item as out-of-print (OP). On occasion, a jobber can supply out-of-print material, and a few jobbers will even try to find out-of-print items for their best customers. This is a special service that is never advertised and is offered only to favored customers.

Beyond fast, accurate service, jobbers should provide personal service. A smooth working relationship is based on mutual understanding and respect. When those are present, it is much easier to solve problems, even the difficult ones. The jobber, because of the smaller base of customers, normally can provide answers more quickly than a publisher's customer service department. Even the small account customer receives a jobber's careful attention (in order to hold the account), something that seldom happens with publishers.

No single jobber can stock all of the in-print items that a library will need. However, most large firms do carry the high-demand current and backlist items. Book trade folklore says that 20 percent of the current and backlist titles represent 80 percent of total sales. All of the good jobbers try to stock the right 20 percent of titles. Some are more successful than others. Bookstores find this useful for maintaining their stock of bestsellers. Libraries, on the other hand, must acquire a broader range of titles. Thus, the opinion of bookstore owners about the best jobbers is useful only if librarians and bookstores agree about whether 20 percent of all titles will fill 80 percent of all needs.

One problem with a jobber that has limited stock is in invoicing and billing procedures. A small jobber may ship and bill for those items in stock, then backorder the remainder of the titles. In this case, the jobber expects to receive payment for the partial fulfillment of the order. However, some funding authorities allow payment only for complete orders. That is, the library must receive or cancel every item on an order before the business office will issue a check. This procedure can cause problems for small jobbers and libraries. Few small vendors are able or willing to wait for payment until a particular order is complete. For small libraries with small materials budgets, the problem is to find a jobber that will accept complicated procedures and delays despite low volume. It is becoming harder to find such firms, and libraries are attempting to persuade their funding authorities to simplify ordering and payment procedures.

Jobbers may handle thousands of different publishers and may maintain an inventory of more than 200,000 titles. One useful service that many large jobbers offer is a periodic report on the status of all of a library's orders. Many provide a monthly report on all items not yet shipped. They provide a list of backordered items along with the reason why each item is unavailable. A timely and complete status report will save both library and jobber unnecessary letter-writing campaigns and telephone calls. Most large jobbers offer a flexible order and invoicing system; that is, they try to adapt to the library's needs, rather than force the library to use their methods.

Status reports are an area of concern for both the acquisitions and collection development staff. Almost everyone in the field has been frustrated by these reports. Does a report stating a book is out of print mean the book is really out of print? It should, but occasionally, by contacting the publisher, the library may have the item in hand in less than 30 days. This happens often enough to keep alive doubts about the quality of jobber reports. Perhaps two of the most frustrating reports are out-of-stock (OS) and temporarily out-of-stock (TOS) reports. Exactly what these two reports mean varies from jobber to jobber. The basic meaning is clear: the book is not available at present. Beyond that, however, there is doubt. How long will the title be out of stock? Some cynics suggest that these reports really mean "We are waiting until we get enough orders from buyers to secure a good discount from the producer." The cynics propose that the difference between the two reports is that TOS means "We expect to have enough soon," and OS means "Don't hold your breath." Those interpretations are much too harsh, but they do indicate that there are problems with the quality and content of the reporting system. (Note: Not all blame for faulty reporting lies with jobbers; sometimes, producers change their plans after reporting a status to a jobber.) An article in a 1989 issue of *School Library Journal* reported 10 percent of all school library orders and 7 percent of public library orders are unavailable for some reason.[2]

Does it really matter how accurate the reports are? Yes, it does matter, and the result can have an impact on collection development. An item on order encumbers (sets aside) the necessary funds for payment. The acquisitions staff cannot determine the precise cost of the item until the invoice arrives; the price may change, the exact discount is unknown, and shipping and handling charges vary. One hopes to set aside slightly more than the total cost. Most libraries and information centers have annual budgets and operate in systems where any unexpended monies at the end of the fiscal year revert to the general fund (that is, the funds do not carry forward into the next fiscal year). In essence, the library loses the unspent money. Having large sums of money tied up (encumbered) in outstanding orders that are undeliverable before the end of the fiscal year can result in a real loss for the collection. In a sense, the library loses twice: wanted items go unreceived, and the library loses funds.

Another problem commonly encountered is the paperwork involved in cancellations and reordering. Many people have estimated the cost of normal library paperwork; these estimates range from $4 for a simple, two-paragraph business letter, to more than $21 for placing an order, to even more, depending on the complexity of the task, the organization, and the cost elements included in the calculation. Regardless of how one calculates the costs, one must consider the staff time, forms, letters, and postage involved in each transaction. Though these costs do not come out of the acquisitions budget, they represent a loss in the sense that the order did not result in the library receiving the desired material.

Finally, the library does lose some buying power as funds remain encumbered. Unlike money in a savings account, which earns a small amount of interest each day, encumbered funds lose a small amount of purchasing power each day. If inflation is rapid or if one is buying foreign books and the currency's value is fluctuating widely, losses can be large. Producers raise prices without notice, and in times of inflation, one can count on regular price increases. The less time funds remain encumbered, the more purchasing power the library has. Thus, the accuracy of vendor's reports is important. If the vendor cannot supply an item (OP, OS, or TOS) in time, and so informs the library, the library can cancel the order and use the funds for something that is available for delivery. Monitoring of vendor performance in report accuracy and speed of delivery can help control the problem.

A typical jobber, in addition to supplying books at wholesale prices, may offer libraries some or all of the following services:

cataloging and processing

continuation services

approval plans

automated ordering programs (some including book reviews)

book rental plans

media other than books

library furniture

library supplies

As this list suggests, the jobber attempts to offer most of the supplies and services necessary for library operation.

Many small libraries (and perhaps, in the future, large libraries) may find it beneficial to buy books already processed. Future studies may show this approach to be very cost-effective, if the public service staff and users find that the material supplied is adequate. Normally, the technical services offered by jobbers allow the library a number of choices. Processing kits that include catalog cards, pockets, labels, jackets, and so forth, are available for purchase; the library staff uses the kit to complete the processing routines. Some firms offer completely processed, ready-for-shelf products. Because U.S. libraries use several different classification systems, jobbers offer processing for all the major systems. In other countries, for example, the Scandinavian countries, there are central acquisitions, cataloging, and processing services that most (if not all) public libraries use to acquire and prepare their stock. Flexibility is essential in these services; yet, to make them cost-effective or profitable for the jobber, there must exist either a high degree of uniformity or, at least, a high sales volume for each variation. Thus, one can expect to receive a degree of personalized customer service but not custom processing.

Standing orders or continuations are a problem for most libraries. Publishers start a series with a number of books, each with a different number. Often, such a numbered series will last for many years. Ordering each title will waste staff time, assuming the library wants the entire series. Most jobbers offer some type of standing order plan that allows the automatic shipment of each new title in a series. Status reports on standing orders are as important as in regular orders. If the jobber includes all orders in the status report, this will save everyone time; next best is a status report issued at monthly, bimonthly, quarterly, or other standard interval. Any reputable dealer will explain just how much service to expect. No single jobber will be able to handle all standing order needs, and some titles are available only on a direct order or membership basis. Nevertheless, jobbers can provide excellent service for a large percentage of a library's needs.

Most book jobbers offer only a monographic continuation service. For journals and other serials, a serials jobber is preferable (for example, EBSCO's replacement copy bank). A basic difference between the two is that serials jobbers seldom offer any service except order placement. As with monographic continuations, there are some journals and serials that the library must order directly from the publisher. All of the questions the library asks of a book jobber are just as valid for serials jobbers. Of special concern is the size of the handling charges levied and to what they apply. By placing one order, or more typically, renewing subscriptions once a year for hundreds of serial titles, the library will save a large amount of staff time. When the firm provides fast, accurate service and a good reporting system, both the library and the jobber benefit.

One jobber, Brodart, offers a rather unusual service, the McNaughton Plan, to help solve the problem of providing an adequate number of high demand titles. Most libraries have suffered the problem of high demand for a popular book, with the demand lasting only a few months. Should the library buy many copies and discard all but one or two after the demand subsides, or buy only a few copies and take reservations? The McNaughton Plan offers another alternative: rent multiple copies for the duration of the title's popularity. Brodart describes the plan as a leasing program. The plan offers high demand items that Brodart's staff selects. One cannot order just any book; it must be on Brodart's list of high demand titles. Savings occur in several areas. There are no processing costs because the books come ready for the shelf, and the leasing fee is considerably lower than the item's purchase price. Patrons will be happier about shorter waiting times for the high interest books. All in all, anyone involved in meeting recreational reading interests will find the program worth investigating. College and university libraries may use it to stock a variety of materials for recreational reading without taking too much money out of the book fund. Currently, Brodart has plans for children's hardcovers, paperback books, and adult hardcovers.

Other services many vendors offer are electronic ordering and, especially useful for serials, electronic invoicing. Access to an electronic version of *Books in Print* is often part of the service as well. With electronic ordering, acquisitions staff have dial-in access to the vendor's inventory database. This allows one to learn the availability of a title, place an order, receive confirmation of receipt of the order, and receive the invoice electronically, with the entire process taking only a few seconds. One problem with electronic ordering is that most acquisitions departments use many different vendors, and each vendor offering this type of service seems to develop a number of variations in their systems. This is an area where standards could be beneficial to everyone. Learning and remembering, or consult manuals for several different electronic ordering systems, cuts into the possible time saved that are possible from using such systems. Some vendors offer useful management reports based on their electronic systems. An example from a serials vendor is illustrated in figure 13.4, on page 359. This report shows the library's average annual price increase for several years.

Another electronic service offered by several book jobbers (for example, Majors and Blackwell North America) is producing tables of contents of books in an electronic format for mounting on the library's OPAC. (The tables of contents are provided only for books the library has purchased.) This may also become a service option for serials vendors in the future.

What Does a Jobber Expect from the Librarian?

Librarians have responsibility for helping to maintain good working relationships with vendors. Simply stated, a vendor's profits are the difference between the price it pays producers and the resale price. Is this any different than for any other type of business? Not in the fundamentals, but there are some special aspects to the book trade and library market. One such variation is that any buyer can buy directly from the materials producer. This is seldom true in other fields. Another difference is that, to a large degree, libraries can determine what is the maximum price of any item by checking in-print lists, such as *Books in Print,* or by consulting the producer. When every buyer knows the maximum price as well as any producer discount, vendors must at least match the maximum price and provide superior service to hold customers.

Volume buying and selling is the only way a jobber can make a profit. Efficient plant operations and low overhead can help, but no matter how efficient the operation, it will fail without high volume. One order for 15 or 20 titles in quantities will yield a high discount for the jobber, perhaps as high as 60 percent. Even after giving a 20-25 percent discount to the library, the jobber has a comfortable margin with which to work. In the library market, such orders are usually the exception rather than the rule. More often, the jobber's discount is 50 percent. A smaller margin is still acceptable if all the items sell. But all of them do not! Many publishers have a return policy (in which a publisher buys back unsold books). However, many producers are changing or dropping the return policy, thus increasing the risk for the vendor. Returns normally result in credits against the current account or future purchases. They seldom result in a cash refund for book jobbers.

Jobbers, being dependent on volume sales, must know their markets very well to project sales and maintain proper stock in their warehouses. When a vendor representative stops by, the purpose is not mere public relations or, necessarily, an attempt to sell more books. Rather, it is an attempt to determine the library's plans for collection development. It is not curiosity nor an attempt to make conversation that generates questions like "How does next year's materials budget look?" The collection development librarian should take time to explain new programs and areas to be worked on or describe how budget prospects look for the next year. This type of information helps vendors plan their buying policies for the coming months.

Selection officers should ask jobbers' representatives about what is available in any field the library is developing, even if the selection officers think they know. The answers may be surprising. One should ask what the vendor could do to supply the items. Is it a field the vendor carries as part of the normal inventory, or is the field one for which the jobber has listed publishers? (Listed publishers indicate the vendor has an established relationship with the publisher but does not stock its titles. If the library uses a vendor for listed publishers, there will be a delay in receiving the material, because the jobber must forward the order to the publisher.) Such discussions take time but result in better service.

To get the maximum discount, some librarians dump their problem orders on vendors and order easy items directly from the publishers. Nothing could be more shortsighted. Without the income from easy, high-volume items, no jobber can stay in business. Someone has to handle the problem orders, and most vendors will try to track down the difficult items, especially for good customers. However, libraries should give jobbers easy orders as well. Almost all of the problems facing jobbers involve cash flow. Lack of cash has been the downfall of many businesses, and it becomes critical for jobbers when they handle only problem orders; staff expenses go up, but income does not. Failure of jobbers would lead to higher labor costs for most acquisitions departments as a result of having to place all orders directly with publishers.

Whenever possible, the library should use the order format preferred by the vendor and not plead legal or system requirements for a particular method of ordering, unless it is impossible to change the requirement. Most vendors and publishers go out of their way to accommodate the legal requirements of library ordering procedures. If libraries could come closer to a standardized order procedure, jobbers could provide better service, because they would not have to keep track of hundreds of variations. If libraries keep all paperwork to a minimum, everyone will benefit.

Though most jobbers accept a few returns from libraries, even if the library is at fault, returns create a lot of paperwork. If an item serves no purpose in a library's collection, perhaps it would save time and money to accept the mistake and discard it rather than return it, assuming mistakes are infrequent. Frequent mistakes signal a problem in the acquisitions department or selection procedures. (Note: This discussion refers to items sent in error; the library should return any defective copy.)

Finally, libraries should process invoices promptly; the acquisitions department should not hold them longer than necessary. Most library systems require at least two approvals before issuing a payment voucher: the library's approval and the business office's approval. Some systems have three or more offices involved in the approval process. The collection development officer should know the system, from approval to final payment. If payment takes longer than six weeks, the library should inform any new jobber of that fact so the firm can decide whether it can do business with the library. There is also a need to inform jobbers of any changes in the system that may have an impact on the speed of payment. Most jobbers would like to receive payment within 30 days because they are on a 30-day payment cycle with publishers.

Jobbers provide a valuable service to libraries. Given a good working relationship, both parties benefit. Following is a summary of the basic factors at work in establishing such a relationship:

What libraries expect from jobbers

large inventory of titles

prompt and accurate order fulfillment

prompt and accurate reporting on items not in stock

personal service at a reasonable price

What jobbers expect from libraries

time to get to know what the library needs

cooperation in placing orders

keeping paperwork to a minimum

prompt payment for services

There are a number of jobbers offering their services to U.S. libraries. Some of the larger and more active firms in marketing their programs are Brodart, Baker and Taylor, Ingram, Yankee Book Peddler, Ballen, Coutts, and Blackwell North America. There also exist specialized jobbers, such as Majors, a leading firm for medical, science, and technical books. Serials jobbers include EBSCO, Faxon, and Readmore.

Almost every jobber offers a variety of services, including some automated order placement and fulfillment services. Several offer information about average price increases, which can be helpful in budget preparation. Jobbers outside the United States appear in lists such as *Books in Other Languages,* published by the Canadian Library Association, and R. R. Bowker's *International Literary Market Place.*[3]

Vendor Evaluation

Acquisitions departments and collection development officers should monitor vendor performance. In the past, monitoring vendors was time-consuming and difficult, and it still is if one is working with a manual acquisitions system. Automated acquisitions systems can produce a variety of useful management/vendor reports very quickly. Knowing what to do with the quantity of data the systems can produce is another matter.

One obvious issue that arises in evaluation is which vendor performs best on a certain type of order (examples are conference proceedings, music scores, or video recordings). The first thing to do is to decide what *best* means. Highest discount? Fastest delivery? Most accurate reports? Highest percentage of the order filled with the first shipment? All of the above? The answer varies from library to library depending on local needs and conditions. Once the library defines *best*, it knows what data to get from the system. Other questions to consider are:

Who handles rush orders most efficiently?

Who handles international orders most effectively—a dealer in the country of origin or a general international dealer?

Are specialty dealers more effective in handling their specialties than are general dealers?

Figure 12.1, on pages 324-28, is a systems report covering two years' performance of some of Loyola Marymount University Library's vendors. It shows quantities of titles ordered, total expended, average delivery time, percentage of the order received, average cost of each order, what, if any, shipping/handling charges, and the discount for each of the vendors. In addition to system reports based on normal operating procedures, one can conduct some experiments by placing a random sample of a type of order with several vendors to assess their performance. When doing a test or experiment one must be certain that each vendor receives approximately the same mix of titles, that no vendor receives more or less easy or hard items to handle. Often, the normal procedure data reflects the use of a particular vendor for only one type of order. This makes comparing vendor performance rather meaningless because one is not comparing like groups. One can use the test method to select a vendor for a particular type of order and use the operating data approach to monitor ongoing performance.

Checking on the performance of serials vendors is more difficult. Most libraries use only domestic serials vendors because of the complexity of changing ongoing subscriptions. A library that is just establishing a current subscription list, or starting a large number of new subscriptions, might consider splitting the list between two or more vendors for several years to determine which would be the best sole source for the long term.

A limited amount of checking is possible through comparisons with other libraries. Often, this type of checking is done in a casual manner, that is, by merely asking a colleague in another library, "Do you use vendor X? How do you like them?" or "How much is your service charge?" To make valid and useful comparisons, one needs to know the other library's title mix. Recent developments of union catalogs based on OPAC data suggest that collections, even in apparently similar libraries, have surprisingly different holdings. Recently, the monograph holdings of Loyola Marymount, Santa Clara, University of San Francisco, and the University of San Diego libraries for a 10-year period were compared using the AMIGOS CD-ROM collection analysis software. The university librarians thought the collections would have a large percentage of overlap because the institutions are similar in size and programs. All were surprised to learn more than 80,000 titles of the 159,000 titles in the database were unique; that is, only one of the four schools held the title. Although the results were not as striking for serials holdings, the number of titles held by just one library was a surprise. These discoveries served to reinforce the idea that casual impressionistic assessments are suspect.

One way to compare serials vendors is to take a sample of commonly held titles. Check on the service charges on those titles, on the effectiveness of claims processing, and on issues like vendor follow-up and handling of credit memos.

In any vendor evaluation, keep in mind some of the problems vendors have with producers. These bear repeating:

changes in title, or not publishing the title

not being informed when publishing schedules change or when publishers suspend or cease publication

incorrect ISBNs or ISSNs

producers refusing to take returns

producers refusing to sell through vendors

producers reducing discounts or charging for freight and handling when those were free in the past

poor fulfillment on the producer's part

constantly changing policies on the producer's part

producer price increases without prior notice

Several years ago, a student in one of my collection development classes asked as we were discussing vendors, "Why are you so pro vendor? They are our enemies, with all their high prices and low discounts." Perhaps I am a little more aware of the vendor problems, having had work experience in both publishing and libraries. However, I am not "so pro vendor." Libraries depend on vendors; they offer services that save libraries time, effort, and staffing. Libraries need vendors and need to understand their problems. That said, one must monitor their performance, question charges, and challenge charges that seem inappropriate. Maintaining good relations is everyone's business. If librarians, vendors, and producers take time to learn about one another's business, working relationships will be better. We had a new regional manager of our serials vendor who

Text continues on page 328.

Fig. 12.1. Vendor Performance Statistics—Amounts
Review file record : 1 to 0
Count orders placed in period 07-01-92 to 05-31-94

		Est Price Orders	Est Price Recpts	Est Price Cancls	Est Price Orders	Amt Paid
1	abc	$11,426.92	$11,426.92	$0.00	$0.00	$12,405.34
2	acs	$620.00	$620.00	$0.00	$0.00	$866.00
3	ala	$75.99	$75.99	$0.00	$0.00	$59.22
4	amb	$15,365.92	$15,365.92	$0.00	$0.00	$14,346.38
5	amdta	$145.50	$145.50	$0.00	$0.00	$165.05
6	amece	$41.50	$41.50	$0.00	$0.00	$44.92
7	arl	$0.00	$0.00	$0.00	$0.00	$43.30
8	aufo	$39.95	$39.95	$0.00	$0.00	$47.93
9	auxam	$135.00	$135.00	$0.00	$0.00	$77.96
10	bakea	$101,166.54	$101,166.54	$0.00	$0.00	$77,823.50
11	baker	$131,411.76	$131,411.76	$0.00	$0.00	$118,973.50
12	bakev	$1,407.06	$1,407.06	$0.00	$0.00	$951.92
13	balbi	$492.36	$492.36	$0.00	$0.00	$473.34
14	bh	$7,846.32	$7,846.32	$0.00	$0.00	$7,838.64
15	blk	$405.30	$405.30	$0.00	$0.00	$391.99
16	bowk	$2,092.49	$2,092.49	$0.00	$0.00	$2,372.96
17	cam	$406.65	$406.65	$0.00	$0.00	$370.54
18	cing	$1,015.00	$1,015.00	$0.00	$0.00	$1,218.97
19	clali	$37.00	$37.00	$0.00	$0.00	$43.95
20	conqi	$90.00	$90.00	$0.00	$0.00	$106.37
21	crome	$599.00	$599.00	$0.00	$0.00	$280.63
22	cusms	$17.45	$17.45	$0.00	$0.00	$21.64
23	danbc	$219.70	$219.70	$0.00	$0.00	$254.19
24	dir	$18,855.63	$18,855.63	$0.00	$0.00	$19,834.11
25	dover	$511.15	$511.15	$0.00	$0.00	$433.46
26	easba	$179.95	$179.95	$0.00	$0.00	$195.77
27	eduvn	$79.95	$79.95	$0.00	$0.00	$9.72
28	euro	$890.99	$890.99	$0.00	$0.00	$1,293.00
29	eveps	$648.55	$648.55	$0.00	$0.00	$492.49
30	fanli	$413.00	$413.00	$0.00	$0.00	$475.18
31	fbc	$1,099.76	$1,099.76	$0.00	$0.00	$1,328.85
32	ffh	$4,153.09	$4,153.09	$0.00	$0.00	$4,680.85
33	gale	$2,434.85	$2,434.85	$0.00	$0.00	$2,465.73
34	geri	$631.75	$631.75	$0.00	$0.00	$2,135.64
35	gjrau	$578.00	$578.00	$0.00	$0.00	$572.66
36	grerp	$214.45	$214.45	$0.00	$0.00	$245.45
37	hacab	$214.75	$214.75	$0.00	$0.00	$240.86
38	harap	$45.00	$45.00	$0.00	$0.00	$13.64
39	harr	$54.00	$54.00	$0.00	$0.00	$65.87
40	hssc	$42.00	$42.00	$0.00	$0.00	$45.47
41	hunli	$45.00	$45.00	$0.00	$0.00	$23.85
42	ieee	$214.90	$214.90	$0.00	$0.00	$281.36
43	insm	$5,627.99	$5,627.99	$0.00	$0.00	$5,759.38
44	isi	$9,775.00	$9,775.00	$0.00	$0.00	$8,170.26
45	jwpla	$1,431.00	$1,431.00	$0.00	$0.00	$1,601.82
46	lacma	$144.95	$144.95	$0.00	$0.00	$162.91
47	limbc	$219.10	$219.10	$0.00	$0.00	$242.17
48	ling	$60.00	$60.00	$0.00	$0.00	$72.85
49	loc	$138.00	$138.00	$0.00	$0.00	$149.39
50	mapli	$9.95	$9.95	$0.00	$0.00	$13.50
51	meckl	$391.50	$391.50	$0.00	$0.00	$445.23
52	medfa	$164.85	$164.85	$0.00	$0.00	$191.65
53	mid	$6,617.09	$6,617.09	$0.00	$0.00	$6,949.43

Vendor Performance Statistics—Quantities
Review file record : 1 to 0
Count orders placed in period 07-01-92 to 05-31-94

		# Order Records	# Copies Ordered	# Orders Recd	# Copies Recd	# Orders Cancld	# Outstd Orders	# Claims	# Orders Claimed
1	abc	292	292	292	292	0	0	61	47
2	acs	4	4	4	4	0	0	1	1
3	ala	3	4	3	4	0	0	1	1
4	amb	417	417	416	416	1	0	38	27
5	amdta	12	12	12	12	0	0	12	6
6	amece	2	2	2	2	0	0	0	0
7	arl	1	1	1	1	0	0	1	1
8	aufo	1	1	1	1	0	0	0	0
9	auxam	3	3	3	3	0	0	0	0
10	bakea	2494	2494	2494	2494	0	0	0	0
11	baker	3065	3068	3065	3068	0	0	232	215
12	bakev	19	19	19	19	0	0	0	0
13	balbi	14	14	14	14	0	0	0	0
14	bh	133	134	133	134	0	0	1	1
15	blk	9	9	9	9	0	0	2	1
16	bowk	7	7	7	7	0	0	0	0
17	cam	8	8	8	8	0	0	0	0
18	cing	4	4	4	4	0	0	0	0
19	clali	6	6	6	6	0	0	0	0
20	conqi	1	1	1	1	0	0	2	1
21	crome	2	2	2	2	0	0	0	0
22	cusms	2	2	2	2	0	0	0	0
23	danbc	7	7	7	7	0	0	0	0
24	dir	327	333	325	331	2	0	12	11
25	dover	38	38	38	38	0	0	0	0
26	easba	17	17	17	17	0	0	0	0
27	eduvn	1	1	1	1	0	0	1	1
28	euro	15	15	15	15	0	0	9	8
29	eveps	49	49	49	49	0	0	0	0
30	fanli	3	3	3	3	0	0	0	0
31	fbc	31	31	31	31	0	0	14	7
32	ffh	35	35	35	35	0	0	2	2
33	gale	17	17	17	17	0	0	2	2
34	geri	19	19	19	19	0	0	20	15
35	gjrau	14	14	14	14	0	0	0	0
36	grerp	20	20	20	20	0	0	0	0
37	hacab	6	6	6	6	0	0	0	0
38	harap	1	1	1	1	0	0	0	0
39	harr	1	1	1	1	0	0	0	0
40	hssc	1	1	1	1	0	0	0	0
41	hunli	1	1	1	1	0	0	0	0
42	ieee	5	5	5	5	0	0	0	0
43	insm	40	40	40	40	0	0	0	0
44	isi	8	8	8	8	0	0	0	0
45	jwpla	4	4	4	4	0	0	0	0
46	lacma	3	3	3	3	0	0	0	0
47	limbc	12	12	12	12	0	0	0	0
48	ling	2	2	2	2	0	0	0	0
49	loc	4	4	4	4	0	0	0	0
50	mapli	1	1	1	1	0	0	0	0
51	meckl	11	22	11	22	0	0	1	1
52	medfa	4	4	4	4	0	0	0	0
53	mid	157	157	157	157	0	0	22	17

Fig. 12.1 continues on page 326.

Vendor Performance Statistics—Delivery Time
Review file record : 1 to 0
Count orders placed in period 07-01-92 to 05-31-94

		Ave Deliv Time	02 wks	04 wks	08 wks	12 wks	16 wks	17+ wks
1	abc	20.3	0	1	51	90	29	121
2	acs	13.2	0	2	0	0	0	2
3	ala	11.6	1	1	0	0	0	1
4	amb	12.9	0	0	80	183	96	57
5	amdta	32.3	0	0	6	0	0	6
6	amece	15.5	0	0	0	0	2	0
7	arl	27.0	0	0	0	0	0	1
8	aufo	6.0	0	0	1	0	0	0
9	auxam	7.0	0	0	3	0	0	0
10	bakea	0.0	2480	3	5	1	0	5
11	baker	7.9	452	1017	678	453	149	316
12	bakev	7.6	2	5	9	2	0	1
13	balbi	9.3	0	0	7	7	0	0
14	bh	9.8	0	3	96	13	6	15
15	blk	13.7	0	0	4	3	1	1
16	bowk	10.5	0	1	2	3	0	1
17	cam	5.6	0	0	8	0	0	0
18	cing	5.2	0	0	4	0	0	0
19	clali	4.0	0	6	0	0	0	0
20	conqi	47.0	0	0	0	0	0	1
21	crome	2.5	1	1	0	0	0	0
22	cusms	3.0	0	2	0	0	0	0
23	danbc	6.0	0	4	0	3	0	0
24	dir	4.7	145	80	65	9	4	22
25	dover	5.3	0	0	37	1	0	0
26	easba	3.2	9	2	6	0	0	0
27	eduvn	22.0	0	0	0	0	0	1
28	euro	19.4	0	0	2	2	3	8
29	eveps	5.7	1	0	48	0	0	0
30	fanli	3.0	0	3	0	0	0	0
31	fbc	21.5	0	0	0	12	2	17
32	ffh	4.0	4	28	0	1	0	2
33	gale	8.7	1	7	4	2	1	2
34	geri	27.0	0	0	0	1	0	18
35	gjrau	4.5	0	10	4	0	0	0
36	grerp	1.0	20	0	0	0	0	0
37	hacab	9.0	0	0	0	6	0	0
38	harap	9.0	0	0	0	1	0	0
39	harr	9.0	0	0	0	1	0	0
40	hssc	7.0	0	0	1	0	0	0
41	hunli	3.0	0	1	0	0	0	0
42	ieee	4.4	0	3	2	0	0	0
43	insm	5.3	1	11	28	0	0	0
44	isi	8.0	0	0	8	0	0	0
45	jwpla	5.0	0	0	4	0	0	0
46	lacma	4.3	2	0	0	1	0	0
47	limbc	2.0	12	0	0	0	0	1
48	ling	11.0	1	0	0	0	0	1
49	loc	12.5	0	0	0	3	0	1
50	mapli	14.0	0	0	0	0	1	0
51	meckl	18.0	0	2	0	0	2	7
52	medfa	6.2	0	1	3	0	0	0
53	mid	13.8	0	3	74	26	11	43

Vendor Performance Statistics—Percentages
Review file record : 1 to 0
Count orders placed in period 07-01-92 to 05-31-94

		# Orders	Ave Est Price/ Order	Ave Est Price Recd Order	Ave Amt Paid/ Order	% Orders Recd	% Orders Cancld	% Orders Claimed	Total Claims
1	abc	292	$39.13	$39.13	$42.48	100.00	0.00	16.09	61
2	acs	4	$155.00	$155.00	$216.50	100.00	0.00	25.00	1
3	ala	3	$25.33	$25.33	$19.74	100.00	0.00	33.33	1
4	amb	417	$36.84	$36.93	$34.48	99.76	0.23	6.47	38
5	amdta	12	$12.12	$12.12	$13.75	100.00	0.00	50.00	12
6	amece	2	$20.75	$20.75	$22.46	100.00	0.00	0.00	0
7	arl	1	$0.00	$0.00	$43.30	100.00	0.00	100.00	1
8	aufo	1	$39.95	$39.95	$47.93	100.00	0.00	0.00	0
9	auxam	3	$45.00	$45.00	$25.98	100.00	0.00	0.00	0
10	bakea	2494	$40.56	$40.56	$31.20	100.00	0.00	0.00	0
11	baker	3065	$42.87	$42.87	$38.81	100.00	0.00	7.01	232
12	bakev	19	$74.05	$74.05	$50.10	100.00	0.00	0.00	0
13	balbi	14	$35.16	$35.16	$33.81	100.00	0.00	0.00	0
14	bh	133	$58.99	$58.99	$58.93	100.00	0.00	0.75	1
15	blk	9	$45.03	$45.03	$43.55	100.00	0.00	11.11	2
16	bowk	7	$298.92	$298.92	$338.99	100.00	0.00	0.00	0
17	cam	8	$50.83	$50.83	$46.31	100.00	0.00	0.00	0
18	cing	4	$253.75	$253.75	$304.74	100.00	0.00	0.00	0
19	clali	6	$6.16	$6.16	$7.32	100.00	0.00	0.00	0
20	conqi	1	$90.00	$90.00	$106.37	100.00	0.00	100.00	2
21	crome	2	$299.50	$299.50	$140.31	100.00	0.00	0.00	0
22	cusms	2	$8.72	$8.72	$10.82	100.00	0.00	0.00	0
23	danbc	7	$31.38	$31.38	$36.31	100.00	0.00	0.00	0
24	dir	327	$57.66	$58.01	$61.02	99.38	0.61	3.36	12
25	dover	38	$13.45	$13.45	$11.40	100.00	0.00	0.00	0
26	easba	17	$10.58	$10.58	$11.51	100.00	0.00	0.00	0
27	eduvn	1	$79.95	$79.95	$9.72	100.00	0.00	100.00	1
28	euro	15	$59.39	$59.39	$86.20	100.00	0.00	53.33	9
29	eveps	49	$13.23	$13.23	$10.05	100.00	0.00	0.00	0
30	fanli	3	$137.66	$137.66	$158.39	100.00	0.00	0.00	0
31	fbc	31	$35.47	$35.47	$42.86	100.00	0.00	22.58	14
32	ffh	35	$118.65	$118.65	$133.73	100.00	0.00	5.71	2
33	gale	17	$143.22	$143.22	$145.04	100.00	0.00	11.76	2
34	geri	19	$33.25	$33.25	$112.40	100.00	0.00	78.94	20
35	gjrau	14	$41.28	$41.28	$40.90	100.00	0.00	0.00	0
36	grerp	20	$10.72	$10.72	$12.27	100.00	0.00	0.00	0
37	hacab	6	$35.79	$35.79	$40.14	100.00	0.00	0.00	0
38	harap	1	$45.00	$45.00	$13.64	100.00	0.00	0.00	0
39	harr	1	$54.00	$54.00	$65.87	100.00	0.00	0.00	0
40	hssc	1	$42.00	$42.00	$45.47	100.00	0.00	0.00	0
41	hunli	1	$45.00	$45.00	$23.85	100.00	0.00	0.00	0
42	ieee	5	$42.98	$42.98	$56.27	100.00	0.00	0.00	0
43	insm	40	$140.69	$140.69	$143.98	100.00	0.00	0.00	0
44	isi	8	$1,221.87	$1,221.87	$1,021.28	100.00	0.00	0.00	0
45	jwpla	4	$357.75	$357.75	$400.45	100.00	0.00	0.00	0
46	lacma	3	$48.31	$48.31	$54.30	100.00	0.00	0.00	0
47	limbc	12	$18.25	$18.25	$20.18	100.00	0.00	0.00	0
48	ling	2	$30.00	$30.00	$36.42	100.00	0.00	0.00	0
49	loc	4	$34.50	$34.50	$37.34	100.00	0.00	0.00	0
50	mapli	1	$9.95	$9.95	$13.50	100.00	0.00	0.00	0
51	meckl	11	$35.59	$35.59	$40.47	100.00	0.00	9.09	1
52	medfa	4	$41.21	$41.21	$47.91	100.00	0.00	0.00	0
53	mid	157	$42.14	$42.14	$44.26	100.00	0.00	10.82	22

Fig. 12.1. continues on page 328.

Vendor Performance Statistics—TOTAL
Review file record : 1 to 0
Count orders placed in period 07-01-92 to 05-31-94

Average Estimated Price per Order : $398,242.96 / 8927 = $44.61
Average Paid Amount of Receipts   : $365,914.14 / 8924 = $41.00
Average Estimated Price for Received Orders : $398,242.96 / 8924 = $44.62
Average Delivery Time : 63142 / 8924 = 7
% Orders Received in 2   weeks : 3187 / 8924 = 35.71 %
% Orders Received in 4   weeks : 1258 / 8924 = 14.09 %
% Orders Received in 8   weeks : 1708 / 8924 = 19.13 %
% Orders Received in 12   weeks : 1481 / 8924 = 16.59 %
% Orders Received in 16   weeks : 457 / 8924 = 5.12 %
% Orders Received in 17+ weeks : 833 / 8924 = 9.33 %
% Cancelled :   3 / 8927 =   0.03 %
% Claimed   :   473 / 8927 =   5.29 %
Average Claims per Claimed Order : 555 / 473 = 1.17
Average Claims per Order   : 555 / 8927 = 0.06

had no prior experience in the library marketing sector. He asked if he could spend a week in our library learning how we handle journals and how our customers use the journals. We said yes, and he spent three days in technical services with the serials acquisition staff and two days in public services. Even if our operations are not completely typical, his experience made him more aware of the problems libraries face in handling serials. Another outcome has been that several of our staff have spent two or more days observing the vendor's operations. Increased understanding of one another's problems solidified an already good working relationship. It is not necessary to go to such lengths, but reading about developments in each other's field and asking informed questions helps build mutual understanding and respect. Having realistic expectations for one another is the key, just as it is in personal relationships. Be professional and ethical in working with vendors and publishers; expect and demand the same from them.

Retail Outlets

How Do New Bookstores Operate?

New bookstores—stores selling new books, not stores that just opened—are interesting places to visit, whether or not one is responsible for collection development. Many librarians started haunting bookstores long before they became librarians. (If there is a bibliographic equivalent to alcoholism, many librarians have it.) Bibliomania is defined as "excessive fondness for acquiring and possessing books."[4] Most bibliomaniacs (librarians included) cannot stay out of bookstores and consider it a great feat of willpower and self-control if they manage to leave one without buying a book or two.

Bookstore owners would be happy if a large percentage of the general population suffered from bibliomania. In the United States, they do not. In fact, the general population appears to have a high level of immunity. On a percentage basis, book buyers are a minority group in most countries, although their actual numbers are large. As a result, bookstores generally exist in somewhat special environments and operate in a certain way. Though most librarians have undoubtedly visited many bookstores innumerable times, one should make a special visit to at least two stores to answer some specific questions. What are the environmental and operating conditions necessary for a good bookstore? How does the store display and market its materials? What is for sale? How wide a range of materials is available? Could this shop be of any value in developing the collection?

One consideration for any bookstore owner is location. Many owners live and work in the community for a long time before they open their stores. Just as the person responsible for library collection development needs to know the community, so does the bookstore owner.

Many librarians harbor the dream of finding a quaint little town somewhere to retire and then open up a small bookstore. Most use it as a nice daydream on the occasional bad day in the library. Of those who go further and try to implement the idea, few succeed. Those who succeed do so by locating the store in a community they know, and the community knows them as a result of frequent visits and extended stays. A successful bookstore is a busy, people-oriented organization. It is not a quiet retreat for persons who do not like working with people, any more than is a library. Furthermore, owning a bookstore requires physical work on the part of the owner and a fairly large population base to support the required volume of sales.

Population base is a key consideration in determining where to locate a bookstore. The American Booksellers Association suggests that a minimum population to support a books-only store is 25,000 persons. Thus, large cities are the most likely locations for books-only stores. The smaller the community, the less likely it is that a books-only store will survive. Cultural activities in a large city help stimulate interest in reading. In major cities, it is even possible to find a variety of specialized bookstores (foreign language and subject matter). Smaller communities adjoining a good-sized academic institution, or that have a high level of tourism, provide the primary exceptions to the rule.

The educational level of the population is another factor in store location. As the average level of education in a community rises, so do the chances of a bookstore's succeeding with a smaller population base. College graduates represent the largest segment of book buyers. Where one finds a high concentration of college-educated people living near a large shopping center, one is also likely to find a bookstore.

A shopping center is a desirable location for a bookstore, if there is a lot of foot traffic. A store tucked away in a remote corner of the busiest center is not likely to do well. If bookstore owners had to survive solely on sales to individuals seeking a particular book, there would be even fewer stores than now exist. Catering to the tastes of middle- and upper-income persons increases a store's chance of success, because a large percentage of book sales result from impulse buying, which requires a location where the bookseller can stimulate the impulse in persons who can afford to indulge themselves. It frequently happens that one goes into a bookstore looking for just one book or something to read and walks out with three or four books. Bookstore owners depend on such impulse buying.

There are striking similarities between a successful bookstore and a successful library. Both require solid knowledge of the community. If librarians could select sites as do bookstore proprietors, library circulation would skyrocket. A public library branch in the center of Stockholm provides an example of an almost ideal bookstore location: on a shopping mall in the center of the main business district, with a high volume of foot traffic, and near a concourse to a main subway station. This branch is the most active of all the service points in a system where high use is the norm. Atlanta, Georgia, has a branch of its public library located in a subway station.

Store owners attempt to stimulate buyers through a variety of sales methods. Owners employ store window and entryway displays to provide clues about the basic stock before a customer enters. Only very large stores can afford to purchase newspaper advertisements on a weekly basis, and radio and television advertising costs are prohibitively high for most owners. An occasional newspaper advertisement and a good storefront display are the best they can do to promote business.

One can make a fair assessment of a bookstore by looking through its windows without walking in the door (of course, this is an assessment of the type of material sold, not the level of service). Observing is not the same as casually looking. One can look closely, but without some guidelines one may not know what to look for or how to interpret what is seen. The following broad generalizations can serve as the most basic guidelines, providing a foundation on which to build as one gains experience. One can use the store marketing techniques in a variety of library settings.

An owner has two basic methods for promoting a store through its windows: One is to focus on a particular topic or on a few bestsellers, the other is a shotgun approach, that is, displaying a wide variety of titles appealing to a wide range of interests. Using a little imagination, some nonbook props, and a good supply of books, successful store owners can create interesting window displays. Such windows can stimulate the inactive reader to come in and buy the promoted title, but such buyers seldom pause to examine other titles in the store. Typically, the display will lead to a good sale of the promoted title or subject. Unfortunately, most buyers, especially those interested only in a certain topic, will not return to the store until the store has another equally striking window display on that topic.

Shotgun window displays are less likely to attract the nonactive reader. If they are well done, however, such displays will stop a reader. A jumble of books in the window will not do the job, but a wealth of titles using some basic graphic techniques will. Store owners know this type of window attracts the steady book-buying customer. Such individuals are as likely to buy four or five titles as one, and all of the titles may be impulse purchases, in the sense that the buyers did not come into the store looking for the specific titles purchased.

If a store has consistently striking windows featuring the latest top sellers, this likely reflects the orientation of the total book stock. Almost everything in such a store will have a proven track record. Backlist titles that have had steady sales (dictionaries, cookbooks, home reference items, and classics) will comprise the majority of items in stock, plus stacks of faddish titles and tables piled high with discount and gift books. Though shops of this type may be willing to order single titles, there will be little advantage for the library. Almost the only reason for a library to patronize such a store is for the discount (remainder) books they offer.

There is a remote chance that an independent (nonchain) store owner would special-order items for the library. In smaller communities, this may be the only type of store available. If the library were to buy $10,000 worth of books each year from the store, this would probably be an adequate incentive for the owner to shift emphasis. (For many small libraries, $10,000 would be 10 years' purchases.) It will still be possible for the store's regular patrons to find their favorite types of books there, and perhaps it will draw in some new steady customers as a result of the change.

If a store's windows do not provide enough clues to its stock, looking in the door can provide another quick visual check. Tables of books with signs such as Top Twenty!, 55% to 75% Off! or Giant Discounts! are almost certain to announce a store of limited value to a library, especially if most of the window displays have favored the latest and best sellers. A store with a good, wide range of stock cannot afford to devote much floor area to such sales methods. All stores have sales from time to time—books that have not sold and may be past their return date, some remainders—and of course, there is always the preinventory sale. However, the store that is always having a sale is never really having a sale and is seldom of value to libraries.

Another quick visual check is for sideline items. A new bookstore selling only new books needs a minimum community population of 25,000, but almost all bookstores now sell some sidelines: greeting cards, stationery and office supplies, posters, art supplies, audio and video recordings, magazines and newspapers, calendars, games, and so forth. Why the sideline? It is difficult to make a good living just selling books because there are few buyers and the margin of profit on books is much smaller than the margin on sideline items.

The possible profit on books is a complex subject given the various discount arrangements available to booksellers. Publishers offer the same general discounts (trade, long, short, new, mass market) to book-stores that they offer to jobbers. Bookstores receive long discounts (40 percent or more) on most trade hardback books. In the case of large orders (multiple copies), discounts of 50 percent or more are possible. Normally, the discount is 40 percent, and even then, the store may have to buy a required minimum number of copies (five or more) to receive this amount. A few publishers offer 33 to 40 percent off an order of 10 different single titles under the Single Copy Order Plan (SCOP). Librarians ordering a sizable number of single copies from one publisher may find bookstores eager to place such orders. However, it is important to remember that such an agreement requires the bookseller to prepay and to do all the paperwork. Thus, if the library is slow in issuing payments, only large bookstores can afford to carry its accounts.

Some stores will order short (20 to 25 percent) discount items but add a service charge. If the order contains enough short discount items from a single publisher, most stores will handle the order without a service charge. On a $20 book with a 25 percent discount, the bookstore has only a $5 margin with which to work. After covering the clerical time and record keeping costs, the owner is lucky if the transaction has not cost the store more money than it received from the customer, so a service charge is not unreasonable.

There are two classes of paperbacks: quality and mass-market. Quality paperbacks (the term does not necessarily apply to the content of the book) generally sell for more than $10 and are found only in bookstores. Mass-market books are those in drugstores, grocery stores, airports, and so forth, that usually sell for $5 to $6. Most publishers give a long discount on quality paperbacks when ordered in groups of five to ten or more. A store must order 25 to 50 assorted titles of the mass-market type to begin to approach a 40 percent discount. Orders for less than that amount will get discounts of 25 to 35 percent.

The book distribution system in the United States is cumbersome and frequently adds to the cost of books. A simplified system would benefit everyone. Perhaps the best illustration of the complexity of the system is in the area of discounts, returns, billings, and so forth. Each year the American Booksellers Association (ABA) publishes a 500-page guide entitled *ABA Book Buyer's Handbook* (American Booksellers Association, 1947-). Pity the poor bookseller, confronted with all of the other problems of a bookstore, who also must work through a mass of legal forms and sales conditions for purchasing from various publishers. It does create extra work for the bookseller and publisher, and they undoubtedly pass their costs to the buyer.

Thus, when a sideline item offers a 70 to 80 percent discount, it is not surprising to find a mixed store; as much as 30 to 40 percent of the total store income comes from nonbook sales. A store that devotes more than one-third of the available floor space to nonbook items probably will not be of much use to a library for developing collections, so the librarian should be sure to observe the percentage of floor space devoted to side-lines. In addition to quick visual checks, some acquaintance with the store's personnel will provide additional information about a store. Although more and more stores must use a self-service arrangement as labor costs rise, getting to know what staff there is can pay dividends in getting service. Most self-service operations emphasize paperbacks, sidelines, and popular trade books. Obviously, such stores offer little that will be of value to the library.

In general, bookstores can be a valuable means of acquiring new books. Carrying out visual inspection of local stores and discussing the library's needs with their owners can form an important link in the selection and acquisition program. Only a few libraries, in large metro-politan areas, have good bookstores nearby. Many libraries are lucky if there is one bookstore in the community. Although most libraries will spend only a small part of the materials budget in such stores, the possibility is worth exploring. Though most bookstores have limited potential as a major source of supply for collection development, when a general bookstore exists nearby, the library ought to talk to the owner to determine what, if any, business relationship might be possible. It may take time for the relationship to fully develop, but it can prove mutually beneficial. (Note: Most of the preceding discussion does not apply to the large national chains, such as Crown Books, B. Dalton, and Waldenbooks. Their operations are very different and they have little to offer in the way of collection development support.)

Out-of-Print, Antiquarian, and Rare Book Dealers

Allowing for overlap, there are two broad categories of out-of-print (OP) dealers. (It should be noted that most of these dealers dislike the label secondhand dealer.) One category focuses primarily on general OP books, that is, with buying and selling relatively recent OP books. Often, these books sell at prices that are the same as, or only slightly higher than, their publication price. The other category of dealer focuses on rare, antiquarian, and special (for example, fore-edged painted, miniature, or private press) books. Prices for this type of book range from around $10 to several thousand dollars per item.

Margaret Landesman provides an excellent, detailed outline of the types of dealers. Her seven types are

Book scouts, working part-time or full-time, searching out desirable books and selling them to dealers and collectors.

Out-of-print dealers, usually working from their homes and not maintaining shops, although they did own a shop when getting established. As overhead expenses go up, working from home becomes more popular among dealers whose primary sales are by mail.

Small, specialized out-of-print shops that issue catalogs and do searching in their specialty.

General out-of-print dealers who have a rather large stock in varied areas; many have specialties as well. Some offer search services, some issue catalogs.

In-print stores that have an out-of-print section; they can be small subject-specialized concerns or larger general bookstores. Some do out-of-print searching and offer catalogs.

Some library in-print wholesalers also offer out-of-print search services.

Rare book dealers specializing in rare and expensive titles. Most established rare book dealers do not handle the more ordinary scholarly out-of-print titles, but many general out-of-print dealers also handle some rare books.[5]

The vast majority of such dealers have small shops in low-rent areas. Because of this diversity, it is difficult to make many generalizations about this group. Sol Malkin paints a cheery picture of at least part of the out-of-print trade:

> Imagine a separate book world within the world of books where dealers set up their businesses where they please (store or office, home or barn); where the minimum markup is 100 percent; where they can call upon 5,000 fellow dealers throughout the world and a stock of over 200 million volumes, practically from the beginning of the printed word; where books are safely packed and mailed with no extra charge for postage; where there is no competition from the publishers and discount houses; where colleagues help one another in time of need to provide fellow dealers with a unique service that makes customers happy all the time—an ideal imaginary book world that never was nor ever will be? Perhaps . . . but the above is 99 percent true in the antiquarian book trade.[6]

Libraries can function without using new bookstores, but they must use the out-of-print and antiquarian dealers for replacement copies if for nothing else. Often, books in poor physical condition but still in demand are no longer in print and are available only in the OP market. Also, there are the many books the library did not buy when they were released and must attempt to purchase sometime later. Libraries do most of their retrospective buying in the OP market. These shops and dealers are the primary sources, although occasional, libraries may buy from collectors.

Every library will have occasion to use the services of these dealers. Collection development officers working with large research collections spend much of their time engaged in retrospective collection development. Changes in organizational goals and programs may result in developing whole new areas of collecting both current and retrospective materials. Public libraries also buy from OP dealers, especially for replacement copies and occasionally for retrospective collection building. School libraries make limited use of this distribution system; scientific and technical libraries rarely need to worry about acquiring retrospective materials.

Several directories to antiquarian or rare book dealers provide information about specialties (for example, *American Book Trade Directory* from R.R. Bowker), and anyone concerned with selection and acquisition needs to get to know these directories. Some major metropolitan areas have local directories or guides to special bookstores. In any case, a person will find it worthwhile to develop a card file on the local shops. The file can provide quick information about search services, hours, and true specialties. One can go to a shop that advertises itself as a Western Americana store only to find the specialty stock very limited or overpriced. Nevertheless, one should examine the shop's stock to identify its true specialties and assess its general pricing polices. Maintaining this private directory can prove well worth the time required to keep it up-to-date. This is not to say that the published sources are worthless. However, owners change emphasis, and their stock turns over and is subject to local economic conditions that often change faster than published sources can monitor.

Many acquisitions librarians and book dealers classify OP book distribution services into three general types: (1) a complete book service, (2) a complete sales service, and (3) a complete bookstore. The first two may operate in a manner that does not allow, or at least require, customers to come to the seller's location. All contact is by mail and telephone. The owner may maintain only a small stock of choice items in a garage or basement. In a complete book service, a dealer actively searches for items for a customer even if the items are not in stock, by placing an ad in a publication like *AB Bookman's Weekly* (Antiquarian Bookman).

Sales service is just what the name implies: a dealer reads the "wanted" sections of book trade publications and sends off quotes on items in his or her stock. Such services seldom place ads or conduct searches for a customer. The complete bookstore is a store operation that depends on in-person trade. Stores of this type often engage in book service and sales service activities as well. Given the unpredictable nature of the OP trade, it is an unusual store that does not need to exploit every possible sales outlet.

AB Bookman's Weekly (*AB*) is a weekly publication devoted solely to advertisements from dealers offering or searching for particular titles. Publications of this type are an essential ingredient in the OP book trade, because they serve as a finding and selling tool. Without services like this, the cost of acquiring an OP item would be much higher (assuming the library could locate a copy without the service).

Selectors also use *AB* in their work. Other useful publications for both dealers and libraries are *AB*'s *Yearbook, Bookman's Price Index* (Gale), Bowker's *Books Out-of-Print*, Ruth Robinson and Daryush Farudi's *Buy Books Where—Sell Books Where* (Robinson Books), *American Book Prices Current* (Bancroft Parkman), and *Library Bookseller* (Antiquarian Bookman). An online service is BookQuest from ABACIS, which is a service connecting dealers, libraries, and some private collectors in a single network.[7]

Both OP and rare bookstores require a high capital investment in a book stock that may not sell immediately. Most owners feel lucky if total sales for a year equal 1½ times the total stock.

Indeed, some items may never sell, and most will remain on a shelf for several years before a buyer appears. Lacking the return rights of the new bookstore owner, a used or rare bookstore owner must be careful about purchases and have inexpensive storage facilities available.

Factors like high investment and low turnover force most owners to locate their businesses in low-rent areas. Rare and antiquarian shops can sometimes exist in high-rent areas, but in such locations the buyer will pay a premium price for the books. Shops in high-rent areas often grew up with the area and seldom resulted from an owner's decision to move into a high-rent area. Several attempts to start antiquarian shops in high-rent areas in Los Angeles failed, despite locations that had a high volume of foot traffic, well-to-do customers with higher-than-average education, and a large university only a few blocks away.

One requisite for an OP dealer is a reputation for honesty, service, and fair prices. To gain such a reputation requires a considerable period of time in this field. Many newcomers to the business do not have adequate capital to carry them through this period, if they locate in a high-rent area. As a result, most OP shops operate in the less desirable areas of a community. This means that a person looking for such shops must make a special trip to visit them. Out-of-the-way, low-rent quarters for such a store also mean that there will be little walk-in trade. This means most customers come looking for specific items and are unlikely to take an interest in nonbook items. Therefore, these stores do not stock sideline items, although a few may have some used phonograph records, old photographs, or posters. Owners can only hope that they have the right items to spark some impulse book buying in the true bibliophile.

One element in the OP trade is very mysterious to the outsider and even to librarians who have had years of experience with these dealers. That element is, how do dealers determine the asking price? As Malkin indicates, the markup is at least 100 percent, but how much more? One may find a book in an OP store with no price on it, take it to the salesperson (often the owner), ask the price, and receive, after a quick look, the answer, "Oh, yes. That is X dollars." Sometimes the amount is lower than one expects, other times much higher, but most of the time it is close to the price the library is willing to pay. Some salespersons seem to be mind readers, to know exactly how much a customer is willing to pay. Malkin sums up the outsider's feeling about pricing in the OP trade: "Many new book dealers think of the antiquarian bookseller as a second-hand junkman or as a weird character who obtains books by sorcery, prices them by cabalistic necromancy, and sells them by black magic."[8]

It may appear that magic is the essential ingredient in successful OP operations. Actually, the mystery fades when one understands the inter-action of three central issues concerning this trade: the source of supply, the predominant sales methods, and the way dealers set prices. Fortunately for those who enjoy the OP trade, the magic remains. With an excellent memory, a love for books, the ability and time to learn books, enough capital to buy a basic stock of books, and finally, the patience to wait for a return on capital, anyone can become an OP bookseller.

To a large degree, dealers set prices after they know the answers to the questions of supply and potential sales. The OP dealer has several sources of supply, but only two consistently produce new stock. One major source is personal or business collections. Placing an ad in the telephone directory (saying "I buy old books") will generate a number of inquiries. Two of the most frequent reasons a private collection comes onto the market are household moves and the settling of estates. Only when outstanding private collections of a well-known collector come on the market will dealers enter into a bidding contest. They may come to look at a collection, but only after determining by telephone that it is large and has potential value. After a quick review of the collection, they make a flat offer with a take-it-or-leave-it attitude. A person who has no experience with the OP trade is usually unhappy with what that person believes is too low an offer. After one or two such offers, a prospective seller might conclude that there is a conspiracy of OP dealers to cheat owners out of rare items.

Nothing could be further from the truth. Experienced OP dealers know how long most of the items they have bid on will occupy storage space in their shops. They also know how few of the seller's treasures are more than personal treasures. Grandfather's complete collection of *National Geographic* from 1921 to 1943 may be a family heirloom but to most OP dealers it is so much fodder for the 25-cent table.

Time is the central theme in the OP trade. In time, every edition of a book will become OP; in time, most of the world's printed materials should return to pulp mills for recycling. In time, the few valuable books will find a buyer. But when is that time? Knowing the time factor as well as they do, OP dealers must buy for as little as they can or they will go out of business. Knowledgeable dealers know the local and the national market; therefore, it is not surprising that several bids on the same collection are almost identical. They read the same trade magazines, they see the same catalogs, and to some extent, they see the same local buyers. If they are to stay in business, they must know the market.

Walk-in sales are only a small segment of OP sales income. Mail-order sales—buying and selling items through publications such as *AB* and catalogs—is the major source of income. Most dealers prepare catalogs of selected items in stock and mail them to other dealers, libraries, and book collectors. Often, the catalog will list only one type of material (for example, Western Americana, European history, first editions, or autographed books); at other times, it will list a variety of titles that the dealer hopes will appeal to many different buyers.

Just as the contents of catalogs vary, so does the quality of the item descriptions and the care taken in preparing the catalog. Some catalogs are nothing more than hard-to-read photocopies of text typed on a typewriter in need of cleaning. At most, one can decipher an author, title, and price. On the other end of the spectrum are catalogs that are so well done and contain so much bibliographic information that research libraries add the catalog to their permanent bibliography collection. Catalogs of high quality are less and less common today, and the trend is likely to continue because of rising printing costs. To recover the cost, it is necessary to sell the catalog to buyers who are not regular customers, which also usually means that the prices for all the items in the catalogs will be rather high ($100 and up).

When a librarian sees a catalog that contains something the library needs and can purchase, he or she should run, not walk, to the nearest telephone, fax, or e-mail computer and place the order. It will probably be too late, and the telephone offers almost the only chance of getting the order in quickly enough to secure the item. A mailed order is almost certain to arrive too late. Out-of-print folklore says that if one librarian wants an item, so do 30 others.

Dealer catalogs and magazines, such as *AB*, provide both a sales mechanism and a major means of establishing prices. If an OP dealer in London offers an autographed copy of the first edition of Richard Adams's *Watership Down* for £10, other dealers will use this information as a guide in setting prices for copies of the book that they have in stock. An unautographed copy of the first edition would be something less than £10, assuming that both copies were in approximately the same physical condition. Other editions, including foreign first editions, also would sell for less. The foreign first editions might come close to the English first edition in price, but the *first* first edition usually commands the highest price.

Prices are based on a number of interrelated factors: (1) how much it costs to acquire the item; (2) the amount of current interest in collecting a particular subject or author; (3) the number of copies printed and the number of copies still in existence; (4) the physical condition of the copy; (5) any special features of the particular copy (autographed by the author or signed or owned by a famous person, for example); and (6) what other dealers are asking for copies of the same edition in the same condition. Without question, the current asking price is the major determining factor—given equal conditions in the other five areas—thus making sales catalogs and *AB* major pricing tools.

A few additional facts about the condition of OP books are important for beginning librarians to know because these bear directly on price. The condition of the book has an impact on its price. One may assume most OP dealers sell their stock as described or as is. If there is no statement about the item's condition, one may assume it to be good or better condition. A common statement in catalogs is "terms—all books in original binding and in good or better condition unless otherwise stated." An example of such a condition statement appears in figure 12.2 on page 339.

One should carefully study the examples of OP dealer catalog entries in figures 12.1 through 12.7. These are examples of the basic catalogs that a librarian concerned with retrospective buying would check. The sample from the William H. Allen catalog represents more expensive materials but is still well within the limits from which a beginner might select. All the catalogs give information about the condition of the items offered. What does the "t.e.g." indicate about item 6438 in the Oriental and African Books catalog (fig. 12.3, page 340)? What is the difference between "VG" (very good) (item 3) and "fine" (item 9) in the Janice Bowen catalog (fig. 12.4, page 341), or between "exceedingly rare" (item 847) and "scarce" (item 852) from The Jenkins Company (fig. 12.5, page 342)? "T.e.g." means "top edges gilt." Some of the meanings will become clear only from knowing the particular dealer, but some guidance can be found in books like John Carter's *ABC for Book Collectors* and *The Bookman's Glossary*.[9] (New editions of such works appear periodically, but initially, any edition will be suitable.) Carter provides illuminating and entertaining notes about dealer adjectives describing the condition of a book:

> *General.*—As new, fine, good, fair, satisfactory (a trifle condescending, this) good second-hand condition (i.e., not very good), poor (often coupled with an assurance that the book is very rare in any condition), used, reading copy (fit for nothing more and below collector's standard), working copy (may even need sticking together).

Text continues on page 345.

No. 275 Autumn 1986

American & European History
Art, Science, Philosophy, Etc.

Unless otherwise noted, books are 12mo or 8vo, bound, and in good second-hand condition. Prices are net; carriage extra. **Send no money; you will be billed.** Pennsylvania residents are liable to the 6% sales tax. All bills are payable **only** in U.S. dollars, drawn on a U.S. bank, or by postal money order.

William H. Allen, Bookseller

2031 Walnut Street   **Philadelphia, Pa. 19103**
(Area Code 215) 563-3398

A. Anderton, James. **The Protestants Apologie for the Roman Church, by John Brereley, Priest.** St. Omar 1608. 4to. New half morocco. Small piece out of corner of title-page. $150.00

The author, a Roman Catholic controversalist and probably a priest, quotes passages from the works of Protestants which admit the claims of the Roman church.

B. Bacon, Sir Francis. **The Elements of the Common Lawes of England, branched into a double tract.** 1639. Old calf, one cover detached. Small piece torn from one margin. Name cut from title. $200.00

The third issue of this work, containing Bacon's proposed restatement of English law.

C. Bible. Whole. **The Self-interpreting Bible: containing the sacred text of the Old and New Testaments.** With marginal references by John Brown. New York 1792. Folio. 20 engr. pl. by Doolittle, A. Godwin, & others. Old leather, front cover detached, 2 leaves, the margins of which are quite frayed, supplied. Some tears into text. $300.00

The second illustrated Bible printed in America.

D. ——. **Biblia, das ist: die ganze goettliche Heilige Schrift alten und neuen Testaments.** Reading, Pa. 1805. 4to. Old calf, quite worn, stitching on spine torn, leather partly covered with scotch tape. Contents very good. $65.00

The fourth edition of the Bible in German printed in America.

E. Bilson, Thomas, Bp. **The True Difference betweene Christian Subjection and Unchristian Rebellion: wherein the princes lawful power to command for truth, and indeprivable right to beare the sword, are defended against the popes censures and the Jesuits sophismes.** 1586. Royal coat-of-arms on verso of title. Lacks first blank. Stamped leather of the 19th century. One joint starting. $200.00

A defense of the English Reformation and an assertion that the English Church is the true Catholic Chjurch.

F. Bungus, Petrus. **Numerorum mysteria ex abditis plurimarum disciplinarum fontibus hausta.** Paris 1618. 4to. Vellum, one joint cracked, edges mouse-eaten. Worm-holes in corner of about 150pp. Title-page mounted. $125.00

The author, a Catholic theologian, devoted much of the work to the mystical number 666 which he equated with Luther, thus proving that he was the Antichrist. Other sections are devoted to other numbers in which he found mystical powers.

Fig. 12.2. William H. Allen, Bookseller. Reproduced by courtesy of William H. Allen.

30

6431 (Cont.) with a full description of the Sudd, and of the measures which have been taken to clear the navigation of the river.'

6432 GIDEIRI, Y.B.A. <u>A Guide to the Perciform Fishes in the Coastal Waters of Suakin</u>. K.U.P., 1968. Oblong 8vo., pp. 52, illus., a v.g. copy.   £8.50

6433 GLADSTONE, P. <u>Travels of Alexine</u>. Alexine Tinne 1835-1869. John Murray, 1970. Bds., pp. xii, 247, illus., 2 maps, v.g. in rubbed d.w.   £12.50

6434 GREENER, L. <u>High Dam over Nubia</u>. Cassell, 1962. Illus., maps, v.g. in d.w.   £5

6435 GWYNN, C.W. <u>Imperial Policing</u>. Macmillan, 1934. pp. ix, 366, 13 maps; a working copy only with front hinge weak and bds. spotted and creased; internally good.   £8.50

6436 HAKE, A.E. <u>The Story of Chinese Gordon</u>. Remington, 1884 rep. (1884). Port. frp., plate, 2 folding maps, orig. dec. cloth gilt; 2 vols., and a very good set.   £65

6437 Ditto, another set, both vols. first edn.; cloth rubbed and faded, o/w good.   £45

6438 HAKE, A.E. <u>The Story of Chinese Gordon</u>. With additions, bringing the narrative to the present time. Worthington, N.Y., 1884. Orig. pict. cloth gilt, t.e.g., frp., illus., pp. 358, a v.g. copy.   £25

6439 HALLAM, W.K.R. <u>The Life and Times of Rabih Fadl Allah</u>. Stockwell Ltd., Ilfracombe, 1977. Bds., pp. 367, 3 mpas, illus., a v.g. copy in d.w.   £15

6440 HARTMANN, Dr. R. <u>Reise des Freiherrn Adalbert von Barnim durch Nord-Ost-Afrika in den Jahren 1859 und 1860</u>. Georg Reimer, Berlin, 1863. Lge. 4to., orig. cloth, pp. xvi, 651, XI, + appendix of 111 pp.; tinted lithographic frp., 28 woodcut illus. in the text, (some full-page), 2 other plates, sketch map, 2 folding maps; some foxing to text and fore-edge, faint waterstain to bottom margin, (but not affecting the text), and a v.g. clean copy. With the accompanying Atlas : <u>Reise in Nordost Africa</u>, 1859-1860. Skizzen nach der Natur gemalt von Adalbert Freiherrn von Barnim und Dr. Robert Hartmann. Oblong folio, (48 x 32 cms.), orig. cloth, cold. lithographic title-page, double page panorama, 23 other lithographic plates, (of which nine are cold.), by W. Loeillet after sketches by the author and von Barnim, an exceptionally fine copy.   £2500
      Hartmann, a naturalist who ended his career as Professor of Anatomy at Berlin University, accompanied the young Baron A. von Barnim on the latter's journey to the Sudan. Crossing the Bayuda Desert from Old Dongola to Khartoum, they continued up the Blue Nile valley via Sennar to Fazughli. After von Barnim died of fever at Roseires, Hartmann took the body to Europe for burial. The work he later produced about this ill-fated tour ranks with those of Tremaux and Lejean as one of the most beautifully produced travel books relating to the Sudan in the mid-Nineteenth Century. Far from being a simple description of the tour, it is a primary source for the period, a major and immensely detailed contribution to the study of Sudan's natural history and ethnography, particularly regarding the Upper Blue Nile, Dar Funj and Sudan-Ethiopian borderlands. The quality of the text is matched by that of the accompanying plates, illustrating the natural history, landscapes and peoples en route, and of which this copy is an exceptional example.

6441 HASSAN, Y.F. & DOORNBOS, P. <u>The Central Bilad Al Sudan</u>. Tradition and Adaptation. Essays on the Geography and Economic and Political History of the Sudanic belt. K.U.P., Sudan Library Series No. 11, 1977. Sm. 4to., wraps, pp. v, 316, maps, tables etc., a v.g. copy.   £15

6442 HENDERSON, K.D.D. <u>Sudan Republic</u>. Benn, 1965. Cloth, pp. 233, 2 maps, (1 folding), a v.g. copy.   £22.50
      In the series 'Nations of the Modern World' ; provides a good general survey of the later Condominium period and early years of the independent Sudan.

Fig. 12.3. Oriental and African Books catalog sample. Reproduced by courtesy of Oriental and African Books.

ANTHROPOLOGY & TRAVEL

THEORETICAL & COMPARATIVE
AFRICA
MIDDLE EAST
ASIA
AUSTRALASIA & PACIFIC
AMERICAS & CARIBBEAN
POLAR REGIONS
EUROPE
ADDENDA

THEORETICAL & COMPARATIVE

1   BANTON (Michael) - Race Relations. Tavistock Pubs., 1967. Pp. xiv+434,
     brown clothgilt, d-j. (snagged). VG. (Analyses of the history and oper-
     ation of different patterns of racial tension.)   £10

2   BETTANY (G.T.) - Red, Brown & Black Men & Their White Supplanters / The
     Inhabitants of America & Oceania. Ward Lock, n.d. (c.1890.) Pp. xi+221,
     numerous ills., grey pictorial clothgilt. Lacks 1 page, o/w VG. Manners,
     customs, racial characteristics and drawings of many tribes.   £10

3   BINDER (Pearl) - Magic Symbols of the World. Hamlyn, 1972. Pp. 127, ills.
     (some coloured), cloth, silvergilt. VG in worn d-j. (Study by artist
     Fellow of the R.A.I. discussing fertility symbols, magical protection
     of body and dwelling, family and livelihood, death and afterlife.) £4.50

4   BOISSEVAIN (Jeremy) - Friends of Friends: Networks, Manipulators and
     Coalitions. Oxford, Blackwell, 1974. Pp. xv+285. Tan clothgilt. Fine,
     in d-j.   £9.50

5   CHAPPLE (Eliot Dismore) & Carlton Stevens Coon - Principles of Anthropology
     New York, Holt, 1947, reprint. Pp. xii+718, blue cloth, VG. (Includes
     operational method, development of personality, symbolism.)   £14

6   COON (Carleton S.) - The Hunting Peoples. Book Club Associates, 1974, rpt.
     Pp. 413, maps, ills., brown clothgilt. VG in chipped d-j.   £9

7   COTLOW (Lewis) - In Search of the Primitive. Robert Hale, 1967 (first Eng-
     lish edn). Pp. 454, col. & b/w plates. Green clothgilt. Bumped at base
     of spine. Good, in chipped d-j. (Ituri Forest pygmies, Watusi, Masai,
     Babira, Jivaro, Matto Grosso Bororo, Yaguas, Eskimo.)   £8

8   DOUGLAS (Mary) - Evans-Pritchard: His Life, Work, Writings & Ideas. Har-
     vester Press/Fontana, 1980. Blue clothgilt, d-j. Mint.   £6

9   DOUGLAS (Mary) - Purity & Danger / An Analysis of the Concepts of Pollution
     & Taboo. Routledge & Kegan Paul, Ark Paperback, 1984. (First pub. 1966.)
     Pp. 188. Paperback, fine.   £2.75

10   DOUGLAS (Mary) - Natural Symbols / Explorations in Cosmology. Barrie &
     Jenkins, 1978, 2nd edn, rpt. Pp. 218. Black clothgilt, d-j. VG.   £7.50

11   EPSTEIN (A.L.) Ed. - The Craft of Social Anthropology. Intro. Max Gluckman.
     Tavistock Pubs., 1969, rpt. Pp. xx+276. Contributors include Mitchell,
     Barnes, Turner, Marwick. Paperback; signature, some scuffmarks and
     scratched erasing on back cover - o/w clean and fresh.   £6

12   EVANS-PRITCHARD (E.E.) - Social Anthropology. Cohen & West, 1960, rpt.
     Pp. vii+134, blue cloth, d-j. (embrowned). Good.   £6.50

Fig. 12.4. Janice Bowen catalog sample. Reproduced by courtesy of Janice Bowen.

- Dec. 6, 1879. Volume I, nos. 1-18 complete. Elephant folio, bound in original cloth, pictorial gilt on front cover. Illus. An interesting collection including military reminiscences of various wars, especially the Civil War, each issue 16 pages in length. Very scarce. (V27-20774) 125.00

MCKENNEY AND JACKSON ON INDIANS

847. [NEW YORK] McKenney, Thomas L. *DOCUMENTS AND PROCEEDINGS RELATING TO THE FORMATION AND PROGRESS OF A BOARD IN THE CITY OF NEW YORK FOR THE EMIGRATION, PRESERVATION, AND IMPROVEMENT OF THE ABORIGINES OF AMERICA*. N.Y.: Vanderpool & Cole, 1829. 48pp. Sewn. First printing. S. & S. 39083. Includes a lengthy address by McKenney, an address from Pres. Andrew Jackson to the Creek Indians, an address from John H. Eaton to John Ross and the Cherokees, the Constitution of the Indian Board for the Emigration, Preservation, and Improvement of the Aborigines of America, and a report by Eaton on the Indians in Georgia. Exceedingly rare, with very fine content. (V27-20797) 125.00

848. [NEW YORK] Murphy, William D. *BIOGRAPHICAL SKETCHES OF THE STATE OFFICERS AND MEMBERS OF THE LEGISLATURE OF THE STATE OF NEW YORK*. N.Y., 1861. 298pp. Original cloth. First edition. A nice copy of the principal reference work on the state legislature of the Civil War's first year. (V27-20731) 35.00

849. [NEW YORK] *THE NEW YORK DEMOCRACY AND VALLANDIGHAM: THEY ENDORSE THE TRAITOR AND WINK AT THE TREASON*. N.p., 1861. 4pp. First printing. "By the time of his return to Ohio he was suspected of treasonable intent and had become one of the most unpopular and most bitterly abused men in the North....Whatever his policy at any time, he advocated it with the ardor and sincerity of a fanatic. In 1871 he was retained as counsel for the defendant in a murder case and while demonstrating the way in which the victim had been shot he mortally wounded himself." (V27-20638) 20.00

850. [NEW YORK] [WEST POINT] *WEST POINT LIFE: AN ANONYMOUS COMMUNICATION, READ BEFORE A PUBLIC MEETING OF THE DIALECTIC SOCIEY, U.S. MILITARY ACADEMY, MARCH 5, 1859*. N.p., 1859. 16pp. Original printed wrappers. In verse form, this fascinating pamphlet details the intense social life at West Point on the eve of the Civil War with amusing accounts of balls and dances and courtships, as well as learning soldiering. George A. Custer and many other future generals were at the Point at this time. (V27-20811) 65.00

851. [NEW YORK] Wilkins, William, et al. *ADDRESS OF THE FRIENDS OF DOMESTIC INDUSTRY, ASSEMBLED IN CONVENTION, AT NEW YORK, OCTOBER 26, 1831, TO THE PEOPLE OF THE UNITED STATES*. Baltimore, 1831. 44pp. Much on developing American industry and on cotton mills. With a complete list of the delegates. S.& S. 5637. (V27-15106) 25.00

852. Nicollet, Joseph Nicolas. *REPORT INTENDED TO ILLUSTRATE A MAP OF THE HYDROGRAPHICAL BASIN OF THE UPPER MISSISSIPPI RIVER*. Wash.: SD237, 1843. 237pp. Calf and boards. First edition. Huge folding map in facsimile by J. C. Fremont. Holliday 820: "Scarce and most interesting." Howes N152. Buck 339: "The report contains also a sketch of the early history of St. Louis." Graff 3022. Wagner-Camp 98: "Nicollet gives many details regarding his expedition to the upper Missouri in 1839 with Fremont." Overlooked by Clark. (VW1-5101) 100.00

853. Noble, Samuel H. *LIFE AND ADVENTURES OF BUCKSKIN SAM, WRITTEN BY HIMSELF*. Rumford Falls, Maine, 1900. 185pp. Original cloth. Fine copy. Frontis. Recollections of his travels throughout the world. His hunting trips, being captured by Indians in South America, and his experiences with Custer during the Civil War. (VW5-12817) 100.00

854. [NORTH CAROLINA] *AN ACT TO INCORPORATE THE NORTH CAROLINA TRANSPORTATION COMPANY*. [Raleigh], 1866. Broadside, 1p., octavo. Creating a steamboat company for the Chesapeake Canal. (VW14-6601) 15.00

855. [NORTH CAROLINA] Alderman, Ernest H. *THE NORTH CAROLINA COLONIAL BAR [AND] THE GREENVILLE DISTRICT, BY E. MERTON COULTER*. Chapel Hill: Univ. of N.C., [1913]. 56pp. 1st ed. Orig.ptd.wrp. Articles in the Sprunt Historical Series (Vol.13 #1). (VW14-15868) 35.00

856. [NORTH CAROLINA] Arthur, John P. *WESTERN NORTH CAROLINA: A HISTORY (FROM 1730 TO 1913)*. Raleigh, 1914. 709pp.+errata. First edition. Illus. An early scholarly survey. CWB II, 210: "Sheds light on civil and military affairs [during the Civil War]." Thornton 317. Howes A342. (VW14-9597) 100.00

857. [NORTH CAROLINA] *A BILL CONCERNING THE FAYETTEVILLE & CENTRE PLANK ROAD COMPANY*. Raleigh, 1854. 4pp. (VW14-2-6595) 15.00

858. [NORTH CAROLINA] *A BILL TO IMPROVE THE PUBLIC ROADS IN NORTH CAROLINA*. Raleigh, 1850. [8]pp. (VW14-6596) 15.00

859. [NORTH CAROLINA] *A BILL TO INCORPORATE THE FAYETTEVILLE AND NORTHERN PLANK ROAD COMPANY*. Raleigh, 1850. [8]pp. (VW14-6594) 15.00

860. [NORTH CAROLINA] Boyd, William K. [ed.]. *SOME EIGHTEENTH CENTURY TRACTS CONCERNING NORTH CAROLINA*. Raleigh, 1927. 508pp. Illus. Facs. Index. An excellent scholarly edition of 14 early North carolina-related printed sources, including politics, religion, economics, Indians, and law. Boyd provides and introduction and good notes for each work. Scarce. (VW14-9598) 65.00

61

Fig. 12.5. The Jenkins Company catalog sample. Reproduced by courtesy of The Jenkins Company.

19. CALLIMACHUS. Callimachi Cyrenæi Hymni (cum scholis Græcis) & Epigrammata. Eivsdem Poemativm Decoma Berenices, a Catullo versum. Nicodemi Frischlini Balingensis interpretationes duæ Hymnorum . . . Henrici Stephani Partim emendatione partim Annotationes . . .

[Geneva] Excudebat Henricus Stephanus, 1577.

Tall quarto, nineteenth century vellum, soiled, light waterstain to edges, title dust soiled, quite decent.

As noted on the title, the translation of the Coma Berenices is by Catullus; both Frischlin and Estienne edited the text, though some work was done by others including Florido. This important edition includes a number of fragments for the first time and because of its completeness and scrupulous editing, became the basic text for all subsequent editions.

Renouard 1,145, =3; Brunet I, 1480; not in Schreiber. **$475.**

20. CANNING (Stratford, *Viscount* Stratford de Redcliffe). Shadows Of The Past. In Verse.

London, MacMillan, 1866.

Octavo, original red morocco gilt presentation binding, corners and edges a bit worn, all edges gilt, complete with the half title. Inscribed by the author to Lady Alford, the brilliant spouse of the Bridgewater heir: "For the Lady Marian Alford from her grateful neighbor and servant the author, Stratford de Redcliffe. October 15th, 1866."

His first full-length book of poems; the uncommon first edition. **$150.**

21. COOPER (Thomas). Thesavrvs Lingvae Romanae & Britannicae . . . Accessit Dictionarivm Historicum & poeticum . . .

Londini, In AEdibus quondam Berthelet, per Henricum Wykes, 16 March 1565.

Folio, neat new half calf, title cut close and mounted, no text lost, title and following leaf somewhat soiled and worn but not badly so. In all, a decent example of a work rarely found in acceptable condition.

Cooper, the tutor of William Camden, first gained fame for his continuation of Thomas Lanquet's *Chronicle*; indeed that work usually is better known as "Cooper's Chronicle." But it was his great dictionary, the *Thesaurus*, which brought him his greatest fame and the recognition of Queen Elizabeth. For scholars, the greatest interest lies in the English idioms of the Elizabethan period. The *Thesaurus* was the standard reference work during the formative years of Spenser, Marlowe, Sidney, Shakespeare, and Jonson, and a copy of the 1573 edition exists with notes identified by Collier as in the hand of Milton. Adapted to the needs of its time, the *Thesaurus* was unique and its influence on English lexicography far reaching.

STC 5686. The rare first edition. **$1250.**

Fig. 12.6. G. W. Stuart, Jr. Catalogue 49.

1 AUDEN, WYSTAN HUGH

ABOUT THE HOUSE.
London: Faber & Faber, 1966.

FIRST ENGLISH EDITION. 8vo. Pp. [viii],
[9-12]13-94. With the four-line errata slip
tipped in on the Acknowledgements page.
Bloomfield & Mendelson A495.

Original light purplish-blue cloth with gold
lettering down the spine, in dust-jacket.

Excellent copy. $85

2 AUDEN, WYSTAN HUGH

CITY WITHOUT WALLS, AND OTHER
POEMS.
New York: Random House, 1969.

FIRST EDITION. 8vo. [x], [1-2]3-
124[125-126]. NCBEL Vol IV, 209.

Fine copy in the original cloth, in very
good dust-jacket with tape-closed tear
on the inside of front cover. $50

3 AUDEN, WYSTAN HUGH

EPISTLE TO A GODSON AND OTHER
POEMS.
London: Faber & Faber, 1972
FIRST EDITION. 8vo. Pp. [viii], 9-72.

Fine copy in the original brown cloth-backed
stiff boards; spine lettered in gold. In fine
dust-jacket. $75

4 AUDEN, WYSTAN HUGH

HOMAGE TO CLIO.
London: Faber & Faber, 1960.

FIRST EDITION. 8vo. Pp. [viii], 9-91[92].
NCBEL Vol IV, 208.

Fine copy in the original purple cloth
lettered in gold along the spine, in fine
price-clipped dust-jacket. $100

5 AUDEN, WYSTAN HUGH

THANK YOU FOG.
London: Faber & Faber, 1974.
FIRST EDITION. 8vo. Pp. [vi], 7-57[58].

Fine copy in the original blue cloth-
backed stiff boards lettered in gold
along the spine, in fine price-clipped
dust-jacket.

These are Auden's last poems, completed
after his return to England in the Spring
of 1972. Also included is his last piece for
the stage, "The Entertainment of the
Senses," written in collaboration with
Chester Kallmann in 1963. He died in
September 1973. $75

6 BATES, HERBERT ERNEST

SEVEN TALES AND ALEXANDER.
London: The Scholartis Press, 1929.

FIRST EDITION. 8vo. Pp. [xii], [1-2]3-
166[167-168]. One of 1,000 copies,
printed on *Antique de Luxe* paper.
NCBEL Vol IV, 520.

Fine copy in the original white stiff
boards and blue cloth spine lettered
in gold, in very good plus dust-jacket.

An early book of stories published three
years after the author's first book. $100

7 BELLOC, HILAIRE

THE POSTMASTER GENERAL BY
HILAIRE BELLOC WITH THIRTY
DRAWINGS BY G. K. CHESTERTON.
London: Arrowsmith, 1932.
FIRST EDITION. 8vo. Pp. [viii]9-10, 11-286.

Original green cloth with gold-lettering on
the spine. Fine copy in near-fine pictorial
dust-jacket.

Another delightful Chester-Bellow satire
with a futuristic plot about the 1960s
television age. $275

8 BETJEMAN, JOHN

A FEW LATE CHRYSANTHEMUMS.
London: John Murray, 1954.
FIRST EDITION. 8vo. Pp. [vi], [1-2]3-95[96].
NCBEL Vol IV, 233.

Fine copy of one of the late poet laureate's
best titles, in the original purple cloth, in
near-fine lightly soiled dust-jacket. $100

T.S. VANDOROS
RARE BOOKS

Fig. 12.7. T. S. Vandoros. Rare Books—British Modern Firsts. March 1994.

Of exterior.—Fresh, sound (probably lacks "bloom"), neat (implies sobriety rather than charm); rubbed, scuffed, chafed, tender (of *joints),* shaken, loose, faded (purple cloth and green leather fade easily), tired (from the French *fatigue),* worn, defective (very widely interpreted), binding copy (i.e., needs it).

Of interior.—Clean, crisp, unpressed, browned (like much later 16th century paper), age-stained, water-stained (usually in the depreciating form, "a few light water stains"), foxed (i.e., spotted or discolored in patches: often "foxed as usual," implying that practically all copies are), soiled, thumbed (in the more lyrical catalogue notes, "lovingly thumbed by an early scholar"), and (very rare in English or American catalogues, but commendably frank), washed.[10]

A careful review of the sample catalog pages in figures 12.2-12.7 reveals many terms, which are to a large degree subjective. What one dealer describes as fine another may call good. An experienced special collections librarian suggests one buy on approval whenever possible, especially when buying from a dealer for the first time.

Because dealer catalogs are so important and the manner in which they describe an item's condition is central to a buying decision, I worked with a student on an "experiment" in describing some out-of-print books. The student worked for an antiquarian book dealer and helped prepare sales catalogs. The student selected three items that were to appear in a forthcoming catalog prepared by the dealer. The dealer's description of each book was one element in the study. Two other antiquarian dealers who worked in the same subject areas were then given the three items to describe as if they were going to list the books in one of their catalogs. In addition, we gave the books to two librarians (both were in charge of large rare book collections in major research libraries) to describe the condition of each item. The student and I identified five major conditions (water stains, mildew, tears, and so forth) present in each book before we had the librarians and other dealers describe the items. Both librarians noted all of the conditions for each book and gave precise information. We had to combine all three dealers' descriptions to have a complete list of all the conditions for each item. No one dealer described all the conditions for all the items. It was also interesting, but not surprising, to find that the dealer descriptions tended to downplay the faults. One would expect this, because their goal is to sell the items. Professional associations (such as ALA) and antiquarian dealer associations attempt to develop guidelines to help reduce the tensions that often arise between libraries and dealers as a result of catalog descriptions.

This section, like the one on new bookstores, can only briefly outline some of the more significant points about the OP book trade. It provides some basic information upon which one can continue to build while buying and collecting books for oneself or a library.

Other Media Retail Outlets

Because of the variety of their formats and purposes, it is not possible to generalize about retail outlets for other media. Libraries acquire most of the formats directly from their producers or from an educational media jobber.

The most common retail outlets for media other than books are the record shop and video store. Many small communities that do not have a bookstore have a record store and a video outlet. One reason for their popularity is that each record has a relatively low sales price (video cassettes are often rented), and a fairly large market exists for both formats. The top 20 recordings (records and tapes) of popular music may outsell the top 20 books by a 20-to-1 margin, at least in the United States.

Other than record shops, it is almost impossible to describe other media retail outlets, primarily because there are so few that it is hard to generalize. There are a few map shops in larger cities, most metropolitan areas have at least one sheet music store, and there are museums that sell slides and art reproductions. Sometimes, one can locate needed educational models and games at a teacher supply store. Libraries frequently purchase microforms from the producers.

Summary

The distribution system for books and other library materials is varied and complex. One must know something about the system before beginning to develop a library collection. This chapter provided highlights of what one needs to know; it portrays just the beginning of a long, enjoyable learning process. Jobbers, book dealers, and media vendors are more than willing to explain how they modify their operations to accommodate library requirements, when they know that a librarian has taken time to learn something about their operations.

Notes

[1] A jobber buys merchandise from manufacturers and sells it to retailers. A wholesaler is a person or business that sells large quantities of goods to a retailer. A drop shipper is a person or company that orders materials from manufacturers after receiving an order from a retailer (or library). Unlike jobbers and wholesalers, a drop shipper does not have a stock of materials, just a telephone.

[2] Lotz Wendall, "Here Today, Here Tomorrow: Coping with the OP 'Crisis,' " *School Library Journal* 35 (July 1989): 25-28.

[3] *Books in Other Languages* (Ottawa: Canadian Library Association, 1976); *International Literary Market Place* (New York: R. R. Bowker, 1966-).

[4] *Random House Dictionary of the English Language* (New York: Random House, 1967), 145.

[5]Margaret Landesman. "Out-of-Print and Secondhand Market," in *Understanding the Business of Library Acquisitions*, edited by K. A. Schmidt, 189 (Chicago: American Library Association, 1990).

[6]Sol Malkin, "Rare and Out-of-Print Books," in *A Manual on Bookselling*, 208 (New York: American Booksellers Association, 1974).

[7]Janet Bales, "In Search of Out-of-Print Materials," *Computers in Libraries* 11 (September 1991): 46-47.

[8]Malkin, "Rare and Out-of-Print Books," 208.

[9]John Carter, *ABC for Book Collectors*, 4th ed. (New York: Knopf, 1970); *The Bookman's Glossary*, 6th ed. (New York: R. R. Bowker, 1983).

[10]Carter, *ABC for Book Collectors*, 67-68.

Further Reading

General

Alessi, D. L. "Me and My Shadow: Vendors As the Third Hand in Collection Evaluation." *Journal of Library Administration* 17, no. 3 (1992): 155-60.

Alley, B. "ACQUIRE, Electronic Book Ordering." *Technicalities* 8 (September 1988): 3-4.

Barbato, J. "Small Press Struggle for Distribution." *Publishers Weekly* 238 (November 15, 1991): 25-34.

Barker, J. W., et al. "Organizing Out-of-Print and Replacement Acquisitions for Effectiveness, Efficiency and the Future." *Library Acquisitions: Practice and Theory* 14, no. 2 (1990): 137-63.

———. "Vendor Studies Redux." *Library Acquisitions: Practice and Theory* 13, no. 2 (1989): 133-41.

Barker, J. W.; D. Tonkery; and C. Flansburg. "Unbundling Vendor Costs." *Library Acquisitions: Practice and Theory* 15, no. 3 (1991): 399-406.

Basch, N. B. "Department Stores to Boutiques: How Many Serial Vendors and What Kind of Services Does Your Library Need?" *Serials Librarian* 12, nos. 3/4 (1990): 81-85.

Boissonas, C. M. "Out-of-Print Searching and Buying: BookQuest vs. Typed Lists." *Library Acquisitions: Practice and Theory* 16, no. 2 (1992): 103-8.

———. "When We Buy Books, We Know What We Pay For—Or Do We?" *Library Acquisitions: Practice and Theory* 13, no. 3 (1989): 87-101.

Boss, R. W., and J. McQueen. "Uses of Automation and Related Technologies by Domestic Book and Serials Jobbers." *Library Technology Reports* 25 (March/April 1989): 125-251.

Bottomley, L. "Changing Role of the Vendor." *Serials Librarian* 23, nos. 3/4 (1993): 245-47.

Coe, G., et al. "Book Distributors and Automation." *Library Technology Reports* 26 (July/August 1990): 497-501.

Demaris, N. "Electronic Book and Serials Acquisitions: The Medium Is the Message." *Computers in Libraries* 13 (January 1993): 25-27.

Gilbert, D. L. *Complete Guide to Starting a Used Book Store.* Chicago: Chicago Review Press, 1986.

Gordon, V. L. "An Overview of the OP Trade from the Book Dealer's Perspective." *Library Acquisitions: Practice and Theory* 15, no. 1 (1991): 53-62.

Grant, J. "Librarian and the Purchasing Function." *Library Acquisitions: Practice and Theory* 9, no. 4 (1985): 305-6.

Ivins, O. "Library Acquisitions: Budget Strategies, Vendor Selection, Vendor Evaluation." *Library Acquisitions: Practice and Theory* 16, no. 3 (1992): 257-63.

Kent, P. "How to Evaluate Serial Suppliers." *Library Acquisitions: Practice and Theory* 18 (Spring 1994): 83-87.

McQueen, J., and N. B. Basch. "Negotiating with Subscription Agencies." *American Libraries* 22 (June 1991): 532-34.

Miller, H. S. "Out-of-Print but Not out of Mind." *Bottom Line* 5, no. 4 (1992): 11-17.

Morris, J. H. "Library Sales and Wholesalers." *Small Press* 11 (Summer 1993): 20-27.

Phelps, D. "Publishers' Discounts but at What Price?" *Library Acquisitions: Practice and Theory* 14, no. 3 (1990): 289-93.

Presley, R. L. "Firing an Old Friend, Painful Decisions: Ethics Between Librarians and Vendors." *Library Acquisitions: Practice and Theory* 17, no. 1 (1993): 53-59.

Quinn, J. "New Approval Plans: Surrendering to the Vendor, Or in the Driver's Seat?" *Library Journal* 116 (September 15, 1991): 38-41.

Richards, D. T. "Library/Dealer Relationships: Reflections on the Ideal." *Journal of Library Administration* 16, no. 3 (1992): 45-55.

Serebnick, J. "Selection and Holding of Small Publishers' Books in OCLC Libraries: A Study of the Influence of Reviews, Publishers, and Vendors." *Library Quarterly* 62 (July 1992): 259-94.

Shafa, Z. M., et al. "Regional Study of Vendor Performance for In-Print Monographs." *Library Acquisitions: Practice and Theory* 16, no. 1 (1992): 21-29.

Shrik, G. M. "Contract Acquisitions." *Library Acquisitions: Practice and Theory* 17 (Summer 1993): 145-53.

Academic

Anderson, J. "Order Consolidation: A Shift to Single Vendor Service." *Serials Librarian* 17, nos. 3/4 (1990): 93-97.

Brugger, J. M. "Automated Acquisitions and the Quality Database." *Library Acquisitions: Practice and Theory* 16, no. 1 (1992): 79-83.

Calhoun, J., et al. "Modelling an Academic Approval Plan." *Library Resources & Technical Services* 34 (July 1990): 367-79.

Ferguson, A. W. "British Approval Plan Books: American or British Vendor?" *Collection Building* 8, no. 4 (1988): 18-22.

Johnson, M. A. "Collection Development Today: Coping with Reality." *Technicalities* 12 (June 1992): 5-8.

Kaatrude, P. B. "Approval Plan vs. Conventional Development." *Collection Management* 11, nos. 1/2 (1988): 145-51.

Womack, K., et al. "An Approval Plan Vendor Review." *Library Acquisitions: Practice and Theory* 12, nos. 3/4 (1988): 363-78.

Public

Anichiarico, M., and A. Boaz. "Distributor Connection: Responding to Demand." *Library Journal* 118 (February 1, 1993): 129-36.

Baker, J. F. "Hard Times, Hard Choices." *Publishers Weekly* 240 (January 4, 1993): 45-48.

"1990: A Year of High Drama." *Publishers Weekly* 238 (January 4, 1991): 23-24.

Prete, B. "Publishing for Literacy." *Publishers Weekly* 237 (November 30, 1990): 27-28+.

Schiller, J. G. "Appraising Rare and Collectible Children's Books." *AB Bookman's Weekly* 86 (November 1990): 1861-71.

Strickler, D. "What I Learned Working in a Bookstore." *Library Journal* 117 (June 15, 1992): 47-48.

Tuttle, M. "Magazine Fulfillment Centers." *Library Acquisitions: Practice and Theory* 9, no. 1 (1985): 41-49.

"Weathering the Storm: Publishers, Booksellers, and Wholesalers Discuss the Effect of the Recession on Children's Books." *Publishers Weekly* 239 (February 12, 1992): 7-9.

School

Eaglen, A. B. "Book Wholesalers: Pros and Cons." *School Library Journal* 25 (October 1978): 116-19.

———. "Shell Game: Publishers, Vendors and the Myth of the Backlist." *School Library Journal* 38 (November 1992): 24-28.

Hass, E. "Librarians and Booksellers Working Together in the Year of the Young Reader." *School Library Journal* 35 (January 1989): 24-27.

Mandell, P. L. "Audiovisual Buyer's Directory." *School Library Journal* 35 (August 1989): 44-46.

Scilken, M. H. "Breaking the Bind." *School Library Journal* 37 (March 1991): 160.

See, L. "Biting the Hand That Feeds You." *Publishers Weekly* 238 (December 13, 1991): 28-29.

Stafford, P. "One-Stop Shopping with Your Paperback Wholesaler." *School Library Journal* 32 (September 1985): 39-41.

Stefani, J. "Using Vendors as Educational Resources." *Southeastern Librarian* 40 (Spring 1990): 9-11.

Special

Cather, J. P. "Librarians and Booksellers: Forming a Durable Bond." *AB Bookman's Weekly* 86 (June 18, 1990): 2624-32.

Front, T. "Music As an Antiquarian Trade Specialty." *AB Bookman's Weekly* 86 (December 10, 1990): 2289-97.

Hook, W. J. "Approval Plans for Religious and Theological Libraries." *Library Acquisitions: Practice and Theory* 15, no. 2 (1991): 215-27.

St. Clair, G., and J. Treadwell. "Science and Technology Approval Plans Compared." *Library Resources & Technical Services* 33 (October 1989): 382-92.

Schwalb, R. "Distributors: Religious and General Wholesalers." *Publishers Weekly* 237 (October 5, 1990): 58-64.

Stave, D. G. "Art Books on Approval: Why Not?" *Library Acquisitions: Practice and Theory* 7, no. 1 (1983): 5-6.

13
Fiscal Management

Controlling expenditures and securing adequate funding are two activities involved in collection management. Monies spent on materials for the collection constitute the second largest expense category for the majority of libraries and information centers. Traditionally, in United States libraries, salaries represent the largest percentage of the total budget, followed by the materials ("book") budget, and finally, all other operating expenses. That order remains today, but the percentage spent on materials has gone down as salaries rise. Although percentages vary, the order also remains the same in any type of information environment or any size collection. As is often the case, most of the literature on the topic of collection budgeting reflects a large research library orientation. However, the same issues exist in other libraries. Similarly, most of the ideas and suggestions contained in such articles apply equally well to other information settings.

In the recent past, there has been a constant pressure on the materials budget of most libraries. This pressure resulted in a decline in the percentage of the total budget spent on acquiring items for the collection. The almost yearly double-digit inflation of serials prices further skewed the traditional balance in collection fund allocations. In many libraries in the United States, serials expenditures exceed monographic purchases, even in institutions that have traditionally emphasized book collections.

If one compares the total amount of money expended on materials 30 years ago with the current funding levels, today's total is considerably higher. Unfortunately, the total expenditures do not tell the entire story. When one looks at the number of items acquired for the money, one sees that the increase in acquisitions is not proportional to the funding increases. We are spending more and acquiring less. Since the 1970s, many libraries, along with many other organizations, have dealt with budgets that some persons call steady state, others call zero growth, and still others call static. Generally, budgeting of this type uses the previous year's inflation rate as the base for the next fiscal year's increase. An average inflation rate, like all averages, contains elements that increase at both above and below the average rate. For libraries this is a problem, because the inflation rate for information materials has been running well ahead of the overall inflation rate.

Problems in Fiscal Management

Over the years, collection development staffs in the United States have faced several problems. Book and journal prices have generally increased, and continue to increase, at rates well above the country's average inflation rate as measured by the Consumer Price Index (CPI). As a result, most libraries experienced some decline in acquisition rates. Serials prices increased even more rapidly than did monographic prices. To maintain serials subscriptions, libraries took monies from book funds, thus further reducing the number of monographs acquired. Eventually, libraries started canceling subscriptions. Thus, differential inflation rates and the use of national average rates as the basis for calculating budgets have contributed to declining acquisition rates for many libraries.

A second problem was, and still is, that the materials budget is vulnerable in periods of tight budgets. Expenditures on materials are somewhat discretionary in that (in theory) one could wait to buy an item this year. Institutions set staff salaries on an annual basis, and staff reductions are rare during the middle of a fiscal year, unless the organization faces a major financial crisis. In essence, salaries are the last item organizations cut when attempting to save money. Without heat, light, and water (utility bills) the organization cannot remain open. So, those generally are not cut during a fiscal year. There are some operating expenses that are discretionary: pens, pencils, paper, typewriter ribbons, and so on (office supplies). Institutions may achieve small savings, in terms of percentage of the total budget, by cutting back in such areas. Institutions with relatively large library collections view the materials budget as one of the largest available pools of funds that could be cut in an emergency. (Even a medium-sized library, such as the Von der Ahe Library at Loyola Marymount University, has a materials budget of more than $1 million. This amount is large enough to make the financial officers look at it as a source of significant funds if needed.) Further, the reality is that the monograph materials budget is the only place where significant cuts are easy to make because of the non-ongoing nature of the material. All too often, the long-term impact of such decisions does not receive enough consideration, and the other choices appear, at least in the short run, to be even less acceptable. These issues are institutional and apply to corporate and special libraries as much as to publicly funded libraries.

What happened in collecting in the 1970s and 1980s was a shift in emphasis from monographs to maintaining periodical collections. Today that shift is slowly reversing, and through careful library budget preparation and presentation, funding authorities appear to be more willing to accept differential budget increases that more closely reflect actual expense experience. If nothing else, the problems of the past 30 years caused collection development officers to become better planners and to develop more accurate methods for calculating budgetary needs. As a result, they have more credibility with funding authorities.

This chapter covers several budget and fiscal topics: (1) library accounting systems (a brief discussion), (2) estimating costs of materials, (3) allocating funds available, (4) monitoring expenditures (encumbering), and (5) special budgeting problems.

Library Fund Accounting

The vast majority of libraries and information centers are part of not-for-profit (NFP) organizations. Being not-for-profit affects how the library maintains its financial records, particularly when contrasted with for-profit organizations. For libraries that are part of a governmental jurisdiction, most revenues are received through an annual budget. Collection development officers must have accurate information about the monies available, and they need accurate data to assist in the preparation of budget requests. The funding authorities review the budget requests and authorize certain levels of funding for various activities. The two most common forms of income for libraries are appropriations (monies distributed by the governing body to its agencies to carry out specific purposes) and revenue generated by the library as a result of fees and fines.

Because of the nature of the financial activities, certain accounting terms and concepts are different for NFP organizations than for for-profit organizations. However, some general accounting rules and practices do apply. One special term for NFP accounting is *fund accounting*. (Fund accounting has been defined as a set of self-balancing account groups.) Another difference is that the profit-oriented bookkeeping system equation uses assets, liabilities, and equity; in NFP accounting, the elements used are assets, liabilities, and fund balance. One of the equations for NFP bookkeeping is that assets must equal liabilities plus the fund balance; another is that the fund balance is the difference between assets and liabilities. Substituting equity for fund balance would make the equation apply to for-profit organizations. A difference between these equations is that an increase in fund balance carries with it no special meaning, whereas an increase in equity is a positive signal in a for-profit organization. Other terms, such as *debit, credit, journalizing, posting,* and *trial balance* have the same meaning, regardless of the organization's profit orientation.

In most libraries, the major fund is the operating fund. Other funds may be endowment and physical plant funds. The operating funds are the group of accounts used to handle the day-to-day activities of the library for a given time, usually one year, covering such items as salaries, materials purchases, and utility bills. Within the operating fund there may be two categories of accounts: restricted and unrestricted.

Restricted accounts require that one uses the monies only for specific purposes. Collection development and acquisition staff often work with such accounts (frequently referred to as funds in the monetary rather than the accounting meaning of the term). More often than not, these accounts are the result of donations by individuals who have definite ideas about how the library may spend the money. Some libraries have endowments that are a combination of individual and corporate or foundation gifts; an example are endowments developed under the National

Endowment for the Humanities Challenge Grant program. (Sometimes gifts are for current use, and sometimes they are for an endowment. Endowments should generate income for the library indefinitely. The normal procedure for endowments is to make available some percentage of the interest earned. The balance of the interest is returned to the endowment to increase its capital base. Private libraries, and an increasing number of publicly funded libraries, have one or more endowments.) Often, the donor's restrictions are narrow. When the restrictions are too narrow, it is difficult to make effective use of the available monies. Most collection development officers prefer unrestricted book accounts (used for any appropriate item for the collection) or broad-based restricted accounts.

The purpose of the accounting system is to assure the proper use of monies provided and to make it possible to track expenditures. That is, one must record (charge) every financial transaction to some account, and a record exists of what the transaction involved. With a properly functioning fund accounting system, it is possible to tie every item acquired to a specific account and to verify when the transaction took place. With a good accounting system, one can easily provide accurate reports about all financial aspects of collection development activities. Furthermore, it is a great planning aid. It takes time to understand accounting systems, but one must understand them if one wishes to be an effective and efficient collection development officer. A good book to consult on this topic is G. Stevenson Smith's *Managerial Accounting for Libraries and Other Not-for-Profit Organizations*.[1]

Estimating Costs

Several factors influence the funding needs for collection development. Changes in the composition of the service community may have an important impact in either a positive or negative sense (see chapter 2). Another factor is changes in collecting activities, such as the scope or depth desired in a subject area (see chapter 3). The two cost factors that come up year in and year out are the price of materials and inflation.

From time to time, libraries have had some problems establishing the credibility of collection development funding requirements. Though a good accounting system will assist in justifying budget requests, additional data about book expenditures is necessary. One example of the problems caused by inflation, stable budgets, and rapidly rising prices for materials (and perhaps limited credibility), is what happened to the expenditures and acquisition rates for the Association of Research Libraries between 1986 and 1991. Libraries of every type and size experienced similar problems during this time. A *Publishers Weekly* article clearly demonstrated the impact of inflation and limited funding on acquisitions activities.[2] Between 1986 and 1991, monograph expenditures rose 25 percent, the unit price rose by 47 percent, and the number of volumes acquired dropped by 15 percent. For serials the picture was much the same, except the costs were higher: expenditures up 70 percent, unit price up 72 percent, and titles purchased down 2 percent. This pattern of prices rising faster than funding level continued for most U.S. libraries into 1994.

Data about price increases has been available for some time. During the 1970s, the profession made an all-out effort to create useful library price indexes that measure rates of change. A subcommittee of the American National Standards Institute, the Z39 Committee, was able to develop guidelines for price indexes.[3] By the early 1980s it was necessary to revise the guidelines. Another group effort was that of the Library Materials Price Index Committee (Resources Section, Resources and Services Division of ALA). The committee has produced a price index for American materials and some international publications. These efforts provide consistent data on price changes over a long period, which, when averaged, is as close as one can come to predicting future price changes.

One finds the most recent data in journals; historical data appear in *The Bowker Annual*. Using *The Bowker Annual* may be adequate for some purposes, but one needs to be aware that the information is almost two years old. Preliminary data for books published during a calendar year appear in *Publishers Weekly* (often in late February or early March). Final data appear some months later (September or October). The major problem with the published indexes is, when one must prepare a budget request, up-to-date data may not be readily available. Vendors can sometimes provide more current data. Some vendors will provide custom pricing information, and others may provide a booklet, such as Baker & Taylor's *Academic and Research Book Price Report*. This publication has price data about books handled in the approval plan program. At the time of preparation of this chapter, the current edition covered titles processed between July 1, 1992, and June 30, 1993. Figures 13.1, on page 356, and 13.2, on page 357, illustrate the type of information one can find in such reports. Figure 13.3, on page 358, illustrates information from Yankee Book Peddler for the same type of material but for a slightly different time period.

It is also possible to secure information about serials subscriptions from a vendor. Figure 13.4, on page 359, is a report for the LMU library based on subscriptions with EBSCO. Figure 13.5, on page 360-61, is reproduced from EBSCO's *At Your Service* quarterly, which shows a five-year cost history for serials. Note the difference between the LMU percentages and the national averages. Figures 13.6 on pages 362-63, 13.7 on pages 364-65, and 13.8 on pages 366-67, reproduced from EBSCO's *Serials Price Projections—1995*, illustrate the differences among types of libraries as well as the relationship between subscription prices and exchange rates.

Just as libraries prepare budget requests at different times of the year, pricing data appears at various times during the year in a variety of sources. The challenge is to find the most current data, which may determine whether the library receives requested funding.

Text continues on page 368.

LIBRARY OF CONGRESS CLASSIFICATION

SUBJECT STATION NUMBER	LC CLASS	SUBJECT STATION NAME	1993 NBR OF TITLES SHIPPED	1993 AVERAGE LIST PRICE	1993 TOTAL LIST PRICE	1992 NBR OF TITLES SHIPPED	1992 AVERAGE LIST PRICE	1992 TOTAL LIST PRICE	VARIANCE 1992-93
A01	A	General Works	323	$91.38	$29,516.18	303	$73.27	$ 22,201.91	24.71%
A10	B	Philosophy	710	45.25	32,124.80	698	43.70	30,503.34	3.54%
A11	BF	Psychology	792	43.90	34,770.95	808	39.37	31,810.14	11.52%
E10	BJ	Ethics	104	36.02	3,745.70	109	37.76	4,115.50	-4.61%
A13	BL	Religion	2,384	30.74	73,282.79	2,393	28.54	68,305.13	7.69%
A18	C	Auxiliary Historical Sciences	77	42.84	3,298.98	89	40.02	3,561.35	7.07%
A17	CC	Archaeology	168	50.10	8,416.93	188	46.38	8,719.03	8.03%
A14	D	History	658	40.99	26,974.03	651	41.11	26,760.45	-0.27%
A15	D	History of Spec Areas and Countries	652	41.99	27,374.43	700	39.20	27,436.62	7.12%
TOTAL	D	TOTAL D	1,310	41.49	54,348.46	1,351	40.12	54,197.07	3.42%
A94	TP	Chemical Engineering	180	123.01	22,140.95	200	104.00	20,800.20	18.27%
B94	TP	Biotechnology	113	98.18	11,094.05	130	94.70	12,310.57	3.68%
TOTAL	TP	TOTAL TP	293	113.43	33,235	330	100.34	33,110.77	13.05%
A06	TR	Reprographics	307	37.28	11,445.53	302	34.31	10,362.70	8.65%
A96	TS	Manufacturing	101	64.72	6,536.33	71	55.14	3,915.00	17.37%
A98	TX	Home Economics	261	29.01	7,571.04	327	25.76	8,424.35	12.60%
A44	U	Military Science	635	34.22	21,726.86	751	31.35	23,543.51	9.14%
N44	V	Naval Science	107	35.59	3,807.79	105	34.11	3,582.00	4.32%
A89	VM	Marine Engineering	36	60.42	2,175.05	51	41.98	2,140.90	43.93%
A28	Z	Publishing and Printing	150	59.19	8,878.77	153	54.57	8,349.83	8.46%
A29	Z	Library and Information Science	263	46.15	12,136.40	311	41.77	12,991.62	10.47%
TOTAL	Z	TOTAL Z	413	50.88	21,015.17	464	45.99	21,341.45	10.63%
		TOTALS	48,660	48.17	2,344,182.66	48,572	45.03	2,186,978.85	6.99%

Fig. 13.1. Price of information materials by Library of Congress Classification. From *Academic and Research Book Price Report, 1992-1993*. Reproduced by courtesy of Baker & Taylor.

PHYSICAL FORMAT

SUBJECT STATION NUMBER	LC CLASS	SUBJECT STATION NAME	1993 HARDBOUND TITLES SHIPPED	1993 AVERAGE LIST PRICE	1993 PAPER TITLES SHIPPED	1993 AVERAGE LIST PRICE	1993 SPIRAL TITLES SHIPPED	1993 AVERAGE LIST PRICE	1993 LOOSELEAF TITLES SHIPPED	1993 AVERAGE LIST PRICE	1993 MULTIMEDIA TITLES SHIPPED	1993 AVERAGE LIST PRICE	1993 PAMPHLET TITLES SHIPPED	1993 AVERAGE LIST PRICE
A49	HF	International Economics	223	$59.27	117	$36.03	1	$25.00	8	$189.38			7	$11.82
A50	Q	Science	120	60.11	44	23.61	1	10.00						
A51	QA	Mathematics	578	80.87	258	39.70	1	54.95			11	$58.80		
A52	QB	Astronomy	128	78.93	29	33.25							1	18.00
A53	QC	Physics	573	95.88	87	57.64	2	45.98			3	65.98		
A54	QD	Chemistry	317	128.91	39	48.03	1	59.95			1	59.95		
A55	QE	Mineralogy	16	106.70	1	39.95					1	75.00		
P55	QE	Petrology	8	75.55	4	81.13								
A56	QE	Geology	102	103.56	55	36.54					2	57.25	2	10.00
A57	GC	Oceanography	26	75.85	10	51.15								
A58	QC	Meterology	54	78.06	20	29.01							1	5.00
A59	QE	Paleontology	29	84.12	16	26.86	1	9.95					3	20.00
A60	QH	Biology	303	77.31	104	29.12	17	48.16			1	80.00	1	9.95
B60	QH	Biophysics	12	134.64	1	34.50								
C60	QP	Biochemistry	147	121.94	24	28.78	11	53.48	1	195.00	1	78.00		
M60	QR	Microbiology	81	122.91	12	28.38	3	44.28					10	15.27
A84	TH	Building Engineering	114	52.28	142	36.09	1	16.95	2	44.50	7	33.57	2	30.50
A85	TJ	Mechanical Engineering	127	94.62	55	62.59					4	76.36		
N85	TJ	Machine Engineering	22	107.60	4	33.48					1	74.95		
A86	TL	Automotive Engineering	86	55.81	242	26.21	1	36.00	3	89.30			2	18.00
A87	TL	Aeronautical Engineering	70	63.10	49	29.79	2	32.48	1	190.00			1	5.95
S87	TL	Space Engineering	25	96.87	8	53.11							1	24.95
A89	VM	Marine Engineering	17	91.85	19	32.30							1	24.95
A90	TK	Electrical Engineering	189	75.63	144	60.05	5	22.86	1	55.00	5	176.97	9	30.44
A91	TK	Electronic Engineering	182	81.18	121	66.94	1	37.95			3	116.00	2	42.75
A92	TK	Nuclear Engineering	23	108.81	17	61.35							7	26.71
D93	QA	Computer Science	641	66.99	1,342	35.31	60	20.30	1	225.00	389	35.69	12	35.02
A94	TP	Chemical Engineering	147	136.11	26	64.38	1	95.00	2	80.88	1	149.00	3	17.67
B94	TP	Biotechnology	85	112.76	25	49.90	1	64.00			1	150.00	1	48.00
A95	TN	Petroleum Engineering	35	120.20	21	73.91	1	45.00	1	24.95				
M95	TN	Mining Engineering	21	113.34	6	46.63					3	106.63		
A96	TS	Manufacturing	49	84.30	49	45.03	1	22.50	1	150.00			1	27.00
A98	TX	Home Economics	137	37.68	115	19.04	5	28.18	1	34.95	1	27.50	2	7.85
		TOTAL	30,380	$59.69	16,674	$27.80	368	$41.23	165	$125.90	547	$45.11	526	$12.71

BAKER & TAYLOR'S APPROVAL PLAN MANAGEMENT REPORT

Fig. 13.2. Price of information materials by format. From *Academic and Research Book Price Report, 1992-1993*. Reproduced by courtesy of Baker & Taylor.

VBP
999 MAPLE STREET
CONTOOCOOK, NH 03229
800-258-3774

TITLES PROFILED BY PRESS TYPE
ADULT TITLES
PRESS TYPE—ALL PRESS TYPES
(EXCLUDE ALTERNATE PAPER)

////// N JOV N UZ N PAGE 1
ADV-AC Y POP Y
GEN-AC Y PROF Y
4/20/94
23 : 42 : 51

ALL VALUES BASED ON LIST PRICE PERIOD 1: 07/92 – 06/93 – – –   – – – PERIOD 2: 07/93 – 04/94 – – –   PERIOD 1 VS PERIOD 2

LC	LC DESCRIPTION	TITLES PROFILED	TOTAL $ VALUE	AVG $/ TITLE	TITLES PROFILED	TOTAL $ VALUE	AVG $/ TITLE	PRICE COMPARISON $/TITLE	%/TITLE
AC	COLLECTIONS	11	255.35	23.21	4	89.90	22.48	.73-	3.15%-
AE	ENCYCLOPEDIAS	3	102.90	34.30	5	132.75	26.55	7.75-	22.59%-
AG	DICTIONARIES	16	494.40	30.90	17	557.00	32.76	1.86	6.02%
AI	INDEXES	2	235.00	117.50	0	.00	.00	117.50-	
AM	MUSEUMS	9	633.85	70.43	12	444.55	37.05	33.38-	47.39%-
AS	LEARNED SOCIETIES	5	272.90	54.58	5	343.85	68.77	14.19	26.00%
AY	YEARBOOKS	5	84.30	16.86	4	542.61	135.65	118.79	704.57%
AZ	HISTORY OF SCHOLARSHIP	7	367.90	52.56	5	105.15	21.03	31.53-	59.99%-
** A		58	2,446.60	42.18	52	2,215.81	42.61	.43	1.02%
B	PHILOSOPHY	417	23,087.30	55.37	322	17,114.66	53.15	2.22-	4.01%-
BC	LOGIC	26	1,356.34	52.17	23	1,511.59	65.72	13.55	25.97%
BD	SPECULATIVE PHILOSOPHY	96	4,430.54	46.15	81	3,426.56	42.30	3.85-	8.34%-
BF	PSYCHOLOGY	587	24,186.30	41.20	477	20,385.80	42.74	1.54	3.75%
BH	AESTHETICS	24	994.78	41.45	13	567.70	43.67	2.22	5.36%
BJ	ETHICS	94	2,907.63	30.93	101	3,366.40	33.33	2.40	7.76%
BL	RELIGION	245	9,109.34	37.18	217	7,353.96	33.89	3.29-	8.85%-
BM	JUDAISM	161	7,394.44	45.93	108	4,121.47	38.16	7.77-	16.92%-
BP	ISLAM	58	2,221.33	38.30	51	1,937.52	37.99	.31-	.81%-
BQ	BUDDHISM	51	1,473.31	28.89	44	1,054.50	23.97	4.92-	17.03%-
BR	CHRISTIANITY	178	7,895.79	44.36	149	7,159.44	48.05	3.69	8.32%
BS	THE BIBLE	257	9,722.47	37.83	295	10,092.99	34.21	3.62-	9.57%-
BT	DOCTRINAL THEOLOGY	199	6,187.66	31.09	190	4,865.48	25.61	5.48-	17.63%-
BV	PRACTICAL THEOLOGY	295	6,233.18	21.13	201	3,753.34	18.67	2.46-	11.64%-
BX	DENOMINATIONS	330	10,372.02	31.43	245	7,948.37	32.44	1.01	3.21%
** B		3,018	117,572.43	38.96	2,517	94,659.78	37.61	1.35-	3.47%-

Fig. 13.3. Yankee Book Peddler, total approval program coverage, primary subject coverage. Reproduced by courtesy of Yankee Book Peddler.

P.O. BOX 92901   FAX (310)322-2558   1-800-683-2726
LOS ANGELES   CA   90009-2901   (310)322-5000

EBSCO
SUBSCRIPTION SERVICES

01/31/94   PAGE 292

HISTORICAL PRICE ANALYSIS BY TITLE CODE

LA   35800-00

LOYOLA MARYMOUNT UNIVERSITY
JANET H LAI-PERIODICALS LIBR
LOYOLA BLVD AT WEST 80TH ST
LOS ANGELES CALIF   90045

TITLE	FREQ	SUB	PRICE 1990 JAN	PRICE 1991 JAN	% INCR	PRICE 1992 JAN	% INCR	PRICE 1993 JAN	% INCR	PRICE 1994 JAN	% INCR	TOTAL INCREASE %
TITLE CODE 973767007												
YOUNG CHILDREN / REGULAR SUBSCRIPTION/ /SURFACE MAIL/ INDICES: ED, CQ, SQ, SM, LQ, ET, SI, AP, AO	BM	AA	25.00	30.00	20.0	30.00	00.0	30.00	00.0	30.00	00.0	5.00 20.0
978540003												
ZEITSCHRIFT FUR DIE NEUTESTAMENTLICHE WISSENSCHAFT /FOR NORTH AMERICA/ INDICES: NG, RI, AP	SA	AA	79.20	88.65	11.9	93.75	05.8	101.40	08.2	101.40	00.0	22.20 28.0
982296006												
ZYGON / JOURNAL OF RELIGION & SCIENCE/ / ALL EXCEPT JAPAN/ INDICES: HU, AJ, BR, HM, HN, NG, OL, PI, RI, SI AP, AO	QR	AA	38.50	42.50	10.4	49.00	15.3	52.50	07.1	56.00	06.7	17.50 45.5
** CUSTOMER TOTAL **			202,455.20	229,869.29		255,542.84		277,453.00		300,068.44		97,613.24
2027 TITLES AVERAGE PRICE			99.87	113.40		126.06		136.87		148.03		48.2
AVERAGE % INCREASE				13.5		11.2		08.6		08.2		

12.0%

DEAR CUSTOMER: BASED ON THE CUMULATIVE TOTAL INCREASE OF FOUR YEARS OF
COMPARATIVE DATA, THE AVERAGE YEARLY INCREASE IS EQUAL TO

Fig. 13.4. EBSCO historical price analysis by title code. Reproduced by courtesy of EBSCO.

COST HISTORY BY LIBRARY TYPE

	Average # Titles	1990 Average Cost Per Title	1991 Average Cost Per Title	Change from 1990-91	1992 Average Cost Per Title	Change from 1991-92	1993 Average Cost Per Title	Change from 1992-93	1994 Average Cost Per Title	Change from 1993-94	Change from 1990-94
ACADEMIC LIBRARY											
U.S. TITLES	4,864	$107.80	$118.66	10.1%	$130.03	9.6%	$140.85	8.3%	$152.15	8.0%	41.1%
NON-U.S. TITLES	2,240	$271.41	$336.64	24.0%	$364.53	8.3%	$411.84	13.0%	$438.22	6.4%	61.5%
ALL TITLES	7,104	$159.39	$187.39	17.6%	$203.97	8.8%	$226.29	10.9%	$242.35	7.1%	52.1%
ACADEMIC MEDICAL LIBRARY											
U.S. TITLES	1,957	$149.11	$164.84	10.6%	$181.98	10.4%	$199.45	9.6%	$216.28	8.4%	45.0%
NON-U.S. TITLES	1,298	$325.65	$399.42	22.7%	$426.78	6.8%	$479.55	12.4%	$503.15	4.9%	54.5%
ALL TITLES	3,255	$219.51	$258.38	17.7%	$279.59	8.2%	$311.15	11.3%	$330.67	6.3%	50.6%
HOSPITAL LIBRARY											
U.S. TITLES	102	$100.27	$113.87	13.6%	$127.07	11.6%	$137.65	8.3%	$150.60	9.4%	50.2%
NON-U.S. TITLES	15	$171.52	$209.66	22.2%	$234.44	11.8%	$237.19	1.2%	$240.85	1.5%	40.4%
ALL TITLES	117	$109.40	$126.15	15.3%	$140.84	11.6%	$150.41	6.8%	$162.17	7.8%	48.2%
LAW FIRM LIBRARY											
U.S. TITLES	986	$190.59	$205.68	7.9%	$217.73	5.9%	$228.83	5.1%	$241.37	5.5%	26.6%
NON-U.S. TITLES	50	$216.40	$249.98	15.5%	$281.17	12.5%	$298.69	6.2%	$327.36	9.6%	51.3%
ALL TITLES	1,036	$191.84	$207.82	8.3%	$220.79	6.2%	$232.21	5.2%	$245.52	5.7%	28.0%

LAW SCHOOL LIBRARY

U.S. TITLES	1,111	$68.97	7.1%	$78.69	6.5%	$83.53	6.1%	$87.95	5.3%	27.5%
NON-U.S. TITLES	332	$114.96	19.8%	$147.20	6.9%	$155.07	5.3%	$158.72	2.4%	38.1%
ALL TITLES	1,443	$79.55	11.3%	$94.46	6.7%	$99.99	5.9%	$104.23	4.2%	31.0%

PUBLIC LIBRARY

U.S. TITLES	3,019	$45.29	6.4%	$51.57	7.1%	$53.55	3.8%	$55.81	4.2%	23.2%
NON-U.S. TITLES	276	$50.27	19.4%	$58.16	-3.1%	$59.69	2.6%	$65.04	9.0%	29.4%
ALL TITLES	3,295	$45.70	7.6%	$52.12	6.0%	$54.06	3.7%	$56.58	4.7%	23.8%

SPECIAL LIBRARY

U.S. TITLES	1,929	$140.36	7.2%	$161.60	7.4%	$171.52	6.1%	$181.38	5.7%	29.2%
NON-U.S. TITLES	308	$214.32	16.5%	$265.88	6.5%	$291.26	9.5%	$305.38	4.8%	42.5%
ALL TITLES	2,237	$150.54	9.0%	$175.96	7.2%	$188.01	6.8%	$198.45	5.6%	31.8%

CORPORATE LIBRARY

U.S. TITLES	1,234	$126.04	8.5%	$146.63	7.3%	$157.27	7.3%	$165.89	5.5%	31.6%
NON-U.S. TITLES	213	$342.32	25.2%	$480.20	12.0%	$525.32	9.4%	$563.81	7.3%	64.7%
ALL TITLES	1,447	$157.88	13.8%	$195.73	8.9%	$211.45	8.0%	$224.46	6.2%	42.2%

Fig. 13.5. Five-year historical price analysis for serials. From *At Your Service*. Reproduced by courtesy of EBSCO.

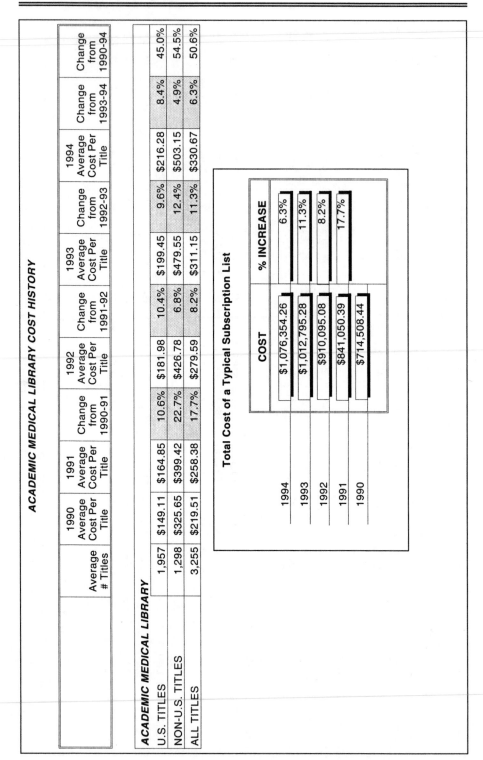

ACADEMIC MEDICAL LIBRARY COST HISTORY

	Average # Titles	1990 Average Cost Per Title	1991 Average Cost Per Title	Change from 1990-91	1992 Average Cost Per Title	Change from 1991-92	1993 Average Cost Per Title	Change from 1992-93	1994 Average Cost Per Title	Change from 1993-94	Change from 1990-94
ACADEMIC MEDICAL LIBRARY											
U.S. TITLES	1,957	$149.11	$164.85	10.6%	$181.98	10.4%	$199.45	9.6%	$216.28	8.4%	45.0%
NON-U.S. TITLES	1,298	$325.65	$399.42	22.7%	$426.78	6.8%	$479.55	12.4%	$503.15	4.9%	54.5%
ALL TITLES	3,255	$219.51	$258.38	17.7%	$279.59	8.2%	$311.15	11.3%	$330.67	6.3%	50.6%

Total Cost of a Typical Subscription List

	COST	% INCREASE
1994	$1,076,354.26	6.3%
1993	$1,012,795.28	11.3%
1992	$910,095.08	8.2%
1991	$841,050.39	17.7%
1990	$714,508.44	

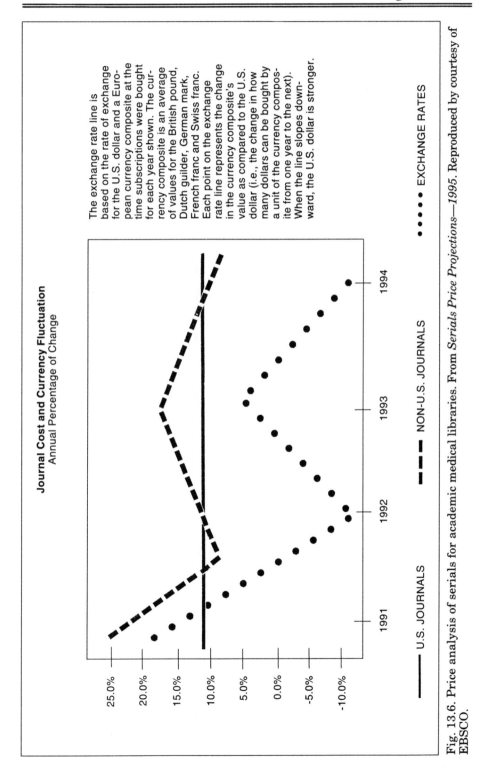

Fig. 13.6. Price analysis of serials for academic medical libraries. From *Serials Price Projections—1995*. Reproduced by courtesy of EBSCO.

PUBLIC LIBRARY COST HISTORY

	Average # Titles	1990 Average Cost Per Title	Change from 1990-91	1991 Average Cost Per Title	Change from 1991-92	1992 Average Cost Per Title	Change from 1992-93	1993 Average Cost Per Title	Change from 1993-94	1994 Average Cost Per Title	Change from 1990-94
PUBLIC LIBRARY											
U.S. TITLES	3,019	$45.29	6.4%	$48.16	7.1%	$51.57	3.8%	$53.55	4.2%	$55.81	23.2%
NON-U.S. TITLES	276	$50.27	19.4%	$60.03	-3.1%	$58.16	2.6%	$59.69	9.0%	$65.04	29.4%
ALL TITLES	3,295	$45.70	7.6%	$49.16	6.0%	$52.12	3.7%	$54.06	4.7%	$56.58	23.8%

Total Cost of a Typical Subscription List

	COST	% INCREASE
1994	$186,460.60	4.7%
1993	$178,147.06	3.7%
1992	$171,762.38	6.0%
1991	$161,990.90	7.6%
1990	$150,610.64	

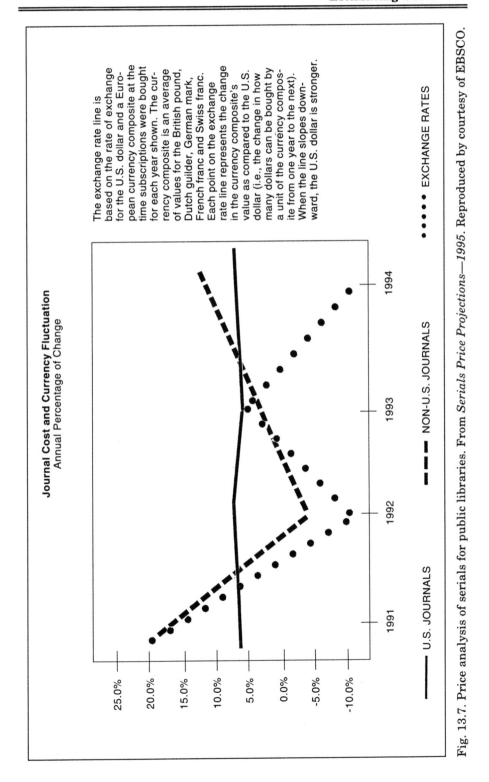

Journal Cost and Currency Fluctuation
Annual Percentage of Change

The exchange rate line is based on the rate of exchange for the U.S. dollar and a European currency composite at the time subscriptions were bought for each year shown. The currency composite is an average of values for the British pound, Dutch guilder, German mark, French franc and Swiss franc. Each point on the exchange rate line represents the change in the currency composite's value as compared to the U.S. dollar (i.e., the change in how many dollars can be bought by a unit of the currency composite from one year to the next). When the line slopes downward, the U.S. dollar is stronger.

U.S. JOURNALS   NON-U.S. JOURNALS   •••••• EXCHANGE RATES

Fig. 13.7. Price analysis of serials for public libraries. From *Serials Price Projections—1995*. Reproduced by courtesy of EBSCO.

SPECIAL LIBRARY COST HISTORY

	Average # Titles	1990 Average Cost Per Title	Change from 1990-91	1991 Average Cost Per Title	Change from 1991-92	1992 Average Cost Per Title	Change from 1992-93	1993 Average Cost Per Title	Change from 1993-94	1994 Average Cost Per Title	Change from 1990-94
SPECIAL LIBRARY											
U.S. TITLES	1,929	$140.36	7.2%	$150.41	7.4%	$161.60	6.1%	$171.52	5.7%	$181.38	29.2%
NON-U.S. TITLES	308	$214.32	16.5%	$249.67	6.5%	$265.88	9.5%	$291.26	4.8%	$305.38	42.5%
ALL TITLES	2,237	$150.54	9.0%	$164.07	7.2%	$175.96	6.8%	$188.01	5.6%	$198.45	31.8%

Total Cost of a Typical Subscription List

	COST	% INCREASE
1994	$443,949.50	5.6%
1993	$420,586.60	6.8%
1992	$393,626.80	7.2%
1991	$367,046.06	9.0%
1990	$336,769.31	

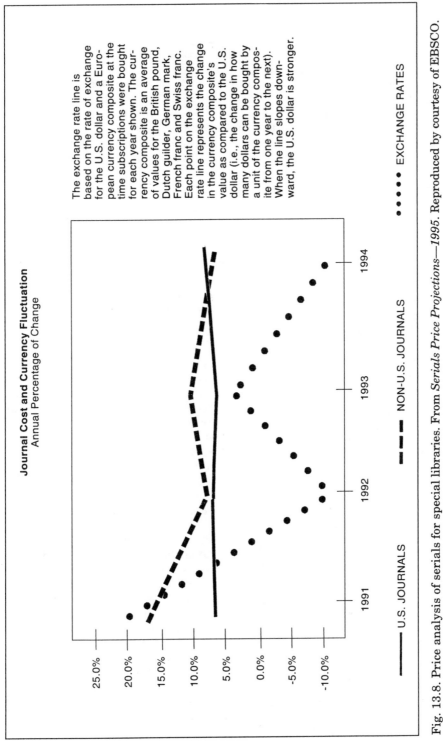

Journal Cost and Currency Fluctuation
Annual Percentage of Change

The exchange rate line is based on the rate of exchange for the U.S. dollar and a European currency composite at the time subscriptions were bought for each year shown. The currency composite is an average of values for the British pound, Dutch guilder, German mark, French franc and Swiss franc. Each point on the exchange rate line represents the change in the currency composite's value as compared to the U.S. dollar (i.e., the change in how many dollars can be bought by a unit of the currency composite from one year to the next). When the line slopes downward, the U.S. dollar is stronger.

U.S. JOURNALS — — — NON-U.S. JOURNALS •••• EXCHANGE RATES

Fig. 13.8. Price analysis of serials for special libraries. From *Serials Price Projections—1995*. Reproduced by courtesy of EBSCO.

For libraries that purchase a significant number of foreign publications, there is a need to estimate the impact of exchange rates. Volatile exchange rates affect buying power almost as much as inflation. For example, in January 1985, the pound sterling was at $1.2963 (U.S.); in January 1988 it was up to $1.7813 (U.S.); in 1992 it was $1.7653 (U.S.); and by January 1994 it was down to $1.4872 (U.S.). During the same period, the Canadian dollar went from $0.6345 to $0.7693 (U.S.), then to $0.7913 (U.S.) and back to $0.736 (U.S.). Although it is impossible to accurately forecast the direction and amount of fluctuation in the exchange rates for the next 12 months, some effort should go into studying the past 12 months and attempting to predict future trends. Naturally, one must have good data about the amounts spent in various countries during the past year. The country of publication may be less important than the country in which the vendor is located. For example, if the library uses the vendor Harrassowitz, prices will be in deutsche marks, regardless of the country of origin of the items purchased. After collecting the data, one can use them as factors in estimating the cost of continuing the current acquisition levels from the countries from which the library normally buys.

Allocation of Monies

Collection development funds may be restricted or unrestricted. For most libraries, the unrestricted allocation represents the majority of monies available for collection development. Libraries employ internal allocation systems in an attempt to match monies available with needs and to assure all collecting areas have some funding for the year. These systems provide guidelines for selection personnel; the allocation sets limits on, and expectations for, purchases in subject areas or for certain types of material.

Ordinarily, the method selected reflects the collection development policy statement priorities. If the library employs a collecting intensity ranking system in the collection development policy, it is reasonable to expect to find those levels reflected in the amount allocated to the subject or format. Almost all allocation methods are complex, and how one goes about matching the needs and monies available requires that the library consider several factors.

Among the factors one must consider are past practices, differential publication, unit cost and inflation rates, level of demand, and actual usage. Implementing a formal system takes time and effort. Some professionals question whether it is worthwhile allocating the monies. Opponents to allocation claim it is difficult to develop a fair allocation model, and it is time-consuming to calculate the amounts needed. They also claim that, because the models are difficult to develop, libraries tend to leave the allocations in place too long and simply add in the next year's percentage increase rather than recalculate the figures annually. They suggest that selectors may not spend accounts effectively because there is too much or too little money available. Finally, they argue it is difficult to effect transfers from one account to another during the year. Proponents claim allocations provide better control of collection development, and are a more effective way to monitor expenditures.

Some allocation does take place, regardless of the presence or absence of a formal allocation process. When there is no formal system, selectors engage in informal balancing of needs and funds available for various subjects or classes of material. (In the worst case, the more influential selectors have greater access to the funds, regardless of actual collection or user needs.) It seems reasonable, if the process is going to take place one way or another, that the formal process provides the best opportunity for achieving a fair balance.

A good allocation process provides at least four outcomes. Obviously, its overall purpose is to match available funds with needs. Second, it provides selectors with guidelines regarding how they should allocate their time. That is, if one is responsible for three selection areas with funding allocations of $15,000, $5,000, and $500, it is clear which area requires the most attention. (In some cases, it is harder to spend the smaller amount, because one must be careful to spend it wisely.)

Third, the allocation process provides a means of assessing the selector's work at the end of the fiscal year. Finally, it provides clients with a sense of collecting priorities, assuming the allocation information is made available to them. The library can communicate the information in terms of percentages rather than specific monetary amounts if there is a concern about divulging budgetary data.

The allocation process should be collaborative, with input from all interested parties. Two things are certain: whether the library uses a formal or informal approach to gaining the input, the process has political overtones, and the outcome will invariably disappoint an individual or group. This is particularly true when introducing a revised allocation when the budget is static. Those who receive more money will be happy, but those who lose funds will object to the method used to reallocate the funds. Unfortunately, sometimes the objectors are influential enough to get the allocations changed, which defeats the purpose of the process—matching funds to needs.

What allocation method the library selects is influenced, in part, by internal library practices, institutional needs, and extra-institutional requirements (such as those of accreditation agencies). Internal factors include operational practices that determine what type of information is readily available to those making the allocation decisions (vendor's country of origin, number of approval titles versus firm orders, format and subject data, and use are some examples). How the library organizes its services—centralized or decentralized—also plays a role in the selection decision. Other internal factors affecting which allocation method is used include past practices for allocation and the purpose of allocation (that is, its use as a control mechanism or guideline). Institutional factors, in addition to the obvious importance of the institution's mission and goals, include the type of budget control it employs, its organization, and its overall financial condition. Extra-institutional factors are the political atmosphere (for example, the degree of accountability), economic conditions, social expectations and values regarding information services (such as equal access and literacy levels), and outside agencies (such as accreditation bodies or governmental bodies) that monitor or control the institution.

One can think of allocation methods as being a continuum with impulse at one end and formula at the opposite end. Between the two extremes are several more-or-less structured methods. Impulse allocation can take the form of allowing active selectors to have greatest access to available funds or, a slightly more structured approach, to allocate on the basis of perceptions of need. History of past use and some annual percentage increase for each allocation area is a little more formal; it is probably one of the most widely employed methods. Allocating on the basis of organizational structure (main and branch units) is still more formal (often, the allocation is a fixed percentage of the fund pool). If one adds to that method some incremental funding based on work load (such as circulation data), one moves even closer to the formula end of the continuum. Also, somewhere in the middle of the continuum is the format allocation method (including books, serials, audiovisual, electronic, and reference).

Format allocation may be as simple as dividing monies between monographic and serials purchase accounts. Even this easy division is no longer easy, because serials prices increase more rapidly than other materials costs. How long can one shift monies from other accounts to maintain serials subscription levels without damaging the overall collection? Libraries employ several category allocation methods in addition to format, such as subject, unit, users, language, and formula. Most libraries that use a format allocation system use several approaches. Many small libraries, including most school media centers, employ the format system with monographs, serials, and audiovisuals being the broad groupings. The library divides these funds by subject (language arts), grade level (fifth grade), or user group (professional reading). Occasionally, libraries divide monograph funds into current, retrospective, and replacement categories. In libraries using approval, blanket order, or standing order plans, it is normal practice to set aside monies for each program before making any other allocations. A typical approach would be to set aside an amount equal to the prior year's expenditure for the category with an additional amount to cover expected inflation. The reason for setting aside these funds first is that they are ongoing commitments.

Formula allocations have become more and more popular, especially in large libraries. Librarians have proposed many formulas over the years, but no one formula has become standard. Each library must decide which, if any, formula is most appropriate for its special circumstances. A 1992 article by Ian R. Young described a project that compared seven formulas.[4] His results showed that, though each formula employed one or more unique variables, there were no statistically significant differences among the formula results in terms of a single institution. He concluded that there was a high degree of similarity among the seven formulas, at least when applied to his institutional setting. Based on my experience with formulas and the selection of a formula in several institutional settings, I would say the library selects the formula that contains all the variables necessary to satisfy all the interested parties. (Thus, political rather than practical considerations dictate which formula is used.) Only quantifiable factors (for example, average price, number of titles published, and use data) can be used as variables in formulas. This does not mean that subjective judgments do not play a role, but the allocation process as a whole depends on weightings, circulation data, production figures, inflation and exchange rates, number of users, and so forth. Figure 13.9 on page 372 shows the allocation formula used at Loyola Marymount University.

ALA's *Guide to Budget Allocation for Information Resources* indicates there are six broad allocation methods: historical, zero-based (no consideration of past practice), formulas, ranking (a variation of formulas), percentages, and other modeling techniques.[5] The book also outlines some of the variations in formulas by type of library. For example, academic libraries might consider enrollment by major or degrees granted in a field (the factors used in figure 13.9 are widely used in academic libraries as well). Public libraries might factor in differences in the service communities being served, the ratio of copies per title of bestsellers to general titles, or the demand (in terms of use or requests) in popular subject fields. Special libraries employ factors like delivery time expectations of the clients, service charge backs, and the number of clients or departments served. Many school media centers use factors like changes in curriculum, number and ability of students by grade level, and loss and aging rates of various subject areas in the collection. The guide provides a starting point for anyone thinking about changing the allocation process their library uses.

Allocating funds is an involved process, and changing an existing method is almost more difficult than establishing a new method. Often, past practices and political issues keep the process from moving forward or evolving. Serials inflation rates (almost 700 percent since 1970[6]) make it difficult to provide both ongoing subscriptions and a reasonable level of monographic acquisitions. How much to allocate to current materials and how much to allocate to retrospective purchases is related, in part, to the serials inflation rate. If the decision is to maintain serials at the expense of monographs, in time, there will be a significant need for retrospective buying funds to fill gaps in the monograph collection. Subject variations also complicate the picture: Science materials are very expensive; social science materials are substantially less costly but are more numerous. Electronic access, rather than local ownership, also clouds the picture, especially because, often, electronic access involves cost at the individual level, something with which allocation models have not dealt. Although allocation work frequently involves political issues and occasionally involves upset individuals, in the long run careful attention to this process will produce a better collection for the organization the library or information center serves.

Department	Use	Average Cost	Cost-Use	Percent Cost-Use	Formula Allocation	Present Allocation
Psychology (BF& RC 435-577)	4,674	$38.55	180,183	0.07	$12,693	$15,033
Sociology (HM-HX)	5,311	$37.85	201,021	0.09	$14,542	$6,587
Theater Arts (PN 1600-1989, 2000-3310)	144	$38.14	5,492	0.003	$361	$3,908
Theology (BL-BX)	6,503	$36.49	237,294	0.1	$16,258	$7,409
Totals			2,491,436		$181,342	$180,652

Use = Circulated use of the class numbers associated with the department
Average Cost = Price listed as average for that discipline in *Choice*
Cost-Use = Average cost times use for the field
Percent Cost-Use = Percentage of library's total cost-use for the field
Formula Allocation = Amount of new allocation under new formula
Present Allocation = Amount of current allocation

Fig. 13.9. Loyola Marymount University library book allocation formula. Courtesy of Loyola Marymount University.

Encumbering

One aspect of accounting and financial management in collection development that differs from typical accounting practice is the process of encumbering. This is a process that allows one to set aside monies to pay for ordered items. When the library waits 60, 90, or 120 or more days for orders, there is some chance that the monies available will be over- or underspent if there is no system that allows for setting aside monies.

The following chart shows how the process works. Day 1, the first day of the fiscal year, shows the library with an annual allocation of $1,000 for a particular subject area. On day 2, the library orders an item with a list price of $24.95. Though there may be shipping and handling charges, there probably will be a discount. Because none of the costs and credits are known at the time, the list price is the amount a staff member records as encumbered. The unexpended column reflects the $24.95 deduction, though there is still nothing in the expended category. Sixty-two days later, the item and invoice arrive; the invoice reflects a 15 percent discount

($3.74) and no shipping or handling charges. The bookkeeper records the actual cost ($21.21) under expended and adds the $3.74 to the unexpended amount. The amount encumbered now is zero.

	Unexpended	Encumbered	Expended
Day 1	$1000.00	0	0
Day 2	$975.05	$24.95	0
Day 62	$978.79	0	$21.21

Needless to say, this system is much more complex than the example suggests, because libraries place and receive multiple orders every day. With each transaction the amounts in each column change. *One seldom knows the precise balance, except on the first and last day of the fiscal year.* If the funding body takes back all unexpended funds at the end of the fiscal year (a cash accounting system), the collection development staff will want to know their fund(s) balances as they enter the final quarter of the year.

Several factors make it difficult to learn the exact status of the funds, even with the use of encumbrance. One factor is delivery of orders. Vendors may assure customers they will deliver before the end of the fiscal year but fail to do so. Such a failure can result in the encumbered money being lost. With a cash system, the collection development staff must make some choices at the end of the fiscal year if there are funds in the encumbered category. The main issue is determining if the items still on order are important enough to leave on order. An affirmative answer has substantial implications for collection development. Using the foregoing example and assuming day 62 comes after the start of a new fiscal year and that the new allocation is $1,000, on day 1 of the new fiscal year, the amount unexpended would be $975.05 ($1,000 minus $24.95), encumbered $24.95 and expended zero. In essence, there is a reduction in the amount available for new orders and the library lost $24.95 from the prior year's allocation. (I once took over as head of a library on June 25, and the system financial officer told me the entire acquisitions allocation was encumbered for the coming fiscal year, July 1. To have some funds for collection development over the next twelve months, it was necessary to cancel 347 orders.)

With an accrual system, the unexpended funds carry forward into the next fiscal year. Under such a system, using the example, the day 1 figures would be unexpended $1,000, encumbered $24.95, and expended zero.

The staff also needs to consider how reliable the vendor or producer is because occasionally, an item never arrives. How long should one wait? The answer varies from producer to producer and country to country. If the library buys substantial amounts from developing countries, waiting several years is not unreasonable. Because print runs tend to be very close to the number of copies on order, the chance of never being able to acquire the item makes it dangerous to cancel the order.

There is a problem in leaving funds encumbered for long periods under either system, especially when there is rapid inflation or exchange rates are unfavorable. These are two reasons why a firm but reasonable date for automatic cancellation of unfilled orders is important.

Other factors making it difficult to know the precise fund balance during the year are pricing and discounts. Prices are subject to change without notice on most library materials, which means the price may be higher on delivery than when ordered. In addition, discounts are unpredictable. Because of the uncertainty, most libraries encumber the list price without freight charges and hope the amount will be adequate. Exchange rates enter the picture for international acquisitions, and the question of when the rate is set can be a critical issue. Certainly, the rate is not firm on the date the order is placed, but is it firm at the time of shipment, the date of the invoice, the date the library receives the invoice and items, the date the financial office makes out the check, or even the date the supplier deposits the check? With international orders, one can expect four months or more to elapse between order placement and delivery. (Tozzer Library had orders arriving five years after placing the order.) In periods of rapid rate changes, even a four month difference can significantly affect the amount of money available for purchases.

Moving monies back and forth, especially in a manual system, can lead to errors, so the acquisitions department needs a good bookkeeper. Automated accounting systems speed the recording activities and provide greater accuracy, as long as the data entry is correct. Despite the uncertainty that exists with the encumbering system, it is still better than having unexpended and expended categories, because without it one would not know how much of the unexpended balance was actually needed for items on order.

Special Problems

Shipping and handling rates and taxes on items purchased have taken a toll on the funds available for additions to the collection. Vendors that in the past paid for shipping now pass the cost to customers. The U.S. Postal Service has reduced the difference between postal rates such as the library rate and parcel post. For example, in 1970 it cost $0.18 to ship a 2-pound book; in 1980 it cost $0.80; by 1994 the rate was $1.47. There are suggestions in the press that the Postal Service will request a 47 percent increase in the rate in the near future. All the charges on the invoice (postage, handling, shipping, taxes, and so forth) must come from the acquisitions budget. As these charges mount there is less money for the items the library wishes to add.

Some publishers and vendors employ a freight pass-through (FPT) charge. Originally, in 1981, publishers intended FPT to create a two-tier pricing system to enable bookstores to pass on freight charges to the customer. That is, the publisher charged the bookstore an invoice price and the dust jacket carried the higher FPT price. Some publishers used a percentage of the invoice price (3 or 4 percent), and others used a flat fee ($0.50). The problem for libraries buying from jobbers is determining what price the jobber used in calculating the library discount. Most contracts with jobbers call for discounts on list price. What is the list price, the invoice price or the FPT price printed on the dust jacket? Jobber practice varied from one extreme to the other. Though the percentages are small, as are the amounts of money for any one title, the cumulative effect on an acquisition budget is great. The FPT problem is not as important today as it once was, but the growing cost of shipping and postage is an ongoing concern.

Summary

One must be constantly aware of changes in prices and in invoicing practices to gain the maximum number of additions to the collection. Watch for changes, and demand explanations of freight and handling charges, inappropriate dual-pricing systems, or other costs that may place additional strain on the budget. By understanding basic accounting principles and using the reports and records generated by the library's accounting system, one will be better able to monitor the use of available monies and use them effectively to meet the needs of the public.

Selected Sources for Library Materials Price Information

"Average Book Prices." *School Library Journal*. Annual article, usually March, author varies (in the mid-1990s it was L. N. Gerhardt).

"Book Title Output and Prices, Final Figures 19*XX*." *Publishers Weekly*. Annual article, September or October, title varies from year to year.

"British Book Production, 19*XX*." *The Bookseller*. Annual review of British book production and prices, various issues, usually January.

"College Book Price Information 19*XX*." *Choice*. Annual article, April or May.

Higher Education Prices and Price Indexes: 19XX. Washington, DC: Research Associates of Washington. Annual publication lists a variety of higher education costs, including library costs.

"Periodical Prices 19*XX*-19*XX*." *Serials Librarian*. Annual survey of serial prices; author and issue vary.

"Prices of U.S. and Foreign Published Materials." In *The Bowker Annual: Library and Book Trade Almanac*. New York: R. R. Bowker.

"The Year in Review. Title Output and Prices." *Publishers Weekly*. Annual article, usually March.

Notes

[1]G. Stevenson Smith, *Managerial Accounting for Libraries and Other Not-for-Profit Organizations* (Chicago: American Library Association, 1991).

[2]Ann Okerson and Kendon Stubbs, "ARL Annual Statistics 1990-91: Remembrance of Things Past, Present—and Future?" *Publishers Weekly* 239 (July 27, 1992): 22-23.

[3]American National Standards Institute, Z39 Committee, *Criteria for Price Indexes for Library Materials* (New York: American National Standards Institute, 1974). ANSI Z39.20.

[4]Ian R. Young, "A Quantitative Comparison of Acquisitions Budget Allocation Formulas Using a Single Institutional Setting," *Library Acquisitions: Practice and Theory* 16, no. 3 (1992): 229-42.

[5]*Guide to Budget Allocation for Information Resources,* edited by Edward Shreeves, Collection Management and Development Guides, no. 4 (Chicago: American Library Association, 1991).

[6]Frank W. Goudy, "Academic Libraries and the Six Percent Solution: A Twenty-Year Financial Overview," *Journal of Academic Librarianship* 19 (September 1993): 212-15.

Further Reading

General

Alley, B. "Increasing Demands, Shrinking Budgets and the Alice's Restaurant Mentality." *Technicalities* 12 (November 1992): 1.

Barker, J. W. "What's Your Money Worth?" *Journal of Library Administration* 16, no. 3 (1992): 25-43.

Budd, J. "Allocation Formulas in the Literature." *Library Acquisitions: Practice and Theory* 15, no. 1 (1991): 95-101.

Bustion, M., et al. "Methods of Serials Funding: Formula or Tradition?" *Serials Librarian* 20, no. 1 (1991): 75-89.

Carrigan, D. P. "Improving Return on Investment: A Proposal for Allocating the Book Budget." *Journal of Academic Librarianship* 18 (November 1992): 292-97.

Christianson, E. "When Your Parent Dictates Your Accounting Life." *Bottom Line* 7 (Summer 1993): 17-21.

Christianson, E., and S. Hayes. "Depreciation of Library Collection: Terminology of the Debate." *Bottom Line* 5, no. 3 (1991): 35-37.

Cubberly, C. "Allocating the Materials Funds Using Cost of Materials." *Journal of Academic Librarianship* 19 (March 1993): 16-21.

Enikhamenor, F. A. "Formula for Allocating Book Funds." *Libri* 33 (June 1983): 148-61.

Guide to Budget Allocation for Information Resources. Collection Management and Development Guides, no. 4, edited by Edward Shreeves. Chicago: American Library Association, 1991.

Hamon, P., et al. *Budgeting and the Political Process in Libraries.* Englewood, CO: Libraries Unlimited, 1992.

Kruger, B. "Basic Acquisitions Accounting." In *Understanding the Business of Library Acquisitions,* edited by K. A. Schmidt, 261-85. Chicago: American Library Association, 1990.

Lee, S. H. *Budget for Acquisitions: Strategies for Serials, Monographs and Electronic Formats.* New York: Haworth Press, 1991.

Lowry, C. B. "Reconciling Pragmatism, Equity, and Need in the Formula Allocation of Book and Serial Funds." *College & Research Libraries* 53 (March (1992): 121-38.

Lynden, F. C. "Strategies for Stretching the Collection Budget." *Journal of Library Administration* 16, no. 3 (1992): 91-110.

McPheron, W. "Quantifying the Allocation of Monograph Funds." *College & Research Libraries* 44 (March 1983): 116-27.

Niemeyer, M., et al. "Balancing Act for Library Materials Budgets: Use of a Formula Allocation." *Technical Services Quarterly* 11, no. 1 (1993): 43-60.

O'Neill, A. L. "Evaluating the Success of Acquisitions Departments." *Library Acquisitions: Practice and Theory* 19, no. 3 (1992): 209-19.

Rein, L. O., et al. "Formula-Based Subject Allocation: A Practical Approach." *Collection Management* 17, no. 4 (1993): 25-48.

Ring, R. "Budgeting for Collection Development: A Suggestion." *Collection Building* 9, nos. 3/4 (1988): 25-28.

Schmitz-Veitin, G. "Literature Use As a Measure for Funds Allocation." *Library Acquisitions: Practice and Theory* 8 (1984): 267-74.

Sellen, M. "Book Budget Formula Allocations: A Review Essay." *Collection Management* 9 (Winter 1987): 13-24.

Stanley, N. M. "Accrual Accounting and Library Materials Acquisitions." *Bottom Line* 7, no. 2 (1993): 15-17.

Williams, S. F. "Reporting Book Prices." *Book Research Quarterly* 1, no. 4 (1986): 85-88.

Academic

Jones, P. A., and C. L. Keller. "From Budget Allocation to Collection Development: A System for the Small College Library." *Library Acquisitions: Practice and Theory* 17 (Summer 1993): 183-89.

Kohut, J. "Allocating the Book Budget: Equity and Economic Efficiency." *College & Research Libraries* 36 (September 1975): 403-10.

Werking, R. H. "Allocating the Academic Library's Book Budget: Historical Perspectives and Current Reflections." *Journal of Academic Librarianship* 14 (July 1988): 140-44.

Public

Bender, A. "Allocation of Funds in Support of Collection Development in Public Libraries." *Library Resources & Technical Services* 23 (Winter 1979): 45-51.

McCabe, G. B., and R. N. Bish. "Planning for Fund Management in Multiple System Environments." *Library Administration and Management* 7 (Winter 1993): 51-55.

McGarth, S. "A Pragmatic Book Allocation Formula for Academic and Public Libraries." *Library Resources & Technical Services* 19 (Fall 1975): 356-69.

Missineo, L. "Supply-Side Measurement: A Formulation for the Allocation of Book Funds in Public Libraries." *Technical Services Quarterly* 2 (Spring/Summer 1985): 61-72.

School

Callison, D. "A Review of the Research Related to School Media Collections." Part 1. *School Library Media Quarterly* 19 (Fall 1990): 57-62.

———. "A Review of the Research Related to School Media Collections." Part 2. *School Library Media Quarterly* 19 (Winter 1991): 117-21.

Miller, M. L., and M. L. Schontz. "Expenditure$ for Resources in School Library Media Centers." *School Library Journal*. This annual review of acquisitions and price data appears in an issue near the end of the year; in 1993, the article appeared in the October issue on pages 26-36.

Wright, R. J. "Selected Acquisition Statistics." *School Library Media Annual* 10 (1992): 222-23.

Special

Burdick, A. J. "Citation Patterns in the Health Sciences: Implications for Serial/ Monograph Fund Allocation." *Bulletin of the Medical Library Association* 81 (January 1993): 44-47.

Norton, R., and D. Gautschi. "User-Survey of an International Library's Resource Allocation." *Aslib Proceedings* 37 (September 1986): 371-80.

14
Deselection

Selection in reverse is one way to think about weeding or collection control. Deselection, or weeding, is something most librarians think about but seldom do. However, this process is as important as the other steps in collection development. Without an ongoing weeding program, a collection can quickly age and become difficult to use. The major function of a library is to acquire, store, and make available knowledge resources; obviously, no library can acquire and store the world's total production of knowledge resources for any current year.

Some of the world's largest libraries (the Library of Congress, the British Library, Bibliotheque Nationale, and others) do acquire most important items. Nevertheless, even these giants of the library world cannot do it all. Eventually, when they reach the limit of their growth, they confront, as the smallest library does, three alternatives: (1) acquire new physical facilities, (2) divide the collection (which also requires space), or (3) weed the collection (which may or may not require new space). Only with a new adequate storage area can a librarian avoid selecting items for relocation.

The need to find space for collections is an old problem for libraries. One of the earliest references to the problem in the United States was a letter from Thomas Hollis to Harvard College's Board of Governors in 1725. He wrote, "If you want more room for modern books, it is easy to remove the less useful into a more remote place, but do not sell them as they are devoted."[1] More than 100 years passed before Harvard followed Hollis's advice; today, like most major research libraries, remote storage is part of everyday collection development activities at Harvard.

What Is Deselection, or Weeding?

H. F. McGraw defined *weeding* (called stock relegation in the United Kingdom) as "the practice of discarding or transferring to storage excess copies, rarely used books, and materials no longer of use."[2] He defined *purging* as "officially withdrawing a volume (all entries made for a particular book have been removed from library records) from a library collection because it is unfit for further use or is no longer needed."[3] The word *purging* applies more to the library's files than to items in the collection. Libraries seldom destroy purged items. Disposal takes several forms: gifts and exchange programs, Friends of the Library book sales, or sale to an out-of-print dealer for credit against future purchases. Occasionally, the material goes into a recycling program. The result is that a patron who may later request a purged item will have to use interlibrary loan to secure a copy.

Storing, on the other hand, retains the item at a second level of access. Second-level access normally is not open to the client and is frequently some distance from the library. Most second-level access storage systems house the materials as compactly as possible to maximize storage capacity. Compact shelving for low-use material is coming into widespread use as libraries attempt to gain maximum storage from existing square footage. Generally, a staff member retrieves the desired item from the storage facility for the user. Depending on the storage unit's location and the library's policy, the time lapse between request and receipt ranges from a few minutes to 48 hours. Nevertheless, this arrangement is normally faster than interlibrary loan.

Before implementing a deselection program, the collection development staff should review deselection policies and goals. This review should include an analysis of the present staffing situation, consideration of alternative approaches, the feasibility of a weeding program in terms of other library operations, user interest and cooperation in such a project, types of materials collected, and cost. Some of the data for the program should come from collection evaluation projects that the selection officers and others undertake on a regular basis. An active (i.e., ongoing) deselection program should be part of the library's collection development policy.

Selection and weeding are similar activities: first, they are both necessary parts in an effective collection development program, and second, both require the same type of decision-making rules. The same factors that lead to the decision to add an item lead to a later decision to remove the item. Book selection policy should determine deselection activities.

Collection policies, if properly prepared, help reduce space problems by controlling growth. Nevertheless, the time eventually comes when collection space no longer accommodates additional material. When this happens, some hard, costly decisions confront the library: build a new building, split the collection and use remote storage, or reduce the collection size. All three alternatives involve time-consuming and expensive processes. A policy of continuous deselection is more effective in the long run. Lazy librarians, like lazy gardeners, will find the weeding problem only gets larger the longer they wait to do the job.

One piece of library folklore helps slow or stop many deselection programs. That is, no matter how strange an item may seem, at least one person in the world will find it valuable—and that person will request the item 10 minutes after the library discards it. I have never met anyone who has had it happen, but everyone agrees that it does.

One of collection development's proverbs is: one person's trash is someone else's treasure. This is the fundamental problem confronting collection development staffs every day. When the library bases its collection building on current user needs, deselection can be a major activity, because those needs change.

Some years ago, in *Current Contents,* Eugene Garfield noted that weeding a library is like examining an investment portfolio. Investment advisors know that people don't like to liquidate bad investments. Just like frustrated tycoons, many librarians can't face the fact that some of their guesses go wrong. They continue to throw good money after bad, hoping, like so many optimistic stockbrokers, that their bad decisions will somehow be undone. After paying for a journal for 10 years, they rationalize maybe someone will finally use it in the eleventh or twelfth year.[4]

Type of Library

Because different types of libraries have significantly different clientele and goals, they approach deselection from different points of view. Although the basic problems, issues, and methods of deselection apply to all libraries, variations occur in how they select the weeds and what they do with the weeds after pulling them.

Public Libraries

Public libraries may be viewed as supplying materials that meet the current needs and interests of a diverse community of users. In the public library, user demand is the important factor influencing selection and deselection. Therefore, materials no longer of interest or use to the public are candidates for storage or disposal. Usually, only large municipal public libraries consider storage, because their collections include research materials. As for discarding, a public library rule of thumb is that collections should completely turn over once every 10 years. Actual practice probably falls far short of that goal. Storage, when undertaken, usually involves separating little-used books from the high-use working collection and discarding duplicates, worn-out volumes, and obsolete material. Some people claim a collection containing many items of little interest is less useful because high demand items are not readily visible or accessible. Costs involved in maintaining a large collection are also a consideration.

Two books are especially useful in planning public library weeding projects: Stanley J. Slote's *Weeding Library Collections II* and Joseph P. Segal's *Weeding Collections in Small and Medium-Sized Libraries: The CREW Method.*[5] Both draw on circulation data, with Slote's system relying almost exclusively on circulation data to identify candidates for weeding. Segal's system uses age of the publication, circulation data, and several subjective elements he labels MUSTY (M = misleading, U = ugly [worn out], S = superseded, T = trivial, and Y = your collection no longer needs the item). The CREW in Segal's title represents Continuous Review Evaluation and Weeding. Ideas and methods described in both books are useful in all types of small libraries, especially school media centers.

Special Libraries

Special libraries have had to exercise the most stringent deselection programs because of strict limits on collection size, usually the result of a fixed amount of storage space. Paula M. Strain examined the problem of periodical storage and cost of industrial floor space and found that the cost is so high that libraries must make efficient use of each square foot.[6]

The special library must operate with the businessperson's eye toward economy and efficiency. Also, the collections of such libraries usually consist of technical material, much of it serial in character and often with a rapid and regular rate of obsolescence, at least for the local users.

The major concern of special libraries is meeting the current needs of clients. In such a situation, deselection is easier because of the comparatively straightforward and predictable use patterns, the small size and homogeneous nature of the clientele, and the relatively narrow service goals for the library. Deselection takes place with little hesitation because costs and space are prime considerations. Many of the bibliometric measures described in chapter 7 can be valuable in setting up deselection programs in special libraries. A book addressing the special requirements of weeding in some types of special libraries is Ellis Mount's *Weeding of Collections in Sci-Tech Libraries.*[7]

Academic Libraries

Traditionally, the purposes of the academic research library have been to select, acquire, organize, preserve (this has had special emphasis), and make available the full record of human knowledge. Collection development officers in these institutions seldom view demand as a valid measure of an item's worth. Potential or long-term research value takes highest priority. Why are deselection programs part of academic library collection development?

The role of the college and university library is changing. Whenever librarians discuss the changing role, they cite the information explosion as one cause. It is clear to most collection development staffs that it is futile to expect any one institution to locate and acquire all of the printed matter that comes into existence. Nor can they organize it, house it, or make it readily accessible to their public. No one person can manage to absorb all the relevant material that would be available, even if libraries could collect and preserve everything. A discussion of several articles that can be of assistance in developing a deselection program in an academic library appears on pages 398-99.

School Media Centers

School libraries and media centers employ highly structured collection development practices. In most schools and school districts, the media center expends its funds with the advice of a committee consisting of teachers, administrators, librarians and, occasionally, parents. The need to coordinate collection development with curriculum needs is imperative. Typically, media centers lack substantial floor space for collections. Thus, when there is a major shift in the curriculum (new areas added and old ones dropped), the library must remove most of the old material. To some degree, the media center's deselection problems are fewer because there usually are other community libraries or a school district central media center that serve as back-up resources.

In addition to the Slote and Segal books, two excellent articles about weeding school media collections are Anita Gordon's "Weeding: Keeping Up with the Information Explosion," and the Calgary Board of Education, Educational Media Team's "Weeding the School Library Media Collection."[8] Gordon's article, though short, provides a good illustration of how one may use some standard bibliographies (*Senior High Catalog,* for example) in a deselection program. The Calgary article provides a detailed, step-by-step method for weeding the school collection.

Reasons for Deselecting

Four reasons for implementing a deselection program appear regularly in the literature:

to save space

to improve access

to save money

to make room for new materials

If the volume of literature on the subject reflected the degree to which libraries practiced deselection, there would be no need for conferences and workshops on the subject. Librarians spend more time writing about deselection than they do implementing the concepts. In part, this is because theory and the real world do not coincide. Often, from a realistic point of view, no other solution to space problems suggests itself except thinning the collection. When existing space fills up, and there is no additional collection space, the staff must do something.

In 1944, Fremont Rider determined that between 1831 and 1938, American research libraries doubled the size of their collections every 16 years, an annual growth rate of 4.25 percent.[9] Since then, studies have shown a gradual decrease in the annual growth rate (to 2.85 percent); nevertheless, libraries often quickly reach their limits of growth. The implications of an annual growth rate are obvious. In addition to the problem of limited shelf space, rapid growth of library collections leads to several other problems: (1) existing space is often not used efficiently, (2) obtaining additional space is expensive, and (3) servicing and using the collections becomes difficult.

Do theory and practice concerning saving space coincide? Definitely! Compact storage systems save space. The conventional rule of thumb allows 15 volumes per square foot (500,000 volumes would require more than 33,000 square feet). A compact shelving system using a sliding shelf arrangement can store 500,000 volumes in slightly more than 14,000 square feet (an average of about 35 volumes per square foot)—a savings of more than 50 percent. Using a rail system of moving ranges, such as Space Saver, some libraries achieve savings of more than 80 percent. Less than 7,000 square feet can house 500,000 volumes. The compact system recently installed at Loyola Marymount University will store 92,000 volumes in the same area that contained 24,000 volumes on conventional shelving.

Obviously, one pays a price for saving space, such as the extra cost of the compact system. However, Ralph Ellsworth, in *Economics of Book Storage in College and Research Libraries,* noted that conventional systems are also very expensive.[10] Although his 1969 cost figures have not been updated, the relationships still hold: conventional shelving costs $1.31 per volume; sliding shelves, $1.24; and a moving range system, $0.91. Thus, one can lower the unit cost for stored items by using a compact storage system. However, the cost cited covers only the building and shelving; one should consider several other cost factors.

One basic theme of this book is that libraries exist to provide service. Archival libraries provide service, so our discussion naturally includes them, since they, too, eventually run out of space. However, service and size frequently do not go together. Anyone who has used a major research library knows that it takes time and effort to locate desired items. Often, such a library will be the only location for certain materials, which is clearly an important service. However, few clients claim that such libraries are easy or convenient to use. Most people still like everything to be convenient and easy-to-use. Thus, it is possible that a smaller, well-weeded collection provides better service than a larger collection—as long as the smaller collection contains popular items.

Does deselection improve access? Here theory and practice start diverging. Some staff members and customers give enthusiastically positive answers. Others give equally definite negative responses. For those who require quick, easy access to high-use, current materials, the thoughtfully maintained collection becomes the ideal. However, for older, seldom-used materials housed in a remote storage facility, it may take some time to determine whether or not the library owns the item as well as to retrieve it. Thus, the answer to the question of whether weeding improves access is sometimes yes, sometimes no.

Finally, does weeding save money? Here the answer is probably no. Theory and reality are far apart at this point. As indicated, the cost per volume stored is usually lower using a compact storage system. However, one should consider several other important costs. For example, it is possible to quickly reduce the size of a collection by some arbitrary figure (5,000 volumes) or percentage (20 percent). One method of weeding in a public library would be to withdraw all books published before 1920 (or some other date) that have not circulated in the past five years. Just withdrawing the items from the shelves does not, however, complete the process. Staff must also change all the public and internal records to reflect the new status of the withdrawn books. Though online catalogs and databases allow rapid record updating, there are still labor costs to consider.

In addition to the cost of record modification, one must consider:

- the cost of deciding which items to remove;
- the cost of collecting and transporting them to their new location; and
- the cost of retrieving items when needed.

Even if the storage system is less expensive per volume than conventional stacks, these hidden costs can quickly mount well beyond the apparent savings.

Another cost, often overlooked, is the cost to customers. Delayed access to desired materials carries a user cost, if nothing more than negative public relations. Almost every customer wants items now, not in a few hours, much less days. In a research and development environment, retrieval delays may cost researchers valuable time and, perhaps, cost the organization money. Though difficult to determine or measure accurately, customer cost should be taken into account when evaluating the costs of deselection.

Gary Lawrence's "A Cost Model for Storage and Weeding Programs" details a cost model for an academic storage program at the University of California.[11] Anyone planning a large-scale deselection and storage project should read the article.

Barriers to Deselection

A story of questionable veracity, but highlighting the major deselection barrier, concerns a collection development teacher. The teacher insisted that there was only one possible test to determine a person's suitability for becoming a collection development officer. Candidates would visit a doctor's office, where office staff would immediately take the candidate's blood pressure. The doctor would then hand the candidate a new book and tell the person to rip out one page and throw the book in a wastebasket. If the candidate's blood pressure rose above the initial reading, the individual would fail the test. True or not, the story does emphasize one of the most significant barriers to deselection—the psychological one.

Parents and teachers teach most of us to treat books and magazines with respect. In fact, we learn a great respect for anything printed. The idea of tearing pages or otherwise damaging a book goes against all we have learned. The problem is that we are again confusing the information contained in a package with the packaging (see chapter 1). Some material becomes dated and must go, or people will act on incorrect information (a prime example is a loose-leaf service with superseding pages). Travel directories and telephone books are other examples of materials that should go. Long-term value of other materials is less clear, and it is easy to find reasons to save them. In essence, our childhood training adds to the difficulties in removing items from the collection. If the library's goal is to purge rather than store the item, the problem is even bigger.

Some of the more common excuses for not thinning a collection are

lack of time

procrastination

fear of making a mistake

fear of being called a book burner

These reasons are, to a greater or lesser extent, psychological. No matter how long the candidate for storage or removal has remained unused, a collection development officer's reaction is, "someone will need it tomorrow." Also, an unused book or audiovisual raises two questions: Why wasn't it used? and, Why did the library buy it? Like anyone else, collection officers are reluctant to admit to making a mistake. The possibility of erroneously discarding some important items always exists. But to use fear of making a mistake as the reason for not engaging in deselection is inexcusable.

Another barrier, which is political as well as psychological, is created by patrons and governing boards. An academic library staff may feel that it needs to institute a weeding and storage program but fails to do so because of faculty opposition. If experience is any indication, one can count on everyone being in favor of removing the dead wood—but not in their areas of interest.

Sometimes, librarians never suggest deselection because they assume there will be opposition from faculty, staff, general users, board members, or others. Naturally, there will be opposition. However, if no one raises the issue, there is no chance of gaining customer support. The possibility also exists that the assumed opposition will never materialize and that customers one least expects turn out to be strong supporters. Fear of possible political consequences has kept libraries from proposing a deselection program.

Loyola Marymount University's library recently completed an extensive deselection project, reviewing 82,000 volumes still classified in Dewey class numbers (DDC) and in the collection for at least 14 years. The librarians responsible for collection development had solid working relationships with the academic departments, so had no trouble gaining support for the project. Gaining active participation in the process was another matter. Because the library was running out of collection space, the collection development staff hoped to remove at least four year's growth space: 40,000-50,000 volumes. Three categories were identified for the DDC volumes (1) high-use, reclass to Library of Congress Classification as soon as possible; (2) low-use, store; and (3) discard. To gain faculty involvement, the librarians told them all material that had circulated at least four times would be reclassed as quickly as possible. The faculty were asked to recommend what should be done with the other materials (see fig. 14.1). As an additional incentive, the librarians warned the faculty that, after a certain date, the librarians would decide what to store and what to toss. Needless to say, every department claimed nothing in its subject area should go. The library was able to discard fewer than 20,000 volumes and garnered less than 25 percent faculty participation—but there was no faculty opposition to the project.

Charles Von der Ahe Library, Loyola Marymount University
Deselection Project Faculty Letter

TO: ALL FACULTY
FROM: Marcia Findley, Head, Collection Development

RE: Weeding Library Books

As you know, the Library has been planning a large scale weeding project affecting books still classified in the Dewey Decimal system. A copy of the twenty-page report outlining the rationale and procedures for this project was sent to each department head and each dean in early December. The Library Committee approved the report in their meeting of February 12 and set the dates for its implementation from March 15 to May 15, 1992.

The faculty will play an important part in weeding these books. Your expertise is necessary in deciding whether they will be kept for storage or discarded. The procedure for faculty is as follows: stop at the Circulation Desk in the Library to pick up boxes of colored adhesive dots; proceed to the subject area to review books (outline of Dewey class attached); examine each book, noting circulation use, and indicate whether to keep, store, or discard it on the brief Book Review Form stapled to each date due card; put the appropriate colored dot on the book spine: blue = keep, yellow = store, red = discard. Books which have circulated during the past 5 years will already have blue dots and will not require examination.

It is important that all faculty participate in this project, so that your decisions reflect your present and future resource needs. Although a university library collection the size of LMU should have a significant number of retrospective materials, these titles should also have a recognized value. At present we have many old, outdated, inappropriate books that have never circulated which should be weeded out to make room for new books. Even for those books you wish to keep, the costs of storage are high: up to $50,000 per year in rent alone to store in a temperature and humidity-controlled building. This money will be taken from the acquisitions budget for the coming year. Also, remember that some books may be discarded with the knowledge that, if needed, they may be borrowed on Inter Library Loan. These are some of the things to keep in mind as you are making weeding decisions.

Sections not reviewed by faculty will be weeded by librarians.

Attached is a copy of the Book Review Form found in each book. Please call me about any questions you may have.

Thank you,

Fig. 14.1. Deselection project faculty letter.

Related to the political barrier is the problem of size and prestige. Many librarians, library boards, and customers rate libraries by size: the bigger the better. This brings us back to the epigraph of this book: "No library of a million volumes can be all BAD!" Quantity does not ensure quality. Collecting everything and throwing nothing away is much easier than selecting and deselecting with care. Librarians risk no political opposition, their prestige remains high, and only the taxpayers and customers pay the price of maintaining everything the library ever acquired.

Practical barriers to deselection also exist. Time can be a practical as well as a psychological barrier. The processes of identifying suitable deselection criteria, developing, and selling a useful program require significant amounts of time. Beyond those steps, time is required for staff training, as is time to identify and pull the candidate items, to change the records, and, finally, to dispose of the weeds. (Loyola Marymount University estimates indicated the library committed a minimum of 2.5 FTE (full time equivalent) for 10 months to its deselection project. That estimate covers all staff time; no staff member was full-time on the project.)

With a small library staff, it is difficult to mount a major deselection project because there are too many things to do with too few people. Starting a program is, inevitably, a major project for any size library. After completing the first project, the library should establish an ongoing deselection procedure and incorporate it into the normal workflow. The ideal approach to a major project is to seek special funds and temporary staff to support the work.

Occasionally, libraries encounter legal barriers. Although not common problems, when they do arise, they are time-consuming. The problem arises in publicly supported libraries where regulations may govern the disposal of any material purchased with public funds. In some cases, the library must sell the material, even if only to a pulp dealer. Any disposal that gives even a hint of government book burning will cause public relations problems; this stems from general attitudes toward printed materials. The library should do all it legally can to avoid any such appearance.

Deselection Criteria

Deselection is not an overnight process, and it is not a function that one performs in isolation from other collection development activities. Persons involved in deselection must consider all library purposes and activities, such as library goals, the availability of acquisition funds for new titles, the relationship of a particular book to others on that subject, the degree to which the library functions as an archive, and potential future usefulness of an item. Only when one considers all the factors can one develop a successful deselection program.

After the staff recognizes the need for a deselection project, several lists of criteria can help in the deselection process. H. F. McGraw developed the following fairly comprehensive list:

duplicates

unsolicited and unwanted gifts

obsolete books, especially science

superseded editions

books that are infested, dirty, shabby, worn out, juvenile (which wear out quickly), and so forth

books with small print, brittle paper, and missing pages

unused, unneeded volumes of sets

periodicals with no indexes[12]

The mere fact that a book is a duplicate or worn out does not necessarily mean one should discard it. Past use of the item should be the deciding factor. Also, consider whether it will be possible to find a replacement copy. The books and articles cited earlier provide additional criteria.

Three broad categories of deselection criteria exist, at least in the literature: physical condition, qualitative worth, and quantitative worth. Physical condition, for most researchers, is not an effective criterion. In most cases, poor physical condition results from overuse rather than nonuse. Thus, one replaces or repairs books in poor physical condition. (There is little indication in the literature on deselection that poor condition includes material with brittle paper. As discussed in chapter 18, brittle paper is a major problem.) Consequently, if the library employs physical condition as a criterion, it will identify only a few items, unless brittle paper is part of the assessment process.

Qualitative worth as a criterion for deselection is highly subjective. As a result of variations in individual value judgments, researchers do not believe this is an effective deselection method. Getting people to take the time to review the material is difficult. As noted above, Loyola Marymount University's library staff were only moderately successful in enlisting faculty input. Also, the faculty did not always agree about what to reclass and what to store, and few faculty recommended the library discard anything. When all is said and done, the same factors that govern the buying decision should govern deselection judgments.

Any group assessment will be slow. Researchers have shown that a library can achieve almost the same outcome it would from specialists reviewing the material by using an objective measure, such as past circulation or use data, if one wishes to predict future use. Also, the deselection process is faster and cheaper when past-use data are available. (This is explored in depth on pages 392-95 in the review of major deselection studies.)

C. A. Seymour summed up the issues regarding deselection as follows:

When the usefulness and/or popularity of a book has been questioned, the librarian, if the policy of the library permits discarding, must decide

a. if the financial and physical resources are present or available to provide continuing as well as immediate housing and maintenance of the book;

    b. if the book can be procured, within an acceptably short time, from another library at a cost similar to, or lower than, the cost of housing and maintenance within the library;

    c. if allowing the book to remain in the collection would produce a negative value.[13]

The problems that plague monograph weeding also apply to serials. A major difference, however, is that journals are not homogeneous in content. Another difference is that the amount of space required to house serial publications is greater than that required to house monographs. Thus, cost is often the determining factor in weeding (that is, although there may be some requests for a particular serial, the amount of space that a publication occupies may not be economical or may not warrant retaining the full set in the collection).

Of course, one should not forget the customer. Considering the benefits and disadvantages, in terms of customer service, that result from an active deselection program is a step in the process. Based on personal research projects, the percentage of librarians who think that a customer should be able to decide which materials to use out of all possible materials available (that is, no deselection) is much smaller than the percentage of librarians who strongly believe that a no-weeding policy is detrimental to the patron. Even academic faculty members lack complete familiarity with all the materials in their own subject fields; faced with a million volumes or more in a collection, how can we expect a student to choose the materials most helpful to his or her research without some assistance?

Criteria for Deselection for Storage

Large libraries, particularly research libraries, deselect for storage rather than for discarding. These are two different processes. Often, criteria useful in making discarding decisions do not apply to storage decisions. It is important to recognize that the primary objective of these two different forms of treatment is not necessarily to reduce the total amount of money spent for library purposes. Instead, the primary objective is to maximize, by employing economical storage facilities, the amount of research material available to the patron. The two main considerations for a storage program are: (1) What selection criteria are most cost-effective? and (2) How will the library store the items?

Although it is more than 30 years old, a Yale University Library project, the Selective Book Retirement Program, has value for today's deselection project planners. The project funding came from the Council on Library Resources with the expectation that the results would be useful to other libraries. Project staff were to determine how best to cope with the problem of limited shelf space while continuing to build quality research collections and provide good service. The council outlined the following objectives for Yale in *Yale's Selective Book Retirement Program:*

a. to expedite the Yale University Library's Selective Book Retirement Program (from 20,000 to 60,000 volumes per year) and to extend it to other libraries on the campus;

b. to study (in collaboration with the faculty) the bases of selection for retirement for various subjects and forms of material;

c. to study the effects of the Program on library use and research by faculty, graduate and undergraduate students;

d. to ascertain what arrangements may compensate for the loss of immediate access caused by the program;

e. to explore the possible effectiveness of the Program toward stabilizing the size of the immediate-access collection;

f. to publish for the use of other libraries the policies, procedures, and results thus discovered.[14]

According to the report, the project staff fulfilled all the objectives but "d."

The Yale staff based their decisions about which books to move to storage on several factors:

1. A study of books on the shelves.

2. Value of a title as subject matter.

3. A volume's importance historically in the field.

4. Availability of other editions.

5. Availability of other materials on the subject.

6. Use of a volume.

7. Physical condition.[15]

Clearly, the selection process depended upon the *subjective judgment* of individual librarians, some of whom were subject bibliography specialists. The librarians determined that general policies regarding weeding were easier to formulate than those that applied to specific fields, that it was easier to recommend weeding of specific titles than groups or kinds of books in specific fields, and that unanticipated mechanical problems greatly affected weeding procedures. The last problems included:

1. Lack of regularity in weeding (i.e., finding an adequate number of faculty and staff members and the time to keep the process going satisfactorily).

2. Diminishing returns over a long period (i.e., the longer the program existed, the more difficult the weeding process became).

3. The "Ever-Normal-Granary" theory (one of the purposes of the selective retirement program was to discover whether a library can control the growth of its collection by annually removing from the stacks the same number of volumes it adds); it was discovered that in order for the theory to be practical, either fragmentation into department libraries must occur, or the library administration must be willing to manage its collection and facilities solely on the principle of stabilization—neither of which Yale was willing to do.

4. Disagreement among weeders (i.e., the narrower viewpoint of faculty because of subject specialty versus the broader viewpoint of the librarian).[16]

Another unforeseen problem was a general feeling of discontent among faculty members and students. Neither group really understood the storage problem, and both objected to any change. Students particularly disliked the fact that they could not browse in the storage area.

In *Patterns in the Use of Books in Large Research Libraries*, Fussler and Simon reported some interesting ideas and statistical findings concerning the use factor in selective weeding of books for storage.[17] Although they recognized that frequency of circulation or use of books is not always an accurate measure of the importance of books in large research libraries, Fussler and Simon hoped to determine whether some statistical method could identify low-use books in research library collections. One of their goals was to sort the collection into high- and low-use materials. High-use items would remain in the local collection, and low-use items would go to a remote storage facility. They found use and circulation data was effective for the first cut, that is, to identify potential materials. The final judgment of what to send to storage or discard remained with the collection development staff and other interested persons. Blindly following the use data can create more problems than it solves.

The authors concluded that past use of an item was the best predictor of future use. Given the nature of a large research library, they thought a 15- to 20-year study period provided the best results, but a 5-year period provided adequate data.

Fussler and Simon's study is valuable because it outlines the factors that affect the validity of comparing criteria (for example, between two research collections) for removing books for storage, and because of their findings concerning the advantages of libraries devising similar rules.

These factors are helpful reminders to any library considering a deselection program:

1. Differences among libraries in composition of the collection in specific subject areas.

2. Differences in size of collections.

3. Differences in size of university populations.

4. Differences in nature of university populations.

5. Differences in kind of record-of-past-use.[18]

In addition to factors that affect comparisons, Fussler and Simon's findings indicate that their methods would produce similar percentages of use in libraries regardless of type, clientele, and collection size. They concluded that scholars at various institutions have similar reading interests. Finally, they identified three practical alternatives for selecting books for storage:

1. Judgment of one or a few expert selectors in a field.

2. An examination of past use of a book and/or its objective characteristics.

3. A combination of these two approaches.[19]

Of these alternatives, they concluded that an objective system (that is, a statistical measure) ranks books more accurately in terms of probable value than does the subjective judgment of a single scholar in the field. They did recommend, however, that subject specialists and faculty review the candidate books identified using objective means before moving the books to remote storage.

Richard Trueswell quantitatively measured the relationship between the last circulation date of a book and user circulation requirements, and their effect on weeding.[20] He hoped to determine a quantitative method of maintaining a library's holdings at a reasonable level while providing satisfactory service to the user. (One can also use his method to determine the need for multiple copies, thus increasing the probability of a user's finding the needed books.)

Trueswell's basic assumption was that the last circulation date of a book is an indication of the book's value. He determined the cumulative distribution of the previous circulation data, which he assumed represented the typical circulation of a given library. Next, he determined the 99th percentile, which he used as the cutoff point for stack thinning. By multiplying the previous monthly circulation figures and the distribution for each month after establishing the 99th percentile, he was able to calculate the expected size of the main collection.

In applying this method to a sample from the Deering Library at Northwestern University, Trueswell predicted that a library could satisfy 99 percent of its circulation requirements with just 40 percent of its present holdings. That is, the library could move 60 percent of its collections to storage without significantly affecting the majority of users.[21] Trueswell did admit that many of his basic assumptions were questionable and that future research would yield more reliable data. Additional research, including that by Trueswell, supported his initial results.

Another study of note is Aridamen Jain's *Report on a Statistical Study of Book Use.*[22] This quantitative study of book use is based on extremely different assumptions from the two studies described previously. Though his statistical manipulations may completely baffle a nonstatistician, the theory behind Jain's method of measuring book use is easy to understand. The purpose of his study was to examine mathematical models and statistical techniques for determining the dependence of circulation rate on a book's age and on certain other characteristics. He hoped to indicate that the age of a book is the most significant variable in both predicting rates of monograph usage and in deciding which books to transfer to storage. He reviewed other studies concerned with determining whether the frequency with which groups of books with defined characteristics were likely to show use in a research library when identified through statistical methods. He hoped to establish, through comparative methods, that the probability of a book not being used is an efficient method of predicting use by taking into account the age of the book.

Jain's model seems to be particularly valuable in deselection projects for two reasons. One is that, contrary to the total library collection sampling method used by Fussler and Simon, Jain, like Trueswell, derived his data from all of the books checked out for a specific time period (that is, without regard to the total library collection). Jain felt that this method was superior to that used by Fussler and Simon. Although their method ensures the gathering of information on the same books over a longer time, Jain's method is much more conducive to a statistical design and data collection—missing data and lack of control are no longer problems. A second reason for this model's importance is that by using the specific time period sampling method, one can determine relative use of books within the library. Using the method of Fussler and Simon, this is not possible. Jain felt that the relative use concept was more efficient in studying the usage of books than the collection method.

Many other deselection studies exist, and they all generally agree that deselection based on past-use data provide the most cost-effective results. Although most of the studies were from academic libraries, Stanley Slote found that the method also worked in public libraries. (A British study by J. A. Urquhart and N. C. Urquhart has taken exception to these findings, especially for serials.[23]) Past use is a reasonable criterion if one is selecting for storage. On the other hand, the questions raised by the Urquharts would seem to indicate that librarians should go slowly in applying the past-use criterion when selecting items for purging.

Researchers have investigated almost every conceivable combination of objective criteria at one time or another in hope of finding the best. For example, they have examined language; date of publication; subject matter; frequency of citation; and listing in bibliographies, indexes, and abstracting services. Citation analysis and presence or absence of indexing or abstracting are most effective for serials and periodicals.

An interesting method for deselecting periodicals is to calculate a density of use value. The method requires establishing a unit of space occupied (perhaps one linear foot of shelf space) for each periodical title. Next, one determines the number of uses the title receives during a fixed time (perhaps one month). A ranking of the titles by use will produce one list, while a ranking by space occupied probably will result in a different list. Because one common objective of deselection programs is cost-effective use of existing collection space, calculating a ratio of space occupied to use (density of use) will help determine which periodicals to move to storage.

The preponderance of evidence points to the past-use criterion as the one most reliable for storage purposes. If the library has a circulation system that leaves a physical record of use in each book or in a database, one can easily collect the needed data. Today's automated circulation systems can provide detailed information about items, including frequency of circulation, class of borrower, use by class number, age of the item, language, producer, as well as almost any other physical or intellectual content characteristic.

Though circulation data is as sound a predictor of future use as one can find, it does rest on several assumptions that staff must understand and accept. One assumption is that circulated use is proportional to in-house use. What that proportion is depends on local circumstances. A second assumption is that current use patterns are similar to past and future patterns. (Trueswell restudied the same library over a period of 10 years with the same results from each study. Of course, that does not mean that the patterns would be the same 50 or 100 years from now.) A third assumption is that statistically random samples provide an adequate base for determining use patterns. A known limitation of circulation data is that a few customers can have a major impact on circulation (the 80/20 rule). Failure to take in-house use into account in a deselection program dependent on use data as the main selection criterion will have skewed results.

Records Retention

Some information professionals in a special library or information center environment find themselves in charge of the organization's paper files, or archive. Some academic libraries also have responsibility for the campus archive. Just as print and audiovisual collections eventually exceed the space available, so do company files. When this happens, the equivalent of the library environment deselection process takes place.

In the business setting, and when dealing with the organization's records, the term used for the process is *retention*. A records retention program, developed by the person in charge of the files (who may be an information specialist, librarian, or records manager) is designed to meet several objectives:

assure protection of the organization's vital records

retain records of value or historical interest for the appropriate amount of time, meeting both legal and business needs for the records to be available

restrict storage equipment and floor space, in expensive areas, to active records

store inactive records in inexpensive storage facilities

release reusable materials—audiotapes, magnetic tapes, or floppy disks—as quickly as possible

destroy records that have served their purpose

With only slight rewording, these objectives apply to almost any library setting.

Records managers classify documents in several ways: as record or nonrecord, as active or inactive, and by value or use. A record is an official document of the organization; nonrecords are convenience copies. With a multiple-part order form, the original, or top copy, of the order is a record and all the other copies are nonrecord. Photocopies and carbon copies are almost always nonrecord items. Active records are those needed for current operating activities and consulted on a regular basis. The organization determines the cutoff period between active and inactive. (Perhaps one consultation in six months keeps a record active.) Factors influencing the organization's decision include the amount and cost of available storage space and the cost of active space. Storage of inactive records normally occurs away from the main facilities of the organization in special warehouses designed to store the inactive records of many organizations. Records managers determine value by the way people use the records. Typical categories of value are legal, operating, administrative, fiscal, research, and historical.

In many cases, the question of when the organization may destroy a record is a function of various federal and state laws. In other cases, the retention period is related to business or needs. Records managers estimate that only about 10 to 20 percent of all records retained are in storage for legal reasons. Determining the laws and regulations covering record retention can be a challenge. Several guides assist in making retention decisions: *Guide to Record Retention Requirements* (Government Printing Office, 1994); *Disposition of Federal Records* (Government Printing Office, 1992); and *Record Keeping Requirements* and *Records Retention Procedures*, both by Donald Skupsky (Association of Records Managers and Administrators, 1991). An organization develops a master retention schedule that lists the record series, where it comes from (that is, the office of record), how long to retain it, where to store it, in what form (according to law, some records must be originals, but others may be copies), and how and when the organization may dispose of it (either by destroying it or transferring it to an archive).

While not all the issues are the same, there are some striking parallels between records retention and collection deselection. The Association of Records Managers and Administrators (ARMA) and the National Archives and Records Administration (NARA) are the best sources for further information about records management.

Summary

One way to overcome some of the psychological barriers to deselection is to develop cooperative programs like that of the Center for Research Libraries (see chapter 16). As long as there is a continuing emphasis on independence and size, customers suffer. Too much material to buy, too little money to spend, too little space to service and store adequately what we do buy, too few staff members to help bewildered patrons find what they need, and too little time and money to maintain collections on a human scale—these are but a few of the problems that librarians face. Clearly, any solution will require cooperation.

Notes

[1]Kenneth E. Carpenter, *The First 350 Years of the Harvard University Library* (Cambridge, MA: Harvard University Library, 1986), 122.

[2]H. F. McGraw, "Policies and Practices in Discarding," *Library Trends* 4 (January 1956): 270.

[3]Ibid.

[4]Eugene Garfield, "Weeding," *Current Contents* 15 (June 30, 1975): 26.

[5]Stanley J. Slote, *Weeding Library Collections II,* 2d rev. ed. (Littleton, CO: Libraries Unlimited, 1982); Joseph P. Segal, *Evaluating and Weeding Collections in Small and Medium-Sized Public Libraries: The CREW Method* (Chicago: American Library Association, 1980).

[6]Paula M. Strain, "A Study of the Usage and Retention of Technical Periodicals," *Library Resources and Technical Services* 10 (Summer 1966): 295.

[7]Ellis Mount, ed., *Weeding of Collections in Sci-Tech Libraries* (New York: Haworth Press, 1986).

[8]Anita Gordon, "Weeding: Keeping Up with the Information Explosion," *School Library Journal* 30 (September 1983): 45-46; Calgary Board of Education, Educational Media Team, "Weeding the School Library Media Collection," *School Library Media Quarterly* 12 (Fall 1984): 419-24.

[9]Fremont Rider, *The Scholar and the Future of the Research Library* (New York: Handen Press, 1944), 17.

[10]Ralph Ellsworth, *Economics of Book Storage in College and Research Libraries* (Washington, DC: Association of Research Libraries, 1969).

[11]Gary S. Lawrence, "A Cost Model for Storage and Weeding Programs," *College & Research Libraries* 42 (March 1981): 139-41.

[12]McGraw, "Policies and Practices in Discarding," 269-82.

[13]C. A. Seymour, "Weeding the Collection," *Libri* 22 (1972): 189.

[14]L. Ash, *Yale's Selective Book Retirement Program* (Hamden, CT: Archon, 1963), ix.

[15]Ibid., 66.

[16]Ibid.

[17]H. H. Fussler and J. L. Simon, *Patterns in the Use of Books in Large Research Libraries,* rev.ed. (Chicago: University of Chicago Press, 1969), 4.

[18]Ibid., 125.

[19]Ibid., 208.

[20]R. Trueswell, "Quantitative Measure of User Circulation Requirements and Its Effects on Possible Stack Thinning and Multiple Copy Determination," *American Documentation* 16 (January 1965): 20-25.

[21]Ibid., 20.

[22]A. Jain, *Report on a Statistical Study of Book Use* (Lafayette, IN: Purdue University, 1968).

[23]J. A. Urquhart and N. C. Urquhart, *Relegation and Stock Control in Libraries* (London, Oriel Press, 1976).

Further Reading

General

Barnett, L. "The Enemy Is Us." *Collection Building* 11, no. 3 (1991): 25-27.

Broadus, R. N. "Materials of History: Saving and Discarding." *Collection Building* 10, nos. 1/2 (1989): 3-6.

Carpenter, E. "Depreciation of Library Collections." *Library Administration & Management* 5 (Winter 1992): 41-43.

Egghe, L., and I. K. Ravichandra Rao. "Citation Age Data and the Obsolescence Function." *Information Processing Management* 28, no. 2 (1992): 201-17.

Guide to the Review of Collections: Preservation, Storage and Withdrawal. Edited by L. Clark. Chicago: American Library Association, 1991.

Kennedy, J. R., and G. Stockman. *The Great Divide: Challenges in Remote Storage.* Chicago: American Library Association, 1991.

Miller, E. P., and A. L. O'Neill. "Journal Deselection and Costing." *Library Acquisitions: Practice and Theory* 14, no. 2 (1990): 173-78.

Nolan, C. W. "Lean Reference Collection." *College & Research Libraries* 52 (January 1991): 80-91.

Oberhofer, C. M. A. "Information Use Value." *Information Processing & Management* 29 (September/October 1993): 587-600.

Pao, M. L., and A. J. Warner. "Depreciation of Knowledge." *Library Trends* 41 (Spring 1993): 545-709.

Wezeman, F. "Psychological Barriers to Weeding." *ALA Bulletin* 52 (September 1958): 637-39.

Academic

Fang, X. "A Study of the Problems of Aging Books in University Libraries." *Journal of the American Society of Information Science* 43 (August 1992): 501-5.

Miller, J. W. "Problem Librarians Make Problems for Humanists." *Collection Building* 10, nos. 3/4 (1989): 11-19.

Milne, S. J. "Periodicals and Space Constraints." *Indiana Libraries* 9, no. 2 (1990): 55-58.

Osheroff, S. K., and M. C. Knittel. "Team Weeding in a University Library." *College & Research Library News* 51 (September 1990): 723-25.

Rider, F. *The Scholar and the Future of the Research Library.* New York: Handen Press, 1944.

Sam, S., and J. A. Major. "Compact Shelving of Circulating Collections." *College & Research Library News* 54 (January 1993): 11-12.

Seaman, S., and D. DeGeorge. "Selecting and Moving Books to Remote Depository." *Collection Management* 16, no. 1 (1992): 137-42.

Turner, S. J. "Trueswell's Weeding Technique: The Facts." *College & Research Libraries* 41 (March 1980): 134-38.

Public

Albsmeyer, B. "Danger—Our Books Contain Outdated Information." *Unabashed Librarian* 73 (1989): 5-6.

Bazirjiian, R. "Ethics of Library Discard Practices." In *Legal and Ethical Issues in Acquisitions,* edited by K. Strauch and B. Strauch, 213-34. New York: Haworth Press, 1990.

Ehrlich, M. "Criteria for Not Discarding from a Public Library." *Unabashed Librarian* 78 (1991): 26.

Futas, E., and J. S. Tryon. "Scheduled Reference Collection Maintenance." *Reference Librarian* 29 (1990): 69-76.

Mahoney, K. "Weeding the Small Library Collection." *Connecticut Libraries* 24 (Spring 1982): 45-47.

Roy, L. "Weeding Without Tears." *Collection Management* 12, nos. 1/2 (1990): 83-93.

Slote, S. J. *Weeding Library Collections,* 3d ed. Englewood, CO: Libraries Unlimited, 1989.

Wallace, D. P. "The Young and the Ageless: Obsolescence in the Public Library Collection." *Public Libraries* 29 (March/April 1990): 102-5.

School

Brown, C. "Selection for Rejection." *School Librarian* 40 (November 1992): 135-36.

Cerny, R. "When Less Is More: Issues in Collection Development." *School Library Journal* 37 (March 1991): 130-31.

Gordon, A. "Weeding—Keeping Up with the Information Explosion." *School Library Journal* 30 (September 1983): 45-46.

Kahler, J. "Dated, Tattered, and Ugly." *Texas Library Journal* 65 (Fall 1989): 100-102.

"Weeding Media." *School Library Workshop* 14 (November 1993): 8-9.

"Weeding the School Library Media Collection." *School Library Media Quarterly* 12 (Fall 1984): 419-24.

Special

Bedsole, D. T. "Formulating a Weeding Policy for Books in a Special Library." *Special Libraries* 49 (May 1958): 205-9.

Burdick, A. J. "Science Citation Index Data As a Safety Net for Basic Science Books Considered for Weeding." *Libraries & Technical Services* 33 (October 1989): 367-73.

Diodato, V. P., and F. Smith. "Obsolescence of Music Literature." *Journal of the American Society of Information Science* 44 (March 1993): 101-12.

Drake, C. S. "Weeding of a Historical Society Library." *Special Libraries* 83 (Spring 1992): 86-91.

Fisher, W. "Weeding the Academic Business/Economics Collection." *Behavioral and Social Sciences Librarian* 4 (Spring 1985): 29-37.

Goldstein, C. H. "Study of Weeding Policies in Eleven TALON Resource Libraries." *Medical Library Association Bulletin* 69 (July 1981): 311-16.

Hulser, R. P. "Weeding in a Corporate Library As Part of a Collection Management Program." *Science and Technology Libraries* 6 (Spring 1986): 1-9.

Hurt, R. K. "Journal Deselection in a Biomedical Research Library." *Bulletin of the Medical Library Association* 78 (January 1990): 45-48.

Index to Federal Record-Keeping Requirements. New York: National Records Management Council, 1981.

"Jury Rules Corporate Library Willfully Destroyed Documents." *Library Journal* 118 (February 1, 1993): 14.

Kidd, Y. M. "New Regulation Relaxes Federal Records Management Requirements." *Inform* 5 (March 1991): 9-10.

Mount, Ellis, ed. *Weeding of Collections in Sci-Tech Libraries.* New York: Haworth Press, 1986.

Triolo, V. A., and D. Bao. "A Decision Model for Technical Journal Deselection with an Experiment in Biomedical Communications." *Journal of the American Society for Information Science* 44 (April 1993): 148-60.

Williams, R. F. "Document Disposition of Optically Stored Records." *Inform* 7 (February 1993): 35-45.

———. "Is It Legal?" *Document Image Automation* 12 (Fall 1992): 10-12.

15
Evaluation

What are the strengths of the collection? How effectively have we spent our collection development monies? How useful are the collections to the service community? How do our collections compare to those of our peers? These are but a few of the questions one may answer by conducting a collection evaluation assessment project. Evaluation completes the collection development cycle and brings one back to needs assessment activities. Though the term *evaluation* has several definitions, there is a common element in all of them related to placing a value or worth on an object or activity. Collection evaluation involves both objects and activities, as well as quantitative and qualitative values.

Dozens of people have written about collection evaluation—Stone, Clapp-Jordan, Evans, Bonn, Lancaster, Mosher, McGrath, and Broadus, to name a few. While the basics remain unchanged, the application of the basics has become more and more sophisticated over the years. Computers make it possible to handle more data, as well as a wider variety of data. Bibliographic and numeric databases can provide valuable data that in the past would have been exceedingly difficult, if not impossible, to obtain (see, for example, Metz's older but still interesting *Landscape of Literatures*[1]). Bibliographic utilities, such as WLN, and regional groups, such as AMIGOS, offer CD-ROM products for assessing and comparing collections. Despite the assistance of technology and increasingly sophisticated systems of evaluation, as Betty Rosenburg, a long-time teacher of collection development repeatedly stated, the best tool for collection evaluation is an intelligent, cultured, experienced selection officer with a sense of humor and a thick skin. Because there are so many subjective and qualitative elements in collection development, Betty Rosenburg's statement is easy to understand and appreciate. Though this chapter will not help one develop the personal characteristics she identified as important, it does outline the basic methods available for conducting an evaluation project and provides a few examples.

Background

Before undertaking any evaluation, the library must carefully define the project's purposes and goals. One definition of evaluation is "a judgment as to the value of X, based on a comparison, implicit or explicit, with some known value, Y." If the unknown and the (presumably) known values involve abstract concepts that do not lend themselves to quantitative measurement, there are bound to be differences of opinion regarding the value. One has many methods for determining the value of a book or of an entire collection: economic, moral, religious, aesthetic, intellectual, educational, political, and social, for example. The value of an item or a collection fluctuates depending on which method one employs. Combining several methods is effective as long as there is agreement as to their relative weight. So many subjective factors come into play in the evaluation process that one must work through the issues before starting. One important benefit of having the goals defined and the criteria for the values established ahead of time is that interpretation of the results is much easier. It may also help minimize differences of opinion about the results.

Libraries and information centers, like other organizations, want to know how they compare with similar organizations. Comparative data can be useful, but it can also be misleading. Like all other aspects of evaluation, comparative data present significant problems of definition and interpretation. What, for example, does library A gain by comparing itself with library B, except, perhaps, an inferiority complex—or a delusion as to its own status. Without question, some libraries are better than others, and comparisons may well be important in discovering why this is so. Two key issues in interpreting comparisons are: (1) one assumes there is a close approximation of needs among the comparative groups and (2) one assumes the existence of standards or norms that approximate optimum conditions. Neither assumption has a solid basis in reality. If the library or its parent organization is considering starting a new service or program, comparative data from libraries already supporting similar services can provide valuable planning information. Though comparisons are interesting and even helpful in some respects, one should be cautious in interpreting the significance of the findings.

Based on many years of experience in surveying library resources, Robert B. Downs suggested,

> From the internal point of view, the survey, if properly done, gives one an opportunity to stand off and get an objective look at the library, to see its strengths, its weaknesses, the directions in which it has been developing, how it compares with other similar libraries, how well the collection is adapted to its clientele, and provides a basis for future planning.[2]

Downs believed that, in addition to their internal value, surveys are an essential step in preparing for library cooperative acquisitions projects and resource sharing.

Organizations conduct evaluations for several reasons, including:

to develop an intelligent, realistic acquisitions program based on a thorough knowledge of the existing collection

to justify increased funding demands or for particular subject allocations

to increase the staff's familiarity with the collection

Accreditation standards usually address the library, and many of the evaluative criteria apply to collection evaluation. J. H. Russell, in "The Library Self-Survey," stated that a survey provides "a check of the effectiveness of the library; . . . a kind of psychological security for the library staff and for the college faculty; . . . a valuable instrument in public relations for the library; . . . [and it would] force the library staff to formulate clearly the objectives of the library itself."[3] By changing the environmental context, the statement could apply to any library.

It is possible to divide collection evaluation purposes into two broad categories: internal reasons and external reasons. The following lists provide a variety of questions or purposes for each category.

Internal Reasons

Collection development needs

What is the true scope of the collections (that is, what is the subject coverage)?

What is the depth of the collections (that is, what amount and type of material comprises the collection)?

How does the service community use the collection (that is, what is the circulation and use within the library)?

What is the collection's monetary value? (This needs to be known for insurance and capital assessment reasons.)

What are the strong areas of the collection (in quantitative and qualitative terms)?

What are the weak areas of the collection (in quantitative and qualitative terms)?

What problems exist in the collection policy and program?

What changes should be made in the existing program?

How well are collection development officers carrying out their duties?

Provide data for possible cooperative collection development programs.

Provide data for deselection (weeding) projects.

Provide data to determine the need for a full inventory.

Budgetary needs

Assist in determining allocations needed to strengthen weak areas.

Assist in determining allocations needed to maintain areas of strength.

Assist in determining allocations needed for retrospective collection development.

Assist in determining overall allocations.

External Reasons

Local institutional needs

Is the library's performance marginal, adequate, or above average?

Is the budget request for materials reasonable?

Does the budget provide the appropriate level of support?

Is the library comparable to others serving similar communities?

Are there alternatives to space expansion (for example, weeding)?

Is the collection outdated?

Is there sufficient coordination in the collection program (that is, does the library really need all those separate collections)?

Is the level of duplication appropriate?

Is the cost/benefit ratio reasonable?

Extra-organizational needs

Provide data for accreditation groups.

Provide data for funding agencies.

Provide data for various networks, consortia, and other cooperative programs.

Provide data to donors.

Having undertaken numerous evaluation projects, as a staff member and a consultant, the reasons stated above have surfaced in one form or another. Not all the reasons apply to every type of information environment, but most have wide applicability.

After the library or evaluators establish the purposes for carrying out the evaluation, the next step is determining the most effective methods of evaluation. A number of techniques are available, and the choice depends, in part, upon the purpose and depth of the evaluation process. George Bonn's "Evaluation of the Collection" lists five general approaches to evaluation:

1. Compiling statistics on holdings.

2. Checking standard lists—catalogs and bibliographies.

3. Obtaining opinions from regular users.

4. Examining the collection directly.

5. Applying standards [which involves the use of various methods mentioned above], listing the library's document delivery capability, and noting the relative use of a particular group.[4]

Most of the methods developed in the recent past draw on statistical techniques. Some of the standards and guidelines of professional associations and accrediting agencies employ statistical approaches and formulas that give evaluators some quantitative indicators of what is adequate. Standards, checklists, catalogs, and bibliographies are other tools of the evaluator.

The ALA's *Guide to the Evaluation of Library Collections*[5] divides the methods into collection-centered measures and use-centered measures. Within each category are a number of specific evaluative methods. The *Guide* summarizes the major techniques currently used to evaluate information collections.

Some years ago, I was part of a team that reviewed the effectiveness of library evaluation through the literature. The team examined more than 750 articles and research reports. From that pool, the team established six categories of measures employed to evaluate library effectiveness. They are accessibility, cost, user satisfaction, response time, cost/benefit ratio, and use.

Four surprising features emerged from the examination. First, almost none of the 750-plus studies provided a clearly stated purpose for the project. We also found evidence of dissatisfaction with the outcome of some of the studies; where dissatisfaction existed there was also a lack of a clear statement of purpose.

Second, none of the methods employed was sufficiently sensitive to both quantitative and qualitative issues. No method was completely satisfactory from either the librarians' or nonlibrarians' point of view. (Perhaps part of the problem was that there had been no agreement as to the purposes of the projects before they were begun).Third, most methods placed high value on circulation and accessibility. Often, this high value was at the expense of quality and breadth. The method that generated the most questioning was document delivery time. Finally, a most surprising finding was that none of the measures then in use, even in combination, took into account a total service program—this is more or less true today. For example, none of the measures took conservation and preservation issues into account. (Chapter 17 discusses preservation, a major issue in collection management.)

Impressionistic Methods

As its name implies, this method depends on personal impressions for making the assessment. What are the impressionistic techniques? (Impressionistic measures are part of ALA's collection-centered measures.) Some evaluators suggest examining a collection in terms of the library's policies and purposes and preparing a report based on impressions of how well the collection meets those goals. The process may involve reviewing the entire collection using the shelf list; it may cover only a single subject area; or, as is frequently the case, it may involve conducting shelf examinations of various subject areas. Normally, the concern is with estimating qualities like the depth of the collection, its usefulness in relation to the curriculum or research, and deficiencies and strengths in the collections.

Very rarely is the impressionistic technique used alone. It occurs most frequently during accreditation visits, when an accreditation team member walks into the stacks, looks around, and comes out with a sense of the value of the collection. No consultant who regularly uses this technique limits it to shelf reading. Rather, consultants prefer to collect impressions from the service community. Though each person's view is valid only for the individual's areas of interest, in combination, individuals' views should provide an overall sense of the service community's views. (This approach falls into the category of user satisfaction.) Customers make judgments about the collection each time they look for something. They will have an opinion even after one brief visit. Thus, the approach is important, if for no other reason than that it provides the evaluator with a sense of what the customers think about the collection. Further, it encourages customer involvement in the evaluation process.

Frequently, an outside consultant, an experienced librarian, or an accrediting committee uses this approach. The evaluation draws on information compiled from various sources—personal examination of the shelves, qualitative measures, and the impressions of the service community. Subject specialists give their impressions of the strengths and weaknesses of a collection. Sometimes, the evaluator employs questionnaires and interviews to collect the data from many people. Less frequently, specialists' impressions may constitute the entire evaluation. Library staff member opinions about the collection add another perspective to the assessment; often, these views differ sharply from those of the users and those of an outsider.

Library self-studies make effective use of the impressions of subject specialists and librarians in combination with list-checking and other evaluative methods. An example of application of the impressionistic method was a project undertaken by the librarians at the State University of New York at Buffalo. The library's subject bibliographers formed an evaluation team that developed an impressive set of project guidelines. The bibliographers prepared a preliminary evaluative statement for their areas of responsibility. They then checked the collection holdings against various bibliographies. They were to use their ingenuity in approaching the research collection, and they were to evaluate the book selection procedures, as well as faculty interest and assistance in the selection process. After gathering the objective data (that is, the results of bibliography checks), the evaluators reexamined their original statements. They found that, though some adjustments were necessary, their initial assessment was reasonably close to the checklist results. Because many large public libraries employ subject specialists, most special libraries have in-depth subject specialists available, and school libraries can draw on teachers for subject expertise, this method is viable in any library environment.

The major weakness of the impressionistic technique is that it is overwhelmingly subjective. Obviously, the opinions of those who use the collection regularly and the views of subject specialists have importance. Impressions may be most useful as part of an evaluation when used in connection with other methods of examining a collection, but their value depends on the objectives of the individual evaluation project, and their significance depends on their interpretation.

Checklist Method

The checklist method is an old standby for evaluators. It can serve a variety of purposes. Used alone or in combination with other techniques—usually with the goal of coming up with some numerically based statement, such as "We (or they) have X percentage of the books on this list," it provides objective data. Consultants frequently check holdings against standard bibliographies (or suggest that the library do it) and report the results. Checklists allow the evaluator to compare the library's holdings against one or more standard lists of materials for a subject area *(Business Journals of the United States)*, for a type of library *(Books for College Libraries)*, or class of customer *(Best Books for Junior High Readers)*.

When I am asked to assess a collection, I use checklists as part of the process. Whenever possible, I ask a random sample of subject experts at the institution to identify one or two bibliographies or basic materials lists in their specialty that they believe would be reasonable to use in evaluating the collection. The responses, or lack of responses, provide information about each respondent's knowledge of publications in her or his field and indicates the degree of interest in the library collection. When appropriate, I also use accreditation checklists, if there is doubt about the collection's adequacy.

Accreditation committees frequently use checklists in evaluation, particularly for reference and periodical collections. Such committees strive to apply standards for various kinds of libraries. The College Library Standards Committee's "Standards for College Libraries" recommends, "Library holdings should be checked frequently against standard bibliographies, both general and subject, as a reliable measure of their quality. A high percentage of listed titles which are relevant to the program of the individual institution should be included in the library collections."[6]

As collections increase in size, there is less need to worry about formal checking or standard bibliographies. However, it is worthwhile for selectors to occasionally take time to review some of the best-of-the-year lists published by various associations. Such reviews will help selectors spot titles missed during the year and serve as a check against personal biases playing too great a role in the selection process. Selectors quickly identify items not selected and can take whatever steps are necessary. Often, such lists appear in selection aids; it takes little extra time to review the list to conduct a mini-evaluation.

Self-surveys by the library staff frequently make use of checklist methods. M. Llewellyn Raney conducted the first checklist self-survey, at least the first reported in the literature, in 1933 for the University of Chicago libraries. This survey used 300 bibliographies to check the entire collection for the purpose of determining future needs. There is little question that this pioneering effort demonstrated the value of using checklists to thoroughly examine the total collection.

Obviously, one can use a variety of checklists in any situation. The major factor determining how many lists to employ is the amount of time available for the project. Today's OPACs make checking an easier process, but it still requires a substantial amount of time. Many evaluators have their favorite standard lists, but there is a growing use of highly specialized lists in an effort to check collection depth as well as breadth. Most evaluators advocate using serials and media checklists in addition to book checklists. Large research libraries (academic, public, or special) seldom use the basic lists; instead, they rely on subject bibliographies and specially compiled lists. One of the quality control checks employed by the RLG/ARL conspectus project (see pages 85-87) uses the specially prepared checklist technique. Specially prepared bibliographies are probably the best checklist method. However, preparing such lists takes additional time, and many libraries are unwilling to commit that much staff effort to the evaluation process.

Using any checklist requires certain assumptions; one is that the selected list reflects goals and purposes that are similar to the checking institution's. Normally, unless an examination of a collection is thorough, the checklist method merely samples the list. Thus, the data are only as good as the sampling method employed.

The shortcomings of the checklist technique for evaluation are many, and eight criticisms appear repeatedly:

Title selection was for specific, not general use.

Almost all lists are selective and omit many worthwhile titles.

Many titles have little relevance for a specific library's community.

Lists may be out of date.

A library may own many titles that are not on the checklist but that are as good as the titles on the checklist.

Interlibrary loan service carries no weight in the evaluation.

Checklists approve titles; there is no penalty for having poor titles.

Checklists fail to take into account special materials that may be important to a particular library.

To answer these criticisms, the checklist would have to be all things to all libraries. All too often, there is little understanding that all works are not of equal value and equally useful to a specific library. Though some older books continue to be respected for many years, an out-of-date checklist is of little use in evaluating a current collection.

Obviously, the time involved in effectively checking lists is a concern. Spotty or limited checking does little good, but most libraries are unable or unwilling to check an entire list. Checklist results show the percentage of books from the list that is in the collection. This may sound fine, but there is no standard proportion of a list a library should have. How should one interpret the fact that the library holds 53 percent of some list? Is it reasonable or necessary to have every item? Comparisons of one library's holdings with another's on the basis of percentages of listed titles is of little value, unless the two libraries have similar service populations. In a sense, the use of a checklist assumes some correlation between the percentage of listed books held by a library and the percentage of desirable books in the library's collection. This may or may not be a warranted assumption. Equally questionable is the assumption that listed books not held necessarily constitute desiderata, and that the proportion of items held to items needed (as represented on the list) constitutes an effective measure of a library's adequacy.

This lengthy discussion of the shortcomings of the checklist method should serve more as a warning than a prohibition. There *are* benefits from using this method in evaluation. Many librarians feel that checking lists helps to reveal gaps and weaknesses in a collection, that the lists provide handy selection guides if the library wishes to use them for this purpose, and that the revelation of gaps and weaknesses may lead to reconsideration of selection methods and policies. Often, nonlibrary administrators respond more quickly and favorably to information about gaps in a collection when the evaluators identify the gaps by using standard lists than when they use other means of identifying the weaknesses.

Statistical Methods of Collection Evaluation

Quantitative methods of evaluating a book collection assume that a sufficient quantity of books is one valid indicator of quality. For example, this method compiles statistics concerning the number of volumes in the total collection as well as its component parts, the expenditures for acquisitions, the relation of this amount to the size of the collection or to the total institutional budget, as well as similar statistics.

The standard checklists developed for opening-day collections operated on this premise. When J. W. Pirie compiled *Books for Junior Colleges,* he stated that a junior college library needed 20,000 volumes to support a liberal arts curriculum.[7] *Books for College Libraries* assumes a four-year college must have a minimum of 150,000 volumes, 20 percent of which should be bound periodical volumes and the other 80 percent monographic titles.[8] Similar assumptions appear in the ALA Public Library Association's shorter list, *Books for Public Libraries: Nonfiction for Small Collections.*[9]

One source of data (in the United States) for comparative purposes is the national shelf list count. The basis of the count is the Library of Congress, which suggests its primary use is in large research libraries. A shelf list project provides three types of data: the actual title count for a class number, the percentage of holdings within a class number range, and the relationship of the holdings to that of other participating libraries and to the Library of Congress holdings. A good review article describing the project and its utility is "The National Shelflist Count Project: Its History, Limitations, and Usefulness," by Joseph Branin, David Farrell, and Mariann Tiblin.[10]

The quantitative method has obvious limitations when applied to collections larger than the standard's minimum. Though quality requires a certain minimum quantity, quantity alone does not guarantee quality. As Guy Lyle unequivocally stated, "The adequacy of the college library's book collection cannot be measured in quantitative terms. To judge a collection as superior or inferior on the basis of the volume of holdings is as absurd as rating a college on the basis of its enrollment."[11] Librarians and information professionals in other environmental settings would agree with Lyle, though their words may vary. The basic weakness in the quantitative method of evaluation lies in interpretation of the statistics when making value judgments about the collection. People often use those data to compare one library with other libraries or with fixed, external standards. Neither comparison provides information about what areas of the collection are strong or weak.

Comparison with Other Institutions

Comparisons among institutions offer limited useful data for evaluation because institutions differ in their objectives, programs, and service populations. For instance, a junior college with only a liberal arts program requires one type of library, whereas a community college with both a liberal arts curriculum and strong vocational programs requires a much larger collection. Comparing the first library to the second would be like comparing apples and oranges. There simply is no basis for comparison, and no point in it.

Comparing libraries is difficult, if not impossible, because of the way some libraries generate statistics about their collections. On paper, two libraries may appear similar, yet their book collections may differ widely. Some years ago, Eli Oboler documented this problem:

> One library, without any footnote explanation, suddenly increased from less than twenty-five thousand volumes added during 1961-62 to more than three times that number while the amount shown for books and other library materials only increased approximately 50 percent. Upon inquiry the librarian of this institution stated that, "from storage in one attic we removed forty thousand items, some of which have been catalogued, but in the main we are as yet unsure of the number which will be added. The addition of a large number of volumes also included about one-fourth public documents, state and federal, and almost fifty thousand volumes in microtext."[12]

No one suggests it is possible to determine the adequacy of a library's collection solely in quantitative terms. Number of volumes is a poor measure of the growth of the library's collection in relation to the programs and services it provides. However, when standards fail to provide quantitative guidelines, budgeting and fiscal officers, who cannot avoid quantitative bases for their decisions, adopt measures that seem to have the virtue of simplicity but are essentially irrelevant to the library's function. Therefore, it is necessary to develop quantitative approaches for evaluating collections that are useful in official decision making and that retain the virtue of simplicity while being relevant to the library's programs and services.

Formulas

Formulas have been employed to assess the worth of library collections. Among the formulas receiving considerable attention are those of Clapp-Jordan, Washington State, California State, the ACRL formula for college libraries, and Beasley's formula for public libraries. Advantages associated with formulas include a greater potential for in-depth comparison between libraries and greater ease in preparation and interpretation. The disadvantage is an inability to assess qualitative factors that are important in the relationship between the library collection and patron needs. Furthermore, there is a lack of standard definitions of what to measure (for example, no uniformity in use of the terms *titles* and *volumes*).

Clapp-Jordan Formula

Because of widespread disagreement with existing standards, some librarians developed additional criteria for determining the adequacy of a collection. One example of this type of formula is the Clapp-Jordan formula. One can secure data from the formula to use for planning, budgeting, and with appropriating bodies. Although formula approaches like Clapp-Jordan have gained acceptance, there are always arguments as to whether these approaches provide the best fit in a given library environment. An empirical study of the validity of the formula by R. M. McInnis (using linear regression analysis) concluded that: (1) minimal levels of adequacy cannot be conclusively determined, (2) over prediction or too high results are not produced, and (3) the Clapp-Jordan Formula can serve as a computed guide to minimum levels of library size.[13]

Washington State Formula

Using this formula, a modification of Clapp-Jordan, it is possible to establish baselines for both colleges and universities, because it takes into account both enrollment and program factors. The Washington formula does not include two Clapp-Jordan elements: an allowance of 335 volumes per undergraduate major and 12 additional volumes per honors student. Both elements are subject to wide variation of interpretation, which makes their usefulness in interinstitutional comparisons questionable. The formula used for determining quantitative adequacy appears in table 15.1.

Table 15.1.

Units of Library Resources

1. Basic or Opening Day Collection	85,000
2. Allowance per FTE Faculty	100
3. Allowance per FTE Student	15
4. Allowance per Masters Field When No Doctorate Offered in Field	6,100
5. Allowance per Masters Field When Doctorate Is Offered in Field	3,050
6. Allowance per Doctoral Field	24,500

From Washington State Universities and Colleges, The Interinstitutional Committee of Business Officers, *A Model Budget Analysis System for Program Libraries* (Olympia, WA: Evergreen State College, Office of Interinstitutional Business Studies, March 1970).

California State Formula

Based on U.S. Office of Education standards, the California State formula takes into consideration opportunities for resource sharing by libraries in close proximity to one another. The formula uses specific allocations for approved fields of graduate study and for the number of FTE (full-time equivalent) students:

1. To a basic allowance of 75,000 volumes, for the opening day allowance of new college libraries and the first 600 FTE students.

2. *Add* 10,000 volumes for each additional 2,000 FTE students.

3. *Add* 3,000 volumes for each subject field of graduate study listed by the Office of Education in application for Title II funds.

4. *Add* 5,000 volumes for each approved joint doctoral program.

5. *Subtract* from the total computed 5 percent of such allowance when the college is closer than 25 miles from the nearest public institution of higher education, as determined by the chancellor.[14]

Formula A—Association of College and Research Libraries Standards for College Libraries

An ad hoc ACRL committee on revision proposed the following standards:

The library's collection shall comprise all corpuses of recorded information owned by the college for educational, inspirational, and recreational purposes, including multidimensional, aural, pictorial, and print materials.

The library shall provide quickly a high percentage of such materials needed by its patrons.

The amount of print materials to be thus provided shall be determined by a formula (Formula A) which takes into account the nature and the extent of the academic program of the institution, its enrollment, and the size of its teaching faculty. (A volume is defined as a physical unit of any printed, typewritten, handwritten, mimeographed, or processed work contained in one binding or portfolio, hardbound or paperbound, which has been cataloged, classified, or otherwise prepared for use. For purpose of this calculation microform holdings should be included converting them to volume-equivalents. The number of volume-equivalents held in microform should be determined either by actual count or by averaging formula which considers each reel or microform as one and five pieces of any other format as one volume-equivalent.)[15]

Formula A used the Clapp-Jordan formula as a base and is similar to the Washington State formula. Formula A excluded the Clapp-Jordan allowance of 12 volumes per honor student. It added one element that was in neither the Clapp-Jordan formula nor the Washington State formula—6,000 volumes per "6th year specialist degree field."

The standards state that "libraries which can provide promptly 100 percent as many volumes or volume-equivalents as are called for in this formula shall, in the matter of quality, be graded 'A'. From 80-99 percent shall be graded 'B'; from 65-79 percent shall be graded 'C'; and from 50-64 percent shall be graded 'D'."[16]

Beasley's Formula

As one can see from the examples of formulas, academic libraries make extensive use of statistical tools for the purposes of evaluating collections. However, statistical tools are also used in public libraries. Perhaps the outstanding example of a public library formula is K. Beasley's "Theoretical Framework for Public Library Management Measurement."[17] Beasley indicated that a statistical reporting system for libraries must have the following features:

1. The expressions should be stated in such a way that they themselves do not set value.

2. There should be a statistical or mathematical formula for each discrete element of a library program.

3. Enough variables must be used to delineate clearly the total pattern.

4. The statistics should state clearly the characteristics of the present—where we are now—and in such a manner as to facilitate forecasts of the future.[18]

Beasley's formula elements are familiar to most librarians, and are as follows:

Potential Service = B/P x C/P x S

Where

B = all resource materials (perhaps) weighted

P = population served

C = circulation

S = study or research factor[19]

This formula makes no attempt to measure quality and bases this on the assumption that quality is primarily a function of individual assessment of the worth of an item.

CD-ROM Products

During the late 1980s, another type of qualitative assessment became popular, a CD-ROM database drawing on bibliographic utility holdings records. Two widely used products are produced by AMIGOS and WLN. The AMIGOS product employs data from OCLC, and the WLN product uses its own bibliographic database. Loyola Marymount University uses the AMIGOS product, with two disks. One disk has a peer group consisting of 40 libraries that are comparable to the LMU library or to which the library could be compared. The other disk contains data for all four California Catholic universities. The disks are used for several projects. One project is to assist the collection development officer in working with individual departments in examining the book collection to identify areas of strength and weakness. Another project is exploring the possibilities for resource sharing and cooperative collection development among the California Catholic universities. A third use is to assist in assessing the collection to support proposed new academic programs. The library also uses the material, in combination with other data, to respond to various accreditation and self-study reports that arise every year.

Using these products takes time, because the manual is large and learning how the product works and how to interpret the results has a steep learning curve. It also takes time to teach the recipients of the data how to use the material effectively. Table 15.2 presents a sample of the type of data one can secure from such a product. An article by Marcia Findley (LMU's collection development officer) describes in detail a project assessing the art history collection.[20]

The term *peer* in table 15.2 refers to the group LMU is comparing itself to; the term *evaluator* refers to LMU. The Subcollection Counts notes that in the areas denoted BL1-BL9999, the peer group of 40 libraries holds 2,821 titles with a total 18,774 copies. There are 922 unique titles (that is, only one library has a copy); of those, 672 are at LMU. In addition, LMU has 647 titles that other libraries in the peer group hold. For the Subcollections Proportions for B1-B68, LMU has 80 titles; the average peer library holds 54. LMU's collection is 48.15 percent larger than the average size for these class numbers. The Subcollection Gap Table shows that LMU does not own 131 books that 80-89 percent of the peer libraries (in this case, three libraries) hold. If LMU were to buy the 131 titles, its comparative rank would increase to 73 percent of that of the peer group. The Bibliographic Lists portion of the CD-ROM program allows LMU to generate a list of the 131 books it does not own.

Table 15.2.

	Subcollection Counts Peer Group: PEER GROUP 1 (40) LC Division: BL-BX Religion					
	Peer Group		Evaluator		Overlap	
NATC	Titles	Holdings	Unique	Titles	Titles	Holdings
BL1-BL9999	2,821	18,774	922	672	647	8,520
BM1-BM9999	1,157	6,680	324	204	189	2,242
BP1-BP9999	746	4,539	274	94	88	1,359
BQ1-BQ9999	710	3,293	284	93	89	976
BR1-BR9999	2,626	16,205	862	643	626	8,529
BS1-BS9999	4,166	23,597	1,274	946	914	10,564
BT1-BT9999	3,194	17,957	1,239	760	737	8,785
BV1-BV9999	3,341	12,412	1,447	458	444	4,314
BX1-BX0799	344	1,323	153	36	36	382
BX0800-BX4795	4,144	20,951	1,635	924	903	10,368
BX4800-BX9999	1,774	7,904	752	287	277	3,012
Totals	25,023	133,635	9,166	5,117	4,950	59,051

Table 15.2 continues on page 416.

Subcollection Proportions
Peer Group: PEER GROUP 1 (40)
LC Division: B-BJ Philosophy/Psychology

| NATC | Titles | | Comparative | | % of Subcollection |
	Evaluator	Avg Mbr	Size	Peer Group	Evaluator
B1-B68	80	54	148.15	2.23	2.09
B69-B789	386	241	160.17	9.96	10.08
B790-B5739	937	606	154.62	25.00	24.47
BC1-BC9999	60	49	122.45	2.01	1.57
BD1-BD9999	336	196	171.43	8.08	8.78
BF1-BF1000	1,500	939	159.74	38.71	39.17
BF1001-BF1400	48	37	129.73	1.54	1.25
BF1401-BF1999	38	37	102.70	1.51	0.99
BH1-BH9999	68	44	154.55	1.81	1.78
BJ1-BJ1800	372	217	171.43	8.95	9.72
BJ1801-BJ2195	4	5	80.00	0.19	0.10
Totals	3,829	2,425	157.88	100.00	100.00

Subcollection Proportions
Peer Group: CALIFORNIA CATHOLIC (3)
LC Division: D-DZ History: General & Old World

| NATC | Titles | | Comparative | | % of Subcollection |
	Evaluator	Avg Mbr	Size	Peer Group	Evaluator
D1-D0899	470	823	57.11	15.62	16.50
D0900-D2009	16	37	43.24	0.70	0.56
DA-DA9999	469	654	71.71	12.41	16.47
DAW1001-DAW	1051	0	0	0.00	0.00
DB-DB9999	31	53	58.49	1.01	1.09
DC-DC9999	133	262	50.76	4.96	4.67
DD-DD9999	152	191	79.58	3.62	5.34
DE-DE9999	20	19	105.26	0.36	0.70
DF-DF9999	140	103	135.92	1.95	4.92
DG-DG9999	137	183	74.86	3.47	4.81
DH-DH9999	4	8	50.00	0.15	0.14
DJ-DJ9999	5	0	100.00	0.09	0.18
DJK-DJK9999	7	50	14.00	0.94	0.25
DK-DK9999	130	373	34.85	7.07	4.56
DL-DL9999	9	22	40.91	0.42	0.32
DP1-DP0500	39	94	41.49	1.78	1.37
DP0501-DP0900	3	8	37.50	0.15	0.11
DQ-DQ9999	2	1	200.00	0.03	0.07
DR-DR9999	14	60	23.33	1.13	0.49
DS1-DS0040	31	69	44.93	1.30	1.09
DS0041-DS0329	278	659	42.19	12.50	9.76
DS0330-DS0500	67	211	31.75	4.00	2.35
DS0501-DS0937	368	857	42.94	16.25	12.92
DT-DT9999	294	433	67.90	8.21	10.32
DU-DU9999	28	96	29.17	1.81	0.98
DX-DX9999	1	3	33.33	0.05	0.04
Totals	2,848	5,271	54.03	100.00	100.00

Division	Holdings Range	Gap Titles In Range	Gap Titles Cumulative	Comparative Size
	Subcollection Gap Peer Group: CALIFORNIA CATHOLIC (3)			
D1-D0899	90-100%	0	0	57.09%
History: General	80-89%	131	131	73.00%
	70-79%	0	131	57.09%
Current:	60-69%	0	131	57.09%
LMU Titles 470	50-59%	300	431	93.52%
Comparative Size	40-49%	0	431	57.09%
	30-39%	0	431	57.09%
	20-29%	0	431	57.09%
	10-19%	0	431	57.09%
	1-09%	0	431	57.09%
Unique		718	1,149	144.29%
Total	0-100%	1,149	1,149	196.64%

Customer Perceptions

Another evaluation technique is worth mentioning, although it is not primarily a collection development tool. Some years ago T. Saracevic and others reported on a study of the causes of customer frustration in academic libraries.[21] Since that time, many researchers have used variations of the original methodology in a variety of institutional settings. Whatever form the project takes, it requires substantial staff effort as well as customer cooperation. This method requires a staff member or researcher to look over the customer's shoulder as she or he searches for material. The focus is on material availability and reasons for its not being available.

There are two types of searches that one studies with this method: a search for a specific item (called a known search) and a search for material on a topic (a subject search). Within each search there are six decision points, or errors:

- Bibliographic error. (Customer has incorrect citation; the correct citation is verifiable in some source and the item is correctly listed in the catalog.)

- Acquisition error. (Customer has correct citation and library does not own the title.)

- Catalog use error. (Customer has correct citation but fails to locate the call number that is in the catalog or fails to record the number properly.)

- Circulation error. (The desired item is identified but it is in circulation or being held for someone else.)

- Library malfunction error. (Library operations or policies block access to the desired item; such errors include items that are lost or missing and no replacements are on order, or the items are misshelved, at the bindery, or waiting to be reshelved.)

- Retrieval error. (Customer has correct call number or location but cannot find the properly shelved item.)

For the subject search, instead of acquisition and bibliographic errors there are:

- Matched query error. (This occurs at the start of the search when the customer fails to find a match between search topic and library subject headings or matches the topic to Library of Congress subject headings but the library has no listings under that heading.)

- Appropriate title error. (This occurs at the end of the search when the customer does not select any of the items listed under the matched subject heading or does not borrow any items after examining them.)

Clearly, this technique goes well beyond collection assessment, but it has obvious collection development implications in terms of specific titles needed, subject area weakness, and the issue of how many copies to have of a title.

A final note on statistical data. As noted in chapter 10, many electronic products provide, as part of the package or as an optional addition, report software that allows one to easily monitor who is using what when. An example is InfoTrac's "EF Library Report." LMU uses such information when making decisions about new periodical subscriptions based on the number of times customers printed abstracts from the title. LMU also uses the data to identify candidates for cancellation.

Use Methods of Collection Evaluation

Studying collection use patterns as a means of evaluating collections is increasingly popular. Two basic assumptions underlie user/use studies: (1) the adequacy of the book collection is directly related to its use by students and faculty, and (2) circulation records provide a reasonably representative picture of collection use. Such pragmatic evaluations of collections or services are distasteful to some professionals. As L. Carnovsky stated,

> In general surveys of college and university libraries, where surveyors have devoted attention to use, they have focused on rules and regulations, physical convenience of facilities, and stimulation of reading through publicity, browsing rooms, open stacks and similar matters. They have not been concerned with circulation statistics, and in fact, the statistics for college and university libraries issued by the Library Services Branch do not include them at all. This is tacit recognition of the fact that circulation is largely a function of curriculum and teaching methods,

and perhaps also of the realization that the sheer number of books a library circulates is no measure at all of its true contribution to the educational process. In spite of the fact that Wilson and Tauber advocated the maintenance of circulation records, Wilson and Swank, in their survey of Stanford University reported: "Because statistics of use are kept for only a few of the University libraries and those that are kept are not consolidated and consistently reported, it is impossible for the surveyors to present any meaningful discussion or evaluation of this significant aspect of the library program."[22]

Use data, normally circulation figures, are objective, and the legitimate differences in the objectives of the institution that the library serves do not affect the data. As with the Clapp-Jordan formula, one can tailor use studies to fit the library, rather than forcing the library into a standard mold.

Use studies serve as a useful check on one or more of the other evaluation methods. They also are helpful in deselection projects. An important factor is to have adequate amounts of data on which to base a judgment. With today's computer-based circulation systems, use data becomes relatively easy and inexpensive to gather. An example of an early study that made extensive use of circulation data is Paul Metz's *Landscape of Literatures: Use of Subject Collections in a University Library*.[23]

Certainly, there are problems in interpreting circulation data in terms of the value of a collection. Circulation data cannot reflect use generated within the library, such as reference collections and noncirculating journals. Even for circulating items, there is no way of knowing how the material was used; perhaps the volume was used to prop open a window or press flowers. Also, the value derived by a customer from a circulated item is unknown, making it difficult to accurately assess the collection's worth. Use factors are only a small part of the overall mission of research and archival libraries.

In the public library setting, circulation and use data can be useful in determining the need for multiple copies as well as subject areas of high use in which the library has limited holdings. Automated circulation systems allow one to gather such data quickly with little staff effort. The staff time goes to assessing the data and deciding what to do about the results.

Summary

There is much research to do before collection evaluation becomes an objective science. Everyone agrees that collection evaluation is a difficult task, and the results are highly subjective. Thus, the evaluator must be willing to live with what are, at best, tentative results.

Because no one evaluation method is adequate by itself, a combined approach is most effective. Most evaluation projects employ several methods to take advantage of the strengths of each technique. Karen Kruger prepared a guide for the Illinois State Library to aid in cooperative collection development activities; it also provides an effective evaluation technique.[24] D. V. Loertscher and M. L. Ho's *PSES: Computerized Collection Development for School Library Media Centers* offers a multiple approach for examining school media center collections.[25] A comprehensive plan is outlined in Blaine Hall's *Collection Assessment Manual.*[26] When I serve as a consultant on collection evaluation projects, I employ the following steps after determining the library's goals and objectives:

1. Develop an individual set of criteria for quality and value.

2. Draw a random sample from the collection and examine the use of the items (shelflist sample).

3. Collect data about titles wanted but not available (ILL requests).

4. Keep a record of titles picked up from tables and in stack areas (in-house use).

5. Keep a detailed record of interlibrary loan activities.

6. Find out how much obsolete material is in the collection (for example, science works more than 15 years old and not considered classics).

7. If checklists have some relevance to the library, check them; but also do some research concerning the usefulness of these checklists.

8. Relate findings to the library's goals and objectives.

Collection evaluation is time-consuming, but only after completing the task does the staff know the collection's strengths and weaknesses. Having this knowledge, the collection development staff can formulate a plan to build on the strengths and correct the weaknesses. This assumes that the assessment of strengths and weaknesses took place in the context of the library's goals, objectives, and community needs. After the first effort, if the process is ongoing, the work will be less time-consuming, and with each assessment the judgments will come closer to accurately assessing the collection's true value.

Notes

[1]P. Metz, *Landscape of Literatures: Use of Subject Collections in a University Library* (Chicago: American Library Association, 1983).

[2]Robert B. Downs, "Techniques of the Library Resources Survey," *Special Libraries* 23 (April 1941): 113-15.

[3]J. H. Russell, "The Library Self-Survey," *College & Research Libraries* 17 (March 1956): 127-31.

[4]George Bonn, "Evaluation of the Collection," *Library Trends* 22 (January 1974): 265-304.

[5]B. Lockett, ed., *Guide to the Evaluation of Library Collections* (Chicago: American Library Association, 1989).

[6]Association of College and Research Libraries, College Library Standards Committee, "Standards for College Libraries," *College & Research Libraries News* 47 (March 1986): 189.

[7]J. W. Pirie, comp., *Books for Junior Colleges* (Chicago: American Library Association, 1969).

[8]*Books for College Libraries,* 3d ed. (Chicago: American Library Association, 1988).

[9]*Books for Public Libraries: Nonfiction for Small Collections,* 3d ed., ed. C. Koehn (Chicago: American Library Association, 1981).

[10]Joseph Branin, David Farrell, and Mariann Tiblin, "The National Shelflist Count Project: Its History, Limitations, and Usefulness," *Library Resources & Technical Services* 29 (October 1985): 333-42.

[11]Guy Lyle, *Administration of the College Library,* 4th ed. (New York: H. W. Wilson, 1974), 399.

[12]Eli Oboler, "Accuracy of Federal Academic Library Statistics," *College & Research Libraries* 25 (September 1964): 494.

[13]R. M. McInnis, "Formula Approach to Size: An Empirical Study of Its Efficacy in Evaluating Research Libraries," *College & Research Libraries* 33 (May 1972): 191.

[14]California State Colleges, Office of the Chancellor, Division of Academic Planning, *Report on the Development of the California State Libraries: A Study of Book, Staffing and Budgeting Problems* (Los Angeles, November 1970).

[15]American Library Association, "Standards for College Libraries," *College & Research Libraries* 20 (July 1959): 277.

[16]Ibid.

[17]K. E. Beasley, "Theoretical Framework for Public Library Management Measurement," in *Research Methods in Librarianship,* edited by H. Goldhor (Urbana, IL: University of Illinois, Graduate School of Library Science, 1968).

[18]Ibid.

[19]Ibid.

[20]M. Findley, "Using the OCLC/AMIGOS Collection Analysis Compact Disk to Evaluate Art and Art History Collections," *Technical Services Quarterly* 10, no. 3 (1993): 1-15.

[21]T. Saracevic et al. "Causes and Dynamics of User Frustration in an Academic Library," *College & Research Libraries* 38 (January 1977): 7-18.

[22]L. Carnovsky, "Survey of the Use of Library Resources and Facilities," in *Library Surveys,* edited by M. F. Tauber and I. R. Stephens, 68 (New York: Columbia University Press, 1967).

[23]Metz, *Landscape of Literatures.*

[24]Karen Kruger, *Coordinated Cooperative Collection Development for Illinois Libraries* (Springfield, IL: Illinois State Library, 1982).

[25]D. V. Loertscher and M. L. Ho, *PSES: Computerized Collection Development for School Library Media Centers* (Castle Rock, CO: Hi Willow Publishing, 1986).

[26]Blaine Hall, *Collection Assessment Manual for College and University Libraries* (Phoenix, AZ: Oryx Press, 1985).

Further Reading

General

Aguilar, W. "Application of Relative Use and Interlibrary Demand in Collection Development." *Collection Management* 8 (Spring 1986): 15-24.

Bremer, T. A. "Assessing Collection Use by Surveying Users at Randomly Selected Times." *Collection Management* 13, no. 3 (1990): 57-67.

Britten, W. A. "A Use Statistic for Collection Management." *Library Acquisitions: Practice and Theory* 14, no. 2 (1990): 183-89.

Comer, C. "List-Checking As a Method for Evaluating Library Collections." *Collection Building* 3, no. 3 (1981): 26-34.

Dannelly, G. N. "National Shelflist Count: A Tool for Collection Management." *Library Acquisitions: Practice and Theory* 13, no. 3 (1989): 241-50.

Downs, R. B. "Technique of the Library Resources Survey." *Special Libraries* 32 (April 1941): 113-15.

Evans, G. E. "Review of Criteria Used to Measure Library Effectiveness." In *Reader in Library Management,* edited by R. Shimmer. London: Clive Bingley, 1976.

Francq, C. "Bottoming Out the Bottomless Pit with the Journal Usage/Cost Relational Index." *Technical Services Quarterly* 11, no. 4 (1994): 13-26.

Gabriel, H. R. "Online Collection Evaluation." *Collection Building* 8, no. 2 (1986): 20-24.

Lancaster, F. W. *If You Want to Evaluate Your Library.* Champaign, IL: University of Illinois, Graduate School of Library and Information Science, 1988.

Lockett, B., ed. *Guide to the Evaluation of Library Collections.* Chicago: American Library Association, 1989.

Miller, A. H. "Do the Books We Buy Get Used?" *Collection Management* 12, nos. 1/2 (1990): 15-20.

Mosher, P. H. "Quality and Library Collections: New Directions in Research and Practice in Collection Evaluation." *Advances in Librarianship* 13 (1984): 65-76.

Osburn, C. B. "Collection Evaluation and Acquisitions Budgets: A Kaleidoscope in the Making." In *Collection Assessment and Acquisitions Budgets,* edited by S. H. Lee, 3-11. New York: Haworth Press, 1992.

Paskoff, B. M., and A. H. Perrault. "A Tool for Comparative Collection Analysis." *Library Resources & Technical Services* 34 (April 1990): 199-215.

Powell, R. R. *Relationship of Library User Studies to Performance Measures: A Review of the Literature.* Champaign, IL: University of Illinois, Graduate School of Library and Information Science, 1988.

Rao, S. N. "Meeting Modern Demands of Collection Evaluation." *Collection Building* 13, no. 1 (1992): 33-36.

Rossi, P. H., and H. E. Freeman. *Evaluation: A Systematic Approach.* Beverly Hills, CA: Sage Publications, 1985.

Sandler, M. "Quantitative Approaches to Qualitative Collection Assessment." *Collection Building* 8, no. 4 (1987): 12-17.

Steffy, R. J., and N. Meyer. "Evaluating User Success and Satisfaction with CD-ROM." *Laserdisk Professional* 2 (September 1989): 35-45.

Vellucci, S. L. "OCLC/AMIGOS Collection Analysis CD: Broadening the Scope of Use." *OCLC Systems and Services* 9, no. 2 (1993): 49-53.

Wiemers, E., et al. "Collection Evaluation: A Practical Guide to the Literature." *Library Acquisitions: Practice and Theory* 8, no. 1 (1984): 65-76.

Academic

Barstow, S. "Quickly Selecting Serials for Cancellation." *Technical Services Quarterly* 10, no. 4 (1993): 29-40.

Broadus, R. N. "Use Studies of Library Collections." *Library Resources & Technical Services* 24 (Fall 1980): 317-24.

Gaylor, R. H. "Collection Analysis at a Junior College Library." *OCLC Systems and Services* 10, no. 1 (1994): 9-12.

Harloe, B. "Achieving Client-Centered Collection Development." *College & Research Libraries* 50 (May 1989): 344-53.

Hyman, F. B. "Collection Evaluation in the Research Library." *Collection Building* 9, nos. 3/4 (1989): 33-37.

Kountz, J. "What's in a Library?" *Library Hi Tech News* 9, no. 2 (1991): 31-61.

Kreyche, M. "BCL3 and Notis: An Automated Collection Analysis Project." *Library Acquisitions: Practice and Theory* 13, no. 4 (1989): 323-28.

Lucas, T. A. "Verifying the Conspectus: Problems and Progress." *College & Research Libraries News* 46 (March 1990): 199-201.

Mosher, P. H. "Collection Evaluation in Research Libraries." *Library Resources & Technical Services* 23 (Winter 1979): 16-32.

Porter, M. A., and F. W. Lancaster. "Evaluation of a Scholarly Collection in a Specific Subject Area by Bibliographic Checking." *Libri* 38, no. 2 (1988): 131-37.

Siverson, S. E. "Fine-Tuning the Dull Roar of Conspectors." In *Collection Assessment*, edited by R. J. Wood and K. Strauch, 45-64. New York: Haworth Press, 1992.

Stelk, R. E., and F. W. Lancaster. "Use of Textbooks in Evaluating the Collection of an Undergraduate Library." *Library Acquisitions: Practice and Theory* 14, no. 2 (1990): 191-93.

Stone, E. O. "Measuring the College Book Collection." *Library Journal* 66 (June 1941): 941-43.

Walch, D. B. "1986 College Library Standards: Applications and Utilization." *College & Research Libraries* 54 (May 1993): 217-26.

Public

Beasley, K. E. "Theoretical Framework for Public Library Measurement." In *Research Methods in Librarianship,* edited by H. Goldhor. Urbana, IL: University of Illinois, Graduate School of Library Science, 1968.

Goldhor, H. "Analysis of an Inductive Method of Evaluating the Book Collection of a Public Library." *Libri* 23, no. 1 (1973): 6-17.

————. "A Report on an Application of the Inductive Method of Evaluation of Public Library Books." *Libri* 31 (August 1981): 121-29.

Griffen, M. A. "Collection Development to Information Access." *RQ* 24 (Spring 1985): 285-89.

Koehn, C., ed. *Books for Public Libraries.* 3d ed. Chicago: American Library Association, 1981.

Kruger, K. *Coordinated Cooperative Collection Development for Illinois Libraries.* Springfield, IL: Illinois State Library, 1982.

Magrill, R. M. "Evaluation by Library Type." *Library Trends* 22 (Winter 1985): 267-91.

Moore, C. M. "Taking the Measure: Applying Reference Outputs to Collection Development." *Public Libraries* 25 (Fall 1986): 108-11.

Newhouse, J. P., and A. J. Alexander. *An Economic Analysis of Public Library Services.* Lexington, MA: Lexington Books, 1972.

Palmour, V. E., et al. *A Planning Process for Public Libraries.* Chicago: American Library Association, 1980.

Stielow, F. J., and H. R. Tibbo. "Collection Analysis in Modern Librarianship: A Stratified, Multidimensional Model." *Collection Management* 11, nos. 3/4 (1989): 73-91.

Wiemers, G. *Materials Availability in Small Libraries.* Occasional Papers, 149. Urbana, IL: University of Illinois, Graduate School of Library and Information Science, 1981.

Zweizig, D. "So Go Figure It: Measuring Library Effectiveness." *Public Libraries* 26 (Spring 1987): 21-24.

Zweizig, D., and B. Dervin. "Public Library Use, Users, Uses." In *Advances in Librarianship,* edited by M. J. Voigt and M. H. Harris, 231-55. New York: Academic Press, 1977.

School

Aaron, S. L. "Current Research." *School Library Media Quarterly* 10 (Winter 1982): 185-89.

Bertland, L. H. "Collection Analysis As a Tool for Collection Development." *School Library Media Quarterly* 19 (Winter 1991): 90-97.

Daniel, E. H. "Evaluation of School Library Media Centers." *Bookmark* 38 (Winter 1980): 287-91.

Evaluating the School Library Media Program. Chicago: American Association of School Librarians, 1980.

Garland, K. "Circulation Sampling As a Technique for Library Media Program Management." *School Library Media Quarterly* 20 (Winter 1992): 73-78.

Latrobe, K. H. "Evaluating Library Media Programs in Terms of 'Information Power,'" *School Library Media Quarterly* 21 (Fall 1992): 37-45.

Loertscher, D. V., and M. L. Ho. *PSES: Computerized Collection Development for School Library Media Centers.* Castle Rock, CO: Hi Willow Publishing, 1986.

"Performance Measures for School Librarians." In *Advances in Librarianship,* edited by M. J. Voigt and M. H. Harris, 1-51. New York: Academic Press, 1976.

Roy, L. "Collection Evaluation As Research." *Journal of Youth Services* 5 (Spring 1992): 297-300.

Thomason, N. W. "Evaluating a School Media Center Book Collection." *Catholic Library World* 53 (Spring 1981): 87-88.

Special

Berger, M., and J. Devine. "Serial Evaluation: An Innovative Approach." *Special Libraries* 81 (Summer 1990): 183-88.

Carpenter, K. H. "Evaluating Library Resources for Accreditation." *Bulletin of the Medical Library Association* 80 (April 1992): 131-39.

Gottlieb, J., ed. *Collection Assessment in Music Libraries.* New York: Music Library Association, 1994.

McClure, C. R., and B. Reifsnyder. "Performance Measures for Corporate Information Centers." *Special Libraries* 75 (July 1984): 193-204.

Norton, R., and D. Gautschi. "User Survey of an International Library: Expectations and Evaluations." *Aslib Proceedings* 37 (April 1985): 195-206.

O'Connor, D. O., and E. R. Dyer. "Evaluation of Corporate Reference Collections." *Reference Librarian* 29 (1990): 21-31.

Rashid, H. F. "Book Availability As a Performance Measure of a Library: An Analysis of the Effectiveness of a Health Science Library." *Journal of the American Society for Information Science* 41, no. 7 (1990): 501-7.

Rice, B. A. "Science Periodicals Use Study." *Serials Librarian* 4 (Fall 1979): 35-47.

Snow, M. "Theatre Arts Collection Assessment." *Collection Management* 12, nos. 3/4 (1990): 69-81.

Strain, P. M. "Evaluation of a Special Library." *Special Libraries* 73 (July 1982): 165-72.

Wender, R. W. "Counting Journal Title Usage in Health Sciences." *Special Libraries* 70 (May/June 1979): 219-26.

Zachert, M. J. K. "Qualitative Evaluation of Law School Library Services." *Law Library Journal* 81 (Spring 1989): 269-76.

16
Cooperative Collection Development and Resource Sharing

Some years ago, Richard Dougherty wrote an article titled "Library Cooperation: A Case of Hanging Together or Hanging Separately."[1] The title reflects a widely held view about library cooperation. Several hundred later articles call for some form of cooperative or coordinated collection building or resource sharing. Regional and local groups with various types of resource sharing arrangements exist, but there has been no progress in establishing a coordinated national program that will assure one copy of almost any research item will be available somewhere in the United States. Technology helps us know who has what, but other tools, such as the RLG conspectus, help librarians know who thinks they have strong collections in various subject fields.

Webster's Third New International Dictionary defines *cooperative* in part as "given to or marked by working together or by joint effort toward a common end"; it defines *coordinate* as "to bring into a common action, movement, or condition; regulate and combine in harmonious action."[2] Cooperative collection development programs are likely to grow, but the future of coordinated collection development appears dim.

A few years ago, John Berry wrote an editorial about how the then-current tight funding situation was causing cooperative ventures to cease. Unfortunately, the situation has changed little since Berry wrote:

> The pressure is reported by public, academic, and school librarians from across the United States. One state's fine multitype systems are near collapse. Cooperative county systems in another have been reduced to bickering disarray from years of no-growth funding. Consortia members are scrapping over slices of a shrinking pie. New, harsh limitations on interlibrary loan crop up. Stiff nonresident fees and interlibrary charges proliferate. Old battles between small and large libraries in shared jurisdictions flare anew. State agency and cooperative system operating budgets are openly attacked by constituent librarians. . . . Librarians, torn between professional commitment to library cooperation and local pressure to provide service with deeply diminished resources, have to make the choice to cut service to outsiders.[3]

The Nature of Cooperative Systems

Library cooperation is like the weather—we all talk about it, but none of us can control it. As with weather modification, some individuals work on the problem with little success. In library cooperation, a primary reason efforts fail is that we do not really understand what we are trying to accomplish. Figure 16.1 presents a general overview of the possible combinations of cooperative collection development.

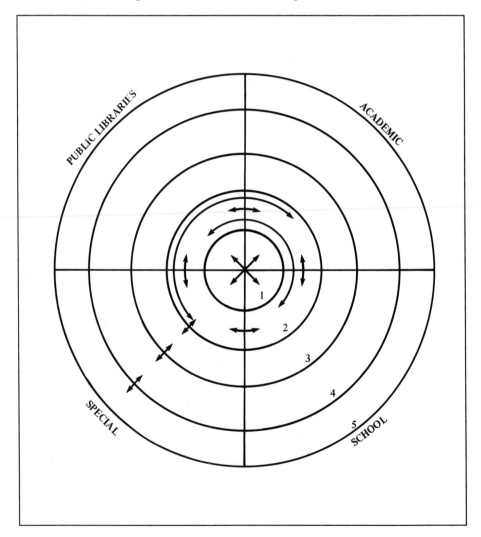

Fig. 16.1. Ideal of interlibrary cooperation (networking). Adapted from Mary Dugan, "Library Network Analysis and Planning," *Journal of Library Automation* 2, no. 9: 157-75.

This figure represents the hope we all have of reaching the librarian's millennium of total cooperation among libraries and access to all of the world's information resources. (See discussion of UNESCO's Universal Availability of Publications [UAP] project on page 455.)

This ideal is a long way off, even at the local level. Many classes of patrons still get various levels of service in various libraries in the same community. Even personality differences among chief librarians can create minor but real barriers to effective cooperation at any level. As one moves farther afield, it is harder to work out major cooperative programs. No longer do only library and patron needs decide the issue of whether to cooperate or not. Legal, political, and economic issues tend to dominate the decision-making process.

Models of Cooperative Activity

Michael Sinclair, in "A Typology of Library Cooperatives," proposed four theoretical models of cooperative activity (see fig. 16.2 on page 430).[4] Although the concepts are Sinclair's, the following interpretation is mine. (One should read Sinclair's article in its entirety to gain a full understanding of his model.)

Type A is a bilateral *exchange model,* in which two participating libraries exchange materials. In practice, libraries calculate the exchange rate according to some agreed-upon value (for example, one for one, two for one); frequently, there is an annual review of the actual results as part of the formal exchange agreement. All of Loyola Marymount University's reciprocal borrowing agreements contain the annual review clause. Resource sharing, reciprocal borrowing, and interlibrary loans employ the exchange model concept.

Type B, a multilateral development of Type A, is the *pooling model.* In this model, more than two libraries contribute to and draw from a common pool of materials. Many of the early cooperative library systems were of this type; in a sense, OCLC started as a pool.

In Type C, the *dual service model,* two or more participating libraries take advantage of the facilities of one of the participants to produce a common output—for instance, a shared online public access catalog (OPAC). The term *dual service* distinguishes this model from the next and emphasizes the fact that *all* participants, including the facilitator, contribute to the common output. Many of the early library systems evolved into this type; frequently, they refer to the facilitator as the flagship library. An example of this type of model is the Research Library Information Network (RLIN).

In type D, the *service center model,* a number of libraries employ the services of a facilitating organization to input and process materials for the individual libraries, rather than for common output. Today's bibliographic utilities, such as OCLC and the Western Library Network (WLN), are of this type.

These four types are adequate to cover all existing systems; however, new systems under consideration may not fit this classification system.

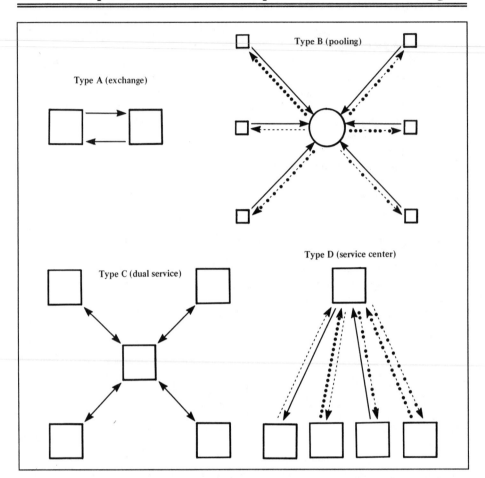

Fig. 16.2. Models of library cooperative activities. A graphic interpretation of M. P. Sinclair, "A Typology of Library Cooperatives," *Special Libraries* 64, no. 4: 181-86.

The Something for Nothing Syndrome

Library cooperative systems operate on a series of assumptions that one should examine with considerable care. Perhaps the most important assumption, although the one least often stated, is that all of the participants in the system are or will be equally efficient in their operations involving the cooperative activities. No one assumes that every member will achieve the same benefits or contribute materials that are equally valuable. Rather, the assumption is each library is somewhat unusual, if not unique (that is, each library has different clientele, collections, and service programs). Why assume that each is equally efficient? It is clear that one cannot legitimately make such an assumption. However, if libraries do not make that assumption, it is difficult to believe that every library will gain something, or, at least, receive a value equal to its contribution. In a sense, librarians assume that each library will get something for nothing by joining a cooperative system. Each library hopes that it will be the one to receive more than it puts into the system. During periods of low funding from outside sources, libraries have a tendency not to cooperate. According to Boyd Rayward, "Networks (cooperatives) are a phenomenon of relative affluence. They cannot be created unless each member at the local level has sufficient resources of time, staff, materials, and basic equipment and supplies to participate."[5]

If a library enters into a cooperative program with the something for nothing goal in mind, there is little hope of success. There are always substantial costs, which any accountant could determine. In addition, there are many costs of cooperation that no cost accounting system can identify, much less control. Two of the most important uncontrolled costs, from a collection development point of view, are ease of access and speed of delivery. Any cooperative system will place a higher cost on these two factors, in comparison to local ownership. That is, it will always take as long, if not longer, to gain access to a desired item, and it will entail more work for both the patron and the library. Libraries seldom consider these costs, because it is difficult (if not impossible) to translate them into monetary units. Often, then, this difficulty means ignoring costs and assuming that benefits will be high.

Librarians seldom consider patron costs; the assumption is that cooperation will result in only increased benefits for the users. Cooperative planners sometimes factor in the extra work of filling out one or more forms or answering extra questions for the library, but almost never do so for the customer. Too often, the planners think of these as small, insignificant increases for an individual to absorb. However, while a single increase may be small, in time or in aggregate, such increases become significant. Nevertheless, a true cooperative collection development program can provide customers with a much broader range of materials than would be possible for one library working in isolation.

Two examples of these problems will illustrate the point. First, in the United States, the traditional postal service-based interlibrary loan (ILL) system is becoming slower and more costly to operate. The early ILL assumption was that everyone would gain as a result of the free exchange of resources. An increased workload was predicted for some of the libraries with larger collections, but they would be doing some borrowing, and the added volume of work would not be too great to handle. Today, the workload in larger institutions is tremendous—so great that major lenders now charge for their services. Today, librarians discuss ways to develop agreements to allow for free ILL services to one another. Recently, the library directors at U.S. Jesuit colleges and universities completed such an agreement after three years of discussion. In essence, the libraries are returning to the original concept of interlibrary loans. It will be interesting to see how long the agreement remains in effect, because the stumbling block to reaching an agreement was concern about the workload. At research libraries, such as Harvard's Tozzer Library, the ILL lending-to-borrowing ratio is high (Tozzer's is 34 to 1, with one staff member devoting 30 percent of the work week to filling incoming ILL requests). The British National Lending Division arose as a direct result of the same problem;

unfortunately, such a system is much harder to establish in the United States. It is important to note that it is not just the large research libraries that are net lenders; LMU lends two items for every one borrowed, and the library has one full-time person handling ILL activities.

The second example is from Denmark. Copenhagen's public library established a system for reciprocal borrowing rights with suburban public libraries. A high percentage of the persons living in the suburbs work in the central city. Danes are avid readers, and, like anyone else, prefer to use a convenient rather than inconvenient service. So, it was not surprising to find them using the most convenient public library for their general library needs. Apparently, for a great many suburbanites, the most convenient location is the Copenhagen public library, with its branches near bus and train stops, and not their local library. The cost for providing this free service rose so much that several politicians suggested either dropping the arrangement or charging a nonresident fee. Certainly, the librarians did not like the idea of charging a fee. We see similar problems in the United States with reciprocal borrowing agreements and a growing trend to impose substantial fees on nonresident borrowers. The original planning projections assumed it would be possible to expand service without increasing costs (something for nothing). That assumption has been proven false.

What Can Be Gained Through Cooperation

One can identify six general benefits that could arise from any library cooperative effort. First is the potential for improving access—improving in the sense of making available a greater range of materials or better depth in a subject area. This seldom means more copies of a particular title, at least, not significantly more. It rarely results in faster service—typically, it takes longer to secure an item. The delay in securing an item is offset by the increase in the number of titles available in a system.

A second benefit is that it may be possible to stretch limited resources. One danger in suggesting that cooperation may benefit the public or the professional staff is that the idea of getting something for nothing becomes ingrained. Too often, people view cooperation as a money-saving device. In truth, however, cooperation does not save money for a library. If two or more libraries combine their efforts, they will not spend less money; an effective cooperative program simply divides the work and shares the results.

Sharing work results leads to some benefits, such as greater staff specialization. A person can concentrate on one or two activities rather than on five or six. The resulting specialization should produce better overall performance. Naturally, better performance should lead to better service, and thus, greater customer satisfaction. Reducing unnecessary duplication is a second result of sharing work. The reduction may be in work performed or materials purchased, but planners should study just how much duplication they can eliminate before developing a formal cooperative agreement. Vague discussions about reducing duplication, without an in-depth study of the situation, usually lead to high expectations and, all too often, dashed hopes. Nevertheless, reduced duplication is a real potential benefit.

By actively advertising its presence and services, a cooperative program may reduce the number of places a customer will need to go for service. However, in most systems, this benefit is more theoretical than real. In the past, a lack of union lists generally negated this potential benefit. Today, networked OPACs provide a real benefit in terms of better directing clients to the correct source of information.

A final benefit, one not frequently discussed, is an improvement in the working relationships among cooperating libraries. This is particularly true in a multitype system. Persons can gain a better perspective about others' problems as a result of working together on mutual problems. Also, learning about the special problems that another type of library encounters helps one to know what its staff can or cannot do. Some systems have found this to be so important that they have set up exchange internships for staff members, both professional and nonprofessional.

More specific examples of what might result from a cooperative arrangement include better or additional public services. For example, it may be possible, by shifting workloads, to extend the hours of reference service or to increase the number of children's programs. Another possibility is to expand the service area. Perhaps the combined resources of the system will allow it to provide service to persons or areas that no one library could reach.

As for many other areas of collection development, ALA's Resources and Technical Services Division has a set of guidelines for cooperative collection development. Paul H. Mosher and Marcia Pankake discuss these guidelines in "A Guide to Coordinated and Cooperative Collection Development."[6] The guidelines provide details about benefits, problems, and recommendations that fit easily into this chapter's more general concepts.

In terms of collection development, cooperative programs force libraries to have better knowledge of their collections. In a cooperative program, a library must know both what it has and what the other member libraries have. The RLG conspectus (discussed in chapter 3) and ARL's National Collection Inventory Project (NCIP), which uses the conspectus model, attempt to identify who has what and in what strength. Although developed for academic library use, the conspectus concept is now in use in all types of libraries. When most libraries complete their conspectus work, they should have the information they need to begin to develop meaningful cooperative collection development programs. However, this is still some distance in the future, and local needs will dominate in times of limited funding. If there is to be a division of collection responsibility by subject area, each library must have an in-depth knowledge of its own collection before entering into a meaningful cooperative agreement. Even if there is no final agreement, the process of examining the collection will be of great value. Also, the opportunity to share problems and solutions should improve each participant's capabilities.

Figure 16.3, on page 434, is an example of how a cooperative program using the conspectus approach might draw together data from a variety of libraries. How a library uses and interprets the data is another matter, but using some form of standardized subject list to identify collection strength is a first step toward possible cooperative or coordinated collection development.

SUBJECT AREA	SPECIFIC SUBJECT	COLLECTION SIZE BOOKS	COLLECTION SIZE OTHER	BUDGET	CIRCULATE YES	CIRCULATE NO	MACHINE READABLE YES	MACHINE READABLE NO	CATALOGED YES	CATALOGED NO	WILL PARTICIPATE YES	WILL PARTICIPATE NO	LIBRARY
Art	Fiber arts	700		n/a	x		x		x		x		JeffCo-Arvada
	Drawing and decorative	1040		Gen. b.	x		x		x		x		Arapahoe Reg.
	Geo. E. Burr		etching etc.	n/a		x		x		x			Denver Public
	Blunt Art Print		1250 prints	n/a				x		x	x		Canon City Pub.
	Fore-edge Pnt	55		Gen. b.		x	x		x		x		Univ. Col. -B
Asian Studies	Model coll.	275 misc.		LSCA		x	x		x		x		JeffCo-Villa
Bibles	Foreign lang.	246		Gen. b.		x							Univ. Col. -B
Blind/Deaf	Large print	430		Gen. b.	x			x	x		x		Canon City Pub.
	Hearing impaired	40		Gen. b.	x		x		x		x		Arapahoe Reg.
	Large print	1000		n/a	x		x		x		x		JeffCo-Arvada
	n/a	700		Endowed	x			x	x			x	Colo. School Deaf & Blind
Botanical	n/a	10760		Sales, etc.	x			x	x		x		Denver Bot. Garden
Business	n/a	4000		Gen. b.	x		x		x		x		JeffCo-Villa
	n/a - tax	456		Gen. b.	x		x		x		x		Weld Co.
	& career info	350		Gen. b.	x		x		x		x		Englewood

Fig. 16.3. Colorado State Library subject strength survey.

In addition, cooperative systems may free time for such things as more in-service training, more and better public relations, or more planning. All of these activities require much time to be effective, but, depending on the nature of the cooperative, a considerable amount of time may become available for such activities. Again, the something for nothing syndrome comes out. Cooperative systems do not mean someone else is doing one's work for free, because, if that were the case, the system would eventually fail. Cooperative systems do mean a librarian will do something for other member libraries and librarians at other member libraries will do things for him or her.

A cooperative program, properly organized, allows for more specialization, more service, and more time to do things effectively. Remember, there are trade-offs. One gets nothing for nothing! Good service costs time and money, and there are no magic formulas for gaining extra time or services. What is necessary is hard work to identify areas in which each potential member has something to gain and something to contribute. In the long run, the give and take must be equitable for all members of a system or the system will fail.

Barriers to Cooperation

The second edition of this book discussed eight barriers to cooperation. This edition groups the barriers in six broad categories: 1) institutional, 2) legal, political, and administrative, 3) technological, 4) physical, 5) people, and 6) knowledge-based issues. This section reviews the changes that have or have not taken place in cooperative collection development in the past eight years. In 1992 Richard Hacken suggested perhaps the changes are not as great as one might expect. He was describing the results of a study of the use of the conspectus among RLG libraries:

> Although small efforts have been made in light of the Conoco Study findings, acquisitions in the vast majority of institutions, both inside and outside RLG, proceed in the traditional manner. When requests for interlibrary loan materials are made, it is overwhelmingly on the basis of "somebody somewhere must have this title," rather than from foreknowledge of pre-planned cooperative or collaborative collecting.[7]

Many of the barriers are minor, from a theoretical point of view; however, there are real, practical problems. Knowing what issues or barriers are likely to arise during attempts to create a cooperative venture helps one anticipate areas of potential difficulty and perhaps forestall problems. Another benefit of knowing what may come up is peace of mind—one will not become too disillusioned with the slow progress, surprised by opposition , or upset with individuals trying to formulate a working agreement that represents both local and group needs.

Institutional Issues

A traditional goal for libraries, especially academic libraries, has been to be locally self-sufficient. While that remains a goal, librarians know it is impossible to achieve. Bendik Rugaas, the national librarian of Norway, presented a paper titled, "The End of All and Forever"[8] at a meeting of national librarians. In the paper, Rugaas outlined the reasons why no national library can hope to collect and preserve all the information materials created within its country's boundaries. All the participating librarians agreed it was an impossible task. Evidence that national libraries are coming to act on their knowledge appeared in the front page article of the September 19, 1994, *Library Hotline*. The article stated that the British Library is giving up collecting every edition of every book, magazine, and journal printed in Great Britain.) If the giants of the library world are giving up local self-sufficiency, what can other libraries of more modest means hope to accomplish? Librarians know there always will be items a client will someday need but the library does not have the funds to buy. As a result, librarians look to interlibrary loan or some form of document delivery to fill most of the gaps. Customers never have been fond of ILL, and they are a constant source of pressure on the library to be self-sufficient.

Customer pressure is particularly strong when there is a proposal to share collection development responsibilities among libraries. A frequent customer reaction to such a proposal is, "What will happen to my area of interest? I do not want the library to stop buying my materials. I cannot afford to wait months for ILL!" If the library has developed the collection carefully in terms of service community needs, what can be given up? How does one respond to customer inquiries about the impact of the proposed cooperative? How can a library be an effective member without giving up some areas? Almost always, the library's level of funding will be insufficient to buy as much as was purchased before, while taking on new cooperative obligations. Therefore, some areas will have to be given up or sharply reduced.

Tom Ballard's provocative article, "Public Library Networking: Neat, Plausible, Wrong," raises a number of points regarding patrons.[9] He makes a strong case, with data supporting his arguments, that, for public libraries and others in a multitype library system, the idea of cooperative collection development with an eye toward resource sharing (ILL, generally) is fine, but it does not work. Drawing on data from a number of systems across the United States, he shows that interlibrary lending accounts for very little of the total circulation, almost always representing less than 2 percent of the total. He cites studies that indicate people tend to select from what is available at the time they come in, even if it is a second or third choice, rather than seek the desired material. (This is another clear example of the law of least effort [see chapter 2].)

Although Ballard emphasizes public libraries and provides examples relating to them, his statements hold some truth for anyone who works in a school media center or an academic library serving undergraduates. Undoubtedly, part of the explanation is that many people are not aware of the possibility of getting needed items somewhere else, so more active marketing by the library may be necessary. A more important factor is that people tend to wait until the last minute to seek out needed information and cannot wait even a few days to get the precise information. Perhaps a third factor is that most people do not really need or want the material enough to pay the price we place on its delivery. If it is immediately available, fine; if not, forget it. All these make a strong case for local self-sufficiency.

In academic institutions, even small ones, there are two primary collecting goals: curriculum and research support. At smaller institutions, though faculty seldom face pressure to engage in research, peers and administrators tend to hold greater regard for those faculty who do engage in research. Usually, there is the expectation that the library will provide some support for scholarly activities beyond the classroom. Today, for many schools, that support is more moral than substantive. Occasionally, the motivated faculty member will slip through purchase requests for items that are more research than instructional in character. This is especially true when the teaching departments control the bulk of the materials budget. They do this because other means of access—ILL, document delivery, or reciprocal borrowing—are too slow for them. One reason ILL is so slow is that most libraries do not recall items in circulation to fill an ILL request, even if they might do so if a local customer needs the item. What is usually easily available through ILL and other resource sharing arrangements is low-use material.

For ARL libraries, low-use material forms a large percentage of the collection. It also consumes a significant portion of the materials budget. For most other libraries, the vast majority of the collection is reasonably high-use material, at least compared to research library collections and use patterns. As the funding gets tighter, the amount of potentially useful as opposed to known to be useful material any library can buy becomes smaller and smaller. Tight budgets also mean there is less money to offer for pooling or sharing collecting categories; low-use items have been the staple of shared collecting projects. Hacken indicated that interest in considering, much less implementing, shared collection building was for items thought to be of potential research interest as opposed to demonstrated interest.[10] Although his comments focused on ARL libraries, the idea of sharing high-demand items is not a common part of any resource sharing proposal.

Some accrediting agencies, for example, the Western Association of Schools and Colleges (WASC), include statements in their standards regarding ownership of the instructional collection. The following is from the WASC *Handbook of Accreditation*:

> 6.B.1 Basic collections *held* by the institution are sufficient in quality and quantity to meet *substantially all* of the needs of educational programs on and off campus.

and

> 6.B.2 Interlibrary loan or contractual use arrangements may be used to *supplement* basic holdings *but are not* to be used as the main source of learning resources."[11]

Though such statements do not preclude cooperative collection building, they certainly add another layer of complexity to an already complex issue.

Twenty years ago, the pressure was strong among all the customers to maintain self-sufficiency. Today, many are willing to let electronic services provide some access, if that access is more convenient than going to the library. On the other hand, funding officials pressure their libraries to find ways to cooperate and reduce the costs of collection building. Unfortunately, as noted in John Berry's editorial (see page 427), given current economic conditions, what libraries and customers mean by local self-sufficiency is more and more restricted in scope. Libraries are lucky to meet all the local high-demand needs, much less acquire material for low-demand areas. That, in turn, reduces the pool of low-use material that might be fodder for a cooperative program. In such circumstances, it is not surprising to find libraries having a difficult time identifying areas they can forego having locally available.

In a pre-agreement stage, two institutions may have overlapping low-use material and overlapping interests in some areas in which neither is currently collecting. A post-agreement situation may show how the two institutions might share their collecting activities in such a manner that not only do they cover their current low-use areas, but expand slightly into new areas. That is the theory, which makes it seem simple, logical, and reasonable to engage in such projects; in practice, it is not at all simple.

Another institutional issue is size and status. They are less important in cooperative collection building than in selection. They were more a factor in the past than they are today; however, they do arise. Today, most librarians think they are doing well if the library receives enough funding to maintain last year's buying. Librarians seldom need to concern themselves with worries about gaining enough size to surpass another library they consider comparable but slightly ahead in terms of collection size. Where status, size, and cooperative collection building cross is that not all subject areas grow at the same rate. If a library gives up an area of moderate growth for one that is slow growing, there may be a decline in the overall collection growth. In addition to the growth rate within a subject area, one must consider the cost of materials. Many science and technology items cost 25 to 50 percent more than social sciences and humanities items, so a library can acquire fewer titles for the same amount of money, which, obviously, affects the growth rate. For some institutions, this can be a problem, because for many individuals, bigger is better, which also means higher status. That may then make it difficult, if not impossible, to find an agreeable breakdown of collecting responsibilities. Realistically, today status and size are minor issues for groups attempting to develop an agreement for a cooperative or coordinated collection building program.

Institutional history and past and current practices also affect efforts to develop a cooperative venture. Examples of historical and traditional barriers that may arise are: institutional competition, special access rules (who may use the service), funding problems, library operating practices, and inability to satisfy local needs. The last problem is and always will be there. No matter how much money is available to develop local collections, some imaginative customer or staff member will think of a new collecting area that will use up all available funding. A variation of both Maslow's needs hierarchy and one of Parkinson's laws is that organizations, like people, always have wants slightly in excess of their ability to satisfy those wants. If local need combines with the desire for local self-sufficiency, librarians will never be able to agree to any cooperative effort.

One obvious historical library practice is the library's classification system. Early in any effort toward developing a cooperative collection building program, the planners must face the task of determining who has how much of what. A common way of doing that is to use existing, or undertake developing, conspectus data (see chapters 3, 14, and 15) for the libraries. Anyone who has done a conspectus project knows the time and effort it takes. The commitment increases when the libraries use different classification systems. The RLG conspectus is built on the LC system, with conversion tables for DDC. Based upon personal experience of doing a conspectus at Tozzer Library, which used its own classification system at the time, I know the problems of converting shelf list data from one classification scheme to another. For many libraries, in today's tight budget and staffing environment, the cost of converting the data is too high.

Another library practice or regulation is who has access to the collection. Many private institutions employ restricted access to help control operating costs. Outsiders, when they are allowed to use the library, are charged a fee. Charging the outside customer was started by the "privates" (that is, privately held institutions). In many cases, the private library must include an expected revenue from outsider use in its budget request; some libraries must make up any shortfall from operating funds. This tends to make the library firm about enforcing fees and reluctant to give up a source of income for an unknown benefit from a cooperative project. Today, larger public libraries are following suit with often substantial use fees. In 1992, the University of California (UC) campus libraries started charging non-UC and non-state college and university system students a minimum of $100 a year for a borrowing card; the fee goes up to $500 for a card that provides the full range of use privileges (borrowing more than five books at a time and ability to recall or place holds on a desired item). Even without fees, there will be questions about loan periods, who can borrow what, and fines, all of which probably vary with each potential participant.

The fee issue brings up the issue of competition for funding and, secondarily, for customers. Traditional practice was that public institutions received their funding from taxes and government grants. Private institutional fund-raising turf was individuals, foundations, government granting agencies, and private business. Today that division no longer exists. Public institutions are very active raising funds from what were primary sources for the privates. One sees this trend most clearly in higher education; however, it is occurring in all areas. The *Chronicle of Higher Education* from time to time publishes lists of the top fund-raising higher education institutions. Fifteen years ago, it would have been unusual to see a public institution appearing on the list, much less in the first position. Over the past six years, more often than not, large public institutions occupy most of the top 10 positions. As the publics become increasingly dependent on such funding, it becomes difficult for the smaller privates to get a hearing, much less funding. Most cooperatives require some start-up capital, and foundations and government granting agencies are the most likely source of support, if one can get one's foot in the door.

The issue of never being able to completely satisfy local needs with local resources is also an institutional competition and funding problem. Often, at the local level, public, school, and community college libraries compete for the same local tax money. Each type of library may have a certain legal minimum due it, but beyond the minimum, the situation is very competitive. In some manner, though, the community will establish a maximum total amount that it is willing to devote to library services. If the allocation process does not use a formula or weighting system, the politics of the budgetary process will determine the final allocation; that is, the best library politician will get the largest share. Furthermore, each type of library will count as customers a large number of persons who also use other types of libraries. While the count of users is correct, the duplication in counting distorts the actual number in the service population. Collections, in fact, reflect the multiple activities and interests of customers. Educational libraries have recreational materials and recreational (public) libraries have educational materials. The competition in trying to meet the needs of the same customer causes a sizable duplication of materials in some cases. In turn, that can result in significant funding problems. Attempts to extract additional monies for cooperative activities from local funding authorities are not likely to be successful unless the funding authorities see the request as a device for stabilizing, if not reducing, total local funding.

Returning to issues related to library practice, incompatibility of procedures is a fact that all cooperatives must address at some point. "We have *always* used *this* procedure, and it works" is a statement heard over and over again in cooperative planning meetings. Some of these compatibility problems are reasonably easy to overcome if everyone is really interested in forming a system. Not so easy to resolve are certain other operational problems, such as differences in classification systems used.

Finally, there are problems of rules and regulations to be overcome—usually a matter of who may use a certain type of library. As long as the cooperative membership consists of one type of library, there are few problems of this kind. However, when several different types of libraries join a system, there may be significant problems. Archival and special collection libraries may have a number of restrictions on who may use the material, just as do some professional libraries (for example, law and medicine). Normally, this is not a major barrier, although it is time-consuming to make certain that the agreement takes into account all the rules and regulations.

Legal, Political, and Administrative Barriers

Legal, political, and administrative barriers each can be complex and unique. One can imagine some of the legal and political barriers that may arise by referring to figure 16.1 (page 428).

Each circle in the figure represents a different level of government and political concern. To develop a library system that combines all four major types with the least amount of waste, in the sense of not duplicating resources and services unnecessarily, planners must cross several jurisdictional lines. Crossing such lines raises questions like: Where do the funds come from for a multi-jurisdictional system? Who will control the funds?

Will there be a lessening of local control? Is it legal to take money from one jurisdiction to spend in another? What are the politics of securing enabling legislation for such a system? Attempts to start at the local level and work upward in the hierarchy of government sometimes succeed because the persons involved are more familiar with the way that local programs relate (for example, levels of funding and interest) to the political system.

Crossing governmental jurisdictional lines can mean the project will have to develop one or more joint power agreements, which allow using funds from two or more jurisdictions for a joint purpose. Usually, this process is a matter of time rather than of getting the agreement, but it involves politicians, and one never really knows how long it will take them to act.

Starting at the national level usually reduces the number of jurisdictional questions and results in better funding. Although the national approach has some major advantages, it also has significant disadvantages. One of the most frequent responses to a national plan from the local authorities is "What do the bureaucrats in the capital know about our problems? No one on the planning committee ever asks us what we need, much less comes to see our program." Suspicion is the key word here, followed by possessiveness. ("What is the real motive for this project, and why should we give up local control?") These problems, of course, are not just library problems; they are part of the political process. Another problem is that the many national plans, to allow for local variation, do not contain enough detail to make them functional. At times it seems as if reporting results to national authorities consumes more administrative time than the library saves through cooperative activities. Finally, regional jealousies and a desire for political gain may dominate the entire process, thus negating most of the advantages that the project may achieve for library customers across the country.

As mentioned earlier, there can be problems when the project involves public and private institutions, particularly when the funding comes from public sources. Certainly, a major concern of the directors of private academic libraries in California (California Private Academic Libraries [CAL PALS]) about a proposed statewide cooperative relates to administrative control and the amount of influence privates will have. Apparently, because the funds would be state or federal, legally only public institutions may decide on how to expend the money. Several CAL PALS directors have stated that they could not agree to participate unless there were greater sharing of administrative and policy decision making.

Accrediting bodies may play a role in the process because of their standards (see page 437). For small and medium-sized educational institutions (secondary as well as higher education), the accrediting agencies can play a significant role in institutional decision making. Top administration can change their minds almost overnight about funding priorities based on an accreditation report.

The role of the WASC as an institutional accrediting body has had a mixed influence on cooperative collection building. WASC's accreditation standards, particularly 6.B.1 (see page 437), were designed, in part, to control institutions that were establishing widely scattered off-campus programs. One concern was that students were not receiving proper support, in particular, library support, at the off-campus sites. The standard has proven to be a two-edged sword for cooperative collection building. There are a few instances where it motivated the library and its parent institution to enter into formal agreements with the libraries near the off-campus instructional sites. Usually, such agreements take the form of the institution needing access to material to pay an annual fee, which the receiving library agrees to use to subscribe to certain journals or to buy books about certain subjects. Given that most libraries do not have large amounts of excess collection growth space, it appears clear that the receiving library believes its primary customers will also benefit from the acquired material. This form of cooperative collection building is often overlooked.

On the negative side, the standard also resulted in libraries acquiring technologies that would allow the remote sites to have access to the main campus library. Undoubtedly, for many of the libraries, the accreditation pressure regarding off-campus students having access to library support resulted in funding for online catalogs, fax machines, CD-ROMs, and networking capabilities. In many cases, most of the technology would have been much slower in arriving in the library if it were not for the accreditation concerns. The technologies, in essence, reduced the need to enter into cooperative agreements. The standard also resulted in lost opportunities to work at developing true cooperative collection building programs. Perhaps with the technologies in place, it will be easier to undertake a cooperative project.

In some cases, there is a need to maintain two systems for a time. Dual operations are always a part of the start-up procedure in any cooperative system, but, normally, the two systems operate simultaneously for only a short period of time. However, even two or three months of dual operation may create a real economic burden for some members with tight operating budgets. All the cooperative can do is to keep the transition period as short as possible. Finally, complex systems require extensive staff training, and thus, some loss of normal productivity will occur while the staff is in training. In addition, a complex system usually means more mistakes will occur and means a longer transition period.

Technological Issues

Faith that new technological developments will vastly increase the storage capacity of a library is an important issue to consider. In some instances, pressure for cooperative collection development comes from a lack of physical space in which to store the collection. Eliminating unnecessary duplication of low-use items can result in more space for high-use materials. However, if new technology will allow storage of the equivalent of the Library of Congress or British Museum Library collections in space no larger than an office desk or less, why worry about running out of space? In addition, the potential for local self-sufficiency may again arise. If one can purchase microfiche collections for less than hard copies, the book budget will stretch farther. Increased acquisition rates will increase the title count and thus raise the status of the library. Increased depth and scope in the collection, plus almost immediate satisfaction of patron needs, are what libraries are all about, right?

Technological developments (for example, CD-ROM) that were mere speculations 15 years ago hold out the hope of being able to store large quantities of full-text material in little space. Long-term costs of such technology are a serious consideration. Most of the new technologies are costly, and many require additional fees when a library wishes to provide simultaneous user access, or, in some cases, even to print a screen. In the past, the only major high-density format was microforms that were (and are) unpopular with customers. For some reason, people are willing to sit for much longer periods at a CRT than they are willing to sit at a microform reader. (This is most probably because of the greater flexibility in accessing the desired information.) If the primary reason for exploring cooperative collection building is slowing collection growth, then the new technologies hold out the hope for self-sufficiency while not running out of storage space. On the other hand, most librarians desire to expand access for customers while not expending more money. (If the same program buys the library or institution time before having to face a remodeling or construction project, so much the better.)

For some, the new technologies might take on a form of cooperative collecting, if a group of libraries could share the full-text database cost. In all likelihood, the cost of such an arrangement would be greater than the combined material budgets of the cooperating libraries. This is because the vendors base their charges on the total number of potential simultaneous users. For example, LMU explored mounting a scientific indexing and abstracting service on a local area network (LAN). The database owner wanted a fee for every university student, faculty, and staff member, rather than a more realistic number of likely simultaneous users. The difference was more than 5,000 users.

Twenty years ago, it was difficult to know who held what material. Bibliographic utilities (such as OCLC, WLN, and RLIN) were still developing, and their databases were small compared to actual library holdings. Union catalogs had proven to be expensive to develop and maintain as well as cumbersome to use. The utilities were slowly replacing the union catalogs, but few libraries could afford the costs of membership and equipment to belong to more than one such service. Today, with the utilities and libraries allowing dial-in access to their OPACs, it is much easier to determine who owns what.

New technologies provide additional ways of expanding access for the customer. Are they also a form of resource sharing? If two or more neighboring libraries agree to share some journal titles, that is a form of cooperation. When several libraries engage in online recording of the journals' tables of contents, is this resource sharing? Probably not. However, if there is the added element of delivering the indexed articles to any customer of the cooperating libraries, resource sharing is clearly present. CARL (Colorado Alliance of Research Libraries) does just that and CARL Corporation markets its efforts to other libraries with CARL UnCover. Is the UnCover program a form of resource sharing or a sound entrepreneurial move? Does the view change when a purely commercial entity offers a similar service?

Technology is blurring the lines of what constitutes resource sharing. Does one really care, as long as the customer's access expands to material the library cannot afford to acquire? A short-term answer is probably not.

However, taking a longer view, perhaps librarians should care. As discussed in chapter 6, information pricing practices, like other commodities, factor in the number of units sold or likely to sell. Shared resources projects may in fact drive prices up, thus negating any financial gain from cooperating.

Without question, technology offers us more opportunities to cooperate than it presents barriers to cooperation. The major concern is what the ultimate costs will be.

Physical Issues

Physical concerns (for example, lack of seating capacity, lack of parking) were moderately important in the past. In a sense, staffing was another physical barrier; one public service person can handle only so many people in a given time. Today, these problems are as great, if not greater, than they were 15 years ago. This may make it more difficult to establish reciprocal borrowing agreements.

Local customers use the collection and the reader stations to the maximum, so acquiring additional customers would result in long waits or no service. Small archival libraries and special libraries, where one must use the materials in the library, often face this problem. Even large facilities, especially academic libraries, often face this problem. For example, not long ago UC-Berkeley decided to close its undergraduate library to outsiders, including non-UC students and faculty. This will mean that resource sharing will have to focus on ways of supplying the needed information to the customer at his or her home institution. Without question, this will raise the cost of cooperation.

Insufficient storage space for materials is not easy to resolve. Cooperative collection development proposals may reduce the need for storage space in some subject areas in the future, but they will add demands in other areas. Normally, such proposals do not address the issue of older materials already in a collection. If there is to be a new central storage unit for low-use items (for example, the Center for Research Libraries), then libraries may gain some space, but this usually does not solve the long-term space problem.

Geographic and transportation issues also can create problems, although technology is making distance less of a problem. Distance is a well-known issue in collection building. People are prone to follow the law of least effort. Often, this translates into using what is easily accessible as opposed to what is most appropriate. When thinking about distance, especially in urban areas such as Los Angeles, think about time rather than distance. Saying item X is available at a library that is only 10 miles away means one thing to a person in Boston or Los Angeles and quite another to someone in Peoria or Colorado Springs. Depending on the time of day and day of the week, that 10-mile drive can turn into a lengthy and challenging commute. The distance issue and the law of least effort means librarians must think and plan in terms of document delivery in any cooperative project.

People Issues

Perhaps the biggest barrier to cooperative collection building is people. Avoiding (but not discounting) such factors as ego, the need to control discussion, or the need to get (or take) credit for a successful project, this discussion focuses on institutional people issues.

There are a variety of psychological barriers planners of a cooperative program must overcome. Change is almost always threatening to at least a few people. Both customers and staff become uneasy when talk of cooperative collection building begins. During the early exploratory discussions, no one knows whether the program will start or what its precise form will be; thus, almost everyone raises a concern or an open objection. Sometimes, the sum total of the concerns is such that heeding all of them would mean no project.

A related issue is the potential loss of autonomy. Staff, and sometimes faculty, worry abut this, and their concerns take the form of questions like: Who will decide? What voice will we have? Won't X dominate the process? Certainly, when it comes to multitype cooperatives or public/private ventures, there are some reasonable grounds for concern. The larger libraries probably would dominate, unless the governance arrangements were carefully thought out. When the bulk of the funding is from public sources, there is a danger that the public institutions may have or may want too much control for private institutions to take part in the project. Carefully formulated agreements can handle these problems in most cases.

Passive resistance, as well as inertia and indifference, can be a serious problem at both the planning and implementation stages. Staff may view the project as resulting in more work with little or no benefit to themselves. For such individuals, passive resistance is the easiest course of action. As with selling any change, planners must be honest and forthright about possible modifications in the workload. If it is likely there will be an increase in work, the planners should try to identify some project benefit that will come to the affected person or unit. An abstract benefit for the library, library customers, or institution all too often is insufficient to effectively combat resistance.

Like staff, customers can engage in passive resistance. An academic library should not undertake a cooperative collection building program without gaining tacit faculty approval. This may require more than a library committee's blessing. Securing approval by the faculty governing body is wise, even if it is not required. Lacking such prior approval, any faculty opposition to the plan is likely to delay the project because of the need to consult widely with all the faculty. A related obstructionist tactic is, "This is a wonderful idea, but we need assurance that there is an equitable distribution of funds for our instructional needs before. . . ." In any situation, consulting with customers during the planning process is wise. By carefully planning and taking the time to consult and inform all interested parties as the work progresses, planners have an excellent chance of overcoming user resistance.

Because selection decisions are subjective, there are concerns about how the process will take place in the cooperative system. Who will and how will they make the decision to buy? Certainly a carefully formulated joint collecting policy statement will help allay worries on this count, but interpretation of the policy is still subjective. In the University of California shared acquisitions program (see pages 452-53), individual campuses suggest titles to acquire, but a committee representing some of the campuses makes the final decision. (Committee membership rotates, so all campuses have representation from time to time.) Such a process can help overcome worries about losing control over the funds and the collection. It does not completely remove subjectivity, but it is based on a group discussion and decision.

A final obstructionist tactic is questioning the quality or reliability of one or more of the proposed cooperative partners. This is a strategy some staff members may employ to slow down the planning process. Errors, especially in an electronic database, present problems for everyone. One of the long-standing complaints about OCLC has been that its quality control is too lax. A point like that is certain to be made by staff members who oppose the project. Sharing access to any database is likely to raise concerns about quality control. However, with proper planning and control, this should not be a major stumbling block.

The bottom line in cooperative collection building should be better service to customers. If customers fight the project and the library staff has doubts as well, there is little reason to think the project will succeed. These issues existed 15 years ago, and they remain strong today.

Knowledge or Lack of Knowledge Issues

Lack of knowledge about customer use patterns can present a barrier to coordinated collection development. As librarians, perhaps we thought we would have time some day to collect use data but have not found the opportunity to do so. Do we have adequate knowledge about what patrons need and want? Furthermore, even if we know the current situation, needs and wants can change quickly. Certainly, selection officers deal with these two issues every day. Why is it any greater a problem for a cooperative? Lacking knowledge about the customer base, we have little or no basis for accurately projecting how the proposed cooperative would affect service. Every member of the cooperative faces the same issues. Collecting data about customer needs can delay the project indefinitely.

A major difficulty with cooperative plans is the speed with which one can make adjustments to changing needs in a network of more than two members. It is much easier to respond to changing local needs when one does not have to worry about the impact the adjustments will have on other libraries. Of course, any proposed change may require modification of the original agreement. While most changes would be minor, each requires discussion with other member libraries.

The specter of the failure of the Farmington Plan (see page 449) will haunt planners. However, people learn from past projects and mistakes. Most people who studied the rise and fall of the Farmington Plan suggest that one factor that caused it to fail was constantly changing institutional needs. Though librarians might hope things have improved, given today's need to control growth and effectively manage limited collection building funds, institutions are seldom willing to make long-term commitments. Experience tells us that institutions change and their libraries must change as well. The problem is that no one knows when the change will take place or what form it will take. As a result, each institution tries to protect its right to respond to unknown, but inevitable, changes.

Another problem is that the literature seldom fully reports how and why a cooperative project failed. Usually, journals publish articles about successful projects. Although this is understandable, information about failed efforts might be even more useful to planners. Announcements about new cooperative projects may appear in the news section of journals like *Library Journal, Wilson Library Bulletin,* or *College & Research Libraries News.* If the project succeeds, an article explaining how and why the project succeeded may appear at a much later date. More likely, there will be no follow-up article. Did the project succeed or fail? Short of tracking down someone from one of the libraries involved in the project, if that information exists, there is no way to know. Most libraries do not have the time or staff to engage in this type of investigation. Thus, lack of knowledge about past efforts is a barrier to success.

Even those projects that are reported change over time. Such changes almost never appear in print, and often, these changes, especially during the first two or three years of operation, are key elements in a successful project. About the only way to learn about such changes is to conduct a survey. Locating individuals who have detailed knowledge about how and why the changes occurred is time-consuming. Using a questionnaire for this type of information is a waste of time, energy, and money. The only effective way to obtain the information is through in-person or telephone interviews; even then, one senses that critical data is missing. (Ten years ago, I served as co-advisor for a doctoral student studying innovation and change in academic libraries. He spent more than $3,000 attempting to get information from 45 individuals through telephone interviews. In addition, he went to eight conferences and conventions to conduct interviews. By the time he completed his research, we both knew he had all the data anyone could collect, yet neither of us felt satisfied that all the critical data was available.)

One other important piece of information is almost impossible to collect: the actual costs of the project. Because a major motivation in initiating a cooperative project is to stretch limited funding, knowing project costs is important. When there is a special grant to start the project, it is easy to get that cost information. What you do not find is information about staff costs not covered by the grant. Anyone with grant experience knows that, even with cost-sharing grants, the institutional contribution is always larger than what appeared in the grant proposal. Getting start-up cost information is simple compared to getting ongoing operational cost data. With excellent contacts in a successful cooperative project, you may be able to get some sense of the direct costs. However, it is often the indirect costs that ultimately eat up the savings that the cooperative generates in other areas. For example, tracking the extra cost in ILL staff time, buried in the overall ILL operations, or calculating ILL indirect costs becomes so burdensome that few institutions undertake such studies. When one does get cost data, one must remember to factor in regional differences in salary. One will also want to know whether there was any consideration of overhead costs and, if so, what the group included as overhead.

Thus, 15 years ago librarians had problems with lack of knowledge. There is little change in the situation today. Pressures to cooperate are perhaps stronger than ever before, yet libraries do not have an adequate base of knowledge about what did and did not work.

Despite what may seem to be a litany of problems, it is possible to establish cooperative projects, and it is becoming more and more a matter of economic necessity.

What to Avoid

The following six points about what to avoid to establish a successful cooperative come from the literature on the topic. Avoid these pitfalls and a system has an excellent chance of succeeding:

- Do not think of the cooperative as supplementary and something it is possible to do without.

- Planners should spend time working out operational details.

- The system should cause major operational changes in the member libraries.

- Do not think of the system as providing the library with something for nothing.

- Have the cooperative's funding and operation handled by an independent agency.

- Realize it takes time; careful, complete communication; and one or two persons who take on the leadership role with patient understanding. Above all else, forming a cooperative is a political process.

An indication of the difficulties associated with developing resource sharing is found in a classic article by Maryann Dugan, "Library Network Analysis and Planning."[12] She asked a group of 109 head librarians to indicate what type of cooperative activities would be appropriate to develop. Based on the responses, she identified 10 important activities; the librarians ranked their desirability and the need to develop cooperatives. Their ranking is indicative of the attitudes we have been discussing:

1. Union list	6. Regional centers
2. Interlibrary loan	7. Central facility
3. Facsimile transmission	8. Type of library centers
4. Networking	9. Central processing
5. Reference service	10. Collection management

In one sense, resource sharing was both first and last; union lists, interlibrary loan, and facsimile transmission are all forms of resource sharing. However, for these to be most useful, in terms of both cost-effectiveness and gaining access to the full universe of knowledge, coordinated collection management must occur. Without cooperative collection management, the situation is the same as it has always been. Certainly today, with hundreds of OPACs available on the Internet, customers can locate material quickly. However, if everyone is buying basically the same materials, is there any useful gain? For years we have used interlibrary loan and variations of facsimile transmission. The attitude in 1969 (when Dugan's survey was conducted) was to cooperate, so long as doing so did not have a negative impact on local autonomy and self-sufficiency. To a large extent, that attitude remains strong today.

The ALA guidelines identify seven models for cooperative collection development: the Farmington Plan, the National Program for Acquisition and Cataloging (NPAC) system, the Library of Congress system, the Center for Research Libraries model, the mosaic overlay of collection development policies, the status quo, and the combined self-interest models.

The Farmington Plan, a valiant but unsuccessful effort, was an attempt by major American research libraries to have one copy of any currently published research work available somewhere within the United States. After years of effort it was abandoned in the 1970s. The plan originally assigned acquisition responsibility on the basis of institutional interests. In 20 years, those interests changed, but the goal of one copy remained. Another problem was that some areas were not a major area of interest to any institution. Sufficient national interest existed to warrant coverage, but deciding which institution should have the responsibility for buying such materials was a constant problem. A careful study of why the Farmington Plan failed provides invaluable data for future cooperative ventures. In the final analysis, it failed as a result of not avoiding the pitfalls discussed earlier.

A European example was the Scandia Plan, implemented in the Scandinavian countries, which experienced similar problems. This plan never achieved the same level of activity as the Farmington Plan, primarily because of problems of changing needs and the assignment of responsibilities.

The NPAC system was another attempt at acquiring quantities of research materials from outside the United States and assuring cataloging data would be available for the material. (Cataloging was a stumbling block to the Farmington Plan.) The Library of Congress was the focal point in NPAC, but there was consultation with other research libraries in the United States about what subjects to include in the program. Public Law 480 (PL 480) was an element of the NPAC program. Again, the Library of Congress was responsible for operating the program, including cataloging, and distributing the materials to participating academic libraries. PL 480 was not a cooperative collection development project in the usual sense of the term; it was a centralized acquisition and cataloging program.

A related, joint acquisition program that also failed was the Latin American Cooperative Acquisition Plan (LACAP). LACAP was a commercial undertaking designed to share costs and problems of acquiring quantities of research material, on a regular basis, from Latin American countries. Although some research libraries in the United States still collect extensively from Latin America, they could not sustain the program. Three factors played an important role in the demise of LACAP. First, most of what the libraries acquired was low-use material. Tight funding requires hard choices, and low-use items are always a prime area for cutting. Second, the plan started in a period when many institutions were developing area study programs and there was an expectation that this would be a growing field. Economic conditions changed, and institutions stopped planning for new programs and often cut some of the most recently established programs. As a result, there were not as many institutions interested in participating in LACAP. Finally, the book trade in many Latin American countries matured, and it was no longer as difficult to locate reliable local dealers. If one can buy directly and reliably at a lower cost, it is reasonable to buy the most material possible with the funds available.

The ALA guidelines describe the Library of Congress system as "a variation of the Farmington Plan." In general terms, it is a centralized (coordinated) system in which the national library and the research libraries in a country work together to ensure that at least one copy of all relevant research material is available.

Two of the most successful cooperative programs are the Center for Research Libraries (CRL) in the United States and the British National Lending Division (BLD). One reason for their success is that they operate as independent agencies. Their purpose is to serve a diverse group of member libraries; in essence, they have no local constituency to serve. Another major difference for CRL is that there is no attempt to acquire high-use items; in fact, just the opposite is true. With no local service population, the fiscal resources can go to acquiring low-use items of national interest.

The CRL does face some major decisions regarding its collection policies. One issue is whether it should build a broad-based selective collection, with many subjects and areas, or whether it should attempt to be comprehensive in a few areas. A second issue relates to the need for a single source for low-use periodicals (National Periodicals Center concept) and what role CRL should play. An interesting article by Sarah E. Thomas, "Collection Development at the Center for Research Libraries: Policy and Practice," suggests that the number of the Center's periodical holdings is not as unique as many members would like (only 20.66 percent of the Center's titles were unique).[13] Local needs of member libraries would account for some of the duplication. Also, the project looked at title holdings in the United States, not just at CRL member libraries, so some of the duplication undoubtedly occurred in nonmember libraries. What of the future? One would hope the center will continue to develop as the holder of unique materials. With better delivery systems, perhaps libraries can supply low-use items quickly enough from CRL and let patrons know about the system, which would allow for less duplication of low-use items.

"Mosaic overlay of collection development policies" is what the RLG conspectus and ARL National Collection Inventory Project (NCIP) are trying to accomplish. The purpose is to assure national coverage; to identify collection gaps nationally; to serve as a basis for libraries taking on collecting responsibilities (primary collecting responsibility, or PCR); to assist in directing scholars to strong collections; to create a consistent basis for collection development policies; to function as a communication device signaling changes in collection activities; to serve as a link among collecting policies and processing and preservation policies; to serve as a possible fund-raising tool; and finally, to stimulate interest in and support for cooperative programs. Whether NCIP and RLG efforts will succeed in achieving that long list of purposes, only time will tell. The final product will be an assessment of collection strength in almost 7,000 subject categories by the participating libraries, giving each appropriate subject category a value of 0 to 5. When that is done, we shall know which libraries think they have strong or weak collections in each area, but we will not know exactly what is in each collection. The assessment will identify gaps and will be useful for referral purposes, and perhaps for ILL if the library is online and the library seeking the information can tap that database. The possibility of each of some 200 or so research libraries (a generous estimate of potential participants) accepting its share of the potential 5,000 PCRs, about 25 PCRs each, is grand. Will it happen? It would be wonderful if it did; however, it has not happened yet.

The status quo approach, as the label implies, would keep things as they are. This model assumes that the sum total of current collecting activities, primarily by research libraries and archives, achieves the comprehensiveness needed. By sharing in-process and catalog files, online of course, adequate access is available to allow individual purchase decisions with the knowledge of who has or has not ordered an item. It is doubtful that many research librarians really believe that the current system is achieving the needed level of coverage.

The combined self-interest plan is something of a multitype system, in that a significant number of libraries would combine with one or more major libraries. In a sense, this is what the Collection Development Committee of the Colorado Council on Library Development attempted to create with the Denver Public Library and the University of Colorado Library System serving as the major libraries. The committee goals and objectives, as outlined in "Developing Collections in Colorado," were:

GOALS:

1. To work toward coordinated collection development policies for all libraries in the state to give greater access to materials for all Colorado citizens.

2. To assess budgetary constraints affecting local and statewide collection development and to work for increased funding and resources to overcome restraints.

OBJECTIVES:

1. To have individual libraries recognize their role in collection development and to prepare their own collection development policy in terms of their own clientele and role within the state.

   A. Each library should define who it serves as its primary client.

    B. Each library should determine and define the needs of that client.

    C. Each library should have a mission statement or goal.

    D. Each library should establish written priorities for allocation of resources.

2. To raise the awareness of individual librarians about collection development, including an understanding of what collection development is and the training needed for it.

3. To determine what materials the state does not have and to make recommendations for providing those needed resources within [Colorado].

4. To encourage preparation of regional and statewide collection development plans.

    A. Identifying local and state responsibilities.

    B. Assisting libraries to delineate responsibilities for materials.

5. To coordinate current collection development activities within the state and provide a clearinghouse for collection development information.[14]

Again, the RLG conspectus and the ALA policy guideline concepts were the basis for the combined policy statements. With all types of libraries involved, problems developed and, in some cases, remain unresolved, and not everyone views the concept with enthusiasm.

Another Colorado cooperative is CARL. Joel Rutstein and Donnice Cochenour's article provides an excellent description of how the project came into being and operates today.[15] Any group thinking about undertaking the development of a proposal for coordinated or cooperative collection building should read this article.

Yet another good paper to consult is Sue Medina's description of the Network of Alabama Academic Libraries.[16]

On a more limited scale is the University of California Library System's "Shared Purchase Program." The program has a 15-year history of shared buying; its purpose is

> to acquire materials which, because of their high cost (or anticipated frequency of use), should be shared among the campuses without unnecessary duplication. The program has also been instituted to reduce competition for, and to promote sharing of, manuscript and subject area collections among the various campuses of the University of California. Stanford University is a full member of the program. However, state funds will not be used to acquire materials housed at Stanford (except for necessary indexes). Materials acquired with shared funds are to be shared among the campuses either statewide or on a regional (North and South) basis.[17]

Any campus library can recommend items for the committee to acquire, and membership on the committee rotates so every campus has representation from time to time.

Local and International Projects

A current project illustrates most of the points discussed in this chapter. Los Angeles County has a number of libraries with theology collections that support one or more degree programs. None of the libraries are well-off financially, and combining acquisition budgets would be of assistance to all customers. Certainly, there is interest in cooperative work at the directors' level. Thus, there is enough institutional and library support to at least explore cooperative ventures. It is still much too early to know how many, if any, of the specific institutional barriers will arise.

Because all of the schools are private institutions, they should not encounter any legal barriers. Because we are in the what-if stage, it is unknown whether any administrative barriers may crop up. It seems likely that administrative barriers could be quickly resolved.

Technology is on our side, at least so far. A year ago, those of us (23 theology libraries) who use EBSCO as our serials agent agreed to have the firm produce a union list of our serials subscriptions (quarterly or more frequent titles). The listing is comprehensive, not just theology and philosophy titles, so we have a fairly sound knowledge of our joint serials holdings. Naturally, there are a few direct-order titles that do not appear on the list. We could use this listing as the starting point for cooperative serials collection management. We have agreed to an annual update of the listing. This could not have been done 15 years ago, without the expenditure of large sums of money. The next step will be to agree that any theology or philosophy title held by only one of us would not be cancelled without first consulting the other libraries.

Most of us have a fax machine, and for those that do not, an investment of a few hundred dollars would provide a Los Angeles-area theological library fax network. Assuming the libraries could agree to giving member libraries priority ILL fax service for theology or philosophy articles, they would achieve a journal document delivery service that should satisfy most customers.

All but a few of the libraries have OPACs. For a relatively modest cost, each could provide dial-in access, at least by member library staff. This would allow the libraries to share information about what each library has in its monograph collections. Certainly, it would be ideal to have a union OPAC, but that is unrealistic at this time. Without question, having to dial into 10 or more individual OPACs to determine whether a library owns a desired title would be time-consuming. Nevertheless, it would appear that such an approach would provide better service than the libraries now provide. Even without entering into formal subject buying agreements, this approach would allow the libraries to make some selection decisions on the basis of knowing who has what in the local area. Some of the libraries have automation systems that reflect information about items on order in the OPAC. This would provide additional data for selectors, if all the libraries could agree to activate such capability in their systems.

Though making the OPACs available to individual faculty members would be ideal, such a move would probably overload dial-in access ports. (Most of the libraries did not plan on heavy off-campus dial-in access.) There would be problems in educating faculty members about the capabilities of five or six different types of OPACs. In the case of LMU, where the law school is in downtown Los Angeles and the main campus is in Westchester, 12 miles away, the library has a simple but difficult problem to solve. Both libraries have the same automation systems. We want the faculty on both campuses to have access to both systems. Currently, access is via telephone dial-in, but there are plans to link the two campuses with a fiber optic network. Our problem is: How do we make certain that the person accessing a catalog knows whether she or he is looking at the law school or the Westchester campus catalog? Both menu screens look very much alike, and, when you are viewing a specific record, there is nothing on the screen to indicate in which library the item is located. Reprogramming is expensive, and so far, we have not come up with a cost-effective solution. While various OPAC systems do format the screens in a variety of distinctive ways, only the experienced user is likely to remember this screen is LMU or that one is the University of Judaism. With proper planning, these problems should be overcome.

Lacking a union catalog will make it more difficult for the L.A.-area theology libraries to determine strengths, weaknesses, and, perhaps of greatest importance, degree of overlap. One option that exists to solve this problem, for the libraries using OCLC, is to use one of the existing CD-ROM products, such as the OCLC/AMIGOS CD-ROM, for collection evaluation. This system provides data about comparative holdings, unique titles, and overlap. The major drawback to the AMIGOS product as it now stands is that you cannot determine which library in the peer group holds which titles. Nevertheless, it could be a useful tool if the project goes forward.

As noted in the discussion of barriers, document delivery (distance) is a stumbling block in developing satisfactory (from the customer's point of view) cooperative collections of books, monographs, and audiovisual materials. Immediate, or at least quick, access is what every customer desires. We may have something of a solution to this problem. The LMU library has a courier service program for faculty to receive research material from UCLA. A person who works 26 hours a week makes the trip (12 miles) to UCLA three times a week to pick up and return material. The person uses a library-owned station wagon. It is possible, with support from proposed member libraries, that this courier service could be expanded to five or six days a week among the libraries. Using this approach, we might be able to promise, and deliver on the promise, a maximum delay of 48 hours between request and book-in-hand.

Thus, we have most of the necessary pieces available to set up a cooperative collection building program:

managerial interest

institutional interest (unknown as to strength)

union list of serials

OPACs

collection assessment tool

document delivery capability

fax capability

courier service

limited geographic service area

Why am I not very optimistic about our chances of success? Lack of knowledge and people are to blame. We have not progressed far enough in our thinking to know exactly what we do and do not know. I doubt that many of us have much data about our collection use patterns. We probably would be hard-pressed to produce much data about our core collections, much less our high- and low-use research material. There is no sense of the costs involved. Thus, lack of knowledge and the time and money to collect the information are serious barriers.

However, the people concerns will pose the major problems. Customer resistance will be particularly hard to overcome. During the early spring of 1993, I approached a member of the LMU faculty library committee who is in the theology department about this project. I gave him a brief outline of the major points. He presented it to his department colleagues at their last meeting of the academic year. His report on the outcome of the discussion was depressing. The faculty said that they would prefer a mediocre collection in all areas at LMU rather than having certain areas of great strength while depending on other libraries in the area for in-depth, non-curriculum or course subjects. If other institutional faculty respond in a similar way, it will be difficult to get the project off the ground, even if the library staffs are fully supportive. Will it succeed? It will depend on how much we want it to work and how well we market the idea to our customers and our funding authorities.

At the international level, there is the ambitious UNESCO program, Universal Availability of Publications (UAP). Although it is not actually a cooperative collection development plan, it must be mentioned. In concept, UAP is grand. It proposes that all published knowledge, in whatever form it is produced, should be available to anyone whenever he or she wants it. Every information professional knows there is a long way to go in achieving that goal, even in countries with strong library systems and economies, let alone in developing countries. As Maurice Line has stated,

> One of the main reasons why the situation with regard to UAP is so unsatisfactory is that availability has been approached piecemeal; particular aspects such as acquisitions and interlending have been tackled by individual libraries or groups of libraries, but uncoordinated piecemeal approaches can actually make things worse. . . . UAP must ultimately depend on action with individual countries.[18]

If the concept is to succeed, it will be necessary to develop coordinated collection development plans in all countries and develop effective delivery systems, because everyone cannot buy, process, and store everything everywhere.

Summary

A midsummer 1994 listserv discussion summed up the major points about cooperative collection development. First, the concept of cooperation is subject to many varying interpretations, even among the library staff—public service staff see it as more access, selection officers have both positive and negative views, and, often, top administrators see it as a way to save money. Second, status and budgets are still major issues, if there is a chance cooperating might have a negative impact on size. Finally, multitype or multisize library efforts are unlikely to succeed because of the libraries' different goals and what each library can contribute to the cooperative venture.

Cooperative collection development is difficult. Local needs often seem to be at odds with broader needs of the area or nation. However, problems of funding and local practices can be overcome. As new delivery systems become available, we may be able to break down the need for local self-sufficiency. It will be a long, slow process, but it is necessary to keep striving for the UAP goal.

Notes

[1]Richard Dougherty, "Library Cooperation: A Case of Hanging Together or Hanging Separately," *Catholic Library World* 46 (March 1975): 324-27.

[2]*Webster's Third New International Dictionary* (Springfield, MA: G & C Merriam, 1976).

[3]John Berry, "Killing Library Cooperation: Don't Let Professional Principles Become the Economy's Next Victim," *Library Journal* 117 (August 1992): 100.

[4]Michael P. Sinclair, "A Typology of Library Cooperatives," *Special Libraries* 64 (April 1973): 181-86.

[5]Boyd Rayward, "Local Node," in *Multiple Library Cooperation*, edited by B. Hamilton and W. B. Ernst, 66 (New York: R. R. Bowker, 1977).

[6]Paul H. Mosher and Marcia Pankake, "A Guide to Coordinated and Cooperative Collection Development," *Library Resources & Technical Services* 27 (October/December 1983): 417-31.

[7]Richard Hacken, "RLG Conoco Study and Its Aftermath: Is Resource Sharing in Limbo?" *Journal of Academic Librarianship* 18 (March 1992): 22.

[8]Bendik Rugaas, "The End of All and Forever," a paper presented at IFLA Conference, Sydney Australia, 1988.

[9]Tom Ballard, "Public Library Networking: Neat, Plausible, Wrong," *Library Journal* 107 (1 April 1982): 679-83.

[10]Hacken, "RLG Conoco Study," 21-22.

[11]Western Association of Schools and Colleges, *Handbook of Accreditation* (Oakland, CA: Western Association of Schools and Colleges, 1988), 62.

[12]Maryann Dugan, "Library Network Analysis and Planning," *Journal of Library Automation* 2 (1969): 157-75.

[13]Sarah E. Thomas, "Collection Development at the Center for Research Libraries: Policy and Practice," *College & Research Libraries* 46 (May 1985): 230-35.

[14]"Developing Collections in Colorado," *Colorado Libraries* 8 (December 1982): 7-8.

[15]Donnice Cochenour and Joel Rutstein, "A CARL Model for Cooperative Collection Development in a Regional Consortium," *Collection Building* 12, nos. 1/2 (1993): 34-53.

[16]Sue O. Medina, "The Evolution of Cooperative Collection Development in Alabama Academic Libraries," *College & Research Libraries* 53 (January 1992): 7-19.

[17]University of California, Library Council, Collection Development Committee, *Guidelines for University of California Library Acquisitions with Shared Purchase Funds* (Berkeley, CA: University of California, 1984), 1.

[18]Maurice Line, "Universal Availability of Publications: An Introduction," *Scandinavian Public Library Quarterly* 15 (1982): 48.

Further Reading

General

Dunn, R. T. "Sharing the Wealth." *PNLA Quarterly* 57 (Fall 1992): 25.

Ferguson, A. W. "Conspectus and Cooperative Collection Development." In *Collection Assessment,* edited by R. J. Wood and K. Strauch, 105-14. New York: Haworth Press, 1992.

Hannesdottir, S. K. *Scandia Plan.* Metuchen, NJ: Scarecrow Press, 1992.

Johnson, M. A. "When Pigs Fly: Or When Access Equals Ownership." *Technicalities* 12 (February 1992): 4-7.

Luquire, W., ed. *Coordinating Cooperative Collection Development: A National Perspective.* New York: Haworth Press, 1986.

Mosher, P. H. "A National Scheme for Collaboration in Collection Development." In *Coordinating Cooperative Collection Development,* edited by W. Luquire, 21-35. New York: Haworth Press, 1986.

Networks for Networkers: Critical Issues in Cooperative Library Development. New York: Neal-Schuman, 1980.

O'Connell, J. B. "Collection Evaluation in a Developing Country." *Libri* 34 (March 1984): 44-64.

Sohn, J. "Cooperative Collection Development: A Brief Overview." *Collection Management* 8 (Summer 1986): 1-10.

Thompson, A. "Getting into a Cooperative Mode." In *Collection Management for the 1990s*, 127-34. Chicago: American Library Association, 1993.

Walters, D. H. "Distributed National Collection, Conspectus, Resource Sharing and Cooperative Collection Development." *Australian Academic & Research Libraries* 23 (March 1992): 20-24.

Weech, T. L. "Networking and Cooperative Collection Management." *Collection Building* 10, nos. 3/4 (1989): 51-57.

Academic

Brill, P. J. "Cooperative Collection Development." In *Collection Management in Academic Libraries,* edited by C. Jenkins and M. Morley, 235-58. London: Gower, 1991.

Edelman, F. "Death of the Farmington Plan." *Library Journal* 98 (April 15, 1973): 1251-53.

Erickson, R. "Choice for Cooperative Collection Development." *Library Acquisitions: Practice and Theory* 16, no. 1 (1992): 43-49.

Glicksman, M. "Some Thoughts on the Future of the Center for Research Libraries." *Journal of Academic Librarianship* 10 (July 1984): 148-50.

Higginbotham, B. B., and S. Bowdowin. *Access Versus Assets.* Chicago: American Library Association, 1993.

Holickey, B. H. "Collection Development vs. Resource Sharing." *Journal of Academic Librarianship* 10 (July 1984): 146-47.

Munn, R. F. "Cooperation Will Not Save Us." *Journal of Academic Librarianship* 12 (July 1986): 166-67.

Rutstein, J. "Cooperative Collection Development Among Research Libraries: The Colorado Experience." In *Coordinating Cooperative Collection Development*, edited by W. Luquire, 65-79. New York: Haworth Press, 1986.

Schwartz, C. A. "Social Science Perspective on Cooperative Collection Development." In *Impact of Technology on Resource Sharing*, edited by T. C. Wilson, 47-60. New York: Haworth Press, 1993.

Thomas, S. E. "Collection Development at the Center for Research Libraries." *College & Research Libraries* 46 (May 1985): 230-35.

Public

Abbott, P., and R. Kavanagh. "Electronic Resource Sharing Changes Interlibrary Loan Patterns." *Library Journal* 111 (October 1986): 56-58.

Atkinson, H. "Resource Sharing." In *Collection Management in Public Libraries,* edited by J. Serebnick, 38-48. Chicago: American Library Association, 1986.

Ballard, T. H. *Failure of Resource Sharing in Public Libraries and Alternative Strategies for Service.* Chicago: American Library Association, 1986.

———. "Public Libraries and Resource Sharing." *Encyclopedia of Library and Information Science* 44, supplement 9, 257-74.

Devenish-Cassell, A. "Electronic Impacts on Library Resource Sharing." *Catholic Library World* 57 (March/April 1986): 221-24.

English, J. "Resource Sharing: A Promise Worth Fulfilling." *American Libraries* 22 (May 1991): 446.

Fiels, K. M. "Coordinated Collection Development in a Multitype Environment." *Collection Building* 7 (Summer 1985): 26-31.

Grabill, C. "Children's Materials: Resource Sharing in Action." *Public Libraries* 25 (Winter 1986): 135-36.

Hanson, C. D. "Commitment to Access: Resource Sharing in Public and School Libraries." *Library Administration & Management* 6 (Winter 1992): 21-25.

Rayward, W. B. "Local Node." In *Multitype Library Cooperation,* edited by B. Hamilton and W. B. Ernst, 60-66. New York: R. R. Bowker, 1977.

Scott, S. "Cooperative Collection Development: A Resource Sharing Activity for Small Libraries." *Colorado Libraries* 18 (June 1992): 27-28.

Turlock, Betty S. *Public Library in the Bibliographic Network.* New York: Haworth Press, 1986.

Yelland, M. *Local Library Co-operation.* London: British Library, 1980.

School

Bright, S. K. "New York City School Library System: Resource Sharing Network." *Bookmark* 50 (Fall 1991): 54-55.

Dickinson, G. K. "Effect of Technology on Resource Sharing in a School Media Program." In *Advances in Library Resource Sharing,* edited by J. S. Cargill and D. J. Graves, 97-105. Greenwich, CT: Meckler, 1992.

Doan, J. K. "School Library Media Centers in Networks." *School Library Media Quarterly* 13 (Summer 1985): 191-99.

Dyer, Ester R. *Cooperation in Library Service to Children.* Metuchen, NJ: Scarecrow Press, 1978.

Guthrie, D. "Experience in Resource Sharing." *Illinois Libraries* 72 (October 1990): 556-57.

Kulleseid, E. "Cooperative Collection Development in the School Library Revolution." *Bookmark* 50 (Fall 1991): 21-23.

Meizel, J. "High School Education and the Internet." In *Impact of Technology on Resource Sharing*, edited by T. C. Wilson, 127-40. New York: Haworth Press 1993.

Special

Cotter, G. A.; R. W. Hartt; and D. J. O'Connor. "Integrated Bibliographic Information System: Concept and Application for Resource Sharing in Special Libraries." *Information Reports and Bibliographies* 17, no. 5 (1988): 12-20.

Freitag, W. M. "Cooperative Collection Development Among Art Libraries." *Art Libraries Journal* 11, no. 2 (1986): 19-32.

Klimley, S. "Taking the Next Step: Directions and Requirements for Cooperative Collection Development Among Academic Geology Libraries." In *User and Geoscience Information,* edited by R. A. Bier, Jr., 69-76. New York: Geoscience Information Society, 1987.

Ladner, S. J. "Effect of Organizational Structure on Resource Sharing in Sci-Tech Libraries." *Science & Technology Libraries* 12 (Winter 1991): 59-83.

Lanier, D., and K. H. Carpenter. "Enhanced Services and Resource Sharing in Support of New Academic Programs" (medical libraries). *Journal of Academic Librarianship* (March 1994): 15-18.

Millson-Martula, C. A. "Greater Midwest Regional Medical Library Network and Coordinated Cooperative Collection Development." *Illinois Libraries* 71 (January 1989): 31-39.

Roberts, E. P. "Cooperative Collection Development of Science Serials." *Serials Librarian* 14, nos. 1/2 (1988): 19-31.

Ward, S. M. "Resource Sharing Among Library Fee-based Information Services." In *Advances in Library Resource Sharing,* edited by J. S. Cargill and D. J. Graves, 124-38. Greenwich, CT: Meckler, 1992.

17
Protecting the Collection

A major premise of this book is that collection development is the central function of collection management. However, collection management involves several other functions, including the preservation and conservation of the collection. As there should be a concern for preservation and conservation throughout the collection development process, it is appropriate to place responsibility for preservation with the collection managers. More and more libraries are placing preservation and binding under the direction of the chief collection development officer.

Libraries invest substantial amounts of money in their collections. (For example, the Loyola Marymount University library, a medium-sized library, spends $1.2 to 1.3 million each year on the collections.)

There are several aspects to protecting the collection, including proper handling of materials, environmental control, security (to protect against theft and mutilation) and disaster preparedness planning, conservation (binding and preservation), and insurance. Most of these issues are broad concerns; detailed discussion of them is beyond the scope of this book; however, this chapter briefly touches on each topic. In a sense, all these topics work together to prolong the useful life of the materials in the collection. Even insurance fulfills this function, because claims payments help the library replace lost or damaged items.

Proper Handling

Storage and handling are the two first steps in protecting the collection. Neither step requires extra expenditures on the part of the library. Libraries purchase storage units from time to time; the purchaser needs to give some thought to what is the most appropriate type of storage unit. (This does not necessarily translate into the most expensive unit.)

Too narrow and/or shallow a shelf will result in items being knocked off and damaged. Filling shelves and drawers too tightly is a poor practice. Equally harmful is allowing the material to fall over on the shelf (because proper supports are lacking) or slide around in a drawer, because either practice will lead to damage in time. Buying adjustable storage units provides the library a measure of flexibility.

Anyone with extensive experience in shelving books (except, perhaps, a preservation specialist) probably has found a way to squeeze "just one more book" onto a shelf when good practice calls for shifting the material to provide proper space. This often happens when shelvers are under pressure to finish a full book truck within a certain time period. Having performance standards is proper management; however, libraries must be certain the shelving standard includes time for shifting materials. Not factoring that in will result in cracked and damaged book spines, as well as torn headbands resulting from patrons' attempts to pull a book out from a fully packed shelf. Books should be vertical or horizontal on the shelf, not leaning this way and that. Fore-edge shelving should be avoided because it places undue strain on the binding (which is designed for horizontal or vertical storage). Proper supports and bookends help to keep materials in good order. Poorly constructed or finished supports can be more damaging to materials than having none at all.

Teaching people how to handle material properly is important. Training public service staff is an ongoing task; teaching proper handling techniques, if not already taught, will cost some time but will pay off in longer-lasting materials. Training must be offered to patrons as well as staff. Some librarians regard housekeeping concerns as bad for the library's image. If the library makes it clear that monies spent on the repair and replacement of materials ultimately means less money to buy new material, people understand the importance of housekeeping. It does not take more than two or three items sent for rebinding to equal the cost of a new book. And bindery fees are constantly increasing.

Environmental Control

Climate control in the library is essential to conservation. Few libraries are able to follow the example of the Newberry Library in Chicago, where a stack area 10 stories high is double-shelled, windowless, and is monitored by a computerized environmental system. Something less complex, however, will help extend the useful life of most materials. The major concerns for environmental control are humidity, temperature, and light. Architects and librarians should take these issues into account when planning a library building. This is often easier said than done because the ideal environmental conditions for human comfort and for preserving materials don't match. For example, the design of new book stacks for the Newberry Library calls for a constant temperature of 60°F +/-5°F.

Few people would be happy to engage in sedentary work all day at that temperature. Most library designs place human comfort ahead of material preservation. The only time designers can effectively meet both sets of requirements is in situations like the Newberry, where the stacks are closed to the public and even employees are in the stacks only for short periods. Still, this arrangement does not answer all concerns about the environment for preserving materials. There also are differences in the ideal conditions to preserve various types of material. Thus, building design characteristics may present some problem for implementing a good conservation program. (See pages 463-64 for some climate control recommendations.)

Institutional emphasis on energy conservation can lead to cooler winter temperatures and warmer summer temperatures. Cooler winter temperatures are better for materials, but normally the temperature is well above 65 degrees. The greatest damage occurs in summer, when reducing air conditioning costs becomes an institutional priority. (A related problem is that changes in air temperature affect relative humidity.) One way to reduce air conditioning costs is to turn off the system when the library is closed, but overnight shutdowns are damaging to materials. When the system is off for some time, such as the weekend, the temperature can rise. When the air conditioning is turned on, the temperature falls fairly quickly. This "roller coaster" temperature swing is more damaging to materials than storing them at a steady, somewhat higher temperature. Temperature cycling is damaging (it ages paper prematurely), but so are high temperatures. For every rise of 10°C, book paper deteriorates twice as fast. With rapid fluctuations in temperature, the primary problem is the humidity level, which causes damage to the materials.

The Library of Congress Preservation Leaflet no. 2 recommends a temperature of 55°F in book storage areas and a maximum of 75°F (below 70°F, if possible) in reading areas, all with a 50 percent relative humidity. Paul Banks, a well-known preservation specialist who set the standards for the Newberry storage area, also recommended 50 percent relative humidity. For most libraries constructed after World War II, there is little chance of having temperature differentials in storage and reading areas because the design concept called for integrating readers and materials. Also, in most libraries, the temperature and humidity range is much greater than +/-5°F.

Why are library conservationists concerned with humidity? Because changes in humidity can physically weaken materials, which, in turn, can create added costs for repair or replacement. Books (including bound periodicals) consist of a number of different materials—paper, cloth, cardboard, thread, manmade fabrics, adhesives, and sometimes, metal (for example, staples). Often, a single book is made up of several different types of material from each category, for example, heavy endpapers, a moderate weight paper for the text, and coated paper for illustrations. Each component absorbs and loses water vapor (humidity) at a different rate. Materials expand as they absorb moisture and shrink as the humidity falls. As the amount of water vapor in the air goes up or down, there is constant shrinking and swelling of the materials. With each expansion and contraction, the material weakens slightly. Overall, paper deterioration is the main problem with cycling. Humidity and heat combine to accelerate paper acidity.

The differences in the rates of expansion and shrinkage for the different components in the book weaken the bonds between the components, making the book more likely to fall apart. Constant humidity stabilizes the materials. How much water vapor is normally present is important; paper fibers are subject to deterioration when humidity is somewhere below 40 percent. At 65 percent or higher, the chances of mildew and mold formation increase. The musty smell of the antiquarian bookshop may contain more than a hint of mildew or mold, something one does not want in the library.

Other materials (microfilms, videotapes, photographs, and so forth) have somewhat different ideal temperature and humidity storage needs. The ideal range for microforms is 70°F +/-5° with humidity at 40% +/-5%. The same ranges apply to still photographs and safety motion picture film. On the other hand, nitrate-based motion picture film must be stored below 55°F but can tolerate humidity up to 45 percent. Videotapes do best at 65°F +/-5° and no more than 45 percent humidity. Audiodiscs (LPs, 45s, and so forth) can handle temperatures up to 75°F and 50 percent humidity. However, the upper limits for audiotapes are 70°F and 45 percent humidity.

The National Archives has set even higher standards for its new facility in College Park, Maryland. Text and map storage areas call for 70°F and 45 percent relative humidity. Black-and-white film, audiotapes, and sound recordings have a 65°F and 30 percent relative humidity limit. Glass negative, black-and-white photographs, slides, negatives, posters, and electronic materials will be in areas with 65°F temperature and 35 percent relative humidity. Storage areas for color photography film, slides, and photographs will be still cooler—38°F and 35 percent relative humidity. Coldest of all will be storage areas for color motion picture film and color serial film at 25°F and 30 percent relative humidity.

Recalling basic chemistry, we know that increasing the temperature also increases chemical activity. Roughly, chemical reactions double with each 10°C increase in temperature. Freezing books would be the best way to preserve them; however, it is not likely that readers would be willing to sit about in earmuffs, overcoats, and mittens. One is fortunate to achieve a controlled temperature below 70°F in areas where people work for extended periods. One reason for wanting the lower temperatures is to slow down the chemical decomposition of wood pulp paper, which the majority of books and journals contain. However, lower temperatures only slow the process, they do not stop it.

All formats are sensitive to temperature variations, and the ideal storage condition is in an environment with minimal changes.

Lighting, both natural and artificial, influences conservation in two ways. First, it contributes to the heat buildup in a building. Naturally, designers take this into account when specifying the building's heating, ventilating, and air conditioning system. Fluorescent lighting is not a major heat contributor, but in older libraries where incandescent fixtures exist, the heat generated by the fixtures can be a problem. If the light fixtures are close to materials (i.e., in exhibit cases), there can be significant temperature differentials from the bottom to the top shelf in a storage unit. Windows and sunlight generate heat as well, and they create mini-climates. The Newberry Library's windowless storage unit eliminates the sunlight problem. Many libraries have designs featuring numerous windows to provide natural lighting (thus reducing electric costs) and to satisfy patrons' desire to see outside. The cost of these designs has been high in terms of money spent after a few years to reduce the sunlight problem and to repair damaged materials.

The second concern is ultraviolet radiation, a result of sunlight and fluorescent and tungsten lights. Ultraviolet light is the most damaging form of light because it quickly causes materials to fade, turn yellow, and become brittle. Windows and fluorescent light fixtures should have ultraviolet screens or filters built in or installed. Tungsten lighting has the lowest levels of ultraviolet radiation, but even these lights should have filters. The longer one exposes materials to unfiltered light, the more quickly damage occurs. Nonprint materials are even more sensitive and they require greater protective measures than do print materials.

Air filters that reduce the gases in the air inside the library are useful, if expensive. Urban activities pump a variety of harmful gases into the air every day. Some enter the building as people come and go. Few buildings have airlocks and ventilating systems that remove all harmful gases. Whenever it is economical, the ventilation system should remove the most harmful substances. Sulfur dioxide is a major air pollutant and a concern for library conservation programs, because it combines with water vapor to form sulfuric acid. Hydrogen sulfide, another common pollutant, also forms an acid that is harmful to both organic and inorganic materials. In addition to gases, air filters can also reduce the amount of solid particles contained in the building air. Dust and dirt include mold spores, which can cause problems if the air conditioning fails in warm, humid weather. Solid particles act as abrasives, contributing to the wearing out and wearing down of materials. Dusty, gritty shelves wear away the edges of bindings, and, all too often, dusting book shelves is not in anyone's job description.

Finally, insects contribute to the destruction of books and other items in the collection. Silverfish enjoy nothing more than a feast of wood pulp paper, flour paste, and glue. Cockroaches seem to eat anything but have a taste for book glue. Termites prefer wood, but wood pulp paper is a good second choice. Larder beetle larvae (book worms), while lacking intellectual curiosity, can devour *War and Peace* in a short time. Finally, book lice enjoy the starch and gelatin sizing on paper. Other, less destructive insects can infest collections in the temperate zones; in a tropical setting, the numbers and varieties increase dramatically. Control of insects presents a few challenges, because pesticides create pollution problems. Naturally, the best control is to keep the insects out. One way to control insects, especially cockroaches, is to keep food and drink out of the library. A second step is to keep the temperature and humidity as low as possible, because insects multiply faster and are more active at higher temperature and humidity levels. If the library faces a significant insect infestation, it is better to call on a commercial service rather than attempt to handle the problem with library staff.

Gifts to the library require careful examination before storing them in an area where insects could get into the general collection. Shipments that arrive by sea mail also need careful study. As the concern for the environment increases, many of the in-library fumigation units have ceased to operate or been extensively (and expensively) modified. This may mean using commercial systems with additional costs and delays in getting and keeping material on the shelf.

Security

A full library security program involves several elements. Broadly, the program's goals are to assure the well-being of people and to protect the collections and equipment from theft and misuse. This discussion emphasizes the collections with only passing mention of the people and equipment issues; topics covered include theft, mutilation, and disaster preparedness. (For a fuller discussion of security programs, see chapter 14 in *Introduction to Library Public Services,* 5th edition.[1])

I have told students, only half in jest, that if a library wishes to identify its true core collection, all it has to do is prepare a list of all the lost and missing books and mutilated journal titles.

Normally, these are the items that, for one reason or another, are (or were) under pressure from users, including high-use or, in the case of missing books, potentially high-use materials.

Every library loses books each year to individuals who, if caught by the security system, say they forgot to check the material out. Journals and other noncirculating material are subject to some degree of mutilation. Each incident of theft and mutilation means some small financial loss for the library, if nothing more than the cost of the material and the labor expended to make the item available. Other costs are the cost of staff time to search for the item, to decide how or whether to replace it, and the replacement and processing costs. Though one incident seldom represents a significant cost, the total annual cost may be surprising, even if one calculates only the amount paid for replacement materials. The Loyola Marymount University library spends about $10,000 per year on replacement materials, and few of those replacements are for items that have become too worn to remain in circulation. This rate of loss occurs despite a high quality electronic security exit system and targeting every book and every issue of every journal that goes into the collection. Needless to say, time and money expended to prevent theft or replace materials is time and money not spent on expanding the resources available to customers.

There are several givens to any security program. First, there will be some level of loss no matter what the library does. Second, the systems help basically honest people stay honest. A professional thief will circumvent almost any library security system, as Stephen Blumberg demonstrated a few years ago.[2] Therefore, the library must decide how important the problem is and how much loss it can tolerate. The goal is to balance the cost of the security program against the losses. The less loss the library will accept, the higher the security costs, so finding the proper balance is important.

Most libraries employ some mix of people-based elements and electronic systems for security. Door guards or monitors who check every item taken from the library are the most effective and most costly option. It works well only when the person doing the checking is not a peer of the people being checked. That is, using students to check fellow students, much less their teachers, does not work well. Retired individuals are most effective. They interact well with users but also do the job without favoring anyone. The major drawback to exit monitors, after the cost, is, when there are peaks and valleys in the exit flow, there can be long queues during the peaks.

Electronic systems are common and may give a false sense of security. Every system has a weakness that the person who regularly "forgets to check out books" eventually discovers, and the professional thief knows. Also, some materials, for example, magnetic tape and videotape, cannot be deactivated, and some materials simply do not have a place for a target. Such systems are susceptible to electronic interference, such as frequencies generated by computers or even fluorescent light ballasts. Finally, the inventive thief can jam the operating frequency and no one on the staff will know the difference.

Mutilation is another ongoing problem, which, during a year, can generate a surprisingly large loss for the library. There are few cost-effective options for handling this problem. Having copy services available and at competitive prices will help. Monitors walking through the building will solve or reduce many other security problems but will do little to stop mutilation. Studies suggest that even customers who see someone mutilating library materials will not report the activity to library staff.[3] One option that customers do not like, but that does stop the mutilation of journals, is to supply only microform back files of journals that are subject to high mutilation. This option does not safeguard the current issues, and it requires providing microform reader-printers, which are more expensive than microform readers. There is also the occasional title that does not make its back files available in a microformat. Perhaps sometime in the future, full-text CD-ROMs or online services will provide an answer to the problem, because there is little user resistance to electronic material. However, at present, there is little full-text material available, and there is the possibility people will not like sitting in front of a CRT to read their favorite journal any more than they like the microform reader screen. Another option is to acquire multiple copies of high-use titles. Here again, one trades some breadth in collection possibilities for a possible reduction in mutilation.

Theft and mutilation are a part of doing business. How much they cost the library depends on the local situation. Those costs come at the expense of adding greater variety to the collections and, in the long run, they hurt the customer.

Disaster preparedness planning is vital for the protection of people, collections, and equipment. Planners must think in terms of both natural and man-made disasters. Earthquakes, hurricanes, tornadoes, heavy rains, and floods are the most common natural disasters for which one should plan. The most common man-made disaster is water damage, which can be caused by a broken water pipe or sprinkler head, a faulty air conditioning system, or broken windows. In the case of a fire, water may cause more damage than the flames.

The following are the basic steps to take in preparing a disaster plan:

1. Study the library for potential problems. Often, the institution's risk management officer (insurance) is more than willing to help in that assessment.

2. Meet with local fire and safety officers for the same purpose.

3. Establish a planning team to develop a plan. This team may become the disaster handling team.

4. Establish procedures for handling each type of disaster and, if appropriate, form different teams to handle each situation.

5. Establish a telephone calling tree, or other fast notification system, for each disaster. A telephone tree is a plan for who calls whom in what order.

6. Develop a salvage priority list for the collections. If necessary, mark a set of floor plans and include them in the disaster planning and response manual. Most plans do not have more than three levels of priority: first priority is irreplaceable or costly materials, second priority is materials that are expensive or difficult to replace, and third priority is the rest of the collection. The LMU plan includes a category for hand-carrying one or two items from the immediate work area, if the disaster strikes during normal working hours. Establishing priorities can be a challenge for planners, because everyone has some vested interest in the subject areas with which they work.

7. Develop a list of recovery supplies the library will maintain on site, for example, plastic sheeting and butcher paper.

8. Include a list of resources—people and companies—who may assist in the recovery work.

Needless to say, after the planners finish the disaster plan, the library must put copies in the hands of each department and in the homes of the disaster team. It is also important to practice some of the procedures before disaster strikes. The LMU plan has been in place for six years and has been used three times, twice for water problems and once for an earthquake. With the water problems, the library was able to save all but eight books out of more than 15,000 that got wet. Had the staff not practiced its disaster response plan ahead of time, the loss rate would have been much higher. The library did not fare as well in the earthquake, because it is impossible to practice having book stacks collapse. Though LMU certainly fared better than libraries closer to the epicenter, it lost 1,237 books. Unfortunately, these losses could have been avoided if the shelving had been properly braced. The library staff knew where the problem stacks were and was waiting for funds to have the stacks retrofitted; however, the earthquake was quicker than the funding authorities.

Locating water, gas, and electrical system shut-offs is a good starting point for training the disaster team.

Next, the team should check fire extinguisher locations to determine whether the units are operational and are inspected on a regular basis.

The team also should implement a program to train staff in the use of the extinguishers. Usually, the local fire department will do this at no charge. There are three types of fire extinguishers: "A" for wood and paper fires, "B" for oil and electrical fires, and "C" for either type of fire. Match type to location and anticipated problems. Prepare floor plans, clearly identifying locations of shut-offs and extinguishers.

Salvage operations require careful planning and adequate personnel and materials. It is a good idea to develop a list of potential volunteers if the situation is too large for the staff to handle within a reasonable time. Keep in mind that the library can count on only about 72 hours of assistance from volunteers—that is, 72 hours from the time the first request for assistance goes out. Thus, there should be planning for what to do after 72 hours, if the disaster is major.

Water damage is a potentially destructive problem, as is the development of mold and mildew. Mold can develop in as little as 48 hours, depending on the temperature. What basic steps should one follow in a water emergency? The best way to handle large quantities of water-soaked paper is to freeze it and process the material as time and money allow. Planners should identify companies with large freezer facilities and discuss with them the possibility of using or renting their freezers in case of emergency. Often, such companies are willing to do this at no cost because of the publicity they gain from such an act. Large grocery store chains and meat packing plants are possible participants. Refrigerated trucks can be most useful, if costly to rent. Getting wet materials to the freezing units is a problem: milk crates, open plastic boxes, or clothes baskets work well, because they allow water to drain. Cardboard boxes absorb water. Plastic interlocking milk crates are ideal, because they are about the right size for a person to handle when three-fourths full of wet material. Sometimes, local dairies are willing to assist by supplying free crates for the duration of the emergency. Freezer or butcher paper is best for separating the materials; never use newsprint, because it tends to stick and the ink comes off. Finally, find some drying facilities. There are three primary methods of drying wet books: 1) freezing/freeze-drying, 2) vacuum drying, and 3) vacuum freeze-drying. Vacuum freeze-drying is the best way to handle wet items. Often, vacuum drying facilities are difficult to locate and can handle only a small volume of material at a time, so materials may be in the freezer for a long time while a small quantity is done whenever the source and funding permit. A variety of disaster-related online information, including Peter Waters' *Procedures for Salvage of Water-Damaged Library Materials*, is available from Conservation OnLine (CoOL) (see page 477).

Two other steps are important when designing a disaster preparedness plan. One is to identify the nearest conservation specialist(s). Most are willing to serve as a telephone resource, and often, they will come to the scene. A second important step is to arrange for special purchasing power. Although some groups, organizations, and companies may be willing to assist free of charge, many will not, and there may be a need to make a commitment quickly to a specific expense. Having to wait even a few hours for approval may cause irreversible damage.

Although most disasters are minor—a few hundred water-damaged items—a large disaster is always possible. One example was the April 1986 fire that struck the Los Angeles Public Library. For more than 10 years, there had been concern about the fire danger, but the hope that a new building would be constructed forestalled major modifications in the existing building. According to *Library Hotline,* it took 1,700 volunteers working around the clock to shrinkwrap and freeze the 400,000 water-soaked books (about 20 percent of the Central Library's collection).[4] In addition, the city paid a salvage contractor $500,000 for his firm's services. One can only speculate what the costs and problems might have been with no disaster preparedness plan.

Conservation Factors

By having the collection properly stored and handled in a controlled climate, and with sound security practices as well as a disaster preparedness plan in place, the library will lengthen the useful life of its materials in addition to reducing preservation problems. However, if the library fails to employ good conservation methods, much of what it gains from those practices becomes lost as items fade, decompose, or become unusable. Conservation should start with the purchase decision (which ought to include consideration of how well the material will stand up to the expected use) and should end with the question of what to do about worn, damaged materials and items identified in the weeding process.

One element in a library's conservation program is the basic binding and repair program. In-house repairs are fine as long as they employ good conservation methods and use materials that will not cause more harm. Repairers should do nothing that cannot be undone later, if necessary. For example, one should avoid using any adhesive tape other than a reversible adhesive, nonacidic tape to repair a torn page.

Most commercial binderies follow sound practices and employ materials that will not add to an already serious problem of decomposing books. An excellent overview of library binding practices, in a commercial setting, is Paul Parisi's "An Overview of Library Binding: Where We Are, How We Got Here, What We Do."[5] Selecting a commercial binder should involve the chief collection officer, if the bindery operation is not under the supervision of that person. Most libraries spend thousands of dollars on bindery and repair work each year, and having a reliable and efficient binder, who uses the proper materials, benefits the library and its customers. Knowing something about bindery operations and the process the materials undergo can help the library staff responsible for selecting materials for binding to make better judgments about the type of binding to order, given the probable use of the material. Most commercial binders are pleased to explain their operations and give customers and new library employees tours of their plant.

At present, the source of many conservation and preservation problems is acidic wood pulp paper. William J. Barrow is the person most often associated with identifying acid as the cause of the deterioration of wood pulp paper. The problem is not new, but people are now seeing the full implications of the findings of Barrow and other researchers. Estimates vary as to just how big the problem is. One project estimated there were more than 600,000 brittle or moderately brittle books in a collection of two million books in the UCLA library system in 1979. (A brittle book is one in which a corner of a page breaks off when folded back and forth two or fewer times.) The estimate was based on a random sample of books in the collection. An estimated one million volumes in Widener Library (Harvard University) are in similar condition.[6] In the early 1980s, the Library of Congress estimated it had six million brittle volumes.[7] According to Richard Dougherty, the Commission on Preservation and Access estimated, "more than 25 percent of the world's greatest monographic collections are already embrittled beyond redemption."[8]

In the case of brittle books, short fibers and chemical residues from the paper manufacturing process are the culprits. The longer the fibers in the paper, the stronger it is. When ground wood pulp became the standard source for paper manufacturing, the long-term strength of paper dropped sharply. A weak paper with the acidic residue from sizing and bleaching as well as lignin (a component of the wood used for paper) combine to create self-destructing material. At one end of the scale is newsprint, which is very acidic; at the other end is nonacidic paper that more and more publishers are using in books. The Council on Library Resources' efforts to establish some guidelines for publishers, manufacturers, and librarians regarding the use of alkaline paper in book production are beginning to pay off. The CLR report states that "alkaline paper *need not be more expensive* than acidic paper of the quality normally used in hardbound books."[9]

The guidelines provide standards for both performance (acid content) and durability (folding and bending) as well as long-term book binding for the initial commercial binding.

Though the guidelines will reduce future problems, they cannot help the present situation. Each year, the number of brittle items already in the collection increases. What can be done about materials that are self-destructing in the stacks? Maintaining environmental factors (temperature, humidity, and light) at the recommended levels slows the chemical processes; thus, this is a first step to take. For the brittle materials in the collection, the two concerns are permanence (shelf life) and durability (use). Permanence is the first issue, and there are several ways to stop the acidic activity. After the acidic action is under control, several options exist to enhance durability.

Several mass deacidification systems on the market are designed to process large numbers of books at one time. The only one with a reasonably long history of use is the Wei T'o process developed by Richard Smith. Probably the second best known system is the DEZ system. Developed with the support of the Library of Congress, the process received widespread press coverage after it encountered several problems, the most notable being an explosion at the test site. A good review of the history of deacidification systems is found in Michèle V. Cloonan's "Mass Deacidification in the 1990s."[10]

Options for Handling Brittle Materials

Given the magnitude of the acid paper problem, almost every library will be faced with a variety of decisions regarding what to do. Here, if nowhere else, collection development staff must enter the preservation picture. When an item in the collection deteriorates to the point that it cannot be rebound, what should one do? Ten options exist:

Ignore the problem and return the item to storage.

Withdraw the item from the collection and do not replace it.

Seek a reprint edition on alkaline paper.

Convert the material to microfilm and decide what to do with the original.

Convert the material to an electronic format.

Photocopy the material on alkaline paper, and decide what to do with the original.

Seek a replacement copy in the out-of-print trade.

Place it in an alkaline protective enclosure made for the item and return it to the collection.

Withdraw the item from the main collection and place in a controlled access storage facility.

Deacidify and strengthen the item and return it to use.

Ignoring the problem is the most reasonable alternative for materials about which one is confident that long-term retention is unnecessary or undesirable and only a limited amount of use is probable. If there is little or no probability of use in the near future, withdrawing the item is probably the most effective option.

Seeking a reprint edition printed on alkaline paper is the least expensive option for materials that are worth long-term storage and probably will experience moderate to heavy use. Reprints are not available for all the items that are self-destructing; only the high-demand titles are reprinted. Several companies exist to serve the reprint market, for example, AMS, Scholarly Reprints, Kraus, Harvester Press Microform Publications, and Research Publications. *Guide to Reprints* (Guide to Reprints, Inc.), *Books on Demand* (University Microfilms), and *Guide to Microforms in Print* (Microform Review) are three sources of information about a broad range of titles. (Note: Just because an item is a reprint does not mean it is available on alkaline paper. Be certain to specify alkaline paper when ordering.)

Microformat and electronic storage of the brittle material are other options. Until the mid-1980s, microfilming was the most common way of storing the content of brittle materials in a secondary format. The cost of making the master negative is high, but once made, duplicate copies are relatively inexpensive to produce. Thus, if the primary collection development concern is with preserving the intellectual content of the brittle material and not with the item as an artifact, a microformat is a good solution. It may be possible to locate a master copy of an item, thereby reducing costs. Two places to check are the *National Register of Microforms Masters* (Library of Congress) and *Guide to Microforms in Print* (Meckler). The *Register* covers more than 3,000 library and publisher holdings worldwide and is produced by the Library of Congress. *Guide to Microforms in Print* is similar to *BIP*; it lists titles from commercial publishers around the world.

The Directory of Library Reprographic Services (Meckler) can be of assistance in identifying libraries with the capability of making a master. The Library of Congress has the most experience in working with analog videodisc technology as a preservation format. The advantages of the technology are high-density storage (54,000 graphic images stored on one disc) and random access to those images. On the other hand, optical disks are used to store print material. A disk can hold about 3,000 pages of text or 200,000 catalog cards. Both technologies have potential for assisting in solving preservation problems. As one might expect, there is a relatively high cost associated with these systems, but as more organizations use optical or analog disk technology, it is reasonable to expect the cost to decline.

Some publishers (and even the Copyright Office) have questions about the legality of converting copyrighted material to a disk format. How this differs in principle from microfilming, which no one seems to question, is unclear. Under U.S. Copyright Law (Sec. 108 [e]), it is possible for a library to make a single complete copy of an out-of-print item after making a reasonable search for the item.

A photocopy of the original may be the best option when the library anticipates moderate use and cannot locate a reprint. There are commercial firms that will produce a bound photocopy on alkaline paper from an individual volume on demand. This is an especially good alternative when it is not necessary to preserve the original item. Photocopying and microfilming cause physical wear on bound materials, and a bound item may need to be taken apart to duplicate properly. Generally, in the photocopy process, there is some loss in image quality; obviously, this is unacceptable for items with photographs and illustrations. Several paper manufacturers (for example Hollinger, Process Materials, and Xerox) offer buffered (alkaline) paper for use in photocopy machines. When binding the photocopies, it is necessary to specify that the binder use buffered materials.

If alkaline paper or deacidified paper comes into contact with acidic material, the acid will migrate into the alkaline paper, and the process starts all over.

The staff should think carefully before going to the out-of-print market for replacement copies. Although a replacement copy may be available at the lowest price of any of the options, will the replacement be in any better condition than the one it is to replace? Unless the replacement copy had better storage conditions than the library's copy, both will be in about the same state of deterioration. It is probable that the replacement copy will be less worn (as long as it is not an ex-library copy), but there will be little difference in the acidic state. Normally, the replacement copy's storage history is worse than the library's copy, and thus, the replacement copy will be in greater need of preservation. Locating a replacement copy in the out-of-print market will take months or even years. During the search, the library must decide what to do with the item in hand. If it is brittle, should customers continue to use it while the library is waiting for a replacement copy that may or may not exist? Additional use may make it difficult, or perhaps impossible, to exercise other options, if the library fails to find a replacement. Although the out-of-print market is a frequent first choice, it is probably the least suitable for long-term preservation purposes.

Protective enclosures or containers provide a stopgap treatment. Enclosing the brittle item in an alkaline container (made of paper, plastic, cardboard) protects it from unnecessary handling and light. This is a common method of storage for the original (hopefully deacidified) item when a surrogate copy is available for general use. The most common approach is to make custom-sized phase boxes for the item using alkaline cardboard. Bindery supply firms and commercial binderies offer a wide range of prefabricated standard-sized phase boxes, as well as materials for constructing custom-sized boxes. Unfortunately, the materials, including alkaline mending tapes and adhesives, are expensive. To save a small amount of money, some libraries decide not to use the proper materials. Certainly, there is no need to use expensive mending materials on items that the library is likely to discard in time, but, all too often, librarians do not know which items will be kept and which will be discarded.

Secondary storage is a stopgap measure in most cases. It may become the most common first option when the quantity of brittle materials escalates beyond the library's ability to handle it. A controlled environment with limited handling would slow the destructive process and buy some time to determine which of the more permanent solutions can be implemented. The essential element is controlling the storage environment; merely placing the materials in a remote storage area with the same or worse climate control accomplishes little and may cause further deterioration. Another danger of remote storage is that, all too often, the adage "out of sight, out of mind" applies. Without a preservation officer or someone on the staff charged with supervising preservation activities, the storage area can become a dumping ground for materials that no one wants to think about. Even in a controlled environment, the disintegration continues day and night until something is done to stop it.

The following are some basic guidelines for preparing materials for storage:

1. Remove extraneous materials, such as paper clips, rubber bands, wrapping material, old folders, and any other material that is not pertinent. If foreign matter, such as pressed flowers, must be saved as documentary evidence, place it in a separate enclosure.

2. Unfold and flatten papers wherever possible without causing damage to the folds. If the paper is brittle or inflexible, it may need to be humidified before unfolding. Remove surface soil with a soft brush.

3. Isolate newsprint because it is highly acidic and will stain adjacent paper. Newspaper clippings can be replaced with photocopies on alkaline paper or placed in a separate envelope. Fax copies are similarly unstable and should be reproduced or isolated, unless they are plain paper faxes.

4. Note any badly damaged items, place them within individual folders, and set them aside for professional conservation treatment. Do not undertake any first aid unless you have received training and are qualified to do so.

5. If it is necessary to place identifying information on the object itself, use a soft (no. 2) pencil and write on the verso or in the lower right margin. Repeat the identification on the storage folders and envelopes in pencil or typing. Never use ballpoint or felt-tip pens that might stain or bleed.

6. Identify boxes with labels that contain adequate information about the contents. This curtails unnecessary browsing and rifling though documents.[11]

If materials need to be humidified (see step 2), one should consult Mary Lynn Ritzenthaler's *Preserving Archives and Manuscripts*.[12]

Restoration is expensive, and libraries will never be able to restore all or even most of the brittle items they own. As noted earlier, the deacidification process is also expensive, and added to that are costs of restoring strength to the individual pages and binding. For a good description of the advantages and disadvantages of the various methods of preservation, see Robert Mareck's "Practicum on Preservation Selection."[13]

Nonpaper Preservation Issues

Although this chapter emphasizes books and paper, other library materials also require conservation care. In many cases, librarians do not fully understand how long the format may last without loss of information or what problems may arise. However, various groups, such as the Council on Library Resources (CLR), the Mellon Foundation, and the National Endowment for the Humanities, are actively exploring the area.

Like paper products, all photographic products (microfilm, photographs, motion picture films) are self-destructing on the shelves and in the cabinets of libraries and archives. There is some hope that electronic technologies will provide a more stable storage medium for older materials, but little testing has been done on their longevity. The Library of Congress is using analog videodiscs to store images from old glass lantern slides, photographs, motion picture publicity stills, and architectural drawings.

Current estimates are that CD-ROMs will have a 30-year life. This may not be a major problem, because one can restore digital information. However, no one can predict what it will cost to periodically check the data and restore it as necessary. Librarians do have some recommended guidelines for checking some of these special formats. Staff should inspect and rewind motion picture film once every three years, inspect and rewind videotape and audiotape every two years, and inspect still photographs every three years. Peter Graham's paper dealing with electronic preservation is an excellent source of information about the issues related to preserving the intellectual content in an electronic environment.[14] The Commission on Preservation and Access published a mission and goals statement for digital consortia that should help resolve some of the unanswered questions about digitized data and long-term retention. The goals are:

1. Verify and monitor the usefulness of digital imagery for preservation and access.

   a. Establish the convertibility of preservation media.

   b. Foster projects to capture special types of documents.

   c. Insure the longevity of digitized images.

   d. Cultivate research on the application of intelligent character recognition.

2. Define and promote shared methods and standards.

   a. Sponsor forums to define production quality standards.

   b. Promote the development and use of the document structure file.

   c. Create appropriate bibliographic control standards.

   d. Address copyright issues.

   e. Organize a document interchange project.

3. Enlarge the base of materials.

   a. Encourage the involvement of service bureaus.

   b. Focus on the conversion of thematically related materials.

   c. Mount a large inter-institutional collaborative project.

4. Develop and maintain reliable and affordable mechanisms to gain access to digital image documents.

   a. Involve a broad base of constituents in technology development.

   b. Forge effective support structures for end-users.

   c. Determine the efficacy of access to digital materials in the context of traditional library collections.[15]

These goals are very similar to those for the paper preservation efforts that started almost 10 years ago. If these goals are as successful as the earlier ones, there is reason to think the profession will resolve the digital preservation problems in time to save at least many valuable materials.

Cooperation

Because of the magnitude of the problems confronting libraries and scholars, it seems clear that cooperative preservation is essential. In the mid-1980s, under the leadership of CRL, the profession created the Commission on Preservation and Access. Two groups, ARL and RLG, have been collecting statistics on research library preservation activities and developing guidelines. The National Endowment for the Humanities has provided funding for microfilming projects. A program for educating preservation librarians was started at the Columbia University Library School, and, after that school closed, the preservation program was transferred to the University of Texas Library School. Many large libraries are hiring full-time preservation specialists. Two newsletters that allow one to keep up-to-date on conservation matters are *The Abbey Newsletter* (7105 Geneva Drive, Austin TX 78723) and *CAN: Conservation Administration News* (Graduate School of Library and Information Science, University of Texas, Austin, TX 78712). The American Institute for Conservation of Historic and Artistic Works (AIC) provides a forum for concerned individuals to discuss preservation and conservation issues. Naturally, ALA and many of its divisions have an active interest in this area, as do most other library associations around the world. One online source of information is Conservation OnLine (CoOL), optimally accessed via the World Wide Web. Using a Web client (Mosaic, Netscape, etc.) open the following URL: http://palimpsest.stanford.edu—otherwise, gopher to: palimpsest.stanford.edu and 'Browse by Topic'.

In addition to national efforts, several regional preservation cooperatives exist. One such group project is the University Center of Georgia. This group started by educating staff members and raising the awareness of preservation issues and concerns and what to do to help reduce the problems. The group's operating premises are reflective of the message this chapter attempts to convey:

> There are some areas in preservation that do not require a team of experts. Self-reliance should be developed in these areas. One area in which this could be done is basic housekeeping.

> Prevention is more cost-effective than treatment. Prevention will be stressed as a priority. (For example, preservation thinking will be built into the collection building process.)

> Preservation is an ongoing activity that is part of normal work flow. Awareness of this, and a sense of individual responsibility, will be fostered. (Again, this emphasizes the basic activities each staff can perform that will help protect the collections.)

> Library and archival collections represent an investment that preservation can protect. (Preservation is an essential function, like cataloging or acquisitions, and should be funded as such.)

> Low-cost preservation activities are possible and desirable, but no-cost preservation is unrealistic.[16]

Another example of a regional cooperative is MAPS (**M**icrogr**A**phic **P**reservation **S**ervice), a service established by Columbia, Cornell, and Princeton, the New York Public Library, and the New York State Library.

> MAPS' focus is to assist libraries, archives, museums, and historical societies prepare their preservation microfilm for the digital present and future. . . . To simply reformat endangered

materials into a form resistant to scanning or one that complicates scanning is a serious disservice to scholars and researchers of the future."[17]

Efforts like these will help solve future preservation problems. All library professionals should do their part to avoid adding to these problems.

Insurance

Careful planning, proper handling, and the other elements discussed in this chapter will help prolong the useful life of collections. A good disaster preparedness plan will help reduce the scope of loss when disaster strikes. Because the odds are rather high that a disaster will strike, where will the library get the funds to replace the materials damaged beyond salvaging? In fact, where will the library get the funds to salvage what it can? The obvious answer is some type of insurance. The section on developing a disaster preparedness plan suggests that one early contact for the planning team should be the institution's risk manager. This is the person who monitors the safety conditions in the work place and oversees the insurance programs that cover various loss situations, from fires to slippery floors to actions of the institutional officers. The risk manager for LMU visits the library once a year to discuss any new or outstanding problems as well as to review the values assigned to the collections, equipment, and building.

The LMU risk manager and library staff have discussed and clarified the fact that there will be insurance coverage for salvage operations, after the institution's deductible limit is surpassed. Discussions regarding the collection valuation have been interesting, especially when it comes to what to do about coverage for special collections and archives materials. If a Shakespeare folio is stolen or destroyed by fire, it is most unlikely the library could ever replace it, even if the library insured each folio for several million dollars. The risk manager sees no point in paying an extra premium for something that cannot be replaced. That moved the discussion to facsimile works and the appropriateness of replacing an original with a top-of-the-line facsimile. To date, this is a topic of ongoing debate. Anyone who has dealt with homeowners' or renters' insurance representatives and policies can understand the complexities involved. Does the collection valuation increase or decrease over time? What does *replacement* mean? Will there be funds to process the material or merely to acquire it? What damage is covered? In 1989, twelve ranges of shelving containing 20,000 volumes collapsed at the Columbia University library annex. Many, if not most, of the volumes were brittle, so the fall was very damaging. However, the embrittlement was a pre-existing condition. After some long negotiations, the insurer agreed to pay for volumes with damage to the cover or text block attachments, but not for volumes with broken pages. There were questions about serial runs as well; this was finally resolved with the insurer paying for the entire run of back files, if more than one third of the run was damaged.[18]

Working out reasonable arrangements in advance, such as who pays for salvage work, will reduce the pressure on everyone during a disaster. One cannot anticipate everything, but some issues are bound to arise, and, to the extent one can deal with those concerns ahead of time, there will be fewer distractions during the recovery phase. Another element that needs pre-disaster discussion is how to value the collection. One common way is to use averages, such as one finds in the *The Bowker Annual*, and multiply that by the number of units held. The problem with that approach, as was noted in an unsigned comment on the collection development listserv, is that local circumstances also determine the value of an item; "a single volume of *JAMA* from 1952 is probably worth $2.00, but as part of a set that is missing from 1952, it's worth $500!"[19]

For a good discussion about replacement, actual cash value, average replacement cost, valuable papers and records coverage, as well as other basic insurance topics and libraries, see Judith Fortson's "Disaster Planning: Managing the Financial Risk."[20] Having insurance is a sound practice, because almost every library at some time will have a disaster of some type and size. Having insurance is one more step in protecting the library's and institution's investment.

Summary

This chapter highlights the many aspects of protecting the collections on which libraries and information centers expend large sums of money. Many of the issues raised are ones virtually any library staff member can implement without major changes in duties or in training. Preparing for trouble always makes it easier to handle the trouble when, or if, it happens. Knowing what type of financial help one can expect to assist in recovering from a disaster can provide some peace of mind, if nothing else. Long-term preservation, though the primary responsibility of the large libraries, is also a concern, or should be, of all libraries and information centers. Working together, we will solve preservation problems, even if it takes a long time and great effort.

Notes

[1] G. Edward Evans, Anthony Amodeo, and Thomas Carter, *Introduction to Library Public Services*, 5th ed. (Englewood, CO: Libraries Unlimited, 1992).

[2] Susan Allen, "The Blumberg Case: A Costly Lesson for Librarians," *AB Bookman's Weekly* 88 (September 2, 1991): 769-73.

[3] Terri L. Pederson, "Theft and Mutilation of Library Materials," *College & Research Libraries* 51 (March 1990): 120-28.

[4] *Library Hotline* (May 12, 1986): 2.

[5] Paul A. Parisi, "An Overview of Library Binding: Where We Are, How We Got Here, What We Do," *The New Library Scene* 12 (February 1993): 5-9.

[6]*Harvard Crimson* (October 23, 1986): 1.

[7]*Book Longevity* (Washington, DC: Council on Library Resources, 1982).

[8]Richard Dougherty, "Redefining Preservation and Reconceptualizing Information Service," *Library Issues* 13 (November 1992): 1.

[9]*Book Longevity*, 9.

[10]Michèle V. Cloonan, "Mass Deacidification in the 1990s," *Rare Books & Manuscripts Librarianship* 5, no. 2 (1990): 95-103.

[11]*Gaylord Preservation Pathfinder No. 2, Archival Storage of Paper* (Syracuse, NY: Gaylord Brothers, 1993): 5.

[12]Mary Lynn Ritzenthaler, *Preserving Archives and Manuscripts* (Chicago: Society of American Archivists, 1993).

[13]Robert Mareck, "Practicum on Preservation Selection," in *Collection Management for the 1990s*, edited by J. J. Brain, 114-26 (Chicago: American Library Association, 1993).

[14]Peter Graham, *Intellectual Preservation: Electronic Preservation of the Third Kind* (Washington, DC: Commission on Preservation and Access, 1994).

[15]*Digital Preservation Consortium: Mission and Goals* (Washington, DC: Commission on Preservation and Access, 1994).

[16]Laurel Bowen and Nan McMurry, "How Firm a Foundation: Getting Cooperative Preservation Off the Ground," *Collection Building* 13, no. 4 (1993): 28.

[17]"MAPS—Preservation for the Future," *PAC-News* 45 (June 1993): 2.

[18]Janet Gertz, "Columbia Libraries Annex Disaster," *Archival Products News* 1 (Summer 1992): 2.

[19]"Number 570—Collection Valuation (Summary of Responses)" COLLD-L@USCVM, August 8, 1994. [listserv.]

[20]Judith Fortson, "Disaster Planning: Managing the Financial Risk," *Bottom Line* 6 (Spring 1992): 26-33.

Further Reading

Conservation

Bansa, H. "New Media: Means for Better Preservation or Special Preservation Problem?" *Restaurator* 12, no. 4 (1991): 219-32.

Brittle Books: Reports of the Committee on Preservation and Access. Washington, DC: Council on Library Resources, 1986.

Child, M. *Directory of Information Sources on Scientific Research Related to the Preservation of Sound Recordings, Still and Moving Images and Magnetic Tape.* Washington, DC: Commission on Preservation and Access, 1993.

————. "Preservation Issues for Collection Development Staff." *Wilson Library Bulletin* 67 (November 1992): 20-21.

Clark, L., ed. *Guide to Review Library Collections; Preservation, Storage and Withdrawal.* Chicago: American Library Association, 1991.

Cloonan, M. V. "Preservation of Knowledge." *Library Trends* 41 (Spring 1993): 594-605.

Cunha, G., and D. Cunha. *Library and Archives Conservation: 1980s and Beyond.* 2 vols. Metuchen, NJ: Scarecrow Press, 1983.

Eden, P.; J. Feather; and L. Graham. "Preservation Policies and Conservation in British Academic Libraries." *British Journal of Academic Librarianship* 8, no. 2 (1993): 65-88.

Fortson, J. *Disaster Planning and Recovery.* New York: Neal-Schuman, 1992.

Fox, L. L. *A Core Collection in Preservation.* Chicago: American Library Association, 1988.

Gertz, J. E.; C. B. Brown; and J. Beebe. "Preservation Analysis and the Brittle Book Problem." *College & Research Libraries* 54 (May 1993): 227-39.

Greenfield, J. *Books, Their Care and Repair.* New York: H. W. Wilson, 1983.

Henderson, K. L., and W. T. Henderson. *Conserving and Preserving Materials in Nonbook Formats.* Urbana, IL: University of Illinois, Graduate School of Library and Information Science, 1991.

Higginbotham, B. B., and M. E. Jackson, eds. *Advances in Preservation and Access.* Greenwich, CT: Meckler, 1992.

Kueppers, B., and C. Coleman. "Preservation of Performing Arts Materials in Los Angeles." *Conservation Administration News* 54 (July 1993): 12-13.

Lienardy, A. "Evaluation of Seven Mass Deacidification Treatments." *Restaurator* 15, no. 1 (1994): 1-25.

Lowry, M. D. "Preservation and Conservation in the Small Library." *Public Library Quarterly* 11, no. 3 (1991): 58-60.

McCabe, C. "Photographic Preservation." *Restaurator* 12, no. 4 (1991): 185-200.

Manns, B. "The Electronic Document Format." In *Preservation of Electronic Formats & Electronic Formats for Preservation*, edited by J. Mohlhenrich, 63-81. New York: Highsmith Press, 1993.

Merrill-Oldham J., and P. Parisi. *Guide to the Library Binding Standard for Library Bindings.* Chicago: American Library Association, 1986.

Mohlhenrich, J., ed. *Preservation of Electronic Formats & Electronic Formats for Preservation.* New York: Highsmith Press, 1993.

Morrow, C. C., and C. Dyal. *Conservation Treatment Procedures*. 2d ed. Littleton, CO: Libraries Unlimited, 1986.

Nelson-Strauss, B. "Preservation Policies and Priorities for Record Sound Collections." *Notes* 48 (December 1991): 425-36.

Oakley, R. L. "Copyright and Preservation." *Bookmark* 50 (Winter 1992): 121-24.

"Preservation Treatment Options for Law Libraries." *Law Library Journal* 84 (Spring 1992): 259-79.

Reilly, B., and J. Porro, eds. *Photograph Preservation and the Research Library*. Stanford, CA: Research Library Group, 1991.

Silberman, R. M. "Mandate for Change in the Library Environment." *Library Administration & Management* 7 (Summer 1993): 145-52.

Sitts, M. *A Practical Guide to Preservation in School and Public Libraries*. Syracuse, NY: Information Resources Publications, 1990.

Slide, A. *Nitrate Won't Wait*. New York: McFarland, 1992.

Environmental Control

Applebaum, B. *Guide to Environmental Protection of Collections*. Madison, CT: Sound View Press, 1991.

Davis, M. "Preservation Using Pesticides: Some Words of Caution." *Wilson Library Bulletin* 59 (February (1985): 386-88.

Dean, S. T., and S. R. Williams. "Renovation for Climate Control." *Conservation Administration News* 56 (January 1994): 12-13.

Gwin, J. E. "Preservation and Environmental Control Issues." In *Academic Libraries in Urban and Metropolitan Areas,* edited by G. McCabe, 187-94. Westport, CT: Greenwood Press, 1992.

Stranger, C., and L. Brandis. "Insect Pests and Their Eradication." *Australian Library Journal* 41 (August 1992): 180-83.

Swartzburg, S.; H. Bussey; and F. Garretson. *Libraries and Archives: Design and Renovation With a Preservation Perspective*. Metuchen, NJ: Scarecrow Press, 1991.

Thomson, G. *Museum Environment*. 2d ed. Stoneham, MA: Butterworths, 1986.

Valentin, N., and F. Preusser. "Insect Control by Inert Gases in Museums, Archives and Libraries." *Restaurator* 11, no. 1 (1990): 22-33.

Housekeeping

Dibble, B. "Conservation in the Stacks." *Idaho Librarian* 42 (January 1990): 7-8.

Ristau, H. "Keep Your Shelves in Order." *School Library Journal* 35 (May 1988): 39-43.

Insurance

Berges, C. "Risk Management: The Unrecognized Necessity." *Rural Libraries* 13, no. 1 (1993): 53-66.

Brawner, L. B. "Insurance and Risk Management for Libraries." *Public Library Quarterly* 13, no. 1 (1993): 5-15.

Delong, L. R. "Valuating Library Collections." In *Conference on Acquisitions, Budget, and Collections,* 89-95. St. Louis, MO: Genaway & Associates, 1990.

Parsons, J. "Insurance Implications of Crime and Security." In *Security and Crime Prevention in Libraries,* edited by M. Chaney and A. P. MacDougall, 203-16. New York: Ashgate, 1992.

Ungarelli, D. L. "Are Our Libraries Safe from Losses?" *Library & Archival Security* 10, no. 1 (1990): 55-58.

———. "Insurance and Prevention: Why and How?" *Library Trends* 33 (Summer 1984): 57-67.

Security

Bahr, A. H. "Electronic Collection Security Systems Today." *Library & Archival Security* 11, no. 1 (1991): 3-22.

———. "The Thief in Our Midst." *Library & Archival Security* 9, nos. 3/4 (1989): 69-74.

Collver, M. "Subsequent Demand for Ripped-off Journal Articles." *Reference Librarian* 28, nos. 27/28 (1989): 347-66.

Cunha, G. M. "Disaster Planning and a Guide to Recovery Resources." *Library Technology Reports* 28 (September/October 1992): 533-623.

Harris, C. L. "Preservation Considerations in Electronic Security Systems." *Library & Archival Security* 11, no. 1 (1991): 35-42.

Hulyk, B. R. "Rare and Valuable Documents: Identification, Preservation, and Security Issues." *North Carolina Libraries* 48 (Summer 1990): 118-21.

Lilly, R. S.; B. F. Schloman; and W. L. Hu. "Ripoffs Revisited." *Library & Archival Security* 11, no. 1 (1991): 43-70.

McDonald, A. C. "Book Detection Systems." In *Security and Crime Prevention in Libraries,* edited by M. Chaney and A. P. MacDougall, 289-97. New York: Ashgate, 1992.

Morris, J. *Library Disaster Preparedness Handbook.* Chicago: American Library Association, 1986.

Smith, F. E. "Door Checkers: An Unacceptable Security Alternative." *Library & Archival Security* 7 (Spring 1985): 7-13.

Stoker, D. "The Case of the Disappearing Books." *Journal of Librarianship and Information Science* 23 (September 1991): 121-24.

Wall, C. "Inventory: What You Might Expect to Be Missing." *Library & Archival Security* 7 (Summer 1985): 27-31.

Wyly, M. "Special Collections Security." *Library Trends* 36 (Summer 1987): 258-59.

18
Legal Issues

National laws and regulations influence collection development activities. Two of the topics discussed in this chapter are of concern only to U.S. libraries. However, most of the chapter addresses copyright, lending rights, licensing agreements, and other concepts of interest to libraries around the world. Two additional legal issues relating to U.S. libraries concern Internal Revenue Service (IRS) regulations.

IRS Regulations

Valuing Gifts

One of the IRS regulations relevant to libraries has to do with gifts and donations to a library or not-for-profit information center. Any library, or its parent institution, that receives a gift in-kind (books, journals, manuscripts, and so forth) with an appraised value of $5,000 or more must report the gift to the IRS. A second regulation forbids the receiving party (in this case the library) to provide an estimated value for the gift in-kind. A third disinterested party or organization must make the valuation. The latter requirement grew out of concern that recipients were placing unrealistically high values on gifts. The donor received a larger tax deduction than was warranted, and it did not cost the receiving organization anything to place a high value on the gift. Normally, an appraiser charges a fee for valuing gifts, and the donor is supposed to pay the fee. Most often, the appraisers are antiquarian dealers who charge a flat fee for the service unless the collection is large or complex. If the appraisal is complex, the appraiser either charges a percentage of the appraised value or an hourly fee. Typically, with gifts small in value, the library writes a letter of acknowledgment indicating the number and type of items received. The donor can set a value on the gift for tax purposes. If asked, the library can provide dealer catalogs for the donors to see retail prices for items similar to their donation. However, the final value of the gift is established by the donor and her or his tax accountant. Note: The collection development staff should be involved in the acceptance of gifts and must have some sound knowledge of material prices. Just because the gift is small in number of items does not mean the fair market value is below $5,000. Recently, Loyola Marymount University (LMU) received a gift of 483 books about Japanese art, architecture, and landscape design; its appraised value was $39,743. The donor might well have accepted a letter stating the number of books given and thus have lost a substantial tax deduction. (For additional discussion about gifts, see chapter 11.)

Publishers' Inventories

Another IRS regulation or ruling (the Thor Power Tool decision, *Thor Power Tool Company* vs. *Commissioner of Internal Revenue*, Jan. 16, 1979, 439 U.S. 522) has had some influence on acquisition practices in the 1980s and early 1990s. The ruling held illegal a practice common to business (including the publishing industry), which was writing down the value of inventories to a low level each year. The practice produced a paper loss that the firm deducted from its income, thus reducing tax liability. The U.S. Supreme Court, deciding that this was taking a current deduction for an estimated future loss, said the practice was inappropriate. Only if the inventory is defective or if there is objective evidence that the firm offered the inventory for sale below cost could it employ the write down.

What does the Thor decision have to do with collection development? Publishers who followed the write down practice claimed it was the only way they could afford to publish small runs of books expected to sell slowly (four to five years to sell out the first printing). Publishers talked about destroying some of their stock, and some did. In 1981 and 1982, jobbers indicated they received increased OP and OS reports from publishers. Blackwell North America stated in a promotional flyer in mid-1981, "[W]e are receiving more o.p., o.s. and generally non-reports, than ever before. In fact, our reports to libraries on unavailable titles have increased 47 percent over a year ago."

There was some hope that the U.S. Congress might pass some legislation exempting publishers. What probably helped resolve the concern was the 1987 tax reform act. While not addressing the question of inventories, the act did reduce corporate tax rates, thus reducing the need to find deductions. Concern has decreased, but publishers appear to declare items out of print more quickly now than before the Thor decision. No one is certain whether there has been a decline in short-run titles published or whether such a decline, if it exists, is the result of the Thor decision or the result of a changing economy. The decision means librarians should not count on finding this year's imprints available in a year or two. In the past, a library might well have decided not to buy some current items, thinking that they could be ordered in a year or two, when funding would be better. Today, it is probably best to buy materials now rather than wait.

In 1990, Ambassador Book Service (a book jobber located in New York state), in response to librarian concerns about the increasing problem of OP and OS reports, issued some fact sheets. One sheet, based on data from the online version of *Books in Print (BIP)*, showed books published, in print and out-of-print for an 11-year period (1979-1989). The table illustrated what everyone knows, the percentage of out-of-print materials increases the farther back in time one goes. However, 81.9 percent of the titles listed in the 1979 *BIP* were available in 1984, and 46.9 percent were available in early 1990. Acquisition or collection development common knowledge was that most books go out-of-print within four to five years.

Which was right, the vendor's data or librarians' common knowledge? Both are right and wrong. The vendor's data is correct, as far as it goes—that is, items listed in *BIP*. When one considers libraries acquire a wide range of items not in *BIP*, including small and regional press titles, report literature, scholarly society publications, and so forth, the picture changes. Without doubt, there has been an increase in items going OP. In many cases, the slowing economy and library cutbacks on monographic purchases caused small publishers (private or professional) to reduce press runs. An article by Margaret McKinley, "The Thor Inventory Ruling: Fact or Fiction,"[1] provides a good review of the issue. It leaves the reader with the impression that there was and still is some impact of the Thor decision, but not nearly as much as librarians believed.

Copyright

Is copyright an issue in collection development? Yes. Cooperative collection development efforts depend on sharing resources through interlibrary loan or some reciprocal borrowing agreement. How does the copyright law affect these programs? The Information Industry Association formed a task force to look at the issue of library resource sharing. Only time will provide the definitive answer to the question of what changes will be necessary to comply with the present law. Clearly, libraries have modified copying policies as well as interlibrary loan practices. For example, under the new law, a library in a not-for-profit setting may borrow no more than five articles per year from any given journal. If the library borrows more than five articles, the assumption is that the borrowing is in lieu of placing a subscription and thus, a violation of the law. If libraries may not freely exchange books, periodicals, or photocopies of copyrighted items, it will be difficult to develop effective cooperative systems.

Copyright grants the creators of works certain rights that protect their interest in the work. Originally, copyright's purpose was to provide protection against unauthorized printing, publishing, importing, or selling of multiple copies of a work. In essence, it was protection from the unauthorized mass production and sale of a work. It was a straightforward and seemingly reasonable method of encouraging individuals or businesses to take a financial risk to produce and distribute information. Libraries, on the other hand, exist to disseminate information on a mass, usually free, basis. Until photocopiers appeared on the scene, the relationship between copyright holders and libraries was cordial, if not friendly.

With the development of fast, inexpensive photocopying, problems arose. Though the library might make only a single copy for a customer, the aggregate number of copies could be very high. By the mid-1960s, the volume of copying became so great that copyright holders thought that libraries, schools, and individuals were violating their rights and, in some cases, they were correct.

In the past, copying printed matter for personal use was no problem. Word-for-word hand copying of extensive sections of books or complete magazine articles was uncommon—people took notes. Today, quick, inexpensive copy services exist everywhere. All of us have made photocopies of complete journal articles rather than take notes, and many of the articles were from current issues of periodicals that we could have purchased for not much more than the cost of the copied item. All of us have done it and, if we thought about it at all, thought that just one copy isn't going to hurt anyone. Unfortunately, as the number of such copies mounts, so does the problem.

With audiovisual materials (for example, videotapes and audiotapes), the problem is acute. Institutions and individuals who own the hardware to play these materials also have copying capabilities. Control of copying is even more difficult to achieve for audiovisual materials than for books or journals. Preview copies help control the institutional buying situation, because they tend to show wear to such an extent that many persons would not want to reproduce a copy. If the preview copy shows too much wear, however, the library's buyer may decide not to buy the item because it lacks technical quality.

Library patrons in general have certain rights to gain access to and to use copyrighted material. Where to draw the line between creators' and users' rights is a complicated problem. A 1975 editorial by J. Berry in *Library Journal* summed up the complex issues involved in library copying. Today, the issues are as complicated, if not more so, than they were when he wrote the editorial.

> Here at *LJ* we are often asked why the magazine has not come out strongly on one side or the other of the copyright issue. We are after all a library magazine. . . . In the case of copyright, however, our library-mindedness is somewhat blunted by the facts of our existence as a publication which is in copyright and is published by an independent, commercial publisher. Not only is copyright protection fundamental to our continued fiscal health, [but] we believe that authors and publishers deserve compensation for their creative work and for the risks taken to package and deliver that creative effort to users of it.
>
> Like any magazine publisher we have winced when it was obvious our rights in our published material have been violated. . . . Yet there is the other side, the flattery in the notion that people want to read what we print, and the gratification that so many share our view of its importance.
>
> So the issue of copyright, particularly of library copying, is deeply complicated for us. . . . We don't believe that "fair use" should be eliminated, but we can't subscribe to the view that wholesale copying should be allowed for "educational purposes."
>
> The answer has to be compromise.[2]

Several points about copyright need emphasis. First, the problem of how to handle the rights of creators and users is worldwide in the sense that each country has to deal with both its own copyright problems and international copyright issues. Second, much of the controversy centers on educational and library copying. Third, copyright disputes divide authors, publishers, and producers from libraries, schools, and users, almost destroying what were once friendly working relationships. The relationship has not yet deteriorated to the point of hostility, but unless true compromises emerge, hostility may be the result. Finally, there is concern over what new technological developments may bring. All of the parties to the copyright controversy view online systems as both a threat and a promise. (This issue is discussed in more detail later in the chapter. Following is an introduction to basic points of present law.)

Most librarians agree that creators' rights need protection and that there have been violations of those rights in and by libraries. However, direct daily contact with users and their needs temper that recognition. Often, copyright infringement occurs because an item is not readily available or because an article or book reports the results of work carried out using government funds. Because government documents are public domain (not under copyright), many persons believe that reports of work funded by the government *should be* public property (even if published by private enterprise). This is especially true when the journal or book publisher charges the author a page charge for publishing the work.

Historical Background

As noted above, producers need encouragement to risk creating something new and making it available. Without adequate incentives, the producer will not produce. For publishers and media producers, copyright is one of the most important incentives. In essence, copyright states: "Person(s) X owns this creation; if you are not person(s) X, before you make copies of this creation for more than your own personal use, you must get written permission from person(s) X."

England was the first country to legalize creative ownership; in 1710, the English Parliament passed the Statute of Anne, the first copyright bill. This law did two things: It gave Parliamentary recognition to a royal decree of 1556, and it gave legal recognition to a work's author as the ultimate holder of copyright. While contemporary copyright laws exist to encourage the creation of new, original works and encourage their wide public distribution, the 1556 decree had a less noble purpose: repression of the freedom of religion, in this case, the Protestant Reformation. Censorship, rather than free public dissemination of information and thought, was the goal. By investing all publishing rights with the Stationers' Company, which represented all major English publishers, the Star Chamber (which controlled the Stationers' Company), hoped to control the flow of information to the English people.

Without question, the Statute of Anne was a notable piece of legislation that did more than merely give legal sanction to censorship. In the two centuries preceding the statute, many changes had taken place in

English society. Although by 1710 authors and publishers were allies in the fight to retain or gain more control over the use of their creations, it was an uneasy alliance, because the authors were the true creators of the copyrighted works. As the creators, authors thought they should have a greater share and say in the distribution of their works, and they thought the profits should be more evenly divided. Before 1710, all rights resided with the publisher. With the enactment of the Statute of Anne, authors received a 14-year monopoly on the publication of their works. An additional 14-year monopoly was possible, if the author was still living at the end of the first term. Thus, for 28 years, the creator of a work could benefit from the publication of it.

The American colonies developed a copyright concept based on the English model. Indeed, the concept was so much a part of American legal thought that it became part of the U.S. Constitution, wherein Congress has the power "to promote the Progress of Science and Useful Arts, by securing for limited Times to Authors and Inventors the exclusive Right to their Respective Writings and Discoveries." Starting in 1790 and ending in 1891, Congress passed legislation granting exclusive rights to American authors and their representatives, but it refused to grant copyright to nonresident foreign authors. The original act covered only books, maps, and charts.

In 1831, Congress passed an act extending the copyright term—the new first term was for 28 years, and the second term remained 14 years. Extension of the exclusive rights has been of concern in all countries since the start of the nineteenth century. Today, it is the heart of the matter: how far and for how long should the copyright owner control the use of the item? By 1870, copyright also covered art prints, musical compositions, photographs, "works of fine arts," translation rights, and the right to dramatize nondramatic works. In 1887, performance rights for plays and musical compositions received coverage. The Chace Act of 1891 finally granted copyright to nonresident foreign authors, if their work, published in English, was printed in the United States. In 1909, Congress passed a new copyright act.

The 1909 act was a matter of extended debate from 1905 to 1909. Several important issues remained unresolved in 1909, including libraries' rights to import books printed in foreign countries and the use of copyrighted music on mechanical instruments, such as phonograph records and piano rolls. After considerable debate, libraries and musicians received the desired rights. Libraries could import a limited number of copies of a foreign work, and copyright owners were to receive payment for the use of their music in mechanical devices. (The later development of jukeboxes, not covered by the 1909 law, caused a problem. The problem was that a new technology, the jukebox, appeared on the scene and there was no legal mechanism for requiring payment to copyright owners for the repeated use of their works in jukeboxes, which were making substantial profits for jukebox owners.) Composers worried about technological developments in 1909; in the 1970s, authors and publishers worried about technological developments. The entire issue of new technologies complicates copyright.

Other provisions of the 1909 law (as passed and amended over the years) include coverage of motion pictures; allowance to the owner of a nondramatic literary work to control public renditions of the work for profit and to control the making of transcriptions or sound recordings of the work; granting of full copyright protection to foreign authors (this done so the United States could join the Universal Copyright Convention in 1954); coverage of all sound recordings; extension of copyright terms to two terms of 28 years each, with a renewal requirement for the second term; and requirement of a notice of copyright displayed on all works. Several of these provisions created barriers for American and foreign producers and made it difficult for the United States to be an effective member of a worldwide copyright program. The three major stumbling blocks have been term of protection, the renewal requirements, and the manufacturing clause (i.e., the requirement that works of foreign authors be printed in the United States in order to be protected). The 1909 Act remained in force until January 1, 1978, when the present copyright law was enacted.

International Copyright Conventions

At the international level, there have been two important copyright conventions, the Berne Convention (1886) and the Universal Copyright Convention (1952). Until the signing of the Berne Convention in 1886, international copyright was in chaos, with reciprocity only on the basis of bilateral treaties. Some countries, like the United States, made no such agreements. As a result, during the nineteenth century, a new form of piracy appeared: literary piracy. Some countries signed the Berne Convention, notable exceptions being the United States and Russia. Basically, the signatories agreed to give one another the same copyright protection they provided their citizens. A 1908 revision required this coverage to be automatic—copyright owners did not have to file any forms to secure coverage. As the convention now stands, the minimum term of copyright is the lifetime of the creator plus 50 years; this term of copyright protection holds for translations as well as the original work.

There are several reasons the United States refused to be a party to the Berne Convention. Automatic coverage of a work (with no need for forms) means that the U.S. requirement that copyright notice appear on or in the work could not apply. Surprisingly, one of the most vocal and effective groups requesting retention of the notice requirement was librarians, who claimed that it would create problems and hardship if the notice were not there. Another problem was the term of coverage: the United States granted a total of only 56 years, while the convention's term is life plus 50 years. The manufacturing clause was a problem because of the U.S. copyright law requirement for U.S. manufacturing of English-language books and periodicals written by foreign authors. Two other issues also played a role in keeping the United States from signing the Berne Convention: One was the need to give retroactive coverage to foreign works that the United States now considers to be in the public domain; the other was the moral protection right for the copyright owner. Moral rights deal with protecting the copyright owner from misuse of the work and prevent "any action in relation to said work which would be prejudicial to the author's honor or reputation."

The United States did sign the Universal Copyright Convention (UCC) in 1954. How is it that the United States is able to sign one international convention but not the other? There are two important differences between the conventions. First, the UCC does not provide automatic copyright without formalities. The formalities, however, are that a work carry the copyright symbol (©), the name of the owner, and the date of first publication. This satisfies the U.S. notice requirement and, presumably, makes life easier for American librarians. The second difference is that the term of copyright may be whatever term the country granted its citizens at the time of signing; the only minimum is 25 years for all works other than photographs and applied arts. (Photographs and applied arts must have at least 10 years' protection.) There are penalty provisions for a Berne Convention signer withdrawing from the Berne Convention to belong to the UCC. (There is no penalty for being a member of both conventions.) To date, 40 of the Berne members have joined the UCC.

In 1971, modifications to both the Berne Convention and the UCC ensured that developing countries would receive certain licensing rights. The revisions provide a mechanism for forcing a copyright owner to grant the use rights to developing countries under certain conditions, in effect, compulsory licensing. Most of the signatories of the two conventions approved the revisions by 1990. Certainly, the revisions helped control what was becoming the second era of international piracy of literary and creative works. Nevertheless, some countries are not party to any copyright agreement, nor do the publishers in those countries bother to seek a license; so piracy is still alive in the 1990s.

PL94-553

Congress passed the new U.S. copyright law on October 19, 1976, following 15 years of debate. On January 1, 1978, Public Law 94-553 went into effect. Unfortunately, the issues causing the most disagreement remain unresolved by the law. The three major issues for libraries were and still are:

1. What is fair use?

2. What types of service may a library offer without infringing on copyright?

3. What, if any, compensation is due the copyright owner for use of the material, and how is the fee to be paid?

The following discussion, which highlights the current copyright law, is adapted from ALA's *Washington Newsletter* (not copyrighted).[3] The discussion provides an accurate summary of the major points in the law as they may affect libraries. Many sections of the law are ambiguous; producers read the law one way, but users (including librarians) read it another. In particular, librarians worry about how the law affects them as intermediaries between producers and users. There were questions about the impact of the law on interlibrary loan practices as well as on cooperative acquisition and collection development programs. Seventeen years after the passage of the law, many of the issues still are unclear.

Copyright holders demand greater enforcement and narrower user rights. Users demand more freedom of access and easier or faster permissions. Everyone agrees that, in the last analysis, the courts will decide the issues. Certainly, copyright holders have been vigorous and successful in their efforts to enforce their rights.

Highlights of the 1978 Copyright Law

Copyright protection is for the life of the author plus 50 years. The Register of Copyright is to maintain current records of the death dates of authors of copyrighted works. Effective January 1, 1978, existing copyrights under the old system were extended to span a total of 75 years, automatically in the case of copyrights already renewed for a second term, but only if renewed in the case of first-term copyrights (Sec. 302).

The fair use doctrine is given statutory recognition for the first time. Traditionally, fair use has been a judicially-created limitation on the exclusive rights of the copyright owner, developed by the courts because the 1909 copyright law made no provision for any copying. In the law, fair use allows copying of a limited amount of material without permission from, or payment to, the copyright owner, when the use is reasonable and not harmful to the rights of the copyright owner (Sec. 107).

The law also extends copyright protection to unpublished works. Instead of the old dual system of protecting works under common law before publication and under federal law after publication, the law also establishes a single system of statutory protection for all works, whether published or unpublished (Sec. 301).

The manufacturing clause finally died in 1987, but not without an extended Congressional fight. This cleared the way for the United States to be a member of both international conventions; however, questions about moral rights still prevent the United States from signing the Berne Convention.

Copyright liability extends to two previously exempted groups—cable television systems and the operators of jukeboxes. Both will have a right to compulsory licenses (Sec. 111, 116).

A five-member Copyright Royalty Tribunal exists to review royalty rates and to settle disputes among parties entitled to several specified types of statutory royalties in areas not directly affecting libraries (Sec. 801).

Every librarian should have some knowledge of all of the following sections of the law. The sections of the law and the content of handbooks on the law can be helpful in developing a collection; however, when questions arise, the best source of information is an attorney who handles copyright cases. What follows *is not* legal advice, merely an outline of the sections and their content:

(Sec. 102-105) defines works protected by copyright.

(Sec. 106) defines the exclusive rights of the copyright owner.

(Sec. 107) provides the basis of the right of fair use.

(Sec. 108) authorizes certain types of library copying.

(Sec. 108 [g]) identifies library copying not authorized by the current law.

(Sec. 602 [a] [3]) relates to the importation of copies by libraries.

Works Protected by Copyright

Copyright protection extends to *literary* works; *dramatic* works; *pantomimes* and *choreographic* works; *pictorial, graphic,* and *sculptural* works; *motion pictures* and other *audiovisual* works; and *sound recordings* (Sec. 102).

Unpublished works by U.S. and foreign authors receive protection under the copyright statute, as do published works by U.S. authors. The published works of foreign authors are subject to copyright under certain conditions, including coverage under national treaties such as the Universal Copyright Convention (Sec. 104).

United States government works are not copyrightable. The law did not change the basic premise that works produced for the U.S. government by its officers and employees are not subject to copyright (Sec. 105).

There is no outright prohibition against copyright in works prepared under government contract or grant. The *Conference Report on General Revision of the Copyright Law 94-553* stated:

> There may well be cases where it would be in the public interest to deny copyright in the writings generated by Government research contracts and the like; it can be assumed that, where a Government agency commissions a work for its own use merely as an alternative to having one of its own employees prepare the work, the right to secure a private copyright would be withheld. However, there are almost certainly many other cases where the denial of copyright protection would be unfair or would hamper the production and publication of important works. Where, under the particular circumstances Congress or the agency involved finds that the need to have a work freely available outweighs the need of the private author to secure copyright, the problem can be dealt with by specific legislation, agency regulations, or contractual restrictions.[4]

Exclusive Rights of Copyright Owners

Section 106 states the exclusive rights of copyright owners. Subject to sections 107 through 118, the owner of copyright under this title has the exclusive rights to do and to authorize any of the following:

1. To reproduce the copyrighted work in copies or phonorecords.

2. To prepare derivative works based upon the copyrighted work.

3. To distribute copies or phonorecords of the copyrighted work to the public by sale or other transfer of ownership, or by rental, lease, or lending.

4. In the case of literary, musical, dramatic, and choreographic works, pantomimes, and motion pictures and other audiovisual works to perform the copyrighted work publicly.

5. In the case of literary, musical, dramatic, and choreographic works, pantomimes, and pictorial, graphic, or sculptural works, including the individual images of a motion picture or other audiovisual work, to display the copyrighted work publicly.

It is important to understand the significant limitations to the exclusive rights stated in Section 106, which are stated in Sections 107 through 118.

Fair Use

Even the most adamant copyright holder advocate acknowledges that at least some kinds of copying are fair and permissible. The problem lies in defining what constitutes fair use. The law codifies the fair use doctrine in general terms. The statute refers to such purposes as criticism, commentary, news reporting, teaching, scholarship, or research, and it specifies four criteria to use in determining whether a particular instance of copying or other reproduction is fair. The statutory criteria (Sec. 107) are:

1. the purpose and character of the use, including whether such use is of a commercial nature or is for nonprofit educational purposes

2. the nature of the copyrighted work

3. the amount and substantiality of the portion used in relation to the copyrighted work as a whole

4. the effect of the use upon the potential market for or value of the copyrighted work.

Depending on the circumstances, fair use might cover making a single copy or multiple copies. For example, the statute specifically states that multiple copying for classroom use may fall within the category of fair use copying. In deciding whether any particular instance of copying is fair use, one must always consider the statutory fair use criteria.

Guidelines for Copying

Guidelines developed by educators, publishers, and authors provide some indication of what various parties believe reasonable for fair use. The guidelines were not part of the statute, but they are part of the House Judiciary Committee's report on the copyright bill. They are *Guidelines for Classroom Copying in Not-For-Profit Educational Institutions* and *Guidelines for Educational Uses of Music.*

Library Copying Authorized by Section 108

In addition to copying that would fall within the fair use section of the statute, certain types of library copying that may not be considered fair use are authorized by Sec. 108. Sec. 108 in no way limits the library's fair use right (Sec. 108 [f] [4]).

Section 108 (a) contains general conditions and limitations that apply to the authorized copying outlined in the rest of the section. These general conditions apply:

1. The copy is made without any purpose of direct or indirect commercial advantage.

2. The collections of the library are open to the public or available not only to researchers affiliated with the library but also to other persons doing research in a specialized field.

3. The copy includes a notice of copyright.

The House Judiciary Committee's report clarified the status of special libraries in for-profit institutions with respect to the criterion "without direct or indirect commercial advantage" (Sec. 108 [a] [1]). It is the library or archives within the institution that must meet the criteria, not the institution itself.

In addition to the general conditions of Section 108 (a), it is possible for contractual obligations between a publisher or distributor and a library to limit copying that would otherwise be permissible under Section 108. In addition, the limited types of copying authorized by Section 108 can be augmented by written agreement at the time of purchase (Sec. 108 [f] [4]).

Possible Contractual Limitations on Section 108

Section 108 (f) (4) states that the rights of reproduction granted to libraries do not override any contractual obligations assumed by the library when it obtained a work for its collection. In view of this provision, librarians must be especially sensitive to the conditions under which they purchase materials, and before executing an agreement that would limit their rights under the copyright law, they should consult with legal counsel. *This is the key section with regard to licensing agreements.*

Single Copy of Single Article or Small Excerpt

The Library's Collection

Section 108 (d) authorizes making a single copy of a single article or a copy of a small part of a copyrighted work in the library's collections, provided that (1) the copy becomes the property of the user; (2) the library has no notice that the use of the copy would be for any purpose other than private study, scholarship, or research; and (3) the library both includes on its order form and displays prominently at the place where users submit copying requests a warning about copyright in accordance with requirements prescribed by the Register of Copyrights.

On November 16, 1977, the *Federal Register* published the new regulation and provided the form for the warning signs that the library must post near all library copy machines (see fig. 18.1).

NOTICE: WARNING CONCERNING COPYRIGHT RESTRICTIONS

The copyright law of the United States (Title 17, United States Code) governs the making of photocopies or other reproductions of copyrighted material.

Under certain conditions specified in the law, libraries and archives are authorized to furnish a photocopy or other reproduction. One of these specified conditions is that the photocopy or reproduction is not to be "used for any purpose other than private study, scholarship, or research." If a user makes a request for, or later uses, a photocopy or reproduction for purposes in excess of "fair use," that user may be liable for copyright infringement.

This institution reserves the right to refuse to accept a copying order if, in its judgment, fulfillment of the order would involve violation of copyright law.

Fig. 18.1 Official text of the required copyright warning sign. From *Federal Register* (November 16, 1977).

The *Federal Register* (February 26, 1991) printed the text for a second warning sign for computer software. The warning is similar to the first warning, but the wording differs (see fig. 18.2).

NOTICE: WARNING CONCERNING COPYRIGHT RESTRICTIONS

The copyright law of the United States (Title 17, United States Code) governs the reproduction, distribution, adaptation, public performance, and public display of copyrighted material.

Under certain conditions specified in law, nonprofit libraries are authorized to lend, lease or rent copies of computer programs to patrons on a nonprofit basis and for nonprofit purposes. Any person who makes an unauthorized copy or adaptation of the computer program, or redistributes the loan copy, or publicly performs or displays the computer program, except as permitted by Title 17 of the United States Code, may be liable for copyright infringement. This institution reserves the right to refuse to fulfill a loan request if, in its judgment, fulfillment of the request would lead to violation of the copyright law.

Fig. 18.2. Official wording of the required copyright notice for computer software. From *Federal Register* (February 26, 1991).

Copying for Interlibrary Loan

Section 108 (d) authorizes making a single copy of a single article or a copy of a small part of a copyrighted work for purposes of interlibrary loan, provided that it meets all of the above conditions regarding a single copy of a single article from the library's own collections, and further provided (Sec. 108 [g] [2]) that requests for interlibrary loan photocopies are not in such aggregate quantities as to substitute for purchases or subscriptions. The wording of the statute places responsibility for compliance on the library requesting the photocopy, not on the library fulfilling the request. The National Commission on New Technological Uses of Copyrighted Works (CONTU), in consultation with authors, publishers, and librarians, developed guidelines to assist libraries in complying with this provision. A library or archive may receive no more than five photocopies per year of articles published in the restricted issues of a periodical. (They may be five copies of one article or single copies of five different articles.) The restriction applies only to issues published within the last five years. Duplication of older issues is limited only by the broad provisions of Section 108 (g) (2) that prohibit copying which by its nature would substitute for a subscription.

Coin-Operated Copying Machines

Section 108 (f) (1) and (2) make clear that *neither libraries nor library employees* are liable for the unsupervised use of reproducing equipment (this does include microform reader printers) located on library premises, provided the machine displays the required notice (see fig. 18.1). The person making the copy is, of course, subject to liability for copyright infringement, if his or her copying exceeds the provisions of Section 107.

Library Copying Not Authorized by Section 108

With the exception of audiovisual news programs, Section 108 does not authorize a library to make multiple copies. Two general types of library copying that are not clearly defined in the statute are specifically not authorized by Section 108. Stated only in the most general terms, the definitions of these types of library copying are susceptible to many interpretations.

The first is "related or concerted reproduction or distribution of multiple copies." This related or concerted copying by libraries is illegal, whether the library makes the copies all on one occasion or over a period of time, and whether intended for aggregate use by one individual or for separate use by individual members of a group (Sec. 108 [g] [1]).

The second type of library copying not authorized by Section 108 is "systematic reproduction or distribution of single or multiple copies." Because many librarians feared that this term might preclude a wide range of interlibrary lending systems, Congress amended this section of the bill to clarify that whatever may be meant by the term *systematic,* copying for purposes of interlibrary loan as specifically authorized by Section 108 (d) was not illegal under Section 108 (g) (2) as long as it does not substitute for purchases or subscriptions. The wording of the statute places responsibility for copyright compliance on the library requesting the photocopy, not on the library filling the request (Sec. 108 [g] [2]).

It is important to remember that the copyright law does not establish licensing or royalty payment schemes for library copying. It focuses primarily on the kinds of copying that libraries can do without such schemes. Section 108 (g) merely states the two types of library copying that are *not* authorized by Section 108.

Importation of Copies by Libraries

In general, the law prohibits the importation of copies of works without the permission of the copyright holder. There are, however, certain exceptions to this general prohibition, one of which directly relates to libraries. Section 602 (a) (3) states that a nonprofit scholarly, educational, or religious organization may import no more than one copy of an audiovisual work for archival purposes only, and no more than five copies of any other work "for its library lending or archival purposes, unless the importation of such copies or phonorecords is part of an activity consisting of systematic reproduction or distribution, engaged in by such organization in violation of the provisions of Section 108 (g) (2)."

Guidelines in Relation to the Statute

Libraries should consult the statute to exercise fully what rights they have under the copyright law. Look first in the statute and the accompanying congressional reports to determine whether a library or archives may make a copy in a given situation:

audiovisual	108 (f) (3)
audiovisual work other than news	107, 108 (h)
book	107, 108
graphic work	107, 108 (h)
importing copies from abroad	602 (a) (3)
instructional transmission	107, 110
motion picture	107, 108 (h)
musical work	107, 108 (h)
periodical article	107, 108
pictorial work	107, 108 (h)
public broadcasting program	107, 108 (d) (3)
sound recording	107, 108, 114

Many organizations, especially educational institutions, issued their own guidelines based on the House Judiciary Committee's report (see fig. 18.3). A number of books will help the staff understand and explain the law. (None of the books, including this one, constitutes legal advice. When in doubt, consult a copyright lawyer.)

Books and Periodicals

The following guidelines for the copying of books and periodicals under the Copyright Law Revision Act were established by agreement between national educational and authors' and publishers' groups for the purposes of setting minimum standards of educational fair use.

I. *Single Copying for Teachers*

A single copy may be made of any of the following by or for a teacher at his or her individual request for his or her scholarly research or use in teaching or preparation to teach a class:

A. A chapter from a book;

B. An article from a periodical or newspaper;

C. A short story, short essay, or short poem, whether or not from a collective work;

D. A chart, graph, diagram, cartoon, or picture from a book, periodical, or newspaper.

II. *Multiple Copies for Classroom Use*

Multiple copies (not to exceed in any event more than one copy per pupil in a course) may be made by or for the teacher giving the course for classroom use or discussions, provided that:

A. The copying meets the tests of brevity and spontaneity as defined below;

B. The copying meets the cumulative effect test as defined below; and

C. Each copy includes a notice of copyright.

Definitions

Brevity

(i) Poetry: (a) A complete poem if less than 250 words and if printed on not more than two pages or, (b) from a longer poem, an excerpt of not more than 250 words.

(ii) Prose: (a) Either a complete article, story or essay of less than 2,500 words, or (b) an excerpt from any prose work of not more than 1,000 words or 10% of the work, whichever is less, but in any event a minimum of 500 words.

(Each of the numerical limits stated in "i" and "ii" above may be expanded to permit the completion of an unfinished line of a poem or of an unfinished prose paragraph.)

(iii) Illustration: One chart, graph, diagram, drawing, cartoon or picture per book or per periodical issue.

(iv) "Special" works: Certain works in poetry, prose or in "poetic prose" which often combine language with illustrations and which are intended sometimes for children and at other times for a more general audience, and fall short of 2,500 words in their entirety. Paragraph "ii" above notwithstanding, such "special works" may not be reproduced in their *entirety;* however, an excerpt comprising not more than two of the published pages of such special work and containing not more than 10 percent of the words found in the text thereof, may be reproduced.

Spontaneity

(i) The copying is at the instance and inspiration of the individual teacher, and

(ii) The inspiration and decision to use the work and the moment of its use for maximum teaching effectiveness are so close in time that it would be unreasonable to expect a timely reply to a request for permission.

Cumulative Effect

(i) The copying of the material is for only one course in the school in which the copies are made.

(ii) Not more than one short poem, article, story, essay, or two excerpts may be copied from the same author, nor more than three from the same collective work or periodical volume during one class term.

(iii) There shall not be more than nine instances of such multiple copying for one course during one class term.

(The limitations stated in "ii" and "iii" above shall not apply to current news periodicals and newspapers and current news sections of other periodicals.)

III. *Prohibitions as to I and II above*

Notwithstanding any of the above, the following shall be prohibited:

A. Copying shall not be used to create or to replace or substitute for anthologies, compilations, or collective works. Such replacement or substitution may occur whether copies of various works or excerpts therefrom are accumulated or reproduced and used separately.

B. There shall be no copying of or from works intended to be "consumable" in the course of study or of teaching. These include workbooks, exercises, standardized tests and test booklets, answer sheets, and like consumable material.

C. Copying shall not:

a. substitute for the purchase of books, publishers' reprints or periodicals;

b. be directed by higher authority;

c. be repeated with respect to the same item by the same teacher from term to term.

D. No charge shall be made to the student beyond the actual cost of the photocopying.

Fig. 18.3. Guidelines for copying. From the Copyright Law Revision Act.

Infringement

A person who violates the rights of the copyright owner is a *copyright infringer*. Remedies available to the copyright holder for infringement include damages (actual or statutory, the latter set by statute at from $100 to $50,000), injunction, and recovery of court costs and attorney's fees. There is also criminal infringement (done willfully for commercial advantage or private financial gain), which is subject to a $10,000 fine and/or one year imprisonment.

There is a waiver of statutory damages for a library or nonprofit educational institution when the institution or one of its employees acting within the scope of his or her employment "believed or had reasonable grounds for believing that his or her use of the copyrighted work was a fair use under Sec. 107" (Sec. 504 [c] [2]).

Librarians and media specialists have a professional responsibility to learn about the provisions of the copyright law that relate to libraries and to frequently review their practices in light of such provisions. If current practices seem likely to constitute infringement, librarians should plan now for needed changes and make sure library users understand the reason for such changes. Above all, it is important to take the time and trouble to master the basic provisions of the statute so the library will fully exercise the rights it has under the copyright law. Anything short of this would be a disservice to library users.

Mandated Five-Year Reviews

Although the library community as a whole worked hard to get a flexible copyright law that would neither harm publishers and authors nor curtail the public's access to information, there was no assurance the law would achieve such a balance. The law requires a review of the library copying provisions every five years by the Register of Copyrights in consultation with librarians and representatives of authors and publishers. If a five-year review determines that the balance between the rights of copyright owners and the rights of the public is tilting too far in one direction, the register may make recommendations for legislative or other changes to correct the balance (Sec. 108 [i]).

As one might expect, the five-year reviews, especially the 1982 review (the first after enactment of the law), generated controversy with producers on one side and users on the other. After a lengthy debate in 1983 and 1984, the Copyright Office asked Congress to pass additional legislation to achieve a better balance between the rights of creators and the needs of users of copyrighted works in libraries and archives. The view was that the creators were not adequately protected. The four areas identified as needing legislative action were: reproduction of out-of-print musical works (made illegal, although libraries were engaging in this type of copying), an umbrella statute (a proposed statute for forced licensing), copyright notice (this would require libraries to post the statutory notice on all photocopies they provide), and unpublished works (to make it clear that unpublished works are exempt from Section 108 provisions). The office also called for additional voluntary guidelines and for all parties to participate in developing licensing agreements. Areas suggested for additional study were a copyright compensation scheme based on a surcharge on photocopying equipment, copyright compensation based on a percentage of the photocopying impressions made using sampling techniques, and issues relating to the impact of new technological developments on library use of copyrighted works. One set of guidelines resulted from the Copyright Office Report. *American Libraries* (February 1986) published the full text of "Library and Classroom Use of Copyrighted Videotapes and Computer Software." Certainly, it is required reading for most public service personnel.

Subsequent reviews generated equally vigorous debates. As one would expect, the last review (1992) suggested changes to the law focus on the electronic environment. Probably, the most critical issue is whether electronic transmission is the same as distribution under terms of the copyright act. The Working Group on Intellectual Property Rights stated, "It is not clear that transmission can constitute a distribution of copies of the work under the current law."[5] Because of the lack of clarity, the group is recommending Congress amend the law to reflect that copies distributed by electronic transmission are the exclusive right of the copyright holder. Several other recommendations deal with the same concept in various sections of the existing law. The Working Group on Intellectual Property Rights also indicated they had "concerns about fair use, library exemptions and educational uses limitations on the copyright owners' exclusivity" and planned to call a conference later in the year to explore these issues.[6] In 1992, Congress ended the review requirement.

Enforcement

Copyright holders are quick to enforce their rights. One of the more notable suits started on February 5, 1980, when a group of book publishers filed a complaint against the Gnomon Corporation for alleged copyright infringements. Gnomon operates a number of photocopy stores in the eastern United States, many located near academic institutions. The publishers claimed the company encouraged copyright violations by promoting its Micro-Publishing service with university and college teachers. By May 1980, publishers had their first favorable ruling and announced that their next target would be large for-profit corporations with libraries that did not use the Copyright Clearance Center (see page 505 for more about the Copyright Clearance Center). Although the publishers won their case against Gnomon, many photocopy service firms continued to promote similar services. By the early 1990s, publishers and commercial copy services worked out a system for providing academic institutions with custom readers. The system uses an electronic copyright approval procedure that permits a Gnomon, Kinko's or other company to quickly secure the requisite permissions and legally produce the reader in the needed quantities. Many academic campus bookstores offer similar services, and most of them use the services of the Copyright Clearance Center.

In 1982, various publications carried announcements that the Association of American Publishers (AAP) had moved forward with infringement suits against several corporate libraries. They had an out-of-court settlement with E. R. Squibb and Sons Corporation, a large pharmaceutical company, after filing suit. Squibb agreed to pay royalty fees when copying articles from technical journals, including the corporation library subscriptions. Before the Squibb suit, the publishers had also been successful in a suit against the American Cyanamid Company.

After their success against for-profit organizations, AAP turned to the not-for-profit sector. On January 5, 1983, the *Chronicle of Higher Education* published an article about an AAP suit in the New York district court against New York University, nine faculty members, and a photocopy shop near the university. New York University settled out of court, agreeing to follow the 1976 guidelines and agreeing that faculty members who did not do so would not receive legal assistance from the institution if they were parties in a future copyright infringement suit. At about the same time, a Los Angeles secondary school teacher lost an infringement suit on the same grounds, failure to follow the 1976 guidelines. In 1984, the National Music Publishers Association persuaded the University of Texas at Austin to stop alleged illegal photocopying of music by its music department.

When will the suits stop? Probably not until copyright holders believe, or know, that libraries, educational institutions, corporations, teachers, and other users are following the guidelines. It would not be surprising to see suits against some large school districts and one or two large public libraries. Though it is true that copyright holders do have rights, the law clearly states that libraries and other users do, too. As Scott Bennett wrote:

> We should respect the copyright law. This means understanding the law so that we can obey it and benefit from it. It means a refusal to wink at violations of the law, however widespread, just as it means advancing no untenable claims either to copyright protection or to fair use. Most important, it means acknowledging there are many genuinely debatable issues before us that will need to be resolved through negotiation, legislation, and litigation. Respecting the copyright law means making judicious use of these methods of resolving differences.
>
> We should keep the Constitutional purposes of copyright in view; honor those purposes; and work to give them vitality.[7]

Without question, the most contentious issue is the electronic environment and who owns what, where, and how. The professional literature is full of articles exploring this or that aspect of the problem. Certainly, licensing of information, be it a CD-ROM, an online service, or an electronic journal, is at issue. Sometimes, changes in the law assist in library operations, such as the amendment (PL 96-517 Section 7 (b) that amends Section 117 of Title 17) that authorizes libraries to make back-up copies of computer programs (for example, programs on disks, which accompany more and more books). On the other hand, one reads articles asking: "Will electronic journals fulfill the current role of assessment that print-on-paper does?" and "How are electronic journal publishers to make money out of document delivery?" These articles leave one wondering how the voice of the user can be heard.[8] One speculates whether librarians ever read licensing agreements, much less ask the institution's legal counsel to review the document. Some agreements come in wrapped packages, meaning one cannot read the full text until after opening the package, but the package carries words to the effect that "opening this package constitutes acceptance of the licensing agreement." A particularly good article discussing these issues is Laura Gasaway's "Copyright in the Electronic Era."[9]

Contractual Compliance

Following the various guidelines is one obvious way to achieve compliance. For some libraries, the guidelines are too narrow and the cost of acquiring, processing, and housing the needed copyrighted material is high. Are these libraries and information centers cut off from needed information? Not if they have enough money.

The Copyright Clearance Center (CCC) is a not-for-profit service designed to serve libraries and other users of copyrighted material by providing a central source to which to submit copying fees. It is, in a sense, a licensing system; CCC does not copy documents but functions as a clearinghouse. Several thousand organizations are members; many, if not most, of these are libraries and information services. The CCC handles both U.S. and foreign publications (more than 4,000 titles).

The fees can be substantial when one realizes that the charge is for one article; however, the cost of a lawsuit would be higher, and, if the organization lost, it could be forced to pay as much as $50,000 plus other costs and fees. Another service is the Television Licensing Center, which assists in legal off-the-air videotaping, an area of concern for school media centers as well as other educational institutions.

Where next with copyright? It is difficult to predict, but it is certain that copyright holders are not satisfied with the status quo. A new group, the American Copyright Council, was formed in mid-1985; its purpose is to lobby Congress against things it believes would undermine the copyright law. "Copyright is more and more at risk these days, under challenge, attack, and erosion. 'It is becoming an endangered species,' said Stanley M. Gortikov, president of the Recording Industry Association of America and chairman of the new council."[10] Some of the 18 members of the council are the American Federation of Musicians; the AFL-CIO; the American Society of Composers, Authors, and Publishers; the Association of American Publishers; the Authors Guild, Inc.; Computer and Business Equipment Manufacturers Association; the Motion Picture Association of America; and Time Warner Communications. The ALA and other groups representing the interests of the user will have their hands full; it seems likely that fair use rather than copyright is the endangered species.

Finally, there is some pressure from not-for-profit organizations about their copyrights. Of greatest concern to libraries, archives, and information centers around the world is the question of who owns the data in various cooperative bibliographic utilities. Late in 1982, OCLC claimed copyright of its database, which was built by the MARC database from LC and records contributed from member libraries. Member libraries quickly began to claim copyright to their contributed copy. A 1982 study by IFLA of 35 national libraries or national bibliographic agencies around the world noted that nine of the organizations claimed copyright for their machine-readable records.[11] If additional royalty charges are made for the use of such records, it will become ever more costly to attempt reasonable cooperative collection development programs.

Public Lending Right

Public lending right (PLR) is a system that allows an author to be compensated for the circulated use of his or her copyrighted work from libraries. Many Americans, including librarians, are not fully aware of this right. Elsewhere in the world it is better known, and in most countries where it exists, it operates successfully.

Authors are compensated in some manner for the circulated use or presence of their works in a library. Where does the money come from? There are only three logical sources: the user, the library, or the funding authority. In most countries, the money comes from a separate fund established for that purpose by the national government. Does the presence of a lending right program have any negative impact on library budgets? No one really knows, but it seems likely that there is some spillover that ultimately reduces library funding. However, a 1986 report from England indicated no adverse effects on library budgets as a result of PLR. Collections built using the demand principle will increase the pressure on the PLR fund, and a self-feeding cycle may begin which makes less money available to buy low-use titles.

The PLR system started in the Scandinavian countries after World War II. Initially, it was considered a way to encourage writers to write in languages that had a small number of native speakers, for example, Danish, Finnish, Icelandic, Norwegian, and Swedish. For more than 20 years, the concept did not spread beyond Scandinavia. Starting in the early 1970s, the idea spread to the Netherlands (1972), the Federal Republic of Germany (1972), New Zealand (1973), Australia (1974), the United Kingdom (1983), and Canada (1986). Although some legislation contains the provision that all libraries are to be included, in most countries only public libraries are involved in data collecting. Details of the systems vary, but some form of sampling is used to collect the data, unless there is a single source from which the public libraries buy their books. A good but somewhat dated source of detailed information about PLR is a 1981 issue of *Library Trends*.[12]

In Canada, the system is called Payment for Public Use (PPU). A $2.5 million fund was established by the national government to compensate authors for the circulation of their books by Canadian public libraries. In 1985, the Council of Writers Organizations was able to get U.S. Senator Charles Matthias of Maryland to submit PLR-enabling legislation. Nothing has happened in the intervening nine years. Does such legislation have much chance of becoming law? Assuming the plan would copy other countries' practice of federal funding, and as long as the federal deficit and budget cutting remain congressional priorities, establishment of a PLR system is unlikely. This assumption may not be valid for several reasons. First, two other sources of funding are possible: the user and the library. Second, the worrisome Section 106 of the copyright law lists as an exclusive right of the copyright owner "to distribute copies or phono-records of copyrighted works to the public by sale or other transfer of ownership, or by rental, lease or *lending*" (emphasis added). Third is the attitude exemplified by a statement in *Publishers Weekly* (1983): "The fate of a book after it is sold is an important one for the book industry, reflecting as it does the possibility of lost sales; pass-along readership of a book, unlike that of a magazine, does not translate into potential revenue."[13] If publishers, authors, and others, such as music producers (audio collections) and motion picture producers (video collections), join forces, we might well see another cost imposed on libraries and their users.

Summary

Copyright assures the right to seek tangible rewards for persons or organizations from the production of creative or informative works. Without users of copyrighted materials, the producers would realize little or nothing from their efforts. Producers and users need to work together or everyone will lose. It would be desirable if once again we became partners in the dissemination of information and knowledge, rather than antagonists. Whatever does develop will not change the fact that it will not be possible to develop a library collection without considering the impact of copyright laws. Librarians should work to maintain a fair balance, but they work for the users because users have few spokespersons.

Notes

[1]Margaret McKinley, "The Thor Inventory Ruling: Fact or Fiction," *Serials Librarian* 17, no. 3/4 (1990): 191-4.

[2]J. Berry, "Copyright: From Debate to Solution," *Library Journal 100* (September 1, 1975): 1459.

[3]American Library Association, *Washington Newsletter* (November 15, 1976).

[4]U.S. House of Representatives, *Conference Report on General Revision of the Copyright Law 94-553* (September 29, 1976): 55.

[5]"Copyright Act Changes Suggested for Electronic Transmission," *Weekly Record* 241 (July 11, 1994): 11.

[6]Ibid.

[7]Scott Bennett, "Copyright and Innovation in Electronic Publishing," *Library Issues* 14 (September 1993): 4.

[8]Jamie Cameron, "The Changing Scene in Journal Publishing," *Publishers Weekly* 240 (May 31, 1993): 24.

[9]Laura N. Gasaway, "Copyright in the Electronic Era," *Serials Librarian* 24, nos. 3/4 (1994): 153-62.

[10]"Copyright Holders Unite in Face of Growing 'Risk'," *Rocky Mountain News* (June 6, 1985): 85.

[11]D. D. McDonald et al., *International Study of Copyright of Bibliographic Records in Machine-Readable Form* (Munich: K. G. Saur, 1983).

[12]"Public Lending Right," *Library Trends* 29 (Spring 1981): 565-719.

[13]"The Pass-Along Market for Books: Something to Ponder for Publishers," *Publishers Weekly* 224 (July 15, 1983): 20.

Further Reading

Copyright

Clark, C. "100 Years of Berne." *The Bookseller* 4209 (August 23, 1986): 788-92.

Cooke, E. D. "Copyright Issues: Computer Software." *School Media Quarterly* 19 (Winter 1991): 125-26.

Fields, H. "Congress Acts to Clarify the Fair Use Doctrine." *Publishers Weekly* 239 (October 19, 1992): 10.

Johnston, D. F. *A Copyright Guide.* 2d ed. New York: R. R. Bowker, 1982.

McDonald, D. D.; E. J. Rodger; and J. L. Squires. *International Study of Copyright of Bibliographic Records in Machine-Readable Form.* Munich: K. G. Saur, 1983.

Rocca, J. "New Law Makes Copyright Renewal Optional." *Library of Congress Information Bulletin* 51 (September 7, 1992): 381-82.

Sievers, R. "Congress Passes Several Amendments to Copyright Act: Architecture, Software Rental, Visual Artist Rights Affected." *Library of Congress Information Bulletin* 49 (December 17, 1990): 437-38.

U.S. House of Representatives. *Conference Report on General Revision of the Copyright Law 94-553.* Washington, DC: Government Printing Office, 1976.

"White Paper on Copyright Backs Licensing, Retains Fair Dealing." *The Bookseller* (April 9, 1986): 1553, 1565-66.

"White Paper Opens Way to Accord on Copyright." *The Bookseller* (June 21, 1986): 2411-12.

Wilson, P. "Copyright, Derivative Rights, and the First Amendment." *Library Trends* 39 (Summer/Fall 1990): 92-110.

Public Lending Right

"Britain's Public Lending Right Is Manna to Authors: Gets No Library Complaints." *American Libraries* 17 (May 1986): 862.

Hyatt, D. "Public Lending Right in the U.S.: An Active Issue." *Public Libraries* 27 (Spring 1988): 42-43.

Lariviere, J. "Le Droit de Pret Public au Canada." *Documentation & Bibliotheques* 37 (April/June 1991): 53-58.

Morrison, Perry D., and Dennis Hyatt, eds. "Public Lending Right." *Library Trends* 29 (Spring 1981): 565-719.

Shimmon, R. "Public Lending Right Changes." *Library Association Record* 92 (August 1990): 540.

Shyu, J. "Preliminary Study on the Issue of Public Lending Right." *Journal of Library & Information Science* 17 (October 1991): 64-92.

Staves, T. "Pay As You Read: Debate over Public Lending Right." *Wilson Library Bulletin* 62 (October 1987): 22-28.

Thor Inventory Decision

Biblarz, D. "Growing Out of Print Crisis." *Technical Services Quarterly* 7, no. 2 (1989): 3-12.

Habecker, J. "Thor Power Tool Decision and O.P. Rates." Master's thesis, University of North Carolina, 1988.

Loe, M. K. H. "Thor Tax Ruling After 5 Years." *Library Acquisitions: Practice and Theory* 10, no. 3 (1986): 203-18.

———. "Study Shows Thor Ruling Still Causes Book Dumping." *Publishers Weekly* 230 (September 5, 1986): 19.

Schrift, L. "After Thor, What's Next?" *Library Acquisitions: Practice and Theory* 9, no. 1 (1985): 61-63.

Selth, J. P. "My Say: OP Books: A Popular Delusion." *Publishers Weekly* 235 (January 6, 1989): 78.

19
Censorship, Intellectual Freedom, and Collection Development

All of the collection development topics discussed thus far are complex, and some touch on a wide variety of social issues and concerns. However, none is more complex than intellectual freedom and censorship. *Intellectual freedom, free speech, freedom to read,* and *open access to information* are alternative terms. First Amendment rights are the cornerstone on which librarians and information managers build collections.

There is not enough space in this chapter to fully explore all the aspects of intellectual freedom and free speech. Although they are interesting and important concepts for anyone involved in collection development, they are so complex that each has been the subject of numerous books and articles. (The bibliography at the end of this chapter provides a starting point for exploring these topics in more depth.) *All* librarians must have an understanding of these areas, but it is essential that all selection personnel fully comprehend the issues relating to censorship.

Many library associations have membership-approved statements and public positions on the questions of free speech and intellectual freedom. The ALA's "Freedom to Read" statement is a classic example. Most of the statements contain fine-sounding phrases. The statements look useful when one is discussing the theory or philosophy of intellectual freedom in the classroom or in a meeting. However, on a daily basis, these statements provide little assistance in collection development and provide only limited assistance in fighting off a censor.

Usually, intellectual freedom and free speech controversies revolve around interpretations of points of law and possible violations of existing law. Therefore, usually, the fight involves attorneys and judges rather than librarians and the community. We hear about the cases that reach the courts but seldom about daily local problems. Cases start as local problems between the library and an individual or group from the community and are usually settled quickly. Most often, the problem starts because someone objects to an item already in the collection. Depending on the nature of the material, the level of emotional involvement, and the prior administrative actions (that is, policies), the library may be able to quickly resolve the issue or the problem may escalate until it reaches the courtroom.

If the library successfully resolves a controversy without the aid of attorneys, it will be a result of one or more of the following:

- staff with an excellent background in interpersonal relations
- a plan of action for handling complaints
- a lack of strong feelings on the part of the person making the complaint
- lack of concerted pressure from special interest groups
- back-up material from library associations

If the individual making a complaint believes very strongly about the matter, it is likely the library's attorney will become involved. From that point on, depending on the emotional involvement and financial resources, the issue may go from the lowest to the highest court in the country before the problem is resolved.

The local issue usually is censorship. Charles Busha provided a satisfactory definition of censorship as it concerns the library: "The rejection by a library authority of a book (or other material) which the librarian, the library board or some person (or persons) bringing pressure on them holds to be obscene, dangerously radical, subversive, or too critical of the existing mores."[1] (Beginning selection officers should read the Busha article.) Censorship has been a problem for libraries as long as there have been libraries. Generally speaking, librarians attempt to resist censorship. (No one knows how many times a librarian or information officer responds to a complaint by removing the offensive item because he or she agrees it is offensive.) Evidence suggests there is a difference between librarians' attitudes toward the concept of censorship and their behavior in handling censorship problems. Librarians' success in fending off censors' efforts varies—there are both notable successes and spectacular failures. The sad truth is that there are no rules or guidelines that ensure success. It is possible to forestall many complaints and quickly resolve those that do occur; however, there is always a chance that the procedures and processes will fail and a legal battle will ensue.

Causes of Censorship

What causes or motivations underlie the actions of a censor? Motivations may be psychological, political, or social. Psychological motivations stem from the desire to restrain others from expressing ideas or creating works that the censor finds offensive. Political motivation underlies the actions of governments that attempt to maintain control over the communication systems that may threaten the government or its policies. Social motivations result from a desire to preserve a wholesome social setting or to reduce crime, both of which the censor may consider related to the presence of objectionable material in the library. Frequently, the censor (government, groups, or an individual) claims to be acting for protective reasons. Censorship is a paternalistic act in that it limits the experiences of both adults and children and limits environments to influences acceptable to the censor.

Freedom and censorship exist in opposition. At one extreme, some persons believe there should be no controls; if they could, they would eradicate all laws, rules, and regulations. At the other extreme are those who think everyone needs protection and outside control. Between these extremes lies the necessary balance between freedom and restraint. Freedom must be restrained so that social institutions intelligently protect citizens' rights and ensure individuals' free choice. Librarians work on a daily basis to achieve an appropriate balance in their collections and services.

The ALA adopted a *Library Bill of Rights* in 1948. ALA's Office for Intellectual Freedom vigorously promotes and publicizes the concepts contained in that statement. Because the *Library Bill of Rights* is not law, the statement provides no legal protection for libraries or librarians. What legal protection exists is primarily in the freedom of speech provisions of the First Amendment. The First Amendment grants every U.S. citizen the right to freely express opinions in speech, writing, or with graphics; to distribute them; and to seek information from public sources without unnecessary restraint. The *Library Bill of Rights* outlines the basic freedom of access concepts that ALA hopes will guide library public service. It states persons should be able to read what they wish without intervention from groups or individuals—including librarians. Since its adoption in 1948, the provisions of the *Library Bill of Rights* have assisted librarians in committing their libraries to a philosophy of service based on the premise that users of libraries should have access to information on all sides of all issues. The text of the document, as amended February 2, 1961; June 27, 1967; and January 23, 1980, by the ALA Council appears in figure 19.1.

The *Library Bill of Rights* is an important guide to professional conduct in terms of intellectual freedom. It is a standard by which one can gauge daily practices against desired professional behavior in the realms of freedom of access to information, communications, and intellectual activity.

Despite the *Library Bill of Rights,* there is pressure to limit or exclude certain types of material from a library's collection. Occasionally, someone suggests labeling material with warnings or some kind of rating system rather than removing it. This practice usually takes the form of placing special marks or designations (stars, letters, and so forth) on certain classes of materials. The practice of labeling is prejudicial and creates bias.

The American Library Association affirms that all libraries are forums for information and ideas, and that the following basic policies should guide their services.

I.   Books and other library resources should be provided for the interest, information, and enlightenment of all people of the community the library serves. Material should not be excluded because of the origin, background, or views of those contributing to their creation.

II.   Libraries should provide materials and information presenting all points of view on current and historical issues. Materials should not be proscribed or removed because of partisan or doctrinal disapproval.

III.   Libraries should challenge censorship in the fulfillment of their responsibility to provide information and enlightenment.

IV.   Libraries should cooperate with all persons and groups concerned with resisting abridgment of free expression and free access to ideas.

V.   A person's right to use a library should not be denied or abridged because of origin, age, background, or views.

VI.   Libraries which make exhibit spaces and meeting rooms available to the public they serve should make such facilities available on an equitable basis, regardless of the beliefs or affiliations of individuals or groups requesting their use.

Fig. 19.1. *Library Bill of Rights.* Adopted June 18, 1948; Amended February 2, 1961; June 27, 1967; and January 23, 1980 by the ALA Council. Reprinted by permission of the American Library Association.

Labeling is a defensive method that says, in effect, "This item may not meet with full community approval." Labeling is contrary to the principles of intellectual freedom. It is not the librarian's duty to warn readers against such things as obscene language; descriptions of explicit sexual acts; or unorthodox political, religious, moral, or economic theories. Librarians are preservers and providers rather than censors. Librarians must always bear in mind that many intellectual advances, in all fields, involve controversy. A librarian's primary responsibility is to provide, not restrict, access to information. Thus, ALA's position is against labeling materials, in the sense of warning people about the content of items. In 1951, ALA adopted an antilabeling statement, which it last amended on June 26, 1990 (see fig. 19.2 on page 514).

Labeling is the practice of describing or designating materials by affixing a prejudicial label and/or segregating them by prejudicial system. The American Library Association opposes these means of predisposing people's attitudes toward library materials for the following reasons:

1. Labeling is an attempt to prejudice attitudes and as such, it is a censor's tool.

2. Some find it easy and even proper, according to their ethics, to establish criteria for judging publications as objectionable. However, injustice and ignorance rather than justice and enlightenment result from such practices, and the American Library Association opposes the establishment of such criteria.

3. Libraries do not advocate the ideas found in their collections. The presence of books and other resources in a library does not indicate an endorsement of their contents by the library.

A variety of private organizations promulgate rating systems and/or review materials as a means of advising either their members or the general public concerning their opinions of the contents and suitability or appropriate age for use of certain books, films, recordings, or other materials. For the library to adopt or enforce any of these private systems, to attach such ratings to library materials, to include them in bibliographic records, library catalogs, or other finding aids, or otherwise to endorse them would violate the *Library Bill of Rights*.

While some attempts have been made to adopt these systems into law, the constitutionality of such measures is extremely questionable. If such legislation is passed which applies within a library's jurisdiction, the library should seek competent legal advice concerning its applicability to library operations.

Publishers, industry groups, and distributors sometimes add ratings to material or include them as part of their packaging. Librarians should not endorse such practices. However, removing or obliterating such ratings—if placed there by or with permission of the copyright holder—could constitute expurgation, which is also unacceptable.

The American Library Association opposes efforts which aim at closing any path to knowledge. This statement, however, does not exclude the adoption of organizational schemes designed as directional aids or to facilitate access to materials.

Fig. 19.2. "Statement on Labeling: An Interpretation of the *Library Bill of Rights*." Reprinted by permission of the American Library Association.

The ALA statements provide a philosophical base for resisting censorship. However, in the long run, success or failure depends on the individual librarian's personal beliefs and attitudes.

Forms of Censorship

A librarian or information professional may encounter three forms of censorship: legal or governmental, individual or group, and self-censorship. The first two are easier to respond to than the third. For the first type, there are two choices: comply or fight. Usually, fighting to change a law or interpretation of a law is time-consuming and expensive. Because of the time and cost, a single librarian or library seldom attempts it. Even at the community level involving a local ordinance, if there is to be a modification, there must be community-wide support. The library staff working alone has little chance of success.

Literary censorship has existed for a long time. The United States has seen an interesting mix of individual and governmental censorship. Anthony Comstock was a person of strong beliefs and personality whose efforts to control the reading materials of Americans were so vigorous and successful that his name is now part of the lexicon of intellectual freedom and censorship discussions—Comstockery.

Indeed, Comstock was so vocal in his efforts that, in 1873, Congress passed a law that attempted to create a structure for national morality. For almost 75 years, this law went unchallenged, with the U.S. Postal Service designated as the government agency primarily responsible for enforcement at the national level. At the local level, several elements were at work. State and local governments passed similar regulations, and, thus, local police departments became involved in the control of vice. Law enforcement agencies had ample help from two citizen groups: the Society for the Suppression of Vice and the Watch and Ward Society. The Society for the Suppression of Vice was the vehicle Comstock used to gain popular support and to show the depth of national support for his views. A primary activity of the society was to check on printed material available to local citizens, whatever the source (bookstores, newsstands, and libraries both public and private). Occasionally, when the society felt that local law enforcement officials were not moving quickly enough, it took matters into its own hands. Book burnings did take place, and the society applied pressure to anyone involved in buying or selling printed material to stock only items it deemed moral. The phrase *banned in Boston* originated as a result of the society's activity.

From 1873 until well into the twentieth century, the United States experienced a mix of all three types of censorship: official censorship because of the 1873 law; group pressure from organized societies concerned with the moral standards of their communities; and self-censorship on the part of publishers, booksellers, and librarians. A public or even a private stance by librarians against such censorship was almost unheard of; in fact, professional groups sponsored workshops and seminars to help librarians identify improper books. Most of the notable librarians of the past are on record (in ALA proceedings, speeches, or writings) in favor of this type of collection development. As E. Geller noted, Arthur Bostwick suggested it was reasonable to purchase books like *Man and Superman* for the New York Library's reference collection (noncirculating) but not for branch libraries.[2] Bostwick's inaugural speech as president of ALA (1908) was about the librarian as censor; as censor the librarian performed a positive act, if not an act of "greatness," Bostwick said.[3]

An interesting situation arose with foreign language titles. Many authors were available in their own languages, but not in English. Apparently, if one could read French, German, Spanish, Russian, or any other language, one was reading a moral book, but that same work in an English translation was immoral. The censorial atmosphere caused a few American authors to live abroad, and some had a larger foreign readership than English-speaking readership. (Henry Miller is a prime example.) At the time, librarians were no more vocal in protesting this situation than anyone else in the country.

The period between 1873 and the mid-1950s exhibited all of the censorship problems one can encounter. From the 1930s to the mid-1950s, various federal court decisions slowly modified the 1873 law, including several by the U.S. Supreme Court. The 1873 Comstock Act remains a part of the U.S. Code, but it is so modified as to be a completely different law. Most court cases dealing with censorship were between the government and publishers or booksellers. Librarians and their associations occasionally entered the suits as *amici curiae* (friends of the court) but seldom as defendants or plaintiffs.

Major changes in the interpretation of the law began with the 1957 U.S. Supreme Court *Roth* decision. This decision established a three-part test for obscenity. First, the dominant theme of the work as a whole had to appeal to prurient interest in sex. Second, the work had to be patently offensive because it affronted contemporary community standards in its representation of sex. Third, the work had to be utterly without redeeming social value. With that interpretation, more sexually explicit material became available in the open market. Not unexpectedly, some people objected to the new openness, and in 1973, the Supreme Court, in deciding the *Miller* case, modified the three-part test. The court suggested a new three-part test. First, would an average person applying contemporary community standards find the work as a whole appealed to prurient interest in sex? Second, does the work depict or describe in a patently offensive way sexual conduct specifically prohibited in a state's law? Third, does the work, as a whole, lack serious literary, artistic, political or scientific value? The effect of the decision was to reduce the impact of national mores by employing tests that emphasize local standards. This test is in place today.

Does the shift in emphasis matter? Yes, especially in terms of production and distribution of materials. One example of what the changed interpretation could do to distribution occurred in 1982. *Show Me,* a children's book about sex, was taken out of distribution by its American publisher/distributor, St. Martin's Press. They stopped distribution because the U.S. Supreme Court upheld a New York state child pornography law. The book contains photographs of naked children. The New York law contains a strict provision barring the use of children in all sexually explicit films and photographs, obscene or not. St. Martin's had already successfully defended *Show Me* in Massachusetts, New Hampshire, and Oklahoma. However, the publisher decided that determining which of the

50 states it could legally ship the book to, as well as keeping track of individual orders, was much too difficult, and it stopped all distribution. Perhaps the most interesting aspect of this incident is that the book was written by a Swiss child psychologist (Helga Fleischhauer-Hardt) and the photographs were taken by an American photographer (Will McBride). They prepared the book for a Lutheran church-sponsored children's book company in West Germany in 1974. The English language edition appeared in 1975, and St. Martin's stated that it had sold almost 150,000 copies in hardback and paperback before it ceased distribution.[4]

Some distributors and book clubs started using labeling systems in an attempt to protect themselves from lawsuits. For example, one book club uses labels that state: "Warning: explicit violence" or "Warning: explicit sex and violence." A few people speculated the purpose was to increase sales rather than avoid a lawsuit. Perhaps it serves a dual purpose. For a time, one of the library distributors that serves many school media centers included warnings with "problem" books it shipped.

For example, in children's books acquired for courses in children's literature, librarians at Loyola Marymount University have found slips bearing the warning, "This book is not up to our usual standards." (The standards referred to do *not* relate to the quality of the physical volume itself.) Such labeling violates the ALA statement on labeling, but it does reflect a growing concern with social values and with pressures to influence those values.

Today, just as during the period 1873-1950, most of the problems libraries encounter are with individual and group attempts to censor material. While no active Society for the Suppression of Vice exists today, librarians increasingly face organized pressure groups. What may at first seem to be a person's objection to one book can become a major confrontation between a library and an organized pressure group. Much depends on the energy and time that the would-be censor is willing to devote to the issue. Influential persons may be able to organize a group to generate even greater pressure than the average person could. A librarian may encounter organized pressure groups based on local interests and views (often, views that are religious or politically oriented), but seldom does a librarian face a challenge from a local group with broad national support. If such a group were to exist, it would be extremely difficult to avoid at least an occasional debate (if not all-out battle) over some materials in the collection. Policy statements about controversial materials, ALA's Freedom to Read documents, and other support materials will help to slow the process, but they will not stop it. Local groups are particularly hard to resist, because they can have a fairly broad base of community support and their existence indicates some active interest in certain problems.

A few examples illustrate the problems facing many librarians in the United States during the 1990s. One example was a 1993 report about censorship in U.S. schools. The report, released by People for the American Way, indicated that in 41 percent of the 395 reported attempts at censorship, censors succeeded in having the objectionable material removed or restricted in some manner.[5] The report indicated the majority of the reported attempts were by groups identified as religious right or pro-family. It went on to report school personnel acknowledged that they were being careful in what they added to the collections, a form of self-censorship. A 1983-1984 study indicated that school media centers resolved most challenges without removing the item or restricting access.[6] In 1992, ALA's Office for Intellectual Freedom recorded 653 incidents; however, it believes libraries report less than 15 percent of all attempts.[7]

Much of the censorship pressure arises from a concern about children, and the concern is not limited to sex. Some parents do not believe they are capable of judging the materials that their children are exposed to in school or the library. As a result, several organizations review materials for worried parents. These groups include Educational Research Analysts, Inc.; Mr. and Mrs. Gabler; America's Future, New Rochelle, N.Y.; the John Birch Society; and Parents of New York United (PONYU). These reviewers are particularly active in the area of elementary school textbooks and required reading material, but they also assess what is in the general collections that supports the curriculum.

Supporters of biblical creationism suggest that libraries are censoring Christian materials and especially creationism literature (or creation science). Anyone thinking about going into school media center work needs to be fully aware of what is taking place and to beware the dangers and pitfalls. The *Island Trees Union Free School District* decision of the U.S. Supreme Court (*Board of Education* vs. *Pico*, 1981. *United States Reports* v457, page 853.), which limited the power of school boards to limit access to materials, did not solve all the problems.

Not all censors are concerned about children's welfare. Challenges to materials based on their racist or sexist content arise fairly often. One of the more unusual cases was "The Incredible Case of the Stack o' Wheat Murders" photograph incident in 1980.[8] The case illustrates that censorship battles are not limited to public and school libraries. The Stack o' Wheat incident occurred at the University of California, Santa Cruz, library, in the special collections room. Ten 4-x-5-inch photographs, called "The Incredible Case of the Stack o' Wheat Murders," were taken by photographer Les Krims. The collection was a parody of theme murders intended for use in a marketing project. Each photograph showed a "gruesomely" murdered nude woman dripping blood alongside a stack of wheat pancakes. The dripping blood was chocolate syrup; the chocolate represented the "epitome of the series humor," according to the text that accompanied the photographs. A young woman who viewed the photographs demanded their removal from the library's collection on the grounds they represented the sexploitation of women. When the library took no action, she went to the special collections room, ripped up the photographs and accompanying material, and poured chocolate syrup over the debris. The case quickly escalated into a significant problem for the campus, encompassing many complex issues, such as freedom of expression, censorship, status of women, vandalism, and social justice.

A more recent case involving photographs, one that gained national attention, was the Robert Mapplethorpe controversy. This case went to trial and led to the resignation of a museum director, as well as an individual who had once won ALA's intellectual freedom award.[9, 10]

If nothing else, this case illustrates how deeply a censorship issue can divide a community. When local pressure groups exist, the librarian may ask, "How will they react if I buy this item?" Thinking along these lines allows one to deal with one's worries. The real danger in the situation is when the thought is unconscious. At that point, the pressure group has almost accomplished its purpose, that is, control over what goes into the collection. Further, the group has accomplished it through the librarian's self-censorship.

Self-censorship is our greatest problem as librarians and information professionals. We all feel that we would never censor ourselves, but it is difficult to prevent. A few librarians would agree with Walter Brahm; it is better to retreat and fight another day.[11] He reasons that censorship falls victim to the times; public opinion can only dampen censorship; that over time, no one can lead society's mores in directions the population opposes. Certainly, libraries and librarians cannot accomplish this alone; and generally, libraries are not the main battleground of intellectual freedom. Most librarians would take a public stance against Brahm's position, when stated in a theoretical sense and when it does not affect them directly. When it becomes a real issue and there is personal involvement, it becomes another matter.

The following are but a few of the hundreds of attempts at censorship in libraries and information centers in the United States. ALA's *Newsletter on Intellectual Freedom* provides an ongoing source of news about this field.

Examples of Censorship

Journals

In the late 1960s, two periodicals, *Ramparts* and *Evergreen Review (ER)*, caused libraries and librarians to confront the censorship issue head-on. These confrontations illustrate the variety of ways libraries deal with controversy. In Los Angeles, the public library had to fight a city councilman's efforts to have *ER* removed from the library.[12] The councilman was unsuccessful, but the library removed the current *ER* issues from public areas while the controversy raged. Eventually, the journal was returned to the open shelves after the parties reached a final decision. This was a short-term victory for censorship, but in the end, a victory for free access.

Not all librarians were so lucky. Richard Rosichan lost his position as director of the Kingston Area (New York) Public Library because he fought to keep *ER*, despite both library board and John Birch Society pressure to drop it.[13] At the same time, the American Legion demanded he remove *Ramparts* because of what the legion considered its un-American stance. Groton (Connecticut) Public Library managed to retain its staff but lost its subscription to *ER;* after a four-month fight, the library's board of trustees ordered the removal of all issues from the library and the subscription canceled. This was done under the threat of fines and jail sentences for both the library board and staff. Head librarian John Carey issued a statement to the effect that this decision would affect the general acquisition policy.[14] One can only hope that he was wrong.

Between keeping an item on the shelves and removing it is the compromise position to which librarians sometimes resort—restricted availability. The Philadelphia Free Library used this approach for *ER* when pressure began to be applied. The library renewed the subscription for the main building and one regional branch, but it kept the issues in closed stack areas and no one under 18 could examine the title.[15] Emerson Greenaway, director of libraries for the Philadelphia Free Library, said this was done because *ER* was "important sociologically." Who was the winner here, the censor or the librarian?

The foregoing are a small sample of the problems that arose with *Evergreen Review* and *Ramparts,* and they are only two of hundreds of periodicals that have been attacked over the years. In fact, groups frequently question *Newsweek* and *Time.* Some other journals that have been questioned by an individual or group in the early 1990s are: *Not-for-Profit* (a school magazine), *People, Playboy, Playgirl, Reader's Digest, Rolling Stone,* and *Young Miss.*

Books

The list of books that have caused trouble is immense. The short list at the end of this section illustrates the range of titles while indicating that one can never really tell what will cause trouble. Some topics are more sensitive than others, and one might expect difficulty with certain acquisitions but not encounter any. However, sex, religion, and politics are always potential problems.

Several school districts and public libraries faced complaints about *I Know Why the Caged Bird Sings* (Maya Angelou) because of passages dealing with child molestation and rape. In most instances, the objectors were successful in forcing its removal or restricting its use by requiring parental approval in writing.

Adventures of Huckleberry Finn (Mark Twain) has a long history of complaints. The complaints are a perennial problem. The usual complaint is the book contains racist material. Complaints are frequently filed over J. D. Salinger's *Catcher in the Rye.* Here the usual issue is profanity; occasionally, someone objects to sexual references. Another book that people think contains inappropriate language is *One Hundred Years of Solitude* by Nobel prize winner Gabriel Garcia Marquez.

Other books draw complaints because of the point of view they present, for example Dee Brown's *Bury My Heart at Wounded Knee.* Still others encounter problems for reasons that are hard to understand. Try to find the offending nudity in *Where's Waldo?* or decide why some school media centers have *Snow White* on the list of books that may be read only with signed parental approval.

Music and Recordings

Though in the past there were fewer problems with music than with other formats, that is no longer the case. Rap music, hard rock, and music lyrics in general now generate controversy. Recently, 2 Live Crew recordings and performances have drawn national attention. Early in 1990, the recording industry instituted a labeling program similar to the motion picture rating system. This occurred after years of debate, even in Congress, and opposition from a variety of groups, such as ALA. Anna Thompson's article "Lyric Censorship" provides some good insights into this area.[16]

One older musical recording that still raises problems from time to time is *Jesus Christ, Superstar*. Some years ago, Rockford High School (Michigan) was the location of one such disagreement over both the music and text. At the end of the debate, the school removed all materials relating to *Jesus Christ, Superstar* from the school system—both the library and the music department—because the musical was "sacrilegious."[17]

A good article that gives one a sense of how long people have been trying to censor music in the United States is Edward Volz's "You Can't Play That."[18]

Games

Nothing in the collection is immune from challenge, as several libraries have learned the hard way. Aurora Public Library (Colorado) had to deal with controversy over *Dungeons and Dragons (D&D)* players' books. (*D&D* is a popular role-playing game with an estimated three million players, mostly young people.) A woman presented an official complaint and a petition with 150 signatures supporting the complaint. She claimed the game promotes "violence, Satanism and blasphemy of Christian terms." The complaint was withdrawn a short time later because the woman said she feared reprisals against her and her widowed mother. However, the publicity sparked a rash of complaints about other items in the library, and a local evangelist began checking area public library collections for *D&D* players' books. He tried to pursue the Aurora complaint, but, because he did not live in the community, he could not file a complaint. At about the same time, in Hanover, Virginia, the parents of a 16-year-old who committed suicide sued a public school system. The parents alleged the suicide was a direct result of his playing *D&D* in a school building. Wrongful death lawsuits related to games, movies, and television programs have been increasing. None has involved libraries, but there is no reason to suppose libraries will be immune from a suit, particularly when many collections have materials about suicide. The November 1983 issue of *American Libraries* published some responses to the ALA Ethics Committee question, Should you give a student a copy of *Suicide Mode D'Emploi?* The book is said to be linked to at least 10 suicides. If one believes in freedom to read, what should one do?

Film and Video

As library collections of theatrical videos grow, so do the odds that someone will demand the removal of one or more titles. Educational videos, especially those dealing with reproduction, abortion, and alternative lifestyles, also present problems.[19] Even foreign language videos, such as a Portuguese language film can draw protests.[20] During the Gulf War, some libraries rejected an antiwar video, raising the question of whether the librarians were acting as censors and not providing both sides of an issue.[21] A short but informative article about issues of accessibility to video collections is by John Hurley.[22]

Some years ago, librarians put on an amazing performance of self-censorship. The situation surrounding the film *The Speaker* provides almost every element one is likely to encounter in any censorship case. To fully understand all of the paradoxes that this event represents, one must review the background of the situation and view the film.

The problem with *The Speaker* began when ALA's Committee for Intellectual Freedom received funds to produce a film about the issues of censorship and intellectual freedom. Shown for the first time to membership at the June 1977 annual convention, the film generated one of the longer debates in ALA history. Seldom has there been as long or as bitter a debate within ALA about an issue that is, presumably, an article of faith in the profession. Many of the African American members labeled the film racist. Many other members agreed the film was a problem for that or other reasons. An attempt to have ALA's name disassociated from the film failed, but not by much. Is that a move to censor? How does that differ from the definition given at the beginning of this chapter? Does that really differ from a publisher's deciding not to release a title because the work is found not to be in the best interest of the owner of the company?

As with every other problem of this type, we have no objective data on which to base a judgment. Not all African Americans or other persons of color who viewed the film saw it as racist. Just because one (albeit large) group claims that an item is this or that, does the claim make it so?

Is this really different from the Citizen's Committee for Clean Books saying that *The Last Temptation of Christ* is sacrilegious or the John Birch Society claiming that *Ramparts* and the *Evergreen Review* are anti-American? One hopes that most librarians will agree with Dorothy Broderick regarding *The Speaker:*

> Let librarians across the country decide for themselves: If they find the film boring, let them not buy it. If they feel that using it will stir up trouble in their community—as if they had invited "The Speaker"—let them ignore its existence. If the film is as bad as its opponents claim, it will die the natural death of an inadequate work in the marketplace."[23]

Many persons believed that if ALA removed its name from the film, the association would have taken the first step toward suppressing the film, thus practicing censorship, the very thing it tries to avoid.

Happily, ALA has produced, or taken part in the production of, an excellent video, *Censorship vs. Selection: Choosing Books for Public Schools.*[24] Though the focus is on public schools, the issues covered are broad enough to make the film useful to use with any group to generate a discussion of intellectual freedom and censorship.

Special Cases

Sometimes, there are unusual circumstances surrounding a book or other item of controversy, and there are major efforts to suppress the distribution of the item by governments or other groups. An extreme example was that of Salman Rushdie's *Satanic Verses*. Although Rushdie was alive but in hiding at this writing, several translators and publishers around the world who played some role in the publishing of the book are dead. Bookstores stocking the book received threats, as did those involved in the distribution of the book. To the best of my knowledge, no library received threats for adding the title to the collection. OCLC holdings statements indicate only 218 OCLC libraries hold a copy.

A good review article about the Rushdie situation and why *Satanic Verses* was condemned is John Swan's "*Satanic Verses*, the Fatwa, and Its Aftermath,"[25] which describes the major events through mid-1991.

Librarians and Censorship

Realistically, all the situations discussed so far are of the type that one can easily identify and choose to fight or not. Given the foregoing sample of the problems that one may encounter, it should not be surprising to find librarians acting in a self-protective manner. How great a problem is this? Several researchers have studied this phenomenon, but this discussion will explore the findings of only two of the more widely known studies, those of Fiske and Busha.

Marjorie Fiske shook the library profession some years ago when she reported that a high percentage of librarians decided not to buy an item because it might cause a problem.[26] Some titles are likely to cause trouble, for example, *The Joy of Sex* or Madonna's *Sex,* and these are easy to identify. However, an examination of the sample list of titles that have caused trouble makes it evident that some items are not easy to identify. After establishing the habit of not selecting a title that has the potential for controversy, it will be difficult to break the habit. Unfortunately, as with so many other habits, it is easy to slip into a behavior pattern without recognizing it.

Reasons like "lack of funds," "no demand," or "poor quality" may be true, or they may be rationalizations for not selecting an item that might make life troublesome. Other excuses, such as "I will buy it when someone asks for it" or "I don't like that author or producer; he or she never has anything worthwhile to say," clearly signal danger. Just because a librarian does not like an author or a subject does not mean he or she has the right to keep others from access. This may not be self-protective in the sense of job security, but it may be self-protective in terms of one's own psyche. In any case, the result is the same—censorship.

One way to raise the level of self-awareness is to periodically check one's holdings against various lists of problem items. How many does the library have? Holdings of less than 50 percent should cause one to question what is happening in the selection process. There may be perfectly good reasons why there are so few of these items in the collection, but until the librarian can give good reasons, he or she cannot complacently say, "I am not a censor."

Charles Busha's study examined librarians' attitudes toward censorship and intellectual freedom. He compared his findings to scores on a standardized test that is an indirect measure of antidemocratic trends. His concluding sentence is probably a reasonable picture of all librarianship in the United States: "It is evident, as a result of opinion research, that Midwestern public librarians did not hesitate to express agreement with cliches of intellectual freedom but that many of them apparently did not feel strong enough as professionals to assert these principles in the face of real or anticipated censorship pressures."[27]

The data from a 1982 survey by Woods and Perry-Holmes indicate the pattern of self-censorship continued, at least for small and medium-sized public libraries.[28] Other reports (cited earlier in this chapter) show the situation remains unchanged today.

A Sampling of Problem Books

The following list comprises books that have been attacked for a host of reasons:

Daddy's Roomate	*Limerick*
Changing Bodies, Changing Lives	The Nancy Drew series
Exposing the AIDS Scandal	*Rabbit Wedding*
Forever	*Robots of Dawn*
The Hardy Boys series	*Tom Sawyer*
Intimacy Between Men	*Wizard of Oz*
Last Picture Show	

What to Do Before and After the Censor Arrives

Knowing the dangers of censorship and having a commitment to avoid it is not enough in today's world. Information professionals must prepare for the censor long, long before there is a perceived threat or before the threat becomes real. The first step in preparing for the censor is to expect to have to face a censor. Prepare a policy statement about how the library will handle complaints, and have the policy approved by all the appropriate authorities. There is nothing worse than having no idea of what to do when facing an angry person who is complaining about library materials. Even with policies and procedures, the situation may escalate into physical violence; without procedures, the odds of violence occurring increase.

A typical procedure is to have the individual(s) file a formal complaint or fill out a form that specifies what is at issue. (Figure 19.3 on page 526 is one such form.) Several organizations, such as ALA and the National Council of Teachers of English, have recommended forms that are equally effective.

After the library develops the policies and procedures and they are approved, everyone working in public services needs to understand the system and receive training in implementing the system. (Sometimes role-playing is helpful in reinforcing the training.) ALA's Office for Intellectual Freedom has an excellent manual that provides details about what to do before censors arrive. Another good source is Frances Jones's *Defusing Censorship: The Librarian's Guide to Handling Censorship Conflicts.*[29]

ALA's organizational structure for dealing with intellectual freedom concerns is somewhat confusing. The Intellectual Freedom Committee (IFC) is responsible for making recommendations to the association regarding matters of intellectual freedom. The Office for Intellectual Freedom (OIF), which has a full-time staff, has the charge of educating librarians and others about intellectual freedom and censorship matters. It also is the support service for the IFC, and it implements the association's policies related to intellectual freedom. As part of the educational function, OIF produces several publications: *Newsletter on Intellectual Freedom* (news and current developments relating to intellectual freedom), *OIF Memorandum* (addressed to local library association intellectual freedom committees), and the *Intellectual Freedom Manual.*

Although OIF does not provide legal assistance when a library faces a complaint, it does provide telephone consultation (occasionally with the addition of written statements or names of persons who might be able to testify for intellectual freedom). Very rarely, the OIF comes to the library to provide moral and professional support. Often, librarians are surprised to learn that OIF does not provide legal aid. Legal assistance *might* be available from the Freedom to Read Foundation (FRF). FRF is not part of ALA (it is a separate legal entity), but the two are so closely affiliated many people have difficulty drawing the line between the two. The executive director of FRF is also the director of the OIF; with such an arrangement, it is not surprising that people think FRF is part of ALA. Be aware there is no assurance of receiving financial or legal aid from FRF; there are too many cases and insufficient funds to assist everyone.

Anyone interested in becoming involved in intellectual freedom activities should consider joining the Intellectual Freedom Round Table, which is the general membership unit of ALA related to intellectual freedom. Though ALA offers a variety of support services for handling censors' complaints, the best support is preparing before the need arises.

Since people differ, citizens may register their complaints by filling out the following form:

Author:

Title:

Publisher (if known):

Request initiated by _____
Name   Telephone No.

_____
Address

Complainant represents: Himself/Herself _____ Organization _____
If organization, give name:_____

1. Specify what you object to in the book (cite pages)_____
    _____

2. For what age group would you recommend this book?_____

3. What do you think might be the effects of reading this book?_____
    _____

4. What do you think is good about this book?_____
    _____

5. Did you read the whole book or just parts of it?_____

6. Do you know the literary critics' view of this book?_____

7. What is the theme of the book?_____

8. What action would you like the library to take about this book?
      Withdraw it from the shelves?_____
      Do not permit it in the children's room?_____
      Do not permit my child to sign it out?_____

9. What book would you recommend in its place?_____
    _____

_____
Signature of Complainant

_____
Date

Fig. 19.3. Patron's request for reconsideration of a book.

Bibliotherapy

A common statement used when defending a book or other library material is that there is no definitive cause-effect relationship between reading or viewing and behavior. The ALA's Freedom to Read statements and the Educational Film Library Association's Freedom to View statements support this view. However, there is a body of literature about the use of reading in the treatment of illness. Some medical professionals believe there is a cause-effect relationship. In addition, a variety of lawsuits allege that reading or viewing caused someone to do something.

John Berry explored this area in a 1992 *LJ* editorial.

> If words don't incite action, I'm in the wrong line of work . . . if they don't motivate people to act, antisocially or otherwise, then our First Amendment is of little value and less importance.

> This is a tough contradiction for those of us who must argue the case against censorship. . . . We can't support free expression by saying it won't do any harm. It is obvious that action triggered by words and pictures can do harm and often does.[30]

Librarians' do not spend enough time learning about the circumstances in which reading or viewing may cause someone to harm a person or property. Perhaps a course or two in bibliotherapy should be required of any professional working in public service areas of a library or information center.

A standard definition of bibliotherapy is "use of literature to bring about a therapeutic interaction between participant and facilitator."[31] Some believe a healing process takes place through reading, that is, that "thoughtful suggestions provide a reader with just the right book, a book that triggers a significant and growth producing feeling in response to some need."[32] Most bibliotherapists operate on the basis of several assumptions:

The process is interactive; it involves both participant and facilitator.

Literature encompasses all forms of writing.

The process is both clinical and developmental.

The process can be one-on-one or group-based.

The outcome is improved self-esteem and better assimilation of appropriate psychological or social values for the participant(s).

The process is a therapy but draws heavily on the healthy aspects of the mind.

The process depends on the facilitator's ability to select the appropriate material for the participant to read and consider.

To date, data about the effectiveness of bibliotherapy are inconclusive. (As a library intern in a Veterans Administration hospital while in library school, I took books and magazines to the locked psychiatric ward for patients to read. Before I delivered the books, a doctor examined every item on the book truck. Often, the doctor removed some items. Was I giving in to censorship? Was I violating the ALA's Freedom to Read statements?)

There is much we do not know about reading or viewing and behavior. Perhaps when we know more, our freedom to read statements may need revision.

Determining the effectiveness of bibliotherapy or the effect or lack of effect of reading, viewing, and listening on behavior should be a high priority. The field makes the case for free and open access to all material for anyone at any time, yet there is some evidence that reading, viewing, and listening to certain items by certain people at certain times does affect behavior in a positive or negative way.

Summary

The problem of censorship is complex, and it is necessary to do a lot of reading and thinking about this topic. A final example may help to illustrate just how complex the issue is. Assume that a librarian is responsible for selecting materials for a small public library. Naturally, he or she needs this job to cover living expenses. A small group of persons in the community wants the librarian to buy certain items for the library collection; but he or she also knows of a large group of vocal and influential persons who would be upset, and might even demand that he or she be fired, if the items were purchased. Should the librarian buy the item and risk his or her family's welfare and own career over this? If he or she does not buy the item, what can be said to the people who asked for its purchase? Does telling them they can get it somewhere else, or get it through interlibrary loan, really address that librarian's problem?

Finally, an article in *American Libraries* raised the question: Is it censorship to remove all copies of *The Joy of Gay Sex* because it advocates sex practices that are now felt to be dangerous in light of the AIDS epidemic?[33] Several librarians responded to the question, and there is some difference of opinion. One wonders how the respondents would have answered had the question been: Is it censorship not to buy copies of Madonna's *Sex?* As with all real problems, there is no simple, completely satisfactory answer.

Notes

[1]Charles Busha, "Intellectual Freedom and Censorship," *Library Quarterly* 42 (July 1972): 283-84.

[2]E. Geller, "The Librarian As Censor," *Library Journal* 101 (June 1, 1976): 125.

[3]A. Bostwick, "The Librarian As Censor," *ALA Bulletin* 2 (September 1908): 108.

[4]"Children's Sex Book Removed from Sale," *Rocky Mountain News,* (September 21, 1982): 49.

[5]"Censors Succeed in 41% of School Cases," *Library Hotline* 22 (September 27, 1993): 2.

[6]*Library Hotline* (March 12, 1984): 1.

[7]"Besieged by Book Banners," *Los Angeles Times* (May 10, 1993): 1, 20a.

[8]"Stack o' Wheat Photos Uproar," *Los Angeles Times,* (May 25, 1980): pt. 8, 1, 22-24.

[9]"Director of Corcoran Resigns," *Newsletter on Intellectual Freedom* 39 (March 1990): 73.

[10]"Mapplethorpe Defender Wins Downs Award," *Newsletter on Intellectual Freedom* 41 (March 1992): 68.

[11]"Knights and Windmills," *Library Journal* 96 (October 1, 1971): 3096-98.

[12]*Wilson Library Bulletin* 48 (September 1969): 18.

[13]Ibid.

[14]*Wilson Library Bulletin* 50 (April 1971): 717.

[15]*Newsletter on Intellectual Freedom* 18 (January 1969): 5.

[16]Anna Thompson, "Lyric Censorship: The Risks of Dirty Disks," *Unabashed Librarian* 62 (1987): 5-7.

[17]*Newsletter on Intellectual Freedom* 23 (May 1974): 54.

[18]Edward J. Volz, "You Can't Play That: A Selective Chronology of Banned Music, 1850-1991," *Colorado Libraries* 19 (Summer 1993): 22-25.

[19]Gordon Flagg, "Protesters Fail to Block Gay Videos at Tallahassee Library," *American Libraries* 23 (July/August 1992): 548-49.

[20]L. Kniffel, "N.C. County Commissioner Defends Effort to Ban Video," *American Libraries* 24 (January 1993): 14.

[21]B. Goldberg, "Librarians Called Censors for Declining Gulf War Video," *American Libraries* 22 (July/August 1991): 615-16.

[22]J. Hurley, "Free Access Issues and Video Collections," *New Jersey Libraries* 22 (Fall 1989): 8-10.

[23]D. Broderick, "Son of Speaker," *American Libraries* 8 (October 1977): 503.

[24]*Censorship vs. Selection: Choosing Books for Public Schools* (New York: Media and Society Seminars, 1982).

[25]John Swan, "*Satanic Verses*, the Fatwa, and Its Aftermath," *Library Quarterly* 61 (October 1991): 429-43.

[26]M. Fiske, *Book Selection and Censorship* (Berkeley, CA: University of California, 1958).

[27]Charles Busha, "Intellectual Freedom and Censorship," 300.

[28]L. B. Woods and C. Perry-Holmes, "The Flak If We Had *The Joy of Sex* Here," *Library Journal* 107 (September 15, 1982): 1711-15.

[29]Frances Jones, *Defusing Censorship: The Librarian's Guide to Handling Censorship Conflicts* (Phoenix, AZ: Oryx Press, 1983).

[30]John Berry, "If Words Will Never Hurt Me, Then —?" *Library Journal* 117 (January 1992): 6.

[31]Arleen M. Hynes and Mary Hynes-Berry, *Bibliotherapy: Interactive Process* (Boulder, CO: Westview Press, 1986).

[32]Ibid., 10-11.

[33]"Censorship in the Name of Public Health," *American Libraries* (May 1986): 306.

Further Reading

General

Asser, P. N. "Freedom and Copyright." *Logos* 4, no. 1 (1993): 45-49.

Berman, S. "Hot Stuff: Getting Sex in the Library." *Collection Building* 13, no. 1 (1993): 45-47.

Bosmajian, H. A. *Freedom of Expression.* New York: Neal-Schuman, 1988.

——. *Freedom of Religion.* New York: Neal-Schuman, 1987.

——. *Freedom to Read.* New York: Neal-Schuman, 1987.

Brahm, W. "Knights and Windmills." *Library Journal* 96 (October 1, 1971): 3096-98.

Branin, J. J. "Collection Management and Intellectual Freedom." In *Collection Management for the 1990s,* edited by J. J. Branin, 148-55. Chicago: American Library Association, 1993.

Broderick, D. "Son of Speaker." *American Libraries* 8 (October 1977): 503.

Busha, C. H. "Intellectual Freedom and Censorship." *Library Quarterly* 42 (July 1972): 283-84.

Bushman, J. "Librarians, Self-censorship, and Information Technologies." *College & Research Libraries* 55 (May 1994): 221-28.

Cornog, M. "Is Sex Safe in Your Library?" *Library Journal* 118 (August 1993): 43-46.

de Grazia, E., and R. K. Newman. *Banned Films*. New York: R. R. Bowker, 1982.

Downs, R. B., and R. McCoy. *The First Freedom Today*. Chicago: American Library Association, 1984.

Foerstel, H. N. *Banned in the U.S.A.: A Reference Guide to Book Censorship in School and Public Libraries*. Westport, CT: Greenwood Press, 1994.

Haight, A. L. *Banned Books*. 4th ed. New York: R. R. Bowker, 1978.

Heckart, R. J. "The Library As a Marketplace of Ideas." *College & Research Libraries* 52 (November 1991): 491-505.

Lack, C. R. "Can Bibliotherapy Go Public?" *Collection Building* 7 (Spring 1985): 27-32.

Manley, W. "Does Intellectual Freedom Protect the Politically Incorrect?" *American Libraries* 24 (December 1993): 1003-4.

Noble, W. *Book Banning in America: Who Bans Books and Why*. Middlebury, VT: Eriksson, 1992.

Pedersen, M. "They Censor, I Select." *Publishers Weekly* 241 (January 1994): 34-36.

Poppel, N., and E. M. Ashley. "Toward Understanding the Censor." *Library Journal* 111 (July 1986): 39-43.

Robotham, J., and G. Shields. *Freedom of Access to Library Materials*. New York: Neal-Schuman, 1982.

Selth, J. P. *Ambition, Discrimination, and Censorship in Libraries*. Jefferson, NC: McFarland, 1993.

Shields, G. R. "Censorship, Social Violence, and Librarian Ethics." *Library Quarterly* 62 (April 1992): 217-22.

Smolla, R. A. "Freedom of Speech for Libraries and Librarians." *Law Library Journal* 85 (Winter 1993): 71-79.

West, C. "Secret Garden of Censorship: Ourselves." *Library Journal* 108 (1 September 1983): 1651-53.

Woodward, D., ed. "Intellectual Freedom." *Library Trends* 39, nos. 1/2 (Summer/Fall 1990): 1-185.

Academic

Bosmajian, H. A. *Academic Freedom*. New York: Neal-Schuman, 1989.

Hippenhammer, C. T. "Patron Objections to Library Materials: A Survey of Christian College Libraries." *Christian Librarian* 37 (November 1993): 12-17.

Hood, E. "Academic Library Censorship in a Conservative Era." In *Association of College and Research Libraries, National Conference*, 4th ed., 15-17. Chicago: Association of College and Research Libraries, 1986.

Houbeck, R. L. "Locked in Conversation." *Journal of Library Administration* 17, no. 2 (1992): 99-131.

Metz, P., and B. Obenhaus. "Virginia Tech Sets Policy on Controversial Materials." *College & Research Libraries News* 54, no. 7 (July/August 1993): 386-88.

Podrygula, S. "Censorship in an Academic Library." *College & Research Libraries News* 55, no. 2 (February 1994): 76-78.

Schrader, A. M.; M. Herring; and C. De Scossa. "Censorship Phenomenon in College Libraries." *College & Research Libraries* 50 (July 1989): 420-32.

Public

Bright, L. "Censorship in a Small Town." *Colorado Libraries* 19 (Summer 1993): 15-17.

Caler, S. L. "Library Will Soon Be Offering Sex." *Colorado Libraries* 19 (Summer 1993): 9-11.

Geler, E. *Forbidden Books in American Public Libraries*. Westport, CT: Greenwood Press, 1984.

Katz, J. "Revisionist History in the Library." *Canadian Library Journal* 48 (October 1991): 319-24.

Kniffel, L. "Justify My Purchase: To Buy Madonna's *Sex* or Not." *American Libraries* 23 (December 1992): 902-4.

LaRue, J. "Reading with the Enemy." *Wilson Library Bulletin* 68 (January 1994): 43-45.

Saunders, K. C. "Factors Affecting the Outcome of Challenges to Library Materials." *Texas Library Journal* 68 (Fall 1992): 84-86.

Serebnick, J. "Book Reviews and the Selection of Potentially Controversial Books in Public Libraries." *Library Quarterly* 51 (October 1981): 390-409.

School

American Library Association. Office for Intellectual Freedom. *Censorship Litigation and the Schools*. Chicago: American Library Association, 1983.

Arbetman, L. "Reviewing the Books School Children Read: Censorship or Selection?" *Georgia Social Science Journal* 14 (Spring 1983): 1-4.

Bosmajian, H. *Censorship, Libraries and the Law*. New York: Neal-Schuman, 1983.

Burress, L. *Battle of the Books: Literary Censorship in the Public Schools (1950-1985)*. Metuchen, NJ: Scarecrow Press, 1989.

Flagg, G. "*Snow White* Is the Latest Title Under Attack in Schools." *American Libraries* 23 (May 1992): 359-60.

Hamilton, C. "Censorship and Intellectual Freedom in Schools." *Book Report* 11 (March/April 1993): 5-29.

Hopkins, D. M. "A Conceptual Model of Factors Influencing the Outcome of Challenges to Library Materials in Secondary School Settings." *Library Quarterly* 63 (January 1993): 40-72.

Krug, J., and A. E. Penway. "School and Library Censorship." *Show-Me Libraries* 44 (Winter/Spring 1993): 3-6.

McDonald, F. B. *Censorship and Intellectual Freedom: A Survey of School Librarians' Attitudes and Moral Reasoning.* Metuchen, NJ: Scarecrow Press, 1993.

Mosley, M. "The School Library in Court." *School Library Journal* 27 (October 1981): 96-99.

Reichman, H. *Censorship and Selection: Issues and Answers for Schools.* Chicago: American Library Association, 1993.

Sorenson, G. P. "Removal of Books from School Libraries 1972-1982." *Journal of Law and Education* 12 (July 1983): 417-41.

Bibliotherapy

Allen, B., and L. O'Dell. *Bibliotherapy and the Public Library.* San Rafael, CA: San Rafael Public Library Bibliotherapy Project, 1981.

Anderson, M. "Literature in the Pediatric Setting." In *Many Faces, Many Voices,* edited by A. L. Mana and C. S. Brodie, 79-86. Fort Atkinson, WI: Highsmith Press, 1992.

"Bibliotherapy Exchange." *Ohio Libraries.* (An ongoing column in various issues of the journal, each dealing with a different topic, such as death and dying, self-esteem, and divorce.)

Brett, D. *More Annie Stories: Therapeutic Storytelling Techniques.* Pasadena, CA: Magination Press, 1992.

Cecil, N. L., and P. Roberts. *Developing Resiliency Through Children's Literature.* Jefferson, NC: McFarland, 1992.

"Counseling in Public Libraries." In *Public Librarianship*, edited by V. L. Pungitore, 115-32. Westport, CT: Greenwood Press, 1989.

Coville, B. "Magic Mirrors." *Bookmark* 49 (Fall 1990): 35-36.

Gubert, B. K. "Sadie Peterson Delaney: Pioneer Bibliotherapist." *American Libraries* 24 (February 1993): 124-30.

Lack, C. R. "Can Bibliotherapy Go Public?" *Collection Building* 7 (Spring 1985): 27-32.

Mohr, C.; D. Nixon; and S. Vickers. *Books That Heal.* Englewood, CO: Teacher Ideas Press, 1991.

Pearl, P. *Helping Children Through Books.* Portland, OR: Church & Synagogue Library Association, 1990.

Smith, A. G. "Will the Real Bibliotherapist Please Stand Up?" *Journal of Youth Services* 2 (Spring 1989): 241-49.

Steele, A. T. "Raising the Issue: Read Two Books and Call Me in the Morning." *Wilson Library Bulletin* 68 (June 1994): 65-66.

20
Collection Development and the Future

Looking to the future is not as risky as predicting the future. In the last edition, I speculated about possible short-term developments. Here, I will review that material and look to the future.

Perhaps someday in the future, the book as we know it will cease to exist except as a museum piece or a collector's curiosity. Certainly, video formats have made tremendous strides; they are the fastest growing part of many collections and command high use. Probably, multimedia is the next high growth area for the collection.

Control of Information

At some time in the future, we may see the end of the library as a facility to which customers come to use materials. Certainly that time is closer than it was at the time the last edition was published. However, the production of print materials remains at levels far above those of 40 years ago, suggesting the demise of the physical library is still far off. Regardless of what happens—changes in formats, services, physical locations—it seems likely there always will be some system for disseminating information to users. There will be just as much need for selectors who are capable of building appropriate collections then as there is today.

There is an ongoing debate over public versus commercial firms' control of information as well as the cost of information. Outsourcing continues to grow, especially for technical service functions. Because of the need to know the local users very well, little outsourcing is taking place in collection management, other than in acquisitions. Special or corporate libraries are encountering increased pressure to reduce operating costs, even in the area of information retrieval. As a result, information brokers are finding an ever-growing market for their services.

In the last edition I wrote that I hoped the individuals who wrote the following would be correct. So far, their view prevails:

> Society's need to collect, preserve, and maintain the integrity and availability of records in all media is permanent, which is why it makes perfect sense for a public institution to be given the responsibility. Business can go bankrupt, merge, and be swayed by social and economic factors. And a business, no matter what

it does, must ultimately be profitable. When the profit margin for a product or service declines, either a solution is found to stabilize or reverse the trend or the product is withdrawn. Even the most idealistic publishers do not reprint books that have stopped selling. Consider then, that since records of information and knowledge never cease to grow, average use per record must steadily decline. In the long run, profit cannot be made from permanently storing records. Some records must be purged. Any permanent collection/archive/database of records can only exist in the not-for-profit sector.[1]

Herbert Schiller made a strong case against depending on private companies for information services. Schiller suggests that there are two different approaches to information collecting and management.

One is to regard information as a central element in the development and creation of a democratic society. Under this premise, information serves to facilitate democratic decision-making, assists citizen participation in government, and contributes to the search for roughly egalitarian measures in the economy at large.[2]

Schiller's approach is "to view information collection, organization, and dissemination as a neutral activity, absent of social direction. . . . This is the equivalent of information for information's sake."[3] What we have witnessed during the past several years is a steady increase in the commercialization of information. The view seems to be that any company has a right to charge what it wishes for information, often, information that in the past was free. As noted in several chapters in this book, pricing information does not follow traditional pricing processes, which results in substantial costs for libraries and information centers and their customers. Schiller comments on this in terms of government information: "The national informational system especially has borne the brunt of the privatization pressure. The national government has been, and remains, the largest generator, collector, and disseminator of information. The drive to privatization has cut deeply into these functions."[4] His view as to what will happen is similar to mine: "Information has become increasingly significant in the organization and performance of the national economy. This has forced the effort to defend American librarianship's longstanding democratic goals to be fused with the need to make the overall economy more responsive to the citizenry and less attractive to powerful corporate interests. Right now, at best, the outcome is uncertain."[5]

Given the economic picture and inevitable growth in the output of information materials, the management aspect of selecting information will become more important in the future. As the volume of information and the forms in which it is available increase, libraries and information centers must be more selective. Emphasis is likely to shift to an evaluation of the cost or value of the information as opposed to the cost of the package. In the immediate future, the push/pull between buying serials or monographs will continue and perhaps increase in intensity. Over the longer run, it seems likely that the integration of information technologies will make the distinctions among various formats, including print and nonprint formats, increasingly blurred. Electronic information will continue to grow in importance and information professionals will slowly resolve the issues of access and ownership for their organizations. Balancing these costs will be an ongoing challenge as we confront technologies that become out-of-date in less and less time.

Legal aspects of collection development probably will increase in importance. Copyright holders' efforts to enforce their rights will continue. Costs to libraries for compliance activities will increase, and libraries and information centers will meet these costs in one of two ways: by setting aside additional funds to purchase low- or moderate-use items (because ILL activity must decrease) or by allocating more funds to pay copyright holder use fees. As information formats become integrated, libraries will acquire more and more material that involves contracts or leases. Negotiating the terms of these contracts may become an important duty of collection development officers. Multimedia development facilities for educators and marketing staffs will present new challenges for users and copyright holders.

Public Access

Public lending right legislation probably will be adopted sometime in the far distant future in the United States. If and when that happens, it probably will not have a government-supplied national fund but will be some form of user tax. For a while, American libraries debated who should pay for ILL and online search charges. In the end, the customer usually pays the costs. I see little likelihood that public lending rights will evolve differently.

Early efforts at cooperative acquisitions failed for many reasons. One reason was that a period of large book budgets occurred, and vendors offered approval or blanket order plans that allowed rapid collection growth. Collection growth, though, is not the same thing as collection development. As noted in chapter 16, the barriers to cooperative collection development are as strong as they were when the second edition of this book was written. Future prospects do not appear much better, because of the lure of technology solving all the local access requirements without the need to cooperate with other institutions.

Internationally, the concept of Universal Availability of Publications (UAP) will continue to be a global goal, and in time, librarians and government officials will take steps to assure some degree of implementation. Ultimately, the program will improve cooperation as countries improve distribution channels, have a better picture of demand, and thus produce the needed number of publications. Steps will be taken to properly preserve and conserve existing resources, and interlibrary lending will be recognized as a central function of adequate information access. A sense of hope for the future appears in the proposed requirements for a national UAP system.

A national system should ensure:

1. Provision of all national imprints.
2. Provision of additional material to meet at least 70 percent of national needs.
3. Supply to remote users within three weeks.
4. Retention of material to meet future needs.
5. Access to international resources.
6. Minimum cost for levels of efficiency set.
7. Simplicity and convenience in use.
8. Regular monitoring of performance.[6]

Though Western European and North American countries already come close to these standards, every country has some work to do to achieve all of them. The changing world economy in the late 1980s and early 1990s has slowed the movement toward UAP but has not diminished interest in the concept.

Whatever the future holds, one thing that is not likely to change is the intellectual challenge of creating the most appropriate resource collection for a community. Whether in a virtual or physical library, collection officers will continue to strive to have the right information at the right time for the right person. To do this they will need the abilities that collection officers have always needed; these are the skills to balance quality, quantity, and costs. Individuals with great curiosity about what is happening in the world, in-depth knowledge of information resources and their producers, and knowledge of the problems and issues in building a library collection in their community will find a rewarding and exciting career in collection management.

Notes

[1]C. P. Briscoe, et al., "Ashurbanipal's Enduring Archetype," *College & Research Libraries* 47 (March 1986): 123.

[2]H. Schiller, "Public Information Goes Corporate," *Library Journal* 116 (October 1, 1991): 43.

[3]Ibid.

[4]Ibid., 44.

[5]Ibid., 45.

[6]*U.A.P. Newsletter*, no. 7 (January 1986): 1.

Further Reading

Anigilaje, M. A. O. "Universal Availability of Publications and Copyright Laws." *Third World Libraries* 3 (Spring 1993): 63-64.

Butler, M., and H. Davis. "Strategic Planning As a Catalyst for Change in the 1990s." *College & Research Libraries* 53 (September 1992): 393-403.

Dole, W. "Acquisitions and Collection Development: 2001—The End User." *Library Acquisitions: Practice and Theory* 12, no. 2 (1988): 249-53.

Iwe, J. I. "Universal Availability of Publications in the Developing World." *Information Development* 7 (April 1991): 81-85.

Line, M., and S. Vickers. *Universal Availability of Publications.* Munich: K. G. Saur, 1983.

Otero-Bosivert, M. "Role of the Collection Development Librarian in the 90s and Beyond." *Journal of Library Administration* 18, nos. 3/4 (1993): 159-70.

Plassard, M. "Universal Availability of Publications: A Bibliography." *IFLA Journal* 16, no. 3 (1990): 357-62.

Rutstein, J. S. "Collection Development Confronts the 90s." *Colorado Libraries* 16 (March 1990): 5-22.

Stam, D. H. "Think Globally—Collection Development." *Collection Building* 5 (Spring 1983): 18-21.

Index

A Woman of Independent Means

331 - 3rd street Apt 2
Atlanta, GA 30308

① Fedex — 271440049
(800) 463-3339

② DHL — 965712073

Gail Vaz-Oxlade

A Woman of Independent Means

~

A WOMAN'S GUIDE TO FULL FINANCIAL SECURITY

REVISED EDITION

Stoddart

Published in 2001 by Stoddart Publishing Co. Limited
895 Don Mills Road, 400-2 Park Centre, Toronto, Canada M3C 1W3
180 Varick Street, 9th Floor, New York, New York 10014

Distributed by:
General Distribution Services Ltd.
325 Humber College Blvd., Toronto, Ontario M9W 7C3
Tel. (416) 213-1919   Fax (416) 213-1917
Email cservice@genpub.com

10 9 8 7 6 5 4 3 2 1

Canadian Cataloguing in Publication Data
Vaz-Oxlade, Gail E., 1959–
A woman of independent means: a woman's guide to full financial security

Rev. ed.
Includes bibliographical references and index.
ISBN 0-7737-6247-7

1. Women — Finance, Personal.
I. Title.

HG179.V393 2001   332.024'042   C2001-901362-0

Every reasonable effort has been made to contact the holders of copyright for
materials quoted in this book. The author and publisher will gladly receive
information that will enable them to rectify any inadvertent errors
or omissions in subsequent editions.

Cover Design: Angel Guerra
Text Design: Tannice Goddard

THE CANADA COUNCIL | LE CONSEIL DES ARTS
FOR THE ARTS | DU CANADA
SINCE 1957 | DEPUIS 1957

*We acknowledge for their financial support of our
publishing program the Canada Council, the Ontario Arts
Council, and the Government of Canada through the
Book Publishing Industry Development Program (BPIDP).*

Printed and bound in Canada

To my husband, Ken, who taught me that the pursuit of fortune is a fool's game, that love is the root of happiness, and that happy is the richest a woman can be.

I am the richest woman in the world. Thank you.

Contents

Thank You

The past five years have been very interesting. Why stop at five? The past ten years have been mind-blowing. The most significant events were certainly the births of my two children, but running a close second is the work I have been doing trying to help people come to terms with money and the role it plays in their lives. From the self-publication of my first book, *The RRSP Answer Book*, through my run at the magazine industry with *FinancialXPress*, through to the co-operative effort it took to get this book to the shelves, the entire experience has been fantastic. I have been especially energized by the willingness of individuals to give of their time and knowledge, of themselves in so many ways, in order to further the cause. There are a lot of people to thank.

To my dear friend Victoria Ryce, who listened when I had to work things out, read my drafts, and gave me balanced and invaluable comments. Thank you for always being on the other end of the phone and listening to my endless ideas. I value your advice and your friendship more than I can say.

To my husband, Ken, who listened as I worked through my battles with this book, encouraged me, and helped me sort the wheat from the chaff. Again, thank you for your soft honesty and enduring patience.

Thank you Gwin Gill. It was kind of you to let me into your busy day to listen to my plan and give advice. Your questions changed the direction of this book and made it the work I am so proud of now.

Thank you to Bruce Cohen, Ellen Roseman, and Tessa Wilmot for pointing me to some of the women who would become my friends in the writing of this book. Tessa, a special thanks to you for all the extra gabbing we've done.

Thank you to all the women who shared their stories with me — many of whom are not directly identified. You have been kind in letting me into your lives and sharing many difficult memories and experiences with me.

And to the women who shared their knowledge, advice, and experience with me, thank you. You were terrific. And smart too!

Finally, to Marnie Kramarich, thank you for your patience, wisdom, and stick-to-it-iveness in editing this book. Boy, are you tenacious!

Introduction

Our pursuit of money, or any enduring association with it, is capable of inducing not only bizarre, but ripely perverse, behaviour.

JOHN KENNETH GALBRAITH

The greatest crimes are caused by excess and not by necessity. Men do not become tyrants in order that they may not suffer cold.

ARISTOTLE

When I set out to write this book, one of my main objectives was to help women put money in perspective. It seems money has become far more important than it should be, and it makes us behave in unhealthy ways, whether that means single-mindedly pursuing wealth for its own sake, blindly spending beyond our means, or enduring sleepless nights over the possibility of a bounced cheque.

On September 3, 1997, *USA Today* published a bar graph that described what people worry about in terms of their money. When divided by gender, the results were very telling. An overwhelming 70% of women feared not having enough money when they were old. They wanted safer or insured investment products (73% women, 56% male), they were unnerved by stock fluctuations (50% women, 33% male), and they tended to avoid making decisions for fear of making a mistake (33% women, 22% male). This bears out other research that shows women are more risk-averse and afraid of being poor in old age. And so we should be.

When Statistics Canada released its report "Growing Old in Canada," an alarming 40% of women over the age of 75 who were living on their own had incomes below the poverty line. And since a woman 75 or older has a greater chance of being disabled than her male counterpart, this can paint a grey picture of the future. But we have the ability to brighten that picture, by taking charge of our present financial situation and making plans for the future. We just have to understand how money works to do it.

Unfortunately, many people have an irrational fear of what is a very basic economic tool. If we can forget, just for a moment, the more complex issues — investing, retirement planning, writing a business plan — and look to the simple tasks, we can see the extremes to which some people will go to avoid taking care of their finances. They would rather buy overdraft protection, one of the most expensive forms of credit, or keep a float of money in their accounts earning next to no return, than reconcile their cheque books. They don't save. Using credit cards, they spend their yet-to-be-earned income without much thought to future implications. They don't have enough or the right kind of insurance. They don't have wills. They just don't want to think about it.

The Wealthy Barber sold millions of copies by delivering a simple set of messages in a simple way. David Chilton successfully opened people's eyes to the most basic steps of money management, including the importance of saving and accepting personal responsibility for retirement planning, home ownership, and risk management. In *Balancing Act*, Joanne Thomas Yaccato delivered the message that anyone can do it. Using her own experiences in coming to terms with the role money plays in her life — and with the mistakes she had made — Joanne went a long way toward demystifying money and showing how it can be controlled.

But despite the best efforts of many financial writers to put money in perspective, the language of money remains extreme. We talk about "worshipping money" and about being "money crazy." We consider money to be dirty: "filthy" rich, "stinking" rich, "money laundering," "dirt cheap." We worry about being "ripped off" or "taken to the cleaners." We are loath to the idea of talking to our children about money, fearing we will imbue them with an immoral love (or is it lust?) for money.

Most financial discussions fail to help people understand how they feel about money. While they may demonstrate how to budget, stress the importance of saving, and describe the various investments available, they seem incapable of motivating people to put these simple ideas into practice. What little that has been written on the psychology of money often doesn't integrate the practical information.

This book has been designed to deal with both the psychological and the practical. And rather than providing all the information in one voice, which is also traditional for books on personal finance, this book will offer the perspective of a dozen women who have expertise in money management. Each of these women has been carefully selected not only for her expertise and knowledge, but for her integrity.

This book will not solve your financial problems. I know that is the implicit promise of most books on money, but that promise is unrealistic. Just as money — or more money — is not the solution to most people's needs for love, security, power, freedom, status, or comfort, so this book cannot miraculously take you from where you are now to where you want to be. Only you can do that.

What this book will do, if you are a willing participant in the process, is help you uncover your personal feelings and attitudes toward money. It will provide you with information and proven techniques for positive money management. It will be a guide to what you must think about to stay on an even keel and keep money in perspective. It will ask you many questions that prompt you to find out for yourself how to achieve financial health. By answering these questions, you will find that money management is easy. You will learn new ways of dealing with money. And you will achieve the results you want.

LIFE-CYCLE FINANCIAL PLANNING

In addition to helping you understand *who* you are when it comes to money, this book emphasizes the importance of *where* you are on the road of your life. Life-cycle issues have been used for years to help manufacturers and retailers decide how to target their customers. If you're a single woman without children, you probably read a different magazine, eat different food, and wear different clothes than a woman who is mired in rug-rats. When I was single, I ate out more often, I wore high-heeled shoes, and I hardly ever thought about spot removers for my carpet, my couch, or my clothes.

Just as where we are in our life cycle influences the commodities we buy, so too does it affect which financial products we should own. As I've moved through my life cycle, I've gone from shopping for GICs to shopping for mutual funds. I've had to think about divorce, stepchildren, and financial commitments to ex-spouses. And I've been forced to face my own mortality and make a will.

Perhaps the single change in my life that has most affected me is the birth of my children. I had no idea that it would be such an all-consuming, over-the-top, fantabulous experience. I've found in talking with women that I'm not the only one completely blown away by motherhood. In fact, one of the questions I'm most often asked is, "How can I stay home with my baby and still help make ends meet?" This is just one example of how a change in life cycle can throw a spanner in the works of the best-laid plans.

It is also one of those issues that's so new that women haven't had any long-term practice dealing with it. Our liberation has given us many new opportunities, and with those opportunities has come the need to make choices. I often suggest to new preggies, for example, that they try living on one income while they are pregnant to see how the family copes, should the sweet smell of baby addle their brains and leave them longing to remain prisoners of their love. It would be a dry run at living on one income, just in case one income is all there will be in the future. And it's a great way to actively pay down debt and build up reserves for emergencies, even if they do decide to return to work after the baby is born.

The life-cycle issue has become increasingly complicated as our norms have changed. In her book *New Passages*, Gail Sheehy says that until recently, "Chronological age has served as a uniform criterion for normalizing the roles and responsibilities that individuals assume over a lifetime . . . age norms have shifted and are no longer normative." In today's fast-moving, ever-changing, nothing's-the-same-as-it-was world, age has little to do with stage, and it's less clear where we should be when. While only one in 10 people lived to age 65 for most of human history, eight in 10 people in North America today will see their sixty-fifth birthday. No longer are 40-somethings delivering their 60-something parents into the care of old-age homes; now it is the 70-something delivering her

90-something mother. And the old demarcations we've grown used to — adulthood at 21, retirement at 65 — have no place in our current reality.

The traditional life sequence — school, job, marriage, child-rearing, empty-nesting, widowhood — has become jumbled. Many women complete their degrees well after the traditional school age. Many delay having children until their careers are well established. And divorce has changed the family structure so that many women now must raise children on their own, or help to raise stepchildren when they may never have expected to be parents at all. Just thinking about the various forms a family can take is enough to boggle the mind. And with these new social structures come new financial considerations.

Since there is no such thing as a normal life cycle anymore, does that mean we have to throw out the concept of life-cycle planning? I don't believe it does. After all, whether you are 20 or 40 and having your first child, the issue of educational savings becomes important. And whether you are widowed at 55 or divorced at 30, you'd better have your own credit history established if you want to be able to function within the financial world.

Think about financial planning as a trip through the supermarket. First there are the essentials you must have to keep body and soul together. What you put in your basket will be a direct reflection of your needs and the needs of those around you. If you are single, your essentials may be few and your fridge quite empty. If you're married with children, you'll need a larger larder. Once you're stocked with the core stuff, then you have to look at changes in the normal weekly routine that will affect what you're buying. If you're planning to have the folks over for turkey dinner, you'll be adding cranberry jelly and stuffing to your basket. If you're throwing a birthday party, oooh, now we're getting to the good stuff: ice cream and cake.

Then there's the shopping you do just in case . . . just in case friends drop in and you need pâté and crackers for a light nosh, or just in case you get a cold and need a steaming bowl of chicken soup.

The financial life cycle is similar. First there's the core stuff, the basics of your financial larder. Just about everyone needs a chequing account and a banking card. Everyone needs to establish a credit history. And everyone should begin investing as soon as they have an extra $25. (Yes, that's all it takes to get started, and the longer you wait the harder it is to convince yourself you can live without spending that 25 bucks.)

As you move through your life cycle, you'll need to add or delete from your financial basket. Early on, you'll be adding. As soon as you have some assets, you'll need a will. As soon as you have dependents, you'll need insurance. And as you increase your income, you'll need to buy more and different types of investments to meet your long-term goals. Later, you'll be deleting. Once you've established a good asset base and most of your dependents have gone their own ways, you can get rid of most, if not all, of your life insurance. As you move closer to retirement, you will consolidate your retirement savings for convenience and ease of conversion. You may even shift some of your assets to your children's hands, or to a trust, to reduce your estate and the taxes payable on death.

Finally, there are the financial precautions you take just in case . . . just in case you lose your job; just in case you become disabled; just in case you suddenly find yourself the primary breadwinner in your family.

WHY A BOOK ABOUT WOMEN AND MONEY?

This is the question I heard most when people asked me what my next book would be about. After all, money can't tell the difference between X and Y chromosomes. That's true, but apparently society, our work environment, our legal system — just about every social construct you can imagine — has yet to catch up. If you don't believe me, ask yourself these questions:

- Why do women still make less than men for work of equal value? Yes, the gap has closed, but why are we still not equal?
- Why are elderly women and women with children the poorest members of our society?
- Why is it that when a couple divorces, a woman's income goes down and a man's goes up?
- Why did a vice-president at a mutual-fund company once tell me that "women are not our market"?

This book isn't just about money. If it were, then the advice would be gender neutral. This book is about women taking control of a part of life that until now they may have wished away or ignored.

Most financial planning books assume a person will continue to earn an income, without snags, for the majority of her life. They seem to abandon women who must deal with significant changes like motherhood, divorce, widowhood, disability, and the like. Yet, it is at these very moments that we need guidance, support, and information. It is then, when our life plan changes, that we must make adjustments to our financial plan so we remain proactive in managing this thing called money.

That's why we need a book for women specifically. And that's why I wrote this book. I hope that you will be able to take from it the information you need as you move through your life, adjusting your plan for significant changes, tweaking it for small ones. You can look to Part I for a general exploration of what money means to you; to Part II for the solid goods on all the basic aspects of financial planning and management; to Part III for the details on how to adapt financially to the events that most of us encounter in life, such as parenthood, partnering, and retirement; and to Part IV to learn how to handle those just-in-case scenarios that tend to send our finances on a detour.

The other reason I wrote this book is that I sometimes despair at women's unwillingness to be authors of their own fate. More often than not, the reason given for not taking control of the money is, "I just can't." Yes, you can. If you choose not to take control, that's your choice. If you choose to write your own script and direct your own future, read on.

SOME DEFINITIONS

When I use the term "marriage," I mean it in the broadest sense: your desire to have a continuing relationship, regardless of your specific family structure. When I use the terms "spouse" and "partner," again, it's in the broadest sense. This is the person with whom you have, and want to continue to have, a relationship. Recognizing that families have changed — having lived in just about all kinds, I'm a first-hand witness — my definition of a family is *everyone* you love who loves you back (even if they also hate you periodically), and with whom you have to relate for the common good of all.

I

WOMAN, KNOW THYSELF

Money is both real and not real, like a spook.
We invented money and we use it, yet we
cannot either understand its laws or control
its actions. It has a life of its own which it
properly should not have.

LIONEL TRILLING

One of the very first questions I was asked when I set out to write this book significantly changed my approach and focus. The question was, "Why do some women do absolutely nothing to take care of their finances, despite the fact that they know better?" For several weeks I rolled the idea around in my head. Why are some women good at planning for the future, while others are not? Why do some people save, while others spend every cent they make, and then some? Why is it easier for some to defer gratification, while others must immediately have it . . . whatever "it" is?

Most financial planning books tell you what you need to know to achieve the results you want. And if you look at the financial planning section in most bookstores, you'll be amazed at the way the shelves sag with advice. But what good is it to know what you should do if you don't do it? We say we want to be secure, but we do little to take care of the what-ifs. We think we'd like to own a home of our own, but we never save a cent for the downpayment. We say we know it's silly to pay loads of interest on a credit card, but we continue to carry a balance.

The next few chapters are about sorting out these contradictions. While subsequent parts of this book will explore the practical details of personal finance — details you may be anxious to get to so you can fix what's wrong with your current financial picture — I recommend that you spend some time thinking through the issues we're about to explore. It is an exercise that may have a profound and lasting impact on the way you look at money.

1

The Importance of Money

Money means in a thousand minds a thousand subtly different, roughly similar, systems of images, associations, suggestions, and impulses.

H. G. WELLS

Everyone's seeking financial freedom. But ask 50 people what constitutes financial freedom and you can expect 50 different definitions. Often it's associated with having enough money to never worry again. But that raises the question, "How much is enough?" The fact is, financial freedom has absolutely nothing to do with how much money you have. Read that last sentence again. Financial freedom comes when you have control — when money anxieties and fears no longer creep into your thoughts as you lie in bed late at night. We can all have financial freedom, regardless of how much we make, if we put money in its proper perspective.

Unfortunately, some people fail to recognize that they are worth more than the car they drive, the home they live in, or the clothes they wear. They use money to create the image they want others to see. Then they spend all their energy maintaining the image. Perhaps they want to be seen as generous, and spend lavishly on children, lovers, and friends. Perhaps it's the desire to be seen as successful that drives them to spend more than they make. Some even work to cultivate a negative image without realizing it. Rather than accepting responsibility for their lives and their money, they continue to play the role of victim, battered by their circumstances.

In researching this book, I heard and read many stories about the influence of childhood experiences on our money values. One of the saddest was the story Suze Orman told in her book, *The 9 Steps to Financial Freedom*.[1] She tells of arriving at her dad's restaurant with her mother just in time to watch flames engulf the building. Her father had escaped unscathed when, realizing that all his money was in the metal cash register inside the building, he ran back in to retrieve it. "He literally picked up the scalding metal box and carried it outside. When he threw the register on the ground, the skin on his arms and chest came with it." Orman relates the experience to the early money values she developed: "That was when I learned that money is obviously more important than life itself. From that point on, earning money, lots of money, not only became what drove me professionally, but also became my emotional priority."

Financial freedom doesn't begin with making more money. It doesn't start in a financial planner's office. And it doesn't begin with investing to earn a return of 32%. *Financial freedom begins in your head*. It begins with understanding what money is, what it means to you, and how you developed the feelings you have about money.

WHAT IS MONEY ANYWAY?

"Papa! what's money?"

The abrupt question had such immediate reference to the subject of Mr Dombey's thoughts, that Mr Dombey was quite disconcerted.

"What is money, Paul?" he answered. "Money?"

"Yes," said the child, laying his hands upon the elbows of his little chair, and turning the old face up towards Mr Dombey's; "what is money?"

Mr Dombey was in a difficulty. He would have liked to give him some explanation involving the terms circulating-medium, currency, depreciation of currency, paper, bullion, rates of exchange, value of precious metals in the market, and so forth; but looking down at the little chair, and

---

1   Suze Orman, *The 9 Steps to Financial Freedom* (Random House Inc., 1997), p. 3.

seeing what a long way down it was, he answered: "Gold, and silver, and
copper. Guineas, shillings, half-pence. You know what they are?"
"Oh yes, I know what they are," said Paul. "I don't mean that, Papa.
I mean what's money after all?"

CHARLES DICKENS, *DOMBEY AND SON*

Apparently it is easier to use money than it is to define it. Money has
as many meanings as there are people and their personal perceptions. As
British economist Sir Ralph Hawtrey once said, "Money is one of those
concepts which, like a teaspoon or an umbrella, but unlike an earthquake
or buttercup, are definable primarily by the use or purpose they serve."
Marshall McLuhan said, "Money is a language for translating the work of
the farmer into the work of the barber, doctor, engineer, or plumber . . .
Money is the store of other people's time and effort." Aristotle said,
"Money has been introduced by convention as a kind of substitute for
need or demand . . . its value is derived, not from nature, but from law,
and can be altered or abolished at will."

Trying to define money is as difficult as trying to define love. Yes, it
is the paper and coin of which it is made, and it represents value. But
currency itself has no intrinsic value. You can't eat it, wear it, or hold it
close late at night. And there are parts of the world where you can't even
use it to buy what you need.

At its most basic level, money is a means of completing financial transactions. It is a measure of value that can be traded for goods or services.
Most financial planning books try to deal with this aspect of money: how to
get it, how to use it, how to keep it. And most promote the belief that more
is better. Seldom do they ask you to quantify the cost of attaining more.

Thanks to the natural resources of the country, every American, until quite
recently, could reasonably look forward to making more money than his
father, so that, if he made less, the fault must be his; he was either lazy or
inefficient. What an American values, therefore, is not the possession of
money as such, but his power to make it as proof of his manhood.

W. H. AUDEN

But the emotional and psychological costs of making money are as
important as the pedestrian what-to-dos. Money causes confusion. It has

a special meaning to each of us based on our childhood experiences. We all have our own money myths — it may represent security, power, acceptance, love, evil — which we then wear like hair shirts.

As a culture, we recognize that money is the basis of our economy and our means for survival and growth. We read about the monster "inflation" and worry about outliving our money. We watch as our cost of living increases and immediately feel poorer. We worry about whether we are in a depression or a recession. We personalize those economic indicators without really understanding them.

Let's take the Consumer Price Index (CPI) as a case in point. No matter how often it is referred to as a measure of your cost of living, it isn't, and here's why. It is calculated based on a sample of prices of goods and services that people tend to buy regularly; however, it doesn't account for the fact that you do not buy a new car every month or every year, or the fact that today's car is much more energy-efficient than previous years' cars. It also doesn't account for changing buying habits after the base period it uses as a comparator. After all, the price of everyday items such as orange juice, coffee, and gas fluctuate based on a variety of factors, but the CPI does not. As Andrew Hacker puts it:

> If wages seemed to go further in 1970, one reason is that shopping lists were simpler. Those were the days of Keds and typewriters and turntables. Today, the Index includes Nikes, laser printers, and multiple-CD changers that cost more because they do more. Even bread has been upgraded: croissants and exotic grains have replaced blander white loaves; Starbucks costs more than Maxwell House. Since cars have so much high-tech gear, a new one costs about half a young couple's income, visibly up from 38 percent in 1970.[2]

That's not to say that economic indicators are invalid and should be ignored. We need to understand them so we can put them in context. What we should not do is panic about economic statistics that have little bearing on our day-to-day lives. Yes, inflation, the CPI, and our gross national product all affect our money and its worth, but it's more important to ask how they affect you personally. If they don't, chill out.

---

2   Andrew Hacker, *Money: Who Has How Much and Why* (Scribner, 1997), p. 61.

Stop worrying. Relax. If they will have an impact on you, stop worrying and do something about it. It's all in your hands. You have the control, and with this book, you'll have the know-how.

Human beings are motivated by strong social drives. Just ask any teenager to name the most important thing in her life, and she'll say it's her friends. Ask her what the second most important thing is, and she'll say it's money. Why money? Because it lets her be with her friends.

As long as we recognize that money is a tool — a means of acquiring the things we need — we've got money in perspective. The problem comes when we see it as the source of all the other things in our lives, such as love, happiness, control, or security.

BEYOND SKILL

If managing money were only a skill, we could learn it and be done with it. But there's more to it than that. After all, some of the most skillful money managers in business are pathetic when it comes to managing their personal finances. Years ago I worked with a woman who was a credit-card maniac. As the office manager, she was wonderful at keeping the books, keeping the spending in check, keeping the bank at bay. At home, her personal finances were a disaster. I remember sitting at her kitchen table watching her play what she called "credit-card roulette." This was a monthly game where she decided who would get their minimum monthly payment. Every card she had — there were more than 40 cards in her wallet — was run up to the limit. Her decisions about who to pay were based on which card she would need to use during the upcoming month.

This was a dreadful place to be. She ached physically from the stress. She couldn't see any way to clear her debts so she resolved to live month to month until the whole thing just caved in. She had new living room furniture, a new stereo, and heaps of other stuff. She also had headaches, backaches, and a short temper.

The cards were taken away, one by one, sometimes at the bank, where the teller would simply keep the card with little explanation. She really didn't need an explanation. Sometimes her plastic was repossessed in stores where she was mortified to find the store clerk instructed by the card company to cut up the card right in front of her. I was with her on one such occasion and she was a wreck. Whenever she was sent a new card — credit-card companies are notorious for lending to people they shouldn't — she would sign the back and proceed to spend herself out of her blues.

Eventually she took control of the situation and started using the skills she had all along. She dumped the cards, got a consolidation loan, and paid off her debts. It took years, but she got better.

This story may seem extreme or all too familiar. It illustrates the point that women often feel incompetent and inadequate in managing their money, often in sharp contrast to their competence in other areas. And some women feel guilty and ashamed around money, or resentful of their inability to get more and keep it.

How Do *You* Feel About Money?

Your attitudes toward money speak volumes about how you have dealt with this part of your life so far. For all the savers I have met, there have been as many spenders. For all those who have worried about money, there are those who avoid dealing with it completely. For all the risk-takers, there are those who are terrified of losing. For as many people who believe that money is the key to happiness, there are just as many who think it leads to misery and corruption.

I have met a lot of these people as I have travelled the country promoting *The Money Tree Myth: A Parents' Guide to Helping Kids Unravel the Mysteries of Money.* One of the most oft-asked questions is, "But what about the morality of money?" Does a car have morality, or is it the person behind the wheel who decides not to drive drunk? Can any inanimate object have a morality or is it the onus we put on that object that gives it such human characteristics? We have to separate the emotional from the practical when we set about teaching our kids about money. If we send our children messages that imply that money has power beyond its role as a means of exchange, we do them a disservice.

Regardless of the impressions you have grown up with, *money does not have a morality.* Money is paper and coin, nothing more.

The best way to develop a healthy attitude toward money is to understand why you have the attitudes you do and then find ways to build on your strengths and minimize your weaknesses. That usually involves taking an inventory and thinking some deep thoughts.

Identify the following statements as true or false based on your first reaction to them:

True False) I have a good relationship with money.

True False   If I had more money, I wouldn't have to think about it as much.

True False) When I feel low I buy myself something nice. Even if I have to charge it, I feel much better.

True False Whoever has the most money has the most power.

True False   It's irresponsible to spend money frivolously. Saving is the key to security.

True False   I'd rather go shopping than save money.

True False) My retirement is taken care of, so I don't have to worry about it.

True False / I'd bet $20 for a 1-in-100,000 chance to win $1 million.

Okay, done? Good. Now answer the questions in *italics*:

True False) I have a good relationship with money. *Can you have a relationship with an inanimate object?*

True False   If I had more money, I wouldn't have to think about it as much. *How much money is enough to eliminate your concerns?* 21,000,000

True False   When I feel low I buy myself something nice. Even if I have to charge it, I feel much better. *How do you feel when the bill comes in?* I don't wanna pay it.

True False   Whoever has the most money has the most power. *In what areas of your life do you feel powerful?* none

True False   It's irresponsible to spend frivolously. Saving is the key to security. *Saving is more important than . . . (what?) What are your priorities for* spending?

True False   I'd rather go shopping than save money. *Do you have a financial safety net? If not, how will you deal with an emergency?* The

True False   My retirement is taken care of, so I don't have to worry about it. *If your external supports (marriage, job, government support) changed, would you still be all right in retirement? What are you doing to take care of yourself?*

True False   I'd bet $20 for a 1-in-100,000 chance to win $1 million. *What if the odds were 1 in 1,000,000? What if the odds were 1 in 10? Is it your chance of winning or the cost of participating that influences your decision?*

It is by challenging your own attitudes in this way that you can take control of how you feel about and deal with money.

Where Did Your Attitudes Come From?

Who we are with money is a direct result of what we learned as children. Answer the following questions to see what pictures emerge for you. It might be helpful to jot down some notes as you think about these questions:

- What are your impressions of how your mother dealt with money? How did she feel about her work inside and/or outside the home? What did she explicitly teach you about money? How did you feel about those money lessons?
- What are your impressions of how your father dealt with money? How did he feel about his work inside and/or outside the home? What did he explicitly teach you about money? How did you feel about those money lessons?
- How did your parents relate to each other when it came to financial matters? What did they feel about each other's money habits? Did they fight about money?
- If you have siblings, did your parents treat you all similarly when it came to money? If not, what were the differences? How do your siblings deal with money now?
- Did anyone else — a teacher, religious leader, grandparent, or other relative — influence the way you think about money today? What messages did you get from them?
- Did your friends have things you didn't? Did you get more or less allowance than your peers? Did you live in a nicer home? Did they

have nicer clothes? What was cool to have back then, and did you have it?

- Did you have to be good to receive special treats? Did you receive money as gifts?
- Did you feel ashamed of having more or less than your friends?
- Did you steal from the corner store, your mother's purse, your father's pocket, your sister's piggy-bank?
- Was your family rich or poor? Why do you feel you were either rich or poor?

Most children feel powerless. Someone else decides when they will eat, sleep, and play. Someone else decides what they will wear and what they will watch on TV. All too often, people carry that sense of powerlessness into their adulthood, even though they manage to take on jobs, raise families, and meet their commitments. The lessons they learned about money run like tapes in their heads, controlling their financial behaviour. Or worse, there were no childhood money lessons, and they feel helpless and scared to death of making a mistake. Money means many things to many people. What does it mean to you?

Money Means Power

They who are of the opinion that Money will do every thing, may very well be suspected to do every thing for Money.

GEORGE SAVILE

"I don't care, as long as you're under my roof, we'll do things my way." That's one of the most familiar power plays. It means, "Since I have the money, I make the rules." But there are other things parents do that send the power message just as clearly. Allowances or support cheques that are promised but rarely delivered without a reminder; constant financial bail-outs with verbal reminders of how lucky you are to have been saved; regular lectures on the respect, duty, or gratitude you owe for having been cared for.

Of course, as with any myth, there's always a grain of truth that allows the myth to survive. The fact is that money does represent power for many people. After all, who among us has a boss who makes less than we do? Most supervisory power comes from the fact that the boss can take your money away. Within families, the spouse who makes the money often feels the right to choose how that money is handled.

Having more money also often leads to more choices: a better education, the opportunity to start and support a new business, the freedom to pursue creative outlets. Money can buy you better health care, a better table in a restaurant, and more acquaintances.

Money Means Love

Love buyers love to play Santa Claus. Money and gifts are to them the means of making others happy and thus winning their friendship and affection . . .

In the final analysis, love buyers get what they pay for — a substitute.

HERB GOLDBERG AND ROBERT T. LEWIS

Turn on your television and you'll be faced with myriad commercials trying to convince you that by spending your money to buy long-distance gift certificates, a new car, or the latest brand of toothpaste, you'll be better loved. If you go shopping when you're lonely or unhappy, if you buy things for others that you can ill afford, or if you shop regardless of your ability to pay for those items, the likelihood is you've got the money-equals-love virus. Women who shower their mates with expensive presents are often using money as a symbol of love. People who lend money to friends may be giving to secure their friendships. Listen to the words of anger often spoken when a love or friendship is betrayed — "you owe me," "I gave you everything," "you stole the best years of my life" — and you'll recognize the language of money.

If you don't believe that people equate love with money, just look at what happens when love disappears from a relationship — especially when divorce isn't a joint decision — and all that's left is to work out the financial dissolution. The communication can get downright ugly. And look at the way we relate to our children: "If you're good, I'll buy you a toy." Will those children then form the habit of rewarding themselves with material things when they feel down or stressed out? Or will they choose to reject money because they see it as a means of control?

Money Means Security

If a person's attitude toward money is essentially a defense against poverty, then this person may never truly experience wealth. The experience of wealth is, after all, a subjective thing.

THOMAS MOORE

For many people, money represents security. These people place great emphasis on preparing for the future and their money management style is cautious and well planned. However, when faced with a threat to that security, these people can panic, or become depressed or angry. While they seldom spend capriciously, they also seldom enjoy what they have. They are constantly squirrelling away a little more, denying today's wants in favour of tomorrow's needs. For them, money offers no pleasure, other than in its acquisition. Each dollar spent represents a dollar they will not have in the future. Women often make this link, partly because of their socialization. Since women have traditionally been dependent on men — fathers, husbands, male bosses — for their security, they have learned to prize that security greatly. They anticipate desertion and disaster and try to prepare for it. On the flip side, of course, are the women who still believe these "heroes" will provide them with security for the rest of their lives. By being good little daughters, wives, and employees, they hope to keep the income streams to which they have become accustomed. Witness the number of women who remain in abusive relationships (marital, familial, or work-related) because they believe they have no other way to support themselves.

Take the case of Yvonne, who quit her job after 20 years. She wasn't independently wealthy. She wasn't anywhere near retirement age. She was just fed up. Having worked at a hospital where constant financial cutbacks had resulted in a significant change in the emotional atmosphere, she was worn out and angry. She watched as people with whom she had worked for decades were laid off. She felt they had been shafted, shuffled off, and sideswiped by "the new economic reality." The expectations for those who remained were enormous: more hours, less room for promotion; more productivity, less socializing; more input, less corporate loyalty. Even after she left she continued to hear from old friends about the horrors of the new work environment. Women who were dependent on their jobs to support themselves and their children were being bullied into doing more, staying later, working harder. The general response to the unfairness of it all was that, if you didn't like it, there were plenty of people who would be happy with the job.

This kind of emotional abuse is pervasive in today's corporate culture and it's a shame. Ultimately, money becomes the means by which we can escape. If we just had more money, we could tell the boss just what to do with the job. Once again, money becomes the answer.

Money Means Happiness

Money is human happiness in the abstract; and so the man who is no longer capable of enjoying such happiness in the concrete, sets his whole heart on money.

ARTHUR SCHOPENHAUER

When we equate money with happiness we put too much stock in what money can do for us. When what you want (more money) is different from what you need (a sense of safety, a pat on the back, a sense of personal accomplishment), you will never feel satisfied. It's like trying to eat carrot sticks when all you really want is a big bowl of ice cream. No matter how much of the good orange stuff you eat, you can't fill the hole and the hunger drives you to seek another substitute; in the end, you'll have your spoon in the ice-cream container — exactly where you wanted to be all along.

If happiness is elusive, money isn't the answer. Perhaps you should look at what your spirit is seeking. In *Happy People*, Jonathan Freedman reports that material wealth has little bearing on a person's sense of happiness.[3] We are fooling ourselves when we use money to try to replace the things we feel are missing from our lives, such as family, meaningful work, a sense of community, and creative play. In *The Poverty of Affluence*, Paul Wachtel says:

Our economic system and our relation with nature have gone haywire because we have lost track of what we really need. Increasing numbers of middle-class Americans are feeling pressed and deprived not because of their economic situation per se — we

---

3   Jonathan Freedman, *Happy People* (Harcourt Brace Jovanovich, 1978), p. 136.

remain an extraordinarily affluent society — but because we have placed an impossible burden on the economic dimension of our lives.[4]

HOW IMPORTANT IS YOUR STUFF?

For over six months I lived without furniture in my living room. I swore I'd never spend another cent to put furniture in until our children, Alex and Malcolm, were of an age when the couches wouldn't be at constant risk. Then, of course, I envisioned the animal tracks the dog and two cats would make when they decided to get comfortable in the cushions, on the cushions, and behind the cushions. I was quite happy offering family and friends the floor, although Ken, my husband, was distressed. But he was brave. He understood my reluctance to spend money we didn't really have since I was on maternity leave and the cash wasn't exactly overflowing.

After six months and a short consulting project I changed my mind. With some money in the bank, the room seemed a little emptier. When I had no money, it had been easy to justify not spending any. Now that we were flush again, it was harder to see Ken try to deal with my frugality. So I acquiesced and we bought two love seats just in time for Malcolm's first birthday party. Imagine the surprised looks on the family's faces when they saw a place to sit! Ken was pleased. I was happy.

This story has three morals (a lot for such a short story, don't you think?). The first is, I've reached the stage in my life when acquiring stuff just doesn't do it for me anymore. There was a time when I would have had to have those couches immediately. That time has passed as my life has filled with other things that have more meaning. The second moral is, spending money you don't have is dumb. You can always go a few weeks, months, even years, putting a little aside each week, until you have the money. The third moral is that we don't live in isolation and we have to consider the other people we affect with our decisions.

How important are things to you? Do you often spend money you don't have acquiring things you feel you must have? Perhaps it's a new

---

4   Paul Wachtel, *The Poverty of Affluence* (New Society Publishers, 1989), p. 2.

suit, or a new pair of shoes. Perhaps it's a new car. Maybe it's new living room furniture. Why do you have to have it? What will happen if you don't acquire it immediately?

I remember when we moved my son Malcolm from his crib into a big bed. We didn't have anywhere to store his toys, and I wanted to buy the shelves I'd chosen. But money was tight that month. I pondered the idea of charging the shelves on my card — I wanted my son's room to be beautiful — feeling sure I would have the money the following month when the bill came in. Ken, whom I'd always considered much more of a spender, was the voice of reason. "His room looks fine," he said. "Let's wait." Since by nature I'm a debt-avoider, it didn't take a lot to convince me. But for a few moments there, my desire to give my son what I thought he should have was way ahead of my good sense. It happens to the best of us.

Research shows that our possessions say a lot about how we feel about ourselves.[5] They help us define who we are and make statements about how we wish to be perceived by others. Most of us are quite skilled at reading the meaning of objects. We make judgments about people based on what they are wearing, what kind of car they drive, and where they live.

People who lose their possessions — those who are forced to flee their country of birth, or who face physical disasters such as earthquakes and fires — often feel they have lost something of themselves. To see how important your stuff is to you, take some time to think about the following question: If a fire threatened to destroy all your personal possessions, and you could save only three things, what would they be, and why?

I'm not sure why, but I've asked myself this question many times over the years and it's interesting how my answers have changed. Now, I'd have to save Beri-Bear, my daughter's favourite plush toy. I'd want my memories boxes that have mementos from my husband and many photos from my life. What else? I'm not sure. At one time I would have included my hippo collection (I've been collecting hippos for years). At another, it was my poetry book, which recorded all the angst I'd felt through my youth. The pillow I've had since childhood always made the list. Not anymore.

---

5 Peter Lunt and Sonia Livingstone, *Mass Consumption and Personal Identity* (Open University Press, 1992), p. 59–85.

As life has changed, so have my priorities.

The close connection between who we are and what we own carries over to money. Since money is our means for acquiring what we then use to define ourselves, the money itself becomes a part of our definition of self. Here are some more questions to ponder:

- How important is your stuff to you?
- If you could have another person's stuff, whose would you choose?
- How many things do you currently have on your "I wish I could have" list?
- How much money would you need to acquire the things to make your life perfect?
- How much of what you have would you sell to help someone else buy food or shelter?

WHERE TO GO FROM HERE

So, what have you learned so far? Do you have more of a sense of why you feel as you do about money? Do you have the skills, but not the emotional competence? If you don't have the skills, the rest of this book will help you. If you don't have the emotional competence, you're going to have to do some soul searching to come to peace with how you feel about money. You may want to see a psychologist who deals with money issues. You may want to talk more about it with friends and family. The very fact that you are reading this book means you want something to change. But you're the only person who can make that change.

Next we'll look more closely at how being a woman can and should affect how you deal with your money. Guess what? We have special obstacles to overcome. But guess what else? We are uniquely equipped to overcome them.

2

Women and Money

*Moreover, it is equally useless to ask what might have happened if
Mrs. Seton and her mother and her mother before her had amassed great
wealth and laid it under the foundations of college and library, because, in
the first place, to earn money was impossible for them, and in the second,
had it been possible, the law denied them the right to possess what money
they earned. It is only for the last forty-eight years that Mrs. Seton has had
a penny of her own. For all the centuries before that, it would have been
her husband's property — a thought which perhaps may have its share in
keeping Mrs. Seton and her mother off the Stock Exchange.*
         VIRGINIA WOOLF, *A ROOM OF ONE'S OWN*

Women and men relate to money differently. We have different fears,
different concerns, and different perspectives. Is this news to you?
It probably isn't. But do you know why?

**Women are comfortable expressing their feelings
and their vulnerability.**
That's because women are traditionally raised in an atmosphere of accom-
modation and co-operation. While men have been socialized to hunt,
women were the gatherers. We are much more open to communication,
to sharing ideas, to asking questions. We are less afraid of appearing

foolish. We would rather ask the question and get an answer than sit quietly in ignorance forever. It may take a while to work up the gumption to interrupt, ask, inquire, find out, but women want knowledge and they'll take it from any number of sources. This all bodes well for women increasing their financial know-how.

Many women still believe that dealing with finances is a man's job. Even as I write this I can hardly believe it myself. Just how far have we come, baby? Time and again I speak with women who have completely relinquished financial control to their husbands, fathers, or sons. I continue to be astounded. You might think that this is a characteristic of older women — women who haven't been educated in the finer points of feminism. You'd be dead wrong.

Who's in a better position to have a handle on personal finances than an accountant or a financial planner? Yet, I have a story for you that clearly demonstrates that "knowing" and "doing" are two distinctly different things. My girlfriend Marla, a financial adviser, had been married for several years when she and her accountant husband separated. At that point Marla decided to take a long, hard look at the money situation. She was surprised to discover that despite the fact that both she and her husband had been saving and investing aggressively, their portfolio had not done much in the past few years. Marla had left all the investing up to her husband, who, as it turned out, had chosen financial products that performed badly. Marla ended up paying for her husband's mistakes. Now, you might ask, what would motivate a well-educated, professional money manager to leave the decision making to someone else? The answer is all too familiar to many women. First, if money creates a conflict, and you want to avoid conflict, you choose the route of least resistance and let him do it all. If you have different investment strategies, and you've been convinced that doing it your way will take too long, you let him have his way. If you trust him implicitly, you let him make the decisions and live with the consequences, good or bad. No one is always right, after all. If you don't have the time, don't have the energy, don't have the desire to do it for yourself, it's easy to give the responsibility to someone else.

If money is so important in terms of keeping a roof over our heads and food in our children's tummies, then why are so many of us still willing to let our partners do the "dirty work"? And how are we going to cope when he goes away?

The incidence of divorce has increased dramatically since the late 1960s, mostly because legislation has made it easier to get divorced. The first time I divorced, I had to wait for three years to pass before I could file. The second time, a one-year separation was all it took.

Out of a population of approximately 30 million, just over 1.4 million Canadians are divorced, with the numbers skewing higher for women than for men (800,000 to 625,000, respectively). That seems like a small number when compared with the population at large, but consider the fact that only 17 million people have entered a communal state at all (that is, they have been married, widowed, or divorced). When the number of divorced Canadians is expressed as a percentage of this 17 million (we've eliminated all the die-hard singles and the children), we see that almost 8.25% of the once-married population are wed no more. As a population, we stand a 1-in-12 chance of divorce. And as women we're more likely to stay divorced.

The difference between the life expectancies of women and men also means women tend to be left on their own. Girls born in 1991 can expect to live to a ripe old age of 81, while their brothers born the same year will likely live to age 75. The older we get, the longer we can expect to live, and the smaller the gap between us and our brothers. So if you were 65 in 1991, you can expect to live to 85, and your male counterpart can expect to live to 81.

The incidence of women heading a single-parent family in Canada has risen dramatically since 1971. Then it was only 10%. By 1991, 16% of all families with children were headed by a woman alone, and 80% of all single-parent families were headed by women.

So, what's the point of all these statistics? Well, we patter around the concept of taking personal responsibility by talking about the "divorce rate" and "life expectancies." But to be perfectly blunt, if you think you'll always have someone to take care of your money for you, you're wrong. He may die. He may leave you. Ultimately, you'll have to do it for yourself. You might as well start now.

Other people believe that dealing with finances is a man's job.
How better to illustrate this point than with a story about shopping for a car? Barb Godin, a former senior vice-president of credit for the Bank of

Nova Scotia, remembers going to the dealership to buy a new car. She began by warning her husband, on pain of death, not to open his mouth. In they went.

"Immediately, they greeted my husband. He said, 'My wife is here,' and they said, 'Oh hello, how are you?' I was looking at several cars and as I was off looking, they were selling to him. No one was paying any attention to me. He said, 'I think you want to speak to my wife, not to me.' So they came to me, but the look on their faces said, 'We really don't want to speak to you because you don't know anything about cars,' not knowing that I look after the automotive finance portfolio so I know a tad about them. They paid me no respect. They talked down to me. They treated me as if this was something I would have to seek the counsel of my husband on before I could make the purchase. I was incensed and ended up walking out of three dealerships. Finally I walked into a dealership where I dealt with a female salesperson. We had a wonderful time."

This kind of treatment is not restricted to car dealerships. Women constantly complain about not being taken seriously, not being treated with respect, and not being seen as able and competent. So while the times are changing, it may not be happening quickly enough for some women.

Women are less likely to take credit for their successes, but are completely willing to accept all responsibility for their mistakes.
This goes back, once again, to our socialization: to the fact that men want to *win* and women want to *win together*. Our very language demonstrates our commitment to keeping the field even so that everyone saves face. While a man might say, "Sit down and have a cup of coffee," a woman would say, "Let's sit down and have a cup of coffee." This socialization toward the group, the team, the together approach means women seldom see themselves as the driving force behind a "win."

According to Olivia Mellan,

When men make money in the stock market . . . they tend to take the credit, attributing the successful outcome to their own cleverness and financial acumen. Where they lose money on their investments, they tend to put the blame on their advisers. When women make money in the stock market, they credit outside influences, such as their advisers, or sheer good fortune. When they lose money, they tend to blame themselves. Since men are raised to be competitive "winners" and to hide their vulnerability, it is easy to see why they project their blame on others. And since women are raised to be accommodators, and to accept a stance of vulnerability and dependency, it is understandable that their first impulse is to swallow blame and to deflect credit.[6]

Women earn less.

For a wide variety of reasons, women have less money than do men. First, they earn less. According to Statistics Canada, in 1993, the average annual pretax income for all women was just $16,500, a whopping 42% less than for men. This is a reflection of the fact that women not only earn less than men, but that many women have no income at all. In 1993, 12% of all women had no income at all, compared with only 5% of men. In 1994, 42% of women did not participate in the labour force. So any income they derived was in the form of earnings from investments, pensions, or government support. Of the 58% of women who earned an income, 26% did so on a part-time basis. In the prime earning years, far more women than men work part-time. While 20% of women aged 25 to 44 worked part-time, in the same age group only about 4% of men were employed part-time. Of women 45 to 54, 24% worked part-time, while only 6% of men worked part-time in this age group. Needless to say, less time on the job means less income, so it's not surprising that women continue to make less than men. Part-timers also have little or no access to company benefits. In 1989, only 26% of part-time employees in the service sector were covered by company medical insurance plans. And only 22% had company pension plans. These exclusions are significant for women's present and future economic security.

If you think women choose to work part-time, you may be surprised. When you look at the reasons why women work part-time, the picture is startling. Of the part-timers between the ages of 25 and 44, 40% of the women (compared with 18% of the men) said they worked part-time because that was the only type of work they could find. For those 45 and over, 32% of women could only find part-time work (compared with

---

6   Olivia Mellan, *Money Harmony* (Walker and Company, 1994), p. 122.

men whose numbers register as too small to be expressed). Personal and family responsibilities also play a big part in women's decisions to work part-time. Of women aged 25 to 44, almost 23% work part-time because of personal and family responsibilities — a category where again, the numbers for men are too small to be reported.

Of those women who were employed on a full-time, full-year basis, women's average income was $28,400, or just 72% of their male counter-parts' salaries. But not all the news is bad. For the next generation, things are looking up. Women who are 24 and younger, working full-time, earned 91% of the average male salary for that age group. The wage gap may be narrowing, but we still have a long way to go in equalizing incomes, particularly for older women.

As we progress up the age scale, women regress in terms of their ability to cope financially. Fifty-six percent of women 65 and older who were not living with their families had low incomes (see the following table). Imagine it. More than half of all women who are retired and alone are in the low-income category.

WHAT IS LOW INCOME?

Statistics Canada's definition of low income is based on the number of people in a family and the size of the population.

NO. OF PEOPLE IN FAMILY	SIZE OF POPULATION				
	500,000+	100,000–499,999	30,000–99,999	<30,000	RURAL
1	16,482	14,187	14,039	13,063	11,390
2	20,603	17,671	17,549	16,329	14,238
3	25,623	21,978	21,825	20,308	17,708
4	31,013	26,604	26,419	24,583	21,435
5	34,671	29,739	29,532	27,479	23,961

Women leave the workforce sooner and more often.

Sad to say, our greatest gift is also a major contributor to our economic insecurity. Our desire to nurture gets in the way of our ability to build our wealth. Whether we are taking time off to have and raise our children, to care for our elders, or to accompany our spouses into retirement, women spend far less time in the workforce than do men.

Having and raising children is one of life's great joys. The birth and care of my children changed me dramatically. I went from a 17-hour-a-day, seven-day-a-week worker to a woman who cannot bear to be away from her kids. I still work — from home. And I choose my work carefully so that I don't have to be away from the kids for too long. It has affected my income stream dramatically. I earn about 50% of what I used to. And I've had to restructure my priorities in order to manage. But I manage. Other women are far less fortunate.

One of the issues I had to deal with was the interruption in my income stream while I was pregnant, and during my "maternity leave." Having two pregnancies-from-hell gave me a whole new appreciation for women who work through their pregnancies. But I found I was not alone. In sharing my horror stories with other women, I found many who barely dragged themselves through their pregnancies, and whose work and careers had to be put on hold temporarily. Since I have always been self-employed, I also had no maternity benefits during my time off with the babies. Here, again, I was not alone. While 89% of mothers on maternity leave received some form of monetary compensation, 77% of women received only EI (employment insurance) benefits. In spite of the fact that most parents receive less than 57% of their regular earnings during their leave, parents choose to take the time off. That commitment to the family is in direct conflict with a woman's desire to be financially independent. The way things are now, it's a choice. And unfortunately, it is our financial security that suffers when we put the family first.

Work absences due to personal or family-related responsibilities rose from 1.9 to 5.2 days a year between 1977 and 1990. That figure may seem low until you consider that parents use their own vacation or sick days to care for kids. Employed mothers surveyed by the Conference Board of Canada in 1989 were four times more likely than fathers to report that they stayed home from work when their children were ill. And according to Donna S. Lero's "Canadian National Child Care Study," child-care problems were three times more likely to affect a mother's productivity or involvement in the workforce than a father's. The most common effect of child-care problems reported included:

- not being able to work overtime when requested or desired
- worrying about children's care while at work
- reduction in commitment to job due to child-care problems

- reduction in work hours
- turning down job offers
- leaving a job because of child-care problems

As our parents age, elder care becomes more of an issue. And since the responsibility for elder care has traditionally fallen on the shoulders of women, we can expect even more interruptions in income. Only a small number of employers surveyed by the Conference Board of Canada provided benefits to employees to assist with the care of elderly or disabled family members. Only 10% offered information on care for family members with disabilities, and only 6% offered elder-care information or referral services.

Women are chronically afraid because of their lack of economic security.
Even women who are well heeled have fears of losing everything and ending up on the street. This is known as the "bag-lady syndrome," and it stems from women's deep-set insecurity about their ability to support themselves and their children in times of trouble. And there are good reasons for women's sense of financial insecurity that go beyond their lower salaries and more sporadic workforce participation patterns.

One factor affecting women's income is their family status. As we've seen, women make up the large majority of single parents in Canada. And single-parent households headed by women have by far the lowest incomes of all. This is reflected in the number of children living in low-income households. While 13.7% of all Canadian children lived in low-income households in 1993, 41% of those low-income kids lived in single-parent families headed by women. It's no wonder we fear for our children and ourselves.

Divorce treats women and men very differently. Typically, a man's income rises after divorce, while a woman's usually falls. For many women, alimony and child support form a significant part of their family income. According to the 1990 General Social Survey, in that year support payments (for single-parent households headed by women) accounted for 18% of the family income. The most alarming statistic of all is the fact that in 1994, of all the support orders in Ontario, only 24% were in full compliance with no arrears. So, not only do women have to face the full emotional responsibility of raising their children, but they often receive little consistent financial support from their children's fathers. Compounding the problem that women have less money to deal with challenges and crises is the fact that we are more likely than men to encounter these challenges. Because women live longer than men, we have to cope for more years on less money, and we are more vulnerable to disabilities, since disabilities increase with age. In 1991, 48% of women 65 and older had disabilities. My husband was absolutely right when he summed up the statistics this way: "Men die, women get sick." In 1991, 36% of women over 65 had severe disabilities, compared with 27% of men. Disability in later years puts more pressure on financial resources. At a younger age, a disability can completely wipe us out because it eliminates or severely hampers our ability to earn an income. Even here, men and women play on different fields. While 11% of men aged 55 to 64 with disabilities were unemployed, 18.4% of women of the same age with disabilities were unemployed. Of all disabled men and women with an income, men's average income was $20,625, while women's average income was only $14,365.

Women seem less willing than men to take risks with their money. There is a debate raging about whether or not women are naturally more risk-averse than men. Some say yes, as witnessed by women's reluctance to take chances, go for the gold, shoot the hoop. The investment statistics bear out this reluctance to take risk. According to research published by the Toronto Stock Exchange in 1996, women are almost twice as likely to think the stock market is too risky. Men, on the other hand, seem to revel in taking chances.

The proponents in the "no" camp believe that women have been socialized, rather than born, to engage in different risk-taking behaviour. Since they have traditionally been less financially secure, they are less willing to take a risk with what they do have. Since they have always earned less, lived longer, been dependent, they want to shore up the resources they have, and keep them safe.

In his book *Galen's Prophecy*, Jerome Kagan provides research to support both positions. In his studies, Kagan found a greater female susceptibility to a fear state. He also cites epidemiological surveys revealing that extreme fearfulness is less frequent in boys. Kagan suggests that because men have been socialized over the centuries to face fear regularly through hunting and combat, their negative reaction to fear has been biologically reduced. Women, on the other hand, who were socialized as gatherers, had less exposure to the fear factor and, therefore, continue to react more strongly to fear. In other words, because men are more accustomed to dealing with fear, they have adapted biologically to deal with fear. Women didn't need to make the same adaptations. The result: girls are more fearful than boys at every age. In fact, according to Kagan's studies, "among the distressed infants who showed high fear at both fourteen and twenty-one months, 86 percent were girls." [7]

As women we can accept the fact that we are biologically less willing to take risk. However, when that unwillingness creates its own risk — the risk of not having enough money to meet our needs when we no longer have a steady income — it becomes clear that we need to get beyond our biology. Perhaps it is time for us to begin reconditioning ourselves so that we accept the fear we feel and move beyond it to achieve the goals we seek. We need to do this not only for ourselves, but also for our children.

In *The Money Tree Myth*, I suggest that parents introduce their children to the world of investing early. One way is to track the performance of a group of stocks chosen for their interest to children — McDonald's, Nike, Disney, Coke — over the long term. Children who are socialized to the ups and downs of the market, who have the opportunity to watch stock prices as they move through their natural rise-and-fall cycles, will be less concerned with short-term volatility when they become adult investors.

Women choose advisers differently.

If you look at financial decision making as having two parts — the thinking (logical) part and the feeling (intuitive) part — then women lean toward the feeling side, while men tend to lean toward the thinking side. The mistake many women make is that they choose to deal with an adviser because they feel comfortable with that person, rather than looking at the individual's track record and experience. Men, on the other hand, seldom ask themselves how they feel about a person. They are more likely to make a decision based on the company's reputation and the adviser's past performance.

---

7   Jerome Kagan, *Galen's Prophecy* (WestviewPress, 1994), p. 195.

Women live longer than men.

While the statistics speak for themselves, we seem unwilling to hear what they have to say.

Intellectually, we know that we will outlive our husbands. Emotionally, we're not willing to face it. Intellectually, we know we have to be able to take care of ourselves. Emotionally, we avoid the subject entirely. It seems to take a major event in our lives to bring the significance of the statistics home to our own reality.

After Kathy Farrell's mother died in 1996, she and her husband were walking through Mount Pleasant cemetery. "I was looking at the grave markers when I noticed that on family plots the date the male died was say, 1850, and the date his female partner died was some 15 or 20 years later. It was such a punctuation of something I had just experienced personally.

"The most profound thing for me was my mother's death. Through that, I got a whole new perspective on financial planning. Her situation was so typical of most. While we know statistically that women live longer than men, until you experience this in your life, you don't really understand what the implications are.

"In my case, my father died about 10 years before my mother. He, like many men, did not believe in life insurance because he believed the insurance company always won. He was well-off relative to most people and he felt there was plenty of money. But after he had been dead for several years my mother started to feel very poor. She needed to take a lot of drugs, and the drug costs were exceeding her income so she began eating into capital.

"The house was paid for, but there were still the basic costs such as taxes and upkeep. I see it time and again. People think that once the house is paid for, it's an expense-free item. It's not. My mother was no longer able to do the gardening. If she wanted to make a capital improvement, that was a separate cost. Even with help from myself and my sister, my mother got to the point where she stopped buying things such as clothes for herself because she simply didn't feel she could afford it.

"The process of my mother's financial deterioration started well before she began to die. When she did become very ill, it went on and on.

"In the movies, people die. But that's just true for men. I used to think how lucky my father was to have just died. No pain, no struggle. My mother had to deal with the loss of dignity. After about a year and a half, I was so drained emotionally."

When Kathy spoke of the strain of her mother's ordeal on both her mother and the rest of the family, there was a sadness in the realization that, at the very least, all the financial stress could have been avoided. The idea of financial planning took on a whole new meaning for Kathy. It isn't about acquiring the most, or having the most. It's about taking care of the details so that the financial issues don't come as a shock. It's taking care of the day-to-day so the tomorrow isn't a horror. As Kathy says, "Life's difficult enough — you experience so many stresses psychologically and emotionally." If you have your financial act together it's one less thing to worry about. Kathy is right when she says, "A lot of the other things you can't do anything about. They just happen. You might as well do something about the things you can control."

It's a woman's world.
Thankfully, women are becoming so much more powerful as an economic force that our special needs are being recognized. And our unique approaches — our desire to be fully informed, our team-oriented styles, our cautious optimism — prepare us to move forward, building on our strengths. Since we are so willing to look at both our skills and our emotional baggage when it comes to money, we are well positioned to learn, develop confidence, and take control. So are you convinced and ready to take charge of your financial well-being? Because now we'll go through the steps you need to take to do just that. You'll be surprised at just how un-money-related they actually are.

3

Seven Steps to
Financial Well-Being

You are responsible, forever, for what you have tamed.
ANTOINE DE SAINT-EXUPÉRY

Financial freedom is a state of being that has far more to do with attitude and approach than quantity. That's what this chapter is about: understanding your attitudes and qualifying your approach so no matter how much money you have, you can view it and use it positively. By taking steps to come to terms with money's role in your life and by committing to change, you can figure out what your personal barriers have been and vault them. You can face your fears, get back in touch with money as it really exists, and take responsibility so you can be free from worry. Ultimately, to change, you've got to *do something differently*.

It's strange, but money is one of our deepest, darkest secrets. While we may feel comfortable talking about many intimate and personal issues — our marital problems, our sex lives, health issues — we are hugely resistant to talking about money truthfully and openly. In the most profound sense, money says absolutely nothing about us, yet we hold our money secrets closest to our hearts.

If you're interested in how you perceive money, and in how to put money in perspective so you can understand your own reactions, you'll find the next exercise interesting.

Step One: Find Out What Influences You

The first step toward financial freedom involves determining your "financial style." Read through the following categories and see how many you rate as true for yourself. Remember, styles may not be exclusive. And you may have shifted styles as you moved through the different stages in your life. What's your predominant style now? To which group of questions did you most often answer "True"? Do you see yourself the way others see you?

Are You a Miser?

True False   I enjoy holding on to my money.
True False   I find it difficult to spend on myself.
True False   I find it difficult to give to others.
True False   I seldom give to charity.
True False   I'm always on the lookout for the least expensive gift.
True False   I'm afraid I won't have enough money.
True False   I often put off buying because I'm sure I can get it cheaper elsewhere.
True False   My family often gets angry with me because I refuse to spend money.
True False   I could never trust anyone else with my money.
True False   I often say, "I can't afford it."

What drives the Miser? It's not really meanness, although it may appear that way to others. It's fear — of not having enough, of being poor, of catastrophe. In order to protect themselves, misers make sure they never run out of money. The best way to have money is to not spend any. These people have no confidence in their ability to make more money. They think the gravy train is about to end and they'll be left destitute.

What the Miser has to learn is that money is just a symbol of security. And she has to learn to stop imagining all those worst-case scenarios that make her feel even more fearful.

If you fear poverty so much that you create poverty in your daily life, you are living your worst nightmare. Stop. Instead of focusing so much on the future, live each day as if you have enough money. Remember, it's not money that makes you rich. It is what you choose to do with your money that will determine the richness of your life.

Help Yourself

- Make a list of five things you would like to buy for yourself: flowers, books, a new blouse, candles, hippos. Ask a friend or family member to look at your list and add two things she has heard you say you want. For each of the next seven weeks, buy one item on your list.

- Make a list of the people closest to you. Beside each name, write one item you know that person wants to buy, or that she or he would enjoy receiving. If you can't think of anything, write in "a card and some flowers." Then, each week for the next few weeks, buy one of the items on the list and present it to your loved one.

- Each time a catastrophic image comes into your mind, write it down on a piece of paper. Put it in a box created specifically for this purpose. At the end of each week, take those bits of paper and tear them up, burn them, or bury them in the garden. Do one piece at a time, reminding yourself with each that you will not give up control of your happiness to this Demon Worry.

Are You a Spender?

True False   I love to shop.
True False   I have a hard time saving.
True False   I find it difficult to defer gratification.
True False   I am not working toward any long-term financial goals.
True False   I never seem to have enough to pay my bills.
True False   My credit cards are maxed out.
True False   I often pay for dinner and buy gifts for friends.
True False   I cannot go into a store without buying something.
True False   I can't resist a bargain.
True False   I get angry if confronted about my spending.

What drives the Spender? The first type of Spender is the person who spends to create an image and has an enormous desire to be noticed. She buys designer clothes, jewelry, expensive cars, luxury items. She needs to be noticed to feel validated or approved of. She wants to impress. She craves preferential treatment and is vulnerable to any pitch that treats her as special. And she likes to shock people by being outrageous. Success is important to the image spender and she is easily impressed by power and fame. She wants to be a part of the "in group," and is prepared to spend her way in. And she wants to be perceived as generous. She competitively races for the bill, buys the most expensive present, and does anything to maintain the facade.

The second type of spender is the bargain seeker. She's in it for the hunt. When she finds a bargain, she feels victorious. While she can often afford to pay full price, the satisfaction comes from adding up how much she has saved. Often bargain hunters buy things they don't need simply because the deal was too good to pass up.

Then there's the compulsive shopper. Whether she has five dollars or $500 in her wallet, she has to spend it as quickly as possible. Often after spending, she feels guilty or ashamed that she didn't handle her money better. She hits the shopper's low and feels anxious. But she shops again, just as wildly. She shops to hide from her misery. She shops for the excitement. She shops to escape loneliness. She shops to enrich her life. She absolutely itches to shop. And because the buying is more important than the having, she may have clothing with the tags still on hanging in the closet, or household items still in their original boxes stacked in the cupboard. She buys not because she needs the item, but to satisfy her urge to shop.

Help Yourself
- Admit that your shopping is having a negative effect on your life. Don't beat yourself up, just recognize that you have to take the problem seriously.
- Keep a journal of your spending. Write down every item you buy, the amount you spent, and how you felt. Don't "forget" your ledger and don't leave anything out. *This is a tough job.* Don't judge your spending, just note your purchases. At the end of the week, total up how much you've spent.
- Shift your source of enrichment from "getting" to "doing." Look for activities you really enjoy and spend more time doing them: potluck dinners with friends, long walks in the early evening with your partner, going to the park with your son.
- The next time you want to buy something, write it on your list and write the current date beside it. Tell yourself you will buy the item

in two weeks if you still need or want it.

- Stay out of the mall. Turn off the shopping channel. Throw out the catalogues *before* you browse through them. Leave your credit cards at home. Carry only a small amount of cash with you.

- Do your shopping like a purchasing department. Usually before a purchasing department will buy an item, it must be convinced that the item to be bought is of benefit to the company, that it is of good value, and that there is money available to pay for it. Before you buy anything, make sure the item meets these criteria.

- Switch from buying consumable items to buying investments. Buy some stock. Buy an RRSP. Buy a mutual fund. Shop around, compare rates, bargain hunt. Make sure you get yourself an adviser to ensure you aren't just buying — but buying wisely. You'll be spending money to increase, instead of deplete, your net worth.

Are You an Avoider?

True False   I don't reconcile my statement and cheque book.
True False   I don't look at my financial statements when they arrive, I just stick them in a drawer for another time.
True False   I don't know how much money I have in my wallet.
True False   I don't know how much money I have in my bank account.
True False   I don't pay my bills on time.
True False   I don't have a will.
True False   I don't read the financial press.
True False   I don't feel very competent about handling my money.
True False   I don't know how much I owe on my credit cards.
True False   I don't do my taxes until the very last minute.

Women avoid handling their personal finances for all sorts of reasons. They feel overwhelmed by the prospect of managing their money. They may feel ashamed because of their lack of skill. But in almost all cases, the longer they avoid dealing with their money issues, the lower their self-respect. One way of overcoming this sense of dread is to hand the responsibility over to a financial planner. Unfortunately, giving over responsibility for your money is a dangerous game. It's one thing to seek advice, and another to give up all control.

An Avoider who is married will often leave all the money management to her spouse. He'll take care of everything. These Avoiders are often unaware of the family's assets and shocked to find out how well-off or destitute they are when forced by divorce or death to face the realities of their financial lives.

Help Yourself

- Once a week, do something to deal with your money such as balancing your cheque book. Set up a filing system for your financial statements and sort them out.
- Stop procrastinating. Pay your bills as they come in. Sit down and do your taxes before the deadline.
- If your spouse handles all the money issues, start communicating about what you have and which responsibilities you can assume. Don't be surprised if he is hesitant to give up control. You have empowered him and he may feel at risk by divulging financial information. Be firm and persistent, but gentle.
- If you do not have one, establish your own financial identity. Open up a bank account in your name. Establish credit in your name. Get yourself an adviser — a broker, financial planner, or accountant — that is yours alone (as opposed to yours and your mate's).

Are You an Acquirer?

True/False I love having lots of money at my disposal.
True/False I'm very focused on increasing my net worth.
True/False I often compare the amount of assets I have with others.
True/False I feel in greater control when I have more money.
True/False I often take a flyer to try to get ahead financially.
True/False People who have less than me are lazy or stupid.
True/False I spend a great deal of my time working.
True/False Money is power.
True/False Time is money.
True/False I feel in greater control when I have more money.

While a healthy attitude toward money means you will use it to experience life and to enrich the lives of those around you, an Acquirer relates to money as if the acquisition is the ultimate goal. She believes it's not what you do with your money, it's how much you have. And since greed makes people vulnerable to dubious get-rich-quick schemes, the desire to acquire doesn't always translate into wealth.

The desire does, however, translate into effort. Acquirers are notorious workaholics. Their motto is "time is money." Spouses and children are ignored, and evenings and weekends are spent on the phone doing deals or managing projects. And their perception of money becomes distorted: no amount is ever enough.

Hard-core Acquirers will go to any lengths to increase their net worth. They will take from others. They will cheat, steal, or involve themselves in shady schemes. The end justifies the means. The goal is to get as much as possible, in any way possible. All that matters is money.

Help Yourself

- Look beyond your financial assets to the other "assets" in your life: spouse, children, friends, personal time, self-development, gratifying work, creative release, spirituality, relaxation, community. Are you expending as much effort to increase your net worth in those areas? List the things that you consider to be "assets" in your life. How can you increase those assets?

- Look realistically at the role money plays in your life. How does your acquisitional behaviour work against your personal well-being? Long commutes, long workdays, lost vacations, few interactions with your loved ones are all costs associated with your drive to acquire. Today, decide you will spend one hour with a child, mate, or friend, just shooting the breeze. Talk about life, dreams, loves, adventures, a good book, a fine meal. Don't mention money.

- What skills do you have that could benefit your community? Choose a community project and volunteer. Keep your commitments to the group.

Are You a Depriver?

True False   I am always broke.

True False   I feel unworthy if given a promotion or other form of recognition.

True False   Even though I have a low-paying job, I often take work home or put in lots of unpaid overtime.

I often dream about ways to make more money.
True False   I lose valuable items.
True False   Each time I feel as if I'm getting ahead, something
             happens to put me back at square one.
True False   If I enjoy what I do, like fixing cars, sewing, or paint-
             ing, I can't charge for it.
 I do not feel capable of handling my money.
True False   I'm not willing to buy into the system and give up my
             freedom.
True False   Money just isn't important.

Why does the Depriver constantly sabotage her efforts to get ahead financially? She may feel undeserving. She may prefer that people not expect too much from her. She may not know a lot about finances, and she may be unwilling to learn. To her, money is incomprehensible. Or perhaps it is dirty. To some, having money will make them spiritually bankrupt or politically incorrect. They think it is virtuous to be broke. Or perhaps they simply want to stay within their peer group, believing that rich people are greedy, arrogant, power-mad, and selfish. To want money is to want all those other characteristics.

Some Deprivers seem 'to want to achieve financial security. They are dreamers, thinking of ways to get money, working out elaborate schemes to make their fortunes. Unfortunately, they never quite get the plane off the ground. They procrastinate or sabotage themselves. Or perhaps they fail in order to reject their parents' obsession with money.

Another reason for depriving is to avoid the grief of loss that will accompany failure. Remaining poor feels safer. By not drawing attention to themselves, they can avoid being hurt. If they achieve success, others will envy them and want to hurt them.

Help Yourself
- Just for today, don't deprive yourself. Pat yourself on the back for a job well done. Treat yourself to a nice lunch.
- Set some goals. What do you like to do? How can you use your skills to improve your financial picture?
- Stop thinking and speaking about money as if it were evil or dirty. Money is paper and metal. What you decide it represents is a

reflection of your morals — not of the morals of money itself. Remember, an inanimate object can't have a morality.

- Find a money mentor, someone knowledgeable and experienced who doesn't share your dread of money. Look for someone who will share your successes joyfully.

Are You a Debtor?

True	*False*	I get a thrill out of using my credit cards.
True	False	I like having access to credit — the more I have, the happier I am.
True	*False*	You don't have to have money to spend money.
True	*False*	I only pay the minimum amounts on my credit-card balances, and my cards are usually maxed out.
True	*False*	Creditors are always overreacting.
True	*False*	My cheques often bounce.
True	*False*	I don't pay bills on time, even when I have the money.
True	*False*	I feel uneasy just walking into a bank.
True	*False*	When I divvy up the dinner bill with friends, I put the bill on my charge card and pocket the cash.
True	*False*	I've taken a consolidation loan and then run my cards right back up again.

Debtors dig themselves into a hole by borrowing excessively and misusing credit. Regardless of whether they can afford to or not, Debtors borrow, mainly because they can't face the limitations of their budget. They find it easy to delay paying bills, and often blame others when the natural consequences occur: "How dare my bank bounce this cheque."

While consolidation loans often work for people who get into debt solely as a result of a change in their personal and economic circumstances — for example, people who are laid off, become disabled, or face sudden, unforeseen expenses — they seldom work for the chronic debtor. Instead of offering a way to get out of the abyss, the loan frees up other credit that is then immediately used up again. And since Debtors traditionally set unrealistic expectations for themselves when they do try to eliminate their debt, they often rein themselves in too tightly. They are then forced to use credit just to make ends meet.

Help Yourself
- Admit to yourself, and to someone else, that you have a problem. Recognize that you cannot get out of debt by taking on new debt. More credit just exacerbates the problem. Become a critic of debt. Do you really want to pay interest on that dress, stereo, or dinner for the next three years? If you only pay the minimum amount each month, you could end up paying twice as much as the original cost for the item.
- Decide that you will not take on any new debt today. By going one day at a time, you'll move closer to freeing yourself from the Debtor's cycle. Join a support group such as Debtors Anonymous.
- Cut up your credit cards and close the accounts. Paying cash ensures you won't take on new debt and makes you more conscious of what you are spending.
- Don't spend more than you make. Make a spending plan that shows how you intend to use your money (as opposed to a budget that is restrictive and constraining). Include a few of the frills that make life more bearable: an occasional meal out, fresh flowers, a movie, a new book. If you do not enjoy the quality of your life, you won't stick to your spending plan.
- Accept responsibility for your debts. That doesn't mean being harsh with yourself. Accept that what is done is done and get on with life. Call your creditors and work out a repayment schedule you can live with. Pay off your most expensive debt first, then apply more money to the next most expensive as it becomes available.

STEP TWO: MAKE PEACE

We would all do well to heed this ancient Chinese proverb: "He who knows he has enough is rich." The second step in achieving financial freedom is to make peace with how much you have.

Whether you make $20,000, $60,000, or $200,000 a year, few people can say honestly that they're happy with their financial lot. Witness all the people who never have time for a holiday, who miss school pageants, or who never take the day off in the middle of the week. It seems we always want more.

After my daughter was born and I started to pull back from corporate consulting, my accountant asked me how concerned I was about lower billings. He was trying to help me plan my income for the future. As I tried to explain to him that my life was changing, I suddenly realized that I was no longer prepared to do the things I had done in the past just for the money.

During my second pregnancy, these feelings grew even stronger. During one particularly tedious project where the client was being petulant, my mind drifted to my daughter at home and I realized my priorities had shifted and I wasn't prepared to put up with the corporate nonsense anymore. I still enjoy working on fast-paced projects where my expertise is valued. But I won't take just any job. I have to trust the client, and the client has to trust me. If not, I've found no amount of money compensates for the aggravation. I realize this is a luxury I've worked for and a choice I make to have less.

To free yourself of the self-doubt and the need to keep up with the Joneses, accept your current situation and set a realistic goal for when enough is enough.

John Stuart Mill said, "Men do not desire to be rich, only to be richer than other men." To cut through the Gordian knot of debt, quantify for yourself how much is enough. In their book *Your Money or Your Life*, Joe Dominguez and Vicki Robin have charted what they refer to as the "Fulfillment Curve":

> At the peak of the Fulfillment Curve we have enough. Enough for our survival. Enough comforts. And even enough little "luxuries." We have everything we need; there's nothing extra to weigh us down, distract or distress us, nothing we've bought on time, have never used and are slaving to pay off. Enough is a fearless place. A trusting place. An honest and self-observant place. It's appreciating and fully enjoying what money brings into your life and yet never purchasing anything that isn't needed . . . [8]

Which brings us to the question of what a "need" is. In my book *The Money Tree Myth*, I describe the various types of needs and how important it is to distinguish between them.

---

8 Joe Dominguez and Vicki Robin, *Your Money or Your Life* (Penguin Books, 1992), p. 25.

First there are the wants, which come about because you simply don't have something right now. It's the need to remedy the lack of a specific item or a state. I want a new dress. I want a new set of dishes. I want to be left alone. Next there are the concerns. These relate to things we worry about. I'm concerned about keeping my money safe, so I need a bank account. I'm worried about how my friends will see me, so I need the latest fashion item. I'm worried I won't be loved, so I buy my children plenty of presents. Then there are the problems. Something has happened that has created a need. My house is too small, so I need a new one. My car just died, so I need a loan to buy a new car. I can't make ends meet so I need to make more money. Finally, there are the desires. These are the "I wish I had" or "I wish I could have" statements. I wish I could take the kids to Disney World. I wish I could buy a new coat. I wish you would listen to me.

The distinctions between these types of needs are not always easy to see. Even professional salespeople have difficulty distinguishing between a want, concern, problem, or desire. But there are differences, and the differences relate to value.

Don't get me wrong. Sometimes it's perfectly appropriate to get something just because you want it. I collect hippos. I buy them because I want them. They don't satisfy any concern or problem and it's not a matter of desire. It's straight out want. I have no goal in buying a hippo, except for the gratification it brings. I have quite the hippo collection, but if I see another one I like, I'll probably buy it just because I want it.

Understanding the motivation to buy goes a long way toward determining the value of the purchase. Without this understanding, people will inappropriately place the same value on one purchase as on another. That hinders their ability to judge the appropriateness of the buying decision.

There are three questions you can ask yourself whenever you find you need something. The first relates to your level of fulfillment. How will the satisfaction of this need make me feel more fulfilled? The second relates to your purpose — your goals, your image of your life, what you want to accomplish. How will the satisfaction of this need move me closer to my purpose? The final question relates to responsibility, and a sense of how your life fits in with those around you. How will the satisfaction of this need affect those around me?

STEP THREE: FIND YOUR MONEY SET-POINT

Dietitians know that people who use only a diet to change their weight usually return to the same weight because we each have a preset internal metabolic rate. The only way to truly change our weight is to reset our internal thermostat by increasing that metabolic rate. Consider the fact that we may also each have an internal thermostat that measures our comfort level with our savings and net worth. When we seem to be moving above this point, we do whatever is necessary to return to equilibrium: go shopping, change jobs, leave the workforce, acquire some debt. I have a girlfriend who can't sleep at night if her savings account drops below $1,800. It's a marker she has set for herself based on absolutely nothing. But no matter how much she and I have talked about the importance of setting up an emergency fund, she can't get her savings *beyond* the $1,800 level. Each time the account rises above her marker, off she goes on a holiday, or there's a new painting, or there's a spiffy new outfit.

If you allow your set-point to be determined by some illogical internal gremlin, *you* are not in charge. If you want to take control, you must either evict the gremlin and reset your set-point, or trick her. If you plan to evict, know the task won't be easy. To begin, sit down and determine what your set-point is. Next, figure out if it works for you. Is it livable? If not, what should it be?

If you can't evict the gremlin then you'll have to trick her. There are all sorts of ways to do this. For example, I know one woman who has four or five bank accounts. Each time she gets to her set-point, she walks away from the bank account and opens another. It's not a very convenient or efficient system, but it works for her. A friend of mine reset her set-point by convincing her gremlin that it was appropriate to have a different set-point for each of her objectives. The more objectives she had, the higher her overall set-point. At last count, she was saving for retirement, a return to school, a downpayment for a second home, her three children's educations (separately), and a fund to care for her parents should the need arise later in life.

STEP FOUR: FACE THE FEAR

Yes, we're all very busy. We're running the kids to day care, running to work, running to our next appointment. No matter what job you have, whether you are selling real estate or coffee, working as a vice-president or a secretary, focusing on your career or on your family, you manage to make time for the things that are important to you. As a wise man once said to me, "If I spent as much time taking care of my money as I do others', I'd be rich." Time, or a lack of it, doesn't prevent you from dealing with your money. Fear does.

As a young adult, I remember reading a book entitled *Feel the Fear and Do It Anyway*, by Susan Jeffers. The premise of the book was that we all carry fears that stop us from doing what we want. As children, we are constantly faced with fear: "Be careful!" "Don't run into the street, you'll be squashed like a bug-a-bug!" These messages stay with us, heightening our anxiety and creating barriers to our achievement. The only way around them is to face them head on and get over them. If we do not, those fears will grow like weeds, suffocating our ability to achieve peace.

What are your fears? Do you worry that you won't have enough when you grow old and will end up a bag lady? Even the very rich describe this fear, so it isn't related to how much money you have in the bank. Do you lose sleep worrying about whether your children will be okay, should something happen to you? Do you think about what you'd have to do to keep a roof over your head and food in your children's stomachs if something happened to your husband? Do you worry that you just can't keep up, or that there's no other job you could ever do?

We all have fears that creep into our minds and steal away our serenity. But if you don't know what you're afraid of, you can't come to terms with it. So, if you're prepared to try dealing with your fears, begin by asking yourself, "What am I afraid of?" If nothing comes to mind immediately, give it time. Make sure you write down your fears. Looking back at the questions on pages 12–13, can you see a connection between your fears and the messages you received as a child? If you don't immediately see a connection, that's not unusual, since many of our earliest memories are deeply buried. Just keep thinking about it, and I'm sure the picture will become clear for you.

Step Five: Get Back in Touch with Money

Go into your wallet and take out a five-dollar bill. Now tear it up. Could you do it? Most people can't. Yet every day we toss money in the garbage:

the books we buy but never read; the leftovers we scrape into the garbage can; the dress we get for a steal but wear only twice. We can fool ourselves in dozens of ways when it comes to "stuff," but it's a lot harder when it comes to the actual money. That's why it's important to start touching the real stuff again.

If you feel a little divorced from money, it's not really surprising. Each technological advance has distanced us from our money, making it more convenient for us to spend. Cheques, for example, are a representation of money: a promise to pay. But if you've ever written a cheque you knew would bounce (or written one that bounced unexpectedly), you know that a cheque and money are two separate animals. Another technological advance is the credit card. Looking back over the purchases you made in the past month, how many fewer would you have made if you didn't have your credit card with you? Sometimes we don't even call it a credit card; instead we refer to it as plastic, distancing ourselves even further from what it actually represents: money. The same holds true for debit cards, except in this case, the money actually has to be there. But a debit card gives us easy access to our cash, and that convenience has made the system successful beyond all expectations. On May 15, 1997, *The Financial Post* reported that in just over two years, since the national launch of the debit system, 50% of Canadians were using their bank cards to pay for groceries, gas, retail purchases, and most other products and services. In fact, direct debit achieved in five years what it took credit cards 25 years to do in terms of broad consumer acceptance. Why? Simple. Debit cards make it easier to spend money. They are faster and more convenient than writing cheques. They are more widely accepted than are credit cards. And they are one of the cheapest ways to pay. (Nothing beats cash for minimizing transaction costs.)

Auto debits, direct payments, telephone banking, on-line banking — these conveniences all stand between you and the actual paper and coin that is money. To get back in touch with your money, for the next month or so, spend nothing except cash. At the end of the month, compare your expenditures with those of the previous month. Is there a difference? How inconvenient was it for you? How did you feel about spending each time you took cash from your wallet? How much money do you have in your wallet now?

Step Six: Be Responsible

"I *am* responsible," you say vehemently. Great. So you have a will and a power of attorney. And you have enough insurance so your family will manage if your income is suddenly gone. And you've taken precautions in case you become disabled. And you have a retirement plan so your children won't have to support you. And you have six months' savings put aside so if the unexpected occurs, your kids can sleep peacefully in their own beds. You also have a pay-yourself-first plan because you know the importance of investing.

A big part of financial freedom is having all the i's dotted and t's crossed so you can free yourself from worrying about the what-ifs of life. Saying you'll get to it isn't enough. Merely knowing you've taken care of your loved ones will move you a long way along the path to financial freedom. If you really love your spouse and your children, you must do more than say you love them. You must act as if you love them. And if you truly love yourself, you must prove it by doing the responsible thing. When you use money to take care of those around you, you have your priorities straight: people first, then money. If you fail to take care of your responsibilities, how much happiness, love, laughter, and joy will the money bring?

Step Seven: Do It!

To be financially free, you can't just think about it, you've got to act. And while people are more important than money, the money won't take care of itself. That's your job. It's not up to your accountant, broker, banker, lawyer, husband, son, financial planner, or mother. If you don't respect and tend to your money, you'll find little available when you need it. So take control — and find the financial freedom you're seeking.

Taking action is precisely what we're going to talk about next: doing the things you can — the things you must — in order to have the control you need to achieve financial freedom. See you in Part II.

II

TELESIS

The business of life is to go forward.
SAMUEL JOHNSON

Where I am today has everything to do with the years I spent hanging on by my fingernails.
BARBARA ARONSTEIN

E ach year as I do the media rounds for RRSP season I am asked, "When should I start contributing to my RRSP?" For young people, the question implies they have lots of time and can wait. For older individuals, the question should really be, "Is it too late for me?"

It is never too soon or too late to begin taking care of your money, no matter how your bottom line reads today. If you find you are in debt and see no way of getting out, take heart and take control, starting today. If you've been busy paying your mortgage, paying for your children, paying for your lifestyle and haven't managed to build yourself a nest egg, you can take control, starting today. If you feel overwhelmed, inexperienced, inept, you can take control, starting today. You just have to understand telesis.

Telesis is defined as the "deliberate, purposeful utilization of the process of nature and society to obtain particular goals."[9] It is progress that is intelligently planned and directed. It is what you must do to get to where you want to be. Instead of planning to save, you save. Instead of planning to pay off those debts, you simply start paying them off. It doesn't mean you will achieve all ends immediately. It does mean you will no longer delay starting. You won't wait until your next raise to open up your pay-yourself-first monthly savings plan. You'll do it immediately. And you won't wait until you have a "decent" contribution to begin using an RRSP; you'll start with that $50 you managed to squirrel away.

I started contributing to an RRSP when I was 22. I wasn't prescient. I didn't know back then that there would be controversy surrounding government pensions, or that I would never benefit from a corporate pension plan. I just knew that I was supposed to save. So save I did. And I used an RRSP because I just couldn't believe the tax man would give me his money to do with as I wished, simply for choosing an RRSP over another savings vehicle. I had been saving since I was a little girl when my dad had offered the incentive of a savings-matching program. Seems the government had a similar deal going, so I took it. And in doing so, I implemented telesis and formed a habit I never intend to lose.

Telesis and inertia go hand in hand. Most people associate inertia with

---

9 *The Random House College Dictionary, Revised Edition,* 1975.

an inability to move. But, in fact, inertia is "a property of matter by which it remains at rest or in uniform motion in the same straight line unless acted upon by some external force."[10]

Now, think about inertia as it applies to the theory of telesis. Once you're moving, it'll take a 10-foot-wide brick wall to stop you. Having established your pay-yourself-first plan, you will keep saving and investing every month for the rest of your life. A comrade-in-writing of mine, Victoria Ryce, refers to it as "painless portfolio building." As she says, "You only miss the money in the first month. By the second month, the pain is gone." That's the beauty of inertia. Once on a roll, you'll continue to roll unless some remarkable force gets in your way. Another Victoria-ism: "Getting rich is boring." Since you don't have to think about it, you can just keep investing monthly — same-old, same-old — until you are rich. That's telesis at work!

The best way to get telesis working for you is to put in place your financial basics: the strategies and habits you'll need to keep your finan-cial body and soul together. Where to start? First you need a plan . . . a spending plan.

---

10 *Merriam-Webster Collegiate Dictionary, Tenth Edition*, 1996.

4

Establishing a Spending Plan

If hippos are on sale, two for a dollar, that's a bargain . . . but only if you have a dollar and need two hippos!

WHO KNOWS

The best things in life are free, but the next best things are expensive.

ME

Every mickle makes a muckle.

OLD JAMAICAN SAYING

I remember a time when I thought that if I could just make $30,000 a year, I'd be set. Since I was only making $10,000 a year at the time, I couldn't imagine what I'd do with all that money. The reality was that by the time I was earning $30,000 I had higher expenses. I had to pay more tax, buy a new car, dress in more expensive business attire.

It's easy to spend money once you get used to having it. And it doesn't take long to get used to it. Like a gas expanding to fill a container, your expenses grow in proportion to your new income. And if you're not careful, you may find your spending plan popping like a balloon.

A spending plan is a way of keeping track of the money you get and the money you spend. The best thing about a spending plan is that it gives you a very clear picture of your financial reality. Many people cringe when I talk about the need for a spending plan. They relate being pro-active about what they're spending with having to give up things they enjoy. In reality, a spending plan gives you the freedom to enjoy yourself, because you don't have to worry about how you'll pay the bill when it comes in. You'll know right from the start whether you can afford the purchase or not.

How does a spending plan differ from a budget? Budgets feel restrictive and are often set unrealistically so, like diets, they seldom work. With a spending plan, you decide how to spend your money so it does you the most good.

One of the truths of money is that the more you have, the more you'll spend. People who let the spending just happen inevitably end up drowning in a sea of debt. Exhausted from bailing to try and get back into the black, they finally give up and sink into credit oblivion.

The trick with any spending plan is to not let it be the tail that wags the dog. Without a keen sense of where you're going, and what you want to achieve, it's very easy to fall into the trap of spending more and more. As Mr. Micawber says in Charles Dickens's *David Copperfield*, "Annual income twenty pounds, annual expenditure nineteen six, result happiness. Annual income twenty pounds, annual expenditure twenty pounds ought and six, result misery." What most people don't know is that this is a version of something Charles Dickens's daddy said to him from debtors' prison.

Have you ever made a large cash withdrawal from a banking machine, only to wonder a few days later where all the money went? Where did the last $100 you withdrew go? Stop for a minute and write it down. Chances are you can account for most of it, but there may be five, 10, or 20 dollars missing from your list.

What does it cost you to live each month? Most people underestimate their expenses because they forget the things that don't occur every month. Did you include your gym costs even though you pay them once a year? How about your house or car insurance? Did you include the cost of your haircuts, your contact lenses, or your vacation? Do you pay someone to shovel your snow, clean your windows and carpets, or do your taxes? Did you buy one or two cords of wood last winter? Did your kids go to camp? What about your vet bills, the flowers for your garden or patio, your coworker's going-away present? Or how about those maga-zines you picked up at the supermarket checkout, the batteries for Tickle-me-Elmo, or the charcoal for the barbecue? And what about the bottle of wine you gave your friends when they had you over for dinner, or the five dollars here and 10 dollars there your son or daughter hit you up for?

When you do all your money management in your head, it's very easy to forget things — sometimes important things — that will have an impact on your overall financial life. If you write cheques without record-ing what you've paid for, it's easy to forget how much you've spent. You're always guessing how much you have left. And you shouldn't really be surprised when your account is overdrawn. After all, if you don't know how much you have, how can you know how much you can spend?

People who barely make it from one paycheque to the next are often surprised when they take the time to do a spending plan. They may not have realized just how much they spend on impulse purchases, lunches or drinks with friends, parking tickets, candy bars, or lottery tickets. Just as importantly, they usually find it much easier to reach their goals when they have a plan to work with. One of the best ways to gain a perspective on your spending habits is to keep a log of everything you spend, each time you do the transaction. Now, hold on a second. Don't go all cross-eyed on me. The idea is to figure out where you're spending all those five-, 10-, and 20-dollar bills that seem to go missing each month. It's also about learning more about yourself and where you place your priorities. This isn't about shame, blame, or deprivation. You don't have to change anything you don't want to change. But you should at least know. By keeping a spending log, you will have a clear picture of your expenses so you can see what you're getting for your money.

Another important concept that is often drowned out by the sound of the credit card swishing through the machine is that of relative value. Relative value refers to the relationship between what an item costs and what you have to do to pay for it. It's not a new concept. Adam Smith talked about it in *The Wealth of Nations* in 1776 when he wrote, "The real price of everything, what everything really costs to the man who wants to acquire it, is the toil and trouble of acquiring it."

What does it cost to buy that new coat? The absolute cost relates to how long you have to work to come up with the cash. If it costs $260 and your *disposable hourly income* is $4.25, you'll have to work for about 61.5 hours to earn enough money. That can put a whole new perspective on the real cost of the coat.

The idea of a disposable hourly income is not one most people are familiar with. It is your gross income less your fixed total expenses (including income tax) divided by the number of hours you work. Let's say you make $30,000 a year, have two weeks' vacation, and work a 45-hour week. Assuming your average tax rate is 29%, you'll net $21,300. Let's also say that your fixed monthly expenses (things like rent, mortgage, loan payments, food, utilities, phone, drugs, transportation) total $1,500 a month, or $18,000 a year. Your disposable hourly income would be $1.47:

$$\frac{21,300 - 18,000}{45 \text{ (hours) x } 50 \text{ (weeks)}} = \frac{3,300}{2,250} = \$1.47 \text{ / hour}$$

Yeech! You probably don't even want to do this exercise, right? It looks pretty depressing. But if you don't do it, you won't see how hard you have to work to pay for the item you're thinking about buying.

Many people who make what seems to be an extremely good living get themselves into holes precisely because they are not aware of their disposable hourly income and their spending patterns. Let's take the case of Margaret and her husband, Frank. Frank is an executive who makes $180,000 a year. That's a lot of money, right? So Margaret could never figure out why they never had any money. After taxes, Frank's income dropped to $96,000 a year. But as Margaret saw it, that was still $8,000 a month. What was the problem? When they did their spending plan, they discovered that their monthly expenses were very high: a $2,000-a-month mortgage, a huge food bill to feed themselves and four kids, clothing, school fees — it all added up to about $6,000 a month. Then, of course, there was Frank's penchant for buying whatever took his fancy. And Margaret, though she considered herself a smart shopper, found that she loved to shop and would use any excuse to buy: new drapes, new clothes for the kids, and fresh flowers for the house. It all added up. After keeping track of their spending patterns for three months, they became far more aware of where their money was going. Then Margaret calculated Frank's disposable hourly income. Since he travelled quite a bit and

worked hard, she tracked his hours for three months ar
weekly average of 57 hours. It turned out that Frank's
income was just $8.42.

You might find it useful to go through the exercise you
Dominguez and Vicki Robin say in *Your Money or Your Life:*

> Money is something we choose to trade our life energy for . . .
> When we go to our jobs we are trading our life energy for money.
> This truth, while simple, is profound . . . While money has no
> intrinsic reality, our life energy does . . . Life energy is all we have.
> It is precious because it is limited and irretrievable and because our
> choices about how we use it express the meaning and purpose of
> our time here on earth.

Think of a spending plan as an architectural drawing. Without one, you
may build too big a bathroom and end up not having enough space for all
the bedrooms you need. Or you might put the staircase in the wrong
place. Maybe you won't remember to put in enough windows. Your
rooms will be dark and you'll have to spend more money on lighting.
With a spending plan, as with an architectural drawing, the first thing you
do is think about all the must-haves. Then you have the flexibility to build
in the want-to-haves. You'll know your rent is covered each month, so
you won't be evicted and have to spend extra money moving. You'll know
just how much you can afford for food, so you won't eat steak for the first
three days of the month and then live on macaroni and tuna for the
remainder. You'll know just how much you can afford to spend on transportation, so you can decide whether you can afford to indulge in a cab
ride without having to walk to work for the next four days. Once you
make a spending plan, you will feel better for knowing the truth about
where your money is going. And you will be in control of the money that's
controlled you for too long.

COMING OUT EVEN

A spending plan is made up of two parts: income and expenses. *Income* is
the money that comes in. It's your salary or commission, dividend or
interest income, alimony, child support, pension, or disability income. It

is all the money you receive, whether it comes in monthly, quarterly, or in some other time frame. It does not include money you think you *might* get. So, if your bonus is not guaranteed, then don't include it in your spending plan. After all, if it doesn't flow in when you expect it to, and you've already planned to spend it, you'll be up the creek. Better to not include it, and then use it to boost your savings or cover a long-wished-for treat.

The term *expenses* refers to money going out. Expenses represent your monthly costs in after-tax dollars. When you pay amounts annually — insurance, camp fees, tuition — divide these amounts by 12 to come up with a monthly amount so you can work these expenses into your plan.

The best way to figure out your expenses is to gather all your bank statements, credit-card bills, and whatever other records you have of how you spent your money for the past two years. (If you do it only for one year, your figures may be skewed by unusually high or low bills in that particular year.) Make a category for each bill: telephone, food, vet bills, gym fees, child care, health, gifts — *everything*. Total each category and divide by 24; that's your monthly average. Now add all the category averages together. This is the amount you spend each month.

Are you surprised? Is it more or less than you thought? Chances are it's more, since most people underestimate. Are you spending more than you are bringing in? Well, if you have a negative gap, there are two things you can do about it: make more or spend less. Look back over your categories and think about how much you *want* to spend for each. Notice that I used the word "want." *You're* in charge of this. *You* say how much you will or will not spend. You can keep right on digging a hole, or you can decide to take control.

The thing about a spending plan is that it isn't carved in stone. It would be nice if life were predictable, but it isn't. Here's just one example of how the unpredictability of life can make your knees weak and your temper flare. One winter, it seemed as though every heat-producing appliance in our house went kaput. First it was the furnace. Imagine two days with no heat. Then the dryer blew, just when I had the biggest, wettest load of towels (could that have been it?). Then the microwave. I prayed that the gremlins would find a new place to live, checked with my Feng Shui book to see if things were in the wrong place, and started sprinkling the house with lavender. The VCR blew next.

Since we could never have predicted that these appliances would all give up the ghost in the same month, there was no way to plan for their repair or replacement. Not in the traditional sense, anyway. But a smart spending plan makes allowances for the unexpected. Spending plans should have a repairs-and-maintenance or supplies-and-services category that accounts for these kinds of expenses and ours did. We call ours "unusual expenses."

Once you've done all the work to come up with the numbers for your spending plan, get ready for the really tough part: the discipline of using it. A spending plan has three columns:

- "Planned" is the money you expect to spend on each of these areas. You may plan to spend $25 a month on prescription drugs, $150 on food, and $10 on books and magazines.
- "Actual" will show the amount you had to lay out. Your spending plan may call for you to put aside $200 a month for children's clothes. It's unlikely you'll spend $200 each and every month. However, in September as you ready the kids for school, you may find you spend considerably more than $200. If you spend $375, this is the figure that would go in the actual column.
- "Difference" is the difference between what was planned and the actual amount spent. If you intended to spend $5 a day on lunch but brown-bagged it three days each week because your horrendous workload meant you couldn't leave your desk, your "planned" would be $100, your "actual" would be $40 (for the two days each week that you escaped from the office), and the "difference" would be $60 followed by a plus (+) sign to show you've spent less than you planned. On the other hand, if you planned to spend $25 on a gift for a friend, but spent $40 (which would go under "actual"), the "difference" would be $15 followed by a minus (–) sign to indicate you exceeded your spending plan.

If you go off track in a particular category one month, don't panic and think you've blown the whole deal. Look at other categories and see where you can adjust to make up the difference. If you planned to spend $3,000 a year on clothes, but blew your budget by September, you could either stop buying clothes, or you could steal the money from your vacation category. It's your choice.

If you're saying to yourself, "Get real, there's no way I can keep up this record-keeping stuff" or "I'd rather be poor than be a slave to this stupid form," I understand completely. The idea is not to become a slave to the plan. It's to go through the process so you can see on paper where your money is coming from and where it's going. It's to get it out of the nebulous grey zone of "I think I spend . . ." to the black-and-white facts.

If you don't believe a spending plan can make a significant difference in your life, I challenge you to use one for just three months and prove me wrong. Then write me and tell me how little use it was. I believe that once you do the plan and use it for three months, you'll find real value in having gone through the exercise.

If you don't believe you can find the time to do this for even three months, I've heard this before too. It is a sad statistic that shows that Canadians, on average, spend 10 hours a year taking care of their money and 1,000+ hours a year watching TV. You'll have to decide where your priorities lie.

LOOKING AT AVERAGES

While averages don't mean a hoot to some people, others want a benchmark against which to measure their financial dealings. For those who like to know what the rest of Canada is doing, here are some numbers you may find interesting. These numbers are all based on the 1992 year, the last year for which data was available at the time of writing.

The average family income before tax in Canada is $46,076 and, on average, Canadians manage to spend 98.85% of that income on household expenditures. Shelter costs about $8,102 a year — or about 17.6% of the average income. Food runs at about $5,686 — about 12.3%. Transportation is a whopping $5,640, with the cost of private transportation ($5,198) far outstripping public transportation ($442). Household costs, including utilities, furnishings, and equipment, are about $4,779. Clothing comes in at $2,222; personal care is about $844 and health-care costs are approximately $867. And despite all that's written about the need for Canadians to take responsibility for their financial futures, the amount spent on financial security — pensions, life insurance, and employment insurance — is a measly $2,289, or 5% of the average income. Compare that with the $2,300 spent on recreation. While Canadians spend about $1,400 a year on tobacco and alcohol, they spend less than half of that — only $678 — on reading and education. Of course, as you probably already expected, the biggest part of our expenses is the whopping tax bill each year — an average of $9,378, or 20% of our average income.

Of course, the numbers vary significantly from one province to the next and from one income group to the next. And averages are just averages. But it is interesting to look at where we place our priorities. If you want the latest numbers, look for Statistics Canada, Catalogue No. 62-555. The data are nicely presented at the Statistics Canada website.

TRIMMING EXPENSES

Many categories of your spending plan will have fixed amounts, but many others can be fiddled. If you buy lunch at work every day, you could decide to skip the lunch out twice a week and save. If you get a haircut every eight weeks, schedule it for every 10 weeks instead and save yourself some money. If you buy magazines off the rack, you could subscribe and save 50% or more. Or go to your local library every second week and binge in the periodical section. Decide to trim, a little here and a little there, until what you spend matches with what you want to spend.

Here are 9,999,999,999 ways to save. Just kidding!

- If you smoke, quit. If you smoke a pack of cigarettes a day at $3.50 a pack, you'll save $1,277.50 a year. If you put $600 of that in an RRSP for the next 15 years and earn an average return of just 7%, you'll end up with $15,500. Put it all away and you'll have $34,394.49. Another reason to quit: If you don't smoke you'll pay 10% to 15% less in premiums on most life insurance and disability insurance policies. That's like getting a month of coverage free each year.
- Take your lunch to work, at least some of the time. If you save $15 a week on lunch, in a year you'll save $780. Invest half that in an RRSP and earn 7% on it, and in 15 years you'll have $9,000.
- Share newspapers with coworkers. If you buy a paper twice a week, instead of five times, you'll save $117 a year.

- Subscribe to magazines. If you buy a monthly magazine costing $3.50 at the newsstand, it'll cost you $42 a year. Buy it by subscription, and you'll pay only $21. Even better: share subscriptions with friends.
- Use the library. Check out books, magazines, tapes, and CDs instead of buying them.
- Buy your phone. Pick one up at a garage sale and save the monthly cost of renting.
- Use a long-distance package. Do the research and choose the package that saves you the most. If your phone habits change (when your daughter goes off to university in another city), check to make sure your plan still works for you.
- Pay your life insurance premiums a year in advance if the company offers a one-month discount.
- When it comes time to renew your mortgage, negotiate. If you can shave just a half-percent off your mortgage, you'll save $500 a year on a $100,000 mortgage.
- Accelerate your mortgage payments. Paying your mortgage on an accelerated basis means an extra payment every year that goes directly to your principal. On a $100,000 mortgage at 11%, amortized over 25 years, you'll save $62,486 in interest over the life of the mortgage.
- Check the blue-book value of your car to determine whether you should still be insuring for comprehensive and collision.
- Are you insuring heirlooms that you could never replace even if they were lost or stolen? Weed out the things you don't need covered anymore.
- Ask your insurance agent for the various discounts available: claims-free policyholders, those who insure both home and car in the same place, and people with security systems all get a break on their rates.
- Increasing the deductibles on your home and car insurance can save you big bucks. You have to be sure you'll have the money to pay the deductible yourself. Sticking it on your credit card and carrying it for months defeats the purpose. But if you don't intend to make a claim for under $500 or $1,000 because you're concerned about how it'll affect your premiums, then you might as well raise your deductible and save.

- Don't buy extended warranties on household appliances. Instead, use a credit card that automatically extends the warranty.
- Set up a co-op baby-sitting service with other parents in your neighbourhood. You take care of three kids once a week, and you'll have two days off.
- Grocery shop with a list and stick to it. If you run out, wait until your next planned shop. Buy in bulk, if you'll use the items, and buy generic (at least try the generic alternative). Buy in bulk with friends and split the savings.
- Buy off-season, providing you can reasonably estimate your child's next size. Your son's next winter wardrobe will be considerably cheaper at the end of this winter.
- Don't even go into convenience stores. Almost everything is more expensive.
- Buy gifts when they are on sale and put them away for birthdays, anniversaries, and other special holidays.
- If you're carrying a balance on a credit card, switch to a card that charges lower interest. On a $3,600 balance, switching from a 17% card to a 9.9% card will save you over $250 a year in interest. Dump the cards from which you've transferred the balance. If you give in to temptation and run those balances up again, you'll be in even worse shape.
- Review your bank statements to see how much you pay per month in service charges. Would you be better off with an all-inclusive monthly fee? Do you have the option of free transactions if you maintain a minimum monthly balance? Shop around for the right account.
- Don't bounce cheques. A friend of mine regularly bounces cheques and each time she does it costs her $19.95 in service fees — never mind what she's doing to her credit rating. And it's not that she doesn't make enough money. She's just a bad money manager.
- At the grocery store, comparison shop and buy on sale. And buy seasonal items in season; what is plentiful will be cheaper.
- Check unit prices to see what it actually costs. Those little calculators on the grocery store shelves serve a purpose. I've often been surprised to find that the bulk items are sometimes more expensive than the regular items on sale. When your favourite products go on

sale, buy enough to last until the next sale.

- Buy second hand. It's amazing what you can get in a garage sale or thrift shop: good quality at a great price. My stepdaughter once outfitted herself for an entire season at the Goodwill store for $35. And I've scored big at garage sales and second-hand shops: beautiful baby clothes for a fraction of their original cost; a mountain of Duplo for $30; lovely books that my children and I still enjoy together.
- Leave your credit cards at home except when you plan to spend. Taking them with you leaves you open to impulse purchases.
- Use public transportation. Figure out what it's costing for the convenience of having a car and decide if it's worth it. Here's a case in point. Julie owns a car. Her loan payment is $236 a month and her insurance payment is $416 a month for a total of $652, which is exactly one-third of her take-home pay. She doesn't live in the car. She doesn't use the car for work. She has the car in case she needs it. Wow!
- Go to the movies on Cheap Tuesdays or when matinees are less costly. Or wait for the film to move to a second-run house and see it there for half the price.
- Write letters instead of making long-distance telephone calls. Or get on the Internet and e-mail. My cousin Van and I discovered e-mail. She's in Florida and I'm in Toronto. Boy, what a difference that has made to our telephone bills. We could spend up to an hour on the phone talking about the kids. Now we e-mail and it takes less than a minute to send the same message. We "talk" more often too.

Look at your spending at least once a year to see where you may have formed some habits you no longer need or want. Think back to a few years ago and ask yourself if you ate out as often, went to as many movies, spent as much on clothes. What's changed? Would it make sense to return to your previous standard, or is your new standard of spending right for the time?

The whole idea is to make sure your needs, wants, and desires are in the right perspective and that you're fully aware of where your money is going. After all, if you feel it is your right to go to that concert, lease a new car, or eat out a couple of nights a week because you work so hard, just remember that because you work so hard you also have the right to be debt-free, well balanced in terms of saving and spending, and on your way to achieving your financial and life goals. It's your money. It's your life. It's your peace of mind.

SETTING GOALS

Whatever money represents for us, it should never become the centre of our lives. But the management of money should become one of the tactics we use to achieve our goals. Whether we want to buy a home, provide for our children's schooling, or retire to a small island in the South Pacific, money is one of the means we will need to achieve our ends.

Life is full of choices. We make them every day. Monday we had the choice of going to work or staying home. Most of us went to work. Tuesday we chose to see a movie. And Friday, we'll either go dancing or put some music on the stereo and catch up on that John Grisham novel.

How we choose to use our money is, in large part, dependent on what we envision for ourselves. However, if you feel it's the money that's giving the orders, you may not be able to see beyond your immediate circumstances to the dreams you want to achieve.

A dream is a gift we give ourselves

Had any good dreams lately? What's stopping you? Maybe you can't remember how. Ask yourself, "If I could have anything I wanted — no holds barred — what would it be?" Grab a pencil and paper and write them down. And don't just limit yourself to financial goals. Remember, no holds barred. Keep going. Think! Absolutely anything you want. How's your list coming? You should have 10, 27, 50 things by now.

Having listed all your dreams, now categorize them as short-, med-ium-, and long-term:

- If you want to realize your dream within the next year, write "ST" beside it.
- If you expect your dream to be realized in the medium term (two to five years), write "MT" beside it.
- If your dream will take longer than five years to happen, write "LT" beside it.

The next step is to prioritize your dreams. Start by creating a shortlist of six dreams that are most important to you. Even within your shortlist you will have priorities. To decide which goals are most important, weigh them against each other. Is having a home more important than taking that trip to the other end of the country to see your ailing grandmother? Is buying a car more important than paying off your credit-card debt? Is taking a trip to see your grandmother more important than paying off your credit card? What's your priority? Reorder and number your dreams 1 through 6 in order of priority.

Goals are dreams with a deadline
Now it's time to set a date for achieving your dreams. This doesn't mean that the date won't change. That's just a tad too optimistic. But without a date there is no sense of urgency and no commitment to moving forward. Go ahead, set your dates.

Now you know where you want to go and you have an ETA. That's the hard part. The rest is easy. It just takes a plan, a commitment, and, perhaps, a guide to help you through the maze of alternatives and information. Use all the resources at your disposal: books, seminars, friends. Talk to your banker, your broker, your financial planner — whomever you trust to act as a guide. And remember, you won't get there just by dreaming about it. *Telesis* will take you there.

5

Establishing an Emergency Fund

A gem is not polished without friction, nor a person perfected without trials.

CHINESE PROVERB

When written in Chinese, the word crisis is composed of two characters. One represents danger and the other represents opportunity.

JOHN F. KENNEDY

An emergency fund is used to meet unexpected expenses. (If you're in debt now this may sound unrealistic to you, but read on to see why you need an emergency fund and how to get one.) Financial media often talk about emergency funds in the context of unforeseen unemployment, that is, you need an emergency fund just in case you are "outplaced" and it takes more than a day to get another job. This is true, but it doesn't matter if you're self-employed, working for the greatest company in the world, or have the most airtight employment contract ever seen. Everyone needs an emergency fund. Unforeseen medical expenses not covered by insurance or a new roof can put a serious crimp in your budget, even when you're fully employed.

The size of your emergency fund will depend on your financial commitments. If your spending plan is tight, you'll need to establish a fairly significant emergency fund. One rule of thumb is that you have the equivalent of six months' income set aside for emergencies.

Of course, to set up an emergency fund, you have to save. Some people find it easy to save, many others don't. Think about how much you have saved right now. Do you think it is enough? Do you feel safe? How do you feel about saving? Are you for it or against it? Why? What did you learn about saving as a child? From your parents? From your spouse? Does saving seem like an impossible dream because of your current financial circumstances? How do your religious beliefs affect your savings habits? If you got a $100-a-week raise today, how much of it would you save?

If you've never been a saver, you'll need to figure out your attitude toward saving before you can change your habits. If you don't believe savings are important, you won't save. It's that simple. Unfortunately, the other reality is that not saving can have some nasty repercussions.

The reason most people don't bother with an emergency fund is that they figure nothing terrible is ever going to happen to them. Optimism is fine to a point, but not when it puts you and your family in jeopardy. Here's a scary story.

Madelaine found herself unable to work. She was experiencing a variety of weird physical symptoms and was severely depressed. She had a disability plan at work and, under the instructions of her psychiatrist, decided the pressure and stress of the job were too much and stayed home. She claimed her disability benefits, only to find that she was declined because the insurance company's representatives felt she could work — if not at her present job, then somewhere else. She had no diagnosis to support her physical complaints. Madelaine went through hell. With no emergency fund, she found herself even more stressed out and, worse, feeling like she was nuts. It took almost 10 months for the doctors to locate the problem. And it was a serious one too. In the meantime, Madelaine had no recourse. Luckily, her husband was able to fill the gap. But the strain on the relationship was obvious. And the strain on Madelaine only made her physical condition worse.

If you don't think bad things can happen to you, here's a statistic to wake you up: Regardless of your current age, there's a one-in-three chance that you'll become disabled before you turn 65. If it happens, you'll probably experience a cash-flow crunch — either you'll receive less money than you are accustomed to or you'll have to live through the wait period before your benefits kick in. Disability isn't the only potential problem we face. There's the car that dies at the most inopportune moment or the emergency trip you must take to deal with a family crisis. It's all the what-ifs you've imagined, and their potential cost. If you don't have an emergency fund, you may get through the crunch, but you'll probably use a very expensive form of credit to do so. And you'll end up paying heavily for not having been prepared.

Once you have your emergency fund set up, keep it in conservative, highly liquid assets. There's no point in having an emergency fund in a five-year GIC where you can't get at it. A money-market fund is a safe bet. If the idea of having $10,000 sitting in a money-market fund earning a low rate of interest makes your blood run cold, the following strategy may be for you. First, apply for a personal line of credit equal to your emergency fund. Next, invest your emergency fund as you would any other investment dollars. (Okay, okay, perhaps with a little less risk.) In the best-case scenario, should you need to access your emergency fund, your investments will be at their all-time high and you can sell them, reap a nice capital gain, and cover your emergency. However, should the timing be all wrong for liquidating your investment, you could buy yourself the time to let your investment do its thing by first calling on your personal line of credit.

Whichever route you choose, make sure you build an emergency fund for unforeseen expenses into your spending plan. Make like a boy scout: Be prepared.

SAVING VERSUS INVESTING

I can't believe there was ever a debate about the difference between "saving" and "investing," but there was. At one point, I had to write an educational piece for a financial institution describing the difference. Unfortunately, some of the mist is still swirling. Here are my definitions.

Saving is the act of accumulating money by setting aside a portion of your income. Saving is what you do when you take cash out of your cash flow and set it aside. Let's say you have an automatic savings plan that deducts $50 from your chequing account and puts it into an investment for you. Let's also say you go out and charge $50 on your credit card that you can't afford to pay off this month. Have you saved anything? NO. Since you didn't take the money out of your cash flow (you used your credit card to put it back into your cash flow once it was deducted from your chequing account), you haven't saved a thing. Don't fool yourself. If you have "savings" and "debt," you've got less than you think.

Investing is what you do to earn a return on the money you've saved. So if you have $500 in a savings account earning .25%, it's invested — not particularly well, but it's invested. And if you have $500 in mutual funds, GICs, bonds, debentures, stock, or anything else of a financial nature, it's invested too. As long as it's potentially earning a return, it's invested.

SAVING STRATEGIES

Do I have to say that saving regularly is an important part of your overall financial strategy? Unfortunately, for many people, saving doesn't come naturally. According to an Angus Reid Group survey published in July 1997, almost one-third of Canadians do not save. The theory is, and statistics bear out, that a person's stage of life is pivotal in determining her savings goals. If you're under 35, there's a 41% chance that you are not saving. There's also a 58% chance that you make less than $30,000 a year. With as little as $100 a month, or $23.08 a week, you would be right on track with your savings. If you're over 35 and you're not saving, you're in the minority. Seventy-two percent of people aged 35 to 54 have accumulated some investments, while 77% of those over 55 are taking care of themselves. With homes to buy, children to raise, and expenses at their peak, the under-35 set just doesn't have the money to save.

Hogwash! If you don't save, it's because you don't want to save. After all, I'm not talking about hundreds of dollars a month. Take $5 from your cash flow for savings and you're doing better than you were in terms of taking care of yourself. And since Canadians feel travel is more important than an emergency fund,[11] I don't think I'm being harsh.

We Canadians have become a spendthrift bunch. We haven't always been. As a country we saved 10% or more for 20 years — from 1973 to 1993 — more than enough time to have established the habit. Our

---

11 "Investment Issues," Angus Reid, Ernst & Young, July 1997.

savings rate reaching a peak of 18.5% in 1982 (in our enthusiasm, did we overdo a good thing?), we bounced around the 10% mark for about a decade, and then in 1993 we began our great slide. By 1999 we'd hit an all-time low (our earliest savings rate records are for 1969) of 3.6%. That's a long way off 10%, and an even longer way off the RRSP contribution limit calculation, which is based on putting aside 18% of earned income.

So why aren't we saving? It really doesn't matter what reason we give — too much debt, high cost of living, exorbitant taxes; the real reason we aren't saving is that we've forgotten how important it is to save.

Why save? Because saving gives us a sense of security and mastery over our finances. As our savings grow — be they in a run-of-the-mill savings account or invested in equities — we can take pride in our sense of discipline and increased ability to weather a storm. And, besides, the more we've accumulated in savings, the harder those savings work for us. It can be truly rewarding to see substantial sums of money generated solely by our savings. Saving also takes us closer to our goals. We have the resources to cover unexpected expenses without incurring debt at high rates of interest. We have the flexibility to take advantage of investment opportunities as they arise. We can change jobs, change homes, change countries without the sense of anxiety that comes with existing from paycheque to paycheque.

Fundamentally, though, if you don't save, you're asking for trouble. The goal should be 10% a year. That's 10% of your gross family income. That may not always be achievable. Some years, you may come up short. But if you never put anything away for the future — just in case, for your children's education, for your own retirement — then you're not taking care of yourself. And if you delay starting until you'll have more disposable income, the cost to your cash flow will be enormous.

Here are some ideas that may help:

- Open up a pay-yourself-first plan that deducts money from your chequing account each month and automatically invests it for you. You'll be surprised how quickly you get used to living without that money.
- To avoid impulse spending, move your savings to a money-market fund. You'll need 24 hours' notice to transfer the money back to

your chequing account. Don't use a savings account (see pages 76–77).

- Purchase CSBs through a payroll deduction plan.
- Invest part or all of any windfall such as tax refunds or gifts you receive.
- Find out about any deferred profit-sharing or share-purchase plans offered by your employer.
- Practise being thrifty. When you save money on an item, immediately put the savings in your money-market fund. If you save on an item and then just spend that money on something else, you haven't saved a thing.
- When a regular expense such as a loan payment or tax installment is eliminated from your budget, continue putting that amount into savings.
- When you get a raise, save half your increased earnings.
- If you have consumer loans or credit-card debt, make paying off those debts a priority. Take the amount you would have spent on interest and save it.
- Contribute to an RRSP and use your tax refund to increase your next RRSP contribution or to start an unregistered investment account for a downpayment on a home, for your children's education, or some other goal.

Saving doesn't come naturally to a large percentage of the population. If you're not turned on by watching your money grow in a savings or investment account, you'll have to find some other motivation for saving. How about this: You're supposed to do it, and if you don't do it you'll have no one but yourself to blame when you find yourself up to your armpits in alligators. Just for one moment, be a pessimist. Yes, you could lose your job, get sick, smash up your car, have a tree fall on your house. Those are good reasons to save. A more important reason is that taking care of yourself and those you care for is your responsibility. Saving should be a part of life. It's necessary to save if you want to be financially healthy. Remember *telesis*? *Do it!*

6

Cash Management

It is better that a man tyrannize over his bank balance than over his fellow-citizens.

JOHN MAYNARD KEYNES

M ost people find that their financial lives revolve around their bank. They have a chequing account and a savings account. When they buy a house, their bank provides the mortgage. When they apply for a credit card, it's their bank's version of MasterCard or Visa. And when they begin investing, they often start with the GICs, mutual funds, and other investments offered at their local branch. For the purpose of this section, it doesn't matter whether you deal with a bank, trust company, credit union, or caisse populaire — we're talking about the place where you do your banking.

ALMOST EVERYONE NEEDS A CHEQUING ACCOUNT

Choosing the right chequing account can be a real test in today's complicated banking world. And the banks haven't made it any easier for us. With the introduction of new-and-improved-this and better-than-ever-that, we now have an overwhelming variety of account features from which to choose.

In the past, the main consideration in choosing a bank was convenience. We chose a branch that was close to home or close to work. But you don't have to buy from the bank on the corner anymore. Telephone banking and banking machines are making it easier to choose a bank based on the products it offers and the service you get for the money you pay.

Start by looking at the services you are now using to make sure you aren't paying for things you don't need. Make a list of the services you use regularly and not-so-regularly so you aren't paying for the ones you use only once in a blue moon. Then shop around to see who has the best package for you. Review brochures in the sanity of your home and at your own pace. Once you've identified the accounts and services you like, make a list of questions to ask the banker to make sure the package does what you expect. And make sure there aren't any hidden costs. Take the time to read the fine print.

Many banks offer no-charge chequing and no-charge use of banking machines (usually referred to as ABMs or ATMs) if you maintain a specific minimum balance. Consolidate your existing accounts to get to the minimum. If you wish to keep your accounts separate, ask your bank to link the accounts so you meet the minimum balance requirement and only pay one set of fees. Many institutions also offer a package of services with a single monthly fee. Compare the individual fees with the cost of the package. If you use quite a number of services, you may be able to save by buying a packaged account. My account allows me to do almost everything for $14 a month. My accounts are all linked, so I pay only one fee. And I can even do two transactions at another bank's ABM at no cost each month. It also includes my telephone banking.

Compare the interest you're earning with the cost of running the account. There's no point in earning minimal interest if the service charges on that account are more than you would pay on another non-interest-bearing account. And there's no point in keeping scads of cash earning little or no interest just to minimize fees. You could be better off paying a fixed monthly fee and investing that chunk of cash.

Use the banking machine to do your routine transactions since this can save you the cost of individual fees. Deposits, withdrawals, and bill payments made at your bank's ABM are often cheaper than those done at a teller's wicket. Plan for your cash needs and make your withdrawals from your own bank's network. Each time you withdraw cash from an ABM belonging to another financial institution, you may be charged a fee, which can be as high as $1 per withdrawal for machines in Canada and $2 or more for withdrawals in the U.S. You would think that such a high charge would be an automatic deterrent. Not so. In a recent two-year study of women's banking habits, up to 25% of women regularly used an ABM from another financial institution.[12]

Another alternative is to use your banking card as a debit card since, most often, the transaction fees are less than the cost of writing a cheque. This is a popular option, with almost 31% of women using debit cards. And the convenience is undeniable: In 1997 alone, Canadians swiped their debit cards more than one billion times.

Do not use the ABM to keep track of your account balance. If you do, you may find yourself counting on a balance that isn't really there because a cheque you've written has still to clear. Use your cheque-book register to keep track of your account — regardless of whether those transactions are cheques, debit-card transactions, cash withdrawals, or credit-card charges — and reconcile it monthly against your bank statement to make sure you're working with an accurate balance.

If you run your account to the limit each month, consider overdraft protection. This is an automatic loan that kicks in when you don't have enough in your account to cover a cheque. The interest rate is high, however, so you should only use it for emergency shortfalls — not as a line of credit. Not having overdraft protection can be expensive too. At one bank, the cost of an NSF (not sufficient funds) cheque is $19.25. And that doesn't include the cost of having an NSF show up on your credit bureau report.

Check your statement when you receive it each month. I can't tell you how many times I've found extra fees on my statement that, with a single call, I've had removed. If you aren't watching the pennies, the dollars can go missing pretty quickly.

If you travel to the U.S. regularly, consider opening a U.S.-dollar account. Keeping your funds in U.S. dollars, as opposed to switching back and forth, can save you money on the exchange fees.

If you find that your cheques are being held for several days after you

---

12 "1997 PMB Two-Year Readership Study," Print Measurement Bureau.

deposit them, go in and tell the bank manager you want the hold removed. Banks hold cheques for as long as seven business days — longer if the cheque is drawn on a foreign account — to ensure the cheque clears before the funds are released. If you're a good customer, you shouldn't have to wait.

If you have a mortgage, an RRSP, and other investments at several institutions, consider consolidating so you can throw your weight around. Banks love to have all your business and you can use the economic power of consolidation to lower your mortgage rate, earn higher interest on investments, and reduce service charges. Shopping for a bank is like shopping for anything else. If you want to get the best deal going, you have to compare and you have to negotiate. Above all, you should only buy what you need.

If you have money on deposit at a bank that also happens to be your credit-card issuer, the bank can go into your account and take those funds if you become delinquent on your credit card. Avoid this by keeping your deposit accounts at an institution other than the one that issued your credit card.

Finally, if you're charged for something that you think is unfair, complain. You'd be amazed at how many times fees will be waived because of your relationship with a branch staff member or because you have a big mouth.

SAVINGS ACCOUNTS

Canadians have millions of dollars sitting in savings accounts earning a pittance in interest. Most haven't even considered the options. If you have money sitting in a savings account, your money is idling. It's probably not even earning enough to offset the service fees you pay for your overall banking needs. There are alternatives.

The most obvious options are the high-interest accounts offered by institutions such as President's Choice Bank, ING Bank, and Citizens Bank, or money-market funds or Treasury-bill (T-bill) funds. These alternatives offer most of the benefits of a savings account. Since unit values are managed to remain stable, there is little or no risk. You can access your money with as little as 24 hours' notice. And the increased return means your money is working considerably harder to offset those bank fees and help make ends meet. Money-market funds sometimes even beat short- and medium-term guaranteed investment certificates (GICs) without the restriction of locking up your money for a specific term. In fact, you can earn 3% or 4% more on a money-market fund if you shop carefully. Check the mutual-fund listings in the newspaper to see where you'll get the best deal and then weigh the return against the convenience of being able to access your funds quickly at your local financial institution.

Some people think the process of getting into and out of a money-market or T-bill fund is complicated. A money-market transaction can take less time than lining up at a teller to make a deposit. What about access to your money? Most financial institutions will allow you to transfer funds from your money-market fund to your chequing account with a signed request by fax. That means you can have your chequing account credited without going into the bank. Others give you access through their telephone banking service.

You might think that for an investment that pays better than a GIC, you would need a mountain of money. Not so. With as little as $500, you can move your savings (and short-term deposits) into a money-market or T-bill fund and earn more. You'll also have the added convenience of receiving your statements at home so you don't have to line up to get your passbook updated with a disappointing amount of interest.

VIRTUAL BANKING

Virtually everyone is talking about it, and if you're not already doing it, might I suggest it's only a matter of time. Whether you bank through the ABM network, by telephone, or by using your computer, you're participating in the world of virtual banking.

My girlfriend Cookie is a perfect example of how virtual banking is changing the way Canadians get at their money. When she moved, she chose to keep her account at her original branch and bank in new ways. She liked the people there and she really liked the service they gave. How astute of her to realize that you don't get the same service at every branch. So she maintained her relationship with the branch even though the location was no longer convenient.

If you can order a pizza, you can bank by phone. Telephone banking is easy and convenient, and if you do it often enough, you can hit the buttons pretty quickly so you don't have to listen to the irritating instructions. Using telephone banking, I've transferred money from one account to another, paid all my monthly bills, checked my balances, and transferred money to my mutual-fund account. And I can do it all at three in the morning. Telephone banking is immediate, and you're given a transaction number to confirm what you've done. You can do it from any touch-tone telephone, so you can even cover your bills when you're on holiday.

The attraction of virtual banking is that it makes your life easier. With more demanding schedules and the ever-increasing challenge of balancing home and work, people who don't have the time to run to a branch to apply for a mortgage, pay bills, or make routine transactions can do their banking on their own terms. And they can save money too.

The field is virtually exploding as people seek easier access to their accounts, more control, and up-to-the-minute information. Here are a few questions to ask so you choose the service and the bank that's right for you:

- What transactions can I make? Services differ by bank. Figure out what you're looking for, what stage you are at, and what services you need. How much of your information can you access? How many different types of transactions can you make? What are the limitations?
- Which bills can I pay? When I first started banking by telephone, I was frustrated when I tried to pay my realty tax bill at the Bank of Montreal and they couldn't accept it. I had to make a special trip to the ABM. Some banks are more aggressive than others in arranging to handle the payment transactions of creditors.
- Do I want to be able to see my account information? Cookie chose computer banking because, as she says, "I can see it in front of me. Right away my account balances change. That's why I like it. I feel more secure that it's been done and is registered."
- Is the system available 24 hours a day, seven days a week? Nothing can be more frustrating than finally finding the time to do your banking only to be greeted with a message that says the system is down.

- When I access my accounts, is the information up-to-date? It's no good working with an old balance. That's why we're into technology, right?
- From where will I want access? If you're on the road without a laptop or access to a computer, the telephone service may make more sense.
- Will I want to download financial information into a software package that lets me track my spending and manage my finances? Some banks provide software so there's no need to export information to a separate financial planning package such as Quicken.
- Can I use my existing account number and access this information from my branch as well as by virtual banking? If it's simplification you're after, the last thing you need is a whole new set of account numbers and passwords.
- Can I do everything from one place? If the bank's systems don't all talk to each other (and sometimes they don't), you may end up reentering information.
- Does the service allow me to use my equipment? Every existing dial-up system is compatible with Windows 3.1 or 95. Few are able to interface with Macintosh. Check before you sign up.
- What's the cost and how much can I save? The costs and potential savings are all over the map. Do a little telephone shopping before you start virtual banking.

How Safe Is Virtually Safe?

Information is transferred to and from a banking network in two ways: through a direct dial-up to your bank's network, or via the Internet. While many people worry about the security of information transferred via the Internet, sophisticated encryption procedures mean the information is scrambled so it's virtually impossible for someone else to get at the private details of your life. And someone would have to tap your private phone line to get the information sent via direct dial-up. Want to protect yourself further? Here are some do's and don'ts:

- Do keep a back-up of your information.
- Do keep a record of transaction numbers given at the completion of

each activity in case there's a mix-up.
- Don't access your personal information via your company's intranet (the company's internal computer network) without completely erasing your records from the caching.
- Don't give your access code to anyone else.
- If you complete a transaction at a call centre, don't assume the transaction has been completed. When I transferred money from my money-market fund to my chequing account through a call centre, the human factor came into play. The transaction was never processed. I had to call my branch to get the job done right.

It makes sense to look over your financial services from time to time to see if the products you're using still match your needs. The banking world is constantly changing and the banks are very competitive. But don't think that just because the service is offered, you need to have it. Review how you use your bank account so you only buy based on what you're actually using. Don't be lured into buying a product just for the prestige. Shopping for financial services is like shopping for anything else. If you want to get the best deal going, you have to compare and you have to negotiate. Above all, you should only buy what you need. All that shopping around and comparing can get mighty confusing (and many of the features offered may seem pretty attractive) so you must be careful not to buy bells and whistles you don't need.

FINANCIAL RECORD KEEPING

Staying in control of your financial life is infinitely easier if you're organized. Whether you invest in a software program such as Quicken or do it all on paper, knowing where everything is will make it easier to keep a handle on your money.

To keep your paperwork organized, you need a place to put all that paper that comes pouring in through the mail: bank statements, bills, credit-card statements, warranties, investment records, and the like. Organize it by category so that should you need to find something you won't have to go wading through reams of paper looking for a single item.

Set aside a filing drawer or get a filing box for keeping your financial stuff. Make up as many file folders as you need to organize your information. If you have three separate bank accounts, it's a good idea to set up a folder for each. Some typical folder headings are Automobile, Bank Statements, Credit Card, Home Purchase, Home Improvements, Household Bills, Income (tax, salary stubs, bonus statements), Insurance (separate files for house, life, disability), Investments, Mortgage, Pension, Personal Papers (birth certificates, marriage and divorce documents, wills, powers of attorney, passport, SIN, etc.), RRSP, Warranties/Equipment Booklets, Work (performance reviews, memos on job performance). An alternative to file folders is to use a three-ring binder with tabs. My husband likes this much better. He's a minimalist and keeps just the important stuff. I use a drawer, folders, and save *everything*.

If you're a pack rat like me, you'll have to cull your files from time to time so you aren't overwhelmed. Hold on to receipts for anything that's tax deductible or required for a warranty. Keep receipts for anything you'll need for insurance purposes. Hold on to your bank statements and cheque stubs for at least three years in case you're audited.

Financial record keeping also involves monitoring your accounts. If you aren't balancing your cheque book against your statement each month, you're not paying enough attention. For some reason, people hate this job, even though it isn't particularly difficult. But unless you're wealthy enough to keep so much cash in your account that you never have to worry about covering all your cheques, you've got to reconcile your cheque book.

It helps if you carry your cheque-book register around with you and write in everything you spend as you spend it, including your debit-card and credit-card transactions. Then, when your statement comes in, you can quickly check all the transactions because they are all in the register. And when your credit-card bill comes in, there are no surprises. Simply write the cheque number for all the transactions on the bill beside the transactions in the register. You won't be tempted to spend money you don't have — even if those transactions haven't come in on the latest bill — because the money has already been deducted from your register.

One good habit I picked up from business is to record my cheque number and date on the bills that I'm paying. When I pay my bills by telephone banking, I write the date of payment and confirmation number on my bill. It's dead easy to find stuff when I must.

Financial record keeping, like most money management, isn't hard. But it does require discipline. If you skip an entry, toss an important piece of paper, misplace a warranty, it'll cost you. It's a pain in the derrière finding the time to file those little pieces of paper, reconcile those statements, check those credit-card bills before you write the cheque, but you have to do it if you want to be financially healthy. So *do it!*

7

Putting a Roof Over Your Head

I want a house that has got over all its troubles; I don't want to spend the rest of my life bringing up a young and inexperienced house.

JEROME K. JEROME

Shelter is one of life's basic necessities and it takes a variety of forms: apartments, town houses, basement flats, houses, condominiums. Most people start off by renting. If you're at this point in your life, make sure you read your lease. Yes, I know that most of it sounds like gobbledygook, but if you don't read the fine print you may be in for a shock.

If you have roommates, make sure they are all listed on the lease and have them all sign the lease. This ensures you will all share legal responsibility in case of a problem. It also protects you if a roommate suddenly changes her mind and decides to move out.

If a security deposit is required, find out how it works. Landlords sometimes ask for a sum of money up front to protect themselves from the cost of repairing any damage you might do. However, the security deposit should not be used to pay for basic maintenance on the unit. Get a receipt for the security deposit, and ask for a letter stipulating what the money will be used for. And find out whether or not you will be paid interest on the money while it remains unused. When your lease is up and you move out, the landlord should refund your deposit if you did not cause any damage. Take pictures of how you got the unit and how you left it so you have some physical proof should there be a dispute with your landlord.

Other key things to watch for in a lease:

- Can you have pets?
- What are the rules regarding noise?
- What happens in the case of non-payment of rent?
- What rights of entry does the landlord or his representative have?
- What are the rules for rent increases?
- What about upkeep; who's responsible for what?
- Can you have roommates? Do they have to sign the lease?

Know your rights. The law protects renters in many ways. But if you don't know your rights, you won't know when someone is taking advantage of you.

THE RENT-VERSUS-OWN QUESTION

At some point the rent-versus-own question may come up. The considerations are not all financial, so the decision will involve more than just comparing your monthly rent with the monthly mortgage you would pay.

Home ownership requires a certain commitment and responsibility not only in terms of money, but also in terms of time, and not everyone is up to the challenge. Once you own your first home, you'll quickly realize that there is always something that needs to be fixed: the roof, the wiring, the plumbing, the eavestroughs, the furnace. If it's not the inside of the house, it's the outside. A couple who live in my neighbourhood bought a home with a pool. First they had a termite problem. Then the skylights had to be fixed. The pool lining went. There seemed to be a constant onslaught of things needing repair.

Then, of course, there are the lifestyle issues. Some people are just too busy living to be bothered with the ongoing maintenance of a home. Painting, caulking, trimming, mowing, and shovelling are furthermost from their minds. Avid travellers who find themselves away from home for long spells may have problems with security issues. People who move often because of work may find their equity eaten up by real estate and legal fees. If you find yourself selling your existing home in a down market and buying in an up market in your new location, you may have less than you need for the downpayment that would make it an even trade.

If you like the idea of having your own place to do with as you wish, ownership might be right up your alley. If you're handy around the house and like puttering about, go for it. If you want to put down roots, if you want to become part of a community, owning your own home could be a very rewarding experience.

Often when people start thinking about buying a home, their focus shifts from simply providing shelter to making a profit. One home-ownership myth is that a house is a good investment. This isn't always so. Witness all those people who bought into the market during the boom of the 1980s and then saw their equity evaporate as the real estate market took a dive. Many were left owing more than their homes were worth.

While conventional wisdom says that renting is throwing your money away because you're developing no equity, renters don't have to worry about taxes or major home repairs. And if you have the discipline to invest the extra you would have had to pay if you owned, you could end up ahead. On the flip side, no matter how small the principal portion of your mortgage payment (and it's incredibly small in the early years), as long as the market is stable or rising, every month you will be building equity and increasing your net worth. A short-term view often makes the owning picture appear somewhat bleak. But as you pay off more of your mortgage, more of your payments will go toward building equity.

If you're doing a calculation to determine which route — renting or buying — would put you further ahead financially, let me warn you that there is a lot to consider. First, you'll need a crystal ball to see where the housing market will be in five, 10, or 25 years. As I write this, the housing market has been brisk and has been termed a "seller's market," but the reality is that a home I bought in 1989 is still worth only 84% of my purchase price. It may be a seller's market, but only if the price is exactly what the buyer is prepared to pay. The standard calculation used for illustrative purposes usually compares the amount the home has appreciated over the years with the growth in assets that would have been realized had the homeowner invested in the equities market instead, but the answer is often misleading. There are a number of factors to be taken into account to make the calculation truly realistic. Consider the costs associated with home improvements and maintenance. When my good friend Victoria bought her new home in the Gatineau, she had to hire no less than eight repair people for plumbing, painting, heating, chimney cleaning, appliance repair, carpet cleaning, wiring, and floor replacement. A house is a constant source of expenditure. Also take into account the property tax you must pay, as well as things such as the real estate commission due if you sell the home (and the capital gains if the home is a second property).

This might sound like I am against home ownership. I'm not. But for almost everyone I've spoken with, the decision to buy or rent has had as much to do with emotion as with money. It is a decision based on a desire to put down roots, to have a place to call one's own. If you do not take these important elements into consideration, the cold hard figures can lead you astray. You might end up ahead financially, but with significantly less personal satisfaction than if you had a home to call your own.

A HOUSE OF YOUR OWN

Owning a home is not an impossible dream. If you're just toying with the idea of buying your own home, you may feel fear, or even dread, at the idea of making such a huge commitment.

There are two things you have to think about when you decide you want to buy property: First, how much can you afford to spend? Second, how large a mortgage payment can you handle?

A starting point in figuring out how much you can afford is to multiply your gross annual income (your income before taxes) by 2.5. Include only income you're sure you will receive, and if you and your spouse both have incomes, add them together. This is referred to as your household income. Let's say your gross salary is $32,000. Your honey makes $26,000 a year gross. You could afford to buy a house with a price tag of $145,000 ($32,000 + $26,000 = $58,000 x 2.5) or less. Remember, however, this is only an estimate. Not only do you have to think about the price of house you can afford, you must also consider how you will work those mortgage payments into your spending plan.

Financial institutions use a calculation called "debt service ratio" to determine how much they'll lend you based on how much you can afford to repay each month. Your debt service ratio is your before-tax income divided by the necessary monthly payment. From the bank's perspective, 30% is the upper limit. You, too, can use this as a starting point to determine how much you can afford. Of course, to calculate the total amount you'll be spending, you have to figure in the downpayment you'll need to get into the house.

So let's see how it would work. Let's say you and your partner make $6,000 a month before taxes. Thirty percent of that would be $1,800 a month, which is what the bank will say you can afford in mortgage payments. At a rate of 10%, according to the mortgage amortization tables, that means you could afford a mortgage of $200,000. Add on your downpayment and voilà . . . you've got the total cost of the house you can afford.

The amount you can afford to spend each month will also depend on whether you have other debts such as a car loan, credit-card balances, a student loan, or alimony and child-support payments. The amount you spend on items such as clothing, transportation, food, entertainment, and so on would also have to be considered. Add up how much you spend, except for housing, and deduct the total from your monthly take-home pay.

Next, consider what it will cost to live in your new home. Ask friends or family what their heating, electricity, water, insurance, repair, and maintenance bills are like for similar homes.

The safest way to find out exactly how much you can afford to spend and what your payments will be is to be pre-approved for a mortgage. Have a lender work out all the figures to tell you how much you will be able to afford to spend on a house, and how much your monthly mortgage payments will be.

When interest rates are rising, most people also want some way of protecting their interest rate. Most mortgage pre-approvals offer an interest rate guarantee for anywhere from 30 to 90 days. To get the guaranteed rate, you must complete the transaction (i.e., close the house and have the mortgage funds disbursed) within the guaranteed period. If the period expires, the guarantee is gone. If interest rates are lower at closing than the rate guaranteed, make sure you get the lower rate.

With pre-approved financing, your offer to purchase may be more attractive to the seller. But despite the implication, just because you're *pre-approved* doesn't mean you're *guaranteed* financing, so make your offer conditional on financing. Your pre-approval is based on your credit-worthiness, downpayment, and ability to service the debt. However, since you haven't chosen the house you're going to buy yet, the mortgage is only approved in principle. Final approval is subject to the property qualifying. An appraisal is needed to determine this. Once you have located the house you want to buy, the normal mortgage application procedure is followed, but with much of the qualifying information already on hand, your application should move quickly.

Just because you've been pre-approved by one lender doesn't mean you have to borrow from that company. You should still shop around even if it is easier to be pre-approved by your existing financial institution. Lenders are constantly coming up with new and improved product features as a way to lure you into their stores. Make sure you know what you want, and shop till you find it.

THE LANGUAGE OF MORTGAGES

Mortgages come with a language all their own, and to the uninitiated it can be quite confusing. Here are some of the most common terms you'll meet when you go shopping for a mortgage:

- *Amortization* refers to the number of years it will take to repay the entire amount of the mortgage based on a set of fixed payments. The *term* is the amount of time that the mortgage agreement covers, usually anywhere from six months to five years.
- A *first mortgage* is a debt registered against a property that is secured by a first call on the property. If you don't make the required payments — referred to as *defaulting* — the first lender has first right to the property. A *second mortgage* comes next in line and carries a higher interest rate, reflecting the increased risk to the lender.
- An *open mortgage* allows you to repay the loan on any payment date without penalty. A *closed mortgage* cannot be pre-paid in total or renegotiated prior to the end of the term.
- A *fixed-rate mortgage* has an interest rate that remains the same throughout the term, regardless of whether rates move up or down. A *variable-rate* (also called *floating-* or *adjustable-rate*) *mortgage*'s rate is based on the prime lending rate and can be adjusted monthly to

reflect changes in current rates.

- A downpayment of 25% or more qualifies you for a *conventional mortgage*. With between 5% and 25%, you'll be dealing with a *high-ratio mortgage*.

COMING UP WITH THE DOWNPAYMENT

Once you get over being a scaredy-cat and decide you want to own a home, the next question you'll ask is, "How am I ever going to save enough for a downpayment?" The answer is simple: *telesis*.

It's easy to look at the real estate market and be overwhelmed by the size of the downpayment you'll need. Don't be put off. With a sound plan and a commitment to making your dreams a reality, you can put yourself in a home of your own.

First, decide how much you are prepared to spend and how large a mortgage payment you can handle. Next, figure out your expected downpayment and how long you're prepared to wait before you jump into the market. The longer you can wait, the more you can accumulate. The less time you have, the more you'll have to put aside each month to meet your goal. Finally, get saving.

The best way to build your downpayment? Sign up for a periodic investment plan. Offered through most financial institutions, these plans make setting aside a specific amount each month very convenient. Once you've determined how much you want to invest, each month you can have that amount automatically transferred from your account to purchase the investment of your choice, be it a mutual fund, term deposit, or what have you. Over time you accumulate a substantial nest egg while minimizing the pinch; after all, your money is taken before you can even think about how to spend it.

Of course, you have to find the money before you can put it aside or allow it to be whisked into a periodic investment plan. While most of us live up to our means — we spend almost every cent we make — if you're determined to find the money for a downpayment, you will. It may mean tightening your belt or, at the very least, reviewing how you spend your money to see where you can cut corners. Track your spending for a couple of months. You may be pleasantly surprised at how much you can set aside once you eliminate all the little frivolities that, in the long run, add very little to your life. There are dozens of things you can do to save money (see the suggestions in Chapters 4 and 5), but if you can't seem to find a place to cut, show your budget to your mother. In minutes she'll find a dozen places where you are wasting money. In lieu of your mom, turn to a close friend for help.

When it comes to deciding how to invest the money you're accumulating for a downpayment, depending on your time frame, you may want to be somewhat aggressive. After all, if you rely on a GIC paying 4% interest, following the Rule of 72 (which says that you divide the interest rate into 72 for the number of years it will take to double the investment) it'll take 18 years for your money to double. If you invest in a balanced mutual fund and manage an average return of 9%, you'll shorten your doubling time to just eight years. Look to an aggressive-growth mutual fund and you may see your return jump to 12%, and your money double in six years.

If you've been paying premiums on a whole life insurance policy, you've probably accumulated a cash value against which you can borrow. Check it out with your insurance company. Some people turn to parents, grandparents, or other relatives to help if they are able. In the U.S., in 1991, almost a quarter of all first-time home buyers relied on loans and gifts from relatives to make up their downpayments. Note well: Your financial institution will want to know where the money came from (they'll check your bank records to see if it was really yours), so you'll need a letter from your benefactor explicitly stating that the money is a gift and that there is no expectation of repayment.

Planning to get married? Ask for cash in lieu of yet another small appliance. Explain that this will help you into your first home, and be explicit about how important it is that this dream come true. If you are buying a new home because you are divorcing, consider asking for your alimony payments as one lump-sum amount to be paid from the proceeds of the sale of your principal residence. This will get you back into the housing market as fast as possible — and maximize the real value of every dollar you receive.

Don't forget about the RRSP Home Buyers' Plan. Under this plan you can withdraw up to $20,000 from your RRSP as a tax-free loan toward a downpayment on a home. The loan must be repaid in annual installments or the amount not repaid will be included in your income for that year and taxed! Check my website, www.gvomoney.com, to see how the plan works.

Consider a partner. Can you find a friend or relative who would also like to get into the housing market, and with whose help you can manage the downpayment? Alternatively, if your partner has the cash and you don't, you can assume a larger percentage of the mortgage as your responsibility. Treat this transaction as a business arrangement, and take the appropriate legal steps to ensure you are both well protected.

WHAT FLAVOUR IS YOUR MORTGAGE?

The size of your downpayment will dictate the type of mortgage for which you will qualify. With 25% or more of the purchase price down, you can finance your new home using a fixed-rate conventional mortgage. This is the vanilla type of mortgage, which charges a fixed amount of interest for a specific period of time and is restricted to a maximum of 75% of the loan-to-value ratio.

Loan-to-value ratio is exactly what it sounds like: the ratio between the loan amount and the value of the property. So a 75% loan-to-value ratio means that 75% of the value of the property can be financed, while the other 25% must come from your resources. The value is usually defined as the lesser of the appraisal value and the purchase price.

For uninsured variable-rate mortgages (VRMs), financing is restricted to a maximum of 70% of the loan-to-value ratio, so you'll have to come up with at least 30% of the purchase price as your downpayment. For insured VRMs, financing is restricted to a maximum of 85% of the loan-to-value ratio, so the minimum downpayment required is 15%.

If you can only arrange a downpayment of between 10% and 24% of the purchase price of the property, then you'll need a high-ratio mortgage. These mortgages are insured through the Canada Mortgage and Housing Corporation, or CMHC, and are usually restricted to a maximum of 90% of the first $180,000, and 80% of the balance of the loan-to-value ratio. So a minimum of 10% of the equity must come from your own resources. You should also note that an application fee and insurance premium are applicable for high-ratio mortgages. This insurance premium is calculated as a percentage of the loan amount, and the percentage depends on the loan-to-value ratio. The higher the loan-to-value ratio, the higher the premium cost. This premium may be paid in cash or added to the mortgage amount. The following table shows examples of the insurance premium that is usually added to the mortgage:

LOAN-TO-VALUE RATIO	COST
0.0% to 65%	0.50% of loan amount
65.1% to 75%	0.75% of loan amount
75.1% to 80%	1.25% of loan amount
80.1% to 85%	2.00% of loan amount
85.1% to 90%	2.50% of loan amount

In 1992, CMHC introduced "First Home Loan Insurance," designed to assist first-time home buyers. In 1998, the program was broadened to include all home buyers. This program requires a minimum downpayment of only 5%. The maximum loan amount is calculated as 95% of the lesser of the sale price, the appraised value, or the maximum house price.

HOUSE HUNTING

When it comes to buying a house, do-it-yourselfers may think they can save a ton of cash handling the details on their own and negotiating away the commission the seller would have paid, but it ain't necessarily so. Home buying is a complicated legal and financial business. A guide who has been around the block a few times can help substantially in assuaging your fears, calming your nerves, and keeping you on the straight and narrow in terms of your home-ownership priorities.

"The first thing you have to do is choose an agent and a mortgage person to work with," says Karen Bryce, a real estate agent with Sutton Group. Ask friends and family who they've dealt with, what they liked, and whom they think would be a good fit for you. You should get great service from both these individuals as you go through this exciting and somewhat frightening experience. "That means you get callbacks and lots of information. I have clients come in for a three-hour appointment before we start looking at houses," Karen says. "They have to feel comfortable with me. And after 15 years of doing business, I've only had two people not prepared to work exclusively with me.

"I like to get everything on the table before I start. I explain that I only work on commission and that I don't get paid until the house closes. Some people have no idea how this works so it's best to talk about it.

PUTTING A ROOF OVER YOUR HEAD   93

I need to know how much they are qualified for — how much mortgage they will get, what downpayment they have, and, by extension, how much they can spend — so I don't even take them to see a house until they have been to the bank and pre-qualified. Of course, just because you're pre-qualified for a mortgage doesn't mean you can just go out and buy a house. You still have to fulfill certain conditions.

"Ninety-nine percent of people have never seen an offer before," says Karen. "So in my first meeting with a client, I explain about agent relationships — the relationship between the buyer and her agent and the seller and her agent — and how I'm compensated. The contract clients sign is usually for a two-month term." According to Karen, if the agent is listening and the buyer's requests aren't outrageous, it should take between two and three weeks to find the house.

That's exactly how it happened to me. When I was shopping for my semi-detached home, I was prospected by an agent who said she was willing to work with me. I told her that I was just looking around, getting familiar with the market in the neighbourhoods I was interested in, and wouldn't be ready to buy until the summer (it was early February). She said that was fine and

The top producer in her office in her first year in real estate, Karen Bryce has been managing her clients' expectations and fulfilling their dreams since 1985. As associate broker with Sutton Group–Bayview Realty Inc., Karen sold more than 40 homes in 1998. Karen believes there's usually no reason people should be helping pay their landlords' mortgages because "you could be investing that money in your own home." Real estate is a seven-day-a-week job, but Karen and her husband like to take time out to go to the movies or vacation abroad — when they aren't jumping through hoops for their two grown children.

that she would help me look around. We looked at lots of houses, just to get a good idea of which of my must-haves and which of my want-to-haves were likely to show up together. Then we found it. It was the perfect little house. I fell in love. We put in an offer and it was accepted to close in April. "Whew," I said. "That was fast!" While I was happy with my new house, I was breathless with the speed of it all. The lesson here: Don't go shopping before you're ready to sign an offer.

"The next thing we talk about," says Karen, "is location. Location and price are the two most important factors." You have to decide where you want to live and how much you're willing to pay. "More than once I've asked clients if they are going to change the amount they'll spend, or change the location in which they look."

People always have priorities in terms of what they're looking for in a house. They usually write down a wish list. But they often don't have a specific mental picture of what the house should look like. That's for the best, since Karen suggests that buyers should not be too tied to many of the things people typically put on their lists: air conditioning, central vacuum, finished basement. You can always rig in these types of extras. Even an open-concept feeling can be created post-purchase. It is more important when you go house shopping to be clear on the elements that *can't* be changed. Don't be unduly influenced by the nice-to-haves. They can become the conditions, in your own mind, that will affect which house you choose over another, and how much you pay.

"Even if you fall in love with the first house you walk into," says Karen, "I'd still want you to look at 10 to 12 other houses so you can see what else you can get for the same money." The kitchen in the first house might be the best, but the second house may have a perfectly finished basement. You then have to ask yourself: What's more important, the kitchen or the basement, and what will it cost to remedy what's lacking? If it costs twice as much to get the kitchen you want than the basement you want, then buying the perfect kitchen and doing the basement later probably makes the most sense.

The other important thing to talk about is the offer. "When you do an offer, the agents do not read you the clauses that are standard — the fine print. So you should go over the offer and make sure you understand it before the time comes to sign," says Karen.

At the offer stage Karen explains the waivers and the fact that in most cases there will be two conditions present: inspection and financing. "If there are any structural problems with the house, if the roof is about to go or termites have invaded, then an inspection will tell you that." The other thing the inspection will do is highlight all the little things you'll need to fix. "You will never get a perfect house," says Karen, "not even if you buy brand new." And she's right. By its very nature, home ownership means you'll always be fixing something.

As a first-time home buyer, you might think that you would somehow be involved in the offer process. Perhaps you've imagined negotiating with the vendor. Even if you expected simply to be present when the offer was presented, you'd be wrong. "I review the offer with my clients who wish to buy, and then I alone take that offer to the vendor's agent and the vendor. If there is negotiating to be done, I move between the seller and the buyer. When the offer is accepted by the vendor, the property is sold except for any outstanding conditions." Assuming all goes well, your agent will have you sign waivers for all the conditions of the offer.

"The closing date also has to be negotiated," says Karen. Flexibility is often the key to working this issue out quickly. Sometimes a vendor has no choice on the closing date, so the purchaser may have to be flexible. I remember when we were buying our house on Carlaw, in Toronto, I was pregnant and expanding quickly. I was determined to be in my new home before I was too big to walk up the stairs under my own power. And since we needed to have access to the house for a couple of weeks before we moved in so we could paint, an early closing date was important. But as Karen points out, "as first-time buyers, if you can give multiple closing dates, you have a better chance when there are a number of people making offers."

What else gives you an edge in the multiple-offer situation? Ultimately, the only way to win this game is to pick the right price. "Lots of people say they don't want to get into a multiple-offer situation," says Karen. In reality, it's not that big a deal. Go with your best shot and resolve yourself to the outcome. You'll be no further behind than having made no offer at all.

HIRING YOUR HOME TEAM

Buying a home involves a host of middlemen, all of whom can offer real value to the process or jimmy up the works. Whom you choose for your home team will make all the difference in terms of how smoothly that process goes and how secure you can feel in your final decision.

Quarterbacking the whole process is the real estate agent. Watch out for agents who are representing both the seller and the buyer. In such a situation, no real negotiation may ever take place, and that should give you pause. After all, you want to be sure that your real estate agent is acting in your best interest.

Look for an agent who knows the neighbourhood you're interested in, so he's familiar with whether there are endemic termite problems or leaky basements. He should also be able to provide you with information on local services, such as transportation and schools. Stick with an agent who is at the job full-time.

The lawyer may be the most important person in the transaction, but all too often she is brought in too late to be truly useful. If she receives the offer — which is a valid and binding contract — after it's been negotiated and signed, she's bound to follow whatever is provided in the agreement. So even if she spots a problem, you'll likely have to live with it.

Real estate law is a specialty. Your lawyer should be familiar with the type of property you're buying. So, if you're buying a cottage, a referral to a lawyer who knows the ins and outs of rural properties will be the best advice your city lawyer can give you.

Your existing relationship with a financial institution may stand you in good stead when it comes time to negotiate your mortgage. Start with a pre-approval. That'll not only let you know what you can reasonably afford, it can make your offer more attractive for sellers. However, just because you've been pre-approved doesn't mean you should eliminate the "conditional on financing" clause from your offer, since your pre-approval is in turn conditional on your home passing muster with an appraiser.

The appraiser is the middleman who works behind the scenes and out of your control. But what he has to say will have an impact on your home-buying decision. Most appraisals are "drive-bys," which do not require a detailed home inspection. However, if the home is priced significantly above or below market prices, the appraiser may want to do a more detailed inspection. The appraisal cost is paid by the lender and passed on to you, unless you negotiate otherwise with the lender up front.

Home inspectors — be they engineers or contractors in a previous life — are the only people who can identify structural defects within a house, and what it will cost to make the required replacements or repairs. However, since anyone can call himself an inspector, a personal reference is important. You should also look for someone who is certified or registered with a provincial or national association, such as the Provincial Association of Certified Home Inspectors (PACHI) in Ontario. A home inspection should take about three hours, and you should be there to see what's being done. And a good real estate agent will be there too, since she'll want to hear what the problems are.

PREPARING FOR THE MORTGAGE INTERVIEW

Once you've found the perfect house, it's time to nail down your mortgage. To do so, you'll have to go to your preferred financial institution for an interview.

There's a great deal that goes into being prepared for the mortgage interview. My book *Shopping for Money* includes everything you need to know about all types of credit, and it tells you what lenders look for. When applying for a mortgage, you have to provide specific information about your financial circumstances. Take the following documentation with you to the interview:

- personal identification, such as your driver's licence or social insurance card, as well as a list of personal information, including your address, the name of your landlord or present mortgage holder, and the amount you are now paying in rent or for your mortgage
- a list of all your assets and liabilities, with a realistic value set for each; also a list of all your credit cards, as you'll probably be asked for the numbers (to check your credit history)
- written confirmation of employment income from your employer, and confirmation in writing of income from any other sources, showing a consistent amount from year to year; take your notices of assessment from CCRA as proof of your income history
- for self-employed people, the last three years' income-tax returns and/or financial statements
- a copy of the accepted purchase agreement, along with a statement regarding urea formaldehyde foam insulation (this statement is normally included on the standard offer-of-purchase forms used by real estate brokers) and a photograph of the house or a copy of the listing
- your lawyer's name, full address, and telephone number
- the name, address, and telephone number of someone who can provide access to the property for the appraisal (this may be the realtor or the vendor)
- heating cost estimate and property tax estimate (usually found on the listing) and condominium fees, if applicable
- for properties that do not have municipal services, well and/or septic tank certificates
- confirmation of downpayment. If it is a gift, a letter confirming that

it is a gift with no repayment terms is needed. If the downpayment is to come from a second mortgage, a written confirmation of the terms and conditions of this mortgage must be provided by the second mortgagor.

CHOOSING A TERM YOU CAN LIVE WITH

What term should you take? That's a good question. Before you look at the issue of term specifically, there are things you should consider so you can manage your mortgage to your best advantage.

When you're looking at term and interest rates, you also need to look at payment amounts and amortization. Interest rate, payment amount, and amortization period are directly related. If you take a $100,000 mortgage at 10% with a 20-year amortization period, your monthly payment would be $951.67. If the rate was 11%, your monthly payment would be higher, at $1,015.64. If the rate was 9%, your monthly payment would be $889.19. So the lower your interest rate, the lower your payment amount.

Now let's look at how the amortization period affects your payment. A $100,000 mortgage at 10% with a 20-year amortization period has monthly payments of $951.67. Choose a 25-year amortization period, and your payments would be $894.49. A 15-year amortization period would give you payments of $1,062.27. So the longer your amortization period, the lower your payment amount, and the shorter the amortization period, the higher your payment amount.

Putting these two factors together will help you figure out what you can live with. The first place to start is to figure out the payment amount with which you'll be comfortable over the long term. Since interest rates are beyond your control, you only have the option of playing with the amortization period to get the payment amount you want. Having done that, you have to consider what will happen if rates go up or down. Since the "up" is the one we all hate, let's look at it first.

If rates go up, you have two choices. First, you can work the increased payment amount into your budget. Second, you can increase your amortization to bring your payment amount back in line. Now, that may mean moving your mortgage to another financial institution, so be prepared for the cost of writing a new mortgage.

What if rates go down? Great! Now you could benefit from a lower payment amount. But think about this a minute. You've already worked the payment into your budget. If you keep your payment amount the same, you'll be paying off your mortgage a lot faster. So don't pocket the difference. Keep applying it to your mortgage.

One final point on managing your mortgage: Rather than locking yourself into a high payment amount that you have to struggle to make each month, do yourself a favour. If you can, choose a payment amount you find easier to live with. Then make sure you have pre-payment options that allow you to make additional payments when you have the cash available. That way, you'll have a payment amount you can manage comfortably, and you can still aggressively pay down your mortgage.

Now, back to the term. You still have to decide what term is best for you. Here are some questions to ask yourself:

- *Where are rates now and where are they going?*

  Trying to predict where rates are going is a tough job. You can twist yourself into knots worrying about what will happen. At the end of 1992, we saw interest rates fall to their lowest point in 35 years. No one ever thought they'd get that low again. Wrong! 1997 brought even lower rates. It would be equally wrong to assume that rates can't skyrocket again. I know it's bad economics, but if anyone had told us in the seventies that interest rates would be in the upper teens in the eighties, we'd have said they were crazy.

  If you feel rates are at a point you can live with and you want to guarantee that rate for as long as possible, you'd choose a long term; this is referred to as "going long." This is a good strategy if rates appear to be rising.

  But what if rates are falling? You may want to remain flexible to take advantage of future lower rates. One way is to choose a short term — referred to as "going short." Then, when your term is up, you can renew at the lower rate. Another option is to go for an open mortgage. You'll pay a higher rate of interest, but you'll have the flexibility to pre-pay or renew at any time. You could also choose a variable-rate mortgage so that as rates come down you benefit from the lower rate. Or you could choose a convertible mortgage, which lets you take advantage of lower rates and then lock in when you feel the rates have bottomed out.

- *Do you want a fixed payment amount?*
  Some people choose a long-term mortgage to ensure they'll have a fixed payment amount they can live with for as long as possible. This makes it much easier to plan for your mortgage payments and everything else in your life — particularly when your cash flow is tight and even a small upward movement in interest rates would be disastrous.

- *Are you a gambler?*
  Some people don't mind the stomach turning associated with fluctuations in rates. Others can't stand the stress. If you're not comfortable with the game, pick a payment amount you can live with and lock in.

- *Are you prepared to keep a close eye on the market?*
  If you're going to choose a short-term, open, variable-rate, or convertible mortgage, then be prepared to keep a careful watch on what interest rates are doing so you can lock in when rates bottom out. If you're not prepared to do this, go with a mid- to long-term rate.

PAYMENT FREQUENCIES

Financial institutions offer a variety of payment frequencies so you can choose when and how often you wish to make your regular payments. The traditional monthly payment amount is calculated using the amortization tables available in libraries and most bookstores. However, if you're paid semimonthly, biweekly, or weekly, you may wish to use a payment frequency that matches your cash flow.

Some people want to take advantage of the savings made available by using a faster-pay or accelerated frequency. With this, you make extra payments against your mortgage, but in such small amounts that those extra payments fit easily into your cash flow. With accelerated payments, in one year you make the equivalent of 13 months of payments in the space of 12 months. That extra payment reduces your principal, so you save on your interest costs in the long term. Based on a mortgage of $100,000 at a rate of 11% amortized over 25 years, you would save $62,486 in interest over the life of the mortgage using a faster-pay biweekly or weekly frequency.

Many financial institutions allow you to change your payment frequency as your needs change. Be aware that there may be a charge for interest adjustment from your current payment due date to the revised date.

MAKING EXTRA PAYMENTS AGAINST YOUR PRINCIPAL

The best way to pay your mortgage off fast is to pour any extra money you have into the mortgage whenever you can. However, this is one area in which all mortgages are not created equal. While some banks offer very flexible options, others still think you should fit with their schedules. If extra payments are a priority for you, shop carefully for the mortgage that offers you the level of flexibility you're looking for.

At least one bank offers an option that will let you make an additional payment up to 12 times a year (or once a month) up to your normal payment amount. If your regular monthly payment amount is $900, you could make an additional payment of anywhere from $100 to $900 every month and that money would go directly to your principal. Back when I was consulting on a regular basis, I found this feature extremely useful. In those months when billings were good, I could double my regular monthly payment and pay down my mortgage while saving bags and bags of interest. An additional feature that came attached to this one was the fact that each time I doubled, I had the right to skip a future payment. What's the point? Well, in those months when the projects weren't coming fast and furiously, I could take pressure off my cash flow by skipping a monthly payment. Yes, I effectively negated the time and interest savings, but boy did that flexibility ever give me peace of mind. I still believe the options of doubling up and skipping are the best features in the marketplace.

While this next feature isn't as flexible as the first, it has its benefits. Some institutions let you increase your monthly payment up to double the original amount. So, if your regular monthly payment is $1,200, you could increase it to as much as $2,400. The drawback with this alternative is that with some financial institutions, once you raise your repayment amount, you can't go back.

Almost every lender lets you make a lump-sum payment of 10% to

20% of your original principal once a year. While some institutions want it on your anniversary date, others will let you do it on any payment date.

Balancing Mortgage Paydown with Other Goals

Did you know that 58% of Canadians with a mortgage don't have an RRSP? It seems that once that mortgage note is signed, getting rid of what can be the single largest debt we ever take on becomes of paramount importance. But the building of retirement assets is just as important. It all comes down to time. The longer you have your mortgage, the more interest you'll pay. And the earlier you begin saving for retirement, the more money you'll have accumulated through tax-deferred compound growth.

There are other parts of your financial life that also need to be managed. In coming up with a downpayment for a home, many people tap all their available resources. They even dip into their emergency fund (if they have one at all) to minimize the amount of mortgage they have to take, or to qualify. But an emergency fund is an important part of the plan, and without it you leave yourself open to all sorts of dire consequences.

Doing anything to the exclusion of everything else is not healthy. You need an emergency fund for the near future. And you need to sock away money regularly for your long-term future needs. So, if you're asking yourself whether you should contribute to an RRSP or pay down your mortgage, here are some factors to consider.

If your income is particularly high one year, then your marginal tax rate will also be high, and a contribution to an RRSP may significantly reduce your tax liability. But if your income is low one year, the tax savings from a small contribution limit and lower marginal tax rate might be outweighed by the interest savings from paying down your mortgage. Remember, too, that the further you are from retirement, the more valuable are contributions to an RRSP, since the money has a longer period to benefit from compounding. The closer retirement is, the less impact an RRSP contribution will have in terms of compounding, and the more important it is to get rid of your debt.

The amount of time left on your mortgage amortization schedule is also important. The faster you repay your principal, the more interest you save in the long run. So, you'll save more interest by paying down a mortgage with a 20-year amortization remaining than one with a 5-year amortization remaining.

Avoid falling into the RRSP carry-forward trap. You may be tempted to carry forward your unused deduction room indefinitely for use in later years, but remember that delaying contributions means your RRSP won't have had the time to do greatest justice to your contributions in terms of compounded return. One $5,000 contribution delayed for just five years will cost your RRSP over $16,000, assuming a rate of return of just 8% — another good reason to reflect carefully on the decision.

Of course, there will always be circumstances when you'll want to swing your decision in favour of a mortgage paydown. If the interest paid on the mortgage is significantly higher than the return being earned on an RRSP, paying down the mortgage may be appropriate.

The answer to the RRSP-versus-mortgage paydown question does not have to be either/or. You can make your maximum RRSP contribution and use the proceeds from your tax refund to pay down your mortgage. Let's say you decided to contribute $8,000 a year to your RRSP. With a marginal tax rate of 45%, you would receive a tax refund of $3,600 each year. Let's also say you apply that refund against your $100,000 mortgage (with an interest rate of 10%). Assuming an average return of 10% each year on your RRSP portfolio, in 30 years your retirement savings will have grown to about $1.4 million. And by applying your refund to your mortgage, you will save almost $89,000 in interest and have your mortgage paid off in 12 years instead of 25. This strategy lets you save for retirement and secure your future, earn tax-sheltered income, reduce the amount of current income tax paid, and reduce the amount of interest to be paid on the mortgage, not to mention the amortization. Many financial institutions have software programs that can show you how much you will save by applying your tax refund as a payment against your mortgage principal. Ask for some examples to see how much you can save. It makes a lot more sense to work toward both objectives than to grapple with the issue of which should be a priority. With the right balance, you can have it all!

MOVIN' ON UP

If you're considering upgrading to a new house, you may also be considering one or more of the following questions:

- How do I get the same great rate on my new mortgage as I have on my existing mortgage?
- Should I discharge the mortgage and take out a new mortgage? What will that cost me in penalty interest?
- Should I let the purchaser assume the mortgage and take out a new mortgage on the new house?

If you decide you want to take your mortgage with you when you move, then it's time to learn all about the portability option on your mortgage. By porting your mortgage, you can continue taking advantage of your existing mortgage rate. If you find you need additional financing, you can blend your existing mortgage with a new one, eliminating the need for a much costlier second mortgage.

The biggest benefit of porting your mortgage is that it eliminates the interest penalties that apply to a straight early discharge of an existing mortgage. This can mean major savings, particularly when the interest rate on your existing mortgage is higher than the rate currently available for a new mortgage.

You can port your mortgage in one of three ways:

1. If you're taking your remaining mortgage term, interest rate, and principal balance to your new property without increasing or decreasing the principal, that's called a straight port.
2. If you're an empty nester, or simply downgrading to a less expensive home, you'll be interested in porting and decreasing. The mortgage is ported, but the principal is reduced. A penalty for lost interest, also referred to as an interest-rate differential, or IRD, may be payable when a smaller loan amount is requested.
3. If you're upgrading and need more financing on your new home than originally existed on the home being sold, then you'll port and increase. The mortgage is ported, the principal is increased, and your interest rate is blended so that you still have the advantage of the original rate on at least a portion of the mortgage.

If you plan to port your mortgage, both you and the new property will still have to meet normal lending guidelines, so a full mortgage application and property appraisal will be completed. And you can only execute your portability option if your existing mortgage is in good standing. Since a new mortgage document must be drawn and registered on title, normal appraisal charges, legal fees, and an administration fee may apply.

Setting the price on your existing home

Once you decide to put your house on the market, one of the first things you'll have to think about is where you'll set your asking price. This is probably the most crucial issue when it comes to listing your home. It entails a financial strategy, along with all the emotion that accompanies selling — and buying — a home. Price is the primary motivation for long hours of negotiation and for the eventual decision to buy or not to buy.

House prices are closely tied to fluctuations in our economy. Prices soar and plummet on a variety of factors including inflation, where interest rates are, where they are going and, of course, demand and supply. And price has two sides in dire opposition. Buyers always want to know if the market has reached the bottom. Sellers want to know if prices are going up.

So, where do you start if you're planning to sell your home and have to set a price? Begin by checking the market value of your property. Ask at least two real estate agents for appraisals. Check the multiple listings for prices of similar homes in your area. Carefully assess how market conditions have changed in the last six months and how they may affect your asking price. Then set your price within 3% to 5% of the average price you've come up with. If the market indicates that your home is worth about $189,000, set your price no higher than about $198,450. Of course, you could set your price at the bottom end of the scale — $179,500 — if you want to get lots of offers and close quickly. You might even benefit from a bidding war that drives up the price slightly.

If you set your price high because you *feel* your house is worth more, don't be surprised if it takes a while for an offer to come in, or if you then have to drop your price once, twice, or even several times in order to interest buyers. Don't be insulted by low-ball offers. And don't think that just because you need the money to get you into a more expensive home that buyers will be willing to fund your dreams. In a buyer's market — one where buyers set the tone for sales because there are fewer of them — buyers are much more likely to win in negotiations because there's so much available, and they usually have time on their side. In a seller's market — one where sellers write the ticket and buyers often bid it up — buyers will go to lengths to make their offer attractive.

Setting the right price may just be the most important aspect of selling your home. Even with the ideal location, the perfect features, and the home in tiptop condition, the price has to be right for buyers to bite. And since most purchasers already have a price in mind when they set about house hunting, pricing too high could take your home right out of their "viewing" range. Also keep in mind that the right price means your house will spend less time on the market, so you'll have to spend less time keeping it in "show" condition and negotiating.

When the time comes to sell, resist the urge to overprice your house. Setting a reasonable price that intrigues potential buyers into your home will, over the long run, save you money, disappointment, and time.

8

Establishing Your Credit Identity

The human species, according to the best theory I can form of it, is composed of two distinct races, the men who borrow, and the men who lend.

CHARLES LAMB

A money lender. He services you in the present tense; he lends you in the conditional mood; keeps you in the subjunctive; and ruins you in the future.

JOSEPH ADDISON

L ots of books have been written about the evils of borrowing (never borrow), how to get out of debt (stop borrowing), and how to stay out of debt (never ever borrow again). I've even written one myself: *Shopping for Money*. In it, I explain how credit works and how to make it work better. It has been the least popular of the five books I've written so far. Yet, clearly people have a problem with borrowing. In 1997, bankruptcies in Canada were at their highest level ever, with a total of 97,497 bankruptcies (that's 2.9 bankruptcies for every thousand Canadians). In fact, the bankruptcy rate has more than quadrupled since 1984.[13]

The fact is, credit is a way of life and if we try to live without it, it becomes very hard to accomplish our goals. After all, does anyone you

---

13 "The Credit Line," Credit Counselling Service of Metropolitan Toronto, June 1997.

A recognized leader in the field of credit risk management, Barb Godin spent 14 years with the Bank of Nova Scotia, where her most recent position was senior vice-president responsible for retail lending and automotive finance. Previously Barb was a member of the Management Advisory Board for the Office of the Superintendent of Bankruptcies and two-term president of the Canadian Credit Risk Management Association. In 1998 Barb moved her model cars, husband, and kids to the United States, where she is now executive vice-president and chief credit risk management officer for KeyBank USA.

know have the cash to buy their first home without borrowing? Credit isn't bad. How we use credit is the problem.

Priorities have shifted dramatically over the past several decades. People who grew up during the thirties, forties, or fifties believed that they had to save. They paid cash for almost everything they bought. They were willing to wait until they were well established and had all the necessities before splurging on the extras.

Barbara Godin talks about growing up in a strict European home. She says, "We saved all of our milk bottles. My father made his own wine and beer at home. We even churned our own butter. We learned the value of every single cent. And when we did spend money, it wasn't on candy or pop, the non-necessities of life. It was on a good, sturdy pair of shoes." When she wanted a new bicycle, her dad said, "You can't afford the bicycle until you have the good shoes."

The lesson was well learned. Barb and her husband worked hard to buy their first car. "We worked every day in the office until 6:00 p.m. Then we travelled for two hours by bus to a factory and cleaned toilets. We did 200 toilets each night. We'd get home at 1:00 a.m. We did this seven days a week. We saved every single dollar. When we went into the dealership, we paid for the car in cash. We were just kids, in our early twenties. I'll never forget that. That to me was a much better experience than saying, 'Oh, put it on a charge card or I'll pay for it over time.'"

The sixties, seventies, and eighties saw a significant shift in people's attitudes toward borrowing. Then it was considered the only way to get ahead. People leveraged investments. They took on huge debt loads. They wanted it all — immediately. The idea of working, saving, and then buying was a thing of the past; the new approach was to charge the purchase and pay it off over time. The result: huge debt loads that have kept growing year after year, resulting in phenomenal levels of personal bankruptcy.

There's a balance that has to be struck between the I-want-it-now camp and the I-need-to-save-for-it camp. "That's where the credit trade-off comes in," says Barb. "It's very difficult to say to someone applying for credit, 'Why are you trying to get a loan for a $20,000 entertainment centre when you haven't bought a home yet and you haven't built up any assets? Where are your priorities?'" But even if the lender isn't saying it aloud to you, rest assured that he or she is thinking it. It's all part of the credit analysis that allows lenders to determine whether you're a good risk. As Bulwer Lytton wrote in 1864, "There is no test of a man's character more generally adopted than the way in which his money is managed. Money is a terrible blab; she will betray the secrets of her owner whatever he do to gag her. His virtues will creep out in her whisper — his vices she will cry aloud at the top of her tongue."

"The privacy issue," says Barb, "is a big deal. People don't want to be counselled anymore. While previously I might have asked, 'Are you sure this is what you want?' now it's simply a matter of do they qualify." On the credit side, lenders have lost their advisory role. "Credit has become a commodity," says Barb. "When I grew up, credit was not a commodity. It was something you sought advice on. Today people say, 'What's your price. I demand it. I expect it. Give it to me.' Now investments are the strong advisory product."

While the installment loan used to be the credit of choice for most people, the focus has shifted to revolving credit — credit cards and personal lines of credit. Unfortunately, if you choose to use revolving credit, you miss the checks and balances that lenders typically use to validate your reason for borrowing. Instead, because the credit is readily available, it's easy to use without thought of the other aspects of your financial life.

Most people don't understand how to use credit to their advantage. They react to their circumstances, and they keep reacting, as they get further and further into debt. When the debt becomes unmanageable, they throw up their arms in despair and say that credit is evil. Well, it's not. Well-planned borrowing can be a useful way to realize dreams and achieve financial goals. Well-planned borrowing can get you where you want to be. But it takes a good understanding of how credit works, when to use credit, and which type of credit will make borrowing work for you.

ESTABLISHING A CREDIT RATING

If you are a good risk and have qualified to use it, it's credit. If you've used it, it's debt. It's funny how a single concept can have such different meanings depending on which end of the stick you're holding. If you've got credit, you're great. You're responsible. You're worthy. You're an up-and-comer. If you've got debt, exactly the opposite is true. Yet we're talking about the same thing: your ability to use someone else's money to achieve your goals.

You can't develop a credit rating until you have paid back a loan. A credit rating is your reputation in terms of your ability to pay back money you've borrowed in a responsible and timely way. If you've been consistently late in making your payments, you'll have a bad credit reputation. If you've ever missed a payment completely, you'll have an even worse rep. If you've always made your payments on time, you will have a great credit rating and just about anyone will be willing to lend to you under the right circumstances.

One way to start building a credit reputation is to borrow some money to contribute to an RRSP. You can pay back the loan over a five- or six-month period and you'll have started saving for the future. And you don't have to worry about whether or not they'll give you the loan. As long as you take the RRSP out with that lending institution, you'll get the loan.

Barb Godin talks about the process of lenders granting credit. "When you sign a credit application form, you give the lender permission to check your credit rating. If you have no credit history, we don't know if you would be a good credit risk or not. So immediately, you become an unknown commodity and that's harder to deal with."

A credit card is one of the easiest ways to establish a credit rating. Apply for a card with a low limit, make small purchases, pay off the card each month, and become a credit star. Another way to establish a credit rating is to take out a loan. If you are a first-time borrower, you may need a guarantor to get the loan (the guarantor is a person who has established a credit reputation and who guarantees to repay the loan if you don't). When you pay back that money promptly, you establish your credit rating. If you have assets such as a car, investments, or a home to use as collateral, you can use that collateral to secure the loan. If you don't repay the loan, the financial institution will seize the asset pledged as collateral and sell it or cash it in order to collect its money.

Some people have difficulty establishing that they even exist when it comes to getting credit. If you are a married woman and all the cards are in your husband's name, even if you make the payments on the card, you're contributing to his credit rating, not your own. The card company doesn't care who signed the cheques. They base their reports to the credit bureau on who holds the card. Women who are recently divorced or widowed often face the shock that they don't exist in the world of credit, simply because all the credit reporting was done in their husbands' names. If you are a married woman, make sure you have at least one credit card in your own name. And use it. You'll have to apply for it and qualify for it on your own. Initially, you may have to use a secured credit card. A secured credit card is one that is fully secured, meaning there's no risk to the credit card company because you provide the company with enough cash to cover your balance. Financial institutions typically want twice the amount of credit you're asking for. So if you want a credit card with a $500 balance, you must put up $1,000 in cash. After you've made regular payments for about a year or so, the financial institution will drop the security requirement and return your deposit.

Barb Godin says that prior to the early 1990s all reporting for a couple was done in the man's name. Now, however, credit bureaus have separated the reporting for men and women. To make sure you establish a credit history, she suggests that when you go to borrow money, make sure you borrow it in your own name. And if you do borrow with your husband, insist that the credit granter report the information to the credit bureau in your name. Typically, credit granters report only in the name of the first person who signed on the credit application. If that happens to be the man — and typically, men are handed the paperwork first — all the credit history for that loan is reported in his name. So if you want the credit history for the loan, insist on signing first.

CHOOSING THE RIGHT CREDIT CARD

To know which credit card is best for you, you'll first have to decide how you plan to use the card. If you usually carry a balance from one month to the next, then a low-interest card is your best bet. If you pay your card off in full every month, look for a card that doesn't charge an annual fee and provides the longest grace period. If you want to take advantage of some of the "rewards" available, you'll have a lot to choose from, but you'll end up paying for the privilege.

Every specialty credit card has a list of features as long as your arm. Wading through the options — points for travel or gift selections, cash rebates, and myriad insurance coverages — can bewitch even the most cautious shoppers into believing they are getting good value. Some cards give you points toward the purchase or lease of a new car, assuming you already know you want to drive that kind of car. I have a girlfriend who continued to carry a balance on her Visa card because she'd accumulated so many points toward the purchase of a new truck she couldn't see giving up the card. If she'd saved the interest in a separate account, she'd have the truck by now. Some cards provide cash back on travel arrangements, providing you use their travel service. Or you can use your credit card to work toward a rebate on the purchase of your first home, which is a terrific head start as long as you're sure that institution will have the best mortgage deal when the time comes to sign the offer.

The real test of the value of a credit card is in what it does for you. Collision damage waiver on car rentals saves about $12 a day. Trip cancellation or interruption insurance, baggage insurance, and emergency travel or medical assistance provide you with peace of mind as you set off. Free traveller's cheques eliminate the usual 1% fee. And medical insurance benefits can look pretty attractive to holiday travellers. If you don't travel enough for these features to at least cover the cost of your card, you'll have to take a good look at the other bells and whistles that are meant to justify the fee.

Most specialty cards offer to extend for an additional 12 months the manufacturer's warranty on items purchased with the card. Some let you replace items bought on your credit card if they are lost or damaged within 90 days of purchase. Both these insurance features are a good deal, if you use them. If the only reason you have your card is to take advantage of the rewards (the banks' term for accumulating points to buy merchandise from a catalogue), make sure you claim your points and that you're not paying more for the merchandise from a catalogue than you would in a store. If you're looking for a card that will pay for itself, look for a card that will give you a cash rebate.

If you think you have to pay more for a snazzy credit card just to get a higher limit, save yourself some money. With a good credit history, you can simply write to your card issuer and ask for a credit increase. And it won't cost you a cent more in annual fees.

Whether you are a binge shopper or a model of self-control, limiting your access to credit is a smart move. No one needs more than two credit cards: one Visa, one MasterCard. Make one a no-frills, no-fee card and pack as many special features on the other as you'll use. If you carry a balance, make sure it's on the cheaper card.

While most credit cards allow you to take cash advances, don't. Advances accrue interest the moment they are taken.

TO BORROW OR NOT TO BORROW

Credit is a part of life. Whether you are financing the purchase of new appliances, replacing your furnace, or financing your children's education, borrowing can offer real benefits. After all, it'd be tough on the family to have to wait out a winter while you save the money you needed to buy a new furnace. Borrowing money, putting in the furnace, and paying off the loan in easily manageable payments makes a lot more sense. The question isn't simply whether or not to borrow. Sometimes we have to. Instead, ask yourself:

- Do I really need it?
- What's the mark-up?
- What's this going to cost me in total, including all the interest I'll have paid?
- What else do I have to give up to buy this?

If you need a car to keep your job, my best guess is that your answer to the first question is a resounding yes. The next question is a very important one. The cost of borrowing can vary significantly. The higher the interest rate you pay, the greater the cost. So are you going to buy a new car or a used one? Will you use bank financing, dealer financing, or will you lease? Also, the longer the term of the loan, the greater the cost to you. And what could be worse than having your loan outlive the item you borrowed to buy? By negotiating the lowest possible rate and taking the shortest possible term, you can pay off the loan faster while reducing the overall costs.

This leads to the third question. Since the longer you take to pay off the debt and the higher the mark-up, the more you'll pay, it's a worth-while exercise figuring out what that item will cost you in total. Let's say you buy a new car for $23,000, and your loan is for five years at 6%. That car will have cost you approximately $27,000. Do the same calculation on your credit-card purchases and you may not be quite so willing to charge ahead with your purchase. If you buy $2,500 worth of new furniture on a credit card that charges 17% interest, and you pay the minimum require-ment of 5% per month, it'll take you almost two years to pay off the charge, and that furniture will end up costing you almost $3,000.

Don't overlook the last question. The more the payments restrict your cash flow, the greater the cost to you in terms of stress and having to go without other things you feel contribute to a comfortable lifestyle. If you choose to make higher payments over a shorter term, you have to be sure your other important living needs can still be met. Resist the urge to steal from Peter to pay Paul. Paying off your loan quickly won't do you any good if you run up your credit cards during the process. If you choose instead to take a slightly longer term so that your payments are lower and fit more comfortably into your cash flow, remember this will mean a longer commitment and more interest over the full term of the loan. Weigh the answers to each of these questions carefully in deciding how you'll manage your credit needs.

Whether or not you qualify for a loan, you should question your borrowing motivation and rationale if:

1. You aren't sure the usefulness of a purchase will outlast the repay-ment period. It's bad enough when we spend cash on impulsive purchases, but when we have to pay for those impulsive actions way beyond the item's life, that can be really hard to take. Ask yourself, and answer honestly, "Will I be severely handicapped without the item?"

2. An installment plan makes it seem too good to pass up. That's not the right place to start. Begin by deciding whether you need the item at all, and then calculate how much you'll be paying in interest.

3. You're adding more debt to your already high debt load. Piling new debt on top of old is dangerous. It can lead you to the point where all your discretionary income is spent making loan payments. Avoid

this scenario by setting priorities before borrowing.

4. You haven't told anyone you intend to borrow. Making unilateral decisions about financing is a great way to put a strain on your relationships. And if you haven't worked up the guts to tell the most trusted people in your life, maybe it's because you know you won't be able to justify the decision to them. Perhaps you'd like to reconsider?

5. You're buying something to cheer yourself up. Lots of people go shopping to lift their spirits. Unfortunately, shopping, like drinking, can create a hangover. Ask yourself how you'll feel when the bill comes in. Adjust your perspective. Maybe a smaller, less-expensive treat will make you feel just as good.

6. You're trying to impress others. Some people need to keep up an image of success. Others shop together to build or strengthen their relationships — my stepdaughter, Amanda, refers to it humorously as "female bonding." But when it comes to paying off the card or repaying the loan, it isn't so funny. Ask yourself if it's really worth it.

KNOW THE COST OF BORROWING

People with credit cards fall into one of two categories: those who pay off their balances in full every month, and those who don't. If you're in the former category, you're using your credit card as a convenience and a short-term borrowing opportunity (because of the time between when you charge and when you have to pay). You're smart. It costs you little or nothing for the convenience (depending on the type of card you have) and you can accumulate all sorts of extra benefits by using your card — things like travel miles, extra purchase insurance, and the like. If you're in the second category, you have plenty of company. It's been estimated that approximately 60% of Canadian women carry a balance on their cards. Unfortunately, you are paying heavily for the privilege.

If you don't pay your balance off completely and on time, you'll be charged interest which is typically calculated on a daily basis. Interest calculations begin on the day the transaction is posted to your account, usually within a few days of having made the purchase. So, if you charged $1,000 last month and made a partial payment of $400 on the due date, you will still be charged interest on the full $1,000 up to the day the

$400 was credited, since you didn't pay off your balance completely. The remaining balance of $600 will become the "retail revolving balance," which will continue to accrue interest until it is repaid.

Financial institutions have done research showing that most people will go out of their way to earn .5% to .75% more on a GIC. Yet they will pay 7% to 14% more interest than necessary, just because it's a credit card. If you have an outstanding balance of $1,000 on which you're paying 17%, that's costing you more than $14 a month, or almost $169 a year. And that's after-tax dollars! You'd have to have a $1,000 GIC paying better than 24% to break even. If you can find a GIC paying 24%, let me know!

Instead of carrying a balance on your credit card, you'd be better off using an installment loan or personal line of credit to pay off your credit card. If you'd go out of your way to earn .5% more in interest, how far out of your way would you go to save 7% in interest costs? Fact is, you don't have to go far — just to your nearest financial institution. What are you waiting for?

The other thing to know about collecting credit cards and higher credit limits is that it can affect your ability to borrow money when you really do need it. If you're applying for a mortgage, the amount of credit you already have access to will be taken into account when deciding how much more you can borrow. Even if your cards are completely paid off, because you have those seven cards, each with a $3,000 credit limit, you have already been granted $21,000 in credit. Should you choose to, you could run all those cards to the limit, severely affecting your ability to repay your mortgage. So don't accumulate cards indiscriminately. Instead, choose the cards that do you the most service, and stick with one or two. You don't need store cards. They charge the highest interest. Go into your wallet now and cut them up. Everyone accepts Visa or MasterCard.

Did you know that when you borrow money to make an investment, the interest on that money is tax deductible? Let's say you sold some stock to pay off a $2,500 debt at 17%. You'd be saving $450 a year in interest costs. If you borrowed $2,500 to buy back that stock and paid 10% interest on the loan, that loan would cost you about $250 a year. And since the interest on a loan for investment purposes is tax deductible, you'd actually end up paying far less — up to 50% less — in after-tax dollars. Assuming a marginal tax rate of 40%, you could pay off your high-cost debt, have your stock, and still save $300 in interest.

Don't be so concerned about having a security net that you fail to use your resources to your best advantage. Start thinking about your money in terms of your overall net worth, rather than just two categories: how much you owe and how much you've saved. Get rid of that high-cost debt in small steps or large, and then you can reallocate the money you would have paid in interest to asset accumulation. Look at the big picture and then make the decisions necessary to paint that big picture black.

It's not unusual for people to borrow for what they feel are good reasons, only to find that over time they have grown a nasty amount of debt they find hard to cope with.

If your debt is costing you more than your savings are earning, cash out and pay off. If it sounds like I'm repeating myself, that's because I am. This is a crucial point. I do not mean to say that you should use your RRSP savings to pay off your debt, since the tax bite to cash out would make the whole exercise far too expensive. However, if you have unregistered savings such as a savings account, GIC, Canada Savings Bonds, or mutual funds that you've been putting aside, pay off your debt and start saving again. If you're still not convinced, here's my last shot at getting you to see your assets and your debts as belonging in the same pot.

Let's say you have a $5,000 loan and $5,000 in a GIC. The loan has an annual interest rate of 9%, and you're earning 4% on the GIC. If you keep the GIC for a year, you'll earn $200 in interest. But you'll have to pay tax on that money. Assuming your average tax rate is 30%, you'll pay $60 in tax so you'll end up with $140 in your pocket. The loan will cost you $450 this year, so you'll end up paying more than three times more in interest on the loan than you earned on your GIC. But if you used the $5,000 GIC to pay off your $5,000 loan, while you'll earn no interest, you'll also pay no interest and you'll end up ahead by $310. Got it?

Another way to reduce the cost of your debt is to *transfer your high-cost debt to a lower-rate loan.* This is called refinancing, and there are many ways to do it. You can take a consolidation loan and pay off all your existing loans so you have a single monthly payment each month. You can refinance by renegotiating an existing loan to a lower rate. Or you can apply for a lower-interest-rate credit card and transfer the balance on an existing card to the new card. It doesn't matter how you do it, just *do it!* It is obviously better to pay 10% on a loan than 17%. Yet so many people carry high-cost debt. Take the case of Paula. When she came to me to ask for advice, she had a $3,000 Visa balance, on which she was paying about 17%. She wasn't even aware that other cards charged as little as 9.9%. I told her to apply for a Canada Trust MasterCard and transfer her balance. She did and now she's working on becoming debt-free. Of course, this strategy only works to your advantage if you put those credit cards on ice until the loan is repaid. If you go out merrily charging away, in no time at all you'll find yourself in an even deeper hole with both a loan and a balance on your cards.

HAVING TROUBLE MAKING PAYMENTS?

Personal debt is an enormous problem in North America, and the level of debt continues to grow dramatically. In the U.S., the outstanding amount of installment credit in 1945 was $3 billion. By 1959, it had risen to $39 billion, and by 1973 it was $148 billion. By 1989, personal debt in the U.S. was at $674 billion. But that's the U.S., right? Canadians aren't nearly as debt-oriented as Americans, right?

In 1971, the per capita personal debt in Canada was $2,205. By 1990 it had risen to a whopping $15,467 — an increase of over 700%. In 1995 Visa and MasterCard balances rose 13% over the previous year to $17.4 billion.[14] And according to a report entitled "Canadian Economy: Personal Savings Rate," put out by Industry Canada, in 1998 total accumulated debt per household in Canada was equal to 114% of after-tax income. (Yep, we're actually spending more than we're making servicing our debt.) Clearly, Canadians are in much the same boat as our American cousins when it comes to accumulating debt.

Laurie Campbell of the Credit Counselling Service in Toronto says it is a myth that low-income earners are the ones spiralling out of control financially. "It is Canadians as a whole," she says. "We're neck and neck with the U.S. in terms of bankruptcies." Even more startling is that "104% of Canadians' [net] income is going toward paying off debt. We're in a credit crisis." And since Statistics Canada says that about 50% of people pay off their credit cards each month, those who don't must have huge credit balances to produce such high average levels of debt. Laurie says there is a

14 Angus Reid, *Shakedown* (Doubleday Canada Limited, 1997), p. 207.

direct correlation between the number of credit cards a person has and the amount of debt being carried. "The more credit cards, the more debt. It's obvious. Very few of us can walk around with 10 credit cards in our pockets and have them all at zero balances."

It's far easier to get into debt than to get out of debt. Consider how you think about your debt. When your credit-card statements come in, are you more concerned about how much you owe in total on all your credit cards, or how much your monthly payments will be each month? Do you even know how much you owe on all your credit cards? Here's an interesting observation made by David Benner in his book *Money Madness and Financial Freedom* about the level of control debtors feel:

Laurie Campbell is the program manager of the Credit Counselling Service of Toronto. Laurie has been with the agency for ten years and speaks often on the issues of credit and debt. She was involved extensively in the development of the education department within the agency and recently helped in the publication of How Chuck Taylor Got What He Wanted, *a credit primer geared to high school students. Laurie is on the board and a vice-president of the International Credit Association. She, her husband, and their two small children live in Toronto and love walking Chloe, their big, wonderful mutt.*

> The more a person owes, the more they tend to believe that the events in their life depend on external circumstances rather than on their own efforts and abilities. This means that their financial affairs are experienced as beyond their control. Those more in debt also tend to not manage well under stress. They report a corresponding lack of confidence in their ability to manage their affairs.[15]

Clearly, financial freedom means being in control. Financial freedom also means freedom from financial stress. But to achieve this when it comes to debt, you must understand the difference between being reactive — waiting for the worst to happen — and being proactive — taking control of the situation and getting on with life.

---

15 David Benner, *Money Madness and Financial Freedom* (Detselig Enterprises Ltd., 1996), p. 133.

If you run into trouble making your credit-card (or any type of credit) payments, *you can get out*. It may take some time, but you can do it.

Begin by calling the credit company and explaining the problem. If you've lost your job, or become ill and are not working, tell the credit company. If you are simply in over your head, tell the credit company. The important thing is to *tell the credit company*. They would much rather talk to you than send you nasty letters and wonder if they will ever be paid. You will probably be able to work out a repayment plan. You may even be able to negotiate with them to reduce the total amount you owe if you make a full payment. So here are the steps:

1. Contact your creditors and tell them what's happening.
2. Try to work out a payment plan that fits with your cash flow.
3. See if the creditor will take less if you agree to make a single repayment.
4. See if your bank will agree to give you a consolidation loan. By doing this you can save a good deal of interest.
5. Put yourself on a spending plan.

Whenever you fall off track, your credit rating gets bruised. If you want to be considered a good risk, you have to work at reestablishing your credit rating. One way is to get a secured credit card and make your payments faithfully.

What happens if you don't deal with the problem?

Debt collection practices vary from one creditor to another. Legal steps that can be taken are regulated by provincial law. As a general rule, repossession (seizure) of goods, garnishment, and other court actions are covered under provincial law, while bankruptcy is covered by federal legislation.

If you default and have offered collateral, creditors have the right to seize the goods and sell them to try to recoup their losses. Even if you haven't offered collateral, creditors may be allowed to seize other goods in order to recover the debt. You usually have plenty of notice and are given one last chance to clear up the debt.

A creditor may also apply for a court order to garnishee your wages or bank accounts. If a garnishment is issued, the creditor claims the money you owe directly from your employer or from the financial institution where your accounts are held. You may also be required to pay any court costs.

If the amount owed is quite small, the creditor may choose to sue you in small claims court to recover the debt. Larger amounts usually mean the lender may have to go to a higher court.

If you simply cannot carry on, you may have to declare bankruptcy, or you may be forced to do so by your creditors (see Chapter 24).

PAY OFF YOUR STUDENT LOAN

On the day that I spoke with Barb Godin, she had spent the morning looking over the bankruptcy numbers. She says that a lot of the bankruptcies today are the result of student loan problems. "I don't believe that our youth today really understand what they are doing to themselves. They have a live-for-today attitude and believe that student loans are funny money and that you really don't have to repay them."

My husband, Ken, tells the story of repaying his student loan. The bank manager expressed surprise that he had bothered. He said, among his peers, practically no one repaid a student loan, so he was an anomaly. But Barb warns, "The rules of the game have changed. It really does matter. By defaulting — not paying — they take themselves out of the credit arena for up to seven years."

Aileen has experienced what Barb is talking about. When she and her husband married, she didn't give much thought to the $48,000 he owed coming out of dental school. He was a great guy and she loved him. When he defaulted on the loan and declared personal bankruptcy to get rid of the debt, she understood. She had watched him agonize about how he was ever going to be able to afford his own practice with this debt hanging over him. Five years later, life looked good. He was working as an associate at a walk-in clinic, she was well established in her marketing career and three months pregnant. They decided to buy a home. He would convert the ground floor to a dental office and set up on his own. She would go back to work after her maternity leave and everything would go on as usual. Aileen was stunned when she and her husband were declined for a mortgage. When they asked why, the bankruptcy was raised. But that was five years ago, she said. Yes, but it stays in the record for seven years and it's out of our hands, they said. No one would touch them.

Barb believes that part of the debt-load problem stems from the fact that people aren't aware of just how much of an impact a default has on their financial life. Another contributing factor: the cost of going to school has increased so dramatically that young adults are leaving school with enormous financial burdens. Yet another contributor to the problem relates to personal responsibility. "Young adults are not understanding or accepting the responsibility that comes with borrowing — the explicit promise of repayment," says Barb. And as if all that wasn't wreaking enough havoc, banks jump into the fray. "If you are a student doing undergraduate or postgraduate work, everyone wants to give you credit. No one knows if you're going to repay or not, but everyone assumes that because you have this long work life ahead of you, you will continue to deal with the person who first granted you credit. So, without asking, you're inundated with credit offers. Or you fill out this credit form on campus and you check 12 boxes for 12 different credit cards and you get them all. And you think, 'My goodness, this is easy.' Everyone has the best intentions; everyone thinks he can handle it. Slowly the credit balances rise. It's easy to say, 'Well, the minimum payment is only $50 and I know I owe $100, but I'll catch up next month.' Next month never comes. And you get used to that. While you're in school you don't have to make any payments against your student loan either." So there it is, a pattern that begins to set: credit is easy. Repayment can be postponed.

"Then you graduate," says Barb, "and no one wants to give you credit. You've turned into a pariah because you only have a month or two on the job. And look at how much debt you're carrying." And remember you have to start repaying your student loans. And get that Visa bill paid down. So now you've finally entered the working world, and the bottom falls out. On top of rent, food, and all the other life-sustaining bills, there's a horrendous debt to repay.

There's no easy answer to this problem. Part of the responsibility clearly lies with the credit grantors in preparing students for their future need to repay. Barb says that lenders are now sitting down with students and their parents to "make it a three-way obligation." By having parents also sign, it increases the pressure on the young adult to repay the loan or, by default, the parents will be on the hook.

That may be the answer for the banks, but it certainly doesn't give parents or students any great sense of peace. Really, the question of whether or not to use credit — and how best to manage that credit — are the keys to staying financially healthy. Yes, it may be difficult to work and go to school at the same time. But will it be any more difficult than graduating $20,000, $30,000, or $40,000 in debt? How will a newly employed graduate deal with life's costs, which stubbornly continue to rise, and repay such a heavy financial burden? And we can expect the burden to grow even heavier. While the Association of Universities and Community Colleges reported that the average debt load for students who graduated in 1996 was $22,000, as tuition and other costs increase, that debt will increase. According to Statistics Canada, between 1985 and 1995, university tuition increased 134%. If costs continue to rise at the same rate, the current cost of about $9,000 a year is expected to spiral to a whopping $16,000 a year by 2005. That's almost $65,000 for a four-year degree. Then, of course, there are the costs of keeping body and soul together while your child is expanding his mind. We'd better start teaching our children about credit, how it works, and what it costs if we expect them to be able to use it successfully.

A FINAL WORD ON USING CREDIT WISELY

Sometimes it's easy to forget that you have to pay for what you buy, particularly when you use credit cards for the majority of your purchases. If you want to stay in control of your finances and use credit wisely, here are some guidelines:

- Make a spending plan and stick to it. Make sure you know how much is coming in and how much is going out each month. Remember to include items that are paid less frequently (such as car and house insurance) or irregularly (such as dental bills).
- Get rid of extra credit cards. Everyone needs a credit card or two. No one needs three, four, seven, nine, or 12. If you have a department store credit card — approximately 52% of Canadians do, and women are more likely to than men[16] — cut it up. The interest rate is staggering, and you don't need the extra temptation.
- Avoid impulse shopping. If you had to use cash to buy the item,

---

16 "Canadians and Credit," Ernst & Young, May 1996.

would you still buy it? Will you still want it tomorrow? Next week? Next month? Next year?

- Comparison shop for both the items you're buying and the financing you're using. Never buy anything without comparing costs and value.
- Always read and understand any financing arrangements you are signing, particularly store financing arrangements. Understand how much the financing will cost, any fees attached, and any penalties you'll have to pay. Know how much interest you'll be paying in dollars.
- Be wary about co-signing or guaranteeing a loan for someone else. If that person defaults, you will be called upon to pay off the loan. Lenders are supposed to advise you of the risks involved in a separate meeting, but ultimately you are responsible for where you put your signature.
- Keep track of all your credit purchases. Save your receipts or keep a written record of credit-card purchases so you can compare them with your statement. Never just pay the statement off without checking it carefully. Mistakes can be made and you may be double-charged, or charged for items you did not buy.

9

Establishing a Pay-Yourself-First Investment Plan

If a person was wholly rational there would be no drive to wealth, only a drive to meet the requirements for living.

OTTO FENICHEL

Men do not desire to be rich, but to be richer than other men.

JOHN STUART MILL

Money is one of the most useful contrivances ever invented; it is not its fault that some people are foolish enough or miserly enough to be fonder of it than of their own souls.

GEORGE BERNARD SHAW

The single best investment you'll ever make is in yourself. It doesn't matter how much money you make in your lifetime, how much stuff you accumulate, how rich you *feel*, if you don't have some money put away for the future, you'll be in a pickle when it comes time to retire. That's where the pay-yourself-first investment plan comes in. Maybe you've already established one. It's either in your RRSP (my favourite; see the last section of this chapter) or in an unregistered investment account.

Now, I know that everyone likens a pay-yourself-first plan to a periodic investment plan that's invested in mutual funds of some kind. When I talk about a pay-yourself-first (PYF) plan, I'm talking about taking money out of your cash flow (to create savings) and putting it somewhere it can work for you (investing). That "somewhere" doesn't have to be a mutual fund. It can be a CSB. It can be a GIC. It can be an individual stock or bond. *It has to be something you are knowledgeable about and comfortable with.*

One of the biggest complaints I hear about the world of investing is that the jargon is stifling. Strips aren't malls. Convertibles aren't cars. TIGRs aren't wild animals. Why the whole different language? Two reasons: first, most professions use jargon to make life easier for the players in the game. Abbreviations are the main offenders in this department. It's easier to say MBS than mortgage-backed security, or GIC than guaranteed investment certificate. Some of the abbreviations, like GIC and DRIPs (Dividend Reinvestment Plans), have become pretty well known so most people aren't baffled. Others, like ADR (American depository receipt), PEAC (payment-enhanced capital security), and SPEC (special capital-gains security), are still used only within the industry and are sure to boggle the minds of "outsiders." And new shortforms are coming along all the time as new investment alternatives are created. Do you know what a BOOM is? How about WEBS, RTUs, or REITs? Take heart. Even the people closest to the products find it hard to keep up sometimes. That's one of the reasons you need a really good investment adviser by your side as you wade through the jargon and the proliferation of products available for investing your money.

To understand even the basics, you must take the responsibility to educate yourself. This is one of my biggies when it comes to taking control of your financial life. If you don't know what you're doing, the answer isn't to do nothing — or worse still, to give the control to someone else. The answer is to find out, get educated, read and learn, and then read and learn some more. You can't expect someone else to take care of your money as well as you would yourself. And you can't blame someone else when your investments go awry. *It's your money, so it's your job.*

After years of emphasizing that RRSPs are a form of registration, not an actual investment, I still have people telling me they *invested* in an RRSP. You can *contribute* to an RRSP, but since an RRSP is not a financial instrument, you can't invest in one. An RRSP is simply a form of registration. It's like having a big umbrella labelled "RRSP," under which you put all the financial instruments (stocks, bonds, mutual funds, GICs) that you're buying to make your retirement savings grow.

Why are people still confused? After all, each RRSP season we are absolutely deluged with RRSP information. Magazines, newspapers, radio, and television cover the topic in great detail, and we swim in advertisements and promotions from financial institutions that are scrambling to win our RRSP dollars. There are also dozens of good books explaining how RRSPs work and why you should have one, the best of which is *Registered Plans* (CCH Canada) written by . . . ME! So if there's so much "education" out there, why are there still so many questions?

While banks, insurance companies, and mutual-fund companies have paid great lip service to educating consumers, that education has been neither broad enough nor deep enough. Most educational material is presented in a highly promotional context, leaving out the issues or concepts that are perceived to be — and I quote one bank executive — "too complicated for the unsophisticated investor" — doublespeak for "they don't need to know that" or worse, "they just won't get it." Apparently, as consumers, we have more money than brains!

Advertisements are misleading, delivering only part of the information needed to make an informed decision. When the strategy of taking a large, long-term loan to catch up unused RRSP contribution room was initially being flogged, none of the advertisements addressed the difference between the interest costs on a single 10-year loan for $50,000 and several one-year loans for $7,000 each. As consumers, we're expected to be sophisticated enough to figure that out for ourselves. How about the cost to our cash flow and its impact on our ability to make current contributions to our RRSPs? Why bother? After 10 years, you could just borrow again and spend another $16,000 in interest catching up for the contributions you didn't make because you were busy paying off the first loan.

Everyone has to take some responsibility for Canadians' lack of education on money matters. Consumers aren't allowed to say "It's the banks' fault" because heaven knows you just have to visit the library and you'll find dozens of books on the financial topic you're interested in. But we also can't say that the financial services sector is totally without blame. After all, the rapidity with which new financial instruments are being launched, and the media blitz used to entice us into these derivative and often very complicated products is unprecedented in terms of dollars spent and influence on consumers. If consumers are going to be bombarded with BOOMs and intrigued by IPOs, these great new, wonderfully improved, fabulously whiter-than-white investments had better be accompanied by some clear, complete, and concise communication designed to educate consumers.

In some ways things are getting better. With the growth in mutual-fund sales, more people are beginning to understand what mutual funds are and how they work. And they are becoming less concerned about short-term volatility and more focused on long-term returns. This was clearly seen in the October 1997 slide and rebound in the market. Spurred by a fall in Hong Kong, markets in North America, Europe, and Australia took a nosedive. The following day, while Hong Kong continued to plummet, the other markets recovered quickly. No panic. No pain. When I asked my stock broker, Ann Richards, how much her phone had rung, she said, "Only about three times." Mind you, she was busy calling her clients to make sure they were okay. "Even those who were retired and living on a fixed income," she said, "seemed fine. They said, 'Ann, I'm not worried about this. Markets go up and down. I'm in it with a plan.'"

Ann is a really good broker and her clients' lack of panic is a testament to the time she takes to make sure she understands their objectives. And it's a testament to the time she takes to ensure her clients understand what they're investing in, what ups and downs they can expect, and how to stay on track to meet their objectives.

Thankfully, there are lots of good people out there willing to help you with your money. Your job is to find yourself a financial adviser who brings to the client/adviser relationship the experience and expertise, kindness and care, and thoughtfulness and thoroughness you need. (See Chapter 13 for more on how to establish financial relationships.) Thankfully, too, there are many investment options out there that even the most inexperienced consumers can grasp with just a minimum commitment of time and energy.

There's absolutely nothing wrong with starting out with the safe, tried-and-true investments that you're already familiar with. But don't stop there. Branch out. Ask questions of your banker, your broker, your personal adviser, your father, your daughter, anyone who can give you more information and help you spread your investment wings. In this respect, women have it over men, hands down. We're more willing to ask for advice. We're more willing to question, to think about how we feel about something, and to want to know more.

WHERE DO I START?

Having decided to take the plunge and invest, if you're not sure where to start, you're in good company. Gerry Merkley says, "It's very confusing for people. It's very confusing even for people in the business. With so many options, the first question inevitably is, 'How do you begin?'"

PURPOSE

Gerry says your launching point should be to ask yourself, "What am I saving this money for?" Are you planning a holiday, planning to take time off work for school or to raise your family, planning to make sure you have money for retirement? People say one thing, but do another. Take the example of Alison, who religiously put money into an RRSP every year because she said she was planning for her long-term future. But each time Alison had an emergency, the first place she turned to was her RRSP. Out came some cash. So Alison wasn't using the RRSP as long-term savings for the

Gerry Merkley has worked in the financial services sector for over 19 years, in roles ranging from financial counselling to investment product management, from retirement planning and education to vice-president of mutual funds. The mom of two young boys, Gerry knows first-hand that financial solutions must be both convenient and flexible. Gerry's work on developing risk-profiling programs gives her keen insight into the emotional barriers women face. "It's okay to be intimidated or overwhelmed by the choices, but it's not okay to let those emotions stop you from planning for your financial future."

future; instead, she was using it as an emergency fund. Alison told me how frustrated she was that no matter how diligent she was, her long-term savings weren't growing fast enough. She figured she was investing in the wrong things and needed to be more aggressive. She needed one of those mutual funds that would get her a zillion percent a year.

I asked her to show me her statements for the previous six years. There, in black and white, were all those small cash withdrawals Alison had made. The problem wasn't what Alison was investing in, the problem was that she wasn't leaving the money invested at all. She kept dipping in.

She hadn't firmly decided what this money was for, or worse, she had decided that it was for emergencies.

To rectify the problem, I suggested that Alison put half her normal contribution into her RRSP, and contribute the other half to her newly established emergency fund, until she built up the emergency fund that she felt comfortable with. Now, Alison has an emergency fund that she keeps at about $3,500 (less than recommended but in keeping with her personal money set-point), and is back to making full contributions to her RRSP. Interestingly, since she established her emergency fund, Alison hasn't dipped into her RRSP once.

Commitment to purpose

Gerry says the next question to ask is, "Is the investment touchable or untouchable?" This goes back, in part, to the purpose of the money (as in Alison's case). "The answer to this question will depend on your personality," says Gerry. Let's take saving for a child's education as an example. Some people may say it's touchable while others do not. "You really have to be truthful with yourself," says Gerry. When I asked if that's one of the areas where people often fall short — they're not as honest with themselves as they could and should be — Gerry replied quite tactfully and with a smile, "I would say so."

TIME HORIZON

Time frame is also very important. If you're saving for a child's post-secondary education, whether your child is two or 12 will have an impact on the investments you choose. The longer you have until you will need to use the money — the longer your time horizon — the more time your investment has to even out its return. So you have to match your time horizon to the investment you are choosing.

What does the time horizon of your investment have to do with what investment you choose? GICs have no volatility and the return is guaranteed. You can't lose your principal and you know exactly what you'll earn in interest on the day your GIC matures. The same holds true for a bond or mortgage investment. So it doesn't matter whether you go long or short, you're guaranteed your return as long as you hold to the end of the term you choose. Equity mutual funds and direct investment in equities are a whole different kettle of fish. They can be quite volatile, with some offering more price stability and others offering more opportunity for growth. Either way, they don't work as short-term investments since they may be at a low just when you need the money and must sell them. They work as medium- and long-term investments, where you have time to ride out the highs and lows and average out your return.

Less than three years is considered a *short-term* investment horizon. Three to seven years is considered *medium term*, and seven years or beyond is considered *long term*. I tend to agree with those people, like James P. O'Shaughnessy, author of *What Works on Wall Street*, who see 10 years as the marker for long-term investments. That would make a seven-, eight-, or nine-year investment medium term and anything over 10 years long term.

Short-term investors should avoid putting the majority of their money in equity investments where the risk of losing that money is greater. Choosing fixed-income investments that generate a steady return while offering a higher level of security is a better idea. Medium-term investors can balance their investment portfolios by using both equity and fixed-income alternatives. Long-term investors have the luxury of time and can therefore choose an asset mix that is weighted more heavily with stocks and stock-based mutual funds. They have the time to ride out the natural volatility associated with the equities market.

Since no single investment offers the perfect opportunity for a high return, liquidity, security, tax advantages, income generation, and convenience, keep your specific goals and investment objectives clearly in mind. And as you get older, or as your personal circumstances or economic conditions change and your investment horizon shortens, you'll need to rebalance your portfolio's asset mix.

RISK PROFILING

The proviso to all this is that you have to buy investments with which you're comfortable. You may have a long-term investment horizon, but if you're uncomfortable with the thought of your investment fluctuating in value, you may not be an equity investor.

"Once you decide your purpose — 'what am I trying to achieve here? what is my goal?'" says Gerry, "then it's a matter of doing a needs

analysis [Gerry's term for what others in the industry refer to as risk pro-
filing]. You have to find an analysis that's comprehensive, because what
happens, and I'll use myself as an example, is that what you think you are,
you aren't really. When I've gone through a superficial risk profile I've
come out high on the tolerance scale. Like I'm a cowboy. But I'm not. I'm
quite conservative, based on my detailed needs analysis."

Those quickie, four-question profiles that are administered by some
financial institutions don't really help you to better understand yourself.
After all, if a financial service's profiler tells you that you're growth-
oriented and quite aggressive, you believe, right? You want to believe. But
what happens when you're challenged by a slip-sliding market or a
change in personal circumstances? Will you panic and bail out? If you're
comfortable with your risk profile, you'll be comfortable with your
choices, and you won't even look at the market."

Remember, too, that everyone is a "person" first — even brokers.
While we believe that those who we think are better educated, more
in tune, or anesthetized to the volatility of the market should know
better, they are people first and so they may act emotionally. I remember
speaking with an investment adviser in late 1997 about how gold was
doing. "It's in the toilet," she replied. I suggested that meant it was a good
time to buy. (Remember the old adage, "Buy low, sell high.") Her
response: "But it's in the toilet." She couldn't get past her own personal
bias — her emotional baggage — to look at the opportunity a low gold
price offered. As Gerry puts it, "The logic and the emotion just don't
come together."

THE RELATIONSHIP BETWEEN RISK AND RETURN

I'm often asked to recommend investments — I never do this, because
there is no way to follow up when investments or the person's circumstances change — and the request is always for something that pays a
huge return with no risk. There is an old investment saying: "The greater
the risk, the higher the potential return; the lower the risk, the lower the
potential return." And there is no such thing as a risk-free investment. It's
really all a matter of degree.

What is risk?

Understanding risks and how to come to terms with them will take you a long way toward being a smart investor. Here are some examples of the risks associated with some pretty traditional investments:

- Stocks and stock-based investments like equity mutual funds can be volatile. *Volatility* is the investment's penchant for fluctuating in value over the short term. High-flying equity investments are typically associated with volatility, though you may be surprised at where volatility raises its ugly head. Industry-specific mutual funds, such as mining or technology, or funds that invest in small-capitalization companies can be very volatile. And even bonds can be volatile investments if interest rates start to swing up and down.

- All equity investments have some capital risk associated with them. *Capital risk* is the potential for losing some or all of the original capital investment.

- GICs and other fixed-income investments such as bonds and mortgages seem relatively risk-free, right? Think again. Interest-bearing investments suffer *interest-rate risk*. One risk is that interest rates will rise and you will be locked in to a lower rate (or that you'll have to sell your bond at a capital loss). Another is that if you've invested at a high rate, interest rates may be significantly lower when it comes time to renew.

- Well, at least there's your risk-free savings account. Wrong again! If your investment's rate of return is the same as or lower than the current rate of inflation, this is called *inflation risk*, and the end result is that your investment will lose value year after year. Your money will be worth less.

Everyone measures risk differently since it is relative to our personal circumstances. While one woman may think investing $5,000 in a stock is an okay thing to do, another may balk. If $5,000 represents the second woman's total savings, or if it represents a substantial portion of her annual disposable income, she will be less willing to throw caution to the wind. On the other hand, if that $5,000 represents only 5% of an overall investment portfolio, the risks can seem a lot less serious.

When a loss would be deeply felt financially, the level of risk is much higher. Interestingly, however, the sense of risk decreases as the pot grows bigger and the odds improve. Would you invest $50 if you had the chance of winning $5,000? What if the jackpot were $500,000? Or $5,000,000? See what I mean? The bigger the pot, the more willing most people are to take the shot. Now, what about the odds? Would you invest $50 to win $5,000,000 if your odds were 100 to 1? If your odds were 10 to 1? What about 2 to 1? Most people would have no problem investing $50 for a 50% chance of winning $5,000,000. What would you do?

It's human nature to measure risk against the opportunity to win. The bigger the risk or potential downside, the bigger the opportunity for return needed to persuade us to go for the gusto. But we've seen that risk has another face that is not widely understood. What's the risk to you personally in not taking any chances, in always playing it safe? What's the risk in being so conservative that you end up losing ground year after year in terms of the real value of your money?

DIVERSIFICATION

The key to building a healthy investment portfolio that gives a good return while minimizing risk is *diversification*: a little of this, and a little of that. Some stocks, some bonds, some GICs. A touch of foreign investment, a little tucked away in a money-market fund where it is easily accessible. By hedging your bets you'll protect yourself from negative swings in any one type of investment. When the stock market dumps and bonds glow, your bond portfolio will pull you along. When bonds dive and the market soars, your equity investments will save the day. And when Canada spirals while Europe, South America, or Asia skyrockets, you'll have enough invested internationally to keep your return balanced.

Whether you call it "asset mix," "investment mix," or "asset allocation," it's the same thing. It means diversifying by dividing your money among a variety of different types of investments. Asset mix usually falls into one of three groups: conservative, balanced, or growth-oriented. But within each of those three groups, there are many different sub-groups defined by very subjective criteria.

To illustrate my point: I consider myself to be fairly conservative. I'm more likely to buy blue-chip stock or a large-cap mutual fund than a mutual fund that focuses on emerging industries. Yet, if you put me beside a woman who wouldn't dream of investing in anything but GICs, I look pretty risk-tolerant. Stick me beside Gerry Merkley, who considers herself to be somewhat conservative but who believes small-cap U.S. is the way to go, and you have to ask, "What does conservative actually mean?"

It's also interesting to think about the fact that men and women do not benefit from the same asset allocation models in the same ways. While these models typically lump men and women together, our needs are different, so our models should also be different. Because women are more at risk for becoming principal providers of elder care and child care, because women live longer on a fixed income during retirement, and because women usually do not have the income expectations of their male counterparts, we *must* be more growth-oriented right off the bat. And we have to maintain a growth orientation for as long as possible. Equally as important is that we continue to save throughout our lives using new savings to rebalance our asset allocation as we age.

One misconception about asset allocation is that if you buy stock in several different companies, you will automatically be well diversified. This ain't necessarily so. To effectively diversify, not only do you have to buy stocks of different companies, those companies should be in different industries and in different countries. Here are five ways to diversify a portfolio:

- by the types of investments — using bonds, deposits, stocks, mutual funds, and real estate
- by the quality of the investments — the lower the quality, as rated by the industry (e.g., A bonds versus AAA bonds), the higher the return offered to offset the higher potential for loss
- by region (in Canada, North America, or global markets)
- by currency
- by levels of liquidity — holding some long-term deposits such as strip bonds or equity funds, along with some shorter-term investments such as Treasury bills

An illustration that is widely used to help investors visualize the relationship between the risk an investment holds and the return it generates is called the investment pyramid. Rather than use the pyramid, however, I'd like to present you with the following chart that more clearly shows the relationship between risk and return.

RISK VERSUS RETURN

As you can see, most of the investment options that are traditionally used, such as savings accounts, GICs, and CSBs, are really low on the risk scale, and equally low on the return scale. Increasingly, investors are coming to understand that safety of capital should not be their only objective since the potential that the assets will not grow sufficiently to keep pace with inflation is as significant a risk. Assuming you invest $100,000 at 4%, you'll earn about $4,000 in interest a year. At an average tax rate of 30%, you'll end up with only $2,800. Your return would fall from 4% to 2.8%. In 10 years' time, at an average inflation rate of 4%, that $2,800 will be worth only $1,900. And inflation will eat away at the principal too — $100,000 will be worth only $68,000 in 10 years, and only $46,000 in 20 years.

As you move up the scale, the investments take on a higher risk profile, but also offer opportunity to enjoy higher returns. At the top of the scale are the most risky, with the highest potential return. Only the most astute and experienced investors, those with cast-iron stomachs, should play in this arena. But there is plenty in the middle for us common folk.

The asset mix you choose will have a direct impact on the return you earn on your portfolio. The more risk you are willing to take, the more return your portfolio may potentially generate. A typical conservative investment portfolio might hold 20% in cash, 60% in fixed-income investments such as bonds or mortgages, and 20% in equities. It's a portfolio that is geared more toward capital preservation and income than it is toward growth. A balanced portfolio would hold 10% in cash, and 45% each in fixed income and equities. Investors who want both income and growth, and split their portfolios 50–50 between fixed income and equities, are balanced in their asset mix. A typical growth portfolio would hold 10% in cash, 30% in bonds, and 60% in equities. Investors with this kind of portfolio are not as interested in generating income and are willing to risk far more in capital in order to potentially earn a much higher return.

Here are some figures to help put the whole thing in perspective. If you had $10,000 to invest from January 1970 until June 1995, here's how much you would have earned[17] if:

- you were a conservative investor, and went the route of complete capital safety with a high level of liquidity: $69,815.
- you were willing to take a little more risk and went the route of a balanced portfolio: $89,082.
- you picked the growth portfolio: $100,263.
- 20% of the equities in your growth portfolio were in foreign investments: $110,510.

The perceived level of risk associated with an investment depends on your personal ability to handle risk. Since risk is a trade-off for good return, you have to ask yourself how much sleep you are prepared to lose for the opportunity to wake up richer. Of course, there are some who choose to stay at the bottom of the scale, never venturing into alternatives such as fixed-income mutual funds, individual corporate bonds, or equity mutual funds. If you're one of these people, and you're doing it for the right reason — you have no stomach for volatility or for the potential capital loss, and you aren't concerned about inflation — then you should stay just where you are. As Gerry points out, most tools for risk profiling will

17 Indices used — for cash: 90-day Canada Treasury bills; for bonds/fixed income: Scotia McLeod Long-Term Bond Index; for stocks/equities: Toronto Stock Exchange 300 Total Return Index; for foreign: The Centre for Research in Security Prices (USA) total return index in Canadian dollars. Source: 1995 Andex Chart.

emphasize the need for you to diversify, but there are always some investors who "need GICs because [they] just don't have the stomach for anything else, even though there is risk associated with that choice." For these investors, the risk that their return may be less than needed is a risk they can bear. What they can't bear is the idea of losing any of their money. These people, and those who are not aware of what they are investing in, don't understand the associated risks, or have good reason to avoid the risks we've been talking about, should stay out of investments such as equities. The lure of the potential return shouldn't be the focus of the decision. Remember what Gerry said right off the bat: Know your purpose in investing, understand your commitment to your purpose, know your time horizon, and perhaps most importantly, know yourself (your investment personality).

After a media blitz during the 1996 RRSP season, I received a call from a woman who wanted some advice. She had seen me on TVO's *Studio 2*, where I had been answering caller questions about mutual funds. She thought I was down to earth and wanted the real scoop on mutual funds. "Should I be investing in mutual funds?" she asked.

"Tell me about your situation," I responded.

"I'm retired," she said, "living on a fixed income. I have no dependents, no family at all. I'm getting about 2.5% on my money right now, and I'm not very happy with that."

"How much do you have to invest?"

"$400,000."

Wow, I thought. "How much are you falling short in terms of meeting your day-to-day needs?"

"Oh, I'm all right," she said. "I'd like more of a cushion, but I'm not touching my capital."

Again, wow. "Have you ever invested in mutual funds before?" I asked.

"No," she said.

"Why do you want to invest in mutual funds?" I asked.

"My friends are all into mutual funds. They think I'm stupid to be stuck in GICs at 2.5% when they're getting 15% or 20% in [equity] mutual funds. And my insurance adviser says that he can double my money in six years. He's recommending mutual funds really strongly. But I'm not sure about this at all. I need some help. Will you tell me what to do?"

"How old are you?" I asked.

"Eighty-seven," she replied.

I was stunned. She was 87 with $400,000 in capital and enough income to meet her normal needs. Before I even realized what I had said I asked, "And how rich do you want to be when you die?"

Looking back, it was a pretty blunt question. But she'd already heard me being pretty blunt for an hour on TVO so I guess she wasn't surprised. She laughed. "I knew you'd cut right to the chase," she said. "I guess I shouldn't bother with the mutual funds."

"Stay out of mutual funds," I said. "They are not for you. At your age, with your circumstances, all you need to do is get a slightly better return. You can get 5.5% on a CMHC bond. Would 5.5% be enough?"

"That would be perfect."

This conversation was interesting for a few reasons. First, she was thinking about investing in mutual funds without knowing what they are or how they work. The recent popularity of mutual funds has meant that more of our investment dollars have flooded into these investment vehicles. However, many people know little about how mutual funds operate. They don't understand the basic premise of mutual funds, or the types of investments different mutual funds hold. And they don't understand how changes in market or economic conditions will affect their mutual-fund holdings. They do know the results can be spectacular. They do know their brother, cousin, best friend, and next-door neighbour are buying them. They don't know that some of these people have no idea what they are doing. The result is that many people rush into investments and then rush out when the investment doesn't perform to their expectations, not realizing that mutual funds usually perform best in the long term.

ECONOMICS 101

Whether you're thinking about investing or trying to decide if this is the right time to go shopping for a house, a basic understanding of economics will help in your decision making. According to a study done by the Canadian Bankers Association, approximately 67% of Canadians feel that if they knew more about the economy, they'd make better financial decisions.[18]

---

18 "The Economy and You," Canadian Bankers Association, 1998.

Patti Croft was ranked #2 economist in Canada in a 1995 survey and was the youngest ever female economist of a major financial institution. In 1997, she joined Sceptre, where she wears two hats: chief economist and portfolio manager for over 100 high-net-worth clients. Patti appears frequently in the media as an economic commentator, and is on the board of Women in Capital Markets, which helps women network and become more aware of the opportunities in capital markets. Patti is a single mom of two boys and a girl. She enjoys all kinds of activities — aerobics, boxing, and Ashtanga yoga — but says, "The reality is, beyond work and the kids, there isn't much time left!"

Patti Croft, vice-president of Sceptre Investment Counsel Limited, says investors "don't need to fixate on indicators such as quarterly growth rates, but should understand how those economic factors affect things like inflation, interest rates, foreign exchange rates and the Canadian dollar, and financial markets."

Economics seems to be a big mystery for most. I may go into the bank and hear that mortgage rates have just increased. They tell me that's because they're worried about inflation. But how are all these ideas linked and what do they mean to me?

As Patti says, "The beauty of economics is in its sheer logic." That logic isn't immediately apparent to those who are not initiated in economic theory. Patti draws a distinction between predictability and logic, which in part explains why no one ever seems to be able to say what will happen next. And Patti likes to talk about global economics because "Canada represents only about 3% of the global economy. The reality today is that what happens in Frankfurt, Tokyo, or Thailand affects us in Canada."

Inflation is one of the economic indicators that most worry investors. "Inflation is simply a measure of how fast the prices of goods or services that we buy are rising," says Patti. So when you hear on the radio or read in the newspaper that the inflation rate this month is 1.8%, that means the cost of a basket of goods and services as selected by Statistics Canada is 1.8% higher than it was a year ago. Of course, not everyone buys the goods in that basket. And a big change in one item in the basket can take the average up or down without actually affecting consumers' budgets. Take, for example, what happened to the Consumer Price Index (CPI) when the heavy taxes on cigarettes were removed. We actually experienced a period of disinflation — inflation was negative for that period of time — because the price to consumers went down. However, if you did not smoke, you would have experienced no drop in the cost of your own personal basket of goods and services.

For those living on a fixed income, inflation means a reduction in your ability to meet your needs over time. A dollar worth 100 cents in 1971 saw its purchasing power fall to less than 25 cents by 1991. Increases in inflation often also signal increases in interest rates because lenders don't want to be left out of the loop when it comes to collecting rent on the money you've borrowed. But inflation can be battled, and your chief weapon is diversification. With a mix of investments, you can reduce your exposure to inflation risk by focusing on your real return.

Real return is the return you earn on an investment after you've accounted for taxes and inflation. Let's say you invested $10,000 in a GIC paying 4.25%. During the second year of your five-year term, inflation rose to 5%. While your certificate will earn $425 in interest each year (assuming it isn't compounding), your net return would be less than you would need to keep pace with inflation. To be able to have the same purchasing power, you would have had to earn $500. Now we have to figure in the taxes. With a tax rate as low as 20%, you would need a return of 6.25% on your certificate just to keep pace with inflation ($10,000 x 6.25% = $625 in interest – 20% for tax = $500). If you earned a return of 7.25%, your real return would be only 1%.

There's no point in patting yourself on the back for earning 12% if inflation is running at 10%, because your real return is only 2%. On the other hand, if inflation is only running at 2% and you have an investment paying a measly 6%, you're cool because although at first glance your return looks pathetic, your real rate of return is higher than in the first example.

People are also in the dark about interest rates and why they go up and down. As savers, we want to earn the highest possible interest. As borrowers we want to pay the lowest. High interest rates are good for people living on a fixed income. Low interest rates are good for businesses. Whether you're shopping for a loan or trying to decide where to invest, you need to consider not only the current rate, but also the direction in which rates are headed. That's demonstrated through what is called the yield curve.

"Yield curve is another thing that scares people," says Patti. The yield curve is a graphic representation of interest rates, at a certain point in time, for various financial instruments with different terms, from three-month Treasury bills to 30-year Government of Canada bonds. When long-term rates are higher than short-term rates, this is referred to as a *normal* yield curve. When long-term rates are lower than short-term rates, the yield is referred to as *inverted*. And when there's little difference, economists refer to that as a *flat* yield curve.

Where we are in the yield curve — normal, inverted, or flat — has implications for making our money grow through investing and managing our debt, as well as for the economy as a whole. For example, when interest rates are falling (when the yield curve is inverted), bond prices will rise, which is great for bond investors. An inverted curve means that money is in short supply, that there is great short-term demand, but that there is also a fear of assuming long-term commitments. "If you're shopping for a mortgage and the yield curve is steep, there will be a big difference between what you pay for a six-month mortgage and a five-year mortgage. That's how it affects people in their day-to-day lives," says Patti.

In late 1997, Canada was experiencing a steep normal yield curve. Three-month rates were under 3% and long bonds — those with terms of 10 years or higher — were at about 6.5%. So there were 350 basis points (100 basis points equals 1%) between short and long rates. "Historically that's a very steep yield curve," says Patti. "A steep yield curve usually indicates that with short-term rates low, the economy will grow fast down the road. We don't have to worry unless the curve flattens or inverts."

Canadian rates have wobbled from a high of over 21% in 1981 to a low of 3.25% in 1997. Why all the variability? Several factors affect rates, including global market forces, inflation, and monetary policy. From a market forces perspective, when more people want to lend than to borrow, the price of money falls. This drop in rates makes it less attractive to save and more attractive to spend. When more people want to borrow than to lend, then the price of renting someone else's money goes up. That makes it more attractive to save and far less attractive to spend, particularly if purchases are being financed.

Current rate and direction also influence how people invest their money. When rates are low, GICs, term deposits, and savings bonds are much less attractive, driving people to look for returns other than interest. The result: people turn to the market for capital gains and dividends. When rates skyrocket, people are less willing to assume the risk associated with equities because they feel they can get a comparable return on a completely secure interest-based investment.

Which brings us to another interesting question: Who the dickens are the "central bankers" we hear so much about, and do they have a purpose other than to make life miserable for investors? A central bank, like the Bank of Canada, is responsible for setting interest rates and controlling the money supply. When the bank tightens the money supply by raising rates, it wants to slow down the economy. When it relaxes the money supply by lowering rates, it is trying to stimulate the economy.

The bank rate is the lowest rate at which the Bank of Canada lends money to members of the Canadian Payments Association — our six major chartered banks and four other financial institutions. This rate sets the tone for all other short-term interest rates such as the rates your bank charges for things like your mortgage, your car loan, or your personal line of credit. The central bank monitors the state of the Canadian economy through numerous market indicators, including inflation, the exchange rate for the Canadian dollar, and employment figures, and decides when conditions warrant a change. In response to a change in the bank rate, the major banks usually alter their prime rate — the rate they charge their most creditworthy customers — which in turn affects the rate they offer everyone else for loans and fixed-term investments.

How does a change in the bank rate affect the economy? Well, when it costs more to borrow money, that cost at once slows spending and is a major factor in the increase in the price of goods. Consumers spend less because it costs more to buy the item on credit. Big-ticket items like cars are a perfect example of how even a small increase in interest rates can significantly affect the price. Manufacturers have to pay more interest on their credit facilities to carry on manufacturing and they pass that increased cost on through the increase in the price of their products. That increase in the price of the widget increases the price of the doodads being built with those widgets, which in turn increases the price of the whatchamacallits being manufactured from those doodads. Then consumers make the decision not to buy that whatchamacallit because they don't want to spend that much more on it. "Consumer spending is two-thirds of economic activity," says Patti. "If that slows, it means much more moderate economic activity." Let's follow the whatchamacallits a little further to see how this works. Okay, no one's buying whatchamacallits, so the people who make them decide to slow production, cut a line, lay off some workers. That means the people who make the doodads end up in the same position. Ditto the people making the widgets. Then, with scads of people out of work, there's not enough money going around to buy even the few whatchamacallits being made. Eventually, the whole economy slooows dooown too.

"As an economist," smiles Patti, "you have to combine psychology with science." The economics textbooks will tell you that the economy is c + i + g + (x – m). The "c" represents consumer spending. In theory, consumers have jobs, they get income, they spend. "The psychology is the unquantifiable element: why they buy what they buy." Historically, consumer spending has been a key driver of the economy. That's why in the 1970s and 1980s when boomers were young and buying houses — and just about everything else in sight — they drove inflation up.

The "i" in the economic formula is investment spending — primarily business investment spending on things like machinery and equipment — that increases the productive capacity of the economy. The "g" is government spending. "While government spending used to make up quite a large percentage of the economy, in the past few years we've seen a downsizing of our government at all levels. If government spending is in decline, the economy goes with it." And Patti believes that "government spending isn't coming back any time soon." The last part of the formula, "(x – m)," stands for exports minus imports. That's our net trade. "Exports are critical for Canada," says Patti. "We're called an 'open economy' because so much of our economic activity is export-related. But while we're exporting we're also importing the many things we don't produce in this country." In the best of worlds, we'd have a trade surplus, meaning we'd export more than we import. Trade surpluses and deficits have an impact on the currency values of different countries.

Currency issues also have a tremendous impact on our economy. There is no predetermined value for the loonie, so it is simply one more commodity that can be bought or sold. If more people want to buy it than sell it, the dollar goes up. If more people want to sell, it goes down.

Economists use something called purchasing power parity (PPP) to help determine the value of a currency. "PPP looks at two countries and asks, 'At what exchange rate could I buy a Big Mac in the United States and a Big Mac in Canada and have those expenditures be equal given the current rate of inflation in both countries?'" Patti explains. However, the perceived value of the currency doesn't always bear any resemblance to the actual value in real life. Let's take the example of the Canadian dollar. In September 1997, the Canadian dollar was perceived to be undervalued. While most people believed, based on PPP, that the Canadian dollar was worth about 80 cents, it was trading at only 72 cents. The outlook: a higher Canadian dollar, just about anytime soon. But it wasn't to be. By June 1998, the dollar had dropped even further, into the 68-cent range, and was still headed south. It would hit the very low 60s before heading up again. "While we uniformly predict that the dollar is undervalued," said Patti, "no one can predict when it will go back to the neutral value" — the point at which it is neither under- nor overvalued. Periods of undervaluation and overvaluation can last for many years because currencies are affected by psychology. If the rest of the world senses any instability in Canadian politics or the economy — as when there's talk about Quebec separation — the dollar takes a beating. The other things that affect the value of our dollar include our trade balance, government policies, unemployment rate, national debt, and level of productivity, to name just a few.

In our yakety-yak about the value of the Canadian dollar, we're always comparing it with the U.S. dollar. Economists also closely watch the difference between the two countries' inflation rates. In September 1997, inflation in the U.S. was at about 2% to 2.5%, while in Canada we were under 2%. "We had been below the U.S. for about seven years. Historically, it is extremely unusual for us to maintain an inflation rate below the U.S.," says Patti. At the same time, interest rates in Canada were below U.S. rates right out to the 30-year area of the yield curve. "Implicit in the fact that interest rates are below the U.S. is a call on the Canadian dollar," says Patti. That "call" comes from the expectation that the value of our dollar would rise.

Another factor that determines exchange rate is based on the trade situation. The "capital account" is an estimate of how much interest and dividends we owe the rest of the world. Canada's large budgetary deficit of the past has been significantly reduced. But we still have a lot of foreign-held debt. "Every month we owe foreign investors the interest on the debt so we end up exporting capital." There is also something called the "current account," which includes the trade and the capital account flows. "The current account for Canada had been, until recently, in surplus. A current account surplus is usually associated with a strong currency."

To tie up some loose ends, let's look at how the central bank uses currency rates and interest rates to guide the economy. First, it is important to note that the central bank does not control where 10-year bond rates trade. Long-term interest rates are primarily a reflection of where investors believe inflation is going. If they think inflation is rising, they will demand a higher return on their fixed-term investments to compensate for inflation's erosion of their return and that, in turn, will push up long-term rates. But the central bank does "control call money rates and very short-term interest rates," says Patti.

"The head of the central bank worries when the Canadian dollar gets too weak, because it increases import price inflation, and gives too much juice to the export side of the economy." Exporters love a cheap currency because it drives up their business. But from a central banker's perspective it could make the economy overheat too fast, which could drive up inflation down the road. So when the Canadian dollar gets too weak, historically the Bank of Canada has stepped in and raised short-term interest rates in an effort to support the dollar.

So what economic factors specifically affect stock market investors? "The stock market is affected by growth of the economy. And by interest rates: with their decline they have really helped improve corporate earnings. But the other factors are more company-specific or industry-specific," says Patti. "If oil prices are weak and going lower, then you'll see the oil and gas sector being hit. If high technology is the flavour of the week, as we've seen in the United States, then that sector will do particularly well."

We often wonder what on earth is happening when we see a period of escalation in prices followed by corrections or falls in prices. "What's probably changed," says Patti, "is the expectation for the outlook for that sector or something that we call valuation: is the stock cheap or is it expensive?" According to Patti, the fundamental measurements we have used to say whether a market is overheated or not didn't apply to the market boom in the late 1990s simply because there had been fundamental changes in the economy. While many people have expounded on the overvaluation of stocks based on their high P/E ratios, Patti counters that "during periods of low inflation, the P/E ratio can rise very rapidly and still represent good value." The P/E ratio, or price-to-earnings ratio, is the relationship between the price of a stock and the company's earnings. Patti continues, "So when you hear that the market looks rich, it's expensive so you shouldn't get in, it's not just the market that's the issue." You have to look at industries individually, and then companies within the industry. You could have an industry that's flatlined — the sector as a whole isn't growing — but within that industry one or two companies are skyrocketing based on their individual financial pictures.

Looking at the details of the industry and company is essential, but you also need to take a macro perspective by watching the global economy. What happens in Japan, Europe, and elsewhere is reflected in the direction taken in New York. While countries once employed a certain amount of protectionism — supporting their own economies first — most of those protections are gone. Patti cites the currency problems in Southeast Asia as an example of how globalization comes into play. "Those are competitive devaluations. The Southeast Asian economies could no longer operate in the old regimes so their currencies had to fall in order for things to be balanced and for the countries to compete." The world truly is a global market and as investors we have to take that into account.

Since the market as a whole is not a good indicator of where money can be made, and unless you're buying an index you're not buying the market as a whole anyway, then how do you decide where to invest? Because no single investment offers the perfect opportunity for the highest return, full liquidity, and most security, we have diversification.

Remember diversification? One misconception people often hold is that if they buy several different companies' stock or several mutual funds, they will automatically be well diversified. This isn't necessarily so. To effectively diversify, you have to invest not only in different companies, but also in different industries and different countries. The same theory holds true for mutual funds. If you don't, you could suffer "deworsification" — an errant sense that you are diversified if you hold lots of different stocks but you haven't been judicious about spreading your assets over several industries, types of investments, or economies. All you have done is rendered your portfolio unmanageable.

GAIL VAZ-OXLADE'S DOZEN GOLDEN RULES OF INVESTING

There are hundreds of different investment options from which you can choose when starting an investment portfolio. I've come up with twelve rules to help you decide among all these financial products. I'll begin at the beginning, with the most important rule of all:

GVO Golden Rule #1: *Know what you're investing in.* If you want to expand your investment horizons, learn all about the investments you're interested in before you buy them. That means you also have to understand the factors that affect your investments. Invest your time before you invest your money and you're more likely to be successful.

GVO Golden Rule #2: *Know yourself.* If you want to be able to buy the right types of investments for your specific needs, you must also understand your personal comfort level with regard to both risk and volatility. If you don't know who you are, the stock market can be an expensive place to find out!

GVO Golden Rule #3: *What you don't know can be just as important as what you do know.* But how do you know what you don't know? Good question. That's the Catch-22 most investors face when they are entering a new investment arena. The answer is simple: Ask tons of questions and read masses of information. Unfortunately, investing isn't the breeze most people would like to believe it is. If it were that easy, all the people working in the investment world would be stinking rich and living in Bora Bora.

GVO Golden Rule #4: *Accept the responsibility for your decisions.* If you can't live with a trade gone bad, don't make it. And be prepared to put a little work into the decision. You can't expect other people to take care of your money as well as you would. Remember, it's your money. And you shouldn't blame others for decisions you make — because ultimately, they are your decisions. So, follow the first three rules carefully, and make this rule the cornerstone of your relationship with all your advisers.

GVO Golden Rule #5: *Have a plan.* It's surprising how many people invest by the seat of their pants. Perhaps they rely on a broker's advice. Maybe they follow the financial press and buy what's hot. Unfortunately, without a specific plan many people may find themselves playing it safe or putting too much money in high-risk investments. Without a specific plan, achieving any goal at all is a hit-or-miss proposition.

You don't have to be a financial whiz to develop a plan. What you have to do is take a good look at what your priorities are, and then make some decisions about what you'll have to do to meet those priorities. If you don't have gobs of money to invest, a plan is even more important.

Planning begins with setting some goals. This may seem like an obvious first step. But do you have a written set of goals for your investment portfolio? If you don't, you should. Once you've set your goals, the next step is to develop an action plan to meet those goals.

GVO Golden Rule #6: *Invest monthly.* It's much easier to find $25 a month than it is to find $400 all at once. So let's say you're determined to make your maximum RRSP contribution of $6,000. Instead of borrowing from the bank at the last minute because you just couldn't save it all up, and then paying it back monthly with interest, pay yourself first. Open up a monthly contribution plan and slide money away in smaller increments that you won't miss quite so much.

Most monthly investment programs will allow you to contribute as little as $25 a month. My friend Victoria Ryce says that when she used to ask people if they could find just $25 in their spending plan that they could recycle to their "painless portfolio building," there were always lots of nods in her audience. In the case of the objective "to invest $1,200 in equities this year," you might choose to put yourself on an investment plan where you contribute $100 a month so that, at the end of the year, you will have accumulated your $1,200 almost painlessly.

GVO Golden Rule #7: *Make sure your objectives are realistic.* There's a great saying on Wall Street: Both bulls and bears can make money in the market, but hogs get slaughtered. While most people get excited when they see returns of 18%, 24%, or 36%, and the media love to highlight the 66% or 130% returns, expecting to achieve those kinds of returns year after year is unrealistic. If your objectives aren't realistic, you'll never be satisfied. Part of making peace with money is setting realistic objectives that are attainable, so you can pat yourself on the back. A realistic objective for investing is to earn an average of 12% over the long term. That's not 12% every year — it's an average return of 12%. If you beat yourself up over a couple of bad years, or raise your expectations after a couple of stellar years, you're not being realistic. Nor are you being kind to yourself. Remember, balance is the keyword of achieving financial freedom.

Investing is hard work. To be good at it you have to learn a lot of stuff, keep up to date with changes in products and economic trends, and have a strategy. By working hard, anyone can become relatively good at investing. And by setting realistic objectives, anyone can feel good about investing.

GVO Golden Rule #8: *Don't do it just because everyone else says you should.* If you follow the herd you're sure to step in a lot of cowpies. If you make an investment simply because it seems like the right thing to do, you're making the wrong decision. If you make an investment just because people say you should, you're making the wrong decision. If you ask plenty of questions and listen carefully to the answers, understand the investment well, understand your priorities, and weigh them carefully against the information you're getting, and make a decision that fits with your overall strategy, chances are you'll make the right decision. Remember the 87-year-old woman whose friends were cajoling her into investing in mutual funds? They had her fully prepared to make an investment that wasn't right for her, but with a little research (she called me!) and resistance to peer pressure, she avoided making the wrong decision.

GVO Golden Rule #9: *Don't try to time the market.* Yes, there can be a right and a wrong time to buy most types of investments. Buying equity-based investments after the market has been steadily rising for some time may not be prudent. Similarly, when interest rates are poised to go up, that's not the time to buy bonds. But market timing is a risky business and far too sophisticated and time consuming for us regular folk. Far better you invest regularly and average out the market swings. You can do that by dollar-cost averaging.

Dollar-cost averaging is a complex name for a simple investment technique. Rather than accumulating a large sum of money before making an investment, it is wiser to invest small amounts at regular intervals. Dollar-cost averaging means you don't have to worry about investing at the right time. However, for it to work effectively, you should use it as a long-term strategy — and stick with it! Don't let market performance shake your trust. It's a great system.

GVO Golden Rule #10: *Diversify*. Don't put all your eggs in one basket. Heavens, how sick are you of this saying? But it's true. If you spread the money around, you don't have to worry about losing it all in one fell swoop. And don't invest all your money in the Canadian economy. Investment in the world economy will help to reduce your dependence on our economic growth and a sometimes volatile Canadian dollar. It'll also allow you to benefit from strong economic growth in other countries or regions. By purchasing several different investments, you can build a well-diversified portfolio to reduce exposure to investment risk; if one investment doesn't do particularly well, the others may make up the difference.

GVO Golden Rule #11: *Stay the course*. If you find you are a little shy of the stock market, or you rank as conservative but decide to go into the market anyway, get yourself a buddy (preferably a financial adviser) who can hold your hand through the rough spots. A knowledgeable adviser will be able to remind you of your initial objectives and reassure you of what is happening so you don't make the fatal leap out of the market at just the wrong time.

And now, the final and most important rule of all.

GVO Golden Rule #12: *Keep a level head*. It's easy to get carried away, to forget the plan, to launch into an investment you don't really understand because someone else has made a killing. And it's easy to get scared, to want to run when everything seems to be turned the wrong way. It's good to keep reminding ourselves that the things we feel aren't real; they are just feelings. If you think your plan's gone awry, then sit down and review it logically. If you wish you were doing a little better, look at investments that might get you there: learn all about them, know the upsides and the downsides, and then make a levelheaded decision.

During one RRSP portfolio review, Ann Richards pointed out that while the market was up significantly, my portfolio had grown a measly 1%. Easy to get upset about, right? I didn't. I had a plan and I was sticking to it. I was holding Korea, which had gone right into the tank, and I wasn't about to sell. So I suffered a much lower average return than I normally would have. We did a four-year review to see how the plan was doing overall, and the figures showed I was earning about 12% on average over the last four years. That was my goal, so there was no reason to panic. Keeping a cool head let me look beyond the immediate circumstances of my portfolio. Looking at my long-term plan made it easy to see that I wasn't off by a mile. Looking beyond the immediate results, sticking with the plan, and keeping a cool head would all allow me to profit nicely as Korea recovered.

RETIRE RICHER SOONER PLAN (RRSP)

One of the best vehicles for long-term savings is an RRSP. An RRSP is a tax-deferral plan registered with Canada Customs and Revenue Agency (CCRA), formerly known as Revenue Canada. With an RRSP, you can deposit a portion of your earned income and claim the contribution as a tax deduction. Not only are the contributions made to an RRSP tax deductible, but the income generated by the investments inside an RRSP is not taxed until withdrawn from the plan. This means you can accumulate a much larger investment for your retirement than you could by investing outside an RRSP.

When you make an RRSP contribution, you receive a tax receipt to be filed with your tax return in order to claim your deduction.

Many people think an RRSP is an investment. It isn't. It is simply a way of registering your investments so they receive preferential tax treatment. Think of an RRSP like an umbrella. The investments you buy with your RRSP dollars — whether they are guaranteed investment certificates, mutual funds, stocks, bonds, or Treasury bills — are all held under this umbrella. As long as they remain under this RRSP umbrella, they continue to be treated in a special way. However, if you take these investments or cash out from under the umbrella — if you deregister them — they no longer benefit from this special tax treatment.

Anyone 69 or younger at the end of the year who has earned income may contribute to an RRSP. There is no minimum age restriction for establishing an RRSP, which means that even children may have RRSPs as long as they have earned income. If you are over 69 but still have earned income for RRSP purposes, remember you can contribute to a spousal RRSP up to the end of the year in which your spouse turns 69.

Contributions to an RRSP may be made at any time during the year, or within the first 60 days of the following calendar year. However, if you're turning 69, you must contribute before December 31, since your RRSP must be matured before year-end. Your RRSP contribution limit is the lesser of 18% of your previous year's earned income and the current year's RRSP dollar limit (set by the government). If you belong to a company pension plan or deferred profit-sharing plan (DPSP), your contribution limit may be reduced by your Pension Adjustment (PA) and, possibly, your Past Service Pension Adjustment (PSPA).

The notice of assessment you receive from CCRA after you file your tax return shows your RRSP limit. If you can't find your notice of assessment, call CCRA's computerized TIPS service. The telephone number is listed in the blue pages of the phone book.

If you decide to take the money out of your RRSP, you will have to pay tax on both the initial contribution and the income earned. Financial institutions are required to withhold tax. Outside Quebec, the rate is 10% on the first $5,000, 20% on withdrawal amounts between $5,000 and $15,000, and 30% for amounts over $15,000. You'll have to include any amounts withdrawn in your income for the year withdrawn. The tax withheld is remitted to CCRA and you will receive a T4RSP slip that you must file with your tax return showing the total amount of the withdrawal and the tax withheld. Once you file your tax return, the true taxes owing based on your marginal tax rate will be calculated, so consider yourself warned: you may end up owing more tax.

What is a locked-in RRSP?

When an employee leaves an employer, taking accumulated pension benefits from the ex-employer's plan before retirement, those funds are usually transferred to a locked-in RRSP (also referred to as a "locked-in retirement account" or "LIRA"). This type of RRSP has limiting provisions attached to it. For example, locked-in RRSP funds cannot be withdrawn all at once. These funds can only be used to purchase a life annuity, Life Income Fund (LIF), or Locked-in Retirement Income Fund (LRIF) and cannot currently be used to purchase a Registered Retirement Income Fund (RRIF). These restrictions are in place to ensure the funds provide a retirement income as originally intended by the pension plan that provided them.

What is a spousal RRSP?

A spousal RRSP is an RRSP to which one spouse (usually the higher income earner) contributes for the other. CCRA recognizes both common-law and same-sex relationships for the purposes of these contributions.

A spousal RRSP belongs to the individual in whose name the plan is registered, not to the contributor. You can contribute as much as you wish to a spousal RRSP, up to your annual RRSP deduction limit, and your contributions to a spousal RRSP do not affect your spouse's contribution to his or her own RRSP.

Spouses who are eligible to make RRSP contributions should not contribute to their own spousal RRSPs. Since there may be significant tax consequences for making withdrawals from a spousal RRSP, spouses who wish to make contributions to RRSPs should set up regular RRSPs for themselves.

Between the tax-deferred compounding return and the tax deferral on the investment (often referred to as your tax refund), an RRSP puts your savings way ahead of the game. And you can use your tax refund to help supplement the growth of your annual contribution. Let's say you can afford to save $50 a month in an RRSP. Go ahead, put it away. At the end of your first year you'll have contributed $600. Assuming a marginal tax rate of 30%, you'll receive a tax refund of $180. When you get your tax refund, stick it in your RRSP for next year. At the end of next year, you'll have contributed $780 (your $600 plus the $180 refund you received). Assuming your tax rate hasn't increased, you'll get a refund of $234. Roll that into your RRSP, and in year three you'll have a total contribution of $834, for a refund of $250. And so on, and so on. All that growth without taking another nickel out of your cash flow!

GETTING ONSIDE WITH ONLINE TRADING

The Internet has completely changed the way the world works, and the world of investing isn't immune. There's a wealth of information available on the net — perfect for those of us who just love to do our research before making a decision. And now we also have the option of buying and selling our own securities, paying a fraction of the price charged by traditional brokers and eliminating our exposure to those high-pressure sales tactics we all hate.

But online investing has its own traps. Without an adviser acting as a sounding board for your investment ideas, you could go off half-cocked or be lured by the ever-enticing investment rumour. Going online? Here are some rules to keep you onside.

- Start small. As a newcomer, don't put your whole portfolio online right from the start. Choose a sum that you can easily manage (remember, you're going to have to keep track of this yourself). As your confidence grows you can add more money to your online account.
- Stay diversified. Don't fall into the trap of focusing on one type of investment (such as stocks) to the exclusion of everything else. Keep your portfolio balanced. The investments you choose should be based on your investment time horizon (how long you plan to stay invested) and your investment risk tolerance (how well you sleep at night when the market is moving and shaking).
- Don't dump all your mutual funds. Yes, I know the idea of trading stock on the Internet is very sexy. And I know a $25 trade is way less expensive than a 6% back-end load. But there's a good reason why you went into mutual funds: professional management and built-in diversification. And once the initial excitement of online trading wears off, you'll be stuck managing the portfolio. Wouldn't it be nice to have at least some of your money invested in an alternative that you don't have to monitor constantly?
- Watch your costs. If you trade often, your costs will add up, even though they may be a lot cheaper than full-service brokerage commissions. Make sure that you're also fully aware of any additional fees or charges associated with your online account. And watch the tax trap. All that trading will result in capital gains that must be reported.
- Learn about "limit orders." A limit order is your instruction to buy a security at a specific price. The buy can only be made if the market price hasn't moved beyond a certain level. So, if you want to buy

ABC Stock at or under $10 and the price of ABC Stock moves up over $10, your trade won't be executed. Why do you want to do this? So you know how much you're spending. If you stick with a market order, regardless of how high the stock goes, your buy order will be executed, so you might end up paying considerably more than you intended.

- Learn about "stop-loss orders." Another important trading technique is the stop-loss order. This sets the price at which the security will be sold. So, if a stock is currently trading at $15, and you set a stop-loss order at $12, the stock will automatically be sold if the price hits $12, preventing any further losses. A word of warning, however: the stop-loss price has to actually be hit for the trade to execute. If the value of the stock drops from $14 to $10 in a single trade, your stop-loss won't work because the $12 marker was never hit.

- Be prepared for problems. Trading online isn't foolproof. There'll be times when you can't get into your account to trade. Your Internet connection might go down. The online brokerage firm's server might crash due to heavy trading or unexpected software problems. Find out if your online trading provider has alternative trading options, such as an automated phone trading system, or person-to-person trading during problem periods. If you aren't prepared for the inevitable problems associated with using technology, then don't go here.

Since information is power, and the web provides a vast amount of information, going online means you could have the investment world at your fingertips. But if you're going to buy and sell investments online, you're going to have to keep yourself as well informed as possible about what is going on with the companies you buy. You can use their sites to download prospectuses, financial statements, and other important information. You can use other sites to read about how analysts feel about your chosen companies. And you can take advantage of free services that allow you to receive automatic e-mail messages whenever your stocks are in the news. Going online to execute "hot tips" will have you offside in no time. Going online to open up your investment world, to learn more, to take control of your portfolio, now that's smart.

Want to learn more about the world of online investing? Pick up a copy of my book, *Dead Cat Bounce: The Skinny on E-vesting.* You'll love it!

10

Risk Management: Your Income and Your Life

The value of money is that with it you can tell anyone to go to the devil.

ATTRIBUTED TO W. SOMERSET MAUGHAM

To achieve financial peace of mind, we need to prepare for the risks of everyday life. To a certain extent, we are quite good about protecting our "stuff," spending buckets of money on property and contents insurance. The risks we tend to overlook, however, are those associated with our economic earning power. If you or your partner were to die or become disabled and unable to work, would your family have the resources to meet their day-to-day needs? It's a tough question to face, but the consequences of not facing it can be even tougher on your family.

Whether you're looking at disability insurance or life insurance, what you are really buying is cash when you need it most. You're buying replacement for the income you would have had if you had not become disabled or had not died. And you're shifting the risk to the insurance company instead of assuming the risk yourself.

It's not unlike what happens within the life insurance industry when one insurer turns to another — called a re-insurance company — so that it does not have to bear all the responsibility and financial risk of a policy payout, particularly for large policies. By purchasing insurance you're doing much the same thing — reducing the risk to your own financial plan. While your emergency fund may be able to replace your income for the first six months, past that point you know there's no way you can support yourself and your family. So you shift the risk to the insurer and you pay a premium for this.

That's the objective in a nutshell. If you have no form of income-replacement insurance, you're betting that you'll just keep chugging along until you're a ripe old age. Wake up! If you're 30 years old, there's a 23% likelihood that you'll die before you reach age 65. And there's a 52% probability that you'll be disabled for 90 days or more.

Unfortunately, people seem to be completely unaware of the impact of not having coverage, the right coverage, or enough coverage. When you consider the media exposure of investments such as mutual funds, or the deluge of promotion that accompanies the RRSP deadline, the area of disability insurance is one that is pathetically underrepresented. One reason may be people's unwillingness to look at the potential downsides of life. This can't happen to me, right? Yet I know six women who are about my age who have been diagnosed with debilitating diseases such as multiple sclerosis and lupus. The growth of an RRSP, the phenomenal performance of the stock market, these are happy stories. Thinking about getting sick or dying is a bummer — so we don't do it.

But we should. It's part of our responsibility to those we love, and it's part of a healthy financial life. Think of insurance, any kind of insurance, as protection against two things:

1. The financial loss resulting from an event that has a high probability of occurring.
2. The financial loss resulting from an event that may not have a high probability of occurring, but which would be financially devastating if it did occur.

"Most people don't appreciate the assets that they have in the form of their future earnings," says insurance specialist and financial planner Leslie Macdonald Francis. "If someone is earning $60,000 with a very modest annual increase, over 30 years that's a multi-million-dollar asset. It sounds corny, but it's like the old fable: *We* are the goose that lays the golden eggs."

So, let's look at risk. What's the probability of your dying or becoming disabled: one in 100; one in 80; one in 50? Do you know? Regardless of that probability, how adversely affected financially would you and your family be if the unthought-of, unprepared-for happened?

You have fire insurance, right? You've insured your car, your possessions, your home. Yet if you don't insure your ability to keep those home fires burning by insuring your income, your goose will be cooked. Quit procrastinating. You can't assume that it won't happen to you. And if your significant other is the primary breadwinner, you can't assume his continued health is guaranteed. Men like to think of themselves as invincible. My husband refers to it as feeling "bulletproof." Like Superman, right? Yet every day we hear stories of men who keel over in the prime of their lives. You had better make sure he has enough insurance so that you can take care of him, and the family, while he recovers.

If you're not convinced yet, here's a statistic to blow your socks off: According to the Society of Actuaries and the National Centre of Health Statistics and Transactions, each year, one in eight people become disabled. One in eight! What would your family do if one of the people bringing home the bacon couldn't anymore? Could you live on your savings? How long would that last, and what would the cost be to the future? Could you borrow the money? Your lender is more likely to call your existing loans, including your mortgage, than to lend you more money. Put all the pressure on your spouse? That's a great way to get a divorce. Tap your RRSP? What will you do when retirement arrives? Rely on the government? Yeah, right!

Leslie Macdonald Francis was awarded the Calgary Life Underwriter of the Year award in 1994. She's been the chairperson for the Canadian Institute of Chartered Life Underwriters and the president of the Calgary Life Underwriters Association. She played an integral role in the formation of the University of Calgary's insurance and risk management program in 1990. A founder of Francis McLachlan Financial Group in Calgary, she's also a member of the Estate Planning Council of Calgary, the Pastoral Institute of Calgary, and the Business and Professional Women's Club. Leslie has two stepdaughters and a stepson, with whom she shares her passion for anthropology.

DISABILITY INSURANCE

Leslie Macdonald Francis is absolutely passionate about women's needs for disability insurance, largely because, as she says, after more than 21 years in the biz, "I've dealt with lots of disability claims but I've only had one death claim."

According to the Society of Actuaries' Commissioner's Individual Disability Tables, for the top occupation class, at age 35 the claim incidence rate is three times greater for women than for men. After 40, the gap in incidence of claims begins to close, narrowing to six percent higher for women by age 60.

The other frightening issue for women is that the incidence of divorce seems to rise sharply for women who become disabled. "This is something I heard in an industry seminar that really had an impact on me," says Leslie. "The probability [of divorce] is far greater when a wife is disabled than when a husband is disabled." You could put this down to men not having been socialized to be nurturers. More important than the why — because there's little we can do about the fact — is the realization that disability puts a significant strain on marriages, so every woman needs to be prepared to cope financially with this devastating situation should it arise. *Do it!* You owe it to yourself so you don't end up poor and alone. You owe it to your spouse so your sweetheart has the means to get the help needed to make your life more comfortable. Your partner should not have to bear the full financial and emotional responsibility alone. And you owe it to your children too. Is it important to you that they see you deal with your setback with dignity? Being prepared can only help. And it will send them the right message: that they must take personal responsibility for their own lives.

Choose four female friends that you know well, that are all around the same age as you. Write their names on a sheet of paper along with your own. There's a 65% to 75% chance that one of the people on that list will die before she's 65. Worse still, there's a 92% to 98% chance that one person on your list will become disabled. How sure are you that it won't be you?

When Leslie was reviewing my material on disability insurance, she was struck by how appropriate this illustration was and offered her own story. "I belong to a study group of four women who are all financial planners," says Leslie. "I'm the one that's most into disability, but we all offer it to clients and we all think about it. One of those women — a dear friend of mine — was diagnosed with breast cancer recently. Now she's had a full mastectomy and has done her chemo treatments. Here I am a perfect example of the one-in-five statistics."

According to the Commissioner's Table on Disability, at most ages there's a one-in-three chance of becoming disabled for at least six months before age 65. When that disability occurs, if it lasts 90 days, then the average length will likely be about five years. According to the U.S. Housing and Home Finance Agency, 48% of all mortgage foreclosures on homes result from disability. With the right coverage, you can avoid this. You'll be able to continue making your mortgage payments without having to use up savings or liquidate investments. Being prepared means those assets are protected, so you, your family, and your long-term financial future are protected.

What to look for in a disability plan

There's no question that you need the help of a qualified insurance adviser when you go shopping for disability insurance. Why? Because there are so many sizes and styles out there, it's very easy to buy one that looks good on the hanger but just doesn't fit. There is a lot involved in arranging an individual disability contract. Using a generalist will get you in trouble. Remember, too, that with insurance, as with just about everything else, you get what you pay for.

Leslie says that you should make sure, above all, that your disability insurance policy is *non-cancellable* and *guaranteed renewable*. It would be useless to buy a policy if the insurance company could refuse to renew it after one or two years. "This is such a fundamental issue," says Leslie, "because you don't want your contract to be changed. The definition of disability might become more restrictive, premiums might increase, or entire benefits, such as cost-of-living increases, might be eliminated." You would have bought a pig in a poke because despite all your comparison shopping, you could end up with a policy that looks significantly different from the one you bought.

The *definition* of disability is also extremely important. "If you think about a life insurance policy," says Leslie, "no one needs to define death. But when it comes to disability, the variables are almost unlimited as to what is or is not a disability, and how you define it, and when it begins and ends."

Maria was playing field hockey with her daughter's team when she fell and shattered her left wrist, thumb, and index finger. After several operations it became clear she would never recover the full use of her hand. As a left-handed endodontist, Maria was no longer able to perform dentistry so she decided to take a position at the local university. How does the change of occupation affect her disability insurance? Is she still entitled to a monthly income benefit even if she is working at something other than what she was originally qualified to do? Well, that depends.

The insurance industry basically offers three definitions of total disability, and they come with different price tags. The narrowest definition, and the one that carries the steepest price, is "own occupation," which considers an individual totally disabled if she is unable to engage in her own occupation, even if she is working at something else. Next down the price scale is "regular occupation," which considers an individual totally disabled if she is unable to engage in her own occupation and is also not working at anything else. "Any occupation" is the least expensive, as well as the broadest and least likely to pay should something go wrong. It considers an individual totally disabled if she is unable to work in any occupation for which she is reasonably suited by education, training, or experience.

While Maria may be earning a substantial income, under an own-occupation definition of total disability, she would be entitled to full benefits for total disability regardless of the fact that she is gainfully working in another occupation. If she had taken out disability insurance with a regular-occupation definition, her university employment would preclude her from receiving monthly income benefits because even if she remained totally disabled from her own occupation as a dentist, she is gainfully employed. If she had disability insurance with an any-occupation definition of disability, she would not qualify for monthly income benefits, except during the initial acute treatment phase of her recovery because, by virtue of her training, education, and experience she would be considered suitably trained and educated to hold a variety of other jobs such as lecturing at a university, consulting for an insurance company, or working for a pharmaceutical company.

Disability is a grey area. It is a matter of degree and debate. Are a fractured wrist and fingers totally disabling? It depends on your job. Will you receive monthly income benefits? It depends on the definition. Make sure you know what your insurance does or does not cover.

So find out how your plan defines disability. Must it be total? Is the determination made by your doctor or the insurer's doctor? How long must you be disabled before you'll begin receiving benefits?

Equally important is the *residual disability* feature. While some people become totally disabled, it is much more likely that you will be able to do some work, but at a lower income. In the case of a slow recovery or a slow deterioration from a progressive disease, this becomes very important. "If you don't have residual disability insurance, it could take five or 10 years before your claim can begin because you must have total disability," says Leslie. "I have a friend with MS and she's far from totally disabled. Some days she can walk better than others. It fades in and out. She seems to get much more exhausted than the rest of us. And a flu bug seems to affect her much more severely. But she's not totally disabled. If you're in this situation and do not have residual or partial disability coverage, you have no claim until you reach the point where you are totally disabled." Think of it on a scale ranging from black to white. If your ability to work whole hog is white, and total disability is black, residual disability represents all the shades of grey in between. Since most group plans have limited or no benefits for residual disabilities, you can be up a creek even though you think you're covered.

Some individual policies require earnings loss only, without requiring any loss of time or duties, which is much more restrictive. "This is a very important point," says Leslie. "The question becomes, 'what is the definition of residual disability?' One company might say it requires a loss of time or duties plus income. Another might say it only requires a loss of income. Look for a contract in which the payout is based on a loss of your income." Leslie cites the example of a young dentist who injured her back. She was still practising, but because she was not as effective due to her pain, she was only seeing half the usual number of patients each day. She had a loss of earnings, but no loss of time or duties. "Whether you are a doctor who can see only half the patients or a realtor who can handle only half the number of clients, your reduction in income should be the qualifier. If you bought a policy several years ago which required both definitions at the time, as long as you're in good health you should try to have the definition changed to 'loss of income.' Most newer, better-quality policies now base payout on a loss of income."

Make sure you also understand the *qualification period* in the plan. This is the number of days of total disability required before the insurer will pay residual disability benefits. A policy with a zero-day qualification period is best and means there is no requirement of total disability. Multiple sclerosis is a good example of an illness that may take years to create total disability. However, as the disease progresses, this could cause significant loss of income. The requirement for, say, a 30-day period of total disability would prevent you from ever being eligible for residual benefits, making your policy almost useless.

We all know that inflation is an evil monster that eats away at our money's purchasing power. Having an *inflation rider* or a *cost-of-living rider* is a good way to increase your monthly benefits. While this is an expensive "addition" to a basic policy, it is critical when you look at the long-term cost to your purchasing power when inflation is taken into account. At an inflation rate of 5%, today's $1,000 will be worth only $613.90 in 10 years, $376.90 in 20 years, and $231.40 in 30 years. So what looks like a healthy payout today may seem paltry in a couple of decades.

"An inflation or cost-of-living rider is different from a policy which is indexed, although they sound much the same," says Leslie. The cost-of-living rider is meant to increase your claim cheques after you've been disabled. Indexing keeps the protection level of your coverage up to what it should be while you are healthy. Sometimes called an update benefit, it is a way of keeping your protection level current.

Another way benefits might increase is under a *future insurability rider*. With this option, the insurance company periodically allows you to increase your benefits by quite large sums without additional health questions. "This is important for the young healthy person who anticipates there will be significant increases in income in the future," says Leslie. "While there are no additional health questions, and you don't have to disclose that you've taken on a more dangerous hobby, the increases do have to be financially justified."

There are a lot of i's to dot and t's to cross when it comes to making sure you have the best policy for your needs. Here's a case in point. When Maya bought her disability plan in her early thirties, she checked on the definition, the residual disability feature, and the qualification period. About 10 years later, Maya went through a difficult divorce and sought counselling from a psychiatrist. She was prescribed antidepressants, and over time, everything fell back into place for her. In her mid-forties, Maya decided to increase her disability coverage to keep up with her increased income stream. She was in for a shock. The insurance company felt Maya was too high a risk because she had been treated for depression, so her request for increased benefits was declined. Maya couldn't understand it. She was well past that. It had been almost five years since she had taken any drugs. Why was this coming back to haunt her now?

Are there exclusions for *pre-existing conditions* on the policy? If you are a diabetic, how would that affect claims for disability arising from conditions that could be linked to your diabetes? In the case of individual disability coverage you must declare all your health issues and then you will be covered, if you are accepted for coverage, that is. Nearly all group policies have pre-existing condition clauses. If you have a disorder before buying a policy, usually you will not be covered for disabilities related to this disorder. It's just as important to know what you're not covered for as what you are.

Another thing to look for is an *integration clause*. Some policies deduct the amount of benefits paid by Employment Insurance, Canada Pension Plan, or car insurance from the amount they pay out in benefits. This has advantages and disadvantages. It can mean that the premiums are lower. However, low-income individuals might end up with no benefits at all from their insurance policy until Employment Insurance sick benefits run out. "Also look for the use of the terms 'payable' and 'paid,'" says Leslie. If the term "payable" is used in your policy, then the insurance company can hold back the portion they expect you to receive from other sources. If it turns out that you do not receive that other income, the company will pay, but you'll have been out-of-pocket for the six months it takes the government to come to a decision.

Another way to reduce the cost of your premiums is to eliminate short duration claims or claims for periods when you are covered by an employer or by government benefits. Know that if you choose this route, you will not be able to make a claim until the waiting period in your policy — usually three or six months — has expired.

Do you smoke? Quit and you'll pay 10% to 15% less in premiums. To qualify as a nonsmoker, you must not have used any tobacco products for 12 consecutive months prior to applying for coverage. Another good reason to give up the evil weed!

I don't have to worry about this, I'm covered at work
How much do you know about your company disability coverage? Can
you answer these questions?

- How much are you covered for? Will your income from disability
  be taxed? Group policies paid for by an employer generate income
  that is taxed. If you pay the premiums directly from your after-tax
  income, your benefits are tax-free. Is your coverage sufficient once
  tax is taken?
- Is there a maximum? Group plans usually cover a percentage of your
  salary, but some also have a specified maximum.
- For how long will your benefits be paid? Most plans cover you for
  only two years if you can't work in your own occupation, shutting
  off completely if you are deemed by the insurance company to be
  able to do any type of work at all.
- If you leave your company, will you be able to take the plan with
  you, or would you have to requalify at your new employer? If you
  developed a problem in the interim, would you qualify?
- Are your benefits indexed to inflation?
- What's your policy's definition of "disabled"? If you can't do the job
  you were hired to do, will you be paid your benefits regardless of
  what other work you find?
- Can the insurance company deny you your benefits because they see
  you as fit to do any other type of work? Let's say you're currently a
  salesperson who must drive as part of your duties. If you cannot
  drive because of a sight problem, can the insurance company deny
  you your claim on the basis that, according to them, you could do
  any other work? Will partial benefits be paid if you can only work
  for a few hours a day?
- Can the company raise the premiums for one group of insured
  people and not for another? How will you be affected?
- What are the exclusions on the policy? Travel outside Canada?
  Pre-existing conditions? Previously treated mental, nervous conditions? Alcoholism?

One of the biggest distractions from individual disability coverage is the
fact that many people who benefit from company coverage think that

they're fully covered. And they figure that since the coverage is free, it's fine. Remember, you get what you pay for. The question you should be asking yourself is, "Does this come anywhere close to meeting my needs?" If you find your group plan lacking, look to an individual policy to supplement it. "Then you have a non-cancellable, totally portable policy you can take with you regardless of where you work," says Leslie, "along with rates that are fixed."

It can't happen to me
According to Statistics Canada, one in seven Canadians today have a disability. If you think accidents are the primary cause of disability, think again! Accidents represented only 21% of claims for long-term disability of three years or longer, according to Aetna Canada. Bone, muscle, and back problems caused 21% of claims. Circulatory system problems caused 8% of claims. Nervous system disorders caused 7% of claims. And mental disorders resulted in a whopping 15% of claims. Then there's a miscellany of problems like digestive disorders, ulcers, and the like that make up another 27%. Of course, there are many more causes — don't worry, I won't list them all — but you get the picture. Anything that has the potential to keep you from earning a living is a threat to your family's financial health. And you don't have to live with the threat. You can protect yourself. *Do it!*

CRITICAL ILLNESS INSURANCE
So, you've been out shopping like a mad fiend, trying to lay your hands on disability insurance coverage. It's expensive. It's tough to get. You give up. You're never going to qualify! Or, worse, because you're currently not employed (maybe you're a mom or dad at home, or maybe you're just between careers) you can't even apply.

While you may not be able to qualify for that disability plan I've convinced you that you need, I have another suggestion that might be at least a partial solution: critical illness insurance. With this insurance, you buy a policy to cover specific types of diseases and if you're subsequently diagnosed with one of them, you'll receive a payout the size of which depends on the amount of coverage you bought.

CI insurance is a relatively new offering, having only come to Canada in 1995. It originated in South Africa in the early 1980s, the brainchild of a cardiologist who watched as the financial stress exacerbated his patients' health problems.

According to the Heart and Stroke Foundation of Canada, one in four Canadians will be diagnosed with a critical illness by the age of 65. But with the tremendous strides that have been made in medical technology, you're far less likely to die than you would have been decades ago. You might even make a full recovery. Thirty percent of people with cancer are completely cured, while 75% of stroke sufferers and 95% of heart attack patients survive the initial occurrence. The problem most people face is that they are unprepared for the financial crunch they experience while they're undergoing lengthy and expensive treatments. CI insurance can fill that gap until they can get back on their feet and start earning a living again.

Critical illness insurance pays a lump sum on either diagnosis of the conditions you've bought coverage for, or on their progress to an agreed state. While a heart attack is a heart attack and requires no further definition, multiple sclerosis might not actually impair your lifestyle for many years.

There are no strings attached to the payout — you're diagnosed and 31 days later you've got a cheque — so you can use the money in any way you see fit. Unsure our overburdened medical system will make space for you? Put your CI money to use seeking private treatment. Or use the money to provide an income while you convalesce. Clear up debts. Keep your small business running. Make physical changes to your home or vehicle. Ready yourself for the rest of your life. It's your money so it's your call how it's used.

The ailments covered aren't the same on every plan. While cancer, heart disease, and stroke are pretty standard, there is considerable variance on conditions such as multiple sclerosis, paralysis, kidney disease, loss of speech or hearing, and so on. Look for a plan that covers the highest number of variables. And watch the definitions used for critical illness conditions, which also tend to vary from plan to plan. Don't let the medical terminology baffle you into buying something you don't understand. Be clear on when you'll be covered and for what.

Buying CI insurance is a lot like buying life insurance except, of course, you don't have to die to collect — which makes it seem more like "life" insurance than life insurance. First you select the amount you wish to be covered for. That can range from about $25,000 to the millions. Next, you provide medical evidence of good health. (Be warned: a strong emphasis is placed on your family's health history, and a tendency toward a hereditary disease such as cancer could result in its omission from your coverage.) That, along with your age, your gender, and whether or not you smoke gives you an annual premium amount.

And that premium ain't no small potatoes. CI insurance can be expensive. As an offset, policies offer a full refund of premiums to your estate if you die without making a claim. And some policies allow you to purchase a special rider that will kick your premiums back to you if you haven't made a claim within a specified time period.

If you haven't been able to lay your hands on disability insurance, CI insurance can help ease your mind by providing a lump-sum payout when you most need it. And with medical science making life-saving advances in treating major illnesses, this might be the time to insure your wallet, as well as your body.

LONG-TERM CARE INSURANCE

Here's another relatively new insurance product that I predict will be a big seller: long-term care, or LTC, insurance. As institutions jump into selling this product, buyers need to be aware that early product offerings tend not to have all the bells and whistles of a more developed product. Time makes the product better as customers make more demands. Here are some of the key issues to keep in mind when buying LTC coverage either for your folks or for yourself so you are not short-changed in your enthusiasm to get covered.

As with any insurance product, you're betting you'll need the benefits, and the insurance company is betting that you won't. A study by the U.S. Department of Health and Human Services indicates that people at age 65 face at least a 40% lifetime risk of entering a nursing home. About 10% will stay there five years or longer. (And while LTC insurance is often associated with elder care, you don't have to be elderly to benefit; a tragic car accident or debilitating illness can create the need for long-term care.)

In trying to determine the need for LTC insurance, your first stop will be at your family's medical history. You might be a ready buyer if you've

As the former director of the Women's Financial Planning Centre, and with more than 20 years of broadcasting experience, Kathy Farrell is especially well qualified to communicate with women and show them how to make the most of their money. While working, Kathy added the rigours of an MBA program to her hectic schedule. She is past-president of the Fellow Life Management Institute and a former member of the board of the International Association of Business Communicators. Kathy is wild about gardening and fiction writing, and is now focused on the pursuit of her personal dreams, surrounded by her Siberian irises.

watched relatives suffer Alzheimer's or some other form of senile dementia. But if your elders have passed on peacefully and in reasonable health, you may wish to opt for a return-of-premium option, which may help you get over the "it's a waste of money" mindset. This option would return all premiums paid to your estate if you never have need of your insurance, effectively eliminating the cost of your unneeded insurance.

One of the choices in selecting a LTC policy is the amount of daily cost you choose to buy. If you decide to buy a policy that will cover only a part of the cost of a day's care, will you be able to cover the difference in cost out of your own pocket? Also check to see if the insurance company specifies a maximum total payout. Many companies do. Are there caps on the cost of individual service providers you may need? While you may be entitled to, say, $100 a day, you'll be dipping into your own pocket pretty quickly if the policy will only pay a maximum of $25 a hour for an RN.

The big problem with trying to predict the cost of long-term care 10, 15, or 20 years from now is that it's hard to anticipate what impact inflation will have on health-care costs. Does the policy you're looking at carry an inflation rider to protect the future value of your benefits? Also ask about the waiting period — the amount of time you must cover costs yourself before your insurance kicks in. Extending the waiting period will reduce the costs of your premiums but will leave you picking up all the costs until your plan kicks in.

Are there different rules for home care and for institutional care? Often there's a difference in the age at which you can purchase coverage, and the length of time the coverage will last. This latter point is one of the most important considerations when buying LTC insurance. If the average time spent in a nursing home is about three years, you'll need to decide whether to gamble on the average, or buy less or more protection. Remember, once your period of coverage is over, you're back to footing the total costs on your own.

Make sure you understand the rules surrounding pre-existing conditions — conditions for which medical advice or treatment was recommended or received within a specific period of time before your LTC insurance purchase. While you're at it, find out whether any specific illnesses are not covered.

Be clear on when benefits will begin; for example, must you be hospitalized in order to receive benefits? And check to see if there is protection against increases in premiums. The last thing you need is to have a policy lapse after years of premiums simply because you can't keep up with increases in costs.

It's been estimated that the chances of using homeowners' insurance are about 1 in 88, that the odds of using car insurance are about 1 in 47, and the chances of using LTC insurance are about 2 in 5. The use of a long-term care policy addresses not only the direct cost of care but also the psychological issues for both patient and caregiver.

LIFE INSURANCE

The protection of your assets is one of the cornerstones of a healthy financial plan. That includes your ability to earn an income. But the hot button of RRSPs — the chance to reduce your annual taxable income — is something people identify with much more easily. When people have, let's say, $200 to put away toward their financial health, they will tend to contribute all of it to their RRSP because of the immediate gratification. According to Kathy Farrell, former director of the Women's Financial Planning Centre, those people do not have a well-rounded financial plan. Instead, she says, "They should be allocating a certain portion of it to good-quality protection." Protection of what? Protection of your future income.

The term "life insurance" is a misnomer. After all, you're not insuring your life, you're insuring the economic value of your life, or your ability to earn an income in the future. It's a matter of taking care of one of the most important details of your life: your responsibility to make sure that those who count on you have been wise in their judgment.

A survey conducted by the Life and Health Insurance Foundation for Education showed that more than half of Canadians think they don't know enough about life insurance. Even more alarming is that one-third of those with life insurance don't know what kind of policy they have. This is a perfect example of being so afraid, resistant, unwilling to deal with a difficult issue that we'd rather just stick our heads in the sand.

People seem far more willing to spend a mint insuring their stuff than to spend a much smaller amount insuring their future economic stability. Look at car insurance as just one example. My young friend Judy pays approximately $300 a month for her car insurance. At just 23 years old, Judy could buy a universal life policy for $300,000 for a premium of just $50.50 monthly.[19] And by the time she reaches 60, Judy will have accumulated $235,350 in assets through her plan.

Kathy Farrell sees four main reasons for people's resistance to life insurance. First, she says, "people don't want to face their own mortality." It's the same story with wills. People don't want to make a will because superstitiously they believe that once they take care of the details, the hand of fate will strike them down.

The second reason is that life insurance is intangible. It's not like buying an investment, where you walk away with a share certificate or an investment statement that shows what you have. The idea of creating a source of income to replace your contribution to the family coffers should you die seems far less concrete for many people.

The third reason is that people are very suspicious of the product, of the industry, and of the people within the industry. There's an image that remains from years ago, where life insurance representatives hounded you. Since life insurance is difficult to sell, that very well could have been the case. In fact, there's a saying in the industry that "life insurance is never bought, it is sold." People are afraid to deal with insurance people because they are afraid they are going to be coerced into doing something they don't want to do. And while it's often sold on the fear factor, that's just the kind of tactic that has people running away from the product.

The fourth reason for people's resistance is the fact that life insurance seems complicated. Will you need to have a physical? What special terms

---

19 Figures provided by Kathy Farrell as at May 1998.

and conditions do you have to watch for? Will the amount you buy now be enough for the future? How much should you buy?

In combination, these concerns prevent people from addressing this key component of their financial health. Everyone pretty well accepts the fact that the worst time to buy something is when you need it — when it is *always* more expensive, or worse, unavailable. Life insurance fits this truism to a T. The best time to buy life insurance is when you don't need it: when you're young, when you're healthy, and when it costs less. It will be an asset that you will much appreciate many years down the road.

The thing about insurance — whether it is life or disability insurance — that makes it different from any other financial instrument is that you can't always get it when you want it. With practically everything else you can go out and buy it if you're willing to spend the money. With life insurance, if your health should deteriorate, as it tends to do when you get older, you may not qualify. Health underwriting is also more rigorous for higher-value plans.

Kathy Farrell says the single most important part of buying insurance is sitting down with a financial adviser that you trust. Because life insurance is a fairly complicated product, you need someone who can explain the differences. According to Kathy, you should be suspicious of anyone who starts off with a set amount you should have: "You need $100,000." And you need someone who begins by trying to understand your needs and concerns. What are the risks you are trying to cover? What are your issues? This person should be both able and willing to guide you through the alternatives.

Kathy and her husband first bought insurance when they purchased their home and wanted mortgage insurance. Kathy says, "At the time, I wondered if I had been swindled because, in my mind, we only had a short-term need. Our insurance representative was considered to be one of the best in the industry and he said it would give long-term value and we would always have a need. I more or less just went along, always questioning it in my own mind. Now that we're at this point in our life, it has very significant cash value. What I like best about it is that if our best-laid plans are sideswiped because we end up with unexpected financial needs, we can always access that policy. It's something you can literally take to the bank and they will give you 90% of the cash value. Or you can borrow against the cash value."

If you take care of the details, you may not end up rich, but you will end up with more options to help minimize the stress in your life and increase your personal freedom. Kathy believes that no one vehicle is better than another. "In my opinion, this is the single largest problem today. Because mutual-fund companies do a lot of advertising, people are solely focused on asset accumulation and on returns. They want the single best. There is no one single best. It's like mix-and-match clothes. You want to have a nice collection of things that complement one another and can perform double duty. Using a holistic approach like that gives you the benefits of synergy." Kathy likens the concept of investment diversification to the issue of life insurance and its place in your whole financial picture. We know it makes sense to hold a variety of investment types within our portfolios so that the underperformance of any one asset type doesn't have too much impact on the entire portfolio. Kathy says, "Insurance is such an important part of the formula because you are protecting your most important asset: your ability to make a living."

Whether or not you need to buy life insurance depends on a lot of things, such as:

- how much you currently have in the way of assets
- how much debt you have
- how much your family will need to make ends meet
- whether you're concerned about minimizing the tax impact on your estate.

The first thing to consider is why you even need insurance. You may not. However, if your death would cause economic hardship to others, you probably do. As a quick test, read through the following questions. If you answer no to any, you'll likely need some insurance.

Will your estate have sufficient funds to:

- take care of your funeral expenses?
- pay your accounting, legal, and probate fees?
- pay taxes owing at death?
- provide sufficient income to meet your family's day-to-day needs?
- eliminate any debts you have at death?

- provide for other areas of priority, such as the education of your children/grandchildren?

How much insurance will I need?

Here's a quick formula you can use to calculate how much insurance you'll need:

$A - (B + C + D + E) = $ insurance needed

A = your family's Assets and income
  (including existing insurance, a spouse's income, government benefits, pension income, income from investments [e.g., GICs, CSBs, mutual funds], income that could be realized from the sale of assets, etc.)

B = your family's monthly Budget needs
  (including shelter, food, and household supplies, clothing, utilities, car maintenance, insurance [home and car], child care, entertainment, etc.)

C = Costs associated with your death
  (including funeral expenses, accounting and legal fees, probate costs, estate taxes, etc.)

D = Debts to be paid off
  (including credit-card balances, mortgages, loans, etc.)

E = Exceptional expenses
  (including educational costs, vacations, major purchases [e.g., new car, medical equipment], etc.)

Begin by calculating the income your family would have, based on the current income (from pension, spouse's employment, etc.). To that, add the income that would be generated from your assets. A $25,000 GIC at 10% would generate an annual income of $2,500. And if you have an existing insurance policy that would pay out $100,000, if that money is then invested, earning a return of, let's say, 12%, it would provide an annual income of $12,000.

Once you know how much income your family will have, you then have to calculate the expenses it will face. Some of those expenses are one-time costs, such as your funeral or the payoff of existing debt, while others are ongoing, such as monthly expenses and educational costs. The discrepancy between what your family has and what it will need must be covered in some way if you wish to minimize the financial impact of your death. That's where the insurance comes into play.

In deciding whether or not to buy insurance, or how much insurance you should buy, look at each of these areas to analyze its impact on your family.

What type of insurance should I buy?
Whether you buy "term," "whole life," or "universal life" insurance will be dependent on two primary factors:

- the amount of insurance you need, and
- how long you need that insurance to be in place.

Term insurance provides protection for a predetermined period of time (perhaps five, 10, or 20 years) or until a certain age, such as 65, 70, or 75. Think carefully before you buy insurance with age cut-offs: statistics show that you can reasonably expect to live past the age of 75, so if you're looking for longer-term protection, term insurance may not be for you.

With term insurance, when the term of the contract expires your coverage ends unless you renew the term. Each time the term is renewed, the premium is adjusted, usually upward. For example, you may buy term insurance that covers you until you're 65. Your policy may dictate that the term must be renewed every five years, so in five, 10, 15 years (and so on), you will receive notice of your new, adjusted amount. If you renew, you're still covered until you turn 65. If you don't, your protection is gone. The benefit paid by term insurance can be level, increasing, or decreasing; however, in most cases the face value remains level while the premiums increase with the risk of death.

When it comes to insurance with decreasing benefits, there are a couple of ways to go. Sometimes people choose bank-offered mortgage life insurance, the benefit of which is full payment of the mortgage upon death of the insured mortgage-holder. With traditional mortgage life insurance, while the premium remains the same for the term of the insurance, the benefit goes down as the mortgage balance decreases. As well, since mortgage life insurance is always paid to the mortgagor (usually the bank), you give up the control of how the money will be used. (Kathy Farrell says mortgage life insurance should be called "group creditor insurance," since the creditor is the person who is protected by the policy.) If your spouse should die, wouldn't you rather have a lump sum of money that you can then use to either pay off the mortgage or do something else? Perhaps you'll continue to make the mortgage payments from the proceeds of the insurance. Perhaps you'll move to a smaller home, or to a home closer to family. The ability to have your options open to you should be factored into your decision.

If freedom of choice is important to you, a private "decreasing" or "declining" term insurance policy might suit you more than a mortgage life insurance policy. Decreasing term insurance is similar to mortgage life insurance in that the benefit declines over the life of the policy. However, when premiums are reevaluated at the end of each term, they typically decrease; and what's more, you or your family, and not the bank, are always the beneficiary.

Think of term insurance as an expense. While it will give you comfort and peace of mind, it accumulates no residual value. If you're only after peace of mind, term insurance may be the ticket. If you're looking at the longer term, if you want coverage to last your lifetime or want to use insurance to build assets, term insurance isn't the right choice. And with term insurance, the statistics are all in favour of the insurance company.

Whole life and universal life insurance are permanent, remaining in place until death. With whole life policies, the insurance company does the investing. With universal life, you have much more control over the types of investments the money is going into.

With both these types of policies, the premium is generally the same for the life of the policy, so the annual cost can be low if taken early in life (when the risk of death is low), or very high if taken late in life. Most whole life policies have a "reserve," which can be refunded if you cancel the policy before your death. This reserve is referred to as the cash value of the plan. You can also borrow against this cash value at an interest rate set in the policy. However, if you haven't paid it back, the money owed will be deducted from the death benefit.

At a certain point, both whole life and universal life can become self-funding: the assets built up in the policy can be used to pay for the policy so that the cost to you is eliminated. That was one of the reasons why I bought my whole life policy at 30. I wanted to set the rate before I got any older or any sicker, and I wanted the benefit of having a policy that would eventually pay for itself. Since I had no idea at the time that I would end up with two children eight years later, in retrospect, my decision was brilliant. But over the years I've taken a pile of flack for having bought a whole life policy. Mostly the criticisms have centred on how much more I am paying for my insurance than I would have if I had purchased a term policy. To see the realities of the situation, I asked Kathy to do a calculation for me.

Let's say that Jane and Suzie, nonsmoking twins aged 30, are evaluating the costs and benefits of a $200,000 life insurance policy. Jane is considering a 10-year-term renewable and convertible policy with premiums of $294 a year. Suzie is looking at a whole life policy with premiums of $2,710 a year. Both want their plans to remain in effect for their whole life. Suzie's whole life plan is projected to become self-funding after 12 years. Here's how the numbers look:

Age	Insurance Costs	
	Term	Whole Life
30–39	$ 2,940	$27,100
40–49	$ 4,400	$ 5,420
50–59	$ 8,720	0
60–65	$13,236	0
Total costs	$29,296	$32,520

Since Jane will likely live well past 65, she will need to switch to a whole life policy to avoid the age cut-off. At age 65 it would cost her $11,754 a year to convert her term policy to a whole life policy. Assuming Jane's whole life policy becomes self-funding in 11 years, Jane will have paid a total of $158,050 for the same benefits Suzie got for $32,520.

When I purchased whole life insurance, like Suzie I chose a $200,000 policy which was projected to be self-funding after 12 years. When I purchased my policy back in 1989, the premiums were calculated at just under $1,200 a year (less than half the amount Suzie would pay today). So my policy is projected to cost me approximately $14,400 for coverage for life. Compare that with the quote given to a woman shopping for term insurance coverage for her husband because they have a new family (her first, his second): they would have to pay $4,800 a year. And if he renews the term at 62 (his children will then be just 15 and 18), his annual premium for the next 10 years would be approximately $14,000 a year.[20]

So, back to the question, "What kind of insurance should I buy?" The best place to start is with the amount of coverage you need. Let's say you'll need $125,000 to pay off your mortgage, $5,000 to cover your funeral expenses, $15,000 to cover legal and accounting bills, and an additional $100,000 to cover the capital gains your estate will be hit with. All told, you'll need about $245,000. Buying a policy with a lower payout clearly won't serve your needs.

The next thing to look at is how long you'll need the coverage. Some of your needs may be short term, in which case declining term insurance may be the most cost-effective way to cover yourself. On the other hand, the need to meet your funeral expenses and minimize the tax hit on your estate is permanent. Whole life insurance will be your best bet here, because you won't die after your coverage ends.

Remember, the premium on your whole life policy will remain the same, while the premium on most term insurance will rise each time the policy is renewed. So while the cost of term insurance will appear far less expensive in the early years of a policy (if taken at an early age), you have to look at the long-term costs. Have your insurance salesperson compare the lifetime cost of both types of policies (remember to compare similar features and benefits), and then make your decision.

Another interesting fact: With some policies, you can buy the right to convert your term policy to a whole life policy at a later date. So if you decide to start off with term insurance to protect your young family, and then wish to convert to a whole life policy when your needs change and you have more money, your health won't be a factor in setting the premiums. However, your age *will* be considered: The older you are, the more your insurance will cost.

Many people don't shop around for individual life insurance plans because they are covered by "group insurance" offered by their employer. But don't assume the group plan gives you the type of insurance or coverage that you need. One of the critical differences between a group

---

20 TD Insurance, quoted May 1998.

plan and an individually owned plan is that with a group plan, you don't own the plan (your company does) even though you're paying a taxable benefit on that policy. Since you don't own the plan, you can't take it with you, and you can't convert it. So while you're covered for as long as you remain with the company, if you're wholly dependent on your group policy, you may find yourself out in the cold if you are terminated from your job (unless your group plan has a provision that allows you to purchase your insurance privately upon termination).

With more than 150 insurance companies in Canada, you *must* shop around when looking for life insurance. Get several quotes, make sure you're comparing apples with apples, and buy the policy that best meets your needs. Resist the urge to overbuy, but don't sell yourself, and your family, short either. Evaluate your future earning potential and your family's ongoing needs realistically, take inflation into account, and then buy enough insurance to meet your requirements.

When deciding which options, or "riders," to add to your policy, remember that each option will increase the cost of your premiums. Here are a few you may be presented with:

- *Waiver of premium*. If you become disabled (sick or injured), this option will waive your premiums but keep your coverage in place. Often this option is of little value because the definition of "disabled" is extremely restrictive, so few people qualify. Before you buy this option, make sure the definition of disability suits you. Also, see how the option is priced; it's usually very expensive. Rather than purchasing this option, consider buying disability insurance coverage — which you should have anyway — that makes allowance for maintaining your life insurance premiums.
- *Accidental death benefit*. This is often referred to as "double indemnity," because it doubles the benefit if death is caused by an accident. However, since your family needs a certain level of insurance coverage regardless of how you die, double indemnity often creates a false sense of security. Don't be tempted to buy only half as much insurance as you need, relying on the fact that if you die it will be by accident. Fewer than 8% of deaths among people 25 to 65 are the result of an accident.
- *Guaranteed insurability*. This is a guarantee that in the future you will

be able to buy more insurance at standard rates despite a change in your health. The amount you can buy, and when you can buy it, are spelled out in the policy. Your option to purchase additional insurance usually cannot exceed the original face value of the policy. Remember that while you have the option of buying more insurance, you should only do so if your circumstances have changed and you need more insurance.

- *Increasing face value.* This option allows you to increase the benefit of your policy by a set amount each year; your premium increases with each increase in the benefit. Since the increases are provided automatically, you will be assured that your coverage has some inflation protection. And since there is no need for proving your insurability, even if your health circumstances change, you can still benefit from an ever-increasing face value. As well, with a locked-in schedule of premium increases, you can take advantage if rates are competitive, or decline the option if you feel you can arrange separate, less expensive insurance. This rider usually has an annual administrative fee, so it's only economical on larger policies.
- *Insuring the cash value of your plan.* If you chose this option, the death benefit paid will also include the cash value of the plan. This means that the policy provides an increasing benefit over time — good for inflation protection.

Who owns what?

So you've decided that insurance is an important part of your basket of goods, but you just can't get your better half to move toward the purchase. What now? I asked Kathy Farrell if you can take out insurance on a spouse. (This sounds like the plot for a murder mystery, as opposed to a financial book, doesn't it?) Kathy says that as long as your spouse is aware and is in agreement, you can take out the policy, name yourself the beneficiary, and pay the premiums. You'll own the policy so any cash value will accrue to you. It is simply his life that is insured.

If you haven't yet considered the importance of insuring your future earning potential from the rigours of disability or death, I hope you're convinced now. Find a professional to help you assess how much and what type of insurance is just right for you. Remember, you'll need a person who is knowledgeable and experienced in the type of insurance you are seeking. That person should be willing to provide you with quotes from more than one insurer, and should be willing to explain the ins and outs of the wide variety of features available.

Ultimately, we all hope to live long, healthy lives that are challenging and full of joy. When circumstances change in ways that threaten to rob us of that joy, or present us with challenges we never imagined, the last thing we need is to be financially challenged at the same time. If you haven't yet faced the possibility that you might become disabled or die, the time has come to take a long, hard look at the statistical realities. The cost of insurance is nothing compared with what your family will pay, both emotionally and financially, if you are not insured and your worst nightmare becomes a reality.

11

Taxes, Taxes, Taxes

Taxes are what we pay for civilized society.

OLIVER WENDELL HOLMES, JR.

Taxes are the sinews of the state.

MARCUS TULLIUS CICERO

Everybody pays too much tax. It doesn't matter how much or how little you pay, it's too much. Since the introduction of personal income tax in 1917 as a temporary measure to pay for the expense of World War I, our income-tax burden has increased steadily. But taxes, like a lot of other things in life, are a reality. Everyone in Canada who earns income above a certain level is taxed on their Canadian income, as well as any income received from outside the country. Knowing how to deal with taxes is the ticket to ensuring you keep more of your hard-earned money in your own pocket.

While Canadians report tax on a calendar-year basis, the deadline for filing a personal tax return is April 30 of the following year. Scads of people leave it to the very last minute. You shouldn't. Leave yourself some breathing space to make sure you've claimed everything to which you're entitled and to check your arithmetic. And if you owe money, you'll need to figure out where that money will come from. Minimizing your taxes isn't something you do on April 30. It takes planning. Tax planning should start in January, not April. While you'll have to deal with last year's taxes in a few months, you still have all of this year to plan for your next year's tax bill.

Canada uses a progressive tax rate system. As your income increases, the rate of tax you pay also increases. Your taxable income is calculated by adding up all your sources of income and then subtracting certain deductions to come up with your net income.

And it's not only the feds who tax our income. The provinces also take their slice of the pie. Since the rates vary by province, check with an accountant for the rates and special surtaxes applicable to your province.

There are a number of deductions and credits that can be claimed to reduce the amount of tax you have to pay; it is by taking advantage of these claims that you can avoid tax. *Avoid* is a very important word. While tax *avoidance* is a perfectly acceptable way to minimize tax, tax *evasion* is a violation of the law. Since the tax laws become increasingly more complex with each passing ruling, it is very important that you check and recheck to ensure you're reporting fully and accurately.

A word of warning: Just because you get advice from Canada Customs and Revenue Agency doesn't mean that you can go ahead and follow that advice, assured that you're well within the rules. *CCRA's representatives can't be held accountable for the information they provide.* The idea of seeking advice from those closest to the whole process seems like a logical one. If you aren't sure whether your deductions or your business setup are within the confines of the tax man's rigorous restrictions, it would seem natural to go straight to the horse's mouth for the answer. And you would assume, of course, that you could bet the farm on that answer. However, there is a long-established principle of law that disallows taxpayers from seeking refuge from a negative assessment simply because they were guided by CCRA's advice. Comments from officials are not binding. So, if you're not sure where you stand, you would be well advised to check with someone who really knows the answer: an accountant or a well-experienced tax lawyer.

The way to pay less tax is to keep more of your taxable income in the lower tiers, so you pay a lower percentage of tax and you don't get hit by the surtaxes. You do that by maximizing your deductions. One of the best ways is to contribute to an RRSP. If you're making $50,000 a year, you have an RRSP contribution limit of $9,000. If you contribute the full $9,000 to an RRSP, you'll essentially reduce your taxable income by that amount. Instead of paying over $16,500 in tax, you'll end up paying only $12,781.50 — a tax saving of $3,718.50 — and your $9,000 can remain on a tax-deferred basis inside your RRSP for when you need it. You'll also have an additional $3,718.50 that you've kept out of the tax man's hands to do with as you wish. You can take a well-deserved vacation, make a principal pre-payment on your mortgage, start an unregistered investment plan, or roll it right into next year's RRSP contribution. Whatever you decide, you'll have been smarter to keep the money for yourself than to send it to CCRA. I bought my first car using the tax refund from two years' RRSP contributions. From my perspective, the government bought me the car. I paid cash. No finance charges. The cost to me: a little deferred gratification. The benefit: I still have the RRSP which provides a nice little nest egg for the future.

The most common mistakes people make when filing their returns are in not claiming all deductions and credits for which they are eligible. The information you need to make sure you pay as little tax as possible is laid out in CCRA's tax guide. Take the time to read it, from cover to cover, highlighting those things that are applicable to you. If you don't read the whole thing, you won't know what you may be missing. It's not the most stimulating reading in the whole world, but you have lots of time if you start now. Keep a copy in the bathroom along with a highlighter pen, and when you get 10 minutes away from the kids, start highlighting. If you're not a bathroom reader, pick another place where you spend 10 minutes a day and work through the guide slowly. Having read it through at least once, you're more likely to identify opportunities for taking advantage of the credits and deductions that come up when you change jobs or make changes in your personal circumstances.

A deduction reduces your taxable income. A $200 deduction for moving expenses may be worth between $54 and $100 in tax savings depending on your marginal tax rate. A credit is a direct reduction of tax, so a $200 credit is worth exactly $200 to you. However, most credits are included in calculating your basic federal tax. Since provincial tax and sur-tax are calculated as percentages of your federal tax, credits end up being worth more than their face value because they reduce these "secondary" taxes as well. Now, some credits are refundable and some are non-refundable. If credits are refundable, they are always worth what they say they are. So even if you end up paying no tax and you have an outstanding credit, the tax man will send you some moolah. However, non-refundable credits work more like deductions because they become non-existent if it ends up that you pay no tax at all. Note, though, that some credits are transferable, so your spouse may be able to use them if you can't. (Also, in some cases, if a dependent child can't use a credit it may be transferred to a supporting parent.)

FILE A RETURN EVEN IF YOU DON'T OWE ANY TAX

People often think that because they don't have to pay any tax, they shouldn't bother to file a tax return. If you're one of those people, you may be losing out on an opportunity to build yourself some RRSP deduction room, which you can use to offset any tax you might have to pay in the future. To build RRSP contribution room, you must file a tax return to show earned income. It doesn't matter how small your income is, and it doesn't matter that there's no tax owed. As long as you have earned income, you will have eligible RRSP contribution room that you can carry forward, at this point, indefinitely. That can translate into a deduction when you do have sufficient income to pay tax. Making the contribution is even better. While there's little point in claiming the RRSP deduction when you owe little or no tax, you will benefit in two ways. First, any contribution can compound to produce what can seem like a magical amount. Second, the RRSP tax deduction can be carried forward and claimed when your tax bracket goes up so you get the biggest bang for your buck. Most young people who are just starting out at their first jobs have little extra income to make an RRSP contribution. But small amounts are all that are needed. An annual contribution of just $200 (from age 21 to 65) to an RRSP compounding at 12% will generate a tidy sum of over $300,000.

Suppose you did your return and then found out about credits or deductions you could have claimed but didn't. The first thing you should do is check your Notice of Assessment to see if the smart people at CCRA caught your mistake. *You should always review your Notice of Assessment in case a mistake was made.* Remember, they're human too. Assuming your error wasn't caught, the next step is to call CCRA and see if you can recover those deductions or credits. This may entail filing a Notice of Objection (a time limit of one year applies, so heads up). Ask the CCRA people to guide you through the process, or consult a tax specialist for help.

Waiver of interest and penalties

Believe it or not, there are times when the tax man leads with his heart instead of his hammer. CCRA recognizes that there may be times when extraordinary circumstances prevent a person, despite his or her best efforts, from complying with the Tax Act. So, at his discretion, the Minister (and, of course, his representatives) may waive any interest or penalties that may have accrued. What qualifies as an extraordinary circumstance? Natural disasters, civil disturbances, disruptions in services — read postal strikes — and the like. Also included are more humanitarian issues such as a serious illness or accident or serious emotional or mental distress such as that caused by a death in the immediate family. It also applies to situations where the tax department messed up: processing delays, errors in publications, incorrect written information, departmental errors, or delays in providing information to taxpayers. It's also interesting that if the tax man thinks you won't be able to pay your back taxes because you just don't have the bucks, he may waive the penalties and interest as part of his collection efforts. And if you might be able to pay back the principal, but the penalties and interest are so big that they prevent you from even starting, voilà . . . they can be wiped away, providing you keep to the agreed-upon repayment schedule.

INSTALLMENTS

Lots of folks don't realize that they may be required to remit tax in installments during the year. Since most people have their tax deducted at source, they figure they're always on the right side of the tax man and are astounded when they are charged interest on tax owing. After all, how do you know you're going to owe tax before you complete your return? Under the law, you have to remit installments if the difference between the amount of tax you owe and the amount of tax that's been withheld at source is more than $2,000 in both the current year and either of the two preceding years (the three-year rule). So if you have alternative sources of income from which no tax is deducted — let's say tips earned, a second job, income from self-employment or, in my case, royalties — it's your job to make sure the tax man has his fair share on time. And on time doesn't mean when you file the return. It means quarterly: on the 15th of March, June, September, and December.

To figure out how much your installments should be, calculate how much income you'll have from your other sources from which tax hasn't been withheld. Let's say you earn an additional $7,000 a year in tips and your marginal tax rate — the rate at which you pay tax on the last dollar you earned, or your highest rate — is 30%. Then you'd owe $2,100 for the year. Divide that by four, and you'll see that your quarterly remittances should be $525. Another alternative is to take the balance you had to pay last year, and pay that amount in four equal installments. Remember, no matter how it shakes out, if you owe, CCRA collects. So if you guess wrong and still owe tax you'll have to pay interest on the difference between the amount you owed and the amount you paid, based on the three-year rule. The only time you won't owe interest is if you made installment payments according to the notices sent to you by CCRA.

VOLUNTARY DISCLOSURE OF UNFILED RETURNS

The tax department, in an attempt to encourage taxpayers to come forward and correct deficiencies in past tax filings, has a set of rules relating to voluntary disclosure. If you've never filed a tax return, and you do so voluntarily, you will only be required to pay tax owing on your reported income along with interest. In other words: you will incur no penalties and no prosecution. You'll have to pay the total amount of tax and interest owing according to an agreed-upon schedule.

WHAT TO DO IF YOU ARE AUDITED

Could there be anything that strikes more fear in a taxpayer's heart than the word "audit"? Almost everyone has heard a horror story about a friend of a friend being reviewed with a fine-toothed comb. And, unfortunately, even people who have had advice directly from CCRA can find that advice overruled when the tax man cometh.

Most people file their returns without anticipating that anything more will be said. In 1996, 214,519 people found out just how an audit feels. And 1.3 million people were subject to a variety of other verifications.

Cumulatively, they had to pony up over $5 billion more in tax.

So, what exactly is an audit and should you be petrified? What we think of as an audit can be as simple as a request for additional documentation to support a deduction or as complex as a full-fledged review of your taxes for the previous five years. In fact, the audit can start long before you're contacted, such as when doctors' incomes are compared to provincial health plan payouts, or waiters' tips are compared to the average tips on credit-card slips in the restaurant where they work. If something looks suspicious to the tax man, an audit ensues.

If you're informed that your taxes are being reviewed, the first thing to do is ask for a letter of notification from the Audit Group so you can see what they want. If you have a tax adviser, get advice immediately. Respond promptly to your notification since CCRA allows a specific number of days for your response. Need additional time? Ask for it. Whatever you do, don't ignore the request. It won't just go away. And if they think you're obfuscating, watch out.

If it comes down to a meeting with the auditor, your behaviour will be a critical factor in the outcome. Don't be confrontational. Co-operation and credible presentation of the facts will go a long way in your favour. Be frank and open in your responses but do not volunteer information. Give the tax man what he asks for and no more.

If it ends up that CCRA disallows a deduction and sends you a notice of reassessment stipulating the amount you owe, you can challenge the reassessment by filing a notice of objection with the Appeals Division. You must file your appeal within 90 days of the date on the notice of reassessment or within one year of the original filing date for your return, whichever is later. However, you'd be wise to pay the amount for which you've been assessed in the interim to avoid the accumulation of interest should things not go your way. Don't worry, paying up is not an admission of any sort so it won't prejudice your appeal.

Back to the question of how scared you should be. That depends on how honest you've been thus far. You're not likely to be prosecuted for tax evasion if your claim has been based on an honest difference in opinion on how the rules apply. But if the tax man concludes that you deliberately under-reported your income or overstated your deductions, you're in for it. Tax evasion is punishable by a fine of up to twice the tax evaded — that's in addition to the tax you owe — and a prison sentence of up to two years.

12

Wills and Powers
of Attorney

*I loved you, so I drew these tides of men into my hands and wrote my will
across the sky in stars.*

T. E. LAWRENCE

A man's dying is more the survivors' affair than his own.

THOMAS MANN

Almost everyone should have a will. Unfortunately, many people think
they don't need one. Research done by the Trust Companies Institute
in 1992 showed that only half of Canadians have a will. Some people think
their wishes will be carried out by a family member. Others feel they don't
have sufficient assets to justify the cost of making a will. And some people
simply avoid making a will because their personal circumstances — marriages, divorces, and accumulated children and stepchildren — just seem
too complex to unravel. If you've delayed seeing a lawyer about a will
because you believe it's not worth the expense, let me assure you that dying
without a will is far more expensive than the cost of drawing one up.

Few people understand the estate rules set out by provincial governments, and the implications and costs associated with dying *intestate*
(without a will). It is enough to say that if you die without a will, trying
to figure out who gets what, and when, is often an unholy mess.

Consider making a will as soon as you begin to accumulate assets. This will ensure that your assets are distributed as you would wish. If you are married or in a non-traditional partnership, you and your spouse or partner may want to have your wills drawn up together so that they reflect an integrated estate plan. Your will may need to be amended or redrawn whenever there are changes in your personal or financial circumstances or if you wish to name new executors or beneficiaries. Review and update your will every three or four years or when:

- family circumstances change. Weddings, divorces, births, and deaths all result in changes in family structure.
- financial circumstances change. Increases or decreases in financial assets may necessitate changes to the will.
- new legislation is implemented. This may have a significant impact on the existing will.
- there are changes in residence. If you change your province of domicile, update your will to ensure compliance with the rules and regulations of your new province.

If you die intestate, your estate is distributed according to the laws of the province in which you were domiciled. (Your domicile refers to the location of your chief residence, where you intended to remain for the rest of your life.) Your probatable assets are frozen until the courts appoint an administrator to oversee the sale of the assets and distribution of the estate. Your funds can be frozen for months while the estate issues are being resolved; these delays can cause financial hardship for surviving family members, who would be deprived of the use of those funds during that time.

A will can minimize delays in the administration and distribution of your estate, since your executor can begin to take action immediately. You can specify who gets what and when. (In some cases, the provincial family law legislation can override provincial distribution formulas, or even override your will. In Ontario, the terms of a will can be frustrated by certain spousal rights under the Family Law Act.) You choose the best person or trust company to represent you as executor of your estate. You're in control, even from the grave.

Your executor or estate trustee is the person (or trust company) you appoint in your will to ensure your testamentary wishes are honoured and your instructions are followed. Your executor or estate trustee must be of sound mind and must have obtained the age of majority to act. Trust companies are the only organizations eligible to be named as executors. An executor can be a beneficiary or a witness. However, a beneficiary should not also be a witness because, while the will is still valid, any gift to the beneficiary will be void.

Through your will, you can also appoint guardians for children who are minors. While such an appointment is only temporary, without it the appropriate government agency may become the guardian of your children until an application to the court is made to appoint a relative or other person. This can be painful for the kids and a sure cause of fights within a family.

To make a will, you must have reached the age of majority — among the exceptions to this are people under the age of majority who are married or who have been married — and have "testamentary capacity." This means that you must have sound mind, memory, and understanding, and must clearly understand that you are making a will that is disposing of your assets. You must understand and recollect the nature and relative value of your assets and understand the claims of those you may be excluding from the will.

There are several circumstances that may affect the validity of your will. Your will may not be valid if:

- you made your will while under the influence of alcohol or drugs (so that you no longer have testamentary capacity)
- undue influence is exerted on you in making the will
- the will was executed under duress or coercion.

WHO SHOULD DRAW UP THE WILL?

Although you can draw up your own will, or use a standard form, don't. While some may feel that lawyers are simply being protective of their industry when they say you need professional help, the fact is that estate law is a complex beast.

Hilary Laidlaw has seen many cases where home-executed wills have been invalidated because of the way they were executed. While a holograph will (one that is completely in your handwriting and signed by you) does not have to be witnessed, a formal will must be witnessed by at least two people. Hilary says, "I've seen cases where a preprinted will form has been filled in and signed, but has not been witnessed. It is neither a formal will, because it has not been witnessed, nor is it a holograph will because it is not wholly in your handwriting." Then there are the cases where people have typed and signed what they believe to be a holograph will so that everyone will be able to read it, totally invalidating it as a holograph will. Another common mistake: Nothing written after the signature forms part of any will, so a postscript doesn't count.

While the language of a will may seem opaque and redundant, Hilary says that it is used largely because much of it has been around for years and its effect is tried and true. However, there is a move afoot to put the language of wills into plain English. Until then, you're still better off letting a professional who is familiar with the technical rules and requirements draw up your will so you can be sure it is valid. An estate lawyer can also help you focus on the important issues, so that your real intentions are translated into the legal language required. "The mistake made most often," says Hilary, "is that the testator's wishes are not clearly expressed and the time it takes to sort them out can be interminable." Let's say I draw up my own will and indicate that I want my husband, Ken, to have all my money by writing, "I want all my money to go to my husband, Ken." Hilary asks, "What do you mean by 'money'? Do you mean your cash? Do you intend to include the money in your RRSP? Do you want to include any debts owing to you? If you mean all the money in your bank chequing account, what happens if you move banks?" As you can see, "money" can have myriad meanings. That's where the guidance of

Hilary Laidlaw has focused her professional life as a lawyer on estates and trusts. A former partner at McCarthy Tétrault, where she practised for 10 years, Hilary now works with Canada Trust as managing director of estate and trust development. Motherhood has strengthened her commitment to educating both the public and her professional peers about the consequences of poor planning. She is a frequent lecturer, writer, and media guest, but it is with her husband and son — at home, travelling, or sailing — that she's the real star.

someone who does this day in and day out can be invaluable.

Just as "money" can mean a dozen different things, so can the term "household contents." Do you mean to include your grandmother's antique pearl brooch? What about the collection of paintings hanging on your walls? Perhaps you don't mean to include the car in your garage as part of your household contents. "It is a matter of context," says Hilary, "including the testator's personal circumstances. One person's financial status may be such that those paintings are simply considered part of their household effects. For another, the collection may be their primary investment — in effect, their 'money.' Either way, intentions must be clearly stated to avoid ambiguity."

The naming of a beneficiary is another area where lack of clarity can cause problems. Imagine you haven't seen your sister Laura for 20 years. If you choose to leave a bequest to your sister Martha, but in your will you simply refer to your "sister" without using her name, guess what? You can't assume that it is implied that you are leaving the bequest to Martha just because Laura isn't really in your life anymore. But with an experienced estate lawyer at your side, you'll be able to avoid these ambiguities.

When you hire a lawyer to draw up your will, you are reducing the risk of misunderstandings and minimizing the delays and costs associated with sorting out those misunderstandings. Here's another example: Hilary warns that when you use a term like "children" or "issue" in your will, it applies not only to your children and remoter descendants born within marriage, but those born outside marriage as well, even if you don't know about them. And it applies to children who have not yet been born at the time of your will, unless you state otherwise.

A lawyer will also help you plan for how beneficiaries will respond to the will. If you have two children to whom you are leaving your family cottage, will one want to sell while the other wants to keep the property? How will you structure your will to eliminate the fighting over what should be done with the property? The same holds true for a business that is being passed on to children. If only one child has taken an active interest in the business, but you leave it to all the children equally without further clarification, who will decide if the business is to continue being run or be sold? How will the child who has invested time and energy in running the business feel if the business is sold "out from under her"?

Often a lawyer can help you in choosing your executor and in deciding the breadth of powers you wish your executor to have. If you've established a trust under your will, your trustee will need to be able to invest that money. However, there are restrictions on what trustees can do in terms of investing if you do not broaden the scope of their authority. For example, without clearly stating that mutual funds are permissible investments for your trustee to make, mutual funds may be forbidden for two reasons. First, most mutual funds are not exclusively invested in trustee-authorized investments (read bank-issued investments such as GICs). Second, by investing in mutual funds, the trustee is arguably delegating the authority for investing to the mutual-fund manager, working against the maxim of law that says, "A delegate cannot delegate further." While there is a bill before the legislature which would remove the legal list (which outlines what investment alternatives are legally allowed), replace it with "a prudent investor" standard, and specifically authorize investment in mutual funds, if you wish your executor to have this authority under current legislation, you should include explicit wording to this effect.

If you're well prepared for your meeting with a lawyer, the process should go smoothly and the cost should be quite manageable. Before you start, do a little research. Most large law firms have a will booklet that will guide you through the process. Trust companies, too, have similar materials you can use as a primer. These booklets often include a list of the information you need to bring with you so that you are well prepared. Call ahead and ask that one be mailed to you.

In preparing for your will meeting, you and your spouse should discuss your financial details together before you go to see a lawyer. You each have a right to know where you stand, and you should both have a say in how your joint assets will be distributed. Make a list of your personal information, including your full legal name, any other names by which you are known, your address, social insurance number, date and place of birth, name and date of birth of spouse and children, marriages (all of them), and existing wills, trusts, and powers of attorney. List your assets, estimating their value. Indicate assets for which a beneficiary designation has been made, or assets that are held in joint tenancy (since these will be distributed on your death independent of your will). If special bequests are to be made, prepare a list of items to be left to particular individuals or organizations. List your liabilities and any insurance provisions you've made to eliminate those liabilities.

NAMING YOUR EXECUTOR

Before the meeting, think about who your executor should be. Your executor is the individual appointed to administer the terms of your will, and is responsible for assembling and protecting your assets, handling tax requirements and filings, and distributing your estate, among other things.

You can appoint a sole executor to act alone or two or more coexecutors. And you can make a contingent or alternate appointment in case the first appointed executor cannot act. Some people choose to name a friend or family member because these people are familiar with the personal details of their lives. Since Aunty Val knows and loves the kids, she's the perfect person. However, rather than being an honour, being named as executor can be quite an imposition. It can be an extremely time-consuming job. Without financial or investment knowledge, some executors feel out of their depth. If your executor is too emotionally involved, that can impede the whole process. Also, get the agreement of the person you plan to name before you do so, since an executor can give up the right to act at any time before the will is probated and before he or she begins administering the estate.

The person you select must be of sound mind and must have obtained age of majority in order to act (a minor may be appointed as an executor, but can only act after having attained the age of majority).

Here are some of the people you might consider as your executor:

- *Partner*. Your spouse or life partner may be a good choice if the assets being transferred under the will are relatively uncomplicated. An estate made up of bank accounts, term deposits, a house, an RRSP, and pension benefits would not be difficult to administer if it were going directly to the surviving spouse. With complex assets (unless your spouse has special skills), or if there are testamentary trusts involved (particularly a trust that will pass on to your children after your spouse dies), consider appointing a coexecutor with expertise in investments, accounting, and tax. Remember, too, that this will be a very stressful time for your partner. Think about how able he or she will be in dealing with the emotions while dealing with the legalities of managing your estate.

- *Children.* Appointing adult children, either alone or with the surviving spouse, can have some advantages. Mature children may be familiar with the assets. Keep in mind, however, that unless they have had specific training in a profession such as law or accounting, children may lack the expertise to complete the administration of the estate. As well, appointing one, but not all, could lead to friction, even if you have good reasons for the decision.
- *Friends and business associates.* Age is a factor in choosing friends and business associates. Inevitably, these individuals tend to be about your age and may find themselves acting as executor at a time when they themselves may require help to manage their own affairs. Older friends may die before you, leaving you to name a new executor — another trip to the lawyer. Worse still, your executor may die during the administration period, in which case his executor — someone you may not even know — would take on the administration of your estate if you have not made provision for an alternate.
- *Family lawyer/accountants.* The family lawyer is often seen as a logical choice to be either an executor or coexecutor. Lawyers may be an appropriate choice if they have the time to devote and have a sound knowledge of estate law. However, unless they are set up to carry out estate administration, these professionals may not be equipped to manage investments and run complex trust accounting systems. Moreover, some lawyers prefer not to act as executors.
- *Corporate executors.* For an institution to act as executor, it must be a corporation licensed to do fiduciary, or trust, business. One of the main advantages of a corporate executor is that these companies have the expertise to handle the obligations. They also have the neutrality to make objective decisions that affect beneficiaries. Company representatives are available 52 weeks of the year so the estate administration won't be delayed because of illness, vacation, or business commitments. As well, these professionals have a wealth of experience, having handled thousands of estates. However, unless you have a pre-existing relationship with a trust company, they won't know your family. You may feel that a friend or family member would offer a more personal touch. Where there's good

reason for a corporate executor, don't let the lack of a relationship deter you. Instead, make it clear that you expect your corporate executor to devote the time and energy necessary to get to know you and your personal circumstances so that when the time comes, they can deal with your family on a very personal level.

Choosing an executor requires a high degree of trust. You must be sure in your own mind that your executor will carry out your wishes as you intended them. And you should regularly reevaluate your choice as your life progresses and things change. Choosing the wrong executor can have serious ramifications.

Sally was a successful actress who, like many other artists, had given over the management of her financial affairs to a financial adviser. She felt she had neither the time nor the expertise to be bothered with the money part of her life. Unfortunately, she later discovered that her trusted financial adviser had been neglecting her affairs. Worse still, Sally didn't have nearly as much invested as she thought. When confronted, the financial adviser disappeared with most of Sally's remaining savings. Not long after, Sally died unexpectedly. Her will named as executor none other than the same rogue who had stolen from her. She had been so busy trying to sort through her financial mess that she completely forgot her will. Her family was left with the stress and complication of having this man removed as executor and dealing with the countless debts and liabilities that had been ignored. The whole process took several years, during which time the estate was virtually in limbo.

Estate planning also means thinking about whom you feel would be most appropriate as a guardian for your children. A guardian is someone who assumes the responsibility for your child until he or she reaches the age of majority. Hopefully, the person you name will never need to do the job. But that's no reason to ignore this detail. While your children may be minors, this is anything but a minor consideration. If you are a single parent, or if you and your spouse were killed in a common disaster, who would care for your babies?

The guardian you name is granted temporary guardianship of your kids. To make the custody legally permanent, the guardian must apply to the court. While the court is not required to appoint the guardian you have named, it usually does so unless there is a challenge to the appointment or a valid reason not to. If your kids are old enough to express their opinions, the courts often ask them where they would like to go before a final decision is made. If you have strong feelings about whom you would want or would not want as guardian for your children, make them clear in your will. That may help the court reach a decision that more closely reflects your wishes. Make sure you check with your intended guardian before you write it into your will to be sure that person is willing to accept the responsibility. Think about the kind of home life this guardian would provide. Would your children want to live with this person? Can this person afford to raise your children, and will your estate provide sufficient financial support to ensure no stress on the guardian's own financial resources? Remember, raising your own children is tough enough. Raising someone else's is an act of supreme kindness. This is particularly true in cases where children are physically or mentally challenged. Check back from time to time to see if the person you have appointed remains willing and able to do the job.

Of course, you will spend most of your energy thinking about how your estate will be distributed. This used to be pretty straightforward. But with divorces and remarriages, half-siblings, stepchildren, and all the other family permutations that are now part of almost everyone's life, the question can be considerably more complicated. Who will be your heirs? When will they receive their bequests — immediately or in the future? How will the bequest be handled if your beneficiary predeceases you?

PLAN YOUR FUNERAL

Just as making a will can be difficult for many people, so too can making funeral arrangements. But planning your funeral is part of estate planning. Funerals are a rite of passage. They bring conclusion to an episode of life. While you may not want an elaborate funeral that rivals a marriage or other significant ceremony in your life, think about the fact that there is little time to prepare for even a simple funeral — at most a few days. And this is a time when your family is most vulnerable both financially and emotionally. The last thing you should want is for them to be spending money in an emotional state, without direction. Better that you spend a couple of minutes thinking about it, and putting it on paper, so there's no debate about how fancy or simple the whole thing should be. If you want a party, plan the party. Some people even identify the guests with prepared invitations. They choose the music to be played, and the food to be served. Others want to keep the whole thing simple. I want to be cremated. It's fast, simple, and doesn't use up valuable land resources.

Your funeral instructions aren't binding, but they're likely to be followed in most cases and will ease the burden on your family members.

WHAT ARE YOU WAITING FOR?

If you haven't thought about these things yet, now is the time. If you don't have a will, make arrangements to make one. If you haven't designated a guardian for your children, start thinking about who is worthy of the job. Don't allow your emotions to get in the way of your responsibility. Hilary talks about redoing her will when she was pregnant. "Just before John was born," she said, "I redid my will and had to think about issues like guardianship. I sat and cried. How could I be thinking about my own death when I was awaiting the birth of my baby? It gave me a whole new appreciation for how difficult it is to go through the exercise; but how absolutely necessary."

It all comes back to the responsibility issue. If you don't do the detail work, the financial and emotional repercussions can be dreadful for those you leave behind. The point of executing a well-thought-out, well-executed will is to make the whole process of tying up the ends as neat and painless as possible for those you love.

Now is also a good time to think about how your affairs should be handled if you become incapacitated physically and/or mentally.

MORE POWER TO YOU

While lawyers and financial planners have been calling attention to the importance of having a Power of Attorney (PoA) for years, for many people the question remains, "Do *I* need a power of attorney?" *Everyone* should take the time to execute this relatively simple document.

A power of attorney is a legal document that authorizes another person to act on your behalf. The most common type of power of attorney deals with property and gives the person you choose the legal authority to deal with your assets. If you become mentally incapacitated, a "continuing" power of attorney would allow your representative to act for you. Note that it must be "continuing" to be binding if you become mentally incompetent. By executing a continuing power of attorney, you eliminate the likelihood of your family facing a cash-flow crisis because they cannot access your chequing or savings accounts, or liquidate investments in your name in the event that you cannot act on your own behalf. If you become incapacitated without a power of attorney, certain family members could obtain authority to act, but might have to post a security bond first and would also be required to file a management plan for your assets.

The person you choose to act for you can be your spouse, another family member, your lawyer, or a trust company. Since the person who has your power of attorney can do anything you can do (except make your will), you should have implicit trust in this person. If a relationship is shaky, don't test it by adding the burden of a power of attorney to it.

A power of attorney can be "general" or "restricted" in nature. With a general power of attorney, all your assets are covered. With a restricted power of attorney, you set out the specific conditions you want met.

Since a power of attorney is legally binding, consult your lawyer to have one prepared.

In the spring of 1995, Ontario introduced new legislation to allow you to also make your wishes known with regard to medical and non-medical care. While this had been the domain of the "living will" for some time, living wills were not legally binding. The new personal care power of attorneys executed under the Substitutes Decisions Act are. Ontario joins British Columbia, Manitoba, Quebec, and Nova Scotia in having legislation (either passed or pending) to give you the power to choose who speaks for you if you are unable to speak for yourself.

Within the power of attorney for personal care you can appoint someone to make decisions on your behalf and can establish in written form your instructions regarding medical treatment and non-medical personal care issues. You can also establish the specific medical treatments you do or do not want, including the specific circumstances in which you want medical treatment to cease. You don't have to include instructions — you can leave it up to your personal care attorney to make the appropriate care decisions based on your wishes and preferences.

13

Building Financial Relationships

If you don't know your jewels, know your jeweller.

UNKNOWN

Don't ask a barber if you need a haircut.

DANIEL GREENBERG

One of the questions I'm asked most often is how to find someone to trust in helping with financial matters. Whether you're looking for a banker, a broker, a financial planner, an insurance agent, a lawyer, or an accountant, you must establish a *relationship*. Now, relationships don't just happen. You have to work at them. And if you have yet to establish a relationship with any one of these advisers, you're starting from ground zero.

The first place to look is in your own backyard. Speak with friends and family. Ask them what adviser they deal with. Do they trust him? Do they like her? Does the adviser give good feedback? If none of your friends or family members knows of anyone, ask the people at work. If your peers don't know of someone, your boss may. The fact that you're looking for an adviser will look good on you, so don't be bashful.

You've got a name at last. Now what do you do? You interview. The only way to get to know the person is to talk to them, preferably in person. And the only way to find out if they can do the job is to ask plenty of questions. Some of the questions you'll ask are basic service questions to see if the level of service the adviser gives matches your expectations:

- how many times a year will you meet?
- what kind of information will you receive on a regular basis?
- how quickly will your calls be returned?
- when can you reasonably expect to receive information that you've requested, or answers to questions you've asked?

You must also ask about the person's credentials and experience. While credentials will give you an educational overview, experience is far more important in terms of your day-to-day activities. If you are looking for an insurance agent to handle a disability insurance request, you need someone who has specialized in disability insurance. A life insurance agent who dabbles in disability insurance won't do the job well enough. The financial world is just too complex to expect one person to know it all. Of course, you may choose to use a financial planner as your quarterback; he or she could then refer you to specialists as you need them.

I'm quite opinionated when it comes to choosing advisers. I believe in the specialist. After all, you wouldn't go to an ob/gyn to have bunions removed, and you wouldn't seek advice from a car mechanic about how your furnace is running. So why would you go to a commercial or real estate lawyer to draw up a will? Or a generalist financial planner for information on insurance? Or a banker for help with your investment portfolio? When you choose an adviser, you need one with lots of experience in the area for which you're seeking advice. If you need help with your current account, ask a banker. If you need help with investments, ask an investment specialist such as a broker or an investment manager. Asking a mutual-fund seller about how the underlying investments in the mutual fund work will likely leave you knowing a lot less than you should. It's not fair to those people, because they can't possibly keep up with the day-to-day activities in the market. And most don't understand how economic conditions will affect your portfolio. If you don't believe me, the next time you're in your branch, ask the mutual-fund specialist the question, "What factors do I need to think about when trying to decide which areas to focus on in broadening my foreign content?" and watch the eyes glaze over.

Another good question to ask is, "What types of investments do you hold, and why?" A financial adviser should be able to explain the rationale for her own investment portfolio, insurance coverage, or whatever instrument she specializes in so you can understand it. All too often, I read about advisers who suggest clients buy a product they would never consider for themselves. Then there are the advisers who use a strategy they would never suggest for their clients. You have to wonder why the disparity. If there's no good answer, find another adviser.

Next you should ask about fees. How will you be billed? By the hour? Will the person receive compensation from any other sources? Financial planners who are compensated by investment companies such as mutual-fund companies obviously have a vested interest in selling you a particular product. That's not bad if the product suits your needs. But you may find yourself questioning just how unbiased their financial advice is. If you're uncomfortable with such an arrangement, go for a relationship with a fee-only financial planner. They'll guide you financially, recommend the types of investments you should have, and offer advice on where to get those products.

Which brings us to the next thing you need to do when seeking financial advice: check references. Know that the adviser is only going to give you his or her happiest clients as references. But even knowing that, you can uncover interesting information about the adviser just by chatting with a couple of clients. Don't ask too many direct questions. Questions such as "Did she make you any money?" deserve a one-word answer. Instead, ask about the relationship. Talk about the kinds of expectations the client had and how they were met. Ask about areas where the adviser added value by delivering more — information, service, time commitment — than was expected.

If you and your spouse will be using the same adviser, get the ground rules straight right from the start. First, you must both feel comfortable talking to him intimately about your money. It's no good working with someone your spouse thinks is great if you have doubts. Second, make sure the adviser knows that you are two separate clients. Yes, you will have similar needs. But you should expect all your information to be kept confidential at all times, unless you say otherwise.

It is equally important that you feel comfortable with the kinds of investments your adviser recommends, and the way those recommendations are delivered. I met Ann Richards when I was publishing my financial magazine and she agreed to be a contributing writer. Working with her on the magazine gave me insight into her values and how she operated. When the magazine stint ended, I asked Ann to take over the management of my self-directed RRSP. I've not been disappointed. Ann not only takes the time to understand what I'm trying to accomplish, when she thinks I'm going off half-cocked, she says so. And if she doesn't know how to do something, such as when Ken and I decided to put our mortgage in our self-directed RRSPs, she finds out and gets back to me. She managed the resources on her end so that from my perspective the whole thing went smoothly. My husband uses Ann's services as well. And despite the fact that we are completely different in our investment and communication styles, Ann bridges the gaps. She makes it easy for us to deal with her. When my husband decided to do a little speculating, Ann requested that he complete a new "know your client" form. It's not only required, but it helped to bring home to Ken just how far he was stepping out of his original investment strategy.

That's what you want from a financial adviser. Whether the person is drawing up your will, helping you with your taxes, or arranging your mortgage, you should feel you are the most important person in that adviser's life at that point in time. You want someone who will watch your back, even if the enemy lies within!

Does everyone need a financial adviser? Probably. And at some point in your life you may need two or three at the same time, depending on what you're doing. The number of people on your financial roster depends on the circuit your life takes. Conceivably, you may need an accountant, an estate lawyer, a real estate lawyer for your home purchase, a banker, a broker for your investment advice, and a financial planner for your overall financial health. You might also seek specialized help in retirement planning, if your financial planner has chosen not to be an expert in this area.

III

ADAPTING YOUR PLAN AS YOUR LIFE CHANGES

*Even in slight things the experience
of the new is rarely without
some stirring of foreboding.*
ERIC HOFFER

There is no greater constant in life than change. No matter how well you plan, how carefully you prepare, how tenaciously you hold on, at some point, everything nailed down comes loose. That's life.

Many years ago, I came across a beautiful saying that I've held close to my heart. I can't remember where I read it, or whom to attribute it to, but it goes like this: "To grow is to change and to change often is to have grown much." I really like the idea that I'm not fickle (as Virgil would have us believe), scatterbrained, vacillating, shifty, warped, flip-flopping, or bent. I'm much happier thinking of myself as growing, metamorphosing, remodelling, reorganizing, moving, improving, bettering. The bottom line: I'm changing. And a good thing too since my life continues to evolve and if I didn't keep up, it would sure be a funny picture. Or a sad one.

As my girlfriend Brownie says, the golden rule is "Get Up." No matter how often you're flattened, you can only move forward if you get up. Of course, it's easier to get up if you have some tools at your disposal. And it's easier to stay financially healthy if you have a road map of what to watch for as you move along life's glorious, muddy, winding, uphill, rocky path. That's what this section is all about. Change.

Since your priorities as a young adult will be different from your priorities as a parent or a retiree, it's important that you repaint your financial canvas to reflect the changes in your life. No one thinks about saving for their kid's education before they actually have a child. And few people can contemplate retirement at the sweet young age of 24. But as you progress, morph, move forward, you need to reorganize and remodel. If you don't take the time to reassess, you may waste a lot of time working to old plans.

14

When You Partner

Keep from your wives the actual amount of your income — because the management of the money should not be put into the wife's hands. It is a popular error which is the cause of many misunderstandings between married people.

HONORÉ BALZAC

When you're young, you think of marriage as a train you simply have to catch.

ELIZABETH BOWEN

There are almost as many different ways to partner as there are people to partner with. When it comes to partnering, life's changed a lot in the past two or three decades. Fewer women marry. In 1992, there were only 5.8 marriages for every 1,000 people, down from 9.2 in 1972. Women are also marrying at older ages. In 1992, the average age for first marriage for brides was 26.5 years, up from 22.1 years in 1971. There's also been a substantial increase in the number of remarriages. In 1992, about 23% of the women who married had been married before. That's up from just 10% in the 1960s. And divorced women make up almost nine out of 10 women who remarried in 1992. Again, that's a significant shift from the 1960s when most women who remarried were widowed.

While the percentage of women who are spouses in the traditional sense has declined, the number living in common-law relationships has increased. In 1981, only 4% of women were in a common-law relationship. By 1991, that had risen to 7%. The net result is that while fewer women marry, the share of all women living with a partner has changed only marginally.

Each time I've partnered, I've done it differently and I've done it better. The only common factor was that in each case I lived with my partner before I married. Having been married three times, I can tell you from experience that no one way is the right way. It's a matter of where you are in your own personal development, and what is important to you at that particular point in your life.

When I partnered with my first spouse, I was very young. I left home abruptly and went to live with him in his flat. Then we moved into an apartment together. A few months later, we married. It was fast and short-lived. I made some significant mistakes — my choice of partner being just one of them.

Recently, I was interviewed by a journalist asking about the financial issues people should think about when they begin living together — married or not. My first response was, "No joint accounts, unless he puts in and you take out."

My first experience with a joint account was negative. I was the only one working. My husband planned to return to Australia, where he felt he would be in a better position to contribute to the family coffers. I was to join him shortly thereafter. Before he left, he emptied the joint account of the $600 we had managed to save and bought me a television to keep me company. I was aghast! Six hundred dollars may not seem like much money now, but in 1979 it was all the money we had in the world. And it had been hard to scrape together. My security was gone. I was going to end up alone, and without a safety net. From his perspective he was doing something nice for me. From my perspective, he had placed me in a horrible position. To him, money was for spending. To me, money was for saving in case something dreadful happened and you needed it. And in his mind, $600 wasn't a lot of money. In mine, it was a fortune.

The point of this story is that you have to talk about what you expect of your spouse, and what he expects of you if you plan to have a successful relationship. You have to talk about it all. How you will live together. How you will share responsibilities. How you will cope with challenges. How you will deal with financial issues. Things one partner does shouldn't come as a shock to the other. That's not to say that as you live together, you won't uncover new, wonderful, challenging aspects to your spouse's personality and ways of seeing things. That's natural. What's destructive is not to have an open line of communication so you can discuss the things that make you sad, mad, crazy, and over-the-top frustrated. While the early months of shared life can be very exciting, they can also bring some very interesting discoveries. You have to be able to talk about them.

If you or your partner are reluctant to talk in a straightforward way about money, you're in trouble. Since every family is faced with challenges, the ability to put the issues on the table, talk openly about them, and come to some resolution is absolutely crucial to your relationship.

As cynical as this may sound, the reality is that money and power have a very close relationship. The partner with the most money is far more likely to control most of the key decisions in the relationship — from which house you'll buy, to where the kids will go to school, to who will stay home with a sick child. In fact, conflicts about money prompt more divorces than any other single issue, regardless of income.[21]

Assuming you and your partner agree to communicate openly about money, your first task will be to set the ground rules. Set aside an hour or so when you will not be interrupted — no kids, no friends, no background distractions. Your first order of business should be to agree on the time and place for your next meeting. Some couples run these meetings like board meetings. Others use them as an excuse to get out of the house for a quiet dinner. Whatever your choice, start your meeting by setting the time, date, and place for the next meeting so no matter what the outcome of this one, you will have already agreed to continue the process.

Begin by talking about the things you agree on so you set a positive tone. Decide how you are going to arrange your money matters: who will pay the bills, who will save toward the downpayment on the home, who will make the contributions to the kids' educational fund, and who will make the investment decisions. If you've already identified a habit your spouse has that makes you nuts, put it on the table. Ask your spouse to do the same. The rule should be that anything is up for discussion providing it is being handled without acrimony. Your discussion should

---

21 Victoria Felton-Collins with Suzanne Blair Brown, *Couples and Money* (Bantam, 1990).

also bring clearly into focus the things that are very important, somewhat important, and a little important to each of you. This may take some thought and may be deferred to your next meeting, but don't skip this step. If making sure you maintain a $500 safety cushion in your chequing account is important to one spouse, and the other runs the account to within a hair's breadth of zero every month, you'll drive each other nuts. Knowing the rules will help you not to break them.

One reason many couples fight about money is that each person has different priorities. One wants to save madly, the other is a shopper; one wants to pay down debt, the other continues to charge purchases and take out loans; one wants to own a home, the other wants to invest the money in the market. And as time goes by, each position becomes more polarized as the individuals attempt to balance the other's "wrong."

Another reason couples fight is because their expectations are not met. Implied promises are hard to escape. A new mother may feel she was implicitly promised time to stay home and take care of her baby, but her spouse may insist she return to work. A husband may believe his wife should stay within the household budget, while she continues to use her already stressed credit card to buy clothing and toys for the kids. One spouse may be disappointed that the other doesn't make more. The other may feel embarrassed, ashamed, or angry at not being able to live up to expectations.

MARRIAGE CONTRACTS AND COHAB AGREEMENTS

While no one ever gets married with the intention of getting a divorce, each year thousands of couples in Canada call it quits. Most people would prefer an amiable separation, but, anger and disappointment being what they are, this hardly ever happens. And while less than 4% of divorces are finalized by a contested hearing, the squabbling confrontations of an out-of-court settlement are no less messy.

Suppose there was a way to clarify how the money would be divvied up before all the hissing started. Suppose there was a way to find out just how much trust and good faith you were entering your marriage with. Suppose you could set down in black and white who would get what and when so there would be nothing to fight over. Just suppose . . .

Well, there is a way to do all that. You can sign a cohabitation agreement or marriage contract to make it perfectly clear how your stuff will be divided if you and your partner go your separate ways. While these are sometimes referred to as prenuptial agreements, under Canadian legislation they're referred to as marriage contracts and cohabitation agreements.

A marriage contract is a contract between two people who are going to be married or who are married. It tends to focus on organizing financial affairs differently than the way they would be organized if spouses were to separate under current family law (which differs from province to province in Canada).

A cohabitation agreement is entered into by two individuals who are living together but not married. Since cohabiting couples have fewer rights legally (i.e., current legislation doesn't allow for equalization of assets), the range of options in negotiating a cohab agreement is narrowed. Often in a cohab agreement, familial partners seek to set down support obligations, with less focus on the division-of-property front, unless they plan to marry at some point in the future.

The number one reason people sign on the dotted line is to protect themselves, or, more specifically, their assets. While it would be nice to think that custody or access issues could be settled before the acrimony of divorce leaves a sour taste in parents' mouths, these areas are beyond the purview of cohabitation agreements or marriage contracts. Nor are these contracts allowed to specify that, in the event of a relationship breakdown, you can boot your ex out of the matrimonial home. With a matrimonial home — defined as "property ordinarily occupied as a family residence at the time of separation" — both partners have special rights of possession. However, as far as the assets go, you can set down how they will be divided in the event of a split.

Let's say you're bringing significant liquid assets into a relationship. Under most divorce rules the income on that pool of money would be divisible, but you might not like the idea of that one little bit. After all, why should your ex share in the increase in the value of an asset he or she did not contribute to in any way? Think previous divorce settlements. Think insurance benefits. Think inheritances. And this is the usual reason contracts are entered into — to exclude specific assets from being equalized.

Of particular interest to people who are entering into second marriages and have children by a previous marriage, a marriage contract organizes the individuals' finances so that everybody knows from the get-go what's happening. Gone are the secrets. Instead, both partners enter the union knowing exactly where the chips will fall, if they do.

This can be particularly important if one of the parties is currently receiving spousal support. Let's face it, if you're receiving a very comfortable level of spousal support from husband number one, and you're contemplating hitching up with husband number two, you're taking a big risk financially. Should the new relationship not work out, you will have given up the income stream from your first ex-husband — an income stream that may not be replaced by your second ex.

Then there are the people who are widowed. If you come to a relationship with inherited assets, you may need to protect those assets for the children you had with your late spouse. Even young, first-time marrieds who anticipate inheritances from their family may have need of a contract. Or so their parents think. Having watched many of their friends, or children of their friends, go through divorces, they want to make sure that the family money isn't vulnerable.

Two scenarios that cry out for a cohab agreement or marriage contract are when one partner has significantly more assets than the other, or when there are children on one side and not on the other. Then the partner with the mostest may want to protect assets accumulated prior to the relationship. Or the partner with children may want to ensure that assets meant for their kids remain that way.

If you think you're a candidate for a marriage contract, don't try springing the idea on your soon-to-be partner in the eleventh hour. If you know you are getting married on June 18, May 1 is not the time to introduce the topic. You need to put the discussions and the contract into place well before the date you do the deed. The closer you are to the wedding, the less likely it is that the contract will stand up to a challenge.

Before you bring it up, be very clear on why you want a contract. Is it your idea or your family's idea? And be absolutely truthful with your partner. Whether you want to make sure your children from a first marriage are protected, or you want to protect your new partner from the barbs of family members who see him or her as a fortune seeker, explain your reasons. There's nothing wrong with saying, "I ran my business for 10 years without any interference or ownership by others. I want to keep that autonomy."

Getting a potential spouse or partner to sign one of these documents is no walk in the park. Many a bride or groom has been left holding the moneybag while an irate buddy headed off in a huff. It takes the highest level of trust and a good understanding of both parties' interests for a marriage contract to happen. It's not unusual for marriage plans to come to a grinding halt over the negotiation of a marriage contract. If one side is feeling mistrustful or suspects the other side is out to pull a fast one, the whole negotiation can collapse.

What if your spouse won't sign? That's perhaps the biggest benefit of the contract negotiation: you get things out in the open before it's too late.

YOUR SPENDING PLAN

Consolidating your spending plans will be one of the first challenges you face when you begin living together. Will you pool your money, or will you manage separate accounts? Who will pay which bills? Who will be in charge of saving? Who will maintain the emergency fund?

The most challenging part of your early conversations about money management may be coming to terms with the fact that you have different money personalities. Your partner may be a charge-ahead spender. You may be a careful saver. Your partner may be illiterate when it comes to investing. You may be well read and enthusiastic. Both you and your partner may be take-charge money managers who struggle over the power to make decisions. Whatever the case, you'd better get to know each other and come to some agreement about how you will handle this aspect of your relationship. The worst thing you could do is simply settle into a financial relationship that pleases neither cf you. In the end, fights, tears, and, ultimately, resentment will be the dividend of your unwillingness to talk it out.

So, today, it's time for a chat. Talk about your attitudes. Talk about your expectations. And disclose. I know this isn't easy for everyone, but if you can't trust the person with whom you are partnering, think twice about this life-changing decision. Begin by talking about what you own and what you owe. It may be difficult admitting debt and listening to someone else's asset-building saga, but you have to know each other's circumstances fully to start off right. And don't assume you know your partner simply because you've been acquainted for years. You don't know anything about anybody until they choose to tell you. So there may be some significant gaps you aren't aware of. Talk about your goals. Do you want to buy a house? When? Do you want to have children? How will you share the care, nurture, and rearing of your babies? How much will you put away for the future? How will you decide where that money will be invested? If you and your partner have different expectations as you start out, it would be a good idea to come to an understanding of each person's position. Talk through your financial arrangements so that for each, the process and the outcome are fair.

Barb Godin says that when she and her husband started out together, they didn't have much money. "We had jars labelled 'food money,' 'gas money,' et cetera. On payday, we put the cash in the jars and when the cash was gone we stopped spending. If the food money jar was empty, that was too bad, unless there was anything in the entertainment jar, which almost always went unfilled."

Once upon a time, men brought home the bacon and women fried it up in the pan. But the times, they are a-changin'. One of the most dramatic changes in Canadian society has been the increase in the number of women who are employed. In 1994, 52% of all women 15 and over had jobs — up from 42% in 1976. In 1994, women represented 45% of all paid workers in Canada, up from 37% in 1976.

So there are more women working now than ever before. In *Money: Who Has How Much and Why*, Andrew Hacker charts the wives' share of combined income in dual-income marriages.[22] At the lowest income levels, wives contribute the most. At an income level of $10,000 to $20,000, wives contribute 47.7% — almost half — of the family income. As the family's income increases, wives' contributions represent a smaller share. At the $20,000 to $30,000 level, wives' income represents 38.9% of the family pool. And at $30,000 to $40,000, wives' incomes make up 34.3% of the family's income.

For many women the question of whether or not to work isn't really a question. They have to work to help their family attain or maintain a certain standard of living. For women who are now better educated than ever before, the choice to work is also a personal one. Women want the

---

22 Andrew Hacker, *Money: Who Has How Much and Why* (Scribner, 1997), p. 174.

option of being able to contribute to the world at large in a meaningful and productive way.

When it comes time to set up a joint household, the fact that many women come into the relationship already financially responsible for themselves is something both they and their significant others have to deal with. For many partners, this is a welcome change. For others, it is a challenge to their ability to take care of the family ("Don't I make enough to support us?") and to maintain their primary-breadwinner status.

The tack you take in consolidating your households will be a reflection of how similar or different your circumstances, attitudes, values, and objectives are. Here are five approaches that can work.

- *Pool your resources.* All your income would go into a joint account, and all bills and spending money would be paid out of this pool. The remainder would be invested in both names. This works best when both people earn approximately the same income, have the same goals, and can agree to merge everything. One downside to this approach is that it's unclear what happens when one person's income significantly outstretches the other's. Will that person, at some point, feel they are unfairly carrying too much of the burden?
- *Contribute proportionately.* Each person puts part of his or her income into the common pot. If both choose to contribute 50%, the actual dollar amounts can be quite different. If you earn $60,000 a year after taxes and your partner earns $35,000 after taxes, your share of the pool would be $30,000 a year, while your partner would contribute $17,500 a year.
- *Split expenses 50/50.* Let's say you determine that your joint living expenses will be $50,000 a year and you decide to split that 50/50. Assuming the same incomes as in the previous example, you would end up paying $25,000 a year, leaving you with $35,000 a year to do with as you wished. Your partner would end up with only $10,000 in his or her pocket.

    This is the way my husband and I did it while I was working full-time. We each contributed a set dollar amount to a joint house-account every month, from which all the joint bills were paid: mortgage, utilities, insurance, children's educational savings. What remained of our money was ours to do with as we pleased. One year, I'd pay for the vacation, another he would. We each did our investing separately. When I stopped working full-time so I could spend time with my babies, we tried to maintain this for as long as possible. Some months would be fine. Others I'd come up short and he'd make up the difference.

- *Split the bills.* Decide who pays what bills. Perhaps you'll pay the mortgage, while your spouse pays the utilities and entertainment costs. Often, people choose this route to split the financial responsibility, as well as the responsibility for getting things done. (There's nothing more aggravating than this conversation: "Did you pay the phone bill?" "No, I thought it was your turn to pay the phone bill.")
- *Go month by month.* If you particularly enjoy keeping the records or are an absolute control freak, this method may be for you. You would pay all the bills each month, total them up, and then give your partner the total of his or her share.

The fact that women are marrying later also means they may bring assets — sometimes considerable assets — to the family. The question of how those assets should be identified in the event of a relationship breakdown is becoming more of an issue. The same is true for people who are remarrying and integrating their families and their family assets.

KEEPING A ROOF OVER YOUR HEAD

Where will you live? Your place? His place? A new place? In my mother-in-law's early married years, couples often lived in apartments, flats, or rental units for years as they accumulated a downpayment for a home of their own. It wasn't unusual for people to buy their first home in their forties. Now, everyone wants a house, a bigger house, more stuff. But taking on a big mortgage can be daunting for young couples. And it is often done at the expense of other parts of their financial lives: emergency fund, insurance, pay-yourself-first investment plan, retirement savings. The thing about having a healthy financial life — and a balanced life overall — is to have reasonable expectations that are in sync with your overall objectives. That's not to say you shouldn't buy a house. But it should be part of the equation — not the sum.

REVIEWING YOUR GOALS

If this hasn't happened as part of your financial discussions, it still needs to be done. When you partner, you have a whole new set of inputs — financial and otherwise — that need to be accommodated. While one would hope that you have similar goals toward which you're jointly working, that doesn't mean giving up your own dreams. Perhaps you'd like to go into business for yourself one day. How will marriage affect that? Will you move toward your goal more quickly or more slowly? Perhaps your goal is as simple as getting away for a couple of weeks every winter. Will you go together? Will you go with friends? Maybe your goal is to move to the country. Does your partner share your love of nature? Will your partner still work in your present locale? What about the commute?

Partnering requires a series of compromises to work. But that doesn't mean compromising yourself. Your personal goals are important. What you want to achieve is important. If you give up your lifelong dreams to make the marriage work, you'll only end up feeling resentful. When my second marriage ended — he is a lovely man, but our different objectives were too much to overcome — I realized that I had compromised my way right out of our relationship. To make him happy and keep him happy, I kept changing who I was. There was a significant difference in our ages and I had to compensate so people would stop referring to me as his daughter. I wore different clothes. I always wore makeup. I gave in, and gave in, and gave in, until I had nowhere to move. I had compromised myself right into a corner: I didn't like who I wasn't, and I didn't like where I was. When it suddenly occurred to me that we were on different paths — I was just getting started with a wonderful career, while he was beginning to wind down and wanted to spend more time out of the city — I realized we weren't going to end up in the same spot.

I'm not the only person with a story like this. I've met scads of people who suddenly realized they had to change. They were losing themselves. It comes as a huge shock to the partner. It seems like a betrayal. The only way to avoid the you-don't-know-who-I-am-or-what-I-want outcome is to talk. Talk about your dreams: what you want from life; what's important to you; how you feel and what you would like to change. And keep talking about your dreams and goals until you feel they are being recognized and accommodated. You have them, whether or not you realize it now. And if you don't share them, they'll overtake you. It's a matter of riding the wave, or being completely washed away by it.

Cash-Management Strategies

Having established a new spending plan, how you will deal with day-to-day transactions should be part of your discussions. If you've decided to set up a joint account, might I suggest you use it only for your joint expenses. When couples pool their money and things go wrong, inevitably one spouse is shocked when the other empties the joint account. You shouldn't be shocked. Anger, bitterness, and resentment make people do things they would never do when they are happy. The first rule of coexistence is to maintain your personal identity. That means having your own accounts, your own investments, and your own credit card. It also means not losing touch with the financial world.

I hear from couples in which one does all the money management and the other hasn't a clue about what's going on. This was often reported of women, particularly women of a certain age. But I've also met women who worry about their husbands' lack of attention. They worry that if something should happen to them, their hubbies would be lost. So it's not strictly a gender thing. And I've met young people who were shocked to find that when their partner left they had no idea of where anything was, or how much they had. So it isn't an age thing. It's a matter of taking personal responsibility for your own financial well-being.

Naturally, there are some things you can benefit from as you consolidate your lives. Throwing double your weight around could get you a lower rate on a loan. Even more significantly, if one of you doesn't have a credit rating, you're more likely to qualify as combined borrowers, but you'll both be on the hook for repayment. Joint bank accounts will let you keep a higher balance on a single account to avoid service charges. The flip side of this is that if your spouse bounces cheques on your joint account, the NSF will be reported in both names, and will affect your credit record. If this seems to be a routine event, then separate your accounts to protect your credit history.

KEEPING A HEALTHY CREDIT IDENTITY

Even thought there are two to a couple, you may be perceived as one as far as your credit identity is concerned unless you do something about it. I recently read a story on an Internet bulletin board entitled "Married Women Beware." I was intrigued. The story was from a young woman who had asked her mother to co-sign a loan for her. She chose to ask her mother, because since her mom made more than her dad she figured she stood a better chance of getting the loan. Imagine their surprise when they found out that mom had no credit history whatsoever. Even though she had been using credit cards and paying them off promptly for years, all her credit history was under her husband's name because her cards were secondary cards on his account.

"Married Women Beware" indeed. If you do not apply for your own credit cards, loans, or personal lines of credit, you're not building your own credit history. And no matter how well you manage your money, it won't be reflected anywhere. In essence, you won't exist from a credit perspective. Don't let this happen to you. You have to take care of yourself and your credit identity now so that you can take care of yourself in the future should you end up on your own. Your best bet is to have your own credit card, in your name alone. Remember Barb Godin's advice: When you borrow money, make sure you borrow it in your own name. If you borrow with your husband, insist that the credit granter report the information to the credit bureau in your name. Better yet, be the first one to sign on the application so the reporting is done automatically to your file.

Call your credit-card company and make sure that *your* accounts are set up in your name only. You're not Mrs. Edward Johnston. You're Jane Johnston. Make sure you keep your nose clean so your credit bureau report is a shining example of good financial management. And check your credit report every year or so to make sure no mistakes have been made that might tarnish your credit glow.

"I can't tell you how many women I've dealt with who have signed unlimited guarantees for their husband's business," says divorce lawyer Sandy Morris (see her bio on page 309). A smarter approach would be to limit your exposure to half of the debt, or to a specific time period. Get independent legal advice — your own lawyer telling you the implications and ramifications — so that you can make unbiased, informed decisions.

The bank should require this as part of the process. If no one has told you to get independent legal advice, consider yourself informed as of today.

Getting the advice is only half the equation. The other half is taking it seriously. If you don't understand what an unlimited guarantee is, ask. And keep asking questions until you're quite sure you do understand. After all, you should not be finding out for the first time that you are primarily liable for your husband's debt on the day he declares bankruptcy.

YOUR PAY-YOURSELF-FIRST INVESTMENT PLAN

As you start out together, keep your eye firmly on the future. Without kids, your living expenses are probably on the low side. You're young, healthy, and, very likely, focused on your career. With two incomes, you have more disposable income now than you will once you start a family. While you can enjoy that discretionary spending power to travel, accumulate your stuff, and have fun, you should also be using a part of it to establish an asset base. Invest in your future.

If you plan to have children, you will experience significant shortfalls in income, and a considerable drop in your disposable income, once the babies start arriving. Your early years are the perfect time to establish a savings plan that will help bridge this gap. Whether or not you intend to become a full-time mother, those savings will come in handy. They can also cushion the financial shock when, having held your warm, cuddly bundle, you decide you can't leave her to go back to work — at least for a year, two years, six years. Invested wisely, those savings can protect your family's standard of living, create more peace of mind, and offer you options for how to live your life.

YOUR EMERGENCY FUND

Once you get married, you only need to cover one person's income so you can cut back on your emergency fund. True or False? FALSE. If you think that your spouse's income is your safety net, might I remind you that there are many couples who have found themselves both out of work at the same time in our new economy. Might I also remind you that with most people living to the edge each month, it's unlikely that any one salary would be able to take care of all the costs associated with your joint lifestyle. Marriage should not be your excuse for giving up your financial responsibility.

Both members of a partnership should have emergency funds established to ensure that should the worst happen, they'll be covered. Trying to accumulate an emergency fund during a divorce, when your spouse is laid off and has exhausted his, or when the world has come crashing down on both of you is next to impossible. If you haven't already done so, start today, putting a little away each week. You'll sleep better for it.

REVIEWING YOUR INSURANCE

If either you or your spouse has health, life, or other insurance benefits at work, partnering is a good time to take another look at the plan. Most people have no idea what their company plans cover. Remember your first day of work? Remember receiving that little handbook of benefits? Where did you put it? Most people never bother to look at it until something comes up that they need to check. But not knowing what you're covered for may mean you're missing several things you could be claiming. And if your partner is paying for coverage, adding him or her as a beneficiary of your plan is one way to save some money.

Under an employer's benefit plan, a spouse usually receives all the health-related coverage that the employee receives. In some cases, same-sex couples are also covered — you can expect to see more equality in this area as time goes by. Even if they are not covered formally, benefit administrators may turn a blind eye when the forms are being filled out. However, currently pension benefits do not apply to same-sex couples because of income-tax regulations.

If both you and your spouse have benefits, pick the best plan and opt out of the other to save money. Since most plans only allow you to claim the portion not covered under another plan, dual coverage often means you're paying more than you should.

A common perk for most employees is life insurance. If you have no children, the minimum may be enough. However, remember that if you plan to have children, or one spouse will be dependent on the other, trying to get insurance when you need it could be harder than you anticipate, since even a small change in health may disqualify you. And it will definitely cost more as you get older. If your company plan offers you the ability to buy more insurance at the group rate, take the time to compare the rate with insurance you can buy on your own. And make sure that before you buy insurance through your company plan, you can take that insurance with you when you leave your employer.

The same rules apply to disability insurance. While many companies offer disability insurance as part of their package, you may want to consider topping it up with a private plan to ensure you are covered even if you are laid off. If your employer allows you to opt out of the company plan, consider buying your own plan with your after-tax dollars so that your disability income will be tax-free. If you are self-employed, disability insurance is absolutely, positively, without question *a must*. It's unlikely that your business can survive a long-term disability, which means you'll have no source of funds with which to support yourself through the disability. Premiums are expensive, but disability insurance must be a priority. If you don't believe it can happen to you, remember the statistics: One in eight people become disabled each year.

TAX IMPLICATIONS

Under the Income Tax Act, unmarried and same-sex couples are treated exactly the same as those who have signed the licence. As far as CCRA is concerned, you are considered married if you have lived together in a conjugal relationship for at least 12 months, or are the natural or adoptive parents of a child. Now, even if you haven't taken a trip down the aisle, you can contribute to an RRSP for your spouse, claim the married credit, lump your medical and charitable donations together, and transfer credits between your returns. You can also leave assets to a common-law spouse without capital-gains attribution.

Here's a question just about everybody in financial planning hears: "How do I minimize my taxes?" Now that you're partnered, you have some more options. You can maximize your tax savings by combining the claim for medical expenses (including your premiums for health and dental insurance) incurred by you, your spouse, and your eligible dependents, for any 12-month period. The lower-income spouse should make the claim. You can also maximize your tax credit for charitable donations by combining your claim on one return.

Income Splitting

Income-splitting strategies aim to reduce the amount of tax you have to pay and increase your family's cash flow. The objective is to have two equal incomes for tax purposes. Many of us can only work to narrow the gap as much as possible.

One way to minimize taxes and keep more money is by rigging the system so that all the family's investments are held in the name of the lower-income earner. When income (interest, dividends, or capital gains) is generated there it will be taxed at a lower rate. Canada Customs and Revenue Agency's response to income splitting and the tax reduction it brings was the introduction of attribution rules. So, if you *give* your spouse money for investment, CCRA will tax you on the interest, dividends, or capital gains earned. In other words, they attribute the return earned on the gifted money back to the person who gave it. The one small loophole: "second generation" return — or the income earned on income — is taxed in the hands of the person holding the investment. So, if you give your partner a $50,000 bond earning $5,000 interest income (10%), the $5,000 will be taxed in your hands. However, the $5,000 payment becomes your partner's property, and any subsequent income generated will be taxed in his name. Over five years he will have accumulated $25,000 (5 x $5,000), which may also generate $2,500 (10%) a year, taxable at his lower rate.

One way to avoid the attribution rules is to have the higher-income earner pay for all household and operating expenses. Then the lower-income earner can invest some or all of his or her net income directly. CCRA doesn't have a problem with that. And interestingly enough, it also doesn't have a problem with one spouse paying the other's taxes. So if the lower-income spouse owes money, the higher-income spouse should pay the taxes, and the lower-income spouse should invest.

One of the best options for income splitting is available to people who own their own business. You can hire your spouse to work for you and pay a regular salary. The only condition is that the amount you pay must be a reasonable salary for the work being done. If you need a family income of $4,000 a month, and you split the income between you and your honey, you'll pay much less tax overall. This will also give a stay-at-home parent the CPP contribution credits, and the ability to build RRSP assets, which will allow you to split your income when you retire.

Attribution ceases for years when you become a non-resident for tax purposes, when there is a marriage breakdown, or when you die.

Lending money to a spouse and charging CCRA's prescribed interest rate is yet another effective way of income splitting. At the time of writing, the prescribed rate was 5%. Let's look at an example to see how this would work. Let's say Mark's been working on a novel for the last two years, during which time he's made about $15,000 a year as a part-time handyman. His wife, Laticia, who works as a dental hygienist, makes $65,000 and has accumulated a nifty little nest egg of unregistered investments. Now, let's say Laticia lent $25,000 to Mark, who in turn invested those funds and earned a return of 12%. Here's how the income-splitting strategy would work.

Laticia would have to charge Mark the prescribed rate of 5% on the loan to keep everything kosher with the tax man. Yes, the money would actually have to change hands and be reported on the tax return of everyone involved. So Laticia would have to pay tax on the $1,250 in interest income from the loan at her marginal tax rate of 50% for a total of $625 in tax. Mark would earn $3,000 on his investment, and have an interest expense deduction of $1,250, on which he would pay tax at his lower rate of 27% ($473). In the end, after all was said and done, the couple would pay $402 less by taking this route than by earning all the return in Laticia's hands and paying the $1,500 in tax at her higher marginal rate.

Another popular way to income split is to use a spousal RRSP to accumulate retirement assets. A spousal RRSP makes oodles of sense for income splitting if your projected retirement income will be significantly higher or lower than your spouse's. It is a good way to get more income into the lower-income spouse's hands where the tax paid will be at a lower marginal rate.

A spousal RRSP works like a regular RRSP except for one difference: One spouse contributes for the other. The spousal RRSP belongs to the individual in whose name the plan is registered, but the contributor receives the tax deduction for having made the contribution. You can contribute as much as you wish to a spousal RRSP, up to your annual RRSP deduction limit. So, if you are allowed to contribute $7,500 to an RRSP, your total contributions to your own RRSP and the spousal RRSP cannot exceed $7,500. How you split the contributions is up to you. If you decide to contribute $4,000 to a spousal RRSP, then you will be able to contribute only $3,500 to your own RRSP.

While your contributions to a spousal RRSP do not affect your spouse's contribution to his or her own RRSP, spouses who are eligible to make their own RRSP contributions should not contribute to the spousal plan. Keep the non-spousal RRSP contributions in a separate plan so that the attribution rules that apply to a withdrawal from a spousal plan don't affect the non-spousal contributions. What "attribution" rules, you might ask?

CCRA has very specific rules for the withdrawal of funds from a spousal RRSP. When funds are withdrawn from a spousal RRSP, they will be taxed in one of two ways:

1. If no contribution has been made to any spousal RRSP in the year of withdrawal or the two preceding calendar years, the funds will be taxed as the plan holder's (the spouse's) income. The word "any" is particularly important. It doesn't matter which spousal RRSP account a withdrawal is taken from, the attribution still applies. Trying to take the money from a spousal RRSP set up five or six years ago at one institution doesn't work if you contributed to a spousal RRSP at another institution at some later point.

2. If a contribution has been made at any time during the year of withdrawal or the two preceding calendar years to any spousal RRSP, all or part of the money withdrawn will be taxed as part of the contributor's income, depending on how much is withdrawn.

Let's say your spousal RRSP is worth $20,000 and that in each of the years 1997, 1996, and 1995, your spouse contributed $2,000 to the plan for you. If you were to withdraw $8,000 from the plan in 1997, $6,000 of the withdrawal would be taxed as part of the contributor's income since those contributions were made "in the year of withdrawal" (1997) and "two preceding years" (1996 and 1995). The remaining $2,000, which represents contributions made before 1995, will be taxed as part of your income.

Again, as with everything else in the tax legislation, the wording is very specific and the use of the term "calendar year" is important. If you made a contribution in January 1996, your spouse would have to wait until January of 1999 before a withdrawal would not have any tax impact on you. However, if you made the contribution in December 1995, your spouse could withdraw without attribution as early as January 1998.

To ensure that withdrawals do not inadvertently work against your income-splitting objectives, it is extremely important to consider the impact of this three-year period before making any withdrawals from a spousal RRSP.

The three-year rule does not apply if the spouses are living apart due to relationship breakdown or if the contributing spouse died in the year of the withdrawal. Other circumstances where there is no attribution include: if either spouse becomes a non-resident of Canada; if the plan holder transfers money directly from the RRSP to an annuity or Registered Pension Plan that cannot be commuted for at least three years; or if the plan holder transfers money to a registered retirement income fund (RRIF) and does not withdraw more than the minimum amount.

When it comes to income splitting, retirement planning specialist Ann Eynon says that people often overlook their company pensions as one factor in the calculation. She says, "People often don't see the relationship between the RRSP and the pension income. The name of the game is to have equal income, including the pension. Spousal contributions may be appropriate by the spouse with a pension even if that means the non-pension spouse ends up with more RRSP assets." It's one way of evening the playing field. Rather than one individual having a huge retirement income with the other partner getting little or nothing, a spousal RRSP can be used to redistribute income evenly between both. That means less tax for the family.

On a total income of $70,000 earned in only one person's hands, there would be a tax liability of about $25,000. However, split that income equally between a couple, and the family tax bill drops to about $20,500. That's a savings of almost 20% for simply having chosen to use a spousal RRSP.

By income splitting, you will also make your spouse eligible for the non-refundable tax credit upon reaching 65 if your spouse receives income from a RRIF or annuity purchased with the proceeds from the spousal RRSP. And it may help you avoid the Old Age Security (OAS) and Age Tax Credit clawbacks. (See Chapter 16 for details on clawbacks.)

Consider, too, the fact that a spousal RRSP is the only way to continue benefiting from an RRSP's tax-deferred growth once you've passed the age of contribution. If your spouse is younger than you and you have earned income or unused contributions carried forward from previous years, you can continue deferring tax by contributing to a plan in your spouse's name even after you are required to stop contributing to your own RRSP.

Too often people are reluctant to use a spousal RRSP because they are concerned about marital breakdown. What they don't realize is that under family law each spouse owns half of the other's RRSP anyway. So just because your name is on the plan doesn't mean it won't be divided when you divorce. Scarlett Ungurean, a chartered accountant and financial planner with William M. Mercer Limited, warns that these same laws don't apply to common-law spouses. "If you're in a common-law relationship, the provincial family law act may not provide for property rights and equalization."

Insurance specialist Leslie Macdonald Francis suggests that people who have been once bitten and are twice shy consider using an RRSP with an irrevocable beneficiary clause from an insurance company. "You can make spousal contributions and have your spouse name you as the irrevocable beneficiary. Your spouse won't be able to make a withdrawal without your signature because you are the irrevocable beneficiary." An additional benefit: You won't unknowingly be removed as beneficiary of the RRSP even in the event of a divorce.

Scarlett Ungurean is a consultant with William M. Mercer Limited. She has 18 years of experience advising individuals on personal tax, personal financial planning, estate and investment planning, and general business matters. A member of the Canadian Tax Foundation, she's a chartered accountant with a degree in mathematics. Scarlett is a Registered Financial Planner, the former vice-president of the Canadian Association of Women Executives and Entrepreneurs, and former treasurer of the Toronto Symphony Women's Committee. With her wry sense of humour and eclectic training and experience, she's proof that accountants aren't all boring and women aren't all mathematically challenged.

YOUR ESTATE PLAN AND OTHER LEGAL ISSUES

"When you marry," says estate specialist Hilary Laidlaw, "Your will is automatically revoked, unless you made the will in contemplation of marriage." So whether you are marrying for the first time, or for the fourth, you will need to make a new will.

Common-law relationships are recognized as legal marriages for certain purposes but not for others. So, if you wish to contribute to a spousal RRSP, you can, as long as you have "cohabited in a conjugal relationship for a period of at least one year, or less than one year if the two individuals are the natural or adoptive parents of a child." However, according to Hilary, under estate law, if you're in a common-law relationship — no matter how long-standing it is — your partner has no rights on intestacy. So if you die without a will, your 20-year partner would have no rights under the succession laws. "In this situation, the common-law spouse's only course of action," says Hilary, "is to make a claim against the estate for support as a dependent, providing they have been in a common-law relationship for not less than three years or for a lesser period if there is a child of that relationship." So the common-law spouse would have to go through the process — and the cost — of making a claim against the estate through a formal proceeding in the court. That's a rough road to walk emotionally, but particularly so when you're also dealing with a family from a first marriage. To protect your spouse, or to ensure you are protected, a will with specific designations must clearly state who gets what and when.

In terms of property rights, legally married spouses can opt into the elective regime so if they don't like what they are getting under the will, they can say, "Forget it, I'll elect for an equalization," which is a 50/50 split of the property amassed during the marriage. Common-law spouses don't have this option. Nor do same-sex spouses.

When it comes to estate planning for same-sex couples, says Bernadette Dietrich, a lawyer with McCarthy Tétrault in Toronto, "There's so little law that it's easy to fall into traps. It's important to look around and see who survives the same-sex spouse at death," says Bernadette. "There may be a legally married spouse who comes forward as a dependent or as a claimant under the Family Law Act if they were never divorced." People often don't think of this because once the relationship is history and there are no present support obligations they just don't think of the future implications. They never get around to a divorce. Bernadette warns, "But that can then mean that the legally married spouse is the first person who is technically entitled to apply to be the administrator of the estate."

There is no precedent for a same-sex spouse to make a claim for support due to dependency (as can be done by a common-law spouse) upon death. "What we have seen is one case that basically said that same-sex spouses ought to be entitled to support in the same way as common-law spouses on relationship breakdown," says Bernadette. "It would be hard to imagine that if it is found acceptable on marriage breakdown it won't be at death."

There is a move to have same-sex couples recognized under the Family Law Act, where same-sex couples could list themselves as "registered domestic partners" so they would be entitled to the same rights as spouses. "But that's been out there for a long time," says Bernadette, "and nothing much has happened with it."

Under the Estates Act, there's no provision for same-sex spouses to be appointed as an estate trustee without a will. "That can be a real problem because there's often conflict between the same-sex spouse and the deceased's family. The family has a prior right, leaving the same-sex spouse in a very weak position." So if you are in a same-sex relationship, you have a responsibility to have a will that protects your partner, since there are so many areas in which she simply has no rights.

"It's unfortunate that our society just hasn't evolved to the point where everybody accepts same-sex couples. We tell clients that when we're taking instructions for the will, we don't want the same-sex spouse in the room, which we don't do with heterosexual couples," says Bernadette. She admits it takes a bit of explaining before this is usually agreed on. The purpose: to ensure that no claim can be made down the road that undue influence was placed on the person whose will is being made. "If we know that the person is HIV-positive or suffering from any kind of illness including depression, we get a letter from a doctor stating that 'these are the drugs being taken and the effect of those drugs, and in my opinion

Bernadette Dietrich is a partner at McCarthy Tétrault, where she specializes in personal tax, estate planning and succession, trusts, estate litigation, and charitable organizations. For a number of years, she taught estate administration courses for the Institute of Law Clerks of Ontario and for the Law Society of Upper Canada Bar Admission Course. She is also the secretary and an executive member of the Trusts and Estates section of the Canadian Bar Association (Ontario). Former editor of the publication Deadbeat, Bernadette is a frequent speaker and writer on estate-planning issues. She enjoys spinning, cycling, running, and skiing and is an avid reader and movie devotee.

they don't affect testamentary capacity,' because that's something the family likes to bring up." That letter guards against a challenge based on testamentary capacity.

Another way to help protect a will from successful challenge is to make sure that everyone who should be taken care of is mentioned in the will. "A will leaving everything to a same-sex spouse will be vulnerable to challenge. If there are children or a former spouse, they should be taken care of." You can designate your same-sex spouse as beneficiary of your insurance and RRSPs, name her as a joint tenant on property, and hold bank accounts jointly to have assets pass directly to a partner without having to be probated. According to Bernadette, "Sometimes it's just a question of optics. If the family can look at a will and it says, 'the residue of my estate to my mom and my dad or to my brothers and sisters,' even if there is no residue they feel better. It's the publicity they don't like. They know wills are public documents and they don't want their neighbours and friends to know that this kind of relationship existed."

While you don't need independent legal advice to sign a power of attorney, don't do so without (a) knowing what you're signing, and (b) keeping a copy for your records. "You wouldn't believe the number of women who come in to talk about divorce and have absolutely no idea what they've signed," says Sandy Morris. You trust your partner, right? You love him or her. Why wouldn't you do it if asked? There's no reason not to, as long as you know what you're signing and you keep a copy. If you don't, then you're asking for big trouble.

PARTNERING AGAIN

You know the saying, "Love is better the second time around"? I can attest to that. And the third time, it's even better. But the fact is, remarriage brings its own complications. There may be one or two ex-spouses. Perhaps you have children, or he has children. Maybe you plan to have children together. Then there are all the habits you've established that you want to keep, but that drive your partner nuts.

Being a stepmother is probably the hardest voyage I've ever undertaken. The waters have been very rough from time to time, and more than once I've been thoroughly seasick. Yet despite my resolve never to repeat it, I've embarked on stepmotherhood again. Happily I can report the sailing is much smoother this time out. But navigating the merging of our families has meant that my husband and I have had to deal with some important financial issues.

Whether through spousal support, child support, or everyday existence, former spouses have a way of docking at the stepfamily jetty. And while many new spouses are at least somewhat aware of the prior financial obligations of their partners, the dollars-and-cents significance can never be completely clear until they start living with it.

New legislation in Ontario on the role of "family income" is laying the groundwork for changes that have some new spouses worried. Now "total household income" — yep, his and yours — is considered in awarding support. So if an ex runs into rough waters, the new spouse's income can be factored into the equation in providing support to the previous family unit.

Stepparents can also be held financially responsible for stepchildren's support in the event that the new marriage ends on the rocks. As long as the stepparent contributed to the upkeep of the stepchild, divorce will not end the stepparent's financial obligation.

Individuals often come to a second marriage bearing assets. Whether those assets are the result of a settlement from a previous marriage, or the assets accumulated prior to the marriage, individuals sometimes want to keep them separate from the new family's assets. Add children to the mix and ownership issues become very complicated.

Equally complicated is how those assets should be distributed when one or both parents sail off to Valhalla. If you die *sans* will — referred to as dying intestate — the money may not be distributed as you intended. My husband, Ken, has two children from his former marriage, and together we have two children. So we have had to ask ourselves, how do we structure our estates so that the little kids are taken care of, in light of the fact that the big kids have already been cared for to adulthood? Sitting with a lawyer is a must when dealing with this type of question, since you can take steps to create pools of money for the benefit of one or another child.

In the case of inheritance, most children expect money and property to follow a bloodline, not a wedding band. My first stepson was outraged at the thought that I would inherit his house. This is a particular concern of adult children. Mistrust, and a human tendency to think the worst, comes when there is a lack of information. If you have a good relationship with your adult stepchildren, make time to talk over their concerns and expectations — and yours. At the same time, consider whether you have clearly identified your position to your new spouse. Ethical commitments do not have to conflict with new love. But sometimes they do require future adjustments and, perhaps, compensations.

Most people are not aware that divorce financial settlements are not binding on creditors. Your family's financial plan can be wrecked by an ex-spouse's personal bankruptcy. And if an ex fails to make payments, the creditor may turn to your family to collect. It's wise to take an inventory of all your financial obligations and take steps to mitigate any risks you can.

Now that you have children, post-secondary education is going to be an issue. While my husband chose to fund his big kids' university costs from cash flow, I've decided we have to set aside money from day one to take care of the little kids. After all, we might not have a cash flow when the time comes for our four-year-old to head off to university.

Does your family need a new insurance policy? Probably, since many divorce agreements assign benefits from existing policies to the former spouse as a guarantee of spousal or child support. If you've started a new family, then the answer is "definitely," since those new babies need to be protected for a long and expensive time to come.

A ready-made family can seem like a blessing or a curse depending on the day of the week. Some women must come to grips with their roles as parents for the very first time. Others must find ways of combining vastly different personalities under the same roof. Hardly ever do merging families create the Brady Bunch. Perhaps the most important lesson I've learned is that nothing stays the same. I change. He changes. The children's needs change. The financial and legal rules change. And so the stepfamily financial discussion is not a "talk" you can have once. Staying on an even keel means constantly monitoring the weather for signs of storms ahead. But if you're willing to balance each other off, to heave when he says ho, it can work out just fine.

15

When You Have a Baby

When the first baby laughed for the first time, the laugh broke into a thousand pieces and they all went skipping about, and that was the beginning of fairies.

SIR JAMES BARRIE

Perhaps the single largest source of conflict for women is in reconciling their roles as caretakers and nurturers with the need to do everything else: keep a job, further their careers, achieve financial independence, just to name a few. I know that until my children were born, I had no trouble deciding what my first priority should be: Me! While a lot has been written about women's innate need to nurture — to put others at the centre of their lives and before themselves — little can prepare us for the impact of a baby. The best description I've ever found was a story by Dale Hanson Bourke in *Chicken Soup for the Woman's Soul*:

I look at her carefully manicured nails and stylish suit and think that no matter how sophisticated she is, becoming a mother will reduce her to the primitive level of a bear protecting her cub. That urgent call of "Mom!" will cause her to drop a soufflé or her best crystal without a moment's hesitation. I feel I should warn her that no matter how many years she has invested in her career, she will be professionally derailed by motherhood. She might arrange for child care, but one day she will be going into an important business meeting and she will think about her baby's sweet smell. She will have to use every ounce of discipline to keep from running home, just to make sure her child is all right . . . I want to assure her that eventually, she will shed the pounds of pregnancy, but she will never feel the same about herself. That her life, now so important, will be of less value to her once she has a child.[23]

When Alexandra was born, I was broadsided on my career track. Until then, I could work 17 hours a day, seven days a week when the situation demanded it. With a sweet angel waiting for mommy upstairs, I was loath to make those kinds of commitments anymore. When Malcolm came along, I was hit by a two-by-four, never to be the same again. My shift in priorities was final and, without question, the kids came first.

That's not to say that I didn't continue to want a career. I did. But now I was going to have to fight with myself each time I contemplated a job of any size. It was no longer a question of, "What do I do to get this job?" Now it was, "How badly do I want this job and what am I willing to give up to do it?" Often what I was willing to give up was sleep. I've spent hundreds of 3:00-to-7:00 mornings (just as I am today) trying to get a decent amount of work done before the kids get up. Thank goodness those early months of motherhood and the accompanying lack of sleep prepared me so well for the rest of my life.

YOUR SPENDING PLAN: INCORPORATING THE COSTS OF RAISING A KID

Kids are expensive. There are diapers, the crib, bum-cream, and child care, the "big bed," breakage, and the footprints on the furniture. Try taking a holiday with two children and suddenly your travel costs have doubled. Go out for a meal and, wham, there's another bill that just went up. Then there are the medical and dental costs. There's the cost of sheltering their wee bodies, summer and winter. The birthdays, the

---

23 Karen Wheeler in Dale Hanson Bourke, *Chicken Soup for the Woman's Soul* (Health Communications, Inc., 1996), p. 164.

holiday season, the parties they'll attend for which you have to supply a gift. If you opt for enrichment lessons such as music or gymnastics, or sports such as hockey, skiing, or anything of a competitive nature that requires travel, you're looking at a whopping bill. And when they become susceptible to the triple whammy of advertising, brand power, and peer pressure, watch out.

While the costs of raising kids can be daunting if looked at all together, it's surprising how you manage to get by with a little less of this or that so Molly can have that new Beanie Baby. And there are strategies you can use to minimize the cost of things such as toys and clothing.

When you get pregnant, you'll be overwhelmed with the desire to provide the best of everything for your new lassie or laddie. The first thing to do is hunt up all your old friends who have had kids and ask them what you'll need. Make a list. Check a baby book to see what's missing. Then start shopping, slowly. Put the word out and you'll be amazed at the number of people who will offer things you'll find useful. Mommies are the most sharing of all creatures.

If you want an idea of what it will cost to raise your child, talk to your friends. Do up a budget for your new expenses and then confirm your figures with those who are in the know. One useful resource is a fact sheet study put out by the home economics section of Manitoba's agriculture ministry. Each fall, they compile a list of basic goods and services used to keep kids healthy and happy. Then they go to popular stores and price the list. The figures they come up with may be slightly lower or higher than in your area, but they're a good starting point. Call the ministry or hit their website (www.gov.mb.ca) for the most recent numbers.

When it comes to shaving dollars off your kid budget, buying second-hand can save you scads of money. Hunt up the secondhand stores in your neighbourhood, or ask friends for the names of good stores. Shop the garage sales. When Alexandra was about 18 months old, I was an avid garage sale shopper. It got me out of the house on my own and for just a few dollars I participated in a great shopping experience. I got an enormous bucket of Lego for $30. My husband and I bought a $200 climber for the backyard for $65. I bought toy cars, books (one of my favourites came from a garage sale), clothes, and dress-up supplies such as beads, necklaces, and scarves at a fraction of the store price.

Secondhand stores are also great places to recycle stuff you want to get rid of if you don't know of anyone who can use it. After Malcolm outgrew his bassinet, I took it to a secondhand store and got 60% of what I paid for it. That's not bad. And I used the money from his crib to pay part of the cost for his new big-boy bed.

My greatest savings have probably been in clothing my daughter. Her cousins who live in Florida are two and four years older than Alex. The timing couldn't be better. Twice a year, my cousin boxes up her girls' outgrowns and sends them to me. Alex wears the most beautiful dresses. I have to do winter, but summer is taken care of each year. Until now, I've never had to buy my daughter a bathing suit because Vanessa sends two or three every year. And Malcolm benefits too from the tee-shirts, shorts, and other non-girlie stuff.

MAKING SPACE FOR BABY

One decision most new parents face is that of making room for a new baby. If you're already in a house or a large apartment, chances are you can just clear out that room you've been using for storage. But if you're out of space or starting to consider things such as school locations and recreational facilities, you'll be planning to move. If it's your first home purchase, you'll have to start thinking about downpayments and mortgages. If you're considering upgrading to a new house, you'll have to figure out what to do with your existing mortgage. See Chapter 7, "Putting a Roof Over Your Head," for details.

REVIEWING YOUR GOALS

Now that you have a new dependent, this is a natural time to review your goals. Things like retirement planning and vacations tend to take a back-seat to raising a baby. But it's not always a good idea to put your own financial goals on hold completely. After all, raising kids is an 18-year proposition.

Let's say you can currently contribute $7,500 to an RRSP. You decide to forgo the RRSP for the next 18 years. At just 8%, that'll cost you $296,000 — and a whopping $161,000 in growth (translation: money you didn't have to contribute). Okay, so you can't contribute $7,500 a year. We'll drop the figures and see the result. If you could contribute $5,000 a year, you'd be out of RRSP-pocket $182,251. If you could contribute $2,000, you'd be out of RRSP-pocket $72,900.

While you will have to trim expenses in some places, and your RRSP may be one of them, it's worthwhile to continue contributing as much as you can because of the magic of compounding return.

Saving for Your Child's Education

If you think raising kids is expensive now, wait until you see what it's going to cost to send them to university. According to Statistics Canada, between 1985 and 1995, university tuition increased by 134%. If costs continue to rise at the same rate — and there's no reason to doubt they will, given recent government spending cuts — the 1996 cost of about $9,000 a year is expected to spiral to a whopping $16,000 a year by 2006. That's almost $65,000 for a four-year degree. The average debt load for students who graduated in 1996 was $22,000. While you may believe it is at least partly your child's responsibility to pay for their education, no one likes to think about their children graduating from school with an albatross of debt around their necks. So what can you do to ensure your little ones have all the educational advantages you think they should? Start planning, and start now!

RESPs

One of the most popular ways to save for future educational costs is with a Registered Education Savings Plan or RESP. An RESP is a savings plan, registered with the federal government, that allows money to be saved for a beneficiary's postsecondary education. Like an RRSP, all income earned within the plan is tax-deferred. Unlike an RRSP, there is no deduction for money going into an RESP. You can set up a single family plan, in antic-ipation of educating more than one child from the same fund, or individual plans for each child.

You can invest up to $4,000 a year in an RESP for each beneficiary (regardless of whether the beneficiary has an individual plan or is named as one beneficiary of a family plan), to a lifetime maximum of $42,000. Contributions can be made for up to 21 years and the plan must be collapsed within 25 years of the starting date; otherwise you will lose the income earned on the plan. That expiry date is sometimes a bummer for parents with kids who are far apart in age, or who are part of a family plan. If the parents wish to pass on their older child's unused RESP savings to a much younger child, timing could become a tricky issue.

If you want to get around the 25-year limit, open up a new RESP every five years or so. With several RESPs you won't have all your money in one plan. If there is a delay in using your RESP because your daughter decides to take time to travel or work before entering university, you won't have to forgo all the income earned because the 25-year time limit has expired. You'll still have two or three other plans to draw on.

Overcontributions to an RESP are subject to a penalty tax of 1% per month. Penalty tax is charged proportionally against all contributors. While overcontributions may be withdrawn at any time, the overcontribution amount will be included in the calculation of the lifetime limit of $42,000, so don't do it.

To use the total accumulated in an RESP, beneficiaries must attend an accredited postsecondary institution on a full-time basis. The program must be no shorter than three consecutive weeks, with at least 10 course hours per week. Correspondence courses qualify, as do universities, community colleges, junior vocational and technical colleges, as well as many universities outside Canada. If an alternate beneficiary is named (another child, or anyone else related by blood, adoption, or marriage), the RESP money must still be used within the original 25-year time frame.

Should your child decide not to pursue a postsecondary education and no other beneficiary will be named, you can withdraw the full amount contributed to an RESP without tax ramifications. As long as the plan has been in existence for at least 10 years, up to $50,000 of the income earned in an RESP to which you have contributed can be transferred to your own RRSP, or to a spousal RRSP, providing you have sufficient contribution room to claim a deduction for the contribution. If you do not have sufficient contribution room, or you wish to withdraw more than the allowable $50,000, the withdrawal will be subject to tax at your marginal tax rate, and the excess above $50,000 will be subject to an additional penalty tax of 20%. Ouch!

If you do withdraw the RESP savings yourself, note that an RESP must be terminated before March 1 of the year following the year in which you make your first withdrawal. You'd be wise to spread the withdrawals over two calendar years so you can take advantage of accumulated RRSP contribution room and avoid penalty tax. Another benefit: Canada's graduated marginal tax rates may mean less in tax since the income is taken over two years instead of in a single year.

Whether or not the child ends up using the income earned on the RESP for school, the principal contributed to an RESP can be withdrawn at any time without penalty, since there was no tax deduction for having made that contribution. Having been a diligent parent and saved, saved, saved, once you're comfortable that your child will have enough, you can take back what you've given without tax consequence. The RESP will have cost you nothing at all. You can put a downpayment on a nice condo in Florida while your child uses the earned income (taxed in his or her hands, not yours) to investigate the halls of higher learning.

Personally, RESPs are not my favourite education savings tool. Even though there are provisions to allow you to withdraw the funds if your child does not end up using them, these plans are far too restrictive. This is particularly true of pooled or group plans where you have no say in how your money is being invested. All investments are made by the plan administrator and tend to be conservative. I get very cranky when I see brochures for these "scholarship trusts" in places they don't belong, such as the doctor's office, the dentist's office, medical labs, hospitals, and the like — places that offer no competitive information or advice and that lend them an air of authority that I don't think they deserve.

The most recent change made to RESPs was the proposed Canada Education Savings Grant (CESG), which will assist parents by adding 20% of the annual amount contributed to an RESP up to a maximum of $400 a year. To get the maximum grant, you'd have to contribute at least $2,000 to an RESP. These grants only apply to contributions made after 1997, and only to children under 18. And there is a maximum total: $7,200. Children who turn 16 or 17 in a year a contribution is made to an RESP on their behalf will only get the grant if there have been contributions of $300 or more for at least four years prior to the year the child turned 16 or if there was a total of $4,000 contributed on behalf of that child prior to the year he or she turned 16.

Unused grant eligibility can be carried forward until the age 17 cut-off, so if you can't make the annual contribution of $2,000 to receive the full $400 grant in a single year, any amount not claimed can be claimed with a later contribution. Let's say that this year I made a contribution of $1,500 on behalf of my son, Malcolm. The maximum grant I'd receive is $300, representing 20%. Since the maximum grant in any given year is $400, it means I can carry forward $100 of the grant to next year, for a total eligibility amount of $500. As long as I made a contribution of $2,500 or more, I'd be able to claim a grant of $500. While grant room accumulates from year to year and can be carried forward, the maximum grant that can be *earned* in any one year is $400. In other words, if you contribute more than $2,000 to an RESP, you do not earn additional grant room that can be carried forward, so keep your flow of contributions even.

Grants must be repaid if beneficiaries do not attend an eligible post-secondary institution or if RESP contributions are withdrawn before a beneficiary is eligible to receive the payments from the RESP (which are called Educational Assistance Payments, or EAPs). Grants cannot be transferred to beneficiaries other than a sibling or blood relative (including adoptive relatives) under the age of 21, and cannot be transferred to another RESP, except if there is no change in beneficiary under the new plan. If a CESG balance remains in an RESP after all eligible beneficiaries have received their lifetime maximum, as may occur with a family plan where all beneficiaries earned CESGs but not all pursued qualifying postsecondary education, that balance must be repaid. Grants must also be repaid if a contribution is removed from the plan. Whenever a withdrawal is made for non-educational purposes, an amount equal to 20% of the withdrawal must be repaid to the government, up to the total of the CESGs that were received. As well, if more than $200 of non-CESG-eligible contributions are withdrawn, RESP beneficiaries under that plan will not qualify for the grant for the remainder of the year or the two subsequent years. And, they will not accumulate grant room for those years.

The upside to an RESP — aside from that enticing grant — is that the income generated, regardless of whether that income is interest, dividends, or capital gains, grows on a tax-sheltered basis. Some people aren't aware of this, and continue to choose traditional interest-bearing investments such as CSBs, savings accounts, or GICs to save for their children's or grandchildren's education, in the mistaken belief that they, as contributors, won't be taxed on anything that accumulates. In fact, whenever an investment earns its return in the form of interest, the person who buys the investment has to pay the tax on the interest earned at their marginal tax rate. So for every $1,000 in interest earned, assuming a marginal tax rate of 45%, you would have to pay $450 in tax. The tax man is earning almost as much as your child! Only the second-generation interest — the interest earned on the interest through compounding — is taxable in your child's hands. The exception to this is an investment bought with funds solely provided from Family Allowance and Child Tax Benefit payments or an inheritance; this money is already classified for tax purposes as your child's money, so tax on *all* income earned must be paid by your child. Take care to keep these investments separate from any you may buy your child with your own funds.

If you're only comfortable with interest-bearing investments as the option for your child's educational savings, an RESP is a good idea because the interest earned within the RESP is tax-deferred. Remember, though, during periods of low interest rates, the plan will struggle to earn a return. If you're willing to step outside the realm of the tried-and-true interest-bearing investment, then take a look at mutual funds. With thousands of mutual funds now available in Canada, you have many options, ranging from the relative security of a money-market fund, through to the income-producing mortgage and bond funds, ending with the most aggressive of all: equity funds.

In-trust accounts

If RESPs are not for you, consider establishing an in-trust account. An in-trust account is set up with a financial institution to invest funds for a minor. The account is set up in trust because kids aren't allowed to enter into binding financial contracts, so an adult has to be responsible for providing the investment instructions and signing the contract on the child's behalf. Most in-trust accounts are informal since setting up a formal trust is expensive. To make the fees for setting up and managing a formal trust worthwhile, you need a minimum of $100,000. Most of us just don't have that kind of change in our pockets. For us, there's the informal in-trust account.

Creating an informal in-trust account that keeps Revenue Canada happy isn't difficult, but it does require you to take some specific steps. First, make sure the account is set up as "Gail Prue in trust for Alex Prue" as opposed to "Alex Prue in trust." This clearly states who the trustee is

(Gail Prue) and who the beneficiary is (Alex). Next, write out the terms of your trust and make sure you clearly spell out:

- who is giving the money (whether that is a father, mother, grandparent, aunt, or other relative), referred to as the "donor"
- who is controlling the trust, referred to as the "trustee"; this cannot be the person who is giving the money
- that the property is "irrevocable," which means that the person who gave it cannot get it back, and has no control over how it is invested or used.

In the case of a couple, decide ahead of time who will be providing the money to the trust and who will be managing the investments, since this cannot be the same person.

Having set up the informal trust, you now have to decide what to invest in. While the attribution rule we saw in the context of earned interest (which dictated that the donor must pay tax on first-generation income, while the account holder pays tax on any second-generation income) also applies to dividend income, it doesn't apply to capital gains. A very important benefit of investing in equities is that there is no income-tax attribution on capital gains earned in an in-trust mutual-fund account, so every dollar earned by way of a capital gain is taxable in your child's hands. And by declaring some capital gains each year, you reduce the gain that will be recorded when the funds are withdrawn, so little or no tax will have to be paid at that time.

If you're choosing a mutual-fund investment for the in-trust account, don't be enticed by enormously high rates of return for the last year or two. Look at the long-term results. And don't look simply at the average rate of return — great years can mask the losses suffered in rotten years. Instead, check out the year-over-year returns. Since it's important not to stick all your raisins in one cookie, choose a good fund family. If you decide to switch from one fund to another as performance and economic conditions change, being in a family of funds will minimize the cost of switching from one type of fund to another. Also consider holding some foreign equities in your child's portfolio. Since Canada accounts for less than 3% of the world's stock market capitalization, diversifying globally will let you take advantage of the economies in other regions around the world. And as your child closes in on graduation, and you decide to get a little more conservative with the portfolio, you'll be able to switch from one fund type to another without incurring additional commissions.

The closer your child is to using the money, the more conservative you'll have to be with how you invest. If you start on your child's savings soon after she's born, you'll have plenty of time to ride out the highs and lows of the equity market to come up with a decent average return, so you can afford to be more aggressive. However, if your child is only five years away from university, you'll have to be more cautious. Fixed-income funds may be the ticket.

The closer your child is to needing the money, the more likely you will be to choose interest-bearing investments. So this might be a good time to catch up on all those CESGs you've not yet gathered by contributing future savings to an RESP.

There's no question that saving for your child's education is important. The trick is to use the option that creates the best possible return while offering the most flexibility. Your child's education savings program shouldn't penalize you for decisions that won't be made for many years yet. The idea of forfeiting income earned should be repulsive, as should the idea of paying a 20% penalty tax. Let's face it, the next best thing to an education is probably a downpayment on a home or the money to set up a new business. Whatever your child decides in the future, your decision now boils down to this: Who would you rather have the money? The RESP administrator, the tax man, or your child? Rhetorical question, right?

PREPARING FOR THE INTERRUPTION IN YOUR INCOME

If you're planning to have a baby, there are steps to take to assure your financial health, just as you take steps to ensure your physical health. Women who want to get pregnant often change their own life patterns in anticipation of creating a new life. They change the way they eat, how much sleep they get, take extra vitamins, stop smoking — lots of stuff to prepare themselves for the blessed event. However, fewer people take into account the cash-flow crunch they'll experience during their maternity leave. Fewer still are prepared for the strong desire to remain at home caring for that sweet little bundle of joy, even after the maternity leave period has expired.

If you want your maternity leave to go smoothly, if you want to be able to focus on the baby without having to worry too much about money, then you have to do some planning. It's like everything else in life. Look ahead, see what has to be done, and just do it.

MATERNITY BENEFITS

Nothing puts a crimp in a couple's cash flow like the arrival of a baby. And while most people feel that the financial offset provided by the Employment Insurance (EI) program is small, the idea of being able to return to a career without penalty for taking parental time is very reassuring to couples planning to start a family.

Early in 2001, you no doubt saw all those ads on television explaining the government's new maternity and parental leave provisions. Under EI, parental leave benefits have been extended from 10 weeks to 35 weeks. EI will also provide 55% of insurable earnings, up to $413 a week, for 15 weeks of maternity (which, of course, is available only to birth mothers) for a combined maternal/parental leave of up to 50 weeks. That would provide children with almost a whole year of parental care.

The federal increase in benefits comes as countries the world over recognize and legislate the time families need to set their babies off on the right foot. Over 100 countries, including most of the industrialized nations, have enacted some form of parental leave policy. In France, parents get up to three years of unpaid parental leave, during which their jobs are protected. In the Netherlands, parental leave can last up to six months. Parents in Britain are entitled to up to 40 weeks of unpaid family leave. In contrast, the United States provides up to 12 weeks of parental leave.

Despite the reassurances in EI advertisements that Canada is committed to providing children with the best care — the care of their parents — for up to one year, for many moms and dads anticipating spending a year with junior, disappointment lurks in the wings. While federal legislation, with its cash benefits, grants men and women the means to make their child a priority in their lives, at least for that baby's first year, in the end our various provincial labour codes do not serve all Canadians equally. It's just one more example of federal and provincial legislation being at loggerheads. For even though EI benefits are provided for approximately one year, some provinces do not give employees the option to take that much time away from work and actually use those benefits.

If you live in Alberta, you're the worst off. Under existing legislation, you're entitled to 18 weeks combined maternity and parental leave and you're not entitled to the maintenance of your employee benefits. There is a draft bill that would increase combined maternity and parental leave to 27 weeks, still well below the federal promise. If you live in Quebec, you've got the highest level of protection, with up to 18 weeks of maternity protection and another 52 weeks of parental leave. And your employer must continue to provide benefits coverage at its expense if your benefits were 100% employer-paid. If those benefits required your contribution, they must be maintained as long as you pay your share. The remaining provinces fall somewhere in the middle.

Employment-benefit entitlement varies greatly, with seven provincial jurisdictions providing for no continuation of employer-provided benefits, some would say just when employees need them the most. In order to be eligible to take maternity leave, an employee must have worked for a specific number of months for the employer granting the leave, except in British Columbia, New Brunswick, and Quebec, where length of service is not an issue. Maternity leave is awarded in Newfoundland, PEI, and Saskatchewan after 20 weeks of employment, and in Ontario after just 13 weeks. Everywhere else you'll need to have been employed for at least 12 months. So if you're pregnant and work in one of the provinces where a 12-month stint is required before you can collect mat benefits, it will be up to you to negotiate that as part of your employment contract. In order to qualify for maternity or adoption benefits under EI, claimants must have accumulated 600 hours of insurable employment. The EI system uses hours, rather than days or weeks, to measure insurable time in order to ensure that all types of employment — full-time, part-time, and seasonal work — contribute to qualify individuals for benefits. Parental leave is available to both mothers and fathers, and under the new EI rules, while a two-week waiting period applies to the first person who seeks to claim parental benefits, there's no waiting period for the second parent. And parents can switch back and forth in taking benefits without penalty.

Parents may also work part-time while receiving parental benefits. (This is not allowed with maternity benefits.) Parents can earn up to 25% of their weekly benefit or $50 a week, whichever is higher. Greater earnings than that and you'll find the difference deducted from your EI benefits on a dollar-for-dollar basis.

People who adopt are also entitled to the stated parental leave (but not the maternity leave) in most provinces. Alberta provides an adoption leave of up to eight weeks. Newfoundland and Saskatchewan offer both adoption and parental leave, with adoption leave mirroring their maternity leave benefits.

Keep in mind that while maternity and parental leave benefits may help with cash flow in the short term, in some cases the money — as little as it may be — won't be yours to keep. If your net income for income tax purposes is $48,750 or more a year, you'll end up having all or part of your EI maternity benefits clawed back. The clawback is now limited to 30% of your net income in excess of the $48,750. However, it is expected that legislation will be introduced shortly to end the clawback on maternity benefits.

Lots of women think of maternity leave as the prime time to dip into their RRSPs to support themselves while they aren't earning a regular income. If you've contributed to your RRSP with this in mind, then you've been using your RRSP as a savings account with a special tax advantage. You haven't been planning for retirement (which you'll still have to do), so don't fool yourself. Every cent you take out of your RRSP is out for good. There's no way to get that money back into the plan. And the long-term growth . . . poof, that's gone, if there's no money in the plan to grow.

I received an e-mail one day from a woman who was in a panic. She was about five months from her maternity leave, her husband was not working, and she had no idea how much income she'd have while she was off work. She hadn't checked to see what her EI benefits would be, but she was already sure they wouldn't be enough to cover her rent, never mind her food and everything else that comes with a new baby.

Okay, so she didn't plan. It's not unusual to see a woman surprised by the fact that the strip turned pink, or blue, or whatever the going colour is. The thing is, panicking won't help. It'll add stress to your life, not to mention your partner's life. It'll stress the baby. But it won't solve anything. It's time to sit down, have a talk about how you're going to cope — what are you going to *do* — so that you can move from panic to planning. Remember *telesis*. A little creativity will go a long way toward getting you through the tight spots. Remember, too, that women aren't the only caregivers in the world. If a child has two parents, both are equally capable of nurturing, cuddling, and caring for that child. And no, he doesn't have to do it the way you'd do it, he just has to do it well.

Here's another tip to consider when planning your maternity income. Just because you make an RRSP contribution doesn't mean you have to claim the deduction in the same year. You can claim that deduction when it suits you most. That's usually when you're in the highest tax bracket because that's when you'll get the biggest refund. Choosing the right time to claim is particularly important for people who are planning on having a family, or anyone who has left the workforce for a period of time or who has income that rises and falls from year to year. Let's take the example of Sue who worked all through 1995 and had an income of $55,000. In 1996, Sue was eligible to make a contribution of $9,900. Smart Sue was on a periodic investment plan, and had socked away all her eligible contribution. In June of 1996, Sue gave birth to Michaela and did not work for the rest of the year so she only earned $25,000 that year. If she claimed her full deduction, she'd get a deduction at her current marginal tax rate of only 25%, so her refund would be $2,475. But let's say Sue held on to the deduction for another year. When she returned to work in 1997, she'd be back to her $55,000 income so she could claim the deduction at a much higher marginal tax rate of 38%: that's $3,762 in tax back. Planning when to take the deduction is an important part of using an RRSP as a tax-reduction strategy. Plan carefully, and you'll get a bigger bang for your buck!

KEEPING A HEALTHY CREDIT IDENTITY

Since having babies is very expensive, rest assured your cash flow will be tested. And since the income interruption associated with having kids is almost a guarantee, you might decide to fill those shortfalls in your cash flow by utilizing some of that wonderful credit you've been granted. According to a study done by Ernst & Young on credit use in Canada (1996), 46% of people aged 18 to 34 have an outstanding balance on at least one of their credit cards. And half of Canadians who had outstanding balances said their balances were higher than they had been three years previously.

In the best of all worlds, you'll have enough set aside to stay in the black while you're off work having and caring for your kids. But most people don't live in that world, and credit becomes one tool for helping to make ends meet. I have a girlfriend who is a single mom. She's chosen to work only part-time so that she can be at home with her little one as much as possible. Working only three days a week, she has seen her income plummet and her debt rise. She's frustrated. She's worried. She's sometimes even angry. And she's always looking for ways to get to the end of the month without getting any further into debt. But there's always something. When she came to me with the problem, she was $12,000 in debt, including her car loan and several credit-card balances. We talked about what she could do to ease the pain. She was carrying a lot of money on a credit card that charged 17% in interest. The first thing I told her to do was apply for a cheaper card and transfer the balance. "You can do that?" she said. Like many people, she didn't realize credit-card companies allowed this kind of transfer. Last year when she was hit with a tax bill, she chose to take an advance on her credit card to pay the government. She didn't ask me first. I would have told her that the government is very happy to accept postdated cheques for taxes, and the interest rate they charge is lower than she's paying on her credit cards.

Sometimes when people get into debt, they can see no way out and everything they do gets them in deeper and deeper. They don't know the rules so they don't know how to play the game to their advantage. They start to bounce cheques. The miss their minimum monthly payments on their credit cards. They skip mortgage payments or car payments, figuring it won't have any long-term impact or that they'll catch up later. Out the window goes the emergency fund, followed closely by the spending plan. Unfortunately, the long-term impact can be quite severe since our credit history tends to show all our financial indiscretions. And it can take a long time to repair the damage done.

It's important when you hit any financial crunch that you keep your credit picture in mind. Credit mistakes aren't quickly erased so you must be careful about what you do and how it will be perceived by a lender in the future. Bouncing cheques may only carry a small penalty now, but the black mark on your record can have significant consequences when it becomes really important to qualify for a loan.

In my girlfriend's case, her car died. She needed her car to do her job. When she went to the bank to get a loan for a new car she was astounded to find that she was denied the loan. It wasn't a huge loan, but her credit history was blotchy and she was already in debt to the tune of about $20,000. She felt trapped. Thankfully, her wonderful parents stepped in and co-signed for her, so she could get a car and get back on her feet. But she felt ashamed and embarrassed in having to turn to them.

Don't do this to yourself. Remember, money is a tool that can be used well or not. So is credit. Learn the rules. Play the game to your advantage. Don't assume little mistakes will be overlooked — they often won't be. Keep your credit record clean so that each time you need it, it will serve you well.

YOUR EMERGENCY FUND

Now that you have a baby, your emergency fund is even more important. You're not just responsible for yourself anymore. You've got a baby to feed, clothes to buy, and a roof to keep over his head. If your husband were to die, if you were to become unemployed, if you were to become disabled, you would need your emergency fund. If your roof were damaged in a storm, if your furnace were red-tagged, if you separated from your spouse, you would need your emergency fund. This is no time to give up your safety net.

If you've established an emergency fund already, you may have to top it up to cover the additional expenses associated with your kids. Major changes in lifestyle such as divorce, widowhood, and illness have their own traumas. You and your children do not need the additional worry about where the groceries will come from next week, or how you'll pay the phone bill.

INSURING YOUR DEPENDENTS' SECURITY

The arrival of a little one brings many added responsibilities, not the least of which is your need to make sure that child can be cared for in the event you are no longer around, or are unable to earn a living because of disability.

Babies are beautiful, aren't they? They are the most innocent of creatures. And it takes longer for a human baby to reach maturity than for any other animal on earth. That means our roles as parents and providers are extended far beyond the other animals. Thank goodness we have the good sense to take steps to protect them.

Or do we? Ask yourself this question: If you or your spouse were to die tomorrow, would there be enough money available to raise your sweet innocent to maturity? Would there be enough for food, clothing, a roof over her head? Would he be able to take piano lessons, travel, get a university education? Or are you depending on the kindness of family and friends, and the hope that if the worst happened, your little angel would be taken care of?

If you don't have enough protection for your children, *now* is the time to do something about it. It would be bad enough having to deal with the loss of a mom or dad — or even worse, both parents. But no child should have to deal with the repercussions of not having any money. It's too much for a single spouse to have to deal with too. Imagine the stress of suddenly being forced back into the workforce to put food on the table, or of finding the additional income to hire a caregiver for the children whose stay-at-home parent has died.

Money doesn't solve all the world's problems. But having sufficient insurance to protect the family gives your loved ones the breathing room and financial resources to cope, adapt, and move forward. And it takes the jeopardy out of the future. Joseph Heller says it perfectly in *Catch-22*:

> Mrs. Daneeka had been widowed cruelly again, but this time her grief was mitigated somewhat by a notification from Washington that she was sole beneficiary of her husband's $10,000 GI insurance policy, which amount was obtainable by her on demand. The realization that she and the children were not faced immediately with starvation brought a brave smile to her face and marked the turning point in her distress.[24]

How much life insurance should you have? That's a good question that has a couple of answers. The most straightforward approach is to ensure you have sufficient insurance coverage to provide the level of income your family will need until your dependents are on their own.

Many people worry about how they'll work the premiums into their

---

24 Joseph Heller, *Catch-22* (Simon and Schuster, 1996), p. 353.

cash flow. Don't start there. If you look at the barriers first, you'll never see the end. Look instead at the opportunities. If you are young, you have an opportunity to establish an insurance policy at a premium rate that will cost less and less, as a proportion of your cash flow, as your income increases. If you're healthy, you'll find it easier to get coverage. The later you leave it, the greater the risk that you won't be covered, and the higher the cost of the insurance.

Now, more than ever, you must insure your ability to create an income stream. By the time you're 40, there's a 21% chance you'll die and a 48% probability that you'll be disabled for at least 90 days before you turn 65. Think of the impact of losing your income for even just five years. If you make $30,000 a year, that's $150,000. Clearly, the risk to you and your family is huge. Besides the mounting debt as you watch bills go unpaid month after month, there are also all the increased costs associated with being treated for your condition. With the appropriate disability coverage, not only will you be able to meet your financial commitments, you'll be protecting your assets.

TAX IMPLICATIONS

According to Manitoba's Agriculture Ministry, it can cost upwards of $150,000 to raise a kid today. So claim all the deductions and credits you can to help make ends meet each year.

Claim all your child-care costs. Child-care expenses include everything from a nanny to occasional baby-sitting. Regardless of your baby-sitter's age, as long as you get a receipt you can claim the expense. And child-care expenses can be claimed for children up to the age of 15. While you don't have to submit those receipts with your return, you must keep them in case they are requested by Revenue Canada for verification. Make sure that all your payments for the year will be made by December 31.

Want to income split with your kids? Do you have older kids to whom you're paying an allowance? Well, get them to give you a receipt each time they spend an evening looking after the younger children. They'll be building up RRSP contribution room, while you get to claim the allowance as a child-care expense. Children and RRSPs? What am I talking about?

Anyone with earned income in Canada can contribute to an RRSP, regardless of age. Whether your baby is a model or your 12-year-old is shovelling snow or baby-sitting, as long as your child files a tax return, and has qualifying earned income, she can begin to contribute to an RRSP. And when you look at the numbers, the story can be quite compelling. A single RRSP contribution of $300 at age 12, compounding at an average return of just 9%, will grow to over $28,800 by the time the child turns 65. Have your child make those $300 contributions every year until age 19, and the figure jumps to over $159,700. While overcontributions can't be made for children under 19, if your child adds the overcontribution amount of $2,000 at 19, the RRSP will grow to over $273,800 by age 65. Any way you cut it, an investment of $4,400 that grows to over a quarter of a million dollars is a good idea.

To be eligible for an RRSP contribution, your child must file a tax return to show earned income. He'll need a social insurance number to do that. And he'll need to keep all his financial information — receipts from baby-sitting or snow-shovelling, and tax slips from part-time jobs and summer employment — as proof of income. While there's little point in claiming the deduction since your child will likely owe little or no tax, the benefits of contributing to an RRSP are two-fold. First, any contribution can compound to produce what can seem a magical amount. Second, the RRSP tax deduction that most people make in the year of contribution can be carried forward indefinitely so that when your child does start working, he will have deductions he can use to offset the tax on his income.

Most young people who are just starting out at their first jobs have little extra income to make an RRSP contribution in their first few years of working. It can be a challenge just making ends meet. But a habit started at age 12 can be one that lasts a lifetime. And small amounts are all that are needed. If children don't start out enthusiastic about putting their hard-earned dollars away for the future, don't be surprised. It's difficult for children to see benefit in such long-term savings. You can help them get started with an RRSP by offering to buy the dress or pay for the ski trip if your child contributes the equivalent amount to her RRSP.

Part of your child's financial education will come when you discuss what types of investments to hold in the RRSP. Younger individuals have time on their side and time gives you the most flexibility over your investment choices.

Keep in mind that the RRSP must be set up in the minor's name. Some institutions won't even accept an RRSP for a child. But some will. They'll likely ask for a letter indicating who has the authorization to make investment decisions since minors aren't allowed to trade.

What about kids who want to cash in their plans? It's their money, so that's their prerogative. The best you can do is show them the long-term cost of making the withdrawal in terms of both the lost growth and the tax that will have to be paid. Remember, even if the deduction hasn't been claimed, the withdrawal is still considered income and, therefore, taxable.

So why don't more parents and children do this? From my experience as a writer trying to find experts to comment on it, the reason is simple. Few people have thought about it. Once you do the math, it's hard to deny the benefits. You don't have to be wealthy to make an RRSP work for you. Putting time on your side — along with the magic of compounding return — and a healthy discipline of long-term savings can do the trick.

If you have children in university, make sure they file their own returns. According to Scarlett Ungurean, "If your children do not need all their tuition fees to reduce their federal tax payable to zero, those fees may then be transferred to you. But this is only possible if your children file returns." If you have kids in private school, check with the school to see if part of the tuition is eligible for the tuition fee credit. It will be if there are courses that apply to the postsecondary school level. If your spouse or child has tuition fees of more than $5,000, income splitting may create enough income to allow him or her to use any non-transferable tuition and education credit.

Remember that money you receive through the Child Tax Benefit is considered your child's for tax purposes. By depositing that money into a bank account in your child's name, the income earned will be taxed in your child's hands.

REVIEWING YOUR ESTATE PLAN

At any point in your life after you've accumulated assets it's important to have a will. At no point is it more important than when you have children. If you don't have one yet, go and get one today. The peace of mind is well worth the money.

I remember the first trip I planned to take away from the children. My girlfriend Leslie asked me how I was feeling about going. I answered that the only thing I was worrying about was the flight (I'm not a frightened flyer, just a dumb mom) and what would happen to my children if both my husband and I were to drop from the sky. Leslie smiled. "Do you have a will?" she asked. "Yes," I replied. "Then nothing can happen," said Leslie with a huge grin. "You only die without a will. Once you get a will, you'll live forever!" I laughed myself silly and felt much better. The point: If you take the right steps to protect your family, you have much less to worry about.

EMPLOYING A CAREGIVER

I always knew I'd go back to work after my children were born. I know my personality type; if I'm not meeting people, learning new stuff, being stimulated I get lazy and cranky. So when it came time to find someone to take care of my children, my husband and I quickly agreed that in-home care was the way to go. We hired ourselves a nanny.

Little did I know back then that becoming an employer is a complicated business. If you thought labour took your breath away, try finding out what your responsibilities are as a new employer. Whether that person looks after your children 14 hours a week or 40, as long as you've established regular working hours for a body for whom you assign and supervise tasks performed, you're an employer.

Your first step will be to register with the Canada Customs and Revenue Agency to get a business number. You'll need this number for remitting any tax you deduct, and for remitting and matching Canada Pension Plan (CPP) and employment insurance (EI) premiums for your employee. (If you don't, you'll be on the hook for both portions of the CPP and EI premiums — your share and your nanny's share.)

You'll be required to pay 1.4 times the employee rate for EI, and you must match your employee's CPP contributions to the annual maximum ($1,329.90 for 2000). You have to send those deductions to CCRA monthly (or pay them at a bank), on the 15th of the month following the pay month, and you'll have to prepare a T4 to report the amounts you paid, withheld, and remitted. Keep a written record of your caregiver's employment, and with each paycheque provide a statement of earnings, which details the gross and net pay, deductions, and total number of hours worked during the pay period.

If your nanny lives in, you will also be responsible for a Workers' Compensation premium based on a percentage of the salary or a minimum rate. Each province sets its own rates. Links to provincial board websites can be found on the website of the Association of Workers' Compensation Boards of Canada at http://www.awcbc.ca/english/wcb_links.htm. Health tax is another issue related to employment, but here you've drawn the long straw. For while some Canadian provinces have chosen to supplement their income tax revenue with a medical plan tax on behalf of employees, you'll be exempt because of your very small payroll.

Find out the labour regulations for your province. In Ontario, for example, the minimum wage is $6.85 unless you're hiring a student who works 28 hours a week or less, in which case you must pay a minimum of $6.40 per hour. So all those shared nanny situations where you offer a few bucks to the next-door neighbour's caregiver to supplement her increased responsibility are technically offside.

After one year of service, your employee is entitled to two weeks' vacation with pay (at least 4% of your caregiver's total wages for the year). You get to choose when your nanny goes on vacation, but you must allow him or her to take vacation within 10 months after he or she has earned it. And if you terminate your employee, unused vacation pay must be paid within one week of termination.

While this all sounds like it may cost you more than you thought, there is a bright side. You can claim a portion of your child-care expenses on your tax return. (These deductions are also applicable for those who choose the daycare route.) For kids who are under seven at the end of the year, you can claim up to $7,000. For kids over seven but under 17, you can claim up to $4,000. Usually the lower-income spouse must make the claim, and total claims are limited to two-thirds of your earned income.

If you're a single parent and in school, you get a bigger break: you can deduct your child-care expenses, whether in-home or daycare, to a maximum of $175 for children under seven and $100 for children seven to 16 for each week you're in school full-time. If you're only going to school part-time the numbers are $175 and $100 per *month* respectively.

TEACHING KIDS ABOUT MONEY

I've written a whole book on this topic entitled *The Money Tree Myth: A Parents' Guide to Helping Kids Unravel the Mysteries of Money*. I wrote the book because I believe strongly that educating children about money — what it is, how it works, its value, and its place in our lives — is a vital part of raising healthy and responsible children. Without your guidance, how will your children learn to do it right? Where will they learn to do it at all?

There's no safer place to learn about money than at home. And there's no one better equipped to teach it than you. Never mind that you're not a financial expert. You can learn too. What's important is that you know your child. You know how she learns best. You understand what motivates her. And you know what won't work. *You* are her best teacher.

You taught him to walk, to talk, to use the toilet (though you may have thought yourself a little out in left field on that one). You taught him to read, to sing, and to dance. You helped him shape his view of himself. Now help him shape his view of money so he learns where it fits in his life, that it is a tool, that it is manageable.

Barb Godin works hard to help her kids see money as an "enabler." Like Barb, I believe that kids have to learn that the money itself shouldn't be the issue. It's what you do with that money, and for that money, that defines how good you are at managing this tool. Barb and her family roll coins together and when they have enough, they take a vacation — once every four or five years. "My kids know that a vacation isn't something that you're due," she says. "You have to work hard for it." And apparently the lessons are well learned.

Barb tells the sweetest story about her son's special gift to her for Mother's Day. "Matthew gave me a gift I'll never in my life forget. He knows that I like model classic cars." She reached behind her and took from her bookshelf a small blue car. "I was looking at this in a store one day, and Matthew said, 'Mommy, aren't you going to buy it?' and I said, 'No, Mommy doesn't have the money right now, it's not something I really need. It's pretty and I like to look at it.' We left it at that. Well, for Mother's Day, he went through his room and said to his father, 'I really want to get Mom that car, I really do. I've got some toys I don't use a lot. Would it be okay if I sold them?' He took toys I knew he liked to school, sold them, and used the money to buy me this car. That is the sweetest, nicest thing. When he gave it to me he was bursting with pride. I was bursting with pride."

Learning about money prepares children for the future. By teaching your children about what money is, how it works, and how it enables you to do what you really want, you're giving your kids one of the most useful lessons of all. And it's a lesson that will serve them for a lifetime. Learning about money doesn't steal the magic from childhood. It gives children an opportunity to make their own magic.

16

As You Approach Retirement

I like work; it fascinates me. I can sit and look at it for hours. I love to keep it by me: the idea of getting rid of it nearly breaks my heart.

JEROME K. JEROME

Retirement is just around the corner and you can hardly believe it. With five years or less left working full-time, you've got to start thinking about a lot of the issues you thought you'd have plenty of time to contemplate. Where will you live? What will you do with your time? How will you structure your finances so you don't have to spend the next 30 years worrying about money?

Thirty years? That's right. One little-known reality of retirement is that the majority of Canadians retire before 65 — the age we traditionally associate with retirement. In fact, according to the General Social Survey (GSS) conducted by Statistics Canada in 1994, 67% of people who retired did so prior to age 65, with as many as 14% retiring prior to age 55. Add to that the fact that life expectancies are increasing. A woman aged 50 today can expect to live to about age 82, while her male counterpart can expect to live another 26.5 years.[25] When you combine earlier retirements and longer life spans, the result for most people is more time

25 Roger Sauvé, *Canadian People Patterns* (Western Producer Prairie Books), 1990.

to fill, more inflationary pressure on fixed incomes, and more concern about how to make the money last at least as long as they do.

But retirement shouldn't be a time of stress and worry. Put your mind at rest by planning for the financial and sociological impacts of retirement. What will you do with your time? How will you maintain your friendships? Where will you live? Look at the big picture as well as the individual pieces of the puzzle. By developing new skills as a rehearsal for retirement, you can set the stage for a more orderly transition. And, if you happen to be forced into retirement before you're ready, you'll be better able to deal effectively with your change in circumstances.

While many people look forward to escaping the rat race well before age 65, retiring early requires some careful planning. You'll be retired for a longer period of time, so your savings will have to last longer. But leaving the workforce early will also mean that you'll have less time to accumulate your asset base. By looking ahead, you can adapt your plan while there's still time to accumulate and organize assets, and plan the transition to the next phase in your life.

In order to retire when you want and live the way you want, take a good look at what retirement will cost. One rule of thumb, according to retirement specialist Ann Eynon, is to estimate that you will need approximately 70% of your income just prior to retirement. "But this is just a starting point," she warns. "You actually have to live in retirement for a couple of years to see what your needs and desires are before you can come up with a fixed amount." She says money is as much an emotional issue as it is a financial issue. "When you retire, some of your emotional needs — that you may have set aside for many years — come to the forefront."

Another way to figure your expenses is to do a budget for what you're spending now, and then project what it will cost when you retire. Some costs will go down. You'll probably spend less on clothing and transportation. And if you've planned carefully, you'll have made all your major purchases (such as a new car, new appliances, etc.) and you may also have eliminated most, if not all, of your debt. But some of your expenses will increase. Premiums on life and health insurance, costs for medical and dental care, and travel and entertainment costs may rise. Don't worry about being too precise in your projections. The point of the exercise is to gain some insight into what your retirement lifestyle will cost, compared with your current costs.

Ann Eynon is an associate of The Rogers Group in Vancouver and has been working in financial services for over 20 years. She offers clients comprehensive and pragmatic advice on retirement planning, investing, and estate planning. She's an active member of both the Canadian Association of Insurance and Financial Advisors and the Canadian Association of Financial Planners, and also belongs to the Women's Insurance Network. She's been a single mom for 20 years, raising two children to share her love of Hawaiian holidays.

Next you need to add up how much income you'll receive. Your retirement income will come from a combination of sources, including government pensions, employer pension, RRSP savings, and your unregistered assets.

Finally, determine if there is a gap between income and expenses. If you have a positive gap (i.e., your expenses are less than your income), you're in great shape and can let your RRSPs continue to grow tax-sheltered. If there is a shortfall, you'll have to look to your unregistered assets and retirement savings to supplement your income. If you're unsure of all your holdings, do a net-worth statement. It will help you see how healthy you are financially and it will help when the time comes to decide where income will be drawn from, and how investments must be structured to maximize your cash flow, minimize your taxes, and protect your estate.

Whether or not you think you have enough will partially depend on your money personality. Ann says she sees three distinct types of retirees: those who are fearful of not having enough and spend little or nothing; those who want to maintain their capital and strive to live on the return their investments generate; and those who plan to draw on their capital to enjoy their retirement. How much you need will depend on how willing you are to spend your money.

YOUR SPENDING PLAN

Developing a spending plan for retirement begins before you retire. As with most things in life, a little planning goes a long way toward making the transition easier to manage. Not thinking about it will only leave you grappling to pull the threads together on the final day. Planning will let you determine when exactly that day should be.

You have to be prepared to make the important decisions that come with such a major life change. That means knowing where you are right now, and where you need to be in the coming months. Review your current spending plan to ensure your expenses are nicely in hand, and that you are on target with your savings goals. If you're not, you'll need to do some belt-tightening while you accumulate the extra savings you need. Better now than later. One of the best ways to see how you'll likely do is by preparing an estimated spending plan for your retirement years.

Review your current expenses and look for ways to eliminate little costs here and there. Brown bagging it, eating out two times a week instead of three, and taking the bus instead of parking the car are all ways of taking money out of your cash flow so you can put it into your retirement nest egg. You might also decide to delay your retirement. The later you retire, the more time you have to save, the higher your company and government pensions will be, and the more time your money has to grow before you have to start pulling on it. And if you also plan to work during retirement, you'll stretch your retirement savings even further. Do you have an interest or hobby you could turn into a moneymaker? Would you consider working part-time in a completely new field? Be creative. Don't underestimate the value of your skills. If you're in a position to take an extra job, you can boost your savings by increasing the money currently coming in.

Use your equity. Whether you decide to sell and rent, or use a reverse mortgage (more on that in the next chapter), your home equity is a good source of additional retirement income.

Remember that your retirement savings are made up of both your principal and the income earned on your savings. Does this sound obvious? Many people resist drawing on their principal during retirement for fear that they will outlive their money. If necessary, take your figures to a financial adviser who can show you exactly how long your principal will last. And for those of you who deny yourself even the smallest of pleasures because you are hell-bent on leaving an estate for your children, who was *your* benefactor?

When it comes to figuring out what your income will be in retirement, the key is to gather lots of information. While we often take for granted our entitlement to government pensions, neither CPP (Canada Pension Plan) nor OAS (Old Age Security) benefits are automatic. You have to apply for them. You'd be wise to send in your application about six months before you wish to receive income (age 65 for OAS and as early as age 60 for CPP), so you're sure to begin receiving your benefits when you need them. Get CPP to determine what your benefits would be if you were to decide to take them early or late. If your CPP benefits are lower than your spouse's, consider splitting your benefits so you will receive more income. This may help to eliminate or reduce the OAS clawback for your spouse. And it may also put each of you in a lower tax bracket so you'll lower your total family bill.

Next, look to your corporate pension plan, if you have one. Find out exactly how it works. If your spouse has a plan, make sure you understand the benefits of that plan too, especially the death benefits. Often pension plans pay out more when a woman signs away her survivor benefits. You may think that makes sense in the early years. But how will you cope if your husband dies before you do — which statistics show he very well might — and your income is drastically reduced? Don't just sign away your rights. Do the math. Understand the implications. Stay in control.

Check to see if your company plan or that of your spouse is integrated. This is important because an integrated plan means the corporate pension is reduced when government pension benefits kick in. This can affect your decision to take CPP early or late. And it can throw a real spanner in your budgetary works if you have not made allowance for it. If the plan promises to provide $1,200 monthly and is integrated with CPP and your monthly benefit from CPP is $650, you'll end up receiving one cheque for $650 from the government and another from the pension plan for $550, for a total of $1,200. For integrated plans, when you get pension income estimates from your employer, make sure these are the "integrated" amounts, so that you don't double-count your CPP benefits. If your integrated-plan benefits are reduced once you start receiving OAS, make sure that if your OAS is clawed back you will not lose out twice. Have a chat with the plan administrator to check the likelihood of this and then discuss how to avoid the problem with your employer. Find out if your pension is indexed to provide protection against inflation. While most pension plans have eliminated this feature, there are still some people who will benefit from indexing. Also check to see if your existing benefit programs continue into retirement. Will your health and life insurance remain intact? Do your benefits include a dental plan? Extended health care? Know where you stand, then make provision for these items yourself if you are not covered when you retire.

Ann also suggests that you ask your corporate pension plan administrator for quotes at a variety of ages. "Do your homework," she says. "Find out year by year what your pension will be approximately so you can decide when it's the right time to retire."

The role your RRSP savings play will be dependent on your other sources of income during retirement. If you'll be depending on your RRSP throughout your retirement, you'll want a steady stream of monthly income that will last at least as long as you do (and perhaps as long as your spouse as well). But you'll also need flexibility so that as your needs change, you can adjust the amount you take or how often you receive your income. Since this will be your primary source of income, inflation protection will be important. Choose investments that will help you preserve your capital (to protect your future income) while maximizing your yield (to cover inflation).

For some people, RRSP assets will be supplemental to the income they'll receive from other sources such as a company pension plan or rental property. If you are one of these fortunates, wait until you're 69 to convert your RRSP so you aren't forced to take income before you need it. The next chapter provides more detail on your options when it comes time to make decisions on RRIFs, annuities, and other strategies.

KEEPING A ROOF OVER YOUR HEAD

It's time to set the date for your mortgage-burning party. If you eliminate this single largest debt from your cash flow, you'll find yourself with a substantial increase in disposable income. But just getting rid of the debt isn't the only thing to look at. Since your income will likely be reduced during retirement, you'll need to do any repairs that may be required while you still have a strong income. Look at your house objectively. Does it need painting? A new roof? How's the furnace?

Look at the expenses associated with running your home so you can get a clear picture of your fixed expenses during retirement. What does it cost to maintain your home? What are your costs for taxes, heating, electricity? Think about the amount of space you'll be using when you retire. If your home is larger than you will need, consider converting the basement to a separate apartment to provide some additional income during retirement — or to provide a home for wayward children as they return to the once-empty nest.

If you plan to stay in the home long term, make sure that you take care of anything that will become difficult to manage as you age. Large lawns are tough to cut. Slippery floors, long driveways that have to be shovelled in the winter, and too many stairs can become real encumbrances, draining the pleasure from staying in your home.

Also think about how much of your time will be spent at home, in the neighbourhood, or out of town. If you plan to spend lots of time at the cottage, do you really want to keep two houses going? If all your friends are in Florida in the winter, how will you feel? How many of your interests and activities take place close to your home? How close do you live to other family members?

REVIEWING YOUR GOALS

For now, you'll mainly be focused on preparing for that all-important and fast-approaching retirement date. You'll want to have most, if not all, of your debt paid off. You'll want to make sure you're maximizing your RRSP contributions and growth so you can accumulate as much as possible before you stop working. But those shouldn't be your only goals. After all, you'll likely live as long in retirement as you spent working.

One of the biggest mistakes people make is thinking that at retirement everything becomes fixed in time and space. There's a real sense that the accumulation of assets will end (what about investment income?) and that inflation will cease (what about the inflation that will erode your income throughout the 20 or 30 years that you are retired?). It's a mistake to see your retirement date as the end. It isn't. It's the beginning of a whole new stage of life. And it brings its ups and downs just as in every other stage of your life.

Since retirement is a new beginning, think about how you will restyle your life. In my *Retirement Answer Book*, I offer suggestions on how people can mentally prepare for the shift from working to retirement. Many people skip this important step. Once you've spent some time on the psychological stuff, and you've made plans for what you'll do during retirement, you have to make sure you'll have enough money to fund your excursion into a new lifestyle. And remember, since that new lifestyle will probably last almost as long as the old one did, you had better be prepared for some long-term financial planning.

CASH-MANAGEMENT STRATEGIES

Holding bank accounts jointly is one of the first things you should consider as you move closer to retirement. It's one way to simplify your life and your estate plan. Another way to simplify is to consolidate all those savings and chequing accounts into a single account. "Bring it under one or two roofs," says Ann Eynon, "so you don't have to worry about what your money is doing." Ann says that for people who have moved into retirement, "a common mantra is 'I cannot be bothered with watching the money anymore. I am retired. I have other interests. I need this to be as simple as possible.' Other people see themselves spending more time charting their money's growth, monitoring their portfolios on their computers. But eventually, even these people find the whole thing overwhelming and move to simplify."

One of your primary objectives in planning for retirement should be to do so debt-free. Ongoing credit-card or loan payments can create a real strain on a fixed income. And if interest rates should rise, you could find more and more of your food money going to interest costs. If you have outstanding debt that is not tax-deductible, make sure you're working to pay off that debt as quickly as possible. Your investment strategy should balance your need to reduce your debt with your need to grow your assets. If you have a low-return investment (say, a GIC earning 5%) and a high-cost credit balance (your Sears card has a balance and you're paying exorbitant interest), you'll be way better off cashing in your pre-tax GIC to pay off your post-tax Sears card. Another good strategy is to use your tax refund from an RRSP contribution to pay off a part of your debt.

KEEPING A HEALTHY CREDIT IDENTITY

You're likely to be well past your major borrowing needs at this point in your life. Now you're looking to get rid of all your debt. But the fact remains that a healthy credit history and the ability to borrow money when you need it are part of a sound financial plan. You just never know when you might need a bridge for your cash flow. If the car suddenly needs major repairs and your GIC doesn't mature for six months, being able to access credit could make the difference. Since one of the only sure things in life is change — and the most significant changes are seldom predictable — having the flexibility to adapt will give you a greater sense of control.

Keeping a healthy credit history as you approach retirement means continuing to borrow money and pay it off to maintain your credit history. Use your credits cards to make purchases, and pay them off every month on time. With each payment, you'll keep your credit history current. If you have a line of credit, draw on it from time to time, as the need arises, and pay it off quickly. That'll keep it in good standing.

YOUR PAY-YOURSELF-FIRST INVESTMENT PLAN

Your registered assets will likely be one of the mainstays of your investment portfolio, so it's very important that you stay on top of them. Monitor the overall rate of return you're getting, and take a little time each year to evaluate your plan to ensure it's achieving your objectives. A small increase in annual return can mean a significant increase in your portfolio's growth over the long term. Two percent may not sound like much, but it is. Over time, even a small difference in your rate of return can have a tremendous impact on how long your retirement nest egg lasts. The following chart shows the difference in growth for $10,000 invested at various rates of return. As you can see, the differences are significant.

	RATE OF RETURN			
YEARS	2%	4%	7%	11%
5	$11,040	$12,161	$14,025	$16,851
10	12,189	14,802	19,672	28,394
15	13,459	18,009	27,590	47,846
20	14,859	21,911	38,679	80,623
25	16,406	26,658	54,274	135,855
30	18,114	32,434	76,123	228,923

Assuming you choose a portfolio of investments that gives you only a 2% higher rate of return, over 30 years your investments would have earned an extra 78%.

If you think these differences are only applicable when you are building your assets, here's more good news. Once you retire and begin to make withdrawals, even a small difference in return can extend the life of your retirement portfolio. A portfolio of $100,000 invested at 7% with an annual payout of $12,000 would last approximately 14 years, for a total payout of approximately $167,000. By increasing your return just 2%, the same portfolio would last just over 17 years, for a total payout of approximately $205,000. With a return of 11%, the $100,000 portfolio would last almost 25 years, for a total payout of approximately $298,000.

There's no better way to get a big-picture perspective of your financial position than by completing a net-worth statement. Start by listing your assets. Be realistic about their value. Assets will include your cash on hand, in accounts, and on deposit. Check the value of investments such as stocks, bonds, and mutual funds in the financial section of the newspaper or with a broker. The cash-surrender value of your insurance should be stated in your policy. To estimate cars, boats, and trailers, refer to comparables in the classifieds. And remember, while you paid the retail price for many of your possessions, you'll likely only receive the wholesale value if you decide to sell them. Now add up everything you owe. This will include your mortgage, outstanding balances on your line of credit and credit cards, and any loans you may have. It'll also include yet-to-be-paid bills (referred to as your "accounts payable"), as well as taxes owing. Subtract your total liabilities from your total assets and you have your net worth.

Once you've completed your net-worth statement, take some time to look over your assets. Are you satisfied with their quality? Are they earning the return you expected? Are you satisfied with your total asset base? Perhaps you have a large amount of cash in a savings account. By moving that money to a term deposit or money-market fund you'll very likely earn a higher rate of return. Next, have a look at your liabilities. Are you paying the lowest possible interest? Can you renegotiate? How quickly can you eliminate these debts? Perhaps you have an underperforming investment that you could sell to eliminate all or part of your debt. Even a small payment toward your mortgage principal will move you closer to freedom from a mortgage during retirement.

Your Emergency Fund

Don't forget your emergency fund. An unexpected big bill can put a serious crimp in your spending plan. The size of your emergency fund will depend on your financial commitments and the amount of income you have regularly flowing in. If it looks like things may be tight during retirement, establish a fairly significant emergency fund before you retire. If you know for certain that you will have more income than you'll need, your emergency fund can be smaller. Also consider the source of your income. A pension that is indexed is more reliable than income from interest-bearing investments, since a decline in interest rates could mean significantly less income.

Reviewing Your Insurance

At the very least, have enough insurance to cover your funeral expenses. However, you may also need to have enough insurance to protect a dependent or two. With family structures changing, it's no longer fair to assume that all your dependents will be self-sufficient before you take leave of this world.

I tease my lovely husband quite often about the fact that he'll have to mature his RRSP assets before his youngest son reaches 21. Just because Ken decides to retire at 60, 65, or 70 doesn't mean that Malcolm's needs for support will have disappeared. And with university costs set to explode, it's unlikely he'll be able to put himself through under his own steam. We'll have to help.

Another important consideration that will have an impact on the amount of insurance you'll need is how your retirement income cash flow will change after the death of one partner. Let's say your spouse has a great pension and after he dies, you'll receive 60% of the pension income. That's the typical survivor's benefit. Have you thought about whether or not this will be enough? I know that you'll have fewer expenses with only one person to feed, clothe, and the like. But inflation will have done its dirty work in terms of reducing the purchasing power of your money. The question to ask yourself then is, "If my spouse dies 20 years after we retire, will there be sufficient cash flow from all sources to allow me to live comfortably?" If the answer is no, speak to an insurance agent about getting extra life coverage. At this point, you'll probably only want to look at term insurance. And prepare yourself for some pretty stiff premiums.

The alternative, of course, would be to put yourself on a savings plan — perhaps investing the amount you would have spent in premiums. Over the long term, you might end up ahead. You'll have to feel fairly secure in terms of how long you and your spouse will live. An unexpected death would cramp the plan.

TAX IMPLICATIONS

Your income-splitting strategies should be well established at this point. But this is a good time to check how much retirement income you and your spouse will be receiving to make sure you're on the mark. If you find that one of you has significantly more projected pension income than the other, you can make all future contributions to a spousal RRSP to even the playing field. Registered assets will be taxed as they are withdrawn from an RRSP or RRIF. If you also plan to use unregistered assets, or to liquidate investments for cash flow, consider how these will be taxed. Remember, the trick is for each of you to pay the same amount of tax so that, as a couple, you pay the lowest amount of tax possible. You also need a strategy to maximize your government benefits.

When the feds announced in 1989 that people with annual incomes over $50,000 must repay part or all of their Old Age Security (OAS), there was an uproar. Despite the hullabaloo, no one did anything about it, so now if your income exceeds the threshold (which was $53,215 in 1998 because it was partially indexed for inflation) you'll be assessed a tax on any income above that threshold, at a rate of 15%, up to the total of all the OAS you've received. In plain English: For every $100 in income you receive above the threshold amount, you have to pay back $15 of your OAS benefits.

One way to reduce the impact of the clawback is to split your income as evenly as possible between you and your spouse. As a couple, you could have a joint income of over $100,000 and not be affected by the clawback. Another is to delay receiving your CPP/QPP benefits until you absolutely need them to meet your expenses.

If you are subject to the OAS clawback, proactively manage your income to claim at least some benefits. A particularly high income in one year and a lower income the next may allow you to keep your OAS benefits at least every other year. How so, you say? Try this. If you plan to draw income from your registered investments, withdraw the amount you need from your RRIFs, above and beyond any minimum withdrawal amounts required by law (see the next chapter for details), for two years at once. You will be taxed on the full amount in the present year. Then the next year, you won't need to withdraw any income beyond the minimum amount. Ta da! Your income won't surpass the clawback threshold, so you'll keep your OAS for that year. By making a larger-than-normal withdrawal in one year and a smaller withdrawal the next, you'll be able to take advantage of OAS every other year.

One of the things many people are concerned about as they approach retirement is how their estate will be taxed. My mother-in-law is a perfect example. She wants to make sure that she passes as much of her remaining assets on to her kids as she can and so, inevitably, the following question came up: "Does it make more sense to use my registered assets first, leaving my unregistered assets to my children, or should I do it the other way?" Good question. And not an easy one to answer. Advisers often say you should leave your registered assets within the plan as long as possible so they can continue to compound on a tax-deferred basis. However, as soon as you die, providing you do not have a spouse to whom to pass those assets, the full amount of the registered assets will be included in your income for the year of your death and you'll likely pay a whopping amount of tax. The other option is to draw down on your registered assets first so you're paying a lower rate of tax over a longer term, while leaving your unregistered (previously taxed) assets intact for passing on.

So what should you do? As with most things about money, it all depends. It depends on your specific circumstances: how much you have, how long you think you'll live, what the mix is between registered and unregistered assets. If the amount you draw from your registered assets moves you into the highest marginal tax rate so you'll be paying the maximum tax anyway, it makes sense to leave the registered assets intact and have your estate pay the tax at the end when you no longer need the money. If you want to mitigate the loss to your beneficiaries, you can always use a portion of the money you pull each year from the registered pool to purchase a life insurance policy to help offset the loss to the tax man. For the average Canadian, however, life insurance at age 60 or 70 is very, very expensive and the cost often outweighs the benefit. Ann Eynon suggests that you "look at your RRSPs and RRIFs as your money, and use it."

ESTATE PLANNING

It's time to review and, perhaps, update your will and get all the legal and financial information in order. If you haven't already done so, put your powers of attorney in place. If you're still hesitating about making a will, might I suggest a small shift in perspective. While estate planning is often seen as a discussion about death, it really isn't. It is a way to make the lives of the people you leave behind less stressful. It's also the only way to ensure your assets are distributed as you would want them to be.

Don't fall into the trap of thinking that your estate isn't big enough to warrant the time and money of bothering with an estate plan. And don't think that your lawyer, accountant, or financial planner will be able to step in and deal with the issues. Once you leave this beautiful earth, everything financial stops until your estate is probated. If you die without a will, you just prolong the agony.

Immediately upon your death, the government will deem that your capital property has been disposed of (watch for the term "deemed disposition" in this context.) Any increase in value on a stock, bond, your cottage, or any other asset that can increase in value will be subject to tax at the current capital-gains rate. There are some exceptions. You can transfer capital property to a spouse without paying tax. This defers the tax until your spouse dies. If you have U.S. assets such as stocks, bonds, a business interest, or a condo in Florida, you might also have to pay estate tax on these assets. The problem that arises from deemed disposition is that while tax may be payable, it may not be the best time to sell the asset because to do so would be to get less than fair value. Or perhaps you don't want to sell the asset at all. It may break your heart to think about your art collection, painstakingly acquired over the years, being sold off to pay the taxes on your family cottage. Whatever your feelings, your estate will have to deal with the legalities of your move from this world to the next.

If you don't have a will, you've effectively given up control over your hard-earned money to the government. You wouldn't do that in life, so why would you do it in death? I know you won't be here, but your spouse, your children, and your grandchildren will. Don't put them through that discomfort and aggravation. If you don't have a will, put down the book, go to the telephone, and call your lawyer. If you don't know whom to call, ask the Law Society for a recommendation. If that doesn't sit well with you, e-mail me at getgvo@interlog.com or write me care of my publisher and I'll try to help. It doesn't matter what it takes. *You need a will.* Get moving!

17

When You Retire

Money can't buy happiness, 'tis true, but it certainly quiets the nerves.

IRISH PROVERB

An aged man is but a paltry thing.
A tattered coat upon a stick, unless
Soul clap its hands and sing, and louder sing
For every tatter in its mortal dress.

W. B. YEATS

Oh, joyous retirement! They've presented you with the gold watch, feted you with wine and cheese, and packed you off home. Now what? It's a question lots of people have as they watch the hands on their newly acquired timepiece slowly count off the seconds, minutes, and hours.

Hello! Now you get to do all the things you've always dreamed of but never had time to do. If you've planned for this first day of the rest of your life, that's great — your date book is jammed, and you have the money you need to pay for all your activities. If you haven't, it's time to get moving.

YOUR SPENDING PLAN

Your retirement income will come from a variety of sources: government pensions, employer-sponsored pensions, personal retirement savings, unregistered investments, and the sale of assets. You and your spouse should keep your figures separate so that you'll be ready when you get into a discussion of how much either one of you will have individually. You'll also need separate figures to calculate your income tax. Check with CCRA to see what the most current income-tax brackets are for your province.

To retire when you want, and to live the way you want during retirement, you have to know just what it will cost to live. Costs will go up or down depending on what stage of retirement you're in. If you are still working part-time or if you are travelling extensively, your expenses will be higher than they will be when you choose to sit on the porch watching the sunset.

You'll also have to make a decision about what to do with your RRSP money. You must mature your RRSP assets by the end of the year in which you turn 69. You can do so earlier if you find you need additional retirement income.

If you think your RRSP savings will be your primary source of retirement income, ensure the retirement income option you choose provides a steady stream of monthly income that will last at least as long as you do (and perhaps as long as your spouse as well). Registered Retirement Income Funds (RRIFs) are usually my first recommendation because they provide the flexibility to design an income stream that meets your specific needs — in terms of both amounts and frequency — as well as the ability to increase or decrease your income as your needs change. More about RRIFs shortly.

If you benefit from a nice company pension plan or you'll be using your unregistered assets to provide an income stream, delay converting your RRSP to keep the tax-deferred growth going for as long as possible. Converting before absolutely necessary means you'll be forced to take income when you don't need it. If you find that you do need some of your retirement savings to make ends meet, you can always make a withdrawal from your RRSP. If you have no other source of pension income (which you need to claim the $1,000 pension-income tax credit), then roll only as much as you will need each year to a RRIF (it'll be the $1,000 plus the applicable withholding taxes if the $1,000 is above your minimum annual payout amount) and take the full year's amount as a lump-sum withdrawal.

With sufficient income from your company and government pension plans to meet your basic needs, allocate your RRSP money to special needs: to travel, to supplement your family's income when pension benefits are reduced due to death of the primary pensioner, or to offset the impact of inflation on your purchasing power. If you don't need to draw on your RRSP savings at all, focus on minimizing the income you need to withdraw and, by extension, the tax you must pay. As we'll see below, you can mitigate your tax liabilities by using your younger spouse's age to determine how much you are required to withdraw or by taking the income annually at the end of the year.

ANNUITIES AND RRIFS

Okay, so now it's time to mature your RRSP. You could simply withdraw the money in cash. Careful, though. What may seem like the easiest option can have negative tax ramifications. When you take cash from your RRSP, that money is included in your income. This can push you into a higher tax bracket and result in your having to pay considerably more tax. The best way to minimize the tax implications is to convert your retirement savings to a regular stream of income using either an annuity or a RRIF.

When you buy an annuity, you give an insurance company, bank, or trust company your money in exchange for a promise of a specific amount of income each month. There are two basic types of life annuities: a straight life annuity provides a regular income payout over your entire life; a joint-and-last-survivor annuity provides income over your life and/or that of your spouse. The amount you receive depends on several factors, including how much money you have, your life expectancy, your sex, and the interest rate in effect when you buy the annuity. Low interest rates mean low monthly incomes, which is one reason why annuities are less popular when interest rates are low. Assuming you buy a $100,000 joint-and-last-survivor annuity with a 60% residual for your spouse and no other guarantees, a 65-year-old man would receive $8,787.68 a year for life. A woman purchasing the exact same annuity would receive $8,500 a year.

There's a potential downside to an annuity: you'll be living on a fixed income, since the monthly payments remain the same. What seems a princely sum at the outset may feel like a pauper's allowance in 20 years. An annual income of $8,500 would have a purchasing power of only $4,700 in 20 years. Remember, too, that surviving spouses will receive less income. The death of the first spouse usually means a 40% drop-off, so the survivor receives only 60% of the original income amount. While you may find $8,787 a year to work for you as a couple, the question you have to ask yourself is, "How comfortable would my spouse be on only $5,272?"

The retirement income alternative that has become most popular with Canadians is conversion of RRSP savings into a RRIF, to create a flow of income during retirement. Your money remains tax-sheltered as long as it remains in the plan, and you pay tax only on the money you take out each year. Basically, a RRIF is a continuation of your RRSP so you can hold the same investments. You can open a RRIF at any age and roll over as much or as little of your RRSP dollars as you wish. You can choose from a variety of investment types so you can use an investment strategy that will help you preserve your capital (to protect your future income) while maximizing your yield (to cover inflation).

A legislated minimum annual payout (MAP) must be paid from the RRIF each year, with one exception: it is not necessary to take a minimum amount in the year the RRIF is opened. In the year in which the plan is set up, the MAP is considered to be zero.

The MAP is calculated using one of two rules: the minimum-amount formula and the minimum-amount schedule of percentages. The formula calculation applies when you open a RRIF before you reach 71, and stays in effect until you turn 79. The formula is: the value of the RRIF at the beginning of the year, divided by 90 less the age of the planholder at the beginning of the year. You can also use your spouse's age for this calculation, provided you make that decision before the first payment is made. So, if on January 1 your RRIF was worth $165,000 and you were 64, your calculation would look like this: $165,000 \div (90 - 64) = $6,346.15$.

The schedule-of-percentages calculation applies in all other circumstances. The difference is that you need to consult a table of values for the calculation (see the next page). To determine your minimum amount using this schedule of percentages, choose the percentage that corresponds with your age at the beginning of the year. Multiply that percentage by the value

Schedule of Percentages	
Existing Age	Percentage of RRIF
71	7.38
72	7.48
73	7.59
74	7.71
75	7.85
76	7.99
77	8.15
78	8.33
79	8.53
80	8.75
81	8.99
82	9.27
83	9.58
84	9.93
85	10.33
86	10.79
87	11.33
88	11.96
89	12.71
90	13.62
91	14.73
92	16.12
93	17.92
94+	20.00

of your RRIF at the beginning of the year. So, if on January 1 your RRIF was worth $45,000 and you were 81, your calculation would look like this: $45,000 x 8.99% = $4,045.50.

Be sure to structure the assets in your portfolio so that you will have enough cash available each year for the withdrawal.

The main advantage to a RRIF is flexibility. As Ann Eynon puts it, "With a RRIF, you have not made a lifelong decision. You've made a decision that can be changed at almost any time, depending on the underlying investments you're holding." You can change your asset mix at any time and, if desired, you can take out more than the minimum amount. And, as you get older, if you decide an annuity suits you more because you no longer want to be concerned with the management of your investments, you can buy one using your RRIF assets. Alternatively, if you want to lock in interest rates because they have risen dramatically, buying strip bonds is another option that guarantees the rate for the term you choose, while giving you the flexibility to sell the investment should you need the cash.

So, a RRIF gives you the flexibility to receive more income in years when you need it and less in years when you don't. It gives you the flexibility to change your mind and change your investment strategy. And if you decide to take only the MAP each year, your RRIF is guaranteed to last a lifetime (the size of the fund may get very small as years go on, but it will never be completely depleted). Ultimately, it gives you more control over your money.

Besides your RRSP investments, you may also have a portfolio of investments that are unregistered. Perhaps you have been buying CSBs through a payroll deduction plan. Maybe you've been investing in mutual funds. Or perhaps you have GICs, or a rental property or two, which can provide a regular income. Having established an investment portfolio to supplement your retirement income needs, you may now be looking for ways to manage the income from those investments to supplement your cash flow in retirement.

Consider a GIC that pays monthly interest. Each month, you'll receive a steady flow of interest income that you can use to supplement your other retirement income. And since the interest rate is guaranteed for the term of the GIC, you'll know exactly how much you're going to get. "Taking monthly interest from your GIC," says Ann, "gives more of a sense of steady cash flow so you can plan your expenses and life." You'll lose about 0.25% (or 25 basis points, if you're talking bankese) by choosing a monthly payout, but your financial life will be more predictable.

In setting up your GICs, stagger your maturities. Instead of buying a single five-year GIC, split your money between a one-, two-, three-, four-, and five-year investment. Referred to as "laddering," this will help to protect against fluctuations in interest rates at renewal time. Also consider investing a portion of your nest egg in a redeemable GIC. This will provide you with the flexibility to get extra cash, should you need it. While the interest rate on the redeemable GIC is a little lower, it's often worth it to have access to cash — just in case.

If most of your investments have been in mutual funds and you need some way of taking a steady income to supplement your other retirement income, ask about a systematic withdrawal plan. Each month you can redeem a specific dollar amount in mutual-fund units, with the cash being deposited directly to your account. This strategy also allows you to use a dollar-cost averaging strategy, but instead of buying regularly, you'll be selling regularly. This will even out the ups and downs in the market so you'll end up with an average selling price. "This often gives tax-preferred income," says Ann, "because the withdrawals are a combination of dividend and capital gain, both of which receive special tax treatment."

Anyone over 60 should also take full advantage of the special rates offered by most banks. For GIC investors, it usually means an extra 0.25% in interest on GICs. And it can mean lower account fees. Once you've retired, you know how important it is to take care of those pennies. Start by figuring out what you want, and then go shopping for the products and services that will help you meet your needs. That's the way to make your investments pay for retirement.

Keeping a Roof Over Your Head

Where do you plan to live? In the same house or apartment, or will you sell and move to a smaller home? For most people, the bulk of their financial assets is tied up in their homes. Folks figure that when they retire, they'll sell, buy a smaller place, and have lots of money left over. But do you really want to move away from your family, your neighbours, and everything that's familiar?

For some people the decision to move is easy. Perhaps they're attracted by warmer climes. For some the lure of a small town or being part of a retirement community is very attractive. Or maybe the house is just too big or inappropriate for their needs. How much more income would you have if you sold your house, eliminated your maintenance/tax costs, and rented? Here's a calculation that may help.

Approximate value of home	$ _____
Less sales-related costs	$ _____
Balance to invest	$ _____
Return expected at _____%	$ _____
Tax payable on return	$ _____
Net return	$ _____
Net return	$ _____
Plus savings on maintenance•	$ _____
Less estimated cost of rental••	$ _____
Balance	$ _____

• When you sell your home, you'll likely eliminate many of your expenses, such as property tax, snow removal, house maintenance, heating, and hydro. Remember, though, that you may still have to pay utility costs if you rent.

•• Make sure you choose a comparable home, one you'll be happy to live in. Check the newspaper for the prices of rentals in areas where you'd feel comfortable living. Investigate subsidized-housing alternatives. Don't underestimate your space requirements. Often people who move from houses to apartments feel "squeezed."

You also have the option of living in your home while using the equity to finance your retirement. This is done with a reverse mortgage, which draws on the equity in your home to generate a monthly income. No interest or principal is due until the home is sold, the reverse mortgage comes due, or the homeowner dies. At this point, if the appreciated value of the property is greater than the amount of the accrued reverse mortgage, the excess goes to the estate. If the value of the property is less than the amount owed, the financial institution that gave you the mortgage has to eat the difference. This is one reason financial institutions don't allow you to use the full value of your home for a reverse mortgage. They limit the amount they will "reverse mortgage" to protect themselves from a decline in the value of your property.

There are two basic types of reverse mortgages: a straight reverse mortgage and a reverse annuity mortgage. A straight reverse mortgage provides a monthly amount for a specified term while building a mortgage against your home. When the agreed-upon term has expired (that is, the mortgage comes due), you must repay the mortgage, usually through the sale of the home. If the property has increased in value, you may be able to finance another loan. If the property has decreased in value, this can leave you with no equity and no place to live.

With a reverse annuity mortgage, a portion of your equity is used to purchase an annuity with a term that matches the mortgage's. The income you receive (as with any annuity) is based on your life expectancy, sex, marital status, and the prevailing interest rates. When your home is sold, or at your death, you or your estate will receive the difference between the sale price of the home and the income you received from the reverse mortgage. If you live longer than the insurance company expected, you'll continue to receive payments for life. The repayment to the insurance company will come from the proceeds of the sale of the home. Your estate will not be liable for more than that.

A reverse mortgage is a "rising debt" loan. This means that the total amount you owe grows over time. Let's say you have a house that is currently worth $189,000. You decide to use a reverse mortgage for $30,000 over 10 years at 11% to supplement your income. You receive $250 a month, or $3,000 a year. At the end of 10 years you will have been paid $30,000, and you will owe the lender $30,000 plus the accumulated interest ($23,970), for a total of $53,970.

In trying to decide if a reverse mortgage is for you, think about whether housing prices in your neighbourhood will likely appreciate or depreciate. Consider, too, interest rates and the various fees (legal, administration, and so on) associated with a reverse mortgage.

If you want to generate some extra income on a temporary basis, a reverse mortgage may be just the ticket. But be prepared to sell your home or be certain that you'll be coming into a whack of money that will allow you to repay the debt you've built up. If you're looking for long-term income, know that at your death there may be no residual value from the home payable to your estate. If you can live with these facts, then a reverse mortgage may give you the financial flexibility to ensure a comfortable retirement.

Many lower-cost housing alternatives exist that you may wish to look into. Subsidized dwellings are not limited to public housing; non-profit housing and co-operative housing developments also offer alternatives geared to a retiree's income. Canada Mortgage and Housing Corporation (CMHC) has information that may help you decide how you want to live in retirement. Contact your local CMHC office for copies of *Housing Choices for Older Canadians* and start learning about your alternatives. You can also get information on subsidized housing from non-profit and co-operative housing agencies.

If you decide your present home isn't suitable for retirement, you'll have to decide whether you will move within your community, divide your time between two communities (perhaps your cottage in the summer and autumn, and a warm climate in the winter and spring), or move to a whole new area. Keep in mind that there are special considerations that must be given to moving to a whole new community and to spending all or part of your time in another country. These are covered in more detail in my *Retirement Answer Book*.

CASH-MANAGEMENT STRATEGIES

The key to keeping your cash flow working during retirement is to know when the money is coming in and when it has to go out. This is something of an adjustment for people who have been on the payroll for years and have received their salary every month on the second Friday or on the 15th and the 30th. During retirement, it may take a little more planning.

You may receive income quarterly, if you'll be earning dividends, or annually, if you're earning interest. And depending on how you structure your RRSP or RRIF payouts, your cash may flow in monthly, semi-annually, or even annually. You need to know specifically when the money will come in and when money will flow out. Some expenses such as your tax bill will come up quarterly. Others, such as insurance, may be on an annual basis. The whole idea of setting up a cash flow is to have the income when you need it.

A cash flow typically lists all the sources of income and expenses down the left side of the page. Each month has a column of its own going across the top. For each month, the sources of income and the expected expenses are written in so that you know exactly when the money is arriving and when it is departing. It gives a clear picture of what you can expect, and shows you where the potential holes may be so you can adjust your income stream to meet your needs. If you know you'll have an insurance bill in December, you could arrange to take extra from your RRIF in November to cover the cost. Similarly, if you're concerned about meeting your quarterly tax payments, even if you're receiving a monthly income from your pension or annuity, you can arrange to have extra income — perhaps from dividends or from GIC interest — paid to you to cover your tax bill.

KEEPING A HEALTHY CREDIT IDENTITY

The same rules that apply just prior to retirement carry through to retirement. Keeping a healthy credit identity is one part of a sound financial plan. Without it, you could find yourself in trouble. You may not ever need it, but if you do, it'll be there.

YOUR PAY-YOURSELF-FIRST INVESTMENT PLAN

You'll likely spend as long in retirement as you did working. And since retirement means different things to different people, and has its own series of stages, you need to keep planning for the next stage. You may begin by semiretiring. Stage One could include working part-time, starting a new business, or working as a consultant. In Stage Two of your retirement, you may plan to stop working completely while you remain very active in other areas. Your active retirement might include extensive travel, activities such as golfing, skiing, or cycling, or active volunteering. Stage Three would be your less active years — the years when you plan to remain in your home, with or without help from others. Stage Four may be the years when you choose to move to a retirement home that provides you with the help you need in managing day-to-day activities, as well as specialized medical attention.

Since your RRSP contribution limit is based on your previous year's earned income, you can make an RRSP contribution during your first year of retirement based on your last year of working (providing you and/or your spouse are under the age of 69). Make sure you adjust your income during your first year of retirement to take advantage of this tax-deferral opportunity.

If you receive a retiring allowance (a kind of lump-sum bonus payment) when you retire from work, you can transfer a large portion of it to an RRSP in order to shelter it from tax. The eligible amount is limited to $2,000 for each year of employment plus an additional $1,500 for each year of employment prior to 1989 for which employer contributions were not made to the company pension plan or were not vested (or made a permanent, unrescindable part of the pension). For the purpose of calculating retirement allowance rollovers to an RRSP, any part of a calendar year is considered a full year.

Your employer will determine the amount that qualifies for the rollover, and if you have the transfer done directly (using a TD2 form, or NRTA1 form if you are a non-resident), no tax will be withheld at source on the funds that have been rolled over. If you receive your retiring allowance directly, you have until 60 days after the end of the year in which the payment is received to contribute the amount allowed to your RRSP.

Accumulated vacation pay and pension benefits are not eligible for this rollover. Your retiring allowance can be transferred only to your own RRSP, not to a spousal plan.

Even after you retire, you can continue to contribute to an RRSP, providing you or your spouse is under 69 and has a source of earned income. Rental income and income stemming from employment, such as disability payments, are forms of earned income.

Another way to maximize your RRSP investments' growth is to allow them to grow in their tax-sheltered environment for as long as possible. Even if you retire before 69, you can continue to maximize your retirement assets by leaving the money invested in the RRSP for as long as possible. Use your unregistered investments as a source of income first. Then, when necessary, take only as much as you need from your plan each year, leaving the remaining amount to continue to grow on a tax-deferred basis.

A lot has been said about the importance of diversifyng your investment portfolio. Since different types of investments earn varying rates of return depending on economic conditions, by holding a mix of investments you can reduce your exposure to the poor performance of any one type of investment to produce a steady rate of growth. That steady rate of growth, in turn, helps to keep the impact of inflation in check. As you move into retirement, you may be asking yourself, "Should I change my asset mix?" Rules of thumb abound in the financial world, and a common one for asset mix is that it should be adjusted based on your age: The percentage of equities in your portfolio should be equal to 100 minus your age. That would mean that at age 60, you'd hold 40% of your investments in equities.

Ann Eynon has a different philosophy. She says, "I don't think any rule of thumb can be used for adjusting the basket of investments since money personality is number one." It's a difficult thing to explain, this idea of money personality, because feelings come into it. "On the day you retire, if you have a good asset mix and it's been working for you, if you can sleep and if your tummy says it's okay, stick with it. After all, every single person has their own comfort level or sleep factor. Some people want to be so cautious that they will only invest in term deposits and Canada Savings Bonds, and that's absolutely correct for them. They shouldn't be criticized for doing that." She stresses, however, that it is important that you regularly review your investment mix to ensure that as your life and priorities change, your asset allocation continues to satisfy your needs. If you find there are significant changes to your lifestyle, at that point, "you may want to make changes to your financial picture."

YOUR EMERGENCY FUND

By this time you probably feel you no longer need an emergency fund. You may be right. It really depends on how often you receive your retirement income, how accessible your assets are, and how likely you are to hit an emergency at this point in your life. You know you won't be laid off. But what would happen if interest rates took a significant downturn for a few months and you were forced to start dipping further into your capital to make ends meet? Or what if a sudden illness required you to lay out money for a nurse? How would you and your cash flow cope? As one person said to me as we sat together in a hospital, waiting for our children to be diagnosed, "Life is an emergency."

At this point in your life, make sure every dollar is working as hard as possible for you — since you're not doing any work yourself! Having the equivalent of three or six months' income set aside for an emergency may be too much of a burden on your overall investment portfolio. Instead, look to other ways of coping. If you have your credit cards, you could use them in the short term. A line of credit would be better because the cost is usually lower. Or you could use investments that can be easily liquidated. Canada Savings Bonds come to mind. One of the nice things about CSBs is that the rate is guaranteed not to decline during the year. However, if interest rates are increasing, the government generally increases the rate on the bonds to discourage people from cashing in their bonds. In this respect, they beat short-term GICs hands down.

REVIEWING YOUR INSURANCE

One reason for having insurance at this point in your life is to provide enough money to meet the tax liability your estate will incur at your death. Since market or economic conditions may make it an inopportune time to sell assets immediately after your death — and since some assets, such as the family cottage, have a lot of sentimental value — having a lump-sum benefit from an insurance policy would provide the flexibility needed.

Let's take the example of a couple who have RRSP assets. When the first spouse dies, the assets can be transferred to the surviving spouse on a tax-deferred basis. In two words: No Tax. But when the second spouse dies, guess what? Tax — and big-time! Let's say you and your spouse each have $100,000 in RRIF assets. Your spouse dies, and so his $100,000 rolls into your plan. Now you have $200,000. Assuming you live on air and die with $200,000 remaining, and the highest marginal tax rate in your province is 48%, your estate will have to pay $96,000 in tax to the government. Ouch! If you have three children to whom you would leave this money equally, they'll each get just under $35,000. Now let's say you had an insurance policy that covered those taxes owed, along with any other taxes calculated on your estate. Instead, each of your three children would be able to split the full $200,000, receiving almost $67,000 a piece. The question to think about is, How much estate protection will you need to cover your assets? If you feel you'll have sufficient cash to pay the taxes directly from your estate, that's cool. You won't need insurance. But if your estate will be eaten away by taxes, leaving far less than you imagined for your heirs, insurance could be the solution.

TAX IMPLICATIONS

Here are 16 tips to help ensure that when you retire, you're not paying more tax than is absolutely necessary.

1. Once you are 65, make sure you have enough pension income to take advantage of the $1,000 pension-income tax credit, which allows you to earn the first $1,000 in pension income tax-free (see pages 278–79).

2. People 65 and older also qualify for the age credit. If one spouse can't use this tax credit fully, the unused portion can be transferred to the other spouse's return.

3. The government has broadened its definition of disability, so more people now qualify for the disability credit. If you think you may, have your doctor complete the Disability Credit Certificate (Form 2201). For more information, check the rules in the General Tax Guide. If you find that either you or your spouse can't claim all the tax credits available to you because you don't have enough income, you can transfer some of these credits to the other spouse. The pension income, age, and disability credits all qualify to be transferred. Since this can save you a lot on your taxes, be careful not to overlook it.

4. Claim the GST tax credit. Since your income in retirement will probably be less than when you were working, you may be eligible for this. In 1998, you were entitled to a GST rebate if your family's net income was less than $25,921. Don't assume you won't get it; check it out.

5. Maximize your medical expense credit by having the lower-income

spouse claim all medical costs. Private insurance premiums for coverage both inside and outside Canada qualify for the medical tax credit. The expenses you claim may be for any 12-month period ending in the tax year for which you're filing, so choose the time frame that gives you the largest claim. And since the credit is based on when expenses are paid (as opposed to when the service is rendered), it may make sense to prepay an upcoming expense to maximize your tax benefit.

6. If you receive a retiring allowance, you can transfer a portion (or perhaps all) of that to your RRSP to maximize the tax deferral on those funds.

7. When you retire, you can still make at least one more contribution to an RRSP (based on your previous year's earned income). Take advantage of this. If you have eligible earned income and you and/or your spouse are under 69, you can continue making RRSP contributions.

8. If you have any unused deduction room (that is, if you have not claimed all your allowable RRSP deductions), don't let it go unclaimed.

9. If one spouse has dividend income but has little or no other income and therefore cannot claim the dividend tax credit, the dividends can be reported on the other spouse's return. This transfer is particularly beneficial when it reduces the lower-income spouse's income enough to allow the higher-income spouse to claim the spousal tax credit. Partial claims are not allowed. In most circumstances, whenever there is any opportunity to claim the spousal tax credit, all the lower-income spouse's dividends should be claimed by the upper-income spouse.

10. Take advantage of the tax benefits of income splitting by using a spousal RRSP and, if appropriate, by splitting CPP benefits.

11. Defer tax for as long as possible by first using your unregistered assets to produce an income. Leave your RRSPs intact for as long as possible so they can continue to grow on a tax-sheltered basis.

12. If you have investment income, you can claim a number of expenses against it, including the expense of a safety deposit box and the interest on money borrowed for investment purposes.

13. Let one spouse claim all charitable donations. You get the biggest

break when donations exceed $200, as long as both of you have an income. CCRA doesn't care who makes the claim. Just remember that your claims are limited to a maximum of 20% of your net income. By claiming all donations made over several years in one year, you'll increase your tax benefit. When you make a donation to a registered charity, you'll receive a federal tax credit of 17% on the first $200 and 29% for all donations over that. So if you normally make donations of $100 a year, by combining three or more years of contributions, you'll qualify for a larger tax credit.

14. Remit your installment payments on time. You're responsible for getting tax to CCRA. And there can be heavy penalties for failing to do so. Contact CCRA for the information you need to stay on their good side.

15. If you have a high retirement income (even after income splitting), manage your income to benefit from OAS at least once every two years. (See pages 273–74.)

16. If you plan to help educate a grandchild or help children buy a home, you may want to consider using an inter vivos trust. You would be giving a certain amount of money to a beneficiary (while you are still alive), and the return on that money would be earned, and taxed, in the beneficiary's hands.

REVIEWING YOUR ESTATE PLAN

You can do a lot of estate planning outside a will to bypass the probate and executor fees. Assets that are not probatable bypass your will and go directly to the joint owner or beneficiary. As well, assets that pass through the estate are liable to the estate's creditors, but those that don't cannot be touched. Ann Eynon suggests that "anything that can be held jointly, such as GICs and bank accounts, should be held in joint names."

Once you've decided what you want to do with your estate, the next step is to make or update your will. Minimize the work for your executor by having complete documentation on where everything is. Minimize the stress on your family by planning your funeral. Make sure you have enough income to maintain your current lifestyle; then you can arrange your affairs to maximize the estate for your heirs and make things easier for your executor. If you have assets you do not need to maintain your lifestyle, consider gifting them to children. As long as the person is over 18 there's no attribution. You can also make loans that are forgivable on death.

As your life progresses, you will move through stages that require specific strategies. But it's hard to think about the implications of a stage that seems so far away. Witness the number of grasshoppers who delay planning for retirement despite the foresight and warnings of a great many ants. The best we seem to be able to do is to cope with the stage we're at. The big downside, of course, is that we often miss things, important things, that we could be, should be, would be doing if we just had the benefit of hindsight. But with these chapters on the most common steps and stages — the "highly likelies" — of life, you can consider yourself well equipped to cope financially. Part IV will help you deal with the true "what-ifs."

IV

JUST
IN CASE

There was only one catch and that was Catch-22, which specified that a concern for one's own safety in the face of dangers that were real and immediate was the process of a rational mind.
JOSEPH HELLER

N o matter how well you plan, life has a way of throwing a punch that can knock you flat. If you want to survive, you've got to keep getting up. Life is about being resilient. This section of the book deals with those knockout punches. I wish we all could lay out a plan and then peacefully follow through. That never happens. No matter how it looks from the outside, everyone is dealing with something difficult in her life. There's no such thing as perfect. But there is a zone.

In the zone, you have things in perspective. In the zone, things are neither bigger nor smaller than they should be. It's a fairly quiet place. From time to time things intrude, but you find it relatively easy to rise above them. Changes don't bring panic. Uncertainty doesn't bring sleeplessness. Life seems to flow around you with a certain symmetry and serenity. I've been in the zone and I can tell you it is wonderful. Unfortunately, I can't tell you how to get there. You have to find your own way.

I can tell you that I found my way by being true to myself and to others. I said what I thought, without being mean. I did what I wanted, without being irresponsible. I never said "yes" when I really meant "no." Perhaps most importantly, I knew what I wanted, and focused on that.

Now, this may seem odd coming from a woman writing about money, but I got into the zone when money became less important to me. Once I realized that I had taken care of the details, I let go of the worry and started living every minute of the day. It came right in the middle of writing this book. Interestingly, all the research I did, all the lessons I learned about how money affects us emotionally, came home in a grand sweep and I entered the zone. It wasn't always perfect — I'm not talking about perfect. I'm talking about happy. Some days I still felt frustrated. Some days, I still felt bogged down. But most of the time I felt alive, sunny, and able to share myself with others. I'm telling you, the zone is a great place to be.

Does this seem like a strange place to be talking about the zone? Well, I mention it here because I believe that being in the zone helps you to get through any of the events discussed in the following chapters with grace and a sense of completeness. And it doesn't matter how it looks from the outside. It's how it feels on the inside that counts.

I have found, throughout my life, that the people furthest from the zone are the ones most concerned about how things look to other people. They are very secretive. Who cares what you make? Money doesn't define who you are. Who cares how much debt you have right now? Money is not a measurement of your worth. Who cares how much you've accumulated? A pile of money doesn't make you smarter. Remember, money is a tool that gets us what we need and want so we can get on with our lives. Break the barriers of silence and secrecy and move into the zone. Figure out what you want and move into the zone. Be true to yourself and move into the zone.

When I was a girl, my Aunty Angie told me something that has stayed with me my whole life. She quoted Shakespeare in my autograph book: "To thine own self be true, and it must follow, as the night the day, thou canst not then be false to any man." Will was right. Thanks, Aunty Angie.

18

Just in Case You Become the Sole Breadwinner

You are rich when you can meet the demands of your imagination.

HENRY JOYCE

Being the sole provider for your family is an extremely stressful position to be in. You are responsible for it all: the roof, the food, the emergencies. Without your income, the family would founder. Without your attendance at work every day, day in and day out, your family wouldn't survive. If something went wrong and you became ill, or your income were interrupted for some other reason — well, the consequences are almost too alarming to imagine.

LIVING THROUGH IT

Of all Canadian working women, 55% provide half or more of the household income.[26] So it's not as though we aren't used to bringing home the bacon. But the shock of being the only one on whom the family counts when it hasn't always been so can knock even the most even-minded person off-kilter. And it's not the same as being self-sufficient — suddenly becoming totally responsible for the family is a different story altogether.

---

26 Dun & Bradstreet, 1995.

Several years ago, when my husband was laid off, I was faced with being the sole breadwinner. While I had taken care of myself all my life, the added responsibility of the family sent my face into spasms. I twitched. My husband said it was stress. I denied it. What stress? I could do this. I would just work harder, do more, spend less. I remember thinking to myself, "This is a changing point in my life. I have to look at things differently from now on." It helped me to be more aware of my guy's burdens when we later changed roles again, and he became the primary income-earner while I spent more time with the kids.

More and more women face the stress of being the sole breadwinner each year. Whether it is through divorce, widowhood, or because your partner is suddenly out of work, the strain can compromise your health, your financial life, and your relationships.

Barb Godin has been the sole provider in her family since 1989, when her husband was laid off and decided to stay home and look after the kids. "I worry constantly," she says. "I worry about providing for the family. If I need credit, will I be able to get enough?" Funny coming from a deacon of credit, right?

Traditionally, men have borne this particular burden, and they haven't talked about the stress. They might get snippy, but they rarely say, "I am just so tired of being solely responsible for this." Now that we women are finding ourselves in the role of primary breadwinner, we too are bearing up bravely, dying earlier of stress-related diseases, and snapping at our children.

Recognizing that the stress is there is the first step in dealing with it. You'll have to acknowledge any changes in status. There is a great deal of literature out there about the relationship between money and power. Don't add this demon to the stresses you're already dealing with. Talk about what the change in circumstances will mean to you as a couple, as a family, and as individuals. Continue to talk all the way through it. If you share your worry with your friend, the burden will immediately lighten. If your partner is not behaving like your friend, find someone to listen to your worries until your partner steadies.

You'll need to keep your financial house in order so you don't exacerbate the stress. Reconciling yourself to living on less money is one of the hardest things to do — particularly when the decision is forced. Intellectually, you make all the compromises. Emotionally, you're way behind. Old habits die hard, especially the ones that let you have what you want, when you want. But die they must, because if you try to maintain the status quo, if you behave as though nothing has changed, you will drown in a credit quagmire.

Time to revisit and adjust your spending plan. The rent or mortgage has to be paid. You need to put food on the table. But there may be several areas where you can cut back, cut down, or cut out to get by on a single income. People do it all the time and survive. The challenge is to do it and be happy. Take a copy of your spending plan and work through it to determine which costs will go down. Here are some things to consider:

- Can you eliminate child-care costs for as long as there is only one income? If your partner is actively looking for work, shared day care would be less expensive than the full-time day care used while you were both working.
- Have you reduced the budget for things like transportation, lunches, and ordering in dinner? Add it up and you may find that the savings are substantial. So are the savings on work clothes, after-work entertainment, and income taxes.
- Could part-time employment supplement the family income in the interim? Does your partner have skills that could be used on a free-lance or consulting basis?
- Would a lifestyle change help? Do you still need the second car? Think of what you'd save on maintenance and insurance, never mind the boost to your savings when you sell the car.

Keeping a roof over your head will be one of your top priorities. It is a somewhat simple decision, really. Can you afford to continue living in your home on the income you are making? For how long can you afford to do this? How long do you expect to have to do it on your own? Is there anything you can do to reduce your mortgage expenses, such as renegotiate your mortgage if rates have fallen, or rent a part of your home in the interim? There's no way you will have the answers to all these questions at your fingertips. So this is where a woman's intuition comes into play, along with some good ol' common sense.

If you've been living well within your means as a family, if you've got your emergency fund set up along with a pretty clean credit situation, you're much more likely to make it through intact — home and all — than if you've been living way beyond your means and have run up thousands in credit-card debt. To see just how you'll cope, you'll need to do a new spending plan, one that's a lot leaner.

I can't remember where I first read the phrase "involuntary simplicity," but it applies to all those circumstances in which you are forced to simplify the way you live because of less money. Lately, there has been a wide-sweeping trend toward simplification. The media is full of stories about how people are reducing their consumption and honouring frugality as a way of life. The words "tightwad," "cheapskate," and "miser" used to have very negative connotations, but that's changing; in fact, stories abound about people who were forced into simplicity only to find that they loved it. They move to the country, grow their own food, and try to live on as little money as possible. They reuse and recycle. They share ideas, coupons, and the inside scoop on bargains. While they may be poor of pocketbook, they are rich of spirit.

Now, this may all seem too cloud-with-a-silver-lining-ish to you if your buddy has just been cast to the wolves by his former employer. But don't discount it completely. Yes, you'll have to spend the next few days, weeks, and months managing the bruise to your pocketbook as well as the bruise to his ego. But you will come through it. This is not the time to pick at each other's shortcomings. If you have children at home, this is not the time to scare them to death with threats of never again having two brass farthings. This is a time to take it slowly on the emotional front while moving quickly to shore up your financial situation.

Having reviewed your spending plan and identified areas where you can cut back, next you must ensure that your cash-management strategies continue to work for you. While you may have had two or more accounts before you became a single-income family, having a single account will probably make more sense now, at least for the short term. Consolidate the money you may have in several accounts to see if you can minimize the cost of doing business with the bank. Look hard at the services you will be using. Now is not the time for services you may only use once in a blue moon. Little things like choosing a passbook option (rather than receiving a statement) can save you money. Remember, too, that the banking world is constantly changing and the banks are very competitive.

Shop around to see who has the best "package" for your specific needs. Many banks offer no-charge chequing and no-charge ABM use if you maintain a specific minimum balance. By consolidating your accounts you may be able to take advantage of these features.

If maintaining a monthly balance is a problem, which it very well may be while you learn to live on less income, then you'll have to compare individual service charges — costs for cheques and withdrawals, for statements, and for ABM transactions. Choose the least expensive account for your purposes. If you're attracted to the packaged accounts, compare the individual fees with the package costs to see if you come out ahead. And compare the interest you're earning with the cost of the account. There's no point in earning minimal interest if the service charges on that account are more than you pay on another non-interest-bearing account.

The easiest thing to do when you have a shortfall in your cash flow is to use your credit cards or personal line of credit to fill the gap. For those people who intended to use their PLC as their emergency fund, a word of caution: Don't get complacent about the fact that you are accumulating debt that will eventually have to be repaid. For those who plan to use their credit cards to get over the hump, make sure you're using the cheapest credit card you can find. If you add a 17% interest rate to your existing burdens, you're dooming yourself. Get a cheapie card and if you're already carrying a balance on an expensive one, transfer your balance.

While I don't often advocate overdraft protection because it is so expensive — and because using it is such an easy habit to get into and such a hard habit to get out of — it may be a good idea while you're adjusting to your new cash flow. You won't need it if you are determined to stay within your means and are meticulous about your record keeping. However, if you tend to let things slide a bit, having overdraft protection to avoid NSF cheques will keep your creditors happy and avoid the negative long-term implications of a rotten credit history.

Don't forget to pay yourself first. Yeah, like you really think I'm going to be able to save *anything* while living on one income? Get real!

If you're divorced, widowed, or any other form of single, you must try. It may not happen immediately. You may need time to adjust to your new lifestyle. But if you don't get yourself back on track and start saving, you're asking for trouble. Everyone has to save. That doesn't mean you have to save your maximum RRSP amount, or the amount your sister saves, or the amount the media advocate. But you do have to set something aside for the future. It's your responsibility.

Your current circumstances are the reason you need an emergency fund. If you have one, you're going to feel a lot safer moving through this trying time. As soon as you can, you'll need to start rebuilding it. It may take longer this time, but at least now you're convinced you need one.

As the primary breadwinner, you are now solely responsible for your family's continued peace of mind. And for your own peace of mind, you had better make sure you have enough insurance. If you had been counting on your spouse's work plan for life, disability, or health benefits, these need to be replaced. If you think that this isn't the time to make a cash-flow commitment to new expenses (like insurance, which nobody ever really uses anyway, right?), think again. What would your family do if you became disabled while you were the only one with a job? How would your spouse cope if you died? How will you cover those medical bills when they arrive? Insurance is not the place to skimp.

Some good news: You will end up paying less tax as a family, and if your spouse has no income at all, you'll get a tax break there. Since you're now living on one income, you'll be claiming all the deductions and credits, so make sure you take advantage of everything you can to minimize your tax liability. If your partner has little or no income, remember to take advantage of the spousal or equivalent-to-spousal tax credit. If you have no spouse, you can claim the equivalent-to-spousal credit for any qualifying dependent, including a child or parent.

While a tax refund may seem like a gift from the government, getting one means you aren't planning particularly well. The idea is to keep money in your hands for your own use, not to provide the government with an interest-free loan. Using the tax man as a forced-savings system may work for some, but the alternative makes more sense financially.

PREPARING FOR IT

Sometimes it comes as a surprise when you find yourself the sole breadwinner in the family. Other times it doesn't. If you and your partner have decided that one of you should stay home to be with the children, and it makes more sense that you keep working, then you may have time to plan this change in lifestyle. One of the best ways to see how it will work is to live on only your paycheque for several months leading up to the change. You can use the other paycheque to actively pay down debt or to build a sturdy emergency fund for those unforeseen financial crises.

Remember to check your insurance benefits to be sure you've got enough coverage for life, disability, and health. Redo your spending plan, incorporating the changes necessary for you to live on a single income. If you plan to eliminate your child-care expenses, remember to leave some money in the plan for baby-sitters while your partner attends doctors' appointments or takes some "sanity time." Set some goals for eliminating or significantly reducing your debt before you make the switch to one income. Talk about the money/power shift that may take place, and the warning signals you'll use to cue each other when that shift begins to manifest itself.

19

Just in Case
You Divorce

Money is always there but the pockets change.

GERTRUDE STEIN

Note: All the provincial legislation referred to in this chapter is based on Ontario's Family Law Act. While the Divorce Act is federal and deals with the grounds for divorce, custody, and child and spousal support, each province has separate legislation that deals with property (which is a provincial matter) as well as custody and child and spousal support. People who do not wish to get divorced (for religious or other reasons) but who separate and need the issues of support settled use the provincial legislation to achieve that end. Please seek advice from a lawyer within your jurisdiction for the legislation that applies to your situation.

LIVING THROUGH IT

According to Statistics Canada, people who are currently married and are 20 or younger have a 40% chance of divorce. At age 25, the chance of divorce drops to approximately 35%. At 30, a man's chance of divorce runs at about 33%, at 40 it's about 20%, and at 50 it's about 10%. The probability of divorce is lower for women at all ages because they are more likely to be widowed. Either way, we're going to end up alone and in charge of the money. So we'd better figure out how it works.

Another disconcerting statistic courtesy of StatsCan: after divorce, a woman's economic status generally falls by about 45% (the guy's goes up by about 72%). All sorts of factors come into play: the oft-bewailed discrepancies in income; the fact that more women leave the workforce than do men to look after family, resulting in a loss of skills and financial security for women; women's naiveté in handling their separation and divorce. If women have in fact been socialized to believe money is a man thing, it's time for some new socialization. Women *must* learn how to handle money if they want to be sure they can have a secure future. And we must teach our daughters that marriage is a noble institution, but that they *must* be capable of doing what is needed to survive, take care of their babies, and get on with their lives.

But before we get into the money part of this, I'd like to talk a little about where your head goes when your love (or whatever it is that's been holding you together) walks out the door. As with just about everything else in life, it depends. It depends on whether you are the person leaving, whom I'll refer to as the "leaver," or the person being left — the "leavee."

If you are the leaver, you have time to plan. You can make an appointment with a lawyer, get advice, and ready yourself for the storm. You can learn the rules of the game and practise your moves and countermoves ahead of the starter's gun. That's not to say that you'll be protected from the emotional upheaval and sadness that comes with a marriage breakdown. You will still grieve — dealing with divorce is not unlike dealing with death — but you'll do it at a different pace than the person you are leaving.

If you are the leavee, you have no opportunity to prepare. The starter's gun is a shot to your gut. Your mind careens from one disastrous scenario to another. A very close friend of mine describes her divorce as shaking her foundation. "Suddenly I felt all the societal taboos: a divorcée, oooh, a single mother, ugh. I felt I had lost my position in society. The security issues had to do with a lot more than just money. It was my emotional sense of self that left. It took me a long time to accept and deal with that. For a time, whenever I was in public with my daughter, I wore a fake wedding ring because I couldn't deal with people thinking I was an unwed mother. You have crazy thoughts. Things come into your mind that would never occur to you if you were feeling safe and secure."

Whereas the leaver has had time to prepare herself, the leavee must make time — slow the whole thing down — so she can catch up emotionally. Whereas the leaver has planned carefully, the leavee must put together a plan. If you do it on the fly, it won't be your best plan. Since this divorce will affect you, and perhaps your children, for a long time to come, don't rush, or be rushed, into decisions. Time makes the difference. And the very first thing you should do is see a very good lawyer.

Family lawyer Sandy Morris says that one mistake women make (and she qualifies this as a generalization) is that they have no knowledge of the family's financial affairs. Leavees panic not only because "He's leaving," but also because they realize they don't have access to the bank accounts, or they don't know how and when to make the mortgage payments.

"When they come into my office looking for me to say everything's going to be okay, I can't always say that," says Sandy. "When I try to get the financial picture, it becomes so apparent that they know nothing. The whole divorce procedure is so much more difficult."

Take the case of Paula R. She had a wonderful life. At 54, she drove a very nice car. Every year she went on a vacation. Her son was working and living at home, and her daughter was finishing her last year of university. Paula was well educated, well turned out, and ill prepared for divorce. When the credit check was done on Paula's husband, the results were abysmal. Paula was guarantor on several of her husband's loans. "Oh, yes," she said, "I signed something, but I don't remember much about it." With his high level of debt, Paula's husband fit the definition of bankrupt. His idea of negotiation was to say, "Look honey, if you're not prepared to accept what I'm going to give you, I'll just make an assignment [meaning he would hand over all his assets to a bankruptcy trustee] and I'm done." Since the bankruptcy would extinguish her claim to property division, that would leave Paula holding an empty bag. Paula's lack of knowledge — and lack of interest — in anything financial left her vulnerable to her ex-husband's tactics.

Danita B. is another case in point. Before marrying, she was an independent career woman. After she had her second child, she decided to stay home full time, at least until the last baby was in school full-time. Over the years, her husband Harry encouraged her not to worry about the financial stuff and she lost touch with what was going on. Since Danita came from a traditional family, it seemed natural to hand Harry the reins of their financial lives while she concentrated on nurturing the children and making sure everything ran smoothly at home. Danita was stunned when Harry walked out. He came home one night, packed his bags, and left saying, "You'll be hearing from my lawyer." With her fourth child still in diapers, she felt abandoned. The fact that Harry left for another woman didn't help Danita's self-image. She was furious and wanted revenge. And she'd use any tactic to make him pay.

Madelaine T. is at the other end of the scale. A child of divorce, Madelaine always maintained control over her own money. Hypersensitive to her parents' messy divorce, Madelaine stayed on top of everything. She admitted to even being slightly secretive about her finances. "I don't think Mathew should know everything," she said. "It's just not his business. I don't expect him to tell me everything." Madelaine was shocked to find out that while she had been very successful at wealth accumulation, Mathew hadn't been quite so prudent. "You mean I'm going to have to give him part of my assets? But he's the man. Why would I have to give him money?" she asked, astounded at the prospect. "But I've been the responsible one. He's been the gadfly. Why should he get half?" That's equality, girls!

Another mistake women make is to let emotion carry them away, as in Danita's case. "Many situations can be resolved without the need for protracted litigation if cooler heads prevail," says Sandy, "so that the parties walk out financially intact."

If you've managed to get this far without a spending plan, you'll need one now. And if you're not familiar with how the money flows in and out of the family pocketbook because the other guy's always taken care of it,

Sandy Morris is a lawyer with the Toronto firm Wilson Christen, where she specializes in family law. She is co-author of the family law section of the Law Society's Bar Admissions Course material and has written articles for the Canadian Bar Association (CBA) Continuing Legal Education programs. She is a regular speaker at New Directions, a branch of the Toronto Women's League, and serves on myriad committees, including the Appeal Committee and the Executive Committee of the CBA. Married with a daughter, Sandy is a fan of the Brontë sisters, loves Greek food, and makes a great case for women to know exactly what's going on in their marriages.

it's time to become familiar. Whether you are litigating or negotiating your divorce settlement, you'll have to complete the standard financial statement provided by your lawyer. One section includes a budget with 69 different types of expenditures to help figure out the family's spending pattern and what that spending pattern will likely look like in the future. Of course, if you've never had a spending plan, you probably have no idea what the numbers are. Refer to Chapter 4, where I explain what a spending plan is, how it works, and how to build one.

The budget section of the financial statement you prepare is, in large measure, what the judge looks at to determine your future needs for support. If you can't complete this properly — if you don't know what you're paying for taxes, entertainment, vacations, food, rent, and medical expenses — you won't be able to paint a clear enough picture for the judge. For example, Sandy says that many people don't know how much they spend on medical expenses. "People will say, my husband has a plan. When I ask if it has 100% coverage, a co-payment, whatever, they have no idea. They don't know if there are any limitations on the plan, or how long the plan lasts after divorce." Many people also think that because they have a drug plan, they don't need a drug budget. But what about those items that aren't covered by the plan: headache, cold, and allergy medicine, antibiotic cream and Band-Aids, potions for diarrhea, stomach upset, and nausea? Anything purchased without a prescription is not covered so everyone needs a drug budget. "Your lawyer should give you a document that shows you how to complete the financial statement," says Sandy. That explanation should draw your attention to each of the expenditures, including those you are likely to overlook. Remember, your financial statement is considered evidence under the rules of the court; so if you don't give complete evidence, the judge has less to work with, and that might be reflected in his or her decision.

"If a woman comes to me before she's actually left her husband, I tell her that her mission is to go home and find every scrap of paper that she can and photocopy it. Unless there is physical abuse or serious verbal abuse, even if she has to stay with her spouse for another month, my view is she should stay there because she has to prepare for this next step," says Sandy. That may include scouring the house for his tax returns, investment information, insurance details, everything that may be pertinent to your settlement.

If you're saying to yourself that this feels scummy, that it's an invasion of his privacy, that you're above such behaviour, give your head a shake. It is your right as a member of that family to know everything. If your spouse hasn't shared information with you, or if you haven't been paying attention, it's time to become informed. You must rectify your lack of knowledge to protect yourself, and perhaps your children. "Quite frankly," says Sandy, "you're saving yourself a lot of money because you won't have all the back-and-forthing that comes with a lack of disclosure. The financial statement is supposed to be a complete disclosure." If your spouse has purposely or inadvertently left something out, and you know about it because you have informed yourself, then it's a relatively easy situation to fix. If you don't know what's going on, you don't know when you're being had. It is healthy to be informed.

Don't forget to budget in your legal costs. The first thing you'll have to do is provide your lawyer with a retainer. People often look suspiciously at lawyers when they ask for a retainer, but the reality is that the exchange of that money — even if it is only one dollar — is what establishes the client-lawyer relationship. "Technically speaking," says Sandy, "in order for there to be that solicitor-client privilege, you need money to change hands."

In order to create a realistic budget for your divorce, ask what your lawyer's hourly rate is at the office and in court, since they are often different. If your lawyer uses a law clerk, find out how that person's time is billed. And remember, everything costs money. Your lawyer's time is the commodity you're paying for, so expect to be billed for telephone calls and letters, as well as face-to-face meetings. Remember, too, that the more prepared you are, the better use you can make of your lawyer's time.

Also check on your lawyer's billing procedures. The last thing you need is to go merrily along fighting your ex-spouse, only to find a bill for $20,000 at the end of it all. "I bill every month," says Sandy, "to give clients an ongoing appreciation for what the procedure will cost." If you'll be counting on a settlement to make good on your legal fees, make sure you gain your lawyer's agreement to a payment plan, and ascertain what the interest rate will be on the outstanding balance.

Since there may be interruptions in your income as you go through the divorce, particularly if your husband is ticked off at the amount of spousal or child support granted to you, you need to have a stash at the ready to fill the gaps. That may mean taking money from a joint account, pulling on a joint line of credit, or, in extreme circumstances, taking advances against a supplemental credit card. Yes, I am advocating getting the money from whatever source is available. The road to divorce can be long and bumpy and you may have to lay out a lot of cash along the way. Document all your withdrawals and advances and give the list to your lawyer (and your ex's lawyer), indicating that you know these amounts will be incorporated in the accounting and final division of assets. If you're in the house with the kids, you can't risk missing mortgage payments. Nor can you miss tuition payments for school or other activities. If the furnace goes, the car dies, or some other unforeseen event occurs, you need a way to cope financially. Remember, when it comes to separation or divorce, you rarely know what you're getting into. You can't afford to be left without money while your husband, the lawyers, and the courts try to decide how much it costs for you and your children to live.

Do you think this is extreme? It only seems so because you haven't yet had to live from week to week without money. I had a girlfriend who was left stranded by her ex when he left. For several months, she barely made ends meet while she continued to pay the mortgage (on an asset that was half his), buy the food (for herself and *their* daughter), and meet every other financial commitment. The stress was unbearable and she came within a straw of breaking. You must protect yourself. And that means having a healthy emergency fund *just in case!*

On separation, each party is equally entitled to live in a matrimonial home (that's possession, not ownership), until there's a court order saying one must get out or there's a separation agreement in which one party gives up the right. "I often tell people not to leave the home until they've seen a lawyer," says Sandy, "because there may be strategic reasons why you don't want to leave." Even if your husband tells you to get out and says he owns the house because only his name is on title, you don't have to leave. And if your husband comes home and tells you he's leaving you but not quite yet, you can't toss his stuff onto the lawn and lock him out, because changing the locks bars him from his right to possession of the matrimonial home.

"The matrimonial home," says Sandy Morris, "is any residence in which either party has a legal interest [so that applies to the home you own or rent] and which is ordinarily occupied by the spouses as their family residence at separation or immediately before separation." If you have a city house that you ordinarily occupy, that's a matrimonial home. You don't need a document saying that. If you have a cottage that you ordinarily occupy for a few weeks each year, that's a matrimonial home. You can have as many matrimonial homes as you live in. Investment properties don't count. You have to live on the property at some point in the year.

"Living separate and apart" for the purposes of being "separated" does not mean you have to be living physically apart. There are situations where people cannot immediately find alternative living space. "So living separate and apart can mean living in the same house," says Sandy. "It can even mean sharing the same bed." The objective test for "living separate and apart" is this: Would a third party looking in determine that these people are holding themselves out to the world as husband and wife? The judge looks for evidence to support the separation: not going out socially together, not doing the husband-and-wife things. "In one of my cases," said Sandy, "technically the woman had been separated for about eight years before she came to see me. I explained that to her. When we got to court, her husband claimed that she couldn't apply for equalization of net family property because the limitation period had passed. [You must make your claim within six years of your date of separation.] His claim was that they had been separated for eight years. We're still working to get to the bottom of this.

"Lots of people who grow apart simply carry on together as man and wife while leading totally separate lives," says Sandy. "I have clients who tell me that people are shocked to find out they were even married because those people never saw them with their spouses socially."

To prepare for your visit to the lawyer, make a list of all the real property you own and indicate whose name appears on the title for each. That way your lawyer will be able to register a "matrimonial home designation." This document is registered on title and has no legal effect other than to flag to would-be lenders that the property is a matrimonial home requiring spousal consent for any changes. That means you're protected if your spouse tries to take out a mortgage without your knowledge.

If you're dealing with a violent spouse, while you're not allowed to change the locks, here's at least one good reason to have him charged for assault. One of the terms of the bail order will be to restrict your husband from coming within a certain distance of your home. With this kind of criminal order in place, keeping him away from your doors, judges are likely to overlook it if you changed the locks (which would be a violation of civil law). You could also change the code on the alarm system so that if he enters the house, the police would be notified immediately. You could also change the frequency on your garage door so he can't get in through the garage.

No matter what your husband promises you as he exits stage left, take it with a grain of salt. Emotions and attitudes swing from one extreme to another during marriage breakdown, and today's guilt-induced promise can be easily rescinded tomorrow. Protect yourself. Get to work finding everything you can to take to the lawyer. Remove your name from all forms of joint credit. Fill up your emergency fund, and batten down the hatches.

Regardless of how lost, negative, abandoned, and rudderless you feel when you're going through a divorce, you will have goals to work toward. Or perhaps you're excited at the prospect of setting out on your own journey — one where you read your own map (and get a lot less lost). Whatever the case, *do not make any significant decisions for the first six to 12 months*. This probably isn't the right time to deal with the stress of a new job, start a business, buy a new house, change your investment portfolio significantly, or remarry. It is perfectly fine to dream. Dreaming is good. Imagine all the possibilities. Work through all the scenarios in your mind. Just don't *do* anything drastic. You need time to adjust emotionally as well as financially, and that means cutting yourself some slack. Don't listen to those who try to impose a time frame on you by telling you to "just get on with it." This is a huge change in your life and you have to take some time to get used to it.

If you have someone to whom you can turn for financial advice, great. But you should already have a relationship with this person. Otherwise, deal with someone who comes very, very highly recommended. Follow your instincts. You should feel comfortable and secure. You should like the person. You should feel that person is helping you to understand your options, not pushing you to make a decision.

You shouldn't be in a hurry to make financial decisions that will affect you or your children for the long haul. Instead, take notes, get second opinions, study up on what's what. Create your personal plan of action.

Don't worry if the stock market skyrockets while you're on the sidelines; you'll get another opportunity. What you'll lose by jumping in is sleep, and right now, girl, whether you are the leaver or the leavee, you need all the rest you can get to recover from your wounds.

While you may end up with half the family assets as part of the divorce, you may very well end up with less cash flow and see your standard of living drop. Since women usually earn less than their male counterparts, moving from a dual income to a lower single one means you may not be able to maintain your lifestyle. If you've been an at-home wife who is now dependent on alimony and child support for income, you, too, may find it difficult because you are not able to meet your previous expectations.

As part of your new independent state of being, if you have not already done so, you'll have to establish a financial identity for yourself. That means setting up a chequing account in your own name, applying for credit cards, and the like. If you've never managed money before, let me reassure you that it isn't hard, but it takes some practice.

Start by talking to a girlfriend or female family member who seems to be doing well on her own. Join a support group in your community. Groups like New Directions in Toronto provide a wealth of information to help women make successful transitions and rebuild their lives. New Directions offers workshops on topics ranging from how to make the legal system work for you if you are separating, to how to manage the effects of divorce on young children, to mending your heart and healing your body through meditation. Ask at community centres, look in the Yellow Pages under "Divorce," and ask friends and family.

Part of what you want to find out is how to manage your money efficiently on a day-to-day basis. If you have a relationship with people at your bank, ask them for help. Since they are closest to the subject, they'll have the most expertise. Don't worry about looking foolish. All that matters is getting informed and learning how to take care of yourself.

Do you have a credit card in your own name? Get one. (By the way, why isn't this ever an issue for men?) Supplemental cards — or the credit cards you use that are tied to your husband's cards — do absolutely Jack Squat to build you a credit history. It doesn't matter who pays the bill. If the card is in his name, the reporting is in his name and *you don't exist*.

What would you do if your husband cut off your supplemental card and you were in Zellers buying your kids new boots when your card was declined? First you would be mortified. Then you'd be angry. Save yourself the trouble. Get your own card.

When Janet divorced several years ago, she discovered that all her credit cards were held jointly with her husband. While she had made payments consistently on the cards she had used, he had not been quite so punctual. The result: Her credit history was far less pristine than she had imagined. Janet hadn't written the credit-card companies to have her name removed from the cards her ex was using, so when he was lackadaisical about making payments during the months they were separated, he was also tarnishing her credit history. When she tried applying for her own credit, she found several banks unwilling to extend her credit because she was now living on substantially less income and her credit bureau report showed a shoddy payment record. She was furious. Take a lesson from Janet's case. If you're holding cards on which you are jointly liable with your spouse, call and have those cards cancelled and new cards issued solely in your name. The fact that you're deep in the throes of a nasty divorce is of no interest to your creditors.

If you and your husband had a joint line of credit at the bank, go and have your signature removed, if you can. If you can't, then hand-deliver to the bank a letter that says, "As of today's date, no cheque can be drawn against this line of credit without both signatures." That way, no one is doing anything without the other's knowledge.

Change your PIN number. Remember that Tuesday last year when you asked him to take some money out of the machine for you? He has your PIN number. If you don't change it, you're allowing him the opportunity to mess with your accounts. While you're at it, change all your PIN numbers and passwords. And don't change them to something obvious like your children's names. Use something obscure like the name of the first man who nibbled your ear or your great-aunt Lucy's birth date.

Since you're completely dependent on yourself, if you're not taking care of your future, no one is. If you have earned income, you should be contributing to an RRSP. Get on a periodic investment plan. You can start with as little as $25 a month.

If you think you can't afford to be investing for your future because your present costs so much, ask yourself this question: If I don't save for my future, what will I live on when my future becomes my present? If you think you have plenty of time to catch up, ask yourself what you did with the last five years of your life and how much you would have today if you had started back then. If you think the government is going to take care of your future, a gentle reminder: You thought your husband was going to do that too. You can't depend on anyone but yourself.

The other thing to think about when reviewing your investment strategy is how the divorce has affected your retirement plan. When RRSP assets are divided as part of a divorce settlement, this can significantly alter your retirement plans and colour how you will invest those dollars for the future. The most important question for many people is how to balance their risk tolerance with the need to grow their RRSP assets now that they are on their own. When you're negotiating who gets what in the divorce, women who have stayed out of the workforce to raise a family or have lower-paying jobs should choose to hold on to RRSP assets, particularly if your spouse has a company pension plan to rely on. With little or no RRSP room to catch up, you'll be starting from ground zero if you relinquish RRSP assets totally; this is of greatest concern if you are in your late forties or fifties and have less time to build a strong retirement asset base.

Often women choose to keep the family home, giving up retirement assets in exchange. But this isn't always a smart move. With expensive upkeep and slow increases in real estate values, a home can become an albatross, inhibiting women from building the investment reserves they need to take care of themselves in later years.

Other areas to watch for:

- A 50/50 split of assets may seem fair, but if your spouse also has a company pension plan, that has to be taken into consideration.
- If you won't be entering the workforce immediately, you'll need to negotiate extra income for investment purposes so you don't spend several years contributing zilch to your retirement plan.
- If your spouse has significant unused RRSP contribution room — if he could have made contributions but chose not to — those catch-up contributions aren't divisible after the settlement. Negotiate for a portion of those contributions to be made in your name (as a spousal contribution) prior to the division of assets, and that the spousal RRSP will not be equalized. That way you'll have assets that can continue to grow on a tax-deferred basis.

Keep in mind that once you are living separately, the RRSP rules for withdrawals from a spousal plan change. The money will be taxed in the hands of the planholder — the "spouse" — so if that's you, don't go grabbing money out of your spousal plan thinking your old buddy will get stuck with the tax bill. You'll end up paying the piper.

If you considered your partner to be your disability plan, it's time to get a new one . . . no, not a new partner, a real disability plan; one that will be with you, regardless. You're the only one you can truly count on should you be unable to work. If you have kids, it's even more important. You don't really want to hear your ex say, "Well, since I'm supporting the children completely now, I think they should live with me and my new wife. After all, you have enough on your plate."

Life insurance is just as important. If your ex isn't in the picture a whole lot — some husbands do move away and start new lives, as though their previous lives and families never existed — then you must have life insurance to protect your children.

Another good use of life insurance is to protect the stream of child-support payments you may be receiving from your ex. Any good lawyer will advise you to have it stipulated in your separation agreement that your husband will take out and pay for an insurance policy that will guarantee your children support until a specific age. While the separation agreement and support order are binding on your ex-spouse's estate, if the estate doesn't have enough to fund the support, you're out of luck. And, of course, if your ex agrees, you can insure his life, pay the premiums yourself, and know your kids will be protected should he depart this earth.

If your partner just can't get insurance, don't give up. Insist that you (if you are being paid spousal support) and your children be named as irrevocable beneficiaries on his RRSPs. "While you won't be able to roll the money over on a tax-free basis because you're no longer spouses, you can set up certain types of trusts to minimize the tax consequences," says Sandy. "Every court order or separation agreement should contain some form of risk mitigation." Of course, there's absolutely no point in arguing for these types of provisions unless you are going to follow up to make sure they are in place. Each year you should receive proof that the premiums have been paid and that your interests and those of your children are protected.

Also keep in mind that if your spouse belongs to a group health plan, your joint dependent children should still be covered under that plan. If you just can't get on with your ex, include in your separation agreement the specifics for when you'll receive payment for submitted claims, so the procedure doesn't turn into a power struggle. And since you probably won't be covered under his medical plan, make sure you get a medical plan of your own.

Even if you're the person initiating the separation, there are some things that aren't top of mind: the tax man, for instance. But he should be. After all, how you structure the financial side of your divorce will have an impact on your money management for years to come. Tax planning for divorce starts before you draw up your separation agreement, especially where support is being paid. Spousal support is deductible for the payer, and is included in the income of the payee (and therefore subject to tax), as long as the payee is receiving support as directed by a written separation agreement or court order, and those payments are made on a periodic basis. This only applies to people who have been legally married. If you've just lived in sin, the payer will need a court order to have support payments deemed deductible by the tax man. CCRA will recognize payments made on a periodic basis one calendar year prior to the year your separation agreement is signed. So if you sign a separation agreement in 1998, the payer can claim any periodic payments made as far back as January 1, 1997.

When you're filing your income tax return for the year of separation you can choose between claiming payments made or the spousal credit. So if you legally separated in December, it might be worth more to claim the spousal credit than a single month's support payment. Do the math before you make the choice. Also note that the same flexibility applies if you pull a Liz Taylor; should you and your spouse get back together, you can make either of these claims for the year the reconciliation takes place.

Under new legislation, child support is no longer deductible for the payer or included in the income of the recipient. This applies to support orders made or orders renegotiated after May 1, 1997. For support orders made prior to that date, the old rules still apply: child support is a deductible expense for the payer, and taxable income for the payee. If you're thinking of renegotiating your child support so you don't have to pay tax on the income, be careful. There are new guidelines for child support and some people think the amounts being awarded are abysmally low. For example, if the supporting parent is making $100,000 a year, the base amount for one child is just $773 per month. Amounts payable above this base amount are awarded at the discretion of the judge — and that's not always a good thing.

Remember, too, that if you choose to renegotiate your support and it becomes non-taxable in your hands and non-deductible in your spouse's, your RRSP contribution limit will be affected, since you'll have reduced your earned income. And if you are the payer, and you used to claim a deduction for support but have stopped, make sure you tell your employer so sufficient tax can be withheld from your paycheque.

Divorce gives you a rare opportunity to fiddle with your RRSP or registered pension plan without tax consequence. If RPP or RRSP assets are being split between spouses, the rollover from one spouse's plan to the other's can take place on a tax-free basis using form T2220 for RRSP or RRIF rollovers, and form T2151 for RPPs.

Do either you or your spouse have any unused RRSP contribution room you could catch up on prior to your split of matrimonial assets? Since registered assets can be rolled between spouses on a tax-free basis, you'd do well to maximize those assets ahead of time, perhaps by liquidating some of your unregistered funds, which *would* be taxed on transfer from one spouse to another.

Most people don't even know what "contingent liabilities" are, let alone how to take them into account when splitting their assets. Take for example a situation where registered and unregistered assets are being equalized separately — let's say one person's taking the RRSP and the other is taking the house. There has to be some recognition that the party holding the RRSP will be taxed when those funds are withdrawn, so the RRSP holder will negotiate for those assets to be discounted for the tax that will later be paid on them. The same kind of negotiation would protect the spouse who took the house as settlement if that house had to be sold sometime in the near future. So the true value of the house — and the settlement — is determined by factoring in the reduction in the asset for legal fees, real estate commissions, GST, and incidental expenses.

By the same token, if your settlement does not include an asset that might appreciate and attract capital gains, you don't want to pay the taxes that come with those gains. To make sure you aren't taxed, you must indicate your intent to CCRA by filing the appropriate forms (referred to as filing an election) at the next tax filing after the split of assets. Imagine

Jane takes over an asset such as a painting that is subject to capital-gains tax, and the painting goes up in value. If it's sold within the next year, the tax man would want to tax her ex-husband, John. If John filed an election, the asset would be taxed in Jane's hands.

Of course, most decisions involve more than just money. Many people have a stronger emotional attachment to their homes than to their partner's RRSP. And other issues, such as not wanting to uproot children, come into play.

Once you're divorced and filing your tax return, take full advantage of all credits and deductions. If you are a single parent with children, claim the equivalent-to-married amount and you'll save about $1,400 in tax. Which parent gets to claim? The custodial parent. And a parent required to make support payments is not entitled to claim. If parents have joint custody, and no money is changing hands, only one can claim this deduction. And if you can't come to an agreement as to who should claim, you'll be cutting off your nose to spite your face, since CCRA will simply rule that no one gets the deduction.

Don't overlook the GST and child tax credit. Since they are based on family income, you may not have qualified as a family unit. However, if you are a single income earner supporting a child or you are thinking of skipping filing because you don't have much income, think again. The only way to qualify for these credits is to file, so sharpen your pencil.

Remember, too, to claim all your child-care expenses. You'll need receipts that include the caregiver's social insurance number or day-care address, but you don't have to file them. Hang on to them in case your return is questioned.

Legal fees may be tax deductible if incurred to enforce a support order. So if you have a separation agreement or support order and you had to incur legal fees to get those payments, you can deduct your legal fees. If you had to sue your spouse to get a court order for support payments, you can deduct those expenses too.

Divorce is never easy, but a little planning can make it less painful financially, especially when it comes to paying tax. Working together to resolve many of these issues may be the furthest thing from your mind, so get yourself a good lawyer and tax accountant, and let them do the job for you. The last person you should want to make money from your divorce is the tax man!

Don't forget about your will. "When you divorce," says estate special-ist Hilary Laidlaw, "the law provides that any benefit to your former spouse in your will is revoked. However, that automatic revocation does not apply to designations made with respect to your spouse. So if your spouse has been named beneficiary of an insurance policy or of your RRSP, you have to take steps to remove him as a designated beneficiary."

If you've executed powers of attorney in which you've named your ex to act on your behalf, remember to have them revoked immediately. There's no way I'd leave the decision on whether or not to pull the plug in my ex's hands, would you? The same holds true for a financial PoA. This applies to brokerage accounts where your husband may have been making most of the calls, and you executed a PoA to give him the right to trade on your behalf. "I can't for the life of me understand why a woman would ever do that," says Sandy Morris, "but if you've done it, revoke it immediately."

A reminder about documentation: If you've been married for a long time to a really, really nice guy and have signed lots and lots of paperwork that you have not kept copies of, you have to get to work to collect it all back. "Women come in to see me and have no idea what they've signed," says Sandy. "When you get to litigation, the husband is giving you all these documents and it becomes apparent that she owned this or executed that. But she has no copies and perhaps no recollection."

A final word on keeping the paperwork. When I was divorcing my second husband, I had to come up with the Decree Absolute (final divorce papers) from my first marriage. One would think that once divorced and remarried, there would be no need to hold on to the evidence of your bad judgment. But marriages, like wrinkles, can only be denied, not abolished. And so, since I had gleefully tossed all my pre-husband-number-two stuff when I was post-husband-number-two, my lawyer had to get another copy of my Decree Absolute — at a cost, of course.

20

Just in Case
You Are Widowed

All weddings are similar but every marriage is different. Death comes to everyone but one mourns alone.

JOHN BERGER

I remember being surprised as a child to learn that there was a word for a man whose wife had died: widower. I knew the word widow; I knew widows. I had never met a widower. That's not surprising when you look at the statistics. At every age, women are more likely than men to be widowed. And as we get older, we're even more likely to be left alone. At some point in their lives, nine out of 10 Canadian women will be responsible for the family finances. Since women live longer than men do — 81.1 years compared to 75.1 years, according to Statistics Canada — even if you marry a younger man, chances are you'll end up on your own at some point.

It's not unusual for women to report lapses in memory after the death of a spouse. All the key things seem to get done, but they have little recollection of how. As with other life-changing losses, such as divorce, widowhood demands time to cope. And yet in those early days it seems there is no time at all because there are so many things to take care of: making the funeral arrangements, contacting family and friends, calling the lawyer, finding the will, keeping the house running.

Coping with the financial aspects of widowhood requires that you wear two hats. First, you must close your partner's financial books and deal with what has been left. Second, you have to continue (or start) dealing with your own financial books as you move through the next stage of your life.

In the first instance, there are several financial items you must attend to:

1. You must find your partner's will, if one exists. Ideally, you've both made wills and you are aware of the contents and location of your partner's will.

2. If you are not the sole executrix, you will have to notify the executor. You should also contact an experienced estates lawyer for legal help if the estate isn't absolutely straightforward.

3. You will need to make funeral arrangements. If your partner left specific instructions in his will, you'll probably want to follow those instructions, though you're not legally bound to do so. If there are no instructions, then you'll have to decide how to handle the ceremony and his remains. Although this is technically the job of the executor, if you have not been named executor, the person who has will usually defer to your wishes as long as the cost of the arrangements is reasonable.

4. Get at least eight copies of the death certificate from the funeral home. This will save having to apply for more when you learn you need copies for just about everything.

5. Make sure your immediate cash needs will be met. If you had a joint account at the bank, the assets immediately become yours. You should transfer the funds in that account to an account solely in your name. Wait a few days to do so in case payments to your spouse or automatic deposits in your partner's name are owing and will be made shortly. If your spouse had an account solely in his name into which his income was automatically deposited, you won't be able to get to the money until the estate is settled, since his account will be frozen. You can, however, access his account to pay for his funeral.

6. Contact your husband's employer to find out what final payment (salary, bonuses, vacation pay) will be coming to you. Ask for a summary of his income for tax purposes. Find out which of his benefits you will be entitled to, and for how long. In all likelihood, you

will no longer be covered under his group benefits, which means you'll have to get your own. Since many companies have insurance in place providing death benefits for widows of employees, check this out.

7. If your partner was receiving a pension at the time of his death, you may receive all, part, or none of it. If your sweetheart was not yet retired, you may receive a lump sum from the plan; this sum can be transferred tax-free to an RRSP in your name. The plan administrator can provide you with information on all your options.

8. If you're not up to date with what your husband had and where he kept it, you'll have to start tracking down what might be out there. If your partner belonged to associations or clubs, check with them to see if there was any insurance in place. Ask the credit-card company if the card balance was insured.

Most of the activities related to tying up your partner's estate will be handled by his executor. If you are the executrix of your partner's estate and feel out of your depth handling the legalities, consider either renouncing this role and hiring a substitute (an estates lawyer or a trust company), or retaining a lawyer or trust company to act as an agent to help you through the details.

While your financial circumstances may necessitate your making some important decisions about where and how you'll live, you should resist making any life-changing decisions during the first six to 12 months. There are significant stages through which you will have to pass emotionally. Making big decisions during that first year can be tough not only on you, because of the responsibility of coming to the decision, but also on your family, because you all have to live with the consequences. You want to move as slowly as you can to maintain your own peace of mind and comfort level.

Please, please, give yourself the time to grieve. It's okay to feel sorry for yourself. Whether you've been married for five years or 50, you will feel lonely. Ask for help when you need it. Plan your days. Keep lists (a journal might also be a good idea), since you may find it hard to remember things. You are distracted by your pain, so compensate. Don't give yourself hell for being weak, wussy, or simpering. Be kind to yourself. And don't let someone else try to set the timeline for your "recovery." This is your grief and you must work through it at your own pace in your own way. Finally, don't let anyone push you into a decision with which you are not comfortable. Sadly, there are people who may try to take advantage of your confusion or distraction to satisfy their own ends. If you feel you are being pushed, push back. If you can't, tell a dear friend and let her do the pushing for you. If it is your dear friend giving the unsolicited advice, smile and nod, turn a deaf ear, and let it slip quietly past you.

Use your friends to get the nurturing you need during this difficult time. There are also support groups to which you can turn that will be able to help you pick up the pieces. Meeting other women at various stages of the grieving process will help. So will having someone to listen as you babble on about what you feel, fear, and worry about. You also need to be careful about your health and well-being. Make sure you eat. It's easy to forget, and you might think you could stand to go a few days without eating, but this isn't the time. You need physical strength to deal with your emotional hurt. If friends offer to make you a meal, accept. Don't say, "Oh, no, I don't want to be a bother." I hate that! I wouldn't offer if I didn't mean it, but I don't want to have to fight you in order to help you. Your friends probably feel exactly the same way. Let them help. Try to get some regular exercise and find a way to release the tension that will build up as you cope. Walking while focusing on your breathing can be great, and you can do it at your own pace. Try to avoid too much alcohol, caffeine, sugar, and tobacco. I know my first instinct would be to immediately light a cigarette (I quit smoking years ago) and eat a box of chocolate cookies. But this probably wouldn't help.

LIVING THROUGH IT

While the emotional part of widowhood is never easy, plenty of money makes the financial part of widowhood a lot less scary. Unfortunately, few of us are so fortunate. We may end up with a home, with or without a mortgage, some investments, some debts, and, perhaps, some insurance. But we will also likely end up with a significantly lower income. If you did not work outside the home, the death of a working partner could bring your regular income stream to a complete halt. If your spouse was retired, death could mean that the pension income you were both receiving will be cut back severely. The likelihood is that you will be cash-flow constrained, even if you are asset-rich.

The first thing you need to do is review your spending plan. With a reduced income stream, you may have to liquidate investments as a buffer to your reduced cash flow. Don't forget to apply for death benefits provided by government programs such as Canada Pension Plan, Old Age Security, and Workers' Compensation. You or your partner's executor should file the paperwork for CPP benefits as soon as possible after the death, since there is a one-year limit on the payment of retroactive benefits. It's your job to find everything that is due to you. Look everywhere for hints and clues. Talk to your partner's stockbroker, insurance agent, accountant, lawyer, and employer. Look at his old tax returns to see if capital gains were declared on investments that might now belong to you. Look in the safety deposit box, in his desk at work, in his computer files — everywhere.

On the expenses side, what can you cut? Typical things include cancelling subscriptions and memberships in clubs or organizations, and asking for a prorated rebate. Cancel disability and medical coverage you no longer need. Look at your bank statement. What's being automatically debited that should be stopped? With less regular income coming in, you may have to make some other changes to accommodate your reduced cash flow. While there are some areas in which your expenses will likely go down — now that your family is smaller, you will likely spend less on food, clothing, health, and myriad other items — some costs just don't go away. It'll cost the same to heat, light, and maintain the home.

You may have to sell your home if you find that the costs of keeping it are too high. Unfortunately, many people die without sufficient insurance to cover their outstanding debts, forcing the sale of assets to settle the estate. While a home held jointly will immediately pass to you, if the mortgage is too high for you to manage on your own, and there's not enough in the estate to pay it down, you could wind up selling and moving to a more manageable home.

When? When is the right time to tell the children, put up the sign, and start looking for the new place? That depends. It depends on how long you can maintain the status quo without digging yourself a huge hole of debt. It depends on how long you've been in the home and how attached you and your children are to the house and your neighbourhood. It depends on how willing you are to try other alternatives. Could you rent a part of the house to help carry the mortgage? Would you be willing to share with a friend in a similar position? What are your other options?

There's never an easy, black-and-white answer to any question that involves feelings and money. It's a matter of balancing the need to live within your spending plan with your emotional needs. What's important to remember is that your feelings will be in turmoil, so you should ask someone who doesn't have a vested interest in the decision to help you work through the pros and cons. That's not necessarily your grown children who would love it if you would move closer, or your sister who would love it if you would let her live with you because she loves your cooking, or your best girlfriend who is a real estate agent and knows she can get you a terrific price right now. By definition, this impartial, unbiased other party shouldn't have anything to gain by any decision you make.

If you have not already done so, you'll have to establish a financial identity for yourself. That means setting up a chequing account in your own name, applying for credit cards, and the like. Women who have never had to manage money before sometimes panic at the thought of all they have to do. I remember seeing Joan Rivers being interviewed after the death of her husband. She said she didn't even know the name of her bank. Imagine. She's no dumb bunny, yet she left so much up to her husband that she didn't even know where to begin.

First thing: don't panic. It may take time to figure everything out, but you'll do it. Take it one step at a time. Breathe deeply, and then go through every piece of paper on his desk, in his drawers, in his pockets. Piece the puzzle together so that you have the full picture.

What if you don't like the picture? The accounts are overdrawn. There are bills that haven't been paid in months. The life insurance policy lapsed because the premiums weren't paid. I'm so sorry if you have to live through this, but live through it you will. You will be brave. You must let your friends help if they can. You must come to terms with the fact that you are now in complete control of your destiny.

You have to start somewhere, and somewhere is the bank. Go in and speak with the bank manager with whom your partner was dealing. If you feel that relationship is in the dumpster because of how far in the hole your husband was, then it's time to search for a new, friendly banker. Ask a friend for a referral and a personal introduction. The more sway your friend has, the more willing the new banker will be to accommodate your needs. Be honest. Tell the banker what's happened and what your plans are.

When Rhonda's husband died, leaving her high and dry with no way to meet her expenses (she had a job, but it wasn't enough), Rhonda went to her banker. She described her predicament and explained that she would be selling her house within the next six months. Because she had a good relationship with her banker, she was approved for a loan to get her through the crunch. She made it through, sold the house, repaid the loan, and is completely loyal to her banker.

If you've never written a cheque before, don't know a PIN from an ABM, and can't imagine how you're going to get by, ask for help. Your banker can help. Your best friend can help. Even your children may be able to help. Don't be embarrassed. The fact that you don't know is nothing to be embarrassed about. The only thing you should be embarrassed about is if you are unwilling to learn. It's time to move ahead. Ask for help.

If you think you may be faced with shortages in your cash flow, consider applying for overdraft protection as a way of avoiding NSF cheques. Of course, you won't need overdraft protection if you spend only what you have available. Hah! In a perfect world. The fact is that from time to time people find themselves in a cash-flow squeeze. You can use overdraft protection to ensure that squeeze doesn't have a long-term negative impact on your credit rating. Remember, however, that overdrafts charge significantly higher rates of interest than other forms of credit.

If you've never had to manage money before, you need to establish a credit identity for yourself, and you must keep it healthy. Having a whole bunch of credit cards that you never use doesn't win you brownie points. The only way your credit identity will shine is if you use your credit and repay it on time. And if you use the right kind of credit — credit cards, for example — building a credit history doesn't have to cost you a cent.

Since credit cards only charge interest when your balance has not been paid off in full, if you pay off your balance each month, you pay no interest. You will have used the bank's money for anywhere from 30 days to 60 days — and it will have cost you absolutely nothing. What a deal!

If you don't have any credit history, it may not be easy to qualify for your first card. One way is to use a secured credit card. With a secured credit card, the issuer has to assume no risk — which is why they're willing to give you the card — because you provide the credit-card company with enough cash to cover your balance. Financial institutions typically want twice the amount of credit you're asking for. So if you want a credit card with a $500 balance, you must put up $1,000 in cash. After you've made regular payments for about a year or so, the financial institution will drop the security requirement and return your deposit. And once you've had one credit card and established a good credit rating, you will always be able to get another or have your limit raised.

Remember to cancel your partner's credit cards. While you're at it, check to see if your spouse had creditor life insurance to take care of outstanding balances. If not, the estate will have to settle up.

If you are widowed while you are still working and building that nest egg for the future, you may face one of three scenarios. You may find everything taken care of financially by a smart, well-prepared partner who was insured to the eyeteeth and had dotted all the i's and crossed all the t's. You may find yourself with little or nothing, struggling just to make ends meet. Or you may be somewhere in the middle.

If you are left in sound shape financially, you'll still have to make some decisions about how to invest the money you've been left. If it's in a trust and there's no thinking involved, carry on! Chances are, if you're an in-charge kind of person, you'll want even a modicum of say in how your money works for you. Get educated about investing even as you take the advice of trusted lawyers, financial planners, accountants, and the like. Remember, this is *your* money we're talking about. Don't be passive about it.

If you are struggling to make ends meet, I'm sorry you have to be dealing with your grief and a financial nightmare at the same time. It shouldn't happen that way, but it often does. It is important to do whatever is necessary to get yourself back on track, and then take care of the future.

If you're somewhere in the middle — you have no horrendous debts, but you'll have to continue working for a living — once you've dealt with the pain, anger, and despair of being left, you can get back on track. You, too, will need to take care of your future, one day at a time.

If you always figured you didn't really need an emergency fund because you had your partner, it's time to get an emergency fund. Depending on whether you are working or retired, you will need more or less. If you are retired and have a regular flow of retirement income, the emergency fund will help if something untoward happens. If you are still working, you not only need to protect yourself from unusual expenses, you need to protect yourself from interruptions in your income (due to illness or layoff), so you need a very healthy emergency fund. Failing that, make sure you have a line of credit.

If you have children, parents, or anyone else who is now dependent on your income, you may need life insurance. If you don't have dependents, in most cases, life insurance shouldn't be a consideration. However, if you receive a number of assets from your partner on which no tax had to be paid but on which a whopping amount of tax may be owed at your death, life insurance could help offset the tax bite for your heirs. You'll have to weigh the cost of the insurance against the need to protect your children from the tax man.

If you were covered for health benefits under your spouse's plan, you will probably have to go shopping for coverage for yourself and your kids. You might also consider upping the amount of disability coverage you have, depending on your other financial resources.

Remember to change the beneficiary designations on your own insurance, RRSPs, RRIFs, or anything else on which your partner was your beneficiary.

As a widow, you will inherit your husband's assets without tax consequence. Usually, at death, a person is deemed for tax purposes to have disposed of all their assets at fair market price. So if someone owned 200 shares of a stock bought at $20, and at the time of death the stock was worth $40 a share, the estate would have to declare a capital gain of $20 a share and pay tax on that gain. However, since you, as the widow, may inherit the shares at their original cost, there is no capital gain, so no tax is payable until you sell the shares or die, whichever comes first.

Your spouse's RRSPs or RRIFs can also be rolled to you on a tax-deferred basis. You won't have to pay any tax on the money, provided you roll the funds, referred to as a "refund of premiums," directly to your own RRSP or RRIF. Or you could use the funds to buy a life annuity or a fixed-term annuity to age 90.

A financially dependent child or grandchild under the age of 18 can also be named as the beneficiary of an RRSP or RRIF. To be "financially dependent," the child's income must be less than the basic personal exemption and no one else must have claimed a tax credit on the child's behalf. The assets are then passed to the child, but they must be used to purchase an annuity for a fixed number of years; that number cannot exceed 18 minus the minor's age at the time the annuity is purchased.

In terms of benefits you may receive from government programs, while the CPP widow's benefit is taxable in your hands, the monthly orphan's benefit (paid for children under 25 as long as they are in school) is considered to be your child's income and taxable in his or her hands. If you plan to invest that money for your child, take care to keep it separate and apart from other money so that it is easily identified by CCRA as the child's money. Insurance proceeds are also free of tax.

You'll need to visit your estates lawyer to change your will, powers of attorney, and any other documents in which your spouse was named. As well, decreases or increases in assets resulting from the death of a spouse mean you should review your own estate plan thoroughly.

PREPARING FOR IT

Regardless of whether your partner suffered a terminal illness or the death of your spouse came as a complete shock, the finality will be staggering. If you know you will be widowed — that your partner's passing is only a matter of time — then there are some things you can do to prepare. The obvious ones include things like making sure that all your insurance is paid up, that you have cash readily available so you aren't cash-flow poor while the estate is being probated — this would be a good time to consider a joint account — and that you know where everything is so you're not scrambling to come up with the documentation you may need. You should also begin to assume some, if not all, of the responsibility for the financial side of your family's life so you are well equipped to continue on your own.

However, there are many less obvious things you may need to consider. In some cases, you may find yourself facing huge debt as you also come to terms with your aloneness. If there is no way around this — if it is a matter of care for your beloved — then get yourself emotionally ready for accepting this debt all on your own. Another less obvious issue: Will you remain in your current home on your own? Will you feel secure? How will you cope with the memories? While it is never a good idea to make big decisions so close to an emotionally traumatic event, if you are given time to prepare, this could be one of the things you seriously think about.

The other thing you can do to prepare is get in touch with organizations you may need to use as support. Widows' groups and grief-counselling workshops, for example, will make things easier. You may not feel you need them now, and that's okay. After all, friends are friends no matter where you meet them. Consider too that you may not want to meet new people as you initially work through your grief. By forming those alliances sooner rather than later, however, you eliminate the stress of meeting new people at an already stressful time.

Finally, buy yourself a good book on grief and have a read. Elisabeth Kübler-Ross wrote *On Death and Dying* in 1969 and it is still considered the definitive guide to coping with grief.

21

Just in Case
You Inherit

Men possessed of money, like men earlier favored by noble birth and great title, have infallibly imagined that the awe and admiration which money inspires were really owing to their own wisdom or personality.

JOHN KENNETH GALBRAITH

If you've had to deal with the loss of someone very close to you, then give yourself time before you do anything with your inheritance. Six months to a year is the time frame most often mentioned when we talk about getting over the stress of the loss, and dealing with your head and heart in the same place. For those who inherit without a huge sense of loss, it's still a good idea to let the money rest for 30 to 90 days so you can think clearly and make plans. A money-market fund would be just the ticket. Don't invest in anything you haven't researched, like a new business or unfamiliar investment option. And don't take investment advice from people you don't know or who don't have the expertise.

LIVING THROUGH IT
Of course, part of the fun of getting a windfall is dreaming about what you'll do with it. It's okay to go a little crazy. That's part of the fun of life. But before you blow your stash, remember that this could be a turning point.

Don't forget to have some fun. We have to be so practical most of the time that it's easy to forget that money is simply a tool to help us get the things we need and want. An unexpected windfall is a great excuse to treat yourself and someone you love to something special.

This would be a good time to review your spending plan. If there have been areas where you've been skimping, you may be able to flesh them out now. However, heed this warning: it doesn't take long to get used to a less restrained spending plan, so it will be hard to pull back later. Sure, you can undo the belt a few notches — just don't be tempted to replace it with an elastic waistband.

You have *no* excuse for not establishing or beefing up your emergency fund. No ifs, ands, or buts. *Do it!*

Been hankering for a home of your own? Here's the perfect opportunity to get into your own place. If you have enough to buy outright, good for you. Don't be a fool about how much you spend. Negotiate hard. Every nickel you save today is a nickel you'll have tomorrow (and we all know that life has a way of changing). If your inheritance is sufficient to give you a downpayment on your home, be careful that you don't buy too much simply because you have a decent downpayment. Remember, the smaller your mortgage, the easier it is on your cash flow and the less you'll spend in interest.

Remember to consult your spouse before you go off on a spending spree. When Alice inherited money from her aunt, she decided to surprise her husband, Mark. She knew Mark had always wanted a house with a large porch and a huge garden, so she bought him one. She couldn't understand why he was so angry. He couldn't believe she had made such an important purchase without his input. She thought he was ungrateful. He thought she was being unreasonable.

My husband's always wanted a house with, in his words, "a large footprint." He means he wants lots and lots and lots and lots of space. I just know that if he ever laid his hands on enough money all at once, we'd be moving to a bigger (more to clean) house. I, on the other hand, just want to be mortgage-free. We've talked about this a lot. I told him I'd love a house with a bigger footprint, as long as it didn't have a mortgage. We've agreed on that as a future strategy. Of course, we've never had to put it into practice since no one's dumped a barrel of money in our laps. The important thing is that we've talked about it.

Make a list of the things that are important to you. Then decide which you can affect with your inheritance. Perhaps you want to invest in the future. Use a portion of your cash to do something to enhance your career options. Have you been thinking about upgrading your skills? Want to try your hand at working for yourself? Use part of your stash to get you going or help with your cash flow as you move to the next stage of your career. Retirement is also in your future. You're likely to be retired for more than 30 years, so consider contributing to an RRSP. You may have unused room you can catch up. That'll make for a tidy nest egg and a handsome tax refund.

If you want to invest for your children, use part of your windfall to jump-start an educational fund. With university costs expected to soar in coming years, that's another solid investment in the future. Ten thousand dollars invested in an educational fund at 12% will equal $60,000 in 15 years, just when junior is getting ready to head off to university.

Shopping for the right chequing or investment account is always important, but now that you've got more financial clout, it's time to throw your weight around. Years ago I sold a piece of property my company owned. My broker, Ann Richards, talked me into opening up a Triple A account at Wood Gundy. She convinced me that the fee (a hefty $200 a year) would be offset by the benefits. Well, she was right. The account paid substantially more interest than I was earning on my old Bank of Montreal corporate account. In fact, in just two months, the entire annual fee was covered. After that, it was gravy. And the statements are so detailed and well designed that reconciling has never been easier. I would never have known about this account if Ann had not introduced me to it. And this raises an interesting question: If a brokerage house can afford to pay me substantially more interest than can a bank account, what's wrong with the bank's approach to business?

Ultimately, it is your responsibility to find yourself the best deal going. It helps to have a relationship with someone in the know, but if you don't you aren't stymied. You simply have to do more legwork. Call around. Ask for brochures. Negotiate fees and rates. Demand more and you'll get more.

You may want to use your inheritance to rectify some of your past mistakes. A lump-sum cash influx can help to eliminate or minimize past lapses in judgment or unfortunate financial circumstances. Get rid of as much of your debt as you can. Start with the debt that's costing you the most in interest. Getting rid of your high-cost debt gets you back into the black faster and can save you a whack of interest. Paying off a $5,000 balance on a credit card that charges 17% in interest can mean savings of up to $850 in interest in just one year.

If you have an outstanding RRSP loan or a balance on your personal line of credit, or if you have used expensive financing to buy household items, pay it off. Then use the money you would have made in monthly payments to save for that special purchase or holiday. With a little patience and some planning, you'll still be able to go to Disney World while saving a ton of interest.

Have a mortgage? While interest rates are relatively low right now, over the life of your mortgage you could pay up to double the original cost of your home because of that interest. A one-time pre-payment of $10,000 on a $100,000 mortgage amortized for 25 years at 10% will save up to $52,223 in interest and get you to the mortgage-burning party 6.25 years sooner.

Trying to decide between your mortgage and your RRSP? Most financial institutions have computer programs that can help you see the relative value of each option. Let them do the math for you so you can choose the option that gives the best return. Of course, you could follow a balanced approach and do both. If your marginal tax rate is 40% and you contribute $10,000 to an RRSP (as a regular contribution or to catch up past unused contributions), you'll get a tax refund of $4,000. Use that as a mortgage pre-payment.

To decide what you'll do with the money you have left over for investment, answer the following questions:

- How much do I want to keep easily available just for the fun of spending it (or helping to pay the bills)?
- Do I need an income from my inheritance to make my life more comfortable?
- Do I want my capital to grow to provide for retirement or for an estate for my children?

These questions lead you to the three considerations for investing, aside from your investment personality, which we talked about in Part II. They are your need for liquidity, your need for a regular stream of income, and your desire for growth. If you're an experienced investor, you may feel comfortable figuring this all out on your own. Chances are if you've come into a bundle of cash for the first time in your life, you'll need help figuring out what to do with it. Get yourself an excellent financial adviser before you do much about your money (see Chapter 13).

Do you still need insurance? That depends. You need enough capital so that if you should die, your family would have enough money to pay off all its debts, provide for your children's education, pay your final taxes, and generate enough income to support the family comfortably. If your estate will do that without insurance, scrap your plan. If you plan to invest your inheritance in a business or in some other endeavour where there is a chance the money won't be there if you die prematurely, keep your insurance. You may be able to scale back, but totally eliminating it may mean you would have to buy it again, at more expensive rates, if your financial picture changes.

The same holds true for your disability insurance. If your inheritance provides enough income to support you (and cover your medical expenses) whether you're working or not, then you may no longer need to carry hefty disability premiums. But be quite sure before you cancel your policy that you will no longer need it. With all that money, you can probably afford to maintain the premiums and protect yourself and your family's future, *just in case!*

Several years ago, a young woman in Ontario won an obscene amount of money in the lottery, and the media kept asking me (and several other financial people) the same question: "What should she invest that money in?" Over and over I said the same thing. "She doesn't have to worry about investing, she has $21 million. Now she has to worry about taxes and estate planning."

While an inheritance is usually delivered net of taxes, once it's yours, any income earned on the capital (or any appreciation realized by the sale of the asset) is taxable in your hands. Make sure you have a good tax accountant.

If you plan to pass any of your inheritance on to your children, then you'll need to do some estate planning to protect your newfound wealth. Get thee to an estates lawyer for advice.

22

Just in Case You Lose Your Job

Work is the price you pay for money.

ANONYMOUS

One of the life events that can shake a girl to her very foundation is losing her job. Not only do you have to consider the financial implications — how are you ever going to make the next rent payment? — but significant social and psychological issues come into play. There's the loss of self-esteem associated with being terminated, regardless of the reason for termination. There's the sense of not knowing what to do next. And there's the loss of relationships; all those people with whom you worked will soon forget who you are as they move on with their lives and you with yours. It can seem pretty dismal, but you will live through it. You've got to grit your teeth, believe you will be fine, and keep moving.

LIVING THROUGH IT

Before you can move ahead, you'll have to deal with the personal anxiety of having joined the ranks of the unemployed. First comes the immediate sense of panic. How will you tell your partner? the kids? your mother? While you may find it hard to believe right now, these very people whom you fear telling will provide you with enormous support to help you deal with the trauma and get back on your feet.

If you're feeling a sense of guilt or your self-esteem is lower than the belly of a snake, take a deep breath. There is no point in blaming yourself. You likely had little control over what happened. Today's economic reality is very different from the past, so we can't use the old rules and standards to make judgments about our worth and accountability. Shake loose the feelings that try to invade and focus on the future. Yes, you will get another job. No, you haven't let your family down. Yes, you will be fine, and so will they.

If you're furious at the world, know that this is a part of your response to the situation. You must get past this stage so you can make a convincing show when you go knocking on doors. Don't deny the anger; that will just delay your recovery. Do what you must to get past it. Meditate. Kickbox. Talk, talk, talk.

Perhaps the most important thing you will have to learn to do is ask for help. For many people, this is the most difficult of all. It shouldn't be. People love to help; just ask. And since you're far more likely to get another job because someone you know knows someone else than from the traditional route, tell everyone you know when you're ready to go back to work.

So often, the shock of the announcement throws people into a tailspin and the last thing they feel like doing is sitting down to make a plan. But if you want to be successful in dealing with your unemployment, you'll need a plan. First you'll have to come to terms with your significantly reduced cash flow — forced simplicity, right? Then there's the prospect of going job hunting. You'll need an up-to-date résumé, a good idea of the work you want to do next, and lots of contacts to get you that next job. Will you need to upgrade your skills? This could be the perfect time to do it. Ever considered self-employment? Don't rush into anything, but starting your own business may be the answer to your joblessness. Finally, there are the things you must do to keep yourself healthy as you deal with the stress of the termination and the job hunt. Some turn automatically to exercise routines. Others feed their emptiness with food. What will you use as your outlet?

Typically, when individuals are terminated due to economic factors (i.e., not a performance-related termination), the dark cloud is often accompanied by a silver lining: a severance. Mandatory only in Ontario and in federally regulated industries, severances have become nationally accepted based on legal precedent set in courts across the country. So one of your first questions should be: "How much do I get?"

Severance can be given as either a lump sum or as salary continuance. It's all a matter of whether you want to take the full amount into income in one fell swoop, or use the salary continuance option to provide a regular flow of income that would extend over a longer period of time.

If you decide to take your severance all at once, consider using the retiring allowance provision of an RRSP to shelter some or all of the money. "Retiring allowance" is a misnomer, since it is money received both on retirement and at termination and includes unused sick leave (but not accrued vacation pay). The portion of your severance that you can roll over to your RRSP includes $2,000 for each year of employment up to and including 1995 plus an additional $1,500 for each year of employment, prior to 1989, for which employer contributions to a pension plan or deferred profit-sharing plan on your behalf were not made or have not vested.

If your severance exceeds your rollover room, the next place to look is your unused RRSP contribution room. Now that you have the money, this would be the time to catch up all those contributions not made.

Concerned about rolling money to an RRSP that you might very well need to live on while you look for a job? Don't be. As long as you choose an investment that leaves you the flexibility to pull money from your plan should you need it, you're set. A money-market mutual fund would be perfect. Monthly or quarterly, you can pull the amount you need to cover your living expenses while unemployed. You may have to pay a fee for withdrawals, so check with your financial institution before you decide how often to dip in. Once you get a job, you can deploy the money remaining to more aggressive investment alternatives.

When you cash in all or part of an RRSP, you'll pay withholding tax (a pre-payment of income tax) at the time of withdrawal. Outside Quebec, the rate is 10% on the first $5,000, 20% on withdrawal amounts between $5,000 and $15,000, and 30% for amounts over $15,000. Then when you file your tax return for the year you made the withdrawal, you'll have to include any amounts withdrawn in your income, and your true taxes owing are calculated based on your marginal tax rate. So consider yourself warned: It may turn out that your withholding tax was insufficient to cover the tax you really owe on the withdrawn income, and you'll have to dish out some more.

While you may pay significantly less tax on RRSP withdrawals because your income while unemployed is considerably lower, try to make your withdrawals in denominations of $5,000 or less. You'll pay less withholding tax, and you won't end up with extra money outside the RRSP should the perfect job suddenly appear on the horizon. More on RRSP withdrawals a little later.

Having figured out how much you'll receive from your employer, the next step is to take stock of what you have accumulated. If you set up an emergency fund, and you have the required three to six months' expenses covered, you now have proof that *telesis* works.

Make a list of all the assets you've accumulated: cash in the bank, money in money-market funds, CSBs, GICs, term deposits, investments in mutual funds, stocks, or bonds, as well as any other sources of income you may have.

Unless you're one of the filthy rich (why does the language of money always sound as though it could use a good bath?), you're going to have to cut back. Review your spending plan to see which expenses can be reduced and which can be eliminated. Do you need to keep the kids in full-time day care? Could you make arrangements with friends and family to spell you off when you need to go for an interview? This could save big bucks. What about your transportation and lunch costs? Those will go down. So, too, will your ordering-in and eating-out costs, since you'll have the time to make dinner at home now that you're not running in the door at 7:30 p.m.

Think about the kinds of things you could do on a freelance or part-time basis while you are looking for a full-time job. Would your former employer consider using your services as a freelancer or consultant? What other employers might? Who have you met through your work who has expressed appreciation for or satisfaction with your efforts on their behalf? Offer to buy lunch, tell them what you want to do next, and ask them to help. Network, network, network.

Finally, make a new spending plan incorporating both the reduced income and reduced expenses you've worked through. How much of a shortfall is there? How will you cover it? Will you use your line of credit and hope you get back to work before you're in debt for the rest of your life? Or will you liquidate assets to fill the hole in your plan?

If you're considering tapping your RRSPs, think carefully. Money you take out can never be replaced, so it's gone for good. If the mortgage has to be paid and food put on the table, and the RRSP is the only resource you have, then the answer is self-evident.

If you can delay making the RRSP withdrawal until the calendar year following your layoff and severance (depending on when in the year you got the old heave-ho), you'll be taking that income in a year when you have yet to earn any other income. That may mean a lower marginal tax rate, depending on when you return to work. Think about the timing carefully before you start pulling money out of your RRSP.

By the way, don't be so proud that you forget to apply for EI benefits, and when those run out, any other benefits to which you may be entitled. You've helped to support the system with your taxes and premiums. Now it's your turn to use the benefits. Taking care of yourself and your family means taking advantage of every option available to stay afloat during the storm.

Assuming you don't have an emergency fund, or it has run out, and you are scrambling to come up with enough money to get by each month, here are some things to consider:

- Can you skip a mortgage payment? Some mortgage agreements allow you to skip a payment and have the amount added to your principal. While this increases your loan, it keeps your credit history from becoming tarnished.
- Do you have a line of credit that you can use to help make ends meet? People often don't think about using a line of credit for emergencies until an emergency arises. But you need a job to qualify for the line. If you're a responsible borrower and don't have a history of using your credit to the limit, getting a line of credit before you need it may be a good idea.
- Are there assets you could sell to help make ends meet? This would be the time to sell assets that have appreciated, or to reap the benefits of long-term compounding interest. What's the point of having assets if you can't bring yourself to sell them when you need the money?
- Can you borrow against your life insurance policy? If your life

insurance has a cash-value component, you may be able to borrow against it to supplement your cash flow in the short term.

Okay, so you have no way of paying the mortgage and you're sure you'll end up losing the house. If you rent, you may already be looking for cheaper digs. Relax. Don't allow your emotions to make your decisions for you. Money, as much as we insist on making it an emotional issue, is really best dealt with logically. So before you stick that sign up on the lawn or pack your life's belongings to move, think about what you could do to cope. There are always alternatives.

Perhaps you could convert part of your home and rent it to supplement your current cash flow. Whether you own or rent, a roommate may be one way of reducing your expenses. While the initial idea of having roomers and boarders may be offensive, vile, intrusive, if it means you can stay where you are, if it means you can limit the disruption to your family's life, isn't it worth considering?

After some deliberation, you might decide that selling your home is the best option. It is most likely to work to your advantage if you have built up considerable equity and can use it to get yourself reestablished. If you're swapping a $1,200-a-month mortgage payment for a $1,200-a-month rental payment (yes, there are people who have done this), you may not be seeing the picture clearly. Ask friends for advice, consult a trusted real estate agent, check with your mother. Ultimately, you'll end up doing what feels right for you. But with enough input, you will have considered all the angles and can follow your instincts.

Are there areas you've wanted to explore previously that you've never had time to delve into? Now you have time. But it won't last forever, and there will always be something that could take priority over your dream. If you really want to try something new, *do it!*

Financial advisers often say that you should think carefully before you decide to go into business for yourself. That's true. But if you don't have a job anyway, and you have a good idea for employing yourself, why not go through the process of putting a plan together? What have you got to lose but time, and you've got plenty of that, right?

Make sure you don't get mired in your own misery and stop dreaming. If it's taking longer than you thought to get back into the swim, don't spend the time you have sitting on the couch watching *One Life to Live.*

Remember, one life is all you have, so don't waste it. Volunteer. Get involved with your local school, church, hospital, shelter, library, whatever. Stay busy. Meet people. Give of yourself. And keep telling people what you want. Believe, and you will get what you want.

You probably should consolidate all your money in one place for a couple of reasons. First, it will help you see what you have. Second, it will likely cost less in service charges and fees. You may even earn some interest. If you have a partner, talk about how you're going to handle the day-to-day money management. If you've always done it and you're feeling a little overwhelmed, this might be the time for your partner to spell you off, at least until you feel less shaky. If your partner has been in charge, now that you've got some extra time on your hands, maybe you should take a run at managing the spending plan. Whatever the outcome, the only way you're going to get through this crisis intact as a couple is to talk. Talk, talk, talk, talk, talk. If you're in the unhappy circumstance of not being able to talk to your partner, find a friend with whom you can bounce ideas around. It's important that you not stay bottled up. Some of the worst decisions are made when an issue is seen from only one perspective.

Now is not the time to make large expenditures. If you have committed to buying a new car, investing in your best friend's business, or going on a vacation, back out. If there is a penalty to pay, so be it. You are going to need every red cent you can lay your hands on to get you through the next little while.

So, should you tell your creditors you don't have a job, or should you hold back for fear they may revoke your only source of cash flow? Good question. Like almost everything else in life, it depends. Don't tell creditors who can call the loan, because ten-to-one they will. This is one good reason why it makes sense not to have all your financial business in one place. (Everyone always talks about the benefits of consolidation. Here's a case where it may not be to your advantage.) If you have your mortgage at ABC Bank and your personal line of credit at XYZ Bank, you can call your mortgage company and negotiate a deal without running the risk that your PLC will be revoked. If you're carrying credit-card debt, you should call and work out a payment option. If you owe taxes, you should call CCRA and work out a payment program.

No matter who's holding the paper on you, consider negotiating a reduction of interest and/or principal. In the first case, there's no point in the lender putting you into bankruptcy with astronomically high interest rates. In the second case, if you can pay off three-quarters of the entire balance, the lender may be willing to settle for that rather than losing the whole shebang to bankruptcy. Negotiate. Smile. Be very sweet. Since you are the fairer, more delicate sex, you might as well play it for all it's worth. This is not the time to be argumentative, authoritarian, or sly. You can be firm without sounding like a bully. You can negotiate without threats. Be upfront, honest, and sincere about wanting to work something out. Remember, your circumstances have changed, not your character.

While it may initially seem like a smart thing to do, reducing or eliminating your insurance to save on the premiums while you are unemployed can have long-term negative consequences. Applying for new coverage later may require a medical checkup and a new policy may exclude pre-existing conditions. Never mind the increased cost of premiums based on your new and improved age! Bottom line: don't cancel your insurance.

Check with your benefits coordinator at work to see if you can take on the premiums of your existing insurance benefits in order to continue being covered. If you've had difficulty qualifying for life insurance because of age or health, converting your group policy to an individual policy is one way to start building your insurance portfolio.

Also keep in mind that employment insurance benefits may be clawed back if your net income exceeds a specific amount ($58,500 in 1997). The total amount clawed back will never exceed 30% of the benefits, but the remaining 70% will be taxable in the normal way. While employment insurance benefits may help with cash flow initially, you may find that almost all your benefits are grabbed back when you file your next tax return. Just a warning so it doesn't come as a complete shock.

PREPARING FOR IT

You've just been given notice. You have three weeks, three months, or something in the middle to adjust to the idea that you are going to be out of work shortly. Perhaps it is only the rumour of massive layoffs that has you worried. If you think the axe might fall, and it may be your head that rolls, it's time to start planning.

Start your job search immediately. Get that résumé up to date and put the word out that you're exploring your options.

Prepare a spending plan for surviving should your worst fears be realized. Your spending plan should cover at least six months. Eliminate all discretionary spending for items such as clothing, meals in restaurants, and entertainment. Beef up your emergency fund. Start paying off your debt with vigour. Charge nothing more on your credit cards. Pay cash for everything, or use your debit card, and make sure you keep meticulous records so you stay on track financially. If you have several loans or many credit cards with outstanding balances, this may be the time to consolidate so you have a single payment and are paying lower interest. When the lender asks why you want the loan, say that you want to reduce your interest costs and have the convenience of a single payment. Do not indicate that your job is at risk.

Review your investments to see what may be liquidated easily, and what should be restructured to provide you with some income during your sabbatical.

23

Just in Case You Have to Relocate

I will arise and go now, and go to Innisfree,
And a small cabin build there, of clay and wattles made:
Nine bean-rows will I have there, a hive for the honey-bee,
And live alone in the bee-loud glade.

W. B. YEATS

You've been transferred. Or, perhaps, you've decided that new scenery would be just the ticket for a fresh start. Maybe you're taking a new job that requires a move halfway across the country. Whatever your specific circumstances, it's important to realize that relocating has significant stresses associated with it, many of them financial.

LIVING THROUGH IT

Depending on how far you move and how different your new environment is, you should take stock of what may change in your spending plan. Some expenses seem obvious: the cost of housing may be more or less expensive, as may the cost of things such as food, clothes, and other consumables. Other less obvious expenses: utilities, transportation, and insurance. Is the new neighbourhood school to your liking or will you have to spend extra on private schooling? How far away is the local community centre — a walk or a drive? What about the costs for child care? Since you don't have a neighbour network yet and you may have left your entire support system behind, even getting out for routine tasks may be challenging.

Then, of course, there are all the costs associated with the move itself: the cost to sell and buy a new home or to get out of a lease; the movers; transportation for you, your partner, your kids, and your pets, including meals and lodging. All the little things will add up to a substantial kick to your spending plan. This might be a great time to hold the mother of all garage sales and get rid of unopened wedding presents, baby clothes, school mementos, and all the other paraphernalia you've accumulated.

If you haven't yet considered making a spending plan for moving, consider it now. It's not that things won't come up. They sure will. (Will you ship the car, or sell here and buy a new one there? Will you feed the cat the tranquillizer, or take it yourself?) But you're much more likely to get through it unscathed if you have thought through those what-ifs and created a pool of funds for dealing with the unexpected.

Get copies of the local newspapers for several weeks before the move so you can start to mentally acclimatize to your new area. You'll be able to uncover scads of information if you make like Sherlock and snoop. What are the local prices in the new area compared with those of your current stores? Who are the major retailers? What types of events are held in your neighbourhood? What types of social, community, or religious supports are there? Will there be a climate change that warrants a different wardrobe in your new location? What are houses going for?

If you're moving to a part of the country of which you know little, it can be stressful trying to decide where to live. And if you're working with a fixed budget, as most people are, then your wishes and realities may seem miles apart. Take heart. There are things you can do to make the whole process a little easier.

Enlist the services of a real estate agent who specializes in the areas where you would like to live. That means contacting a national organization that can refer you to a local broker, or asking friends or work acquaintances who live in that area for help. (Remember, people like to help, you just have to ask.) Ask the agent for copies of listings for the area, as well as for specifics relating to schools, health care, child care, transportation, and social facilities (closest supermarket, closest hockey rink, etc.). Visit your new neighbourhood before you buy and scout it out for yourself. Do you like the feel? Does it provide everything you must have or would like to have?

Test your new location before you make the final leap. Perhaps you can sublet an apartment for a few months to see what the area will be like to live in. I stress live, because often people make their decision to move based on their holiday experiences. Visiting a place for weeks can be very different from living there for months. Before you sink money into a permanent place, try it on and see how it feels first.

Don't try setting new goals for a few months. You need time to settle in and get your bearings. There's no point in trying to plot a new course until you've had a good look at the terrain, mapped the stars, and looked at the opportunities. But don't delay doing this forever either. It's easy to get wrapped up in the day-to-day excitement, frustration, and stress of living in a new place and completely lose track of your goals. Allow yourself about six months to settle. You might decide then that you need a little more time. If you've hit a year and you're still working with the old map, time to do some surveying. There's little chance, with all the changes that have taken place over the past year, that you're still perfectly on course.

Depending on where you bank, whether you move across town or across the country you may be able to maintain your existing accounts and simply carry on as usual. Our network of national banks offers us easy access to our money through branches, banking machines, computers, and the telephone. That sounds really great, doesn't it? And it's what our banks would have you believe. When our Aunty Jackie moved from the big city to a small town, she discovered the only branch of her bank in town was completely automated. She was some ticked off, I'll tell you. She didn't want to deal with a machine. She wanted a person.

It can be good to deal with a big bank, because you will likely be able to maintain all your services with little fuss. All you'll have to do is put in notices of address change and keep on trucking. Of course, if you deal with a smaller financial institution and there's no branch convenient to your new location, you'll have to go shopping.

The ultimate test of your worth to any bank will be how willing the branch people are to build a relationship with you when you move to town. After all, as a stranger to the area, you'll need help. If you're what banks refer to as "high value" you may get references to all sorts of resources you can use. If you're further down the value scale, you may find yourself with little attention and fewer services. The smaller your bank balance or use of credit, the more likely you are to need the care and attention of a smaller institution such as a credit union.

Earlier I used the word "shopping" to describe the process of choosing a new bank. You see, when I talk about your relationship with a bank — or whatever type of financial institution — I see you as the client, customer, or buyer and I see the other guy as the service provider or seller. You're spending your money (service charges and interest) to buy products and services, and the other guy is making a big profit. So, as a customer, client, or buyer, you have the right to choices. And if the other guy isn't treating you with the care and respect you deserve, one of the choices you should execute is walking across the street to the competition.

Now, you may think this would be an exercise in frustration since all banks are the same, and each one is as bad as the next. Not so, I say. They are if you paint them with the same big brush and call them by their corporate names. But if you look at the individual branches instead of the Big Name Bank, you'll see some significant differences. Every branch is made up of the people who work in it. Yes, there are corporate rules. Yes, they may even look exactly the same. But they aren't, so don't be fooled. Since no two people on earth are exactly the same, a group of people working in one branch cannot be the same as another group of people working in a different branch. All you have to do is find the right group of people.

When I moved into my current home several years ago, it was the perfect time to go shopping for a new financial institution. I interviewed five branch managers with a simple request. I wanted to pay the least in interest and service charges, earn the most return, and be treated like a queen. All but one manager told me why I could not have what I wanted. I was being unrealistic. One branch manager laughed at me. Mr. Cocky didn't get the biz. Only one manager had the wherewithal to say, "Let me show you what we *can* do for you." He got the biz.

The point of my story: You can have what you want even if four out of five dopes tell you that you can't. Just keep going until you find the one bright person who acknowledges that you are the customer, that it is your contribution to the company's bottom line that pays his wages, and that you deserve to have your needs met.

According to an Ernst & Young survey conducted in 1996, relocation is one of the most common reasons why people have difficulty making monthly credit-card payments. I have to admit I was a little surprised at first. It would make perfect sense if job loss led to missed monthly payments, as would marriage breakup. I had grossly underestimated the stress relocating places on cash flow. There might be an interruption in income. There will certainly be increased costs. The more I thought about it, the more sense it made. Have you thought about it yet?

Our first tendency when our cash flow is squeezed is to jump to the most convenient form of credit to fill the gap: credit cards. And the excitement and uncertainty of a move can create some needs that wouldn't be considered needs under normal circumstances. After all, if you've been driving for the last six hours and the kids are driving you crazy, will you really care if the next bed costs $75 a night or $125 a night? And if everyone is starving, it's a lot more likely that you'll stop at a restaurant than go shopping at a local grocery store for sandwich fixin's. Little costs add up. The king-size bed won't fit up the narrow stairway, so you'll have to buy a smaller bed. Your daughter's carpet is too big for her new room but too small to use in the basement. The coffee machine was broken in the move, and you need your coffee.

The single best way to stay on track with your credit usage is to keep a running log of what you're charging. A spending log is one way of making sure you know where your money is going and that you don't go off track. Don't add the stress of unexpected credit-card bills to the stress of your relocation. Know what you're charging and what it's going to cost you emotionally and financially.

If your expenses go up in your new location, it's a lot easier to save less than to live without, right? And if your expenses go down, it'll be better to have some extra money to spend than to have some extra money to save, right? If you agree with either of these statements, you're probably in the majority. It takes a certain discipline to look at expenses that have grown and commit to not changing the long-term investment plan. It would mean cutting back in some areas to keep 10% going to investments. It may mean giving up some of the things you previously enjoyed. On the flip side, it's a lot easier to spend money than to save it. After all, if your new lifestyle gives you more disposable income, you and your family deserve to be able to enjoy it. But it's also the perfect time to boost your savings. Split the difference. Take advantage of your extra disposable income. Put some extra money to work in investments too. After all, life is about balance.

Relocating may seem like the emergency you've been waiting for. Your expenses may have gone up. Your spending plan may have been blown. Your income may have been interrupted as you changed jobs. Yes, this may have had some emergency elements. Just remember, whatever you take out, you're going to have to put back to top up the emergency fund. It's fine to use it when you need it. After all, that's what it's there for. Just remember, tomorrow is another day, and you may need it again. Remember to restock your just-in-case larder, just in case.

Does your homeowner's insurance policy cover your contents while they are in transit? Do you need extra insurance as protection against the hazards of moving? Call your broker and find out *before* something breaks.

There are tax benefits associated with relocating to take a new job. If you move to a new home that is 40 km closer to your new work location — even if it is your own business — than was your old home, you can deduct substantial amounts for tax purposes. So, if you're planning to move, see if you can arrange to meet the tests for deducting your moving expenses.

Except where you are reimbursed by your employer, you'll be able to deduct:

- reasonable travelling costs to move all members of your household, so keep your receipts
- the moving costs for your stuff, including any storage costs, so keep your receipts
- the costs of meals and lodging near either the old or new home for up to 15 days, so keep your receipts
- the cost of cancelling a lease
- commissions and other sales costs associated with selling your old home, and legal fees and land transfer tax to buy a new home.

24

Just in Case You Have to Declare Personal Bankruptcy

O money, money, how blindly thou hast been worshipped, and how stupidly abused!

CHARLES LAMB

You're broke. After years of university, getting up for work at the crack of dawn, working until late at night, and giving up weekends and holidays, you're flat broke. You tried to save, but everything was so expensive. Or maybe your partner left with the money and you got stuck with the mortgage and all the credit-card bills. Or perhaps you were laid off seven months ago and you've been doing everything possible to make ends meet since then.

No one plans for financial disaster, but it happens. And even if you have been scrupulous with your finances, economic circumstances, family tragedy, and deception can conspire to knock down even the most well-built financial house like a pile of toothpicks. "Unemployment has been a big issue for people who come to us," says Laurie Campbell of Credit Counselling in Toronto. "Often they have been using credit to help them through their circumstances. There are people who may have had a $60,000-a-year job and are now working for $30,000. But they have not adjusted their lifestyle to fit within their new income. They fill the gap with credit."

Another big contributor to financial distress: student loans. Laurie says, "For people between 20 and 30 years of age, student loans are becoming a primary problem. Their debt loads are so high and the interest is accumulating at such a phenomenal rate that by the time they come in to see us they are at the point of insolvency."

So, what do you do now?

A good place to start is at your local credit counselling service. Arrange an appointment with a counsellor to go over your situation and help you unravel the knots. The counsellor may be able to help negotiate a repayment plan with your creditors. But if your income and assets are insufficient to enable you to dig yourself out of debt, the idea of a fresh start may be more to your liking. Keep in mind that the road there isn't easy, but it is doable. Here are some of the most frequently asked questions about bankruptcy, and their answers.

What is bankruptcy? Bankruptcy is a legal proceeding to help individuals cope with financial crisis so they can move ahead financially without being burdened by past problems. To go into bankruptcy, you must be insolvent; that is, you must owe at least $1,000 and be unable to meet your debts as they are due. You can choose to go into bankruptcy, or you can be petitioned into bankruptcy by a creditor.

You must file for bankruptcy using a trustee in bankruptcy — a licensed professional — who will act as an agent for all of your creditors while assuring your rights. At the initial meeting, your trustee will review your financial situation and advise you of your options. Usually there is no fee for this meeting. To file for bankruptcy, you must complete and sign two main documents. The *assignment* gives your trustee all your assets (other than those that are provincially exempt), which will then be sold and used to repay your debts. The *statement of affairs* shows all your assets and liabilities (like a net-worth statement). It also includes basic personal information. Your trustee will file these two documents and then notify creditors of the "meeting of creditors." You must attend this meeting, since creditors may wish to ask questions and get information about your situation. Your trustee will come up with what he or she considers a manageable repayment plan; over the course of your bankruptcy, you must make the agreed-upon monthly payments to the trustee and provide any information necessary to file your tax returns. You will be completely discharged of your debts, if all goes well, at the end of the bankruptcy.

Who will know I've gone bankrupt? If you have significant assets, a notice is placed in the "legals" section of the newspaper, notifying creditors of the date of the meeting of creditors; at the meeting, they will decide whether to accept or reject your proposal for repayment. If there are minimal assets, creditors are notified by mail. A legal filing of a bankruptcy is a public document. The bankruptcy is also recorded on your credit bureau record, and remains part of your credit history for seven years.

Are there assets I can keep? This varies from province to province. In Alberta, you are allowed to retain up to $40,000 in equity in your home. In Ontario, all home equity is assignable (i.e., given over to your trustee) to be used in repaying your debts. Depending on the province in which you go bankrupt, different allowances are available for clothing and personal effects, household furniture, tools of trade, and automobiles. An insurance contract where the designated beneficiary is a spouse, parent, child, or grandchild may be protected from seizure. This includes an RRSP or RRIF with an irrevocable designation. If you make your mortgage payments on time, the mortgagor must allow you to continue to own and live in your home. However, any equity may be assignable.

Are there debts that are not discharged? Yes. You will not be released from debts secured by an asset such as your car or your home (although those debts are limited to the value of the secured assets at the time you declare bankruptcy); nor will you be released from paying alimony, child-support payments, parking tickets, court fines, and debts obtained by fraud. Assets obtained during bankruptcy (an inheritance or lottery winning) will be taken and used to pay creditors. Your bankruptcy will not erase the liability of someone who has co-signed a loan for you. If the bankruptcy occurs while you're still a student, or within 10 years of having been one, debts or obligations for student loans are also not discharged.

When will the bankruptcy be over? For first-time bankruptcies, a discharge is automatic after nine months, if no one opposes and you have received counselling. If creditors do object, or if this is not the first time you have been bankrupt, the discharge must be heard before a judge or registrar. The discharge will usually be granted if you are earning just enough income to reasonably provide for yourself and your dependents, and so have nothing more to offer creditors.

Must I take counselling? Yes, if you wish to be eligible for an automatic nine-month discharge. Your typical cost for this is $85 per session and a minimum of two sessions is required.

What does it cost to go bankrupt? The trustee is usually paid out of the money realized from the sale of your assets. If no assets are available, a retainer is required or the trustee may allow the fees to be paid over time. The minimum cost is approximately $1,025 plus GST.

Alternatives to bankruptcy:

- Contact your creditors. Explain why you cannot make your payments and suggest an arrangement that could work for both of you. Suggest a reduced amount that you can afford to pay, or an extension of the repayment period to give you more time to make good on your debt. You may be surprised at a creditor's willingness to negotiate.

- Apply for a debt-consolidation loan. Pay off your debts with the loan advance. Not only will you then have one single monthly payment to make, but you will likely save interest because this bank loan may carry a much lower rate of interest than, say, your credit cards. Shop around carefully, since interest rates will vary.

- File a proposal. If you want to try to pay off the debts because you don't relish the idea of watching everything you've worked for sold out from under you, consider filing a proposal to your creditors. In it you would indicate how much of your debts you could afford to repay, requesting that creditors cut you some slack on interest, fees, or even principal. You decide who to include in the proposal with the help of an administrator, a person authorized to accept and manage proposals. Since all trustees are also administrators — though not all administrators are trustees — you would most likely use the same shop you would if you went bankrupt.

  If you have debts of $75,000 or less, not including your home mortgage, you can make a *consumer* proposal. This is most often used by salaried employees. Credit counselling is mandatory. If creditors reject your proposal, they may resume collection activities. Only one consumer proposal may be filed, so it should be your best offer since the alternative is usually bankruptcy. An *ordinary* proposal, usually used by those who are self-employed, has no restriction on the amount owed. Counselling is not required, but a rejection of your proposal results in immediate bankruptcy.

LIVING THROUGH IT

When you declare bankruptcy, you will have to prepare a spending plan of your monthly income and expenses. The trustee will review it and decide how much you should pay directly to him or her each month on behalf of your creditors. Trustees use a schedule provided by the superintendent of bankruptcy as a guideline in making their decision. But your trustee has the final say and can adjust your payment based on your actual income and reasonable living expenses.

Since you're going to have to live with the spending plan for at least nine months, this is a good opportunity to learn new habits. You may have already tried a budget (a masochist's word for a spending plan). If the last one didn't work, you'll have to ask yourself why. If you've never used a spending plan before, it'll take some practice, but you have to do it so *do it!*

They can't take your house. They can take all the equity you've built up, but you get to keep the mortgage payments. And as long as you continue to make the payments on time, you get to stay in your home. And you'll start rebuilding equity once your bankruptcy is discharged.

Goals, who has time for goals? I just want to get out of this mess and get my life back. That's a goal. And you have a timeline because your trustee has already explained how long the whole process will take. Now you have to live through it. But what will you do when you get to the end of the nine months and, heaven willing and you able, the bankruptcy is discharged? Now what? Go shopping to celebrate? Throw a party to declare unbankruptcy? What you should do (and I don't mean to sound preachy, but it may not be top of mind for you, and you really should do it) is set yourself some new goals. You may feel whipped. You may feel broken. So you've got to start dreaming again.

Time to make friends with your banker. In all likelihood, when you declared bankruptcy, you became persona non grata at your local branch. This would be a good time to create a relationship with a bank that was not a creditor in your bankruptcy or proposal proceedings. After all, you went through hell and back, so it's time for a fresh start. Spend some time developing the relationship with your banker by explaining what happened, how your circumstances have changed, and how much you are depending on this person to help you reestablish your credit identity.

Set up a chequing account as soon as possible and make sure you keep your nose clean. No NSF cheques. You've already been through the wringer once, don't do it to yourself again. Stick to your spending plan.

When you file for bankruptcy, you have to give up all your existing credit cards — even the ones you've paid faithfully and on which there is no credit balance. Having fulfilled your obligations, you next should visit your local credit bureau. Provide them with a copy of your certificate of discharge or full performance and ensure this is noted on your credit records. All your previous financial dealings should be expunged, and you may even want to put a short note on your own record to explain what has happened.

Once you've managed to accumulate a small amount of savings, take a loan using your investment as collateral and repay the loan over six months. This will create a record of borrowing and repayment — a new credit history.

You might also apply for a store credit card that you could use to reestablish your credit history. Use it for small amounts and repay it promptly when you receive your statement. After six months or so, apply for another card and keep it going. Eventually you will qualify for an Visa or MasterCard, at which point you should dump the store cards to avoid the ongoing temptation to spend. Remember, the more cards you have, the more likely you are to carry debt.

It may take several years to reestablish your credit history, so don't put off getting started.

Start putting aside some money each month using a periodic investment plan. It's not important how much you save each month. What is important is that you get on the bandwagon. It would be a good idea to establish an RRSP as well. Twenty-five dollars a month each to an unregistered mutual-fund portfolio and to an RRSP will create the right impression with your banker and start you back on the road to financial health.

When you declare bankruptcy, your trustee will prepare and file income-tax returns on your behalf. If the previous year's return hasn't yet been filed, that comes first. Then the year in which you go bankrupt is split in two: from January 1 to the date of your bankruptcy (referred to as your pre-bankruptcy return), and from that date to the end of the year (referred to as your post-bankruptcy return). Tax owing on the pre-bankruptcy return is included along with your other debts in the bankruptcy.

If you expected to receive a refund, say "so long" to that. It will be included in the assets the trustee must take on behalf of your creditors. As well, any GST payable to you for approximately 18 months from the bankruptcy will be directed by CCRA to the trustee.

25

Just in Case You Have to Move Back Home

Home is the place where, when you have to go there, they have to take you in.

ROBERT FROST

Thousands of 20- and 30-somethings are boomeranging back home for all sorts of reasons, many of them economic. No matter how independent you may be, circumstances may conspire to send you home to momma. If you are between jobs, spouses, or cities, you may need a place to bunk while you set yourself free of the past and noodle on the future.

If you're thinking of going home, the likelihood is that you'll be welcomed. Research done at Simon Fraser University shows that more than three-quarters of cohabiting parents and adult children surveyed were very satisfied with their situation. Of course, the extent of the satisfaction will be directly related to how well everyone is getting on. And there are some basic rules you can follow to help ensure mom and dad don't up and sell the house and move without telling you where they are going.

Don't expect things to be the way they were when you were a child, unless you want to be treated like a child. You're a grown-up now, so behave like one. That means you won't encourage your mom to do your laundry or your dad to hand over an allowance. And, even before moving in, you will have set your departure date, if at all possible.

Living harmoniously with your folks will be contingent on talking about your expectations of each other. It will be tough to redefine yourself to your parents when they maintain a firm image of you as a freckled, pigtailed 12-year-old. And they'll have a tough time getting used to the new limitations on their privacy. You'll need to be considerate of each other and honest in communicating. After all, if you can't talk to your parents about sex, then you probably shouldn't be having it under their roof.

LIVING THROUGH IT

Assuming you moved home for economic reasons, whether you've lost your job, lost your apartment, or lost your spouse, you'll need to make a new spending plan. While you should insist on paying room and board if you are working, if you are unemployed you could substitute additional housework, run errands, and generally be Helpful Hattie around the house. Chip in to keep yourself on equal footing as an adult in the house. You don't want to be considered a charity case, right? This is a temporary setback, right?

Initially, your parents may be unwilling to accept money. Tell them how important it is to you to maintain your financial independence. While the amount may not be large at first, particularly if you have debt you need to get rid of, even a token amount helps pave the way for future increases.

Your spending plan should include money for your own phone line, entertainment costs when friends come over (why should your folks buy your beer?), as well as small treats for the family as a whole. If you'll be using the family car, budget for things like gas and insurance. If you have children living with you at your parents' home, you'll have to cover all their costs and keep a budget for child care. Don't assume your parents are there to baby-sit. They may be willing, but each opportunity should be presented in a way that gives them the option to say no if it's not convenient. You could say, "Mom, I'm going to catch a movie tonight, so I'm planning to call Sarah to baby-sit, okay?" Mom can then decide to take the job if she chooses, but has an easy out if she wants the night to herself.

Moving home probably means you didn't get to where you wanted when you wanted. You may perceive the move home as a temporary measure, or you may feel that you have completely failed. Whatever you feel, work through those emotions so you can get on with living. I'd give the same advice to you as I give to people going through bankruptcy: Set yourself some new goals. Remember, a goal is a dream with a deadline, and a dream is a gift we give ourselves. You deserve the gift of a dream, and you're worth the time it takes to turn that dream into a goal that you can accomplish and be proud of achieving. It's up to you.

Often people move home when things become unmanageable elsewhere. Divorce, unemployment, and high levels of debt all contribute to the feeling that things are out of control. And if you're carrying a huge debt burden, they may be. Moving home may cut you the slack you need to get back into the black. Of course, you're never going to get there if you keep spending more than you make. If you're unemployed and make nothing, that's just what you can afford to spend.

When Donna P.'s husband left, things got way out of control. To fill the gap between what she was making and what she was spending, she called upon trusty Mr. Credit Card. Within two years her credit cards were playing the tune and she was dancing as fast as she could. As a single mother, Donna wasn't finding it easy to make ends meet. "It was costing me about $5,000 a year more to live than I was making," says Donna. "It had to come from somewhere."

Getting off the credit treadmill isn't easy but it can be done. Good money management is simply a matter of doing what you very likely already know you *should* do. Read the section on using credit wisely on pages 123–24.

Whether it is to reestablish your emergency fund or to launch or relaunch your pay-yourself-first investment plan, you have to start saving. Why? Because you're supposed to. Because if you don't, your parents may have to install a revolving front door. Because goodwill only goes so far, and then it runs out. Because you're a grown-up now and it's *your* responsibility to take care of your future.

Because although you love your parents, you don't want to live with them forever; nor do you want them to have to install a revolving front door. The more you contribute to your nest egg, the sooner you'll be out of their hair and back enjoying the independence you've temporarily left behind.

26

Just in Case Your Kids Move Home

Home again, home again, jiggarty-jig.

CHILDHOOD RHYME

Don't think this won't happen to you. Kids are more likely to move back home with you than you are to move in with them. If it happens in your family, there are some things you should consider.

Probably the most important part of this phenomenon is dealing with the emotional side of the change. If your child has been forced to move home because of a lost job, divorce, or illness, his or her self-esteem has been damaged, and your help is badly needed. Don't think you will be immune to heated moments as you redefine your roles within the new family structure. Your children may at once love you for being there to help and hate you for reminding them of their need — even if you don't say a word. And you may feel compassion for your children even while you resent being put back on duty as caregiver, financial supporter, grown-up.

LIVING THROUGH IT

While it may not be reasonable or even possible to expect a financial contribution initially, there are other solutions. Talk about how your child will help to compensate for the additional financial stress on you. Yes, you are a mommy, but that doesn't negate your child's responsibility to pull his or her load. It may mean contributing to the household in the form of rent, or cooking and cleaning in exchange for room and board — whatever works for your family. But it is important that some compensation be given for three reasons:

1. The last thing you need right now is to create a situation where your child becomes so dependent on you that he can't get his life back on track. Washing his clothes, cooking his meals, paying his way will all diminish his sense of worth as a contributor to the family. You need to have some expectations of him, just as he has some of you.

2. You'll get angry if you see your child sitting on the couch all day eating bonbons and reading magazines while you're off slaving to bring home the bacon. It's human nature. And it's hard to change the rules once they have been established. So set the rules right from the start. Yes, those rules will evolve, but establishing guidelines at the outset creates the sense that everyone has an expectation — not just your kid.

3. Fair is fair. You want to help your child, but she must want to help herself and return your kindness. Parenting may be a lifelong commitment, but financial support isn't part of that. When you choose to (or have to) support adult children, it is going above and beyond the call of duty, and that should be acknowledged.

Several years ago when I was doing a television phone-in show, an elderly lady called in to say that her son was pressuring her to lend him money for a business venture. She wanted to know what I thought about her mortgaging her house to give him a leg up. I asked her this: "Who gave you a leg up when you got started?" There was a long pause — not a good thing on television. I filled it with, "Who helped you get started?"

She said, "No one. I had to do it myself."

I responded, "Give your son the same opportunity. Let him do it for himself so he can experience all the pleasure and pride of having done it on his own."

No child should expect an elderly parent to go into debt to help him or her get started. No parent should allow a child to do that. Yet children's expectations often exceed a parent's ability or willingness. I've heard dozens of stories of children who assumed their parents' home, cottage, or other assets would be theirs some day. Why? Just 'cos! I've never believed that my parents' house, money, or anything else was mine. My retirement plan does not consist of an inheritance from my parents. I fully expect them to spend every cent before they die. It's their money. And my children will know that the same rules apply. What are your rules?

If you own your home or have a place big enough to easily accommodate your returning child (and perhaps a brood of grandchildren), none of this may seem like a big deal to you. But if you have to get a bigger place, your finances will be squeezed, particularly if your child is unable to contribute financially in the short term. Make sure you both understand the ramifications of a change of address. This should be a long-term decision (i.e., you'll be living together forever and ever), not a months-long experiment. You might decide that you and your child will share the purchase of a new home. You could use your assets to provide the down-payment while you and your child split the mortgage 75/25, with your child paying the larger share. Or you might decide to do all the supporting while your child gets back on her feet, in exchange for her doing all the supporting at some other point while you catch up your retirement savings. Talk about what will work. Bounce the plan off a good friend to ensure you're not being too hard or too soft on the kid.

If your expenses go up substantially because of a change of address, you'll need to go back and revisit your spending plan and your goals to see how they are affected. If you stop making contributions to your retirement plan because your expenses have gone up, you'll need to think about how this will affect your long-term strategy. At some point you'll have to decide whether you should change your expectations for retirement, or catch up the unsaved portion of the plan. Visit your banker and plug the figures into the latest retirement software to see the long-term ramifications.

27

Just in Case You Must Care for Your Aging Parents

If one is not going to take the necessary precautions to avoid having parents, one must undertake to bring them up.

QUENTIN CRISP

One of the most damaging myths surrounding aging is that getting old automatically means a decline in mental facilities. Our youth-oriented society makes older individuals feel less vital, less important, less significant because they are less youthful. As the baby-boomer generation ages, this attitude may change; no doubt boomers will continue to rock-and-roll through life in their nonconformist way. For now, though, we must battle our own stereotypical views of aging.

Perhaps it is human nature to be pessimistic, and it is our fear of the worst that drives us to push aside the elderly — to hide them from view so we won't have to deal with our own aging. When we see someone who's had a stroke, suffers from dementia, or is in a wheelchair, we tell ourselves, "That's what it's like to be old." We lump all older people into one demographic group. That approach is neither fair nor realistic. Older Canadians are a diverse group. As we grow older and are seasoned by life's milestones, we become more different from each other and age becomes the only common denominator.

Then there's the myth of mental decline. At 41 I forget things, as I will at 48 and 53. Women blame it on the brain cells we lose during pregnancy, and we laugh. We blame it on the fact that we must hold 17 thoughts at once, and we laugh. It's easy when we're young to dismiss it as just having too much on our minds at any given time. But when we're old and forget things, we automatically blame age. Just because a person can't balance a chequebook doesn't mean she can't handle her own financial decision making. Many young people can't balance a chequebook but would be aghast if a parent attempted to take over their financial management.

Unfortunately, when we project a limiting myth onto our aging parent, it becomes self-perpetuating. If you say anything often enough, you can make it so. Stereotypes rob people of their opportunity to participate and be independent. Ageism is insidious. You can see it in action in indicators like unemployment rates among seniors and in resource allocation decisions such as cutbacks to long-term care facilities.

LIVING THROUGH IT

Studies have shown that children are reluctant to talk to parents about financial topics. A study conducted for Trimark in 1997 showed that 35% of people agreed to the statement, "I avoid discussions about money matters with my family." When presented with the idea that adults may need to assist their aging parents in managing their financial affairs, 31% said they'd never discussed their parents' finances. Tackling the what-if questions with parents can be especially hard. But you must.

There's real danger in not knowing about a parent's financial situation. If you don't know your parents' financial status, it's hard to know what type of care would be affordable if they were to have an accident or get ill. If you don't know how your parents would want matters handled if they couldn't do it themselves, you may find yourself making important decisions in the dark. If you don't know where all the important stuff is — the money, the investments, the insurance, the safety deposit box, the will, the powers of attorney — you'll be scrambling to find them just when you're scrambling to cope with a parent's death or disability.

There are some prevailing attitudes to watch for if you find yourself in the role of caregiver. First, there's the I'll-do-the-thinking-around-here approach that involves taking total control and negating the parents' responsibility for their own lives. If this sounds like you, when did you get so smart? It's the question your mom or dad would ask if they felt up to it. And it's a good question. After all, just because your notion of what should be done is different from your parents' doesn't mean you're right and they're wrong. If you find yourself being very bossy because you're worrying about every little thing, take a deep breath. If there is no evidence that a problem exists with your parent, relax. It may be your own anxiety and guilt that drives you to make decisions for your parents that they are fully capable of making for themselves.

Then there's the it's-your-life-do-whatever-you-want approach that, through frustration or lack of serious concern, leaves parents on their own to cope. This is also sometimes a symptom of denial: Children don't want to see any changes in their parents, so they write off a parent's inability to cope as "just part of getting old," when these things are problems that could be mitigated with proper attention. It would be irresponsible to walk away from issues simply because dealing with them brings conflict or consternation. Ultimately, when you watch your parents flounder, you'll be heartbroken that you didn't step in sooner. And if they will not let you help — if they push you away to maintain their privacy, protect you from their angst, keep their identities separate — that brings its own heartbreak too. The best you can do is be at the ready with information and time when it becomes apparent that you must step in.

A 1995 guide to elder care published by North Carolina State University recommends that the person you're caring for should always be given as much control and involvement in financial decisions as possible. If you must assume full responsibility for a relative's finances, the guide recommends that you continue to share information about your decisions with other family members to reduce the possibility of later recriminations." You may even consider family meetings to discuss finances, just to keep everyone current on spending and income. It's also wise to keep good notes about significant discussions you have with family members and the actions taken as a result.

Consider sharing duties with family and friends. While some regular responsibilities, such as bill paying or deposit making, might be done most efficiently by one person, don't be bashful about asking family, neighbours, and old friends to step in. Those with legal, health-care, or financial training can be particularly helpful with certain tasks.

As life expectancy has increased, so too have the responsibilities adult children must assume in caring for aging parents. In the old days, you were finished taking care of your children by the time your parents needed attention in their final years. But couples are having children at later stages, whether because they delayed starting their families while they focused on their careers, or because they're in second marriages where babies are part of the new union. The result: More people are being crushed between child- and elder-care responsibilities.

According to the Ontario Women's Directorate and Ministry of Community and Social Services publication *Work and Family: The Crucial Balance*, women spend 17 years caring for their children and 18 years helping an elderly parent. Chances are if you're a baby-boomer, you're also a member of the *sandwich generation*. This is Faith Popcorn's term for adults who are caught between caring for their children and caring for their parents. And it only begins to suggest how overwhelming it can be trying to do it right, do it better, do it all.

It's hard to give parents advice. Sometimes it's difficult because parents continue to see their offspring as the wee ones they once cradled on their laps, and are unable to acknowledge their expertise and experience in dealing with life's issues. At other times the adult children have integrated a great deal of knowledge that has escaped their parents, and it seems they come from different worlds. Personality clashes can arise as the child attempts to become mother to the woman.

One way to approach a parent who's unwilling to reveal financial particulars would be to present several options and ask the parent which one she or he would like to pursue. You might choose to use a friend's death as a place to start talking about the what-ifs. Or the death of a celebrity may provide an opening. You might also use your own financial review to ask for parental advice and begin the discussion.

You need to know where to find your parents' personal and financial documents in the event of an emergency. Find out:

- where they bank
- where their investments (RRSPs, RRIFs, mutual funds, etc.) are held
- the names of their accountant, lawyer, broker, financial planner, and so on

- where the will is kept and who they've named as the executor
- where they keep other legal documents, such as powers of attorney
- the names of their insurance agents, companies, and advisers

You're not prying. You don't need to know what's in the will, just where it is. You don't need to know how much insurance, just where it's kept. You simply want to know what documents to look for, and where to find them in an emergency. Being aware of your parent's financial situation may also help you to ensure dividends and interest are received, insurance is paid on time, pensions are administered appropriately, and so on. Approach your parent practically and non-confrontationally in a friendly environment. Having a family meeting where several family members gang up on an aging parent won't make your mom, dad, aunt, or grandmother any more open to your suggestions. And be prepared for the fact that you may have to suggest a discussion several times, or take small steps toward getting them to fully disclose their affairs. If your parents are reluctant to talk to you specifically, offer to help in finding a professional adviser, assuring them you'll back out once they're in good hands.

Once you've got your hands on the goods, you may find stuff you just weren't prepared for: unpaid bills, misplaced documents, unfiled tax returns. Don't panic. Begin by making a list of all the things that must be remedied, write to the people who have been offended, and start cleaning up the mess. There is no point in getting angry. Yes, you will be frustrated, but the job at hand is to fix the problems, and blaming your parents won't fix them any faster.

The other thing to avoid: judging your parents' choices. So what if your mother has a million dollars sitting in a savings account earning 0.25% in interest? That's her choice. Remember, it's her money. You might make suggestions for changes, but the decision should still be hers, at least until you assume full financial responsibility. Remember, older people are often more concerned about keeping their money accessible than about earning a big return.

Cash flow will become an issue for you when your parent or parents can no longer handle the routine transactions themselves. And there are a whole bunch of concerns that you'll have to address, ranging from who will pay the bills to how long the money will last. There may be plenty of expenses too, depending on the parent's health. Consider the costs of a stair lift or bath bench, or a scooter, walker, or cane. It's important that you check with your doctor or tax adviser before you purchase items for a dependent relative, since many items can be deducted only if prescribed by a medical practitioner. More on taxes a little later.

Be prepared for out-of-pocket expenses. Caregivers don't get paid, often don't get thanked, and frequently don't get reimbursed for long-distance phone calls, travel, groceries, medications, personal care items, or other purchases. A recent survey by the National Alliance for Caregiving and the American Association of Retired Persons found that families caring for an elderly relative spend a monthly average of U.S. $171 of their own money on elder care. This doesn't include "hidden" costs, such as unpaid leave from work. Keep your receipts for everything. You may need to produce them at some point to prove a claim.

You've read all those headlines about the trillion-dollar inheritance the baby-boomers can look forward to. That must mean their folks are pretty well heeled, right? The reality for many "wealthy seniors" is that while they quite often have a home and live mortgage-free, they need income for upkeep of the house, food, clothing, and the like. The majority of women living alone have incomes below Statistics Canada's designated "low-income cut-off" (currently $17,000 for one person). Overall, 19% of all seniors aged 65 and over had incomes below the cut-off. In 1994, people aged 65 and over had an average income (from all sources) of just over $19,000.

For many people, a home is their primary capital investment. However, it can be frustrating to be house-rich and cash-flow poor. Parents may need extra cash to take care of health bills, or to modify their home to make it more comfortable. However, they may not want to sell their home just yet, choosing instead to remain in a familiar neighbourhood. The answer to this conundrum may be a reverse mortgage (see pages 284–85 for more on this topic).

If you're worried about the little things falling through the cracks, but want to see your elder remain independent, here are some small steps you can take. Arrange for the automatic payment of important and recurring bills — water, hydro, and other utility bills, along with health insurance, mortgage, and other regular commitments. Pre-authorized and electronic transactions prevent hassles and interruptions in service that arise from late payments. You might also arrange to be notified if your relative misses a payment. Also arrange for the direct deposit of pension and benefit cheques into bank and brokerage accounts. That way there are no delays in getting funds deposited, no cheques are lost in the mail or forgotten at home, and notices about each payment and deposit can be obtained. And if you set up a joint account with telephone banking privileges, you can do a quick check every now and then to make sure everything in the account is going smoothly (no overdrafts!). Caring for an elderly parent will add so many additional thoughts to your already overloaded circuits that you should look for ways to eliminate routine tasks.

A word of warning: If you and your parent both have deposits at the same bank, and your parent adds your name to his or her account, you may find that you're personally exceeding the $60,000 limit for Canada Deposit Insurance Corporation (CDIC) protection. The solution: Since CDIC limits are based on balances within any single financial institution, move your personal accounts to a financial institution that is different from the one that holds your parent's account.

Beware the financial scam! Targeting the sick or the elderly has become a way of life. Since elderly people are often lonely, they may be willing to trust strangers who call on them. They become the ideal prospects for telemarketing fraud, trumped-up home repairs, and other cons. If you discover a problem, don't be critical. Try not to embarrass your parent. Yes, it can make you angry, but don't take it out on mom or dad. Report the potential con man to the authorities. At home, calmly explain that the friendly person supposedly offering great deals may be a crook.

When it comes to taxes, many health- and age-related expenses can be claimed as medical expenses; these can range from a truss for a hernia to a stair lift, bath bench, dentures, and air or water filters or purifiers. You'll need the advice of a tax specialist when dealing with complex medical expense claims. Don't wait until you've incurred the expense, since certain items can only be claimed if prescribed by a medical practitioner. The definition of medical practitioner is not limited to medical doctors but includes dentists, naturopaths, and a whole slew of other practitioners.

The medical expense claim on your parent's tax form may not include the portion of medical expenses that is covered by any medical plan. However, the health insurance premiums will qualify as medical expenses.

You must file original receipts with your income-tax return to support all medical expenses claimed.

There are also several tax credits a child may claim for a parent:

- The equivalent-to-spouse credit is available to a single child who supports a parent.
- In some cases, the child may claim a personal tax credit for an infirm parent. The disability tax credit requires a medical doctor complete a special form certifying that the parent is "disabled," and any portion of this credit not used by the parent may be transferred to the child. There are other rules and restrictions for claiming these credits.
- A child may claim the medical expenses paid for a dependent parent. CCRA publishes an Interpretation Bulletin that lists in detail what types of expenses qualify as "medical expenses" and which of these items must be prescribed by a medical practitioner. This extensive list changes from time to time. Please consult CCRA or a tax specialist. A medical expense claim for a dependent parent will be reduced if the parent had net income for tax purposes above the basic personal tax credit amount ($6,456 for 1998). This reduction may be greater than the value of the medical expenses of the parent and may even reduce the medical expenses that the child is claiming for herself.

If your dependent is in a nursing home, you can claim medical- and attendant-care costs as part of his or her medical expenses. Attendant-care expenses can include the cost of a companion or health-care aide. There are detailed rules concerning the deductibility of attendant-care expenses, including whether the care is on a part-time or full-time basis, the amount paid for an attendant, and whether the parent meets the government's definition of "disability." However, medical and attendant care are the most expensive costs associated with a nursing home, so a well-supported claim can result in a significant tax credit. Most nursing homes identify the portion that is eligible for the credit on their bills. You'll need form T2201 to claim this credit so CCRA can verify that your dependent is under attendant care.

It is very important that your parent execute a will and powers of attorney, if they have not already done so. Since even beginning this discussion means facing difficult issues such as death or incapacitation, people are hugely resistant to talking openly about them. Superstitiously, people may feel they are tempting fate. But there is a very real danger in not having these documents completed.

Parents who are suddenly incapacitated, and have not executed powers of attorney, will have lost their ability to name a trusted representative to be in control of their affairs. And since there's a time lag before an attorney is appointed by the public trustee, during that time, no one has control or authority over things like paying bills or the mortgage, filing tax returns, and the like. Even if you have joint ownership of a home with your parent, you won't be able to make changes until someone is appointed to represent your parent's interest. And if your father has always controlled the finances and your mom has no independent means, should he become incapacitated, she would become totally dependent on your resources while the province appoints an attorney.

Parents who are reluctant to sign a document that they feel reduces their personal control over their finances, and even their lives, should consider naming two children (or a child and lawyer or accountant) to act on their behalf. The two parties named then act as a check on each other. And the power of attorney can be left with a third party, who is given specific instructions as to its release. As well, it can be limited in terms of the specific time period — such as when a parent is hospitalized — or specific acts.

When it comes to preparing the will or power of attorney, it's up to the lawyer to establish mental competence. He or she might ask your mother questions about her estate, her understanding of her assets, and her reason for visiting the lawyer at that particular time. As long as these questions are answered satisfactorily, the individual is usually deemed competent. If the lawyer has concerns about competency, a medical assessment will be done. This can be tough for an aging client to hear, but it may be necessary to ensure the legal documentation is valid.

28

Just in Case You Become Disabled

Illness is the night-side of life, a more onerous citizenship. Everyone who is born holds dual citizenship, in the kingdom of the well and in the kingdom of the sick. Although we all prefer to use only the good passport, sooner or later each of us is obliged, at least for a spell, to identify ourselves as citizens of that other place.

SUSAN SONTAG

My husband often says, of the difference between men and women, that "men die. Women get sick." He's right. And the thought of getting sick and not being able to take care of myself, of being a burden to my husband or my children, of not being able to do what I wanted when I wanted kept me away from this chapter for a long time. Finally I worked up the courage, and here's what I have for you.

Women between the ages of 25 and 55 are far more likely to become disabled than to die. While we have a lower mortality rate than our male contemporaries, our likelihood of disability is higher. Statistics show that if someone becomes disabled for more than three months, that person will likely be disabled five years later. Pricing structures for disability insurance show that women are more often claimants, as reflected in their significantly higher premiums.

Living Through It

I know a woman named Heather who has the fortitude of a brigade. Heather has multiple sclerosis. As a strong, career-oriented woman, Heather refuses to give up. Once when we met at a children's movie — our daughters are about the same age — she was in a walker and expressing frustration at her latest setback. That week she had awoken to find that she would no longer be able to drive. Her concern: How was she going to get to work?

I have to admit that Heather takes my breath away. I can hardly imagine wanting to go to work knowing that my body could no longer direct my car. Heather didn't just want to go. She went. Her husband now drives her to and from work each day. It's just one of the concessions they have had to make to her disease and the disability it has brought to their lives.

Heather's story isn't meant to set a standard to which we must all strive. On the contrary. Heather's story is a prime example of how we must all cope in our own way to make the journey worthwhile. Why didn't she just stay home and rest? She couldn't. That, more than the disease, would have killed her spirit. Each person facing trying circumstances must find her own way. We must each seek the road that suits our step. We must walk gingerly alongside all those other women who are trying their best to make life work. And, wherever we can, we must lend a hand to help.

Regardless of how well insured you are, you will have to make adjustments to your cash flow. And if you have arrived at this spot with little or no disability insurance, how you manage what you do have will have great bearing on how you will live your life.

The first thing you need to do if you have a disability plan is to find out when you will get your first cheque. This may seem quite straightforward. It can be. It can also be a nightmare. A girlfriend of mine was without disability income for well over a year because the company carrying the plan refused to accept that she was at least 60% disabled. Once her employment insurance (EI) benefits ran out, she ran out of money. She had to cash in her RRSPs just to keep the roof over her head. A few weeks, even a few days, spent gathering paperwork for the insurance company can mean the difference between meeting your financial commitments on time and struggling to put food on the table. In a state of general vulnerability, it's easy to let things slide. But you can't.

You must follow up, insist, push to get what you need. If you don't have the strength, get an advocate working on your behalf.

Your insurance company may have very specific wording for how it wants your disability described and your inability to work proven. Before your doctor starts writing letters and making phone calls, find out everything you can to make your case as strong as it can be the first time. Yes, there is usually an appeal process, and you can always add more information. But each delay, each change in your circumstances that must be documented, adds time to the approval process and leaves you without an income for even longer. If your doctor has had no experience dealing with insurance companies, or with claims like yours, ask for a referral to a specialist who will be better able to create a convincing argument on your behalf.

If you think your disability insurance is your right once you make a claim, you're like most people. We figure that since we've paid our premiums in a timely fashion for five, 10, 20 years, we're entitled to our disability payments when we need them. The insurance company sees things a little differently. Since the disability claim can be huge over the life of the disability, they want proof that you're disabled. Medical science's progress in documenting and naming new diseases means insurance companies are being faced with claims for illnesses they never imagined would exist when early policies were written. They are keeping a careful eye on what documentation should be required to support a claim for these new conditions.

If you are not covered by a private disability plan or a group plan through work, you will have to seek social assistance. The Canada Pension Plan (CPP) has a disability program that is applicable for long-term (more than one year) disabilities. The benefits paid are based on the amount of contributions you and your employers have made over the years. If you have made contributions for at least two of the last three years (or four out of the last six, pending legislative approval at the time of writing), you may qualify to receive payments. Benefits may also be paid to your children who are under the age of 18 (or up to age 25 if they are attending school on a full-time basis). This income is taxable in the child's hands. Remember, too, that this amount qualifies for RRSP purposes as earned income, creating RRSP deduction room for you and your children. CPP benefits kick in after a four-month waiting period.

Insurance disability benefits usually kick in after a waiting period too, during which time EI benefits, if you are entitled, may pick up the slack. It won't be as much as you were earning, and you may very well have some additional medical expenses you must meet, so the next step is to review your spending plan:

- Are there expenses you could minimize or eliminate completely — things like transportation, lunches, and ordering in dinner? Shared day care would be less expensive than full-time day care. Do you still need the second car?
- Are there areas in which your expenses will increase? Medical coverage used to be a given in Canada, but with the social safety net slowly unravelling, you may find yourself with more costs to bear, just at the time when you can least cope financially and emotionally.
- If you had a medical plan at work, will it remain in effect while you are disabled? If not, how will you replace the coverage of those medical costs?
- Are there assets you could sell to help make ends meet? Resist the urge to attack your RRSPs. You're going to need that money down the line, since most disability benefits end at age 65.

You're walking a fine line when you're on a reduced income and trying to manage your credit effectively. It's all very well and good to have scads of credit available on cards and to use that credit to make ends meet when you must, but if you have no hope of repayment, it's a fool's game.

There's no question that from time to time emergencies arise that force you to look to credit as the answer. The most important question to ask yourself before you decide to do the swipe is, "When will I pay this off?" If the answer is "Later," then you may be setting yourself up for a future of juggling one card against the other until the bankruptcy police catch up with you. Not a pretty sight. And not the kind of stress you need in your life. If you don't know when you'll be able to pay off your credit card, don't charge it. Pay cash. If you don't have the cash, do without. If you can't do without, you'll have to find another way.

Some forms of credit offer disability insurance in the event that you cannot work and, therefore, cannot pay your bills. I don't recommend this feature since, for the most part, the insurance doesn't pay off your debt; it simply takes care of the interest portion so the financial institution isn't out of pocket and trying to collect from a vulnerable client. It just keeps them from looking bad. It would be better to apply for disability insurance and have personal coverage that paid you directly so you could then redirect the money in the way that would do you and your family the most good.

If you find that you've become disabled while carrying a significant debt load, it's time to get on the phone and make some telephone calls. You're going to have to explain to your creditors that you may be unable to meet your commitments in the short term. Try to work out a payment plan that minimizes the crunch to your cash flow. Negotiate to make a reduced single payment in lieu of taking 10 years to pay the whole thing off.

When Alison became disabled, she had being flying full-force through life, charging up a storm and wreaking havoc at the mall. Suddenly she came to a full stop and found herself with a mountain of debt she could not handle. "I was doing fine," she said. "Then this thing with my hands started and now I can't work. I can't type or input data. Some days I can't hold a pencil or brush my daughter's hair." Alison still had a personal line of credit that was in good shape — she had only used $1,200 of her $5,000 line. But she was maxed out on her credit cards and department store cards, for a total of $7,500 in debt. And she owed Revenue Canada tax from two previous years. "What a mess," she said, as she looked at the papers on the dining-room table. I suggested Alison call the department stores' credit divisions first, since those cards carried the heftiest rate of interest. After several calls, a letter from her doctor, and proof of her reduced income, Alison managed to negotiate a deal where she would pay two-thirds of the outstanding balance all at once and that would clear her bills. Using her line of credit, she wrote cheques for a total of $3,000 and cleared away $5,000 in debt. The next call was to CCRA.

Alison explained her situation and the tax man listened sympathetically. Most people don't realize just how thoughtful the tax man can be when he believes that you are honestly in a bind, particularly when the circumstances are beyond your control. CCRA agreed to waive all interest and penalties, and they worked out a very gentle repayment plan of just $45 a month for the principal tax owed. Finally, she came to the charge cards. More heavy negotiating. More indications that if forced to she would have to declare personal bankruptcy. Finally, Alison won their acceptance of a repayment plan that fit with her cash flow. In the end, the amount of her monthly income that went to servicing her debt dropped from $750 a month to just $325. "I can do this," she sighed with relief. Of course she can!

For women with partners, the prospect of becoming homeless is less overwhelming. For women who are dealing with their disability on their own, it can be a constant worry. And if a woman has children, the stress is even greater. To deal with this situation, you need some unbiased advice. I'm referring to the kind of advice a good friend can give by asking you a bunch of questions you may not yet have thought to ask yourself. And it doesn't hurt if that friend knows how the financial world operates.

The decision to sell or not sell, move and rent elsewhere, or stay where you are is a purely black-and-white decision. Or, at least, it should be. We often let emotion get in the way of logic. Or we react too quickly, not considering all the options, and let opportunities slip past us. Here's an example of what I mean.

When Emma came to me asking for advice on whether or not to sell her home — she was disabled with a drastic reduction in her income — I asked why she wanted to. "I can't afford this house any longer," she said, as she wept into her hands. "I have my daughter to care for and I've little or nothing to live on."

"Where will you go?" I asked.

"I don't know."

"What are you paying for your mortgage and upkeep right now?"

"Just under $900 a month for my mortgage, so I'd estimate about $1,200 a month with taxes, insurance, and the like."

"And how much longer do you have on your mortgage term and at what rate?"

"It was originally a five-year mortgage at 9%, and I've got a year and a half left on it."

"Have you considered renegotiating the mortgage?"

"I'd have to pay an interest penalty, and I have no money."

"Actually," I said, "there's a thing called a 'blend and extend' mortgage, which I have to admit very few people know about or understand. With a blend and extend, in effect, you would continue to pay 9% for the next 18 months, and then the current rate of 6% for the remaining term — I'd suggest you go long, long at these rates. In reality, the two interest rates would be averaged out based on the terms applicable so you'd end up paying less than 9% now, but more than 6% for the rest of the term. Get my drift?"

"I understand that, but how would it help?"

"Cash flow, girl. Let's say you end up with a 7.25% mortgage. Your payments would go from about $900 to about $700 a month. That knocks $200 a month off your housing costs."

"Okay, but that's still too expensive."

"Didn't you tell me earlier that your basement is rentable?"

"Yes, but the house is so small and that's my daughter's playroom."

"Not if you have to move, it won't be. How much could you rent it for, reasonably?"

"About $400 a month."

"So your housing costs would drop another $400 to about $300 a month, right?"

"Yeah," Emma's face brightened, "I see what you mean."

"Okay, so tomorrow, you call the bank and find out the figures for the blend and extend and then you can make some decisions based on the real financial facts. And start putting feelers out for someone for that basement apartment."

Emma could see her way clear for the first time in a long time. And all it took was one conversation, a little application of black and white, and a sense of being able to do something.

What about your investments? Depending on the type of disability you are living with, this may be more or less important. Disability brought on by terminal illness may negate, in your mind and in the minds of most others, your need to build assets for the future. And if you are struggling to make ends meet now, the argument is moot. However, if your disability is one that will not affect your life expectancy, then you will need to make plans for the long-term future. Even a little put away regularly will make a huge difference in terms of the amount of money you will have when you finally reach 65 and your insurance benefits end. If you do not put something away for the future, you may very well find yourself in an awful place at some point down the road. It is important that you save and that you invest. If you are not taking care of you, who will?

You've probably had to use your emergency fund very recently, so you now know the value of this financial tool. If you're living on a much lower income, it's easy to say that you can't afford to rebuild the fund you've exhausted. But the fact is, with less cash flow available, you need one now more than ever. After all, on a restricted cash flow, even the smallest of emergencies can put a severe crimp in your spending plan. It may take longer to rebuild your emergency fund, but you've got to start. Five dollars this month, 10 dollars next; each little step will take you closer to your goal. Without the emergency fund you will constantly have to worry about the what-ifs. Do what you can to protect yourself so you have the money available, *just in case!*

Think you can't afford to maintain your life insurance on your reduced cash flow? You can't afford not to, since a new policy would be prohibitively expensive. Ideally, you had a disability rider for your insurance. The only way to know is to read your policies or check with your broker.

You may be able to get some breaks from CCRA on your current and future taxes. People who suffer from a severe and prolonged mental or physical impairment — one that has lasted or is expected to last for at least a year — that markedly restricts their ability to perform a basic activity of daily life are entitled to a substantial non-refundable tax credit ($4,293 in 2000) that can be claimed by a disabled taxpayer *or* supporting individual for a disabled spouse or other dependents. This credit is for individuals who are considered to be markedly restricted in their activities due to severe and prolonged impairment, including blindness, or who are unable to perform basic functions such as thinking and remembering, speaking in a way that can be understood, hearing, bowel or bladder functions, walking, feeding and dressing themselves. The credit can be claimed regardless of whether the individual is working or not, since working, social and recreational activities, and housekeeping are not considered a basic activity of daily life. This credit is available only if no other claim is being made for this or any other non-refundable tax credit.

Attendant-care expenses can also be claimed but may have an impact on whether or how you can claim the disability amount on the same return. Check with a tax specialist on the best way to ensure you get maximum benefit without forfeiting any disability amounts.

For people who are terminally ill, you must review your estate plan. It is surprising just how long you can delay something that you feel may be an unpleasant experience. But, it will continue to remain an unpleasant must-do for as long as it remains undone. Yes, it will be difficult for you, and it will be difficult for the loved ones with whom you must consult. But to do nothing, to die without a will, can create even more confusion and heartache.

If you are severely ill when you make your will, you must seek the best possible estate-planning advice to ensure that your wishes are acted upon, and not posthumously discredited due to your illness. If there are people you wish to protect, individuals you feel a responsibility toward, friends, lovers, or children you must care for, then you must have a will.

In terms of your wishes while alive, there may come a time when you cannot make decisions — be they financial or personal-care decisions — on your own behalf. You must have a legally executed power of attorney naming a trusted individual to act on your behalf so you can be sure your wishes will be respected.

PREPARING FOR IT

I don't know if you can ever be prepared for disability. That's probably one of the reasons why I waited until D-Day to write this chapter. After all, just the idea of becoming disabled was stomach-wrenching enough. It was excruciating to watch a close friend deal with her own debilitating case of MS, to watch her relationship disintegrate, to watch as she swung from the highs of being able to cope one day to the lows of believing she would never be able to cope again.

The best advice I can give in preparing for a disability — assuming you can prepare because your condition is progressive and you still have time — is to surround yourself with your friends and ask them for help. Get yourself involved in an association that deals with your malady — there are hundreds of associations in Canada dealing with a variety of disabilities — and start to connect with like-minded individuals who can help you understand where you're going. A great place to start is on the Internet. Search by the name of your illness, or simply by the word "disability," and you'll come up with a world of information. You may also want to pick up a copy of *What's Stopping You?: Living Successfully with Disability*, by Mark Nagler and Adam Nagler (Stoddart, 1999), at your local bookstore or library.

My only other advice (and it comes from observing what has worked for my friends): Try to spend at least a part of each week being "other-focused" or, in other words, helping someone else cope. Your disability and its impact on your life can be all-consuming, and financial clouds may seem so thick that they block out the very things we should be focused on: family, love, and enjoyment of the here-and-now. If you can take just a moment from your life to help someone else get over his or her hurdles, your spirit will be enriched and your burden lightened, at least for a little while.

Conclusion

It isn't often that you get to work on a project that can actually change people's lives by helping them see things in a new light. With this book, I hope that I, and my comrades in money, have helped you change how you feel about the green stuff and what you'll do with it as you move through your life.

Good money management isn't magic. And it doesn't require you to be some sort of financial wizard. It's all about doing the right things consistently. It's about being deliberate in the steps you take to attain your particular goals. That means saving some money, investing smartly for your specific needs, and taking care of the what-ifs. It also means understanding who you are with money, and why, so you can shed your emotional baggage. If you face the money demons that inhabit both your soul and your wallet, you can move on from there.

Remember, *telesis* is about making progress. And no matter what comes along to throw you off track, you are the only person who can control what you do next. Sinking into a quagmire of misery and self-pity won't get you into that house, or out of debt, or back to school to build new skills. Now, I'm not saying there aren't some times when a nice thick blanket and a huge box of chocolates can't be your best friends. But if you stay in that place, you can't move forward. Inertia will keep you bogged down. The only way to get out is to make it happen. And you can.

Whether you're a little in debt or a lot, recently widowed or living through a divorce-from-hell, movin' on up or in a job that feels like the same-old, same-old, you can change your life. You need a plan. You must know the rules of smart money management. And you must follow them.

Today, pick one thing you'll do differently. You might choose to stash your cards behind the refrigerator and shop with cash. (If you have to dig through all that gunk under the fridge to get your cards out, you'll think twice about how much you actually *need* those new shoes.) Or perhaps you'll call your insurance agent and find out what it would cost to protect your family should you or your honey meet your Maker. Maybe you'll put yourself on a monthly investment plan. With as little as $25 a month you can start forming a habit that will hold you in good stead forever.

If you're one of those people who believe they're too deep in debt to ever get out, give yourself a good kick. You can if you want to. If you don't really want to, quit whingeing; if you do, ask for some help. There are all kinds of people out there ready and willing to come to your aid. For a start, check out the resources section on the next few pages.

Finally, after spending this much time reading my book, you know enough about me to know that I wouldn't kid you. You can take control. You can be financially at peace, if you want to be. But only *you* can make it happen, so . . . do it!

Resources

The following is a list of books and organizations you may wish to consult when you have questions about money and specific aspects of financial planning.

Banking
Canadian Bankers Association
  199 Bay Street, Suite 3000, P.O. Box 348, Commerce Court West,
  Toronto, ON M5L 1G2
  Tel: 416-362-6092
Canada Deposit Insurance Corporation
  50 O'Connor Street, 17th Floor, P.O. Box 2340, Station D, Ottawa, ON
  K1P 5W5
  Toll-Free: 1-800-461-2342

Credit
Staats, William F., and E. D. Sledge. *How Chuck Taylor Got What He Wanted* (Canadian edition), Credit Counselling Service of Toronto, 1998.
Kisluk, Frank. *Life After Debt*, Doubleday Canada, 1996.
Vaz-Oxlade, Gail. *Shopping for Money*, Stoddart Publishing, 1998.

Access Nova Scotia
   Department of Business and Consumer Services
   Toll-Free: 1-800-670-4357 (only in Nova Scotia) Fax: 902-424-0720
B.C. Ministry of the Attorney General
   Debtors Assistance Branch
   Toll-free: 1-800-663-7867 (only in B.C.)
   Victoria: 250-387-1747 Fax: 250-953-4783
   Burnaby: 604-660-3550 Fax: 604-660-8472
   Kamloops: 250-828-4511 Fax: 250-371-3822
Consumer Services Officer (New Brunswick)
   Consumer Affairs Branch, Department of Justice
   Tel: 506-453-2659 Fax: 506-444-4494
Credit Counselling Service of Toronto
   45 Sheppard Avenue East, Suite 810, Toronto, ON M2N 5W9
   Tel: 416-228-3328
Credit Counselling Services of Alberta
   Toll-free: 1-888-294-0076 (only in Alberta)
   Calgary: 403-265-2201   Fax: 403-265-2240
   Edmonton: 403-423-5265 Fax: 403-423-2791
Credit Counselling Services of Atlantic Canada, Inc.
   Toll-free: 1-800-539-2227 (only in New Brunswick)
   Tel: 506-652-1613 Fax: 506-633-6057
Credit Counselling Society of British Columbia
   Toll-free: 1-888-527-8999 (only in B.C.)
   Tel: 604-527-8999 Fax: 604-527-8008
Equifax Canada Inc.
   Box 190, Jean-Talon Station, Montreal, PQ H1S 2Z2
   Tel: 514-493-2470
Family Services of Fredericton, Inc.
   Tel: 506-458-8211 Fax: 506-451-9437
Fédération des associations coopératives d'économie familiale du Québec
   Tel: 514-271-7004 Fax: 514-271-1036
Manitoba Community Financial Counselling Services
   Tel: 204-989-1900 Fax: 204-989-1908
Newfoundland and Labrador Personal Credit Counselling Service
   Tel: 709-753-5812 Fax: 709-753-3390

N.W.T. Consumer Services
  Municipal and Community Affairs
  Tel: 867-873-7125 Fax: 867-920-6343
Ontario Association of Credit Counselling Services
  Tel: 1-888-7IN-DEBT (746-3328) Fax: 905-945-4680
Option-consommateurs
  Tel: 514-598-7288 Fax: 514-598-8511
P.E.I. Department of Community Affairs
  Consumer, Corporate and Insurance Services
  Tel: 902-368-4580 Fax: 902-368-5355
Port Cities Debt Counselling Society
  Tel: 902-453-6510
Saskatchewan Department of Justice
  Provincial Mediation Board
  Regina: 306-787-5387 Fax: 306-787-5574
  Saskatoon: 306-933-6520 Fax: 306-933-7030
Trans Union of Canada
  P.O. Box 338–LCD1, Hamilton, ON L8L 7W2

Estate Planning
Foster, Sandra E. *You Can't Take It With You*, John Wiley & Sons, 1998.

Financial Planning and Specialty Areas
Cohen, Bruce. *The Money Adviser*, Stoddart Publishing, 1999.
Flynn, Donald. *The Truth About Funerals*, Funeral Consultants International Inc., 1993.
Kerr, Margaret, and JoAnn Kuirtz. *Buying, Owning and Selling a Home in Canada*, John Wiley & Sons, 1997.
McNicol, Barry. *The Severance Package Strategy Book*, Stoddart Publishing, 1996.
Nagler, Mark, and Adam Nagler. *What's Stopping You?: Living Successfully with Disability*, Stoddart Publishing, 1999.
Orman, Suze. *The 9 Steps to Financial Freedom*, Random House, Inc., 1997.
Rhodes, Ann. *The Eldercare Sourcebook*, Key Porter Books, 1993.
Vaz-Oxlade, Gail. *Divorce: A Canadian Woman's Guide*, Prentice Hall Canada, 2001.

Vaz-Oxlade, Gail. *The Money Tree Myth: A Parents' Guide to Helping Kids Unravel the Mysteries of Money*, Stoddart Publishing, 1996.
Vaz-Oxlade, Gail. *The Retirement Answer Book*, Stoddart Publishing, 1997.
Wylie, Betty Jane. *Enough*, Northstone Publishing, Inc., 1998.

Financial Planners Standards Council of Canada (FPSC)
  505 University Avenue, Suite 1600, Toronto, ON M5G 1X3
  Tel: 416-593-8587
Canadian Association of Financial Planners
  60 St. Clair Avenue East, Suite 510, Toronto, ON M4T 1N5
  Tel: 416-966-9928

Insurance

Bullock, James, and George Brett. *Insure Sensibly: A Guide to Life and Disability Insurance*, Penguin Books, 1991.

Insurance Bureau of Canada
  181 University Avenue, Toronto, ON M5H 3M7
  Tel: 416-362-9528
Independent Life Insurance Brokers of Canada
  2175 Sheppard Avenue East, Suite 310, Willowdale, ON M2J 1W8
  Tel: 416-491-9747
The Insurance Institute of Canada
  18 King Street East, Toronto, ON M5C 1C4
  Tel: 416-362-8586
Canadian Life and Health Insurance Association
  1 Queen Street East, Suite 1700, Toronto, ON M5C 2X9
  Tel: 416-777-2221

The Internet as a Resource

Carroll, Jim, and Rick Broadhead. *1999 Mutual Funds and RRSPs Online*, Prentice-Hall, Inc., 1998. (Make sure you get the most recent edition.)

Investing

Canadian Securities Institute. *How to Invest in Canadian Securities*, 1997.
Canadian Securities Institute. *How to Start and Run an Investment Club*, 1998.

Edey, David. *Smart Money Strategies for the Canadian Mutual Fund Investor*, Regine Communications, 1998.

Hartman, George. *Risk Is Still a Four Letter Word*, Stoddart Publishing, 2000.

Moynes, Riley. *The Money Coach*, Addison Wesley, 1997.

Newsome, Mark, and Jeffrey Zahn. *Taking Control: Your Blueprint for Financial Success*, Key Porter Books, 1993.

Vaz-Oxlade, Gail. *Dead Cat Bounce: The Skinny on E-vesting*, Prentice Hall Canada, 2001.

Canadian Shareowners Association
1090 University Avenue West, P.O. Box 7337, Windsor, ON N9C 4E9
Tel: 519-252-1555

Investment Dealers Association of Canada
121 King Street West, Suite 1600, Toronto, ON M5H 3T9
Tel: 416-364-6133

The Investment Funds Institute of Canada
151 Yonge Street, 5th Floor, Toronto, ON M5C 2W7
Tel: 416-363-2158

Investor Learning Centre of Canada
Toronto: 121 King Street West, 15th Floor, Toronto, ON M5H 3T9
Tel: 416-364-6666
Montreal: 1 Place Ville Marie, Suite 2840, Montreal, PQ H3B 4R4
Tel: 514-878-3591
Calgary: 355–4th Avenue SW, Suite 2330, Calgary, AB T2P 0J1
Tel: 403-269-9923
Vancouver: P.O. Box 11574, 650 West Georgia Street, Suite 1350, Vancouver, BC V6B 4N8
Tel: 604-683-1338

Psychology of Money

Boundy, Donna. *When Money Is the Drug*, HarperCollins Publishers, 1993.

Dominguez, Joe, and Vicki Robin. *Your Money or Your Life*, Penguin Books, 1992.

Mellan, Olivia. *Money Harmony*, Walker and Company, 1994.

Sociology of Money

Galbraith, John Kenneth. *A Journey Through Economic Time: A Firsthand View*,

Houghton Mifflin Company, 1994.

Hacker, Andrew. *Money: Who Has How Much and Why*, Scribner, 1997.

Taxes

Cestnick, Tim. *Winning the Tax Game*, Prentice-Hall, Inc., 1998.

Jacks, Evelyn. *Jacks on Tax*, McGraw-Hill Ryerson, 1998.

Rosentreter, Kurt. *50 Tax-Smart Investing Strategies*, Stoddart Publishing, 1999.

Canadian Tax Foundation

    1 Queen Street East, Suite 1800, Toronto, ON M5C 2Y2

    Tel: 416-863-9784

Chartered Accountants of Canada

    277 Wellington Street West, Toronto, ON M5V 3H2

    Tel: 416-977-3222

Index